WileyPLUS with ORION

Quickly identify areas of strength and weakness before the first exam, and use the information to build a learning path to success.

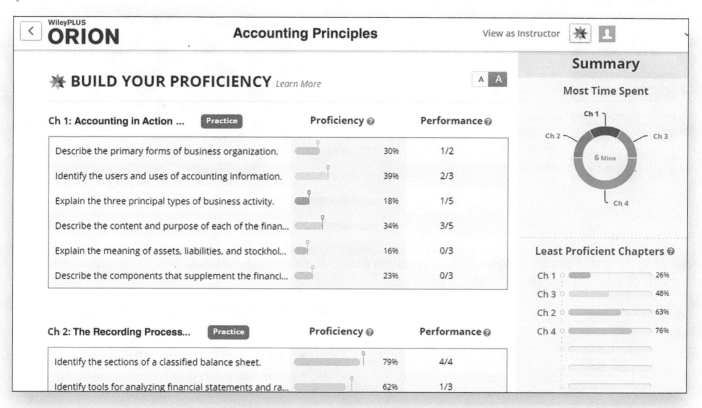

A little time with ORION goes a long way.

Based on usage data, students who engage in ORION adaptive practice—just a few minutes per week—get better outcomes. In fact, students who used ORION five or more times over the course of a semester reported the following results:

86%	80%	81%	70%
better prepared for tests and quizzes	more confident in their ability to learn the material	better able to retain the material	better grades in their course

Streamlined Learning Objectives

Newly streamlined learning objectives help students make the best use of their time outside of class. Each learning objective is addressed by reading content, watching educational videos, and answering a variety of practice and assessment questions, so that no matter where students begin their work, the relevant resources and practice are readily accessible.

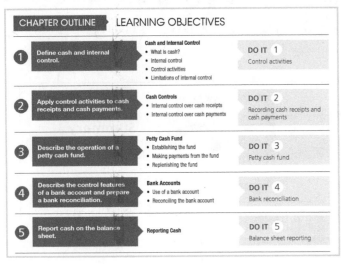

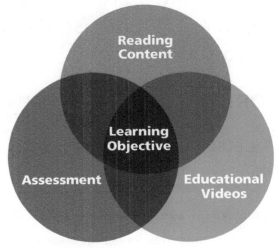

Review and Practice

Developing effective problem-solving skills requires practice, relevant feedback, and insightful examples with more opportunities for self-guided practice.

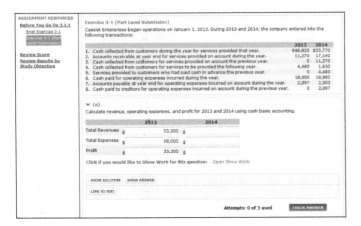

Review and practice opportunities in the text include:

- Learning Objectives Review
- Glossary Review
- Multiple-Choice Questions with Answers
- Do It Problems with Action Plans
- Demonstration Problems

In **WileyPLUS**, the practice assignments include several Brief Exercises and Exercises from the related exercises listed in the Before You Go On section. These exercises give students the opportunity to check their work or see the answer and solution after their final attempt. Algorithmic versions of these questions allow students to revisit these questions until they understand a topic completely.

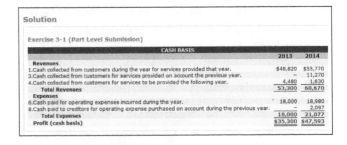

ACCOUNTING PRINCIPLES

SEVENTH CANADIAN EDITION

→ Jerry J. Weygandt *Ph.D., CPA*
University of Wisconsin—Madison

→ Donald E. Kieso *Ph.D., CPA*
Northern Illinois University

→ Paul D. Kimmel *Ph.D., CPA*
University of Wisconsin—Milwaukee

→ Barbara Trenholm *M.B.A., FCA*
University of New Brunswick—Fredericton

→ Valerie R. Warren *M.B.A., CPA, CA*
Kwantlen Polytechnic University

→ Lori Novak *H.B.Comm., CPA, CGA*
Red River College

WILEY

To our students—past, present, and future

Library and Archives Canada Cataloguing in Publication

Weygandt, Jerry J., author

Accounting principles / Jerry J. Weygandt, Ph.D., CPA (University of Wisconsin—Madison), Donald E. Kieso, Ph.D., CPA (Northern Illinois University), Paul D. Kimmel, Ph.D., CPA (University of Wisconsin—Milwaukee), Barbara Trenholm, MBA, FCA (University of New Brunswick—Fredericton), Valerie Warren, B.Comm., M.B.A., CPA, CA (Kwantlen Polytechnic University), Lori Novak, H.B.Comm., CPA, CGA (Red River College).—Seventh Canadian edition.

Includes indexes.
Revision of: Accounting principles / Jerry J. Weygandt, Donald E. Kieso, Barbara Trenholm; in collaboration with Donald C. Cherry.—1st Canadian ed.—Toronto: J. Wiley Canada, ©1999.
ISBN 978-1-119-04850-3 (volume 1: bound).—ISBN 978-1-119-04847-3 (volume 2: bound)

1. Accounting—Textbooks.   I. Kieso, Donald E., author   II. Kimmel, Paul D., author   III. Trenholm, Barbara, author   IV. Warren, Valerie, 1968-, author   V. Novak, Lori, author   VI. Title.

HF5635.W39 2015   657'.044   C2015-906305-1

Production Credits
Executive Editor: Zoë Craig
Vice President and Director, Market Solutions: Veronica Visentin
Marketing Manager: Anita Osborne
Editorial Manager: Karen Staudinger
Developmental Editor: Daleara Jamasji Hirjikaka
Media Editor: Luisa Begani
Production and Media Specialist: Meaghan MacDonald
Assistant Editor: Ashley Patterson
Cover and Interior Design: Joanna Vieira
Production Editing: Denise Showers, Senior Project Manager, Aptara Inc.
Typesetting: Aptara Inc.
Cover Photo: Background: ©raspu/Getty Images. Leaves in iPad: © View Stock/Getty Images. Ipad: © Mattjeacock/Getty Images. Falling leaves: ©bgfoto/Getty Images.

Manufactured in the United States by LSC Communications
3 4 5 LSC 19 18 17

John Wiley & Sons Canada, Ltd.
Suite 300, 90 Eglinton Ave East
Toronto, Ontario, Canada, M4P 2Y3
Visit our website at: www.wiley.ca

BRIEF CONTENTS

CONTENTS – VOLUME TWO

9 LONG-LIVED ASSETS

CHAPTER PREVIEW Under International Financial Reporting Standards, companies have two models they can choose between to account for their long-lived assets: the cost model or the revaluation model. The cost model is the more commonly used method, and is the only model allowed under ASPE. We will cover the cost model in the following sections of the chapter and refer briefly to the revaluation model in a later section.

The **cost model** records long-lived assets at cost of acquisition. After acquisition, depreciation (when applicable) is recorded each period and the assets are carried at cost less accumulated depreciation.

For organizations such as Red River College, making the right decisions about long-lived assets is critical because these assets represent huge investments. Organizations must make decisions about what assets to acquire, how to account for them, and when to dispose of them.

In this chapter, we address these and other issues surrounding long-lived assets. Our discussions will focus on three types of long-lived assets: (1) property, plant, and equipment; (2) natural resources; and (3) intangible assets.

FEATURE STORY ▶ ## CAPITALIZING ON EDUCATION

WINNIPEG, Man.—Chances are that your college or university does not consist of one big building—it's likely a sprawling campus, perhaps with several locations around the city or region. That's certainly the case for Red River College—Manitoba's largest institute of applied learning, with more than 30,000 students—which has eight campuses in Winnipeg and several other communities in the province. Its largest campus, Notre Dame campus in Winnipeg, has 1.3 million square feet (120,000 square metres) of building space spread over 100 acres (40 hectares).

How does a post-secondary institution account for all these buildings, which are usually the largest asset on its books? The accounting treatment varies depending on the ownership. Until 1992, community colleges in Manitoba were part of a provincial government department. After that, they became not-for-profit entities operated by a board of governors, and the colleges started renting their buildings from the province, recording the rent as an operating expense. Gradually, the province has been transferring ownership of campus buildings to the colleges, which record the buildings as capital assets. Red River College expected the transfer of the remainder of its buildings to be completed in 2016, said Ted Maciurzynski, Director of Campus Planning. "We will have the keys to the campus," he said.

For the buildings it owned in 2014, Red River College recorded a net book value (carrying amount) in its financial statements of $97.3 million—by far the largest asset—while its assets under capital leases had a net book value of $2.7 million. The college depreciates the buildings it owns using the straight-line method: a constant rate of depreciating value of 2.5% per year for 40 years. Assets under capital leases are depreciated on a straight-line basis over their expected useful lives.

Red River College has another long-lived asset with an interesting accounting treatment. It recently acquired an unused school in Portage la Prairie, west of Winnipeg, from the local school district. "Essentially, we got the building for $1," said Mr. Maciurzynski. But the college doesn't record the building's value as $1, because it spent about $2.5 million renovating the school for use as college classrooms and offices, he said. The college depreciates the cost of the renovated building at a straight-line rate of 2.5% per year.

What about all the equipment, furniture, and computers inside these buildings? They're not considered long-lived assets, the way buildings are. Their depreciation rates vary depending on their estimated useful lives. Red River College depreciates the cost of equipment and furniture at a rate between 10% and 20% per year, while it depreciates computers and software—which can become obsolete very quickly—at up to 33% per year, according to its financial statements.

CHAPTER OUTLINE

LEARNING OBJECTIVES

1 Calculate the cost of property, plant, and equipment.

Property, Plant, and Equipment
- Determining the cost of property, plant, and equipment

DO IT 1
Cost of plant assets

2 Apply depreciation methods to property, plant, and equipment.

- Depreciation

DO IT 2
Methods of depreciation

3 Explain the factors that cause changes in periodic depreciation and calculate revised depreciation for property, plant, and equipment.

- Revising periodic depreciation

DO IT 3
Revised depreciation

4 Demonstrate how to account for property, plant, and equipment disposals.

- Disposal of property, plant, and equipment

DO IT 4
Plant asset disposal

5 Record natural resource transactions and calculate depletion.

Natural Resources
- Cost
- Depletion
- Disposal

DO IT 5
Calculating depletion for natural assets

6 Identify the basic accounting issues for intangible assets and goodwill.

Intangible Assets and Goodwill
- Accounting for intangible assets
- Intangible assets with finite lives
- Intangible assets with indefinite lives
- Goodwill

DO IT 6
Accounting for intangible assets

7 Illustrate the reporting and analysis of long-lived assets.

Statement Presentation and Analysis
- Presentation
- Analysis

DO IT 7
Asset turnover and return on assets

Property, Plant, and Equipment

Alternative terminology Property, plant, and equipment are also commonly known as *fixed assets*; *land, building, and equipment*; or *capital assets*.

Property, plant, and equipment are long-lived assets that the company owns and uses for the production and sale of goods or services to consumers. They have three characteristics. They (1) have a physical substance (a definite size and shape); (2) are held for use in the production or supply of goods or services, for rental to others, or for administrative purposes; and (3) are not intended for sale to customers. Unlike current assets, these assets are expected to provide services to a company for a number of years.

LEARNING OBJECTIVE   Calculate the cost of property, plant, and equipment.

DETERMINING THE COST OF PROPERTY, PLANT, AND EQUIPMENT

The cost of an item of property, plant, and equipment includes the following:

1. The purchase price, plus any non-refundable taxes, less any discounts or rebates;
2. The expenditures necessary to bring the asset to the required location and make it ready for its intended use;
3. If there are obligations to dismantle, remove, or restore the asset when it is retired, an estimate of these costs is also included in the cost of the long-lived asset. We will assume that these costs, known as **asset retirement costs**, are equal to zero in the examples in this text. (Accounting for these costs will be covered in more advanced courses.)

All of the above-mentioned expenditures are **capitalized** (recorded as property, plant, and equipment), rather than expensed, if it is probable that the company will receive an economic benefit in the future from the asset. Determining which costs to include in a long-lived asset account and which costs not to include is very important. Costs that benefit only the current period are expensed. Such costs are called **operating expenditures**. Costs that benefit future periods are included in a long-lived asset account. These costs are called **capital expenditures**.

Consider the following example:

JJ & Company purchased equipment for its factory; the equipment is expected to be used for 10 years. The following costs were incurred:

Description of expenditure	Amount	Expenditure type
Purchase price	$100,000	Capital expenditure
Shipping	8,000	Capital expenditure
Insurance while the equipment was in transit	1,200	Capital expenditure
Installation in factory	3,500	Capital expenditure
Total	$112,700	

In the above example, JJ & Company would record each of the expenditures as an addition to the Equipment account. The total cost of the equipment is $112,700. All of these costs were necessary to get the equipment to its required location and ready for use.

Continuing with this example, assume that JJ & Company begins using the equipment on July 1. Over the next six months, the following expenditures are made related to the equipment:

Description of expenditure	Amount	Expenditure type
Oil and lubrication	$ 160	Operating expenditure
Repairs required because of normal wear and tear	1,600	Operating expenditure
Total	$1,760	

The above costs are incurred after the equipment is put into use and will only benefit the current period, so JJ & Company would record these costs as Repairs Expense.

However, it is also important to note that companies will expense, rather than capitalize, low-cost long-lived assets. For example, JJ & Company might purchase several stools for its employees while they are working in the factory. The stools cost $500 in total. JJ & Company has a policy that costs incurred below $1,000 for long-lived assets will be recognized as operating expenditures and included in an expense account rather than an asset account. This is an application of a concept known as materiality, which you will learn more about in Chapter 11. It allows companies to immediately record immaterial expenditures as an expense.

Subsequent to acquisition, the same distinction exists between capital and operating expenditures. For example, once the asset is in use, having an insurance policy benefits only the current period and is treated as an expense. But major expenditures that are incurred once the asset is in use that **increase the life of the asset or its productivity are capitalized**. We will discuss expenditures subsequent to acquisition in more depth later in the chapter.

Property, plant, and equipment are often subdivided into four classes:

1. **Land**, such as a building site
2. **Land improvements**, such as driveways, parking lots, fences, and underground sprinkler systems
3. **Buildings**, such as stores, offices, factories, and warehouses
4. **Equipment**, such as store checkout counters, cash registers, office furniture, computer equipment, factory equipment, and delivery equipment

Determining the cost of each of the major classes of property, plant, and equipment is explained in the following sections.

Land

The cost of land includes (1) the purchase price, (2) closing costs such as surveying and legal fees, and (3) the costs of preparing the land for its intended use, such as the removal of old buildings, clearing, draining, filling, and grading. All of these costs (less any proceeds from salvaged materials) are debited to the Land account.

To illustrate, assume that JJ & Company purchases property for $200,000 cash. An old warehouse stood on the property and was removed at a cost of $7,500. Parts of the old warehouse are salvaged and sold for $1,500 cash. Additional expenditures include legal fees of $3,000. The cost of the land is $209,000, calculated as follows:

Land	
Cash price of property	$200,000
Cost of removing warehouse	7,500
Proceeds from salvaged material	(1,500)
Legal fees	3,000
Cost of land	$209,000

When recording the acquisition, Land is debited for $209,000 and Cash is credited for $209,000 (assuming the costs were paid in cash). Land is a unique long-lived asset. Its cost is not depreciated because land has an unlimited useful life.

Land Improvements

Land improvements are structural additions made to land, such as driveways, sidewalks, fences, and parking lots. Land improvements, unlike land, decline in service potential over time, and require maintenance and replacement. Because of this, land improvements are recorded separately from land and are depreciated over their useful lives.

When classifying costs, **it is important to remember that one-time costs required for getting the land ready to use are always charged to the Land account, not the Land Improvements account.**

Buildings

All costs that are directly related to the purchase or construction of a building are debited to the Buildings account. When a building is purchased, these costs include the purchase price and closing costs (such as legal fees). The costs of making a building ready to be used as intended can include expenditures for remodelling, and for replacing or repairing the roof, floors, electrical wiring, and plumbing. These costs are also debited to Buildings. **As noted above, any costs incurred to remove or demolish existing buildings are debited to the Land account and should not be included in the Building account.**

When a new building is built, its cost includes the contract price plus payments for architects' fees, building permits, and excavation costs. The interest costs of financing the construction project are also included in the asset's cost but only the interest costs incurred during the construction phase. In these circumstances, interest costs are considered to be as necessary as materials and labour are. When the building is ready for use, interest costs are once again included in Interest Expense.

Equipment

The "equipment" classification is a broad one that can include delivery equipment, office equipment, computers, machinery, vehicles, furniture and fixtures, and other similar assets. The cost of these assets includes the purchase price; freight charges and insurance during transit paid by the purchaser; and the costs of assembling, installing, and testing the equipment. These costs are treated as capital expenditures because they benefit future periods and are necessary to bring the asset to its required location and make it ready for use.

Annual costs such as motor vehicle licences and insurance on company trucks and cars are treated as operating expenditures because they are recurring expenditures that do not benefit future periods.

To illustrate, assume that JJ & Company purchases a used delivery truck on January 2, 2017, for $24,500 cash. Related expenditures include painting and lettering, $500; a motor vehicle licence, $80; and a one-year insurance policy, $2,600. The cost of the delivery truck is $25,000, calculated as follows:

Delivery Truck	
Cash price	$24,500
Painting and lettering	500
Cost of delivery truck	$25,000

The cost of the motor vehicle licence is recorded as an expense and the cost of the insurance policy is recorded as a prepaid asset. The entry to record the purchase of the truck and related expenditures, assuming they were all paid for in cash, is as follows:

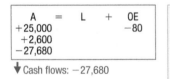

A	=	L	+	OE
+25,000				−80
+2,600				
−27,680				

↓ Cash flows: −27,680

Jan. 2	Vehicles	25,000	
	Licence Expense	80	
	Prepaid Insurance	2,600	
	Cash		27,680
	To record purchase of delivery truck and related expenditures.		

Allocating Cost to Multiple Assets or Significant Components

Alternative terminology A basket purchase is also known as a *lump sum purchase.*

Multiple Assets. Property, plant, and equipment are often purchased together for a single price. This is known as a **basket purchase.** Each asset will have a different useful life (number of years the asset is expected to provide benefit). We need to know the cost of each individual asset in order to journalize the purchase, and later calculate the depreciation of each asset. When a basket purchase occurs, we determine individual asset costs by allocating the total price paid for the group of assets to each individual asset based on its relative fair value.

To illustrate, assume Paradise Manufacturing Company purchased land, a building, and some equipment on July 31 for $400,000 cash. The land was appraised at $135,000, the building at $270,000, and the equipment at $45,000. The $400,000 cost should be allocated based on fair values (i.e., appraised values), as shown in Illustration 9-1.

▶ILLUSTRATION 9-1
Allocating cost in a basket purchase

Asset	Appraised Value (Fair Value)	Percent of Total Fair Value			Total Purchase Price		Cost of Each Asset
Land	$135,000	30%	($135,000 ÷ $450,000)	×	$400,000	=	$120,000
Building	270,000	60%	($270,000 ÷ $450,000)	×	$400,000	=	240,000
Equipment	45,000	10%	($ 45,000 ÷ $450,000)	×	$400,000	=	40,000
Totals	$450,000	100%					$400,000

The journal entry to record this purchase is as follows:

July 31	Land	120,000	
	Building	240,000	
	Equipment	40,000	
	Cash		400,000
	To record purchase of land, building, and equipment.		

A	=	L	+	OE
+120,000				
+240,000				
+40,000				
−400,000				

▼ Cash flows: −400,000

Significant Components. When an item of property, plant, and equipment includes individual components that have different useful lives, the cost of the item should be allocated to each of its significant components. This allows each component to be depreciated separately over the different useful lives or possibly by using different depreciation methods. For example, an aircraft and its engine may need to be treated as separate depreciable assets if they have different useful lives.

Further discussion of calculating depreciation for the different component parts of an asset will be covered in advanced accounting courses. For simplicity, we will assume in this text that all of the components of a depreciable asset have the same useful life, and we will depreciate assets as a whole.

BEFORE YOU GO ON...DO IT   1   **Cost of Plant Assets**

Assume that factory equipment is purchased on November 6 for $10,000 cash and a $40,000 note payable. Related cash expenditures include insurance during shipping, $500; the annual insurance policy, $750; and installation and testing, $1,000. (a) What is the cost of the equipment? (b) Record these expenditures.

Solution

Factory Equipment

Purchase price	$50,000
Insurance during shipping	500
Installation and testing	1,000
Cost of equipment	$51,500

The entry to record the purchase and related expenditures is:

Nov. 6	Equipment	51,500	
	Prepaid Insurance	750	
	Cash ($10,000 + $500 + $750 + $1,000)		12,250
	Note Payable		40,000
	To record purchase of factory equipment and related expenditures.		

Action Plan
• Capitalize expenditures that are made to get the equipment ready for its intended use.
• Expense operating expenditures that benefit only the current period, or are recurring costs.

Related exercise material: BE9–1, BE9–2, BE9–3, BE9–4, E9–1, E9–2, E9–3, and E9–12.

LEARNING OBJECTIVE ❷

> Apply depreciation methods to property, plant, and equipment.

DEPRECIATION

As we learned in Chapter 3, depreciation is the systematic allocation of the cost of a long-lived asset, such as property, plant, and equipment, over the asset's useful life. The cost is allocated to expense over the asset's useful life to recognize the cost that has been used up (the expense) during the period, and report the unused cost (the asset) at the end of the period.

You will recall that depreciation is recorded through an adjusting journal entry that debits Depreciation Expense and credits Accumulated Depreciation. Depreciation Expense is an operating expense on the income statement. Accumulated Depreciation appears on the balance sheet as a contra account to the related long-lived asset account. The resulting balance, cost less accumulated depreciation, is the carrying amount of the depreciable asset, as defined in Chapter 4.

It is important to understand that **depreciation is a process of cost allocation, not a process of determining an asset's real value**. Illustration 9-2 shows this. Under the cost model, an increase in an asset's fair value is not relevant because property, plant, and equipment are not for resale. As a result, the carrying amount of property, plant, or equipment (cost less accumulated depreciation) may be very different from its fair value.

Alternative terminology An asset's *carrying amount* is also called its *carrying value, book value,* or *net book value.*

▶ **ILLUSTRATION** 9-2
Depreciation as an allocation concept

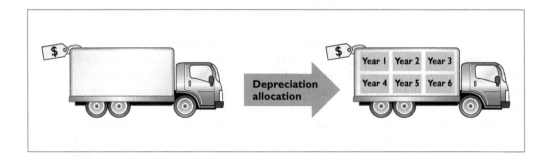

It is also important to understand that **depreciation neither uses up nor provides cash to replace the asset**. The balance in Accumulated Depreciation only represents the total amount of the asset's cost that has been allocated to expense so far. It is not a cash fund. Cash is neither increased nor decreased by the adjusting entry to record depreciation.

During a depreciable asset's useful life, its revenue-producing ability declines because of physical factors such as wear and tear, and economic factors such as obsolescence. For example, a company may replace a truck because it is physically worn out. On the other hand, companies replace computers long before they are physically worn out because improvements in hardware and software have made the old computers obsolete.

Factors in Calculating Depreciation

In Chapter 3, we learned that depreciation expense was calculated by dividing the cost of a depreciable asset by its useful life. At that time, we assumed the asset's residual value was zero. In this chapter, we will now include a residual value when calculating depreciation. Consequently, there are now three factors that affect the calculation of depreciation: (1) cost, (2) useful life, and (3) residual value.

Cost. The factors that affect the cost of a depreciable asset were explained earlier in this chapter. Remember that the cost of property, plant, and equipment includes the purchase price plus all costs necessary to get the asset ready for use. Cost includes an initial estimate of the retirement costs, if there are any.

Useful Life. **Useful life** is either (1) the period of time over which an asset is expected to be available for use or (2) the number of units of production (such as machine hours) or units of output that are expected to be obtained from an asset. Useful life is an estimate based on such factors as the asset's intended use, its expected need for repair and maintenance, and how vulnerable it is to wearing out or becoming obsolete. The company's past experience with similar assets often helps in estimating the expected useful life. Red River College, in the feature story, uses a five- to 10-year useful life for most of its equipment, but only three years for computers because computer equipment can quickly become technologically obsolete.

Residual Value. **Residual value** is the estimated amount that a company would obtain from disposing of the asset at the end of its useful life. Residual value is not depreciated, because the amount is expected to be recovered at the end of the asset's useful life.

Alternative terminology Residual value is sometimes called *salvage value*.

Illustration 9-3 summarizes these three factors in calculating depreciation.

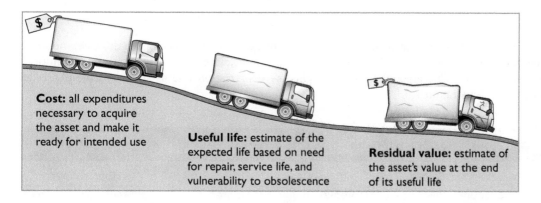

▶ILLUSTRATION 9-3
Three factors in
calculating depreciation

Cost: all expenditures necessary to acquire the asset and make it ready for intended use

Useful life: estimate of the expected life based on need for repair, service life, and vulnerability to obsolescence

Residual value: estimate of the asset's value at the end of its useful life

The difference between an asset's cost and its residual value is called the **depreciable amount**, which is the total amount to be depreciated over the useful life. As we learned in Chapter 3, companies reporting under ASPE may use the term "amortization" instead of "depreciation." Because of this, the depreciable amount is often called the "amortizable cost."

Depreciation Methods

Depreciation is generally calculated using one of the following methods:

1. Straight-line
2. Diminishing-balance
3. Units-of-production

The straight-line method of depreciation is used by the majority of publicly traded companies. But how do companies decide which of the three depreciation methods to use? Management must choose the method that best matches the estimated pattern in which the asset's future economic benefits are expected to be consumed. The depreciation method must be reviewed at least once a year. If the expected pattern of consumption of the future economic benefits has changed, the depreciation method must be changed, and the change disclosed in the notes to the financial statements.

To learn how to calculate the three depreciation methods and to compare them, we will use the following data for the small delivery truck bought by JJ & Company on January 2, 2017:

Cost (as shown earlier in the chapter)	$25,000
Estimated residual value	$2,000
Estimated useful life (in years)	5
Estimated useful life (in kilometres)	200,000

Straight-Line. The straight-line method was first defined in Chapter 3. We will define it again here, this time including the impact of a residual value on the calculation. The **straight-line method** of calculating depreciation has two steps. First, residual value is deducted from the asset's cost to determine an asset's depreciable amount. Second, the depreciable amount is divided by the asset's useful life to calculate the annual depreciation expense.

The depreciation expense will be the same for each year of the asset's useful life if the cost, the useful life, and the residual value do not change. The calculation of depreciation expense in the first year for JJ & Company's delivery truck is shown in Illustration 9-4.

▶ILLUSTRATION **9-4**
Formula for straight-line method

Alternatively, we can calculate an annual percentage rate of depreciation. In this case, the straight-line depreciation rate is 20% (100% ÷ 5 years). The depreciation expense is calculated by multiplying the asset's depreciable amount by the straight-line depreciation rate as shown in the depreciation schedule in Illustration 9-5.

▶ILLUSTRATION **9-5**
Straight-line depreciation schedule

Carrying amount = Cost − Accumulated depreciation

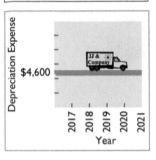

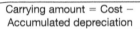

| | | | | | End of Year | |
Year	Depreciable Amount	×	Depreciation Rate	=	Depreciation Expense	Accumulated Depreciation	Carrying Amount
							$25,000
2017	$23,000		20%		$ 4,600	$ 4,600	20,400
2018	23,000		20%		4,600	9,200	15,800
2019	23,000		20%		4,600	13,800	11,200
2020	23,000		20%		4,600	18,400	6,600
2021	23,000		20%		4,600	23,000	2,000
					$23,000		

JJ & COMPANY Straight-Line Depreciation Schedule

Note that the depreciation expense of $4,600 is the same each year. Also note that the column total for depreciation expense is equal to the asset's depreciable amount, and that the carrying amount at the end of the useful life is equal to the estimated $2,000 residual value. The journal entry to record depreciation expense in 2017 is:

A = L + OE
−4,600   −4,600

Cash flows: no effect

2017			
Dec. 31	Depreciation Expense	4,600	
	Accumulated Depreciation—Vehicles		4,600
	To record depreciation expense for delivery truck.		

Straight-line is the most appropriate method of depreciation when the asset is used quite uniformly throughout its useful life. Examples of assets that deliver their benefit primarily as a function of time include office furniture and fixtures, buildings, warehouses, and garages for motor vehicles. Red River College, in the feature story, uses straight-line depreciation for its buildings.

Alternative terminology The diminishing-balance method is sometimes called the *declining-balance method.*

Diminishing-Balance. The **diminishing-balance method** produces a decreasing annual depreciation expense over the asset's useful life. This method is so named because the periodic depreciation is based on a diminishing carrying amount (cost less accumulated depreciation) of the asset. Annual depreciation expense is calculated by multiplying the carrying amount at the beginning of the year by the depreciation rate. **The depreciation rate remains constant from year to year, but the rate is applied to a carrying amount that declines each year.**

The carrying amount for the first year is the asset's cost, because the balance in Accumulated Depreciation at the beginning of the asset's useful life is zero. In the following years, the carrying amount is the difference between the cost and the accumulated depreciation at the beginning of the year. Unlike the other depreciation methods, the diminishing-balance method does not use a depreciable amount in calculating annual depreciation expense. **Residual value is not included in the calculation of either the depreciation rate or the depreciation expense.** Residual value does, however, limit the total depreciation that can be recorded. Depreciation expense entries stop when the asset's carrying amount equals its estimated residual value.

A common diminishing-balance method is double the straight-line rate and is referred to as the **double diminishing-balance method.** Other variations include one time (single) and even three times (triple). In this textbook, we will use the double diminishing-balance method.

Helpful hint The straight-line rate is determined by dividing 100% by the estimated useful life. In JJ & Company's case, it is 100% ÷ 5 = 20%.

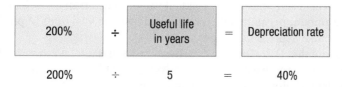

If JJ & Company uses the double diminishing-balance method, the depreciation rate is 40%, as shown in Illustration 9-6.

ILLUSTRATION 9-6
Formula for depreciation rate—double-diminishing-balance method

200%	÷	Useful life in years	=	Depreciation rate
200%	÷	5	=	40%

The rate can also be determined by multiplying the straight-line rate by 2. Illustration 9-7 shows the calculation of depreciation on the delivery truck for the first year.

ILLUSTRATION 9-7
Formula for double diminishing-balance method

Carrying Amount at Beginning of Year	×	Straight-Line Depreciation Rate × 2	=	Annual Depreciation Expense
$25,000	×	40%	=	$10,000

The depreciation schedule under this method is given in Illustration 9-8.

ILLUSTRATION 9-8
Double diminishing-balance depreciation schedule

JJ & COMPANY
Double Diminishing-Balance Depreciation Schedule

						End of Year	
Year	**Carrying Amount Beginning Year**	×	**Depreciation Rate**	=	**Depreciation Expense**	**Accumulated Depreciation**	**Carrying Amount**
							$25,000
2017	$25,000		40%		**$10,000**	$10,000	15,000
2018	15,000		40%		**6,000**	16,000	9,000
2019	9,000		40%		**3,600**	19,600	5,400
2020	5,400		40%		**2,160**	21,760	3,240
2021	3,240		40%		**1,240***	23,000	2,000
					$23,000		

*The calculation of $1,296 ($3,240 × 40%) is adjusted to $1,240 so that the carrying amount will equal the residual value.

Carrying amount = Cost − Accumulated depreciation to date

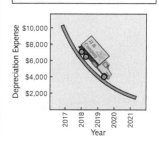

Returning to Illustration 9-8, you can see that the delivery truck is 70% depreciated ($16,000 ÷ $23,000) at the end of the second year. Under the straight-line method, it would be 40% depreciated ($9,200 ÷ $23,000) at that same time. Because the diminishing-balance method produces higher depreciation expense in the early years than in the later years, it is considered an *accelerated* depreciation method. In later years, its depreciation expense will be less than the straight-line depreciation expense. Regardless of the method that is used, the total amount of depreciation over the life of the delivery truck is $23,000—the depreciable amount. The journal entry to record depreciation Expense in 2017 is:

2017 Dec. 31	Depreciation Expense	10,000	
	Accumulated Depreciation—Vehicles		10,000
	To record depreciation expense for delivery truck.		

A	=	L	+	OE
−10,000				−10,000

Cash flows: no effect

The diminishing-balance method, or another accelerated method, should be used if the company receives more economic benefit in the early years of the asset's useful life than in the later years. Examples of assets that deliver more economic benefit in the early years of the asset's useful life are motor vehicles and computer systems.

Alternative terminology The units-of-production method is often called the *units-of-activity method*.

Units-of-Production. Useful life can be expressed in ways other than time. In the **units-of-production method**, useful life is either the estimated total units of production or total expected use of the asset, not the number of years that the asset is expected to be used. The units-of-production method is ideal for equipment whose activity can be measured in units of output, such as kilometres driven or hours in use. The units-of-production method is generally not suitable for buildings or furniture, because depreciation of these assets is more a result of time than of use.

In this method, the total units of production for the entire useful life are estimated. This amount is divided into the depreciable amount (cost – residual value) to determine the depreciable amount per unit. The depreciable amount per unit is then multiplied by the actual units of production during the year to calculate the annual depreciation expense.

To illustrate, assume that JJ & Company's delivery truck has a total estimated life of 200,000 km and that in the first year of the truck's use it is driven 30,000 km. Illustration 9-9 shows the steps involved to calculate depreciation expense in the first year.

▶ **ILLUSTRATION 9-9**
Formula for units-of-production method

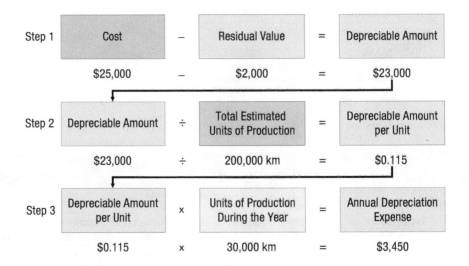

Illustration 9-10 shows the units-of-production depreciation schedule, using assumed units of production (kilometres driven) for the later years.

▶ **ILLUSTRATION 9-10**
Units-of-production depreciation schedule

Carrying amount = Cost – Accumulated depreciation to date

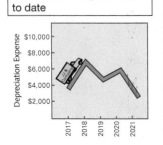

| | | | | | End of Year | |
| **JJ & COMPANY** Units-of-Production Depreciation Schedule | | | | | | |
Year	Units of Production	×	Depreciation Cost/Unit	= Depreciation Expense	Accumulated Depreciation	Carrying Amount
						$25,000
2017	30,000		$0.115	$ 3,450	$ 3,450	21,550
2018	60,000		$0.115	6,900	10,350	14,650
2019	40,000		$0.115	4,600	14,950	10,050
2020	50,000		$0.115	5,750	20,700	4,300
2021	20,000		$0.115	2,300	23,000	2,000
	200,000			$23,000		

In the example in Illustration 9-10, the total actual units of production equals the original estimated total units of production of 200,000 km. But in most real-life situations, the total actual units of production do not exactly equal the total estimated units of production. This means that the final year's depreciation will have to be adjusted—as we saw in the double diminishing-balance method in Illustration 9-8—so that the ending carrying amount is equal to the estimated residual value. The journal entry to record depreciation expense in 2017 is:

2017			
Dec. 31	Depreciation Expense	3,450	
	Accumulated Depreciation—Vehicles		3,450
	To record depreciation expense for delivery truck.		

A	=	L	+	OE
−3,450				−3,450

Cash flows: no effect

The units-of-production method is used for assets whose activity can be measured in units of output. But it can only be used if it is possible to make a reasonable estimate of total activity. Later in this chapter, we will see that this method is widely used to depreciate natural resources. The units-of-production method results in the best matching of expenses with revenues when the asset's productivity varies significantly from one period to another.

Comparison of Depreciation Methods

Illustration 9-11 represents a comparison of annual and total depreciation expense for JJ & Company under each of the three depreciation methods. In addition, if we assume for simplicity that profit before deducting depreciation expense is $50,000 for each of the five years, we can clearly see the impact that the choice of method has on profit.

	Straight-Line		Double Diminishing-Balance		Units-of-Production	
Year	Depreciation Expense	Profit	Depreciation Expense	Profit	Depreciation Expense	Profit
2017	$ 4,600	$ 45,400	$10,000	$ 40,000	$ 3,450	$ 46,550
2018	4,600	45,400	6,000	44,000	6,900	43,100
2019	4,600	45,400	3,600	46,400	4,600	45,400
2020	4,600	45,400	2,160	47,840	5,750	44,250
2021	4,600	45,400	1,240	48,760	2,300	47,700
	$23,000	$227,000	$23,000	$227,000	$23,000	$227,000

▶ILLUSTRATION 9-11
Comparison of depreciation methods

Recall that straight-line depreciation results in the same amount of depreciation expense and therefore profit each year. Diminishing-balance depreciation results in a higher depreciation expense in early years, and therefore lower profit, and a lower depreciation expense and higher profit in later years. Results with the units-of-production method vary, depending on how much the asset is used each year. While the depreciation expense and profit will be different each year for each method, *total* depreciation expense and *total* profit after the five-year period are the same for all three methods.

The balance sheet is also affected by the choice of depreciation method because accumulated depreciation is increased by depreciation expense and owner's equity is increased by profit. There is no impact on cash flow because depreciation does not involve cash.

Partial Period Depreciation

All of the examples so far portray a situation where a property, plant, and equipment asset is purchased on the first day of a fiscal period. Depreciation expense is then calculated for an entire year. But what happens when an asset is purchased part way through the fiscal period? In that case, depending on the depreciation method used, it is necessary to **pro-rate the annual depreciation for the part of the year that the asset was used**. Note that depreciation is normally rounded to the nearest month. Since depreciation is an estimate, calculating it to the nearest day gives a false sense of accuracy.

To keep things simple, some companies establish a policy for partial-period depreciation rather than calculating depreciation monthly. Some other common policies that companies use are:

- Full first year policy: This method records a full year of depreciation expense in the year of acquisition regardless of what point in the year the asset was purchased and put into use and none in the final year of the asset's life.
- Half-year policy: This method records a half year of depreciation expense in the year of acquisition and a half year of depreciation expense in the final year of the asset's life.

Whatever policy is chosen for partial-year depreciation, the impact is not significant in the long run if the policy is used consistently.

To illustrate the techniques used for partial period depreciation, we return to JJ & Company and the purchase of the small delivery truck. The relevant factors for depreciation calculations are reproduced below. This time, let's assume that the truck was purchased on April 1, 2017, and JJ & Company uses the nearest month policy for partial period depreciation calculations.

Cost	$25,000
Estimated residual value	$2,000
Estimated useful life (in years)	5
Estimated useful life (in kilometres)	200,000

Straight-Line Depreciation for a Partial Year. If the delivery truck was ready to be used on April 1, 2017, the truck would be depreciated for nine months in 2017 (April through December). The depreciation for 2017 would be $3,450 ($23,000 × 20% × $\frac{9}{12}$).

The new depreciation schedule is shown in Illustration 9-12.

▶ILLUSTRATION 9-12
Straight-line
depreciation schedule—
partial year

JJ & COMPANY
Straight-Line Depreciation Schedule

Year	Depreciable Amount	×	Depreciation Rate	×	Fraction of a year	=	Depreciation Expense	End of Year Accumulated Depreciation	End of Year Carrying Amount
2017	$23,000	×	20.00%	×	$\frac{9}{12}$	=	$ 3,450	$ 3,450	$21,550
2018	23,000		20.00%		-		4,600	8,050	16,950
2019	23,000		20.00%		-		4,600	12,650	12,350
2020	23,000		20.00%		-		4,600	17,250	7,750
2021	23,000		20.00%				4,600	21,850	3,150
2022	23,000		20.00%		$\frac{3}{12}$		1,150	23,000	2,000
							23,000		

Note that when a partial year is used in the year of acquisition of the asset, a partial year is also used in the final year of the asset's life. This ensures that five full years of depreciation are recorded and the carrying amount is equal to the residual value at the end of the asset's life. The journal entry to record depreciation expense in 2017 would include a debit to Depreciation Expense for $3,450 and a credit to Accumulated Depreciation—Vehicles for $3,450.

Diminishing-Balance Depreciation for a Partial Year. Similar to straight-line, when using diminishing-balance it is also necessary to pro-rate depreciation expense in the year of acquisition.

If JJ & Company uses double diminishing-balance depreciation, depreciation expense in 2017 would be $7,500 ($25,000 × 40% × $\frac{9}{12}$) if depreciation is calculated monthly. The carrying amount for calculating depreciation in 2018 would then become $17,500 ($25,000 − $7,500) and so on as shown in Illustration 9-13.

	Carrying Amount Beginning Year		Depreciation Rate		Fraction of a Year		Depreciation Expense	End of Year	
								Accumulated Depreciation	Carrying Amount
Year		×		×		=			
2017	$25,000		40%		9/12		$ 7,500	$ 7,500	$17,500
2018	17,500		40%				7,000	14,500	10,500
2019	10,500		40%				4,200	18,700	6,300
2020	6,300		40%				2,520	21,220	3,780
2021	3,780		40%				1,512	22,732	2,268
2022	2,268		40%		3/12		268*	23,000	2,000
							$23,000		

JJ & COMPANY
Double Diminishing-Balance Depreciation Schedule

*The calculation of $907 ($2,268 × 40%) is adjusted to $268 so that the carrying amount will equal the residual value.

▸ILLUSTRATION 9-13
Double diminishing-balance depreciation schedule—partial year

The journal entry to record depreciation expense in 2017 would include a debit to Depreciation Expense for $7,500 and a credit to Accumulated Depreciation—Vehicles for $7,500.

Units-of-Production Depreciation in a Partial Year. This method is easy to apply when assets are purchased during the year. The actual units of production already show how much the asset was used during the year. Therefore, the depreciation calculations do not need to be adjusted for partial periods as is done in the straight-line and diminishing-balance methods.

ACCOUNTING IN ACTION
BUSINESS INSIGHT

Why does Morris Formal Wear use the units-of-production method for its tuxedos? The reason is that the Ottawa-based family business wants to track wear and tear on each of its 5,200 tuxedos individually. Each tuxedo has its own bar code. When a tux is rented, a clerk runs its code across an electronic scanner. At year end, the computer adds up the total rentals for each of the tuxedos, then divides this number by expected total use to calculate the rate. For instance, on a two-button black tux, Morris expects a life of 30 rentals. In one year, the tux was rented 13 times. The depreciation rate for that period was 43% (13 ÷ 30) of the depreciable cost.

©istockphoto.com/DNY59

 Is the units-of-production method the best depreciation method for Morris Formal Wear to use for its tuxedos or would you recommend another method?

Depreciation and Income Tax

The Canada Revenue Agency (CRA) prescribes the amount of depreciation that companies can deduct from gross revenues in order to determine taxable income. These prescribed amounts (determined using prescribed rates) are generally different from accounting depreciation methods. The CRA refers to these amounts as **capital cost allowance (CCA)**. Accounting for and determining income taxes will be covered in more advanced courses. For now, be aware that you may see a company deduct depreciation on its income statement, which is required by generally accepted accounting principles, and this amount will generally be different from the amount deducted for income tax purposes.

Helpful hint Depreciation for accounting purposes is usually different from depreciation for income tax purposes.

Action Plan

- Under straight-line depreciation, annual depreciation expense is equal to the depreciable amount (cost less residual value) divided by the estimated useful life.
- Under double diminishing-balance depreciation, annual depreciation expense is equal to double the straight-line rate of depreciation multiplied by the asset's carrying amount at the beginning of the year. Residual values are not used in this method.
- Under the straight-line and diminishing-balance methods, the annual depreciation expense must be pro-rated if the asset is purchased during the year.
- Under units-of-production depreciation, the depreciable amount per unit is equal to the total depreciable amount divided by the total estimated units of production. The annual depreciation expense is equal to the depreciable amount per unit times the actual usage in each year.

BEFORE YOU GO ON...DO IT **2**   **Methods of Depreciation**

On October 1, 2017, Iron Mountain Ski Company purchases a new snow grooming machine for $52,000. The machine is estimated to have a five-year useful life and a $4,000 residual value. It is also estimated to have a total useful life of 6,000 hours. It is used 1,000 hours in the year ended December 31, 2017, and 1,300 hours in the year ended December 31, 2018. How much depreciation expense should Iron Mountain Ski record in each of 2017 and 2018 under each depreciation method: (a) straight-line, (b) double diminishing-balance, and (c) units-of-production?

Solution

	2017	2018
Straight-line	$2,400	$ 9,600
Double diminishing-balance	5,200	18,720
Units-of-production	8,000	10,400

(a) Straight-line: ($52,000 − $4,000) ÷ 5 years = $9,600 per year; 2017: $9,600 × $^{3}/_{12}$ = $2,400
(b) Double diminishing-balance: 200% ÷ 5 years = 40% double diminishing-balance rate; 2017: $52,000 × 40% × $^{3}/_{12}$ = $5,200
   2018: ($52,000 − $5,200) × 40% = $18,720
(c) Units-of-production: ($52,000 − $4,000) ÷ 6,000 hours = $8.00 per hour
   2017: 1,000 × $8.00 × $8,000
   2018: 1,300 × $8.00 = $10,400

Related exercise material: BE9–5, BE9–6, BE9–7, BE9–8, BE9–9, E9–2, E9–3, E9–4, E9–5, and E9–12.

LEARNING OBJECTIVE **3**   Explain the factors that cause changes in periodic depreciation and calculate revised depreciation for property, plant, and equipment.

REVISING PERIODIC DEPRECIATION

During the useful life of a long-lived asset, the annual depreciation expense needs to be revised if there are changes to the three factors that affect the calculation of depreciation: the asset's cost, useful life, or residual value. Thus, depreciation needs to be revised if there are

1. capital expenditures during the asset's useful life,
2. impairments in the value of an asset,
3. changes in the appropriate depreciation method, or in the asset's estimated useful life or residual value,
4. changes in the asset's fair value when using the revaluation model, and/or.

In the following sections, we discuss each of these items and then show how to revise depreciation calculations.

Capital Expenditures During Useful Life

Earlier in the chapter, we learned that companies can have both operating and capital expenditures when a long-lived asset is purchased. Similarly, during the useful life of a long-lived asset, a company may incur costs for ordinary repairs, or for additions or improvements.

Ordinary repairs are costs to *maintain* the asset's operating efficiency and expected productive life. Doing motor tune-ups and oil changes, repainting a building, or replacing worn-out gears on equipment are examples of ordinary repairs. These costs are frequently fairly small amounts that occur regularly. They may also be larger, infrequent amounts, but if they simply restore an asset to its prior condition, they are considered an ordinary repair. Such repairs are debited to Repairs Expense as they occur. Ordinary repairs are operating expenditures.

Additions and improvements are costs that are incurred to *increase* the asset's operating efficiency, productive capacity, or expected useful life. These costs are usually large and happen less often. Additions and improvements that add to the future cash flows associated with that asset are not expensed as they occur—they are capitalized. As capital expenditures, they are generally debited to the appropriate property, plant, or equipment account. The capital expenditure will be depreciated over the remaining life of the original structure or the useful life of the addition. Additions and improvements can also increase the useful life of the original structure. The depreciation calculations need to be revised when a company makes an addition or improvement.

Impairments

As noted earlier in the chapter, under the cost model, the carrying amount of property, plant, and equipment is cost less any accumulated depreciation since its acquisition. And, as already discussed, the carrying amount of property, plant, and equipment is rarely the same as its fair value. Remember that the fair value is normally not relevant since property, plant, and equipment are not purchased for resale, but rather for use in operations over the long term.

While it is accepted that long-lived assets such as property, plant, and equipment may be under-valued on the balance sheet, it is not appropriate if property, plant, and equipment are overvalued. Property, plant, and equipment are considered impaired if the asset's carrying amount exceeds its recoverable amount. The recoverable amount is the greater of the asset's fair value less costs to sell or its value in use, which is determined by discounting future estimated cash flows. When an asset is impaired, an impairment loss is recorded that is the amount by which the asset's carrying amount exceeds its recoverable amount. The rules for determining if an asset is impaired are somewhat differ-ent under ASPE and IFRS. While the details of these differences are left to an intermediate accounting course, it should be noted that under ASPE impairments are recorded less often.

Companies are required to determine on a regular basis if there is any indication of impairment. Some factors that would indicate an impairment of an asset include:

- Obsolescence or physical damage of the asset.
- Equipment used in the manufacture of a product where there is dramatically reduced demand or the market has become highly competitive.
- Bankruptcy of a supplier of replacement parts for equipment.

To illustrate an impairment loss on a long-lived asset, assume that on December 31, Piniwa Company reviews its equipment for possible impairment. The equipment has a cost of $800,000 and accumulated depreciation of $200,000. The equipment's recoverable amount is currently $500,000. The amount of the impairment loss is determined by comparing the asset's carrying amount with its recoverable amount as follows:

Carrying amount ($800,000 − $200,000)	$600,000
Recoverable amount	500,000
Impairment loss	$100,000

The journal entry to record the impairment is:

Dec. 31	Impairment Loss	100,000	
	Accumulated Depreciation—Equipment		100,000
	To record impairment loss on equipment.		

A	=	L	+	OE
−100,000				−100,000

Cash flows: no effect

Assuming that the asset will continue to be used in operations, the impairment loss is reported on the income statement. Often the loss is combined with depreciation expense on the income statement. The Accumulated Depreciation account, not the asset account, is credited for the impairment loss. The Accumulated Depreciation account will increase and the asset's carrying amount will decrease. Recording the loss this way keeps a record of the asset's original cost. Future depreciation calculations will need to be revised because of the reduction in the asset's carrying amount.

IFRS allows the reversal of a previously recorded impairment loss. Under IFRS, at each year end, the company must determine whether or not an impairment loss still exists by measuring the asset's recoverable amount. If this recoverable amount exceeds the current carrying amount, then a reversal is recorded. The **reversal of an asset is limited to the amount required to increase the asset's carrying amount to what it would have been if the impairment loss had not been recorded**. In other words, we cannot simply write the asset up to its recoverable amount—reversals are limited to the impairment loss originally recorded. When an impairment loss is reversed, we simply credit the impairment loss account and debit the accumulated depreciation account. If the asset is depreciable, additional revisions will be made to depreciation calculations. ASPE does not allow an impairment loss to be reversed.

Cost Model Versus Revaluation Model

As mentioned at the start of this chapter, under IFRS, companies can choose to account for their property, plant, and equipment under either the cost model or the revaluation model. We have used the cost model in this chapter because it is used by almost all companies. Only about 3% of companies reporting under IFRS use the revaluation model. The revaluation model is allowed under IFRS mainly because it is particularly useful in countries that experience high rates of inflation or for companies in certain industries, such as investment or real estate companies, where fair values are more relevant than cost. It is not allowed under ASPE.

Under the **revaluation model**, the carrying amount of property, plant, and equipment is its fair value less any accumulated depreciation less any subsequent impairment losses. This model can be applied only to assets whose fair value can be reliably measured. The accounting in the revaluation model will be studied further in more advanced courses. For now, be aware that if this model is used for property, plant, and equipment assets, depreciation will have to be revised regularly.

ACCOUNTING IN ACTION
ETHICS INSIGHT

Finney Container Company has been seeing sales go down for its main product, non-biodegradable plastic cartons. Although some expenses have also declined in line with the reduced revenues, there has been a decrease in profit because some expenses, such as depreciation, have not declined. The company uses the straight-line depreciation method.

The president, Philip Shapiro, recalling his college accounting classes, instructs his controller to lengthen the estimated asset lives used for depreciation calculations in order to reduce annual depreciation expense and increase profit. The president's compensation includes an annual bonus based on the amount of net profit reported in the income statement.

A processing line of automated plastic-extruding equipment that was purchased for $2.9 million in January 2015 was originally estimated to have a useful life between five and nine years. Therefore, the company used the middle of that estimate, or seven years, as the useful life and a residual value of $100,000 to calculate the annual straight-line depreciation for the first two years. However, the president now wants the equipment's estimated useful life to be changed to nine years (total), and to continue using the straight-line method.

The controller is hesitant to make the change, believing it is unethical to increase profit in this way. The president says, "Hey, the useful life is only an estimate. Besides, I've heard that our competition uses a nine-year estimated life on its production equipment. You want the company results to be competitive, don't you? So maybe we were wrong the first time and now we are getting it right. Or you can tell the auditors that we think maybe the equipment will last longer now that we are not using it as much."

 Q **Is the president's requested change unethical? If so, why?**

Changes in Depreciation Method, Estimated Useful Life, or Residual Value

As previously explained, the depreciation method used should be consistent with the pattern in which the asset's future economic benefits are expected to be consumed by the company. The appropriateness of the depreciation method should be reviewed at least annually in case there has been a change in the expected pattern.

Management must also review its estimates of the useful life and residual value of the company's depreciable assets at least at each year end. If wear and tear or obsolescence indicates that the estimates are too low or too high, estimates should be changed. If the depreciation method, estimated useful life, or residual values are changed, this will cause a revision to the depreciation calculations.

Revised Depreciation Calculations

All of the above-discussed factors will result in a revision to the depreciation calculation. In each case, the revision is made for current and future years only. The revision is not made retroactively for past periods. The rationale for this treatment is that the original calculation made in the past was based on the best information available at that time. The revision is based on new information that should affect only current and future periods. In addition, if past periods were often restated, users would feel less confident about financial statements.

Revised depreciation is calculated at the time of the change in estimate. To calculate the new annual depreciation expense, we must first calculate the asset's carrying amount at the time of the change. This is equal to the asset's original cost minus the accumulated depreciation to date, plus any capital expenditures, minus any impairment in value.

To illustrate how to revise depreciation, assume that JJ & Company decides on December 31, 2020—before recording its depreciation for 2020—to extend the original estimated useful life of its truck by one more year (to December 31, 2022) because of its good condition. As a result of using the truck for one additional year, the estimated residual value is expected to decline from its original estimate of $2,000 to $700. Assume that the company has been using straight-line depreciation and determines this is still the appropriate method. Recall that the truck was purchased on January 1, 2017, for $25,000 and originally had an estimated useful life of five years, with annual depreciation expense of $4,600.

The carrying amount at December 31, 2020—before recording depreciation for 2020—is $11,200 [$25,000 − (3 × $4,600)]. This is also the amount shown in Illustration 9-5 as the carrying amount at December 31, 2019. The remaining useful life of three years is calculated by taking the original useful life of five years, subtracting the three years where depreciation has already been recorded, and adding the additional estimated years of useful life—in this case, one year. The new annual depreciation is $3,500, calculated as in Illustration 9-14.

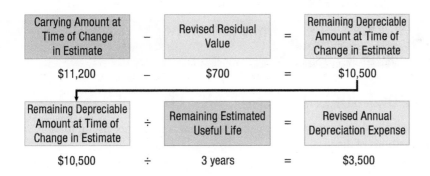

▶ ILLUSTRATION 9-14
Formula for revised straight-line depreciation

As a result of the revision to the truck's estimated useful life and residual value, JJ & Company will record depreciation expense of $3,500 on December 31 of 2020, 2021, and 2022. The company will not go back and change the depreciation for 2017, 2018, and 2019. Accumulated depreciation will now equal $24,300 [($4,600 × 3) + ($3,500 × 3)] at the end of the six-year useful life instead of the $23,000 that was originally calculated.

If the units-of-production depreciation method is used, the calculation is the same as we just saw except that the remaining useful life is expressed as units rather than years. If the diminishing-balance method is used, the revised rate would be applied to the carrying amount at the time of the change in estimate. The rate must be revised because the useful life has changed.

BEFORE YOU GO ON...DO IT **3** | **Revised Depreciation**

Action Plan

- Understand the difference between an operating expenditure (benefits only the current period) and a capital expenditure (benefits future periods).
- To revise annual depreciation, calculate the carrying amount (cost less accumulated depreciation) at the revision date. Note that the cost of any capital expenditure will increase the carrying amount of the asset to be depreciated.
- Subtract any revised residual value from the carrying amount at the time of the change in estimate (plus the capital expenditure in this case) to determine the remaining depreciable amount.
- Allocate the revised depreciable amount over the remaining (not total) useful life.

On August 1, 2002, just after its year end, Fine Furniture Company purchased a building for $500,000. The company used straight-line depreciation to allocate the cost of this building, estimating a residual value of $50,000 and a useful life of 30 years. After 15 years of use, on August 1, 2017, the company was forced to replace the entire roof at a cost of $25,000 cash. The residual value was expected to remain at $50,000 but the total useful life was now expected to increase to 40 years. Prepare journal entries to record (a) depreciation for the year ended July 31, 2017; (b) the cost of the addition on August 1, 2017; and (c) depreciation for the year ended July 31, 2018.

Solution

(a)

July 31, 2017	Depreciation Expense [($500,000 − $50,000) ÷ 30]	15,000	
	Accumulated Depreciation—Building		15,000
	To record annual depreciation expense.		

(b)

Aug. 1, 2017	Building	25,000	
	Cash		25,000
	To record replacement of roof.		

(c)

Cost:	$ 500,000
Less: Accumulated depreciation $15,000 per year × 15 years	225,000
Carrying amount before replacement of roof, August 1, 2017	275,000
Add: Capital expenditure (roof)	25,000
Carrying amount after replacement of roof, August 1, 2017	300,000
Less: Residual value	50,000
Remaining depreciable amount	250,000
Divide by: Remaining useful life (40 − 15)	÷ 25 years
Revised annual depreciation	$ 10,000

July 31, 2018	Depreciation Expense	10,000	
	Accumulated Depreciation—Building		10,000
	To record revised annual depreciation expense.		

Related exercise material: BE9–10, BE9–11, E9–6, E9–7, and E9–8.

LEARNING OBJECTIVE **4** | **Demonstrate how to account for property, plant, and equipment disposals.**

DISPOSAL OF PROPERTY, PLANT, AND EQUIPMENT

▶ **ILLUSTRATION** **9-15**
Methods of property, plant, and equipment disposal

Companies dispose of property, plant, or equipment that is no longer useful to them. Illustration 9-15 shows three methods of disposal.

Retirement
Equipment is scrapped or discarded.

Sale
Equipment is sold to another party.

Exchange
Existing equipment is traded for new equipment.

Steps in Recording Disposals of Property, Plant, and Equipment

Whatever the disposal method, a company must perform the following four steps to record the retirement, sale, or exchange of the property, plant, or equipment.

Step 1: Update Depreciation. Depreciation must be recorded over the entire period of time an asset is available for use. Therefore, if the disposal occurs in the middle of an accounting period, depreciation must be updated for the fraction of the year since the last time adjusting entries were recorded up to the date of disposal.

Step 2: Calculate the Carrying Amount. Calculate the carrying amount at the date of disposal after updating the accumulated depreciation for any partial year depreciation calculated in Step 1 above.

Alternative terminology
Derecognition is a term used under IFRS to describe the removal of a long-lived asset from the accounts after it is disposed of or no longer provides any future benefit.

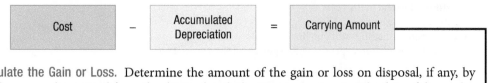

Helpful hint "Proceeds" generally refers to cash or other assets received.

Step 3: Calculate the Gain or Loss. Determine the amount of the gain or loss on disposal, if any, by comparing the proceeds received from the disposal with the carrying amount at the date of disposal.

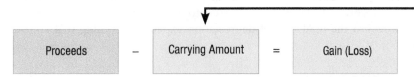

Gains and losses are similar to revenues and expenses except that gains and losses arise from activities that are peripheral to (outside of) a company's normal operating activities. For instance, Burger King's normal operating activities include earning revenue and incurring expenses related to the sale of hamburgers, french fries, salads, etc. If Burger King decided to dispose of a refrigerator, and the amount received is in excess of the carrying amount of the refrigerator, the excess would be recorded as a gain on the income statement.

If the proceeds of the sale are more than the carrying amount of the property, plant, or equipment, there is a gain on disposal. If the proceeds of the sale are less than the carrying amount of the asset sold, there is a loss on disposal.

Step 4: Record the Disposal. The journal entry to record the disposal always involves removing the asset's cost and the accumulated depreciation from the accounts. These are the same amounts used to calculate the carrying amount in Step 2 above. The journal entry may also include recording the proceeds and the gain or loss on disposal. Gains on disposal are recorded as credits because, like revenue, gains increase owner's equity; losses on disposal are recorded as debits because, like expenses, losses decrease owner's equity.

Gains and losses are reported in the operating section of a multiple-step income statement. Why? Recall that depreciation expense is an estimate. A loss results when the annual depreciation expense has not been high enough so that the carrying amount at the date of disposal is equal to the proceeds. Gains are caused because annual depreciation expense has been too high, so the carrying amount at the date of disposal is less than the proceeds. Thus gains and losses are adjustments to depreciation expense and should be recorded in the same section of the income statement.

Retirement of Property, Plant, and Equipment

Instead of being sold or exchanged, some assets are simply retired at the end of their useful lives. For example, some productive assets used in manufacturing may have highly specialized uses and consequently have no market when the company no longer needs the asset. In this case, the asset is retired.

When an asset is retired, there are often no proceeds on disposal. The Accumulated Depreciation account is decreased (debited) for the full amount of depreciation recorded over the life of the asset. The asset account is reduced (credited) for the asset's original cost. Even if the carrying amount equals zero, a journal entry is still required to remove the asset and its related depreciation account from the books, as shown in the following example.

To illustrate the retirement of a piece of property, plant, and equipment, refer to the information below for Andres Enterprises:

- Date of retirement: December 31, 2017
- Equipment cost: $31,200
- Equipment acquisition date: January 2, 2014
- Estimated useful life: 4 years
- Residual value: none
- Depreciation method: straight-line
- Annual depreciation expense: $7,800 per year ($31,200 ÷ 4)

The balance in the Accumulated Depreciation account at Andres' year end, December 31, 2016, was $23,400 ($7,800 × 3). Before recording the disposal, Andres must first record depreciation from the last time it was recorded—December 31, 2016—to the date of disposal—December 31, 2017. The journal entry to record the final year of depreciation expense, assuming that adjusting entries are recorded annually, is:

A	=	L	+	OE
−7,800				−7,800

Cash flows: no effect

2017	Depreciation Expense	7,800	
Dec. 31	Accumulated Depreciation—Equipment		7,800
	To record depreciation expense from last time it was recorded to date of disposal.		

After this journal entry is posted, the Equipment and Accumulated Depreciation accounts appear as follows:

Equipment			
Jan. 2, 2014	31,200		

Accumulated Depreciation—Equipment		
	Dec. 31, 2014	7,800
	Dec. 31, 2015	7,800
	Dec. 31, 2016	7,800
	Balance	23,400
	Dec. 31, 2017	7,800
	Balance	31,200

The equipment is now fully depreciated with a carrying amount of zero (cost of $31,200 − accumulated depreciation of $31,200). As the equipment is being retired, there are zero proceeds, and since the carrying amount is equal to the proceeds, there is no gain or loss on disposal. All that is required is an entry to remove the cost and accumulated depreciation of the equipment, as follows:

A	=	L	+	OE
+31,200				
−31,200				

Cash flows: no effect

2017	Accumulated Depreciation—Equipment	31,200	
Dec. 31	Equipment		31,200
	To record retirement of fully depreciated equipment.		

After this entry is posted, the balance in the Equipment and Accumulated Depreciation—Equipment accounts will be zero.

What happens if a company is still using a fully depreciated asset? In this case, the asset and its accumulated depreciation continue to be reported on the balance sheet, without further depreciation, until the asset is retired. Reporting the asset and related depreciation on the balance sheet informs the reader of the financial statements that the asset is still being used by the company. Once an asset is fully depreciated, even if it is still being used, no additional depreciation should be taken. Accumulated depreciation on a piece of property, plant, and equipment can never be more than the asset's cost.

If a piece of property, plant, and equipment is retired before it is fully depreciated and no proceeds are received, a loss on disposal occurs. Assume that Andres Enterprises retires its equipment on January 2, 2017 instead of December 31, 2017. The loss on disposal is calculated by subtracting the asset's carrying amount from the proceeds that are received. In this case, there are no proceeds and the carrying amount is $7,800 (cost of $31,200 − accumulated depreciation of $23,400), resulting in a loss of $7,800:

Proceeds	−	Carrying amount	=	Gain (Loss)
$0	−	$7,800	=	$(7,800)
		($31,200 − $23,400)		

The entry to record the retirement of equipment in 2017 is as follows:

Jan. 2	Accumulated Depreciation—Equipment	23,400	
	Loss on Disposal	7,800	
	Equipment		31,200
	To record retirement of equipment at a loss.		

A = L + OE
+23,400   −7,800
−31,200

Cash flows: no effect

You should also note that there will never be a gain when an asset is retired with no proceeds. The proceeds would be zero and therefore cannot be greater than the carrying amount of the retired asset.

Sale of Property, Plant, and Equipment

In a disposal by sale, there are proceeds that must be recorded. Both gains and losses on disposal are common when an asset is sold. Only by coincidence will the asset's carrying amount and fair value (the proceeds) be the same when the asset is sold. We will illustrate the sale of furniture at both a gain and a loss in the following sections.

Gain on Disposal. To illustrate a gain, assume that on April 1, 2017, Andres Enterprises sells office furniture for $15,000 cash. The office furniture had originally been purchased on January 2, 2013, at a cost of $60,200. At that time, it was estimated that the furniture would have a residual value of $5,000 and a useful life of five years.

The first step is to update any unrecorded depreciation. Annual depreciation using the straight-line method is $11,040 [($60,200 − $5,000) ÷ 5]. The entry to record the depreciation expense and update accumulated depreciation for the first three months of 2017 is as follows:

2017 Apr. 1	Depreciation Expense ($11,040 × $^3/_{12}$)	2,760	
	Accumulated Depreciation—Furniture		2,760
	To record depreciation expense for the first three months of 2017.		

A = L + OE
−2,760   −2,760

Cash flows: no effect

After this journal entry is posted, the Furniture and Accumulated Depreciation accounts appear as follows:

Furniture	
Jan. 2, 2013 60,200	

Accumulated Depreciation—Furniture	
	Dec. 31, 2013 11,040
	Dec. 31, 2014 11,040
	Dec. 31, 2015 11,040
	Dec. 31, 2016 11,040
	Apr. 1, 2017 2,760
	Balance 46,920

The second step is to calculate the carrying amount on April 1, 2017. Note that the balance in Accumulated Depreciation is now $46,920.

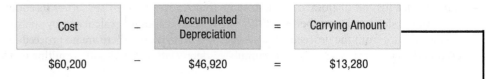

Cost	−	Accumulated Depreciation	=	Carrying Amount
$60,200	−	$46,920	=	$13,280

The third step is to calculate the gain or loss on disposal. A $1,720 gain on disposal is determined as follows:

Proceeds	−	Carrying Amount	=	Gain (Loss)
$15,000	−	$13,280	=	$1,720

The fourth step is the entry to record the sale of the office furniture as follows:

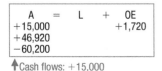

```
A      =   L   +   OE
+15,000            +1,720
+46,920
−60,200
```
↑Cash flows: +15,000

Apr. 1	Cash	15,000	
	Accumulated Depreciation—Furniture	46,920	
	Gain on Disposal		1,720
	Furniture		60,200
	To record the sale of office furniture at a gain.		

Notice that the carrying amount of $13,280 does not appear in the journal entry. Instead, the asset's cost ($60,200) and the total accumulated depreciation ($46,920) are used. **Remember: the carrying amount is simply a calculated amount to determine the gain or loss.** It is not an account and cannot be debited or credited.

Loss on Disposal. Assume that, instead of selling the furniture for $15,000, Andres sells it for $9,000. In this case, a loss of $4,280 is calculated as follows:

Proceeds	−	Carrying Amount	=	Gain (Loss)
$9,000	−	$13,280	=	$(4,280)

The entry to record the sale of the office furniture is as follows:

```
A      =   L   +   OE
+9,000             −4,280
+46,920
−60,200
```
↑Cash flows: +9,000

Apr. 1	Cash	9,000	
	Accumulated Depreciation—Furniture	46,920	
	Loss on Disposal	4,280	
	Furniture		60,200
	To record the sale of office furniture at a loss.		

Exchanges of Property, Plant, and Equipment

An exchange of assets is recorded as the purchase of a new asset and the sale of an old asset. Typically a **trade-in allowance** on the old asset is given toward the purchase price of the new asset. An additional cash payment is usually also required for the difference between the trade-in allowance and the stated purchase price (list price) of the new asset. The trade-in allowance amount is often just a price concession and does not reflect the fair value of the asset that is given up. Consequently, as fair value is what matters, trade-in allowances are only used to determine the remaining cash that must be paid and are not recorded in the accounting records.

Instead of using the stated purchase price, **the new asset is recorded at the fair value of the asset given up plus any cash paid (or less any cash received) unless the fair value of the asset given up cannot be determined reliably, in which case the fair value of the asset *received* should be used.** The fair value of the asset given up is used to calculate the gain or loss on the asset being given up. A loss results if the carrying amount of the asset being given up is more than its fair value. A gain results if the carrying amount is less than its fair value.

Thus, the procedure to account for exchanges of assets is as follows:

Step 1: Update any unrecorded depreciation expense on the asset being given up to the date of the exchange.
Step 2: Calculate the carrying amount of the asset being given up (cost – accumulated depreciation).
Step 3: Calculate any gain or loss on disposal (fair value – carrying amount = gain [loss]).
Step 4: Record the exchange as follows:
- Remove the cost and the accumulated depreciation of the asset that is given up.
- Record any gain or loss on disposal.
- Record the new asset at the fair value of the old asset plus any cash paid (or less any cash received).
- Record the cash paid or received.

To illustrate an exchange of long-lived assets, assume that Chilko Company exchanged an old vehicle for a new vehicle on October 1, 2017. The details for the exchange are:

Original cost of the old vehicle: $61,000
Date of acquisition of old vehicle: January 1, 2012
Depreciation method: straight-line method
Estimated useful life: 6 years
Estimated residual value: $1,000
Fair value of the old vehicle (asset given up) on October 1, 2017: $3,000

The list price of the new vehicle was $51,000. Chilko received an $8,000 trade-in allowance from the vehicle dealership for the old vehicle and paid $43,000 cash ($51,000 – $8,000) for the new vehicle. Chilko's year end is December 31.

The first step is to update the depreciation on the old vehicle for the nine months ended October 1, 2017. Annual depreciation expense is $10,000 [($61,000 – $1,000) ÷ 6], so depreciation for nine months is $7,500 ($10,000 × $^9/_{12}$).

Oct. 1	Depreciation Expense	7,500	
	Accumulated Depreciation—Vehicles		7,500
	To record depreciation expense for the first nine months of 2017.		

A	=	L	+	OE
−7,500				−7,500

Cash flows: no effect

After this journal entry is posted, the Vehicles and Accumulated Depreciation accounts appear as follows:

Vehicles	
Jan. 1, 2012 61,000	

Accumulated Depreciation—Vehicles	
	Dec. 31, 2012 10,000
	Dec. 31, 2013 10,000
	Dec. 31, 2014 10,000
	Dec. 31, 2015 10,000
	Dec. 31, 2016 10,000
	Oct. 1, 2017 7,500
	Balance 57,500

The next step is to calculate the carrying amount of the old vehicle on October 1, 2017. Note that the balance in Accumulated Depreciation of $57,500 is equal to five years (January 1, 2012, to December 31, 2016) at $10,000/year plus $7,500 for 2017.

On October 1, 2017, the carrying amount is $3,500 (cost of $61,000 – accumulated depreciation of $57,500). The loss on disposal on the old vehicle is determined by comparing the carrying amount with the fair value:

Fair Value of Old Vehicle	–	Carrying Amount (Old Vehicle)	=	Gain (Loss)
$3,000	–	$3,500 ($61,000 – $57,500)	=	($500)

The cost of the new vehicle is determined by summing the fair value of the assets given up, that is:

Fair value of the old vehicle	$ 3,000
Cash paid	43,000
Cost of new vehicle	$46,000

The entry to record the exchange of vehicles is as follows:

A = L + OE
+46,000   −500
+57,500
−61,000
−43,000

Oct. 1	Vehicles (cost of new vehicle)	46,000	
	Accumulated Depreciation—Vehicles (on the old vehicle)	57,500	
	Loss on Disposal	500	
	Vehicles (cost of old vehicle)		61,000
	Cash		43,000
	To record exchange of vehicles, plus cash.		

Note that the exchange of vehicles is not netted. That is, it is shown as a separate increase and decrease to the general ledger account Vehicles. Also note that the list price of $51,000 and the trade-in allowance of $8,000 are ignored in determining the recorded cost of the new vehicle.

In the example above, the company recorded a loss on the exchange because the exchange was assumed to have **commercial substance**. An exchange has commercial substance if future cash flows change as a result of the exchange. That is, a company's operations will be altered in some fashion and future cash flows will change significantly.

In some situations, the exchange lacks commercial substance or else the fair value of the asset acquired or the asset given up cannot be determined. In such cases, the new long-lived asset is recorded at the carrying amount of the old asset that was given up, plus any cash paid (or less any cash received).

BEFORE YOU GO ON...DO IT   **4**   ▶ **Plant Asset Disposal**

Overland Trucking has a truck that was purchased on January 2, 2014, for $80,000. The truck had been depreciated on a straight-line basis with an estimated residual value of $5,000 and an estimated useful life of five years. Overland has a December 31 year end. Assume each of the following four independent situations:

1. On January 2, 2019, Overland retires the truck.
2. On May 1, 2018, Overland sells the truck for $9,500 cash.
3. On October 1, 2018, Overland sells the truck for $9,500 cash.
4. On November 1, 2018, Overland exchanges the old truck, plus $60,000 cash, for a new truck. The old truck has a fair value of $9,500. The new truck has a list price of $70,000, but the dealer gives Overland a $10,000 trade-in allowance on the old truck.

Prepare the journal entry to record each of these situations.   *(continued)*

BEFORE YOU GO ON...DO IT   **Plant Asset Disposal** *(continued)*

Solution

$$\frac{\$80,000 - \$5,000}{5 \text{ years}} = \$15,000 \text{ annual depreciation expense}$$

$$\$15,000 \div 12 = \$1,250 \text{ per month}$$

1. Retirement of truck:

Jan. 2, 2019	Accumulated Depreciation—Vehicles		
	($1,250 × 60 months)	75,000	
	Loss on Disposal [$0 − ($80,000 − $75,000)]	5,000	
	Vehicles		80,000
	To record retirement of truck.		

2. Sale of truck for $9,500 on May 1, 2018:

May 1, 2018	Depreciation Expense ($1,250 × 4 months)	5,000	
	Accumulated Depreciation—Vehicles		5,000
	To record depreciation for four months.		
	Cash	9,500	
	Accumulated Depreciation—Vehicles		
	($1,250 × 52 months)	65,000	
	Loss on Disposal [$9,500 − ($80,000 − $65,000)]	5,500	
	Vehicles		80,000
	To record sale of truck at a loss.		

3. Sale of truck for $9,500 on Oct. 1, 2018:

Oct. 1, 2018	Depreciation Expense ($1,250 × 9 months)	11,250	
	Accumulated Depreciation—Vehicles		11,250
	To record depreciation for nine months.		
	Cash	9,500	
	Accumulated Depreciation—Vehicles		
	($1,250 × 57 months)	71,250	
	Gain on Disposal [$9,500 − ($80,000 − $71,250)]		750
	Vehicles		80,000
	To record sale of truck at a gain.		

4. Exchange of truck on Nov. 1, 2018:

Nov. 1, 2018	Depreciation Expense ($1,250 × 10 months)	12,500	
	Accumulated Depreciation—Vehicles		12,500
	To record depreciation for 10 months.		
	Vehicles (cost of new) ($9,500 + $60,000)	69,500	
	Accumulated Depreciation—Vehicles		
	($1,250 × 58 months)	72,500	
	Gain on Disposal [$9,500 − ($80,000 − $72,500)]		2,000
	Vehicles (cost of old)		80,000
	Cash ($70,000 − $10,000)		60,000
	To record exchange of trucks, plus cash.		

Related exercise material: BE9–12, BE9–13, BE9–14, E9–9, and E9–10.

Action Plan

- Update any unrecorded depreciation for dispositions during the fiscal year.
- Compare the proceeds with the asset's carrying amount to determine if there has been a gain or loss.
- Record any proceeds received and any gain or loss. Remove both the asset and any related accumulated depreciation from the accounts.
- Determine the cash paid in an exchange situation as the difference between the list price and the trade-in allowance.
- Record the cost of the new asset in an exchange situation as the fair value of the asset given up, plus the cash paid.

LEARNING OBJECTIVE **Record natural resource transactions and calculate depletion.**

Natural Resources

Natural resources consist of standing timber and underground deposits of oil, gas, and minerals. Canada is rich in natural resources, ranging from the towering rainforests in coastal British Columbia to one of the world's largest nickel deposits in Voisey's Bay, Labrador. These long-lived assets have two characteristics that make them different from other long-lived assets: (1) they are physically extracted in operations such as mining, cutting, or pumping; and (2) only an act of nature can replace them.

Natural resources are tangible assets, similar to property, plant, and equipment. A key distinction between natural resources and property, plant, and equipment is that natural resources physically lose substance, or deplete, as they are used. For example, there is less of a tract of timberland (a natural resource) as the timber is cut and sold. When we use equipment, its physical substance remains the same regardless of the product it produces.

COST

The cost of a natural resource is determined in the same way as the cost of property, plant, and equipment and includes all expenditures necessary in acquiring the resource and preparing it for its intended use. These costs are often referred to as acquisition, exploration, and development costs. The cost of a natural resource also includes the estimated future removal and site restoration cleanup costs, which are often large. Restoration costs are usually required in order to return the resource as closely as possible to its natural state at the end of its useful life.

Detailed discussion on determining the cost of a natural resource will be left for more advanced accounting courses. In this section, we will look at how the acquisition cost of a natural resource is allocated over its useful life.

DEPLETION

Helpful hint Depreciation for natural resources is frequently called *depletion* because the assets physically deplete as the resource is extracted.

The units-of-production method (learned earlier in the chapter) is generally used to calculate the depreciation of natural resources. Under the units-of-production method, the total cost of the natural resource less its residual value is divided by the number of units estimated to be in the resource. The result is a depletion amount per unit of product. The depletion amount per unit is then multiplied by the number of units extracted, to determine the annual depletion expense.

To illustrate, assume that Fox Lake Company invests $5.5 million in a mine that is estimated to have 10 million tonnes (t) of uranium and a $200,000 residual value. In the first year, 800,000 tonnes of uranium are extracted. Illustration 9-16 shows the formulas and calculations.

▶ ILLUSTRATION **9-16**
Formula for units-of-production method for natural resources

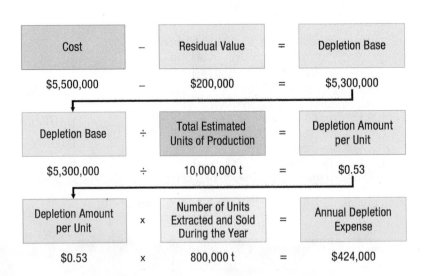

The calculated annual depletion expense is initially debited to an inventory account, a current asset. Note that this is not the same as depreciation for property, plant, and equipment, which is recorded as an expense. Depletion of natural resources is accounted for in this way because the resource extracted is available for sale—similar to merchandise that has been purchased or manufactured for sale, as we learned in Chapter 5.

The entry to record depletion of the uranium mine for Fox Lake Company's first year of operation, ended December 31, 2017, is as follows:

Dec. 31	Inventory ($0.53 × 800,000 t)	424,000	
	Accumulated Depletion—Resource		424,000
	To record depletion expense on uranium mine.		

A	=	L	+	OE
+424,000				
−424,000				

Cash flows: no effect

All costs of extracting the natural resource—both current production costs such as labour and depletion of the natural resource—are recorded as inventory. When the resource is sold, the inventory costs, which include depletion, are transferred to cost of goods sold and matched with the period's revenue. In other words, the depletion is charged to the income statement only in the period in which the related goods are sold. Depletion related to goods not yet sold remains in inventory and is reported as a current asset.

For example, assume that Fox Lake Company does not sell all of the 800,000 tonnes of uranium extracted in 2017. It sells 700,000 tonnes and stores 100,000 tonnes for later sale. In this situation, Fox Lake Company would include $371,000 (700,000 × $0.53) in cost of goods sold in 2017. The remaining depletion of $53,000 ($424,000 − $371,000) is for the 100,000 tonnes kept for later sale and will be included in inventory in the current assets section of the company's balance sheet.

Like depreciation for property, plant, and equipment, the depletion of a natural resource needs to be revised if there are capital expenditures during the useful life. Also, the depletion amount per unit of a natural resource needs to be revised whenever the estimated total units of the resource have changed as a result of new information. Natural resources such as oil and gas deposits and some metals have provided the greatest challenges. Estimates of the total units (also called reserves) of these natural resources are mostly knowledgeable guesses and may be revised whenever more information becomes available.

Natural resources must also be reviewed and tested for impairment annually or more frequently whenever circumstances make this appropriate. As with other long-lived assets, if there is impairment, the natural resource must be written down to its fair value, an impairment loss must be recorded, and current and future depreciation needs to be revised accordingly.

DISPOSAL

At disposal, just as with property, plant, and equipment, any unrecorded depletion of natural resources must be updated for the portion of the year up to the date of the disposal. Then proceeds are recorded, the cost and the accumulated depletion of the natural resource are removed, and a gain or loss, if any, is recorded.

Action Plan
- Use units-of-production depreciation for natural resources.
- Calculate the depletion amount per unit by dividing the total cost minus the estimated residual value by the total estimated units.
- Multiply the depletion amount per unit by the number of units cut to determine the total depletion.
- Allocate the depletion related to the units that have been cut but not yet sold to inventory.
- Allocate the depletion related to the units that have been cut and sold to expense.

BEFORE YOU GO ON...DO IT **Calculating Depletion for Natural Assets**

High Timber Company invests $14 million in a tract of timber land. It is estimated to have 10 million cunits (1 cunit = 100 cubic feet) of timber and a $500,000 residual value. In the first year, 40,000 cunits of timber are cut, and 30,000 of these cunits are sold. Calculate depletion for High Timber's first year of operations and allocate it between inventory and cost of goods sold.

Solution

1. Depletion amount per unit: ($14,000,000 − 500,000) ÷ 10,000,000 cunits = $1.35 per cunit
2. Total depletion for the year: $1.35 per cunit × 40,000 cunits cut = $54,000
3. Depletion allocated to inventory: $1.35 per cunit × 10,000 cunits on hand = $13,500
4. Depletion allocated to expense: $1.35 per cunit × 30,000 cunits sold = $40,500

Related exercise material: BE9–15 and E9–11.

LEARNING OBJECTIVE **6**

Identify the basic accounting issues for intangible assets and goodwill.

Intangible Assets and Goodwill

Similar to property, plant, and equipment, and natural resources, intangible assets provide economic benefits in future periods. They are used to produce products or provide services over these periods and are not intended for sale to customers. However, unlike property, plant, and equipment, and natural resources, which are **tangible assets** because they have a physical substance, **intangible assets** involve rights, privileges, and competitive advantages that have no physical substance. In other words, they are not physical things. Many companies' most valuable assets are intangible. Some widely known intangibles are Apple's trademark logo, Dr. Frederick G. Banting and Dr. Charles H. Best's patent for insulin, the franchises of Tim Hortons, the trade name of President's Choice, and the trade name of BMW.

An intangible asset must be identifiable, which means it must meet one of the two following criteria:

1. It can be separated from the company and sold, whether or not the company intends to do so, or
2. It is based on contractual or legal rights, regardless of whether or not it can be separated from the company.

Goodwill is a unique type of intangible asset. Because it cannot be separated from a company and sold, there are differences in the accounting for goodwill versus other intangible assets. We will discuss goodwill later in this section.

ACCOUNTING FOR INTANGIBLE ASSETS

Like tangible assets (property, plant, and equipment, and natural resources), intangible assets are recorded at cost. Cost includes all the costs of acquisition and other costs that are needed to make the intangible asset ready for its intended use—including legal fees and similar charges.

As with tangible assets, companies have a choice of following the cost model or the revaluation model when accounting for intangible assets subsequent to acquisition. The majority of companies use the cost model for all long-lived assets. So we will leave further study of the revaluation model, as it applies to intangible assets, for a later accounting course.

Under the cost model, if an intangible asset has a finite (limited) life, its cost must be systematically allocated over its useful life. We called this "depreciation" when discussing tangible assets. With intangible assets, we use the term **amortization**.

For an intangible asset with a finite life, its **amortizable amount** (cost less residual value) should be **allocated over the shorter of the (1) estimated useful life and (2) legal life**. Intangible assets, by their nature, rarely have any residual value, so the amortizable amount is normally equal to the cost. In addition, the useful life of an intangible asset is usually shorter than its legal life, so useful life is most often used as the amortization period.

When a company estimates the useful life of an intangible asset, it must consider factors such as how long the company expects to use the asset, obsolescence, demand, and other factors that can make the intangible asset ineffective at helping to earn revenue. For example, a patent on a computer chip may have a legal life of 20 years, but with technology changing as rapidly as it does, the chip's useful life may be only four or five years maximum.

Amortization begins as soon as the asset is ready to be used as intended by management. Similar to depreciation, the company must use the amortization method that best matches the pattern with which the asset's future economic benefits are expected to be consumed. If that pattern cannot be determined reliably, the straight-line method should be used.

Just as land is considered to have an indefinite life, there are also intangible assets with an indefinite life. An intangible asset is considered to have an indefinite (unlimited) life when, based on an analysis of all of the relevant factors, there is no foreseeable limit to the period over which the intangible asset is expected to generate net cash inflows for the company. If an intangible has an indefinite life, it is not amortized.

As with tangible assets, companies must determine if there are indicators of impairment on intangible assets' definite lives. If there are indicators, an impairment test is performed. Under IFRS, intangible assets with indefinite lives must be tested for impairment at least once a year even if no indications of impairment are evident. Under ASPE, this annual test is not required unless indicators are present.

Similar to tangible assets, the amortization is revised if there are changes in cost or useful life, or an impairment loss.

At disposal, just as with tangible assets, the carrying amount of the intangible asset is removed, and a gain or loss, if any, is recorded.

INTANGIBLE ASSETS WITH FINITE LIVES

Examples of intangible assets with finite lives include patents and copyrights. We also include research and development costs in this section because these costs often lead to the creation of patents and copyrights.

Patents

A **patent** is an exclusive right issued by the Canadian Intellectual Property Office of Industry Canada that allows the patent holder to manufacture, sell, or otherwise control an invention for a period of 20 years from the date of the application. A patent cannot be renewed. But the legal life of a patent may be extended if the patent holder obtains new patents for improvements or other changes in the basic design.

The initial cost of a patent is the price paid to acquire it. After it has been acquired, legal costs are often incurred. Legal costs to successfully defend a patent in an infringement suit are considered necessary to prove the patent's validity. They are added to the Patent account and amortized over the patent's remaining life.

The cost of a patent should be amortized over its 20-year legal life or its useful life, whichever is shorter. As mentioned earlier in this chapter, the useful life should be carefully assessed by considering whether the patent is likely to become ineffective at contributing to revenue before the end of its legal life.

Copyrights

A **copyright** is granted by the Canadian Intellectual Property Office, giving the owner an exclusive right to reproduce and sell an artistic or published work. Copyrights extend for the life of the creator plus 50 years. Generally, a copyright's useful life is significantly shorter than its legal life.

The cost of a copyright consists of the cost of acquiring and defending it. The cost may only be the fee paid to register the copyright, or it may amount to a great deal more if a copyright infringement suit is involved.

ACCOUNTING IN ACTION
ALL ABOUT YOU INSIGHT

Getty Images/Moxie Productions

If you copy a song from a CD that has a "digital lock" on it to prevent unauthorized copying to your smart phone, you could be liable for a fine ranging from $100 to $5,000 for breaking the digital lock and copying the CD. This is one of the provisions in Canada's Copyright Modernization Act, passed in 2012. The last time the copyright laws were changed was in 1997, before the first MP3 player came on the market. Since that time, the Internet and other new technologies have changed the way we produce and access copyright material. Supporters of the law argue that companies and individuals in the entertainment and creative fields need to have their songs, videos, TV shows, software, electronic books, and other works protected in order to foster creativity and innovation. But the amendments are also intended to give more flexibility to consumers such as officially legalizing the recording of television programs to watch at their convenience.

Sources: Bea Vongdouangchanh, "Parliament Passes New Copyright Law; Geist Says Feds Caved to U.S. on Digital Locks," *The Hill Times*, July 2, 2012; CBC News, "Copyright Bill Finally Clears Commons," CBC.ca, June 19, 2012; Mary Teresa Bitti, "Chambers: Copyright Lawyers Prepare for New Rules," *Financial Post*, March 26, 2012.

Q **Why is it important that the copyrights of artists, writers, musicians, and the entertainment industry be protected?**

Research and Development Costs

Research and development (R&D) costs are not intangible assets by themselves. But they may lead to patents and copyrights, new processes, and new products. Many companies spend large sums of money on research and development in an ongoing effort to develop new products or processes.

Research and development costs present two accounting problems: (1) it is sometimes difficult to determine the costs related to specific projects, and (2) it is also hard to know the extent and timing of future benefits. As a result, accounting distinguishes between research costs and development costs.

Research is original, planned investigation that is done to gain *new knowledge and understanding*. It is not known at this stage if a future benefit will exist as a result of the research. Therefore, **all research costs should be expensed when they are incurred**.

Development is the *use of research findings and knowledge* for a plan or design before the start of commercial production. Development costs with probable future benefits should be capitalized. Specific criteria must be met before development costs can be recognized as an asset. If the conditions are not met, the development costs must be expensed. Illustration 9-17 shows the distinction between research and development. After development is completed, the capitalized development costs are amortized over the useful life of the project developed.

▶ **ILLUSTRATION** **9-17**
Distinction between research and development

Research

Development

Examples
- Laboratory research aimed at the discovery of new knowledge
- Searching for ways to use new research findings or other knowledge
- Forming concepts and designs of possible product or process alternatives

Examples
- Testing in search or evaluation of product or process alternatives
- Design, construction, and testing of pre-production prototypes and models
- Design of tools, jigs, moulds, and dies involving new technology or materials

INTANGIBLE ASSETS WITH INDEFINITE LIVES

An intangible asset is considered to have an indefinite life when there is no foreseeable limit to the length of time over which the asset is expected to generate cash. Examples of intangible assets with indefinite lives include trademarks and trade names, franchises, and licences. Intangible assets do not always fit perfectly in a specific category. Sometimes trademarks, trade names, franchises, or licences do have finite lives. In such cases, they would be amortized over the shorter of their legal or useful lives. It is more usual, however, for these intangible assets, along with goodwill, to have indefinite lives.

Trademarks, Trade Names, and Brands

A **trademark** or **trade name** is a word, phrase, jingle, or symbol that identifies a particular enterprise or product. Trade names like President's Choice, Starbucks, adidas, the Toronto Maple Leafs, and TSN create immediate brand recognition and generally help the sale of a product or service. Each year, Interbrand ranks the world's best brands. In 2014, it ranked Apple as the most successful brand in the world, followed by Google, Coca-Cola, and IBM. In Canada, the most valuable brands in retail included Shoppers Drug Mart and lululemon.

The creator can get an exclusive legal right to the trademark or trade name by registering it with the Canadian Intellectual Property Office. This registration gives continuous protection. It may be renewed every 15 years, as long as the trademark or trade name is in use. In most cases, companies continuously renew their trademarks or trade names. In such cases, as long as the trademark or trade name continues to be marketable, it will have an indefinite useful life.

If the trademark or trade name is purchased, the cost is the purchase price. If the trademark or trade name is developed internally rather than purchased, it cannot be recognized as an intangible asset on the balance sheet. The reason is that expenditures on internally developed trademarks or brands cannot be distinguished from the cost of developing the business as a whole. The cost cannot be separately measured.

Franchises and Licences

When you purchase a Civic from a Honda dealer, fill up your gas tank at the corner Mohawk station, or buy coffee from Tim Hortons, you are dealing with franchises. A **franchise** is a contractual arrangement under which the franchisor grants the franchisee the right to sell certain products, to provide specific services, or to use certain trademarks or trade names, usually inside a specific geographic area.

Another type of franchise is granted by a government body that allows a company to use public property in performing its services. Examples are the use of city streets for a bus line or taxi service; the use of public land for telephone, power, and cable lines; and the use of airwaves for radio or TV broadcasting. Such operating rights are called **licences**.

When costs can be identified with the acquisition of the franchise or licence, an intangible asset should be recognized. These rights have indefinite lives and are not amortized. Annual payments, which are often in proportion to the franchise's total sales, are sometimes required under a franchise agreement. These payments are called **royalties** and are recorded as operating expenses in the period in which they are incurred.

GOODWILL

Unlike other assets, which can be sold individually in the marketplace, goodwill cannot be sold individually because it is part of the business as a whole. It cannot be separated from the company, nor is it based on legal rights. **Goodwill** represents the value of favourable attributes related to a business such as exceptional management, a desirable location, good customer relations, skilled employees, high-quality products, fair pricing policies, and harmonious relations with labour unions.

If goodwill can be identified only with the business as a whole, how can it be determined? An accountant could try to put a dollar value on the attributes (exceptional management, a desirable location, and so on), but the results would be very subjective. Subjective valuations would not contribute to the reliability of financial statements. For this reason, internally generated goodwill is not recognized as an asset.

Goodwill is recorded only when there is a purchase of an entire business. The cost of goodwill is measured by comparing the amount paid to purchase the entire business with the fair value of its net assets (assets less liabilities). If the amount paid is greater than the net identifiable assets, then the purchaser has paid for something that cannot be separated and sold—goodwill. In this situation, because a transaction has occurred, the cost of the purchased goodwill can be measured and therefore recorded as an asset.

Because goodwill has an indefinite life, just as the company has an indefinite life, it is not amortized. Since goodwill is measured using the company's fair value—a value that can easily change—IFRS requires goodwill to be tested annually for impairment even if there is no indication of impairment. Under ASPE, impairment tests of goodwill are only conducted if there is an indication that impairment exists.

 BEFORE YOU GO ON...DO IT **6** **Accounting for Intangible Assets**

Dummies 'R' Us Company purchased a copyright to a new book series for $15,000 cash on August 1, 2016. The books are expected to have a saleable life of three years. One year later, the company spends an additional $6,000 cash to successfully defend this copyright in court. The company's year end is July 31. Record (a) the purchase of the copyright on August 1, 2016; (b) the year-end amortization at July 31, 2017; (c) the legal costs incurred on August 1, 2017; and (d) the year-end amortization at July 31, 2018.

(continued)

BEFORE YOU GO ON...DO IT **6**   **Accounting for Intangible Assets** *(continued)*

Action Plan

- Amortize intangible assets with finite lives over the shorter of their useful life and legal life (the legal life of a copyright is the life of the author plus 50 years).
- Treat costs to successfully defend an intangible asset as a capital expenditure because they benefit future periods.
- Revise amortization for additions to the cost of the asset, using the carrying amount at the time of the addition and the remaining useful life.

Solution

(a)

Aug. 1, 2016	Copyrights	15,000	
	Cash		15,000
	To record purchase of copyright.		

(b)

July 31, 2017	Amortization Expense ($15,000 ÷ 3)	5,000	
	Accumulated Amortization—Copyrights		5,000
	To record amortization expense.		

(c)

Aug. 1, 2017	Copyrights	6,000	
	Cash		6,000
	To record costs incurred to defend copyright.		

(d)

July 31, 2018	Amortization Expense	8,000*	
	Accumulated Amortization—Copyrights		8,000
	To record revised amortization expense.		

*$15,000 − $5,000 + $6,000 = $16,000 carrying amount; $16,000 carrying amount ÷ 2 years remaining = $8,000

Related exercise material: BE9–16, E9–12, E9–13, and E9–14.

LEARNING OBJECTIVE **7**   **Illustrate the reporting and analysis of long-lived assets.**

Statement Presentation and Analysis

PRESENTATION

Long-lived assets are normally reported in the balance sheet under the headings "property, plant, and equipment," "intangible assets," and "goodwill". Natural resource assets are generally reported under "property, plant and equipment." Some companies combine property, plant, and equipment and intangible assets under the heading "capital assets." Goodwill must be disclosed separately.

The cost and the accumulated depreciation and/or amortization for each major class of assets are disclosed in either the balance sheet or notes. In addition, the depreciation and amortization methods that are used must be described. The amount of depreciation and amortization expense for the period should also be disclosed. As previously explained, gains or losses on disposals of long-lived assets are included in operating expenses on the income statement.

Under IFRS, companies also have to disclose if they are using the cost or the revaluation model for each class of assets, and include a reconciliation of the carrying amount at the beginning and end of the period for each class of long-lived assets in the notes to the financial statements. This means they must show all of the following for each class of long-lived assets: (1) additions, (2) disposals, (3) depreciation or amortization, (4) impairment losses, and (5) reversals of impairment losses. ASPE does not require disclosure of all of these details.

Illustration 9-18 contains an excerpt from Enerflex's 2014 balance sheet (which it calls the statement of financial position). Enerflex is a Calgary-based supplier of products and services to the oil and gas production industry.

▶ILLUSTRATION 9-18
Presentation of
long-lived assets

ENERFLEX LTD. Statement of Financial Position (partial) December 31, 2014 (in thousands)	
Assets	
Property, plant, and equipment (note 11)	$152,898
Rental equipment (note 11)	290,577
Intangible assets (note 13)	42,104
Goodwill (note 14)	707,913

Enerflex provides additional details on the long-lived assets in the notes to its financial statements. For example, in note 11, Enerflex discloses the required information about all of its property, plant, and equipment, which include land, buildings, equipment, assets under construction, assets held for sale, and rental equipment.

Another note, the summary of significant accounting policies, discloses that Enerflex uses straight-line depreciation and provides information on the estimated useful lives of the company's long-lived assets. This note also states that major renewals and improvements in rental equipment and property, plant, and equipment are capitalized. It explains that significant components of property, plant, and equipment that require replacement at regular intervals are accounted for separately. The notes also include information on Enerflex's policies on testing its long-lived assets for impairment. Property, plant, and equipment, rental equipment, and intangible assets are assessed for impairment whenever changes in events or changes in circumstances indicate that the asset's carrying amount may not be recovered. Goodwill is tested for impairment at least annually.

ANALYSIS

Information in the financial statements about long-lived assets allows decision makers to analyze a company's use of its total assets. We will use two ratios to analyze total assets: asset turnover and return on assets.

Asset Turnover

The **asset turnover** ratio indicates how efficiently a company uses its assets; that is, how many dollars of sales are generated by each dollar that is invested in assets. It is calculated by dividing net sales by average total assets. If a company is using its assets efficiently, each dollar of assets will create a high amount of sales. When we compare two companies in the same industry, the one with the higher asset turnover is operating more efficiently. The asset turnover ratio for fiscal 2014 for Corus Entertainment Inc. (dollars in thousands) is calculated in Illustration 9-19. (Note that Corus reports "Revenues" and not "Net Sales" but the two account names can be used interchangeably for the purposes of the ratio calculation.)

▶ILLUSTRATION 9-19
Asset turnover

Net Sales	÷	Average Total Assets	=	Asset Turnover
$833,016	÷	((2,784,582 + 2,167,137) ÷ 2)	=	0.34 times

The asset turnover ratio shows that each dollar invested in assets produced $0.34 in sales for Corus. This ratio varies greatly among different industries—from those that have a large investment in assets (e.g., utility companies) to those that have much less invested in assets (e.g., service companies). Asset turnover ratios, therefore, should only be compared for companies that are in the same industry. According to Reuters.com, the average for Corus's industry is 0.53. This means that generally the diversified entertainment industry as a whole has an asset turnover of 0.53. When compared with the industry, Corus is producing slightly less in sales per dollar invested in assets than the industry as a whole.

Return on Assets

The **return on assets** ratio measures overall profitability. This ratio is calculated by dividing profit by average total assets. The return on assets ratio indicates the amount of profit that is generated by each dollar invested in assets. A high return on assets indicates a profitable company. Illustration 9-20 shows the return on assets for Corus (dollars in thousands).

▶ ILLUSTRATION 9-20
Return on assets

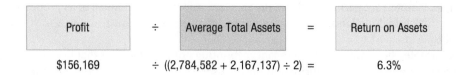

Profit	÷	Average Total Assets	=	Return on Assets
$156,169	÷	((2,784,582 + 2,167,137) ÷ 2) =		6.3%

Corus's return on assets was 6.3% for 2014. As with other ratios, the return on assets should be compared with previous years, with other companies in the same industry, and with industry averages, to determine how well the company has performed.

BEFORE YOU GO ON...DO IT 7 > **Asset Turnover and Return on Assets**

The following information is available for Toni's Sporting Goods for three recent years:

	2017	2016	2015
Total assets	$299,650	$259,700	$223,540
Net sales	521,180	487,150	441,280
Profit	26,390	18,210	13,540

Calculate the asset turnover and return on assets ratios for Toni's Sporting Goods for 2017 and 2016 and comment on any trends.

Action Plan
- Calculate average total assets using the total assets at the beginning and end of the year.
- Divide net sales by the average total assets for that year to calculate asset turnover.
- Divide profit by the average total assets for that year to calculate return on assets.
- Recall if it is better for asset turnover and return on assets to increase or decrease.

Solution

	2017	2016
Average total assets	($299,650 + $259,700) ÷ 2 = $279,675	($259,700 + $223,540) ÷ 2 = $241,620
Asset turnover	1.9 times = $\dfrac{\$521,180}{\$279,675}$	2 times = $\dfrac{\$487,150}{\$241,620}$
Return on assets	9.4% = $\dfrac{\$26,390}{\$279,675}$	7.5% = $\dfrac{\$18,210}{\$241,620}$

In general, it is better to have a higher asset turnover and return on assets. Toni's Sporting Goods' lower asset turnover may indicate it is not using its assets as efficiently in 2017 as compared with 2016. However, the increase in the return on assets indicates improved profitability. Given the decrease in turnover, this is a positive result.

Related exercise material: BE9–17, BE9–18, BE9–19, E9–15, and E9–16.

Comparing IFRS and ASPE

Key Differences	International Financial Reporting Standards (IFRS)	Accounting Standards for Private Enterprises (ASPE)
Valuing property, plant, and equipment	Choice of cost or revaluation model.	Must use cost model.
Terminology	The term "depreciation" is used for allocating the cost of property, plant, and equipment.	The term "amortization" may be used for allocating the cost of property, plant, and equipment. The term "depreciation" is also accepted.
Impairment of property, plant, and equipment, and finite-life intangible assets	Must look for indicators of impairment annually. If they exist, then must test for impairment. Allow for recoveries of previously recorded impairments.	No requirement to look for indicators of impairment annually. Perform tests only if it is apparent they exist. Impairments recorded less often, but cannot later reverse an impairment loss.
Test for impairment of indefinite-life intangible assets	Must perform impairment tests annually. Allows for recoveries of previously recorded impairments.	Same approach as for property, plant, and equipment, and intangible assets with finite lives.
Test for impairment of goodwill	Must be conducted every year.	Conducted only if there is an indication of impairment.
Disclosure	Must provide a reconciliation of the opening and closing carrying amount of each class of assets.	Reconciliation not required.

Demonstration Problem 1

DuPage Company purchases a factory machine at a cost of $17,500 on June 1, 2017. The machine is expected to have a residual value of $1,500 at the end of its four-year useful life on May 31, 2021. DuPage has a December 31 year end.

During its useful life, the machine is expected to be used for 10,000 hours. Actual annual use is as follows: 1,300 hours in 2017; 2,800 hours in 2018; 3,300 hours in 2019; 1,900 hours in 2020; and 700 hours in 2021.

Instructions

Prepare depreciation schedules for the following methods: (a) straight-line, (b) units-of-production, and (c) diminishing-balance using double the straight-line rate.

SOLUTION TO DEMONSTRATION PROBLEM 1

(a) Straight-line method

Year	Amount	×	Rate	=	Expense	End of Year Depreciation	End of Year Amount
							$17,500
2017	$16,000^a		25%^{b} × $^7/_{12}$		$2,333	$ 2,333	15,167
2018	16,000		25%		4,000	6,333	11,167
2019	16,000		25%		4,000	10,333	7,167
2020	16,000		25%		4,000	14,333	3,167
2021	16,000		25% × $^5/_{12}$		1,667	16,000	1,500

^{a} $17,500 − $1,500 = $16,000
^{b} 100% ÷ 4 years = 25%

(b) Units-of-production method

| | | | | | End of Year | |
Year	Units of Production	× Depreciable Amount/Unit	= Depreciation Expense	Accumulated Depreciation	Carrying Amount
					$17,500
2017	1,300	$1.60[a]	$2,080	$ 2,080	15,420
2018	2,800	1.60	4,480	6,560	10,940
2019	3,300	1.60	5,280	11,840	5,660
2020	1,900	1.60	3,040	14,880	2,620
2021	700	1.60	1,120	16,000	1,500

[a] $17,500 – $1,500 = $16,000 depreciable amount ÷ 10,000 total units = $1.60/unit

(c) Diminishing-balance method

| | | | | End of Year | |
Year	Carrying Amount Beginning of Year	× Depreciable Rate (25% × 2)	= Depreciation Expense	Accumulated Depreciation	Carrying Amount
					$17,500
2017	$17,500	50% × 7/12	$5,104	$ 5,104	12,396
2018	12,396	50%	6,198	11,302	6,198
2019	6,198	50%	3,099	14,401	3,099
2020	3,099	50%	1,549	15,950	1,550
2021	1,550	50%	50[a]	16,000	1,500

[a] Adjusted to $50 so that the carrying amount at the end of the year is not less than the residual value.

Demonstration Problem 2

On January 2, 2017, Skyline Limousine Co. purchased a specialty limo for $78,000. The vehicle is being amortized by the straight-line method using a four-year service life and a $4,000 residual value. The company's fiscal year ends on December 31.

Instructions

Prepare the journal entry or entries to record the disposal of the limo, assuming that it is:

(a) retired for no proceeds on January 2, 2020.

(b) sold for $15,000 on July 1, 2020.

(c) traded in on a new limousine on January 2, 2020, for a trade-in allowance of $25,000 and cash of $52,000. The fair value of the old vehicle on January 2, 2020, was $20,000.

SOLUTION TO DEMONSTRATION PROBLEM 2

$78,000 – $4,000 ÷ 4 years = $18,500 annual depreciation expense

Accumulated Depreciation at December 31, 2019: $18,500 × 3 years = $55,500

(a)

Jan. 2, 2020	Accumulated Depreciation—Vehicles	55,500	
	Loss on Disposal [$0 – ($78,000 – $55,500)]	22,500	
	Vehicles		78,000
	To record retirement of limo.		

(b)

July 1, 2020	Depreciation Expense ($18,500 × $^6/_{12}$)	9,250	
	Accumulated Depreciation—Vehicles		9,250
	To record depreciation for six months.		
	Cash	15,000	
	Accumulated Depreciation—Vehicles		
	($55,500 + $9,250)	64,750	
	Gain on Disposal [$15,000 − ($78,000 − $64,750)]		1,750
	Vehicles		78,000
	To record sale of limo.		

(c)

Jan. 2, 2020	Vehicles (cost of new) ($20,000 + $52,000)	72,000	
	Accumulated Depreciation—Vehicles	55,500	
	Loss on Disposal [$20,000 − ($78,000 − $55,500)]	2,500	
	Vehicles (cost of old)		78,000
	Cash		52,000
	To record exchange of limousines, plus cash.		

Marginal notes:
- Calculate any gain or loss by comparing proceeds with the carrying amount.
- Remove the asset's carrying amount by debiting accumulated depreciation (for the total depreciation to the date of disposal) and crediting the asset account for the cost of the asset. Record proceeds and any gain or loss.
- Ignore trade-in allowances.
- Record the new asset in an exchange situation at the fair value of the asset given up, plus the cash paid.

▶ Summary of Learning Objectives

1. **Calculate the cost of property, plant, and equipment.** The cost of property, plant, and equipment includes all costs that are necessary to acquire the asset and make it ready for its intended use. All costs that benefit future periods (that is, capital expenditures) are included in the cost of the asset. When applicable, cost also includes asset retirement costs. When multiple assets are purchased in one transaction, or when an asset has significant components, the cost is allocated to each individual asset or component using their relative fair values.

2. **Apply depreciation methods to property, plant, and equipment.** After acquisition, assets are accounted for using the cost model or the revaluation model. Depreciation is recorded and assets are carried at cost less accumulated depreciation. Depreciation is the allocation of the cost of a long-lived asset to expense over its useful life (its service life) in a rational and systematic way. Depreciation is not a process of valuation and it does not result in an accumulation of cash. There are three commonly used depreciation methods:

Method	Effect on Annual Depreciation	Calculation
Straight-line	Constant amount	(Cost − residual value) ÷ estimated useful life (in years)
Diminishing-balance	Diminishing amount	Carrying amount at beginning of year × diminishing-balance rate
Units-of-production	Varying amount	(Cost − residual value) ÷ total estimated units of production × actual activity during the year

Each method results in the same amount of depreciation over the asset's useful life. Depreciation expense for income tax purposes is called capital cost allowance (CCA).

3. **Explain the factors that cause changes in periodic depreciation and calculate revised depreciation for property, plant, and equipment.** A revision to depreciation will be required if there are (a) capital expenditures during the asset's useful life; (b) impairments in the asset's fair value; (c) changes in the asset's fair value when using the revaluation model; and/or (d) changes in the appropriate depreciation method, estimated useful life, or residual value. An impairment loss must be recorded if the recoverable amount is less than the carrying amount. Revisions of periodic depreciation are made in present and future periods, not retroactively. The new annual depreciation is determined by using the depreciable amount (carrying amount less the revised residual value), and the remaining useful life, at the time of the revision.

4. **Demonstrate how to account for property, plant, and equipment disposals.** The accounting for the disposal of a piece of property, plant, or equipment through retirement or sale is as follows:

   (a) Update any unrecorded depreciation for partial periods since depreciation was last recorded.
   (b) Calculate the carrying amount (cost − accumulated depreciation).
   (c) Calculate any gain (proceeds > carrying amount) or loss (proceeds < carrying amount) on disposal.
   (d) Remove the asset and accumulated depreciation accounts at the date of disposal. Record the proceeds received and the gain or loss, if any.

An exchange of assets is recorded as the purchase of a new asset and the sale of an old asset. The new asset is recorded at the fair value of the asset given up plus any cash paid (or less any cash received). The fair value of the asset given up is compared with its carrying amount to calculate the gain or loss. If the fair value of the new asset or the asset given up cannot be determined, the new long-lived asset is recorded at the carrying amount of the old asset that was given up, plus any cash paid (or less any cash received).

5. *Record natural resource transactions and calculate depletion.* The units-of-production method of depreciation is generally used for natural resources. The depreciable amount per unit is calculated by dividing the total depreciable amount by the number of units estimated to be in the resource. The depreciable amount per unit is multiplied by the number of units that have been extracted to determine the annual depreciation. The depreciation and any other costs to extract the resource are recorded as inventory until the resource is sold. At that time, the costs are transferred to cost of resource sold on the income statement. Revisions to depreciation will be required for capital expenditures during the asset's useful life, for impairments, and for changes in the total estimated units of the resource.

6. *Identify the basic accounting issues for intangible assets and goodwill.* The accounting for tangible and intangible assets is much the same. Intangible assets are reported at cost, which includes all expenditures necessary to prepare the asset for its intended use. An intangible asset with a finite life is amortized over the shorter of its useful life and legal life, usually on a straight-line basis. The extent of the annual impairment tests depends on whether IFRS or ASPE is followed and whether the intangible asset had a finite or indefinite life. Intangible assets with indefinite lives and goodwill are not amortized and are tested at least annually for impairment. Impairment losses on goodwill are never reversed under both IFRS and ASPE.

7. *Illustrate the reporting and analysis of long-lived assets.* It is common for property, plant, and equipment, and natural resources to be combined in financial statements under the heading "property, plant, and equipment." Intangible assets with finite and indefinite lives are sometimes combined under the heading "intangible assets" or are listed separately. Goodwill must be presented separately. Either on the balance sheet or in the notes, the cost of the major classes of long-lived assets is presented. Accumulated depreciation (if the asset is depreciable) and carrying amount must be disclosed either in the balance sheet or in the notes. The depreciation and amortization methods and rates, as well as the annual depreciation expense, must also be indicated. The company's impairment policy and any impairment losses should be described and reported. Under IFRS, companies must include a reconciliation of the carrying amount at the beginning and end of the period for each class of long-lived assets and state whether the cost or revaluation model is used.

The asset turnover ratio (net sales ÷ average total assets) is one measure that is used by companies to show how efficiently they are using their assets to generate sales revenue. A second ratio, return on assets (profit ÷ average total assets), calculates how profitable the company is in terms of using its assets to generate profit.

▶ Glossary

Additions and improvements Costs that are incurred to increase the operating efficiency, productive capacity, or expected useful life of property, plant, or equipment. (p. 483)

Amortizable amount The cost minus the residual value of a finite-life intangible asset that is amortized over its useful life. (p. 496)

Amortization The systematic allocation of the amortizable amount of a finite-life intangible asset over its useful life. (p. 496)

Asset retirement costs The cost to dismantle, remove, or restore an asset when it is retired. (p. 470)

Asset turnover A measure of how efficiently a company uses its total assets to generate sales. It is calculated by dividing net sales by average total assets. (p. 501)

Basket purchase The acquisition of a group of assets for a single price. Individual asset costs are determined by allocating relative fair values. (p. 472)

Capitalized Capital expenditures recorded as property, plant and equipment or other long-lived asset rather than being recorded as an expense. (p. 470)

Capital cost allowance (CCA) The depreciation of long-lived assets that is allowed by the Income Tax Act for income tax purposes. It is calculated on a class (group) basis and mainly uses the diminishing-balance method with maximum rates specified for each class of assets. (p. 481)

Capital expenditures Expenditures related to long-lived assets that benefit the company over several accounting periods. (p. 470)

Commercial substance An exchange of long-lived assets that results in a change in future cash flows of each party to the transaction. (p. 492)

Copyright An exclusive right granted by the federal government allowing the owner to reproduce and sell an artistic or published work. (p. 497)

Cost model A model of accounting for a long-lived asset that carries the asset at its cost less accumulated depreciation or amortization and any impairment losses. (p. 468)

Depreciable amount The cost of a depreciable asset (property, plant, and equipment, or natural resources) less its residual value. (p. 475)

Diminishing-balance method A depreciation method that applies a constant rate to the asset's diminishing carrying amount. This method produces a decreasing annual depreciation expense over the useful life of the asset. (p. 476)

Double diminishing-balance method   A diminishing-balance method of depreciation that uses a rate equal to two times the straight-line rate. (p. 477)

Franchise   A contractual arrangement under which the franchisor grants the franchisee the right to sell certain products, offer specific services, or use certain trademarks or trade names, usually inside a specific geographical area. (p. 499)

Goodwill   The amount paid to purchase another company that is more than the fair value of the company's net identifiable assets. (p. 499)

Impairment loss   The amount by which an asset's carrying amount exceeds its recoverable amount. (p. 483)

Intangible assets   Rights, privileges, and competitive advantages that result from owning long-lived assets that have no physical substance. (p. 496)

Land improvements   Structural additions to land that have limited useful lives, such as paving, fencing, and lighting. (p. 471)

Licences   Operating rights to use public property, granted by a government agency to a company. (p. 499)

Natural resources   Long-lived tangible assets, such as standing timber and underground deposits of oil, gas, and minerals, that are physically extracted and are only replaceable by an act of nature. (p. 493)

Operating expenditures   Expenditures that benefit only the current period. They are immediately charged against revenues as expenses. (p. 470)

Ordinary repairs   Expenditures to maintain the operating efficiency and productive life of the unit. (p. 483)

Patent   An exclusive right issued by the federal government that enables the recipient to manufacture, sell, or otherwise control an invention for a period of 20 years from the date of the application. (p. 497)

Property, plant, and equipment   Identifiable, long-lived tangible assets, such as land, land improvements, buildings, and equipment, that the company owns and uses for the production and sale of goods or services. (p. 470)

Recoverable amount   The higher of the asset's fair value, less costs to sell, and its value in use. (p. 483)

Research and development (R&D) costs   Expenditures that may lead to patents, copyrights, new processes, and new products. (p. 498)

Residual value   The estimated amount that a company would currently obtain from disposing of the asset if the asset were already as old as it will be, and in the condition it is expected to be in, at the end of its useful life. (p. 475)

Return on assets   An overall measure of profitability that indicates the amount of profit that is earned from each dollar invested in assets. It is calculated by dividing profit by average total assets. (p. 502)

Revaluation model   A model of accounting for a long-lived asset in which it is carried at its fair value less accumulated depreciation or amortization and any impairment losses. (p. 484)

Royalties   Recurring payments that may be required under a franchise agreement and are paid by the franchisee to the franchisor for services provided (e.g., advertising, purchasing), and are often proportionate to sales. (p. 499)

Straight-line method   A depreciation method in which an asset's depreciable amount is divided by its estimated useful life. This method produces the same periodic depreciation for each year of the asset's useful life. (p. 475)

Tangible assets   Long-lived resources that have physical substance, are used in the operations of the business, and are not intended for sale to customers. Tangible assets include property, plant, and equipment, and natural resources. (p. 496)

Trade-in allowance   A price reduction offered by the seller when a used asset is exchanged for a new asset as part of the deal. (p. 490)

Trademark (trade name)   A word, phrase, jingle, or symbol that distinguishes or identifies a particular enterprise or product. (p. 498)

Units-of-production method   A depreciation method in which useful life is expressed in terms of the total estimated units of production or use expected from the asset. Depreciation expense is calculated by multiplying the depreciable amount per unit (cost less residual value divided by total estimated activity) by the actual activity that occurs during the year. (p. 478)

Useful life   The period of time over which an asset is expected to be available for use, or the number of units of production (such as machine hours) or units of output that are expected to be obtained from an asset. (p. 474)

▶ Self-Study Questions

Answers are at the end of the chapter.

(LO 1) K   1. Additions to property, plant, and equipment are:
   (a) operating expenditures.
   (b) debited to the Repairs Expense account.
   (c) debited to the Inventory account.
   (d) capital expenditures.

(LO 1) AP   2. Bulyea Company purchased equipment and incurred the following costs:

Cash price	$36,000
Freight—FOB shipping point	1,000
Insurance during transit	200
Annual insurance policy	500
Installation and testing	400
Total cost	$38,100

What amount should be recorded as the cost of the equipment?
   (a) $36,000   (c) $37,600
   (b) $36,200   (d) $38,100

(LO 1) AP   3. Asura Company purchased land, a building, and equipment for a package price of $190,000. The land's fair value at the time of acquisition was $75,000. The building's fair value was $80,000. The equipment's fair value was $50,000. What costs should be debited to the Land account?
   (a) $74,146   (c) $46,341
   (b) $69,512   (d) $75,000

(LO 2) AP   4. Cuso Company purchased equipment on January 2, 2016, at a cost of $40,000. The equipment has an estimated residual value of $10,000 and an estimated useful life of five years. If the straight-line method of depreciation is used, what is depreciation expense on December 31, 2017?

(a) $6,000
(b) $12,000
(c) $18,000
(d) $24,000

(LO 2) AP 5. Kant Enterprises purchases a truck for $33,000 on July 1, 2017. The truck has an estimated residual value of $3,000, and an estimated useful life of five years, or a total distance of 300,000 km. If 50,000 km are driven in 2017, what amount of depreciation expense would Kant record at December 31, 2017, assuming it uses the units-of-production method?

(a) $2,500
(b) $3,000
(c) $5,000
(d) $5,333

(LO 2) AP 6. Refer to the data for Kant Enterprises in question 5. If Kant uses the double diminishing-balance method of depreciation, what amount of depreciation expense would it record at December 31, 2017?

(a) $6,000
(b) $6,600
(c) $12,000
(d) $13,200

(LO 3) K 7. When depreciation is revised:
(a) previous depreciation should be corrected.
(b) current and future years' depreciation should be revised.
(c) only future years' depreciation should be revised.
(d) None of the above.

(LO 4) AP 8. Oviatt Company sold equipment for $10,000. At that time, the equipment had a cost of $45,000 and accumulated depreciation of $30,000. Oviatt should record a:
(a) $5,000 loss on disposal.
(b) $5,000 gain on disposal.
(c) $15,000 loss on disposal.
(d) $15,000 gain on disposal.

(LO 4) AP 9. St. Laurent Company exchanged an old machine with a carrying amount of $10,000 and a fair value of $6,000 for a new machine. The new machine had a list price of $53,000. St. Laurent paid $42,000 cash and was offered $11,000 as a trade-in allowance in the exchange. At what amount should the new machine be recorded on St. Laurent's books?
(a) $42,000
(b) $48,000
(c) $52,000
(d) $53,000

(LO 5) AP 10. Titus Proudfoot Company expects to extract 20 million tonnes of coal from a mine that cost $12 million. If no residual value is expected and 2 million tonnes are mined in the first year, the entry to record depletion will include a:
(a) debit to Accumulated Depletion for $2,000,000.
(b) credit to Depletion Expense of $1,200,000.
(c) debit to Inventory of $1,200,000.
(d) credit to Accumulated Depletion of $2,000,000.

(LO 6) K 11. Which of the following statements about intangible assets is *false*:
(a) If an intangible asset has a finite life, it should be amortized.
(b) The amortization period should never be less than 20 years.
(c) Goodwill is recorded only when a business is purchased.
(d) Research costs should always be expensed.

(LO 7) AP 12. Cross Continental Rail Services reported net sales of $2,550 million, profit of $178 million, and average total assets of $3,132 million in 2017. What are the company's return on assets and asset turnover?
(a) 0.81% and 5.7 times
(b) 5.7% and 1.2 times
(c) 7.0% and 5.7 times
(d) 5.7% and 0.81 times

▶ Questions

(LO 1) K 1. What are the three characteristics of property, plant, and equipment?

(LO 1) K 2. What are some examples of land improvements?

(LO 1) C 3. Blue Hosta Company recently purchased a new vehicle. The company also had to pay for the company's logo to be painted on the vehicle, for a safety inspection, and for an annual insurance policy on the vehicle. Explain how each of these costs should be recorded and why.

(LO 1) C 4. In a recent newspaper article, the president of Altas Company asserted that something has to be done about depreciation. The president said, "Depreciation does not come close to accumulating the cash needed to replace the asset at the end of its useful life." What is your response to the president?

(LO 1) C 5. Jacques asks why the total cost in a basket purchase has to be allocated to the individual assets. For example, if we purchase land and a building for $250,000, why can we not just debit an account called Land and Building for $250,000? Answer his question.

(LO 2) C 6. Victor is studying for the next accounting examination. He asks your help on two questions: (a) What is residual value? (b) Is residual value used in determining periodic depreciation under each depreciation method? Answer Victor's questions.

(LO 2) K 7. Explain the factors that are used to calculate depreciation.

(LO 2) C 8. Contrast the effects of the three depreciation methods on annual depreciation expense.

(LO 2, 3) K 9. What factors should be considered when choosing a depreciation method?

(LO 3) C 10. Explain the difference between operating expenditures and capital expenditures during an asset's useful life and describe the accounting treatment of each.

(LO 3) C 11. Under what circumstances will depreciation need to be revised? Should these circumstances also result in the revision of previously recorded depreciation?

(LO 3) K 12. What factors contribute to an impairment loss?

(LO 3) C 13. In the fourth year of an asset's five-year useful life, the company decides that the asset will have an eight-year service life. How should the revision of depreciation be recorded? Why?

(LO 4) C 14. If equipment is sold in the middle of a fiscal year, why does depreciation expense have to be recorded for the partial period? Doesn't the subsequent journal entry to record the sale remove the accumulated depreciation from the books anyway?

(LO 4) C 15. Ewing Company owns a machine that is fully depreciated but is still being used. How should Ewing account for this asset and report it in the financial statements?

(LO 4) K 16. How is a gain or loss on the sale of an item of property, plant, or equipment calculated? Is the calculation the same for an exchange of a piece of property, plant, or equipment?

(LO 4) C 17. How is the carrying amount of an item of property, plant, or equipment calculated? Why does this amount NOT appear in the journal entry to record the disposition of an item of property, plant, or equipment?

(LO 5) K 18. What are natural resources, and what are their distinguishing characteristics?

(LO 5) C 19. Why is the units-of-production method used frequently to calculate depletion for natural resources?

(LO 6) C 20. Zeus Company's manager believes that all intangible assets should be amortized over their legal lives. Do you agree or disagree? Explain.

(LO 6) C 21. What are the similarities and differences between accounting for intangible and tangible assets?

(LO 6) C 22. What is goodwill? Why can it not be sold to raise cash if a company is planning to expand?

(LO 7) K 23. How should long-lived assets be reported on the balance sheet and income statement? What information should be disclosed in the notes to the financial statements?

(LO 7) C 24. Balpreet believes that when comparing the ratios for one company over a two-year period, it is more important for a company to have an improved asset turnover than it is to have an improved return on assets. Do you agree or disagree? Why?

▶ Brief Exercises

BE9–1   The following costs were incurred by Shumway Company in purchasing land: cash price, $85,000; legal fees, $1,500; removal of old building, $5,000; clearing and grading, $3,500; installation of a parking lot, $5,000. (a) What is the cost of the land? (b) What is the cost of the land improvements?

Determine cost of land and land improvements. (LO 1) AP

BE9–2   Surkis Company incurs the following costs in purchasing equipment: invoice price, $40,375; shipping, $625; installation and testing, $1,000; one-year insurance policy, $1,750. What is the cost of the equipment?

Determine cost of equipment. (LO 1) AP

BE9–3   In the space provided, indicate whether each of the following items is an operating expenditure (O) or a capital expenditure (C):

(a) _____ Repaired building roof, $1,500
(b) _____ Replaced building roof, $27,500
(c) _____ Purchased building, $480,000
(d) _____ Paid insurance on equipment in transit, $550
(e) _____ Purchased supplies, $350
(f) _____ Purchased truck, $55,000
(g) _____ Purchased oil and gas for truck, $125
(h) _____ Rebuilt engine on truck, $5,000
(i) _____ Added new wing to building, $250,000
(j) _____ Painted interior of building, $1,500

Identify operating and capital expenditures. (LO 1) K

BE9–4   Rainbow Company purchased land, a building, and equipment on January 2, 2017, for $850,000. The company paid $170,000 cash and signed a mortgage note payable for the remainder. Management's best estimate of the value of the land was $352,000; of the building, $396,000; and of the equipment, $132,000. Record the purchase.

Record basket purchase. (LO 1) AP

BE9–5   Surkis Company acquires equipment at a cost of $42,000 on January 3, 2017. Management estimates the equipment will have a residual value of $6,000 at the end of its four-year useful life. Assume the company uses the straight-line method of depreciation. Calculate the depreciation expense for each year of the equipment's life. Surkis has a December 31 fiscal year end.

Calculate straight-line depreciation. (LO 2) AP

Calculate diminishing-balance depreciation. (LO 2) AP

BE9–6 Refer to the data given for Surkis Company in BE9–5. Assume instead that the company uses the diminishing-balance method and that the diminishing-balance depreciation rate is double the straight-line rate. Calculate the depreciation expense for each year of the equipment's life.

Calculate units-of-production depreciation. (LO 2) AP

BE9–7 Speedy Taxi Service uses the units-of-production method in calculating depreciation on its taxicabs. Each cab is expected to be driven 550,000 km. Taxi 10 cost $38,950 and is expected to have a residual value of $4,300. Taxi 10 is driven 90,000 km in 2016, and 135,000 km in 2017. Calculate (a) the depreciable amount per kilometre (use three decimals), and (b) the depreciation expense for 2016 and 2017.

Calculate partial-year straight-line depreciation. (LO 2) AP

BE9–8 Pandora Pants Company acquires a delivery truck on April 6, 2017, at a cost of $38,000. The truck is expected to have a residual value of $6,000 at the end of its four-year life. Pandora uses the nearest month method to pro-rate depreciation expense. Calculate annual depreciation expense for the first and second years using straight-line depreciation, assuming Pandora has a calendar year end.

Calculate partial-year diminishing-balance depreciation. (LO 2) AP

BE9–9 Refer to the data given for Pandora Pants Company given in BE9–8. Assume now that the company has a policy of recording a half-year's depreciation in the year of acquisition and a half-year's depreciation in the year of disposal. Using the double diminishing-balance method, calculate the depreciation expense for each year of the equipment's life.

Determine carrying amount and record impairment loss. (LO 3) AP

BE9–10 Cherry Technology purchased equipment on January 4, 2015, for $250,000. The equipment had an estimated useful life of six years and a residual value of $10,000. The company has a December 31 year end and uses straight-line depreciation. On December 31, 2017, the company tests for impairment and determines that the equipment's recoverable amount is $100,000. (a) Calculate the equipment's carrying amount at December 31, 2017 (after recording the annual depreciation). (b) Record the impairment loss.

Calculate revised depreciation. (LO 3) AP

BE9–11 On January 2, 2017, Ares Enterprises reports balances in the Equipment account of $32,000 and Accumulated Depreciation—Equipment account of $9,000. The equipment had an original residual value of $2,000 and a 10-year useful life. Ares uses straight-line depreciation for equipment. On this date, the company decides that the equipment has a remaining useful life of only four years with the same residual value. Calculate the revised annual depreciation.

Record disposal by retirement. (LO 4) AP

BE9–12 On January 3, 2017, Ruiz Company retires equipment, which cost $25,700. No residual value is received. Prepare journal entries to record the transaction if accumulated depreciation is also $25,700 on this equipment. Ruiz has a December 31 fiscal year end.

Record disposal by sale. (LO 4) AP

BE9–13 Wilbur Company sells equipment on March 31, 2017, for $35,000 cash. The equipment was purchased on January 5, 2014, at a cost of $86,400, and had an estimated useful life of five years and a residual value of $2,200. Wilbur Company uses straight-line depreciation for equipment. Adjusting journal entries are made annually at the company's year end, December 31. Prepare the journal entries to (a) update depreciation to March 31, 2017, (b) record the sale of the equipment, and (c) record the sale of the equipment if Wilbur Company received $29,000 cash for it.

Record disposal by exchange of equipment. (LO 4) AP

BE9–14 Demeter Company exchanges an industrial oven for an industrial freezer. The carrying amount of the industrial oven is $31,000 (cost $61,000 less accumulated depreciation $30,000). The oven's fair value is $24,000 and cash of $5,000 is paid by Demeter in the exchange. Prepare the entry to record the exchange.

Record depletion for natural resources. (LO 5) AP

BE9–15 Cuono Mining Co. purchased a mine for $6.5 million that is estimated to have 25 million tonnes of ore and a residual value of $500,000. In the first year, 5 million tonnes of ore are extracted and 3 million tonnes are sold. Record annual depletion for the first year, ended August 31, 2017.

Record acquisition, legal expenditure, and amortization for patent. (LO 6) AP

BE9–16 Mabasa Company purchases a patent for $150,000 cash on January 2, 2017. Its legal life is 20 years and its estimated useful life is 8 years.

(a) Record the purchase of the patent on January 2, 2017.
(b) Record amortization expense for the year ended December 31, 2017.

Identify and classify long-lived assets. (LO 7) K

BE9–17 Indicate whether each of the following items is property, plant, and equipment (write "PPE"), a natural resource ("NR"), or an intangible asset ("I"). If the item does not fit any of these categories, write "NA" (not applicable) in the space provided.

(a) _____ Building
(b) _____ Cost of goods sold
(c) _____ Franchise
(d) _____ Diamond mine
(e) _____ Inventory
(f) _____ Land

(g) _____ Mining equipment
(h) _____ Note receivable, due in three years
(i) _____ Parking lot
(j) _____ Patent
(k) _____ Research costs
(l) _____ Trademark

BE9–18 Information related to property, plant, and equipment; natural resources; and intangibles on December 31, 2017 for H. Dent Company is as follows: land $400,000, building $1,100,000, accumulated depreciation—building $600,000, goodwill $410,000, nickel mine $500,000, and accumulated depletion—nickel mine $108,000. Prepare a partial balance sheet for H. Dent Company.

Prepare partial balance sheet. (LO 7) AP

BE9–19 Agrium Inc., a global agricultural nutrients producer headquartered in Calgary, reports the following in its 2014 financial statements (in millions of US$):

Calculate ratios. (LO 7) AP

	2014	2013
Sales	$16,042	$15,727
Net earnings	720	1,063
Total assets	17,108	15,977

Note: "Sales" can be used in place of "Net sales" and "Net earnings" can be used in place of "Profit" in your ratio calculations.

Calculate Agrium's return on assets and asset turnover for 2014.

▶ Exercises

E9–1 The following expenditures related to property, plant, and equipment were made by Pascal Company:

Classify expenditures. (LO 1) AP

1. Paid $400,000 for a new plant site.
2. Paid $5,000 in legal fees on the purchase of the plant site.
3. Paid $7,500 for grading the plant site.
4. Paid $4,800 to demolish an old building on the plant site; residual materials were sold for $900.
5. Paid $54,000 for a new delivery truck.
6. Paid $200 freight to have the new delivery truck delivered.
7. Paid the $95 motor vehicle licence fee on the new truck.
8. Paid $17,500 for paving the parking lots and driveways on the plant site.

Instructions

(a) Explain what types of costs should be included in determining the cost of property, plant, and equipment.
(b) List the numbers of the preceding transactions, and beside each number write the account title that the expenditure should be debited to.

E9–2 Hohenberger Farms purchased real estate for $1,280,000, which included $5,000 in legal fees. It paid $255,000 cash and incurred a mortgage payable for the balance. The real estate included land that was appraised at $476,000, a building appraised at $748,000, and fences and other land improvements appraised at $136,000. The building has an estimated useful life of 60 years and a $50,000 residual value. Land improvements have an estimated 15-year useful life and no residual value.

Record basket purchase and calculate depreciation. (LO 1, 2) AP

Instructions

(a) Calculate the cost that should be allocated to each asset purchased.
(b) Record the purchase of the real estate.
(c) Calculate the annual depreciation expense for the building and land improvements assuming Hohenberger Farms uses straight-line depreciation.

E9–3 Jeffrey Parker has prepared the following list of statements about depreciation.

Understand depreciation concepts. (LO 1, 2) C

1. Depreciation is a process of asset valuation, not cost allocation.
2. Depreciation provides for the proper matching of expenses with revenues.
3. The carrying amount of a plant asset should approximate its fair value.
4. Depreciation applies to three types of assets: land, buildings, and equipment.
5. Depreciation does not apply to a building because its usefulness and revenue-producing ability generally remain intact over time.
6. The revenue-producing ability of a depreciable asset will decline due to wear and tear and to obsolescence.
7. Recognizing depreciation on an asset results in an accumulation of cash for replacement of the asset.
8. The balance in Accumulated Depreciation represents the total cost that has been charged to expense.
9. Depreciation expense and accumulated depreciation are reported on the income statement.
10. Four factors affect the calculation of depreciation: cost, useful life, residual value, and fair value.

Instructions

Identify each statement as true or false. If false, indicate how to correct the statement.

Calculate depreciation using three methods; recommend method. (LO 2) AP

E9–4 On June 9, 2016, Blue Ribbon Company purchased manufacturing equipment at a cost of $345,000. Blue Ribbon estimated that the equipment will produce 600,000 units over its five-year useful life, and have a residual value of $15,000. The company has a December 31 fiscal year end and has a policy of recording a half-year's depreciation in the year of acquisition.

Instructions

(a) Calculate depreciation under the straight-line method for 2016 and 2017.

(b) Calculate the depreciation expense under the double diminishing-balance method for 2016 and 2017.

(c) Calculate the depreciation expense under the units-of-production method, assuming the actual number of units produced was 71,000 in 2016 and 118,600 in 2017.

(d) In this situation, what factors should the company consider in determining which depreciation method it should use?

Prepare depreciation schedules and answer questions. (LO 2) AP

E9–5 On April 22, 2016, Sandstone Enterprises purchased equipment for $129,200. The company expects to use the equipment for 12,000 working hours during its four-year life and that it will have a residual value of $14,000. Sandstone has a December 31 year end and pro-rates depreciation to the nearest month. The actual machine usage was: 1,900 hours in 2016; 2,800 hours in 2017; 3,700 hours in 2018; 2,700 hours in 2019; and 1,100 hours in 2020.

Instructions

(a) Prepare a depreciation schedule for the life of the asset under each of the following methods:
   1. straight-line,
   2. double diminishing-balance, and
   3. units-of-production.

(b) Which method results in the lowest profit over the life of the asset?

(c) Which method results in the least cash used for depreciation over the life of the asset?

Record depreciation and impairment. (LO 3) AP

E9–6 Bisor Company has a December 31 year end and uses straight-line depreciation for all property, plant, and equipment. On July 1, 2015, the company purchased equipment for $500,000. The equipment had an expected useful life of 10 years and no residual value. The company uses the nearest month method for partial year depreciation.

   On December 31, 2016, after recording annual depreciation, Bisor reviewed its equipment for possible impairment. Bisor determined that the equipment has a recoverable amount of $325,000. It is not known if the recoverable amount will increase or decrease in the future.

Instructions

(a) Prepare journal entries to record the purchase of the asset on July 1, 2015, and to record depreciation expense on December 31, 2015, and December 31, 2016.

(b) Determine if there is an impairment loss at December 31, 2016, and if there is, prepare a journal entry to record it.

(c) Calculate depreciation expense for 2017 and the carrying amount of the equipment at December 31, 2017.

Calculate revised depreciation. (LO 3) AP

E9–7 Lindy Weink, the new controller of Lafrenière Company, has reviewed the expected useful lives and residual values of selected depreciable assets at December 31, 2017. (Depreciation for 2017 has not been recorded yet.) Her findings are as follows:

Type of Asset	Date Acquired	Cost	Total Useful Life in Years		Residual Value	
			Current	Proposed	Current	Proposed
Building	Jan. 1, 2002	$800,000	20	30	$40,000	$60,500
Equipment	Jan. 1, 2015	125,000	5	4	5,000	4,000

After discussion, management agrees to accept Lindy's proposed changes. All assets are depreciated by the straight-line method. Lafrenière Company has a December 31 year end.

Instructions

(a) For each asset, calculate the annual depreciation expense using the original estimated useful life and residual value.

(b) Calculate the carrying amount of each asset as at January 1, 2017.

(c) For each asset, calculate the revised annual depreciation expense and the carrying amount at December 31, 2017.

Record asset addition and revised depreciation. (LO 3) AP

E9–8 On October 1, 2015, Chignecto Manufacturing Company purchased a piece of high-tech equipment for $90,000 cash. Chignecto estimated the equipment would have a six-year useful life and a residual value of $9,000. The company uses straight-line depreciation and has a September 30 fiscal year end.

   On October 1, 2017, Chignecto paid $15,000 cash to upgrade the equipment. It is expected that the upgrade will significantly reduce the operating costs of the equipment. Chignecto also reviewed the equipment's expected useful life and estimated that, due to changing technology, the equipment's total expected useful life will be four years and its residual value will be $5,000.

Instructions

(a) Calculate the annual depreciation expense for the first two years of the equipment's life.
(b) Calculate the carrying amount of the equipment at September 30, 2017.
(c) Record the expenditure to upgrade the equipment on October 1, 2017.
(d) Record the annual depreciation of the equipment on September 30, 2018.

E9-9 The following are some transactions of Surendal Company for 2017. Surendal Company uses straight-line depreciation and has a December 31 year end.

Record disposal of property, plant, and equipment. (LO 4) AP

Apr. 1 Retired a piece of equipment that was purchased on January 1, 2008, for $45,000. The equipment had an expected useful life of 10 years with no residual value.

July 30 Sold equipment for $1,100 cash. The equipment was purchased on January 3, 2015, for $12,600 and was depreciated over an expected useful life of three years with no residual value.

Nov. 1 Traded in an old vehicle for a new vehicle, receiving a $10,000 trade-in allowance and paying $36,000 cash. The old vehicle had been purchased on November 1, 2011, at a cost of $35,000. The estimated useful life was eight years and the estimated residual value was $5,000. The fair value of the old vehicle was $7,000 on November 1, 2017.

Instructions

(a) For each of these disposals, prepare a journal entry to record depreciation from January 1, 2017, to the date of disposal, if required.
(b) Record the disposals.

E9-10 Plessis Company owns equipment that cost $65,000 when purchased on January 2, 2017. It has been depreciated using the straight-line method based on estimated residual value of $5,000 and an estimated useful life of five years.

Calculate gain or loss on disposal. (LO 4) AP

Instructions

Prepare Plessis Company's journal entries to record the sale of the equipment in these four independent situations.

(a) Sold for $31,000 on January 2, 2020
(b) Sold for $31,000 on May 1, 2020
(c) Sold for $11,000 on January 2, 2020
(d) Sold for $11,000 on October 1, 2020

E9-11 On July 1, 2017, Phillips Exploration invests $1.3 million in a mine that is estimated to have 800,000 tonnes of ore. The company estimates that the property will be sold for $100,000 when production at the mine has ended. During the last six months of 2017, 100,000 tonnes of ore are mined and sold. Phillips has a December 31 fiscal year end.

Record depletion for natural resources; show financial statement presentation. (LO 5) AP

Instructions

(a) Explain why the units-of-production method is often used for depleting natural resources.
(b) Record the 2017 depletion.
(c) Show how the mine and any related accounts are reported on the December 31, 2017, income statement and balance sheet.

E9-12 An accounting student encountered the following situations at Chin Company:

Apply accounting concepts. (LO 1, 2, 6) AP

1. During the year, Chin Company purchased land and paid legal fees on the purchase. The land had an old building, which was demolished. The land was then cleared and graded. Construction of a new building will start next year. All of these costs were included in the cost of land. The student decided that this was incorrect, and prepared a journal entry to put the cost of removing the building and clearing and grading the land in land improvements and the legal fees in legal fee expense.

2. The student decided that Chin's amortization policy on its intangible assets is wrong. The company is currently amortizing its patents but not its trademarks. The student fixed that for the current year end by adding trademarks to her adjusting entry for amortization. She told a fellow student that she felt she had improved the consistency of the company's accounting policies by making these changes.

3. One of the buildings that Chin uses has a zero carrying amount but a substantial fair value. The student felt that leaving the carrying amount at zero did not benefit the financial information's users—especially the bank—and wrote the building up to its fair value. After all, she reasoned, you write down assets if fair values are lower. She feels that writing them up if their fair value is higher is yet another example of the improved consistency that her employment has brought to the company's accounting practices.

Instructions

Explain whether or not the student's accounting treatment in each of the above situations follows generally accepted accounting principles. If it does not, explain why and what the appropriate accounting treatment should be.

Record acquisition, amortization, and impairment of intangible assets. (LO 6) AP

E9–13   Karsch Enterprises has a December 31 fiscal year end and uses straight-line amortization to the nearest month for its finite-life intangible assets. The company has provided you with the following information related to its intangible assets and goodwill during 2016 and 2017:

2016

Jan. 9	Purchased a patent with an estimated useful life of five years and a legal life of 20 years for $45,000 cash.
May 15	Purchased another company and recorded goodwill of $450,000 as part of the purchase.
Dec. 31	Recorded adjusting entries as required for amortization.
Dec. 31	Tested assets for impairment and determined the patent and the goodwill's recoverable amounts were $40,000 and $400,000, respectively.

2017

Jan. 2	Incurred legal fees of $30,000 to successfully defend the patent.
Mar. 31	Incurred research costs of $175,000.
Apr. 1	Purchased a copyright for $66,000 cash. The company expects the copyright will benefit the company for 10 years.
July 1	Purchased a trademark with an indefinite expected life for $275,000 cash.
Dec. 31	Recorded adjusting entries as required for amortization.

Instructions

(a) Record the transactions and adjusting entries as required.
(b) Show the balance sheet presentation of the intangible assets and goodwill at December 31, 2017.

Determine balance sheet and income statement presentation for intangible assets. (LO 6) AP

E9–14   Whiteway Company has a December 31 fiscal year end. Selected information follows for Whiteway Company for two independent situations as at December 31, 2017:

1. Whiteway purchased a patent from Hopkins Inc. for $400,000 on January 1, 2014. The patent expires on January 1, 2022. Whiteway has been amortizing it over its legal life. During 2017, Whiteway determined that the patent's economic benefits would not last longer than six years from the date of acquisition.
2. Whiteway has a trademark that had been purchased in 2010 for $250,000. During 2016, the company spent $50,000 on a lawsuit that successfully defended the trademark. On December 31, 2017, it was assessed for impairment and the recoverable amount was determined to be $275,000.

Instructions

(a) For each of these assets, determine the amount that will be reported on Whiteway's December 31, 2016 and 2017, balance sheets.
(b) For each of these assets, determine what, if anything, will be recorded on Whiteway's 2017 income statement. Be specific about the account name and the amount.

Classify long-lived assets; prepare partial balance sheet. (LO 7) AP

E9–15   The North West Company Inc., a leading retailer to underserved rural and urban areas in hard-to-reach markets, reported the following selected information as at January 31, 2015 (in thousands):

Accumulated amortization—buildings	$209,584
Accumulated amortization—leasehold improvements	30,296
Accumulated amortization—fixtures and equipment	186,617
Accumulated amortization—computer equipment	62,074
Accumulated amortization—software	17,032
Accumulated amortization—other intangibles	5,750
Buildings	377,061
Cost-U-Less banner (trademark)	8,902
Computer equipment	73,151
Fixtures and equipment	265,706
Goodwill	33,653
Interest expenses	6,673
Land	16,041
Leasehold improvements	51,845
Other intangible assets	7,989
Other non-current assets	12,555
Software	28,376

Instructions

(a) Identify in which financial statement (balance sheet or income statement) and which section (e.g., property, plant, and equipment) each of the above items should be reported.
(b) Prepare the non-current assets section of the balance sheet as at January 31, 2015.

E9–16 Suncor Energy Inc. reported the following information for the fiscal years ended December 31, 2014, and December 31, 2013 (in millions):

Calculate asset turnover and return on assets. (LO 7) AN

	Dec. 31, 2014	Dec. 31, 2013
Net revenues	$39,862	$39,593
Net earnings	2,699	3,911
Total assets, end of year	79,671	78,315
Total assets, beginning of year	78,315	76,401

Instructions

(a) Calculate Suncor's asset turnover and return on assets for the two years.

(b) Comment on what the ratios reveal about Suncor Energy Inc.'s effectiveness in using its assets to generate revenues and produce profit.

▶ Problems: Set A

P9–1A In 2017, Kadlec Company had the following transactions related to the purchase of a property. All transactions were for cash unless otherwise stated.

Record property transactions. (LO 1) AP

Jan. 12   Purchased real estate for a future plant site for $420,000, paying $95,000 cash and signing a note payable for the balance. On the site, there was an old building. The fair values of the land and building were $400,000 and $40,000, respectively. The old building will be demolished and a new one built.

16   Paid $8,500 for legal fees on the real estate purchase.

31   Paid $25,000 to demolish the old building to make room for the new plant.

Feb. 13   Received $10,000 for residual materials from the demolished building.

28   Graded and filled the land in preparation for the construction for $9,000.

Mar. 14   Paid $38,000 in architect fees for the building plans.

31   Paid the local municipality $15,000 for building permits.

Apr. 22   Paid excavation costs for the new building of $17,000.

Sept. 26   The construction of the building was completed. The full cost was $750,000. Paid $150,000 cash and signed a mortgage payable for the balance.

Sept. 30   Purchased a one-year insurance policy for the building, $4,500.

Oct. 20   Paved the parking lots, driveways, and sidewalks for $45,000.

Nov. 15   Installed a fence for $12,000.

Instructions

(a) Record the above transactions.

(b) Determine the cost of the land, land improvements, and building that will appear on Kadlec's December 31, 2017, balance sheet.

TAKING IT FURTHER   When should Kadlec start to record depreciation and on which assets?

P9–2A In its first year of business, ChalkBoard purchased land, a building, and equipment on March 5, 2016, for $650,000 in total. The land was valued at $275,000, the building at $343,750, and the equipment at $68,750. Additional information on the depreciable assets follows:

Allocate cost and calculate partial period depreciation. (LO 1, 2) AP

Asset	Residual Value	Useful Life in Years	Depreciation Method
Building	$25,000	60	Straight-line
Equipment	5,000	8	Double diminishing-balance

Instructions

(a) Allocate the purchase cost of the land, building, and equipment to each of the assets.

(b) ChalkBoard has a December 31 fiscal year end and is trying to decide how to calculate depreciation for assets purchased during the year. Calculate depreciation expense for the building and equipment for 2016 and 2017 assuming:

1. depreciation is calculated to the nearest month.

2. a half-year's depreciation is recorded in the year of acquisition.

(c) Which policy should ChalkBoard follow in the year of acquisition: recording depreciation to the nearest month or recording a half year of depreciation?

TAKING IT FURTHER   In the year the asset is purchased, should ChalkBoard record depreciation for the exact number of days the asset is owned? Why or why not?

Determine cost; calculate and compare depreciation under different methods.
(LO 1, 2) AP

P9–3A   Payne Company purchased equipment on account on September 3, 2015, at an invoice price of $210,000. On September 4, 2015, it paid $4,400 for delivery of the equipment. A one-year, $1,975 insurance policy on the equipment was purchased on September 6, 2015. On September 20, 2015, Payne paid $5,600 for installation and testing of the equipment. The equipment was ready for use on October 1, 2015.

Payne estimates that the equipment's useful life will be four years, with a residual value of $15,000. It also estimates that, in terms of activity, the equipment's useful life will be 82,000 units. Payne has a September 30 fiscal year end. Assume that actual usage is as follows:

# of Units	Year Ended September 30
16,750	2016
27,600	2017
22,200	2018
16,350	2019

Instructions

(a) Determine the cost of the equipment.
(b) Prepare depreciation schedules for the life of the asset under the following depreciation methods:
  1. straight-line
  2. double diminishing-balance
  3. units-of-production
(c) Which method would result in the highest profit for the year ended September 30, 2017? Over the life of the asset?

TAKING IT FURTHER   Assume instead that, when Payne purchased the equipment, it had a legal obligation to ensure that the equipment was recycled at the end of its useful life. Assume the cost of doing this is significant. Would this have had an impact on the answers to parts (a) and (b) above? Explain.

Account for operating and capital expenditures and asset impairments.
(LO 1, 3) AP

P9–4A   Arnison Company has a December 31 fiscal year end and follows ASPE. The following selected transactions are related to its property, plant, and equipment in 2017:

Jan. 12   All of the company's light bulbs were converted to energy-efficient bulbs for $2,200. Arnison expects that this will save money on its utility bills in the future.
Feb. 6   Paid $5,400 to paint equipment that had started to rust.
Apr. 24   An air conditioning system was installed in the factory for $75,000.
May 17   Safety training was given to factory employees on using the equipment at a cost of $3,100.
July 19   Windows broken in a labour dispute (not covered by insurance) were replaced for $5,900.
Aug. 21   Paid $26,000 to convert the company's delivery vehicles from gasoline to propane. Arnison expects this will substantially reduce the vehicles' future operating costs and consequently improve efficiency, but it will not extend the vehicles' useful lives.
Sept. 20   The exhaust system in a delivery vehicle was repaired for $2,700.
Oct. 25   New parts were added to equipment for $20,000. Arnison expects this will increase the equipment's useful life by four years.
Dec. 31   After recording annual depreciation, Arnison reviewed its property, plant, and equipment for possible impairment. Arnison determined the following:
  1. Land that originally cost $200,000 had previously been written down to $175,000 in 2014 as a result of a decline in the recoverable amount. The current recoverable amount of the land is $220,000.
  2. The recoverable amount of equipment that originally cost $150,000 and has accumulated depreciation of $62,500 is $50,000.

Instructions

(a) For each of these transactions, indicate if the transaction increased (+) or decreased (−) Land, Building, Equipment, Accumulated Depreciation, total property, plant, and equipment (PP&E), and profit, and by how much. If the item is not changed, write "NE" to indicate there is no effect. Use the following format, in which the first one has been done for you as an example.

Transaction	Land	Building	Equipment	Accumulated Depreciation	Total PP&E	Profit
Jan. 12	NE	NE	NE	NE	NE	−$2,200

(b) Prepare journal entries to record the above transactions. All transactions are paid in cash.

TAKING IT FURTHER   Assume that Arnison also purchases equipment with an expected useful life of 12 years. Assume also that the equipment's engine will need to be replaced every four years. Which useful life should Arnison use when calculating depreciation on the equipment? Explain.

P9–5A Slope Style Snowboarding Company, a public company, purchased equipment on January 10, 2013, for $750,000. At that time, management estimated that the equipment would have a useful life of 10 years and a residual value of $50,000. Slope Style uses the straight-line method of depreciation and has a December 31 year end.

Slope Style tested the equipment for impairment on December 31, 2017, after recording the annual depreciation expense. It was determined that the equipment's recoverable amount was $320,000, and that the total estimated useful life would be eight years instead of 10, with a residual value of $10,000 instead of $50,000.

Record impairment and calculate revised depreciation. (LO 3) AP

Instructions

(a) Calculate the annual depreciation expense for the years 2013 to 2017 and the carrying amount at December 31, 2017.

(b) Record the impairment loss, if any, on December 31, 2017.

(c) What will appear on Slope Style's 2017 income statement and balance sheet with regard to this equipment?

(d) Assuming no further impairments or recoveries, calculate the annual depreciation expense for the years 2018 to 2020.

TAKING IT FURTHER Suggest some possible reasons why companies are allowed to record recoveries of previously recorded impairments under IFRS but not under ASPE.

P9–6A NW Tool Supply Company purchased land and a building on April 1, 2015, for $385,000. The company paid $115,000 in cash and signed a 5% note payable for the balance. At that time, it was estimated that the land was worth $150,000 and the building, $235,000. The building was estimated to have a 25-year useful life with a $35,000 residual value. The company has a December 31 year end, prepares adjusting entries annually, and uses the straight-line method for buildings; depreciation is calculated to the nearest month. The following are related transactions and adjustments during the next three years.

Record acquisition, depreciation, impairment, and disposal of land and building. (LO 1, 2, 3, 4) AP

2015

Dec. 31   Recorded annual depreciation.
     31   Paid the interest owing on the note payable.

2016

Feb. 17   Paid $225 to have the furnace cleaned and serviced.
Dec. 31   Recorded annual depreciation.
     31   Paid the interest owing on the note payable.
     31   The land and building were tested for impairment. The land had a recoverable amount of $120,000 and the building, $240,000.

2017

Jan. 31   Sold the land and building for $320,000 cash: $110,000 for the land and $210,000 for the building.
Feb. 1   Paid the note payable and interest owing.

Instructions

(a) Record the above transactions and adjustments, including the acquisition on April 1, 2015. (Round depreciation calculation to the nearest dollar.)

(b) What factors may have been responsible for the impairment?

(c) Assume instead that the company sold the land and building on October 31, 2017, for $400,000 cash: $160,000 for the land and $240,000 for the building. Prepare the journal entries to record the sale.

TAKING IT FURTHER How might management determine the recoverable amount of the land and building at each year end? Would the company need to test the assets for impairment every year?

P9–7A On December 27, 2014, Wolcott Windows purchased a piece of equipment for $107,500. The estimated useful life of the equipment is either three years or 60,000 units, with a residual value of $10,500. The company has a December 31 fiscal year end and normally uses straight-line depreciation. Management is considering the merits of using the units-of-production or diminishing-balance method of depreciation instead of the straight-line method. The actual numbers of units produced by the equipment were 10,000 in 2015, 20,000 in 2016, and 29,000 in 2017. The equipment was sold on January 5, 2018, for $15,000.

Calculate and compare depreciation and gain or loss on disposal under three methods of depreciation. (LO 2, 4) AP

Instructions

(a) Calculate the depreciation for the equipment for 2015 to 2017 under (1) the straight-line method; (2) the diminishing-balance method, using a 40% rate; and (3) units-of-production. (*Hint:* Round the depreciable cost per unit to three decimal places.)

(b) Calculate the gain or loss on the sale of the equipment under each of the three methods.

(c) Calculate the total depreciation expense plus the loss on sale (or minus the gain on sale) under each of the three depreciation methods. Comment on your results.

TAKING IT FURTHER The owner of Wolcott Windows believes that having a gain or loss on sale indicates the company had made a mistake in calculating depreciation. Do you agree or disagree? Explain.

Record acquisition,
depreciation, and disposal of
equipment. (LO 2, 4) AP

P9–8A Express Co. purchased equipment on March 1, 2015, for $95,000 on account. The equipment had an estimated useful life of five years, with a residual value of $5,000. The equipment is disposed of on February 1, 2018. Express Co. uses the diminishing-balance method of depreciation with a 20% rate and calculates depreciation for partial periods to the nearest month. The company has an August 31 year end.

Instructions

(a) Record the acquisition of the equipment on March 1, 2015.
(b) Record depreciation at August 31, 2015, 2016, and 2017.
(c) Record the disposal on February 1, 2018, under the following assumptions:
   1. It was scrapped with no residual value.
   2. It was sold for $55,000.
   3. It was sold for $45,000.
   4. It was traded for new equipment with a list price of $97,000. Express was given a trade-in allowance of $52,000 on the old equipment and paid the balance in cash. Express determined the old equipment's fair value to be $47,000 at the date of the exchange.

TAKING IT FURTHER   What are the arguments in favour of recording gains and losses on disposals of property, plant, and equipment as part of profit from operations? What are the arguments in favour of recording them as non-operating items?

Record property, plant, and
equipment transactions;
prepare partial financial
statements. (LO 2, 4, 7) AP

P9–9A At January 1, 2017, Hamsmith Corporation, a public company, reported the following property, plant, and equipment accounts:

Accumulated depreciation—buildings	$31,100,000
Accumulated depreciation—equipment	27,000,000
Buildings	48,700,000
Equipment	75,000,000
Land	10,000,000

     Hamsmith uses straight-line depreciation for buildings and equipment and its fiscal year end is December 31. The buildings are estimated to have a 50-year useful life and no residual value; the equipment is estimated to have a 10-year useful life and no residual value. Interest on the notes is payable or collectible annually on the anniversary date of the issue.

     During 2017, the following selected transactions occurred:

Apr. 1   Purchased land for $2.2 million. Paid $550,000 cash and issued a three-year, 6% note for the balance.
May 1   Sold equipment for $150,000 cash. The equipment cost $1.4 million when originally purchased on January 1, 2009.
June 1   Sold land for $1.8 million. Received $450,000 cash and accepted a three-year, 5% note for the balance. The land cost $700,000.
July 1   Purchased equipment for $1.1 million cash.
Dec. 31   Retired equipment that cost $500,000 when purchased on December 31, 2010.

Instructions

(a) Record the above transactions.
(b) Record any adjusting entries required at December 31, 2017.
(c) Prepare the property, plant, and equipment section of Hamsmith's balance sheet at December 31, 2017.

TAKING IT FURTHER   The owner of Hamsmith is considering using the revaluation model to account for property, plant, and equipment. What are some reasons to use the revaluation model?

Correct errors in recording
intangible asset transactions.
(LO 6) AP

P9–10A Due to rapid turnover in the accounting department, several transactions involving intangible assets were improperly recorded by Riley Co. in the year ended December 31, 2017:

1. Riley developed a new manufacturing process early in the year, incurring research and development costs of $160,000. Of this amount, 45% was considered to be development costs that could be capitalized. Riley recorded the entire $160,000 in the Patents account and amortized it using a 15-year estimated useful life.
2. On July 1, 2017, Riley purchased a small company and, as a result of the purchase, recorded goodwill of $400,000. Riley recorded a half-year's amortization on the goodwill in 2017 based on a 40-year useful life and credited the Goodwill account.
3. Several years ago, Riley paid $70,000 for a licence to be the exclusive Canadian distributor of a Danish beer. In 2014, Riley determined there was an impairment of $40,000 in the value of the licence and recorded the loss. In 2017, because of a change in consumer tastes, the value of the licence increased to $80,000. Riley recorded the $50,000 increase in the licence's value by crediting Impairment Loss and debiting the Licence account. Management felt the company should consistently record increases and decreases in value.

Instructions

Assuming that Riley reports under IFRS, prepare the journal entries that are needed to correct the errors made during 2017.

TAKING IT FURTHER The majority of the intangible assets reported on a balance sheet have been purchased as opposed to being internally generated. Why? What happens to the cost of an internally generated intangible asset if it is not recorded as an asset?

P9–11A The intangible assets reported by Ip Company at December 31, 2016, follow:

Record intangible asset transactions; prepare partial balance sheet. (LO 6, 7) AP

Patent #1	$80,000	
Less: Accumulated amortization	16,000	$ 64,000
Copyright #1	48,000	
Less: Accumulated amortization	28,800	19,200
Goodwill		220,000
Total		$303,200

Patent #1 was acquired in January 2015 and has an estimated useful life of 10 years. Copyright #1 was acquired in January 2008 and also has an estimated useful life of 10 years. The following cash transactions may have affected intangible assets and goodwill during the year 2017:

Jan. 2   Paid $23,200 of legal costs to successfully defend Patent #1 against infringement by another company.

June 30   Developed a new product, incurring $180,000 in research costs and $60,000 in development costs, which were paid in cash. The development costs were directly related to Patent #2, which was granted for the product on July 1. Its estimated useful life is equal to its legal life of 20 years.

Sept. 1   Paid $12,000 to an Olympic athlete to appear in commercials advertising the company's products. The commercials will air in September.

Oct. 1   Acquired a second copyright for $18,000 cash. Copyright #2 has an estimated useful life of six years.

Instructions

(a) Record the above transactions.
(b) Prepare any adjusting journal entries required at December 31, 2017, the company's year end, and update the account balances.
(c) Show how the intangible assets and goodwill will be reported on the balance sheet at December 31, 2017.

TAKING IT FURTHER Since intangible assets do not have physical substance, why are they considered to be assets?

P9–12A Rivers Mining Company has a December 31 fiscal year end. The following information relates to its Golden Grove mine:

Record natural resource transactions; prepare partial financial statements. (LO 3, 5, 7) AP

1. Rivers purchased the Golden Grove mine on March 31, 2016, for $2.6 million cash. On the same day, modernization of the mine was completed at a cash cost of $260,000. It is estimated that this mine will yield 560,000 tonnes of ore. The mine's estimated residual value is $200,000. Rivers expects it will extract all the ore, and then close and sell the mine site in four years.
2. During 2016, Rivers extracted and sold 120,000 tonnes of ore from the mine.
3. At the beginning of 2017, Rivers reassessed its estimate of the remaining ore in the mine. Rivers estimates that there are still 550,000 tonnes of ore in the mine at January 1, 2017. The estimated residual value remains at $200,000.
4. During 2017, Rivers extracted and sold 100,000 tonnes of ore from the mine.

Instructions

(a) Prepare the 2016 and 2017 journal entries for the above, including any year-end adjustments.
(b) Show how the Golden Grove mine will be reported on Rivers's December 31, 2017, income statement and balance sheet.

TAKING IT FURTHER If the total estimated amount of units that will be produced (extracted) changes during the life of the natural resource, is it still appropriate to use the units-of-production method? Explain.

P9–13A Andruski Company and Brar Company both manufacture school science equipment. The following financial information is for three years ended December 31 (in thousands):

Calculate ratios and comment. (LO 7) AN

Andruski Company	2017	2016	2015
Net sales	$ 552.0	$ 515.9	$ 469.0
Profit	21.4	20.6	18.7
Total assets	702.5	662.8	602.5
Brar Company	2017	2016	2015
Net sales	$1,762.9	$1,588.2	$1,484.3
Profit	96.5	85.4	79.8
Total assets	1,523.5	1,410.7	1,318.4

Instructions

(a) Calculate the asset turnover and return on assets ratios for both companies for 2016 and 2017. Round your answers to two decimal points.

(b) Comment on how effective each of the companies is at using its assets to generate sales and produce profit.

TAKING IT FURTHER   After reading the notes to the financial statements, you have determined that Andruski Company uses diminishing-balance depreciation and Brar uses straight-line. Does this affect your ability to compare these two companies?

▶ Problems: Set B

Record property transactions.
(LO 1) AP

P9–1B   In 2017, Weisman Company had the following transactions related to the purchase of a property. All transactions are for cash unless otherwise stated.

Feb. 7   Purchased real estate for $575,000, paying $115,000 cash and signing a note payable for the balance. The site had an old building on it and the fair value of the land and building were $555,000 and $30,000, respectively. Weisman intends to demolish the old building and construct a new apartment building on the site.

9   Paid legal fees of $7,500 on the real estate purchase on February 7.

15   Paid $19,000 to demolish the old building and make the land ready for the construction of the apartment building.

17   Received $8,500 from the sale of material from the demolished building.

25   Graded and filled the land in preparation for the building construction at a cost of $10,500.

Mar. 2   Architect's fees on the apartment building were $28,000.

15   Excavation costs were $18,000. Construction began on March 20.

Aug. 31   The apartment building was completed. The full cost of construction was $850,000. Paid $170,000 cash and signed a note payable for the balance.

Sept. 3   Paid $40,000 for sidewalks and a parking lot for the building.

10   Purchased a one-year insurance policy on the finished building for $3,750.

Oct. 31   Paid $37,750 for landscaping.

Instructions

(a) Record the above transactions.

(b) Determine the cost of the land, land improvements, and building that will appear on Weisman's December 31, 2017, balance sheet.

TAKING IT FURTHER   When should Weisman begin recording depreciation on this property and on which assets?

Allocate cost and calculate partial period depreciation.
(LO 1, 2) AP

P9–2B   In its first year of business, Solinger Company purchased land, a building, and equipment on November 5, 2016, for $700,000 in total. The land was valued at $262,500, the building at $337,500, and the equipment at $150,000. Additional information on the depreciable assets follows:

Asset	Residual Value	Useful Life in Years	Depreciation Method
Building	$15,000	60	Straight-line
Equipment	15,000	8	Double diminishing-balance

Instructions

(a) Allocate the purchase cost of the land, building, and equipment to each of the assets.

(b) Solinger has a December 31 fiscal year end and is trying to decide how to calculate depreciation for assets purchased during the year. Calculate depreciation expense for the building and equipment for 2016 and 2017 assuming:

1. depreciation is calculated to the nearest month.
2. a half-year's depreciation is recorded in the year of acquisition.

(c) Which policy should Solinger follow in the year of acquisition: recording depreciation to the nearest month or recording a half year of depreciation?

TAKING IT FURTHER Suppose that Solinger decided to use the units-of-production depreciation method instead of diminishing-balance for its equipment. How would this affect your answer to part (c) above?

P9–3B Glans Company purchased equipment on account on April 6, 2015, at an invoice price of $442,000. On April 7, 2015, it paid $4,000 for delivery of the equipment. A one-year, $3,000 insurance policy on the equipment was purchased on April 9, 2015. On April 22, 2015, Glans paid $6,000 for installation and testing of the equipment. The equipment was ready for use on May 1, 2015.

Determine cost; calculate and compare depreciation under different methods.
(LO 1, 2) AP

    Glans estimates that the equipment's useful life will be four years, with a residual value of $20,000. It also estimates that, in terms of activity, the equipment's useful life will be 150,000 units. Glans has an April 30 fiscal year end. Assume that actual usage is as follows:

# of Units	Year Ended April 30
22,600	2016
45,600	2017
49,700	2018
32,200	2019

Instructions

(a) Determine the cost of the equipment.
(b) Prepare depreciation schedules for the life of the asset under the following depreciation methods:
   1. straight-line
   2. double diminishing-balance
   3. units-of-production
(c) Which method would result in the highest profit for the year ended April 30, 2017? Over the life of the asset?

TAKING IT FURTHER Assume instead that, at the time Glans purchased the equipment, it had a legal obligation to ensure that the equipment was recycled at the end of its useful life. Assume the cost of doing this is significant. Would this have had an impact on the answers to parts (a) and (b) above? Explain.

P9–4B Sugden Company has a December 31 fiscal year end and follows IFRS. The following selected transactions are related to its property, plant, and equipment in 2017:

Account for operating and capital expenditures and asset impairments. (LO 1, 3) AP

Jan. 22   Performed an annual safety inspection on the equipment for $4,600.
Apr. 10   Installed a conveyor belt system in the factory for $95,000, which is expected to increase efficiency and allow the company to produce more products each year.
May 6   Painted the interior of the entire building at a cost of $30,500.
July 20   Repaired a machine for $10,000. An employee had used incorrect material in the machine, which resulted in a complete mechanical breakdown.
Aug. 7   Overhauled equipment that originally cost $100,000 for $35,000. This increased the equipment's expected useful life by three years.
15   Trained several new employees to operate the company's equipment at a cost of $1,900.
Oct. 25   Paid $16,700 for the purchase of new equipment and $1,500 to a consultant for testing and installing the equipment.
Nov. 6   Added an elevator and ramps to a building owned by the company to make it wheelchair-accessible for $120,000.
Dec. 31   After recording annual depreciation, Sugden reviewed its property, plant, and equipment for possible impairment. Sugden determined the following:
    1. The recoverable amount of equipment that originally cost $250,000 and has accumulated depreciation of $75,000 is $90,000.
    2. Land that originally cost $575,000 had previously been written down to $500,000 as a result of an impairment in 2014. Circumstances have changed, and the land's recoverable amount is now $600,000.

Instructions

(a) For each of these transactions, indicate if the transaction increased (+) or decreased (−) Land, Building, Equipment, Accumulated Depreciation, total property, plant, and equipment (PP&E), and profit, and by how much. If the item is not changed, write "NE" to indicate there is no effect. Use the following format, in which the first one has been done for you as an example.

Transaction	Land	Building	Equipment	Accumulated Depreciation	Total PP&E	Profit
Jan. 22	NE	NE	NE	NE	NE	−$4,600

(b) Prepare journal entries to record the above transactions. All transactions are on account.

TAKING IT FURTHER   Assume that Sugden also purchased equipment with an expected useful life of 15 years and that the equipment's engine will need to be replaced every five years. Which useful life should Sugden use when calculating depreciation on the equipment? Explain.

Record impairment and calculate revised depreciation.
(LO 3) AP

P9–5B   Short Track Speed Skating, a public company, purchased equipment on January 10, 2013, for $600,000. At that time, management estimated that the equipment would have a useful life of 10 years and a residual value of $25,000. Short Track uses the straight line method of depreciation and has a December 31 year end.

Short Track tested the equipment for impairment on December 31, 2017, after recording the annual depreciation expense. It was determined-that the equipment's recoverable amount was $260,000, and that the total estimated useful life would be seven years instead of 10, with a residual value of $10,000 instead of $25,000.

Instructions

(a) Calculate the annual depreciation expense for the years 2013 to 2017 and the carrying amount at December 31, 2017.
(b) Record the impairment loss, if any, on December 31, 2017.
(c) What will appear on Short Track's 2017 income statement and balance sheet with regard to this equipment?
(d) Assuming no further impairments or recoveries, calculate the annual depreciation expense for the years 2018 and 2019.

TAKING IT FURTHER   Why is it important to recognize impairment losses?

Record acquisition, depreciation, impairment, and disposal of land and buildings. (LO 1, 2, 3, 4) AP

P9–6B   SE Parts Supply Company purchased an industrial robot on July 1, 2015, for $395,000. It paid $100,000 in cash and signed a 5% note payable for the balance. The industrial robot was estimated to have a 20-year useful life with a $15,000 residual value. The company has a December 31 year end and prepares adjusting entries annually. It uses the double diminishing-balance method of depreciation to the nearest month for equipment. The following are related transactions and adjustments during the next three years.

2015

Dec. 31	Recorded annual depreciation.
31	Paid the interest owing on the note payable.

2016

May 21	Paid $2,000 to update robot's software system. The updates are required annually.
Dec. 31	Recorded annual depreciation.
31	Paid the interest owing on the note payable.
31	The equipment was tested for impairment. It had a recoverable amount of $275,000.

2017

Mar. 31	Sold the industrial robot for $240,000 cash.
Apr. 1	Paid the note payable and interest owing.

Instructions

(a) Record the above transactions and adjustments, including the acquisition on July 1, 2015.
(b) What factors may have been responsible for the impairment?
(c) Assume instead that the company sold the robot on September 30, 2017, for $260,000 cash. Prepare the journal entries to record the sale.

TAKING IT FURTHER   How might management determine the recoverable amount of the robot at each year end? Does the company need to test the asset for impairment every year?

Calculate and compare depreciation and gain or loss on disposal under three methods of depreciation.
(LO 2, 4) AP

P9–7B   On January 3, 2016, Ajax Argyle purchased a piece of equipment for $125,000. The equipment's estimated useful life is either three years or 12,000 units, with a residual value of $18,000. The company has a December 31 fiscal year end and normally uses straight-line depreciation. Management is considering the merits of using the units-of-production or diminishing-balance method of depreciation instead of the straight-line method. The actual numbers of units produced by the equipment were 6,000 in 2016, 2,000 in 2017, and 3,800 in 2018. The equipment was sold on January 5, 2019, for $21,000.

Instructions

(a) Calculate the depreciation for the equipment for 2016 to 2018 under (1) the straight-line method; (2) the diminishing-balance method, using a 45% rate; and (3) units-of-production. (*Hint:* Round the depreciable cost per unit to three decimal places.)
(b) Calculate the gain or loss on the sale of the equipment under each of the three methods.
(c) Calculate the total depreciation expense plus the loss on sale (or minus the gain on sale) under each of the three depreciation methods. Comment on your results.

TAKING IT FURTHER   The owner of Ajax Argyle believes that having a gain or loss on sale indicates the company had made a mistake in calculating depreciation. Do you agree or disagree? Explain.

P9–8B   Walker Co. purchased furniture on February 4, 2015, for $70,000 on account. At that time, it was expected to have a useful life of five years and a $1,000 residual value. The furniture was disposed of on January 26, 2018, when the company moved to new premises. Walker Co. uses the diminishing-balance method of depreciation with a 20% rate and calculates depreciation for partial periods to the nearest month. The company has a September 30 year end.

Record acquisition, depreciation, and disposal of furniture. (LO 2, 4) AP

Instructions

(a) Record the acquisition of the furniture on February 4, 2015.

(b) Record depreciation for each of 2015, 2016, and 2017.

(c) Record the disposal on January 26, 2018, under the following assumptions:
  1. It was scrapped and has no residual value.
  2. It was sold for $30,000.
  3. It was sold for $40,000.
  4. It was traded for new furniture with a catalogue price of $100,000. Walker Co. was given a trade-in allowance of $45,000 on the old furniture and paid the balance in cash. Walker Co. determined that the old furniture's fair value was $30,000 at the date of the exchange.

TAKING IT FURTHER   What are the arguments in favour of recording gains and losses on disposals of property, plant, and equipment as part of profit from operations? What are the arguments in favour of recording them as non-operating items?

P9–9B   At January 1, 2017, Jaina Company, a public company, reported the following property, plant, and equipment accounts:

Record property, plant, and equipment transactions; prepare partial financial statements. (LO 2, 4, 7) AP

Accumulated depreciation—buildings	$12,100,000
Accumulated depreciation—equipment	15,000,000
Building	28,500,000
Equipment	48,000,000
Land	4,000,000

Jaina uses straight-line depreciation for buildings and equipment, and its fiscal year end is December 31. The buildings are estimated to have a 50-year life and no residual value; the equipment is estimated to have a 10-year useful life and no residual value. Interest on all notes is payable or collectible at maturity on the anniversary date of the issue.

During 2017, the following selected transactions occurred:

Apr.	1	Purchased land for $1.9 million. Paid $475,000 cash and issued a 10-year, 6% note for the balance.
May	1	Sold equipment that cost $750,000 when purchased on January 1, 2010. The equipment was sold for $350,000 cash.
June	1	Sold land purchased on June 1, 1996, for $1.2 million. Received $380,000 cash and accepted a 6% note for the balance. The land cost $300,000.
July	1	Purchased equipment for $1 million on account, terms n/60.
Dec. 31		Retired equipment that cost $470,000 when purchased on December 31, 2010.

Instructions

(a) Record the above transactions.

(b) Record any adjusting entries required at December 31, 2017, and update account balances.

(c) Prepare the property, plant, and equipment section of Jaina's balance sheet at December 31, 2017.

TAKING IT FURTHER   Why do most companies use the cost model instead of the revaluation model to account for property, plant, and equipment?

P9–10B   Due to rapid employee turnover in the accounting department, the following transactions involving intangible assets were recorded in a questionable way by Hahn Company in the year ended August 31, 2017:

Correct errors in recording intangible asset transactions. (LO 6) AP

1. Hahn developed an electronic monitoring device for running shoes. It incurred research costs of $70,000 and development costs of $45,000. It recorded all of these costs in the Patent account.

2. The company registered the patent for the monitoring device developed in transaction 1. Legal fees and registration costs totalled $21,000. These costs were recorded in the Professional Fees Expense account.

3. The company recorded $5,750 of annual amortization on the patent over its legal life of 20 years [($70,000 + $45,000 = $115,000) ÷ 20 years]. The patent's expected economic life is five years. Assume that for amortization purposes, all costs occurred at the beginning of the year.

Instructions

Assuming Hahn reports under ASPE, prepare the journal entries that are needed to correct the errors made during 2017.

TAKING IT FURTHER   The majority of the intangible assets reported on a balance sheet have been purchased as opposed to being internally generated. Why? What happens to the cost of an internally generated intangible asset if it is not recorded as an asset?

Record intangible asset transactions; prepare partial balance sheet. (LO 6, 7) AP

P9–11B The intangible assets section of Ghani Corporation's balance sheet at December 31, 2016, is as follows:

Copyright #1	$36,000	
Less: Accumulated amortization	24,000	$ 12,000
Trademark		52,000
Goodwill		150,000
Total		$214,000

The copyright was acquired in January 2015 and has an estimated useful life of three years. The trademark was acquired in January 2010 and is expected to have an indefinite useful life. The following cash transactions may have affected intangible assets during 2017:

Jan. 2 Paid $7,000 in legal costs to successfully defend the trademark against infringement by another company.

July 1 Developed a new product, incurring $275,000 in research costs and $50,000 in development costs. A patent was granted for the product on July 1, and its useful life is equal to its legal life.

Aug. 1 Paid $45,000 to a popular hockey player to appear in commercials advertising the company's products. The commercials will air in September and October.

Oct. 1 Acquired a second copyright for $168,000. The new copyright has an estimated useful life of six years.

Dec. 31 Recorded annual amortization.

Instructions

(a) Prepare journal entries to record the transactions.

(b) Show how the intangible assets and goodwill will be presented on the balance sheet at December 31, 2017.

TAKING IT FURTHER Since intangible assets do not have physical substance, why are they considered to be assets?

Record equipment, note payable, and natural resource transactions; prepare partial financial statements. (LO 2, 5, 7) AP

P9–12B Cypress Timber Company has a December 31 fiscal year end. The following information is related to its Westerlund tract of timber land:

1. Cypress purchased a 50,000-hectare tract of timber land at Westerlund on June 7, 2016, for $50 million, paying $10 million cash and signing a 7% note payable for the balance. Annual interest on the mortgage is due each December 31. The note payable is due December 31, 2018. It is estimated that this tract will yield 1 million tonnes of timber. The timber tract's estimated residual value is $2 million. Cypress expects it will cut all the trees and then sell the Westerlund site in seven years.

2. On June 26, 2016, Cypress purchased and installed equipment at the Westerlund timber site for $196,000 cash. The equipment will be depreciated on a straight-line basis over an estimated useful life of seven years with no residual value. Cypress has a policy of recording depreciation for partial periods to the nearest month. The equipment will be scrapped after the Westerlund site is harvested.

3. In 2016, Cypress cut and sold 110,000 tonnes of timber.

4. In 2017, Cypress cut and sold 240,000 tonnes of timber.

Instructions

(a) Prepare the 2016 and 2017 journal entries for the above, including any year-end adjustments.

(b) Show how property, plant, and equipment, natural resources, and related accounts will be reported on Cypress's December 31, 2017, income statement and balance sheet.

TAKING IT FURTHER If the total estimated amount of units that will be produced (extracted) changes during the life of the natural resource, is it still appropriate to use the units-of-production method? Explain.

Calculate ratios and comment. (LO 7) AN

P9–13B Mock Orange Company and Cotoneaster Company both manufacture pruning shears. The following financial information is for three years ended December 31 (in thousands):

Mock Orange Company	2017	2016	2015
Net sales	$9,428.0	$8,894.3	$8,235.5
Profit	627.7	597.8	553.5
Total assets	5,829.1	5,771.4	5,343.9

Cotoneaster Company	2017	2016	2015
Net sales	$3,839.8	$3,656.9	$3,417.7
Profit	143.4	137.9	128.9
Total assets	2,754.5	2,504.1	2,340.3

Instructions

(a) Calculate the asset turnover and return on assets ratios for both companies for 2016 and 2017. Round your answers to two decimal points.

(b) Comment on how effective each of the companies is at using its assets to generate sales and produce profit.

TAKING IT FURTHER   After reading the notes to the financial statements, you have determined that Mock Orange Company uses straight-line depreciation and Cotoneaster uses diminishing-balance. Does this affect your ability to compare these two companies?

CHAPTER 9: BROADENING YOUR PERSPECTIVE

▶ # Financial Reporting and Analysis

Financial Reporting Problem

BYP9–1   Refer to the financial statements and the Notes to Consolidated Statements for **Corus Entertainment Inc.**, which are reproduced in Appendix A.

Instructions

(a) For each type of property and equipment that Corus reports in note 6 to its consolidated statement of financial position, identify the following amounts at August 31, 2014: (1) cost, (2) accumulated depreciation, and (3) net carrying amount.

(b) For the broadcast licences (intangible asset) and goodwill that Corus reports in note 9 and in its consolidated statement of financial position, identify the following amounts at August 31, 2014: (1) cost, (2) impairments, and (3) net carrying amount.

(c) Refer to note 6 again and identify the amount of disposals and retirements for the fiscal year ended August 31, 2014.

(d) What total amount did Corus report for depreciation and amortization expense?

(e) Note 3 includes additional details regarding property, plant, and equipment accounting policies. Read the note and answer the following questions:

1. Does Corus use the cost model or revaluation model for property, plant, and equipment?
2. What depreciation method does Corus use for these assets?
3. For each property, plant, and equipment asset, identify the estimated useful life ranges used by Corus for depreciation.
4. When does Corus derecognize assets and how does it calculate gains and losses?

Interpreting Financial Statements

BYP9–2   **WestJet Airlines Ltd.** is one of Canada's leading airlines, offering service to destinations in Canada, the United States, Mexico, and the Caribbean. The following is a partial extract from its December 31, 2014, notes to the financial statements:

Note. 1 (j) Statement of Significant Accounting Policies—Property and Equipment

Property and equipment is stated at cost and depreciated to its estimated residual value. Expected useful lives and depreciation methods are reviewed annually.

Asset class	Basis	Rate
Aircraft, net of estimated residual value	Straight-line	15–20 years
Engine, airframe and landing gear overhaul	Straight-line	5–15 years
Ground property and equipment	Straight-line	3–25 years
Spare engines and rotables, net of estimated residual value	Straight-line	15–20 years
Buildings	Straight-line	40 years
Leasehold improvements	Straight-line	5 years/Term of lease

Estimated residual values of the Corporation's aircraft range between $2,500 and $6,000 (in thousands of dollars) per aircraft. Spare engines have an estimated residual value equal to 10% of the original purchase price. Residual values, where applicable, are reviewed annually against prevailing market rates at the consolidated statement of financial position date.

Major overhaul expenditures are capitalized and depreciated over the expected life between overhauls. All other costs relating to the maintenance of fleet assets are charged to the consolidated statement of earnings on consumption or as incurred.

Instructions

(a) WestJet uses straight-line depreciation for all of its depreciable property and equipment. For which of the assets shown above might WestJet consider using units-of-production instead of straight-line depreciation? Should WestJet use units-of-production for those assets?

(b) According to this note, major overhaul expenditures are treated differently than other fleet maintenance costs. Explain how WestJet records these items. Is this appropriate? Why or why not?

(c) WestJet depreciates the cost of leasehold improvements over the terms of the leases. Is this appropriate? Are these terms the same as the physical lives of these assets?

(d) Does WestJet use component depreciation for any of its property and equipment assets? Explain.

▶ Critical Thinking

Collaborative Learning Activity

Note to instructor: Additional instructions and material for this group activity can be found on the Instructor Resource Site and in *WileyPLUS*.

BYP9–3 In this learning activity, you will improve your understanding of depreciation by working in small groups to analyze and categorize, on a grid, information about the three methods of depreciation.

Communication Activity

BYP9–4 Long Trucking Corporation is a medium-sized trucking company with trucks that are driven across North America. The company owns large garages and equipment to repair and maintain the trucks. Ken Bond, the controller, knows that assets can be exchanged with or without money being paid or received. The company is considering exchanging a semi-truck with a carrying amount of $100,000 (original cost $165,000) for a garage in a rural area where the company can operate a branch of the repair operation. The garage has a fair value of $90,000 and the semi-truck has a fair value of $75,000. Long Trucking Corporation will also pay the seller an additional $15,000.

 Santé Smoothie Saga

(***Note:*** This is a continuation of the Santé Smoothie Saga from Chapters 1 through 8.)

BYP9–6 Natalie is thinking of buying a van that will be used only for business. She estimates that she can buy the van for $28,400. Natalie would spend an additional $3,000 to have the van painted. As well, she wants the back seat of the van removed so that she will have lots of room to transport her juicer inventory and smoothies and supplies. The cost of taking out the back seat and installing shelving units is estimated at $1,600. She expects the van to last about five years and to be driven for 200,000 km. The annual cost of vehicle insurance will be $1,440. Natalie estimates that, at the end of the five-year useful life, the van will sell for $5,000. Assume that she will buy the van on December 15, 2017, and it will be ready for use on January 2, 2018.

Natalie is concerned about the impact of the van's cost and related depreciation on Santé Smoothies' income statement and balance sheet.

Instructions

(a) Determine the cost of the van.

Instructions

Write an e-mail to Jason Long (the owner) that explains (1) the financial impact of the exchange on assets and profit and (2) how the transaction should be recorded in the accounting records. Suggest appropriate depreciation methods to use for the garage for future recording.

"All About You" Activity

BYP9–5 In the "All About You" feature, you learned about actions that were taken to strengthen Canada's copyright law and the radical changes in technology that drove the need to update the law. You have recently graduated from a music program and have composed two songs that you believe a recording artist may produce. You are wondering how you can best get copyright protection for your songs.

Instructions

Go to the Canadian Intellectual Property Office website at http://www.cipo.ic.gc.ca and search for its publication "A Guide to Copyright." The guide can be found by clicking on "Learn" in the "Copyright" box midway down the page. (Note that the links may change so a basic search of the site may be required.)

Answer the following questions:

(a) What is a copyright and to what does copyright apply?

(b) How can you obtain a copyright for your songs and what do you have to do to be protected?

(c) What are the benefits to you of getting copyright registration for your songs?

(d) How and where do you register a copyright?

(e) When you register a copyright, you are required to pay a fee for the registration. Should the registration fee for the copyright be recorded as an asset or an expense?

(f) Go to the glossary in "A Guide to Copyright." What is infringement of copyright? Provide a specific example of infringement.

(g) Go to frequently asked questions in "A Guide to Copyright." How long does copyright last?

(b) Prepare depreciation schedules for the life of the van under the following depreciation methods:
1. straight-line.
2. diminishing-balance at double the straight-line rate.
3. It is estimated that the van will be driven as follows: 30,000 km in 2018, 37,500 km in 2019, 40,000 km in 2020, 47,500 km in 2021, 35,000 km in 2022, and 10,000 km in 2023.

Recall that Santé Smoothies has a May 31 year end.

(c) Which method of depreciation would result in the highest profit for the year ended May 31, 2019? Over the life of the asset?

(d) Which method would result in the highest carrying amount for the van for the year ended May 31, 2019? Over the life of the asset?

(e) Which method of depreciation would you recommend that Natalie use? Why?

ANSWERS TO CHAPTER QUESTIONS

ANSWERS TO ACCOUNTING IN ACTION INSIGHT QUESTIONS

Business Insight, p. 481

Q: Is the units-of-production method the best depreciation method for Morris Formal Wear to use for its tuxedos or would you recommend another method?

A: Since Morris Formal Wear wants to track wear and tear on each of its tuxedos, the units-of-production depreciation method is the best choice. Rental tuxedos are the type of long-lived asset that will physically wear out with use much faster than they would become obsolete due to changing tuxedo styles. By keeping track of how many times each tuxedo has been used, instead of just how old they are, the business can make better decisions about when to replace the tuxedos.

Ethics Insight, p. 484

Q: Is the president's requested change unethical? If so, why?

A: The president's requested change is unethical because he wants to revise the depreciation calculation solely to increase company profits and therefore his bonus. A change in estimate for an asset's useful life should only be made when management decides that wear and tear or obsolescence require a change. Otherwise, changing the asset's useful life just to boost the president's bonus is unfair to readers of financial statements, competitors, and even employees, who may suffer if the company's reputation were damaged because the marketplace found out. The move would also not be fair to the company's auditors, who have a professional obligation to ensure that such changes in estimates are not made for unethical reasons.

All About You Insight, p. 497

Q: Why is it important that the copyrights of artists, writers, musicians, and the entertainment industry be protected?

A: Just as it is important that you as an individual be compensated in your career, it is important that individuals in artistic, music, entertainment, and literary careers be compensated fairly for their creativity. Without fair compensation, Canada's creativity and innovation will be discouraged. Without copyright protection, it may be difficult to ensure that appropriate individuals are fairly compensated and companies may not be willing to invest in creative ventures if the work is not protected.

ANSWERS TO SELF-STUDY QUESTIONS

1. d   2. c   3. b   4. a   5. c   6. b   7. b   8. a   9. b   10. c   11. b   12. d

10 CURRENT LIABILITIES AND PAYROLL

CHAPTER PREVIEW Whether it is a huge company such as one of Canada's chartered banks, a medium-sized company like Nanotech Security Corp., or a small business such as your local convenience store, every company has liabilities. **Liabilities are present obligations resulting from past transactions that will involve future settlement.** Liabilities are classified as current and non-current. As explained in Chapter 4, current liabilities are obligations that are expected to be settled within one year from the balance sheet date or in the company's normal operating cycle. Obligations that are expected to be paid after one year or longer are classified as non-current liabilities. Financial statement users want to know whether a company's obligations are current or non-current. A company that has more current liabilities than current assets often lacks liquidity, or the ability to pay short-term obligations as they become due. This may signal financial difficulties. Therefore, users want to know the types of liabilities a company has and when they will be due.

In this chapter, we explain current liabilities; non-current liabilities will be discussed in Chapter 15. Payroll creates current liabilities and affects almost every company. It is also explained in this chapter.

FEATURE STORY   BUTTERFLIES BRING ABOUT BETTER BANKNOTES

SURREY, B.C.—How does a Canadian company commercialize the same technology that makes a butterfly glow? Nanotech Security Corp., inspired by nature, has developed a way to imprint hologram-like images on objects as diverse as banknotes and designer purses to prevent counterfeiting.

Nanotech uses nanotechnology—a method of manipulating matter on a molecular scale—to chip holes no bigger than one-billionth of a metre (or one nanometre) on an item's surface. These tiny holes reflect light, mimicking the nanostructures of the blue morpho butterfly, whose wings are luminescent. Nanotech's patented process, first developed by the company founders while at Simon Fraser University, is unlike other anti-counterfeiting processes, which inject dyes or pigments onto the surface and can be more easily copied. Nanotech's machines that make the holes are proprietary and expensive—well beyond the reach of typical counterfeiters.

Nanotech is now signing contracts with foreign countries to produce anti-counterfeit images on bank notes. The company hopes to work with luxury goods manufacturers, which can use the technology to etch their logos onto purse clasps, for example, producing a shimmering image that can't be reproduced.

These contracts require a certain accounting treatment, because Nanotech is often asking for money up front before the service is delivered. This revenue that Nanotech collects, but hasn't earned yet until it produces the anti-counterfeiting images on products, is called unearned revenue (also known as deferred revenue). Deferred revenue is considered a current liability because it is an obligation—to provide services under contract—that will be fulfilled within a year.

The biggest share of Nanotech's current liabilities was accounts payable and accrued liabilities, which amounted to $1.6 million as at September 30, 2014.

Sources: Ivor Tossell, "Famous Butterfly Inspires Anti-counterfeiting Nanotechnology," *Globe and Mail*, April 1, 2013; Jameson Berkow, "Nanotech's Big Break," *Financial Post*, February 13, 2012; Nanotech Security Corp. annual report 2014; Nanotech corporate website, http://nanosecurity.ca.

Ingo Arndt/Getty Images

Determinable (Certain) Current Liabilities

In this section of the chapter, we will discuss liabilities where there is no uncertainty about their existence, amount, or timing. Liabilities with a known amount, payee, and due date are often referred to as **determinable liabilities**.

Examples of determinable current liabilities include accounts payable, bank indebtedness from operating lines of credit, notes payable, sales taxes payable, unearned revenue, and current maturities of long-term debt. This category also includes accrued liabilities such as property taxes, payroll, and interest payable.

The entries for accounts payable and determinable unearned revenues have been explained in previous chapters, but we will provide a brief review in this section. We will also discuss the accounting for other types of current liabilities in this section, including bank indebtedness from an operating line of credit, notes payable, sales taxes payable, property taxes payable, and current maturities of long-term debt. Payroll and employee benefits payable are also examples of determinable liabilities, but as the accounting for payroll is complex, we discuss it in a separate section of this chapter.

Alternative terminology Determinable liabilities are also referred to as *certain liabilities* or *known liabilities*.

ACCOUNTS PAYABLE

Whenever an entity buys goods from a supplier with the agreement to pay at a later date, an **account payable** (sometimes referred to as a "trade payable") is created. Most businesses require payment within 30 days; therefore, accounts payable are classified as current liabilities. For example, recall from previous chapters that when an entity buys supplies, the required journal entry is as follows:

A = L + OE
+500   +500

Cash flows: no effect

Apr. 6	Supplies	500	
	Accounts Payable		500
	To record purchase of supplies.		

When this journal entry is posted, the current liability is now recorded until the payment is made.

Accounts payable, or trade accounts payable, are often the largest current liability on a company's balance sheet, as is the case with Nanotech Security Corp. In another example, as shown on Corus Entertainment's balance sheet excerpt in Illustration 10-1, its trade and other payables amounted to $170,411 thousand, which is almost 97% of its total current liabilities.

▸ ILLUSTRATION 10-1
Corus Entertainment Inc.'s current liabilities

CORUS ENTERTAINMENT INC. Consolidated Statement of Financial Position (partial) August 31, 2014 (in thousands)	
Accounts payable and accrued liabilities (*note 11*)	170,411
Provisions (*note 12*)	5,314
Total current liabilities	175,725

UNEARNED REVENUES

As noted in the feature story on Nanotech, unearned revenues are common for many businesses. This is especially true for entities in the publishing, entertainment, and travel industries. For example, when a magazine publisher, such as Rogers Communications, sells magazine subscriptions to *Sportsnet* or *LouLou*, it receives payment in advance when the customer order is placed. An airline, such as WestJet, often receives cash when it sells tickets for future flights. Season tickets for concerts, sporting events (as we saw in the feature story on Maple Leaf Sports and Entertainment in Chapter 3), and theatre programs are also paid for in advance. How do companies account for unearned revenues that are received before goods are delivered or services are performed?

1. When a company receives the payment in advance, it debits cash and credits a current liability account identifying the source of the unearned revenue.
2. When the company provides the goods or performs the service, the performance obligation is satisfied, and the company recognizes the revenue earned as it debits an unearned revenue account and credits a revenue account.

To illustrate, assume that the Saint John Seadogs hockey team sells 10,000 season tickets at $50 each for its five-game home schedule. The Seadogs make the following entry for the sale of season tickets.

Aug. 6	Cash	500,000	
	Unearned Revenue		500,000
	To record sale of 10,000 season tickets.		

A = L + OE
+500,000 +500,000
↑Cash flows: +500,000

As each game is completed, the team records the recognition of revenue with the following entry.

Sept. 7	Unearned Revenue	100,000	
	Ticket Revenue		100,000
	To record hockey ticket revenue earned.		

A = L + OE
−100,000 +100,000
Cash flows: no effect

The account Unearned Revenue is reported as a current liability. As the Saint John team recognizes revenue, it reclassifies the amount from Unearned Revenue to Ticket Revenue. For some companies, unearned revenue is material. For example, in the airline industry, tickets sold for future flights can represent almost 50% of total current liabilities.

Illustration 10-2 shows common types of unearned and earned revenue in selected types of businesses.

| | Types of Revenue | |
Type of Business	Unearned Revenue	Revenue
Airline	Unearned Ticket Revenue	Ticket Revenue
Magazine publisher	Unearned Subscription Revenue	Subscription Revenue
Hotel	Unearned Rent Revenue	Rent Revenue

▶ ILLUSTRATION 10-2
Common types of unearned and earned revenue

Helpful hint Unearned revenues are the opposite of prepaid accounts. For prepaid assets, the cash is paid out before the service or goods are received. For unearned revenues, the cash is received before the goods or services are provided.

OPERATING LINE OF CREDIT AND BANK OVERDRAFT

Operating Line of Credit

Current assets (such as accounts receivable) do not always turn into cash at the exact time that current liabilities (such as accounts payable) must be paid. Consequently, most companies have an **operating line of credit** at their bank to help them manage temporary cash shortfalls. This means that the company has been pre-authorized by the bank to borrow money when it is needed, up to a pre-set limit.

Security, called **collateral**, is usually required by the bank as protection in case the company is unable to repay the loan. Collateral normally includes some, or all, of the company's current assets (e.g., accounts receivable or inventories); investments; or property, plant, and equipment.

Money borrowed through a line of credit is normally borrowed on a short-term basis, and is repayable on demand by the bank. In reality, repayment is rarely demanded without notice. A line of credit makes it very easy for a company to borrow money. It does not have to make a call or visit its bank to actually arrange the transaction. The bank simply covers any cheques written in excess of the bank account balance, up to the approved credit limit.

Bank Overdraft

Some companies have a negative (credit), or overdrawn, cash balance at year end. This amount is usually called *bank indebtedness*, *bank overdraft*, or *bank advances*. No special entry or account is required to record the overdrawn amount. The Cash account has a credit balance because the dollar amount of cheques written exceeded the dollar amount of deposits. The credit balance in Cash is reported as a current liability with the appropriate note disclosure.

Interest is usually charged on the overdrawn amount at a floating rate, such as prime plus a specified percentage. The **prime rate** is the interest rate that banks charge their best customers. This rate is usually increased by a specified percentage according to the company's risk profile.

SHORT-TERM NOTES PAYABLE

Helpful hint Notes payable are the opposite of notes receivable, and the accounting is similar.

The line of credit described above is similar to a **note payable**. Notes payable are obligations in the form of written promissory notes. Notes payable are often used instead of accounts payable because they give the lender formal proof of the obligation in case legal remedies are needed to collect the debt. Companies frequently issue notes payable to meet short-term financing needs. Notes payable usually require the borrower to pay interest.

Notes are issued for varying periods. **Notes payable due for payment within one year of the balance sheet date are classified as current liabilities.** Most notes payable are interest-bearing, with interest due monthly or at maturity.

To illustrate the accounting for notes payable, assume that Koh Co. borrows $100,000 from the local caisse populaire (credit union) on March 1 for four months, at an interest rate of 6%.

Koh makes the following journal entry when it signs the note and receives the $100,000:

A	=	L	+	OE
+100,00		+100,00		

↑Cash flows: +100,000

Mar. 1	Cash	100,000	
	Notes Payable		100,000
	To record issue of four-month, 6% note to		
	Caisse Populaire Dumoulin.		

Helpful hint Interest is normally calculated using the number of days. In this textbook, we use months in order to simplify the calculations.

Interest accrues over the life of the note; therefore, the company must periodically record the interest accrual. If Koh prepares financial statements annually and it has an April 30 year end, it will have to make an adjusting entry to recognize the interest expense and interest payable at April 30.

Helpful hint Interest rates are always expressed as annual rates, not the rate for the duration of the note.

Recall from Chapter 3 that **interest is calculated by multiplying the principal amount by the annual interest rate by the fraction of the year in the accrual.** The formula for calculating interest for Koh is shown in Illustration 10-3.

▶ **ILLUSTRATION 10-3**
Formula for calculating interest

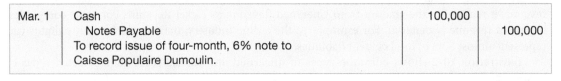

Face Value of Note		Annual Interest Rate		Time in Terms of One Year		Interest
$100,000	×	6%	×	$^{2}/_{12}$	=	$1,000

The adjusting entry to record the interest is:

A	=	L	+	OE
		+1,000		−1,000

Cash flows: no effect

Apr. 30	Interest Expense	1,000	
	Interest Payable		1,000
	To accrue interest to April 30.		

In the April 30 financial statements, the current liabilities section of the balance sheet will show notes payable of $100,000 and interest payable of $1,000. In addition, interest expense of $1,000 will be reported as other expenses in the income statement. **Interest payable is shown separately from the note payable.**

At maturity (July 1), Koh Co. must pay the face value of the note ($100,000) plus $2,000 interest ($100,000 × 6% × $^{4}/_{12}$). Two months ($1,000) of this interest has already been accrued. Interest must also be updated for $1,000 ($100,000 × 6% × ²/₁₂) for the two additional months—May and June—since interest was last recorded.

July 1	Interest Expense	1,000	
	Interest Payable		1,000
	To accrue interest for May and June.		
1	Notes Payable	100,000	
	Interest Payable ($1,000 + $1,000)	2,000	
	Cash ($100,000 + $2,000)		102,000
	To record payment of Caisse Populaire		
	Dumoulin note and accrued interest.		

A = L + OE
+1,000 −1,000
Cash flows: no effect

A = L + OE
−102,000 −100,000
−2,000
Cash flows: −102,000

The calculation of total interest expense over the life of the note is shown in Illustration 10-4.

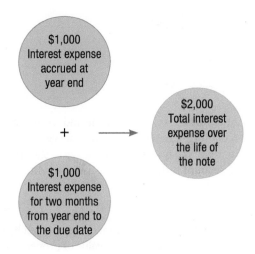

▶ ILLUSTRATION 10-4
Calculation of total
interest expense over
the life of the note

SALES TAXES

As a consumer, you are well aware that you pay sales taxes on most products and services. For businesses, sales taxes are collected from customers on behalf of the government. Taxes collected are therefore a liability. The business has an obligation to pay the amount collected to the appropriate government body.

Sales taxes are expressed as a percentage of the sales price. As discussed in earlier chapters and in Appendix B at the end of this textbook, sales taxes usually take the form of the federal Goods and Services Tax (GST) and Provincial Sales Tax (PST) or a combined Harmonized Sales Tax (HST). The following table summarizes the sales taxes by province or territory at the time of writing:

Province/Territory	GST	PST	HST
Newfoundland and Labrador			13%
Nova Scotia			15%
Prince Edward Island			14%
New Brunswick			13%
Quebec	5%	9.975% (known as Quebec Sales Tax)	
Ontario			13%
Saskatchewan	5%	5%	
Manitoba	5%	8%	
Alberta	5%		
British Columbia	5%	7%	
Northwest Territories/Yukon/Nunavut	5%		

In Ontario, Newfoundland and Labrador, and New Brunswick, the PST and GST have been combined into one 13% HST. Prince Edward Island has a 14% HST and Nova Scotia a 15% HST. Quebec, Alberta, British Columbia, Manitoba, Saskatchewan, Yukon, Northwest Territories, and Nunavut do not have HST.

Whether GST, PST, or HST, the business collects the tax from the customer when the sale occurs. The business then pays (remits) the sales taxes collected to the designated federal and provincial collecting authorities. In the case of GST, HST, and the Quebec Sales Tax or QST, collections may be offset against sales taxes paid by the business on its purchases. In such cases, only the net amount owing or recoverable must be paid or refunded. Depending on the size of the business, the sales taxes must be sent to the government monthly, quarterly, or, for very small companies, annually.

The amount of the sale and the amount of the sales tax collected are usually rung up separately on the cash register. The cash register readings are then used to credit sales or services and the correct sales taxes payable accounts. For example, if the March 25 cash register reading for Comeau Company, in New Brunswick, shows sales of $10,000 and Harmonized Sales Tax of $1,300 ($10,000 × 13% HST rate), the entry is as follows:

<table>
<tr><td>

A = L + OE
+11,300 +1,300 +10,000

↑Cash flows: +11,300
</td><td>

Mar. 25 | Cash | 11,300 |
| Sales | | 10,000
| HST Payable | | 1,300
| To record sales and sales taxes. | |
</td></tr>
</table>

Comeau Company does **not** report the sales taxes collected from customers as revenue; sales taxes collected from customers are a liability. Comeau Company serves only as a collection agent for the government. When the company remits (pays) these sales taxes to the appropriate government collecting authorities, the HST Payable account is debited and Cash is credited.

PROPERTY TAXES

Businesses that own property pay property taxes. These taxes are charged by municipal governments, and are calculated at a specified rate for every $100 of assessed value of property (land and buildings). Property taxes generally cover a full calendar year, although bills are not issued until the spring of each year.

To illustrate, assume that Tantramar Management owns land and a building in Regina. Tantramar's year end is December 31 and it makes adjusting entries annually. On March 1, it receives its property tax bill of $6,000 for the calendar year, which is due to be paid on May 31.

In March, when Tantramar receives the property tax bill for the calendar year, two months of that year have passed. The company records the property tax expense for the months of January and February and the liability owed at that point as follows:

<table>
<tr><td>

A = L + OE
+1,000 -1,000

Cash flows: no effect
</td><td>

Mar. 1 | Property Tax Expense ($6,000 × $^2/_{12}$) | 1,000 |
| Property Tax Payable | | 1,000
| To record property tax expense for January | |
| and February and amount owing. | |
</td></tr>
</table>

On May 31, when Tantramar pays the property tax bill, the company records the payment of the liability recorded on March 1. It also records the expense incurred to date for the months of March, April, and May. As at May 31, five months have passed and should be recorded as property tax expense. The remaining seven months of the year are recorded as a prepayment, as shown in the following entry:

<table>
<tr><td>

A = L + OE
+3,500 -1,000 -1,500
-6,000

↓ Cash flows: -6,000
</td><td>

May. 31 | Property Tax Payable | 1,000 |
| Property Tax Expense ($6,000 × $^3/_{12}$) | 1,500 |
| Prepaid Property Tax ($6,000 × $^7/_{12}$) | 3,500 |
| Cash | | 6,000
To record payment of property tax expense	
for March through May, and amount prepaid	
for June through December.	
</td></tr>
</table>

After the payment of the property tax, Tantramar has a zero balance in its liability account but still has a prepayment. Since Tantramar makes adjusting entries only annually, it would not adjust the prepaid property tax account until year end, December 31. At that time, it would make the following entry:

Dec. 31	Property Tax Expense	3,500	
	Prepaid Property Tax		3,500
	To record property tax expense for June through December.		

A	=	L	+	OE
−3,500				−3,500

Cash flows: no effect

There are other acceptable ways to record and adjust property taxes. Some companies would debit Property Tax Expense when the bill is recorded on March 1 and avoid a later adjusting entry. In addition, companies may prepare monthly or quarterly adjusting entries. Whatever way is used, at year end, the companies would have the same ending balances. In this case, the accounts Prepaid Property Tax and Property Tax Payable should each have a zero balance and Property Tax Expense should have a balance of $6,000.

CURRENT MATURITIES OF LONG-TERM DEBT

Companies often have a portion of long-term debt that will be due in the current year. That amount is considered a current liability. Assume that on January 1, 2017, Cudini Construction issues a $25,000, five-year note payable. Each January 1, starting on January 1, 2018, $5,000 of the note will be repaid. When financial statements are prepared on December 31, 2017, $5,000 should be reported on the balance sheet as a current liability and the remaining $20,000 of the note should be reported as a long-term liability. Companies often present this current liability as **current portion of long-term debt**. The Canadian winery Andrew Peller Ltd. reported almost $7.4 million of such debt (Illustration 10-5).

ANDREW PELLER LTD. Balance Sheet (partial) March 31, 2014 (in thousands)	
Current Portion of Long-Term Debt (note 11)	7,392

▶ **ILLUSTRATION** **10-5**
Andrew Peller Ltd.'s current portion of long-term debt

It is not necessary to prepare an adjusting entry to recognize the current maturity of long-term debt. The proper statement classification of each liability account is recognized when the balance sheet is prepared.

BEFORE YOU GO ON...DO IT **1** ▷ **Reporting Current Liabilities**

Prepare the journal entries to record the following transactions for DiMaria Enterprises. Round any calculations to the nearest dollar.

1. Accrue interest on January 31 (the company's year end) for a $10,000, 30-month, 8% note payable issued on December 1. Interest is payable the first of each month, beginning January 1.
2. The cash register total for sales on April 2 is $250,000. The HST tax rate is 13%. Record the sales and sales taxes.
3. A property tax bill of $12,000 for the calendar year is received on May 1 and is due on June 30. Record the entry on May 1, assuming the company has a January 31 year end.

(continued)

BEFORE YOU GO ON...DO IT   **Reporting Current Liabilities** *(continued)*

Action Plan

- The formula for interest is as follows: principal (face) value × annual interest rate × time.
- Record sales separately from sales taxes. To calculate sales taxes, multiply the sales total by the sales tax rate.
- Record the property tax expense and the property tax payable for amounts incurred (owed) to date.

Solution

Jan. 31	Interest Expense ($10,000 × 8% × $\frac{1}{12}$)	67	
	Interest Payable		67
	To accrue interest on note payable.		
Apr. 2	Cash	282,500	
	Sales		250,000
	HST Payable ($250,000 × 13%)		32,500
	To record sales and sales taxes.		
May 1	Property Tax Expense ($12,000 × $\frac{3}{12}$)	3,000	
	Property Tax Payable		3,000
	To record property tax for February, March, and April.		

Related exercise material: BE10–1, BE10–2, BE10–3, BE10–4, BE10–5, BE10–6, BE10–7, E10-1, E10–2, E10–3, E10–4, E10–5, E10–6, E10–7, E10–8, and E10–9.

LEARNING OBJECTIVE   **Account for uncertain liabilities.**

Uncertain Liabilities

In the previous section, we discussed current liabilities where there was a high degree of certainty. It was known who required payment, the amount to be paid, and when the payment was due. However, this may not always be the case. In this section, we will discuss liabilities that have a lower degree of certainty but are still likely to occur. We will then discuss situations where there is an even greater degree of uncertainty, as sometimes the determination of a liability may depend on a future event.

PROVISIONS

Alternative terminology Provisions are also known as *estimated liabilities.*

A **provision** is a liability that exists but the amount and the timing of the settlement are uncertain. We know we owe someone, but we are not sure how much and when. We may not even know whom we owe. Common provisions include product warranties, customer loyalty programs, and gift cards. We discuss these three provisions in the following sections.

Product Warranties

Product warranties are promises made by the seller to repair or replace a product if it is defective or does not perform as intended. Warranties (also known as guarantees) are usually issued by manufacturers. For a specified period of time after the item was sold, a manufacturer may promise to repair the item, replace it, or refund the buyer's money under certain conditions. As a buyer, it is important to read all warranty contracts carefully because the promises they make can be quite different.

Warranties will lead to future costs for the manufacturer for the repair or replacement of defective units. When goods are sold, it is not known which units will become defective. The company does not know whom it will have to pay, or when. The company does know a liability exists even though the payee and timing are unknown.

There are two possible approaches to accounting for product warranties: the expense approach and the revenue approach. In this chapter, we will illustrate the expense approach. The revenue approach is explained in an intermediate accounting textbook.

Under the expense approach, the warranty liability is measured using the estimated future cost of honouring the product's warranty. At the time the product is sold, the costs are not known, but based on past experience with a particular product, most companies are able to estimate it. Using the estimated amount, the company records a warranty expense and a liability. This ensures the company recognizes the full cost of the sale in the period in which the sale occurs. Recall that this is known as matching expenses with revenues. As the actual costs are incurred in subsequent periods, the liability is reduced.

To illustrate the expense approach of accounting for warranty liabilities, assume that Hermann Company sells 10,000 stereos at an average price of $600 in the year ended December 31, 2017. The selling price includes a one-year warranty on parts. Based on past experience, it is expected that 500 units (5%) will be defective, and that warranty repair costs will average $100 per unit.

At December 31, it is necessary to accrue the estimated warranty costs for the 2017 sales. The calculation is as follows:

Number of units sold	10,000
Estimated rate of defective units	× 5%
Total estimated defective units	500
Average warranty repair cost	× $100
Estimated product warranty liability	$50,000

The adjusting entry is:

Dec. 31	Warranty Expense	50,000	
	Warranty Liability		50,000
	To accrue estimated warranty costs.		

A = L + OE
+50,000 −50,000

Cash flows: no effect

In 2017, warranty contracts were honoured on 300 units at a total cost of $30,000. These costs are recorded when they are incurred, but for our illustration they are being recorded in one summary journal entry for the year:

Dec. 31	Warranty Liability	30,000	
	Repair Parts Inventory (and/or Wages Payable)		30,000
	To record honouring of 300 warranty contracts on 2017 sales.		

A = L + OE
−30,000 −30,000

Cash flows: no effect

As demonstrated in the T accounts below, in 2017, a warranty expense of $50,000 is reported as an operating expense in the income statement. The remaining estimated warranty liability of $20,000 ($50,000 − $30,000) is classified as a current liability on the balance sheet.

Warranty Expense			Warranty Liability		
50,000		Actual	30,000	Estimate	50,000
(Income Statement)				Bal. Dec. 31, 2017	20,000
				(Balance Sheet)	

In 2018, all costs incurred to honour warranty contracts on 2017 sales should be debited to the Warranty Liability account, like what was shown above for the 2017 sales. The Warranty Liability account will be carried forward from year to year—increased by the current year's estimated expense and decreased by the actual warranty costs incurred. It is quite likely that the actual expenses will not exactly equal the estimated liability amount. Every year, as is done with accounts receivable and the allowance for doubtful accounts, the warranty liability is reviewed and adjusted if necessary.

Customer Loyalty Programs

To attract or keep customers, many companies offer **customer loyalty programs.** Loyalty programs are designed to increase sales and are important for many businesses. These programs provide customers with future savings on the merchandise or services the company sells. Customer loyalty programs take varying forms. Some programs, such as airline frequent flyer programs, may require customers to collect points. Other programs may involve a credit reward that provides a cash discount on future sales.

The most successful loyalty program in Canadian retail history is Canadian Tire "money" (CTM), first introduced in 1958. The "money" resembles real currency (although the bills are considerably smaller than Bank of Canada notes) and is issued with no expiry date. CTM is given out by the cashiers for purchases paid for by cash, debit card, or the Canadian Tire Options MasterCard credit card. Customers can use CTM to buy anything at a Canadian Tire store. In fact, some privately owned businesses in Canada also accept CTM as payment since the owners of many of these businesses shop at Canadian Tire. Recently the company broadened the loyalty program and implemented an e-money program. Customers can now earn e-Canadian Tire "money" when store purchases are made. e-money is collected by the customer by showing their Canadian Tire mobile app, program card, or key fob with their payment. Like the paper money, the e-money never expires and it can be transferred to other loyalty program members.

Customer loyalty programs result in a liability to the business in the form of unearned or deferred revenue. When customers purchase goods or services and are awarded a loyalty benefit, there is a promise to deliver further goods or services in the future, either for free or at a discount. This promise results in a performance obligation to the entity. To record this future performance obligation, a portion of the original sales price should be allocated to unearned revenue until the future performance obligation is satisfied. The allocation of the selling price should be based on the stand-alone value of the goods or services sold and the stand-alone value of the goods or services promised. The stand-alone value is the amount at which the entity would sell the goods or services to the customer individually. The portion of the sale allocated to the loyalty program is recorded as unearned revenue. When the loyalty points are redeemed and the promised goods or services are delivered to the customer, the performance obligation is satisfied and the unearned revenue is earned.

To illustrate, assume that Greenville Co-op has a rewards program whereby customers get 1 point for every $10 spent on groceries. Each point is redeemable for a $1 discount towards the future purchase of groceries. During the month of April, the Co-op sells goods worth $100,000 and consequently awards customers 10,000 points. Based on past history, Greenville Co-op estimates that 90% of the rewards will be redeemed. Therefore, it is expected that 9,000 points will be redeemed with a stand-alone value of $9,000. A portion of the $100,000 of sales is to be allocated to the rewards program based on the total stand-alone value of $109,000 ($100,000 + $9,000). The revenue allocation for the current sales and the unearned revenue will be as follows:

Amount related to the revenue earned   = $100,000 ($100,000 ÷ $109,000)   = $91,743
Amount related to the loyalty points   = $100,000 ($9,000 ÷ $109,000)   = $8,257

Greenville will record the following journal entry to record the sale of the goods and the liability relating to the future redemption of the rewards points for the month of April:

A	=	L	+	OE
+100,000		+8,257		+91,743

↑Cash flows: +100,000

April 30	Cash	100,000	
	Sales		91,743
	Unearned Revenue—Loyalty Program		8,257
	To record the sales and unearned revenue related to the loyalty program.		

The account Unearned Revenue—Loyalty Program is a current liability that is reported on the balance sheet. It represents the unearned revenue related to the customer loyalty program. As the loyalty points are redeemed, the unearned revenue becomes earned.

To illustrate this, customers of the Greenville Co-op redeemed 4,500 points during the month of May. That is, half of the rewards issued in April were redeemed in May. This means half of the unearned revenue was earned during the month of May and must be recorded. Therefore, Greenville Co-op makes the following entry at the end of May (ignoring the cost of sales):

A	=	L	+	OE
		−4,129		+4,129

Cash flows: no effect

May 31	Unearned Revenue—Loyalty Program	4,129	
	Revenue from Rewards Program		4,129
	To record the redemption of rewards during May.		

Gift Cards

Gift cards or gift certificates have become an increasingly popular source of revenue for many companies. They are unearned revenues in that the company receives cash in advance of providing the goods or the services. Thus, when gift cards are issued, the Unearned Revenue account (liability) is credited. As the gift card is redeemed (used), the company will then record the sales or service revenue and reduce or debit the Unearned Revenue account.

Alternative terminology Unearned revenue is sometimes called *deferred revenue.*

As with customer loyalty programs, the difficulty with gift cards is that it is unknown when and even if the card will be redeemed. If an entity is able to estimate the gift card balances that will not be redeemed and there is little possibility of a reversal, the amount not expected to be redeemed may be taken into revenue as the gift card revenue is earned. If the entity is not able to estimate how much will remain unredeemed, then it may only recognize the related revenue once the possibility of redemption is remote. As with warranties and customer loyalty programs, a company with a gift card program will need to use past experience to estimate the appropriate balance for the liability.

ACCOUNTING IN ACTION
ACROSS THE ORGANIZATION

Almost every retailer offers some kind of customer loyalty program, through club memberships, discount cards, or points programs. Shoppers Drug Mart was one of the first retailers to take this trend a step further by having its Optimum Points program benefit others as well as customers. Shoppers Optimum Points® Donation Program allows Optimum card holders to donate some or all of their points to one of many registered charitable organizations. The organizations can then use the points to purchase products and supplies they need for their day-to-day activities and ongoing fund-raising events. A wide variety of charitable organizations, both national and provincial, have signed up to receive the points.

LuckyImages/Shutterstock

Q A company's marketing department is responsible for designing customer loyalty programs. Why would Shoppers' marketing department add the option of donating points to charity?

BEFORE YOU GO ON...DO IT **2a** ▶ **Warranty Provisions**

Hockey Gear Company sells hockey skates with a two-year warranty against defects. The company expects that of the units sold each year, 5% will be returned in the first year after they are sold and 2% will be returned in the second year. The average cost to repair or replace a defective unit under warranty is $50. The company reported the following sales and warranty cost information:

	Units Sold	Actual Warranty Costs Incurred
2016	10,000	$20,000
2017	15,000	45,000

Calculate the balance in the Warranty Expense and Warranty Liability accounts at the end of 2017.

Solution

2016: Total defective units = 5% + 2% = 7%
      10,000 × 7% = 700 × $50 = $35,000

Warranty Expense			Warranty Liability		
35,000		Actual	20,000	Estimate	35,000
				Bal. Dec. 31, 2016	15,000

2017: 15,000 × 7% = 1,050 × $50 = $52,500

Warranty Expense			Warranty Liability		
52,500		Actual	20,000	Estimate	35,000
				Bal. Dec. 31, 2016	15,000
		Actual	45,000	Estimate	52,500
				Bal. Dec. 31, 2017	22,500

Action Plan
- Calculate the warranty expense by multiplying the number of units sold by the percentage that is expected to be returned and by the average warranty cost.
- Record warranty expenses in the period of the sale.
- The warranty liability is increased by the expense in each period and decreased by the actual costs of repairs and replacements.

Related exercise material: BE10–8, BE10–9, BE10–10, BE10–11, E10–11, E10–12, and E10–13.

CONTINGENCIES

The current liabilities discussed earlier in this chapter were either definitely determinable or estimable. While it might have been necessary to estimate the timing or amount, in both cases there was no uncertainty about their existence. With **contingencies**, there is much more uncertainty about the timing and amount and even the existence of a liability.

In general, a **contingent liability** is a possible obligation resulting from a past event. Whether an actual liability exists is dependent on a future event that will confirm the liability's existence or non-existence.

Lawsuits are good examples of contingencies. The existence of a loss and the related liability depend on the outcome of the lawsuit. The settlement of the lawsuit will confirm the existence of the liability, the amount payable, the payee, and/or the date payable. Under IFRS, the term contingent liability refers only to possible obligations that are not recognized in the financial statements. A contingency that is considered probable would be classified as a provision and recorded under IRFS. Under ASPE, a liability for a contingent loss is recorded if **both** of the following conditions are met:

1. The contingency is *likely* (the chance of occurrence is high).
2. The amount of the contingency can be *reasonably estimated*.

Therefore, if it is likely that the company will lose a lawsuit, and if the amount can be reliably estimated, then the company must record the loss and the liability.

When a contingent loss is likely, but it cannot be reasonably estimated, or if its likelihood of occurrence is not determinable, it is necessary only to disclose the contingency in the notes to the financial statements. In that case, a liability is not recorded.

If a contingency is unlikely—the chance of occurrence is small—it should still be disclosed if the event could have a substantial negative effect on the company's financial position. Otherwise, it does not need to be disclosed. A loan guarantee is an example of a contingency that should be disclosed even if the chance of having to pay is small. General risk contingencies that can affect anyone who is operating a business, such as the possibility of a war, strike, or recession, are not reported in the notes to the financial statements.

In the sample note disclosure from Bombardier Inc.'s financial statements in Illustration 10-6, the company is unable to reasonably estimate probable losses. Therefore, they are only disclosed in this note.

▶ **ILLUSTRATION** **10-6**
Note disclosure on contingencies by Bombardier Inc.

BOMBARDIER INC.
December 31, 2014
Excerpt: Note 37

Litigation

In the normal course of operations, the Corporation is a defendant in certain legal proceedings currently pending before various courts in relation to product liability and contract disputes with customers and other third parties.

The Corporation intends to vigorously defend its position in these matters.

While the Corporation cannot predict the final outcome of all legal proceedings pending as at December 31, 2014, based on information currently available, management believes that the resolution of these legal proceedings will not have a material adverse effect on its financial position.

S-Bahn claim

On March 4, 2013, S-Bahn Berlin GMBH ("SB") filed a claim against Bombardier Transportation GmbH, a wholly owned subsidiary of the Corporation, in the Berlin District Court ("Landgericht Berlin"), concerning the trains of the 481 Series delivered to SB between 1996 and 2004.

This lawsuit alleges damages of an aggregate value of €348 million ($423 million) related to allegedly defective wheels and braking systems. The claim is for payment of €241 million ($293 million) and also for a declaratory judgment obliging the Corporation to compensate SB for further damages. SB currently alleges such further damages to be €107 million ($130 million).

It is the Corporation's position that this claim i) is filed in absence of any defect, ii) is not founded on any enforceable warranty, iii) is filed after the expiry of any statute of limitations and iv) is based on inapplicable standards. The lawsuit contains allegations against the Corporation which the Corporation rejects as unfounded and defamatory. The Corporation intends to vigorously defend its position and will undertake all actions necessary to protect its reputation.

ACCOUNTING IN ACTION
ACROSS THE ORGANIZATION

Contingent liabilities abound in the real world, and their amounts are often large and difficult to estimate. The cost of government-regulated environmental cleanup of contaminated sites, for example, can run in the millions of dollars. Calgary-based Agrium Inc., a global producer and marketer of fertilizer and other agricultural products and services, reported environmental remediation liabilities for certain facilities and sites of an estimated $169 million as at December 31, 2014. The company is expected to settle those liabilities by 2038. Possible liabilities due to lawsuits are also common. Air Canada, for example, had a provision of $27 million as at December 31, 2014, relating to outstanding legal claims that it and other air carriers had violated European Union rules regarding cargo fees. The provision was an estimate based on Air Canada's assessment of the potential outcome of the legal proceedings.

Sources: Agrium 2014 annual report; Air Canada 2014 annual report.

Q Environmental contingencies are generally considered to be harder to estimate than contingencies from lawsuits. What might be the reason for this difference?

BEFORE YOU GO ON...DO IT **Reporting and Disclosing a Contingency**

A list of possible contingencies follows. Identify whether each of the following should be recorded, disclosed, or not reported:

1. A factory risks being damaged by floods. The building is located on a flood plain but has never experienced any damage from flooding in the past.
2. The government may expropriate a company's assets so that a new highway can be built. So far, there have been no discussions about how much the government might pay the company.
3. A public company is being sued for $1 million for wrongful dismissal of a company executive.
4. A company has guaranteed other companies' loans but the guarantees are unlikely to result in any payments.
5. A private company following ASPE is being sued for negligence and damages by a customer who slipped and broke a leg in the company's store.

Solution

1. No disclosure required.
2. Disclosure required.
3. If it is probable that the company will lose and the amount can be reasonably estimated, then this would be recorded as a provision; otherwise, just disclose.
4. Disclosure required.
5. If it is likely that the company will lose and the amount can be reasonably estimated, then this is recorded as a contingent liability; otherwise, just disclose.

Related exercise material: BE10–12, BE10–13, E10–14, and E10–15.

Action Plan

- Under IFRS, contingent liabilities are disclosed, as once they are recorded, they become provisions.
- Recall that under ASPE, contingent liabilities are recorded if they are likely and can be reasonably estimated.
- If the amounts cannot be estimated, they are only disclosed. Contingencies are not disclosed if they are unlikely unless they could have a substantial negative impact on the entity.

LEARNING OBJECTIVE **Determine payroll costs and record payroll transactions.**

Payroll

Payroll and related fringe benefits often make up a large percentage of current liabilities. Employee compensation is often the most significant expense that a company incurs. For example, Costco recently reported 103,000 total employees and labour and fringe benefits costs that amounted to approximately 70% of the company's total cost of operations. Similarly, Nanotech, our chapter feature story, reports payroll-related expenses that are over 60% of its general and administration expenses.

Payroll accounting involves more than just paying employee salaries and wages. In addition to paying salaries and wages, companies are required by law to have payroll records for each employee, to report and remit payroll deductions, and to abide by provincial and federal laws on employee compensation. There are up to 190 different pieces of legislation and regulations that employers have to consider when doing payroll. In this section, we will discuss some of the basic issues regarding payroll costs, journalizing payroll, and payroll records. In the appendix to this chapter, we explain calculating mandatory payroll deductions.

There are two types of payroll costs to a company: (1) employee costs and (2) employer costs. Employee costs involve the gross amount earned by employees. Employer costs involve amounts paid by the employer on behalf of the employee (employee benefits). We will explore employee and employer payroll costs in the following sections.

EMPLOYEE PAYROLL COSTS

Accounting for employee payroll costs involves calculating (1) gross pay, (2) payroll deductions, and (3) net pay.

Gross Pay

Gross pay, or earnings, is the total compensation earned by an employee. It consists of salaries or wages, plus any bonuses and commissions. The terms "salaries" and "wages" are often used interchangeably and the total amount of salaries or wages earned by the employee is called **gross pay**, or gross earnings.

In addition to the hourly pay rate, most companies are required by law to pay hourly workers for overtime work at the rate of at least one and one-half times the government-regulated minimum hourly wage. The number of hours that need to be worked before overtime becomes payable is based on a standard workweek. A 44-hour standard workweek is fairly common but this will vary by industry and occupation. Most employees in executive, managerial, and administrative positions do not earn overtime pay.

To illustrate gross pay, assume that Mark Jordan works for Academy Company as a shipping clerk. His authorized pay rate is $20 per hour. The calculation of Mark's gross pay for the 48 hours shown on his time card for the weekly pay period ending June 23, 2017, is as follows:

Type of Pay	Hours	×	Rate	=	Gross Pay
Regular	44	×	$20	=	$ 880
Overtime	4	×	30	=	120
Total	48				$1,000

This calculation assumes that Mark receives one and one-half times his regular hourly rate ($20 × 1.5) for any hours worked in excess of 44 hours per week (overtime). Overtime rates can be as much as twice the regular rates.

ACCOUNTING IN ACTION
ETHICS INSIGHT

Robert Eberle owns and manages Robert's Restaurant, with 9 full-time and 16 part-time employees. He pays all of the full-time employees by cheque, but pays all of the part-time employees in cash, taken from the register. Robert says his part-timers prefer cash, and he doesn't withhold or pay any taxes or deductions because they go unrecorded and unnoticed. His accountant urges him to pay his part-timers by cheque and take off all required deductions.

Q **Who are the stakeholders regarding Robert's handling of his payroll?**

Payroll Deductions

As anyone who has received a paycheque knows, the actual cash received is almost always less than the gross pay for the hours worked. The difference is caused by **payroll deductions**. Payroll deductions are also frequently called "withholdings" because these are the amounts that the employer withholds or holds back from the employee. Payroll deductions may be mandatory or voluntary. Illustration 10-7 shows the types of payroll deductions that most employers usually make.

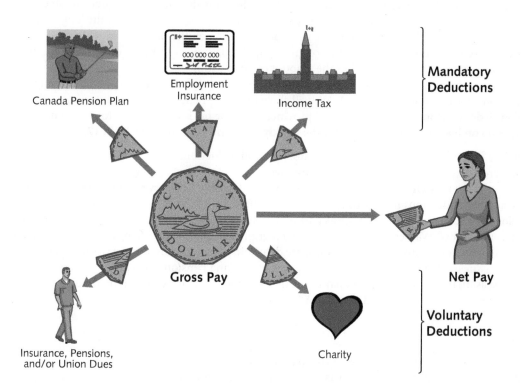

▶ ILLUSTRATION **10-7**
Employee payroll deductions

Payroll deductions are not an expense to the employer. The employer only collects the amounts and forwards the collected amounts to the government at a later date. Required deductions include Canada Pension Plan, Employment Insurance, and income tax. Voluntary deductions may be union dues, extended benefits, or charitable donations.

The designated collection agency for the federal government is the Canada Revenue Agency (CRA), which collects money on behalf of the Receiver General for Canada, the cabinet minister responsible for accepting payments to the Government of Canada.

Mandatory Payroll Deductions. Mandatory deductions are required by law and include Canada Pension Plan contributions, Employment Insurance premiums, and personal income tax. We will discuss these three deductions in the following sections.

Canada Pension Plan. All employees between the ages of 18 and 70, except those employed in the province of Quebec, must contribute to the **Canada Pension Plan (CPP)**. Quebec has its own similar program, the Quebec Pension Plan (QPP). These mandatory plans give disability, retirement, and death benefits to qualifying Canadians.

Contribution rates are set by the federal government and are adjusted every January if there are increases in the cost of living. We will show how to calculate CPP contributions in Appendix 10A. For now, assume that Mark Jordan's CPP contribution for the weekly pay period ending June 23, 2017, is $46.17.

Employment Insurance. The Employment Insurance Act requires all Canadian workers who are not self-employed to pay **Employment Insurance (EI)** premiums. Employment insurance is designed to give income protection (in the form of payments representing a portion of one's earnings) for a limited period of time to employees who are temporarily laid off, who are on parental leave or compassionate leave, or who lose their jobs. Self-employed individuals may choose to pay EI to qualify for special benefits such as maternity or parental and compassionate care benefits. But this will not qualify them for Employment Insurance if they are not able to work.

Each year, the federal government determines the contribution rate and the maximum amount of premiums for the year. We will show how to calculate EI premiums in Appendix 10A. For now, assume that Mark Jordan's EI premium for the weekly pay period ending June 23, 2017, is $18.80.

Personal Income Tax. Under the Income Tax Act, employers are required to withhold income tax from employees for each pay period. The amount to be withheld is determined by three variables: (1) the employee's gross pay, (2) the number of credits claimed by the employee, and (3) the length of the pay period. The amount of provincial income taxes also depends on the province in which the employee works. There is no limit on the amount of gross pay that is subject to income tax withholdings. The higher the pay or earnings, the higher the amount of taxes withheld.

The calculation of personal income tax withholdings is complicated and is best done using payroll deduction tables supplied by the CRA. We will show this in Appendix 10A. For now, assume that Mark Jordan's federal income tax is $114.90 and provincial income tax is $58.15, for a total income tax owed of $173.05 on his gross pay of $1,000 for the weekly pay period ending June 23, 2017.

Voluntary Payroll Deductions. Unlike mandatory payroll deductions, which are required by law, voluntary payroll deductions are chosen by the employee.

Employees may choose to authorize withholdings for charitable, retirement, and other purposes. All voluntary deductions from gross pay should be authorized in writing by the employee. The authorization may be made individually or as part of a group plan. Deductions for charitable organizations, such as the United Way, or for financial arrangements, such as Canada Savings Bonds and the repayment of loans from company credit unions, are determined by each employee. In contrast, deductions for union dues, extended health insurance, life insurance, and pension plans are often determined on a group basis. In the calculation of net pay in the next section, we assume that Mark Jordan has voluntary deductions of $10 for the United Way and $5 for union dues.

Net Pay

The difference between an employee's gross pay, or total earnings, less any employee payroll deductions withheld from the earnings is known as **net pay**. This is the amount that the employer must pay to the employee.

Net pay is determined by subtracting payroll deductions from gross pay. For Mark Jordan, net pay for the weekly pay period ending June 23, 2017, is $746.98, as shown in Illustration 10-8.

▶ILLUSTRATION **10-8**
Employee payroll
deductions

Gross pay		$1,000.00
Payroll deductions:		
CPP	$ 46.17	
EI	18.80	
Income tax (federal and provincial)	173.05	
United Way	10.00	
Union dues	5.00	253.02
Net pay		$ 746.98

Before we learn how to record employee payroll costs and deductions, we will turn our attention to *employer* payroll costs. After this discussion, we will record the total employee and employer payroll costs for Academy Company, where Mark Jordan works.

EMPLOYER PAYROLL COSTS

Employer payroll costs are amounts that the federal and provincial governments require employers to pay. The federal government requires CPP and EI contributions from employers. The provincial governments require employers to fund a workplace health, safety, and compensation plan. These contributions, plus such items as paid vacations and pensions, are referred to as **employee benefits**.

Employer payroll costs are not debited to the Salaries Expense account, but rather to a separate Employee Benefits Expense account.

Canada Pension Plan

Employers must also contribute to the CPP. **For each dollar withheld from the employee's gross pay, the employer must contribute an equal amount.** The CPP Payable account is credited for both the employees' and employer's CPP contributions.

Employment Insurance

Employers are required to contribute 1.4 times an employee's EI premiums. The EI Payable account is credited for both the employees' and employer's EI premiums.

Workplace Health, Safety, and Compensation

Each provincial workplace health, safety, and compensation plan gives benefits to workers who are injured or disabled on the job. The cost of this program is paid entirely by the employer; employees do not make contributions to these plans. Employers are assessed a rate—usually between 0.25% and 10% of their gross payroll—based on the risk of injury to employees in their industry and based on past experience.

> **Helpful hint** CPP contributions and EI premiums are paid by both the employer and the employee. Workers' compensation premiums are paid entirely by the employer.

Additional Employee Benefits

In addition to the three employer payroll costs described above, employers have other employee benefit costs. Two of the most important are paid absences and post-employment benefits. We will describe these briefly here, but leave further details to an intermediate accounting course.

Paid Absences. Employees have the right to receive compensation for absences under certain conditions. The compensation may be for paid vacations, sick pay benefits, and paid statutory holidays. A liability should be estimated and accrued for future paid absences.

Post-Employment Benefits. Post-employment benefits are payments by employers to retired or terminated employees. These payments are for (1) pensions, and (2) supplemental health care, dental care, and life insurance. Employers must use the accrual basis in accounting for post-employment benefits. It is important to match the cost of these benefits with the periods where the employer benefits from the services of the employee.

RECORDING THE PAYROLL

Recording the payroll involves maintaining payroll records, recording payroll expenses and liabilities, paying the payroll, and filing and remitting payroll deductions.

Payroll Records

A separate record of an employee's gross pay, payroll deductions, and net pay for the calendar year is kept for each employee and updated after each pay period. It is called the **employee earnings record** and its cumulative payroll data are used by the employer to (1) determine when an employee has reached the maximum earnings subject to CPP and EI premiums, (2) file information returns with the CRA (as explained later in this section), and (3) give each employee a statement of gross pay and withholdings for the year.

An extract from Mark Jordan's employee earnings record for the month of June is shown in Illustration 10-9. This record includes the pay details shown in Illustration 10-8 for the weekly pay period ending June 23, 2017, highlighted in green.

ACADEMY COMPANY
Employee Earnings Record
Year Ending December 31, 2017

	Name	Mark Jordan		Address	162 Bowood Avenue
Social Insurance Number		113-114-496			Toronto
Date of Birth		December 24, 1985			Ontario, M4N 1Y6
Date Employed		September 1, 2010		Telephone	416-486-0669
Date Employment Ended				E-mail	jordan@sympatico.ca
Job Title		Shipping Clerk		Claim Code	1

2017 Period Ending	Total Hours	Gross Pay				Deductions						Payment	
		Regular	Overtime	Total	Cumulative	CPP	EI	Income Tax	United Way	Union Dues	Total	Net Amount	Cheque #
June 9	46	880.00	60.00	940.00	19,940.00	43.20	17.67	154.15	10.00	5.00	230.02	709.98	974
June 16	47	880.00	90.00	970.00	20,910.00	44.68	18.24	163.15	10.00	5.00	241.07	728.93	1028
June 23	48	880.00	120.00	1,000.00	21,910.00	46.17	18.80	173.05	10.00	5.00	253.02	746.98	1077
June 30	46	880.00	60.00	940.00	22,850.00	43.20	17.67	154.15	10.00	5.00	230.02	709.98	1133

▶ ILLUSTRATION 10-9
Employee earnings record

In addition to employee earnings records, many companies find it useful to prepare a **payroll register**. This record accumulates the gross pay, deductions, and net pay per employee for each pay period and becomes the documentation for preparing paycheques for each employee. Academy Company's payroll register for the weekly pay period ended June 23, 2017, is presented in Illustration 10-10. It shows the data for Mark Jordan in the wages section, highlighted in green. In this example, Academy Company's total payroll is $34,420, as shown in the gross pay column.

ACADEMY COMPANY
Payroll Register
Week Ending June 23, 2017

Employee	Total Hours	Gross Pay			Deductions						Payment	
		Regular	Overtime	Gross	CPP	EI	Income Tax	United Way	Union Dues	Total	Net Amount	Cheque #
Aung, Ng	44	1,276.00		1,276.00	59.83	23.99	257.86	15.00		356.68	919.32	998
Canton, Maggie	44	1,298.00		1,298.00	60.92	24.40	264.72	20.00		370.04	927.96	999
Caron, William	44	1,166.00		1,166.00	54.89	21.92	223.60	11.00		311.41	854.59	1000
Deol, Rejean	44	880.00	60.00	940.00	43.20	17.67	154.15	10.00	5.00	230.02	709.98	1001
Jordan, Mark	48	880.00	120.00	1,000.00	46.17	18.80	173.05	10.00	5.00	253.02	746.98	1,077
Lee, Milroy	47	880.00	90.00	970.00	44.68	18.24	163.15	10.00	5.00	241.07	728.93	1078
Total		32,400.00	2,020.00	34,420.00	1,497.28	629.89	6,722.86	480.00	150.00	9,480.03	24,939.97	

▶ ILLUSTRATION 10-10
Payroll register

Note that this record is a listing of each employee's payroll data for the June 23, 2017, pay period. In some companies, the payroll register is a special journal. Postings are made directly to ledger accounts. In other companies, the payroll register is a supplementary record that gives the data for a general journal entry and later posting to the ledger accounts. At Academy Company, the second procedure is used.

Recording Payroll Expenses and Liabilities

Helpful hint Total Payroll Expense = Gross Salaries and Wages + Employer's Portion of Payroll Costs

Employer payroll expenses are made up of two components: (1) employees' gross salaries and wages and (2) employer's payroll costs. Therefore, when recording, two journal entries are typically required.

1. Employee Payroll Costs.

The first journal entry records the employee gross wages and the related withholding taxes. In the following example, Academy Company records its total payroll for the week ended June 23 as follows:

June 23	Salaries Expense	34,420.00	
	CPP Payable		1,497.28
	EI Payable		629.89
	Income Tax Payable		6,722.86
	United Way Payable		480.00
	Union Dues Payable		150.00
	Salaries Payable		24,939.97
	To record payroll for week ending June 23.		

A	=	L	+	OE
		+1,497.28		−34,420.00
		+629.89		
		+6,722.86		
		+480.00		
		+150.00		
		+24,939.97		

Cash flows: no effect

The above journal entry records the gross pay of $34,420 in Academy Company's Salaries Expense account. Sometimes companies will use separate accounts to record office worker expenses, salary expenses, and hourly wages. In this example, the net pay of $24,939.97 that is owed to employees is recorded in the Salaries Payable account. This is equal to the amount the employees will receive when the payroll is paid. Academy Company uses separate liability accounts for the amounts that it owes for its employee payroll deductions to the government for CPP, EI, and income tax, and amounts owed to third parties like United Way and for union dues.

2. Employer Payroll Costs.

Employer payroll costs are also usually recorded when the payroll is journalized. As discussed previously, employers must record their portion of CPP, EI, workers' compensation, and vacation pay. Therefore, as demonstrated below, Academy Company must record its share of CPP of $1,497.28 ($1,497.28 × 1) and its EI premium of $881.85 ($629.89 × 1.4).

Assume that Academy Company is also assessed for workers' compensation at a rate of 1%. It must also record this expense of $344.20 ($34,420 × 1%). Lastly, assuming that Academy Company employees accrue vacation days at an average rate of 4% of the gross payroll (equivalent to two weeks of vacation), Academy must record $1,376.80 ($34,420 × 4%) to recognize the accrued vacation benefits for one pay period.

Accordingly, the entry to record the employer payroll costs or employee benefits associated with the June 23 payroll is as follows:

June 23	Employee Benefits Expense	4,100.13	
	CPP Payable		1,497.28
	EI Payable		881.85
	Workers' Compensation Payable		344.20
	Vacation Pay Payable		1,376.80
	To record employer payroll costs on June 23 payroll.		

A	=	L	+	OE
		+1,497.28		−4,100.13
		+881.85		
		+344.20		
		+1,376.80		

Cash flows: no effect

Employer payroll costs are debited to a separate expense account, normally called Employee Benefits Expense, so the employer can keep track of these costs. It may be combined with Salaries Expense on the income statement. The liability accounts are classified as current liabilities since they will be paid within the next year.

Recording Payment of the Payroll

Payment of the payroll by cheque or electronic funds transfer (EFT) is made from either the employer's regular bank account or a payroll bank account. Each paycheque or EFT is usually accompanied by a statement of earnings document. This shows the employee's gross pay, payroll deductions, and net pay for the period and for the year to date.

After the payroll has been paid, the cheque numbers are entered in the payroll register. The entry to record payment of the payroll for Academy Company follows:

A = L + OE				
−24,939.97 −24,939.97				

↓ Cash flows: −24,939.97

June 23	Salaries Payable	24,939.97	
	Cash		24,939.97
	To record payment of payroll.		

Note that Academy Company is only recording payments to its employees, and not its payroll deductions, in this entry. Employee and employer deductions will be remitted to government authorities or other third parties when they are due.

Many companies use a separate bank account for payroll. Only the total amount of each period's payroll is transferred, or deposited, into that account before it is distributed. This helps the company determine if there are any unclaimed amounts.

When companies report and remit their payroll deductions, they combine withholdings of CPP, EI, and income tax. Generally, the withholdings must be reported and remitted monthly on a Statement of Account for Current Source Deductions (known by the CRA as the PD7A remittance form), and no later than the 15th day of the month following the month's pay period. Depending on the size of the payroll deductions, however, the employer's payment deadline could be different. For example, large employers must remit more often than once a month, and small employers with perfect payroll deduction remittance records can remit quarterly.

Workplace health, safety, and compensation costs are remitted quarterly to the provincial workers' compensation commission or board. Remittances can be made by mail or through deposits at any Canadian financial institution. When payroll deductions are remitted, payroll liability accounts are debited and Cash is credited.

The entry to record the remittance of payroll deductions by Academy Company in the following month is as follows:

A = L + OE				
−12,203.36 −2,994.56				
−1,511.74				
−6,722.86				
−480.00				
−150.00				
−344.20				

↓ Cash flows: −12,203.36

July 15	CPP Payable ($1,497.28 + $1,497.28)	2,994.56	
	EI Payable ($629.89 + $881.85)	1,511.74	
	Income Tax Payable	6,722.86	
	United Way Payable	480.00	
	Union Dues Payable	150.00	
	Workers' Compensation Payable	344.20	
	Cash		12,203.36
	To record payment of payroll deductions for June 23 payroll.		

Note that the vacation pay liability recorded on June 23 is not debited or "paid" until the employees actually take their vacation.

Other payroll information returns or forms must be filed by the employer with the government by the last day of February each year. In addition, as noted previously, employers must give employees a Statement of Remuneration Paid (called a T4 slip by the CRA) by the same date.

ACCOUNTING IN ACTION
ALL ABOUT YOU INSIGHT

Alex Hinds/Shutterstock

Employers are required by law each month to remit to the CRA mandatory payroll deductions as well as the employer's share of CPP and EI. Failure to do so can lead to interest and stiff penalties.

What happens if you are self-employed and providing consulting services to a company? If you are self-employed, you are required to pay CPP equal to both the employee's and employer's share, and you are also responsible for paying income tax. If you are self-employed, you can choose to pay EI to qualify for special benefits such as maternity or sickness benefits. But this will not qualify you for Employment Insurance if you are not able to work. If you choose to pay EI, you will not be required to pay the employer's portion of the EI premium.

It may seem beneficial to some companies to hire consultants and avoid paying the employer's share of CPP and EI as well as other benefits. However, the CRA has strict guidelines as to whether an individual is considered an employee or a self-employed consultant. If a company inappropriately treats an individual as self-employed and fails to deduct CPP and EI, the company will be required to pay both the employer's and employee's share of CPP and EI as well as penalties and interest.

Sources: Service Canada website, "Frequently Asked Questions: Employment Insurance (EI) Special Benefits for Self-Employed People," available at www.servicecanada.gc.ca/eng/sc/ei/sew/faq.shtml; Canada Revenue Agency website, "Payroll," available at www.cra-arc.gc.ca/tx/bsnss/tpcs/pyrll/menu-eng.html; Canada Revenue Agency, "Employee or Self-Employed?", available at www.cra-arc.gc.ca/E/pub/tg/rc4110/README.html.

Q If you are providing services to a company, what are the advantages and disadvantages of being a self-employed consultant versus an employee of the company?

BEFORE YOU GO ON...DO IT **Payroll**

Prepare the journal entries to record the following transactions. Round any calculations to the nearest dollar.

1. A company's gross salaries amount to $10,000 for the week ended July 11. The following amounts are deducted from the employees' wages: CPP of $495, EI of $183, income tax of $3,965, and health insurance of $950. Assume employees are paid in cash on July 11.
2. The company accrues employer's payroll costs on the same day as it records payroll. Assume vacation days are accrued at an average rate of 4% of the gross payroll and that the health insurance is 100% funded by the employees.
3. Record the payment of the mandatory payroll deductions from the July 11 payroll on August 15.

Solution

July 11	Salaries Expense	10,000	
	CPP Payable		495
	EI Payable		183
	Income Tax Payable		3,965
	Health Insurance Payable		950
	Cash		4,407
	To record payment of wages for week ending July 11.		
July 11	Employee Benefits Expense	1,151	
	CPP Payable		495
	EI Payable ($183 × 1.4)		256
	Vacation Pay Payable ($10,000 × 4%)		400
	To record employer's payroll costs on July 11 payroll.		

Action Plan
- Record both the employees' portion of the payroll and the benefits owed by the employer.
- Employee deductions are not an expense to the employer.
- The vacation pay liability is not "paid" until the employees actually take their vacation.

(continued)

> **BEFORE YOU GO ON...DO IT ❸**   **Payroll** *(continued)*
>
> | Aug. 15 | CPP Payable ($495 + $495) | 990 | |
> |---|---|---|---|
> | | EI Payable ($183 + $256) | 439 | |
> | | Income Tax Payable | 3,965 | |
> | | Health Insurance Payable | 950 | |
> | | Cash | | 6,344 |
> | | To record payment of mandatory payroll deductions. | | |
>
> Related exercise material: BE10–14, BE10–15, E10–16, and E10–17.

LEARNING OBJECTIVE ④ ▶ **Prepare the current liabilities section of the balance sheet.**

Financial Statement Presentation

Current liabilities are generally reported as the first category in the liabilities section of the balance sheet. Each of the main types of current liabilities is listed separately. In addition, the terms of operating lines of credit and notes payable and other information about the individual items are disclosed in the notes to the financial statements.

Similar to current assets, current liabilities are generally listed in order of liquidity (by maturity date). However, this is not always possible, because of the varying maturity dates that may exist for specific obligations such as notes payable. Many companies show bank loans, notes payable, and accounts payable first.

Illustration 10-11 shows how Air Canada presents its current liabilities in traditional order in its balance sheet.

▶ **ILLUSTRATION** **10-11**
Presentation of current liabilities

AIR CANADA
Balance Sheet (partial)
December 31, 2014
(in millions)

Accounts payable and accrued liabilities	1,259
Advance ticket sales	1,794
Current portion of long-term debt and finance leases	484
Total current liabilities	3,537

Companies must carefully monitor the relationship of current liabilities to current assets. This relationship is critical in evaluating a company's short-term ability to pay debt. There is usually concern when a company has more current liabilities than current assets, because it may not be able to make its payments when they become due.

Air Canada had current assets of $3,478 million at December 31, 2014, which results in a current ratio of less than 1. You will recall from Chapter 4 that the current ratio is calculated by dividing current assets by current liabilities.

Air Canada's current ratio is 0.98:1 ($3,478 ÷ $3,537), which indicates that Air Canada does not have quite enough current assets to cover its current liabilities.

Recall also that the current ratio should never be interpreted without also looking at the receivables and inventory turnover ratios to ensure that all of the current assets are indeed liquid. It is also important to look at the acid-test ratio. If we wanted to do a more complete analysis of Air Canada's liquidity, we would need additional information.

<table>
<tr><td>

BEFORE YOU GO ON...DO IT **4**
</td><td>**Current Liabilities on the Balance Sheet**</td></tr>
</table>

The following selected items were included in EastBoat Enterprises' adjusted trial balance at November 30, 2017:

Accounts payable	$ 52,775
Accounts receivable	30,250
Accrued liabilities	18,350
Bank indebtedness	10,400
Merchandise inventory	85,900
Notes payable	100,000
Prepaid expenses	12,000
Unearned revenue	6,500
Warranty liability	8,825

Additional information:

The $100,000 balance in notes payable consisted of: (1) a six-month, 5%, $25,000 note payable due on March 31, 2018; (2) a one-year, 5.5%, $15,000 note payable due on October 31, 2018; and (3) a three-year, 4.5%, $60,000 note payable due on September 30, 2020.

Prepare the current liabilities section of the balance sheet.

Solution

EASTBOAT ENTERPRISES
Balance Sheet (partial)
November 30, 2017

Current liabilities	
Bank indebtedness	$ 10,400
Accounts payable	52,775
Accrued liabilities	18,350
Unearned revenue	6,500
Warranty liability	8,825
Notes payable	40,000
Total current liabilities	136,850

Related exercise material: BE10–14, BE10–15, BE10–16, BE10–17, BE10–18, E10–18, and E10–19.

Action Plan
- Determine which items are liabilities.
- Recall that current liabilities are payable within one year of the balance sheet date.

Appendix 10A: PAYROLL DEDUCTIONS

LEARNING OBJECTIVE **5** Calculate mandatory payroll deductions.

MANDATORY PAYROLL DEDUCTIONS

As discussed in the chapter, payroll deductions may be mandatory or voluntary. Mandatory deductions are required by law and include Canada Pension Plan contributions, Employment Insurance premiums, and income tax. We discuss how to calculate these in the following sections.

Canada Pension Plan (CPP)

CPP contributions are based on a maximum ceiling or limit (called the maximum pensionable earnings) less a basic yearly exemption, and on the contribution rate set each year by the federal government. **Pensionable earnings** are gross earnings less the basic yearly exemption.

As at January 1, 2015, the following amounts were in effect:

Maximum pensionable earnings	$53,600
Basic yearly exemption	$3,500
CPP contribution rate	4.95%
Maximum annual employee CPP contribution	$2,479.95

Illustration 10A-1 shows the formulas and calculations used to determine Mark Jordan's CPP contribution on his gross pay of $1,000 for the weekly pay period ending June 23, 2017.

▶ ILLUSTRATION
Formula for CPP
contributions

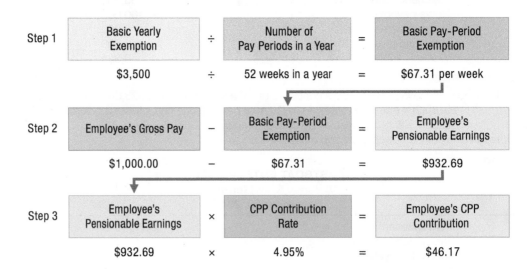

Note that the basic pay-period exemption of $67.31 is a per-week exemption and is used in this case because Academy Company pays its employees weekly. If a company pays its employees monthly, the basic pay-period exemption would be $291.67 ($3,500 ÷ 12).

An employer stops deducting CPP contributions if and when the employee's earnings are greater than the maximum pensionable earnings. In this way, the employee's CPP contributions will not be greater than the maximum annual CPP contribution. Self-employed individuals pay both the employee and employer share of CPP.

Employment Insurance (EI)

EI calculations are based on a maximum earnings ceiling (called the maximum annual insurable earnings) and the contribution rate set by the federal government each year. Different from CPP, there is no basic yearly exemption. For 2015, the following amounts were in effect:

Maximum insurable earnings	$49,500
EI contribution rate	1.88%
Maximum annual employee EI premium	$930.60

In most cases, **insurable earnings** are gross earnings.

The required EI premium is calculated by multiplying the employee's insurable earnings by the EI contribution rate. Illustration 10A-2 shows the formula and calculations to determine Mark Jordan's EI premium on his gross pay of $1,000 for the pay period ending June 23, 2017.

▶ ILLUSTRATION
Formula for EI
premiums

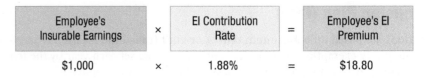

An employer stops deducting EI premiums if and when the employee's earnings are greater than the maximum insurable earnings. In this way, the employee's EI premiums will not be greater than the maximum annual EI premium. Self-employed individuals who have chosen to pay EI pay only the employee's share of EI.

Personal Income Tax

Income tax deductions are based on income tax rates set by the federal and provincial governments. The federal government uses a progressive tax scheme when calculating income taxes. Basically, this means that the higher the pay or earnings, the higher the income tax percentage, and thus the higher the amount of taxes withheld. For example, effective January 1, 2015, the federal tax rates were:

- 15% **on the first** $44,701 of taxable income, plus
- 22% **on the next** $44,700 of taxable income (on the portion of taxable income between $44,701 and $89,401), plus
- 26% **on the next** $49,185 of taxable income (on the portion of taxable income between $89,401 and $138,586), plus
- 29% of taxable income **over** $138,586.

Taxable income is determined by the employee's gross pay and the amount of personal tax credits claimed by the employee. **Personal tax credits** are amounts deducted from an individual's income taxes and they determine the amount of income taxes to be withheld. To indicate to the Canada Revenue Agency (CRA) which credits he or she wants to claim, the employee must complete a Personal Tax Credits Return (known as a TD1 form). In 2015, all individuals are entitled to a minimum personal credit (called the basic personal credit) of $11,327.

In addition, provincial income taxes must be calculated. Each province has its own specific tax rates and calculations.

As you can see, the calculation of personal income tax deductions is very complicated. Consequently, it is best done using one of the many payroll accounting software programs that are available or by using the payroll deduction tools provided by the CRA. These tools include payroll deduction tables and the Payroll Deductions Online Calculator. We will illustrate how to use the payroll deduction tables.

USING PAYROLL DEDUCTION TABLES

Payroll deduction tables are prepared by the CRA and can be easily downloaded from the CRA website (go to www.cra-arc.gc.ca and click on Businesses, then Payroll). There are separate payroll deduction tables for determining federal tax deductions, provincial tax deductions, Canada Pension Plan contributions, and Employment Insurance premiums.

These tables are updated at least once a year on January 1 to reflect the new rates for that year. Income tax tables are also reissued during the year if the federal or provincial governments make changes to income tax rates during the year. It is important to make sure you have the tables that are in effect during the payroll period for which you are calculating deductions.

There are separate sections of the federal and provincial income tax and CPP tables for weekly, biweekly, semi-monthly, and monthly pay periods. Thus, when determining these amounts, it is important to make sure you are using the table prepared for the company's pay period. The Academy Company would use the weekly tables.

Illustration 10A-3 shows excerpts from the CPP, EI, and federal and Ontario income tax tables effective January 1, 2015. You can use these tables to determine the appropriate deductions for Mark Jordan's gross pay of $1,000 during the pay period ended June 23, 2017.

In the CPP table, under the Pay column, find $1,000. The CPP deduction for the pay range $999.93 to $1,000.12 is $46.17. Earlier in the appendix, we showed how to calculate Mark Jordan's CPP and determined it was $46.17. The table has been created in such a way that within the ranges shown, the determination of the CPP will be exactly the same as the calculation carried out above (with a possible maximum rounding error of one cent).

▶ILLUSTRATION 10A-3

Excerpts from CPP, EI, and income tax deduction tables prepared by the Canada Revenue Agency, effective January 1, 2015

In the EI table, under the Insurable Earnings column, find $1,000. The EI deduction in the pay range $999.74 to $1,000.26 is $18.80. This is exactly the same amount we calculated earlier in the appendix.

Canada Pension Plan Contributions
Weekly (52 pay periods a year)

Pay From		Pay To	CPP	Pay From		Pay To	CPP	Pay From		Pay To	CPP	Pay From		Pay To	CPP
998.11	-	998.31	46.08	1012.66	-	1012.85	46.80	1027.20	-	1027.40	47.52	1570.84	-	1580.83	74.67
998.32	-	998.51	46.09	1012.86	-	1013.05	46.81	1027.41	-	1027.60	47.53	1580.84	-	1590.83	75.17
998.52	-	998.71	46.10	1013.06	-	1013.25	46.82	1027.61	-	1027.80	47.54	1590.84	-	1600.83	75.66
998.72	-	998.91	46.11	1013.26	-	1013.46	46.83	1027.81	-	1028.00	47.55	1600.84	-	1610.83	76.16
998.92	-	999.11	46.12	1013.47	-	1013.66	46.84	1028.01	-	1028.20	47.56	1610.84	-	1620.83	76.65
999.12	-	999.32	46.13	1013.67	-	1013.86	46.85	1028.21	-	1028.41	47.57	1620.84	-	1630.83	77.15
999.33	-	999.52	46.14	1013.87	-	1014.06	46.86	1028.42	-	1028.61	47.58	1630.84	-	1640.83	77.64
999.53	-	999.72	46.15	1014.07	-	1014.26	46.87	1028.62	-	1028.81	47.59	1640.84	-	1650.83	78.14
999.73	-	999.92	46.16	1014.27	-	1014.47	46.88	1028.82	-	1029.01	47.60	1650.84	-	1660.83	78.63
999.93	-	1000.12	46.17	1014.48	-	1014.67	46.89	1029.02	-	1029.21	47.61	1660.84	-	1670.83	79.13
1000.13	-	1000.33	46.18	1014.68	-	1014.87	46.90	1029.22	-	1029.42	47.62	1670.84	-	1680.83	79.62
1000.34	-	1000.53	46.19	1014.88	-	1015.07	46.91	1029.43	-	1029.62	47.63	1680.84	-	1690.83	80.12
1000.54	-	1000.73	46.20	1015.08	-	1015.27	46.92	1029.63	-	1029.82	47.64	1690.84	-	1700.83	80.61
1000.74	-	1000.93	46.21	1015.28	-	1015.48	46.93	1029.83	-	1030.02	47.65	1700.84	-	1710.83	81.11
1000.94	-	1001.13	46.22	1015.49	-	1015.68	46.94	1030.03	-	1030.22	47.66	1710.84	-	1720.83	81.60
1001.14	-	1001.34	46.23	1015.69	-	1015.88	46.95	1030.23	-	1030.43	47.67	1720.84	-	1730.83	82.10
1001.35	-	1001.54	46.24	1015.89	-	1016.08	46.96	1030.44	-	1030.63	47.68	1730.84	-	1740.83	82.59
1001.55	-	1001.74	46.25	1016.09	-	1016.28	46.97	1030.64	-	1030.83	47.69	1740.84	-	1750.83	83.09

Employment Insurance Premiums

Insurable Earnings From		To	EI premium	Insurable Earnings From		To	EI premium	Insurable Earnings From		To	EI premium	Insurable Earnings From		To	EI premium
919.42	-	919.94	17.29	957.72	-	958.24	18.01	996.02	-	996.54	18.73	1034.31	-	1034.84	19.45
919.95	-	920.47	17.30	958.25	-	958.77	18.02	996.55	-	997.07	18.74	1034.85	-	1035.37	19.46
920.48	-	921.01	17.31	958.78	-	959.30	18.03	997.08	-	997.60	18.75	1035.38	-	1035.90	19.47
921.02	-	921.54	17.32	959.31	-	959.84	18.04	997.61	-	998.13	18.76	1035.91	-	1036.43	19.48
921.55	-	922.07	17.33	959.85	-	960.37	18.05	998.14	-	998.67	18.77	1036.44	-	1036.96	19.49
922.08	-	922.60	17.34	960.38	-	960.90	18.06	998.68	-	999.20	18.78	1036.97	-	1037.49	19.50
922.61	-	923.13	17.35	960.91	-	961.43	18.07	999.21	-	999.73	18.79	1037.50	-	1038.03	19.51
923.14	-	923.67	17.36	961.44	-	961.96	18.08	999.74	-	1000.26	18.80	1038.04	-	1038.56	19.52
923.68	-	924.20	17.37	961.97	-	962.49	18.09	1000.27	-	1000.79	18.81	1038.57	-	1039.09	19.53
924.21	-	924.73	17.38	962.50	-	963.03	18.10	1000.80	-	1001.31	18.82	1039.10	-	1039.62	19.54
924.74	-	925.26	17.39	963.04	-	963.56	18.11	1001.32	-	1001.86	18.83	1039.63	-	1040.15	19.55
925.27	-	925.79	17.40	963.57	-	964.09	18.12	1001.87	-	1002.39	18.84	1040.16	-	1040.69	19.56
925.80	-	926.31	17.41	964.10	-	964.62	18.13	1002.40	-	1002.92	18.85	1040.70	-	1041.22	19.57
926.32	-	926.86	17.42	964.63	-	965.15	18.14	1002.93	-	1003.45	18.86	1041.23	-	1041.75	19.58
926.87	-	927.39	17.43	965.16	-	965.69	18.15	1003.46	-	1003.98	18.87	1041.76	-	1042.28	19.59
927.40	-	927.92	17.44	965.70	-	966.22	18.16	1003.99	-	1004.52	18.88	1042.29	-	1042.81	19.60
927.93	-	928.45	17.45	966.23	-	966.75	18.17	1004.53	-	1005.05	18.89	1042.82	-	1043.35	19.61
928.46	-	928.98	17.46	966.76	-	967.28	18.18	1005.06	-	1005.58	18.90	1043.36	-	1043.88	19.62
928.99	-	929.52	17.47	967.29	-	967.81	18.19	1005.59	-	1006.11	18.91	1043.89	-	1044.41	19.63
929.53	-	930.05	17.48	967.82	-	968.35	18.20	1006.12	-	1006.64	18.92	1044.42	-	1044.94	19.64
930.06	-	930.58	17.49	968.36	-	968.88	18.21	1006.65	-	1007.18	18.93	1044.95	-	1045.47	19.65
930.59	-	931.11	17.50	968.89	-	969.41	18.22	1007.19	-	1007.71	18.94	1045.48	-	1046.01	19.66
931.12	-	931.64	17.51	969.42	-	969.94	18.23	1007.72	-	1008.24	18.95	1046.02	-	1046.54	19.67
931.65	-	932.18	17.52	969.95	-	970.47	18.24	1008.25	-	1008.77	18.96	1046.55	-	1047.07	19.68
932.19	-	932.71	17.53	970.48	-	971.01	18.25	1008.78	-	1009.30	18.97	1047.08	-	1047.60	19.69
932.72	-	933.24	17.54	971.02	-	971.54	18.26	1009.31	-	1009.84	18.98	1047.61	-	1048.13	19.70
933.25	-	933.77	17.55	971.55	-	972.07	18.27	1009.85	-	1010.37	18.99	1048.14	-	1048.67	19.71
933.78	-	934.30	17.56	972.08	-	972.60	18.28	1010.38	-	1010.90	19.00	1048.68	-	1049.20	19.72
934.31	-	934.84	17.57	972.61	-	973.13	18.29	1010.91	-	1011.43	19.01	1049.21	-	1049.73	19.73
934.85	-	935.37	17.58	973.14	-	973.67	18.30	1011.44	-	1011.96	19.02	1049.74	-	1050.26	19.74
935.38	-	935.90	17.59	973.68	-	974.20	18.31	1011.97	-	1012.49	19.03	1050.27	-	1050.79	19.75
935.91	-	936.43	17.60	974.21	-	974.73	18.32	1012.50	-	1013.03	19.04	1050.80	-	1051.32	19.76
936.44	-	936.96	17.61	974.74	-	975.26	18.33	1013.04	-	1013.56	19.05	1051.32	-	1051.86	19.77
936.97	-	937.49	17.62	975.27	-	975.79	18.34	1013.57	-	1014.09	19.06	1051.87	-	1052.39	19.78
937.50	-	938.03	17.63	975.80	-	976.31	18.35	1014.10	-	1014.62	19.07	1052.40	-	1052.92	19.79
938.04	-	938.56	17.64	976.32	-	976.86	18.36	1014.63	-	1015.15	19.08	1052.93	-	1053.45	19.80
938.57	-	939.09	17.65	976.87	-	977.39	18.37	1015.16	-	1015.69	19.09	1053.46	-	1053.98	19.81
939.10	-	939.62	17.66	977.40	-	977.92	18.38	1015.70	-	1016.22	19.10	1053.99	-	1054.52	19.82
939.63	-	940.15	17.67	977.93	-	978.45	18.39	1016.23	-	1016.75	19.11	1054.53	-	1055.05	19.83

Federal tax deductions
Effective January 1, 2015
Weekly (52 pay periods a year)
Also look up the tax deductions in the provincial table

Pay		CC 0	CC 1	CC 2	CC 3	CC 4
From	Less than					
943 -	951	135.65	103.00	99.85	93.60	87.40
951 -	959	137.35	104.65	101.55	95.30	89.05
959 -	967	139.05	106.35	103.25	97.00	90.75
967 -	975	140.75	108.05	104.95	98.70	92.45
975 -	983	142.45	109.75	106.65	100.40	94.15
983 -	991	144.15	111.45	108.35	102.10	95.85
991 -	999	145.85	113.15	110.05	103.80	97.55
999 -	1007	147.55	114.90	111.75	105.50	99.25
1007 -	1015	149.25	116.60	113.45	107.20	100.95
1015 -	1023	150.95	118.30	115.15	108.90	102.65
1023 -	1035	153.10	120.40	117.30	111.05	104.80
1035 -	1047	155.70	123.05	119.90	113.65	107.40
1047 -	1059	158.35	125.65	122.55	116.30	110.05
1059 -	1071	161.00	128.30	125.20	118.95	112.70
1071 -	1083	163.60	130.95	127.85	121.60	115.35
1083 -	1095	166.25	133.60	130.45	124.25	118.00
1095 -	1107	168.90	136.25	133.10	126.85	120.60
1107 -	1119	171.55	138.85	135.75	129.50	123.25
1119 -	1131	174.20	141.50	138.40	132.15	125.90
1131 -	1143	176.80	144.15	141.05	134.80	128.55

Ontario provincial tax deductions
Effective January 1, 2015
Weekly (52 pay periods a year)
Also look up the tax deductions in the federal table

Pay		CC 0	CC 1	CC 2	CC 3	CC 4
From	Less than					
942 -	950	62.75	53.15	52.10	50.05	48.00
950 -	958	63.45	53.85	52.85	50.75	48.70
958 -	966	64.15	54.55	53.55	51.50	49.40
966 -	974	64.85	55.30	54.25	52.20	50.15
974 -	982	65.60	56.00	54.95	52.90	50.85
982 -	990	66.30	56.70	55.70	53.60	51.55
990 -	998	67.00	57.40	56.40	54.35	52.25
998 -	1006	67.70	58.15	57.10	55.05	52.95
1006 -	1014	68.40	58.85	57.80	55.75	53.70
1014 -	1022	69.15	59.55	58.55	56.45	54.40
1022 -	1030	69.85	60.25	59.25	57.15	55.10
1030 -	1038	70.55	61.00	59.95	57.90	55.85
1038 -	1046	71.30	61.70	60.70	58.65	56.55
1046 -	1054	72.05	62.45	61.40	59.35	57.30
1054 -	1062	72.75	63.20	62.15	60.10	58.05
1062 -	1074	73.70	64.10	63.05	61.00	58.95
1074 -	1086	74.80	65.20	64.15	62.10	60.05
1086 -	1098	75.90	66.30	65.25	63.20	61.15
1098 -	1110	76.95	67.40	66.35	64.30	62.25
1110 -	1122	78.05	68.50	67.45	65.40	63.35
1122 -	1134	79.15	69.60	68.55	66.50	64.45
1134 -	1146	80.25	70.70	69.65	67.60	65.55
1146 -	1158	81.35	71.80	70.75	68.70	66.65
1158 -	1170	82.45	72.90	71.85	69.80	67.75
1170 -	1182	83.55	74.00	72.95	70.90	68.80

Source: T4032 Payroll Deduction Tables, Effective July 1, 2015. Pages B-17, C-7, D-3, D-4, E-3, E4

In the federal tax deduction table, first find $1,000 in the Pay column. Now follow across the table to the Federal Claim Code 1 column. The federal tax deduction in the "from" $999 to "less than" $1,007 range, claim code 1, is $114.90. The same process is used in the Ontario provincial tax deduction table. In the "from" $998 to "less than" $1,006 range, provincial claim code 1, the provincial tax deduction is $58.15. The total of these amounts is $173.05 ($114.90 + $58.15).

Claim code 1 is used for individuals who qualify for only the basic personal credit on the TD1 form discussed earlier in the appendix. You will notice on the federal and provincial tax deduction tables that the higher the claim code, the lower the income tax deduction. These claim codes can be used for employees who have more personal tax credits. We have assumed that Mark Jordan qualifies for only the basic personal credit.

As mentioned earlier, employers may also use the payroll software packages or the CRA's Payroll Deductions Online Calculator to determine payroll deductions. All of these methods will provide correct deductions as long as the correct dates, gross pay, pay period, and claim codes are used.

BEFORE YOU GO ON...DO IT **Employer's Payroll Deductions**

Highland Company pays salaries on a weekly basis. The payroll for the week ended May 26, 2015, includes three employees as follows:

Employee Name	Weekly Earnings	Claim Code
Hudson, James	$ 975	4
Randell, Findley	$ 975	2
Kim, Jaegeun	$1,015	1

Determine the appropriate mandatory payroll deductions and net pay for each employee. Calculate the CPP and EI deductions using the formula provided in Appendix 10A. Use the tables in Illustration 10A-3 to determine federal and provincial income taxes.

(continued)

Action Plan
- The CPP basic pay-period deduction is the annual basic deduction divided by the number of pay periods in a year.
- CPP deductions are equal to an employee's pensionable earnings times the CPP contribution rate.

BEFORE YOU GO ON...DO IT Employer's Payroll Deductions *(continued)*

- EI premiums are equal to an employee's insurable earnings times the EI premium rate.
- The federal tax deduction is the amount in the correct Pay range and Claim Code column on the federal tax deduction table.
- The provincial tax deduction is the amount in the correct Pay range and Claim Code column on the provincial tax deduction table.

Solution

				Deductions			
Employee	Gross Pay	CPP	EI	Federal Income Tax	Provincial Income Tax	Total	Net Pay
Hudson, James	$ 975.00	44.93[1]	18.33[3]	94.15	50.85	208.26	766.74
Randell, Findley	975.00	44.93	18.33	106.65	54.95	224.86	750.14
Kim, Jaegeun	1,015.00	46.91[2]	19.08[4]	118.30	59.55	243.84	771.16

Calculations:

Note: CPP basic pay-period exemption = $3,500 ÷ 52 = $67.31
[1] ($975.00 − $67.31) × 4.95% = $44.93
[2] ($1,015 − $67.31) × 4.95% = $46.91
[3] $975.00 × 1.88% = $18.33
[4] $1,015 × 1.88% = $19.08

Related exercise material: *BE10–19, *BE10–20, *E10–20, and *E10–21.

Comparing IFRS and ASPE

Key Differences	International Financial Reporting Standards (IFRS)	Accounting Standards for Private Enterprises (ASPE)
Conditions necessary to record a liability for a contingent loss.	Chance of occurrence is "probable" or "more likely than not."	Chance of occurrence is "likely."

Demonstration Problem

Benoit Company has the following selected transactions:

Feb. 1 Signed a $50,000, six-month, 7% note payable to the Central Canadian Bank, receiving $50,000 in cash. Interest is payable at maturity.

10 Cash register receipts totalled $37,565, plus 13% HST.

28 The payroll for the month is salaries of $50,000. CPP contributions and EI premiums withheld are $2,475 and $915, respectively. A total of $15,000 in income taxes is withheld. The salaries are paid on March 1.

The following adjustment data are noted at the end of the month:

1. Interest expense should be accrued on the note.
2. Employer payroll costs are recorded. In addition to mandatory costs, the company also pays $800 a month for a dental plan for all its employees.
3. Some sales were made under warranty. Of the units sold under warranty this month, 350 are expected to become defective. Repair costs are estimated to be $40 per defective unit.

Instructions

(a) Record the February transactions. Round your calculations to the nearest dollar.
(b) Record the adjusting entries at February 28.

SOLUTION TO DEMONSTRATION PROBLEM

(a)

Feb.	1	Cash	50,000	
		Notes Payable		50,000
		Issued six-month, 7% note.		
	10	Cash ($37,565 + $4,883)	42,448	
		Sales		37,565
		HST Payable ($37,565 × 13%)		4,883
		To record sales and sales tax payable.		
	28	Salaries Expense	50,000	
		Income Tax Payable		15,000
		CPP Payable		2,475
		EI Payable		915
		Salaries Payable		31,610
		To record February salaries.		

(b)

Feb.	28	Interest Expense ($50,000 × 7% × $^1/_{12}$)	292	
		Interest Payable		292
		To record accrued interest for February.		
	28	Employee Benefits Expense	4,556	
		CPP Payable ($2,475 × 1)		2,475
		EI Payable ($915 × 1.4)		1,281
		Dental Plan Payable		800
		To record employee benefit costs for February.		
	28	Warranty Expense (350 × $40)	14,000	
		Warranty Liability		14,000
		To record estimated product warranty liability.		

ACTION PLAN

- Remember that interest rates are annual rates and must be adjusted for periods of time less than one year.
- Remember that sales taxes collected must be sent to the government and are not part of sales revenue.
- Remember that employee deductions for CPP, EI, and income tax reduce the salaries payable.
- Employer contributions to CPP, EI, and the dental plan create an additional expense.
- Warranty costs are expensed in the period when the sales occur.

▶ Summary of Learning Objectives

1. **Account for determinable or certain current liabilities.** Liabilities are present obligations arising from past events, to make future payments of assets or services. Determinable liabilities have certainty about their existence, amount, and timing—in other words, they have a known amount, payee, and due date. Examples of determinable current liabilities include accounts payable, unearned revenues, operating lines of credit, notes payable, sales taxes, current maturities of long-term debt, and accrued liabilities such as property taxes, payroll, and interest.

2. **Account for uncertain liabilities.** Estimated liabilities exist, but their amount or timing is uncertain. As long as it is *likely* the company will have to settle the obligation, and the company can reasonably estimate the amount, the

liability is recognized. Product warranties, customer loyalty programs, and gift cards result in liabilities that must be estimated. They are recorded as an expense (or as a decrease in revenue) and a liability in the period when the sales occur. These liabilities are reduced when repairs under warranty, redemptions, and returns occur. Gift cards are a type of unearned revenue because they result in a liability until the gift card is redeemed. Because some cards are never redeemed, it is necessary to estimate the liability and make adjustments.

A contingency is an existing condition or situation that is uncertain, where it cannot be known if a loss (and a related liability) will result until a future event happens or does not happen. Under ASPE, a liability for a contingent loss is recorded if it is likely that a loss will occur and the amount of the contingency can be reasonably estimated. Under IFRS, the threshold for recording the loss is lower. It is recorded if a loss is probable. Under ASPE, these liabilities are called contingent liabilities, and under IFRS, these liabilities are called provisions. If it is not possible to estimate the amount, these liabilities are only disclosed. They are not disclosed if they are unlikely unless they could have a substantial impact on the entity.

3. ***Determine payroll costs and record payroll transactions.*** Payroll costs consist of employee and employer payroll costs. In recording employee costs, Salaries Expense is debited for the gross pay, individual liability accounts are credited for payroll deductions, and Salaries Payable is credited for net pay. In recording employer payroll costs, Employee Benefits Expense is debited for the employer's share of Canada Pension Plan (CPP), Employment Insurance (EI), workers' compensation, vacation pay, and any other deductions or benefits

provided. Each benefit is credited to its specific current liability account.

4. ***Prepare the current liabilities section of the balance sheet.*** The nature and amount of each current liability and contingency should be reported in the balance sheet or in the notes accompanying the financial statements. Traditionally, current liabilities are reported first and in order of liquidity.

5. ***Calculate mandatory payroll deductions (Appendix 10A).*** Mandatory payroll deductions include CPP, EI, and income taxes. CPP is calculated by multiplying pensionable earnings (gross pay minus the pay-period exemption) by the CPP contribution rate. EI is calculated by multiplying insurable earnings by the EI contribution rate. Federal and provincial income taxes are calculated using a progressive tax scheme and are based on taxable earnings and personal tax credits. The calculations are very complex and it is best to use one of the Canada Revenue Agency income tax calculation tools such as payroll deduction tables.

▶ Glossary

Accounts payable Accounts payable that result from purchase transactions with suppliers. Also known as trade payables. (p. 530)

Canada Pension Plan (CPP) A mandatory federal plan that gives disability, retirement, and death benefits to qualifying Canadians. (p. 543)

Collateral Property pledged as security for a loan. (p. 531)

Contingency An existing condition or situation that is uncertain, where it cannot be known if a loss (and a related liability) will result from the situation until one or more future events happen or do not happen. (p. 540)

Contingent liability A liability whose existence will be confirmed only by the occurrence or non-occurrence of a future event. (p. 540)

Customer loyalty programs Programs that result in future savings for members on the merchandise or services the company sells. (p. 537)

Determinable liability A liability whose existence, amount, and timing are known with certainty. (p. 530)

Employee benefits Payments made by an employer, in addition to wages and salaries, to give pension, insurance, medical, or other benefits to its employees. (p. 544)

Employee earnings record A separate record of an employee's gross pay, payroll deductions, and net pay for the calendar year. (p. 545)

Employment Insurance (EI) A federal mandatory insurance program designed to give income protection for a limited period of time to employees who are temporarily laid off, who are on parental leave, or who lose their jobs. (p. 543)

Gross pay Total compensation earned by an employee. Also known as gross earnings. (p. 542)

Insurable earnings Gross earnings used to calculate EI deductions. There is a maximum amount of insurable earnings set each year by the government. (p. 552)

Net pay Gross pay less payroll deductions. (p. 544)

Notes payable Obligations in the form of written promissory notes. (p. 532)

Operating line of credit Pre-authorized approval to borrow money at a bank when it is needed, up to a pre-set limit. (p. 531)

Payroll deductions Deductions from gross pay to determine the amount of a paycheque. (p. 543)

Payroll register A record that accumulates the gross pay, deductions, and net pay per employee for each pay period and becomes the documentation for preparing a paycheque for each employee. (p. 546)

Pensionable earnings Gross earnings less the basic yearly exemption. There is a maximum amount of pensionable earnings set each year by the government. (p. 551)

Personal tax credits Amounts deducted from an individual's income taxes that determine the amount of income taxes to be withheld. (p. 553)

Prime rate The interest rate banks charge their best customers. (p. 532)

Product warranties Promises made by the seller to a buyer to repair or replace a product if it is defective or does not perform as intended. (p. 536)

Provisions Liabilities of uncertain timing or amount. Also known as "estimated liabilities." (p. 536)

Note: All questions, exercises, and problems below with an asterisk (*) relate to material in Appendix 10A.

▶ Self-Study Questions

Answers are at the end of the chapter.

(LO 1) C   1. Which of the following statements is the best description of a liability?
   (a) A liability is a commitment to pay an amount in the future.
   (b) A liability arises when an expense is incurred.
   (c) A liability is an amount that should have been paid in the past.
   (d) A liability is a present obligation, arising from past events, to make future payments of assets or services.

(LO 1) C   2. The time period for classifying a liability as current is one year or the operating cycle, whichever is:
   (a) longer.
   (b) probable.
   (c) shorter.
   (d) possible.

(LO 1) AP   3. Gibraltar Company borrows $55,200 on July 31, 2017, from the East Coast Bank by signing a one-year, 5% note. Interest is payable at maturity. Assuming Gibraltar has a December 31 fiscal year end, how much interest expense will Gibraltar record in 2017?
   (a) $0
   (b) $1,150
   (c) $1,380
   (d) $2,760

(LO 1) AP   4. RS Company borrowed $70,000 on December 1 on a six-month, 6% note. At December 31:
   (a) neither the note payable nor the interest payable is a current liability.
   (b) the note payable is a current liability, but the interest payable is not.
   (c) the interest payable is a current liability but the note payable is not.
   (d) both the note payable and the interest payable are current liabilities.

(LO 1) AP   5. On March 1, Swift Current Company receives its property tax assessment of $13,200 for the 2017 calendar year. The property tax bill is due May 1. If Swift Current prepares quarterly financial statements, how much property tax expense should the company report for the quarter ended March 31, 2017?
   (a) $3,300
   (b) $4,400
   (c) $1,100
   (d) $13,200

(LO 2) AP 6. Big Al's Appliance Store offers a two-year warranty on all appliances sold. The company estimates that 5% of all appliances sold need to be serviced at an average cost of $100 each. At December 31, 2016, the Warranty Liability account had a balance of $20,000. During 2017, the store spends $14,500 repairing 145 appliances. An additional 4,500 appliances are sold in 2017. On the 2017 income statement, warranty expense will be:
   (a) $28,000.
   (b) $22,500.
   (c) $14,500.
   (d) $20,000.

(LO 2) K   7. Friendly Department Store has a customer loyalty program in which customers receive points when they make a purchase. The points can be redeemed on future purchases. The value of the points issued should be recorded as:
   (a) revenue when the points are issued.
   (b) an expense when the points are issued.
   (c) revenue when the points are redeemed.
   (d) an expense when the points are redeemed.

(LO 2) K   8. Under IFRS, a contingent loss and the related liability should be recorded in the accounts when:
   (a) it is probable the contingency will happen, but the amount cannot be reasonably estimated.
   (b) it is probable the contingency will happen, and the amount can be reasonably estimated.
   (c) it is highly unlikely the contingency will happen, but the amount can be reasonably estimated.
   (d) it is unlikely that the users of the financial statements will read the notes.

(LO 3) AP   9. In a recent pay period, Blue Company employees have gross salaries of $17,250. Total deductions are: CPP $866, EI $316, and income taxes $4,312. What is Blue Company's total payroll expense for this pay period? Ignore vacation benefits and workers' compensation premiums.
   (a) $17,250
   (b) $18,558
   (c) $11,765
   (d) $18,432

(LO 4) K   10. On November 1, 2017, SSNL Company borrows $120,000 cash from the bank and issues a two-year, 4% note payable. SSNL must make payments of $5,000 plus interest at the end of each month. On December 31, 2017, what amount will be included in current and in non-current liabilities on the balance sheet?

	Current Liabilities	Non-current Liabilities
(a)	$60,000	$ 50,000
(b)	$60,000	$ 60,000
(c)	$10,000	$100,000
(d)	$50,000	$ 70,000

(LO 3, 5) *11. During the first week of May 2017, Emily Marquette
AP   worked 35 hours at an hourly wage of $29.50 per
hour for an employer in Ontario. Using the payroll
deduction tables in Appendix 10A, what was the
amount of federal tax withheld, assuming her only
personal tax credit is the basic personal amount?

      (a) $153.10
      (b) $120.40
      (c) $117.30
      (d) $150.95

▶ Questions

(LO 1) K   1. What is a determinable liability? List some examples.

(LO 1) K   2. Why is a present commitment to purchase an asset
in the future not recorded as a liability?

(LO 1) AP   3. The Calgary Panthers sold 5,000 season football
tickets at $80 each for its six-game home schedule.
What entries should be made (a) when the tickets
were sold and (b) after each game?

(LO 1) K   4. How is interest calculated on a note payable? How is
the amount of interest payable at the fiscal year end
calculated?

(LO 1) K   5. What is the difference between an operating line of
credit and a bank overdraft?

(LO 1) C   6. Your roommate says, "Sales taxes are reported as an
expense in the income statement." Do you agree?
Explain.

(LO 1) C   7. Laurel Hyatt believes that if a company has a
long-term liability, the entire amount should be
classified as non-current liabilities. Is Laurel
correct? Explain.

(LO 2) C   8. The accountant for Amiable Appliances feels that warranty expense should not be recorded unless an appliance is returned for repair. "Otherwise, how do you
know if the appliance will be returned, and if so, how
much it will cost to fix?" he says. Do you agree? Explain.

(LO 2) C   9. Why does issuing a customer some form of future
savings, when the customer purchases goods or
services, result in a liability for the business?

(LO 2) C   10. A restaurant recently started a customer loyalty
program. For all bills in excess of $100, the customer
receives a 2-for-1 voucher for an appetizer for future
meals. How should the restaurant account for the
vouchers?

(LO 2) C   11. In what respects are gift cards similar to unearned
revenues and why are they classified as a liability?
How is a gift card different than an airline's unearned
passenger revenue for flights paid in advance?

(LO 1,2) K   12. What are the differences between determinable,
estimated, and contingent liabilities?

(LO 2) C   13. What is a contingency? How is it different from an
estimated liability?

(LO 2) C   14. If a company is using ASPE, under what circumstances
are a contingent loss and the related liability recorded
in the accounts? Under what circumstances are they
disclosed only in the notes to the financial statements?

(LO 2) C   15. If a company is using IFRS, under what circumstances
are a contingent loss and the related liability recorded
in the accounts? How is IFRS different from ASPE in
this respect?

(LO 2) C   16. When is it necessary to disclose a contingency even
if the chance of occurrence is small?

(LO 3) C   17. What is gross pay? How is it different than net pay?
Which amount (gross or net) should a company
record as salaries expense?

(LO 3) C   18. Explain the different types of employee and employer
payroll deductions, and give examples of each.

(LO 3) K   19. What are an employee earnings record and a payroll
register?

(LO 3) C   20. To whom, and how often, are payroll deductions
remitted?

(LO 4) K   21. In what order are current liabilities generally reported in the balance sheet? Why might this method not
always be possible?

(LO 4) K   22. What information about current liabilities
should be reported in the notes to the financial
statements?

(LO 4) K   23. How can a company determine if its current
liabilities are too high?

(LO 5) K *24. Explain how CPP and EI are calculated.

(LO 5) K *25. How is the amount deducted from an employee's
wages for income tax determined?

▶ Brief Exercises

Identify whether obligations
are current. (LO 1) AP

BE10-1   Jamison Jackets has the following obligations at December 31:
(a) a note payable for $100,000 due in two years
(b) salaries payable of $20,000
(c) a 10-year mortgage payable of $300,000, payable in 10 annual payments of $30,000 plus interest
(d) interest payable of $15,000 on the mortgage

(e) accounts payable of $60,000

(f) sales taxes payable of $6,500

For each obligation, indicate whether it should be classified as a current liability. (Assume an operating cycle of less than one year.)

BE10–2   The Brampton Bullet hockey team sold 2,000 tickets at $120 each for its six-game home schedule. Prepare the entry to record (a) the sale of the season's tickets and (b) the revenue recognized upon playing the first home game.

Journalize unearned revenue. (LO 1) AP

BE10–3   Satterfield publishes a monthly music magazine, *DiscOver*. Subscriptions to the magazine cost $18 per year. During November 2017, Satterfield sells 15,000 subscriptions beginning with the December issue. Satterfield prepares financial statements quarterly and recognizes subscription revenue earned at the end of the quarter. The company uses the accounts Unearned Revenue and Revenue. Prepare the entries to record (a) the receipt of the subscriptions and (b) the adjusting entry at December 31, 2017, to record revenue earned in December 2017.

Journalize unearned revenue. (LO 1) AP

BE10–4   Rabbitt Enterprises borrows $60,000 from LowLand Trust Co. on July 1, 2017 signing a 4%, one-year note payable. Interest is to be paid at maturity. Prepare journal entries for Rabbitt Enterprises to record: (a) the receipt of the proceeds of the note; (b) the journal entry to record the accrued interest at December 31, assuming adjusting entries are made only at year end; and (c) the payment of the note at maturity.

Record note payable. (LO 1) AP

BE10–5   Blue Robin Retail has one store in Ottawa and one in Regina. All sales in Ontario are subject to 13% HST; all sales in Saskatchewan are subject to 5% GST and 5% PST. On March 12, 2017, the Ottawa store reports cash sales of $7,200 and the Regina store reports cash sales of $8,400. (a) Calculate the sales taxes each store charged for these sales. (b) Prepare a journal entry for each store to record the sales on March 12, 2017.

Calculate sales taxes and record sales. (LO 1) AP

BE10–6   Backyard Shed Solutions sells its largest shed for $1,800 plus HST of 13%. On May 10, 2017, it sold 40 of these sheds. On May 17, 2017, the company sold 95 of these sheds. All sales are cash sales. For each day's sales, (a) calculate the HST and (b) prepare a journal entry to record the sales.

Calculate HST and record sales. (LO 1) AP

BE10–7   Dresner Company has a December 31 fiscal year end. It receives a $9,600 property tax bill for the 2017 calendar year on March 31, 2017. The bill is payable on June 30. Prepare entries for March 31, June 30, and December 31, assuming the company adjusts its accounts annually.

Record property tax. (LO 1) AP

BE10–8   In 2017, Song Company introduces a new product that includes a two-year warranty on parts. During 2017, 4,400 units are sold for $450 each. The cost of each unit was $175. The company estimates that 5% of the units will be defective and that the average warranty cost will be $85 per unit. The company has a December 31 fiscal year end and prepares adjusting entries on an annual basis. Prepare an adjusting entry at December 31, 2017, to accrue the estimated warranty cost.

Record warranty. (LO 2) AP

BE10–9   One-Stop Department Store has a loyalty program where customers are given One-Stop "Money" for cash or debit card purchases. The amount they receive is equal to 2% of the pre-tax sales total. Customers can use the One-Stop Money to pay for part or all of their next purchase at One-Stop Department Store. On July 3, 2017, Judy Wishloff purchases merchandise and uses $50 of One-Stop Department Store money. What entry or entries will One-Stop Department Store record for this transaction? Ignore taxes.

Record loyalty rewards issued and redeemed. (LO 2) AP

BE10–10   Metropolis Books sold 50,000 copies of a best-selling novel in July for $8 each. Included in each book was a $2 mail-in rebate if the customer sends in proof of purchase with a completed rebate form. Metropolis estimates that 10% of the purchasers will claim the rebate. (a) Calculate the sales revenue and the unearned revenue related to the loyalty program that Metropolis earned in July on this book. (b) Prepare the journal entry to record the sale and the unearned revenue Metropolis Books should record.

Record estimated liability for a cash rebate program. (LO 2) AP

BE10–11   Rikard's Menswear sells $4,750 of gift cards for cash in December 2017. Rikard's has a December 31 fiscal year end and uses a perpetual inventory system. In January 2018, $2,425 of the gift cards are redeemed for merchandise with a cost of $1,070. Prepare journal entries for Rikard's for December 2017 and January 2018 assuming all gift card balances will be redeemed.

Record gift cards issued and redeemed. (LO 2) AP

BE10–12   For each of the following independent situations, indicate whether it should be (1) recorded, (2) disclosed, or (3) neither recorded nor disclosed. Explain your reasoning and indicate if the accounting treatment would be the same or different under IFRS and ASPE.

(a) A customer has sued a company for $1 million. Currently the company is unable to determine if it will win or lose the lawsuit.

(b) A customer has sued a company for $1 million. The company will likely lose the lawsuit.

(c) A competitor has sued a company for $2 million. The lawyers have advised that there is a 55% chance that the company will lose the lawsuit.

Account for contingencies. (LO 2) C

BE10–13   Athabasca Toil & Oil Company, a public company, is a defendant in a lawsuit for improper discharge of pollutants and waste into the Athabasca River. Athabasca's lawyers have advised that it is probable the company

Discuss contingency. (LO 2) AP

will lose this lawsuit and that it could settle out of court for $50,000. Should Athabasca record anything with regard to this lawsuit? Or should it disclose it in the notes to the financial statements? Explain.

Calculate gross and net pay, and employer costs.
(LO 3) AP

BE10–14   Becky Sherrick's regular hourly wage rate is $12.50, and she is paid time and a half for work over 40 hours per week. In the pay period ended March 16, Becky worked 46 hours. Becky's CPP deductions total $26.99, EI deductions total $11.21, and her income tax withholdings are $94.56. (a) Calculate Becky's gross and net pay for the pay period. (b) What are Becky's employer's costs for CPP, EI, and income tax?

Record payroll. (LO 3) AP

BE10–15   Bri Company's gross pay for the week ended August 22 totalled $70,000, from which $3,330 was deducted for CPP, $1,281 for EI, and $19,360 for income tax. Prepare the entry to record the employer payroll costs, assuming these will not be paid until September.

Identify current liabilities.
(LO 1, 2, 3, 4) K

BE10–16   Identify which of the following items should be classified as a current liability. For those that are not current liabilities, identify where they should be classified.
(a) A product warranty C L
(b) Cash received in advance for airline tickets C L
(c) HST collected on sales
(d) Bank indebtedness
(e) Interest owing on an overdue account payable C L
(f) Interest due on an overdue account receivable
(g) A lawsuit pending against a company. The company is not sure of the likely outcome. C L
(h) Amounts withheld from the employees' weekly pay
(i) Prepaid property tax
(j) A $75,000 mortgage payable, of which $5,000 is due in the next year C L

Calculate current and non-current portion of notes payable. (LO 1, 4) AP

BE10–17   Diamond Dealers has two notes payable outstanding on December 31, 2017, as follows:
(a) A five-year, 5.5%, $60,000 note payable issued on August 31, 2017. Diamond Dealers is required to pay $12,000 plus interest on August 31 each year starting in 2018.
(b) A four-year, 4.5%, $96,000 note payable issued on September 30, 2017. Diamond Dealers is required to pay $2,000 plus interest at the end of each month starting on October 31, 2017. All payments are up to date.

Calculate the amount of each note to be included in current and non-current liabilities on Diamond Dealers' December 31, 2017, balance sheet. Ignore interest.

Prepare current liabilities section and calculate ratios.
(LO 4) AP

BE10–18   **Suncor Energy Inc.** reported the following current assets and current liabilities (in millions) at December 31, 2014:

Accounts payable and accrued liabilities	$5,704
Accounts receivable	4,275
Cash and cash equivalents	5,495
Current portion of long-term debt	34
Current portion of provisions	752
Income taxes payable	1,058
Income taxes receivable	680
Inventories	3,466
Short-term debt	806

(a) Prepare the current liabilities section of the balance sheet.
(b) Calculate the current and acid-test ratios.

Calculate CPP and EI deductions. (LO 5) AP

*BE10–19   Cecilia Hernandez earned $60,100 in 2015 and was paid monthly. She worked for HillSide Tours for all of 2015. Using the formulas, what were her CPP and EI deductions in (a) January 2015 and (b) December 2015?

Calculate payroll deductions.
(LO 5) AP

*BE10–20   In 2015, Viktor Petska was paid a gross salary of $1,075 on a weekly basis. For the week ended May 12, 2015: (a) calculate his CPP and EI deductions and (b) use the excerpts in Illustration 10A-3 to determine his income tax deductions assuming his TD1 claim code is 1.

▶ Exercises

Record various liabilities.
(LO 1, 3) AP

E10–1   Peter's Mini Putt was opened on March 1 by Peter Palazzi. The following selected transactions occurred during March:

Mar. 1   Purchased golf balls and other supplies for $350 from Stevenson Supplies payable in 30 days.
   5   Received a booking for a birthday party to be held the following week. The customer paid the mini golf fees of $200 in advance.

12   Provided the golf services for the birthday party.
15   Wages were paid to hourly workers. A total of $5,000 was paid out, with withholdings as follows: CPP
     $230, EI $94, and income tax $1,400.
30   Wrote a cheque to Stevenson Supplies for the $350 owing to settle the balance due.

Instructions

Journalize the transactions.

E10–2   Udala Uke's had the following transactions involving notes payable.

Record note payable and interest. (LO 1) AP

July 1, 2017	Borrows $50,000 from First National Bank by signing a nine-month, 8% note.
Nov. 1, 2017	Borrows $60,000 from Interprovincial Bank by signing a three-month, 6% note.
Dec. 31, 2017	Prepares adjusting entries.
Feb. 1, 2018	Pays principal and interest to Interprovincial Bank.
Apr. 1, 2018	Pays principal and interest to First National Bank.

Instructions

Prepare journal entries for each of the transactions.

E10–3   On June 1, Merando borrows $90,000 from First Bank on a six-month, $90,000, 6% note.

Record note payable and interest. (LO 1) AP

Instructions

(a) Prepare the entry on June 1.
(b) Prepare the adjusting entry on June 30.
(c) Prepare the entry at maturity (December 1), assuming monthly adjusting entries have been made through
     November 30.
(d) What was the total financing cost (interest expense)?

E10–4   On June 1, 2017, Novack Company purchases equipment on account from Moleski Manufacturers for
$50,000. Novack is unable to pay its account on July 1, 2017, so Moleski agrees to accept a three-month, 7% note
payable from Novack. Interest is payable the first of each month, starting August 1, 2017. Moleski has an August 31
fiscal year end and adjusts its accounts on an annual basis.

Record note payable, interest paid monthly. (LO 1) AP

Instructions

Record all transactions related to the note for Novack Company.

E10–5   On March 1, 2017, Tundra Trees purchased equipment from Edworthy Equipment Dealership in exchange
for a seven-month, 8%, $30,000 note payable. Interest is due at maturity. Tundra Trees has a July 31 fiscal year end.
Edworthy has a May 31 fiscal year end. Both companies adjust their accounts annually. Tundra honours the note
at maturity.

Record note payable and note receivable; interest paid at maturity. (LO 1) AP

Instructions

(a) For Tundra Trees, record all transactions related to the note.
(b) For Edworthy Equipment, record all transactions related to the note. Assume the cost of the equipment to
     Edworthy was $18,000.

E10–6   In providing accounting services to small businesses, you encounter the following independent situations:

Record sales taxes. (LO 1) AP

1. Sainsbury rang up $13,200 of sales, plus HST of 13%, on its cash register on April 10.
2. Montgomery rang up $30,000 of sales, before sales taxes, on its cash register on April 21. The company charges
    5% GST and no PST.
3. Winslow charges 5% GST and 7% PST on all sales. On April 27, the company collected $25,100 sales in cash
    plus sales taxes.

Instructions

Record the sales transactions and related taxes for each client.

E10–7   Scoggin rings up sales plus sales taxes on its cash register. On April 10, the register total for sales is
$80,000.

Record sales taxes. (LO 1) AP

Instructions

Journalize the transactions assuming the sales were made in
(a) Quebec,
(b) Nova Scotia, and
(c) Alberta.

Account for unearned
revenue. (LO 1) AP

E10–8 Charleswood Musical Theatre's season begins in November and ends in April, with a different play each month. In October 2017, Charleswood sold 100 season tickets for the 2017–18 season, for $210 each. Charleswood records all season ticket sales as unearned revenue and adjusts its accounts on a monthly basis. The company has a March 31 fiscal year end.

Instructions

(a) Prepare the entry for sale of the season tickets. Date the entry October 31.
(b) Prepare any required adjusting entries on:
   1. November 30, 2017
   2. March 31, 2018
   3. April 30, 2018
(c) Determine the balance (after any required adjustments) in Unearned Revenue on:
   1. November 30, 2017
   2. December 31, 2017
   3. March 31, 2018

Account for unearned
revenue. (LO 1) AP

E10–9 Satterfield publishes a monthly sports magazine, *Hockey Hits*. Subscriptions to the magazine cost $18 per year. During November 2017, Satterfield sells 15,000 subscriptions beginning with the December issue. Satterfield prepares financial statements quarterly and recognizes revenue earned at the end of the quarter. The company uses the accounts Unearned Revenue and Revenue.

Instructions

(a) Prepare the entry in November for the receipt of the subscriptions.
(b) Prepare the adjusting entry at December 31, 2017, to record revenue earned in December 2017.
(c) Prepare the adjusting entry at March 31, 2018, to record revenue earned in the first quarter of 2018.

Record property tax;
determine financial statement
impact. (LO 1, 4) AP

E10–10 Seaboard Company receives its annual property tax bill of $24,000 for the 2017 calendar year on May 31, 2017, and it is payable on July 31, 2017. Seaboard has a December 31 fiscal year end.

Instructions

(a) Prepare the journal entries for Seaboard on May 31, July 31, and December 31, 2017, assuming that the company makes monthly adjusting entries. (Assume property tax expense in 2016 was $2,200 per month.)
(b) What is recorded on Seaboard's December 31, 2017, balance sheet and income statement for the year ended December 31, 2017, in regard to property taxes?

Record warranty costs.
(LO 2) AP

E10–11 Castellitto Company began selling game consoles on November 1, 2017. The company offers a 75-day warranty for defective merchandise. Based on past experience with other similar products, Castellitto estimates that 2.5% of the units sold will become defective in the warranty period, and that the average cost of replacing or repairing a defective unit is $20. In November, Castellitto sold 30,000 units and 450 defective units were returned. In December, Castellitto sold 32,000 units and 630 defective units were returned. The actual cost of replacing the defective units was $21,600.

Instructions

(a) Prepare a journal entry to accrue for the estimated warranty costs for the November and December sales at December 31, 2017.
(b) Prepare one summary journal entry at December 31, 2017, to record the cost of replacing the defective game consoles returned during November and December.
(c) What amounts will be included in Castellitto's 2017 income statement and balance sheet at December 31, 2017, with regard to the warranty?

Calculate warranty costs for
multiple years. (LO 2) AP

E10–12 Silver Cloud manufactures and sells computers for $2,000 each, with a two-year parts and labour warranty. Based on prior experience, the company expects, on average, to incur warranty costs equal to 5% of sales. The business reports the following sales and warranty cost information:

	Sales (units)	Actual Warranty Costs
2015	500	$30,000
2016	600	46,000
2017	525	53,500

Instructions

(a) Calculate the warranty expense for each year.

(b) Calculate the warranty liability at the end of each year.

E10–13 Steig's Sports Store has a customer loyalty program in which it issues points to customers for every cash purchase that can be applied to future purchases. For every dollar spent, a customer receives three points. Each point is worth one cent. There is no expiry date on the points. Steig's estimates that 35% of the points issued will eventually be redeemed. Steig's has a December 31 year end.

Calculate customer loyalty program liability. (LO 2) AP

    The program was started in 2016. During 2016, 900,000 points were issued. Sales for 2016 were $300,000. In 2017, 1.2 million points were issued. Total sales for 2017 were $400,000.

Instructions

(a) What is the stand-alone value of the points issued in 2016? In 2017?

(b) Prepare the journal entries to record the sales for 2016 and 2017.

(c) When the points are redeemed, how is this accounted for? What is the impact of the point redemptions on profit and cash flow?

E10–14 A list of possible liabilities follows:

Identify type of liability. (LO 1, 2) C

1. An automobile company recalled a particular car model because of a possible problem with the brakes. The company will pay to replace the brakes.

2. A large retail store has a policy of refunding purchases to dissatisfied customers under a widely advertised "money-back, no questions asked" guarantee.

3. A manufacturer offers a three-year warranty at the time of sale.

4. To promote sales, a company offers prizes (such as a chance to win a trip) in return for a specific type of bottle cap.

5. A local community has filed suit against a chemical company for contamination of drinking water. The community is demanding compensation, and the amount is uncertain. The company is vigorously defending itself.

Instructions

(a) State whether you believe each of the above liabilities is determinable, estimable, or contingent, and explain why.

(b) If you identify the liability as contingent in part (a), state what factors should be considered in determining if it should be recorded, disclosed, or neither recorded nor disclosed in the financial statements.

E10–15 Sleep-a-Bye Baby Company, a public company, is the defendant in a lawsuit alleging that its portable baby cribs are unsafe. The company has offered to replace the cribs free of charge for any concerned parent. Nonetheless, it has been sued for damages and distress amounting to $1.5 million. The company plans to vigorously defend its product safety record in court.

Analyze contingency. (LO 2) AP

Instructions

(a) What should the company record or report in its financial statements for this situation? Explain why.

(b) What if Sleep-a-Bye Baby Company's lawyers advise that it is likely the company will have to pay damages of $100,000? Does this change what should be recorded or reported in the financial statements? Explain.

(c) How would your answers to parts (a) and (b) change if Sleep-a-Bye Baby Company were a private company that had chosen to follow ASPE?

E10–16 Hidden Dragon Restaurant's gross payroll for April is $46,600. The company deducted $2,162 for CPP, $853 for EI, and $9,011 for income taxes from the employees' cheques. Employees are paid monthly at the end of each month.

Record payroll. (LO 3) AP

Instructions

(a) Prepare a journal entry for Hidden Dragon on April 30 to record the payment of the April payroll to employees.

(b) Prepare a journal entry on April 30 to accrue Hidden Dragon's employer payroll costs. Assume that Hidden Dragon is assessed workers' compensation premiums at a rate of 1% per month and accrues for vacation pay at a rate of 4% per month.

(c) On May 15, Hidden Dragon pays the government the correct amounts for April's payroll. Prepare a journal entry to record this remittance.

Calculate gross pay; prepare payroll register, and record payroll. (LO 3) AP

E10–17 Ahmad Company has the following data for the weekly payroll ending May 31:

Employee	M	Tu	W	Th	F	S	Hourly Rate	CPP Deduction	Income Tax Withheld	Health Insurance
A. Kassam	9	8	9	8	10	3	$13	$29.17	$ 85.55	$10
H. Faas	8	8	8	8	8	5	14	29.59	87.10	15
G. Labute	9	10	9	10	8	0	15	33.05	102.55	15

Employees are paid 1.5 times the regular hourly rate for all hours worked over 40 hours per week. Ahmad Company must make payments to the workers' compensation plan equal to 2% of the gross payroll. In addition, Ahmad matches the employees' health insurance contributions and accrues vacation pay at a rate of 4%.

Instructions

(a) Prepare the payroll register for the weekly payroll. Calculate each employee's EI deduction at a rate of 1.88% of gross pay.

(b) Record the payroll and Ahmad Company's employee benefits.

Calculate current and non-current portion of notes payable, and interest payable. (LO 1, 4) AP

E10–18 Emerald Enterprises has three notes payable outstanding on December 31, 2016, as follows:

1. A six-year, 6%, $60,000 note payable issued on March 31, 2016. Emerald Enterprises is required to pay $10,000 plus interest on March 31 each year starting in 2017.

2. A seven-month, 4%, $30,000 note payable issued on July 1, 2016. Interest and principal are payable at maturity.

3. A 30-month, 5%, $120,000 note payable issued on September 1, 2016. Emerald Enterprises is required to pay $4,000 plus interest on the first day of each month starting on October 1, 2016. All payments are up to date.

Instructions

(a) Calculate the current portion of each note payable.

(b) Calculate the non-current portion of each note payable.

(c) Calculate any interest payable at December 31, 2016.

Prepare current liabilities section of balance sheet. (LO 4) AP

E10–19 Medlen Models has the following account balances at December 31, 2017:

Notes payable ($60,000 due after 12/31/18)	$100,000
Unearned service revenue	70,000
Mortgage Payable ($90,000 due in 2018)	250,000
Salaries payable	32,000
Accounts payable	63,000

In addition, Medlen is involved in a lawsuit. Legal counsel feels it is probable Medlen will pay damages of $25,000 in 2018. Medlen records contingent liabilities in the account Litigation Liability.

Instructions

Prepare the current liabilities section of Medlen's December 31, 2017, balance sheet.

Calculate gross pay and payroll deductions; record payroll. (LO 3, 5) AP

*E10–20 Kate Gough's regular hourly wage rate is $22.60, and she receives a wage of 1.5 times the regular hourly rate for work over 40 hours per week. For the weekly pay period ended June 15, 2017, Kate worked 44 hours. Kate lives in Ontario and has a claim code of 1 for tax deductions.

Instructions

(a) Calculate Kate's gross pay, payroll deductions, and net pay. Use Illustration 10A-3 to determine her income tax deductions.

(b) Record Kate's salary on June 15, assuming it was also paid on this date.

(c) Record the employer's related payroll costs on June 15, assuming they were not paid on this date.

Calculate gross pay and payroll deductions. (LO 5) AP

*E10–21 In 2017, Donald Green worked for the Green Red Company and earned a gross salary of $57,000 for the year ($4,750 per month). He was paid once a month at the end of each month.

Instructions

Calculate Donald's CPP and EI deductions for the following:

(a) September 2017

(b) October 2017

(c) November 2017

(d) December 2017

(e) In total for 2017

▶ Problems: Set A

P10–1A   Motzer Company had the following selected transactions.

Prepare current liability entries and adjusting entries. (LO 1, 2) AP

Feb.	2	Purchases supplies from Supplies R Us on account for $2,500.
	10	Cash register sales total $43,200, plus 5% GST and 8% PST.
	15	Signs a $35,000, six-month, 6%-interest-bearing note payable to MidiBank and receives $35,000 in cash.
	21	The payroll for the previous two weeks consists of salaries of $50,000. All salaries are subject to CPP of $2,308 and EI of $940 and income tax of $8,900. The salaries are paid on February 28. The employer's payroll expense is also recorded.
	28	Accrues interest on the MidiBank note payable.
	28	Accrues the required warranty provision because some of the sales were made under warranty. Of the units sold under warranty, 350 are expected to become defective. Repair costs are estimated to be $40 per unit.
	28	Pays employees the salaries for the pay period ending February 21.
Mar.	1	Remits the sales taxes to the Province and GST to the Receiver General for the February 10 sales.
	2	Makes the payment to Supplies R Us from the February purchase.
	15	Remits the payroll taxes owing from the February 21 payroll to the Receiver General.

Instructions

Journalize the February and March transactions.

TAKING IT FURTHER   What are some additional employee benefits paid by employers? How are they accounted for?

P10–2A   On January 1, 2017, the ledger of Accardo Company contains the following liability accounts.

Prepare current liability entries, adjusting entries, and current liabilities section. (LO 1, 2, 4) AP

Accounts Payable	$52,000
HST Payable	7,700
Unearned Revenue	16,000

During January, the following selected transactions occurred.

Jan.	2	Borrowed $27,000 from Canada Bank on a three-month, 6%, $27,000 note.
	5	Sold merchandise for cash totalling $20,500 plus 13% HST.
	12	Performed services for customers who had made advance payments of $10,000. The payment included HST of $1,151. (Credit Service Revenue.)
	14	Paid Receiver General for HST invoiced in December 2016 ($7,700).
	20	Sold 900 units of a new product on credit at $50 per unit, plus 13% HST. This new product is subject to a one-year warranty.
	25	Sold merchandise for cash totalling $12,500 plus 13% HST.

Instructions

(a) Journalize the January transactions.

(b) Journalize the adjusting entries at January 31 for (1) the outstanding notes payable, and (2) estimated warranty liability, assuming warranty costs are expected to equal 7% of sales of the new product sold January 20.

(c) Prepare the current liabilities section of the balance sheet at January 31, 2017. Assume no change in accounts payable.

TAKING IT FURTHER   Explain why warranty liabilities are recorded before a customer has any issues with the product.

P10–3A   Crab Apple Tree Farm has a December 31 fiscal year end. The company has six notes payable outstanding on December 31, 2017, as follows:

Calculate current and non-current portion of notes payable, and interest payable. (LO 1, 4) AP

1. A 10-month, 5%, $35,000 note payable issued on August 1, 2017. Interest is payable monthly on the first day of each month starting on September 1.
2. A four-month, 4%, $15,000 note payable issued on September 1, 2017. Interest and principal are payable at maturity.
3. A six-month, 4.5%, $26,000 note payable issued on November 1, 2017. Interest and principal are payable at maturity.
4. A five-year, 3.5%, $60,000 note payable issued on March 31, 2017. Crab Apple Tree Farm is required to pay $12,000 plus interest on March 31 each year starting in 2017.
5. A six-year, 5%, $100,000 note payable issued on October 1, 2017. Crab Apple Tree Farm is required to pay $2,000 plus interest on the first day of each month starting on November 1, 2017. All payments are up to date.
6. A four-year, 5%, $40,000 note payable issued on January 31, 2016. Crab Apple Tree Farm is required to pay $10,000 every January 31 starting in 2017. Interest is payable monthly on the last day of each month, starting on February 28, 2016.

Instructions

(a) Calculate the current portion of each note payable.

(b) Calculate the non-current portion of each note payable.

(c) Calculate any interest payable at December 31, 2017.

TAKING IT FURTHER What are the costs and benefits to the maker and the payee of the note of using a note payable in place of an account payable?

Record note transactions; show financial statement presentation. (LO 1, 4) AP

P10–4A The current liabilities section of the December 31, 2016, balance sheet of Learnstream Company included notes payable of $14,000 and interest payable of $490. The note payable was issued to Tanner Company on June 30, 2016. Interest of 7% is payable at maturity, March 31, 2017.

The following selected transactions occurred in the year ended December 31, 2017:

Jan. 12 Purchased merchandise on account from McCoy Company for $25,000, terms n/30. Learnstream uses a perpetual inventory system.

31 Issued a $25,000, three-month, 7% note to McCoy Company in payment of its account. Interest is payable monthly.

Feb. 28 Paid interest on the McCoy note (see January 31 transaction).

Mar. 31 Paid the Tanner note, plus interest.

31 Paid interest on the McCoy note (see January 31 transaction).

Apr. 30 Paid the McCoy note, plus one month's interest (see January 31 transaction).

Aug. 1 Purchased equipment from Drouin Equipment by paying $11,000 cash and signing a $30,000, 10-month, 6% note. Interest is payable at maturity.

Sept. 30 Borrowed $100,000 cash from the First Interprovincial Bank by signing a 10-year, 5% note payable. Interest is payable quarterly on December 31, March 31, June 30, and September 30. Of the principal, $10,000 must be paid each September 30.

Dec. 31 Paid interest on the First Interprovincial Bank note (see September 30 transaction).

Instructions

(a) Record the transactions and any adjustments required at December 31.

(b) Show the balance sheet presentation of notes payable and interest payable at December 31.

(c) Show the income statement presentation of interest expense for the year.

TAKING IT FURTHER Why is it important to correctly classify notes payable as either current or non-current in the balance sheet?

Record current liability transactions; prepare current liabilities section. (LO 1, 2, 3, 4) AP

P10–5A On January 1, 2017, Shumway Software Company's general ledger contained these liability accounts:

Accounts payable	$40,000
Unearned revenue—loyalty program	3,700
CPP payable	1,320
EI payable	680
HST payable	8,630
Income tax payable	3,340
Unearned revenue	15,300
Vacation pay payable	8,660

In January, the following selected transactions occurred:

Jan. 2 Issued a $46,000, four-month, 7% note. Interest is payable at maturity.

5 Sold merchandise for $8,600 cash, plus 13% HST. The cost of this sale was $4,100. Shumway Software uses a perpetual inventory system.

12 Provided services for customers who had paid $8,000 cash in advance. The payment included HST of $920.

14 Paid the Receiver General (federal government) for sales taxes collected in December 2016.

15 Paid the Receiver General for amounts owing from the December payroll for CPP, EI, and income tax.

17 Paid $14,800 to creditors on account.

20 Sold 1,900 units of a new product on account for $55 per unit, plus 13% HST. This new product has a one-year warranty. It is estimated that 9% of the units sold will be returned for repair at an average cost of $10 per unit. The cost of this sale was $25 per unit.

29 During the month, provided $2,300 of services for customers who redeemed their customer loyalty rewards. Assume that HST of $265 is included in the $2,300.

31 Issued 30,000 loyalty rewards points worth $1 each. Based on past experience, 20% of these points are expected to be redeemed. Cash sales related to the issuance of the loyalty points were $250,000.

31   Recorded and paid the monthly payroll. Gross salaries were $18,750. Amounts withheld included CPP of $764, EI of $343, and income tax of $3,481.

Instructions

(a) Record the transactions.
(b) Record adjusting entries for the following:
   1. Interest on the note payable
   2. The estimated warranty liability
   3. Employee benefits for CPP, EI, and vacation pay (accrued at a rate of 4%)
   4. Estimated property taxes of $8,820 for the 2017 calendar year
(c) Prepare the current liabilities section of the balance sheet at January 31.

TAKING IT FURTHER   Explain how and when the Vacation Pay Payable account balance is paid.

P10–6A   On January 1, 2015, Hopewell Company began a warranty program to stimulate sales. It is estimated that 5% of the units sold will be returned for repair at an estimated cost of $30 per unit. Sales and warranty figures for the three years ended December 31 are as follows:

Record warranty transactions. (LO 2) AP

	2015	2016	2017
Sales (units)	1,500	1,700	1,800
Sales price per unit	$ 150	$ 120	$ 125
Units returned for repair under warranty	75	90	105
Actual warranty costs	$2,250	$2,400	$2,640

Instructions

(a) Calculate the warranty expense for each year and warranty liability at the end of each year.
(b) Record the warranty transactions for each year. Credit Repair Parts Inventory for the actual warranty costs.
(c) To date, what percentage of the units sold have been returned for repair under warranty? What has been the average actual warranty cost per unit for the three-year period?

TAKING IT FURTHER   Assume that at December 31, 2017, management reassesses its original estimates and decides that it is more likely that the company will have to service 7% of the units sold in 2017. Management also determines that the average actual cost per unit incurred to date (as calculated in part [c] above) is more reasonable than its original estimate. What should be the balance in the Warranty Liability account at December 31, 2017?

P10–7A   Save-Always Stores started a customer loyalty program at the beginning of 2016 in which customers making cash purchases of gasoline at Save-Always Gas Bars are issued rewards in the form of grocery coupons. For each litre of gasoline purchased, the customer gets a grocery coupon for 3.8 cents that can be redeemed in Save-Always Food Stores. The coupons have no expiry date. Save-Always Stores began selling gift cards in 2017 that do not have expiry dates.

Record customer loyalty program and gift card transactions; determine impact on financial statements. (LO 2) AP

The following are selected transactions in 2016 and 2017:

1. In 2016, the Gas Bars sold 3.8 million litres of gasoline resulting in gas sales of $4,560,000. Grocery coupons were issued with these sales. The expected redemption rate for the grocery coupons is 80%.
2. In 2016, customers redeemed $46,000 of the grocery coupons in the Food Stores.
3. In 2017, the Gas Bars sold 4.65 million litres of gasoline resulting in gas sales of $6,045,000. Grocery coupons were issued with these sales. The expected redemption rate for the grocery coupons is 80%.
4. In 2017, customers redeemed $53,500 of the grocery coupons in the Food Stores.
5. In 2017, customers purchased $82,000 of gift cards, and $45,000 of the cards were redeemed by the end of the year.

Instructions

(a) Indicate if the following activities will increase, decrease, or have no effect on each of revenues, expenses, and profit:
   1. Issuing grocery coupons when sales are made
   2. Redeeming grocery coupons
   3. Issuing gift cards
   4. Redeeming gift cards
(b) Record the above transactions.
(c) What balances will be included in current liabilities at December 31, 2016 and 2017, regarding the customer loyalty program and gift cards?

TAKING IT FURTHER   What factors should management consider in determining if current liabilities are correctly valued at December 31, 2017?

Discuss reporting of contingencies and record provisions.
(LO 2, 4) AP

P10–8A   Mega Company, a public company, is preparing its financial statements for the year ended December 31, 2017. It is now January 31, 2018, and the following situations are being reviewed to determine the appropriate accounting treatment:

1. Mega Company is being sued for $4 million for a possible malfunction of one of its products. In July 2017, a customer suffered a serious injury while operating the product. The company is vigorously defending itself as it is clear the customer was intoxicated when using the product.
2. In a separate lawsuit, Mega is being sued for $3 million by an employee who was injured on the job in February 2017. It is likely that the company will lose this lawsuit, but a reasonable estimate cannot be made of the amount of the expected settlement.
3. On December 7, 2017, a potential customer injured himself when he slipped on the floor in the foyer of Mega Company's office building. Mega Company did not have appropriate floor mats in place and melting snow from the customer's boots made the floor very dangerous. Mega has negotiated a potential settlement of $200,000 with the individual's lawyer.

Instructions

For each of the above situations, recommend whether Mega Company should: (1) make an accrual in its December 31, 2017, financial statements; (2) disclose the situation in the notes to the financial statements; or (3) not report it. Provide a rationale for your recommendations.

TAKING IT FURTHER   What are the potential benefits and costs of making an accrual for a contingency as opposed to only disclosing it in the notes to the financial statements?

Prepare payroll register and record payroll. (LO 3) AP

P10–9A   Sure Value Hardware has four employees who are paid on an hourly basis, plus time and a half for hours worked in excess of 40 hours a week. Payroll data for the week ended March 14, 2017, follow:

Employee	Total Hours	Hourly Rate	CPP	EI	Income Tax	United Way
I. Dahl	37.5	$17.00	$27.80	11.83	$ 82.25	$ 7.50
F. Gualtieri	42.5	16.50	32.40	13.57	91.20	8.00
G. Ho	43.5	15.50	31.39	13.19	97.50	5.00
A. Israeli	45.0	15.00	31.94	13.40	107.75	10.00

Instructions

(a) Prepare a payroll register for the weekly payroll.
(b) Record the payroll on March 14 and the accrual of employee benefits expense. Assume the company accrues 4% for vacation pay.
(c) Record the payment of the payroll on March 14.
(d) Record the payment of remittances to the Receiver General on April 15.

TAKING IT FURTHER   Does the owner of a proprietorship need to deduct CPP, EI, and income taxes on his or her drawings?

Record payroll transactions and calculate balances in payroll liability accounts.
(LO 3) AP

P10–10A   On January 31, 2017, Cardston Company had the following payroll liability accounts in its ledger:

Canada Pension Plan payable	$ 7,887	Life insurance payable	$ 855
Disability insurance payable	1,280	Union dues payable	1,450
Employment Insurance payable	3,755	Vacation pay payable	20,520
Income tax payable	16,252	Workers' compensation payable	4,275

In February, the following transactions occurred:

Feb.	4	Sent a cheque to the union treasurer for union dues.
	7	Sent a cheque to the insurance company for the disability and life insurance.
	13	Issued a cheque to the Receiver General for the amounts due for CPP, EI, and income tax.
	20	Paid the amount due to the workers' compensation plan.
	28	Completed the monthly payroll register, which shows gross salaries $92,600; CPP withheld $4,281; EI withheld $1,695; income tax withheld $17,595; union dues withheld $1,574; and long-term disability insurance premiums $1,380.
	28	Prepared payroll cheques for the February net pay and distributed the cheques to the employees.
	28	Recorded an adjusting journal entry to record February employee benefits for CPP, EI, workers' compensation at 5% of gross pay, vacation pay at 4% of gross pay, and life insurance at 1% of gross pay.

Instructions

(a) Journalize the February transactions and adjustments.
(b) Calculate the balances in each of the payroll liability accounts at February 28, 2017.

TAKING IT FURTHER Why do employers need an employee earnings record for each employee as well as a payroll register?

P10–11A The following selected account balances are from LightHouse Distributors' adjusted trial balance at September 30, 2017:

Prepare current liabilities section; calculate and comment on ratios.
(LO 4) AP

Accounts payable	$ 90,000
Accounts receivable	182,000
Bank indebtedness	62,500
CPP payable	7,500
EI payable	3,750
HST payable	15,000
Income tax payable	35,000
Interest payable	10,000
Merchandise inventory	275,000
Mortgage payable	150,000
Notes payable	100,000
Prepaid expenses	12,500
Property taxes payable	10,000
Unearned revenue-loyalty program	5,000
Unearned revenue	30,000
Vacation pay payable	13,500
Warranty liability	22,500
Workers' compensation payable	1,250

Additional information:

1. On September 30, 2017, the unused operating line of credit is $75,000.
2. Redemption rewards, warranties, and gift cards are expected to be redeemed within one year. Unearned revenues relate to gift cards sold but not yet redeemed.
3. Of the mortgage, $10,000 is due each year.
4. Of the note payable, $1,000 is due at the end of each month.

Instructions

(a) Prepare the current liabilities section of the balance sheet.
(b) Calculate LightHouse's current ratio and acid-test ratio.
(c) Explain why the company did not report any cash as part of its current assets.

TAKING IT FURTHER The accountant for LightHouse argues that since property taxes are unavoidable, a company should record the full year's worth of property taxes as an expense when it is paid. Is the accountant correct? Explain.

P10–12A Maple Leaf Foods Inc. is a packaged meat producer. It reports biological assets on its balance sheet which consists of hogs and poultry livestock. These are considered current assets somewhat similar to inventory. The company reports the following current assets and current liabilities at December 31, 2014 (in thousands):

Prepare current liabilities section; calculate and comment on ratios.
(LO 4) AP

Cash	$496,328
Accounts payable and accruals	275,249
Accounts receivable	60,396
Biological assets	105,743
Current portion of long-term debt	472
Income taxes payable	26,614
Inventories	270,401
Notes receivable	110,209
Other current liabilities	24,383
Prepaid expenses and other assets	20,157
Provisions	60,443

Hint: Notes receivable are current assets that should be included in the acid-test ratio.

Instructions

(a) Prepare the current liabilities section of the balance sheet. The provisions are due within 12 months of the balance sheet date.

(b) Calculate the current and acid-test ratios.

(c) At December 31, 2013, Maple Leaf Foods Inc. had total current assets of $1,183,171 thousand, which included cash of $506,670 thousand, receivables of $111,034 thousand and notes receivable of $115,514. Current liabilities were $966,522 thousand. Did the current and acid-test ratios improve or weaken in 2014?

TAKING IT FURTHER   What other factors should be considered in assessing Maple Leaf Foods' liquidity?

Calculate payroll deductions; prepare payroll register.
(LO 5) AP

*P10–13A   Western Electric Company pays its support staff weekly and its electricians on a semi-monthly basis. The following support staff payroll information is available for the week ended June 9, 2015:

Employee Name	Weekly Earnings	Claim Code
Chris Tanm	$ 945	2
Terry Ng	1,130	4
Olga Stavtech	1,130	1
Alana Mandell	1,067	1

The electricians' salaries are based on their experience in the field, as well as the number of years they have worked for the company. All three electricians have been with the company more than two years. The annual salaries of these employees are as follows:

Employee Name	Annual Salary for 2015
Sam Goodspeed	$43,440
Marino Giancarlo	64,770
Hillary Ridley	76,880

Instructions

(a) Prepare a payroll register for the June 9, 2015, weekly payroll for the support staff. Calculate the CPP and EI deductions using the formulas provided in Appendix 10A. Use the tables in Illustration 10A-3 to determine federal and provincial income taxes.

(b) Calculate the CPP and EI deductions for each of the electricians for their June 15, 2015, semi-monthly payroll.

(c) In which semi-monthly pay period will each of the electricians reach their maximum CPP and EI payments for 2015?

TAKING IT FURTHER   Why are there separate payroll deduction tables for determining weekly, semi-monthly, and monthly income tax deductions?

▶ Problems: Set B

Prepare current liability entries and adjusting entries.
(LO 1, 2) AP

P10–1B   Vacation Villas had the following selected transactions.

Feb.   1   Signs a $30,000, eight-month, 5%-interest-bearing note payable to CountryBank and receives $30,000 in cash.

8   Sales on account of $14,500, plus 13% HST.

14   The payroll for the previous week consists of salaries of $15,000. All salaries are subject to CPP of $692 and EI of $282 and withholding taxes of $2,700. The salaries are paid on February 21. The employer's payroll expense is also recorded.

15   Purchase furniture worth $1,975 to be paid for in 30 days.

21   Pays employees the salaries for the pay period ending February 14.

28   Accrues interest on the CountryBank note payable.

28   Accrues the required warranty provision because some of the sales were made under warranty. Of the units sold under warranty, 20 are expected to become defective. Repair costs are estimated to be $25 per unit.

Instructions

Journalize the February transactions.

TAKING IT FURTHER   The accountant at Vacation Villas believes a current liability is a debt that can be expected to be paid in one year. Is the accountant correct?

P10–2B   On January 1, 2017, the ledger of Edmiston Software Company contains the following liability accounts:

Prepare current liability entries, adjusting entries, and current liabilities section. (LO 1, 2, 4) AP

Accounts Payable	$42,500
GST Payable	5,800
PST Payable	8,200
Unearned Revenue	15,000

During January, the following selected transactions occurred.

Jan. 1   Borrowed $30,000 in cash from Canada Bank on a four-month, 8%, $30,000 note.
  5   Sold merchandise for cash totalling $10,400, plus GST of 5% and PST 7%.
  12   Provided services for customers who had made advance payments of $9,000. The payment included GST of $402 and PST of $562.
  14   Paid the Province PST invoiced in December 2016 of $8,200 and paid the Receiver General GST invoiced in December 2016 of $5,800.
  20   Sold 900 units of a new product on credit at $52 per unit, plus GST of 5% and PST 7%. This new product is subject to a one-year warranty.
  25   Sold merchandise for cash totalling $18,720, plus GST of 5% and PST 7%.

Instructions

(a) Journalize the January transactions.
(b) Journalize the adjusting entries at January 31 for (1) the outstanding notes payable, and (2) estimated warranty liability, assuming warranty costs are expected to equal 5% of sales of the new product.
(c) Prepare the current liabilities section of the balance sheet at January 31, 2017. Assume no change in accounts payable.

TAKING IT FURTHER   James, an employee of the Edmiston Software Company, believes payroll taxes withheld are an expense to his employer. Is James correct? Explain.

P10–3B   Juniper Bush Farm has a December 31 fiscal year end. The company has six notes payable outstanding on December 31, 2017, as follows:

Calculate current and non-current portion of notes payable, and interest payable. (LO 1, 4) AP

1. A nine-month, 5%, $25,000 note payable issued on July 1, 2017. Interest is payable monthly on the first day of each month starting on August 1.
2. A six-month, 4%, $10,000 note payable issued on September 1, 2017. Interest and principal are payable at maturity.
3. A seven-month, 4.5%, $40,000 note payable issued on November 1, 2017. Interest and principal are payable at maturity.
4. A five-year, 3.75%, $80,000 note payable issued on May 31, 2017. Juniper Bush Farm is required to pay $16,000 plus interest on May 31 each year starting in 2018.
5. A three-year, 4.25%, $126,000 note payable issued on October 1, 2017. Juniper Bush Farm is required to pay $3,500 plus interest on the first day of each month starting on November 1, 2017. All payments are up to date.
6. A four-year, 5%, $50,000 note payable issued on March 31, 2016. Juniper Bush Farm is required to pay $12,500 every March 31 starting in 2017. Interest is payable monthly at the end of the month, starting on April 30, 2016.

Instructions

(a) Calculate the current portion of each note payable.
(b) Calculate the non-current portion of each note payable.
(c) Calculate any interest payable at December 31, 2017.

TAKING IT FURTHER   What are the costs and benefits to the maker and the payee of the note of using a note payable in place of an account payable?

P10–4B   MileHi Mountain Bikes markets mountain-bike tours to clients vacationing in various locations in the mountains of British Columbia. The current liabilities section of the October 31, 2016, balance sheet included notes payable of $15,000 and interest payable of $375 related to a six-month, 6% note payable to Eifert Company on December 1, 2016.

Record note transactions; show financial statement presentation. (LO 1, 4) AP

During the year ended October 31, 2017, MileHi had the following transactions related to notes payable:

2016

Dec. 1   Paid the $15,000 Eifert note, plus interest.

2017

Apr. 1   Issued a $75,000, nine-month, 7% note to Mountain Real Estate for the purchase of additional mountain property on which to build bike trails. Interest is payable quarterly on July 1, October 1, and at maturity on January 1, 2018.
  30   Purchased Mongoose bikes to use as rentals for $8,000, terms n/30.

May 31 Issued Mongoose an $8,000, three-month, 8% note payable in settlement of its account (see April 30 transaction). Interest is payable at maturity.

July 1 Paid interest on the Mountain Real Estate note (see April 1 transaction).

Aug. 31 Paid the Mongoose note, plus interest (see May 31 transaction).

Oct. 1 Paid interest on the Mountain Real Estate note (see April 1 transaction).

1 Borrowed $90,000 cash from Western Bank by issuing a five-year, 6% note. Interest is payable monthly on the first of the month. Principal payments of $18,000 must be made on the anniversary of the note each year.

Instructions

(a) Record the transactions and any adjustments required at October 31, 2017.

(b) Show the balance sheet presentation of notes payable and interest payable at October 31, 2017.

(c) Show the income statement presentation of interest expense for the year.

TAKING IT FURTHER Why is it important to correctly classify notes payable as either current or non-current in the balance sheet?

Record current liability transactions; prepare current liabilities section.
(LO 1, 2, 3, 4) AP

P10-5B On January 1, 2017, Zaur Company's general ledger had these liability accounts:

Accounts payable	$63,700
Unearned revenue—loyalty program	2,150
CPP payable	2,152
EI payable	1,019
HST payable	11,390
Income tax payable	4,563
Unearned revenue	16,000
Vacation pay payable	9,120
Warranty liability	5,750

In January, the following selected transactions occurred:

Jan. 5 Sold merchandise for $15,800 cash, plus 13% HST. Zaur uses a periodic inventory system.

12 Provided services for customers who had previously made advance payments of $7,000. The payment included HST of $805.

14 Paid the Receiver General (federal government) for sales taxes collected in December 2016.

15 Paid the Receiver General for amounts owing from the December payroll for CPP, EI, and income tax.

16 Borrowed $18,000 from Second National Bank on a three-month, 6% note. Interest is payable monthly on the 15th day of the month.

17 Paid $35,000 to creditors on account.

20 Sold 500 units of a new product on account for $60 per unit, plus 13% HST. This new product has a two-year warranty. It is expected that 6% of the units sold will be returned for repair at an average cost of $10 per unit.

30 Customers redeemed $1,750 of loyalty rewards in exchange for services. Assume that HST of $201 is included in this amount.

31 Issued 50,000 loyalty points worth $1 each. Based on past experience, 10% of these points are expected to be redeemed. Sales related to the issuance of the loyalty points were $500,000.

31 Determined that the company had used $875 of parts inventory in January to honour warranty contracts.

31 Recorded and paid the monthly payroll. Gross salaries were $25,350. Amounts withheld include CPP of $1,183, EI of $464, and income tax of $4,563.

Instructions

(a) Record the transactions.

(b) Record adjusting entries for the following:
   1. Interest on the note payable for half a month
   2. The estimated warranty liability
   3. Employee benefits, which include CPP, EI, and vacation pay that is accrued at a rate of 4%

(c) Prepare the current liabilities section of the balance sheet at January 31.

TAKING IT FURTHER Explain how and when the Vacation Pay Payable account balance is paid.

Record warranty transactions.
(LO 2) AP

P10-6B On January 1, 2015, Logue Company began a warranty program to stimulate sales. It is estimated that 5% of the units sold will be returned for repair at an estimated cost of $25 per unit. Sales and warranty figures for the three years ended December 31 are as follows:

	2015	2016	2017
Sales (units)	1,200	1,320	1,420
Sales price per unit	$100	$105	$110
Units returned for repair under warranty	60	70	80
Actual warranty costs	$1,275	$1,600	$1,960

Instructions

(a) Calculate the warranty expense for each year and warranty liability at the end of each year.

(b) Record the warranty transactions for each year. Credit Repair Parts Inventory for the actual warranty costs.

(c) To date, what percentage of the units sold have been returned for repair under warranty? What has been the average actual warranty cost per unit for the three-year period?

TAKING IT FURTHER   Suppose at December 31, 2017, management reassesses its original estimates and decides that it is more likely that the company will have to service 7% of the units sold in 2017. Management also determines that the original estimate of the cost per unit is the appropriate cost to use for future repair work. What should be the balance in the Warranty Liability account at December 31, 2017?

P10–7B   Caribou County Service Station started a customer loyalty program at the beginning of 2016 in which customers making cash purchases of gasoline at the gas bar are issued rewards in the form of coupons. For each litre of gasoline purchased, the customer gets a coupon for 2.5 cents that can be redeemed in the service department toward such things as oil changes or repairs. The coupons have no expiry date. Caribou County Service Station began selling gift cards in 2017 that do not have expiry dates.

Record customer loyalty program and gift card transactions; determine impact on financial statements. (LO 2) AP

The following are selected transactions in 2016 and 2017:

1. In 2016, the gas bar sold 750,000 litres of gasoline resulting in gas sales of $1,050,000. Service department coupons were issued with these sales. The expected redemption rate for the grocery coupons is 70%.
2. In 2016, customers redeemed $5,950 of the coupons in the service department.
3. In 2017, the gas bar sold 810,000 litres of gasoline, resulting in gas sales of $1,255,000. Service department coupons were issued with these sales. The expected redemption rate for the grocery coupons is 70%.
4. In 2017, customers redeemed $9,500 of the coupons in the service department.
5. In 2017, customers purchased $3,950 of gift cards, and $1,500 of the cards were redeemed by the end of the year.

Instructions

(a) Indicate if the following items will increase, decrease, or have no effect on each of revenues, expenses, and profit:
   1. Issuing coupons when sales are made
   2. Redeeming coupons
   3. Issuing gift cards
   4. Redeeming gift cards

(b) Record the above transactions.

(c) What balances will be included in current liabilities at December 31, 2016 and 2017, regarding the customer loyalty program and gift cards?

TAKING IT FURTHER   What factors should management consider in determining if current liabilities are correctly valued at December 31, 2017?

P10–8B   Big Fork Company, a private company that follows ASPE, is preparing its financial statements for the year ended December 31, 2016. It is now February 15, 2017, and the following situations are being reviewed to determine the appropriate accounting treatment:

Discuss reporting of contingencies and record provisions. (LO 2, 4) AP

1. Big Fork is being sued for $3 million for a possible malfunction of one of its products. In March 2017, a customer suffered a serious injury while operating the product. The company is defending itself but it is clear that there was an error in the published operations manual for the product. It is likely that the company will lose this lawsuit, but it is unlikely it will have to pay the full $3 million. At this point, a reasonable estimate cannot be made of the amount of the expected settlement.
2. Big Fork is being sued for $1.5 million by an employee for wrongful dismissal and defamation of character. The employee was fired on August 2, 2017. The company is vigorously defending itself because the employee had a documented history of poor performance at work.
3. On December 16, 2017, a sales representative from one of the company's suppliers injured herself on a visit to Big Fork's offices. She tripped over equipment that had not been properly stored and will be unable to work for

several months as a result of her injuries. A $250,000 claim against Big Fork has been filed by the sales representative's insurance company.

Instructions

For each of the above situations, recommend whether Big Fork Company should (1) make an accrual in its December 31, 2017, financial statements; (2) disclose the situation in the notes to the financial statements; or (3) not report it. Provide a rationale for your recommendations.

TAKING IT FURTHER What are the potential benefits and costs of making an accrual for a contingency as opposed to only disclosing it in the notes to the financial statements?

Prepare payroll register and record payroll. (LO 3) AP

P10-9B Scoot Scooters has four employees who are paid on an hourly basis, plus time and a half for hours in excess of 40 hours a week. Payroll data for the week ended February 17, 2017, follow:

Employee	Total Hours	Hourly Rate	CPP	EI	Income Tax	United Way
P. Kilchyk	40	$15.25	$26.86	$11.16	$76.60	$5.00
B. Quon	42	15.00	28.60	11.80	83.70	7.25
C. Pospisil	40	16.25	28.84	11.90	84.10	5.50
B. Verwey	44	14.50	29.68	12.21	87.10	8.25

Instructions

(a) Prepare a payroll register for the weekly payroll.
(b) Record the payroll on February 15 and the accrual of employee benefits expense. Assume the company accrues 4% for vacation pay.
(c) Record the payment of the payroll on February 17.
(d) Record the payment of the remittances to the Receiver General on March 15.

TAKING IT FURTHER Does the owner of a proprietorship have to deduct CPP, EI, and income taxes from his or her own drawings?

Record payroll transactions and calculate balances in payroll liability accounts. (LO 3) AP

P10-10B On March 31, 2017, Babb Company had the following payroll liability accounts in its ledger:

Canada Pension Plan payable	$ 6,907	Life insurance payable	$ 756
Disability insurance payable	1,134	Union dues payable	1,285
Employment Insurance payable	3,320	Vacation pay payable	3,024
Income tax payable	14,364	Workers' compensation payable	3,780

In April, the following transactions occurred:

Apr.	4	Sent a cheque to the union treasurer for union dues.
	7	Sent a cheque to the insurance company for the disability and life insurance.
	13	Issued a cheque to the Receiver General for the amounts due for CPP, EI, and income tax.
	20	Paid the amount due to the workers' compensation plan.
	28	Completed the monthly payroll register, which shows gross salaries $83,160, CPP withheld $3,799, EI withheld $1,522, income tax withheld $15,800, union dues withheld $1,414, and long-term disability insurance premiums $1,247.
	28	Prepared payroll cheques for the April net pay and distributed the cheques to the employees.
	28	Recorded an adjusting journal entry to record April employee benefits for CPP, EI, workers' compensation at 5% of gross pay, vacation pay at 4% of gross pay, and life insurance at 1% of gross pay.

Instructions

(a) Journalize the April transactions and adjustments.
(b) Calculate the balances in each of the payroll liability accounts at April 30, 2017.

TAKING IT FURTHER Why do employers need an employee earnings record for each employee as well as a payroll register?

Prepare current liabilities section; calculate and comment on ratios. (LO 4) AP

P10-11B The following selected account balances are from Creative Carpentry's adjusted trial balance at March 31, 2017:

Accounts receivable	$184,000
Accounts payable	60,000
Bank overdraft	55,200
CPP payable	2,300
EI payable	1,750
HST payable	12,250
Income tax payable	25,000
Interest payable	8,000
Accumulated depreciation	115,000
Mortgage payable	200,000
Merchandise inventory	120,600
Notes payable	30,000
Prepaid expenses	500
Unearned revenue	9,385
Vacation pay payable	1,200
Warranty liability	12,500

Additional information:

1. On March 31, 2017, the unused operating line of credit is $25,000.
2. Redemption rewards, warranties, and gift cards are expected to be redeemed within one year. Unearned revenues relate to gift cards sold but not yet redeemed.
3. Of the mortgage, $50,000 is due each year.
4. Of the note payable, $5,000 is due at the end of each month.

Instructions

(a) Prepare the current liabilities section of the balance sheet.
(b) Calculate Creative's current ratio and acid-test ratio.
(c) Explain why the company did not report any cash as part of its current assets.

TAKING IT FURTHER   Explain to Peter, the owner of Creative Carpentry, why unearned gift card revenue is a current liability and how the liability will be settled.

P10-12B   BCE Inc., whose offerings include Bell Canada, reports the following current assets and current liabilities at December 31, 2014 (in millions of dollars):

Prepare current liabilities section; calculate and comment on ratios.
(LO 4) AP

Cash	$ 142
Cash equivalents	424
Current tax liabilities	269
Debt due within one year	3,743
Dividends payable	534
Interest payable	145
Inventory	333
Other current assets	198
Prepaid expenses	379
Trade and other receivables	3,069
Trade payables and other liabilities	4,398

Instructions

(a) Prepare the current liabilities section of the balance sheet.
(b) Calculate the current and the acid-test ratio.
(c) On December 31, 2013, BCE Inc. had current assets of $5,070 million. This included cash and cash equivalents of $335 million, and trade and other receivables of $3,043 million. Current liabilities were $7,890 million. Did the current and acid-test ratios improve or weaken in 2014?

TAKING IT FURTHER   What other factors should be considered in assessing BCE Inc.'s liquidity?

*P10-13B   Slovak Plumbing Company pays its support staff weekly and its plumbers on a semi-monthly basis. The following support staff payroll information is available for the week ended May 12, 2015:

Calculate payroll deductions and prepare payroll register.
(LO 5) AP

Employee Name	Weekly Earnings	Claim Code
Dan Quinn	$ 985	1
Karol Holub	1,037	3
Al Lowhorn	1,080	1
Irina Kostra	950	4

The plumbers' salaries are based on their experience in the field, as well as the number of years they have worked for the company. All three plumbers have been with the company more than two years. The annual salary of these employees is as follows:

Employee Name	Annual Salary for 2015
Branislav Dolina	$80,700
Henrietta Koleno	62,500
Aida Krneta	44,120

Instructions

(a) Prepare a payroll register for the May 12, 2015, weekly payroll for the support staff. Calculate the CPP and EI deductions using the formulas provided in Appendix 10A. Use the tables in Illustration 10A-3 to determine federal and provincial income taxes.
(b) Calculate the CPP and EI deductions for each of the plumbers for their May 15, 2015, semi-monthly payroll.
(c) In which semi-monthly pay period will each of the plumbers reach their maximum CPP and EI payments for 2015?

TAKING IT FURTHER   Why are there separate payroll deduction tables for determining income tax deductions for weekly, semi-monthly, and monthly pay periods?

▶ Cumulative Coverage—Chapters 3 to 10

The unadjusted trial balance of LeBrun Company at its year end, July 31, 2017, is as follows:

LEBRUN COMPANY
Trial Balance
July 31, 2017

	Debit	Credit
Cash	$ 16,550	
Petty cash	200	
Accounts receivable	38,500	
Allowance for doubtful accounts		$ 2,000
Note receivable (due December 31, 2017)	10,000	
Merchandise inventory	45,900	
Prepaid expenses	16,000	
Land	50,000	
Building	155,000	
Accumulated depreciation—building		10,800
Equipment	25,000	
Accumulated depreciation—equipment		12,200
Patent	75,000	
Accumulated amortization—patent		15,000
Accounts payable		78,900
Warranty liability		6,000
Notes payable (due August 1, 2029)		124,200
S. LeBrun, capital		124,700
S. LeBrun, drawings	54,000	
Sales		750,000
Cost of goods sold	450,000	
Operating expenses	181,220	
Interest revenue		400
Interest expense	6,830	
Totals	$1,124,200	$1,124,200

Adjustment information:

1. The July 31 bank statement reported debit memos for service charges of $50 and a $650 NSF (not sufficient funds) cheque that had been received from a customer for the purchase of merchandise in July.
2. Estimated uncollectible accounts receivable at July 31 are $3,850.

3. The note receivable bears interest of 8% and was issued on December 31, 2016. Interest is payable the first of each month.
4. A physical count of inventory determined that $39,200 of inventory was actually on hand.
5. Prepaid expenses of $5,500 expired in the year (use the account Operating Expenses).
6. Depreciation is calculated on the long-lived assets using the following methods and useful lives:

> Building: straight-line, 25 years, $15,000 residual value
> Equipment: double diminishing-balance, five years, $2,500 residual value
> Patent: straight-line, five years, no residual value

7. The 6% note payable was issued on August 1, 2009. Interest is paid monthly at the beginning of each month for the previous month's interest. Of the note principal, $1,680 is currently due.
8. Estimated warranty costs for July are $1,975 (use Operating Expenses).

Instructions

(a) Prepare the adjusting journal entries required at July 31. (Round your calculations to the nearest dollar.)
(b) Prepare an adjusted trial balance at July 31.
(c) Prepare a multiple-step income statement and statement of owner's equity for the year and a balance sheet at July 31.

CHAPTER 10: BROADENING YOUR PERSPECTIVE

▶ Financial Reporting and Analysis

Financial Reporting Problem

BYP10–1   Refer to the financial statements of **Corus Entertainment** and the Notes to the Financial Statements in Appendix A.

Instructions

Answer the following questions about the company's current and contingent liabilities:

(a) What were Corus's total current liabilities at August 31, 2014? What was the increase (decrease) in total current liabilities from the previous year?

(b) Which specific current liabilities and in what order did Corus present on the August 31, 2014, statement of financial statement position?

(c) Calculate Corus's current ratio, acid-test ratio, and receivables turnover ratios for 2014 and 2013. Comment on Corus's overall liquidity.

(d) Does Corus report any contingencies? If so, where are they disclosed? Explain the nature, amount, and significance of Corus's contingencies, if any.

Interpreting Financial Statements

BYP10–2   **Loblaw Companies Limited** (which owns Shoppers Drug Mart) reported the following information about contingencies in the notes to its December 31, 2014, financial statements:

LOBLAW COMPANIES LIMITED
Notes to the Consolidated Financial Statements
December 31, 2014

32. Contingent Liabilities (excerpt)
Legal Proceedings The Company is the subject of various legal proceedings and claims that arise in the ordinary course of business. The outcome of all of these proceedings and claims is uncertain. However, based on information currently available, these proceedings and claims, individually and in the aggregate, are not expected to have a material impact on the Company.

Shoppers Drug Mart has been served with an Amended Statement of Claim in a proposed class action proceeding that has been filed under the Ontario Superior Court of Justice by two licensed Associates, claiming various declarations and damages resulting from Shoppers Drug Mart's alleged breaches of the Associate Agreement, in the amount of $500 million. The proposed class action comprises all of Shoppers Drug Mart's current and former licensed Associates residing in Canada, other than in Québec, who are parties to Shoppers Drug Mart's 2002 and 2010 forms of the Associate Agreement. On July 9, 2013, the Ontario Superior Court of Justice certified as a class proceeding portions of the action. While Shoppers Drug Mart continues to believe that the claim is without merit and will vigorously defend the claim, the outcome of this matter cannot be predicted with certainty.

Instructions

Why would Loblaw disclose information about these legal disputes, including the amount of the potential loss, in the notes to the financial statements instead of accruing an amount for these as liabilities in its accounting records?

⏵ Critical Thinking

Collaborative Learning Activity

Note to instructor: Additional instructions and material for this group activity can be found on the Instructor Resource Site and in *WileyPLUS.*

BYP10–3 In this group activity, your group must decide on the best accounting treatment for a contingency. Your instructor will provide the class with a scenario and each group will be required to decide if an accrual should be made and, if so, for how much. Groups will simultaneously report to the class and will be required to defend their decisions.

Communication Activity

BYP10–4 The Show Time movie theatre sells thousands of gift certificates every year. The certificates can be redeemed at any time because they have no expiry date. Some of them may never be redeemed (because they are lost or forgotten, for example). The owner of the theatre has raised some questions about the accounting for these gift certificates.

Instructions

Write an e-mail to answer the following questions from the owner:
(a) Why is a liability recorded when these certificates are sold? After all, they bring customers into the theatre, where they spend money on snacks and drinks. Why should something that helps generate additional revenue be treated as a liability?
(b) How should the gift certificates that are never redeemed be treated? At some point in the future, can the liability related to them be eliminated? If so, what type of journal entry would be made?

"All About You" Activity

BYP10–5 In the "All About You" feature, you learned who is responsible for remitting income tax, CPP, and EI to the Canada Revenue Agency (CRA) if you are an employee or self-employed. You also learned that the CRA has strict guidelines as to whether someone is self-employed or an employee.

Assume that as a new graduate you are accepting a position where you will be providing consulting services to a company. You have agreed to provide the services for $3,000 a month. The company's manager of human resources suggests that you may want to be considered self-employed rather than an employee of the company. Before you make your decision, you need to better understand the CRA's guidelines and the financial implications.

Instructions

(a) Go to the Canada Revenue Agency's website at www.cra-arc.gc.ca and search for document RC4110 "Employee or Self-Employed?"

What are the factors that should be considered when determining if a worker is an employee or self-employed?
(b) Assume you are an employee and you are paid monthly and that the following amounts are deducted from your gross earnings. (*Note:* The following deductions are based on the 2015 payroll tables for Ontario.)

CPP	$134.06
EI	54.90
Income tax	409.35

What is the amount of cash you will receive each month? What is the total amount of cash you will receive in a year?
(c) Based on the information in part (b), what is the total CPP you will pay in a year? What is the total EI you will pay in a year?
(d) Assume you are self-employed, and you have chosen to pay EI. What is the amount of cash you will receive each month from the company? What is the total CPP you will have to pay in a year? What is the total EI you will have to pay in a year?
(e) Assuming that you will pay the same amount of income tax as you would if you were an employee, calculate the amount of cash you will receive for the year if you are self-employed.
(f) Based on your answers to parts (c) and (e), do you want to be self-employed or an employee of the company? Explain.
(g) If you had the opportunity to provide consulting services to another company in your spare time, would your answer in part (f) be different? Explain.

 Santé Smoothie Saga

(***Note:*** This is a continuation of the Santé Smoothie Saga from Chapters 1 through 9.)

BYP10–6 Natalie has had much success with her smoothies business over the past number of months. Some customers have shown an interest in purchasing gift certificates from Natalie. Natalie is considering a gift certificate that would include a recipe book and all of the supplies needed to create two cups of smoothies. Natalie wants to make sure that she has considered all of the risks and rewards of issuing gift certificates. She has come to you with the following questions:

1. From what I understand, if I sell a gift certificate, I need to be recording the money received as "unearned revenue." I am a little confused. How is the use of this account the same as the money that I received from customers that have paid me a deposit for premade smoothies?

2. What if I record the sale of gift certificates as revenue instead of unearned revenue? Technically, I have made a sale of a gift certificate and therefore should be recording amounts received as revenue for the sale of a gift certificate. What if a gift certificate is never used? Does this not justify a sale being recorded?

Instructions

Answer Natalie's questions.

ANSWERS TO CHAPTER QUESTIONS

ANSWERS TO ACCOUNTING IN ACTION INSIGHT QUESTIONS

Across the Organization Insight, p. 539

Q: A company's marketing department is responsible for designing customer loyalty programs. Why would Shoppers' marketing department add the option of donating points to charity?

A: Most customer loyalty programs were designed under the assumption that customers are motivated by cost savings. Shoppers realized that some customers have enough disposable income that cost saving is not a motivation. But many of these customers are motivated by the desire to help others. Thus the option to donate points has the potential to appeal to a wider base of customers and increase the program's success.

Across the Organization Insight, p. 541

Q: Environmental contingencies are generally considered to be harder to estimate than contingencies from lawsuits. What might be the reason for this difference?

A: The requirement to account for environmental contingencies is relatively new compared with the requirement to account for contingencies from lawsuits. Although it is difficult to predict whether the company will win or lose a lawsuit and what type of settlement may be involved, there is a vast history of case law that can be used to help a company form an opinion. Environmental regulations, in contrast, are still evolving and there is often no system (e.g., regulatory compliance audits or environmental site assessment data) that would help a company estimate the possible cost, or even the existence, of environmental contingencies for many years.

Ethics Insight, p. 542

Q: Who are the stakeholders regarding Robert's handling of his payroll?

A: The stakeholders include the part-time employees (who won't be covered by government programs such as EI and workers' compensation), the full-time employees (who are paying more taxes than the part-timers), the accountant (who is violating the professional code of conduct), the government (which is losing out on collecting income taxes, CPP premiums, and EI premiums, among other things), and the justice system (which would want to prosecute Robert for not making the legally required deductions).

All About You Insight, p. 549

Q: If you are providing services to a company, what are the advantages and disadvantages of being a self-employed consultant versus an employee of the company?

A: As a self-employed individual, your monthly cash received from the company would be higher as no CPP, EI, and income tax will be deducted. On the other hand, you will have to make quarterly instalment payments of CPP, EI (if you choose to pay it), and income taxes. If you are self-employed, you may be able to deduct certain expenses to reduce your income tax.

However, some individuals may not manage their cash properly and may be unable to make the remittances when required. In addition, you will have to pay twice as much for CPP and you will not qualify for EI benefits if you are unable to work. If you are self-employed, you would not qualify for other benefits offered to employees by the company, either.

ANSWERS TO SELF-STUDY QUESTIONS

1. d   2. a   3. b   4. d   5. a   6. b   7. c   8. b   *9. b   10. a   11. a

11 FINANCIAL REPORTING CONCEPTS

CHAPTER PREVIEW   In the first 10 chapters of this textbook, you learned the process that leads to the preparation of a company's financial statements. You also learned that users make decisions based on financial statements, and that to be useful, these statements must communicate financial information to users in an effective way. This means that generally accepted accounting principles must be used. Otherwise, we would have to be familiar with each company's particular accounting and reporting practices in order to understand its financial statements. It would be difficult, if not impossible, to compare the financial results of different companies.

This chapter explores the conceptual framework that is used to develop generally accepted accounting principles.

FEATURE STORY ▶ **THE NEED FOR ACCOUNTING STANDARDS**

TORONTO, Ont.—This entire textbook is about how to follow accounting standards for financial reporting. But let's step back for a moment and ask: Why do we need accounting standards?

It's essential that companies follow the same accounting standards so that users can compare their financial statements on the same footing, both between two competing companies and from year to year within one company. Imagine if a company decided its fiscal year ended in January in one year and in November the next year. Its financial statements would not reflect the same 12-month period and would be almost useless to a user looking for changes over time.

Something as basic as using the same period for each financial statement—known as the periodicity concept—is part of the conceptual framework, which is the theory that underlies accounting standards. Standard setters are guided by the conceptual framework when developing new standards or making changes to existing standards. For example, no matter how much a standard might change for the method of accounting for an asset, the definition of an asset—a financial statement element in the conceptual framework—would remain largely the same.

In Canada, the Accounting Standards Board (AcSB) is the independent body responsible for developing accounting standards for private companies. The AcSB develops and makes changes to Accounting Standards for Private Enterprises

(ASPE). It follows a rigorous approach known as "due process," which can include researching standards in other countries, issuing discussion papers to get preliminary input, and issuing exposure drafts to get feedback on proposed standards. Throughout the process, the AcSB consults with stakeholders, including the private companies that would be affected by changes to ASPE. When proposing changes to standards, the AcSB ensures that they meet the requirements in the conceptual framework, such as providing users of financial statements with useful information.

The conceptual framework developed for International Financial Reporting Standards (IFRS) also underpins those standards, and changes proposed by the International Accounting Standards Board (IASB) must follow that framework. The AcSB plays a role in helping the IASB make changes to standards. The AcSB makes the IASB aware of Canadian IFRS users' views on proposed changes to IFRS, keeping in mind that the changes need to meet the IFRS conceptual framework.

Sources: Zivanai Mazhambe, "Review of International Accounting Standards Board (IASB) Proposed New Conceptual Framework: Discussion Paper (DP/2013/1)," *Journal of Modern Accounting and Auditing*, August 2014, Vol. 10, No. 8, 835–845; "IFRS: The New Conceptual Framework—Important, Inconsequential and Very Long," PricewaterhouseCoopers, September 1, 2013; AcSB website, www.frascanada.ca.

ktasimar/Shutterstock

CHAPTER OUTLINE	LEARNING OBJECTIVES

The chapter is organized as follows:

1 Explain the importance of having a conceptual framework of accounting, and list the key components.

The Conceptual Framework of Accounting

DO IT 1

The conceptual framework

---

2 Explain the objective of financial reporting, and define the elements of the financial statements.

The Objective of Financial Reporting
- Elements of financial statements

DO IT 2

Financial reporting

---

3 Apply the fundamental and enhancing qualitative characteristics of the conceptual framework to financial reporting situations.

Qualitative Characteristics of Useful Financial Information
- Fundamental characteristics
- Enhancing qualitative characteristics
- Application of the qualitative characteristics
- Differences in qualitative characteristics under IFRS and ASPE

DO IT 3

Qualitative characteristics of financial information

---

4 Apply the recognition and measurement criteria of the conceptual framework to financial reporting situations.

Recognition and Measurement Criteria
- General recognition
- Revenue recognition
- Other revenue recognition situations
- Expense recognition
- Measurement of elements
- Violation of recognition and measurement concepts: Errors and intentional misstatements

DO IT 4

Two approaches to revenue recognition

---

5 Apply the foundational concepts, assumptions, and constraints of the conceptual framework to financial reporting situations.

Foundational Concepts, Assumptions, and Constraints
- Concepts and assumptions
- Constraints
- Summary of conceptual framework
- Looking ahead

DO IT 5

Foundational concepts

The Conceptual Framework of Accounting

According to standard setters, the **conceptual framework of accounting** is "a coherent system of inter-related objectives and fundamentals that can lead to consistent standards and that prescribes the nature, function, and limits of financial accounting statements." In other words, the conceptual framework of accounting guides decisions about what to present in financial statements, how to report economic events, and how to communicate such information.

A conceptual framework ensures that we have a coherent set of standards. New standards are easier to understand and are more consistent when they are built on the same foundation as existing standards. As a foundation for accounting, the conceptual framework:

- ensures that existing standards and practices are clear and consistent
- provides guidance in responding to new issues and developing new standards
- assists accountants in the application of accounting standards
- increases financial statement users' understanding of and confidence in the financial statements

It is impossible to create a rule for every situation. Canadian and international accounting standards are therefore based mainly on general principles rather than specific rules. It is hoped that, with the help of a conceptual framework and their professional judgement, accountants will be able to quickly determine an appropriate accounting treatment for each situation.

Not every country uses the same conceptual framework and/or set of accounting standards. This lack of uniformity has arisen over time because of differences in legal systems, in processes for developing standards, in government requirements, and in economic environments. The International Accounting Standards Board (IASB), the standard-setting body responsible for developing IFRS, was formed to try to reduce these areas of difference and unify global standard setting.

Helpful hint Accounting principles are affected by economic and political conditions, which change over time. As a result, accounting principles can and do change.

To promote global consistency and comparability, the IASB and its U.S. counterpart, the Financial Accounting Standards Board (FASB), agreed to work together to produce an updated common conceptual framework. The first part of the new joint framework has been issued. The IASB is now working alone on another project to further refine additional components of the framework. This chapter incorporates the concepts of the proposed framework to the extent possible. Canada's Accounting Standards Board (AcSB) has committed to update the conceptual framework used in ASPE to be consistent with the IASB's conceptual framework used in IFRS. This means that, although the conceptual frameworks for IFRS and ASPE are fundamentally similar at the time of writing, they are not identical. Differences between the two frameworks will be identified in sections of this chapter.

The conceptual framework under IFRS was first introduced in Chapter 1. The key components of the conceptual framework are:

1. **The objective of financial reporting and user needs:** These are the goals and purposes of accounting; in other words, why financial statements report what they do to ensure the needs of financial statement users are met.
2. **Elements of financial statements:** The elements are the means used to accomplish the objective of financial reporting. In other words, the elements are the "what" users expect to see, such as assets, liabilities, equity, revenues, and expenses.
3. **Qualitative characteristics:** These are the attributes that ensure the information presented is useful. Qualitative characteristics include relevance and faithful representation. If information is not relevant or it does not reflect the substance of a transaction (it is not faithfully represented), it is not considered useful.
4. **Recognition and measurement criteria:** These criteria provide guidance on what elements are reported and when as well as how much is reported.
5. **Foundational concepts, assumptions, and constraints:** These concepts indicate "how" the objective of financial reporting will be accomplished, in that they represent the foundation or starting point to determine how financial information is reported.

The Conceptual Framework

Indicate if each of the following statements is true or false.

1. The specific rules for accounting for inventory are a component of the conceptual framework.
2. The use of a common conceptual framework will enhance the consistency and comparability of financial reporting in the global environment.
3. The conceptual framework eliminates the need for financial statement preparers to use professional judgement.
4. The conceptual framework includes recognition and measurement criteria.
5. The conceptual framework provides guidance in developing new standards.

Solution

1. F The conceptual framework does not provide specific guidance for any element of the financial statements; it only assists in the application of accounting standards.
2. T
3. F The conceptual framework is intended to supplement professional judgement by supplying a cohesive foundation of theory from which to base decisions.
4. T
5. T

Related exercise material: BE11–1.

Action Plan
- Review the purpose of the conceptual framework.

**LEARNING
OBJECTIVE   2**   Explain the objective of financial reporting, and define the elements of the financial statements.

The Objective of Financial Reporting

The conceptual framework first introduced in Chapter 1 is reproduced in part as a pyramid in Illustration 11-1. We will use this pyramid as a guide throughout the chapter as we discuss each component of the framework.

▶ILLUSTRATION 11-1
The conceptual framework of accounting

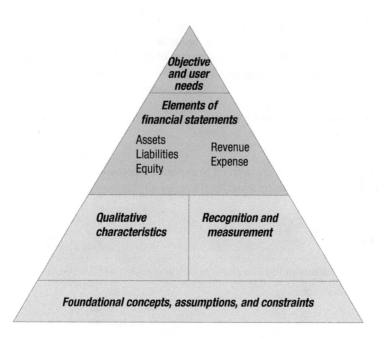

The first step in establishing accounting standards is to decide on the purpose or objective of financial reporting. To decide what the **objective of financial reporting** should be, some basic questions need to be answered first: Who uses financial statements? Why? What information do the users need?

The objective of general purpose financial reporting is to provide users with information that is **useful** for decision-making purposes.

Recall from Chapter 1 that, although a wide variety of users rely on financial reporting, investors and creditors are identified as the key users of financial reporting. Investors and creditors play a fundamental role in the efficient functioning of the economy by providing cash (capital) to businesses. Businesses require this cash or capital to start up, maintain operations, and grow. Cash or capital comes from investors, lenders, and the company's revenue-generating activities.

To make decisions about allocating capital (investing or lending), users look for information in the financial statements about a company's ability to earn a profit and generate future cash flows. To assess this ability, users read the financial statements to determine whether or not management acquired and used the company's resources in the best way possible. This is referred to as **stewardship**. Consequently, financial statements must give information about the following:

1. Economic resources (assets) and claims on the economic resources (liabilities and equity)
2. Changes in economic resources and in claims on the economic resources
3. Economic performance

ELEMENTS OF FINANCIAL STATEMENTS

The **elements of financial statements** are the basic categories used in the financial statements to meet the objective of financial reporting. These elements include assets, liabilities, equity, revenues, and expenses.

Because these elements are so important, they must be precisely defined and applied in the same way by all reporting entities. You have already been introduced to the definitions of assets, liabilities, equity, revenues, and expenses in earlier chapters. For your review, a summary of the definitions is provided in Illustration 11-2.

▶ **ILLUSTRATION 11-2**
Elements of financial
statements

Element	Definition
Assets	An asset is a resource controlled by a business as a result of past events and from which future economic benefits are expected to flow to the business.
Liabilities	A liability is a present obligation, arising from past events, the settlement of which will include an outflow of economic benefits.
Equity	Equity is the residual interest in the assets of the business after deducting all its liabilities. (Assets – Liabilities = Equity)
Revenues	Revenues are increases in assets or decreases in liabilities that result in increases in equity, other than those relating to contributions from owners. Under IFRS, revenues also include gains. Revenues arise in the course of the company's ordinary activities, while gains may or may not arise from ordinary activities.
Expenses	Expenses are decreases in assets or increases in liabilities that result in decreases in equity other than those relating to distributions to owners. Under IFRS, expenses also include losses. Expenses arise from the company's ordinary activities. Losses may or may not arise from the company's ordinary activities.

 Under ASPE, gains and losses are defined in separate categories from revenues and expenses, but the basic definitions are similar to those under IFRS.

BEFORE YOU GO ON...DO IT **Financial Reporting**

The following is a list of some of the components in the conceptual framework:

1. Objective of financial reporting   4. Equity
2. Assets   5. Revenue
3. Liabilities   6. Expense

Identify the component that applies to the following statements:

(a) _____ provides financial information about a business that is useful to existing and potential investors and lenders

(continued)

BEFORE YOU GO ON...DO IT ▸ **Financial Reporting** *(continued)*

(b) _____ an economic resource that is controlled by a business

(c) _____ arises from an increase in assets or a decrease in liabilities, other than those relating to contributions of owners

(d) _____ a present obligation that results in an outflow of resources from a business

(e) _____ Assets minus Liabilities

(f) _____ arises from decreases in assets or increases in liabilities, other than those relating to distributions to owners

(g) _____ requirement to show economic performance in the financial statements

Solution

(a) 1. (b) 2. (c) 5. (d) 3. (e) 4. (f) 6. (g) 1.

Related exercise material: BE11–2 and E11-1.

Action Plan
- Review the objective of financial reporting.
- Review the definitions of the elements of the financial statements.

<table>
<tr><td>**LEARNING OBJECTIVE**</td><td>**3**</td><td>**Apply the fundamental and enhancing qualitative characteristics of the conceptual framework to financial reporting situations.**</td></tr>
</table>

Qualitative Characteristics of Useful Financial Information

How does a company like Corus Entertainment Inc. decide how much financial information to disclose? In what format should its financial information be presented? How should assets, liabilities, revenues, and expenses be measured? Remember that the objective of financial reporting is to provide useful information for decision-making. Thus **the main criterion for judging accounting choices is decision usefulness.**

What makes information useful for decision-making? Accounting standard setters have decided that there are two fundamental characteristics that financial information must have in order to be useful: relevance and faithful representation. In addition, there are other characteristics, complementary to the fundamental characteristics, that enhance the usefulness of financial information. We discuss these qualitative characteristics, shown in green in the diagram below, in the following section.

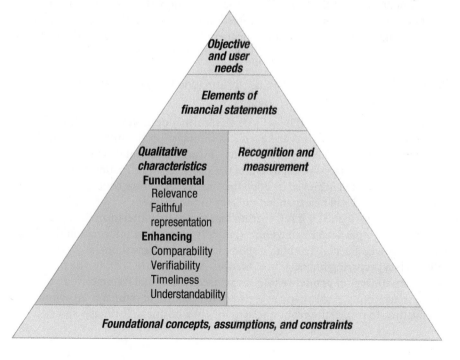

FUNDAMENTAL CHARACTERISTICS

Relevance

Financial information has **relevance** if it makes a difference in a decision. Relevant information has either predictive value or confirmatory value or both. Predictive value helps users forecast future events. For example, the sales and profit reported by Corus in its comparative financial statements may be used along with other information to help predict future sales and profit. Confirmatory value confirms or corrects prior expectations. The sales and profit reported by Corus can also be used to confirm or correct previous predictions made by users.

Materiality is an important component of relevance. An item is material when it is likely to influence the decision of a reasonably careful investor or creditor. It is immaterial if including it or leaving it out has no impact on a decision maker. Materiality and relevance are both defined in terms of making a difference to a decision maker. This does not mean that an immaterial transaction is not recorded or reported at all; it relates to whether or not the item is *separately disclosed* on the face of the financial statements or in the notes to the financial statements. A decision not to disclose certain information may be made because the users do not need that kind of information (it is not relevant) or because the amounts involved are too small to make a difference (they are immaterial). To determine the materiality of an amount, the accountant usually compares it with such items as total assets, total liabilities, gross revenues, cash, and profit.

Materiality is also related to the cost constraint, as illustrated in the following example. Assume that Yanik Co. purchases several inexpensive pieces of office equipment, such as wastepaper baskets. Although it is correct to capitalize these wastepaper baskets and depreciate them over their useful lives, they are usually expensed immediately instead. Immediate expensing is the easiest, and thus the least costly method of accounting for these items and is justified because these costs are immaterial. Making depreciation schedules for these assets is costly and time-consuming. Expensing the wastepaper baskets will not make a material difference to total assets and profit.

Faithful Representation

Once it is determined which information is relevant to financial statement users, then how the information is reported must be determined. To be useful, information must be a **faithful representation** of the economic reality of the events that it is reporting and not just the legal form. This is the concept of **substance over form**. Accounting professionals should always attempt to report the underlying substance of an economic activity, not simply the way it is portrayed in a legal document. For example, a company may sign a lease agreement that requires periodic rental payments to be made over the life of the lease. If a company follows the legal form of the transaction, the periodic rental payments will be recorded as rent expense. However, for certain leases, the economic reality is that an asset is purchased and the periodic payments are loan payments. For these leases, it is necessary to record an asset and a liability to properly report the economic reality. You will learn more about the accounting for lease agreements in Chapter 15.

Faithful representation is achieved when the information is (1) complete, (2) neutral, and (3) free from material error, as explained below.

1. Financial information is **complete** if it includes all information necessary to show the economic reality of the underlying transactions and events. If information is omitted, users will not be able to make appropriate resource allocation decisions. If Corus does not disclose when payments are due on its long-term debt, users would not have the necessary information to predict future cash flows. Completeness is often achieved by applying the full disclosure concept. Full disclosure is a foundational concept and will be expanded on later in the chapter.

2. Financial information is **neutral** if it is free from bias that is intended to attain a predetermined result or to encourage a particular behaviour. Neutrality means that information should not be manipulated in any way. Factual, truthful, unbiased information must be the overriding consideration when preparing financial information. At the time of writing, the IASB had decided to incorporate the concept of **prudence** into the revised conceptual framework. **Prudence** is closely related to neutrality, particularly as it relates to accounting estimates. Accounting estimates are used all the time to record the economic activities of a business. Estimates should be neutral and

Helpful hint "Prudence" has in the past been referred to as "conservatism" and simply means managing with care, economy, and frugality.

reflect the best available information while at the same time ensuring that the accounting treatment or estimate chosen will be the one least likely to overstate assets, revenues, and gains, or understate liabilities, expenses, and losses. Prudence is guidance to exercise caution in situations of uncertainty.

3. If an error in financial information could have an impact on an investor's or creditor's decision, then the error is a **material error**. There will always be some errors in financial information because estimates, such as estimated useful life, are used. If financial information is to be free from material error, estimates must be based on the best available information and be reasonably accurate. Accountants must use professional judgement and caution when using estimates in financial reporting.

The fundamental qualitative characteristics of financial information are summarized in Illustration 11-3.

ENHANCING QUALITATIVE CHARACTERISTICS

Enhancing qualitative characteristics complement the two fundamental qualitative characteristics: relevance and faithful representation. The enhancing characteristics are said to help users distinguish more useful information from less useful information. Comparability, verifiability, timeliness, and understandability are enhancing characteristics.

Comparability

Financial information about a company is most useful when it can be compared with financial information about other companies. There is **comparability** when companies with similar circumstances use the same accounting policies to collect, record, and report financial information. Comparability enables users to identify the similarities and differences between companies.

Comparability is reduced when companies use different policies to account for specific items. For example, recall that there are different methods of determining the cost of merchandise inventory (FIFO, weighted average, specific identification), which can result in different amounts of profit. But if each company states which cost determination method it uses, the external user can determine whether the financial information for two companies is comparable.

Comparability is easier when accounting policies are used consistently. **Consistency** means that a company uses the same accounting policies from year to year. For example, if a company selects FIFO as its inventory cost formula in the first year of operations, it is expected to use FIFO in subsequent years. When financial information has been reported consistently, the financial statements make it possible to do a meaningful analysis of company trends.

This does not mean, however, that a company can never change its accounting policies. Sometimes changes in accounting policies are required by standard setters. For example, when Canadian companies adopted either ASPE or IFRS in 2011, they were required to change some accounting policies. At other times, management may decide that it would be better to change to a new accounting policy. To do this, management must demonstrate that the new policy will result in more relevant information in the statements.

In the year of a change in an accounting policy, the change and its impact must be disclosed in the notes to the financial statements. This disclosure makes users of the financial statements aware of the lack of consistency. In addition, the financial statements for past years must be restated as if the new accounting policy had been used in those years. We will learn more about accounting for, and reporting, changes in accounting policies in Chapter 14.

Verifiability

Verifiability helps assure users that the financial information shows the economic reality of the transaction. Information is verifiable if two knowledgeable and independent people would generally agree that it is faithfully represented. For example, the balance in a bank account can be directly verified by obtaining confirmation of the amount from the bank. Other types of information can be verified by checking inputs to a formula and recalculating the outputs.

Timeliness

Timeliness means that financial information is provided when it is still highly useful for decision-making. In other words, it must be available to decision makers before it loses its ability to influence

▶ ILLUSTRATION **11-3**
Fundamental qualitative characteristics of financial information

I need information to help me make decisions

Relevance
1. Provides a basis for forecasts
2. Confirms or corrects prior expectations

I promise to faithfully represent the economic reality of the situation.

Faithful Representation
1. Is complete
2. Is neutral
3. Is free from material error

Helpful hint Accounting policies are the methods used by a company to record and report economic transactions. In some elements, companies will have a choice between acceptable accounting policies.

decisions. Many people believe that by the time annual financial statements are issued—sometimes up to six months after a company's year end—the information has limited usefulness for decision-making. Timely financial reporting is essential to decision-making.

Understandability

For the information in financial statements to be useful, users must be able to understand it. **Understandability** enables reasonably informed users to interpret and comprehend the meaning of the information provided in the financial statements. Users are expected to have reasonable knowledge of business, economic, and financial activities, and of financial reporting. Users who do not have this level of understanding are expected to rely on professionals who do have an appropriate level of expertise.

Understandability is greater when the information is classified, characterized, and presented clearly and concisely. In making decisions, users should review and analyze the information carefully.

The enhancing qualitative characteristics of financial information are summarized in Illustration 11-4.

▶**ILLUSTRATION** **11-4**
Enhancing qualitative
characteristics of useful
financial information

Comparability	Verifiability	Timeliness	Understandability
1. Different companies use similar accounting principles. 2. A company uses the same accounting policies consistently from year to year.	3. Independent people agree that the economic reality is reported.	4. Information is provided when it is still useful.	5. Information is understandable when it is understood by users who have a reasonable knowledge of accounting concepts and procedures. 6. Information is understandable when it is understood by users who have a reasonable knowledge of business and economic conditions.

APPLICATION OF THE QUALITATIVE CHARACTERISTICS

The qualitative characteristics are complementary concepts; that is, they work together. Nonetheless, they must be applied in a certain order. The qualitative characteristic of relevance should be applied first because it will identify the specific information that would affect the decisions of investors and creditors and that should be included in the financial report.

Once relevance is applied, faithful representation should be applied to ensure that the economic information faithfully represents the economic events being described. Taken together, relevance and faithful representation make financial reporting information useful when making decisions.

Then the enhancing qualitative characteristics—comparability, verifiability, timeliness, and understandability—are applied. They add to the decision usefulness of financial reporting information that is relevant and representationally faithful. They must be applied after the first two characteristics because they cannot, either individually or together, make information useful if it is irrelevant or not faithfully represented.

DIFFERENCES IN QUALITATIVE CHARACTERISTICS UNDER IFRS AND ASPE

Currently, the IFRS and ASPE conceptual frameworks are fundamentally similar, but they are not identical. However, the AcSB has signalled that it will adopt the IASB's revised conceptual framework and in the future there should be no differences between the two. At the time of writing, the revised framework was not yet completed. A list of current differences is in Illustration 11-5.

IFRS	ASPE	Comments
Qualitative characteristics: **Fundamental** • Relevance • Faithful representation **Enhancing** • Comparability • Verifiability • Timeliness • Understandability	Qualitative characteristics • Understandability • Relevance • Reliability • Comparability	In ASPE, the reliability characteristic is similar in many ways to faithful representation in IFRS. Information is considered reliable if it is a faithful representation of transactions and events, is verifiable, and is neutral. ASPE includes conservatism as a component of reliability. Conservatism is similar to the prudence concept discussed earlier for IFRS.

▶ILLUSTRATION 11-5
Qualitative characteristics: Differences between IFRS and ASPE

BEFORE YOU GO ON...DO IT ③ **Qualitative Characteristics of Financial Information**

Presented below are some of the qualitative characteristics of financial information.

1. Relevance
2. Faithful representation
3. Completeness
4. Neutrality
5. Comparability
6. Verifiability
7. Timeliness
8. Understandability

Match the qualitative characteristics to the following statements:

(a) _____ Financial information is available to decision makers before it loses the ability to influence decisions.

(b) _____ Financial information is free from bias that is intended to attain a predetermined result.

(c) _____ Information makes a difference in a decision.

(d) _____ Users are assured that the financial information shows the economic reality of the transaction.

(e) _____ All of the information necessary to show the economic reality of transactions is provided.

(f) _____ Financial information about one company can be evaluated in relation to financial information from another company.

(g) _____ Financial information reports the underlying substance of the transaction, not necessarily its legal form.

(h) _____ Financial information is prepared on the assumption that users have a reasonable understanding of general business and economic conditions and are able to interpret financial statements.

Action Plan
• Review the two fundamental qualitative characteristics.
• Review the enhancing qualitative characteristics.

Solution

(a) 7.   (b) 4.   (c) 1.   (d) 6.   (e) 3.   (f) 5.   (g) 2.   (h) 8.

Related exercise material: BE11–3, E11–3, and E11–6.

Apply the recognition and measurement criteria of the conceptual framework to financial reporting situations.

Recognition and Measurement Criteria

You learned in earlier chapters that financial statements are prepared using the accrual basis of accounting. The **accrual basis of accounting** means that transactions affecting a company's financial statements are recorded in the period in which the events occur, rather than when the company receives cash or pays cash. Therefore, accounting standards are necessary to help accountants answer two questions: (1) when should an event be recorded? and (2) at what amount should it be recorded? **Recognition criteria help determine when an event should be recorded** in the financial statements. When an item is recorded in the financial statements, accountants say that it has been recognized. **Measurement criteria provide guidance on what amount should be recorded** for the event.

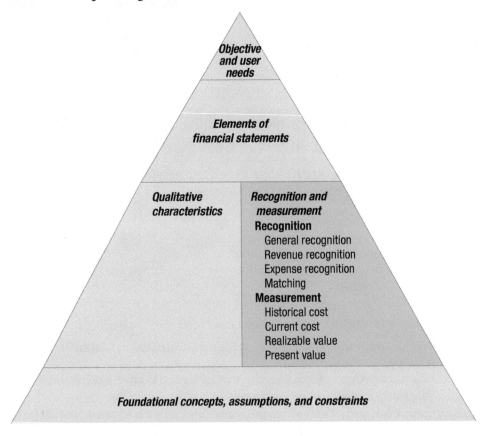

GENERAL RECOGNITION

As mentioned earlier in the chapter, the conceptual framework is being revised. The following section has incorporated the current discussion and preliminary decisions of the planned conceptual framework. Generally an item will be included in the financial statements when all of the following criteria are met:

1. It meets the definition of an element (asset, liability, equity, revenue, or expense).
2. It is probable that any future economic benefit associated with the item will flow to or from the business. (This generally refers to the receipt or payment of money.)
3. The item has a cost or value that can be measured or estimated with a reasonable amount of reliability. If an item cannot be measured, it cannot be recognized.
4. Recognition of the item meets the fundamental qualitative characteristics of relevance and faithful representation.

Recognition of an asset will occur when it is probable that future economic benefit will flow to the business. The term "future" is important because it distinguishes between recording an asset or an expense. If an item can be measured but will only provide economic benefit in the current period, it is recognized as an expense. Recognition of a liability will occur when it is probable that future economic benefit will flow from the business to settle present obligations.

At this point, it is important to understand what the term "probable" means related to recognition criteria. Under IFRS, probable is defined as "more likely than not," which is often interpreted as a greater than 50% chance. Under ASPE, probable is defined as "likely," meaning a high chance of occurrence. A common example of an item being recognized when it is only probable is the recognition of an account receivable. A company does not have to be 100% certain that it will collect an account receivable to record it; it just has to be probable that cash will be collected.

In addition, when a precise dollar amount is not known, an estimate may be used to recognize an item provided that the estimate is based on the best available information, relevance and faithful representation are considered, and prudence is exercised.

A closely related concept to recognition that is included in the revised conceptual framework is derecognition. **Derecognition** is the removal of all or part of a previously recognized asset or liability from a company's balance sheet (statement of financial position). Derecognition is normally a straightforward process. You have already performed derecognition in previous chapters when, for example, a property, plant, and equipment asset was sold: the asset and its accumulated depreciation were reduced to zero to remove them from the balance sheet. There are some transactions that require more guidance on derecognition and, like the general recognition criteria, the criteria to remove an element will be part of the revised conceptual framework.

Although the general recognition criteria provide guidance for recording events, it is necessary to have more specific criteria related to the recognition of revenues and expenses. Should revenue be recorded when a customer places an order with the company, or when the goods are delivered? How should the transaction be recorded if cash collection is uncertain? Revenue recognition criteria are discussed in the following section. Expense recognition will be discussed later in the chapter.

REVENUE RECOGNITION

In the opinion of many people, when to recognize revenue is the most difficult issue in accounting. And it is an issue that has been responsible for many of the accounting scandals of the past decade. For example, when Alexa Life Sciences, the manufacturer of Cold-FX, first started selling its products in the United States in 2006, it failed to recognize that there was considerable risk that a significant amount of the product would be returned by retailers. As a result, the company overstated its 2006 revenues (net sales) by $5.6 million.

Why is revenue recognition such a difficult concept to apply? In some cases, revenue recognition has been intentionally abused in order to overstate profits. However, in most cases, revenue recognition is a difficult concept that requires professional judgement because the activities that generate revenues have become a lot more innovative and complex than in the past. These include "swap" transactions, "bill and hold" sales arrangements, risk-sharing agreements, complex rights of return, price-protection guarantees, and post-sale maintenance contracts—all topics that go beyond an introductory accounting course.

Revenue (or sales) is an important number because it communicates information to users about a company's operational performance. Unless a company can successfully earn revenue and profit, it will not remain in business for very long. Users of financial information need this information to be relevant and faithfully represented, so it is critical that accounting standards provide a robust framework from which to work.

Generally, the revenue recognition criteria state that revenue is recognized when there has been an increase in an asset or a decrease in a liability due to ordinary profit-generating activities that results in an increase in equity. The question that needs to be answered is, when have assets actually increased or liabilities decreased?

There are two approaches to revenue recognition: the contract-based approach (also known as the asset-liability approach) and the earnings approach. The contract-based approach will be required for those following IFRS beginning January 1, 2018; however, early adoption is permitted. The earnings approach is currently used by those following both IFRS and ASPE and will continue to be the standard used in ASPE. We will look at both approaches in this chapter.

Contract-Based Approach

The contract-based approach is based on enforceable rights and obligations obtained upon entering into a contract with a customer. In a contract, the seller promises to deliver goods or services, which is referred to as a **performance obligation**. The buyer agrees to pay some amount of consideration in exchange for the goods or services, which is referred to as an **enforceable right to receive consideration**.

The core principle of the contract-based approach is that a seller will recognize revenue when the promised goods or services are transferred to the buyer and the amount that is recognized reflects the consideration the business expects to receive in exchange for the goods and services.

To determine when and how much revenue is recognized, the five-step model shown in Illustration 11-6 is used.

▶ **ILLUSTRATION** **11-6**
Contract-based
approach five-step model
for revenue recognition

1. **Identify the contract with a customer.** A contract is an agreement between two or more parties that creates enforceable rights and obligations. Generally this means that one party agrees to deliver goods or services in exchange for payment for those goods or services. A contract may be written, verbal, or the result of customary business practices.

2. **Identify the performance obligations in the contract.** A contract includes an agreement to transfer goods or services to a customer. This creates a performance obligation in that the business has committed to provide goods or services to another party. A contract may involve the delivery of one good or service or it may create a commitment to deliver several goods and/or services over a period of time. If more than one distinct good or service is to be delivered, each distinct good or service creates a separate performance obligation that will need to be accounted for separately. A **distinct good or service** is one that may be sold separately as a stand-alone good or service.

3. **Determine the transaction price (overall contract price).** The transaction price is the amount the business expects to receive in exchange for the goods and services promised to the other party. When determining the transaction price, attention must be paid to any variable consideration included in the transaction price. **Variable consideration** is any amount that may change the consideration that is ultimately received. Examples of variable components of the transaction price include discounts, rebates, incentives, price concessions, and a customer's right to return products.

4. **Allocate the transaction price to the performance obligations in the contract.** If the contract consists of more than one performance obligation as identified in Step 2, the entity should allocate the transaction price to each separate performance obligation. This should be done based on the relative stand-alone selling prices of the goods or services promised. The stand-alone selling price is the fair value of what the good or service would sell for on its own.

5. **Recognize revenue when the performance obligation is complete.** Completion of a performance obligation is determined by considering when **control** of the good or service is transferred to the customer. In many situations, control will be transferred to a customer at a point in time but control may also transfer over the period of the contract.

Illustration 11-7 provides guidance to determine when control of the good or service is transferred to the customer.

▶ **ILLUSTRATION** **11-7**
Indications of the
transfer of control

Indications that control of the goods or services have transferred at a *point in time* are:	**Indications that control of the goods or services transfers *over a period of time* are:**
• Customer has the ability to direct the use of and obtain substantially all of the benefits of the goods.	• Customer receives and consumes the benefits as the seller performs (e.g., bookkeeping services).
• Customer has the ability to prevent other businesses from directing the use of, or receiving the benefits from the goods.	• Business creates or enhances an asset that the customer controls (e.g., a contractor providing a service to construct an office building).
• Customer has legal title to the goods.	• Business does not have an alternative use for the asset created or enhanced (e.g., manufacturing customized factory equipment for a customer).
• Business has transferred physical possession of the goods.	
• Customer has accepted the goods or service.	• Business has a right to payment for performance completed to date.
• Business has a right to payment.	

Note that **revenue recognition does not depend on whether or not cash *has been* received**, only that a business has completed its performance obligation and now has an enforceable right to consideration (payment).

While the process listed above may seem daunting, there are some basic revenue transactions that are relatively straightforward and that easily meet the requirements of the above five steps. For example, consider a situation where you enter your local convenience store with the intention of purchasing a snack. Applying the five-step model, we can determine when and how much revenue is recognized, as shown in Illustration 11-8.

Step	Question to ask	Criteria to be met and discussion
1	Is there a contract?	Yes, you are the customer and the local convenience store is the business. Upon entering the store, a contract is implied because a variety of goods are available and displayed for sale at various prices. This indicates that the business will provide the goods in exchange for some amount of consideration.
2	What is the performance obligation?	The performance obligation of the store is to transfer to you, the customer, control of the goods you select. In this case, there is one performance obligation: to transfer the snack to you.
3	What is the transaction price?	The transaction price is the asking price listed on the snack.
4	Is there a need to allocate the transaction price?	In this situation, there is only one performance obligation and the transaction price will be allocated to the one snack you purchase. If you choose more than one item to purchase, the total transaction price will be allocated to the goods based on their stand-alone selling prices (the price listed for each item).
5	Has the performance obligation been satisfied?	Yes, when you pay the asking price, you now have control of the snack. The store has completed its performance obligation because it has transferred the promised good to you. The convenience store can now recognize the revenue from the sale of the goods.

▶ ILLUSTRATION 11-8
Five-step model:
Convenience store example

The above example reflects a straightforward, but common, revenue transaction. In the following section, we will examine additional revenue recognition situations using the contract-based approach.

The following are examples of revenue recognition situations and journal entries required under the contract-based approach.

Sale of goods

On October 2, 2017, Armani Company enters a contract with Karon Industries to transfer 50 classic stainless steel watches at $200 each. Once delivered, the watches cannot be returned. The watches cost Armani $75 each. The watches are delivered to Karon Industries on October 31, 2017. Armani uses a perpetual inventory system. Applying the five-step model, we can determine when and how much revenue is recognized, as shown in Illustration 11-9.

▶ ILLUSTRATION **11-9**
Five-step model:
Watch example

Step	Question to ask	Criteria to be met and discussion
1	Is there a contract?	Yes, Armani and Karon agree that, upon the delivery of the watches by Armani, Karon will pay Armani $10,000 ($200 × 50).
2	What is the performance obligation?	There is only one performance obligation: the delivery of the watches to Karon Industries.
3	What is the transaction price?	The transaction price is $10,000.
4	Is there a need to allocate the transaction price?	In this situation, there is only one performance obligation: delivering 50 stainless steel watches. The entire transaction price will be allocated to the watches.
5	Has the performance obligation been satisfied?	Yes. On October 31, Armani delivers the goods to Karon, which takes control (possession and legal title has transferred) of the goods. Armani now has an enforceable right to payment and will recognize revenue on the same day.

Armani will prepare journal entries to recognize revenue on October 31. No journal entry is required on October 2, 2017, because neither party has performed in the contract. The journal entries are as follows:

A	=	L	+	OE
+10,000				+10,000
−3,750				−3,750

Cash flows: no effect

Oct. 31	Accounts Receivable	10,000	
	Sales (50 × $200)		10,000
	Cost of Goods Sold (50 × $75)	3,750	
	Merchandise Inventory		3,750
	To record the transfer of goods to Karon Industries.		

On November 30, Karon Industries pays the amount in full, and the journal entry to record the payment from Karon is:

A	=	L	+	OE
+10,000				
−10,000				

↑Cash flows: +$10,000

Nov. 30	Cash	10,000	
	Accounts Receivable		10,000
	To record receipt of payment from Karon Industries.		

Provision of services

Gosling Consulting provides information technology support to a variety of clients. On June 1, 2017, Gosling enters into a contract to provide Stallman Company one month of services for a price of $1,000. Gosling completes the services on June 30, 2017. The contract requires Stallman to pay the amount owing to Gosling on July 15, 2017. Applying the five-step model, we can determine when and how much revenue is recognized, as shown in Illustration 11-10.

▶ ILLUSTRATION **11-10**
Five-step model:
IT example

Step	Question to ask	Criteria to be met and discussion
1	Is there a contract?	Yes, Gosling and Stallman agree that one month of information technology services will be provided and total consideration will be $1,000.
2	What is the performance obligation?	There is only one performance obligation: to provide one month of services.
3	What is the transaction price?	The transaction price is $1,000.
4	Is there a need to allocate the transaction price?	In this situation, there is only one performance obligation: completion of one month of services. The entire transaction price will be allocated to the information technology service.
5	Has the performance obligation been satisfied?	Yes. On June 30, Gosling completes the services agreed to under the contract and the customer accepts the services. Gosling has an enforceable right to payment.

No journal entry is required on June 1, 2017, because neither party has completed its performance obligations in the contract. Gosling will recognize revenue on June 30. The journal entry required on this date is:

June 30	Accounts Receivable	1,000	
	Revenue		1,000
	To record completed performance obligation for Stallman Company.		

A = L + OE
+1,000 +1,000

Cash flows: no effect

On July 15, 2017, when Stallman pays the amount owed to Gosling, the following journal entry is prepared:

July 15	Cash	1,000	
	Accounts Receivable		1,000
	To record receipt of payment from Stallman Industries.		

A = L + OE
+1,000
−1,000

↑Cash flows: +$1,000

Multiple performance obligations (separate performance obligations; the provision of distinct goods and services)

Codd Computers is a leading retailer of commercial computer equipment. Codd enters into contracts with clients that need commercial equipment in their businesses. Codd also offers a variety of other services to clients, such as installation, training, and maintenance. Generally, Codd will offer to provide installation services along with the equipment, but this service is also offered separately for a price of $25,000. On February 1, 2017, Codd entered into a contract with Fox Distributing. The contract details are as follows:

- Codd will supply the equipment to Fox for a contract price of $750,000. Codd does not expect any returns and does not offer a warranty.
- This price will include installation if Fox requires it.
- The equipment will be supplied and installed by Codd (as requested by Fox) no later than March 1, 2017.
- Fox agrees to pay the full contract price upon delivery of the equipment (when there is a transfer of control).

The cost of the equipment to Codd is $400,000. The equipment was delivered to Fox's offices on February 16, 2017, and installation was completed on March 1, 2017. Applying the five-step model, we can determine when and how much revenue is recognized, as shown in Illustration 11-11.

▶ ILLUSTRATION  11-11
Five-step model:
Computer equipment example

Step	Question to ask	Criteria to be met and discussion
1	Is there a contract?	Yes, Codd and Fox agree to the provision of equipment and the installation service and the consideration will be $750,000.
2	What is the performance obligation?	There are two performance obligations in this contract. The delivery of the equipment is a distinct good and the installation service is a distinct service.
3	What is the transaction price?	The transaction price is $750,000.
4	Is there a need to allocate the transaction price?	Yes, this contract includes two separate performance obligations and the transaction price must be allocated to each obligation based on the relative stand-alone values of each distinct good and service (see the calculation below this illustration).
5	Has the performance obligation been satisfied?	The performance obligation related to the equipment delivery is completed on February 16 and the second performance obligation related to the installation service is completed on March 1. Codd will recognize revenue on February 16 and March 1.

The following shows the calculation in Step 4—allocation of the transaction price. To allocate the $750,000 transaction price to the separate performance obligations, we use the stand-alone **fair value** of the equipment ($750,000) and the stand-alone **fair value** of the installation service ($25,000). The allocation of the transaction price is shown in Illustration 11-12.

▶ILLUSTRATION 11-12
Allocation of transaction price for multiple performance obligations

Performance obligation	Stand-alone value	% of total stand-alone value	×	Contract price	=	Allocation of contract price
Supply equipment	$750,000	97%[1]		$750,000		$727,500
Install equipment	25,000	3%[2]		$750,000		22,500
	$775,000	100%				$750,000

[1]$750,000 ÷ $775,000
[2]$25,000 ÷ $775,000

You may notice the method used to allocate the transaction price to separate performance obligations is similar to the methods used to allocate a basket purchase price to property, plant, and equipment discussed in Chapter 9 and accounting for rewards programs in Chapter 10.

If the stand-alone amount cannot be determined, two alternative approaches can be used: the adjusted market assessment approach or the expected cost plus a margin approach. You will learn more about these in intermediate accounting courses. For our purposes, we will use the relative fair value approach where fair values are the stand-alone selling prices of the distinct goods and services.

No journal entry is required on February 1 because neither party has completed its performance obligation. Codd will prepare revenue recognition entries on February 16 as follows:

A	=	L	+	OE
+750,000		+22,500		+727,500
−400,000				−400,000

↑Cash flows: +$750,000

Feb. 16	Cash	750,000	
	Sales		727,500
	Unearned Revenue		22,500
	To record completion of first performance obligation for Fox contract and receipt of payment in full.		
	Cost of Goods Sold	400,000	
	Merchandise Inventory		400,000
	To record cost of goods sold for Fox contract.		

On March 1, when the installation is complete, Codd will recognize the revenue for the second performance obligation as follows:

A	=	L	+	OE
		−22,500		+22,500

Cash flows: no effect

Mar. 1	Unearned Revenue	22,500	
	Revenue		22,500
	To record completion of second performance obligation on Fox contract.		

Earnings Approach

Like the contract-based approach, revenue is recognized using the earnings approach when there has been an increase in an asset or a decrease in a liability due to ordinary profit-generating activities that results in an increase in owners' equity. There is no stated core principle for the earnings approach. Instead, specific criteria must be met for revenue to be recognized and generally the criteria provide an indication of when a business has completed the earnings process. The earnings process represents the activities performed by a company to create a valuable product or service.

The following are examples of revenue recognition situations and journal entries required under the earnings approach.

Sale of goods

Revenue from the sale of goods is recognized when *all* of the following conditions have been met:

1. Performance is complete and the seller has transferred the significant risks and rewards of ownership to the buyer. The buyer will have the significant risks and rewards of ownership when the buyer starts receiving the benefits (e.g., cash flows) of the goods and has the risk of loss (e.g., goods decline in value or are damaged).

2. The seller does not have control over the goods or continuing managerial involvement.
3. The amount of the revenue can be reliably measured.
4. It is probable there will be an increase in economic resources (that is, cash will be collected).
5. Costs relating to the sale of the goods can be reliably measured.

The "critical event" is the point in the earnings process that signals that all the criteria have been met.

To illustrate the sale of goods using the earnings approach, we will use the following example. Charisma Company is a retailer specializing in fair trade and specialized merchandise from around the world. On October 18, the company purchases $60,000 in merchandise for resale. The merchandise is received on October 28 and is packaged and ready for resale. On November 10, the goods are sold and shipped at the price of $72,000 to a customer, FOB shipping point, terms n/30. The goods are received by the customer on November 15. Charisma uses a perpetual inventory system and performs credit checks on all of its customers who request credit terms before shipping any merchandise. Charisma does not expect any material returns of the merchandise and no further costs will be incurred.

We can apply the revenue recognition criteria for the sale of goods to determine when and how much revenue is recognized, as shown in Illustration 11-13.

▶ ILLUSTRATION 11-13
Earnings approach: Merchandise example

Criterion	Description	Discussion
1	Performance is complete and the seller has transferred the risks and rewards of ownership to the buyer.	The transfer of the risks and rewards of ownership generally coincides with the date when the customer takes legal title and possession of the goods. In this case, the buyer obtains legal title on November 10 when the goods are shipped. (Recall from Chapter 5 that FOB shipping point generally means legal title transfers to the buyer at the shipping point.)
2	The seller does not have control over the goods or continuing managerial involvement.	The merchandise is transferred in total to the customer and Charisma does not expect any returns. Based on the information in this example, this criterion has been met.
3	The amount of the revenue can be reliably measured.	The amount of revenue can be measured based on the selling price of the merchandise, which is $72,000.
4	It is probable there will be an increase in economic resources (that is, cash will be collected).	Charisma does a credit check for the customer and there is no uncertainty about the customer's ability to pay within 30 days.
5	Costs relating to the sale of the goods can be reliably measured.	As soon as the goods are shipped to the customer, Charisma will incur no further costs associated with this sale.

In this situation, all five criteria have been met as of November 10, with the critical event being the physical shipment of the merchandise to the customer.

The journal entries to recognize revenue are:

Nov. 10	Accounts Receivable	72,000	
	Sales		72,000
	To record shipment of merchandise, FOB shipping point, n/30.		
	Cost of Goods Sold	60,000	
	Merchandise Inventory		60,000
	To record cost of goods sold for the sale on November 10.		

A	=	L	+	OE
+72,000				+72,000
−60,000				−60,000

Cash flows: no effect

Now assume that, although Charisma does credit checks on its customers before shipping, this customer does not have a good credit rating and there is a chance that payment will not be made. Charisma decides to send the goods and risk non-payment because selling to this customer may lead to significant additional sales. The customer makes payment on December 10. In this case, criterion number 3 will not be met until payment from the customer is actually received. Therefore, revenue recognition cannot take place on November 10. Rather, it must take place on December 10.

The journal entries Charisma will make are as follows:

A	=	L	+	OE
+72,000		+12,000		
−60,000				

Cash flows: no effect

Nov. 10	Accounts Receivable	72,000	
	Deferred Gross Profit		12,000
	Merchandise Inventory		60,000
	To record shipment of merchandise, FOB shipping point, n/30.		

On November 10, the goods are physically shipped so an accounting transaction must be recorded. Merchandise Inventory is reduced because it is no longer in the warehouse. The customer has agreed to the price of $72,000, which gives rise to the account receivable. The Deferred Gross Profit account is a type of unearned revenue and is a liability. It represents the gross profit that has not yet been recognized.

On December 10, the customer pays the amount owing and all five criteria have now been met. Charisma will make the following journal entry to record the transaction:

A	=	L	+	OE
+72,000				
−72,000				

↑Cash flows: +72,000

A	=	L	+	OE
		−12,000		+72,000
				−60,000

Cash flows: no effect

Dec. 10	Cash	72,000	
	Accounts Receivable		72,000
	To record receipt of payment for goods shipped on November 10.		
	Cost of Goods Sold	60,000	
	Deferred Gross Profit	12,000	
	Sales		72,000
	To record revenue from sale on November 10.		

Sale of services

Generally, in businesses that provide services, **revenue is recognized when the service has been provided and it is probable that the cash will be collected.**

To illustrate, assume your doctor gives you a routine checkup on September 30, sends an invoice for services to the provincial health care plan in October for the cost of the checkup, which is $105, and receives payment in November. When should your doctor recognize the revenue? The revenue should be recognized in September because that was when the service was performed, the price would have been known, and the receivable was likely to be collected.

The journal entry your doctor will make in September to recognize revenue will be as follows:

A	=	L	+	OE
+105				+105

Cash flows: no effect

Sept. 30	Accounts Receivable	105	
	Revenue		105
	To record revenue from medical checkup on September 30.		

OTHER REVENUE RECOGNITION SITUATIONS

In the previous section, we covered the fundamentals of revenue recognition under both the contract-based approach and the earnings approach. The following section gives two examples of other revenue recognition situations commonly encountered in business. Explanations are given for both recognition approaches.

Right of Return

In many industries, such as retail, companies will often allow customers to return merchandise after a sale. A company can have a stated return policy or it may simply be customary business practice. In situations where returns are material, revenue recognition is complicated. If revenue is recognized for sales without consideration of potential returns, revenue will be overstated.

To illustrate the accounting for a sale where a right of return exists, consider Gold Publishing Company's contract with Verses Books and Music Co. The details of the contract are as follows:

- Gold and Verses enter into a contract for the supply of 1,000 new bestseller books in paperback on June 1, 2017.
- Gold will deliver the books on June 15, 2017, and Verses agrees to pay $4.00 per book.

- Gold has a stated policy that it will accept returns of any unsold books for a period not longer than six months after the date of delivery: December 15, 2017. Based on Gold's experience, 5% of the books will be returned by Verses.
- Gold's cost per book is $2.00.
- Gold and Verses agree that payment for the books will be made on June 30, 2017.
- Gold has done business with Verses in the past and there is no uncertainty about eventual collection.
- Verses returns a total of 50 books on November 30.

The journal entries required are as follows:

	Contract-based approach			Earnings approach		
June 15	Accounts Receivable	4,000		Accounts Receivable	4,000	
	Refund Liability		200	Sales		4,000
	Sales		3,800	Sales Returns and Allowances	200	
				Allowance for Sales Returns		200
June 15	Cost of Goods Sold	1,900		Cost of Goods Sold	2,000	
	Estimated Inventory Returns	100		Merchandise Inventory		2,000
	Merchandise Inventory		2,000			
June 30	Cash	4,000		Cash	4,000	
	Accounts Receivable		4,000	Accounts Receivable		4,000
Nov. 30	Refund Liability	200		Allowance for Sales Returns	200	
	Cash		200	Cash		200
Nov. 30	Merchandise Inventory	100		Merchandise Inventory	100	
	Estimated Inventory Returns		100	Cost of Goods Sold		100

Using the contract-based approach to revenue recognition, the entity will record revenue at **the amount that it expects to receive**. If returns are expected, revenue should be recognized net of estimated returns. In the example above, estimated returns are $200 ($4,000 × 5%). If the amount of returns cannot be estimated, revenue will not be recognized until the return period expires.

Therefore, when recording revenue where there is a right of return, sellers must estimate the amount of expected returns and record a liability for estimated refunds in an account called Refund Liability. The refund liability represents the future obligation to accept returned goods and provide a refund. The seller will also recognize a new asset that we refer to as Estimated Inventory Returns for the cost of the estimated returns. This asset represents a right to receive returned goods.

When goods are returned, the refund liability is credited to reflect the fact that the obligation has been satisfied. The Estimated Inventory Returns asset account is also reduced and the Merchandise Inventory account is increased. The refund liability and the estimated inventory returns accounts will both be reported on a gross basis as current items on the balance sheet to reflect the short-term nature of expected returns. At the end of each reporting period, the entity should review its estimate to ensure it reflects any changes to the return estimates.

Using the earnings approach, a similar transaction is initially recorded. Sales Returns and Allowances is debited and a contra asset account called Allowance for Sales Returns is credited for the selling price of the estimated returns. No refund liability is recorded. The allowance reduces the realizable value of accounts receivable. When goods are returned, the allowance is debited. Returned inventory can be recorded in a separate merchandise inventory account but debiting the Merchandise Inventory account is also acceptable.

Warranties

Many consumer goods come with some type of a warranty that provides assurance that the product will operate as intended. Warranties may also be purchased separately and are often referred to as "extended warranties." Accounting standards define these two types of warranties as assurance and service warranties, respectively. As we saw in Chapter 10, when recognizing revenue for a sale with an assurance warranty, companies are required to recognize an estimated liability (provision) for future warranty costs that may be incurred. The accounting for warranties is the same for the contract-based and earnings approach. When a service warranty is sold to a customer as part of a product purchase, it is accounted for in the same manner as a multiple performance obligation. The accounting for multiple performance obligations was discussed previously. While we did not demonstrate the accounting under the earnings approach for multiple performance obligations, the journal entries and calculations are exactly the same.

EXPENSE RECOGNITION

The basic **expense recognition criterion** states that expenses are recognized when there is a decrease in an asset or increase in a liability, excluding transactions with owners that result in a decrease in owners' equity. This is not necessarily when cash is paid. For example, as supplies are used, the asset Supplies is decreased and an expense is recognized. Alternatively, when Salaries Payable is increased, Salaries Expense is recognized.

Expense recognition is tied to revenue recognition when there is a direct association between costs incurred and the earning of revenue. For example, there is a direct association between cost of goods sold and sales revenue. This process is commonly referred to as the **matching concept. Under matching, revenues and expenses that relate to the same transaction are recorded in the same accounting period.** Other examples of expenses that relate directly to revenue are bad debt expense, warranty expense, and sales salaries.

Other costs are more difficult to directly associate with revenue. For example, it is difficult to match administrative salary expense or interest expense with the revenue they help to earn. Such costs are therefore expensed in the period when the liability arises.

Sometimes, however, there is no direct relationship between expenses and revenue. When it is hard to find a direct relationship and costs incurred are expected to benefit several accounting periods, an asset is recognized. In this case, a rational and systematic allocation policy is used to allocate the cost of the asset to expense over time. For example, the cost of a long-lived asset can be allocated to depreciation expense over the life of the asset because it can be determined that the asset contributes in some way to revenue generation during its useful life. Allocation requires the accountant to use professional judgement in estimating the benefits that will be received from the asset and to determine what method is used to allocate the cost to expense over time.

In other cases, when expenditures are made that do not qualify for the recognition of an asset, an expense is recognized immediately. For example, expenditures for research do not qualify for recognition of an asset because it is impossible to determine the future benefits arising from the research, so research costs are expensed immediately. Another example is expenditures made for advertising, which are also expensed immediately because they generally only provide benefit in the current period.

Sometimes a previously recognized asset ceases to have future benefit, and the asset must be expensed. For example, inventory that is obsolete and cannot be sold is expensed when it becomes apparent it cannot be sold.

Costs that are incurred in a period must be analyzed to determine the appropriate treatment. In most cases, a cost will either be immediately expensed or recorded as an asset, if it meets the definition of an asset. Illustration 11-14 is a summary of the expense recognition criteria.

▶ **ILLUSTRATION** **11-14**
Summary of expense recognition criteria

Recognize costs as expenses when:	Examples
Costs incurred are directly associated with revenue recognized (matching)	Cost of goods sold
Costs incurred benefit only one period	Insurance expense Utilities expense
Costs are difficult to associate with revenue recognized	Administrative salaries expense
The cost of an asset is allocated to expense over time when the asset is expected to benefit several accounting periods	Depreciation expense
Costs do not qualify as an asset	Research expense
Previously recognized assets cease to have future benefit	Obsolete inventory (cost of goods sold)

MEASUREMENT OF ELEMENTS

So far, we have looked at when items should be recognized or recorded in the accounting records. Now we will look at what dollar amounts should be used to record the items. In Chapter 1, we discussed two measurement methods only: historical cost and fair value. In this chapter, fair value is expanded on and includes current cost, realizable value, and present value. The measurement methods discussed in the following section are:

1. Historical cost
2. Current cost
3. Realizable value
4. Present value

Assets are recorded at cost when they are acquired. Cost is used because it is relevant and it provides a faithful representation of the transaction. Cost represents the price paid, the assets sacrificed, or the commitment made at the date of acquisition. After acquisition, cost is referred to as **historical cost**. Historical cost is objectively measurable, factual, and verifiable. It is the result of an exchange transaction. Historical cost is relevant for reporting certain assets in the balance sheet because the assets are intended for use in the business and are not going to be sold.

Most companies use the historical cost model to report property, plant, and equipment where the carrying value on the balance sheet is historical cost less accumulated depreciation. However, you will recall from Chapter 9 that, under IFRS, companies can choose to account for their property, plant, and equipment under either the historical cost model or the revaluation model. Under the revaluation model, the carrying amount of property, plant, and equipment is its fair value less any accumulated depreciation less any subsequent impairment losses.

> Alternative terminology Other common terms for *fair value* are *market value* and *realizable value*.

Current cost measures assets at the amount of cash or equivalent that would have to be paid if the same or an equivalent asset had to be purchased in the current period. This is sometimes referred to as "replacement cost." Liabilities measured at current cost reflect the amount required to settle an obligation currently. Accounts payable are an example of an element that is normally presented at current cost.

Realizable value measures assets at the amount of cash or equivalent that could currently be obtained by selling the asset in an orderly disposal. In reference to assets, we can think of realizable value as the amount that a business can reasonably expect to collect in cash from that asset. Liabilities measured at realizable value report the cash expected to be paid to satisfy the liabilities in the normal course of business. Realizable value also encompasses fair value, which will be defined separately below. Both accounts receivable and inventory are measured at realizable value. This is accomplished by reducing the value of these elements for expected uncollectible amounts and obsolete inventory, respectively.

Present value measures assets and liabilities at the present value of future cash inflows or outflows. Present value measures are generally used for long-term assets and liabilities and will be covered more in Chapters 15, 16 and in Appendix PV.

> Alternative terminology Present value is also referred to as *value in use* or *fulfilment value*.

Fair value is a measure of the current value of an asset or liability at the reporting date. IFRS 13 defines fair value as "the price that would be received to sell an asset or paid to transfer a liability in an orderly transaction between market participants." Fair value is not specifically identified in the conceptual framework but is instead defined in IFRS 13. However, you will notice that all of current cost, realizable value, and present value could also be the fair value of an asset or liability. So why not just include "fair value" in the conceptual framework? In fact, the revised framework, which was anticipated to be issued in 2016, was expected to include fair value as a measurement method, replacing both current cost and realizable value.

Fair values are thought to be more relevant in some financial reporting situations and will provide users with more relevant information to assess the impact of changes in value on the company's liquidity and solvency. As mentioned above, under IFRS, companies can choose to report property, plant, and equipment at fair values when using the revaluation model. Investments and investment properties are generally reported using fair value because historical cost for these types of assets provides little useful information to a user.

It is important to note that, while all of the above measurement methods can be and are used in the preparation of financial statements, they are not simply used whenever or however management feels appropriate. Each element in the financial statement has a related accounting standard that supersedes the conceptual framework and limits the choice. Where no standard exists for an element, management can refer to the framework and, using professional judgement, make the most informed and appropriate decision. The conceptual framework simply outlines each of the methods as acceptable bases to use.

Up to this point in the text, we have used historical cost to record assets and liabilities. As you continue in the text, we will use some of the other measurement bases discussed above.

VIOLATION OF RECOGNITION AND MEASUREMENT CONCEPTS: ERRORS AND INTENTIONAL MISSTATEMENTS

As we discussed earlier in the chapter, revenue recognition is considered the most difficult issue in accounting. In some cases, revenue recognition has been intentionally abused. Incorrect application of the expense and measurement criteria can also result in errors or intentional misstatement of the financial statements. In this section, we will discuss what situations might lead management and accountants to abuse accounting principles and potential misstatements that can be made in applying the recognition and measurement criteria.

Management may be under pressure to report a certain amount of profit to meet owners' expectations, or management's bonuses may be based on the company achieving a specified profit. In these situations, management may be inclined to overstate profits by overstating revenues or understating expenses. Alternatively, management of some private companies may want to reduce the amount of tax paid and consequently may be inclined to understate profits by understating revenues and overstating expenses. Ways in which revenues or expenses may be misstated in error or intentionally are as follows:

1. **Recognition of revenue or expense in the incorrect accounting period.** For example, the seller might recognize sales revenues for goods that are shipped FOB destination when the goods are shipped and not when the customer receives the goods. This would overstate revenues if legal title and physical possession of the goods have not transferred to the customer prior to the end of the fiscal year. Alternatively, a company might delay recording an expense by recording as an asset an expenditure for which there is no future benefit.

2. **Misstatement of estimates.** Earlier in the chapter, we discussed the need to estimate potential returns and reduce sales. If the estimate is understated, sales will be overstated. Alternatively, management might understate the estimate for bad debt expense. Estimates do not need to be 100% accurate. However, professional judgement needs to be used in arriving at the estimate and estimates need to be supported and verifiable. For example, a company may need to estimate the accrual for utilities expense because the invoice has not been received. The accountant might use previous utility invoices to arrive at a reasonable estimate.

3. **Failure to record a revenue or expense.** Due to poor internal controls and record keeping, the accountant may be unaware that revenue should be recognized or an expense incurred.

4. **Failure to apply the correct measurement.** For example, a company may neglect to write down inventory to net realizable value. Or alternatively, land might be reported at fair value when the company is following the cost model for property, plant, and equipment.

It is important that accountants analyze transactions carefully to ensure that accounting principles are applied correctly and the financial statements are a faithful representation of the underlying economic events. When adjusting entries are prepared at the end of an accounting period, accountants must give careful attention to determining the appropriate accounting period in which revenues and expenses should be recognized and to ensuring that appropriate measurements and estimates are made. In addition, care must be exercised to ensure all economic transactions affecting a company are recorded. Professional judgement and ethical reasoning are used to guard against errors or abuse in applying accounting principles.

ACCOUNTING IN ACTION
ETHICS INSIGHT

Mike Slaughter/Getty Images

One of the biggest accounting scandals in Canadian history involved former telecommunications giant Nortel Networks. The company was accused of accruing expenses that did not occur and then reversing these expenses in 2003 in order to turn a profit, after losing money in the 2001 dot-com bust. Nortel allegedly accrued millions of dollars in liabilities related to the company's downsizing, such as lawsuits from suppliers over cancelled contracts and employee severance packages. If the company overestimated the amounts of these liabilities, also known as accruals, reserves, or provisions, it would consider the difference as revenue in the period in which the settlement was reached. Three senior executives were charged with fraud, accused of manipulating earnings in 2003 to trigger millions of dollars in profitability bonuses for themselves. During a six-month trial in 2012, the Crown alleged that the executives ordered extra liabilities to be accrued in 2002, turning a profit into a loss, and then reversed the accruals in 2003, turning a loss into a profit. The Crown argued that the accruals should have been reversed earlier. The company restated its financial information several times in the years thereafter, and filed for bankruptcy in 2009. In early 2013, all three executives were found not guilty on all counts.

Sources: Jamie Sturgeon, "Nortel Executives Found Not Guilty on All Counts of Fraud," *Financial Post*, January 14, 2013; James Bagnall, "Were Senior Executives Scapegoats for Nortel's Demise?," *Postmedia News*, January 14, 2012; Jamie Sturgeon, "'Unsupportable' Reserves Remained on Nortel Books, Court Hears," *Financial Post*, March 5, 2012; Janet McFarland, "Nortel Releases $80-Million in Accounting Reserves to Reach Profit Threshold: Witness," *Globe and Mail*, April 2, 2012; James Bagnall, "Nortel Witnesses Were 'Accomplices' to Fraud," *Ottawa Citizen*, August 7, 2012.

 Accountants are often required to make estimates when preparing financial statements. What is the difference between what the Crown argued happened at Nortel and what we would expect an accountant to do when estimating accruals for adjusting journal entries? (Consider the qualitative characteristic faithful representation.)

BEFORE YOU GO ON...DO IT   4   Two Approaches to Revenue Recognition

The following represent two revenue transactions for Li Xiu Company. Li Xiu uses a perpetual inventory system and has a 60-day return policy. Liu Xiu's terms for all customers are n/30.

1. On July 3, 2017, Li Xiu enters into a contract with Watson Co. to deliver 600 chess sets for a transaction price of $100 each. The chess sets are delivered on July 19, 2017. Li Xiu expects that 1% of the sets will be returned. The sets cost Li Xiu $40 each. There is no uncertainty about Watson's ability to pay the amounts owing.
    (a) Assuming that Li Xiu uses the contract-based approach:
        1. Identify the contract with the customer.
        2. Identify the performance obligation(s).
        3. Determine the transaction price.
        4. Identify when revenue should be recognized and for how much.
        5. Prepare the journal entries to recognize revenue.
2. On December 15, 2017, Li Xiu agrees to deliver 100 violins to Lewis Co. for a total contract price of $12,500. The goods are shipped on December 29, 2017, FOB shipping point, and received by Lewis on January 10, 2018. Li Xiu does not expect any returns for the violins. The violins cost Li Xiu $75 each. Lewis Co. pays the amount owing in full on February 10, 2018.
    (b) Assuming that Li Xiu uses the earnings approach:
        1. Identify the critical event that would indicate that revenue recognition is appropriate.
        2. Identify when revenue should be recognized and for how much.
        3. Prepare the journal entries to recognize revenue.
        4. Assume that Lewis Co. is a new company and that Li Xiu cannot assess its ability to pay any amounts owing. Would your answers to parts (1) and (2) change? Why or why not?

Solution

(1a)

1. Li Xiu Company and Watson Co. agree that, upon delivery of 600 chess sets, Watson Co. will pay Li Xiu $60,000.
2. There is one performance obligation. Li Xiu agrees to deliver the chess sets to Watson Co.
3. The transaction price will be $59,400. This is made up of the selling price of $100 per chess set, or $60,000, less the variable consideration of $600 for potential returns.
4. Li Xiu will recognize revenue on July 19, 2017, when the chess sets are delivered and control of the goods has transferred to Watson Co. Li Xiu now has an enforceable right to payment.
5.

July 19	Accounts Receivable	60,000	
	Refund Liability		600
	Sales		59,400
19	Cost of Goods Sold	23,760	
	Inventory Returns	240	
	Merchandise Inventory		24,000

(2b)

1. The critical event is the transfer of the significant risks and rewards of ownership from Li Xiu to Lewis Co. on December 29, 2017. FOB shipping point indicates that ownership of the goods transfers at the point of shipment.
2. Revenue will be recognized on December 29, 2017, for $12,500.
3.

Dec. 29	Accounts Receivable	12,500	
	Sales		12,500
29	Cost of Goods Sold	7,500	
	Merchandise Inventory		7,500

4. If Li Xiu cannot assess Lewis Co.'s ability to pay the amounts owing, criterion 4 of the revenue recognition criteria (probability of receiving payment) is not fulfilled because the probability of an increase in economic resources (cash payment) cannot be assessed. Revenue would be deferred and recognized on February 10, 2018, when cash collection takes place and criterion 4 is fulfilled. The amount would not change as it was collected in full.

Related exercise material: BE11–4, BE11–5, BE11–6, BE11–7, BE11–8, BE11–9, BE11–10, E11–4, E11–5, E11–7, and E11–8.

Action Plan
- Review the five-step model for revenue recognition under the contract-based approach.
- Review the criteria that must be met for revenue recognition under the earnings approach.

> Apply the foundational concepts, assumptions, and constraints of the conceptual framework to financial reporting situations.

Foundational Concepts, Assumptions, and Constraints

The conceptual framework contains, either directly or indirectly, some foundational concepts, assumptions, and constraints. Many of these were introduced in Chapter 1 and are described again below. Two additional concepts are introduced here: cost constraint and full disclosure. Recall that these concepts, assumptions, and constraints form the bedrock from which we are able to account for and report financial information in a useful manner. This bedrock is shown at the bottom of the conceptual framework pyramid.

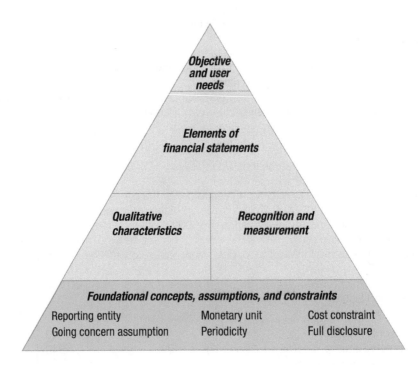

CONCEPTS AND ASSUMPTIONS

Reporting Entity Concept

Financial statements are prepared for a business or economic unit. This is referred to as the **reporting entity concept**. **This foundation concept requires that the accounting for a reporting entity's activities be kept separate and distinct from the accounting for the activities of its owner and all other reporting entities.** A reporting entity can be any organization or unit in society. You will recall that proprietorships', partnerships', and corporations' records of their business activities are kept separate from the personal records of their owners/shareholders. That is because proprietorships, partnerships, and corporations are considered reporting entities for financial reporting purposes.

A reporting entity could be one company or a collection of companies consolidated under common ownership. We will discuss consolidated companies in Chapter 16.

Going Concern Assumption

A key assumption, the going concern assumption, creates a foundation for the financial reporting process. The **going concern assumption assumes that the company will continue operating for the foreseeable future; that is, long enough to carry out its existing objectives and commitments.** Although there are many business failures, most companies continue operating for a long time.

This assumption has important implications for accounting. If a company is assumed to be a going concern, then financial statement users will find it useful for the company to report assets, such as buildings and equipment, at their cost minus accumulated depreciation (carrying amount). If the company is not a going concern, then the carrying amount will not be relevant. Instead, the financial statement user would want to know what amount can be recovered for existing assets. Furthermore, if the company is not a going concern, the classification of assets and liabilities as current or non-current would not matter. Labelling anything as non-current would be difficult to justify. For example, if a company intends to shut down operations and sell off all its assets, the assumption would not apply and GAAP could not be used to report the financial information. A different and more useful method would be to report information using some other appropriate measure, such as market value. If it *cannot* be assumed that the company is a going concern, this also needs to be explicitly stated in the financial statements.

Monetary Unit Concept

Even though it seems obvious that economic activity is reported in terms of the amount of money exchanged, there is a foundational concept that describes the basis of measurement for the collection, recording, and reporting of financial information. **The monetary unit concept means that money is the common denominator of economic activity.** In Canada, financial information is generally reported in Canadian dollars unless a Canadian company trades its shares on a U.S. stock exchange—in this case, the financial information would be reported in U.S. dollars. In the United States, financial information is reported in U.S. dollars; in Japan, in yen; and so on.

The monetary unit concept prevents the recognition of elements that cannot be quantified, such as employee morale, customer loyalty, or health of the owner.

Periodicity Concept

Users require relevant financial information; that is, the information must enhance or complete their understanding of a particular enterprise. In order for financial information to be relevant, users require it on a timely basis. The **periodicity concept** (also sometimes referred to as the time period concept) **guides businesses in dividing up their economic activities into distinct time periods.** The most common time periods are months, quarters, and years.

In Chapter 3, accrual basis accounting was introduced. Recall that accrual basis accounting requires that economic activities be recorded when they occur, not when the money is paid or received. Accrual accounting is closely related to the periodicity concept. The best way to provide relevant information to users is to divide up economic activities into time periods. In this way, the information gives a timely report of the economic performance of the business. In order to do this and give a complete picture, activities have to be recorded when they occur in a particular time period.

Full Disclosure Concept

Earlier in our discussion of faithful representation, we explained that information provided in the financial statements must be complete. This requires that **companies fully disclose circumstances and events that make a difference to financial statement users.** This is known as the **full disclosure** concept. It is important that investors be made aware of events that can affect a company's financial health.

Full disclosure is accomplished in the financial statements by the data (reported amounts) they contain and the accompanying notes. For example, a company will include a note that summarizes its significant accounting policies. The note discloses accounting methods used by the company when there are acceptable alternative choices. Corus's note on its significant accounting policies (Note 3 in Appendix A at the end of this textbook) discloses that "the consolidated financial statements have been prepared on a cost basis." The note further indicates that investments (which Corus refers to as "available-for-sale financial assets") are measured at fair value. These disclosures tell the user that the business mainly uses historical cost to measure the elements in the financial statements and that fair value is used for only certain elements. The information that is disclosed in the notes to the financial statements generally falls into three additional categories. The information can:

1. give supplementary detail or explanation (for example, a schedule of property, plant, and equipment);
2. explain unrecorded transactions (for example, contingencies, commitments, and subsequent events); or
3. supply new information (for example, information about future commitments).

CONSTRAINTS

The cost constraint is a pervasive constraint that ensures the value of the information provided is greater than the cost of providing it. That is, the benefits of financial reporting information should justify the costs. The discussion on qualitative characteristics introduced the requirement that financial information must be complete to be useful. To achieve completeness, accountants could record or disclose every financial event that occurs and every uncertainty that exists. However, providing this information increases reporting costs. The benefits of providing more information, in some cases, may be less than the costs.

In many cases, the IASB and the AcSB will apply this constraint when requiring companies to adopt a new accounting standard. The AcSB applied this constraint when it adopted IFRS for public companies and ASPE for private companies. Users of private companies' financial statements generally require less information than users of public companies' financial statements. The board recognized that the cost to private companies of providing financial statements prepared under IFRS was greater than the benefits. Consequently, the board developed ASPE, which is simpler and requires less disclosure than IFRS.

Recall that financial information should be relevant and faithfully represented in order to help users make decisions with confidence. However, it is not possible to ensure that general purpose financial statements provide all relevant information to all users. The costs of attempting to do so would outweigh the benefits to a small number of users. Note that the ASPE conceptual framework refers to this constraint as the benefit versus cost constraint.

ACCOUNTING IN ACTION
ALL ABOUT YOU INSIGHT

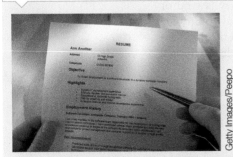

No doubt you have used a resumé to find a job. Your resumé is like a company's annual report, describing your recent accomplishments so others can evaluate your performance and try to predict how you will do in the future. Your resumé must be a faithful representation of your background, education, and experience. The temptation to overstate accomplishments is great, however—even at the highest levels of responsibility, as shown in the case of a former CEO of Yahoo, Scott Thompson. After just four months

at the company's helm, Yahoo announced that Thompson had decided to step down. Although the company did not state the reasons, it was reported that the decision was partly due to an activist hedge fund having publicized the fact that Thompson had misrepresented his education on his resumé. His biography in the company's annual report stated that he had a degree in accounting and computer science, but his degree is in accounting only. Yahoo's annual report is a legal document filed with the U.S. Securities and Exchange Commission, in which CEOs must swear that all information is truthful. Yahoo said the statement was an "inadvertent error" and hired a lawyer to investigate the statement.

Sources: Michael J. de la Merced and Evelyn M. Rusli, "Yahoo's Chief to Leave as Company Strikes Deal with Loeb," *New York Times*, May 13, 2012; Julianne Pepitone, "Yahoo Confirms CEO Is Out after Resume Scandal," CNNMoney, May 14, 2012; Amir Efrati and Joann S. Lublin, "Yahoo CEO's Downfall," *Wall Street Journal*, May 15, 2012.

 What may be the consequences to you if you misrepresent yourself on your resumé?

SUMMARY OF CONCEPTUAL FRAMEWORK

As we have seen, the conceptual framework starts with the objective of financial reporting and defines the elements of financial statements. It then describes the qualitative characteristics of useful information (fundamental and enhancing) along with recognition and measurement guidance. Finally, the foundational concepts, assumptions, and constraints provide the bedrock used to achieve the objective. The complete representation of the conceptual framework is summarized in Illustration 11-15.

▶ ILLUSTRATION **11-15**
Conceptual framework

LOOKING AHEAD

Throughout the textbook, we have referred to upcoming changes to accounting standards that the IASB continues to develop. Recall that accounting principles are affected by economic and political conditions, which change over time. As a result, accounting principles can and do change.

The new IFRS 15 *Revenue from Contracts with Customers* and the revised conceptual framework were two of the bigger changes happening as this textbook was being written. While IFRS 15 had been finalized, it would not take effect until January 1, 2018, and further changes may be required as the market begins to apply the standard. The revised conceptual framework was still in a draft form and, as mentioned, some of the ideas and concepts have been presented in this chapter where appropriate. The IASB was planning to issue the new framework in 2016. However, there are additional revisions that we have not incorporated because they had yet to be finalized at the time of writing. Below is a list of some of these revisions.

1. Measurement: description/terminology of measurement bases to be revised
2. Elements: revised definitions of elements
3. Reporting entity: additional guidance provided
4. Objective and qualitative characteristics: light revisions

Foundational Concepts

Presented below are two foundational concepts in financial reporting:

1. Going concern
2. Full disclosure

Identify the concept that applies to the following statements:

(a) _____ A company includes information in the financial statements about future payments required for long-term liabilities.
(b) _____ Assets and liabilities are classified as current or non-current.
(c) _____ Supplementary information is provided for property, plant, and equipment assets detailing historical cost, accumulated depreciation, and depreciation methods and rates.
(d) _____ Land is recorded at its cost.

Action Plan
- Review the application of the foundational assumption, going concern, and the full disclosure concept.

Solution

(a) 2.   (b) 1.   (c) 2.   (d) 1.

Related exercise material: BE11–11, BE11–12, BE11–13, BE11-14, E11-6, E11-9, E11-10, E11-11, and E11-12.

Comparing IFRS and ASPE

Key Differences	International Financial Reporting Standards (IFRS)	Accounting Standards for Private Enterprises (ASPE)
Conceptual framework	Phase one of the IASB and FASB joint project is finalized and adopted (objectives and qualitative characteristics) Remaining phases were still under development	Deferring adoption of the joint project phase one improvements until further progress has been made by the IASB and FASB on the conceptual framework
Constraint	Uses the term "cost constraint"	Uses the term "benefit versus cost constraint"
Definition of elements: gains and losses	Defined as being part of revenues and expenses	Separate definitions for revenues and gains and for expenses and losses
Qualitative characteristics	Identifies two fundamental characteristics: relevance and faithful representation	Identifies four principal characteristics: understandability, relevance, reliability, and comparability Faithful representation is a component of reliability
Prudence (conservatism)	Not recognized as a qualitative characteristic	Recognized as a qualitative characteristic

Demonstration Problem

Several independent financial reporting situations follow:

1. Young Company uses the contract-based approach and recognized sales revenue for a customer order of merchandise inventory that had not yet been shipped.
2. In preparing its financial statements, Casco Company left out information about its depreciation policy.
3. Kenton Company amortized its patent over 20 years even though it is estimated to provide benefit for only 5 years.
4. Taws Company, a private company reporting under ASPE, reported land that cost $50,000 at its fair value of $100,000.
5. Athwal Company used the cost model in its financial statements that were issued after the company had started liquidation procedures due to bankruptcy. The bankruptcy was not reported in the notes to the financial statements.

6. Yen Yeh Company capitalized the cost and recorded depreciation on its office wastepaper baskets.
7. Mayberry Company used a janitorial service in December to clean its offices. The company recorded the cost of the service when it paid the bill in the following February. Mayberry's year end is December 31.
8. Sims Industries uses the earnings approach and recognized revenue from sales when a customer paid in advance for an order that had not yet been delivered.

Instructions
(a) For each of the above situations, indicate the concept (qualitative characteristic, assumption, constraint, recognition criteria, or measurement) in the conceptual framework that has been violated. If there is more than one, list them.
(b) For each situation, provide a brief explanation of how the concept was violated.

SOLUTION TO DEMONSTRATION PROBLEM

(a) Violation	(b) Explanation
1. Revenue recognition criteria: contract-based approach	Control has not been transferred to the customer because the goods have not been shipped. Revenue should be recognized when the customer has legal title and possession of the goods, which is an indication that control has transferred.
2. Faithful representation: completeness comparability full disclosure	The company should fully disclose information that is relevant to the user. Users would require information on the depreciation policy to enhance comparability with other companies' financial statements. Understanding the depreciation policy may also help users make predictions about the company's future profitability.
3. Expense recognition: matching	The cost of the patent should be allocated to expense over the period for which the company will realize economic benefits.
4. Measurement: historical cost	The company must use the cost model for financial reporting because it follows ASPE. The land should be reported at cost.
5. Going concern assumption	If the company is not a going concern, assets should be reported at realizable value (fair value), not cost. There should be a note in the financial statements disclosing that the company is bankrupt.
6. Relevance: materiality	The carrying value of the wastepaper baskets is likely immaterial and therefore is not useful information to the user. Yen Yeh should expense the cost of the baskets.
7. Expense recognition	The company has a liability at December 31 for services used during December.
8. Revenue recognition criteria: earnings approach	Revenue cannot be recognized because performance is not complete, and therefore, Sims has not completed the earnings process.

ACTION PLAN

- Review the revenue recognition criteria for the sale of goods using the contract-based approach.
- Review the revenue recognition criteria for the sale of goods using the earnings approach.
- Review the qualitative characteristics.
- Review the expense recognition criteria.
- Review the measurement methods.
- Review the going concern assumption.

▶ Summary of Learning Objectives

1. **Explain the importance of having a conceptual framework of accounting, and list the key components.** The conceptual framework ensures that there is a consistent and coherent set of accounting standards. Key components of the conceptual framework are the: (1) objective of financial reporting; (2) elements of the financial statements; (3) qualitative characteristics; (4) recognition and measurement concepts; and (5) foundational concepts, assumptions, and constraints.

2. **Explain the objective of financial reporting, and define the elements of the financial statements.** The objective of financial reporting is to provide useful information for investors and creditors in making decisions in their capacity as capital providers. The elements are assets, liabilities, equity, revenue, and expense. Each element has a specific definition. The definitions provide important guidance on when an element should be recognized.

3. **Apply the fundamental and enhancing qualitative characteristics of the conceptual framework to financial reporting situations.** The fundamental qualitative characteristics are relevance and faithful representation. Financial information has relevance if it makes a difference in a decision. Materiality is an important component of relevance. An item is material when it is likely to influence the decision of a reasonably careful investor or creditor. Information is faithfully represented when it shows the economic reality and is complete, neutral, and free from material error.

   The enhancing qualitative characteristics are comparability, verifiability, timeliness, and understandability. Comparability enables users to identify the similarities and differences between companies. The consistent use of accounting policies from year to year is part of the comparability characteristic. Information is verifiable if two knowledgeable and independent people would generally agree that it faithfully represents the economic reality. Timeliness means that financial information is provided when it is still highly useful for decision-making. Understandability enables reasonably informed users to interpret and comprehend the meaning of the information provided in the financial statements.

4. **Apply the recognition and measurement criteria of the conceptual framework to financial reporting situations.**

General recognition criteria require that elements be recognized in the financial statements when it is probable that any economic benefit associated with the item will flow to or from the business and the item has a cost or value that can be measured or estimated with a reasonable amount of reliability. There are two approaches to revenue recognition: (1) contract-based and (2) earnings. The contract-based approach requires that revenue be recognized when promised goods or services are transferred and the amount reflects the consideration the business expects to receive. The earnings approach requires that revenue be recognized when the earnings process is complete, the risks and rewards of ownership have been transferred, and the amount can be reliably measured. Expenses are recognized when there is a decrease in an asset or increase in a liability, excluding transactions with owners, which result in a decrease in owners' equity. Four measurements used in accounting are (1) historical cost, (2) current cost, (3) realizable value, and (4) present value. Incorrect application of the basic recognition and measurement concepts can lead to material misstatements in the financial statements. Incorrect application can be due to error or intentional misstatement.

5. **Apply the foundational concepts, assumptions, and constraints of the conceptual framework to financial reporting situations.** The foundational concepts, assumptions, and constraints form the bedrock of accounting and are used to achieve the objective of financial reporting. The reporting entity concept requires that accounting for a reporting entity's activities be kept separate and distinct from the accounting for the activities of its owner and all other reporting entities. The going concern assumption assumes that the company will continue operating for the foreseeable future. The monetary unit concept means that money is the common denominator of economic activity. The periodicity concept guides businesses in dividing up their economic activities into distinct time periods. The cost constraint is a pervasive constraint that ensures the value of the information provided is greater than the cost of providing it. The full disclosure concept requires companies to fully disclose circumstances and events that make a difference to financial statement users.

▶ Glossary

Accrual basis of accounting The method of accounting where revenues are recorded in the period when the transaction occurs and not when cash is received or paid. (p. 592)

Comparability An enhancing qualitative characteristic that financial information has if it can be compared with the financial information of other companies because the companies all use the same accounting principles. (p. 589)

Complete The characteristic of financial information when it provides all information necessary to show the economic reality of the transactions. Completeness is part of the faithful representation fundamental qualitative characteristic of financial information. (p. 588)

Conceptual framework of accounting A coherent system of interrelated elements that guides the development and application of accounting principles: it includes the objective of financial reporting, elements of financial statements, qualitative characteristics of financial information, recognition and measurement criteria, and foundational concepts, assumptions and constraints. (p. 584)

Consistency   The use of the same accounting policies from year to year. Consistency is part of the comparability enhancing qualitative characteristic of financial information. (p. 589)

Contract   An agreement between two or more parties that creates enforceable rights and obligations. (p. 594)

Cost constraint   The constraint that the costs of obtaining and providing information should not be more than the benefits that are gained. (p. 608)

Current cost   A measurement method that measures an asset at the amount of cash or equivalent that would have to be paid if the same or an equivalent asset had to be purchased in the current period. This is sometimes referred to as "replacement cost." Liabilities measured at current cost reflect the amount required to settle an obligation currently. (p. 603)

Elements of financial statements   The basic categories in financial statements: assets, liabilities, equity, revenue, and expenses. (p. 586)

Expense recognition criteria   The criteria that state that expenses should be recognized when there is a decrease in an asset or increase in a liability, excluding transactions with owners that result in a decrease in owners' equity. (p. 602)

Faithful representation   A fundamental qualitative characteristic of financial information that shows the economic reality of a transaction and not just its legal form. (p. 588)

Full disclosure   The accounting concept that recognizes that financial statement information must be complete and requires the disclosure of circumstances and events that make a difference to financial statement users. (p. 607)

Going concern assumption   The assumption that the company will continue operating for the foreseeable future; that is, long enough to meet its current objectives and carry out its current commitments. (p. 607)

Historical cost   An accounting concept that states that assets should be recorded at their historical (original) cost. (p. 603)

Material error   An error in the financial information that could impact an investor's or creditor's decision. (p. 589)

Materiality   An important component of relevance in which an item is considered material if it is likely to influence the decision of a reasonably careful investor or creditor. (p. 588)

Neutral   The characteristic of financial information when it is free from bias that is intended to attain a predetermined result or to encourage a particular behaviour. Neutrality is part of the faithful representation fundamental qualitative characteristic of financial information. (p. 588)

Objective of financial reporting   The goal of providing useful information for investors and creditors in making decisions in their capacity as capital providers. (p. 585)

Performance obligation   In a contract with a customer, this is an obligation to provide goods or services to another party. (p. 594)

Present value   A measurement method that measures assets and liabilities at the present value of future cash inflows or outflows. (p. 603)

Prudence   Guidance expected to be included in the revised conceptual framework to exercise caution in situations of uncertainty. Prudence is closely related to neutrality. (p. 588)

Realizable value   A measurement method that measures assets at the amount of cash or equivalent that could currently be obtained by selling the asset in an orderly disposal. Liabilities measured at realizable value report the cash expected to be paid to satisfy the liabilities in the normal course of business. Realizable value also encompasses fair value. (p. 603)

Relevance   A fundamental qualitative characteristic that financial information has if it makes a difference in a decision. The information should have predictive and feedback value and be material. (p. 588)

Reporting entity concept   This foundation concept requires that the accounting for a reporting entity's activities be kept separate and distinct from the accounting for the activities of its owner and all other reporting entities. (p. 606)

Revenue recognition criteria   The criteria that state that revenue should be recognized when there is an increase in assets or decrease in liabilities from profit-generating activities. (p. 593)

Stand-alone selling price   The fair value of what a good or service would sell for on its own. (p. 594)

Stewardship   The ability of management to acquire and use a company's resources in the best possible way. (p. 586)

Timeliness   An enhancing qualitative characteristic that financial information has if it is provided when it is still highly useful to decision makers. (p. 589)

Transaction price   The amount a business expects to receive in exchange for the goods and services promised to the other party. (p. 594)

Understandability   An enhancing qualitative characteristic of financial information that enables reasonably informed users to interpret and comprehend the meaning of the information provided in the financial statements. Understandability is greater when the information is classified, characterized, and presented clearly and concisely. (p. 590)

Verifiability   An enhancing qualitative characteristic of financial information that assures users that the information shows the economic reality of the transaction. (p. 589)

▶ Self-Study Questions

Answers are at the end of the chapter.

(LO 1) K   1. Which of the following is not a reason for having a conceptual framework for financial reporting?
   (a) To provide specific rules for every situation in accounting
   (b) To ensure that existing standards and practices are clear and consistent

   (c) To provide guidance in responding to new issues and developing new standards
   (d) To increase financial statement users' understanding of and confidence in the financial statements

(LO 1) K   2. Which of the following is not a key component of the conceptual framework?
(a) Foundational concepts
(b) Specific recommendations for financial statement presentation
(c) Elements of the financial statements
(d) Recognition and measurement concepts

(LO 2) K   3. Which of the following is not information that is required to meet the objective of financial reporting?
(a) Information about the economic resources and claims on the economic resources
(b) Information about the company owner's personal economic resources
(c) Information about the changes in economic resources and in claims on the economic resources
(d) Information about the economic performance of the reporting entity

(LO 3) K   4. Under IFRS, these qualitative characteristics should be applied in which order?
(a) Relevance, faithful representation, and understandability
(b) Relevance, understandability, and faithful representation
(c) Faithful representation, relevance, and understandability
(d) Understandability, relevance, and faithful representation

(LO 3) K   5. Financial information faithfully represents an economic event when it is reported
(a) on a timely basis.
(b) on a comparable basis to other companies with the same economic events.
(c) on a consistent basis from year to year.
(d) in a way that portrays the economic reality and not just the legal form of the event.

(LO 4) K   6. Which of the following describes the core principle of the contract-based approach to revenue recognition?
(a) Definition of an element is met.
(b) The cost or value of the transaction can be reliably measured or estimated.
(c) Revenue recognized reflects the amount a company expects to collect.
(d) The earnings process is complete.

(LO 4) C   7. Which of the following best describes when an asset will be recognized?
(a) Cash is paid and it is relevant to users.
(b) Meets the definition of an asset, can be reliably measured, and is relevant to users.
(c) An item will benefit one accounting period, can be reliably measured, and is relevant to users.
(d) Future benefits will flow out of the business, the amount can be measured, and it is relevant to users.

(LO 4) C   8. Which of the following is not an appropriate time to recognize an expense?
(a) When cash is paid for the purchase of computer equipment
(b) When an expenditure is made that does not qualify for the recognition of an asset
(c) When the cost of computer equipment is allocated over its useful life
(d) When a previously recorded asset no longer has any future benefit

(LO 4) K   9. Which of the following statements about the historical cost basis of accounting is false?
(a) Cost is relevant for reporting certain assets in the balance sheet because the assets are intended for use in the business and are not going to be sold.
(b) Cost is relevant for reporting all assets on the balance sheet because it is measurable.
(c) Cost is measurable and verifiable.
(d) Cost is not relevant if the business is being liquidated.

(LO 5) K 10. Foundational concepts, assumptions, and constraints include which of the following?
(a) Going concern, cost, periodicity, revenue recognition
(b) Periodicity, monetary unit, going concern, full disclosure
(c) Periodicity, financial statement elements, monetary unit, going concern
(d) Cost, monetary unit, full disclosure, measurement

▶ Questions

(LO 1) C   1. Describe the conceptual framework of accounting and explain how it helps financial reporting.

(LO 2) K   2. (a) What is the main objective of financial reporting? (b) Although there are many users of financial statements, why does the objective identify the specific users?

(LO 2) C   3. (a) Describe the meaning of stewardship. (b) How does the objective of financial reporting help users assess stewardship?

(LO 2) K   4. List the differences between IFRS and ASPE related to the definition of financial statement elements.

(LO 3) K   5. Describe the two fundamental qualitative characteristics of financial information.

(LO 3) C   6. (a) Explain the concept of materiality. (b) How is materiality related to the qualitative characteristic of relevance?

(LO 3) K   7. Describe the four enhancing qualitative characteristics of financial information.

(LO 3) C   8. Mustafa Company purchased tools needed to perform services for a customer. The tools cost the company $500 and are expected to have a useful life of two years. The owner of the company has decided not to record the purchase at all because, as she states, "It is not a material purchase, so I don't have to include it in my accounting records." Explain to the owner what materiality means and how it is applied in financial reporting.

(LO 3) C   9. Identify the differences between the qualitative characteristics identified in the conceptual framework for IFRS and the conceptual framework for ASPE.

(LO 3) K   10. The qualitative characteristics should be applied in a certain order. Identify the order and explain why.

(LO 3,4) C 11. Explain how fair value measurements are related to the qualitative characteristic of relevance.

(LO 4) C   12. Why does the conceptual framework specifically address revenue recognition?

(LO 4) K   13. Describe the revenue recognition steps when using the contract-based approach.

(LO 4) K   14. What are the criteria that must be met for revenue to be recognized from the sale of goods using the earnings approach?

(LO 4) A   15. On January 16, 2017, JRT Company enters into a contract with Beowulf Industries to deliver office furniture. JRT manufactures the products and ships them to Beowulf on March 31, 2017. Beowulf takes possession of the goods on June 10, 2017. Assuming JRT Company has a March 31 year end and uses the contract-based approach to revenue recognition, on what date should JRT recognize revenue? Explain.

(LO 4) A   16. On March 24, 2017, Greenthumb Landscaping Services received $10,000 for five months of landscaping service to be provided from May through September 2017. Greenthumb's year end is April 30 and the company uses the earnings approach to revenue recognition. When should Greenthumb recognize revenue? Explain.

(LO 4) K   17. Refer to question 16 and assume that Greenthumb uses the contract-based approach to recognize revenue. What indications would Greenthumb look for to determine that control of the services has transferred to the customer?

(LO 4) C   18. A company has a return policy that allows customers to return goods within 30 days of purchase and receive a full refund. If the company follows the contract-based approach to revenue recognition, describe how the revenue will be recognized if (a) potential returns can be estimated, and (b) potential returns cannot be estimated.

(LO 4) A   19. Ingvar Company has the following expenditures: newspaper advertising for one month, $400; annual insurance premium, $5,000; salaries paid to employees for one month, $7,000; and an industrial oven used in operations, $15,000. The bookkeeper has recorded all of these as expenses in the same month they were paid. Do you agree with this treatment? Explain.

(LO 2,5) C   20. Xiaoping owns a Tim Horton's franchise, a Snap Fitness franchise, and a Best Western franchise. She records all accounting transactions in one set of accounting records along with all of her personal transactions. Xiaoping would like to borrow money from your bank and brings you her financial statements. Are the financial statements useful to you? Why or why not? Be sure to include in your answer any conceptual framework concepts that apply.

(LO 3,5) C   21. Explain how the cost constraint relates to the quality of completeness.

(LO 5) C   22. (a) Explain the going concern assumption. (b) How does the going concern assumption support the use of the cost basis of accounting and the classification of assets and liabilities as current and non-current?

(LO 5) C   23. Describe the cost constraint on financial reporting.

(LO 5) C   24. Relevance is accomplished in part by applying the periodicity concept. Do you agree with this statement? Explain.

▶ Brief Exercises

BE11–1 Indicate which of the following statements are true or false. (Write "T" or "F" beside each item.)

(a) _____ The conceptual framework includes recommendations on how to analyze financial statements.
(b) _____ The conceptual framework identifies the objective of financial reporting.
(c) _____ The conceptual framework is a temporary framework that provides guidance for accountants until standard setters can develop specific rules for every situation.
(d) _____ The conceptual framework defines assets, liabilities, owner's equity, revenue, and expenses.
(e) _____ The conceptual framework identifies qualitative characteristics of useful information.
(f) _____ The conceptual framework provides guidance for responding to new issues and developing new standards.

Identify items included in the conceptual framework.
(LO 1) K

BE11–2 Here are the basic elements of financial statements that we learned about in earlier chapters:

1. Assets   2. Liabilities   3. Equity   4. Revenues   5. Expenses

Each statement that follows is an important aspect of an element's definition. Match the elements with the definitions. *Note:* More than one number can be placed in a blank. Each number may be used more than once or not at all.

(a) __4__ Increases in assets or decreases in liabilities resulting from the main profit-generating activities of the business
(b) _____ Existing debts and obligations from past transactions
(c) __1__ Resources owned by a business

Identify elements of financial statements. (LO 2) K

(d) __1__ Goods or services used in the process of earning revenue
(e) _____ A residual claim on total assets after deducting liabilities
(f) _____ The capacity to provide future benefits to the business

Identify qualitative characteristics. (LO 3) K

BE11–3 The following selected items relate to the qualitative characteristics of useful information:

1. Comparability
2. Materiality
3. Neutrality
4. Timeliness
5. Faithful representation
6. Feedback value

7. Predictive value
8. Consistency
9. Understandability
10. Verifiability
11. Completeness

Match these qualitative characteristics to the following statements, using numbers 1 to 11.

(a) __4__ Financial information must be available to decision makers before the information loses its ability to influence their decisions.
(b) __6__ Financial information provides a basis to evaluate decisions made in the past.
(c) __3__ Financial information cannot be selected, prepared, or presented to favour one set of interested users over another.
(d) __5__ Financial information reports the economic substance of a transaction, not its legal form.
(e) __7__ Financial information helps reduce uncertainty about the future.
(f) __10__ Financial information must be provided in such a way that knowledgeable and independent people agree that it faithfully represents the economic reality of the transaction or event.
(g) __1__ Financial information about one company can be evaluated in relation to financial information from another company.
(h) __9__ Financial information is provided in a way that enables reasonably informed users to interpret and comprehend the meaning of the information provided in the financial statements.
(i) __8__ Financial information in a company is prepared using the same principles and methods year after year.
(j) __2__ Financial information that is insignificant and not likely to influence a decision does not need to be disclosed.
(k) __11__ Financial information includes all information necessary to show the economic reality of the transaction.

Determine revenue and expense recognition—earnings approach. (LO 4) AP

BE11–4 Howie, Price, and Liu operate an accounting firm. In March, their staff worked a total of 1,000 hours at an average billing rate of $250 per hour. They sent bills to clients in the month of March that totalled $150,000. They expect to bill the balance of their time in April. The firm's salary costs total $75,000 each month. How much revenue should the firm recognize in the month of March assuming the firm uses the earnings approach to revenue recognition? How much salaries expense should it recognize?

Determine revenue to be recognized—contract-based approach. (LO 4) AP

BE11–5 Mullen Manufacturing Ltd. sold $450,000 of merchandise on credit to customers in the month of September. During September, the company collected $250,000 cash from its customers. The company estimates that about 2% of the sales will be returned by customers. How much revenue should the company recognize for the month of September assuming Mullen uses the contract-based approach to revenue recognition?

Determine revenue and expense recognition—earnings approach. (LO 4) AP

BE11–6 Abbotsford Ltd., a sports equipment wholesaler, sold $350,000 of merchandise to a customer on November 14, 2017. The merchandise was shipped on November 29, 2017, FOB shipping point and was received by the customer on December 3, 2017. Full payment was received on November 30, 2017. The cost of the merchandise shipped was $200,000. Assuming Abbotsford Ltd. uses a perpetual inventory system and the earnings approach for revenue recognition, identify the critical event that will trigger revenue recognition. Prepare the journal entry to record revenue in November. What is the gross profit recognized in November?

Determine revenue recognition, collection uncertain—earnings approach. (LO 4) AP

BE11–7 During December, Willow Appliance Company sold appliances to Ragnar Company for $25,000. Willow is unable to determine Ragnar's ability to pay the amount owing. Ragnar pays the full amount due in February of the following year. Willow uses the earnings approach to revenue recognition. Identify the critical event that will trigger revenue recognition. Prepare the journal entry to record the shipment of goods to Ragnar. The goods cost Willow $19,000 and Willow uses a perpetual inventory system.

Determine revenue recognition using five-step model—contract-based approach. (LO 4) AP

BE11–8 Flin Flon Company enters into a contract on April 3, 2017, with Thompson Industries to supply 5,000 microprocessors at a price of $7 each. The microprocessors cost Flin Flon $3 each. The microprocessors will be delivered to Thompson on June 3, 2017. Flin Flon has a three-month return policy and estimates that 5% of the goods will be returned. Flin Flon is confident that Thompson will pay any amounts owing. The goods are delivered on June 3, 2017, and Thompson pays the amount owing on July 3, 2017. Using the revenue recognition model for the contract-based approach, identify the contract, the performance obligation(s), and the transaction price. On what date will Flin Flon recognize revenue? How much revenue will be recognized on this date?

BE11–9 Courtney Company reported total operating expenses of $55,000 on its adjusted trial balance for the year ended November 30, 2017. After the preliminary statements were prepared, the accountant became aware of the following situations:

1. The physical inventory count revealed that merchandise inventory costing $4,000 was damaged and needed to be scrapped.
2. Sales staff were owed $2,500 of sales commissions relating to November sales. The sales commissions were paid in December.

Calculate the total operating expenses that should be reported in the November 30, 2017, income statement.

Calculate expense. (LO 4) AP

BE11–10 The accountant for Ellery Co., a private company reporting under ASPE, recorded the following journal entries:

1. A building with a cost of $75,000 is reported at its fair value. The following entry was made:

Building	85,000	
Cash		75,000
Gain on Fair Value Adjustment of Building		10,000

2. Tickets for a musical production were sold in January and the production runs during March. The following entry was recorded in January.

Cash	5,000	
Admission Revenue		5,000

For each journal entry, indicate which recognition or measurement criterion has been violated. Explain.

Identify recognition and measurement violations. (LO 4) AP

BE11–11 A list of accounting concepts follows:

1. Revenue recognition
2. Matching
3. Full disclosure
4. Historical cost
5. Expense recognition
6. Realizable value

Match these concepts to the following statements, using numbers 1 to 6.

(a) _____ Hirjikaka Company reports information about pending lawsuits in the notes to its financial statements.
(b) _____ Sudin Company reduces prepaid insurance to reflect the insurance that has expired.
(c) _____ Joss Company records revenue when its performance obligation is satisfied.
(d) _____ Law Company records revenue as it completes services for its clients, not when the client pays cash.
(e) _____ Hilal Company reports its land at the price it paid for it, not at what it is now worth.
(f) _____ Rich Company reports accounts receivable less an estimated amount for uncollectible accounts.
(g) _____ Nickel Company depreciates its mining equipment using the units-of-production method.

Identify concepts in the conceptual framework. (LO 4, 5) C

BE11–12 For each of the following situations, indicate if the going concern assumption has been violated. (Write "Yes" or "No" beside each item.)

(a) _____ A company that is going to continue to operate in the foreseeable future reports all of its assets on the balance sheet at the amount expected to be collected if the assets were sold.
(b) _____ A company that is being liquidated reports current assets, non-current assets, current liabilities, and non-current liabilities on its balance sheet.
(c) _____ A company that is going to operate in the foreseeable future reports its merchandise inventory at cost when the net realizable value is higher than cost.

Identify violations of the going concern assumption. (LO 5) C

BE11–13 For each of the following independent situations, indicate whether or not the cost constraint should be applied. (Write "Yes" or "No" beside each situation.)

(a) _____ The manager of a privately held company believes the company should be using IFRS and not ASPE even though using IFRS will not provide any additional relevant information to users.
(b) _____ The CEO of a publicly traded company wants to include a detailed analysis of inventory purchases (not required by IFRS) in the financial statements because one shareholder has requested this information.
(c) _____ The manager of a privately held company discovers a minor error in the financial statements issued three years ago. The manager believes he must reissue all the financial statements with the error corrected. There are no external users of the financial statements with the exception of the Canada Revenue Agency.

Identify application of the cost constraint. (LO 5) C

Identify concepts in the conceptual framework. (LO 5) C

BE11–14   Here are some of the accounting concepts relating to the conceptual framework discussed in this chapter:

1. Going concern assumption
2. Reporting entity concept
3. Full disclosure
4. Monetary unit
5. Cost constraint
6. Periodicity

Identify by number the foundational concept, assumption, or constraint that describes each situation below. Do not use a number more than once.

(a) _____ is why land is reported as a non-current asset.
(b) _____ indicates that personal and business record keeping should be kept separate.
(c) _____ ensures that all relevant financial information is reported.
(d) _____ explains why Canadian companies report financial information in Canadian dollars.
(e) _____ explains how to divide up economic activities into distinct time periods.

▶ Exercises

Identify elements of the financial statements. (LO 2) C

E11–1   The following situations occurred for Mira Company.

1. Purchased a delivery truck to deliver goods to customers.
2. Experienced increased customer loyalty over the past two years.
3. Received the property tax invoice from the municipal government.
4. Saw its sales staff voted best in customer service by the industry.
5. Borrowed funds from DT Bank of Canada.

Instructions

For each of the above situations, indicate what element (if any) would be recorded in Mira's financial statements (asset, liability, equity, revenue, expense). If no element should be recorded, explain why.

Identify qualitative characteristics. (LO 3) C

E11–2   Presented below are selected qualitative characteristics of financial information.

1. Relevance
2. Neutrality
3. Verifiability
4. Timeliness
5. Faithful representation
6. Comparability
7. Understandability

Instructions

For each of the following situations, indicate which qualitative characteristic was violated.

(a) _____ Allen Ltd. reported its merchandise inventory at a net realizable value of $25,000. The company's auditors disagree with this value and estimated the net realizable value to be $20,000.
(b) _____ Owens Corporation does not issue its annual financial statements for the year ended December 31, 2016, until December 2017.
(c) _____ Silver Mining Ltd. is the only company in the mining industry that uses the straight-line method to depreciate its mining equipment.
(d) _____ Chapman Ltd. switches inventory cost formulas from average to FIFO and back to average in a three-year period.
(e) _____ Enco Ltd. intentionally recorded revenue in 2016 for sales made in 2017 to ensure that management would receive their bonuses, which were based on profits.
(f) _____ World Talk Corporation used terminology in its financial statements and notes to the financial statements that is not commonly used in financial reporting and did not provide explanations of the terminology.
(g) _____ Precise Ltd., a multinational drilling company, reported separately its paper, paper clips, and pens in the balance sheet rather than reporting a single line item for office supplies. Total office supplies were $5,000.
(h) _____ Community Health Foods Ltd. signed a legal agreement to finance the purchase of equipment. The agreement required annual payments of $15,000 for five years. The agreement referred to the payments as rental payments. The company records rent expense when the annual payments are made.

Identify components of relevance and faithful representation. (LO 3) AP

E11–3   The following are independent situations.

1. The results for the economic performance confirms Sam's predictions about the company.
2. The manager records the cost of a new building as an asset.
3. A company prepares notes to the financial statements to ensure all relevant information is given to users.
4. After studying the financial statements, Lori determines that the company's earnings will increase 1% to 2% over the next two years.

Instructions

For each of the above situations, indicate which component of qualitative characteristics applies (predictive value, feedback value, neutrality, free from material error, or completeness).

E11–4   Leo Legal Services enters into a written contract to provide one month of legal service to J & J Home Inspections. Leo tells J & J that he can do the work required for a fee of $5,000. At the end of the month, Leo concludes the work and sends appropriate reports to J & J along with an invoice for $5,000.

Identify contract components—contract-based approach. (LO 4) AP

Instructions

Using the five-step model for revenue recognition under the contract-based approach, answer the following questions:

(a) What kind of contract does Leo Legal Services have with the customer?
(b) What is Leo's performance obligation?
(c) What is the transaction price?
(d) Should the transaction price be allocated? If so, how?
(e) When should Leo recognize revenue from this contract?

E11–5   Below is a list of specific revenue recognition terms discussed in the chapter.

Identify terminology—revenue recognition. (LO 4) K

1. _____ Enforceable right to receive consideration   5. _____ Variable consideration
2. _____ Critical event   6. _____ Earnings process
3. _____ Performance obligation   7. _____ Control
4. _____ Allowance for sales returns   8. _____ Refund liability

Instructions

Beside each term above, indicate whether it is related to

(a) the contract-based approach or
(b) the earnings approach.

E11–6   Business transactions for Ellis Company and East Air follow:

Identify violation of conceptual framework and correct entries. (LO 4, 5) AN

1. Merchandise inventory worth $50,000 is acquired at a cost of $42,000 from a company going out of business. The following entry is made:

Merchandise Inventory	50,000	
Cash		42,000
Cost of Goods Sold		8,000

2. The president of Ellis Company, Evan Ellis, purchases a computer for personal use and charges it to his expense account. The following entry is made:

Office Expense	1,000	
Cash		1,000

3. Merchandise inventory with a cost of $280,000 is reported at its fair value of $255,000. The following entry is made:

Cost of Goods Sold	25,000	
Merchandise Inventory		25,000

4. A coffee machine costing $50 is being depreciated over five years. The following adjusting entry is made:

Depreciation Expense	10	
Accumulated Depreciation—Equipment		10

5. East Air sells an airline ticket for $650 in February for a trip scheduled in April. (Assume the earnings approach is used.) The following entry is made:

Cash	650	
Service Revenue		650

Instructions

In each of the situations above, identify the concept that has been violated, if any. If a journal entry is incorrect, give the correct entry.

E11–7   Over the winter months, Lush Lawns Co. pre-sells fertilizing and weed control lawn services to be performed from May through September, inclusive. If payment is made in full by March 31, a 5% discount is allowed. In March, 350 customers took advantage of the discount and purchased the summer lawn service package for $760 each. In April, 300 customers purchased the package for $800, and in May, 100 purchased it for the same price. For customers who pay after May 1, service starts in the month the customer makes the payment.

Determine amount of revenue to be recognized—earnings approach. (LO 4) C

Instructions

How much revenue should be recognized by the Lush Lawns Co. in each of the months of March, April, May, June, July, August, and September? Explain.

Determine amount of expenses to be recognized.
(LO 4) AP

E11–8   Consider the following events for Byer's Innovations Co. that occurred during 2017.

1. Leased factory space from Whole Properties Company for a one-year period starting November 1, 2017. Six months of rent at $3,000 per month was paid in advance.
2. Incurred $35,000 of research costs for new products. No new products were developed but management believes the research will lead to new products.
3. Used power and water during December for manufacturing. Byer's Innovations Co. will receive the bill in January 2018 and pay it in February 2018. Power and water costs totalling $55,000 have been recorded for the period from January 1 to November 30, 2017.
4. New packaging equipment costing $48,000 was installed during November 2017. The equipment was tested in December and will be used for packaging starting in January 2018. The equipment has an estimated useful life of four years and an estimated residual value of $4,000. The company uses straight-line depreciation.

Instructions

For each event, indicate the amount of expense that should be recognized in the 2017 income statement. (*Hint:* Use professional judgement to estimate expense where appropriate.)

Discuss financial reporting objective and cost constraint.
(LO 1, 5) C

E11–9   Susan began an office cleaning business by investing $5,000 cash and cleaning equipment. Her friend, Aristotelis, recommends that she prepare monthly financial statements.

Instructions

(a) Explain why Aristotelis recommends that she prepare monthly financial statements.
(b) Susan knows that, as a private company, she can choose to follow either ASPE or IFRS. Which one should she choose? Explain.

Apply the objective of financial reporting, reporting entity concept, and going concern assumption.
(LO 2, 4, 5) AP

E11–10   The Skate Stop is owned by Marc Bélanger. It sells in-line skates and accessories. It shares rented space with another company, Ride Snowboards. Ride Snowboards is owned by Marc's wife, Dominique Maltais, who was an Olympic bronze medallist in snowboarding. Ride Snowboards sells snowboards and related accessories. The market for in-line skates is growing and Marc wants to expand the amount of inventory The Skate Stop carries. He has asked his bank for a loan to finance the inventory. The bank manager has requested financial statements that are prepared using GAAP.

Instructions

(a) Explain how financial statements will help the bank manager decide whether to lend Marc money for inventory.
(b) Why does the bank manager want the statements to be prepared using GAAP?
(c) Should Marc include Ride Snowboards' financial information in The Skate Stop's financial statements? Explain.
(d) Should Marc report all of the store's assets at cost or what they could be sold for? Explain.

Identify concepts related to the conceptual framework.
(LO 4, 5) C

E11–11   Here are some concepts related to the conceptual framework discussed in this chapter:

1. Going concern assumption
2. Reporting entity concept
3. Completeness
4. Historical cost
5. Cost constraint
6. Materiality

Instructions

Identify by number the concept that describes each situation below. Do not use a number more than once.

(a) _____ Barb Denton runs her accounting practice out of her home. She separates her business records from her household accounts.
(b) _____ The cost to provide financial information should not be more than the benefits.
(c) _____ Significant accounting policies are reported in the notes to the financial statements.
(d) _____ Assets are not stated at their liquidation value. (*Note:* Do not use concept number 4, historical cost.)
(e) _____ Dollar amounts on financial statements are often rounded to the nearest thousand.
(f) _____ Land is recorded at its cost of $100,000 rather than at its market value of $150,000.

Identify violations of the concepts in the conceptual framework. (LO 4, 5) AP

E11–12   Several reporting situations follow:

1. Tercek Company recognizes revenue during the production cycle. The price of the product and how many items will be sold are not certain.
2. In preparing its financial statements, Seco Company left out information about its cost flow assumption for inventories.
3. Martinez Company amortizes patents over their legal life of 20 years instead of their economic life, which is usually about five years.
4. Ravine Hospital Supply Corporation reports only current assets and current liabilities on its balance sheet. Long-term assets and liabilities are reported as current. The company is unlikely to be liquidated.

5. Barton Company reports merchandise inventory on its balance sheet at its current market value of $100,000. The inventory has an original cost of $110,000.
6. Bonilla Company is in its third year of operations and has not yet issued financial statements.
7. Watts Company has merchandise inventory on hand that cost $400,000. Watts reports merchandise inventory on its balance sheet at its current market value of $425,000.
8. Steph Wolfson, president of the Download Music Company, bought a computer for her personal use. She paid for the computer with company funds and debited the computer account.
9. Sagoo Company decided not to implement a perpetual inventory system that would save $40,000 annually because the cost of the system was $100,000 and it was estimated to have a 10-year life.

Instructions

For each of the above, list what concept in the conceptual framework has been violated, if any.

▶ Problems: Set A

P11–1A The following financial statements were provided by Sumsong Electronics Company. The owner, Gillian Sumsong, is applying for a second loan from the bank to buy some new equipment. The bank manager has requested these financial statements before considering a new loan to the company. Gillian has asked you to look at the statements and provide feedback. The company uses a perpetual inventory system and the contract-based approach for revenue recognition. All sales are made with terms of n/30. Sumsong has a 60-day return policy.

Identify violations of the components of the conceptual framework.
(LO 1, 2, 3, 4, 5) AP

SUMSONG ELECTRONICS COMPANY
Balance Sheet
September 30, 2017

Current assets		
Cash	$500,000	
Accounts receivable	2,500	
Merchandise inventory	135,000	
Total current assets		$637,500
Property, plant, and equipment		75,000
Depreciation of property, plant, and equipment		75,000
Total assets		$787,500
Liabilities		
Accounts payable	$ 16,000	
Bank loan owing	160,000	
Total liabilities		$176,000
Equity		
G. Sumsong, capital		546,500
Sumsong Appliance Store, capital		65,000
Total owner's equity		611,500
		$787,500

SUMSONG ELECTRONICS COMPANY
Income Statement
For the year ended September 30, 2017

Sales	$175,000	
Sales—customer deposits	14,000	
Sales—orders to be filled	18,000	
Total sales		$207,000
Expenses		
G. Sumsong, personal credit card expense	45,000	
G. Sumsong, withdrawal expense	24,000	
Vehicle expense (purchased for deliveries)	60,000	
Total expenses		129,000
Net income		$ 78,000

Additional information provided:

1. The cash balance consists of $5,000 in the company chequing account and $495,000 in an investment that Sumsong Electronics made in the common shares of a new social networking company.
2. Property, plant, and equipment assets are being depreciated over 2 years even though they are expected to have a useful life of 10 years. Gillian considers depreciation a fund to purchase additional assets in the future and has the bookkeeper record it as an asset.
3. Merchandise inventory on hand has a realizable value of $25,000 and a cost of $29,000. Gillian does not adjust merchandise inventory on the balance sheet for any items sold.
4. The bank loan reported on the balance sheet represents a mortgage payable to the Bank of Toronto. The term of the mortgage is 15 years and payments of principal and interest are made monthly.
5. Gillian owns an appliance store in addition to the electronics store. The bookkeeper records some of the appliance store's transactions in the electronics store and credits the equity account Sumsong Appliance Store—Capital.
6. All the company's operating costs are paid by Gillian using her personal credit card so that she can accumulate travel points. The bookkeeper records all payments on the card as an expense to the company.

Instructions

Using the concepts in the conceptual framework covered in this chapter, answer the following questions:

(a) Are these statements useful to the bank manager? What information will the bank manager be looking for when Sumsong Electronics applies for a loan?
(b Are the assets, liabilities, revenues, and expenses recognized in the financial statements appropriate? If an element is incorrectly recognized, explain why.
(c) Has Sumsong followed the guidance for relevance and faithful representation? If not, what are the violations?
(d) Are there any revenue recognition problems that you can see? Are there any measurement problems? If so, how would these problems be corrected?
(e) Have the reporting entity and full disclosure concepts been followed? Explain.

TAKING IT FURTHER   Gillian has approached you with a proposition to invest in her company. Based on the financial statements provided, assess Gillian's stewardship of the company assuming she is the manager as well as the owner.

Identify objective of financial reporting, identifying elements, and revenue and expense recognition—earnings approach.
(LO 2, 3, 4) AP

P11–2A   Kamloops Company is a grocery wholesaler and is planning to expand its operations. The company has asked the bank for a loan to finance the expansion. Alphonzo, the company's manager, has prepared the preliminary financial statements. The preliminary financial statements for the year ended December 31, 2017, reported the following:

Current assets	$120,000
Current liabilities	80,000
Sales	560,000
Cost of goods sold	252,000
Total operating expenses	106,000

The bank has requested that Kamloops have an independent professional accountant review the statements. You have been asked to review the statements and during your review you have discovered the following:

1. Kamloops's supplier shipped $15,000 of merchandise inventory to Kamloops on December 31, 2017, FOB shipping point. Alphonzo indicated that he did not record the inventory for the year ended December 31, 2017, because it was not received until January 2, 2018.
2. Included in sales and accounts receivable was $8,400 for merchandise ordered by a customer that was packed and in the warehouse. The customer indicated that they might pick it up on January 10, 2018. The customer will pay for the merchandise within 30 days of pickup. The cost of the merchandise was $4,300 and was included in merchandise inventory because the merchandise was still in Kamloops's warehouse.
3. Kamloops offers its customers a full refund for merchandise returned within 15 days of purchase. Sales recorded from December 17 to December 31 were $26,000. Typically, about 5% of sales are returned. The returned goods are scrapped and not returned to merchandise inventory. Alphonzo said that customers had not returned any merchandise from the December 17 to December 31 sales by the company's year end. Any returns from these sales will be recorded in January when the merchandise is returned and the company knows the exact amount of the returns.
4. During the last week of December, the company had run a promotional campaign in the local newspaper. The cost of the campaign was $3,500. Alphonzo recorded it as a prepaid expense because he anticipates that January 2018 sales will be higher as a result of the campaign.

Instructions

(a) Explain how financial statements help the bank with its decision on whether or not to lend money to Kamloops.

(b) Explain why the bank has requested an independent review of the financial statements.

(c) Calculate the correct amounts for current assets, current liabilities, sales, cost of goods sold, and total operating expenses. Explain each of your corrections. Kamloops Company uses the earnings approach to recognize revenue.

TAKING IT FURTHER   Calculate the current ratio based on (a) the preliminary financial statements and (b) the corrected amounts. Is the current ratio based on the corrected amounts better or worse? Does there appear to be bias in the types of errors that were made? Explain.

P11–3A   Santa's Holiday Farm sells and delivers fir trees over the holiday season. The trees sell for $50 each and the farm also offers a removal service after the holiday season for $20. The trees cost $15 each. In November and December 2017, the farm offers customers a holiday package that costs $60 and includes both a fir tree and removal service. The trees will be removed on January 3, 2018. On December 2, 2017, Santa's Holiday Farm sells 200 holiday packages which are all delivered on the same day.

*Identify contract components and prepare journal entries— contract-based approach, multiple performance obligations.
(LO 4) AP*

Instructions

(a) Using the five-step model for revenue recognition under the contract-based approach, answer the following questions related to the holiday packages sold by Santa's Holiday Farm:

1. Is there a contract? If so, describe the contract.
2. What is Santa's Holiday Farm's performance obligation(s)?
3. What is the transaction price? 60 $
4. Is there a need to allocate the transaction price? Yes for the fir tree (50÷70)x60 / removal - (20÷70)x60
5. Has the performance obligation(s) been satisfied? If so, when? Yes, on Dec 31, 2017

(b) Prepare any journal entries required to record revenue. (Round to the nearest dollar.)

TAKING IT FURTHER   Stephen Forni is the manager of Santa's Holiday Farm. He has found the use of the contract-based approach to revenue recognition very challenging and does not understand why he cannot go back to the old way of doing it. Explain to Stephen why accounting standards change over time.

P11–4A   The following transactions took place in December 2017 for MegaMart. MegaMart uses the contract-based approach to revenue recognition and a perpetual inventory system. MegaMart estimates returns at 1% of sales.

*Identify elements of the financial statements— contract-based approach, revenue transactions.
(LO 2, 4) AP*

Dec. 4   Purchased a building for $200,000 by borrowing $160,000 from the bank and paying the rest in cash.
   10   Received an offer from a competitor to purchase the business for $400,000. unless you sell it
   15   Sold goods that cost $8,000 for $15,000 cash. Asset (15 000 cash) Revenue (sales), Expense (cost of goods sold)
   18   Ordered new office furniture that will be delivered in February 2018.
   20   Sold $18,000 of goods to TinyTown Toys, n/30. The goods cost MegaMart $10,000. There is no uncertainty about TinyTown's ability to pay the amount owing. Acc Rec, Exp (cost of), Rev (sales)
   24   Paid employee wages in the amount of $4,000. Exp (salaries exp) Asset (cash)
   31   Received a $1,200 invoice for electricity for the month of December. Acc pay, Exp (utilities
   31   Recorded depreciation on store equipment of $3,000. Asset (Accum. Dep - Eq), Exp (Dep Exp)

Instructions

For each of the above transactions, indicate what element(s) will be recognized (if any). If no element should be recognized, explain why.

TAKING IT FURTHER   Discuss the importance of having precisely defined elements for the financial statements.

P11–5A   Port Automotive Supply enters into a contract to supply Kelsee Electrocar Company with 300 automotive tires at a price of $40 per tire on August 4, 2017. The tires were delivered to Kelsee on September 18, 2017, FOB destination, and terms are n/30. No returns are expected and Kelsee does not offer a warranty on the tires because one is provided by the manufacturer. The cost of the tires to Port is $20 per tire. Port is unable to determine the collectibility of the amount from Kelsee because it is a new company, but Kelsee pays the amount in full on November 4, 2017.

*Identify revenue recognition criteria and prepare journal entries—earnings approach.
(LO 4) AP*

Instructions

(a) Using the revenue recognition criteria for the earnings approach, answer the following questions:

1. When is Port's performance complete? When do the risks and rewards of ownership of the tires transfer to Kelsee?
2. Does Port have any control over the goods or continuing involvement once the tires are delivered?
3. Can this transaction be measured reliably? If so, how much is the potential revenue?
4. Is it probable that there will be an increase in economic resources to Port?

5. Are the costs associated with the sale known? If so, how much are the costs?
6. What is the critical event that triggers revenue recognition?

(b) Prepare any journal entries required to recognize revenue on the appropriate dates.

TAKING IT FURTHER One of the criteria when using the earnings approach is to determine any costs associated with a sale. Cost of goods sold is one cost that is associated with the sale. What other costs might a business incur after a sale has been concluded?

Identify contract components and prepare journal entries—contract-based approach, right of return. (LO 4)

P11-6A Nicolet Publishers sells textbooks to universities across Canada. On July 10, 2017, Nicolet entered into a contract with Hinton University to supply 300 accounting textbooks at a price of $110 per book to be paid on September 25, 2017. The books cost Nicolet $80 each. Nicolet's return policy states that any unsold books can be returned within 90 days of delivery. The books were delivered on August 25, 2017. Nicolet estimates returns at 10% of sales. Hinton returns 10 books on September 15, 2017, and 20 books on September 30, 2017.

Instructions

(a) Identify the contract with the customer.
(b) Identify Nicolet's performance obligation.
(c) Determine the transaction price.
(d) On what date should revenue be recognized?
(e) Prepare all journal entries required by Nicolet to record the transactions with Hinton University.

TAKING IT FURTHER The contract-based approach requires revenue to be recognized at the amount a business expects to be entitled to. If Nicolet offers cash discounts for early payment, how might this affect its revenue recognition? (*Hint:* Significant cash discounts are a type of variable consideration.)

Identify concept or assumption violated and prepare entries. (LO 2, 3, 4, 5) AN

P11-7A Czyz and Ng are accountants at Kwick Kopy Printers. Kwick Kopy has not adopted the revaluation model for accounting for its property, plant, and equipment. The accountants are having disagreements over the following transactions during the fiscal year ended December 31, 2017:

1. Kwick Kopy bought equipment on January 1, 2017, for $80,000, including installation costs. The equipment has a useful life of five years. Kwick Kopy depreciates equipment using the double diminishing-balance method. "Since the equipment as installed in our system cannot be removed without considerable damage, it will have no resale value. It should not be depreciated but, instead, expensed immediately," Czyz argues.
2. Depreciation for the year was $43,000. Since the company's profit is expected to be low this year, Czyz suggests deferring depreciation to a year when there are higher profits.
3. Kwick Kopy purchased equipment at a fire sale for $36,000. The equipment would normally have cost $50,000. Czyz believes that the following entry should be made:

Equipment	50,000	
Cash		36,000
Gain on Fair Value Adjustment of Equipment		14,000

4. Czyz says that Kwick Kopy should carry its furnishings on the balance sheet at their liquidation value, which is $30,000 less than cost.
5. Kwick Kopy rented office space for one year, effective September 1, 2017. Six months of rent at $3,000 per month was paid in advance. Czyz believes that the following entry should be made on September 1:

Rent Expense	18,000	
Cash		18,000

6. Land that cost $41,000 was appraised at $60,000. Czyz suggests the following journal entry:

Land	19,000	
Gain on Fair Value Adjustment of Land		19,000

Ng disagrees with Czyz in each of the situations.

Instructions

(a) For each transaction, indicate why Ng disagrees. Support your answer with reference to the conceptual framework definition of elements, qualitative characteristics, assumption, constraint, recognition, and measurement criteria.
(b) Prepare the correct journal entry to record each transaction.

TAKING IT FURTHER Discuss the circumstances in which it is appropriate to record property, plant, and equipment at its liquidation value.

P11–8A   During the 2008 and 2009 global economic crisis, several large corporations in Canada and the United States could not meet their financial commitments and filed for bankruptcy protection. Bankruptcy protection gives companies time to reorganize their operations and financial commitments and to develop a comprehensive restructuring plan, which will allow them to continue to operate. While bankruptcy protection is in place, creditors are prevented from taking any action against the company.

Explain assumptions and concepts—going concern, full disclosure. (LO 5) AP

Instructions

(a) What is the potential effect on a company's financial statements if the company files for bankruptcy?

(b) Should companies under bankruptcy protection prepare their statements under the going concern assumption? Explain.

TAKING IT FURTHER   Describe the dilemma that a company's management faces in disclosing that the company may not be able to continue as a going concern.

▶ Problems: Set B

P11–1B   The following financial statements were provided by Zytel Communications Co. The owner, Daniel Zytel, is meeting with an investor who is interested in investing in the company. The investor has requested these financial statements before considering the investment. Daniel has asked you to look at the statements and provide feedback. Zytel uses the earnings approach for revenue recognition. All sales are made with terms of n/30.

Identify violations of the components of the conceptual framework. (LO 1, 2, 3, 4, 5)

ZYTEL COMMUNICATIONS CO.		
Balance Sheet		
March 31, 2017		
Current assets		
Cash	$ 15,000	
Accounts receivable	350,000	
Merchandise inventory	225,000	
Total current assets		$590,000
Property, plant, and equipment		85,000
Depreciation of property, plant, and equipment		85,000
Total assets		$760,000
Liabilities		
Accounts payable		$180,000
Equity		
D. Zytel, capital		485,000
Zytel Music Store, capital		95,000
Total owner's equity		580,000
Total liabilities and owner's equity		$760,000

ZYTEL COMMUNICATIONS CO.		
Income Statement		
For the year ended March 31, 2017		
Sales	$335,000	
Sales—customer deposits	10,000	
Sales—orders to be filled	35,000	
Total sales		$380,000
Expenses		
D. Zytel, personal credit card expense	65,000	
D. Zytel, withdrawal expense	100,000	
Building expense	75,000	
Total expenses		240,000
Net income		$140,000

Additional information provided:

1. The Accounts Receivable balance includes amounts owing from customers of $35,000 and the remaining amount represents an investment in the common shares of a speculative mining company. Daniel believes that he will collect about 95% of the receivables but will wait and see what happens.

2. Property, plant, and equipment assets are being depreciated over two years even though they are expected to have a useful life of five years. Daniel considers depreciation a fund to purchase additional assets in the future and has the bookkeeper record it as an asset.

3. Merchandise inventory on hand has a realizable value of $20,000 and a cost of $18,000. Zytel does not adjust merchandise inventory on the balance sheet for any amounts that are sold.

4. Accounts payable includes a bank loan from the Bank of Quebec. The term of the bank loan is 10 years and payments of principal and interest are made monthly.

5. Daniel owns a music store in addition to the communications business. The bookkeeper records some of the music store's transactions in the communications business and credits the equity account Zytel Music Store—Capital.

6. All the company's operating costs are paid by Daniel using his personal credit card so that he can accumulate travel points. The bookkeeper records all payments on the card as an expense to the company.

7. The building expense reflects the cost of an addition built for inventory storage.

Instructions

Using the concepts in the conceptual framework covered in this chapter, answer the following questions:

(a) Are these statements useful to the investor? What information will the investor be looking for when considering the investment?

(b) Determine if the assets, liabilities, revenues, and expenses recognized in the financial statements are appropriate. If an element is incorrectly recognized, explain why.

(c) Has Zytel followed the guidance for relevance and faithful representation? If not, what are the violations?

(d) Are there any revenue recognition problems that you can see? Are there any measurement problems? If so, how would these problems be corrected?

(e) Have the reporting entity and full disclosure concepts been followed? Explain.

TAKING IT FURTHER   Daniel has heard that property, plant, and equipment assets can be recorded at fair value instead of historical cost. Explain to Daniel how this might be advantageous to current and potential investors.

Identify objective of financial reporting, identifying elements, and revenue and expense recognition. (LO 2, 3, 4) AP

P11–2B   Eugene Company is a small private company that sells computers and provides consulting services. The owner of the company, Eugene, wants to expand and has asked you to become his business partner. Eugene has prepared financial statements for the year ended December 31, 2017. These financial statements reported the following:

Current assets	$ 90,000
Current liabilities	65,000
Net sales and consulting revenue	650,000
Cost of goods sold	475,000
Total operating expenses	106,000

You are trying to decide if you will invest in the business and you are reviewing the financial statements. During your review, you have discovered the following:

1. On December 1, 2017, Eugene signed a $24,000, one-year consulting contract with a new customer starting December 1. Eugene reported the $24,000 in sales and consulting revenue because the customer paid the full amount on December 1.

2. During 2017, Eugene started a new warranty program. Under this program, customers can buy a five-year extended warranty for $500 and 20 customers purchased the warranty. Eugene reported the warranty sales in sales and consulting revenue. No warranty service was provided in 2017.

3. Included in sales is $55,000 for computers that a customer had paid for but had not picked up from the company by December 31, 2017. The customer was picking up the computers on January 2. The cost of these computers is $35,000 and Eugene included this cost in merchandise inventory because the computers were still in the warehouse.

4. During the last week of December, the company ran a promotional campaign in the local newspaper. The cost of the campaign was $4,800. Eugene recorded it as a prepaid expense because he anticipates that January 2018 sales will be higher as a result of the campaign.

Instructions

(a) Explain how financial statements help you with your decision on whether or not to invest in the company.

(b) Calculate the correct amounts for current assets, current liabilities, sales and consulting revenue, cost of goods sold, and total operating expenses. Explain each of your corrections. Eugene uses the contract-based approach to revenue recognition.

TAKING IT FURTHER   Based on your review of the financial statements, would you invest in Eugene Company? Explain. What other information might help with your decision?

P11–3B   Brilliance Holiday Light Services offers commercial and residential lighting services for the holiday season. Brilliance charges a standard rate of $100 per hour. The company also offers a wide variety of holiday lights for purchase separately. In November and December 2017, Brilliance offers customers a holiday package consisting of a box of lights and one hour of service to hang the lights for a total price of $110. The lights in the package normally sell for $35 per box. On November 15, 2017, Brilliance sells 40 light packages. Customers receive the box of lights upon payment and arrange for service on December 5, 2017.

Identify contract components and prepare journal entries— revenue recognition contract-based approach, multiple performance obligations. (LO 4) AP

Instructions

(a) Using the five-step model for revenue recognition under the contract-based approach, answer the following questions related to the holiday packages sold by Brilliance Holiday Light Services:
 1. Is there a contract? If so, describe the contract.
 2. What is Brilliance's performance obligation(s)?
 3. What is the transaction price?
 4. Is there a need to allocate the transaction price?
 5. Has the performance obligation(s) been satisfied? If so, when?

(b) Prepare any journal entries required to record revenue on the appropriate dates. (Round to the nearest dollar.)

TAKING IT FURTHER   Brilliance is considering the addition of a 30-day warranty on the lights offered in its holiday package. What additional information would you require about the warranty before recognizing revenue? Would your answer to part (b) change? Explain.

P11–4B   The following transactions took place in October 2017 for Slim's Organic Food Store. Slim's uses the earnings approach to revenue recognition and a perpetual inventory system. Slim's estimates returns at 0.5% of sales.

Identify elements of the financial statements— earnings approach, revenue transactions. (LO 2, 4) AP

Oct. 4	Purchased a building for $175,000 by borrowing $100,000 from the bank and paying the rest in cash.
10	The owner of Slim's recently announced she was engaged to be married.
15	Sold goods for cash that cost $1,500 for $3,300.
18	Ordered new commercial refrigeration unit that will be delivered in January 2018.
20	Sold $2,000 of goods to TotWorld DayCare, n/30. The goods cost Slim's $1,250. There is no uncertainty about TotWorld's ability to pay the amount owing.
24	Paid employee wages in the amount of $1,500.
31	Received a $300 invoice for Internet and telephone service for the month of October.
31	Recorded depreciation on store equipment of $1,000.

Instructions

For each of the above transactions, indicate what element(s) will be recognized (if any). If no element should be recognized, explain why.

TAKING IT FURTHER   Accounting estimates are a critical part of accrual accounting. Discuss the process that an accountant should go through when making estimates. What would be the impact on the financial statements if the estimate made for returns is erroneous?

P11–5B   Crittenden Cellular enters into a contract to supply Joe's Country Corner Store with 10 smart phones at a price of $45 per phone on March 4, 2017. The phones will be delivered to Joe's on March 15, 2017, FOB destination and terms are n/30. No returns are expected and Crittenden does not offer a warranty on the phones because one is provided by the manufacturer. The cost of the phones to Crittenden is $30 per phone. Crittenden is unable to determine the collectibility of the amount from Joe's, but Joe's pays the amount in full on April 30, 2017.

Identify revenue recognition criteria and prepare journal entries—earnings approach. (LO 4) AP

Instructions

(a) Using the revenue recognition criteria for the earnings approach, answer the following questions:
 1. When is Crittenden's performance complete? When do the risks and rewards of ownership of the phones transfer to Joe's?
 2. Does Crittenden have any control over the goods or continuing involvement once the phones are delivered?
 3. Can this transaction be measured reliably? If so, how much is the potential revenue?
 4. Is it probable that there will be an increase in economic resources to Crittenden?
 5. Are the costs associated with the sale known? If so, how much are the costs?
 6. What is the critical event that triggers revenue recognition?

(b) Prepare any journal entries required to recognize revenue on the appropriate dates.

TAKING IT FURTHER   One of the criteria when using the earnings approach is to determine any costs associated with a sale. Cost of goods sold is one cost that is associated with the sale. What other costs might a business incur after a sale has been concluded?

Identify contract components and prepare journal entries—earnings approach, right of return. (LO 4)

P11-6B Dusky Designs makes and sells custom jewellery and accessories to retail stores throughout Canada. On April 6, 2017, Dusky entered into a contract with Tara's Boutique to supply 50 custom bracelets at a price of $85 each to be paid on June 30, 2017. The bracelets cost Dusky $25 to make and they were delivered to Tara's on June 1, 2017, FOB destination, n/30. Dusky Designs is a relatively new business and in order to promote the brand and encourage retailers to purchase goods, the company has a return policy that states that any unsold jewellery can be returned within 30 days of delivery for a full refund. Dusky estimates that 10% of the bracelets will be returned. Tara's returns five bracelets on June 20, 2017, and pays the remaining amount owing on June 30, 2017.

Instructions

(a) When is Dusky's performance complete? When do the risks and rewards of ownership of the bracelets transfer to Tara's Boutique?
(b) Can this transaction be measured reliably? If so, how much is the potential revenue?
(c) Is it probable that there will be an increase in economic resources to Dusky?
(d) Are the costs associated with the sale known? If so, how much are the costs?
(e) What is the critical event that triggers revenue recognition?
(f) Prepare all journal entries required by Dusky to record the transactions with Tara's Boutique.

TAKING IT FURTHER   If returns cannot be estimated, are the revenue recognition criteria met? Explain.

Identify elements, assumptions, constraints, and recognition and measurement criteria. (LO 2, 3, 4, 5) AN

P11-7B Jivraj and Juma are accountants at Desktop Computers. Desktop Computers has not adopted the revaluation model for accounting for its property, plant, and equipment. The accountants disagree over the following transactions that occurred during the fiscal year ended December 31, 2017:

1. Desktop purchased equipment for $60,000 at a going-out-of-business sale. The equipment was worth $75,000. Jivraj believes that the following entry should be made:

Equipment	75,000	
Cash		60,000
Gain on Fair Value Adjustment of Equipment		15,000

2. Land costing $90,000 was appraised at $215,000. Jivraj suggests the following journal entry:

Land	125,000	
Gain on Fair Value Adjustment of Land		125,000

3. Depreciation for the year was $18,000. Since the company's profit is expected to be lower this year, Jivraj suggests deferring depreciation to a year when there is a higher profit.
4. Desktop bought a custom-made piece of equipment for $54,000. This equipment has a useful life of six years. Desktop depreciates equipment using the straight-line method. "Since the equipment is custom-made, it will have no resale value," Jivraj argues. "So, instead of depreciating it, it should be expensed immediately." Jivraj suggests the following entry:

Miscellaneous Expense	54,000	
Cash		54,000

5. Jivraj suggests that the company building should be reported on the balance sheet at the lower of cost and fair value. Fair value is $15,000 less than cost, although it is expected to recover its value in the future.
6. On December 20, 2017, Desktop hired a marketing consultant to design and implement a marketing plan in 2018. The plan will be designed and implemented in three stages. The contract amount is $60,000, payable in three instalments in 2018 as each stage of the plan is completed. Jivraj argues that the contract must be recorded in 2017 because there is a signed contract. Jivraj suggests the following:

Advertising Expense	60,000	
Accounts Payable		60,000

Instructions

(a) For each transaction, indicate why Juma disagrees. Support your answer with reference to the conceptual framework (definition of elements, qualitative characteristics, assumptions, constraints, and recognition and measurement criteria).
(b) Prepare the correct journal entry to record each transaction.

TAKING IT FURTHER   How would your response in part (a) differ if Desktop adopted the revaluation model of accounting for its property, plant, and equipment?

Comment on application of accounting assumptions and concepts. (LO 5) AP

P11-8B EastJet Airlines reported a $1-million loss for the year ended December 31, 2015. After financial restructuring in 2015, EastJet continued to report losses, and it reported a $900,000 loss for the year ended December 31, 2016. In June 2017, EastJet was preparing to ask the Canadian government to allow it to make reduced cash contributions to one of the company's pension plans as well as to reduce other financial pressures. A spokesperson for the company stated, "It is of critical interest for the company to gain that relief now, thereby assuring its long-term solvency." Solvency refers to the company's ability to repay its long-term debt and survive over a long period of time.

Instructions

(a) EastJet's December 31, 2016, financial statements were prepared using the cost model. What assumption did EastJet make about its operations?

(b) With the uncertainty facing EastJet, should the company's financial statements be prepared under the assumption that it will continue to operate for the foreseeable future? Explain.

TAKING IT FURTHER Explain the implications of the full disclosure concept for EastJet's financial statements in these circumstances.

▶ Cumulative Coverage—Chapters 6 to 11

Johan Company and Nordlund Company are competing businesses. Both began operations six years ago and they are quite similar. The current balance sheet data for the two companies are as follows:

	Johan Company	Nordlund Company
Cash	$ 70,300	$ 48,400
Accounts receivable	309,700	312,500
Allowance for doubtful accounts	(13,600)	0
Merchandise inventory	463,900	520,200
Property, plant, and equipment	255,300	257,300
Accumulated depreciation	(112,650)	(189,850)
Total assets	$972,950	$948,550
Current liabilities	$440,200	$436,500
Non-current liabilities	78,000	80,000
Total liabilities	518,200	516,500
Owner's equity	454,750	432,050
Total liabilities and owner's equity	$972,950	$948,550

You have been hired as a consultant to do a review of the two companies. Your goal is to determine which one is in a stronger financial position. Your review of their financial statements quickly reveals that the two companies have not followed the same accounting policies. The differences, and your conclusions, are summarized below:

1. Johan Company has had good experience in estimating its uncollectible accounts. A review shows that the amount of its write offs each year has been quite close to the allowances the company provided.

 Nordlund Company has been somewhat slow to recognize its uncollectible accounts. Based on an aging analysis and review of its accounts receivable, it is estimated that $20,000 of its existing accounts will become uncollectible.

2. Johan Company has determined the cost of its merchandise inventory using the average inventory cost formula. The result is that its merchandise inventory appears on the balance sheet at an amount that is slightly below its current replacement cost. Based on a detailed physical examination of its merchandise on hand, the current replacement cost of its merchandise inventory is estimated at $477,000.

 Nordlund Company has used the FIFO inventory cost formula. The result is that its ending merchandise inventory appears on the balance sheet at an amount that is close to its current replacement cost.

3. Johan Company estimated a useful life of 12 years and a residual value of $30,000 for its items of property, plant, and equipment, and has been depreciating them on a straight-line basis. Nordlund Company has the same type of property, plant, and equipment. However, it estimated a useful life of 10 years and a residual value of $10,000. It has been depreciating its property, plant, and equipment using the double diminishing-balance method.

 Based on engineering studies of these types of property, plant, and equipment, you conclude that Nordlund's estimates and method for calculating depreciation are more appropriate.

Instructions

(a) Where would you find the above information on the two companies' accounting policies? Be specific about what information would be available and where you would find it.

(b) Using similar accounting policies for both companies, revise the balance sheets presented above.

(c) Has preparing the revised statements in part (b) improved the quality of the financial information for the two companies? If so, how?

CHAPTER 11: BROADENING YOUR PERSPECTIVE

▶ Financial Reporting and Analysis

Financial Reporting Problem

BYP11–1 Refer to the notes to the consolidated financial statements for **Corus Entertainment Inc.** in Appendix A at the end of the textbook.

Instructions

(a) Note 3, Basis of Presentation, states that the financial statements have been prepared on a [historical] cost basis except for derivative financial instruments and available-for-sale financial assets, which are measured at fair value. Corus's available-for-sale financial assets are short-term investments in marketable securities classified as current assets. Why does Corus report these investments at fair value?

(b) Note 3, Revenue Recognition, describes Corus's revenue recognition policy. When does Corus recognize revenue for advertising and subscriptions? These statements are prepared using the earnings approach to revenue recognition. What revenue recognition criteria must be met for this type of revenue?

(c) Note 27, Commitments, Contingencies and Guarantees, discloses that Corus has purchase commitments for future program and film expenditures of approximately $61.7 million as well as $97,000 for future television script productions. Do you think this additional disclosure was necessary? Explain why or why not, referring to the appropriate concepts or items from the conceptual framework of accounting in your answer.

(d) Corus's independent auditors' report is provided in Appendix A with the company's financial statements. What is the purpose of an independent audit? What opinion did Corus's auditors provide in the auditors' report.

Interpreting Financial Statements

BYP11–2 **McCain Foods Limited** is a large multinational private company with $7 billion in sales. It produces both frozen and non-frozen food products and makes one third of the frozen French fries produced worldwide. It has manufacturing operations in 18 countries, sales operations in over 160 countries, and employs more than 17,000 people. Most private companies in Canada have chosen to follow ASPE; however, some private companies like McCain have chosen to follow IFRS. "We believe that we are exactly the type of company for whom IFRS was developed," McCain told the IASB in a letter of comment responding to the IASB's preliminary views on financial statement presentation.

Instructions

(a) Other than the owners of McCain, who might be the users of McCain's financial statements?

(b) McCain has numerous subsidiaries located throughout the globe. How would this type of multinational structure motivate McCain to follow IFRS?

(c) What are the benefits to the users of its financial statements of McCain reporting under IFRS?

▶ Critical Thinking

Collaborative Learning Activity

Note to instructor: Additional instructions and material for this group activity can be found on the Instructor Resource Site and in *WileyPLUS*.

BYP11–3 In this group activity, you will be given a set of financial statements and a list of items that might need correcting. You will be required to (a) decide if an adjusting journal entry is required, (b) justify your decision by referring to the conceptual framework (including revenue and expense recognition criteria), and (c) calculate profit. Your decisions may have an impact on the annual bonuses that senior management members hope to receive.

Communication Activity

BYP11–4 Junk Grrlz (Junk) is a wholesale distributor of goods. Junk purchases goods that are not selling from manufacturers and other wholesalers and sells them to discount retail outlets. You are a professional accountant and are preparing Junk's financial statements for the year ended September 30, 2017. The company had $300,000 of real animal fur coats in merchandise inventory that were not selling. Junk has not had an order for real fur coats for over a year. The president is reluctant to write off the inventory and consequently signed a sales agreement with Cheap But Good (Cheap). Cheap agreed to buy the coats for $350,000 and could return any coats that it had not sold by December 31, 2017. In addition, Cheap was not required to pay Junk for the coats until December 31, 2017. The coats were shipped to and received by Cheap on September 29, 2017.

Instructions

Write a memo to the president of Junk Grrlz answering the following questions:

(a) Assuming returns cannot be estimated and Junk uses the earnings approach, when should revenue be recognized on the fur coats sold to Cheap But Good? Explain.

(b) How should the fur coats be reported in Junk's financial statements for the year ended September 30, 2017? Explain.

"All About You" Activity

BYP11–5 In the "All About You" feature, you learned about the importance of your personal resumé being a faithful representation of your personal background, education, and experience.

To apply this concept further, assume that you are applying for a car loan. The loan application requires that you prepare two reports: (1) a projected cash budget and (2) information about your assets and liabilities. The information in the loan application will be used to determine if the bank manager will approve the loan or not.

Instructions

(a) Why would a bank manager ask you to complete a projected cash budget and provide information about your assets and liabilities in order to decide whether or not to approve your loan? What is the bank manager trying to determine about you?

(b) Describe the qualitative characteristics that the information you provide to the bank manager should have in order for this information to be useful to the bank manager.

(c) The cash budget will be primarily based on future cash inflows and outflows. How might a bank manager verify the reasonableness of the cash budget?

(d) What might be the consequences to you if the bank manager determines the information provided is misleading?

 *Santé Smoothie Saga*

(**Note:** This is a continuation of the Santé Smoothie Saga from Chapters 1 through 10.)

BYP11–6   Natalie's high school friend, Sasha Petrolinski, has been operating a microbrewery for approximately 10 months, which he calls Blazing Skies Brew. Natalie and Sasha usually meet once a month to catch up and discuss problems they have encountered while operating their respective businesses. Sasha wishes to borrow from his bank so he can purchase a new state-of-the-art distillery unit. He recognizes that the bank will be evaluating his financial statements.

Sasha has recently negotiated a one-year contract with Libations Bar to provide 150 cases of craft beer every week. Libations Bar, upon receipt of a monthly invoice, will send Sasha a cheque by the 15th of the following month. Sasha has decided that, because he has signed this contract, he is able to record the total contract price that will be earned over the next 12 months as revenue in his financial statements.

When Sasha negotiated the contract with Libations Bar, he purchased additional brewing supplies to meet the increased demand for his craft beer. He has decided that he will not record the purchase of these supplies until the invoice is due, which is in about 30 days. He argues that the amount to be paid for the purchase of brewing supplies is relatively small and the amount won't really make much of a difference to the bank when it decides whether to lend him the money.

Sasha assures Natalie that this is the right way to account for this revenue and the purchase of additional supplies. He is sure that the bank will lend him the money that he needs to purchase the new distillery unit.

Natalie is confused and comes to you with the following questions:

1. Is Sasha accounting for the contract revenue correctly? (Assume that Sasha uses the contract-based approach to revenue recognition.)

2. Is Sasha accounting for the purchase of the brewing supplies correctly?

3. What other information will the bank be considering when deciding whether or not to extend the loan to Sasha?

4. Do you think that Sasha's income statement will be representationally faithful and provide relevant information to the bank?

Instructions

(a) Answer Natalie's questions.

(b) How should Sasha be recording this revenue? Why?

(c) How should Sasha be recording the purchase of brewing supplies? Why?

(d) How could Sasha ensure that the bank is aware of the contractual arrangement with Libations Bar when it reads his financial statements?

ANSWERS TO CHAPTER QUESTIONS

ANSWERS TO ACCOUNTING IN ACTION INSIGHT QUESTIONS

Ethics Insight, p. 604

Q: Accountants are often required to make estimates when preparing financial statements. What is the difference between what the Crown argued happened at Nortel and what we would normally expect an accountant to do when estimating accruals for adjusting journal entries?

A: When an accountant makes estimates in the financial statements, these estimates should be made using professional judgement and the best information available at the time to arrive at a reasonable estimate. Differences between these types of estimates and actual amounts are considered to be part of the accounting process. In the case of Nortel, the executives were accused of— but found not guilty of—not using professional judgement to arrive at the best estimate but intentionally misstating the accruals in the financial statements for their personal benefit.

All About You Insight, p. 608

Q: What may be the consequences to you if you misrepresent yourself on your resumé?

A: If it is determined that you have misrepresented yourself on your resumé, your credibility will be damaged. If your employer determines that you misrepresented yourself, you may lose your job, or at the very least your employer may always question your trustworthiness. You may also find yourself in a job for which you are not qualified and therefore your reputation will be damaged because of your inability to perform to the level required. In addition, it may be difficult for you to get a good reference from your employer when you apply for jobs in the future.

ANSWERS TO SELF-STUDY QUESTIONS

1. a   2. b   3. b   4. a   5. d   6. c   7. b   8. a   9. b   10. b

12 ACCOUNTING FOR PARTNERSHIPS

CHAPTER PREVIEW It is not surprising that most accountants use the partnership form of organization to start their accounting practice. Most realize that partnerships provide the opportunity to combine expertise and leverage resources. In this chapter, we will discuss why the partnership form of organization is often chosen. We will also explain the major issues in accounting for partnerships.

FEATURE STORY ▶ PARTNERING FOR SUCCESS

TORONTO, Ont.—If you become a professional accountant, you'll have lots of career options. One possibility is to work for a public accounting firm, which offers services to individuals and businesses. Many accounting firms—even the biggest, globally known ones—are organized as partnerships. That means that the owners contribute capital to run the business and share in the profits as partners.

While you would likely begin your accounting career as an employee, you might launch your own firm one day. What form of ownership should it take? Some interesting numbers from CPA Canada might help with that decision. Its survey of members conducted in mid-2015 found that among members who owned accounting firms, those who were sole proprietors earned an average of $136,000 a year, while those who were partners in an accounting firm earned an average of $276,000 a year.

CPA Canada didn't guess as to why there was such a difference in the earnings of a sole proprietor and a partner. One possibility is that a partnership can offer a wider range of its partners' expertise to clients and therefore charge more for their services. Another possibility is that the larger the firm, the greater the opportunity to land larger, possibly multinational, well-paying clients.

On the other hand, being a sole proprietor can bring rewards greater than financial ones. You would have sole decision-making authority to run the business the way you want and be proud of its success. You can also work for as long as you want. An issue in some partnership agreements with professional firms such as accounting and law firms is a mandatory retirement clause, which some partners have been fighting in the Canadian courts. The good news for young accountants is that partners at accounting firms are retiring in large numbers, paving the way for the next generation of partners.

If you earn a CPA designation, what are the odds that you'll be a business owner? They're pretty good. The CPA Canada survey found that 1 in 10 respondents owned a business—either as a sole proprietor or as a partner. Most of these businesses were accounting firms, but some were other types of business. Even if you don't end up owning a business, a CPA designation pays off. The survey found that members who were not business owners earned an average of $141,000 in total compensation, which includes base salary and bonuses. No matter what field you end up working in, an accounting background is an excellent springboard to a rewarding future.

Sources: "2015 CPA Profession Compensation Study Report," CPA Canada, fall 2015; "2016 Salary Guide: Accounting & Finance," Robert Half, 2015; Jeff Gray, "Lawyers Eye Top Court's Ruling on Forced Retirement for Partners," *The Globe and Mail*, May 21, 2014.

Multi-bits/Getty Images

The chapter is organized as follows:

1 Describe the characteristics of the partnership form of business organization.

Partnership Form of Organization
- Characteristics of partnerships
- Advantages and disadvantages of partnerships
- Partnership agreement

DO IT 1
Partnership organization

2 Account for the formation of a partnership.

Basic Partnership Accounting
- Forming a partnership

DO IT 2
Recording partnership investment

3 Allocate and record profit or loss to partners.

- Dividing partnership profit or loss

DO IT 3
Division of profit

4 Prepare partnership financial statements.

- Partnership financial statements

DO IT 4
Statement of partners' equity

5 Account for the admission of a partner.

Admission and Withdrawal of a Partner
- Admission of a partner

DO IT 5
Recording the admission of a partner

6 Account for the withdrawal of a partner.

- Withdrawal of a partner

DO IT 6
Recording the withdrawal of a partner

7 Account for the liquidation of a partnership.

Liquidation of a Partnership
- No capital deficiency
- Capital deficiency

DO IT 7
Recording the dissolution of a partnership

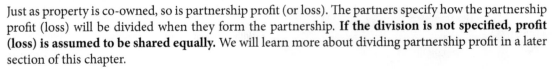

LEARNING OBJECTIVE   **1**   Describe the characteristics of the partnership form of business organization.

Partnership Form of Organization

All provinces in Canada have a partnership act that sets out the basic rules for forming and operating partnerships. These acts define a **partnership** as a relationship between people who do business with the intention of making a profit. This does not necessarily mean that there must be a profit—just that profit is the objective. Partnerships are common in professions such as accounting, advertising, law, and medicine. Professional partnerships can vary in size from two partners to thousands.

CHARACTERISTICS OF PARTNERSHIPS

The main characteristics of the partnership form of business organization are as follows:

Association of Individuals

indeed/Getty Images

The association of two or more individuals in a partnership can be based on an act as simple as a handshake. However, it is much better to have a legal, written agreement that outlines the rights and obligations of the partners. Partners who do not have a written agreement may face difficulties later.

A partnership is a legal entity. For instance, property (land, buildings, and equipment) can be owned in the name of the partnership. The firm can sue or be sued. A partnership is also an accounting entity for financial reporting purposes. Thus, the personal assets, liabilities, and transactions of the partners are kept separate from the accounting records of the partnership, just as they are in a proprietorship.

The profit of a partnership is not taxed as a separate entity. A partnership must file an information tax return that reports the partnership's profit and each partner's share of that profit. Each partner must then report his or her share of the partnership profit on their personal income tax returns. The partner's profit is taxed at his or her personal income tax rate, regardless of the amount of money the partner withdraws from the partnership during the year.

Co-ownership of Property

Jan Stromme/Getty Images

Partnership assets are owned jointly by the partners. If the partnership is dissolved, an asset does not legally return to the partner who originally contributed it. The assets are normally sold and the partners share any gain or loss from the sale according to their profit and loss ratios. After partnership liabilities are paid, each partner then has a claim on any cash that remains: the claim is equal to the balance in the partner's capital account.

Similarly, if, in doing business, a partner invests a building in the partnership that is valued at $100,000 and the building is later sold at a gain of $20,000, that partner does not receive the entire gain. The gain becomes part of the partnership profit, which is shared among the partners, as described in the next section.

Division of Profit

Just as property is co-owned, so is partnership profit (or loss). The partners specify how the partnership profit (loss) will be divided when they form the partnership. **If the division is not specified, profit (loss) is assumed to be shared equally.** We will learn more about dividing partnership profit in a later section of this chapter.

Limited Life

A partnership does not have an unlimited life. Any change in ownership ends the existing partnership. There is a **partnership dissolution** whenever a partner withdraws or a new partner is admitted. When a partnership is dissolved, this does not necessarily mean that the business ends. If the continuing partners agree, operations can continue without any interruption by forming a new partnership.

Mutual Agency

Mutual agency means that the action of any partner is binding on all other partners. If one partner enters into an agreement, provided the act looks appropriate for the partnership, all partners are then bound to that agreement. For example, a partner of an accounting firm who purchases a building that is suitable for the business creates a binding contract in the name of the partnership. On the other hand, if a partner in a law firm decides to buy a snowmobile for the partnership, the act would not be binding on the partnership, because the purchase is unrelated to the business.

Unlimited Liability

Each partner is jointly and severally (individually) liable for all partnership liabilities. If one partner incurs a liability, the other partners are also responsible for it. For repayment, creditors first have claims on the partnership assets. If there are not enough partnership assets to repay the amounts owing, creditors can make a claim against partners' personal assets. Because each partner is responsible for all the debts of the partnership, each partner is said to have unlimited liability.

Jacob Wackerhausen/
iStockphoto

Unlimited liability and mutual agency can combine for disastrous results. An unethical or incompetent partner can commit the partnership to a deal that eventually bankrupts the partnership. The creditors may then be able to claim the partners' personal assets—the assets of all the partners, not just those of the partner who made the bad deal. Consequently, an individual must be extremely cautious in choosing a partner.

Because of concerns about unlimited liability, there are now special forms of partnership organization that modify liability. These include limited partnerships and limited liability partnerships, discussed in the next two sections.

Limited Partnerships (LP). In a **limited partnership**, or "LP," one or more of the partners have unlimited liability. This type of partner is called a general partner. A general partner normally contributes work and experience to the partnership and is authorized to manage and represent the partnership. The general partner's liability for the partnership's debts is unlimited.

Getty Images/Oxford

The other partners have limited liability for the partnership's debts. This type of partner is called a limited partner. Limited partners normally give the partnership cash or assets, but not services. The amount of debt that the limited partner is liable for in the partnership is limited to the amount of capital that he or she contributed to the partnership. In other words, a limited partner's personal assets cannot be sold to repay any partnership debt that is more than the amount that he or she contributed to the partnership.

A limited partnership is identified in its name with the words "Limited Partnership" or the abbreviation "LP." Limited partnerships are normally used by businesses that offer income tax shelters for investors, such as real estate investment trusts, rental properties, and sports ventures.

Limited Liability Partnerships (LLP). Most professionals, such as lawyers, doctors, and accountants, form a **limited liability partnership** or "LLP."

A limited liability partnership is designed to protect innocent partners from the acts of other partners that result in lawsuits against the partnership. That is, partners in an LLP continue to have unlimited liability for their own negligence but have limited liability for other partners' negligence. In addition to being liable for their own actions, partners are also liable for the actions of employees whom they directly supervise and control.

ADVANTAGES AND DISADVANTAGES OF PARTNERSHIPS

Why do people choose partnerships?

One major advantage of a partnership is to combine the skills and resources of two or more individuals. In addition, partnerships are easily formed and face fewer government regulations and restrictions than a corporation. Also, decisions can be made quickly on important matters that affect the firm. This is also true in a proprietorship, but not in a corporation, where some decisions have to be approved by the board of directors.

Partnerships also have some disadvantages: mutual agency, limited life, and unlimited liability in general partnerships. Unlimited liability is particularly troublesome. Many individuals fear they may lose not only their initial investment but also their personal assets if those assets are needed to pay partnership creditors. As a result, partnerships often have difficulty getting large amounts of investment capital. That is one reason why the largest businesses in Canada are corporations, not partnerships.

The advantages and disadvantages of the general partnership form of business organization are summarized below.

Advantages	Disadvantages
• Combines skills and resources of two or more individuals • Is easily formed • Has fewer government regulations and restrictions than corporations • Allows for easier decision-making	Has the following aspects: • Mutual agency • Limited life • Unlimited liability

ACCOUNTING IN ACTION
ACROSS THE ORGANIZATION

Debbi Smirnoff/Getty Images

What should you do when you and your business partner disagree to the point where you are no longer on speaking terms? Given how heated business situations can get, this is not an unusual occurrence.

Unfortunately, in many instances the partners do everything they can to undermine each other, eventually destroying the business. In some cases, people even steal from the partnership because they either feel that they "deserve it" or they assume that the other partners are stealing from them.

It would be much better to follow the example of Jennifer Appel and her partner. They found that, after opening a successful bakery and writing a cookbook, they couldn't agree on how the business should be run. The other partner bought out Ms. Appel's share of the business. Ms. Appel went on to start her own style of bakery, which she ultimately franchised.

Source: Paulette Thomas, "As Partnership Sours, Parting Is Sweet," *Wall Street Journal*, July 6, 2004, p. A20.

Q How can partnership conflicts be minimized and more easily resolved?

PARTNERSHIP AGREEMENT

ETHICS NOTE
A well-developed partnership agreement specifies in clear and concise language the process by which the partners will resolve ethical and legal problems. This issue is especially significant when the partnership experiences financial distress.

Ideally, when two or more individuals agree to organize a partnership, their agreement should be expressed as a written contract. Called a **partnership agreement**, this contract contains such basic information as the name and main location of the firm, the purpose of the business, and the date of inception. In addition, relationships among the partners must be specified, such as:

1. The names and capital contributions of partners
2. The rights and duties of partners
3. The basis for sharing profit or loss
4. Provisions for a withdrawal of assets
5. Procedures for submitting disputes to arbitration
6. Procedures for the withdrawal, or addition, of a partner
7. The rights and duties of surviving partners if a partner dies
8. Procedures for the liquidation of the partnership

The importance of a written contract cannot be overemphasized. A partnership agreement is crucial. If there is no partnership agreement, the provisions of the partnership act will apply, and they may not be what the partners want. For example, as previously discussed, profits and losses are shared equally in the absence of an agreement. The partnership agreement should be written with care so that it considers all possible situations, contingencies, and future disagreements between the partners.

Basic Partnership Accounting

We now turn to the basic accounting for partnerships. Accounting for a partnership is very similar to accounting for a proprietorship. Just as most proprietorships will choose to use Accounting Standards for Private Enterprises (ASPE), many partnerships are private and will also choose to follow these accounting standards. On the other hand, limited partnerships are often public enterprises and these partnerships will follow International Financial Reporting Standards (IFRS). In addition, some large professional partnerships are international and these partnerships must also follow IFRS.

There are three accounting issues where there are differences between partnerships and proprietorships: formation of a partnership, dividing the partnership profit or loss, and preparing partnership financial statements. There are no significant differences in the accounting for these issues between partnerships following ASPE or IFRS. We will examine each of these in the following sections.

LEARNING OBJECTIVE 2   **Account for the formation of a partnership.**

FORMING A PARTNERSHIP

When a partnership is formed, each partner may contribute assets. Each partner's initial investment must be recorded in the partnership records. **These investments should be recorded at the assets' fair value at the date of their transfer to the partnership.** The values used must be agreed to by all of the partners.

To illustrate, assume that M. Gan and K. Sin combine their proprietorships on January 2 to start a partnership named Interactive Software. Gan and Sin each have the following assets before forming the partnership:

	M. Gan		K. Sin	
	Book Value	**Fair Value**	**Book Value**	**Fair Value**
Cash	$ 8,000	$ 8,000	$ 9,000	$ 9,000
Accounts receivable			4,000	4,000
Allowance for doubtful accounts			(700)	(1,000)
Equipment	5,000	4,000		
Accumulated depreciation	(2,000)			
	$11,000	$12,000	$12,300	$12,000

The entries to record the investments in the partnership are:

A	=	L	+	OE
+8,000				+12,000
+4,000				

↑ Cash flows: +8,000

A	=	L	+	OE
+9,000				+12,000
+4,000				
−1,000				

↑ Cash flows: +9,000

Investment of M. Gan

Jan. 2	Cash	8,000	
	Equipment	4,000	
	M. Gan, Capital		12,000
	To record investment of Gan.		

Investment of K. Sin

2	Cash	9,000	
	Accounts Receivable	4,000	
	Allowance for Doubtful Accounts		1,000
	K. Sin, Capital		12,000
	To record investment of Sin.		

Helpful hint The fair value of the noncash assets at the date of acquisition becomes the cost of these assets to the partnership. The fair value is what the assets would have cost if they had been purchased at that time.

Note that neither the original cost of Gan's equipment ($5,000) nor its accumulated depreciation ($2,000) is recorded by the partnership. Instead, the equipment is recorded at its fair value of $4,000. Because the equipment has not yet been used by the partnership, there is no accumulated depreciation.

In contrast, Sin's gross claims on customers ($4,000) are carried into the partnership. The allowance for doubtful accounts is adjusted to $1,000 to arrive at a net realizable value of $3,000. A partnership may start with an allowance for doubtful accounts, because it will continue to track and collect existing accounts receivable and some of these are expected to be uncollectible. In addition, this maintains the control and subsidiary relationship between Accounts Receivable and the accounts receivable subsidiary ledger that we learned about in Chapter 8.

After the partnership has been formed, the accounting for transactions is similar to the accounting for any other type of business organization. For example, all transactions with outside parties, such as the performance of services and payment for them, should be recorded in the same way for a partnership as for a proprietorship.

BEFORE YOU GO ON...DO IT **2**   **Recording Partnership Investment**

On June 1, Eric Brown and Erik Black decide to organize a partnership, E&E Painting. Eric Brown contributes equipment with a cost of $5,000 and $2,000 of accumulated depreciation. Erik Black contributes accounts receivable of $1,200. Eric and Erik agree that the equipment has a fair value of $2,500 and the accounts receivable have a net realizable value of $1,000. Erik Black will also contribute the amount of cash required to make his investment equal to Eric Brown's. (a) How much cash must Erik Black contribute? (b) Prepare the journal entries to record their investments in the partnership.

Action Plan

- Use fair values for the assets invested in the partnership.
- Each partner's equity is equal to the fair value of the net assets he invests in the partnership.

Solution

(a)
Fair value of equipment contributed by Eric Brown	$2,500
Less: fair value of accounts receivable contributed by Erik Black	1,000
Cash investment required from Erik Black	$1,500

(continued)

LEARNING OBJECTIVE **3** ▶ **Allocate and record profit or loss to partners.**

DIVIDING PARTNERSHIP PROFIT OR LOSS

Partners are not employees of the partnership; they are its owners. If a partner works for the partnership, it is to earn profit, not a salary. Thus, like a proprietorship, when a partner withdraws assets from the business these amounts are called drawings. Because these withdrawals decrease a partner's equity, they are not expenses reflected on the income statement. Partnership withdrawals are tracked separately in a drawings account for each partner.

To illustrate, assume that the partners of Interactive Software, M. Gan and K. Sin, had cash drawings of $8,000 and $6,000, respectively, for the year ended December 31, 2017. The journal entries (shown in summary format for the year) to record the partners' drawings are:

Dec. 31	M. Gan, Drawings	8,000	
	Cash		8,000
	Gan's withdrawal of cash for personal use.		
31	K. Sin, Drawings	6,000	
	Cash		6,000
	Sin's withdrawal of cash for personal use.		

A	=	L	+	OE
−8,000				−8,000

↓ Cash flows: −8,000

A	=	L	+	OE
−6,000				−6,000

↓ Cash flows: −6,000

Each partner's share of the partnership's profit or loss is determined according to the partnership's profit and loss ratio as determined in the partnership agreement. The profit and loss ratio can be a simple ratio or a more complicated calculation to recognize the different contributions of service and capital by each partner. **If the profit and loss ratio is not specified in the partnership agreement, profit and losses are shared equally among the partners.**

Sometimes a partnership agreement will refer to salary and interest allowances. Such allowances are not expenses or distributions of cash or other assets. Salary and interest allowances are used as a means to divide any profits or losses among partners. In a partnership, as with other companies, salary expense is the cost of services performed by employees. Likewise, interest expense is the cost of borrowing from creditors. As owners, **partners are neither employees nor creditors**.

The only relationship between salary allowances and cash withdrawals is that under some partnership agreements, partners are allowed to make monthly cash withdrawals based on their salary allowance. But in such cases, as with all withdrawals, the withdrawals are debited to each partner's drawings account, not to salary expense.

Alternative terminology The profit and loss ratio is sometimes called the *profit ratio*, or the *income and loss ratio*.

Getty Images/Jade

Susan and Erin operate a spa as partners and share profits and losses equally. Their business has been more successful than they expected and is operating profitably. Erin works hard to maximize profits. She schedules appointments from 8 a.m. to 6 p.m. daily and she even works weekends. Susan schedules her appointments from 9 a.m. to 5 p.m. and does not work weekends. Susan regularly makes much larger withdrawals of cash than Erin does, but tells Erin not to worry. "I never make a withdrawal without you knowing about it," she says to Erin, "so it's properly recorded in my drawings account and charged against my capital at the end of the year." To date, Susan's withdrawals are twice as much as Erin's.

Q In what ways are Susan's actions unethical? What provisions could be put in the partnership agreement so that the differences in Susan's and Erin's work and withdrawal habits are no longer unfair to Erin?

Profit and Loss Ratios

Helpful hint It is often easier to work with fractions or percentages than proportions when allocating profit or loss. When converting to a fraction, determine the denominator for the fractions by adding the proportions, then use the appropriate proportion to determine each partner's fraction. For example, 2:1 converts to $^2/_3$ and $^1/_3$; 3:5 converts to $^3/_8$ and $^5/_8$; and for three partners using 3:2:1, these proportions convert to $^3/_6$, $^2/_6$, and $^1/_6$.

As previously stated, since partners work to earn profits, profits (and losses) are allocated among the partners, ideally in a way that fairly reflects each partner's capital investment and service to the partnership. There are many ways of allocating the partnership profits. Partners may share profit and loss equally, or the partnership agreement may specify a more complex basis for sharing profit or loss. The following are typical **profit and loss ratios**:

1. **A fixed ratio**, expressed as a proportion (2:1), a percentage (67% and 33%), or a fraction (⅔ and ⅓). A fixed ratio is easy to use, and it may be a fair basis in some circumstances. For example, assume that Hughes and Samford are partners. Each contributes the same amount of capital, but Hughes expects to work full-time in the partnership, while Samford expects to work only half-time. Accordingly, the partners agree to a fixed ratio of two thirds to Hughes and one third to Samford.
2. **A ratio based either on capital balances** at the beginning or end of the year, or on average capital balances during the year. This may be the right choice when the funds invested in the partnership are the critical factor. Capital balances may also be fair when a manager is hired to run the business and the partners do not plan to take an active role in daily operations.
3. **Salary and interest allowances to partners and the remainder in a fixed ratio**. This is discussed in more detail in the section below.

Salaries, Interest, and Remainder in a Fixed Ratio

When a partnership agreement specifies profits are to be allocated based on salary and/or interest allowances, these allowances must be allocated first. Then any remaining profit is divided according to a fixed ratio. This is true even if the salary and/or interest allowances are more than profit. **It is also true even if the partnership has suffered a loss for the year.** The same basic method of dividing (or allocating) profit or loss is used if there is only a salary allowance, or if there is only an interest allowance, or if both are used. In the illustration that follows, we will use a profit and loss ratio that includes both salary and interest allowances before allocating the remainder.

Helpful hint The total of the amounts allocated to each partner must equal the profit or loss.

Assume that Sylvie King and Ray Lee are partners in the Kingslee Partnership. The partnership agreement specifies (1) salary allowances of $8,400 for King and $6,000 for Lee, (2) interest allowances of 5% on capital balances at the beginning of the year, and (3) the remainder to be allocated equally. Capital balances on January 1, 2017, were King $28,000 and Lee $24,000. In 2017, partnership profit is $22,000. The division of profit for the year is shown in Illustration 12-2.

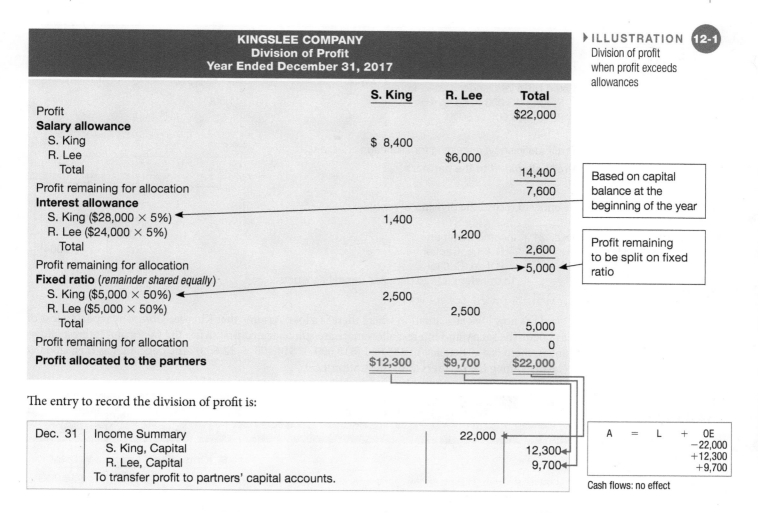

▶ILLUSTRATION 12-1
Division of profit
when profit exceeds
allowances

KINGSLEE COMPANY
Division of Profit
Year Ended December 31, 2017

	S. King	R. Lee	Total
Profit			$22,000
Salary allowance			
S. King	$ 8,400		
R. Lee		$6,000	
Total			14,400
Profit remaining for allocation			7,600
Interest allowance			
S. King ($28,000 × 5%)	1,400		
R. Lee ($24,000 × 5%)		1,200	
Total			2,600
Profit remaining for allocation			5,000
Fixed ratio (*remainder shared equally*)			
S. King ($5,000 × 50%)	2,500		
R. Lee ($5,000 × 50%)		2,500	
Total			5,000
Profit remaining for allocation			0
Profit allocated to the partners	$12,300	$9,700	$22,000

Based on capital balance at the beginning of the year

Profit remaining to be split on fixed ratio

The entry to record the division of profit is:

Dec. 31	Income Summary	22,000	
	S. King, Capital		12,300
	R. Lee, Capital		9,700
	To transfer profit to partners' capital accounts.		

```
A   =   L   +    OE
                -22,000
                +12,300
                +9,700
```
Cash flows: no effect

Note in the above example that the salary allowances are allocated first, followed by the interest allowances. Any **remaining** balance is paid out equally. Remember, this allocation does not reflect salaries for the year but rather the agreed-upon allocation of partnership profits. Also note, a partner's share of profit or loss is recognized through closing entries. This will be reviewed in more detail in the following section.

Let's now look at a situation where the salary and interest allowances are greater than profit. Assume that Kingslee Company reports profit of $14,000. In this case, the salary and interest allowances create a deficiency of $3,000 ($14,000 − $14,400 − $2,600). This deficiency is divided equally among the partners as in Illustration 12-2.

▶ILLUSTRATION 12-2
Division of profit when
allowances exceed profit

KINGSLEE COMPANY
Division of Profit
Year Ended December 31, 2017

	S. King	R. Lee	Total
Profit			$14,000
Salary allowance			
S. King	$8,400		
R. Lee		$6,000	
Total			14,400
Profit (deficiency) remaining for allocation			(400)
Interest allowance			
S. King ($28,000 × 5%)	1,400		
R. Lee ($24,000 × 5%)		1,200	
Total			2,600

	S. King	R. Lee	Total
Profit (deficiency) remaining for allocation			(3,000)
Fixed **ratio** (*remainder shared equally*)			
S. King ($3,000 × 50%)	(1,500)		
R. Lee ($3,000 × 50%)		(1,500)	
Total			(3,000)
Profit (deficiency) remaining for allocation			0
Profit allocated to the partners	$8,300	$5,700	$14,000

Balance of loss to be split on fixed ratio

The entry to record the division of profit is:

A	=	L	+	OE
−14,000				
+8,300				
+5,700				

Cash flows: no effect

Dec. 31	Income Summary	14,000	
	S. King, Capital		8,300
	R. Lee, Capital		5,700
	To transfer profit to partners' capital accounts.		

Let's now look at a situation where there is a loss. Assume that Kingslee Company reports a loss of $18,000. The salary and interest allowances are still allocated first. After the salary and interest allowances, there is a deficiency of $35,000 ($18,000 + $14,400 + $2,600). The deficiency is then divided equally among the partners as in Illustration 12-3.

▶ ILLUSTRATION 12-3
Division of loss

KINGSLEE COMPANY
Division of Loss
Year Ended December 31, 2017

	S. King	R. Lee	Total
Loss			$(18,000)
Salary allowance			
S. King	$ 8,400		
R. Lee		$6,000	
Total			14,400
Deficiency remaining for allocation			(32,400)
Interest allowance			
S. King ($28,000 × 5%)	1,400		
R. Lee ($24,000 × 5%)		1,200	
Total			2,600
Deficiency remaining for allocation			(35,000)
Fixed ratio (*remainder shared equally*)			
S. King ($35,000 × 50%)	(17,500)		
R. Lee ($35,000 × 50%)		(17,500)	
Total			(35,000)
Loss remaining for allocation			0
Loss allocated to the partners	$(7,700)	$(10,300)	$(18,000)

The salary and interest allowances are calculated first, as in the previous examples, whether the partnership reports a profit or a loss. Any remaining excess or deficiency is then allocated to the partners.

The journal entry to record the division of the loss would be as follows:

A	=	L	+	OE
−7,700				
−10,300				
+18,000				

Cash flows: no effect

Dec. 31	S. King, Capital	7,700	
	R. Lee, Capital	10,300	
	Income Summary		18,000
	To transfer loss to partners' capital accounts.		

As previously noted, a partner's share of profit or loss is recognized in the accounts through closing entries. In the following section, we will first review closing entries and then illustrate closing entries when profit and loss is shared equally.

Closing Entries

As in a proprietorship, there are four entries to prepare closing entries for a partnership. The entries are:

1. Debit each revenue account for its balance and credit Income Summary for total revenues.
2. Debit Income Summary for total expenses and credit each expense account for its balance.
3. Debit Income Summary for its balance (which should equal the profit amount) and credit each partner's capital account for his or her share of profit. Conversely, credit Income Summary and debit each partner's capital account for his or her share of a loss.
4. Debit each partner's capital account for the balance in that partner's drawings account, and credit each partner's drawings account for the same amount.

The first two entries are the same as in a proprietorship, as shown in Chapter 4, and are not shown in this chapter. The last two entries are different from closing entries in a proprietorship because (1) it is necessary to divide profit (or loss) among the partners, and (2) there are two or more owners' capital and drawings accounts.

To illustrate the last two closing entries, we will assume that Interactive Software has a profit of $32,000 for the year and that the partners, M. Gan and K. Sin, share profit and loss equally. Recall that drawings for the year were $8,000 for Gan and $6,000 for Sin. The closing entries on December 31 are as follows:

Helpful hint Recall from Chapter 4 the four steps to the closing process: **R-E-I-D.**

1. **Revenue** accounts are closed to the Income Summary account.
2. **Expense** accounts are closed to the Income Summary account.
3. **Income** Summary account is closed to the partnership capital accounts.
4. **Drawings** is closed to the partnership capital accounts.

Dec. 31	Income Summary	32,000	
	M. Gan, Capital ($32,000 × 50%)		16,000
	K. Sin, Capital ($32,000 × 50%)		16,000
	To close profit to capital accounts.		
31	M. Gan, Capital	8,000	
	K. Sin, Capital	6,000	
	M. Gan, Drawings		8,000
	K. Sin, Drawings		6,000
	To close drawings accounts to capital accounts.		

A	=	L	+	OE
				−32,000
				+16,000
				+16,000

Cash flows: no effect

A	=	L	+	OE
				−8,000
				−6,000
				+8,000
				+6,000

Cash flows: no effect

Recall from the previous section that both Gan and Sin had made investments in the partnership of $12,000 at the beginning of the year. After posting the closing entries, Gan has a capital balance of $20,000 and Sin has a capital balance of $22,000 as shown below:

M. Gan, Capital					K. Sin, Capital				
Dec. 31 Clos.	8,000	Jan. 2		12,000	Dec. 31 Clos.	6,000	Jan. 2		12,000
		Dec. 31 Clos.		16,000			Dec. 31 Clos.		16,000
		Dec. 31 Bal.		20,000			Dec. 31 Bal.		22,000

M. Gan, Drawings					K. Sin, Drawings				
Dec. 31		8,000	Dec. 31 Clos.	8,000	Dec. 31		6,000	Dec. 31 Clos.	6,000
Dec. 31 Bal.		0			Dec. 31 Bal.		0		

As in a proprietorship, the partners' capital accounts are permanent accounts, and their drawings accounts are temporary accounts.

BEFORE YOU GO ON...DO IT   **3**   Division of Profit

LeMay Company reports profit of $72,000 for the year ended May 31, 2017. The partnership agreement specifies (1) salary allowances of $30,000 for L. Leblanc and $24,000 for R. May, (2) an interest allowance of 4% based on average capital account balances, and (3) sharing any remainder on a 60:40 basis (60% to Leblanc, 40% to May). Average capital account balances for the year were $40,000 for Leblanc and $30,000 for May. (a) Prepare a schedule dividing the profit between the two partners. (b) Prepare the closing entry for profit.

Action Plan

- First allocate the salary allowances and the interest allowances.
- Then apply the partners' fixed ratios to divide the remaining profit or the deficiency.
- In the closing entry, distribute profit or loss among the partners' capital accounts according to the profit and loss ratio.

Solution

(a)

	L. Leblanc	R. May	Total
LEMAY COMPANY			
Division of Profit			
Year Ended May 31, 2017			
Profit			$72,000
Salary allowance			
L. Leblanc	$30,000		
R. May		$24,000	
Total			54,000
Profit remaining for allocation			18,000
Interest allowance			
L. Leblanc ($40,000 × 4%)	1,600		
R. May ($30,000 × 4%)		1,200	
Total			2,800
Profit remaining for allocation			15,200
Fixed ratio (*remainder shared 60:40*)			
L. Leblanc (60% × $15,200)	9,120		
R. May (40% × $15,200)		6,080	
Total			15,200
Profit remaining for allocation			0
Profit allocated to the partners	$40,720	$31,280	$72,000

(b)

May 31	Income Summary	72,000	
	L. Leblanc, Capital		40,720
	R. May, Capital		31,280
	To close profit to partners' capital accounts.		

Related exercise material: BE12–4, BE12–5, BE12–6, BE12–7, BE12–8, BE12–9, E12–3, and E12–4.

LEARNING OBJECTIVE   **4**   Prepare partnership financial statements.

PARTNERSHIP FINANCIAL STATEMENTS

The financial statements of a partnership are very similar to those of a proprietorship. The differences are due to the additional owners involved in a partnership.

The income statement for a partnership is identical to the income statement for a proprietorship. The division of the partnership profit or loss is not an additional financial statement. It is simply a schedule that shows how the profit or loss was allocated to the partners. It is often disclosed as a separate schedule or in a note to the statement.

The statement of equity for a partnership is called the **statement of partners' equity**. Its function is to explain the changes in each partner's capital account and in total partnership capital during the year. As in a proprietorship, changes in capital may result from three causes: additional investments by owners, drawings, and each partner's share of the profit or loss.

The statement of partners' equity for Kingslee Company is shown in Illustration 12-4. It is based on the division of $22,000 of profit in Illustration 12-1. The statement includes assumed data for the investments and drawings.

KINGSLEE COMPANY
Statement of Partners' Equity
Year Ended December 31, 2017

	S. King	R. Lee	Total
Capital, January 1	$28,000	$24,000	$52,000
Add: Investments	2,000	0	2,000
Profit	12,300	9,700	22,000
	42,300	33,700	76,000
Less: Drawings	7,000	5,000	12,000
Capital, December 31	$35,300	$28,700	$64,000

▶ILLUSTRATION **12-4**
Statement of partners' equity

KINGSLEE COMPANY
Balance Sheet (partial)
December 31, 2017

Liabilities and Partners' Equity

Total liabilities (assumed amount)		$115,000
Partners' equity		
S. King, Capital	$35,300	
R. Lee, Capital	28,700	64,000
Total liabilities and partners' equity		$179,000

▶ILLUSTRATION **12-5**
Partners' equity section of a partnership balance sheet

The statement of partners' equity is prepared from the income statement and the partners' capital and drawings accounts.

The balance sheet for a partnership is the same as for a proprietorship, except for the equity section. In a proprietorship, the equity section of the balance sheet is called owner's equity. A one-line capital account is reported for the owner. In a partnership, the capital balances of each partner are shown in the balance sheet, in a section called partners' equity. The partners' equity section in Kingslee Company's balance sheet appears in Illustration 12-5.

It is impractical for large partnerships to report each partner's equity separately. For reporting purposes, these amounts are usually aggregated in the balance sheet.

 **Statement of Partners' Equity**

The capital accounts of Mindy Dawson and Rania Alam, partners in Best Skate Company, had balances of $80,000 and $95,000, respectively, on January 1, 2017. During the year, Dawson invested an additional $15,000 and each partner withdrew $50,000. Profit for the year was $150,000 and was shared equally between the partners. Prepare a statement of partners' equity for the year ended December 31, 2017.

(continued)

BEFORE YOU GO ON...DO IT 4 > Statement of Partners' Equity *(continued)*

Action Plan

- Each partner's capital account is increased by the partner's investments and profit, and decreased by the partner's drawings.
- Allocate profit between the partners according to their profit-sharing agreement.

Solution

BEST SKATE COMPANY Statement of Partners' Equity Year Ended December 31, 2017			
	M. Dawson	R. Alam	Total
Capital, January 1	$ 80,000	$ 95,000	$175,000
Add: Investments	15,000	0	15,000
Profit	75,000	75,000	150,000
	170,000	170,000	340,000
Less: Drawings	50,000	50,000	100,000
Capital, December 31	$120,000	$120,000	$240,000

Related exercise material: BE12–10, E12–7, and E12–8.

Admission and Withdrawal of a Partner

We have seen how the basic accounting for a partnership works. We now look at how to account for something that happens often in partnerships: the addition or withdrawal of a partner.

LEARNING OBJECTIVE 5 Account for the admission of a partner.

ADMISSION OF A PARTNER

When a new partner is admitted to a partnership, the existing partnership is dissolved and a new partnership begins. From a practical standpoint, the admission of a new partner (or partners) may have only a minor impact on the continuity of the business. For example, in large public accounting or law firms, partners are admitted without any change in operating policies. From an economic standpoint, only a new capital account must be created for each new partner. In most cases, the accounting records of the old partnership will continue to be used by the new partnership.

A new partner may be admitted by either (1) purchasing the interest of an existing partner, or (2) investing assets in the partnership. **The purchase of a partner's interest involves only a transfer of capital among the partners who are part of the transaction: the total capital of the partnership is not affected. The investment of assets in the partnership increases both the partnership's net assets (total assets less total liabilities) and its total capital.**

Purchase of a Partner's Interest

Helpful hint In a purchase of an interest, the partnership is not a participant in the transaction. No cash is contributed to the partnership.

The **admission of a new partner by purchase of a partner's interest** occurs when a new partner personally purchases an ownership interest from an existing partner(s). This is a personal transaction between the new partner and one or more of the existing partners. The price paid is negotiated by the individuals involved. (It may be equal to or different from the partner's capital in the partnership's accounting records.) The new partner pays the existing partner(s) personally. As a result, the total capital of the partnership does not change; there is simply a reallocation of the partners' ownership interests.

Accounting for the purchase of an interest is straightforward. In the partnership, only the transfer of a partner's capital is recorded. The old partner's capital account is debited for the ownership claims that have been given up. The new partner's capital account is credited with the ownership interest purchased. Total assets, total liabilities, and total capital remain unchanged, as do all individual asset and liability accounts.

To illustrate, assume that on July 1, L. Carson agrees to pay $8,000 each to two partners, D. Arbour and D. Baker, for one third of their interest in ABC partnership. At the time of Carson's admission, each partner has a $30,000 capital balance. Both partners, therefore, give up $10,000 (⅓ × $30,000) of their capital. The entry to record the admission of Carson is as follows:

July 1	D. Arbour, Capital	10,000	
	D. Baker, Capital	10,000	
	L. Carson, Capital		20,000
	To record admission of Carson by purchase.		

```
A    =    L    +    OE
                    −10,000
                    −10,000
                    +20,000
```
Cash flows: no effect

Note that the cash paid by Carson is not recorded by the partnership because it is paid personally to Arbour and Baker. The entry above would be exactly the same regardless of the amount paid by Carson for the one-third interest. If Carson pays $12,000 each to Arbour and Baker for one third of their interest in the partnership, the above entry is still made.

The effect of this transaction on the partners' capital accounts is as follows:

D. Arbour, Capital		**D. Baker, Capital**		**L. Carson, Capital**	
	Bal. 30,000		Bal. 30,000		
July 1 10,000		July 1 10,000			July 1 20,000
	Bal. 20,000		Bal. 20,000		Bal. 20,000

Each partner now has a $20,000 ending capital balance and total partnership capital is $60,000 ($20,000 + $20,000 + $20,000). Net assets (assets − liabilities) and total partners' capital remain unchanged. Arbour and Baker continue as partners in the firm, but the capital interest of each has been reduced from $30,000 to $20,000.

Investment of Assets in a Partnership

The admission of a partner by an investment of assets in the partnership occurs when a partner makes a contribution of assets (such as cash) to the partnership. This is sometimes referred to simply as **admission by investment**. **This transaction increases both the net assets and the total capital of the partnership.**

To illustrate when cash is invested, assume that instead of purchasing a partner's interest, as illustrated in the previous section, Carson invests $30,000 in cash in the ABC partnership for a one-third capital interest. In this case, the entry is:

July 1	Cash	30,000	
	L. Carson, Capital		30,000
	To record admission of Carson by investment.		

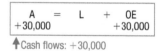

```
A       =    L    +    OE
+30,000                +30,000
```
↑Cash flows: +30,000

Both net assets and total capital increase by $30,000. The effect of this transaction on the partners' capital accounts is as follows:

D. Arbour, Capital		**D. Baker, Capital**		**L. Carson, Capital**	
	Bal. 30,000		Bal. 30,000		
					July 1 30,000
	Bal. 30,000		Bal. 30,000		Bal. 30,000

Remember that Carson's one-third capital interest might not result in a one-third profit and loss ratio. Carson's profit and loss ratio should be specified in the new partnership agreement. It may or may not be equal to the one-third capital interest.

The before and after effects of an admission by purchase of an interest or by investment are shown in the following comparison of the net assets and capital balances:

	Before Admission of Partner	After Admission of Partner	
		Purchase of a Partner's Interest	Investment of Assets in the Partnership
Net assets	$60,000	$60,000	$90,000
Partners' capital			
D. Arbour	$30,000	$20,000	$30,000
D. Baker	30,000	20,000	30,000
L. Carson		20,000	30,000
Total partners' equity	$60,000	$60,000	$90,000

When an interest is purchased, the partnership's total net assets and total capital do not change. In contrast, when a partner is admitted by investment, both the total net assets and the total capital increase by the amount of cash invested by the new partner.

In an admission by investment, complications occur when the new partner's investment is not the same as the equity in the partnership acquired by the new partner. When those amounts are not the same, the difference is considered a bonus to either (1) the old (existing) partners or (2) the new partner.

Bonus to Old Partners. With the admission of a new partner, the existing partners may want a bonus. A bonus may be requested to reflect the fact that the fair value of the partnership's assets may exceed their carrying value and, if a partnership has been profitable, goodwill may exist. Recall that internally generated goodwill is not recorded as part of the company's net assets. Where this is the case, the new partner is usually willing to pay a bonus to become a partner.

A bonus to the old partners occurs when the new partner's investment in the firm is greater than the credit balance in the capital account on the date of admittance. **The partnership allocates the bonus to the existing partners based on their income ratios before the admission of the new partner.** The bonus **increases the capital balances of the old partners**.

To illustrate, assume that on November 1, the Peart-Huang partnership, owned by Sam Peart and Hal Huang, has total partnership capital of $120,000. Peart has a capital balance of $72,000; Huang has a capital balance of $48,000. The two partners share profits and losses as follows: Peart 60% and Huang 40%.

Peart and Huang agree to admit Eden Trent to a 25% ownership (capital) interest in exchange for a cash investment of $80,000. The procedure for determining Trent's capital amount and the bonus to the old partners is as follows.

1. **Determine the total capital of the new partnership.** Add the new partner's investment to the total capital of the old partnership. In this case, the total capital of the new firm is $200,000, calculated as follows.

Total capital of existing partnership	$120,000
Investment by new partner, Eden Trent	80,000
Total capital of new partnership	$200,000

2. **Determine the new partner's capital credit.** Multiply the total capital of the new partnership by the new partner's ownership interest. Trent's capital credit is $50,000 ($200,000 × 25%).
3. **Determine the amount of bonus.** Subtract the new partner's capital credit from the new partner's investment. The bonus in this case is $30,000 ($80,000 − $50,000).
4. **Allocate the bonus to the old partners on the basis of their income ratios before the admission of the new partner.** Given that before the admission of the new partner, Peart held 60% and Huang held 40% of the old partnership, the new allocation is Peart $18,000 ($30,000 × 60%) and Huang $12,000 ($30,000 × 40%).

Therefore, the entry to record the admission of Trent is:

Nov. 1	Cash	80,000	
	S. Peart, Capital		18,000
	H. Huang, Capital		12,000
	E. Trent, Capital		50,000
	To record admission of Trent and bonuses to old partners.		

A	=	L	+	OE
+80,000				+18,000
				+12,000
				+50,000

↑Cash flows: +80,000

The before and after effects of the admission of a partner who pays a bonus to the old partners are shown in the following comparison of the net assets and capital balances:

	Bonus to Old Partners	
	Before Admission of Partner	After Admission of Partner
Net assets	$120,000	$200,000
Partners' capital		
S. Peart	$ 72,000	$ 90,000
H. Huang	48,000	60,000
E. Trent		50,000
Total capital	$120,000	$200,000

In summary, Eden Trent invests $80,000 cash in the partnership for a 25% capital interest of $50,000. The difference of $30,000 between these two amounts is a bonus that is allocated to the old partners based on their profit- and loss-sharing ratio as follows: $18,000 to Sam Peart and $12,000 to Hal Huang.

Bonus to New Partner. A bonus to a new partner occurs when the new partner's investment in the firm is less than the credit balance in his or her capital account. This may occur when a new partner has specific resources or special attributes that the partnership wants. For example, the new partner may be able to supply cash that is urgently needed for expansion or to meet maturing debts. Or the new partner may be a recognized expert or authority in a relevant field. Or the new partner may be a celebrity whose name will draw more customers to the business.

A bonus to a new partner **decreases the capital balances of the old partners. The amount of the decrease for each partner is based on the profit and loss ratios before the admission of the new partner.**

To illustrate, assume instead that on November 1, the Peart-Huang partnership admits Eden Trent to a 25% ownership (capital) interest in exchange for a cash investment of $20,000 (instead of $80,000 as in the previous illustration). The process to determine the bonus to a new partner is the same as when there is a bonus to the existing partners. Trent's capital balance on the new partnership books of $35,000 and allocation of the bonus from the old partners are calculated as follows:

Partnership capital before Trent is admitted ($72,000 + $48,000)	$120,000
Trent's investment in the partnership	20,000
Partnership capital after Trent is admitted	$140,000
Trent's capital in the partnership ($140,000 × 25%)	$ 35,000
Bonus to the new partner ($35,000 – $20,000)	$ 15,000

The bonus from the old partners is based on their profit and loss ratios:

From Peart ($15,000 × 60%)	$ 9,000
From Huang ($15,000 × 40%)	6,000
Total bonus allocated to the new partner	$ 15,000

The entry to record the admission of Trent on November 1 in this case is:

A	=	L	+	OE
				−9,000
+20,000				−6,000
				+35,000

↑Cash flows: +20,000

Nov. 1	Cash	20,000	
	S. Peart, Capital		9,000
	H. Huang, Capital		6,000
	E. Trent, Capital		35,000
	To record Trent's admission and bonus to new partner.		

The before and after effects of the admission of a partner who is paid a bonus by the old partners are shown in the following comparison of the net assets and capital balances:

	Bonus to New Partner	
	Before Admission of Partner	**After Admission of Partner**
Net assets	$120,000	$140,000
Partners' capital		
S. Peart	$ 72,000	$ 63,000
H. Huang	48,000	42,000
E. Trent		35,000
Total capital	$120,000	$140,000

In summary, $20,000 cash was invested in the partnership by Eden Trent for a $35,000 capital credit, and her $15,000 bonus was allocated from the partners' capital accounts as follows: $9,000 from Sam Peart and $6,000 from Hal Huang.

BEFORE YOU GO ON...DO IT 5   Recording the Admission of a Partner

Action Plan

- Recognize that the purchase of a partnership interest is a personal transaction between one or more existing partners and the new partner.
- In an admission by purchase of a partner's interest, no cash is received by the partnership and the capital credit for the new partner is not based on the cash paid.
- Recognize that the admission by investment of assets is a transaction between the new partner and the partnership.
- In an admission by investment, determine any bonus to old or new partners by comparing the total capital of the new partnership with the new partner's capital credit. Allocate the bonus based on the old partners' profit and loss ratios.

I. Shandler and M. Rossetti have a partnership in which they share profit and loss equally. There is a $40,000 balance in each capital account. Record the journal entries on September 1 for each of the independent events below:

(a) Shandler and Rossetti agree to admit A. Rachel as a new one-fourth interest partner. Rachel pays $16,000 in cash directly to each partner.

(b) Shandler and Rossetti agree to admit A. Rachel as a new one-fourth interest partner. Rachel contributes $32,000 to the partnership.

Solution

(a) Sept. 1	I. Shandler, Capital	10,000	
	M. Rossetti, Capital	10,000	
	A. Rachel, Capital		20,000[1]
	To record admission of Rachel by purchase of a partner's interest.		

(b) Sept. 1	Cash	32,000	
	I. Shandler, Capital ($4,000[2] × 50%)		2,000
	M. Rossetti, Capital ($4,000[2] × 50%)		2,000
	A. Rachel, Capital		28,000
	To record admission of Rachel investment of assets.		

[1] Total capital of partnership: $40,000 + $40,000 = $80,000
Rachel's capital credit: $80,000 × ¼ = $20,000
[2] Total capital of partnership: $40,000 + $40,000 + $32,000 = $112,000
Rachel's capital credit: $112,000 × ¼ = $28,000
Bonus to old partners: $32,000 − $28,000 = $4,000 (shared equally)

Related exercise material: BE12–11, BE12–12, E12–9, and E12–10.

LEARNING OBJECTIVE 6 ▶ Account for the withdrawal of a partner.

WITHDRAWAL OF A PARTNER

Let's now look at the opposite situation, when a partner withdraws. A partner may withdraw from a partnership voluntarily, by selling his or her equity in the firm. He or she may withdraw involuntarily, by reaching mandatory retirement age (as mentioned in our opening story), by expulsion, or by dying. The withdrawal of a partner, like the admission of a partner, legally dissolves the partnership. However, it is customary to record only the economic effects of the partner's withdrawal, while the partnership reorganizes itself and continues to operate.

As indicated earlier, the partnership agreement should specify the terms of withdrawal. The withdrawal of a partner may be done by payment from (1) partners' personal assets or (2) partnership assets. Payment from personal assets affects only the remaining partners' capital accounts, not total capital. Payment from partnership assets decreases the total net assets and total capital of the partnership.

After a partner has withdrawn, profit and loss ratios for the remaining partners must be reviewed and specified again. If a new profit and loss ratio is not indicated in the partnership agreement, the remaining partners are assumed to share profits and losses equally.

Payment from Partners' Personal Assets

A withdrawal by payment from partners' personal assets is a personal transaction between the partners. **It is the direct opposite of admitting a new partner who purchases a partner's interest.** Payment to the departing partner is made directly from the remaining partners' personal assets. **Partnership assets are not involved in any way, and total capital does not change.** The effect on the partnership is limited to a transfer of the partners' capital balances.

To illustrate, assume that Javad Dargahi, Dong Kim, and Roberta Viau have capital balances of $25,000, $15,000, and $10,000, respectively. The partnership equity totals $50,000 ($25,000 + $15,000 + $10,000). Dargahi and Kim agree to buy out Viau's interest. Each agrees to personally pay Viau $8,000 in exchange for one half of Viau's total interest of $10,000 on February 1. The entry to record the withdrawal is as follows:

Feb. 1	R. Viau, Capital	10,000	
	J. Dargahi, Capital		5,000
	D. Kim, Capital		5,000
	To record purchase of Viau's interest by other partners.		

A	=	L	+	OE
				−10,000
				+5,000
				+5,000

Cash flows: no effect

The effect of this transaction on the partners' capital accounts is as follows:

J. Dargahi, Capital		D. Kim, Capital		R. Viau, Capital	
	Bal. 25,000		Bal. 15,000		Bal. 10,000
	5,000		5,000	10,000	
	Bal. 30,000		Bal. 20,000		Bal. 0

Net assets of $50,000 remain the same and total partnership capital is also unchanged at $50,000 ($30,000 + $20,000 + $0).

What about the $16,000 paid to Viau? You've probably noted that it is not recorded. The entry debited Viau's capital only for $10,000, not for the $16,000 that she received. Similarly, both Dargahi and Kim credit their capital accounts for only $5,000, not for the $8,000 they each paid. This is because there has only been a reallocation of capital amounts and we are showing the accounting for the partnership, not the partners' personal accounting. After Viau's withdrawal, Dargahi and Kim will share profit or loss equally unless they indicate another income ratio in the partnership agreement.

Payment from Partnership Assets

A **withdrawal by payment from partnership assets** is a transaction that involves the partnership. **Both partnership net assets and total capital decrease as a result.** Using partnership assets to pay for a withdrawing partner's interest is the **reverse** of admitting a partner through the investment of assets in the partnership.

In accounting for a withdrawal by payment from partnership assets, asset revaluations should not be recorded. Recording a revaluation to the fair value of the assets at the time of a partner's withdrawal violates the historical cost principle, which requires assets to be stated at original cost. It would also ignore the going concern assumption, which assumes that the entity will continue indefinitely. The terms of the partnership contract should not dictate the accounting for this event.

To illustrate, assume that instead of Roberta Viau's interest being purchased personally by the other partners, as illustrated in the previous section, her interest is bought out by the partnership. In this case, the entry is:

A	=	L	+	OE
−10,000				−10,000

↓ Cash flows: −10,000

Feb. 1	R. Viau, Capital	10,000	
	Cash		10,000
	To record purchase of Viau's interest by partnership.		

Both net assets and total partnership capital decrease by $10,000. The effect of this transaction on the partners' capital accounts is as follows:

J. Dargahi, Capital		D. Kim, Capital		R. Viau, Capital	
	Bal. 25,000		Bal. 15,000		Bal. 10,000
				10,000	
	Bal. 25,000		Bal. 15,000		Bal. 0

The before and after effects of the withdrawal of a partner when payment is made from personal assets or from partnership assets are shown in the following comparison of the net assets and capital balances:

		After Withdrawal of Partner	
	Before Withdrawal of Partner	Payment from Partners' Personal Assets	Payment from Partnership Assets
Net assets	$50,000	$50,000	$40,000
Partners' capital			
J. Dargahi	$25,000	$30,000	$25,000
D. Kim	15,000	20,000	15,000
R. Viau	10,000	0	0
Total capital	$50,000	$50,000	$40,000

When payment is made from partners' personal assets, the partnership's total net assets and total capital do not change. In contrast, when payment is made from the partnership assets, both the total net assets and the total capital decrease.

In a payment from partnership assets, it is rare for the partnership to pay the partner the exact amount of his or her capital account balance, as was assumed above. When the amounts are not the same, the difference between the amount paid and the withdrawing partner's capital balance is considered a bonus to either (1) the departing partner, or (2) the remaining partners.

Bonus to Departing Partner. A bonus may be paid to a departing partner in any of these situations:

1. The fair value of partnership assets is more than their carrying amount.
2. There is unrecorded goodwill resulting from the partnership's superior earnings record.
3. The remaining partners are anxious to remove the partner from the firm.

The bonus is deducted from the remaining partners' capital balances based on their profit and loss ratios at the time of the withdrawal.

To illustrate a bonus to a departing partner, assume the following capital balances in the RST Partnership: Fred Roman, $50,000; Dee Sand, $30,000; and Betty Terk, $20,000. The partners share profit in the ratio of 3:2:1, respectively. Terk retires from the partnership on March 1 and receives a cash payment of $25,000 from the firm. The bonus to the departing partner and the allocation of the bonus to the remaining partners is calculated as follows:

1. **Determine the amount of the bonus.** Subtract the retiring partner's capital balance from the cash paid by the partnership. The bonus in this case is $5,000 ($25,000 − $20,000).
2. **Allocate the bonus to the remaining partners on the basis of their income ratios.** The ratios of Roman and Sand are 3:2. Thus, the allocation of the $5,000 bonus is: Roman $3,000 ($5,000 × $^3/_5$) and Sand $2,000 ($5,000 × $^2/_5$).

The entry to record the withdrawal of Terk on March 1 is as follows:

Mar. 1	B. Terk, Capital	20,000	
	F. Roman, Capital	3,000	
	D. Sand, Capital	2,000	
	Cash		25,000
	To record withdrawal of, and bonus to, Terk.		

A	=	L	+	OE
−25,000				−20,000
				−3,000
				−2,000

↓ Cash flows: −25,000

The before and after effects of the withdrawal of a partner when a bonus is paid to the departing partner are shown in the following comparison of the net assets and capital balances:

	Bonus to Departing Partner	
	Before Withdrawal of Partner	**After Withdrawal of Partner**
Net assets	$100,000	$75,000
Partners' capital		
F. Roman	$ 50,000	$47,000
D. Sand	30,000	28,000
B. Terk	20,000	0
Total capital	$100,000	$75,000

In summary, both net assets and capital decreased by $25,000 when $25,000 cash was paid by the partnership to Betty Terk to purchase her $20,000 equity interest. The $5,000 bonus was allocated from the remaining partners' capital accounts according to their profit and loss ratios. Fred Roman and Dee Sand, the remaining partners, will recover the bonus given to Terk as the undervalued assets are used or sold.

Bonus to Remaining Partners. The departing partner may give a bonus to the remaining partners in the following situations:

1. Recorded assets are overvalued.
2. The partnership has a poor earnings record.
3. The partner is anxious to leave the partnership.

In such cases, the cash paid to the departing partner will be less than the departing partner's capital balance. **The bonus is allocated (credited) to the capital accounts of the remaining partners based on their profit and loss ratios.**

To illustrate, assume, instead of the example above, that Terk is paid only $16,000 for her $20,000 equity when she withdraws from the partnership on March 1. The bonus to the remaining partners is calculated as follows:

1. The bonus to remaining partners is $4,000 ($20,000 − $16,000).
2. The allocation of the $4,000 bonus is Roman $2,400 ($4,000 × $^3/_5$) and Sand $1,600 ($4,000 × $^2/_5$).

The entry to record the withdrawal on March 1 follows:

A	=	L	+	OE
−16,000				−20,000
				+2,400
				+1,600

↓ Cash flows: −16,000

Mar. 1	B. Terk, Capital	20,000	
	F. Roman, Capital		2,400
	D. Sand, Capital		1,600
	Cash		16,000
	To record withdrawal of Terk and bonus to remaining partners.		

The before and after effects of a withdrawal of a partner when a bonus is paid to the remaining partners are shown in the following comparison of the net assets and capital balances:

	Bonus to Remaining Partners	
	Before Withdrawal of Partner	**After Withdrawal of Partner**
Net assets	$100,000	$84,000
Partners' capital		
F. Roman	$ 50,000	$52,400
D. Sand	30,000	31,600
B. Terk	20,000	0
Total capital	$100,000	$84,000

In summary, both net assets and capital decreased by $16,000 when $16,000 cash was paid by the partnership to Betty Terk to purchase her $20,000 equity interest. The $4,000 bonus was allocated to the remaining partners' capital accounts according to their profit and loss ratios.

Death of a Partner

The death of a partner dissolves the partnership. But there is generally a provision in the partnership agreement for the surviving partners to continue operations. When a partner dies, the partner's equity at the date of death normally has to be determined. This is done by (1) calculating the profit or loss for the year to date, (2) closing the books, and (3) preparing the financial statements.

The death of the partner may be recorded by either of the two methods described earlier in the section for the withdrawal of a partner: (1) payment from the partners' personal assets or (2) payment from the partnership assets. That is, one or more of the surviving partners may agree to use his or her personal assets to purchase the deceased partner's equity. Or, partnership assets may be used to settle with the deceased partner's estate. To make it easier to pay from partnership assets, many partnerships take out life insurance policies on each partner. The partnership is named as the beneficiary. The proceeds from the insurance policy on the deceased partner are then used to settle with the estate.

BEFORE YOU GO ON...DO IT   **6**   **Recording the Withdrawal of a Partner**

Action Plan

- Recognize that the withdrawal by sale of a partnership interest with payment from partner's personal assets is a personal transaction between one or more remaining partners and the withdrawing partner.
- Recognize that the withdrawal by payment from partnership assets is a transaction between the withdrawing partner and the partnership.

S. Hossein, M. Bélanger, and C. Laurin have a partnership in which they share profit and loss equally. There is a $40,000 balance in each capital account. Record the journal entries on March 1 for each of the independent events below:

(a) Laurin withdraws from the partnership. Hossein and Bélanger each pay Laurin $25,000 out of their personal assets.
(b) Laurin withdraws from the partnership and is paid $30,000 of partnership cash.

Solution

(a) Mar. 1	C. Laurin, Capital	40,000	
	S. Hossein, Capital ($40,000 × ½)		20,000
	M. Bélanger, Capital ($40,000 × ½)		20,000
	To record purchase of Laurin's interest with payment from partners personal assets.		

(continued)

BEFORE YOU GO ON...DO IT 6 > **Recording the Withdrawal of a Partner** *(continued)*

(b) Mar. 1	C. Laurin, Capital	40,000	
	Cash		30,000
	S. Hossein, Capital ($10,000[1] × ½)		5,000
	M. Bélanger, Capital ($10,000[1] × ½)		5,000
	To record withdrawal of Laurin by payment from partnership assets and bonus to remaining partners.		

[1]Bonus: $30,000 − $40,000 = $(10,000)

Related exercise material: BE12–13, BE12–14, E12–11, and E12–12.

- In a with payment assets, determine any bonus to the departing or remaining partners by comparing the amount paid with the amount of the withdrawing partner's capital balance. Allocate the bonus based on the remaining partners' profit and loss ratios.

LEARNING OBJECTIVE 7 > **Account for the liquidation of a partnership.**

Liquidation of a Partnership

The liquidation of a partnership ends the business. It involves selling the assets of the business, paying liabilities, and distributing any remaining assets to the partners. Liquidation may result from the sale of the business by mutual agreement of the partners or from bankruptcy. A **partnership liquidation** ends both the legal and the economic life of the entity.

Before the liquidation process begins, the accounting cycle for the partnership must be completed for the final operating period. This includes preparing adjusting entries, a trial balance, financial statements, closing entries, and a post-closing trial balance. Only balance sheet accounts should be open when the liquidation process begins.

In liquidation, the sale of noncash assets for cash is called **realization**. Any difference between the carrying amount and the cash proceeds is called the gain or loss on realization. To liquidate a partnership, it is necessary to follow these steps:

1. Sell noncash assets for cash and recognize **any gain or loss on realization**.
2. Allocate any gain or loss on realization to the partners, based on their profit and loss ratios.
3. Pay partnership liabilities in cash.
4. Distribute the remaining cash to partners, based on their **capital balances**.

Each of the steps must be done in sequence. The partners must pay creditors **before** partners receive any cash distributions.

When a partnership is liquidated, all partners may have credit balances in their capital accounts. This situation is called **no capital deficiency**. Alternatively, one or more of the partners' capital accounts may have a debit balance in the capital account. This situation is called a **capital deficiency**.

To illustrate each of these situations, assume that Ace Company is liquidated on April 15, 2017, when its post-closing trial balance shows the assets, liabilities, and partners' equity accounts in Illustration 12-6. The profit and loss ratios of the partners are 3:2:1 for R. Aube, P. Chordia, and W. Elliott.

ETHICS NOTE
The process of selling noncash assets and then distributing the cash reduces the likelihood of partner disputes. If instead the partnership distributes noncash assets to partners to liquidate the firm, the partners would need to agree on the value of the noncash assets, which can be very difficult to determine.

ACE COMPANY
Post-Closing Trial Balance
April 15, 2017

	Debit	Credit
Cash	$ 5,000	
Accounts receivable	33,000	
Equipment	35,000	
Accumulated depreciation—equipment		$ 8,000
Accounts payable		31,000
R. Aube, capital		15,000
P. Chordia, capital		17,800
W. Elliott, capital		1,200
Totals	$73,000	$73,000

▶ILLUSTRATION 12-6
Account balances
before liquidation

NO CAPITAL DEFICIENCY

No capital deficiency means that all partners have credit balances in their capital accounts prior to the final distribution of cash. An example of the steps in the liquidation process with no capital deficiency follows:

1. Assume the noncash assets (accounts receivable and equipment) are sold on April 18 for $75,000. The carrying amount of these assets is $60,000 ($33,000 + $35,000 − $8,000). Thus, a gain of $15,000 is realized on the sale, and the following entry is made:

A	=	L	+	OE
+75,000				+15,000
+8,000				
−33,000				
−35,000				

↑Cash flows: +75,000

		(1)		
Apr. 18	Cash		75,000	
	Accumulated Depreciation—Equipment		8,000	
	Accounts Receivable			33,000
	Equipment			35,000
	Gain on Realization			15,000
	To record realization of noncash assets.			

2. The gain on realization of $15,000 is allocated to the partners based on their profit and loss ratios, which are 3:2:1 (or $^3/_6$, $^2/_6$, and $^1/_6$). The entry is:

A	=	L	+	OE
				−15,000
				+7,500
				+5,000
				+2,500

Cash flows: no effect

		(2)		
Apr. 18	Gain on Realization		15,000	
	R. Aube, Capital ($15,000 × $^3/_6$)			7,500
	P. Chordia, Capital ($15,000 × $^2/_6$)			5,000
	W. Elliott, Capital ($15,000 × $^1/_6$)			2,500
	To allocate gain to partners' capital accounts.			

3. Partnership liabilities consist of accounts payable, $31,000. Creditors are paid in full on April 23 by a cash payment of $31,000. The entry is:

A	=	L	+	OE
−31,000		−31,000		

↓ Cash flows: −31,000

		(3)		
Apr. 23	Accounts Payable		31,000	
	Cash			31,000
	To record payment of partnership liabilities.			

Illustration 12-7 shows the account balances after the entries in the first three steps are posted. All of the accounts will have zero balances except for cash and the partners' capital accounts.

	Assets			= Liabilities	+ Partners' Equity		
	Cash	Accounts Receivable	Equipment	Accum. Dep. Equipment	Accounts Payable	R. Aube, Capital	P. Chordia, Capital	W. Elliott, Capital
Account balances prior to liquidation:	$ 5,000	$ 33,000	$ 35,000	$8,000	$31,000	$15,000	$17,800	$1,200
1. & 2. Sale of assets and share of gain	+75,000	−33,000	−35,000	−8,000		+7,500	+5,000	+2,500
Balances	80,000	0	0	0	31,000	22,500	22,800	3,700
3. Payment of accounts payable	−31,000				−31,000			
Balances	49,000	0	0	0	0	22,500	22,800	3,700
4. Distribution of cash to partners	−49,000					−22,500	−22,800	−3,700
Final balances	$ 0	$ 0	$ 0	$ 0	$ 0	$ 0	$ 0	$ 0

▶ ILLUSTRATION 12-7
Partnership liquidation—
no capital deficiency

4. The remaining cash is distributed to the partners on April 25 based **on their capital balances** as shown in Illustration 12-7. The entry to record the distribution of cash on April 25 is:

(4)			
Apr. 25	R. Aube, Capital	22,500	
	P. Chordia, Capital	22,800	
	W. Elliott, Capital	3,700	
	Cash		49,000
	To record distribution of cash to partners.		

A	=	L	+	OE
−49,000				−22,500
				−22,800
				−3,700

↓ Cash flows: −49,000

As shown in Illustration 12-7, after this entry is posted, all of the accounts have zero balances and the liquidation of the partnership is complete.

Two points to remember:

- Gains or losses on sale of assets are allocated to the partners based on the profit and loss ratio.

- **The final cash payment to the partners is based on the balances in the partners' capital accounts.**

CAPITAL DEFICIENCY

Capital deficiency means that at least one partner has a debit balance in his or her capital account before the final distribution of cash. This may be caused by recurring losses, excessive drawings, or losses from the realization during liquidation.

To illustrate, assume instead that Ace Company (see Illustration 12-7) is almost bankrupt. The partners decide to liquidate by having a going-out-of-business sale on April 18. Many of the accounts receivable cannot be collected, and the equipment is sold at auction at less than its fair value. Cash proceeds from the equipment sale and collections from customers total only $42,000. The loss on liquidation is $18,000 ($60,000 in carrying amount − $42,000 in proceeds). The steps in the liquidation process are as follows:

1. The entry for the realization of noncash assets is recorded on April 18:

(1)			
Apr. 18	Cash	42,000	
	Accumulated Depreciation—Equipment	8,000	
	Loss on Realization	18,000	
	Accounts Receivable		33,000
	Equipment		35,000
	To record realization of noncash assets.		

A	=	L	+	OE
+42,000				−18,000
+8,000				
−33,000				
−35,000				

↑ Cash flows: +42,000

2. The loss on realization is allocated to the partners based on their profit and loss ratios of 3:2:1 and is recorded as follows:

A	=	L	+	OE
				−9,000
				−6,000
				−3,000
				+18,000

Cash flows: no effect

(2)		
Apr. 18	R. Aube, Capital ($18,000 × 3/6)	9,000	
	P. Chordia, Capital ($18,000 × 2/6)	6,000	
	W. Elliott, Capital ($18,000 × 1/6)	3,000	
	Loss on Realization		18,000
	To allocate loss to partners' capital accounts.		

3. Partnership liabilities are paid on April 23 and recorded:

A	=	L	+	OE
−31,000		−31,000		

↓ Cash flows: −31,000

(3)		
Apr. 23	Accounts Payable	31,000	
	Cash		31,000
	To record payment of partnership liabilities.		

After posting of the three entries, as shown in Illustration 12-8, there is $16,000 of cash remaining. Two of the partners' capital accounts have credit balances: R. Aube, Capital $6,000; and P. Chordia, Capital $11,800. The illustration shows W. Elliott's capital account as a negative number, which represents a debit balance or capital deficiency of $1,800.

▶ ILLUSTRATION **12-8**
Partnership
liquidation—capital deficiency

		Assets				= Liabilities	+ Partners' Equity		
		Cash	**Accounts Receivable**	**Equipment**	**Accum. Dep. Equipment**	**Accounts Payable**	**R. Aube, Capital**	**P. Chordia, Capital**	**W. Elliott, Capital**
	Account balances prior to liquidation:	$ 5,000	$ 33,000	$ 35,000	$ 8,000	$31,000	$ 15,000	$17,800	$1,200
	1. & 2. Sale of assets and share of loss	+42,000	−33,000	−35,000	−8,000		−9,000	−6,000	−3,000
	Balances	47,000	0	0	0	31,000	6,000	11,800	−1,800
	3. Payment of accounts payable	−31,000				−31,000			
	Balances	16,000	0	0	0	0	6,000	11,800	−1,800

W. Elliott's capital deficiency of $1,800 means that he owes the partnership $1,800. R. Aube and P. Chordia have a legally enforceable claim for that amount against Elliott's personal assets. The final distribution of cash depends on how Elliott's deficiency is settled. Two alternatives for settling are presented next.

Payment of Deficiency

If the partner with the capital deficiency pays the amount owed to the partnership, the deficiency is eliminated. To illustrate, assume that W. Elliott pays $1,800 to the partnership on April 24. The entry to record this payment is as follows:

A	=	L	+	OE
+1,800				+1,800

↑ Cash flows: +1,800

(4)		
Apr. 24	Cash	1,800	
	W. Elliott, Capital		1,800
	To record payment of capital deficiency by Elliott.		

As shown in Illustration 12-9, after posting this entry, the cash balance of $17,800 is now sufficient to pay the two remaining partners with credit balances in the capital accounts ($6,000 + $11,800).

▶ILLUSTRATION 12-9
Payment of deficiency

	Assets =		Partners' Equity	
	Cash	R. Aube, Capital	P. Chordia, Capital	W. Elliott, Capital
Account balances after selling assets and paying liabilities:	$ 16,000	$6,000	$ 11,800	$−1,800
Payment of capital deficiency	+1,800			+1,800
Balances	17,800	6,000	11,800	0
Distribution of cash to partners	−17,800	−6,000	−11,800	
Final balances	$ 0	$ 0	$ 0	$ 0

Cash is distributed based on these balances on April 25. This was step 4 in the list when there was no capital deficiency. The following entry is made:

	(5)		
Apr. 25	R. Aube, Capital	6,000	
	P. Chordia, Capital	11,800	
	Cash		17,800
	To record distribution of cash to partners.		

A   =   L   +
−17,800   −6,000
                       −11,800
↓ Cash flows: −17,800

As shown in Illustration 12-9, after this entry is posted, all accounts will have zero balances and the partnership liquidation is finished.

Nonpayment of Deficiency

If a partner with a capital deficiency is unable to pay the amount owed to the partnership, the partners with credit balances must absorb the loss. The loss is allocated based on the profit and loss ratios between the partners with credit balances. Recall that the profit and loss ratios of R. Aube and P. Chordia are 3:2 (or $3/5$, and $2/5$), respectively. The following entry would be made to remove W. Elliott's capital deficiency on April 25:

Helpful hint The profit and loss ratio changes when the partner with the capital deficiency is not included. When allocating the loss from the sale of the assets, the profit and loss ratio was divided among the three partners as 3:2:1 or $3/6$, $2/6$, and $1/6$. When Elliott is excluded, the profit and loss ratio is now 3:2 or $3/5$ and $2/5$.

	(4)		
Apr. 25	R. Aube, Capital ($1,800 × $3/5$)	1,080	
	P. Chordia, Capital ($1,800 × $2/5$)	720	
	W. Elliott, Capital		1,800
	To write off Elliott's capital deficiency.		

A   =   L   +   OE
                         −1,080
                         −720
                         +1,800
Cash flows: no effect

After posting this entry, the cash balance of $16,000 now equals the sum of the credit balances in the capital accounts ($4,920 + $11,080), as shown in Illustration 12-10.

▶ILLUSTRATION 12-10
Nonpayment of deficiency

	Assets =		Partners' Equity	
	Cash	R. Aube, Capital	P. Chordia, Capital	W. Elliott, Capital
Account balances after selling assets and paying liabilities:	$16,000	$6,000	$ 11,800	$−1,800
Write off of capital deficiency	0	−1,080	−720	−1,800
Balances	16,000	4,920	11,080	0
Distribution of cash to partners	−16,000	−4,920	−11,080	
Final balances	$ 0	$ 0	$ 0	$ 0

The entry to record the final distribution of cash is:

	(5)		
Apr. 25	R. Aube, Capital	4,920	
	P. Chordia, Capital	11,080	
	Cash		16,000
	To record distribution of cash to partners.		

A   =   L   +   OE
−16,000   −4,920
                       −11,080
↓ Cash flows: −16,000

After this entry is posted, all accounts will have zero balances, as shown in Illustration 12-10, but Aube and Chordia still have a legal claim against Elliott for the deficiency. If Elliott is able to make a partial payment, it would be split between Aube and Chordia 3:2 in the same way as the deficiency was split.

ACCOUNTING IN ACTION
ALL ABOUT YOU INSIGHT

Many successful businesses start as a simple partnership based on an inspiration, idea, or dream shared by a couple of friends.

In 1968, Bill Gates and Paul Allen met at a computer club meeting at Seattle's private Lakeside School. In Gates's dorm room at Harvard University in 1974, they devised and sold a BASIC platform for the Altair 8800. The university disciplined Gates

for running a business in his dorm. A year later, Gates and Allen formed Microsoft, now the world's largest software company.

Larry Page and Sergey Brin met while working on their doctorates in computer science at Stanford in 1995. Working in their dorm rooms, they created a proprietary algorithm for a search engine on the Net that catalogued search results according to the popularity of pages. The result was Google, arguably the world's No. 1 Internet search engine.

Sources: Steve Lohr, "An 'Unvarnished' Peek Into Microsoft's History," *New York Times*, April 17, 2011; "Larry Page and Sergey Brin," *Entrepreneur*, October 16, 2008; Stacy Perman, "Historic Collaborations—Business Partnerships That Changed the World," *Business Week*, November 21, 2008.

 Q If you and a friend wanted to start a partnership, how might you use a partnership agreement to ensure that your partnership becomes successful, instead of ending in an unhappy liquidation?

BEFORE YOU GO ON...DO IT **7** | **Recording the Dissolution of a Partnership**

S. Anders, J. Haque, and R. Smit, LLP, dissolved their partnership as of August 31. Before liquidation, the three partners shared profit and losses in the ratio of 3:2:4. After the books were closed on August 31, the following summary accounts remained:

Cash	$ 6,000	S. Anders, Capital	$30,000
Noncash assets	110,000	J. Haque, Capital	20,000
Accounts payable	25,000	R. Smit, Capital	41,000

On September 24, the partnership sold the remaining noncash assets for $74,000 and paid the liabilities. If there is a capital deficiency, none of the partners will be able to pay it. Prepare the journal entries to record (a) the sale of noncash assets, (b) the allocation of any gain or loss on realization, (c) the payment of liabilities, and (d) the distribution of cash to the partners.

Action Plan

- Calculate the gain or loss by comparing cash proceeds with the carrying amount of assets.
- Allocate any gain or loss to each partner's capital account using the profit and loss ratio.
- Allocate the capital deficiency, if there is one, using the profit and loss ratio of the other partners.
- Record the final distribution of cash to each partner to eliminate the balance in each capital account. Do not distribute cash using the profit and loss ratio.

Solution

(a) Sept. 24	Cash		74,000	
	Loss on Realization		36,000	
	Noncash Assets			110,000
	To record realization of noncash assets.			
(b) Sept. 24	S. Anders, Capital ($36,000 × $3/9$)		12,000	
	J. Haque, Capital ($36,000 × $2/9$)		8,000	
	R. Smit, Capital ($36,000 × $4/9$)		16,000	
	Loss on Realization			36,000
	To allocate loss to partners' capital accounts.			
(c) Sept. 24	Accounts Payable		25,000	
	Cash			25,000
	To record payment of liabilities.			
(d) Sept. 24	S. Anders, Capital ($30,000 – $12,000)		18,000	
	J. Haque, Capital ($20,000 – $8,000)		12,000	
	R. Smit, Capital ($41,000 – $16,000)		25,000	
	Cash ($6,000 + $74,000 – $25,000)			55,000
	To record distribution of cash to partners.			

Related exercise material: BE12–15, BE12–16, BE12–17, BE12–18, E12–13, E12–14, E12–15, E12–16, and E12-17.

Comparing IFRS and ASPE

Key Differences	International Financial Reporting Standards (IFRS)	Accounting Standards for Private Enterprises (ASPE)
No significant differences.		

Demonstration Problem

On January 1, 2016, the partners' capital balances in Hollingsworth Company are Lois Holly, $26,000, and Jim Worth, $24,000. For the year ended December 31, 2016, the partnership reports profit of $32,500. The partnership agreement specifies (1) salary allowances of $12,000 for Holly and $10,000 for Worth, (2) interest allowances on opening capital account balances of 5%, and (3) the remainder to be distributed equally. Neither partner had any drawings in 2016.

In 2017, assume that the following independent transactions occur on January 2:

1. Halley Richter personally purchases one half of Lois Holly's capital interest from Holly for $25,000.
2. Morgan Mears is admitted with a 25% capital interest by a cash investment of $37,500.
3. Stan Kee is admitted with a 30% capital interest by a cash investment of $32,500.

Instructions
(a) Prepare a schedule that shows the distribution of profit in 2016.
(b) Journalize the division of 2016 profit and its distribution to the partners on December 31.
(c) Journalize each of the independent transactions that occurred on January 2, 2017.

SOLUTION TO DEMONSTRATION PROBLEM

(a)

HOLLINGSWORTH COMPANY
Division of Profit
Year Ended December 31, 2016

	L. Holly	J. Worth	Total
Profit			$32,500
Salary allowance			
L. Holly	$12,000		
J. Worth		$10,000	
Total			22,000
Profit remaining for allocation			10,500
Interest allowance			
L. Holly ($26,000 × 5%)	1,300		
J. Worth ($24,000 × 5%)		1,200	
Total			2,500
Profit remaining for allocation			8,000
Fixed ratio (remainder shared equally)			
L. Holly ($8,000 × 50%)	4,000		
J. Worth ($8,000 × 50%)		4,000	
Total			8,000
Profit remaining for allocation			0
Profit allocated to the partners	$17,300	$15,200	$32,500

ACTION PLAN

- Allocate the partners' salaries and interest allowances, if any, first. Divide the remaining profit among the partners, based on the profit and loss ratio.
- Journalize the division of profit in a closing entry.
- Recognize the admission by purchase of a partnership interest as a personal transaction between an existing partner and the new partner.
- Recognize the admission by investment of partnership assets as a transaction between the new partner and the partnership.
- In an admission by investment, determine any bonus to old or new partners by comparing the total capital of the new partnership with the new partner's capital credit. Allocate the bonus based on the old partners' profit and loss ratios.

(b) 2016

Dec. 31	Income Summary		32,500	
	L. Holly, Capital			17,300
	J. Worth, Capital			15,200
	To close profit to partners' capital accounts.			

L. Holly, Capital				J. Worth, Capital		
	Bal.	26,000			Bal.	24,000
		17,300				**15,200**
	Bal.	43,300			Bal.	39,200

(c) 2017

1. Jan. 2	L. Holly, Capital ($43,300 × 50%)		21,650	
	H. Richter, Capital			21,650
	To record purchase of one half of Holly's interest.			
2. Jan. 2	Cash		37,500	
	L. Holly, Capital ($7,500 × 50%)			3,750
	J. Worth, Capital ($7,500 × 50%)			3,750
	M. Mears, Capital			30,000
	To record admission of Mears by investment and bonus to old partners.			

Total capital after investment: ($43,300 + $39,200 + $37,500)	$120,000
Mears's capital in the partnership: (25% × $120,000)	$30,000
Bonus to old partners: ($37,500 − $30,000)	$7,500

3. Jan. 2	Cash		32,500	
	L. Holly, Capital ($2,000 × 50%)		1,000	
	J. Worth, Capital ($2,000 × 50%)		1,000	
	S. Kee, Capital			34,500
	To record admission of Kee by investment and bonus to new partner.			

Total capital after investment: ($43,300 + $39,200 + $32,500)	$115,000
Kee's capital in the partnership: (30% × $115,000)	$34,500
Bonus to Kee: ($34,500 − $32,500)	$2,000

▶ Summary of Learning Objectives

1. **Describe the characteristics of the partnership form of business organization.** The main characteristics of a partnership are (1) the association of individuals, (2) mutual agency, (3) co-ownership of property, (4) limited life, and (5) unlimited liability for a general partnership.

2. **Account for the formation of a partnership.** When a partnership is formed, each partner's initial investment should be recorded at the assets' fair value at the date of their transfer to the partnership. If accounts receivable are contributed, both the gross amount and an allowance for doubtful accounts should be recorded. Accumulated depreciation is not carried forward into a partnership.

3. **Allocate and record profit or loss to partners.** Profit or loss is divided based on the profit and loss ratio, which may be any of the following: (1) a fixed ratio; (2) a ratio based on beginning, ending, or average capital balances; or (3) salary and interest allowances and the remainder in a fixed ratio.

4. **Prepare partnership financial statements.** The financial statements of a partnership are similar to those of a proprietorship. The main differences are that (1) the statement of owners' equity is called the statement of partners' equity, and (2) each partner's capital account is usually reported on the balance sheet or in a supporting schedule.

5. *Account for the admission of a partner.* The entry to record the admission of a new partner by purchase of a partner's interest affects only partners' capital accounts. The entry to record the admission by investment of assets in the partnership (1) increases both net assets and total capital, and (2) may result in the recognition of a bonus to either the old partners or the new partner.

6. *Account for the withdrawal of a partner.* The entry to record a withdrawal from the firm when payment is made from partners' personal assets affects only partners' capital accounts. The entry to record a withdrawal when payment is made from partnership assets (1) decreases net assets and total capital, and (2) may result in recognizing a bonus to either the departing partner or the remaining partners.

7. *Account for the liquidation of a partnership.* When a partnership is liquidated, it is necessary to record (1) the sale of noncash assets, (2) the allocation of the gain or loss on realization based on the profit and loss ratio, (3) the payment of partnership liabilities, (4) the removal of any capital deficiency either by repayment or by allocation to the other partners, and (5) the distribution of cash to the partners based on their capital balances.

▶ Glossary

Admission by investment Admission of a partner by an investment of assets in the partnership. Both partnership net assets and total capital increase. (p. 647)

Admission of a new partner by purchase of a partner's interest Admission of a partner through a personal transaction between one or more existing partners and the new partner. It does not change total partnership assets or total capital. (p. 646)

Capital deficiency A debit balance in a partner's capital account after the allocation of a gain or loss on liquidation of a partnership. Capital deficiencies can be repaid or allocated among the remaining partners. (p. 655)

Limited liability partnership (LLP) A partnership in which partners have limited liability for other partners' negligence. (p. 635)

Limited partnership (LP) A partnership in which one or more general partners have unlimited liability, and the other partners, known as limited partners, have limited liability for the obligations of the partnership. (p. 635)

Mutual agency The concept that the action of any partner is binding on all other partners. (p. 635)

No capital deficiency A situation where all partners have credit balances after the allocation of a gain or a loss on liquidation of a partnership. (p. 655)

Partnership An association of individuals who operate a business for profit. (p. 634)

Partnership agreement A written contract that expresses the voluntary agreement of two or more individuals in a partnership. (p. 636)

Partnership dissolution A change in the number of partners that dissolves (ends) the partnership. It does not necessarily end the business. (p. 634)

Partnership liquidation An event that ends both the legal and economic life of a partnership. (p. 655)

Profit and loss ratio The basis for dividing both profit and loss in a partnership. (p. 640)

Realization The sale of noncash assets for cash on the liquidation of a partnership. (p. 655)

Statement of partners' equity The equity statement for a partnership that shows the changes in each partner's capital balance, and in total partnership capital, during the year. (p. 645)

Withdrawal by payment from partners' personal assets Withdrawal of a partner by a personal transaction between partners. It does not change total partnership assets or total capital. (p. 651)

Withdrawal by payment from partnership assets Withdrawal of a partner by a transaction that decreases both partnership net assets and total capital. (p. 652)

▶ Self-Study Questions

Answers are at the end of the chapter.

(LO 1) K 1. Which of the following is **not** a characteristic of a partnership?
(a) Taxable entity
(b) Co-ownership of property
(c) Mutual agency
(d) Limited life

(LO 1) K 2. Which of the following is considered to be a disadvantage of the partnership form of organization?
(a) Unlimited life   (c) Mutual agency
(b) Limited liability   (d) Ease of formation

(LO 2) AP 3. Brianne and Stephen are combining their two proprietorships to form a partnership. Brianne's proprietorship has $8,000 of accounts receivable and an allowance for doubtful accounts of $2,000. The partners agree that the fair value of the accounts receivable is $4,800. The entry that the partnership makes to record Brianne's initial contribution includes a:
(a) debit to Accounts Receivable for $8,000.
(b) debit to Accounts Receivable for $4,800.
(c) debit to Bad Debts Expense for $200.
(d) credit to Allowance for Doubtful Accounts for $200.

(LO 3) AP 4. The NBC Company reports profit of $60,000. If partners N, B, and C have an income ratio of 50%, 30%, and 20%, respectively, C's share of the profit is:
(a) $30,000.
(b) $12,000.
(c) $18,000.
(d) No correct answer is given.

(LO 4) K 5. To close a partner's drawings account, an entry must be made that:
(a) debits that partner's drawings account and credits Income Summary.
(b) debits that partner's drawings account and credits that partner's capital account.
(c) credits that partner's drawings account and debits that partner's capital account.
(d) credits that partner's drawings account and debits the partnership's dividend account.

(LO 5) AP 6. R. Ranken purchases 50% of L. Lars's capital interest in the Kim & Lars partnership for $20,000. The capital balances of Kim and Lars are $40,000 and $30,000, respectively. Ranken's capital balance after the purchase is:
(a) $15,000.
(b) $20,000.
(c) $22,000.
(d) $35,000.

(LO 5) AP 7. Capital balances in the DEA partnership are Delano, Capital $60,000; Egil, Capital $50,000; and Armand, Capital $40,000. The profit and loss ratio is 5:3:2. The DEAR partnership is formed by admitting Ramachandran to the firm with a cash investment of $60,000 for a 25% capital interest. The bonus to be credited to Delano, Capital, in admitting Ramachandran is:
(a) $1,500.

(b) $3,750.
(c) $7,500.
(d) $10,000.

(LO 6) AP 8. Capital balances in the Alouette partnership are Tremblay, Capital $50,000; St-Jean, Capital $40,000; and Roy, Capital $30,000. The profit and loss ratio is 5:4:3. Roy withdraws from the partnership after being paid $16,000 personally by each of Tremblay and St-Jean. St-Jean's capital balance after recording the withdrawal of Roy is:
(a) $46,000.
(b) $50,000.
(c) $55,000.
(d) $65,000.

(LO 6) AP 9. Capital balances in the TERM partnership are Takako, Capital $50,000; Endo, Capital $40,000; Reiko, Capital $30,000; and Maeda, Capital $20,000. The profit and loss ratio is 4:3:2:1. Maeda withdraws from the firm after receiving $29,000 in cash from the partnership. Endo's capital balance after recording the withdrawal of Maeda is:
(a) $36,000.
(b) $37,000.
(c) $37,300.
(d) $40,000.

(LO 7) K 10. In the liquidation of a partnership, it is necessary to (1) distribute cash to the partners, (2) sell noncash assets, (3) allocate any gain or loss on realization to the partners, and (4) pay liabilities. These steps should be performed in the following order:
(a) (2), (3), (4), (1).
(b) (2), (3), (1), (4).
(c) (3), (2), (1), (4).
(d) (3), (2), (4), (1).

▶ Questions

(LO 1) K 1. The characteristics of a partnership include the following: (a) association of individuals, (b) limited life, and (c) co-ownership of property. Explain each of these terms.

(LO 1) C 2. K. Nasser and T. Yoko are considering a business venture. They ask you to explain the advantages and disadvantages of the partnership form of organization. Explain these to Nasser and Yoko.

(LO 1) K 3. (a) What items should be specified in a partnership agreement? (b) Why is it important to have this agreement in writing?

(LO 2) K 4. (a) For accounting purposes, when a partner invests assets in a partnership, how is the value of these assets determined? (b) Is this practice consistent with the cost principle? Explain.

(LO 2) K 5. When a partnership is formed, one or more of the partners may contribute equipment as part of their initial investment. How is the amount of accumulated depreciation to be recorded on this equipment determined?

(LO 2) K 6. Franca and Naheed are transferring $8,000 of accounts receivable from each of their sole proprietorships into a partnership. They have agreed that $7,000 of Franca's receivables is collectible but it is likely they will collect only $6,000 of the receivables from Naheed's proprietorship. How should these receivables be recorded in the partnership? Explain why.

(LO 3) C 7. What is the relationship between (a) a salary allowance for allocating profit among partners and (b) partners' cash withdrawals?

(LO 3) C 8. What is the difference between a salary allowance for allocating profit among partners and salary expense? Between an interest allowance and interest expense?

(LO 4) C   9. What is included in a statement of partners' equity? How is it similar to, and different from, a statement of owner's equity?

(LO 4) C   10. The income statement of a partnership includes the details of how the profit or loss is divided among the partners. Do you agree or disagree? Explain.

(LO 4) C   11. The equity section of a partnership's balance sheet shows the total amount invested by the partners separate from the profit earned to date and retained in the business. Do you agree or disagree? Explain.

(LO 5) AP 12 How is the accounting for admission to a partnership by purchase of a partner's interest different from the accounting for admission by an investment of assets in the partnership? In your explanation, also include how the net assets and total capital change after the admission of a partner in each of these two ways.

(LO 5) C   13. R. Minoa decides to invest $25,000 in a partnership for a one-sixth capital interest. Will Minoa's capital balance be $25,000? Does Minoa also acquire a one-sixth profit and loss ratio through this investment?

(LO 5) C   14. What are some reasons why the existing partners may be willing to give a new partner a bonus for joining a partnership?

(LO 6) C   15. What is the impact on a partnership's balance sheet when (a) a partner withdraws by payment from partners' personal assets, and (b) a partner withdraws by payment from partnership assets?

(LO 6) C   16. Under what circumstances will a partner who is leaving a partnership give the remaining partners a bonus?

(LO 7) K   17. Identify the steps in liquidating a partnership.

(LO 7) C   18. What basis is used for making the final distribution of cash to the partners when there is a capital deficiency and the deficiency is paid? And when it is not paid?

▶ Brief Exercises

BE12–1   The following terms were introduced in this chapter:

1. Profit and loss ratio
2. Admission by investment
3. Partnership liquidation
4. Mutual agency
5. Salary allowance
6. Withdrawal by payment from partners' personal assets
7. Capital deficiency
8. Limited liability partnership
9. General partnership
10. Partnership dissolution

Identify partnership terminology. (LO 1) K

Match the terms with the following descriptions:

(a) _____ Partners have limited liability.
(b) _____ Partners have unlimited liability.
(c) _____ It is the basis for dividing profit and loss.
(d) _____ Partnership assets and capital increase with the change in partners.
(e) _____ Partnership assets and capital stay the same with the change in partners.
(f) _____ Actions of partners are binding on all other partners.
(g) _____ It is a compensation for differences in personal effort put into the partnership.
(h) _____ Partnership is changed by the addition or withdrawal of a partner.
(i) _____ There is a debit balance in a partner's capital account.
(j) _____ Partnership is ended.

BE12–2   Barbara Ripley and Fred Nichols decide to organize the ALL-Star partnership. Ripley invests $15,000 cash and Nichols contributes $10,000 cash and equipment with a cost of $7,000 and accumulated depreciation of $5,000 and a fair value of $3,000. Prepare the entries to record each partner's investment in the partnership.

Record formation of partnership. (LO 2) AP

BE12–3   R. Black and B. Rivers decide to organize the Black River Partnership. Black contributes $10,000 cash. Rivers contributes $2,400 of accounts receivable, of which the partners agree that $2,000 is collectible. Rivers will also contribute the amount of cash required so both partners have the same amount in their capital accounts. Prepare the entry to record each partner's investment in the partnership on July 1, 2017.

Record formation of partnership. (LO 2) AP

Convert proportions into fractions and percentages. (LO 3) AP

BE12-4 Fixed profit and loss ratios can be expressed as proportions, fractions, or percentages. For each of the following proportions, determine the equivalent fractions or percentages:

	Proportions	Fractions	Percentages
(a)	2:1		
(b)	6:4		
(c)	3:8		
(d)	4:3:2		
(e)	1:2:1		

Journalize the division of profit. (LO 3) AP

BE12-5 Rod and Dall are partners in R&D LLP. The partnership reports profit of $75,000. There is no partnership agreement. (a) Prepare the entry to distribute the profit between the partners. (b) Prepare the entry to distribute the profit assuming it is a $75,000 net loss.

Calculate division of profit and record closing entries. (LO 3) AP

BE12-6 During the fiscal year ended November 30, 2017, the profit for Scrimger & Woods Partnership was $84,000. The partners, A. Scrimger and D. Woods, share profit and loss in a 3:5 ratio, respectively. (a) Calculate the division of profit to each partner. (b) Prepare the entry to close the Income Summary account.

Calculate division of profit. (LO 3) AP

BE12-7 MET Co. reports profit of $70,000 for the current year. Partner salary allowances are J. Moses $24,000; T. Eaton $30,000; and M. Tung-Ching $5,000. The profit and loss ratio is 6:2:2. Calculate the division of profit to each partner.

Calculate division of profit. (LO 3) AP

BE12-8 The MillStone Partnership reported profit of $60,000 for the year ended February 28, 2017. Salary allowances are $45,000 for H. Mills and $25,000 for S. Stone. Interest allowances of 5% are calculated on each partner's opening capital account balance. Capital account balances at March 1, 2016, were as follows: H. Mills $72,000 (Cr.) and S. Stone $47,000 (Cr.). Any remainder is shared equally. Calculate the division of profit to each partner.

Calculate and record division of loss. (LO 3) AP

BE12-9 Tognazzini Company had a $15,300 loss for the year ended October 31, 2017. The company is a partnership owned by Lilia and Terry Tognazzini. Salary allowances for the partners are Lilia $24,900 and Terry $15,000. Interest allowances are Lilia $5,300 and Terry $9,300. The remainder is shared 75% by Lilia and 25% by Terry. (a) Calculate the loss to be allocated to each partner. (b) Prepare a journal entry to close the Income Summary account.

Prepare financial statements. (LO 4) AP

BE12-10 The medical practice of Dr. W. Jarratt and Dr. M. Bramstrup had the following general ledger account balances at April 30, 2017, its fiscal year end:

Accounts payable	$27,100	M. Bramstrup, drawings	$121,000
Accumulated depreciation—equipment	17,100	Operating expenses	149,400
Cash	36,000	Service revenue	377,000
Equipment	75,100	W. Jarratt, capital	36,900
M. Bramstrup, capital	50,400	W. Jarratt, drawings	127,000

(a) Calculate the profit or loss for the year.
(b) Prepare the statement of partners' equity and the balance sheet, assuming the doctors share profit or loss equally.

Record admission of partner by purchase of interest. (LO 5) AP

BE12-11 In ABC Co., the capital balances of the partners are A. Ali $30,000; S. Babson $25,000; and K. Carter $36,000. The partners share profit equally. On June 9 of the current year, D. Dutton is admitted to the partnership by purchasing one half of K. Carter's interest for $20,000 paid to him personally. Journalize the admission of Dutton on June 9.

Journalize admission by investment of assets. (LO 5) AP

BE12-12 In Eastwood partnership, capital balances are Irey $40,000 and Pedigo $50,000. The partners share income equally. Vernon is admitted to the firm with a 45% interest by an investment of cash of $58,000. Journalize the admission of Vernon.

Record withdrawal of partner. (LO 6) AP

BE12-13 On December 31, 2017, capital balances of the partners in Manitoba Maple are R. Neepawa $45,000; S. Altona $35,000; and T. Morden $25,000. The partners share profit in a 5:3:2 ratio, respectively. Morden decides that she is going to leave the partnership. Journalize the withdrawal of Morden assuming:

(a) Neepawa and Altona both pay Morden $17,000 from their personal assets to each receive 50% of Morden's equity.
(b) Neepawa and Altona both pay Morden $12,000 from their personal assets to each receive 50% of Morden's equity.

Record withdrawal of partner. (LO 6) AP

BE12-14 Data for Manitoba Maple are presented in BE12-13. Instead of a payment from personal assets, assume that Morden receives cash from the partnership when she withdraws. Journalize the withdrawal of Morden if she receives (a) $35,000 cash, and (b) $20,000 cash.

BE12–15 After liquidating noncash assets and paying creditors, account balances in the Mann partnership are Cash $21,000; A, Capital (Cr.) $8,000; B, Capital (Cr.) $9,000; and C, Capital (Cr.) $4,000. The partners share profit equally. Journalize the final distribution of cash to the partners.

Journalize final cash distribution in liquidation. (LO 7) AP

BE12–16 The partners of LR Company have decided to liquidate their partnership. Noncash assets were sold for $125,000. The income ratios of the partners Cisneros, Gunselman, and Forren are 3:2:3, respectively. Complete the following schedule of cash payments for LR Company.

Complete schedule of partnership liquidation payments. (LO 7) AP

P18		*fx*									
	A	B	C	D	E	F	G	H	I	J	K	L
1	Item	Cash	+	Noncash Assets	=	Liabilities	+	Cisneros, Capital	+	Gunselman, Capital	+	Forren, Capital
2	Balances before liquidation	15,000		90,000		40,000		20,000		32,000		13,000
3	Sale of noncash assets and allocation of gain											
4	New balances											
5	Pay liabilities											
6	New balances											
7	Cash distribution to partners											
8	Final balances											
9												
10												

BE12–17 On November 15 of the current year, the account balances in Greenscape Partnership were Cash $8,000; Other Assets $17,000; D. Dupuis, Capital $12,000; V. Dueck, Capital $10,000; and B. Veitch, Capital $3,000. The three partners share profit and losses equally. The other assets are sold for $20,000 cash. Prepare journal entries to (a) record the sale of the other assets, (b) distribute any resulting gain or loss to the capital accounts, and (c) record the final distribution of cash to the partners.

Record partnership liquidation. (LO 7) AP

BE12–18 Data for Greenscape Partnership are presented in BE12–17. Assume that the other assets were sold for $14,000 cash instead of $20,000. Prepare journal entries to (a) record the sale of the other assets, (b) distribute any resulting gain or loss to the capital accounts, and (c) record the final distribution of cash to the partners.

Record partnership liquidation. (LO 7) AP

▶ Exercises

E12–1 Presented below are three independent situations:

Determine form of organization. (LO 1) AN

1. Angelique Gloss and David Deutsch, two students looking for summer employment, decide to open a home meal replacement business. Each day, they prepare nutritious, ready-to-bake meals, which they sell to people on their way home from work.
2. Joe Daigle and Cathy Goodfellow own a ski repair business and a ski shop, respectively. They have decided to combine their businesses. They expect that in the coming year they will need a large amount of money to expand their operations.
3. Three business professors have formed a business to offer income tax services to the community. They expect to hire students during the busy season.
4. Myles Anawak would like to organize a company that buys and leases commercial real estate. Myles will need to raise a large amount of capital so that he can buy commercial property for lease.

Instructions

In each of the above situations, explain whether the partnership form of organization is the best choice for the business. Explain your reasoning.

E12–2 K. Decker, S. Rosen, and E. Toso are forming a partnership. Decker is investing $50,000 of personal cash to the partnership. Rosen owns land with a fair value of $15,000 and a small building with a fair value of $80,000, which she transfers to the partnership. Toso transfers to the partnership cash of $9,000, accounts receivable of $32,000, and equipment with a fair value of $39,000. The partnership expects to collect $29,000 of the accounts receivable.

Record formation of partnership. (LO 2) AP

Instructions

(a) Prepare the journal entries to record each of the partners' investments.
(b) What amount would be reported as total partners' equity immediately after the investments?

Record formation of partnership. (LO 2) AP

E12-3   Suzy Vopat has owned and operated a proprietorship for several years. On January 1, she decides to terminate this business and become a partner in the firm of Vopat and Sigma. Vopat's investment in the partnership consists of $12,000 in cash and the following assets of the proprietorship: accounts receivable $14,000 less allowance for doubtful accounts of $2,000, and equipment $30,000 less accumulated depreciation of $4,000. It is agreed that the allowance for doubtful accounts should be $3,000 for the partnership. The fair value of the equipment is $23,500.

Instructions

Journalize Vopat's admission to the firm of Vopat and Sigma.

Calculate and record division of profit. (LO 3) AP

E12-4   K. Ison (beginning capital, $50,000) and I. McCoy (beginning capital $80,000) are partners. During 2017, the partnership reported profit of $60,000, and Ison made drawings of $15,000 while McCoy made drawings of $20,000.

Instructions

(a) Assume the partnership agreement calls for profit to be divided 55% to Ison and 45% to McCoy. Prepare the journal entry to close the Income Summary account.

(b) Assume the partnership agreement calls for profit to be divided with a salary of $30,000 to K. Ison and $20,000 to I. McCoy, with the remainder divided 55% to Ison and 45% to McCoy. Prepare the journal entry to close the Income Summary account.

(c) Assume the partnership agreement calls for profit to be divided with a salary of $40,000 to K. Ison and $30,000 to I. McCoy, interest of 10% on beginning capital, and the remainder divided 50%–50%. Prepare the journal entry to record close the Income Summary account.

Calculate and record division of profit. (LO 3) AP

E12-5   R. Huma and W. How have capital balances on July 1, 2016, of $62,000 and $58,000, respectively. The partnership profit-sharing agreement specifies:

1. salary allowances of $30,900 for Huma and $21,900 for How,
2. interest at 6% on beginning capital balances, and
3. for the remaining profit or loss to be shared 60% by Huma and 40% by How.

Instructions

(a) Prepare a schedule showing the division of profit for the year ended June 30, 2017, assuming profit is (1) $70,000, and (2) $55,000.

(b) Journalize the allocation of profit in each of the situations in part (a).

Calculate and record division of loss. (LO 3) AP

E12-6   Daisey Brodsky and Jim Leigh began a partnership on February 1, 2017, by investing $62,000 and $88,000, respectively. They agree to share profit and losses by allocating yearly salary allowances of $60,000 to Daisey and $40,000 to Jim, an interest allowance of 8% on their investments, and to split the remainder 55:45. During the year, Daisey withdrew $30,000 and Jim withdrew $22,000. The partnership recorded a loss of $15,000 in its first fiscal year.

Instructions

(a) Prepare a schedule showing the division of the loss for the year.

(b) Prepare the journal entry to close the Income Summary account at the end of the year.

Prepare partial financial statements. (LO 4) AP

E12-7   Copperfield Developments is a partnership owned by Alvaro Rodriguez and Elisabetta Carrieri. On December 31, 2016, the partners' capital balances are Rodriguez $67,140 and Carrieri $78,140. During 2017, Carrieri invested $3,540 cash into the partnership, drawings were $36,010 by Rodriguez and $58,940 by Carrieri, and profit was $77,230. Rodriguez and Carrieri share profit based on a 3:4 ratio.

Instructions

(a) Prepare the statement of partners' equity for the year.

(b) Prepare the partners' equity section of the balance sheet at year end.

Prepare financial statements and closing entries. (LO 3, 4) AP

E12-8   Dr. J. Kovacik and Dr. S. Donovan have been operating a dental practice as a partnership for several years. The fixed profit and loss ratio is 60% for Dr. Kovacik and 40% for Dr. Donovan. The dental practice had the following general ledger account balances at November 30, 2017, its fiscal year end:

Cash	$ 33,900
Supplies	16,150
Equipment	176,300
Accumulated depreciation—equipment	41,450
Accounts payable	15,700
Note payable, due 2021	56,000
J. Kovacik, capital	59,000
J. Kovacik, drawings	142,000
S. Donovan, capital	33,000
S. Donovan, drawings	94,000

Fees earned	$425,000
Salaries expense	80,100
Office expense	83,600
Interest expense	4,100

Instructions

(a) Prepare financial statements for the partnership.

(b) Prepare closing entries.

E12–9 A. Veveris and J. Rubenis share profit on a 2:1 basis, respectively. They have capital balances of $42,000 and $33,000, respectively, when S. Weiss is admitted to the partnership on September 1, 2017.

Journalize admission of a new partner by purchase of an interest. (LO 5) AP

Instructions

(a) Prepare the journal entry to record the admission of Weiss under each of the following independent assumptions:
1. Weiss purchases 50% of Ververis's equity for $25,000. This is a personal transaction between the partners.
2. Weiss purchases 25% of Ververis's and Rubenis's equity for $15,000 and $10,000, respectively. This is a personal transaction among the partners.

(b) For each of these alternatives, indicate the balance in each partner's capital account and total partners' equity after Weiss is admitted to the partnership.

E12–10 Olive Oil Imports is a partnership owned by Magda Stavros and Giannis Metaxas. The partners share profit on a 3:2 basis, respectively. On January 1, 2017, they have capital balances of $95,000 and $65,000, respectively. On that day, Magda and Giannis agree to admit Iona Xanthos to the partnership in exchange for an investment of cash into the partnership.

Journalize admission of a new partner by investment of assets. (LO 5) AP

Instructions

(a) Prepare the journal entry to record the admission of Xanthos on January 1 under each of the following independent assumptions:
1. Xanthos invests $65,000 cash for a 33⅓% ownership interest. This is an investment of assets.
2. Xanthos invests $95,000 cash for a 33⅓% ownership interest. This is an investment of assets.

(b) For each of these alternatives, indicate the balance in each partner's capital account and total partners' equity after Xanthos is admitted to the partnership.

E12–11 Julie Lane, Sara Miles, and Amber Noll have capital balances of $50,000, $40,000, and $30,000, respectively. The profit and loss ratio is 5:3:2. Assume Noll withdraws from the partnership on December 31 of the current year under each of the following independent conditions:

Record withdrawal of partner. (LO 6) AP

1. Miles agrees to purchase all of Noll's equity by paying $35,000 cash from her personal assets.
2. Noll withdraws $30,000 cash from the partnership.
3. Noll withdraws $35,000 cash from the partnership.

Instructions

(a) Journalize the withdrawal of Noll under each of the above assumptions.

(b) Determine the balances in the partners' capital accounts and in total partners' equity after Noll has withdrawn, for conditions 1 and 2 above.

E12–12 Dale Nagel, Keith White, and Issa Mbango have capital balances of $92,000, $74,000, and $6,000, respectively. They share profit or loss on a 4:3:2 basis. White withdraws from the partnership on September 30 of the current year.

Record withdrawal of partner with payment from partnership assets. (LO 6) AP

Instructions

(a) Journalize the withdrawal of White under each of the following assumptions.
1. White is paid $83,000 cash from partnership assets.
2. White is paid $59,000 cash from partnership assets.

(b) Determine the balances in the partners' capital accounts and in total partners' equity after White has withdrawn from the partnership for condition 2 above.

E12–13 Windl, Houghton, and Pahli decided to liquidate their partnership on October 1. Before the noncash assets were sold, the capital account balances were Windl, $87,400; Houghton, $34,500; and Pahli, $50,800. The partners divide profits and losses equally. After the noncash assets are sold and the liabilities are paid, the partnership has $172,700 of cash.

Calculate amounts paid on liquidation of partnership. (LO 7) AP

Instructions

(a) How much cash will each partner receive in the final liquidation?

(b) Assume instead that there is $142,700 of cash after the noncash assets are sold and the liabilities are paid. How much cash will each partner receive?

Calculate amounts paid on liquidation of partnership. (LO 7) AP

E12-14 The Braun Company at December 31 has the following account balances.

			Noncash			
Item		Cash +	Assets =	Liabilities +	Ho, Capital +	Li, Capital
Balances before liquidation		$15,000	$110,000	$60,000	$40,000	$25,000

THE BRAUN COMPANY

Instructions

Calculate how much cash each partner will receive on the liquidation of the partnership under each situation assuming any deficiencies are paid by the partners:

(a) Cash of $110,000 is received for the noncash assets. Ho's and Li's income ratios are 60% and 40%, respectively.

(b) Cash of $60,000 is received for the noncash assets. Ho's and Li's income ratios are 60% and 40%, respectively.

Calculate amounts paid on liquidation of partnership. (LO 7) AP

E12-15 At December 31, Baylee Company has cash of $40,000, equipment of $130,000, accumulated depreciation of $40,000, liabilities of $55,000, and the following partners' capital balances: H. Bayer $45,000 and J. Leech $30,000. The partnership is liquidated on December 31 of the current year and $100,000 cash is received for the equipment. Bayer and Leech share profits and losses equally.

Instructions

(a) How much is the gain or loss on the disposal of the noncash assets?

(b) How much of that gain or loss is allocated to each partner?

(c) How much cash will be paid to each of the partners when the company is liquidated on December 31?

Record partnership liquidation. (LO 7) AP

E12-16 Data for the Baylee Company partnership are presented in E12-15.

Instructions

Prepare the entries to record:

(a) the sale of the equipment,

(b) the allocation to the partners of the gain or loss on liquidation,

(c) the payment of creditors, and

(d) the distribution of cash to the partners.

Record partnership liquidation. (LO 7) AP

E12-17 Ole Low, Arnt Olson, and Stig Lokum decided to liquidate the LOL partnership on December 31 of the current year, and go their separate ways. The partners share profit and losses equally. As at December 31, the partnership had cash of $15,000, noncash assets of $121,000, and liabilities of $22,000. Before selling their noncash assets, the partners had capital balances of $45,100, $59,900, and $9,000, respectively. The noncash assets were sold for $85,000 and the creditors were paid.

Instructions

(a) Calculate the loss on the sale of the noncash assets and the amount of cash remaining after paying the liabilities.

(b) Calculate the balance in each of the partners' capital accounts after allocating the loss from the sale of the noncash assets and paying the liabilities.

(c) Assume that all of the partners have the personal resources to cover a deficit in their capital accounts. Prepare journal entries to record any cash receipts from the partners to cover any existing deficit and to record the final distribution of cash.

(d) Now assume that the partners do not have the personal resources to cover a deficit in their capital accounts. Prepare journal entries to allocate any deficit to the remaining partners and to record the final distribution of cash.

▶ Problems: Set A

P12–1A   The trial balances of two proprietorships on January 1, 2017, follow:

Discuss advantages and disadvantages of partnerships and record formation of partnership. (LO 1, 2) AP

	Domic Company		Dasilva Company	
	Dr.	Cr.	Dr.	Cr.
Cash	$ 9,000		$10,000	
Accounts receivable	13,500		24,000	
Allowance for doubtful accounts		$ 3,000		$ 5,500
Merchandise inventory	11,500		15,500	
Equipment	40,000		31,000	
Accumulated depreciation—equipment		24,000		13,000
Accounts payable		11,000		34,000
I. Domic, capital		36,000		
P. Dasilva, capital				28,000
	$74,000	$74,000	$80,500	$80,500

Domic and Dasilva decide to form a partnership on January 1 and agree on the following valuations for the noncash assets that they are each contributing:

	Domic	Dasilva
Accounts receivable—net realizable value	$ 9,000	$21,000
Merchandise inventory	14,000	13,000
Equipment	18,000	15,000

All of the assets in each of the proprietorships will be transferred to the partnership. The partnership will also assume all the liabilities of the two proprietorships. Domic and Dasilva are also agreed that Dasilva will invest the amount of cash required so their investments in the partnership are equal.

Instructions

(a) What are the advantages and disadvantages for these two individuals of forming a partnership as opposed to setting up a corporation?
(b) Prepare separate journal entries to record the transfer of each proprietorship's assets and liabilities to the partnership on January 1.
(c) Journalize the additional cash investment.

TAKING IT FURTHER   What are some of the advantages of two individuals such as Domic and Dasilva operating as a partnership instead of as two separate proprietorships?

P12–2A   On January 1, 2017, the capital balances in Gablesmith Partnership are as follows:

Calculate and record division of profit. Prepare closing entries. (LO 3) AP

Zoya Gable	$20,000
Matthew Smith	$24,000

Neither partner had any drawings in 2017.

Instructions

Prepare closing entries to allocate the partnership profit under the following situations:

(a) In 2017, the partnership reports profit of $90,000. There is no partnership agreement.
(b) In 2017, the partnership reports profit of $60,000. The income ratio provides for salary allowances of $42,000 for Gable and $30,000 to Smith and the remainder to be shared equally.
(c) In 2017, the partnership reports profit of $60,000. Assume the partnership agreement calls for profit to be divided with a salary of $40,000 to Gable and $30,000 to Smith. Gable is allowed 6% of interest on her beginning capital, and the remainder is divided 70%–30%.

TAKING IT FURTHER   When Gable and Smith were discussing how profit and losses should be divided, they considered waiting to see who worked the hardest before agreeing on how to share the profit. What are the advantages and disadvantages of doing this?

Calculate and record division of profit. Prepare statement of partners' equity. (LO 3, 4) AP

P12–3A   At the end of its first year of operations, on December 31, 2017, CDW Partners' accounts show the following:

Partner	Drawings	Capital
J. Chapman-Brown	$10,100	$30,000
C. Duperé	7,000	40,000
H. Weir	5,000	50,000

The capital balance represents each partner's initial capital investment. No closing entries for profit (loss) or drawings have been recorded as yet.

Instructions

(a) Journalize the entry to record the division of profit for the year ended December 31, 2017, under each of the following independent assumptions:
1. Profit is $40,000. Duperé and Weir are given salary allowances of $8,000 and $12,000, respectively. The remainder is shared equally.
2. Profit is $40,000. Each partner is allowed interest of 5% on beginning capital balances. Chapman-Brown, Duperé, and Weir are given salary allowances of $15,000, $20,000, and $18,000, respectively. The remainder is shared in a ratio of 5:3:2.

(b) Prepare a statement of partners' equity for the year under assumption 2 in part (a) above.

TAKING IT FURTHER   Explain why partnerships such as CDW Partners include an interest allowance in their profit- and loss-sharing arrangements.

Calculate division of profit or loss. Prepare an income statement and a statement of partners' equity, and closing entries. (LO 3, 4) AP

P12–4A   Veda Storey and Gordon Rogers have a partnership agreement with the following provisions for sharing profit or loss:

1. A salary allowance of $30,900 to Storey and $39,700 to Rogers
2. An interest allowance of 5% on capital balances at the beginning of the year
3. The remainder to be divided between Storey and Rogers on a 2:3 basis

The capital balances on January 1, 2017, for Storey and Rogers were $82,000 and $101,000, respectively. For the year ended December 31, 2017, the Storey Rogers Partnership had sales of $340,000; cost of goods sold of $250,000; operating expenses of $130,000; V. Storey drawings of $24,000; and G. Rogers drawings of $28,800.

Instructions

(a) Prepare an income statement for Storey Rogers Partnership for the year.
(b) Prepare a schedule to show how the profit or loss will be allocated to the two partners.
(c) Prepare a statement of partners' equity for the year.
(d) Prepare closing entries at December 31.

TAKING IT FURTHER   Assume that gross profit was lower than expected for 2017 because Rogers sold a significant amount of inventory to friends at substantially reduced prices. These arrangements were made without Storey's approval. She therefore argues that she should be allocated her salary allowance and the remaining loss should be allocated to Rogers. Is this reasonable?

Prepare financial statements and closing entries. (LO 3, 4) AP

P12–5A   Below is an alphabetical listing of the accounts in the general ledger of the Kant-Adder accounting firm at the partnership's fiscal year end, March 31, 2017. Adjusting entries for the year have been posted and included in these balances.

Accounts payable	$ 12,500	Note payable	$ 50,000
Accounts receivable	61,000	Rent expense	36,000
Accumulated depreciation—equipment	12,000	Salaries expense	80,000
Cash	14,000	Salaries payable	8,000
Depreciation expense	8,000	Supplies	1,500
Equipment	42,000	Supplies expense	5,000
Fees earned	255,000	U. Adder, capital	30,000
I. Kant, capital	30,000	U. Adder, drawings	60,000
I. Kant, drawings	90,000	Unearned revenue	5,000
Interest expense	5,000		

Additional information:

1. The balance in Kant's capital account includes an additional $5,000 investment during the year.
2. $1,500 of the note payable is due within the next year.
3. Kant and Adder share profit in the ratio of 2:1, respectively.

Instructions

(a) Prepare an income statement, statement of partners' equity, and balance sheet.
(b) Journalize the closing entries.

TAKING IT FURTHER   Each partner's drawings are larger than their respective capital account balances. Is this a problem? Why or why not?

P12–6A   Tyler Gilligan and Matt Melnyk, two college friends, decided to set up a snow removal business called Ty & Matt Snow Removal Services. At the inception of the partnership, Tyler invested $4,000 cash and Matt invested $11,000 cash. Once formed, the partnership purchased equipment and a vehicle. Tyler estimates that the equipment purchased for $2,000 and the vehicle purchased for $10,000 have five-year useful lives, with no residual value. He used the straight-line method to calculate depreciation expense. At the end of the first year of business, Tyler, who was studying accounting, provided the following information:

Prepare entries to correct errors, allocate profit, and prepare financial statements. (LO 3, 4) AP

TY & MATT SNOW REMOVAL SERVICES		
Income Statement		
Year Ended December 31, 2017		
Service revenue		$50,000
Expenses		
Supplies expense	$ 6,000	
Depreciation expense	2,400	
Salaries expense	30,000	38,400
Profit		$11,600

Additional information:

1. Salaries expense is $20,000 and $10,000 cash that was paid to Tyler and Matt, respectively, during the year.
2. All revenues were collected in cash.
3. All supplies were paid for in cash. At the end of the year, there were no supplies on hand.
4. There is $17,000 in the bank account at December 31, 2017.

Instructions

(a) Prepare journal entries to correct the errors, if any, on the income statement.
(b) Calculate the correct profit and the amount to be allocated to each partner.
(c) Prepare a statement of partners' equity for the year ended December 31, 2017.
(d) Prepare a balance sheet at December 31, 2017.

TAKING IT FURTHER   Tyler is not happy about how the profit was allocated. He says that he works twice as hard as Matt. Matt argues that he made a larger contribution to start the partnership. What should Tyler and Matt do to deal with their concerns?

P12–7A   At April 30, partners' capital balances in DES Partners are Dexter $44,000, Emley $26,000, and Sigle $24,000. The profit-sharing ratio is 5:3:2, respectively. On May 1, the DESW Partnership is formed by admitting Watson to the firm as a partner with 20% equity.

Record admission of partner. (LO 5) AP

Instructions

Journalize the admission of Watson under each of the following independent assumptions.

(a) Watson invests $23,500.
(b) Watson invests $35,000.
(c) Watson invests $10,000.

TAKING IT FURTHER   After joining the partnership, Watson developed concerns over unlimited liability. Watson is now aware that there are partnerships that modify this feature. Explain to Watson these other forms of partnership.

Record admission of partner. (LO 5) AP

P12–8A At April 30 of the current year, partners' capital balances and the profit- and loss-sharing ratio in SOS Enterprises are as follows:

Partner	Capital Balance	Profit and Loss Ratio
R. Short	$38,000	3
K. Osborne	$19,000	2
W. Sanga	$59,000	4

On May 1, the SOSO Company is formed by admitting N. Osvald to the firm as a partner.

Instructions

Journalize the admission of Osvald under each of the following independent assumptions:

(a) Osvald purchases 50% of W. Sanga's ownership interest by paying W. Sanga $31,000 cash from personal funds.
(b) Osvald invests $68,000 cash in the partnership for a 40% ownership interest.
(c) Osvald invests $41,000 in the partnership for a 20% ownership interest.
(d) Osvald invests $29,000 in the partnership for a 20% ownership interest.

TAKING IT FURTHER Why would a new partner be willing to pay a bonus to the existing partners in order to join a partnership? Give an example of a situation where this might happen.

Record withdrawal of partner. (LO 6) AP

P12–9A On December 31, the capital balances and profit and loss ratios in FJA Company are as follows:

Partner	Capital Balance	Profit and Loss Ratio
H. Fercho	$144,000	60%
P. Jiang	$ 59,300	30%
R. Antoni	$ 48,000	10%

Antoni is withdrawing from the partnership.

Instructions

Journalize the withdrawal of Antoni under each of the following independent assumptions:

(a) Using personal funds, Jiang agrees to purchase Antoni's ownership interest for $58,000 cash.
(b) Antoni is paid $58,000 from partnership assets.
(c) Antoni is paid $38,200 from partnership assets.

TAKING IT FURTHER What factors are important in deciding whether the withdrawing partner should be paid from the remaining partners' personal assets or from the partnership's assets?

Record withdrawal and admission of partners; allocate profit. (LO 3, 5, 6) AP

P12–10A Triple A Accountants is a partnership with three partners. On February 28, 2017, the three partners, M. Kumar, H. Deol, and A. Kassam, have capital balances of $85,000, $72,000, and $43,000, respectively. The profit and loss ratio is 4:3:1. On March 1, 2017, Deol withdraws from the partnership and the remaining partners agree to pay him $90,000 cash from the partnership assets.

After Deol leaves, Kumar and Kassam agree to a 4:2 profit ratio. During the year ended February 28, 2018, the partnership earns a profit of $24,000. Neither Kumar nor Kassam makes any withdrawals because the partnership is short of cash after paying Deol. On March 1, 2018, Kumar and Kassam agree to admit C. Mawani to the partnership with a 45% interest for $75,000 cash. After Mawani is admitted, the new profit ratio will be 4:2:5 for Kumar, Kassam, and Mawani, respectively.

Instructions

(a) Journalize the withdrawal of Deol from the partnership.
(b) What are the balances in Kumar's and Kassam's capital accounts after Deol leaves the partnership?
(c) Prepare the journal entry to close the Income Summary account on February 28, 2018.
(d) What is the total partnership capital on March 1, 2018, prior to admitting Mawani?
(e) Prepare the journal entry to record the admission of Mawani into the partnership.
(f) What is the balance in each of the partners' capital accounts after Mawani is admitted to the partnership?

TAKING IT FURTHER Why would the remaining partners agree to pay a bonus to a partner who is withdrawing from the partnership?

P12–11A Partners in Game Tech Partnership decided to liquidate the partnership on June 30, 2017, when the balances in the partnership's accounts were as follows:

Prepare and post entries for partnership liquidation. (LO 7) AP

Item	Cash	Accounts Receivable	Equipment	Accumulated Depreciation	Accounts Payable	A. Hunt, Capital	K. Lally, Capital	D. Portman, Capital
Balances before liquidation	$32,600	$28,000	$48,600	$16,800	$30,200	$42,100	$18,800	$1,300

The partners share profit and loss 5:3:2 for Hunt, Lally, and Portman, respectively.

Instructions

(a) Complete the schedule and prepare the journal entries for the liquidation of the partnership assuming the noncash assets were sold for $59,800, liabilities are paid, and the cash is distributed appropriately.

(b) Complete the schedule and prepare the journal entries assuming the assets were sold for $45,000, liabilities are paid, and any deficiencies will be paid by the deficient partner. Include the journal entries to record the distribution of cash.

(c) Complete the schedule and prepare the journal entries assuming the assets were sold for $30,000, liabilities are paid, and any deficiencies will be absorbed by the other partners. Include the journal entries to record the distribution of cash.

TAKING IT FURTHER   When determining how the cash is distributed to partners in a liquidation, the profit and loss ratio should be used. Is this correct or incorrect? Why?

P12–12A The three partners of Hawkdale Contractors agree to liquidate their partnership on August 8, 2017. At that point, the accounting records show the following balances:

Record liquidation of partnership. (LO 7) AP

Cash	$142,600	H. Brumby, capital	$227,900
Inventory	402,900	R. Criolio, capital	179,900
Bank loan payable	113,000	A. Paso, capital	24,700

The three partners share profit and loss equally.

Instructions

(a) Journalize the liquidation of the partnership on August 8 under each of the following independent assumptions:

1. The inventory is sold for $434,000 cash, the bank loan payable is paid, and the remaining cash is paid to the partners.

2. The inventory is sold for $318,000 cash and the bank loan payable is paid. Assume that any partners with a debit capital balance pay the amount owed to the partnership.

(b) Refer to item 2 above. Assume instead that any partners with a debit capital balance are unable to pay the amount owed to the partnership. Journalize the reallocation of the deficiency and final distribution of cash to the remaining partners.

TAKING IT FURTHER   What can partners do when a partnership is first created to reduce the possibility that one of the partners will have a deficit (debit balance) when the partnership is liquidated?

P12–13A On March 2, 2016, Zoe Moreau, Karen Krneta, and Veronica Visentin start a partnership to operate a personal coaching and lifestyle consulting practice for professional women. Zoe will focus on work-life balance issues, Karen on matters of style, and Veronica on health and fitness. They sign a partnership agreement to split profits in a 3:2:3 ratio for Zoe, Karen, and Veronica, respectively. The following are the transactions for MKV Personal Coaching:

Account for formation of a partnership, allocation of profits, and withdrawal and admission of partners; prepare partial balance sheet. (LO 2, 3, 4, 5, 6) AP

2016

Mar. 2 The partners contribute assets to the partnership at the following agreed amounts:

	Z. Moreau	K. Krneta	V. Visentin
Cash	$15,000	$10,000	$20,000
Furniture		17,000	
Equipment	18,000		13,000
Total	$33,000	$27,000	$33,000

They also agree that the partnership will assume responsibility for Karen's note payable of $5,000.

Dec. 20 Zoe, Karen, and Veronica each withdraw $30,000 cash as a "year-end bonus." No other withdrawals were made during the year.

      31 Total profit for 2016 was $110,000.

2017

Jan. 5 Zoe and Veronica approve Karen's request to withdraw from the partnership for personal reasons. They agree to pay Karen $15,000 cash from the partnership.

      6 Zoe and Veronica agree to change their profit-sharing ratio to 4:5, respectively.

Dec. 20 Zoe and Veronica withdraw $42,750 and $45,000 cash, respectively, from the partnership.

      31 Total profit for 2017 was $123,750.

2018

Jan. 4 Zoe and Veronica agree to admit Dela Hirjikaka to the partnership. Dela will focus on providing training in organizational skills to clients. Dela invests $31,000 cash for 25% ownership of the partnership.

Instructions

(a) Record the above transactions. For the profit earned each year, calculate how it is to be allocated and record the closing of the Income Summary account.

(b) Prepare the partners' equity section of the balance sheet after Dela is admitted to the partnership.

TAKING IT FURTHER   Every time a new partner is admitted to a partnership or a partner withdraws from a partnership, it is necessary to completely close the accounting records of the existing partnership and start new accounting records for the new partnership. Do you agree or disagree? Explain.

▶ Problems: Set B

Discuss advantages and disadvantages of partnerships and record formation of partnership. (LO 1, 2) AP

P12–1B   Here are the post-closing trial balances of two proprietorships on January 1 of the current year:

	Visanji Company		Vanbakel Company	
	Dr.	Cr.	Dr.	Cr.
Cash	$ 9,500		$ 5,000	
Accounts receivable	15,000		20,000	
Allowance for doubtful accounts		$ 2,500		$ 4,000
Merchandise inventory	18,000		15,000	
Equipment	42,500		25,000	
Accumulated depreciation—equipment		22,000		14,000
Accounts payable		25,000		20,000
F. Visanji, capital		35,500		
P. Vanbakel, capital				27,000
	$85,000	$85,000	$65,000	$65,000

Visanji and Vanbakel decide to form the Varsity partnership and agree on the following fair values for the noncash assets that each partner is contributing:

	Visanji	Vanbakel
Accounts receivable	$11,500	$15,500
Merchandise inventory	20,000	15,000
Equipment	18,000	14,000

All of the assets in the two proprietorships will be transferred to the partnership on January 1. The partnership will also assume all the liabilities of the two proprietorships. Further, it is agreed that Vanbakel will invest the amount of cash required so her investment in the partnership is equal to Visanji's.

Instructions

(a) What are the advantages and disadvantages for these two individuals of forming a partnership as opposed to setting up a corporation?

(b) Prepare separate journal entries to record the transfer of each proprietorship's assets and liabilities to the partnership on January 1.

(c) Journalize the additional cash investment.

TAKING IT FURTHER   What are some of the advantages of two individuals such as Visanji and Vanbakel operating their businesses as a partnership instead of as two separate proprietorships?

P12–2B On January 1, 2017, the capital balances in the A&R Partnership are as follows:

Calculate and
of profit. Prepare closing
entries. (LO 3) AP

Khurram Ali	$53,500
Pradjot Ramsey	$44,000

Neither partner had any drawings in 2017.

Instructions

Prepare closing entries to allocate the partnership profit under the following situations:

(a) In 2017, the partnership reports profit of $170,500. There is no partnership agreement.

(b) In 2017, the partnership reports profit of $170,500. The income ratio provides for salary allowances of $82,000 to Ali and $33,000 to Ramsey and the remainder to be shared equally.

(c) In 2017, the partnership reports profit of $90,000. Assume the partnership agreement calls for income to be divided with a salary of $60,000 to Ali and $55,000 to Ramsey. Ali is allowed 5% of interest on his beginning capital, and the remainder is divided 65%–35%.

TAKING IT FURTHER Ali and Ramsey decided to form a partnership and operate a business together. Ali is much more cautious and concerned about keeping expenses to a minimum than Ramsey. Ali also has significantly more personal assets than Ramsey. Should Ali have any concerns about using the partnership form of business organization to operate this business? Explain.

P12–3B At the end of its first year of operations, on December 31, 2017, LBG Company's accounts show the following:

Calculate and record division
of profit. Prepare statement of
partners' equity. (LO 3, 4) AP

Partner	Drawings	Capital
S. Little	$21,000	$65,000
L. Brown	14,000	40,000
P. Gerhardt	9,000	20,000

The capital balance represents each partner's initial capital investment on January 1, 2017. No closing entries have been recorded for profit (loss) as yet.

Instructions

(a) Journalize the entry to record the division of profit for the year ended December 31, 2017, under each of the following independent assumptions:

1. Profit is $55,000. Little, Brown, and Gerhardt are given salary allowances of $5,000, $25,000, and $10,000, respectively. The remainder is shared equally.

2. Profit is $25,000. Each partner is allowed interest of 7% on beginning capital balances. Brown and Gerhardt are given salary allowances of $15,000 and $20,000, respectively. The remainder is shared 3:2:1.

(b) Prepare a statement of partners' equity for the year under assumption 2 in part (a) above.

TAKING IT FURTHER Explain why partnerships such as LBG Company include a salary allowance in their profit- and loss-sharing arrangements.

P12–4B Terry Lam and Chris Tan have a partnership agreement with the following provisions for sharing profit or loss:

Calculate division of profit
or loss. Prepare statement of
partners' equity and closing
entries. (LO 3, 4) AP

1. A salary allowance of $20,000 to Lam and $30,000 to Tan
2. An interest allowance of 5% on capital balances at the beginning of the year
3. The remainder to be divided between Lam and Tan on a 3:4 basis

The capital balances on February 1, 2016, for T. Lam and C. Tan were $100,000 and $120,000, respectively. For the year ended January 31, 2017, the partnership reported a loss of $30,000. The partnership also reported the following: T. Lam drawings of $12,000 and C. Tan drawings of $14,400.

Instructions

(a) Prepare a schedule to show how the profit or loss is allocated to the two partners.
(b) Prepare a statement of partners' equity for the year.
(c) Prepare closing entries on January 31, 2017 to allocate the partnership profit and to close the drawings accounts.

TAKING IT FURTHER In general, what is the relationship between the salary allowance specified in the profit and loss ratio and a partner's drawings?

P12–5B Below is an alphabetical listing of the accounts in the general ledger of Clay and Ogletree, LLP, at the partnership's fiscal year end, September 30, 2017. Adjusting entries for the year have been posted and included in these balances.

Prepare financial statements
and closing entries.
(LO 4) AP

Accounts payable	$ 21,500
Accounts receivable	105,000
Accumulated depreciation—equipment	12,000
Cash	13,500
Depreciation expense	12,000
Equipment	60,000
Fees earned	515,000
G. Clay, capital	75,000
G. Clay, drawings	150,000
Insurance expense	18,500
Interest expense	5,000
M. Ogletree, capital	37,500
M. Ogletree, drawings	100,000
Note payable	22,500
Prepaid insurance	3,500
Property tax expense	15,000
Salaries expense	225,000
Unearned revenue	24,000

Additional information:

1. The balance in Clay's capital account includes an additional investment of $10,000 made during the year.
2. $5,000 of the note payable is due within the next year.
3. Clay and Ogletree share profit and loss in the ratio of 3:2, respectively.

Instructions

(a) Prepare an income statement, statement of partners' equity, and balance sheet.
(b) Journalize the closing entries.

TAKING IT FURTHER   Should the two partners draw equal amounts each year? Both of them work full-time for the partnership.

Prepare entries to correct errors, allocate profit, and prepare financial statements.
(LO 3, 4) AP

P12–6B   Caitlin Maguire and Fiona Whelan, two college friends, decided to set up a house-cleaning business called Maguire & Whelan Cleaning Services. On January 1, 2017, they put their resources together, shook hands, and started their business. Maguire contributed cash of $2,500 and Whelan contributed cash of $8,750. At the end of the first year of business, Caitlin, who was studying accounting, provided the following information:

MAGUIRE & WHELAN CLEANING SERVICES
Income Statement
Year Ended December 31, 2017

Service revenue		$35,000
Expenses		
Supplies expense	$ 3,000	
Depreciation expense	1,900	
Salaries expense	20,000	24,900
Profit		$10,100

Additional information:

1. Salaries expense is $12,000 and $8,000 cash paid to Caitlin and Fiona, respectively, during the year.
2. All revenues were collected in cash.
3. All supplies were paid for in cash. At the end of the year, there were no supplies on hand.
4. Once formed, the partnership purchased equipment with a cost of $1,500 and a vehicle with a cost of $8,000. Caitlin estimates that the equipment and vehicle have five-year useful lives, with no residual value. She used the straight-line method to calculate depreciation expense.
5. There is $13,750 in the bank account at December 31, 2017.

Instructions

(a) Prepare journal entries to correct the errors, if any, on the income statement.
(b) Calculate the correct profit and the amount to be allocated to each partner.
(c) Prepare a statement of partners' equity for the year ended December 31, 2017.
(d) Prepare a balance sheet at December 31, 2017.

TAKING IT FURTHER   Caitlin is not happy about how the profit was allocated. She says that she works twice as hard as Fiona. Fiona argues that she made a larger contribution to start the partnership. What should Caitlin and Fiona do to deal with their concerns?

P12–7B   At April 30, partners' capital balances in HIJ Partners are Ho $174,000, Ishikawa $142,000, and Jay $84,000. The income-sharing ratio is 4:2:1, respectively. On May 1, HIJK Partners is formed by admitting Kai to the firm as a partner with 20% equity.

Record admission of partner. (LO 5) AP

Instructions

Journalize the admission of Kai under each of the following independent assumptions.

(a) Kai invests $100,000.
(b) Kai invests $145,000.
(c) Kai invests $65,000.

TAKING IT FURTHER   Kai is surprised to learn it is possible to purchase a partnership interest with a gain or loss. Explain to him how this may happen.

P12–8B   At September 30 of the current year, partners' capital balances and profit and loss ratios in NEW Company are as follows:

Record admission of partner. (LO 5) AP

Partner	Capital Balance	Profit and Loss Ratio
A. Nolan	$60,000	5
D. Elder	$50,000	4
T. Wuhan	$15,000	1

On October 1, NEWS Company is formed by admitting C. Santos to the partnership.

Instructions

Journalize the admission of C. Santos under each of the following independent assumptions:

(a) Santos purchases 25% of Nolan's ownership interest by paying Nolan $20,000 cash.
(b) Santos invests $80,000 for a 30% ownership interest.
(c) Santos invests $36,000 for a 30% ownership interest.
(d) How much would Santos have to invest in the partnership for a 30% ownership interest so there is no bonus to the existing partners or the new partner?

TAKING IT FURTHER   Why would the existing partners be willing to give a bonus to the new partner? Give an example of a situation where this might happen.

P12–9B   On December 31, the capital balances and profit and loss ratios in VKD Company are as follows:

Record withdrawal of partner. (LO 6) AP

Partner	Capital Balance	Profit and Loss Ratio
B. Vuong	$72,000	50%
G. Khan	50,000	30%
R. Dixon	35,000	20%

Instructions

Journalize the withdrawal of Dixon under each of the following independent assumptions:

(a) Khan agrees to purchase Dixon's ownership interest for $45,000 cash.
(b) Dixon is paid $47,500 from partnership assets.
(c) Dixon is paid $29,500 from partnership assets.

TAKING IT FURTHER   Assume that, instead of any of the above options, Dixon withdraws from the partnership by selling her interest to S. Meyers. Do Vuong and Khan need to approve it? Why or why not?

P12–10B   Ajax Architects is a partnership with three partners. On January 31, 2017, the three partners, Tova Radzik, Sela Kopel, and Etti Falkenberg, have capital balances of $98,000, $79,000, and $47,000, respectively. The profit and loss ratio is 4:3:1. On February 1, 2017, Radzik withdraws from the partnership and they agree to pay her $90,000 cash from the partnership assets.

Record withdrawal and admission of partners; allocate profit. (LO 3, 5, 6) AP

After Radzik leaves, Kopel and Falkenberg agree to a 2:1 profit ratio. During the year ended January 31, 2018, the partnership earns profit of $45,000. Neither Kopel nor Falkenberg makes any withdrawals because the partnership is short of cash after paying Radzik. On March 1, 2018, Kopel and Falkenberg agree to admit Devra Malkin to the partnership with a 45% interest for $110,000 cash. After Malkin is admitted, the new profit ratio will be 4:2:5 for Kopel, Falkenberg, and Malkin, respectively.

Instructions

(a) Journalize the withdrawal of Radzik from the partnership.
(b) What are the balances in Kopel's and Falkenberg's capital accounts after Radzik leaves the partnership?
(c) Prepare the journal entry to close the Income Summary account on January 31, 2018.

(d) What is the total partnership capital on February 1, 2018, prior to admitting Malkin?

(e) Prepare the journal entry to record the admission of Malkin into the partnership.

(f) What is the balance in each of the partners' capital accounts after Malkin is admitted to the partnership?

TAKING IT FURTHER   Why might a partner who is withdrawing from a partnership agree to a cash payment that results in a bonus to the remaining partners?

Prepare and post entries for partnership liquidation. (LO 7) AP

P12–11B   The partners in Omni Services decided to liquidate the partnership on May 31, 2017, when balances in the company's accounts were as follows:

Item	Cash	Accounts Receivable	Equipment	Accumulated Depreciation	Accounts Payable	B. Hally, Capital	H. Lockyear, Capital	A. Vu, Capital
Balances before liquidation	$33,000	$20,000	$75,200	$6,400	$53,160	$39,600	$25,200	$3,840

The partners share profit and loss 5:3:2 for Hally, Lockyear, and Vu, respectively.

Instructions

(a) Complete the schedule and prepare the journal entries for the liquidation of the partnership assuming the noncash assets were sold for $88,800, liabilities are paid, and the cash is distributed appropriately.

(b) Complete the schedule and prepare the journal entries assuming the assets were sold for $60,000, liabilities are paid, and any deficiencies will be paid by the deficient partner. Include the journal entry to record the distribution of cash.

(c) Complete the schedule and prepare the journal entries assuming the assets were sold for $40,000, liabilities are paid, and any deficiencies will be absorbed by the other partners. Include the journal entry to record the distribution of cash.

TAKING IT FURTHER   In a liquidation, why are the liabilities paid before the partners?

Record liquidation of partnership. (LO 7) AP

P12–12B   The three partners of Summer Springs Medical Clinic agree to liquidate their partnership on September 15, 2017. At that point, the accounting records show the following balances:

Cash	$100,000	M. Nokota, capital	$70,000
Supplies	110,000	S. Taishuh, capital	30,000
Accounts payable	90,000	A. Paso, capital	20,000

The three partners share profit and loss 50%, 25%, and 25%, for Nokota, Taishuh, and Paso, respectively.

Instructions

(a) Journalize the liquidation of the partnership on September 30 under each of the following independent assumptions:

1. The supplies are sold for $130,000 cash, the liabilities are paid, and the remaining cash is paid to the partners.

2. The supplies are sold for $25,000 cash and the liabilities are paid. Assume that any partners with a debit capital balance pay the amount owed to the partnership.

(b) Refer to item 2 in part (a) above. Assume instead that any partners with a debit capital balance are unable to pay the amount owed to the partnership. Journalize the reallocation of the deficiency and final distribution of cash to the remaining partners.

TAKING IT FURTHER   For what reasons would a partnership decide to liquidate?

Account for formation of a partnership, allocation of profits, and admission and withdrawal of partners; prepare statement of partners' equity. (LO 2, 3, 4, 5, 6) AP

P12–13B   On February 14, 2016, Isabelle Moretti, Aida Kam, and Channade Fenandoe start a partnership to operate a marketing consulting practice. They sign a partnership agreement to split profits in a 2:3:4 ratio for Isabelle, Aida, and Channade, respectively. The following are transactions for MKF Marketing:

Feb. 14 The partners contribute assets to the partnership at the following agreed amounts:

	I. Moretti	A. Kam	C. Fenandoe
Cash	$ 9,000	$12,000	$18,000
Furniture	15,000		
Equipment		24,000	40,000
Total	$24,000	$36,000	$58,000

They also agree that the partnership will assume responsibility for Channade's accounts payable of $10,000.

Dec. 20 The partners agree to withdraw a total of $72,000 cash as a "year-end bonus." Each partner will receive a share proportionate to her profit-sharing ratio. No other withdrawals were made during the year.

31 Total profit for 2016 was $81,900.

2017

Jan. 5 The three partners agree to admit Carolyn Wells to the partnership. Carolyn will pay Channade $30,000 cash for 50% of her interest in the partnership. The profit-sharing ratio will be changed so that Carolyn is allocated 50% of what was previously allocated to Channade. The partnership's name is changed to MKFW Marketing.

Dec. 20 The partners agree to pay another year-end bonus. The total amount withdrawn is $91,800. Each partner will receive a share proportionate to her profit-sharing ratio. No other withdrawals were made during the year.

31 Total profit for 2017 was $103,050.

2018

Jan. 2 Channade withdraws from the partnership. The partners agree the partnership will pay her $25,550 cash. The partnership's name is changed to MKW Marketing.

Instructions

(a) Record the above transactions. For the profit earned each year, calculate how it is to be allocated and close the accounts to the Income Summary account.

(b) Prepare the statement of partners' equity for 2017.

(c) Calculate the balance in each partner's capital account on January 2, 2018, after Channade has withdrawn.

TAKING IT FURTHER   Moretti, Kam, and Fenandoe discuss the liquidation of a partnership. Moretti argues that all cash should be distributed to partners based on their profit and loss ratios. Is he correct? Explain.

CHAPTER 12: BROADENING YOUR PERSPECTIVE

▶ Financial Reporting and Analysis

Financial Reporting Problem

BYP12–1   Corus Entertainment is a media company that delivers interactive television and radio shows. It was founded by J. R. Shaw and built from the media assets originally owned by Shaw Communications. It was spun off as a separate, publicly traded company in 1999. Since then, the entity has grown through strategic acquisitions and a strong operating discipline.

Instructions

(a) When Shaw spun off Corus Entertainment, it could have operated it as a partnership. What factors might have influenced its decision to form as a corporation?

(b) Look at Corus Entertainment's corporate financial statements reproduced in Appendix A at the back of this textbook. In what ways would partnership financial statements have been different from these corporate statements?

Interpreting Financial Statements

BYP12–2   Crane Cove Seafoods Limited Partnership is a limited partnership set up by the Eskasoni First Nation in Nova Scotia to manage the band's involvement in the commercial fishery. The balance sheet and notes to its financial statements include the following excerpts:

PARTNERS' EQUITY		
Partners' equity	889,036	1,132,522
	$3,268,300	$3,643,405

DESCRIPTION OF BUSINESS

The Crane Cove Seafoods Limited Partnership (the Partnership) is registered under the Partnerships and Business Names Registration Act. The Partnership is a limited partnership. The general partner is the Eskasoni Benevolent General Partner Inc. and the limited partner is the Eskasoni First Nation.

The Partnership operates to represent the Eskasoni First Nation and its residents in all aspects of their involvement in commercial fisheries and management of selected community projects.

Instructions

What are the advantages to the company of operating as a limited partnership rather than as a general partnership?

▶ Critical Thinking

Collaborative Learning Activity

Note to instructor: Additional instructions and handout material for this group activity can be found on the Instructor Resource Site and in *WileyPLUS*.

BYP12–3 In this group activity, you will be given two independent scenarios: one involving the admission of a partner, and one involving the withdrawal of a partner. You will be required to determine the balance in the cash account and in each partner's capital account after the change in ownership.

Communication Activity

BYP12–4 You are an expert in forming partnerships. Dr. Konu Chatterjie and Dr. Sheila Unger want to establish a partnership to practise medicine. They will meet with you to discuss their plans. However, you will first send them a letter that outlines the issues they need to consider beforehand.

Instructions

Write a letter, in good form, discussing the different types of partnership organizations and the advantages and disadvantages of each type so that the doctors can start thinking about their needs.

"All About You" Activity

BYP12–5 In the "All About You" feature, we learned about some famous partnerships. The Beatles and the Rolling Stones were popular music bands that started in the early 1960s. However, the Beatles broke up in 1970 after disagreements, including who should be their financial advisor. In contrast, the Rolling Stones have continued to play together.

You and a couple of friends have decided to form an "indie" band. An indie band records and publishes its music independently from commercial record labels, thus maintaining control over its music and career. You play the guitar and sing; your friends are a bass player and a keyboard player. You have written the lyrics to a couple of songs and the music for the lyrics was composed by the band. After the songs are recorded, the band intends to register the recordings with SOCAN. SOCAN sells access to music registered with it by collecting licence fees from anyone playing or broadcasting live or recorded music. SOCAN then pays the musicians a royalty.

The three of you have decided to get together and discuss some of the issues that may arise and what should be addressed in the band's agreement.

Instructions

(a) Is the band a partnership even if a partnership agreement is never created?
(b) Identify the different types of revenues that the band may earn.
(c) Identify the costs that the band will incur to earn these revenues.
(d) Identify issues that may arise when the band is determining how the revenues and costs should be shared by the members.

(e) Identify issues that may arise if one of the band members wants to leave the band. How might this be addressed in the agreement?
(f) Identify issues that may arise if a new member joins the band after the band has already successfully recorded music and is receiving royalties.
(g) Identify issues that may arise if one of the band members does a solo recording or performance.
(h) Identify issues that may arise if the band decides to split up.

 *Santé Smoothie Saga*

(***Note:*** This is a continuation of the Santé Smoothie Saga from Chapters 1 through 11.)

BYP12-6 Because Natalie has been so successful operating Santé Smoothie, another friend, Jade Wingert, has asked Natalie to become a partner in a new smoothie company. Jade believes that together they will create a thriving smoothie-making business. Jade has been operating a frozen yogourt shop called Gem Frogurt for about a year.

Natalie is quite happy with her current business set-up. Up until now, she had not considered joining forces with anyone. However, Natalie has gathered the following information about Jade's business and compared it with her own results.

The current fair values of the assets and liabilities of both businesses are as follows:

	Gem Frogurt	Santé Smoothie
Cash	$ 1,500	$8,050
Accounts receivable	5,250	800
Merchandise inventory	500	1,200
Supplies	350	450
Equipment	7,500	1,500
Bank loan payable	10,000	0

All assets would be transferred into the partnership. The partnership would assume all of the liabilities of the two proprietorships. Gem Frogurt's bank loan is due on October 31, 2018.

Jade operates her business from leased premises. She has just signed a lease for 12 months. Monthly rent will be $1,000; Jade's landlord has agreed to draw up a new lease agreement that would be signed by both partners.

Jade has no assets and has a lot of student loans and credit card debt. Natalie's assets consist of investments in Canada Savings Bonds. Natalie has no personal liabilities.

Jade is reluctant to have a partnership agreement drawn up. She thinks it's a waste of both time and money. As Jade and Natalie have been friends for a long time, Jade is confident that all problems can be easily resolved over a nice meal.

Natalie believes that it may be a good idea to establish a partnership with Jade. She comes to you with the following questions:

1. Do I really need a formalized partnership agreement drawn up? What would be the point of having one if Jade and I agree on all major decisions? What type of information should the partnership agreement contain?
2. I would like to have Jade contribute the same amount of capital as I am contributing. How much additional cash, beyond the amount in Jade's proprietorship, would Jade have to borrow to invest in the partnership so that she and I have the same capital balances?

3. Jade has a lot of personal debt. Should this affect my decision about whether or not to go forward with this partnership? Why or why not?

4. What other issues should I consider before I say yes or no to Jade?

Instructions

(a) Answer Natalie's questions.

(b) Assume that Natalie and Jade go ahead and form a partnership called Santé Smoothies and More on April 1, 2018, and that Jade is able to borrow the additional cash she needs to contribute to the partnership. Prepare a balance sheet for the partnership at April 1.

ANSWERS TO CHAPTER QUESTIONS

ANSWERS TO ACCOUNTING IN ACTION INSIGHT QUESTIONS

Across the Organization, p. 636

Q: How can partnership conflicts be minimized and more easily resolved?

A: First, it is important to develop a business plan that all parties agree to. Second, it is vital to have a well-thought-out partnership agreement. Third, it can be useful to set up a board of mutually agreed-upon and respected advisors to consult when making critical decisions.

Ethics Insight, p. 640

Q: In what ways are Susan's actions unethical? What provisions could be put in the partnership agreement so that the differences in Susan's and Erin's work and withdrawal habits are no longer unfair to Erin?

A: The stakeholders are Susan and Erin. There are significant differences in their time worked and the amount of drawings made. Sooner or later, Erin is going to become annoyed with Susan. The ethical consideration is primarily a lack of fairness to Erin. The differences here emphasize the importance of a written partnership agreement. Time to be worked by each partner and allowable drawings should be in the agreement. For the differences in time worked, two changes in the partnership

agreement should be considered. First, Erin could be given a higher salary allowance than Susan. Second, because Erin is contributing more to net income than Susan, she could be given a higher percentage of net income after deducting salary allowances. For the differences in drawings, the partnership agreement could be altered to allow for interest on average monthly net partners' capitals. Net partners' capitals is the difference between the balances of the capital and drawing accounts at the end of each month. If Susan does not agree, then the partnership agreement should be changed to limit the drawings of each partner to a fixed amount.

All About You, p. 660

Q: If you and a friend wanted to start a partnership, how might you use a partnership agreement to ensure that your partnership becomes successful, instead of ending in an unhappy liquidation?

A: A partnership agreement should include: Who are the partners? What is each partner contributing? What are each partner's duties? How is profit (loss) shared? How will disputes be resolved? Addressing these items in advance may assist in resolving issues that might arise as the partnership evolves.

ANSWERS TO SELF-STUDY QUESTIONS

1. a   2. c   3. a   4. b   5. c   6. a   7. b   8. c   9. b   10. a

13 INTRODUCTION TO CORPORATIONS

CHAPTER PREVIEW Many incorporated companies start out as unincorporated proprietorships or partnerships and later incorporate. Because of its advantages, the corporation dominates as the most common form of business organization. In this chapter, we will explain the essential features of a corporation, issuing share capital, corporate income tax, cash dividends, and retained earnings. Financial statements for a corporation reporting under ASPE, including an income statement, statement of retained earnings, and the shareholders' equity section of a balance sheet, are also shown. In Chapter 14, we will look at additional topics for corporations and the different corporate financial statements required under IFRS.

FEATURE STORY ▸ ## THE ADVANTAGES OF INCORPORATION

WATERLOO, Ont.—Brick Brewing Co. Limited started in 1984 with just 10 employees, making only 35,000 cases of beer a year. Ontario's first craft brewery steadily grew over the years. Brick now employs more than 140 people and produces more than 3.6 million cases a year of products such as Laker beer, the Seagram's brand of coolers, and beer marketed under the Waterloo brand, named in honour of its hometown.

While a microbrewery might start out as a sole proprietorship or partnership, Brick founder Jim Brickman incorporated the business from the start. Two years later, he took the company public, selling shares to the public on the Toronto Stock Exchange (TSX) to raise capital to pay for expansion.

Brick Brewing has two types, or classes, of shares: common and preferred. It has never issued preferred shares, but as at January 31, 2015 (its fiscal year end), it had more than 34.7 million common shares issued and outstanding. Common shareholders have certain rights of ownership, including the right to vote for members of Brick's board of directors. Brick Brewing reported in its 2015 financial statements cash inflows from issuing shares of $351,900.

While many corporations pay dividends, providing shareholders with regular payments as a portion of profits, Brick Brewing did not issue dividends at the time of writing. "At the present time, the Board of Directors of the Company believes that the cash flow of the Company should be reinvested to finance current activities," Brick said in its 2015 annual report.

Among other investments, Brick recently spent $9 million to expand its brewing facility in nearby Kitchener, Ont.

In addition to raising capital, an advantage to incorporating and selling shares is that companies can use shares to motivate and reward employees. Brick Brewing has a stock option plan for certain executive officers and key employees. They have the option of buying an allotted number of Brick common shares at a 10% discount from the average closing price the shares are trading at on the TSX during the five days before January 15 each year. Employees can then sell their shares at market price and pocket the difference.

In 2015, Brick Brewing reported an increase in net income of 165.6%, despite a decrease in gross sales revenue, as a result of cost controls and a gain on the sale of property, plant, and equipment assets. While Brick Brewing's return on equity of 4.2% was below the five-year industry average of 10.1%, it had increased over the prior year. Perhaps as a result of increased income and return on equity, the company's share price rose from $1.53 per share in April 2015 when the financial statements were issued to $1.85 at the time of writing. Positive financial results make it easier for Brick to raise additional capital for future growth.

Sources: "Brick Refocuses on Its Waterloo Craft Brewing Heritage," *Guelph Mercury*, April 19, 2013; Troy Burtch, "Pioneer Rides into the Sunset," *TAPS: Canada's Beer Magazine*, Spring 2009; Brick Brewing Co. Limited 2015 annual report; Brick Brewing Co. corporate website, www.brickbeer.com.

Stephen C. Host/CP Images

CHAPTER OUTLINE

LEARNING OBJECTIVES

The chapter is organized as follows:

1 Identify and discuss characteristics of the corporate form of organization.

The Corporate Form of Organization
- Characteristics of a corporation
- Operating a corporation

DO IT 1
Corporate organization

2 Explain share capital and demonstrate the accounting for the issuance of common and preferred shares.

Share Capital
- Share issue considerations
- Common shares
- Preferred shares

DO IT 2
Issuance of shares

3 Prepare a corporate income statement.

Retained Earnings
- Corporate income statements

DO IT 3
Recording income tax and preparing an income statement

4 Explain and demonstrate the accounting for cash dividends.

- Cash dividends

DO IT 4
Dividends on preferred and common shares

5 Prepare a statement of retained earnings and closing entries for a corporation.

- Reporting retained earnings

DO IT 5
Retained earnings statement

6 Prepare the shareholders' equity section of the balance sheet and calculate return on equity.

Statement Presentation and Analysis
- Presentation of shareholders' equity
- Analysis

DO IT 6
Shareholders' equity and return on equity

LEARNING OBJECTIVE   **1**   Identify and discuss characteristics of the corporate form of organization.

The Corporate Form of Organization

A **corporation** is a legal entity that is separate from its owners, who are known as shareholders. Corporations can be classified in a variety of ways. Two common classifications are by purpose and by ownership. For example, a corporation may be organized for the purpose of making a profit (such as WestJet) or it may be **not-for-profit** (such as United Way).

In classification by ownership, there is a difference between public and private corporations. A **public corporation** is a corporation whose shares are available for purchase by the general public in an organized securities market, such as the Toronto Stock Exchange (TSX); it may have thousands of shareholders. All public corporations are "publicly accountable enterprises" and, as such, must follow International Financial Reporting Standards (IFRS). Most of the largest Canadian corporations are publicly held. In addition to Brick Brewing Co. Limited in our feature story, examples of publicly held corporations are Suncor Energy, Potash Corporation of Saskatchewan, and, of course, Corus Entertainment Inc., as featured in Appendix A.

In contrast, a **private corporation** is a corporation whose shares are held by a few shareholders and are not available for the general public to purchase. Private corporations are generally much smaller than publicly held corporations, although there are notable exceptions, such as McCain Foods Limited, Moosehead Breweries Ltd., and Home Hardware companies. Generally, a private company has the choice of following IFRS or ASPE.

Alternative terminology Privately held corporations are also referred to as *closely held corporations*.

CHARACTERISTICS OF A CORPORATION

Regardless of the purpose or ownership of a corporation, there are many characteristics that make corporations different from proprietorships and partnerships. The most important ones are explained below.

Separate Legal Existence

As an entity that is separate from its owners, the corporation acts under its own name rather than in the name of its shareholders. A corporation may buy, own, and sell property. It may borrow money and enter into legally binding contracts in its own name. It may also sue or be sued, and it pays income tax as a separate legal entity.

Remember that, in a proprietorship or partnership, the acts of the owners bind the proprietorship or partnership. In contrast, the acts of shareholders (owners in a corporation) do not bind a corporation unless these individuals are also official agents of the corporation. For example, if you owned shares of Corus Entertainment Inc., you would not have the right to purchase or lease a new building in the name of the corporation unless you were an official agent of the corporation.

Shareholders
Legal existence separate from owners

Limited Liability of Shareholders

Since a corporation is a separate legal entity, creditors have access to a corporation's assets only to satisfy any unpaid claims. The liability of each shareholder is limited to the amount that he or she invested in the shares of the corporation. This means that shareholders cannot be made to pay for the company's liabilities out of their personal assets, which can be done in the case of a proprietorship and a general partnership.

Limited liability is a significant advantage for the corporate form of organization, just as it is for a limited, or limited liability, partnership. However, in private corporations, creditors may demand a personal guarantee from a controlling shareholder. This makes the controlling shareholder's personal assets available, if required, for satisfying the creditor's claim—which eliminates or reduces the limited liability advantage.

Shareholders
Limited liability of shareholders

Transferable Ownership Rights

Ownership of a corporation is held in shares of capital. These are transferable units. Shareholders may dispose of part or all of their interest in a corporation simply by selling their shares. In a public corporation, the transfer of shares is entirely decided by the shareholder. It does not require the approval of either the corporation or other shareholders. However, in some private corporations, there may be a shareholders' agreement that limits how, and to whom, a shareholder can sell his or her shares.

The transfer of ownership rights between shareholders has no effect on the corporation's operating activities and it doesn't affect the corporation's assets, liabilities, and total equity. The transfer of these ownership rights is a transaction between individual shareholders. The company is only involved in the original sale of the share capital to investors. Therefore, **whenever a shareholder sells his or her shares to another investor, the company does not record a journal entry**.

Transferable ownership rights

Ability to Acquire Capital

Corporations may issue shares in order to obtain capital (cash) for operations or new investments. Buying shares in a corporation is often attractive to an investor because a shareholder has limited liability and, in a public company, shares are easily transferable. Also, because only small amounts of money need to be invested, many individuals can become shareholders. For these reasons, a successful corporation's ability to obtain capital is almost unlimited.

Note that the "almost unlimited" ability to acquire capital by issuing shares is only true for large, public corporations. Private corporations can have as much difficulty getting capital as any proprietorship or partnership.

Ability to acquire capital

Continuous Life

Corporations have an unlimited life. Because a corporation is a separate legal entity, its continuance as a going concern is not affected by the withdrawal, death, or incapacity of a shareholder, employee, or officer. As a result, a successful corporation can have a continuous and indefinite life. For example, Hudson's Bay Company, the oldest commercial corporation in North America, was founded in 1670 and is still going strong. Its shareholders have changed over the years, but the corporation itself continues. In contrast, proprietorships end if anything happens to the proprietor and partnerships must reorganize if anything happens to one of the partners.

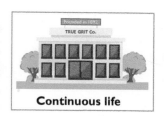

Continuous life

Government Regulations

Canadian companies may be incorporated federally, under the terms of the Canada Business Corporations Act, or provincially, under the terms of a provincial business corporations act. Federal and provincial laws specify the requirements for issuing shares, distributing income to shareholders, and reacquiring shares. Similarly, provincial securities commissions' regulations control the sale of share capital to the general public. When a corporation's shares are listed and traded on foreign securities markets, such as the New York Stock Exchange or the London Stock Exchange, the corporation must also respect the reporting requirements of these exchanges. Respecting international, federal, provincial, and securities regulations increases costs and complexity for corporations.

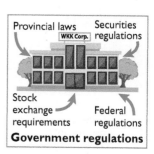

Government regulations

Income Tax

Corporations must pay federal and provincial income tax as separate legal entities. Income tax rates vary based on the type of income and by province. In general, corporate income tax rates are lower than the rate an individual would pay on the same amount of profit, especially in the case of small businesses. Shareholders must pay income tax personally on any dividends (pro rata distribution of profit) they receive from the corporation. While it appears that corporate profits are taxed twice, this is a common misconception. The Canadian Income Tax Act (the regulations that govern income tax) is structured so that profits that are retained by a corporation and those paid to shareholders are taxed overall at approximately the same rate as individual income. There are of course exceptions to this, but in-depth discussions about corporate income tax will be explored further in more advanced courses.

Proprietorships and partnerships, on the other hand, do not pay income tax as separate entities. Instead, profit from these organizations is reported on the owner's or partner's personal income tax return. Income tax is then paid by the individual on this amount. In terms of income tax, it does not matter how much cash a proprietor or partner withdraws from the business. The owner is taxed on the profit, not on the cash withdrawals.

The following list summarizes the advantages and disadvantages of the corporate form of business organization:

Advantages	Disadvantages
• Separate legal existence • Limited liability of shareholders • Potential for deferred or reduced income tax • Transferable ownership rights • Ability to acquire capital • Continuous life	• Increased cost and complexity to follow government regulations

OPERATING A CORPORATION

There are a few differences between operating a business using the corporate form of organization and using a partnership or proprietorship.

Forming a Corporation

Proprietorships and partnerships can be formed and begin operations without any formalities. On the other hand, the process of creating a corporation requires that the organizers submit articles of incorporation to the federal or provincial government for approval.

Articles of incorporation form the company's "constitution." They include information such as (1) the name and purpose of the corporation, (2) the number of shares and the kinds of shares to be authorized, and (3) the location of the corporation's head office. Anyone can apply to incorporate a company, as long as he or she is over the age of 18, of sound mind, and not bankrupt.

After receiving its articles of incorporation, the corporation sets its bylaws. The bylaws are the internal rules and procedures for operations. Corporations that operate interprovincially must also get a licence from each province they do business in. The licence ensures that the corporation's operating activities respect the laws of the province.

The costs of forming a corporation are called **organization costs**. These costs include legal fees, accounting fees, and registration costs. Under both ASPE and IFRS, **these costs are recorded as expenses in the period when they are incurred**.

Ownership Rights of Shareholders

Shareholders purchase ownership rights in the form of shares. Depending on the company's articles of incorporation, it may be authorized to issue different classes of shares, such as Class A, Class B, and so on. The rights and privileges for each class of shares are stated in the articles of incorporation. The different classes are often identified by the generic terms "common shares" and "preferred shares." When a corporation has only one class of shares, this class has the rights and privileges of **common shares**. Each common share gives the shareholder the ownership rights pictured in Illustration 13-1.

► ILLUSTRATION 13-1
Ownership rights of
shareholders

Shareholders have the right to:

1. **Vote:** Shareholders have the right to vote on the election of the board of directors and appointment of external auditors. Each shareholder normally has one vote for each common share owned.

2. **Dividends:** Shareholders share in the distribution of the corporate profit through dividends, proportionate to the number of shares owned, if the board of directors declares a dividend.

3. **Liquidation:** Shareholders share in any assets that remain after liquidation, in proportion to the number of shares owned. This is known as a residual claim because shareholders are paid only if any cash remains after all the assets have been sold and the liabilities paid.

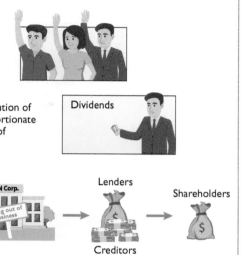

ACCOUNTING IN ACTION
ACROSS THE ORGANIZATION

Erkan Mehmet/Alamy

Travelling to space or embarking on an expedition to excavate lost Mayan ruins is normally the stuff of adventure novels. But for employees of Facebook, these and other lavish dreams moved closer to reality when the world's No. 1 on-line social network went public through an initial public offering (IPO) that may have created at least a thousand millionaires. The IPO was the largest in Internet history, valuing Facebook at over US$104 billion.

With all these riches to be had, what might be some reasons why Mark Zuckerberg, the founder of Facebook, delayed taking his company public? Consider that the main motivation for issuing shares to the public is to raise money so you can grow your business. However, unlike a manufacturer or even an on-line retailer, Facebook doesn't need major physical resources, it doesn't have inventory, and it doesn't really need much money for marketing. So in the past, the company hasn't had much need for additional cash beyond what it was already generating on its own. When Facebook was originally considering going public, the value of similar technology shares was lower than what the company wanted to generate from an IPO, so it delayed the initial offering. Finally, as head of a closely held, nonpublic company, Zuckerberg was subject to far fewer regulations than a public company.

Source: J. O'Dell, "The Real Reason Facebook's IPO Will Be Delayed: 15-30% Drop in New Tech Stocks," Venturebeat.com, April 25, 2012; Douglas MacMillan, "Zuckerberg Controlling 57% of Facebook Seen as Risk to Investors," Bloomberg Business, February 2, 2012; "Status Update: I'm Rich! Facebook Flotation to Create 1,000 Millionaires Among Company's Rank and File," *Daily Mail Reporter*, February 1, 2012.

 Mark Zuckerberg, the CEO and founder of Facebook, owned just 28% of shares but maintained a 57% voting interest in Facebook after it went public. What are some advantages and disadvantages to Facebook that Zuckerberg still had control of the company?

Corporation Management

Shareholders legally own the corporation. But, as just explained, they have limited rights. They manage the corporation indirectly through the board of directors that they elect. The board, in turn, decides on the company's operating policies and selects officers—such as a chief executive officer (CEO) and other executive officers—to execute policy and to perform daily management functions. This structure is shown in Illustration 13-2.

In a small private company, it is possible to have only one shareholder, who elects him- or herself to be the only person on the board of directors. In that capacity, they can appoint themselves as the CEO. On the other hand, the authority structure of a corporation makes it possible for it to hire professional managers to run the business, which is generally the case in public corporations.

ETHICS NOTE
Managers who are not owners are often compensated based on the firm's performance. They thus may be tempted to exaggerate profit by inflating figures.

▶ ILLUSTRATION 13-2
Authority structure
in corporations

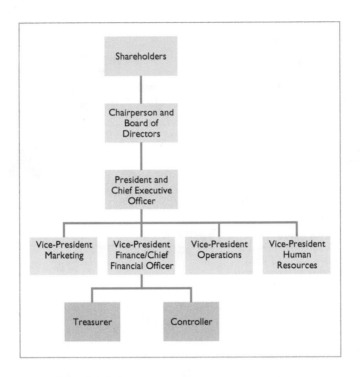

Distribution of Profit—Dividends

Profits can be either reinvested by a company or distributed to its shareholders as dividends. A **dividend** is a pro rata distribution of a portion of a corporation's profits to its shareholders. "Pro rata" means that if you own, say, 10% of a corporation's shares, you will receive 10% of the total dividend paid to all shareholders. Dividends in corporations are somewhat similar to drawings in proprietorships or partnerships.

ACCOUNTING IN ACTION
ETHICS INSIGHT

Greg Kretovic/iStockphoto

The R&D division of Simplex Chemical Corp. has just developed a chemical to sterilize the voracious mountain pine beetles that are invading Western Canada's forests. The president of Simplex is anxious to get the new chemical to market and has already named it PinebeetleX101. Simplex's profits need a boost and the president's job is in jeopardy because of decreasing sales and profits. Simplex has an opportunity to sell this chemical in several Central American countries, where the laws about proving a product's safety before beginning to use it or sell it are much more relaxed than in Canada.

The director of Simplex's R&D division strongly recommends more laboratory testing for side effects of this chemical on other insects, birds, animals, plants, and even humans. He cautions the president, "We could be sued from all sides if the chemical has tragic side effects that we didn't even test for in the labs." The president answers, "We can't wait an additional year for your lab tests. We can avoid losses from such lawsuits by creating a new separate corporation called Simplex Central America Inc., which will be 100% owned by Simplex Chemical Corp., to operate our business in those countries. We will invest just the patent covering this chemical in Simplex Central America Inc. That corporation will have limited liability so we can't lose any more than the assets that we put into it. Since we will own 100% of the shares of Simplex Central America Inc., we can put ourselves on its board of directors, and then we can make it pay dividends to Simplex Chemical Corp. when it makes a profit. We'll reap the benefits if the chemical works and is safe, and avoid the losses from lawsuits if it's a disaster."

The following week, Simplex Chemical Corp. creates the new 100%-owned corporation Simplex Central America Inc., sells it the chemical patent for PinebeetleX101 for $10, delivers a shipload of the chemicals, and watches the spraying begin.

Q Can Simplex Chemical Corp. be certain that it is protected against all losses related to the activities of Simplex Central America Inc.?

BEFORE YOU GO ON...DO IT ❶ Corporate Organization

Indicate if each of the following sentences is true or false:

_____ 1. Shareholders of a corporation have unlimited liability.
_____ 2. A corporation does not journalize the transfer of shares from one shareholder to another.
_____ 3. A corporation does not pay income tax on its profits.
_____ 4. Corporations are separate legal entities and continue to exist after the death of a shareholder.
_____ 5. The articles of incorporation contain information about the shares a corporation is authorized to issue.
_____ 6. The shareholders of a corporation have the right to declare a dividend.

Solution

1. False	3. False	5. True
2. True	4. True	6. False

Related exercise material: BE13–1 and E13–2.

Action Plan
• Review the characteristics and operation of a corporation.

LEARNING OBJECTIVE ❷ **Explain share capital and demonstrate the accounting for the issuance of common and preferred shares.**

Share Capital

You may recall from Chapters 1 and 4 that the shareholders' equity section of a balance sheet includes (1) share capital (contributed capital), and (2) retained earnings (earned capital). **Share capital** is amounts paid or contributed to the corporation by shareholders in exchange for shares of ownership. In the following section, we will look at issuing shares and the two main classes of shares—common shares and preferred shares. We will learn about retained earnings later in the chapter.

Alternative terminology Shares are sometimes referred to as *stocks* or *securities.*

SHARE ISSUE CONSIDERATIONS

A corporation must determine how many different classes of shares it will issue, the specific rights and privileges of each class of shares, and how many of each class of shares can be sold to shareholders. It also has to decide how many to sell and at what price.

Authorized Share Capital

A corporation's **authorized shares**—the total number of each class of shares a corporation is allowed to sell—is indicated in its articles of incorporation. It may be specified as an unlimited number or a certain number (such as 500,000 shares authorized). Most corporations in Canada, including Brick Brewing Co. Limited in our feature story, have an unlimited number of authorized shares. If a number is specified, the amount of authorized shares normally reflects the company's initial need for capital and what it expects to need in the future. **The authorization of share capital does not result in a formal accounting entry, because the event has no immediate effect on either assets or shareholders' equity.**

Issue of Shares

Issued shares represent the number of authorized shares that have been sold to investors. If a corporation has issued all of its authorized shares, it must get approval to change its articles of incorporation before it can issue additional shares. To find out how many shares can still be issued without changing the articles of incorporation, the total shares issued are subtracted from the total authorized.

A corporation can issue common shares in two ways: either directly to investors or indirectly through an investment dealer (brokerage house) that specializes in making potential investors aware of securities. Direct issue is typical in private corporations; indirect issue is typical for public corporations. The first time a corporation's shares are offered to the public, the offer is called an **initial public offering (IPO)**.

Once shares have been issued, investors can buy and sell them to each other, rather than buying them from the company. In public companies, the shares are traded on a **secondary market**, or stock exchange such as the TSX. **When a company's shares are sold among investors, there is no impact on the company's financial position. The only change in the company records is the name of the shareholder, not the number of shares issued.**

Legal Capital

The distinction between share capital and retained earnings is important for both legal and financial reasons. Retained earnings can be distributed to shareholders as dividends or retained in the company for operating needs. On the other hand, share capital is **legal capital** that cannot be distributed to shareholders. Because shareholders have limited liability, legal capital must remain invested in the company for the protection of the corporation's creditors. In a proprietorship or a partnership, there is no such thing as legal capital. Proprietors or partners may withdraw whatever amount they choose because a company's creditor can access the owner's personal assets if the creditor suffers a loss.

Some countries, notably the United States, assign a par or stated value to shares to determine the amount of legal capital. The use of par value shares is rare in Canada, with fewer than 1% of publicly traded companies issuing par value shares. In fact, companies that are incorporated federally, as well as companies that incorporate in most Canadian provinces, are not allowed to issue shares with par values.

In Canada, **no par value shares**—shares that have not been assigned any specific value—are normally issued. When no par value shares are issued, all of the proceeds received from the sale of the shares are considered to be legal capital. In this text, we will assume that all of the shares in the examples and end-of-chapter material have no par value.

Market Value of Shares

As mentioned previously, the shares of public companies are traded on organized exchanges. The market value of a public company's shares changes according to the interaction between buyers and sellers on the secondary market. To some extent, the price follows the trend of a company's profit and dividends. The price also depends to some extent on how well the company is expected to perform in the future. Factors that a company cannot control (such as the recession in 2007 and 2008, changes in interest rates, the outcome of an election, terrorism, and war) can also influence market prices.

ACCOUNTING IN ACTION
ALL ABOUT YOU

When you graduate and start to make decisions on where to invest your money, you may consider buying shares in public companies, including the company you work for. Organized exchanges trade the shares of publicly held companies at dollar prices per share established by the interaction between buyers and sellers. For each listed security, the financial press reports the high and low prices of the shares during the year, the total volume of shares traded on a given day, the high and low prices for the day, and the closing market price, with the net change for the day. You may want to follow the progress of the companies you own shares in, to track how your investment is doing. Our feature company, Corus Entertainment, is listed on the Toronto Stock Exchange. Below is a listing for Corus, whose symbol is CJR.B:

Liangpv/Getty Images

| | 52 Weeks | | | | | | |
Company	High	Low	Volume	High	Low	Close	Net Change
CJR.B	$26.05	$17.42	195,551	$19.23	$18.53	$18.96	$0.20

These numbers indicate the following. The high and low market prices for the past 52 weeks were $26.05 and $17.42. The trading volume for the day was 195,551 shares. The high, low, and closing prices for the day were $19.23, $18.53, and $18.96, respectively. The net change for the day was an increase over the previous day's closing price of $0.20.

 For shares traded on organized exchanges, what factors influence the dollar price per share?

The trading of shares on organized exchanges involves the transfer of already issued shares from an existing shareholder to another investor. These transactions have no impact on a corporation's shareholders' equity. For each listed security, the financial press reports relevant information about trading activity. Shares that are regularly bought and sold on the secondary market are considered to be actively traded. When shares are actively traded, the quoted market value of the share is considered to be a very good indication of the fair value of the shares.

COMMON SHARES

All profit-oriented corporations must issue common shares. Some corporations also issue preferred shares, which have different rights and privileges than common shares. We will look at common shares in this section, and preferred shares in the next.

Issuing Shares for Cash

As discussed earlier, when no par value common shares are issued, the entire proceeds from the issue become legal capital. That means that the proceeds of the share issue are credited to the Common Share account. Most of the time, shares are issued in exchange for cash, particularly in large corporations.

To illustrate the issue of common shares for cash, assume that Urbantech Inc., a private corporation that follows ASPE, is authorized to issue an unlimited number of common shares. It issues 20,000 of these shares for $1 cash per share on January 2. The entry to record this transaction is as follows:

Jan. 2	Cash	20,000	
	Common Shares		20,000
	To record issue of 20,000 common shares.		

A = L + SE
+20,000 +20,000

↑Cash flows: +20,000

Issuing Shares for Services or Noncash Assets

Although it is more usual to issue common shares for cash, shares are sometimes issued in exchange for services (such as compensation to lawyers or consultants) or for noncash assets (land, buildings, and equipment). When this happens, should the transaction be recorded at the fair value of the goods or services received, or at the fair value of the shares given up?

Under IFRS, the fair value of the goods or services received should be used, and it is presumed that this value can be determined except in rare cases. If the fair value of the goods or services received cannot be reliably determined, then the transaction is recorded at the fair value of the shares given in exchange. **Under ASPE, the rules are more flexible; the transaction should be valued at whichever amount can be more reliably measured**—the fair value of the goods or services received or the fair value of the shares issued. Because a private company's shares are not widely traded, it can be very difficult to measure their fair value. Thus it is more likely that the value of the goods or services received will be used in recording the transaction.

To illustrate, assume that on February 25, the lawyer who helped Urbantech Inc. incorporate billed the company $3,900 for her services. If Urbantech has limited cash available, it may offer to issue common shares to the lawyer instead of cash. If the lawyer agrees, the challenge is to determine how many shares to offer in exchange for the legal services. Because Urbantech is a private company, its shares are not actively traded in a stock market. Therefore, it is difficult to determine the fair value per share, which in turn makes it difficult to know how many shares to issue.

Recall from the previous example that Urbantech issued shares for $1 cash each at the beginning of the year. Therefore, it may offer the lawyer 3,900 shares in exchange for the legal services. On the other hand, the lawyer may argue that she wants 4,000 shares because she is not getting paid in cash. The actual number of shares issued will be the result of a negotiation between the company and the lawyer. Regardless of the number of shares issued, the transaction is recorded at the fair value of the lawyer's services received, not at the value of the shares given up, because the fair value of the lawyer's

Helpful hint Fair value is the amount that would be agreed upon in an arm's-length transaction between knowledgeable, willing parties, or as the result of a bargaining process over the value of the good or service.

services can be more reliably determined. For purposes of this example, we will assume that 4,000 shares are issued. Accordingly, the entry is recorded at $3,900 as follows:

A	=	L	+	SE
				−3,900
				+3,900

Cash flows: no effect

Feb. 25	Legal Fees Expense	3,900	
	Common Shares		3,900
	To record issue of 4,000 common shares for legal services.		

Helpful hint The asking or list price of land, buildings, or equipment is rarely the fair value of the asset. Asking or list prices are typically used only to start the bargaining process.

If shares are issued in exchange for land, buildings, or equipment, it is often necessary to use an appraiser to determine the fair value of the asset. Appraised values are often used as a reasonable estimate of the asset's fair value.

To illustrate, assume that Luna Pharma Ltd., a public company that follows IFRS, issues 10,000 shares on October 1 to acquire laboratory equipment. Assuming that an appraisal valued the equipment at $72,000, the following entry is made:

A	=	L	+	SE
+72,000				+72,000

Cash flows: no effect

Oct. 1	Equipment	72,000	
	Common Shares		72,000
	To record issue of 10,000 common shares for equipment.		

If the equipment's fair value could not be determined, and if Luna's shares are actively traded on an organized exchange with a market value of $7 per share, the equipment would be recorded at the fair value of the shares given up, $70,000 (10,000 × $7).

PREFERRED SHARES

A corporation may issue preferred shares in addition to common shares. **Preferred shares** have a preference, or priority, over common shares in certain areas. Typically, preferred shareholders have priority over (1) dividends (distributions of profit) and (2) assets if the company is liquidated. They generally do not have voting rights.

Like common shares, preferred shares may be issued for cash or for noncash assets or services. When a company has more than one class of shares, the transactions for each class should be recorded in separate accounts (such as Preferred Shares or Common Shares).

Unlike common shares, the annual dividend rate that the preferred shareholder may receive is specified in the articles of incorporation. The rate may be expressed as a percentage of the issue price or as a specific dollar amount. For example, if the annual dividend rate on the preferred shares is specified as $5 per share, these shares would be referred to as "$5 preferred shares." The dividend rate is always stated as an annual rate.

To illustrate, assume that Urbantech Inc. issues 500, $5 preferred shares for $100 per share on July 7. The entry to record this transaction is as follows:

A	=	L	+	SE
+50,000				+50,000

↑Cash flows: +50,000

July 7	Cash (500 × $100)	50,000	
	Preferred Shares		50,000
	To record issue of 500, $5 preferred shares.		

Some typical features of preferred shares, including dividend and liquidation preferences, are discussed next.

Dividend Preference

Preferred shareholders have the right to share in the distribution of dividends before common shareholders. This reflects the priority status given to preferred shares. For example, using the case of Urbantech's $5 preferred shares explained above, when the company declares dividends, the common shareholders will not receive any dividends until preferred shareholders have first received $5 for every share they own.

It is important to note that shareholders of both classes of shares (preferred and common) are **entitled to a dividend only when formally approved by the board of directors**. Formal approval will depend on many factors, such as having enough retained earnings and available cash.

Preferred shares may have a **cumulative** dividend feature. This means that preferred shareholders must be paid dividends from the current year as well as any unpaid dividends from past years before common shareholders receive any dividends. When preferred shares are cumulative, preferred dividends that are not declared in a period are called **dividends in arrears**. Preferred shares without this feature are called **noncumulative**. A dividend on a noncumulative preferred share that is not paid in any particular year is lost forever. If a company has both cumulative and noncumulative preferred shares, the cumulative preferred shares will have priority over the noncumulative shares when dividends are declared. We will discuss how to account for these types of dividends a little later in the chapter.

Liquidation Preference

In addition to having a priority claim on dividends over common shares, preferred shares also have a priority claim on corporate assets if the corporation fails. This means that if the company is bankrupt, preferred shareholders will get money back before common shareholders do. The preference to assets can be for the legal capital of the shares or for a specified liquidating value. So, while creditors still rank above all shareholders in terms of preference, preferred shareholders rank above the common shareholders. This is important because the money usually runs out before everyone gets paid.

Because of these two preferential rights—the right to dividends and assets—preferred shareholders generally do not mind that they do not have the voting right that common shareholders have.

Convertible Preferred

As an investment, preferred shares are even more attractive when there is a conversion privilege. **Convertible preferred shares** give preferred shareholders the option of exchanging their preferred shares for common shares at a specified ratio. They are purchased by investors who want the greater security of preferred shares but who also want the option of converting their preferred shares to common shares if the fair value of the common shares increases significantly.

To illustrate, assume that a corporation issues 1,000 convertible preferred shares at $100 per share. One preferred share is convertible into 10 common shares. The current fair value of the common shares is $9 per share. At this point, holders of the preferred shares would not want to convert, because they would exchange preferred shares worth $100,000 (1,000 × $100) for common shares worth only $90,000 (10,000 × $9). However, if the fair value of the common shares were to increase above $10 per share, it would be profitable for shareholders to convert their preferred shares to common shares.

When the shares are converted, the average per share amount of the preferred shares is transferred to the Common Shares account. Because it is seldom possible to determine the original dollar amount of the preferred shares that are involved in the conversion, the average per share amount of the preferred shares is used instead. This is calculated by dividing the balance in the Preferred Shares account by the number of preferred shares issued immediately prior to the conversion.

To illustrate, return to the facts in the example above. Assume all 1,000 preferred shares with an average per share amount of $100 are converted into 10,000 common shares when the fair value of the common shares is $12 per share on July 10. The entry to record the conversion is:

July 10	Preferred Shares (1,000 × $100)	100,000	
	Common Shares		100,000
	To record conversion of 1,000 preferred shares into 10,000 common shares.		

A	=	L	+	SE
				−100,000
				+100,000

Cash flows: no effect

Note that the fair value of the shares is **not** used by the corporation in recording the transaction because the total amount of share capital has not changed. But fair values are used by the preferred shareholders in their decision to convert.

Redeemable and Retractable Preferred

Many preferred shares are issued with a redemption or call feature. **Redeemable (or callable) preferred shares** give the issuing corporation the right to purchase the shares from shareholders at specified future dates and prices. Corporations may redeem shares when it is beneficial for the company's overall capital structure.

Helpful hint The two features benefit different parties. Redeemable shares are at the option of the corporation. Retractable shares are at the option of the shareholder.

Retractable preferred shares are similar to redeemable preferred shares except that the shareholders can redeem shares at their option instead of the corporation redeeming the shares at its option. The retraction usually occurs at an arranged price and date.

When preferred shares are redeemable or retractable, the distinction between equity and debt is not clear. Redeemable and retractable preferred shares are similar in some ways to debt. They both offer a rate of return to the investor, and with the redemption or retraction of the shares, they both offer a repayment of the principal investment.

Recall from Chapter 11 that, in order for accounting information to be useful, it must be presented in accordance with its economic substance rather than its form. Therefore, redeemable and retractable preferred shares may be presented in the **liabilities** section of the balance sheet rather than in the shareholders' equity section if, depending on the exact terms of the redemption or retraction, they have more of the features of debt than of equity. Accounting for these types of shares is left to an intermediate accounting course.

BEFORE YOU GO ON...DO IT **2** **Issuance of Shares**

Turin Corporation, a private company, was incorporated on March 1. The following are selected transactions over the next several months:

Mar. 15   Issued 120,000 common shares for cash at $8 per share.
Apr. 2   Issued 3,200 common shares to its lawyers in settlement of their bill for $25,000. Turin's president and the law firm agreed that the shares had a fair value of $8 each.
May 22   Issued 10,000 preferred shares for $90 each. Each share was convertible into 10 common shares.
Oct. 5   Preferred shareholders converted 2,000 of the preferred shares into common. At that point, it was estimated that the fair values of the common and preferred shares were $10 and $92, respectively.

Record the share transactions.

Action Plan

- Credit the Common Shares account for the entire proceeds of the share issue.
- When shares are issued for services, use the fair value of what is received. If this amount cannot be determined, use the fair value of what is given up.
- Credit the Preferred Shares account for the entire proceeds of the share issue.
- Use the preferred shares average per share amount to record the conversion. Fair values are irrelevant.

Solution

Mar. 5	Cash	960,000	
	Common Shares (120,000 × $8)		960,000
	To record issue of 120,000 shares at $8 per share.		
Apr. 2	Legal Fees Expense	25,000	
	Common Shares		25,000
	To record issue of 3,200 shares for $25,000 of lawyers' fees.		
May 22	Cash	900,000	
	Preferred Shares (10,000 × $90)		900,000
	To record issue of 10,000 preferred shares at $90.		
Oct. 5	Preferred Shares (2,000 × $90)	180,000	
	Common Shares		180,000
	To record conversion of 2,000 preferred shares into 20,000 (2,000 × 10) common shares at an average per share amount of $90.		

Related exercise material: BE13–2, BE13–3, BE13–4, BE13–5, E13–2, E13–3, E13–4, and E13–5.

LEARNING OBJECTIVE **3** **Prepare a corporate income statement.**

Retained Earnings

Retained earnings are earned capital (cumulative profit or loss since incorporation) that has been retained in the company for future use. In other words, it is the cumulative profit that has not been distributed to shareholders. In the following sections, we will learn about two major components of retained earnings: (1) profit, and how it is reported on a corporation's income statement; and (2) cash distributions to owners (dividends) that reduce retained earnings. We will also learn how retained earnings are reported in the financial statements for companies following ASPE, and examine closing entries for a corporation. In Chapter 14, we will discuss the reporting requirements under IFRS.

CORPORATE INCOME STATEMENTS

In a corporation, unlike a proprietorship or partnership, income tax expense must be deducted when determining profit. **Income tax expense is based on profit before income tax**, which is calculated by subtracting all of the other expenses from total revenue. Although there are many complexities in corporate income tax, in this text we will keep it straightforward by simply multiplying profit before income tax by the income tax rate to determine income tax expense.

    Because income tax expense is based on profit before income tax, both of these amounts are shown on the income statement. Using assumed data for revenues and expenses, the condensed, multiple-step income statement for Urbantech Inc. is shown in Illustration 13-3.

URBANTECH INC. Income Statement Year Ended December 31, 2017	
Sales	$800,000
Cost of goods sold	420,000
Gross profit	380,000
Operating expenses	94,000
Profit from operations	286,000
Interest expense	4,750
Profit before income tax	**281,250**
Income tax expense	**56,250**
Profit	$225,000

▶ ILLUSTRATION 13-3
Corporate income statement

    Companies prepare a corporate income tax return (called a T2) annually to determine their taxable income and income tax payable. However, the Canada Revenue Agency requires income tax to be estimated in advance and paid (remitted to taxing authorities) in monthly instalments, rather than waiting until the end of the company's fiscal year.

    After a company determines its total income tax payable at year end, it compares this amount with the total income tax instalments paid during the year. The difference between the income tax paid and income tax payable results in either an additional amount payable or a refund.

    Once the additional liability (or receivable) has been determined, an adjusting entry is required. Assume Urbantech had originally estimated that the amount of income taxes owing would be $42,000 and it remitted instalments of $3,500 per month ($42,000 ÷ 12). At year end, after the corporation's income tax return is completed, the actual amount of income tax owing is $56,250. Urbantech has recorded the monthly instalment payments by debiting income tax expense and crediting cash for $3,500 each month. At the end of the year, the balance in the Income Tax Expense account is a debit balance of $42,000. Urbantech must now prepare an adjusting journal entry to correctly state income tax expense and recognize the remaining amount owing to the taxing authority. The calculation and adjusting entry are illustrated below.

Preliminary balance in the Income Tax Expense account at year end	$42,000 Dr.
Required balance in the Income Tax Expense account for the year	56,250 Dr.
Adjustment required	$14,250

Dec. 31	Income Tax Expense	14,250		A = L + SE
	Income Tax Payable		14,250	+14,250 −14,250
	To adjust estimated income tax expense to actual.			Cash flows: no effect

Urbantech's income statement reports income tax expense of $56,250. The balance sheet reports a current liability for additional income tax owing of $14,250.

BEFORE YOU GO ON...DO IT	3	Recording Income Tax and Preparing an Income Statement

Action Plan
- Determine profit before income tax by deducting expenses from revenues.
- Calculate income tax expense by multiplying profit before income tax by the tax rate.
- Prepare the income statement, deducting income tax expense from profit before income tax.
- Deduct the income tax previously recognized from actual income tax expense to prepare the adjusting income tax entry.

For the year ended June 30, 2017, Neptune Inc. had service revenue of $350,000, operating expenses of $195,000, and interest expense of $14,000. The company has a 25% income tax rate. (a) Determine income tax expense. (b) Prepare an income statement. (c) Prepare the entry to record income tax, assuming that Neptune has already made instalment payments of $30,000.

Solution

(a) Profit before income tax = $350,000 − $195,000 − $14,000 = $141,000
    Income tax expense = $141,000 × 25% = $35,250

(b)

NEPTUNE INC. Income Statement Year Ended June 30, 2017	
Service revenue	$350,000
Operating expenses	195,000
Profit from operations	155,000
Interest expense	14,000
Profit before income tax	141,000
Income tax expense	35,250
Profit	$105,750

(c)

June 30	Income Tax Expense ($35,250 − $30,000)	5,250	
	Income Tax Payable		5,250
	To adjust estimated income tax expense to actual.		

Related exercise material: BE13-6, BE13–7, and E13–6.

LEARNING OBJECTIVE 4 Explain and demonstrate the accounting for cash dividends.

CASH DIVIDENDS

A **cash dividend** is a distribution of cash, on a pro rata basis, to shareholders. Cash dividends are the most common type of dividend in practice but stock dividends are also declared on occasion. We will learn about stock dividends in Chapter 14.

Necessary Conditions to Pay Cash Dividends

For a corporation to pay a cash dividend, it must have all three of the following:

1. **Enough cash.** A company must keep enough cash on hand to pay for its ongoing operations and to pay its bills as they come due. Under the Canada Business Corporations Act, a corporation cannot pay a dividend if it would then become unable to pay its liabilities. Therefore, a company must consider its ongoing cash needs before paying shareholders a cash dividend.
2. **The maintenance of legal capital.** As discussed earlier, in order to protect creditors, a company must maintain its legal capital. Under the Canada Business Corporations Act, a company must

ensure that the dividend does not reduce the realizable value of its assets below the total of its liabilities and legal capital. Under some provincial legislation, a company must also have enough retained earnings before it can pay a dividend. In those cases, a corporation is not allowed to create or increase a deficit (negative retained earnings) by declaring the dividend.

3. **A declaration of dividends by the board of directors.** A company cannot pay dividends unless its board of directors decides to do so, at which point the board "declares" the dividend to be payable. The board of directors has full authority to determine the amount of retained earnings to be distributed as a dividend and the amount to keep in the business. Dividends do not accrue like interest on a note payable. **Even if the preferred shares are cumulative, dividends in arrears are not a liability until they are declared.**

Entries for Cash Dividends

There are three important dates for dividends: (1) the declaration date, (2) the record date, and (3) the payment date. Normally, there are several weeks between each date and the next one. **Accounting entries are required on two of the dates: the declaration date and the payment date.**

On the **declaration date**, a company's board of directors formally declares (authorizes) the cash dividend and announces it to shareholders. Declaring a cash dividend commits the corporation to a legal obligation. The obligation is binding and cannot be rescinded (reversed).

To illustrate a cash dividend, assume that on December 1, the directors of Urbantech Inc. declare a $0.50-per-share quarterly cash dividend on the company's 100,000 common shares. Urbantech does not have any preferred shares and thus does not need to pay them as well. The dividend totals $50,000 ($0.50 × 100,000) and is payable on January 23 to shareholders of record on December 30. The entry to record the declaration is as follows:

	Declaration Date		
Dec. 1	Cash Dividends—Common	50,000	
	Dividends Payable		50,000
	To record declaration of cash dividend.		

$$A = L + SE$$
$$+50,000 \quad -50,000$$
Cash flows: no effect

Note that the balance in Dividends Payable is a current liability and will be paid on January 23. Also note that the Cash Dividends—Common account is similar to the owner's drawings accounts in proprietorships and partnerships in that each is a temporary equity account and must be closed to Retained Earnings at the end of each accounting period.

Instead of debiting a Cash Dividends account, it is also acceptable to debit Retained Earnings when the dividends are declared because dividends reduce retained earnings. The only difference is that, if a Cash Dividends account is debited, then it will have to be closed at the end of the accounting period, as mentioned above. The advantage of debiting a Cash Dividends account, instead of Retained Earnings, is that it is easier to keep track of the dividends declared during the period. We will use the temporary Cash Dividends account to demonstrate accounting for dividends in this textbook.

On the **record date**, ownership of the shares is determined so that the corporation knows who to pay the dividend to. These shareholders are known as the shareholders of record on that date. This date is particularly important for public corporations whose share ownership constantly changes as shares are bought and sold on the secondary market. For Urbantech, the record date is December 30. **No entry is required on this date because the corporation's liability was recognized on the declaration date and is unchanged.**

On the **payment date**, dividend cheques are mailed to shareholders and the payment of the dividend is recorded. The entry on January 23, the payment date, is as follows:

Helpful hint Between the declaration date and the record date, the number of shares remains the same. The purpose of the record date is to identify the persons or entities that will receive the dividend, not to determine the total amount of the dividend liability.

	Payment Date		
Jan. 23	Dividends Payable	50,000	
	Cash		50,000
	To record payment of cash dividend.		

$$A = L + SE$$
$$-50,000 \quad -50,000$$
↓ Cash flows: −50,000

Note that the declaration of a cash dividend increases liabilities and reduces shareholders' equity. The payment of the dividend reduces both assets and liabilities, but has no effect on shareholders' equity. The cumulative effect of the declaration and payment of a cash dividend is to decrease both shareholders' equity (through the Retained Earnings account) and total assets (through the Cash account).

The key dates for dividends are shown in Illustration 13-4.

▶ILLUSTRATION 13-4
Key dividend dates

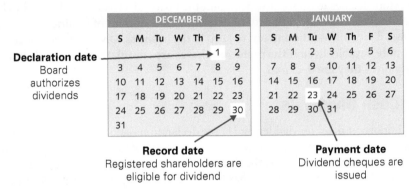

Dividends in a corporation are the equivalent of drawings in a proprietorship or a partnership. Dividends reduce shareholders' equity, just as drawings reduce owner's equity in a proprietorship and partners' equity in a partnership.

Preferred Share Cash Dividends

In the previous discussion, the accounting for cash dividends paid to common shareholders was explored. We now turn to accounting for cash dividends paid to preferred shareholders. Generally, there is little difference in the accounting; cash must be available, legal capital must be maintained, and the board must authorize the dividend. The main differences occur when the preferred shares are cumulative. Recall that preferred shares have priority over common shares.

To illustrate the cumulative dividend feature, assume that Urbantech Inc. has now issued 500, $5 cumulative preferred shares in addition to the common shares already issued. Assume now that in addition to the $0.50 per share common dividend declared by the board, the board also authorizes that the required preferred dividend be paid. Urbantech's annual total preferred dividend is $2,500 (500 × $5 per share). If dividends are two years in arrears, Urbantech's preferred shareholders are entitled to receive the following dividends:

Dividends in arrears ($2,500 × 2)	$5,000
Current year dividends	2,500
Total preferred dividends	$7,500

The journal entry required to recognize the dividend is as follows:

On the **date of declaration:**

A	=	L	+	SE
		+57,500		−57,500

Cash flows: no effect

		Declaration Date		
Dec. 1	Cash Dividend—Preferred		7,500	
	Cash Dividend—Common		50,000	
	Dividends Payable			57,500
	To record declaration of cash dividends to preferred and common shareholders.			

On the **payment date:**

A	=	L	+	SE
−57,500		−57,500		

↓ Cash flows: −57,500

		Payment Date		
Jan. 23	Dividends Payable		57,500	
	Cash			57,500
	To record payment of cash dividends to preferred and common shareholders.			

Dividends in arrears are not considered a liability. There is no obligation to pay a dividend until one is declared by the board of directors. However, the amount of dividends in arrears related to cumulative preferred shares should be disclosed in the notes to the financial statements. This allows investors to assess the potential impact of a future dividend declaration on the corporation's financial position.

BEFORE YOU GO ON...DO IT **4** **Dividends on Preferred and Common Shares**

The board of directors of Juno Corporation met on December 22 and voted in favour of declaring both the annual preferred share dividend and a $1 common share dividend to shareholders of record on January 1. The dividend will be paid on January 15. The company has 30,000, $4 noncumulative preferred shares and 150,000 common shares. Prepare the entries required on each of these dates.

Solution

Dec. 22	Cash Dividends—Preferred (30,000 × $4)	120,000	
	Cash Dividends—Common (150,000 × $1)	150,000	
	Dividends Payable ($120,000 + $150,000)		270,000
	To record declaration of cash dividend.		
Jan. 1	No journal entry		
Jan. 15	Dividends Payable	270,000	
	Cash		270,000
	To record payment of cash dividend.		

Related exercise material: BE13–8, E13-7, and E13–8.

Action Plan
- Remember that as soon as a dividend is declared, the company has an obligation to pay it.
- The date of record is used to determine who will receive the dividend.
- On the payment date, there is no impact on shareholders' equity but assets and liabilities are reduced.

LEARNING OBJECTIVE **5** **Prepare a statement of retained earnings and closing entries for a corporation.**

REPORTING RETAINED EARNINGS

Statement of Retained Earnings (ASPE Only)

All corporations are required to provide information on each of the transactions and events that changed retained earnings during the period and to show how ending retained earnings has been calculated. For companies following ASPE, this information is reported in a **statement of retained earnings**. In Chapter 14, you will learn how companies following IFRS include this information in a statement of changes in shareholders' equity.

A statement of retained earnings is similar to the statement of owner's equity prepared for a proprietorship. The income statement must be prepared before the statement of retained earnings in order to determine the profit that will be added to (or loss that will be deducted from) beginning retained earnings. As in the statement of owner's equity, the statement of retained earnings starts with the beginning balance, and then shows all of the changes in order to calculate the ending balance.

As cash dividends declared reduce retained earnings, this amount is shown as a deduction in the statement of retained earnings. This is similar to deducting drawings in a statement of owner's equity. However, you should note that **the statement of retained earnings reports the amount of dividends declared, not the amount of dividends paid.** Frequently these are the same amounts. But as we saw in the previous section, dividends can be declared in one year and paid in the next; thus dividends declared and dividends paid during the year are not always the same amounts.

To illustrate, assume that Urbantech Inc. had $928,000 of retained earnings at January 1, 2017. During the year, the company declared total cash dividends of $57,500 and its profit after tax was $225,000 for the year. Urbantech's statement of retained earnings for the year ended December 31, 2017, is shown in Illustration 13-5.

▶ILLUSTRATION
Statement of retained
earnings

URBANTECH INC. Statement of Retained Earnings Year Ended December 31, 2017	
Retained earnings, January 1	$ 928,000
Add: Profit	225,000
	1,153,000
Less: Cash dividends	57,500
Retained earnings, December 31	$1,095,500

Closing Entries for a Corporation

As in a proprietorship or partnership, it is necessary to close all of a corporation's temporary accounts at the end of the accounting period to get the accounts in the general ledger ready for the next period. It is also necessary to update the balance in the Retained Earnings account to its year-end balance.

Recall from Chapter 4 that recording closing entries and preparing a post-closing trial balance are the final steps in the accounting cycle. Also recall that in a proprietorship or partnership, each revenue and expense account (which combine to produce profit or loss) is closed to Income Summary, which is then closed to the owner's capital account, and drawings are also closed to the owner's capital account.

▶ILLUSTRATION
Closing process for a
corporation

In a corporation, the process is the same, except that the Income Summary and dividend accounts are closed to Retained Earnings. The closing process for a corporation is shown in Illustration 13-6.

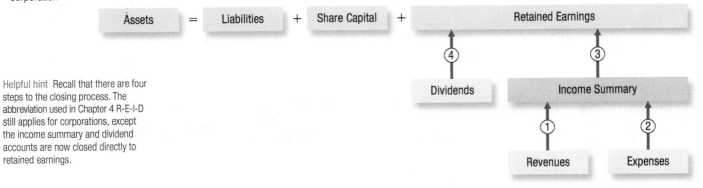

Helpful hint Recall that there are four steps to the closing process. The abbreviation used in Chapter 4 R-E-I-D still applies for corporations, except the income summary and dividend accounts are now closed directly to retained earnings.

Notice that the closing process does not affect assets, liabilities, or share capital accounts.

To illustrate the closing journal entries, use the income statement accounts shown for Urbantech Inc. in Illustration 13-3. Also recall from Illustration 13-5 that Urbantech declared and paid dividends of $57,500 in 2017. The cash dividends accounts will also need to be closed. The closing entries follow:

A = L + SE
−800,000
+800,000

Cash flows: no effect

A = L + SE
−575,000
+575,000

Cash flows: no effect

A = L + SE
−225,000
+225,000

Cash flows: no effect

A = L + SE
−57,500
+57,500

Cash flows: no effect

Dec. 31	Sales	800,000	
	Income Summary		800,000
	To close revenue to Income Summary.		
31	Income Summary	575,000	
	Cost of Goods Sold		420,000
	Operating Expenses		94,000
	Interest Expense		4,750
	Income Tax Expense		56,250
	To close expenses to Income Summary.		
31	Income Summary ($800,000 – $575,000)	225,000	
	Retained Earnings		225,000
	To close Income Summary to Retained Earnings.		
31	Retained Earnings	57,500	
	Cash Dividends—Common		50,000
	Cash Dividends—Preferred		7,500
	To close dividends to Retained Earnings.		

Posting the closing entries to the Income Summary and Retained Earnings accounts follows:

Income Summary						Retained Earnings		
Clos.	575,000	Clos.	800,000				Bal.	928,000
		Bal.	225,000	Clos.	57,500	Clos.		225,000
Clos.	225,000						Bal.	1,095,500
		Bal.	0					

Although not shown, after posting the closing entries, all of the revenue, expense, and dividend accounts will have a zero balance.

After these entries are posted, the Retained Earnings account (a permanent account) is updated in the general ledger to the December 31, 2017, balance of $1,095,500, previously shown in the statement of retained earnings. This ending balance is reported in the shareholders' equity section of the balance sheet.

BEFORE YOU GO ON...DO IT **5** **Retained Earnings Statement**

On January 1, 2017, Minerva Ltd. had a balance of $326,700 in its Retained Earnings account. During the year, it declared $100,000 of cash dividends and paid $75,000. Its profit after tax in 2017 was $115,000, calculated as follows:

Sales		$425,000
Cost of goods sold	$202,500	
Selling expenses	75,000	
Income tax expense	32,500	310,000
Profit		$115,000

(a) Prepare a statement of retained earnings.
(b) Prepare closing entries.
(c) Post closing entries to the Income Summary and Retained Earnings accounts.

Solution

(a)

MINERVA LTD.		
Statement of Retained Earnings		
Year Ended December 31, 2017		
Retained earnings, January 1, 2017		$326,700
Add: Profit		115,000
		441,700
Less: Cash dividends		100,000
Retained earnings, December 31, 2017		$341,700

(b)

Dec. 31	Sales	425,000	
	Income Summary		425,000
	To close revenue to Income Summary.		
31	Income Summary	310,000	
	Cost of Goods Sold		202,500
	Selling Expenses		75,000
	Income Tax Expense		32,500
	To close expenses to Income Summary.		
31	Income Summary	115,000	
	Retained Earnings		115,000
	To close Income Summary ($425,000 – $310,000) to Retained Earnings.		

Action Plan

• A statement of retained earnings shows the changes in the company's retained earnings. It starts with the previous year's retained earnings. Then profit is added and dividends declared are deducted to determine the ending balance.

• Dividends declared are shown on the statement of retained earnings.

• Closing entries are similar to those for proprietorships and partnerships except that the Income Summary and Cash Dividends accounts are closed to Retained Earnings.

(continued)

BEFORE YOU GO ON...DO IT 5 Retained Earnings Statement *(continued)*

31	Retained Earnings		100,000	
	Cash Dividends—Common			100,000
	To close dividends to Retained Earnings.			

(c)

Income Summary					Retained Earnings		
Clos.	310,000	Clos.	425,000			Bal.	326,700
		Bal.	115,000	Clos.	100,000	Clos.	115,000
Clos.	115,000					Bal.	341,700
		Bal.	0				

Related exercise material: BE13–9, BE13–10, E13–9, and E13–10.

LEARNING OBJECTIVE 6 Prepare the shareholders' equity section of the balance sheet and calculate return on equity.

Statement Presentation and Analysis

In this section, we explain the preparation and presentation of the shareholders' equity section of the balance sheet and then learn how to use this information to calculate an important profitability measure—the return on equity ratio.

PRESENTATION OF SHAREHOLDERS' EQUITY

As explained earlier in the chapter, shareholders' equity always includes two parts: (1) share capital and (2) retained earnings. On the balance sheet, share capital may be shown as part of contributed capital, as explained below. Corporations following IFRS may also have a third section called accumulated other comprehensive income, illustrated in Chapter 14. Companies following ASPE do not have accumulated other comprehensive income.

Contributed Capital

Contributed capital is the total amount contributed by the shareholders. Within contributed capital, there are two classifications shown on the balance sheet:

1. **Share capital.** This category consists of preferred and common shares. Because of the additional rights they possess, preferred shares are shown before common shares. The number of shares authorized, number of shares issued, and any particular share preferences (such as convertibility) are reported for each class of shares either on the balance sheet or in a note to the financial statements.

    Private companies following ASPE are not required to disclose the number of shares authorized, only the number issued and their related rights and privileges.

2. **Contributed surplus.** This is another type of contributed capital account. The most common sources of contributed surplus are (1) the amount in excess of the actual share issue price and its par value (where par value shares are allowed), (2) the retirement of shares for less than the average per share amount, and (3) donations of assets to the corporation. We will cover the retirement of shares in Chapter 14. The remaining sources for contributed surplus will be discussed in advanced courses. For now, it is important to note the following about contributed surplus accounts:

    - Contributed surplus is an equity account and is reported on the balance sheet immediately following share capital.
    - A separate contributed surplus account is used for each source for recording purposes.

Alternative terminology Contributed surplus is also known as *additional contributed capital.*

Retained Earnings

Recall that retained earnings are the cumulative profit (or loss) since incorporation that has been retained (that is, not distributed to shareholders). For companies that follow ASPE, the statement of retained earnings provides information on how the account changed during the year. On the balance sheet, the year-end balance in Retained Earnings is shown in shareholders' equity.

The normal balance of the Retained Earnings account is a credit. If total losses and dividends to date are greater than total profit to date, the Retained Earnings account will have a debit balance, which is called a **deficit**. A deficit is reported as a deduction from shareholders' equity, rather than as an addition. The ending Retained Earnings balance becomes the opening balance for the next period.

Sample Shareholders' Equity Section

The shareholders' equity section of Augusta Inc. is shown in Illustration 13-7. Augusta has noncumulative preferred shares with a dividend rate of $6 per year. The company is authorized to issue 50,000 preferred shares and a total of 6,000 have been issued for a total of $770,000.

The company has authorized an unlimited number of common shares; at December 31, 2017, 400,000 shares are issued for $2.8 million. Augusta's ending retained earnings is $1,050,000.

AUGUSTA INC. Balance Sheet (partial) December 31, 2017		
Shareholders' equity		
Share capital		
$6 noncumulative preferred shares, 50,000 shares authorized, 6,000 shares issued	$ 770,000	
Common shares, unlimited shares authorized, 400,000 shares issued	2,800,000	
Total share capital		$3,570,000
Retained earnings		1,050,000
Total shareholders' equity		$4,620,000

▶ ILLUSTRATION **13-7**
Shareholders' equity section

ANALYSIS

There are many ratios determined from the shareholders' equity section of the balance sheet. We will learn about return on equity here. In the next chapter, we will learn about earnings per share and the price-earnings and dividend payout ratios.

Return on equity, also known as return on investment, is considered by many to be **the** most important measure of a company's profitability. This ratio is used by management and investors to evaluate how many dollars are earned for each dollar invested by the shareholders. It can be used to compare investment opportunities in the marketplace. The higher the ratio, the better.

Return on equity is a widely published figure. Illustration 13-8 calculates the return on equity ratio for Corus Entertainment Inc. (in thousands of dollars). (Note that in its financial statements in Appendix A at the end of the textbook, Corus refers to profit as "net income.")

Profit	÷	Average Shareholders' Equity	=	Return on Equity
$156,169	÷	($1,310,126 + $1,220,833) / 2	=	12.3%

▶ ILLUSTRATION **13-8**
Return on equity

Return on equity ratios can be compared with industry averages, which provide users with valuable information when making an investment decision.

BEFORE YOU GO ON...DO IT **6** **Shareholders' Equity and Return on Equity**

Action Plan

- Calculate average shareholders' equity using the total shareholders' equity at the beginning and end of the year.
- Divide profit by the average shareholders' equity for that year to calculate return on equity.
- Recall if it is better for return on equity to increase or decrease.

The following information is available for The Sewing Company Inc. for three recent years:

	2017	2016	2015
Total shareholders' equity	$659,200	$599,822	$558,850
Profit	79,170	54,630	40,620

Calculate return on equity for The Sewing Company for 2017 and 2016 and comment on any trends.

Solution

	2017	2016
Average shareholders' equity	($659,200 + $599,822) ÷ 2 = $629,511	($599,822 + $558,850) ÷ 2 = $579,336
Return on equity	$12.6\% = \dfrac{\$79,170}{\$629,511}$	$9.4\% = \dfrac{\$54,630}{\$579,336}$

The increase in the return on equity indicates improved profitability over the two years.

Related exercise material: BE13–11, BE13–12, E13–11, and E13–12.

Comparing IFRS and ASPE

Key Differences	International Financial Reporting Standards (IFRS)	Accounting Standards for Private Enterprises (ASPE)
Issue of shares for noncash goods or services	Record the transaction at the fair value of the goods or services received. If this value cannot be reliably determined, then the fair value of the shares given up is used.	Record the transaction at the most reliable of the two values—the fair value of the goods or services received or the fair value of the shares. Because private company shares are not traded, it is often difficult to measure their fair value. Thus, in practice, the fair value of the goods or services received is used more often.
Changes in retained earnings	Presented in a statement of changes in shareholders' equity.	Presented in a statement of retained earnings.
Accumulated other comprehensive income	Reported in shareholders' equity on the balance sheet.	Not required under ASPE.
Authorized share capital	Must present the number of shares authorized for each class of shares.	Not required under ASPE.

Demonstration Problem

On January 2, 2017, Rolman Corporation, a private company, began operations. Its articles of incorporation authorize it to issue an unlimited number of common shares and 500,000, $3 noncumulative preferred shares. In its first year, 2017, the company had the following selected transactions:

Jan. 2   Issued 50,000 common shares to Rowena Rolman for $10 cash per share.
Jan. 10   Issued 1,500 common shares to Rowena's brother in exchange for a used vehicle. The vehicle was appraised at $15,000.
June 30   Declared a $0.25 dividend to the common shareholders of record on July 1, payable July 5.

July 5   Paid the common share dividend.

Oct. 1   Issued 1,000 preferred shares to Rowena's grandmother at $60 per share.

Dec. 30   Declared the $0.75 quarterly preferred share dividend, and a $0.25 common share dividend. Both dividends are payable on January 5 to the shareholders of record on January 1.

During 2017, the company had service revenue of $240,000, and operating expenses of $180,000. The company has a 15% income tax rate and did not make any instalments during the year. Rowena has decided the company will use ASPE.

Instructions

(a) Prepare journal entries for the selected transactions.

(b) Prepare an income statement and a journal entry to record income tax expense.

(c) Prepare a statement of retained earnings and the shareholders' equity section of the balance sheet.

(d) Prepare closing entries.

SOLUTION TO DEMONSTRATION PROBLEM

(a)

Jan. 2	Cash	500,000	
	Common Shares (50,000 × $10)		500,000
	To record issue of 50,000 common shares at $10.		
Jan. 10	Vehicles	15,000	
	Common Shares		15,000
	To record issue of 1,500 common shares for a vehicle.		
June 30	Cash Dividends—Common ($0.25 × 51,500)	12,875	
	Dividends Payable		12,875
	To record declaration of a $0.25 common share dividend.		
July 5	Dividends Payable	12,875	
	Cash		12,875
	To record payment of cash dividend.		
Oct. 1	Cash ($60 × 1,000)	60,000	
	Preferred Shares		60,000
	To record issue of 1,000 preferred shares at $60 per share.		
Dec. 30	Cash Dividends—Common ($0.25 × 51,500)	12,875	
	Cash Dividends—Preferred ($0.75 × 1,000)	750	
	Dividends Payable ($12,875 + $750)		13,625
	To record declaration of $0.75 quarterly preferred share dividend and $0.25 common share dividend.		

(b)

ROLMAN CORPORATION
Income Statement
Year Ended December 31, 2017

Service revenue	$240,000
Operating expenses	180,000
Profit before income tax	60,000
Income tax expense	9,000
Profit	$ 51,000

Dec. 31	Income Tax Expense ($60,000 × 15%)	9,000	
	Income Tax Payable		9,000
	To record 15% income taxes for 2017.		

ACTION PLAN

- Credit the Common Shares and Preferred Shares accounts for the entire proceeds of the share issue.
- When shares are issued for noncash assets, use the fair value of what is received.
- Determine profit before income tax by deducting expenses from revenues.
- Calculate income tax expense by multiplying profit before income tax by the tax rate.
- Prepare the income statement, deducting income tax expense from profit before income tax.
- A statement of retained earnings shows all of the changes in the company's retained earnings, which include profit and dividends declared (not dividends paid).
- Closing entries are similar to proprietorships and partnerships except that the Income Summary and Cash Dividends accounts are closed to Retained Earnings.
- On the balance sheet, separate shareholders' equity into share capital and retained earnings.

(c)

ROLMAN CORPORATION		
Statement of Retained Earnings		
Year Ended December 31, 2017		

Retained earnings, January 1		$ 0
Add: Profit for the year		51,000
		51,000
Less: Common share dividends	$25,750	
Preferred share dividends	750	26,500
Retained earnings, December 31		$24,500

ROLMAN CORPORATION		
Balance Sheet (partial)		
December 31, 2017		

Shareholders' equity		
Share capital		
Preferred shares, $3 noncumulative, 1,000 shares issued	$ 60,000	
Common shares, 51,500 shares issued	515,000[1]	
Total share capital		$575,000
Retained earnings		24,500
Total shareholders' equity		$599,500

[1]500,000 + 15,000 = 515,000

(d)

Dec. 31	Service Revenue	240,000	
	Income Summary		240,000
	To close revenue to Income Summary.		
31	Income Summary	189,000	
	Operating Expenses		180,000
	Income Tax Expense		9,000
	To close expenses to Income Summary.		
31	Income Summary ($240,000 – $189,000)	51,000	
	Retained Earnings		51,000
	To close Income Summary to Retained Earnings.		
31	Retained Earnings	26,500	
	Cash Dividends—Common		25,750
	Cash Dividends—Preferred		750
	To close dividends to Retained Earnings.		

▶ Summary of Learning Objectives

1. *Identify and discuss characteristics of the corporate form of organization.* The major characteristics of a corporation are as follows: separate legal existence, limited liability of shareholders, transferable ownership rights, ability to acquire capital, continuous life, government regulations, and corporate income tax. Corporations must be incorporated federally or provincially, and may have shareholders of different classes. Each class of share carries different rights and privileges. The rights of common shareholders are restricted to the right to elect the board of directors, to receive a proportionate share of dividends, if declared, and to receive the remaining assets if the corporation is liquidated. Corporations are managed by the board of directors.

2. **Explain share capital and demonstrate the accounting for the issuance of common and preferred shares.** When shares are issued, the entire proceeds from the issue become legal capital and are credited to the Common Shares account. When shares are issued for noncash assets or services, the fair value of the consideration received is used if it can be determined. If not, the fair value of the consideration given up is used. The accounting for preferred shares is similar to the accounting for common shares.

Preferred shares typically do not have voting rights but do have priority over common shares to receive (1) dividends, and (2) assets, if the company is liquidated. The dividend is specified and may be cumulative or noncumulative. Cumulative preferred shares must be paid dividends for the current year as well as any unpaid dividends from previous years before the common shares receive dividends. Noncumulative preferred shares lose the right to unpaid dividends from prior years. In addition, preferred shares may be convertible, redeemable, and/or retractable. Convertible preferred shares allow their holder to convert them into common shares at a specified ratio. Redeemable preferred shares give the corporation the right to redeem the shares for cash; retractable preferred shares give the shareholder the right to convert the shares to cash.

3. **Prepare a corporate income statement.** Corporate income statements are similar to the income statements for proprietorships and partnerships, with one exception. Income tax expense must be determined based on profit before tax and is reported on the income statement. Profit before tax less income tax expense is equal to profit for the year.

4. **Explain and demonstrate the accounting for cash dividends.** Dividends are similar to drawings in that they are a distribution of profit to the owners (shareholders). Entries for cash dividends are required at the declaration date and the payment date. Cash dividends reduce assets and shareholders' equity (retained earnings). Preferred shareholders are paid their dividends first before the common shareholders are entitled to any dividends.

5. **Prepare a statement of retained earnings and closing entries for a corporation.** Retained earnings are increased by profit, and decreased by losses and dividends. Companies reporting under ASPE are required to prepare a statement of retained earnings showing the beginning balance, changes during the year, and ending balance of Retained Earnings. In a corporation, the Income Summary and dividends accounts are closed to Retained Earnings.

6. **Prepare the shareholders' equity section of the balance sheet and calculate return on equity.** Within the shareholders' equity section of the balance sheet, all corporations will report contributed capital and retained earnings. Within contributed capital, two classifications may be shown if applicable: (1) share capital and (2) contributed surplus. Corporations reporting under IFRS will also have another component in shareholders' equity, which will be introduced in Chapter 14.

Return on equity is calculated by dividing profit by average shareholders' equity. It is an important measure of a company's profitability.

▶ Glossary

Authorized shares The total number of each class of shares a corporation is allowed to sell, as indicated in its articles of incorporation. This amount may be specified or unlimited. (p. 691)

Cash dividends A pro rata (equal) distribution of cash to shareholders. (p. 698)

Common shares Shares where the owners have the right to (1) vote on the election of the board of directors, (2) share in the distribution of profit through dividends, and (3) share any assets that remain after all debts and shares with priority rights have been paid. If the corporation has only one class of shares, they are common shares. (p. 688)

Contributed capital The total amount contributed by the shareholders. Consists of share capital and contributed surplus. (p. 704)

Convertible preferred shares Preferred shares that the shareholder can convert into common shares at a specified ratio. (p. 695)

Corporation A business organized as a separate legal entity, with most of the rights and privileges of a person. Shares are evidence of ownership. (p. 686)

Cumulative A feature of preferred shares that entitles the shareholder to receive current dividends and unpaid prior-year dividends before common shareholders receive any dividends. (p. 695)

Declaration date The date when the board of directors formally declares a dividend and announces it to shareholders. (p. 699)

Deficit A debit balance in the Retained Earnings account created when total losses and dividends to date are greater than total profit to date; it is reported as a deduction from shareholders' equity. (p. 705)

Dividend A distribution of profit by a corporation to its shareholders on a pro rata basis. (p. 690)

Dividends in arrears Dividends on cumulative preferred shares that were not declared. (p. 695)

Initial public offering (IPO) The initial offering of a corporation's shares to the public. (p. 691)

Issued shares The authorized shares that have been sold. (p. 691)

Legal capital The share capital that must be retained in the business for the protection of corporate creditors. (p. 692)

No par value shares Share capital that has not been given a specific value. All the proceeds from the sale of no par value shares are treated as legal capital. (p. 692)

Noncumulative Preferred shares that are entitled to the current dividend, but not to any unpaid amounts from previous years. (p. 695)

Organization costs Costs incurred in the formation of a corporation. (p. 688)

Payment date The date when cash dividends are paid to shareholders. (p. 699)

Preferred shares Shares that have contractual preferences over common shares. (p. 694)

Private corporation A corporation that has only a few shareholders. Its shares are not available for sale to the general public. (p. 686)

Public corporation A corporation that may have thousands of shareholders. Its shares are usually traded on an organized securities market. (p. 686)

Record date The date when ownership of shares is determined for dividend purposes. (p. 699)

Redeemable (callable) preferred shares Preferred shares that give the issuer the right to purchase the shares from shareholders at specified future dates and prices. (p. 695)

Retained earnings Earned capital (cumulative profit less losses and amounts distributed to shareholders since incorporation) that has been retained for future use. If negative (that is, a debit balance), it is called a "deficit." (p. 696)

Retractable preferred shares Preferred shares that give the shareholder the right to sell the shares to the issuer at specified future dates and prices. (p. 696)

Return on equity A measure of profitability from the shareholders' point of view. It is calculated by dividing profit by average common shareholders' equity. (p. 705)

Secondary market A market where investors buy and sell shares of public companies from each other, rather than from the companies. (p. 692)

Share capital The amount paid, or contributed, to the corporation by shareholders in exchange for shares of ownership. It can consist of preferred and common shares. (p. 691)

Statement of retained earnings A financial statement that shows the changes in retained earnings during the year, used only under ASPE. (p. 701)

▶ Self-Study Questions

Answers are at the end of the chapter.

(LO 1) K　1. An important characteristic unique to a corporation is that:
(a) it is separate and distinct from its owners.
(b) owner liability is unlimited.
(c) owners personally manage the company.
(d) ownership rights are not transferable.

(LO 1) AP　2. Ilona Schiller purchased 100 common shares of Air Canada on the Toronto Stock Exchange for $50 per share. Air Canada had originally issued these shares at $33. This transaction will have what impact on Air Canada's Common Shares account?
(a) Increase of $1,700
(b) Increase of $3,300
(c) Increase of $5,000
(d) No effect

(LO 2) AP　3. ABC Corporation issues 1,000 common shares at $12 per share. In recording the transaction, a credit is made to:
(a) Gain on Sale of Shares for $12,000.
(b) Common Shares for $12,000.
(c) Investment in ABC Common Shares for $12,000.
(d) Cash for $12,000.

(LO 2) AP　4. Orcus Corporation issued 1,000 common shares in exchange for land that will be used in operations. The shares are actively trading at $9 per share. The land was advertised for sale at $10,500. The land should be recorded at:
(a) $4,000.
(b) $5,000.
(c) $9,000.
(d) $10,500.

(LO 3) AP　5. In 2017, Lucina Corp. had $480,000 of revenue and $216,000 of operating expenses. The company has a 17% income tax rate. What is the company's profit for the year?
(a) $44,880
(b) $219,120
(c) $264,000
(d) $435,120

(LO 4) K　6. Which of the following statements about cash dividends is **not** true?
(a) Cash dividends are recorded as an expense to the corporation.
(b) Cash dividends ultimately reduce retained earnings.
(c) Cash dividends are a pro rata distribution of retained earnings to shareholders.
(d) Cash dividends are recorded in a temporary equity account.

(LO 4) K　7. The dates on which a corporation will record a journal entry with regard to a cash dividend are the:
(a) record date and payment date.
(b) declaration date and record date.
(c) declaration date, record date, and payment date.
(d) declaration date and payment date.

(LO 5) AP　8. Cyberscape Ltd. began operations on January 1, 2016, and issued common shares for $285,000 cash. On December 31, 2016, the balance in the Retained Earnings account was a deficit of $57,000. In 2017, the company had a profit of $123,000 and declared a $30,000 dividend on December 17 payable on

January 8, 2018. What is the ending balance in
Retained Earnings on December 31, 2017?
(a) ($57,000)
(b) $36,000
(c) $66,000
(d) $30,000

(LO 6) C   9. The shareholders' equity section of a balance sheet for
a company reporting under ASPE will never report:
(a) the total number of shares issued.
(b) accumulated other comprehensive income.

(c) a deficit (debit balance in Retained Earnings).
(d) cumulative preferred shares.

(LO 6) AP 10. If a company's profit is $95,000, its total assets
$1.1 million, its average common shareholders' equity
$950,000, and its net sales $600,000, its return on
equity is:
(a) 3.3%.
(b) 5%.
(c) 8.6%.
(d) 10%.

▶ Questions

(LO 1) C   1. Corporations can be classified in different ways. For
example, they may be classified by purpose (for
example, profit or not-for-profit) or by ownership
(for example, public or private). Explain the difference between each of these types of classifications.

(LO 1) C   2. Patrick Sabine, a student, asks for your help in
understanding the following characteristics of a
corporation: (a) limited liability of shareholders,
(b) transferable ownership rights, and (c) ability to
acquire capital. Explain these characteristics to
Patrick.

(LO 1) C   3. (a) The following terms pertain to the forming of a
corporation: (1) articles of incorporation, (2) bylaws,
and (3) organization costs. Explain these terms.
(b) Donna Fleming believes a corporation must be
incorporated in the province in which its head office
is located. Is this correct? Explain.

(LO 1) C   4. Explain the ownership rights of shareholders and the
authority structure in a corporation.

(LO 2) C   5. Explain the difference between authorized and issued
shares.

(LO 2) C   6. Paul Joyce purchases 100 common shares of TechTop
Ltd. for $12 per share from the company's initial
public offering. Later, Paul purchases 200 more
TechTop Ltd. common shares for $20 each on the
Toronto Stock Exchange, using his own on-line
brokerage account. Explain the impact of each of
these transactions on TechTop's assets, liabilities, and
shareholders' equity.

(LO 2) AP 7. Compare the rights of preferred shareholders with
common shareholders. Include in your answer the
areas in which preferred shares are given priority
over common shares.

(LO 2) K   8. What factors help determine the market price of
shares on an organized stock exchange?

(LO 2) AP 9. Following two years of no dividend payments to
either cumulative preferred or common shareholders,
management decides to declare a dividend for all
shareholders. (a) Is the company required to pay all
shareholders for the previous two years of missed

dividends? (b) Should the company report a liability
for the years of missed dividends or are there any
other reporting requirements?

(LO 2) AP 10. A preferred shareholder converts her convertible
preferred shares into common shares. What effect
does this have on the corporation's (a) total assets,
(b) total liabilities, and (c) total shareholders' equity?

(LO 3) C 11. What is the main difference between income
statements for corporations and income statements
for proprietorships and partnerships? Why does this
difference exist?

(LO 4) K 12. A dividend is a "pro rata" distribution of retained
earnings. Explain what "pro rata" means.

(LO 4) K 13. At what point does a cash dividend become a liability
of a company? What entries are made for cash
dividends on the declaration date, the record date,
and the payment date?

(LO 4) C 14. Jorge is confused about cumulative preferred share
dividends. He believes that dividends that have not
been paid should be accrued as a liability each year.
Explain to Jorge how cumulative preferred share
dividends are accounted for and include the
treatment of dividends in arrears.

(LO 5) C 15. Explain what information is included in a statement
of retained earnings.

(LO 5) C 16. Explain how temporary accounts are closed in a corporation. In what ways are closing entries similar to
those of a proprietorship and in what ways are they
different?

(LO 6) K 17. Shareholders' equity on the balance sheet is divided
into major components. Identify and explain what
each component represents.

(LO 6) C 18. Two independent companies have the same annual
earnings of $100,000; however, the companies
have different amounts of shareholders' equity.
Average shareholders' equity is $300,000 for com-
pany 1 and $350,000 for company 2. Which com-
pany would you consider a better investment and
why?

▶ Brief Exercises

BE13–1   Match the statements in Column A with the appropriate term from Column B.

Column A

1. _____ A company whose shares are not traded on an organized stock exchange like the TSX.

2. _____ Accounting standards that can be used by private companies.

3. _____ The characteristic that allows a corporation to act in its own name rather than in the name of its shareholders.

4. _____ The characteristic that ensures shareholders cannot be made to pay creditors out of their personal assets.

5. _____ The characteristic that allows shareholders to transfer shares without the approval of the corporation.

6. _____ The costs incurred when forming a corporation.

7. _____ The shareholders have a right to elect this group of people.

8. _____ The right to vote, to receive dividends when declared, and to share in assets upon liquidation.

Column B

(a) Transferable ownership rights

(b) Separate legal existence

(c) ASPE

(d) Limited liability

(e) Board of directors

(f) Common shares

(g) Organization costs

(h) Private company

BE13–2   On August 5, Hansen Corporation issued 2,000 common shares for $12 per share. Prepare the journal entry for this transaction.

BE13–3   Juke Joint Ltd., a private company, began operations on March 12 by issuing 5,000 common shares for $20 cash per share. On September 10, the company issued 500 common shares in exchange for equipment with an appraised value of $9,500. Assuming the company uses ASPE, prepare a journal entry to record the September 10 transaction and provide a rationale for the value.

BE13–4   StarLight Ltd. is authorized to issue 10,000, $4 noncumulative preferred shares. On January 13, it issued 3,000 preferred shares for $90 cash per share. (a) Prepare the journal entry to record the transaction. (b) Determine the total amount of dividends that must be paid to the preferred shareholders prior to paying a dividend to common shareholders.

BE13–5   Beauce Incorporated had 45,000, $2.50 preferred shares issued. It did not pay a dividend to the preferred shareholders in 2016 and 2017. (a) What are the dividends in arrears, if any, at December 31, 2017, if the shares are cumulative and if they are noncumulative? (b) How are dividends in arrears reported in the financial statements?

BE13–6   For the year ended June 30, 2017, Viceron Inc. had service revenue of $800,000 and operating expenses of $575,000. The company has a 15% income tax rate. No income tax instalments have been paid or recorded. Prepare the journal entry to record income tax.

BE13–7   Refer to the information for Viceron Inc. and your answer in BE13–6. Prepare an income statement for Viceron Inc. for the year ended June 30, 2017.

BE13–8   On October 14, the board of directors of Celeria Corp. voted to declare the annual preferred share dividend to shareholders of record on November 1, payable on November 21. The company is authorized to issue 100,000, $5.25 noncumulative preferred shares; 25,000 have been issued. Prepare the required entries on each of these dates.

BE13–9   For the year ended December 31, 2017, Grayfair Inc. reported profit of $175,000. During the year, the company declared a total of $120,000 cash dividends and paid $85,000 of these dividends. Prepare a statement of retained earnings for the year, assuming the balance in Retained Earnings on December 31, 2016, was $248,000.

BE13–10   For the year ended December 31, 2017, Huron Lake Enterprises Ltd. had the following revenues and expenses: Sales, $745,000; Cost of Goods Sold, $450,000; Operating Expenses, $135,000; and Income Tax Expense, $35,000. The company also declared $25,000 of dividends to the common shareholders on December 27 to be paid on January 15, 2018. Prepare closing entries for Huron Lake on December 31, 2017.

BE13–11   True Green Nurseries Ltd. is a private company that follows ASPE. It is authorized to issue an unlimited number of both common and $6.50 cumulative preferred shares. On December 31, 2017, there were 15,000 common and 1,000 preferred shares issued with the following balances: Common Shares, $150,000; and Preferred Shares, $100,000. The statement of retained earnings showed retained earnings of $285,000 at December 31, 2017. The dividend on the preferred shares was two years in arrears. Prepare the shareholders' equity section of the balance sheet on December 31, 2017.

Prepare shareholders' equity section. (LO 6) AP

BE13–12   For the year ended December 31, 2014, **WestJet Airlines Ltd.** reported (in thousands) revenue $3,976,552; profit $283,957; beginning shareholders' equity $1,589,840; and ending shareholders' equity $1,777,502. Calculate the return on equity.

Calculate return on equity. (LO 6) AP

▶ Exercises

E13–1   Hana has prepared the following list of statements about corporations:

Identify characteristics of a corporation. (LO 1) C

1. A corporation is an entity separate and distinct from its owners.
2. As a legal entity, a corporation may buy, own, and sell property; borrow money; and enter into legally binding contracts.
3. Shareholders have the right to vote, and to receive dividends on an annual basis.
4. The profit of a corporation is not taxed as a separate entity.
5. Creditors have a legal claim on the personal assets of the owners of a corporation if the corporation does not pay its debts.
6. In a public company, the transfer of shares from one owner to another requires the approval of either the corporation or other shareholders.
7. The board of directors of a corporation is elected by the shareholders.
8. Corporations are subject to fewer provincial and federal regulations than partnerships or proprietorships.

Instructions

Identify each statement as true or false. If false, indicate how to correct the statement.

E13–2   Here are some of the terms discussed in the chapter:

Identify terminology. (LO 1, 2) K

1. Retained earnings	7. Convertible
2. Issued shares	8. Retractable preferred shares (can ask for their money back
3. Legal capital	9. Cumulative
4. Liquidation preference	10. Initial public offering
5. Authorized shares	11. Redeemable preferred shares
6. Public corporation	12. Secondary market

Instructions

For each description, write the number of the term it best matches. Do not use a number more than once.

(a) __8__ Preferred shares that give the shareholder the right to redeem shares at their option
(b) __6__ The type of corporation whose shares are traded in an organized securities market, such as the Toronto Stock Exchange
(c) __11__ Preferred shares that give the issuing corporation the right to repurchase the shares at a specified price and date
(d) __5__ The maximum number of shares a corporation is allowed to sell
(e) __2__ The number of shares a corporation has actually sold
(f) __10__ The first time a corporation's shares are offered to the public
(g) __12__ Where investors buy and sell shares from each other, rather than from the company
(h) __1__ The element of shareholders' equity that is increased by profit and decreased by losses
(i) __4__ A preference to get money back before common shareholders if the company is bankrupt
(j) __3__ The share capital that must be retained in the business for the protection of corporate creditors
(k) __7__ A feature that allows preferred shareholders to exchange their shares for common shares
(l) __9__ A preference to collect unpaid dividends on preferred shares before common shareholders can receive a dividend

E13–3   Santiago Corp., a private corporation, received its articles of incorporation on January 3, 2017. It is authorized to issue an unlimited number of common shares and $1 preferred shares. It had the following share transactions during the year:

Record issue of shares in cash and noncash transactions. (LO 2) AP

Jan. 12   Issued 50,000 common shares for $5 per share.
    24   Issued 950 common shares in payment of a $4,500 bill for legal services.

July 11   Issued 1,000 preferred shares for $25 per share.
Oct. 1   Issued 10,000 common shares in exchange for land. The land's fair value was estimated to be $55,000. Santiago's accountant estimated that the fair value of the shares issued might be as high as $6 per share.

Instructions

(a) Journalize the share transactions.
(b) Calculate the average per share amount for the common shares.

Record issue of shares in cash and noncash transactions. (LO 2) AP

E13-4   Hao Corporation had the following transactions during the current period.

Mar. 2   Issued 5,000 common shares to its legal counsel in payment of a bill for $30,000 for services performed in helping the company incorporate.
June 12   Issued 60,000 common shares for $375,000 cash.
July 11   Issued 1,000, $3 noncumulative preferred shares at $110 per share cash.
Nov. 28   Issued 2,000, $3 noncumulative preferred shares at $95 per share cash.

Instructions

Journalize the transactions.

Determine conversion date and record conversion of preferred shares. (LO 2) AP

E13-5   New Wave Pool Corporation is authorized to issue common and $3 convertible preferred shares. Each preferred share is convertible into four common shares. On July 2, the company issued 100,000 preferred shares for $110 per share. The common shares were trading at $25.00 on September 7, $27.50 on September 19, and $29.00 on September 28.

Instructions

(a) On which date or dates would the preferred shareholders consider converting their shares to common? Why?
(b) Journalize the conversion of the preferred shares using the date chosen in part (a).
(c) Assume also that the preferred shares are redeemable at $115 per share at the option of the company. How, if at all, will this affect the preferred shareholders' decision to convert?

Prepare income statement and entry to record income tax. (LO 3) AP

E13-6   Shrunk Inc. has recorded all necessary adjusting entries, except for income tax expense, at its fiscal year end, July 31, 2017. The following information has been taken from the adjusted trial balance:

Accounts payable	$ 25,500	Interest expense	$ 5,000
Cash dividends—common	60,000	Notes payable	100,000
Common shares	200,000	Retained earnings (Aug. 1, 2016)	352,000
Cost of goods sold	310,000	Salaries expense	140,000
Dividends payable	15,000	Sales	665,000
Income tax expense	30,000	Supplies expense	10,000
Income tax payable	3,000	Unearned revenue	12,000

All accounts have normal balances and total assets equal $817,500. Shrunk has a 20% income tax rate.

Instructions

Prepare a multiple-step income statement and the required journal entry to adjust income tax expense.

Determine split between preferred and common shares and record cash dividend transactions. (LO 2, 4) AP

E13-7   Accentrics Limited has the following information available regarding its share capital at December 31, 2016:

Preferred shares, $3.50 cumulative, 20,000 shares issued	$1,000,000
Preferred shares, $4.50 noncumulative, 10,000 shares issued	500,000
Common shares, 300,000 shares issued	1,500,000

The shares were issued when the corporation began operations on January 1, 2015. No dividends were declared during 2015 and 2016. On October 30, 2017, the board of directors declares the required preferred share dividends and a $0.50 dividend for each of the common shares. The dividends are payable on December 1, 2017, to the shareholders of record on November 16, 2017.

Instructions

(a) How much will be paid to each class of shares?
(b) Prepare journal entries on the appropriate dates for the 2017 dividends.
(c) Assume instead that the maximum cash dividend the company can pay in 2017 is $200,000. Determine how much will be paid to the preferred shareholders and to the common shareholders.

Determine dividends in arrears. (LO 4) AP

E13-8   Windswept Power Corporation issued 150,000, $4.50 cumulative preferred shares to fund its first investment in wind generators. In its first year of operations, it paid $450,000 of dividends to its preferred shareholders. In its second year, the company paid dividends of $900,000 to its preferred shareholders.

Instructions

(a) What is the total annual preferred dividend supposed to be for the preferred shareholders?
(b) Calculate any dividends in arrears in years 1 and 2.
(c) Explain how dividends in arrears should be reported in the financial statements.
(d) If the preferred shares were noncumulative rather than cumulative, how much dividend would the company likely have paid its preferred shareholders in year 2?

E13-9   Refer to the data given in E13-6 for Shrunk Inc.

Instructions

(a) Prepare a statement of retained earnings.
(b) Prepare closing entries and post to the Income Summary and Retained Earnings accounts.

Prepare a statement of retained earnings and closing entries. (LO 5) AP

E13-10   Didsbury Digital Ltd. has a September 30 fiscal year end and a 15% income tax rate. The following information is available for its 2017 year end:

Record income tax; prepare an income statement and statement of retained earnings. (LO 3, 4, 5) AP

1. Earned $529,000 of service revenue and incurred $442,000 of operating expenses. Interest expense was $2,500.
2. On October 5, 2016, paid $50,000 of dividends that had been declared on September 25, 2016.
3. On September 28, 2017, declared $40,000 of dividends payable on October 8, 2017.
4. Retained earnings on September 30, 2016, were $237,500.
5. Issued common shares for $25,000 cash on July 2, 2017.

Instructions

(a) Prepare an income statement.
(b) Journalize the adjustment for income tax assuming no income tax instalments were made during the year.
(c) Prepare a statement of retained earnings.

E13-11   The shareholders' equity section of Charley Corporation is as follows:

Answer questions about the shareholders' equity section. (LO 2, 6) C

CHARLEY CORPORATION
Balance Sheet (partial)
December 31, 2017

Contributed capital
$2 cumulative preferred shares, 10,000 shares
  authorized, 6,000 shares issued $ 300,000
Common shares, 750,000 shares authorized,
  600,000 shares issued   1,200,000
Contributed surplus   10,000

Total contributed capital   1,510,000
Retained earnings   1,858,000

Total shareholders' equity $3,368,000

Instructions

Review the shareholders' equity section and write a memo to the company president answering the following questions.

(a) How many common shares have been issued?
(b) How many preferred shares have been authorized?
(c) What are possible sources of contributed surplus?
(d) Explain what causes retained earnings to change each year.
(e) How much must be paid to preferred shareholders when dividends are declared, assuming the company has not declared or paid dividends in 2016 and 2017?

E13-12   Raiders Limited is a private company that follows ASPE. It is authorized to issue an unlimited number of both common and $5 cumulative preferred shares. On December 31, 2017, there were 35,000 common and 1,000 preferred shares issued. The common shares had been issued at an average per share amount of $10; the preferred shares at $105. The balance in the Retained Earnings account on January 1, 2017, was $287,000. During 2017, the company had profit of $125,000 and declared a total of $75,000 of dividends, of which $56,250 was paid during the year.

Prepare shareholders' equity section and calculate return on equity. (LO 6) AP

Instructions

(a) Prepare the shareholders' equity section of the balance sheet on December 31, 2017.
(b) Calculate return on equity for 2017. Assume there were no changes in the Common Shares and Preferred Shares accounts during the year.

▶ Problems: Set A

Determine form of business organization. (LO 1) AN

P13–1A   Presented below are four independent situations:

1. After passing their final accounting exam, four students put together plans to offer bookkeeping services to small companies. The students have signed an agreement that details how the profits of this new business will be shared.
2. Darien Enns has had so many people ask about the new solar and wind equipment he recently added to his home, he has decided to start a company that will offer planning, design, and installation of alternative power technology. To launch the business, Darien will need substantial funding to purchase a service truck, a special crane, and the solar- and wind-generating equipment. He expects the business to grow quickly and that he will have to hire additional employees and triple the number of trucks and cranes owned by the business. Darien has no way to provide funding for the start of the business, and he also understands that the expected growth will require large additional investments.
3. After working in the construction industry for several years, Joeline Pal has decided to offer her own roofing services to homeowners.
4. Frank Holton owns a small two-seater airplane to fly hunters and hikers to remote areas in northern Ontario. Demand for Frank's services has grown so much that he plans to hire additional pilots and purchase four larger planes. Frank will also purchase liability insurance in case of accidents, and plans to maintain control of the company.

Instructions

In each case, explain what form of organization the business is likely to take: proprietorship, partnership, or corporation. Give reasons for your choice.

TAKING IT FURTHER   Since a corporation is a separate legal entity, what gives employees the authority to complete a transaction on behalf of the company?

Record and post share transactions. Determine balances and answer questions. (LO 2) AP

P13–2A   Wetland Corporation, a private corporation, was organized on February 1, 2016. It is authorized to issue 100,000, $6 noncumulative preferred shares, and an unlimited number of common shares. The following transactions were completed during the first year:

Feb.	10	Issued 80,000 common shares at $4 per share.
Mar.	1	Issued 5,000 preferred shares at $115 per share.
Apr.	1	Issued 22,500 common shares for land. The land's asking price was $100,000 and its appraised value was $90,000.
June	20	Issued 78,000 common shares at $4.50 per share.
July	7	Issued 10,000 common shares to lawyers to pay for their bill of $45,000 for services they performed in helping the company organize.
Sept.	1	Issued 10,000 common shares at $5 per share.
Nov.	1	Issued 1,000 preferred shares at $117 per share.

Instructions

(a) Journalize the transactions.
(b) Open general ledger accounts and post to the shareholders' equity accounts.
(c) Determine the number of shares issued and the average per share amount for both common and preferred shares.
(d) How many more shares is the company authorized to issue for each class of shares?

TAKING IT FURTHER   If Wetland were a public corporation, how might that affect the journal entries recorded for the April 1 and July 7 issues of common shares?

Allocate dividends between preferred and common shares. (LO 2) AP

P13–3A   At the beginning of its first year of operations, Northwoods Limited has 5,000, $4 preferred shares and 50,000 common shares.

Instructions

Using the format shown below, allocate the total dividend paid in each year to the preferred and common shareholders, assuming that the preferred shares are (a) noncumulative, and (b) cumulative.

		(a)		(b)	
Year	Dividend Paid	Noncumulative Preferred	Common	Cumulative Preferred	Common
1	$20,000				
2	15,000				
3	30,000				
4	35,000				

TAKING IT FURTHER Why would an investor choose to invest in common shares if preferred share dividends have a higher priority? *[handwritten: bcoz common shares have voting rights and influence investors]*

P13–4A Pro Com Ltd. issues 8,000, $5 cumulative preferred shares at $66 each and 15,000 common shares at $30 each at the beginning of 2015. Each preferred share is convertible into two common shares. During the years 2016 and 2017, the following transactions affected Pro Com's shareholders' equity accounts:

Allocate dividends between preferred and common shares and record conversion. (LO 2, 4) AP

2016

Jan. 10   Paid $12,000 of annual dividends to preferred shareholders.

2017

Jan. 10   Paid annual dividend to preferred shareholders and a $4,000 dividend to common shareholders.
Mar. 1   The preferred shares were converted into common shares.

Instructions

(a) Journalize each of the transactions.
(b) Are there any additional reporting requirements regarding preferred share dividends in either 2016 or 2017?
(c) What factors affect preferred shareholders' decision to convert their shares into common shares?

TAKING IT FURTHER Why might investors be willing to pay more for preferred shares that have a conversion option?

P13–5A Zurich Limited is a private corporation reporting under ASPE. At December 31, 2017, its general ledger contained the following summary data:

Record dividends; prepare income statement and statement of retained earnings. (LO 3, 4, 5) AP

Cost of goods sold	$1,225,000
Interest expense	35,000
Interest revenue	12,500
Operating expenses	210,000
Retained earnings, January 1	550,000
Sales	1,650,000

Additional information:

1. In 2017, common share dividends of $25,000 were declared on June 30 and December 31. The dividends were paid on July 8, 2017, and January 8, 2018, respectively. *[handwritten: not record bcoz its next year]*
2. The company's income tax rate is 20%.

Instructions

(a) Record the dividend transactions in 2017.
(b) Determine income tax expense and prepare a multiple-step income statement for 2017. *[handwritten: if asked for an entry / Income tax exp Dr / Income tax pay Cr]*
(c) Prepare a statement of retained earnings for 2017.

TAKING IT FURTHER Compare a statement of retained earnings with a statement of owner's equity.

P13–6A Memphis Ltd. is a private corporation reporting under ASPE. It has recorded all necessary adjusting entries at its fiscal year end, October 31, 2017. The following information has been taken from the adjusted trial balance:

Prepare income statement, statement of retained earnings, and closing entries. (LO 3, 4, 5) AP

Accounts payable	$ 18,000	Interest expense	$ 1,400
Cash dividends—common	40,000	Notes payable	55,000
Common shares	150,000	Rent expense	38,800
Depreciation expense	15,250	Retained earnings (Nov. 1, 2016)	610,000
Dividends payable	10,000	Salaries expense	175,750
Income tax expense	29,740	Service revenue	385,000
Income tax payable	2,500	Unearned revenue	14,000
Insurance expense	5,100		

All accounts have normal balances and total assets equal $938,460. Memphis has a 20% income tax rate.

Instructions

(a) Prepare a multiple-step income statement for the year.
(b) Prepare a statement of retained earnings for the year.

(c) Prepare closing entries.

(d) Post the closing entries to the Income Summary and Retained Earnings accounts and compare with the financial statements.

TAKING IT FURTHER   If Memphis Ltd. followed IFRS instead of ASPE, which statements would you prepare?

Record and post transactions; prepare shareholders' equity section. (LO 2, 4, 6) AP

P13–7A   On January 1, 2017, Schipper Ltd. had the following shareholders' equity accounts:

Common shares (1,000,000 issued)	$1,500,000
Retained earnings	1,800,000

The company was also authorized to issue an unlimited number of $4 noncumulative preferred shares. As at January 1, 2017, none had been issued. During 2017, the corporation had the following transactions and events related to its shareholders' equity:

Jan.	2	Issued 100,000 preferred shares for $50 per share.
Apr.	1	Paid quarterly dividend to preferred shareholders.
July	1	Paid quarterly dividend to preferred shareholders.
Aug.	12	Issued 100,000 common shares for $1.70 per share.
Oct.	1	Paid quarterly dividend to preferred shareholders.
Dec.	31	Paid quarterly dividend to preferred shareholders and a $0.25 per share dividend to the common shareholders.
Dec.	31	Loss for the year was $100,000.

Instructions

(a) Journalize the transactions and the entries to close dividends and the Income Summary account.

(b) Open general ledger accounts for the shareholders' equity accounts, enter the beginning balances, and post entries from part (a).

(c) Prepare the shareholders' equity section of the balance sheet at December 31, 2017, including any required disclosures. Assume Schipper is reporting under ASPE.

TAKING IT FURTHER   Schipper incurred a loss in 2017. Are companies allowed to declare and pay dividends during a year when they have a loss?

Record and post transactions; prepare shareholders' equity section. (LO 2, 4, 6) AP

P13–8A   Cattrall Corporation is authorized to issue an unlimited number of $5 cumulative preferred shares and an unlimited number of common shares. On February 1, 2016, the general ledger contained the following shareholders' equity accounts:

Preferred shares (10,000 shares issued)	$ 475,000
Common shares (70,000 shares issued)	1,050,000
Retained earnings	700,000

The following equity transactions occurred during the year ended January 31, 2017:

Feb.	28	Issued 5,000 preferred shares for $275,000.
Apr.	12	Issued 200,000 common shares for $3.2 million.
May	25	Issued 5,000 common shares in exchange for land. At the time of the exchange, the land was valued at $75,000.
Jan.	1	Paid dividend of $2.50 per share to preferred shareholders.
	31	A loss of $50,000 was incurred for the year.

Instructions

(a) Journalize the transactions and the entries to close dividends and the Income Summary account.

(b) Open general ledger accounts for the shareholders' equity accounts and post entries from part (a).

(c) Prepare the shareholders' equity section of the balance sheet at January 31, 2017, including any required disclosures. Assume Cattrall is reporting under ASPE and there were no preferred dividend arrears at January 31, 2016.

TAKING IT FURTHER   What are the difficulties in determining how many shares to issue in exchange for noncash assets as well as how to value the transaction?

Prepare financial statements. (LO 3, 5, 6) AP

P13–9A   Choke Cherry Ltd. is a private company reporting under ASPE. Its adjusted trial balance at its fiscal year end, December 31, 2017, is shown below:

CHOKE CHERRY LTD.
Adjusted Trial Balance
December 31, 2017

	Debit	Credit
Cash	$ 28,000	
Inventory	26,500	
Supplies	5,000	
Equipment	300,000	
Accumulated depreciation—equipment		$ 65,000
Accounts payable		34,000
Income tax payable		8,985
Unearned revenue		21,000
Notes payable ($12,000 is due in 2018)		30,000
Preferred shares ($4 noncumulative, 1,000 issued)		40,000
Common shares (120,000 issued)		60,000
Retained earnings		73,000
Cash dividends—preferred	4,000	
Cash dividends—common	50,000	
Sales		515,000
Cost of goods sold	159,000	
Depreciation expense	20,000	
Income tax expense	14,385	
Insurance expense	8,200	
Interest expense	1,800	
Rent expense	32,600	
Salaries expense	185,000	
Supplies expense	12,500	
	$846,985	$846,985

Instructions

Prepare an income statement, statement of retained earnings, and balance sheet.

TAKING IT FURTHER   Compare dividends paid to owners of corporations with withdrawals by owners of proprietorships or partnerships.

P13–10A   Northwood Architects Ltd. is a private company reporting under ASPE. It is authorized to issue an unlimited number of common and $3 cumulative preferred shares. The following is an alphabetical list of its adjusted accounts at March 31, 2017, its fiscal year end. All accounts have normal balances.

Prepare financial statements and calculate return on equity. (LO 5, 6) AP

Accounts payable	$ 21,350	Income tax expense	$ 16,535
Accounts receivable	38,700	Insurance expense	6,550
Accumulated depreciation—equipment	23,650	Interest expense	3,000
Cash	54,600	Note payable	50,000
Cash dividends—common	40,000	Preferred shares	56,250
Cash dividends—preferred	4,500	Prepaid expenses	6,150
Common shares	75,000	Rent expense	35,800
Consulting revenue	404,500	Retained earnings	64,800
Depreciation expense	11,825	Salaries expense	245,400
Dividends payable	15,000	Salaries payable	2,310
Equipment	224,000	Supplies expense	25,800

There are 1,500 preferred and 75,000 common shares issued.

Instructions

(a) Prepare the statement of retained earnings, and the shareholders' equity section of the balance sheet.
(b) Calculate return on equity. Note: No shares were issued during the year.

TAKING IT FURTHER   Why is it important that retained earnings be tracked and presented separately from share capital in the balance sheet?

Calculate return on assets and equity and comment. (LO 6) AP

P13–11A The following financial information (in millions) is for two major corporations for three fiscal years ended December 31 as follows:

	2014	2013	2012
Canadian Pacific Railway Limited			
Profit	$ 1,476	$ 875	$ 484
Shareholders' equity	5,610	7,097	5,097
Total assets	16,640	17,060	14,727
Canadian National Railway Company			
Profit	$ 3,167	$ 2,612	$ 2,680
Shareholders' equity	13,470	12,953	11,018
Total assets	31,792	30,163	26,659

Instructions

(a) Calculate return on assets and return on equity for each company for 2014 and 2013. Comment on whether their ratios have improved or deteriorated.

(b) Compare Canadian Pacific's ratios with Canadian National's.

(c) The five-year industry average for return on equity is 11.14%. Compare the two companies' performance with the industry average.

TAKING IT FURTHER   Using your findings in this question to illustrate, explain why it is important to use comparisons in evaluating ratios.

Record transactions and adjustments; prepare financial statements. (LO 2, 3, 4, 5, 6) AP

P13–12A Annora Inc., a private company, is authorized to issue an unlimited number of common shares and 100,000 noncumulative $4 preferred shares. It began operations on January 1, 2017, and the following are selected transactions during 2017:

Jan. 1   Issued 300,000 common shares for $150,000 cash.

2   Issued 30,000 preferred shares for $40 cash per share.

Dec. 1   Declared a total of $225,000 in dividends, payable on January 5, to shareholders of record on December 13.

31   Determined that it had total revenues of $915,000 and operating expenses of $610,000.

Annora elected to report under ASPE. It has a 15% income tax rate and paid income tax instalments during the year of $40,000.

Instructions

(a) Record the share issue and dividend transactions.

(b) Prepare a partial income statement starting with profit before income tax and record an adjusting entry for income tax.

(c) Prepare a statement of retained earnings and the shareholders' equity section of the balance sheet.

TAKING IT FURTHER   Why are common shareholders sometimes referred to as "residual owners"?

▶ Problems: Set B

Identify and discuss major characteristics of a corporation. (LO 1) AN

P13–1B Four independent situations follow:

1. Kevin Roberts, President and CEO of Hanley Tools Inc., has just been notified that his company has been sued due to the failure of one of its key products. Although the lawsuit is for several million dollars, Kevin is not concerned that he will have to sell his new house to pay damages if his company is unsuccessful in defending itself against the lawsuit.

2. Salik Makkar has just negotiated a borrowing agreement with a bank. The completed borrowing agreement is a contract between two parties: the bank and the company that Salik works for as an executive officer.

3. Marion Kureshi incorporated her business, Kureshi Fine Furniture Corporation, in 1974. The business has grown steadily every year, and now employs over 2,000 people. Kureshi Fine Furniture's common shares trade on a public stock exchange. Marion is currently the president of the company; however, due to deteriorating health, Marion can no longer be active in the business. Fortunately, Marion has put plans in place for her daughter to assume her role as president.

4. Matthew Antoine has been working on a new technology to improve cell phone reception in remote rural locations. Matthew knows that a significant amount of funding will be required to purchase the production equipment and inventory to manufacture his new antenna. In order to launch his new business, Matthew plans to organize the business as a publicly held corporation and issue shares on the TSX Venture Exchange.

Instructions

In each case, identify the characteristic being described in the situation that separates a corporation from a proprietorship or partnership, and explain how the situation might be different for a sole proprietor or partnership.

TAKING IT FURTHER   How does limited liability help investors sell shares in the secondary markets?

P13–2B   Highland Corporation was organized on January 1, 2017. It is authorized to issue 50,000, $3 noncumulative preferred shares, and an unlimited number of common shares. The following transactions were completed during the first year:

Jan. 10   Issued 100,000 common shares at $2 per share.
Mar. 1   Issued 10,000 preferred shares at $42 per share.
Mar. 31   Issued 75,000 common shares at $3 per share.
Apr. 3   Issued 25,000 common shares for land. The land's appraised value was $74,000.
July 24   Issued 20,500 common shares for $60,000 cash and used equipment. The equipment originally cost $25,000. It now has a carrying amount of $15,000 and a fair value of $12,000.
Nov. 1   Issued 2,000 preferred shares at $48 per share.

Record and post share transactions. Determine balances and answer questions. (LO 2) AP

Instructions

(a) Journalize the transactions.
(b) Open general ledger accounts and post to the shareholders' equity accounts.
(c) Determine the number of shares issued and the average per share amount for both common and preferred shares.
(d) If the preferred shares were cumulative instead of noncumulative, would this have changed the amount investors were willing to pay for the shares? Explain.

TAKING IT FURTHER   If Highland were a public corporation, how might that affect the journal entries recorded for the April 3 and July 24 issues of common shares?

P13–3B   At the beginning of its first year of operations, Backwoods Limited has 3,000, $5 preferred shares and 50,000 common shares.

Allocate dividends between preferred and common shares. (LO 2) AP

Instructions

Using the format shown below, allocate the total dividend paid in each year to the preferred and common shareholders, assuming that the preferred shares are (a) noncumulative, and (b) cumulative.

		(a)		(b)	
Year	Dividend Paid	Noncumulative Preferred	Common	Cumulative Preferred	Common
1	$15,000				
2	12,000				
3	27,000				
4	35,000				

TAKING IT FURTHER   Why would an investor choose to invest in common shares if preferred share dividends have a higher priority?

P13–4B   Kari Corporation issues 5,000, $4 cumulative preferred shares at $80 each and 10,000 common shares at $18 each at the beginning of 2015. Each preferred share is convertible into four common shares. During the years 2016 and 2017, the following transactions affected Kari Corporation's shareholders' equity accounts:

Allocate dividends between preferred and common shares and record conversion. (LO 2, 4) AP

2016

Jan. 10   Paid $12,000 of annual dividends to preferred shareholders.

2017

Jan. 10   Paid annual dividend to preferred shareholders and a $4,000 dividend to common shareholders.
Mar. 1   The preferred shares were converted into common shares.

Instructions

(a) Journalize each of the 2016 and 2017 transactions.
(b) Are there any additional reporting requirements regarding preferred share dividends in either 2016 or 2017?
(c) After the preferred shares are converted, what is the total number of common shares issued?

TAKING IT FURTHER   What are retractable preferred shares and how do they compare with convertible preferred shares?

cord dividends; prepare income statement and statement of retained earnings. (LO 3, 4, 5) AP

P13–5B Hyperchip Limited is a private corporation reporting under ASPE. At December 31, 2017, its general ledger contained the following summary data:

Cost of goods sold	$ 950,000
Net sales	1,425,000
Operating expenses	270,000
Other expenses	30,000
Other revenues	45,000
Retained earnings, December 31, 2016	1,150,000

Additional information:

1. In 2017, common share dividends of $80,000 were declared on June 26 and December 26. The dividends were paid on July 9, 2017, and January 9, 2018, respectively.
2. The company's income tax rate is 20%.

Instructions

(a) Record the dividend transactions in 2017.
(b) Prepare a multiple-step income statement for 2017.
(c) Prepare a statement of retained earnings for 2017.

TAKING IT FURTHER If this company were following IFRS, what statement would have to be prepared instead of the statement of retained earnings?

Prepare income statement, statement of retained earnings, and closing entries. (LO 3, 4, 5) AP

P13–6B Hayden Inc. is a private corporation reporting under ASPE. It has recorded all necessary adjusting entries at its fiscal year end of November 30, 2017. The following information has been taken from the adjusted trial balance:

Accounts payable	$ 23,700	Interest expense	$ 7,500
Cash dividends—common	120,000	Notes payable	125,000
Common shares	150,000	Rent expense	43,500
Depreciation expense	51,650	Retained earnings (Dec. 1, 2016)	339,500
Dividends payable	30,000	Salaries expense	220,000
Income tax expense	13,800	Service revenue	425,000
Income tax payable	1,500	Unearned revenue	19,500
Insurance expense	10,350		

All accounts have normal balances and total assets equal $647,400. Hayden has a 15% income tax rate.

Instructions

(a) Prepare a multiple-step income statement for the year.
(b) Prepare a statement of retained earnings for the year.
(c) Prepare closing entries.
(d) Post the closing entries to the Income Summary and Retained Earnings accounts and compare with the financial statements.

TAKING IT FURTHER Why is the entry to adjust income tax expense usually the last adjusting entry prepared each year?

Record and post transactions. Prepare shareholders' equity section. (LO 2, 4, 6) AP

P13–7B On January 1, 2017, Conway Ltd. had the following shareholders' equity accounts:

Common shares, unlimited number of shares authorized, 1.5 million issued	$1,650,000
Retained earnings	550,000

It was also authorized to issue an unlimited number of $6 noncumulative preferred shares. During 2017, the corporation had the following transactions and events related to its shareholders' equity:

Jan.	2	Issued 100,000 preferred shares at $66 per share.
Mar.	31	Paid quarterly dividend to preferred shareholders.
Apr.	18	Issued 250,000 common shares at $1.30 per share.
June	30	Paid quarterly dividend to preferred shareholders.
Sept.	30	Paid quarterly dividend to preferred shareholders.
Dec.	31	Paid quarterly dividend to preferred shareholders.
Dec.	31	Profit for the year was $160,000.

Instructions

(a) Journalize the transactions and the entries to close dividends and the Income Summary account.
(b) Open general ledger accounts for the shareholders' equity accounts, enter the beginning balances, and post transactions in part (a).

(c) Prepare the shareholders' equity section of the balance sheet at December 31, 2017, including any required disclosures. Assume Conway reports under ASPE.

<u>TAKING IT FURTHER</u>   What conditions must be met to declare dividends in a corporation?

P13-8B   Largent Corporation is authorized to issue 200,000, $4 cumulative preferred shares and an unlimited number of common shares. On January 1, 2017, the general ledger contained the following shareholders' equity accounts:

Record and post transactions. Prepare shareholders' equity section. (LO 2, 4, 6) AP

Preferred shares (8,000 shares issued)	$ 440,000
Common shares (70,000 shares issued)	1,050,000
Retained earnings	800,000

During 2017, the following transactions occurred:

Jan. 1	Issued 10,000 preferred shares for $600,000.
Apr. 14	Issued 40,000 common shares for $560,000.
June 30	Paid a semi-annual dividend to the preferred shareholders.
Aug. 22	Issued 10,000 common shares in exchange for a building. At the time of the exchange, the building's fair value was $150,000.
Dec. 31	Profit for the year was $582,000.

Instructions

(a) Journalize the transactions and the entries to close dividends and the Income Summary account.
(b) Open general ledger accounts for the shareholders' equity accounts and post entries from part (a).
(c) Prepare the shareholders' equity section of the balance sheet at December 31, 2017, including any required disclosures. Assume Largent is reporting under ASPE and there were no preferred dividend arrears at January 31, 2016

<u>TAKING IT FURTHER</u>   What are the difficulties in determining how many shares to issue in exchange for non-cash assets as well as how to value the transaction?

P13-9B   Rupert Engineering Corp. is a private company reporting under ASPE. Its adjusted trial balance at its fiscal year end, March 31, 2017, is shown below:

Prepare financial statements. (LO 3, 5, 6) AP

RUPERT ENGINEERING CORP.
Adjusted Trial Balance
March 31, 2017

	Debit	Credit
Cash	$ 65,400	
Accounts receivable	31,150	
Supplies	7,300	
Equipment	148,000	
Accumulated depreciation—equipment		$ 29,600
Accounts payable		14,200
Income tax payable		1,900
Unearned revenue		2,500
Notes payable ($10,000 is due within the next year)		40,000
Preferred shares ($3.75 cumulative, 500 issued)		18,750
Common shares (35,000 issued)		50,000
Retained earnings		65,000
Cash dividends—preferred	1,875	
Cash dividends—common	53,125	
Consulting revenue		315,500
Depreciation expense	14,800	
Income tax expense	21,200	
Interest expense	2,400	
Rent expense	36,000	
Salaries expense	140,300	
Supplies expense	15,900	
	$537,450	$537,450

Instructions

Prepare an income statement, statement of retained earnings, and balance sheet.

TAKING IT FURTHER Are there any differences between the Retained Earnings account for corporations and the owner's capital account used for proprietorships?

Prepare financial statements.
(LO 3, 5) AP

P13–10B Carlotta's Cakes Inc. is a private company reporting under ASPE. It is authorized to issue an unlimited number of common and $3 cumulative preferred shares. The following is an alphabetical list of its adjusted accounts at May 31, 2017, its fiscal year end. All accounts have normal balances.

Accounts payable	$ 38,500	Income tax expense	$ 11,230
Accounts receivable	15,300	Insurance expense	7,500
Accumulated depreciation—equipment	126,000	Interest expense	4,500
Cash	20,600	Inventory	70,220
Cash dividends—common	50,000	Notes payable	75,000
Cash dividends—preferred	7,500	Preferred shares	150,000
Common shares	50,000	Rent expense	24,500
Cost of goods sold	277,475	Retained earnings	73,000
Depreciation expense	42,000	Salaries expense	67,800
Dividend payable	7,500	Sales	504,500
Equipment	420,000	Supplies expense	5,875

The note payable is due in 2019. There are 10,000 common shares issued and 5,000 preferred shares issued as at May 31, 2017.

Instructions

Prepare an income statement, statement of retained earnings, and balance sheet.

TAKING IT FURTHER What ethical issues may managers face when reporting a company's financial performance?

Calculate return on assets and equity and comment.
(LO 6) AP

P13–11B The following financial information (in millions) is for two major corporations for three fiscal years ended December 31:

	2014	2013	2012
Husky Energy Inc.			
Profit	$ 1,258	$ 1,829	$ 2,022
Shareholders' equity	20,575	20,078	19,161
Total assets	38,848	36,904	35,161
Suncor Energy Inc.			
Profit	$ 2,699	$ 3,911	$ 2,740
Shareholders' equity	41,603	41,180	39,215
Total assets	79,671	78,315	76,401

Instructions

(a) Calculate return on assets and return on equity for each company for 2014 and 2013. Comment on whether their ratios have improved or deteriorated.

(b) Compare Husky's ratios with Suncor's.

(c) The five-year industry average for return on equity is 14.06%. Compare the two companies' performance with the industry average.

TAKING IT FURTHER Using your findings in this question to illustrate, explain why it is important to use comparisons in evaluating ratios.

Record transactions and adjustments; prepare financial statements.
(LO 2, 3, 4, 5, 6) AP

P13–12B Nygren Corporation, a private company, is authorized to issue an unlimited number of common shares and 500,000, $5 cumulative preferred shares. It began operations on January 1, 2017, and the following transactions occurred in 2017:

Jan. 1   Issued 6,000 common shares for $60,000 cash.

     2   Issued 1,000 preferred shares for $62.50 cash per share.

Dec. 10   Declared a total of $17,000 in dividends, payable on January 3, to shareholders of record on December 23.

The following information is also available with respect to the company's operations during the year:

1. Collected $268,000 cash for consulting revenue earned.
2. Paid $164,000 salaries expense; $42,000 rent expense; and $12,000 office expense.

3. Purchased equipment for $130,000 cash.
4. At December 31, determined the following adjustments were required:
   - Depreciation on the equipment, $13,000;
   - Consulting revenue earned but not yet collected in cash, $22,000;
   - Accrued salaries expense, $4,200;
   - Income tax rate, 15%. No instalments were made during the year.

Nygren elected to report under ASPE.

Instructions

(a) Record the share issue and dividend transactions.
(b) Prepare an income statement, statement of retained earnings, and the shareholders' equity section of the balance sheet.

TAKING IT FURTHER Why are common shareholders sometimes referred to as "residual owners"?

CHAPTER 13: BROADENING YOUR PERSPECTIVE

▶ Financial Reporting and Analysis

Financial Reporting Problem

BYP13-1 The shareholders' equity section for **Corus Entertainment Inc.** is shown in the consolidated balance sheet in Appendix A. You will also find data related to this problem in the notes to the financial statements.

Instructions

(a) How many classes of shares does Corus have? For each class of shares, specify how many shares are authorized and issued at August 31, 2014. (*Hint*: Refer to Note 15.)
(b) Refer to Note 15 again. What are the rights of each class of shares?
(c) Did Corus issue any additional shares in fiscal 2014? If so, specify how many were issued, for what dollar amount, and for what purpose.
(d) What was the average per share amount of each class of Corus's shares at the end of fiscal 2014?
(e) Did Corus declare any cash dividends in fiscal 2014? If yes, how much?
(f) Corus's return on equity was calculated for fiscal 2014 in Illustration 13-8. Calculate the company's return on equity for fiscal 2013. Did this ratio improve or worsen from 2013 to 2014?

Interpreting Financial Statements

BYP13-2 **Loblaw Companies Limited,** headquartered in Brampton, Ontario, is a large food and pharmacy retailer. Loblaw's authorized share capital includes an unlimited number of common shares, 1 million first preferred shares, and 12 million second preferred shares, series A. As at December 31, 2014, no first preferred shares had ever been issued.

The following information is also available for the years ended December 31, 2014 and 2013:

	2014	2013
Gross profit margin	24.8%	23.7%
Return on assets	0.19%	3.25%
Return on equity	0.54%	9.38%
Market price per common share	$62.17	$42.38
Market price per second preferred share, series A	$25.85	$26.25

Instructions

(a) Discuss the change in Loblaw's profitability from 2013 to 2014.
(b) Is your assessment in part (a) consistent with the change in market price per share? Explain.
(c) Loblaw issued 133.5 million common shares during 2014 and received proceeds of $6.8 million, but no additional preferred shares were issued during 2014. Was it more advantageous to issue the common shares instead of preferred shares? Explain.
(d) Loblaw has a stock option plan for its employees and directors. What advantages are there to the employees when they receive a portion of their annual compensation in shares? What are the advantages to the corporation?
(e) The preferred shareholders receive a dividend of 5.95% on the face value of the preferred shares. The company has issued a total of 9 million second preferred shares, series A, with total face value of $225 million. What is the dollar amount of the dividend per share? Why is this rate higher than the interest rate on savings accounts paid by banks?
(f) The preferred shares are redeemable for $25 per share (plus unpaid dividends) on or after July 31, 2015. Why might Loblaw choose to redeem the shares?

▶ Critical Thinking

Collaborative Learning Activity

Note to instructor: Additional instructions and material for this group activity can be found on the Instructor Resource Site and in *WileyPLUS*.

BYP13–3 In this activity, students will be provided with information about a corporation over four years (incorporation to dissolution) and will be required to answer some questions and solve a number of problems related to retained earnings. For each of the eight scenarios, two groups will face off (in Family Feud style) in a friendly competition to see which group will answer the questions for that scenario and explain their rationale to the rest of the groups.

Communication Activity

BYP13–4 Your cousin owns 100% of the common shares of a corporation, Ghost River Back Country Limited, a retail company specializing in outdoor clothing and equipment. The company has the opportunity to purchase land and a building in a desirable location that would be used to operate a second store. Your cousin is very excited about this opportunity but is wondering about the best way to finance this purchase because the company currently does not have excess cash. She and the seller are considering the possibility of issuing new shares of Ghost River Back Country Limited to the seller to pay for the land and buildings.

Instructions

Write a memo to your cousin explaining some of the advantages and disadvantages of issuing either common or preferred shares, compared with borrowing money, to purchase the land and buildings. Also include in your discussion any issues in terms of recording the transaction if shares are issued.

"All About You" Activity

BYP13–5 As you learned in the "All About You" feature, possibly buying shares in publicly traded companies is one financial decision you'll need to make when you graduate. Another decision about your finances is whether you'll work for someone else or be self-employed. After you have completed your post-secondary business education, you may be an entrepreneur and may need to decide if and when to incorporate your business. And if you decide to incorporate, you will also need to know more about how.

Instructions

Go to the website of Corporations Canada, part of Industry Canada, at http://corporationscanada.ic.gc.ca. Click on "Frequently Asked Questions."
(a) What are the benefits of incorporating with the federal government?
(b) What kinds of businesses can incorporate under the Canada Business Corporations Act?
(c) Who can form a corporation?
(d) Go to the question "If I decide to incorporate, what next?" When are corporations formed? Describe the information required in the articles of incorporation (forms 1 and 2).
(e) What are the advantages of incorporating on-line?
(f) On the Corporations Canada home page, go to "Business Corporations" and then click on the "Guide to Federal Incorporation." Go to Chapter 6, Other Obligations of the Corporation. Answer the following questions:
   1. By what date do the annual financial statements have to be prepared?
   2. The financial statements are required to be prepared in accordance with generally accepted accounting principles (GAAP). For Canadian corporations, where is GAAP set out?

3. Does a company have to appoint auditors?
4. What corporate records are required to be kept by a corporation?

 *Santé Smoothie Saga*

(*Note:* This is a continuation of the Santé Smoothie Saga from Chapters 1 through 12.)

BYP13–6 Recall (from Chapter 12) that Natalie had been considering forming a partnership with Jade Wingert, one of her friends. Natalie has concluded that she and Jade are not compatible to operate a business together and Natalie has continued on her own.

Natalie's parents, Janet and Brian Koebel, have been operating Santé Sweets Ltd., a private corporation, for a number of years. Santé Sweets Ltd. is a specialty bakery that features organic and gluten-free bakery products including their signature all-natural granola bars. They are very proud of Natalie and the success of Santé Smoothies and have decided that it may be time to get Natalie involved with the operation of the family business.

In anticipation of Natalie graduating, and in hopes of spending a little more time away from the bakery, Janet and Brian have discussed with Natalie the possibility of her becoming one of the shareholders of Santé Sweets Ltd. In addition, once Natalie has graduated, she would assume the full-time position of administrator. Natalie would continue to provide smoothies and sell juicers; however, that would be done by Santé Sweets in future rather than by Natalie's Santé Smoothies.

The share capital and the retained earnings of Santé Sweets Ltd. at June 1, 2017, are as follows:

$6 cumulative preferred shares, 10,000 shares authorized, none issued	
Common shares, unlimited number of shares authorized, 200 shares issued	$ 200
Retained earnings	116,251

Profit before income tax for the year ended May 31, 2018, was $255,823. The company has an 18% income tax rate. A cash dividend of $85,000 was declared on May 15, 2018, to common shareholders of record on May 20, 2018, and was paid on May 31, 2018.

Based on the bakery's success, the Koebels would like to issue 10 shares to Natalie for $1,200 per share. Natalie would contribute the fair value of Santé Smoothies' assets in exchange for the shares of Santé Sweets as follows:

	Santé Smoothies
Cash	$8,050
Accounts receivable	800
Merchandise inventory	1,200
Supplies	450
Equipment	1,500

The sale of shares by Santé Sweets to Natalie is expected to take place on June 1, 2018. Currently, Janet and Brian each own 100 shares. Assume Santé Sweets reports using ASPE.

Instructions

(a) Prepare the journal entries required for the cash dividend declared on May 15 and paid on May 31, 2018. Who received the cash dividend, and for what amount?

(b) Prepare the statement of retained earnings for Santé Sweets for the year ended May 31, 2018.

(c) Prepare the shareholders' equity section of the balance sheet for Santé Sweets at May 31, 2018.

(d) Assume that Natalie purchases the shares of Santé Sweets Ltd. on June 1, 2018, in exchange for the fair value of assets held by Santé Smoothies. Prepare the journal entries required by Santé Sweets Ltd.

(e) Determine the number of shares issued and the average per share amount for the common shares before and after Natalie purchases the shares of Santé Sweets. Why is there a significant change in value?

(f) How do you think a value of $1,200 per share was determined when Janet and Brian were attempting to come up with the number of shares to be sold to Natalie? Do you think that the number of shares Natalie received in exchange for the assets of Santé Smoothies is fair? Why or why not?

ANSWERS TO CHAPTER QUESTIONS

ANSWERS TO ACCOUNTING IN ACTION INSIGHT QUESTIONS

Across the Organization, p. 689

Q: Mark Zuckerberg, the CEO and founder of Facebook, owned just 28% of shares but maintained a 57% voting interest in Facebook after it went public. What are some advantages and disadvantages to Facebook that Zuckerberg still had control of the company?

A: Keeping Zuckerberg at the helm would help Facebook maintain its founder's vision, leadership, and expertise, and provide stability. However, some potential investors might be scared away from buying Facebook common shares if they think Zuckerberg has too much power and their shares don't grant them the majority of voting rights to have a bigger say in how the company is run.

Ethics Insight, p. 690

Q: Can Simplex Chemical Corp. be certain that it is protected against all losses related to the activities of Simplex Central America Inc.?

A: The actions of the president are both irresponsible and unethical. A parent company may protect itself against loss and most reasonable business risks by establishing separate subsidiary corporations, but whether it can insulate itself against this type of action is a matter of international corporate law and criminal law.

All About You, p. 692

Q: For shares traded on organized exchanges, what factors influence the dollar price per share?

A: Factors that can influence the dollar price per share are changes in economic conditions, such as interest rates, as well as war, terrorism, political elections, and interactions between buyers and sellers on an organized exchange.

ANSWERS TO SELF-STUDY QUESTIONS

1. a   2. d   3. b   4. c   5. b   6. a   7. d   8. b   9. b   10. d

14

CORPORATIONS: ADDITIONAL TOPICS AND IFRS

CHAPTER PREVIEW   This chapter builds on the introduction to corporations in Chapter 13. This chapter will cover additional shareholders' equity transactions that are more likely to occur in public companies using IFRS. Therefore, we will focus in this chapter on financial reporting using IFRS and will look at the statements of comprehensive income and changes in shareholders' equity.

FEATURE STORY   ▶   BREWING SHAREHOLDER RETURN

OAKVILLE, Ont.—Public corporations issue shares, but they can buy some of their shares back, as well. One reason why companies sometimes do this is that they may be sitting on a large amount of cash. For example, at the end of its 2013 fiscal year, before it was purchased by Burger King Worldwide Inc., Tim Hortons Inc., the iconic quick service restaurant franchise chain, had cash and cash equivalents of more than $50 million.

With consistently healthy cash flows, a priority for Tim Hortons was to invest in the business. The company reinvested a significant amount of its free cash flow in capital expenditures such as renovating and building restaurants and building manufacturing or distribution centres.

If there was still money left over after making all its desired capital expenditures, then the company tried to make sure it had a solid balance sheet so it could weather any economic storms, like the 2008 global financial crisis, when Tim Hortons did not need to rely on banks for funding. Once the company was assured its balance sheet was strong, it felt it needed to return the rest to shareholders because to sit on cash idly is not a good investment decision. To return money to shareholders, Tim Hortons considered the right balance between issuing dividends to existing shareholders and buying back some of its shares. After becoming a publicly traded company in 2006, Tim Hortons underwent several consecutive

major share repurchase programs. For example, in early 2014, the company announced plans to start a new share repurchase program to buy up to $440 million in common shares.

Tim Hortons had a dividend policy whereby it committed to paying out a certain percentage of its profit to shareholders every year. Since becoming a public company, it had increased its quarterly dividend several times, ranging from an 11% increase to a 31% increase.

Tim Hortons' approach to dividends changed when it merged in 2014 with Burger King to become a new company called Restaurant Brands International Inc. (RBI), still headquartered in Oakville, Ont. RBI does not have a dividend policy. Instead, its board of directors may declare a dividend each quarter at its discretion. For example, in February 2015, the RBI board declared a cash dividend of $0.09 per common share and $1.20 per preferred share to help create shareholder value.

Sources: "Tim Hortons Inc. Announces New Share Repurchase Program for Up to $440 Million in Common Shares," Tim Hortons Inc. news release, February 20, 2014; "World's Third Largest Quick Service Restaurant Company Launched with Two Iconic and Independent Brands: Tim Hortons and Burger King," Tim Hortons and Burger King joint news release, August 26, 2014; Restaurant Brands International Inc. 2014 annual report; Tim Hortons Inc. 2013 annual report.

© Roberto Machado Noa/Getty Images

CHAPTER OUTLINE ⟩ LEARNING OBJECTIVES

The chapter is organized as follows:

1 Explain how to account for stock dividends and stock splits, and compare their financial impact.

Additional Share Transactions
- Stock dividends and stock splits

DO IT 1
Stock dividends and stock splits

2 Explain how to account for the reacquisition of shares.

- Reacquisition of shares

DO IT 2
Reacquisition of shares

3 Prepare an income statement showing continuing and discontinued operations, and prepare a statement of comprehensive income.

Comprehensive Income
- Continuing and discontinued operations
- Other comprehensive income

DO IT 3
Statement of comprehensive income

4 Explain the different types of accounting changes and account for the correction of a prior period error.

Accounting Changes
- Changes in accounting estimates
- Changes in accounting policies
- Correction of prior period errors

DO IT 4
Error correction and statement of retained earnings

5 Prepare a statement of changes in shareholders' equity.

Reporting Changes in Shareholders' Equity
- Summary of shareholders' equity transactions
- Statement of changes in shareholders' equity

DO IT 5
Statement of changes in shareholders' equity

6 Explain earnings and dividend performance and calculate performance ratios.

Analyzing Shareholders' Equity
- Earnings performance
- Dividends record

DO IT 6
Earnings per share and price-earnings ratio

Additional Share Transactions

Recall from Chapter 13 that shares can be issued for cash and for noncash assets or services, and that they can be issued when preferred shares are converted into common shares. Shares can also be issued as the result of stock dividends, stock splits, and stock options. Companies may also decide to reacquire previously issued shares.

LEARNING OBJECTIVE 1 — **Explain how to account for stock dividends and stock splits, and compare their financial impact.**

STOCK DIVIDENDS AND STOCK SPLITS

In Chapter 13, a dividend was described as a pro rata distribution of a portion of a corporation's retained earnings to its shareholders. Cash dividends are the most common type of dividend and are used in both private and public corporations.

Stock dividends are another type of dividend rarely used in private corporations; they are more common in public corporations. Stock splits are not dividends, but have some similarities with stock dividends and are also typically used only in public corporations.

Stock Dividends

A **stock dividend** is a distribution of the corporation's own shares to shareholders. Whereas a cash dividend is paid in cash, a stock dividend is distributed (paid) in shares. And while a cash dividend decreases assets and shareholders' equity, a stock dividend does not change either assets or shareholders' equity. A stock dividend results in a decrease in retained earnings and an increase in share capital, but there is no net change in **total** shareholders' equity.

From the company's point of view, no cash has been paid, and no liabilities have been assumed. What are the purposes and benefits of a stock dividend? A corporation generally issues stock dividends for one or more of the following reasons:

1. To satisfy shareholders' dividend expectations without spending cash.
2. To increase the marketability of the corporation's shares. When the number of shares increases, the market price per share tends to decrease. Decreasing the market price makes it easier for investors to purchase the shares.
3. To emphasize that a portion of shareholders' equity has been permanently reinvested in the business and is unavailable for cash dividends.

The size of the stock dividend and the value to be assigned to each share are determined by the board of directors when it declares the dividend. It is common for companies to assign the fair value (market price) per share for stock dividends at the declaration date.

To illustrate the accounting for stock dividends, assume that on June 30, Blackthorn Corporation declares a 10% stock dividend on its 50,000 common shares, to be distributed on August 5 to shareholders of record on July 20. This means 5,000 (10% × 50,000) additional shares will be issued to existing shareholders. In recording the transaction, **the fair value at the declaration date is used**, not the fair value on the record or distribution dates.

Assuming the fair value of its shares on June 30 is $15 per share, the amount debited to Stock Dividends is $75,000 (5,000 × $15). The entry to record the declaration of the stock dividend is as follows:

A	=	L	+	SE
				+75,000
				−75,000

Cash flows: no effect

Declaration Date		
June 30	Stock Dividends	75,000	
	Stock Dividends Distributable		75,000
	To record declaration of 10% stock dividend.		

At the declaration date, the Stock Dividends account—which is a temporary equity account—is increased by the fair value of the shares to be issued. This will result in a decrease in Retained Earnings, similar to cash dividends, when the Stock Dividends account is closed. Stock Dividends Distributable, a shareholders' equity permanent account, is increased by the same amount. Stock Dividends Distributable is not a liability, because assets will not be used to pay the dividend. Instead, it will be settled with common shares on the **distribution date**, which is August 5 in the above example. If a balance sheet is prepared before the stock dividends are issued, the Stock Dividends Distributable account is reported as share capital in the shareholders' equity section of the balance sheet.

As with cash dividends, no entry is required at the record date. On August 5, the date of distribution, Stock Dividends Distributable is debited and Common Shares is credited as follows:

Helpful hint As with cash dividends, it is also acceptable to directly debit Retained Earnings. This eliminates the need to close the Stock Dividends account at the end of the year but might make it more difficult to track the amount of each type of dividend declared.

Distribution Date		
Aug. 5	Stock Dividends Distributable	75,000	
	Common Shares		75,000
	To record issue of 5,000 common shares in a stock dividend.		

A	=	L	+	SE
				+75,000
				−75,000

Cash flows: no effect

Note that neither of the above entries changes shareholders' equity in total. However, the composition of shareholders' equity changes because a portion of Retained Earnings is transferred to the Common Shares account. The number of shares issued has also increased. These effects are shown below for Blackthorn Corporation using assumed data for Retained Earnings and Common Shares prior to and after the stock dividend.

	Before Stock Dividend	**After Stock Dividend**
Shareholders' equity		
Common shares	$500,000	$575,000
Retained earnings	300,000	225,000
Total shareholders' equity	**$800,000**	**$800,000**
Total number of common shares issued	50,000	55,000

In this example, the Common Shares account is increased by $75,000 and Retained Earnings is decreased by the same amount. Total shareholders' equity remains unchanged at $800,000, the total before and after the stock dividend. After the stock dividend, the company now has 55,000 (50,000 + 5,000) common shares issued.

ACCOUNTING IN ACTION
ETHICS INSIGHT

Flambeau Corporation has paid 40 consecutive quarterly cash dividends (10 years' worth). Increasing competition over the past six months has greatly squeezed profit margins. With only enough cash to meet day-to-day operating needs, the president, Vince Ramsey, has decided that a stock dividend instead of a cash dividend should be declared. He tells Flambeau's financial vice-president, Janice Rahn, to issue a press release stating that the company is extending its consecutive dividend record with the issue of a 5% stock dividend. "Write the press release to convince the shareholders that the stock dividend is just as good as a cash dividend," Ramsey orders. "Just watch our share price rise when we announce the stock dividend. It must be a good thing if that happens."

Q Is there anything unethical about Ramsey's intentions or actions? Explain.

Stock Splits

A **stock split**, like a stock dividend, involves the issue of additional shares to shareholders according to their percentage ownership. A stock split is usually described as a 2-for-1 or 3-for-1 split. Technically, this means that a shareholder will return one share to the corporation and receive two in exchange (for a 2-for-1 split). In practice, the corporation simply issues one additional share to shareholders for every share they own. You can probably deduce at this point that a stock split will substantially increase the number of shares issued.

The purpose of a stock split is to increase the marketability of a company's shares by lowering the market price per share. A lower market price will appeal to more investors and make it easier for the corporation to issue additional shares. For example, after the National Bank of Canada announced a 2-for-1 split, the market price of its shares fell from $90.48 to $41.72, an overall reduction of $48.76. Sometimes, due to increased investor interest, the market price will quickly rise again.

On the other hand, sometimes companies want to increase the market price per share and decrease the number of shares outstanding by doing a **reverse stock split**. In this case, instead of issuing two stocks for one, they issue one stock for two, to increase the market price per share.

In a stock split, the number of shares is increased by a specified proportion. For example, in a 2-for-1 split, one share is exchanged for two shares. **No journal entry is required when a stock split is announced and therefore it does not have any effect on share capital, retained earnings, or shareholders' equity.** Only the number of shares increases and only a memo entry explaining the details of the split is required.

A stock split is illustrated below for Blackthorn Corporation's common shares. For the illustration, we assume that, instead of a 10% stock dividend, Blackthorn announces a 2-for-1 stock split for its 50,000 common shares.

	Before Stock Split	After Stock Split
Shareholders' equity		
Common shares	$500,000	$500,000
Retained earnings	300,000	300,000
Total shareholders' equity	**$800,000**	**$800,000**
Total number of common shares issued	50,000	100,000

Either common or preferred shares can be split. If preferred shares that have a stated dividend rate are split, then the dividend must also be adjusted for the effects of the split. For example, if 10,000, $6 preferred shares are split 3 for 1, then after the split there will be 30,000 preferred shares with a $2 annual dividend. The total dividend before and after the split remains unchanged at $60,000 (10,000 × $6 before and 30,000 × $2 after). After all, it is the same shareholders who held 10,000 shares before the split who now hold 30,000 shares.

Comparison of Effects

Significant differences among stock splits, stock dividends, and cash dividends (after payment) are shown below.

		Shareholders' Equity	
	Assets	Share Capital	Retained Earnings
Cash dividend	Decrease	No effect	Decrease
Stock dividend	No effect	Increase	Decrease
Stock split	No effect	No effect	No effect

Cash dividends reduce assets and shareholders' equity. Stock dividends increase share capital (the Common Shares or Preferred Shares account) and decrease retained earnings. Stock splits do not affect any of the accounts. However, both a stock dividend and a stock split increase the number of shares issued.

Note that, because stock dividends and splits neither increase nor decrease the assets in the company, investors are not receiving anything they did not already own. In a sense, it is like having a piece of pie and cutting it into smaller pieces. They are no better or worse off, as they have the same amount of pie.

To illustrate a stock dividend or stock split for the common shareholders, assume that a shareholder owns 1,000 of Blackthorn's 50,000 common shares. If Blackthorn declares a 10% stock dividend, the shareholder will receive 100 shares (10% × 1,000). On the other hand, if Blackthorn splits its shares on a 2-for-1 basis, the shareholder will receive 1,000 shares. Will the shareholder's ownership interest change? As shown in Illustration 14-1, there is no change.

| | Stock Dividend | | | Stock Split | | |
| | Company | Shareholder | | Company | Shareholder | |
	Total Shares issued	# Shares	Ownership Interest	Total Shares issued	# Shares	Ownership Interest
Before	50,000	1,000	2%	50,000	1,000	2%
New shares issued	5,000	100		50,000	1,000	
After	55,000	1,100	2%	100,000	2,000	2%

▶ **ILLUSTRATION 14-1**
Effect of stock dividend and stock split for shareholders

ACCOUNTING IN ACTION
ACROSS THE ORGANIZATION

© lev radin/Shutterstock

Stock exchanges usually require publicly traded stocks to maintain a minimum value or they will be delisted, meaning a company's shares will no longer be traded. The Nasdaq exchange, for example, requires shares to be worth a daily average of at least US$1 over a consecutive 30-day trading period. The shares of Montreal-based Acasti Pharma Inc., a pharmaceutical company, recently dipped below that minimum. To avoid being delisted on the Nasdaq, Acasti implemented a reverse stock split. It offered shareholders 1 share for every 10 that they owned, as at

October 14, 2015. The consolidation reduced the number of common shares from approximately 106.6 million to about 10.7 million. By increasing the fair value per share, Acasti could continue to trade on the Nasdaq, along with the TSX Venture Exchange. In the days immediately after the 1-for-10 split, Acasti's shares were consistently trading above $2.20.

There was another advantage to doing the reverse stock split. "Acasti also believes the Consolidation will allow the Corporation to attract a broader shareholder base," the company stated.

Sources: "Acasti Announces 1-for-10 Stock Split," company news release, September 29, 2015; "Acasti Pharma Inc. Interactive Stock Chart," Nasdaq website, www.nasdaq.com/symbol/acst/interactive-chart?timeframe=1m, accessed October 26, 2015; Rick Aristotle Munarriz, "Reverse Splits Aren't All Bad," Motley Fool newsletter, March 20, 2012.

 Q If a company announces a reverse stock split, is this considered a positive or negative sign about its future?

 1

BEFORE YOU GO ON...DO IT

Stock Dividends and Stock Splits

Dahlia Corporation has had five years of high profits. Due to this success, the market price of its 500,000 common shares tripled from $15 to $45 per share. During this period, the Common Shares account remained the same at $2 million. Retained Earnings increased from $1.5 million to $10 million. President Bill Zerter is considering either (a) a 10% stock dividend, or (b) a 2-for-1 stock split. He asks you to show the before-and-after effects of each option on the Common Shares and Retained Earnings accounts and on the number of shares.

Solution

(a) With a 10% stock dividend, 50,000 new shares will be issued (500,000 × 10%). The stock dividend amount is $2,250,000 (50,000 × $45). The new balance in Common Shares is $4,250,000 ($2,000,000 + $2,250,000). In Retained Earnings, it is $7,750,000 ($10,000,000 − $2,250,000).

(b) With a 2-for-1 stock split, 500,000 new shares will be issued. The account balances in Common Shares and Retained Earnings after the stock split are the same as they were before: $2 million and $10 million, respectively.

Action Plan

- Calculate the stock dividend effect on Retained Earnings by multiplying the stock dividend percentage by the number of existing shares to determine the number of new shares to be issued. Multiply the number of new shares by the shares' market price.
- A stock dividend increases the number of shares and affects both Common Shares and Retained Earnings.
- A stock split increases the number of shares but does not affect Common Shares and Retained Earnings.

BEFORE YOU GO ON...DO IT Stock Dividends and Stock Splits *(continued)*

The effects on the shareholders' equity accounts of each option are as follows:

	Original Balances	After Stock Dividend	After Stock Split
Common shares	$ 2,000,000	$ 4,250,000	$ 2,000,000
Retained earnings	10,000,000	7,750,000	10,000,000
Total shareholders' equity	$12,000,000	$12,000,000	$12,000,000
Total number of common shares issued	500,000	550,000	1,000,000

Related exercise material: BE14–1, BE14–2, BE14–3, E14–1, and E14–2.

LEARNING OBJECTIVE **Explain how to account for the reacquisition of shares.**

REACQUISITION OF SHARES

Companies can purchase or reacquire their own shares from shareholders. Typically, the reasons for doing this will be different for a private company as opposed to a public company. Private companies reacquire shares when there is a change in business circumstances or a change in the needs of the shareholders. For example, a private corporation may have an agreement in which it must reacquire the shares owned by an employee if the employee leaves the company.

A public corporation may acquire its own shares for any number of reasons. For example, as explained in our feature story, Tim Hortons repurchased its shares as a way of returning cash to shareholders when the cash was not needed to grow the business. Other reasons a public corporation may reacquire shares include the following:

1. To increase trading of the company's shares in the securities market in the hope of increasing the company's fair value.
2. To reduce the number of shares issued, which will increase earnings per share.
3. To eliminate hostile shareholders by buying them out.
4. To have additional shares available so that they can be reissued to officers and employees through stock compensation plans, or used to acquire other companies.

For federally incorporated companies, and most provincially incorporated companies, the repurchased shares must be retired and cancelled. This restores the shares to the status of authorized but unissued shares. In some Canadian provinces, in the United States, and internationally, reacquired shares can also be held for subsequent reissue. If the shares are not retired and cancelled, they are referred to as **treasury shares**. Treasury shares are not common in Canada and the accounting for them will be covered in advanced courses.

Whether the company is private or public, the following steps are required to record a reacquisition of common (or preferred) shares:

1. **Remove the dollar amount of the shares from the share capital account:** The common or preferred share account will be debited for the number of shares reacquired and retired multiplied by the **average per share amount.** The average per share amount is determined by dividing the balance in the share capital account by the number of shares issued as at the date of the reacquisition transaction. Average per share amount is used because it is impractical and often impossible to determine the dollar amount of each individual share that is being reacquired. Illustration 14-2 shows the two calculations required.

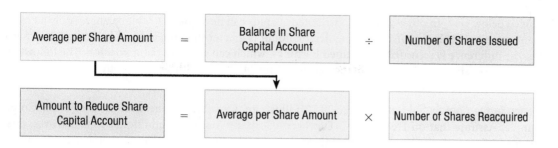

▶ ILLUSTRATION 14-2
Calculations for share retirement

2. **Record the cash paid:** The Cash account is credited for the amount paid to reacquire the shares. Note that a public company has little choice in what it has to pay to reacquire the shares. (It can only decide when to make the reacquisition.) It must purchase the shares on the secondary market by paying the current market price on the date of purchase.

3. **Record any difference between the cost of the shares and the amount paid to reacquire the shares in shareholders' equity:** The difference between the cash paid to reacquire the shares and their average per share amount is either an excess or deficiency that belongs to the shareholders. **It is important to note that, because companies cannot realize a gain or suffer a loss from share transactions with their own shareholders, these amounts are not reported on the income statement.** That is, they will never be recorded as a "gain" or "loss." As a result, the amount is reported as an increase or decrease in shareholders' equity.

The accounting for the reacquisition of shares differs depending on whether the shares are reacquired by paying less than the average per share amount or more than the average per share amount. We will examine each situation in the next two sections.

Reacquisition below Average per Share Amount

When a company reacquires its shares for less than the average per share amount, the company has an excess on reacquisition. The excess is credited to an account called Contributed Surplus—Reacquisition of Shares. Recall from Chapter 13 that contributed surplus is one of the components in shareholders' equity and it can arise from several different sources, including reacquiring and retiring shares. This amount is recognized as additional contributed capital of the company because, effectively, the shareholder has made a contribution to the company equal to the difference between the original cost of the shares and the price the shareholder received when the shares were reacquired.

To illustrate the reacquisition of common shares at a price less than the average per share amount, assume that Dewberry Corp. has an unlimited number of common shares authorized, and a total of 75,000 common shares issued. It has a balance in its Common Shares account of $150,000. The average per share amount of Dewberry's common shares is therefore $2 per share ($150,000 ÷ 75,000).

On September 23, Dewberry Corp. reacquired 5,000 of its common shares at a market price of $1.50 per share. Because the average per share amount of the shares is $0.50 ($2.00 − $1.50) more than the price paid to reacquire them, there is an additional contribution to shareholders' equity. The entry is recorded as follows:

Sept. 23	Common Shares (5,000 × $2)	10,000	
	Contributed Surplus—Reacquisition of Shares (5,000 × $0.50)		2,500
	Cash (5,000 × $1.50)		7,500
	To record reacquisition and retirement of 5,000 common shares.		

A	=	L	+	SE
−7,500				−10,000
				+2,500

↓ Cash flows: −7,500

After this entry, Dewberry still has an unlimited number of shares authorized, but only 70,000 (75,000 − 5,000) shares issued, and a balance of $140,000 ($150,000 − $10,000) in its Common Shares account. The average per share amount is still $2 per share ($140,000 ÷ 70,000).

Reacquisition above Average per Share Amount

If shares are reacquired at a price greater than the average per share amount, then the company has a deficiency on reacquisition. If there is any balance in the Contributed Surplus account from previous reacquisitions, this amount would first be reduced (debited). However, Contributed Surplus cannot be reduced below zero. In other words, Contributed Surplus can never have a debit balance—only a credit balance or a zero balance. Instead, if the debit amount is greater than the balance in Contributed Surplus, the difference is recorded in Retained Earnings, which can go into a debit position. The following two examples show how to record the reacquisition of shares with and without a balance in the Contributed Surplus account.

Balance in the Contributed Surplus Account. To illustrate, we will continue with the Dewberry Corp. example. Assume that on December 5, Dewberry Corp. reacquires an additional 10,000 shares, this time for $2.75 per share. Assuming no additional shares have been issued since September 23, the average per share amount is still $2.00, as previously shown. The result is a deficiency of $0.75 ($2.00 − $2.75) per share. The total deficiency is $7,500 (10,000 × $0.75). There is a balance of $2,500 in the Contributed Surplus account and it will be debited to reduce it to zero. The remaining deficiency of $5,000 ($7,500 − $2,500) will reduce Retained Earnings as follows:

A	=	L	+	SE
−27,500				−20,000
				−2,500
				−5,000

↓ Cash flows: −27,500

		Debit	Credit
Dec. 5	Common Shares (10,000 × $2)	20,000	
	Contributed Surplus—Reacquisition of Common Shares	2,500	
	Retained Earnings ($7,500 − $2,500)	5,000	
	Cash (10,000 × $2.75)		27,500
	To record reacquisition and retirement of 10,000 common shares.		

After this entry, Dewberry still has an unlimited number of shares authorized, but only 60,000 (70,000 − 10,000) shares issued, and a balance of $120,000 ($140,000 − $20,000) in its Common Shares account. The average per share amount is still $2 per share ($120,000 ÷ 60,000).

No Balance in the Contributed Surplus Account. To illustrate, we will continue with the Dewberry Corp. example. Assume that on December 27, the company reacquires an additional 2,000 shares, this time for $2.25 per share. Assuming no additional shares have been issued since the previous transaction on December 5, the average per share amount is still $2.00, as previously shown. The result is a deficiency of $0.25 ($2.00 − $2.25) per share. The total deficiency is $500 (2,000 × $0.25). Because there is no balance in the Contributed Surplus account, the full amount is recorded as a reduction of Retained Earnings, as follows:

A	=	L	+	SE
−4,500				−4,000
				−500

↓ Cash flows: −4,500

		Debit	Credit
Dec. 27	Common Shares (2,000 × $2)	4,000	
	Retained Earnings	500	
	Cash (2,000 × $2.25)		4,500
	To record reacquisition and retirement of 2,000 common shares.		

Note that the reductions to Retained Earnings on December 5 and 27 will never be reversed, even if the company later reacquires shares below cost.

In summary, the only difference in the accounting for a reacquisition at prices below or above the average per share amount is the recording of the difference between the average per share amount for all the shares reacquired and the amount of cash paid to reacquire them. Illustration 14-3 shows a summary of the share reacquisition transactions.

▶ **ILLUSTRATION 14-3**
Summary of accounting for share acquisitions

Share Reacquisition Transaction	Debit	Credit
Shares reacquired at average per share amount	Share Capital	Cash
Shares reacquired at a price below average per share amount	Share Capital	Contributed Surplus Cash
Shares reacquired at a price above average per share amount	Share Capital	Cash
	First, Contributed Surplus (if credit balance already exists, but only debit to zero)	
	Remaining, Retained Earnings	

| BEFORE YOU GO ON…DO IT | 2 | **Reacquisition of Shares** |

Ramsay Corporation reported having 25,000 common shares issued for a total share capital of $100,000 on its December 31, 2016, balance sheet. On February 15, 2017, it reacquired 4,000 of these shares. This is the first time Ramsay has reacquired any of its shares. Record the reacquisition of the shares assuming the company paid (a) $14,000, and (b) $18,000, to reacquire the shares.

Solution

Average per share amount = $100,000 ÷ 25,000 = $4.00

(a)

Feb. 15	Common Shares (4,000 × $4.00)	16,000	
	Contributed Surplus—Reacquisition of Common Shares ($16,000 − $14,000)		2,000
	Cash		14,000
	To record reacquisition and retirement of 4,000 common shares.		

(b)

Feb. 15	Common Shares (4,000 × $4.00)	16,000	
	Retained Earnings ($18,000 − $16,000)	2,000	
	Cash		18,000
	To record reacquisition and retirement of 4,000 common shares.		

Related exercise material: BE14–4, BE14–5, and E14–3.

Action Plan
- Determine the average per share amount by dividing the balance in the Common Shares account by the number of shares issued.
- Reduce the Common Shares account by the number of shares reacquired multiplied by the average per share amount.
- Compare the average per share amount of the shares reacquired with the cash paid to reacquire the shares.
- If the average per share amount is less than the reacquisition price, the company has an excess and records it as contributed surplus.
- If the reacquisition price is above the average per share amount, debit the difference to Retained Earnings unless there is already a balance in a contributed surplus account from previous reacquisitions and retirements.

| LEARNING OBJECTIVE | 3 | **Prepare an income statement showing continuing and discontinued operations, and prepare a statement of comprehensive income.** |

Comprehensive Income

In Chapter 13, we introduced corporate income tax and how to prepare an income statement for a corporation. In the following section, we will build on those concepts and show how to prepare an income statement when a company has gains or losses from discontinued operations. We also introduce the concept of other comprehensive income for companies following IFRS and show how it is combined with profit to determine comprehensive income.

CONTINUING AND DISCONTINUED OPERATIONS

Recall from Chapter 11 that investors need accounting information that is relevant in making decisions about such things as whether or not they should buy (or sell) shares of a company. Creditors need to know if they should lend to a company or not. Thus both investors and creditors use the income statement to evaluate a company's profitability and performance in the previous accounting period. But they are often even more interested in being able to predict or forecast how much profit the company may earn the following year. In order to provide this information, it is necessary to divide the company's profit or loss between its continuing and discontinued operations.

Continuing operations are the revenues, expenses, and profit or loss generated from the company's ongoing activities. **Discontinued operations** include components of an entity that have been disposed of by sale, abandonment, or spinoff, or are classified as a held for sale asset. A **component of an entity** is a separate major line of business or geographic area of operations that is clearly distinguishable from the rest of the entity. That is, it has separate cash flows and operations.

Many large corporations have multiple separate major lines of business. For example, Corus Entertainment Inc. describes its principal business activities as "the operation of radio stations; the operation of specialty, pay and conventional television networks; and the production and distribution of films and television programs, merchandise, licensing, publishing and the production of animation software." These are all related but separate business activities, any one of which could be discontinued in the future.

When a component of an entity is disposed of, the disposal is reported separately on the income statement as a nonrecurring item called discontinued operations. In order to fully separate profit earned (or losses incurred) in a company's continuing operations from its discontinued operations, it is necessary to also allocate income tax expense or savings to the two categories. This is known as **intraperiod tax allocation**. In intraperiod tax allocation, the income tax expense or saving is associated with certain items or categories, and the items are reported net of applicable income tax. The general concept is "let the tax follow the profit or loss."

The profit (or loss) reported in the discontinued operations section consists of two parts: the profit (loss) from these operations and the gain (loss) on disposal of the segment. Both items are presented net of applicable income tax.

To illustrate, assume Canaco Inc. has a 30% income tax rate and that in 2017 it sold its kayak manufacturing division. The following information is available:

- Profit before income tax on its continuing operations (details shown in the income statement in Illustration 14-4) is $156,000.
- The loss from operating the kayak manufacturing division during 2017 (prior to selling it) is $70,000.
- The loss from selling the assets in the kayak manufacturing division is $50,000.

Note that the losses in the kayak manufacturing division will result in income tax savings, as opposed to income tax expense. Income tax expense (or savings) is allocated to each of these items and is calculated as follows:

- Income tax expense on continuing operations is $46,800 ($156,000 × 30%).
- The income tax savings on the loss from operating the kayak manufacturing prior to its sale is $21,000 ($70,000 × 30%).
- The income savings on the loss on disposal of the assets in this division is $15,000 ($50,000 × 30%).

On the income statement, the loss from operation of the kayak division and the loss from the sale of the assets of the kayak division are shown separately, net of tax. Deducting the income tax is referred to as "net of tax."

Illustration 14-4 shows how the continuing and discontinued operations are reported in Canaco's income statement.

▶ **ILLUSTRATION 14-4**
Income statement presentation with discontinued operations

CANACO INC. Income Statement Year Ended December 31, 2017			
Sales		$800,000	Continuing operations
Cost of goods sold		600,000	
Gross profit		200,000	
Operating expenses		40,000	
Profit from operations		160,000	
Other expenses		4,000	
Profit before income tax		156,000	
Income tax expense		46,800	
Profit from continuing operations		109,200	
Discontinued operations			Discontinued operations
Loss from kayak manufacturing operations, net of $21,000 income tax savings	$49,000		
Loss on disposal of kayak manufacturing division, net of $15,000 income tax savings	35,000	84,000	
Profit		$ 25,200	

The loss from kayak manufacturing operations in the amount of $49,000 is determined as follows:

Loss from operating the division before tax	$70,000
Less: income tax savings	21,000
Net loss from operating the division	$49,000

The loss on disposal of the kayak manufacturing division in the amount of $35,000 is determined as follows:

Loss from disposal of division assets before tax	$50,000
Less: income tax savings	15,000
Net loss from disposal of division	$35,000

Note that the captions "Profit from continuing operations" and "Discontinued operations" are used. This presentation clearly indicates the separate effects of continuing operations and discontinued operations on profit. This allows us to separate the effects of operations that are not relevant to the company's ongoing performance.

Companies reporting under both IFRS and ASPE must report discontinued operations separately from continuing operations. The accounting and journal entries for discontinued operations will be covered in advanced courses. For now, you should be able to prepare an income statement showing separate categories for continuing and discontinued operations from given information.

OTHER COMPREHENSIVE INCOME

Under IFRS, there are certain gains (and losses) that are not included in profit but are still added to (or deducted from) shareholders' equity. These gains and losses that are not included in profit are referred to as **other comprehensive income (loss)**. For public companies, this additional component requires the company to report **comprehensive income**. Comprehensive income is determined as follows:

Profit (loss)
± Other comprehensive income (loss)
= Comprehensive income (loss)

Comprehensive income includes all changes in shareholders' equity during a period **except** for changes that result from the sale or repurchase of shares or from the payment of dividends. Companies following ASPE do not report other comprehensive income or comprehensive income.

There are specific sources of gains or losses that are excluded from profit and reported only as other comprehensive income. These gains or losses arise mainly from fair value adjustments to certain types of assets reported on the balance sheet at the end of a period. In Chapter 16, we will discuss one of the types that would be reported separately in other comprehensive income. In this chapter, we will discuss the classification and presentation of these gains and losses on the statement of comprehensive income.

Other comprehensive income is reported separately from profit for two important reasons: (1) it protects profit from sudden changes that could simply be caused by fluctuations in fair value, and (2) it informs the financial statement user of the cash that would have been received for certain types of investment assets if they had been sold at the year end.

Statement of Comprehensive Income

Companies reporting under IFRS must prepare a **statement of comprehensive income** that shows all of the items included in comprehensive income. There are two possible formats for this statement:

1. **All-inclusive format.** A statement of comprehensive income can include all components of profit or loss and other comprehensive income in a single statement. In this case, the traditional profit or loss is shown as a subtotal in arriving at comprehensive income. This is referred to as an "all-inclusive" format. If using this format, the company would not prepare a traditional income statement. Corus Entertainment Inc. in Appendix A uses this format.

2. **Separate statement.** The other option is to present the traditional income statement, followed by a separate statement of comprehensive income. In this case, the statement of comprehensive income starts with the profit or loss that was reported on the income statement. Then the other comprehensive income gains or losses are added to, or deducted from, profit or loss to calculate comprehensive income.

Similar to discontinued operations, other comprehensive income must be reported net of income tax. The Corus Entertainment Inc. consolidated statements of income and comprehensive income in Appendix A report each item in other comprehensive income net of income tax. In this textbook, we will follow the same approach.

To illustrate a comprehensive income statement, we will continue our example with Canaco Inc. Recall that Canaco Inc. has prepared a separate traditional income statement, with profit of $25,200, as shown in Illustration 14-4. Assume that Canaco Inc. also has types of investment assets that require gains or losses on the assets to be recognized as other comprehensive income items, not part of profit or losses for the period. In 2017, Canaco records a loss on these investment assets of $5,000. This will be presented on the statement of comprehensive income at $3,500, which is determined as follows:

Loss on investment	$5,000	
Less: income tax savings	1,500	($5,000 × 30%)
Net loss on investment	$3,500	

This information is presented in Illustration 14-5 in a statement of comprehensive income for Canaco Inc. Note that Canaco is using the separate statement approach for its presentation of comprehensive income.

▶ ILLUSTRATION **14-5**
Statement of
comprehensive income

CANACO INC. Statement of Comprehensive Income Year Ended December 31, 2017	
Profit	$25,200
Other comprehensive income (loss)	
Loss on investment, net of $1,500 of income tax savings	(3,500)
Comprehensive income	$21,700

Accumulated Other Comprehensive Income

The cumulative amount of other comprehensive income and losses over the life of the company is reported as a separate component in shareholders' equity on the balance sheet, called **accumulated other comprehensive income**. This is a similar account to Retained Earnings in that the amounts that make up total other comprehensive income (loss) are "closed" to Accumulated Other Comprehensive Income in a similar way to how revenues and expenses are closed to Retained Earnings. Later in the chapter, we will illustrate how this is reported on the statement of changes in shareholders' equity.

At the end of the year, when closing entries are prepared, the **Retained Earnings account will be updated for the profit portion of comprehensive income** and **Accumulated Other Comprehensive Income will be updated for the other comprehensive income (loss) portion of comprehensive income.** Illustration 14-6 shows the updated balances in Retained Earnings and Accumulated Other Comprehensive Income using assumed data for beginning Retained Earnings and Accumulated Other Comprehensive Income. Notice that Canaco Inc. declared no dividends and there are no other changes to the Retained Earnings account.

Alternative terminology
Accumulated other comprehensive income is sometimes referred to as a *reserve*.

Retained Earnings		
	Beg. Bal.	338,500
	Profit	25,200
	End Bal.	363,700

[1]Other Comprehensive Income

Accumulated Other Comprehensive Income		
OCI (loss)[1] 3,500	Beg. Bal.	31,400
	End Bal.	27,900

▶ILLUSTRATION 14-6
Updated balances in
Retained Earnings and
Accumulated Other
Comprehensive Income

BEFORE YOU GO ON...DO IT **3** ▷ **Statement of Comprehensive Income**

Bluebell Ltd. reports comprehensive income in a single statement of comprehensive income. In 2017, the company reported profit before income tax of $400,000; a pre-tax loss on discontinued operations of $75,000; a pre-tax gain on the disposal of the assets from the discontinued operations of $30,000; and other comprehensive income from a gain on an investment asset of $14,000 before tax. The company has a 25% income tax rate. Prepare a statement of comprehensive income, beginning with profit before income tax.

Solution

BLUEBELL LTD.
Statement of Comprehensive Income (partial)
Year Ended December 31, 2017

Profit before income tax		$400,000
Income tax expense		100,000[1]
Profit from continuing operations		300,000
Discontinued operations		
Loss from operations, net of $18,750[2] income tax savings	$56,250[3]	
Gain on disposal of assets, net of $7,500[4] income tax expense	22,500[5]	33,750
Profit		266,250
Other comprehensive income		
Gain on investment asset, net of $3,500[6] income tax expense		10,500[7]
Comprehensive income		$276,750

[1]$400,000 × 25% = $100,000
[2]$75,000 × 25% = $18,750
[3]$75,000 − $18,750 = $56,250
[4]$30,000 × 25% = $7,500
[5]$30,000 − $7,500 = $22,500
[6]$14,000 × 25% = $3,500
[7]$14,000 − $3,500 = $10,500

Related exercise material: BE14–6, BE14–7, BE14–8, E14–4, and E14–5.

Action Plan
- Allocate income tax between income from continuing operations, income from discontinued operations, and other comprehensive income items.
- Separately disclose (1) the results of operations of the discontinued division, and (2) the disposal of the discontinued operation.
- A statement of comprehensive income presents other comprehensive income amounts, net of income tax, following the profit for the year.

LEARNING OBJECTIVE **4** ▷ **Explain the different types of accounting changes and account for the correction of a prior period error.**

Accounting Changes

Accounting policies and estimates can change from time to time based on new information, new standards, or changes in a business environment. Errors in processing accounting information can also happen—after all, we are only human and computers can't do all the thinking for us. In this section of the chapter, we will look at the specific accounting and reporting requirements that companies must follow when these events happen.

There are three types of accounting changes:

1. Changes in accounting estimates
2. Changes in accounting policies
3. Correction of prior period errors

We will discuss each type below.

CHANGES IN ACCOUNTING ESTIMATES

In accounting, estimates of future conditions and events are often made. For example, in order to calculate depreciation, it is necessary to estimate the useful life of the depreciable asset. Recording bad debt expense also requires estimates to be made. As time passes, it is very possible that there may be a change in circumstances or new information about the estimate is available that indicates the need for a **change in an accounting estimate**.

A change in an accounting estimate does not mean an error was made in the prior period. Because it is not an error, we do not go back and correct the prior periods. Instead, we use the new estimate to change our calculations in the current and future periods. This is referred to as **prospective application**. In Chapter 9, we discussed how to account for a change in estimate when depreciation was revised because of a change in the estimated useful life or residual value of a long-lived asset. The accounting was applied prospectively because of a change in estimate.

CHANGES IN ACCOUNTING POLICIES

To make comparisons from one year to the next easier, financial statements for the current period are prepared using the same accounting policies that were used for the preceding period. This improves comparability, an important characteristic of accounting information that we learned about in Chapter 11.

Up to this point in your accounting education, you are aware that companies will often have a choice of policies that can be used to account for some elements of the financial statements. For example, property, plant, and equipment asset depreciation methods include straight-line, diminishing balance, and units of production. As well, inventory choices include FIFO and weighted average cost. Occasionally companies will change the policy that has been used in the past if the change:

1. is required by new IFRS or ASPE guidance, or
2. results in more reliable and relevant information for users of the financial information (this may be the case if comparability between companies is enhanced).

When there is a **change in an accounting policy**, companies are required to use **retrospective application**. Retrospective application requires a company to apply the new accounting policy as if that policy had *always* been in use. This means the company must recalculate and restate all of the related accounts from prior years. For example, when companies begin using IFRS 15 Revenue from Contract with Customers (discussed in Chapter 11 with regard to revenue recognition principles), the change from the previous standards must be retrospectively applied. Consequently, the financial statements will reflect the new standard for all the years presented.

The only exception to this type of application is when it is impractical to do so. This would be the case when significant estimates are required, or if the required information is not available, or if the amounts involved are not material.

CORRECTION OF PRIOR PERIOD ERRORS

Suppose that a corporation's temporary accounts have been closed and the financial statements have been issued. The corporation then discovers that a material error has been made in a revenue or expense account in a prior year that misstated that year's profit. This also means that the Retained Earnings account is incorrect because the incorrect amount of revenue or expense was transferred to Retained Earnings in the closing entries. Rather than reopening all revenue and expense accounts from the prior year and correcting previous entries (which would be a colossal amount of work), an adjusting journal entry is made directly to Retained Earnings to correct the error because the error is now in this account. This correction of a **prior period error** is referred to as **retrospective restatement** and requires correction to the recognition, measurement, and disclosure of transactions as if the prior period error had not occurred.

Entries to Correct Prior Period Errors Using Retrospective Restatement

To illustrate the entries required to correct a prior period error, assume that Trillium Corporation discovers in 2017 that it overstated interest expense in 2016 by $10,000 as a result of recording payment on a note payable to interest expense. Because interest expense was overstated, profit before income tax was understated by the same amount, $10,000. If we assume that income tax expense was calculated at a rate of 30% on the understated amount, then income tax expense is also understated by $3,000 ($10,000 × 30%). The overall effect on profit was an understatement of $7,000 ($10,000 − $3,000).

The following table details the effect of this error on the prior year's income statement, using assumed data for revenues and expenses:

	Incorrect	Correct	Difference
Revenues	$900,000	$900,000	$ 0
Expenses	**550,000**	**540,000**	**10,000**
Profit before income tax	350,000	360,000	10,000
Income tax expense (30%)	**105,000**	**108,000**	**3,000**
Profit	$245,000	$252,000	$ 7,000

In addition to the error in profit, Notes Payable will be overstated and income tax payable will be understated.

The entry for the correction of this error, discovered on February 12, 2017, is as follows:

Feb. 12	Notes Payable	10,000	
	Income Tax Payable		3,000
	Retained Earnings		7,000
	To adjust for overstatement of interest expense in the prior period.		

A	=	L	+	SE
+10,000		+3,000		+7,000

Cash flows: no effect

It is important to note that **an adjusting journal entry is only prepared for the current period. The error is corrected by correcting beginning Retained Earnings in the current period.** Remember that the revenue and expense accounts from the prior year have been closed.

Presentation of Corrections of Prior Period Errors

Corrections of prior period errors must also be reported in the financial statements. They are added to (or deducted from, depending on the direction of the adjustment) the beginning Retained Earnings balance. They are also reported net of the related income tax in the same way that the correcting entry to Retained Earnings was net of tax. The method of reporting is similar to reporting gains or losses from discontinued operations or other comprehensive income, as shown earlier in the chapter.

To illustrate, using the adjustment we journalized above—the correction for the overstatement of interest expense—assume that Trillium previously reported $750,000 as the balance in Retained Earnings on December 31, 2016. This is also the beginning balance in Retained Earnings on January 1, 2017. It is still necessary to show this as the beginning balance, even though we now know it is incorrect. The phrase "as previously reported" is added so users know this amount was reported as the ending balance in the previous year.

Because the error was found in 2017, it is reported as a correction to beginning retained earnings in the 2017 financial statements. Illustration 14-7 shows how the correction of Trillium's prior period error will be presented in its 2017 financial statements.

Retained earnings, January 1, 2017, as previously reported	$750,000
Add: Correction for overstatement of interest expense in 2016, net of $3,000 income tax expense	**7,000**
Retained earnings, January 1, 2017, as adjusted	757,000

▶ ILLUSTRATION 14-7
Presentation of a correction of a prior period error using retrospective restatement

This is shown on the statement of retained earnings if the company is following ASPE. If the company is following IFRS, as we will see later in the chapter, it is shown in the retained earnings section of the statement of changes in shareholders' equity. The effects of the change should also be detailed and disclosed in a note to the statements. As part of the process of retrospective restatement, any financial information from the prior year that is included in the annual financial statements must also be recalculated and the correct amounts shown as if the error had never taken place.

The accounting for a change in accounting policy using retrospective application is similar to the correction of prior period errors using retrospective restatement. The only difference is the terminology that is used: application vs. restatement. Opening Retained Earnings is adjusted for the effect of the change, net of the applicable income tax.

Action Plan

- Calculate the tax effect of the error by multiplying the error by the tax rate.
- If expenses were overstated in a prior year, that means income tax expense was understated. It also means that profit and retained earnings were understated by the difference between the error and the related tax.
- When reporting the correction of the error, begin with the amount of retained earnings as reported at the end of the previous year.
- Add or subtract corrections of prior period errors, net of applicable income tax, to arrive at the adjusted opening Retained Earnings balance.
- Add profit to and subtract dividends declared from the adjusted opening Retained Earnings balance to arrive at the ending balance in Retained Earnings.

BEFORE YOU GO ON...DO IT   4   Error Correction and Statement of Retained Earnings

Vega Corporation reported retained earnings of $5,130,000 at December 31, 2016. In 2017, the company earned $2 million of profit and declared and paid a $275,000 cash dividend. On March 7, 2017, Vega found an error made in 2016 when it purchased land; the $275,000 cost of the land was debited to Legal Expense in error. Vega's income tax rate is 30%. (a) Prepare the journal entry to correct the error. (b) Prepare a statement of retained earnings for the year ended December 31, 2017.

Solution

(a)

Mar. 7	Land	275,000	
	Income Tax Payable ($275,000 × 30%)		82,500
	Retained Earnings ($275,000 − $82,500)		192,500
	To correct for overstatement of legal expenses in a prior period.		

(b)

VEGA CORPORATION
Statement of Retained Earnings
Year Ended December 31, 2017

Balance, January 1, 2017, as previously reported	$5,130,000
Add: Correction for overstatement of legal expenses in 2016, net of $82,500 income tax	192,500
Balance, January 1, 2017, as adjusted	5,322,500
Add: Profit	2,000,000
	7,322,500
Less: Cash dividend	275,000
Balance, December 31, 2017	$7,047,500

Related exercise material: BE14–9, BE14–10, E14–6, and E14–7.

LEARNING OBJECTIVE 5   Prepare a statement of changes in shareholders' equity.

Reporting Changes in Shareholders' Equity

Companies reporting under IFRS are required to disclose all changes affecting shareholders' equity in a **statement of changes in shareholders' equity**. This statement shows the changes in total shareholders' equity during the year, as well as changes in each shareholders' equity account, including Contributed

Capital, Retained Earnings, and Accumulated Other Comprehensive Income. Under ASPE, companies do not prepare a statement of changes in shareholders' equity. Instead they prepare a statement of retained earnings, with details about changes in other equity accounts disclosed in the notes to the statements.

In the following sections, we will first review the transactions that affect shareholders' equity and then show how to prepare a statement of changes in shareholders' equity.

ASPE

Alternative terminology The statement of changes in shareholders' equity is also called the *statement of shareholders' equity* or *statement of changes in equity.*

SUMMARY OF SHAREHOLDERS' EQUITY TRANSACTIONS

In Chapter 13, and earlier in this chapter, you have learned several transactions and events that affect shareholders' equity accounts. These are summarized in Illustration 14-8.

It is important to review this summary and make sure you understand each of these transactions and their impact on the shareholders' equity accounts. This is the information that is included in the statement of changes in shareholders' equity.

▶ ILLUSTRATION 14-8
Summary of transactions affecting shareholders' equity

Transaction	Impact on Shareholders' Equity Accounts
1. Issuance of share capital	1. Common or Preferred Shares is increased.
2. Reacquisition of share capital	2. Common or Preferred Shares is decreased. Contributed Surplus may be increased or decreased. Retained Earnings may be decreased.
3. Correction of a prior period error that affected the prior year's ending Retained Earnings	3. Opening Retained Earnings is either increased or decreased as required to make the correction.
4. Effect of a change in accounting policy on the prior year's ending Retained Earnings	4. Opening Retained Earnings is either increased or decreased as required to make the adjustment.
5. Profit (loss)	5. Retained Earnings is increased (decreased).
6. Other comprehensive income (loss)	6. Accumulated Other Comprehensive Income is increased (decreased).
7. Cash dividends are declared	7. Retained Earnings is decreased.
8. Stock dividends are declared	8. Retained Earnings is decreased and Stock Dividends Distributable is increased.
9. Stock dividends are distributed	9. Stock Dividends Distributable is decreased and Common Shares is increased.
10. Stock split	10. Number of shares issued increases; there is no effect on account balances.

STATEMENT OF CHANGES IN SHAREHOLDERS' EQUITY

To explain and illustrate the preparation of a statement of changes in shareholders' equity, we will use financial information from Hawthorn International Inc. Illustration 14-9 presents Hawthorn's prior year shareholders' equity section of the balance sheet and its current year statement of comprehensive income.

▶ ILLUSTRATION 14-9
Hawthorn International's financial information

HAWTHORN INTERNATIONAL INC. **Balance Sheet (partial)** **December 31, 2016**	
Shareholders' equity	
Share capital	
Common shares, unlimited number authorized, 1,000,000 shares issued	$2,980,000
Contributed surplus—reacquisition of common shares	20,000
	3,000,000
Retained earnings	190,000
Accumulated other comprehensive income	385,700
Total shareholders' equity	$3,575,700

(continued)

▶ ILLUSTRATION 14-9
(continued)

HAWTHORN INTERNATIONAL INC. Statement of Comprehensive Income Year Ended December 31, 2017	
Profit	$349,800
Other comprehensive income	
Gain on equity investments, net of $132,000 of income tax expense	198,000
Comprehensive income	$547,800

During 2017, Hawthorn International entered into a number of transactions that affected its shareholders' equity accounts, as follows:

1. On January 21, Hawthorn International reacquired 25,000 common shares for $115,000. As you learned previously in this chapter, Common Shares is decreased by $74,500 [($2,980,000 ÷ 1,000,000) × 25,000]. Contributed Surplus—Reacquisition of Common Shares is decreased by its balance of $20,000. Retained Earnings is decreased by $20,500 ($115,000 − $74,500 − $20,000).
2. On March 4, Hawthorn International declared a 4% stock dividend to be distributed on April 10 to shareholders of record on March 20. The fair value of its shares on March 4 was $4.75. As the total shares issued at that point amounted to 975,000 (1,000,000 − 25,000), 39,000 shares are distributed (975,000 × 4%) at $185,250 (39,000 × $4.75).
3. On September 22, Hawthorn International sold 50,000 common shares at $5 per share for a total of $250,000 cash.
4. On November 9, Hawthorn International declared cash dividends of $100,000 to be paid on January 2, 2018, to shareholders of record on December 7, 2017.

It was also determined that expenses had been overstated by $70,000 in 2016. Hawthorn International has an income tax rate of 40%. The income tax impact of the overstatement was $28,000 ($70,000 × 40%). The net impact of the error on opening retained earnings was $42,000 ($70,000 − $28,000).

In the statement of changes in shareholders' equity, this information is organized by shareholders' equity account. For each account, the beginning balance from the prior-year balance sheet is shown, followed by the increases and decreases during the year. The ending balance is calculated for each shareholders' equity account and then the overall total of shareholders' equity is determined.

Remember that comprehensive income is divided into profit and other comprehensive income in terms of its impact on shareholders' equity. Profit is added to Retained Earnings, and Other Comprehensive Income is added to Accumulated Other Comprehensive Income.

The following schedule demonstrates how each component of equity is changed during the year:

Share capital, common shares	
Balance, January 1, 1,000,000 shares issued	$2,980,000
Reacquired 25,000 shares	(74,500)
Stock dividend issued, 39,000 shares	185,250
Issued for cash, 50,000 shares	250,000
Balance, December 31, 1,064,000 shares issued	3,340,750
Stock dividends distributable	
Balance, January 1	0
Stock dividend declared	185,250
Stock dividend distributed	(185,250)
Balance, December 31	0
Contributed surplus—reacquired shares	
Balance, January 1	20,000
Reacquired common shares	(20,000)
Balance, December 31	0

Retained earnings

Balance, January 1, as previously reported	190,000
Correction for overstatement of expenses in 2016, net of $28,000 of income tax expense	42,000
Balance, January 1, as adjusted	232,000
Profit	349,800
Reacquired common shares	(20,500)
Stock dividends	(185,250)
Cash dividends	(100,000)
Balance, December 31	276,050

Accumulated other comprehensive income

Balance, January 1	385,700
Other comprehensive income	198,000
Balance, December 31	583,700
Shareholders' equity, December 31	$4,200,500

In Illustration 14-10, Hawthorn's statement of changes in shareholders' equity for the year ended December 31, 2017, has been prepared using the above information.

▶ILLUSTRATION 14-10
Statement of changes in shareholders' equity

HAWTHORN INTERNATIONAL INC.
Statement of Changes in Shareholders' Equity
Year Ended December 31, 2017

	Common shares	Contributed surplus, reacquisition of common shares	Retained earnings	Accumulated other comprehensive income	Total
Balance, January 1, as previously reported	$2,980,000	$20,000	$190,000	$385,700	$3,575,700
Correction of prior period error			42,000		42,000
Balance, January 1, as adjusted	2,980,000	20,000	232,000	385,700	3,617,700
Issuance of shares	250,000				250,000
Reacquired shares	(74,500)	(20,000)	(20,500)		(115,000)
Stock dividends	185,250		(185,250)		0
Cash dividends			(100,000)		(100,000)
Comprehensive Income			349,800	198,000	547,800
Balance, December 31	$3,340,750	$ 0	$276,050	$583,700	$4,200,500

The end-of-year balances shown in the statement of changes in shareholders' equity are the amounts that will be reported on the December 31, 2017, balance sheet in shareholders' equity.

BEFORE YOU GO ON...DO IT 5 **Statement of Changes in Shareholders' Equity**

Grand Lake Corporation had the following shareholders' equity balances at January 1, 2017:

Common shares, unlimited number authorized, 500,000 issued	$1,000,000
Retained earnings	600,000
Accumulated other comprehensive income	100,000

The following selected information is available for the year ended December 31, 2017:

1. Issued 100,000 common shares for $300,000 cash.
2. Declared dividends of $50,000.
3. Reported profit of $360,000.
4. Reported a loss after tax on equity investments of $25,000 as other comprehensive loss.

Prepare a statement of changes in shareholders' equity for Grand Lake Corporation for the year ended December 31, 2017.

(continued)

BEFORE YOU GO ON...DO IT 5   **Statement of Changes in Shareholders' Equity** *(continued)*

Action Plan

- The statement of changes in shareholders' equity covers a period of time, starting with the opening balances and ending with the ending balances for the period.
- Include all of the changes in each shareholders' equity account, as well as total shareholders' equity.
- Recall that comprehensive income consists of both profit and other comprehensive income.

Solution

GRAND LAKE CORPORATION
Statement of Changes in Shareholders' Equity
Year Ended December 31, 2017

	Common shares	Retained earnings	Accumulated other comprehensive income	Total
Balance January 1	$1,000,000	$600,000	$100,000	$1,700,000
Issuance of shares	300,000			300,000
Cash dividends		(50,000)		(50,000)
Comprehensive Income		360,000	(25,000)	335,000
Balance, December 31	$1,300,000	$910,000	$ 75,000	$2,285,000

Related exercise material: BE14–11, BE14–12, E14–8, E14–9, and E14–10.

LEARNING OBJECTIVE 6   **Explain earnings and dividend performance and calculate performance ratios.**

Analyzing Shareholders' Equity

Shares are generally purchased by investors for potential capital gains (increases in the shares' market price) or for potential income (dividends). Consequently, investors are interested in both a company's earnings performance and its dividend record.

EARNINGS PERFORMANCE

When shareholders want to analyze their investment in a company, they can measure the company's earnings performance, or profitability, in several different ways. We learned about one measure in Chapter 13: the return on equity ratio. Two other ratios are widely used by existing shareholders and potential investors: earnings per share and the price-earnings ratio.

Earnings per share is useful because shareholders usually think in terms of the number of shares they own—or plan to buy or sell—so determining profit per share makes it easier for the shareholder to understand the return on his or her investment. Some companies even communicate to their shareholders their targeted earnings per share for the upcoming year.

Investors and others also link earnings per share to the market price per share. This relationship produces the second ratio: the price-earnings ratio.

Earnings per Share

Earnings per share (EPS) presents the profit earned by each common share. Thus, earnings per share is reported only for common shares. Illustration 14-11 shows the formula for calculating EPS.

▶ **ILLUSTRATION 14-11**
Earnings per share formula

Profit Minus Preferred Dividends	÷	Weighted Average Number of Common Shares Issued	=	Earnings per Share
$150,408	÷	84,993	=	$1.77

To show the calculation of earnings per share, the illustration uses data (in thousands) from Corus Entertainment's financial statements for August 31, 2014. Corus's profit, or net income as Corus calls it, of $150,408 is divided by the weighted average number of common shares issued, 84,993, to determine an earnings per share amount of $1.77. When a company has both preferred and common shares, the current year's dividend declared on preferred shares is subtracted from profit to determine the income available to common shareholders. Corus does not have any preferred shares issued and therefore preferred dividends are not applicable to the calculation.

Calculating Earnings per Share

1. Determine the amount of profit available to common shareholders. As mentioned above, the numerator in the EPS formula is reduced for preferred dividends. These amounts are subtracted from profit to reflect only those amounts that could be paid to common shareholders. Recall that preferred shareholders have priority over common shareholders and would be entitled to any distribution of earnings first. The adjustment made for preferred dividends is as follows:
   (a) If preferred shares are noncumulative, only reduce profit if preferred dividends were **actually declared** during the year. If no dividend on preferred shares was declared, there is no adjustment to reduce profit.
   (b) If preferred shares are cumulative, **reduce profit for the annual dividend amount** the preferred shareholders are entitled to, **whether or not** dividends were declared during the year.
2. Calculate the **weighted average number of common shares** issued. A weighted average number of common shares issued is used instead of the ending balance, or a straight average.
   (a) If there is no change in the number of common shares issued during the year, the weighted average number of common shares issued will be the same as the ending balance.
   (b) If new shares are issued or shares are reacquired in the year, these shares are **adjusted for the fraction of the year** they are outstanding to determine the weighted average number of common shares issued.

To illustrate the calculation of the weighted average number of common shares issued, assume that a company had 100,000 common shares on January 1. It reacquired and retired 7,500 shares on May 1, and issued an additional 10,000 shares on October 1. The weighted average number of shares for the year would be calculated as follows:

Time period	Actual number of common shares	Fraction of the year	Weighted average
January 1 – April 30: beginning number of shares	100,000	$4/12$	$33,333^1$
May 1: reacquired shares	−7,500		
May 1 – September 30: actual number of shares	92,500	$5/12$	$38,542^2$
October 1: issued shares	10,000		
October 1 – December 31 actual number of shares	102,500	$3/12$	25,625
			97,500

1. 100,000 shares were issued for 4 out of 12 months during the year. Multiply 100,000 by $4/12$ and the weighted amount is 33,333.
2. On May 1, 7,500 shares were reacquired and retired, reducing the number of common shares issued. 92,500 shares are now issued for 5 out of 12 months during the year. Multiply 92,500 by $5/12$ and the weighted amount is 38,542.
3. On October 1, 10,000 additional shares are issued, increasing the total number of shares issued to 102,500. This number of shares is issued for 3 out of 12 months during the year. Multiply 102,500 by $3/12$ and the weighted amount is 25,625.

Note that the total number of months should be equal to 12 (4 + 5 + 3). The total weighted average of 97,500 is the sum of each amount calculated above.

We can now calculate an earnings per share figure using an assumed amount of $224,250 profit available to common shareholders:

$224,250 ÷ 97,500 = $2.30

The disclosure of earnings per share is required for companies reporting under IFRS. This disclosure is so important that EPS must be reported directly on the statement of comprehensive income or the income statement if presented separately, and it also has to be explained in the notes to the financial statements. It is the only ratio that is reported in this way. Companies using ASPE are not required to report EPS.

Complex Capital Structure. When a corporation has securities that may be converted into common shares, it has what is called a complex capital structure. One example of a convertible security is convertible preferred shares. When the preferred shares are converted into common shares, the additional common shares will result in a reduced, or diluted, earnings per share figure.

Two earnings per share figures are calculated when a corporation has a complex capital structure. The first earnings per share figure is called **basic earnings per share**, which we calculated above. The earnings per share amount we calculated in Illustration 14-11, of $1.77, is a basic earnings per share amount. The second earnings per share figure is called **fully diluted earnings per share**. This figure calculates **hypothetical** earnings per share as though **all** securities that can be converted into, or exchanged for, common shares have been. Corus Entertainment Inc. reports a diluted earnings per share amount of $1.76 for August 31, 2014.

The calculation of fully diluted earnings per share is complex. Further discussion of these and other earnings per share complexities is left to an intermediate accounting course.

Price-Earnings Ratio

Comparing the earnings per share amounts of different companies is not very helpful, because there are big differences in the numbers of shares in companies and in the share prices. In order to compare earnings across companies, we instead calculate the **price-earnings (PE) ratio**. The price-earnings ratio is a frequently quoted statistic that gives the ratio of the market price of each common share to its earnings per share.

To illustrate, we will calculate the price-earnings ratio for Corus Entertainment Inc. Corus's earnings per share for the year ended August 31, 2014, was $1.77, as shown in Illustration 14-11. Its market price per share for its Class B shares at year end was $24.45. Illustration 14-12 shows Corus's price-earnings ratio.

▶ **ILLUSTRATION** **14-12**
Price-earnings ratio
formula

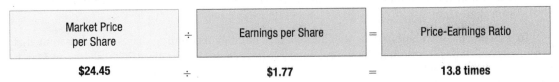

Market Price per Share	÷	Earnings per Share	=	Price-Earnings Ratio
$24.45	÷	**$1.77**	=	**13.8 times**

This ratio indicates that Corus's shares are trading at more than 13 times their earnings. The PE ratio reflects investors' assessment of a company's future earnings. The ratio of price to earnings will be higher if investors think that current income levels will continue or increase. It will be lower if investors think that income will decrease.

The price-earnings ratio is not relevant for private companies. Private companies will not have a readily available market price per share, and, as discussed above, if they follow ASPE, they also do not report earnings per share in their financial statements.

DIVIDENDS RECORD

In order to remain in business, companies must honour their interest payments to creditors, bankers, and debt holders. But the payment of dividends to shareholders is another matter. Many companies can survive, and even thrive, without such payouts. For example, high-growth companies generally do not pay dividends. Their policy is to retain all of their earnings to finance their growth.

On the other hand, some companies, such as Corus, have a dividend policy to pay dividends to shareholders quarterly in amounts approved by the board of directors. In its annual report, Corus states that one of its long-term objectives is maintaining annual dividend payments to shareholders. Presumably, investors who feel that regular dividends are important will buy shares in companies that pay periodic dividends, and those who feel that the share price is more important will buy shares in companies that retain earnings.

One way of assessing a company's dividend-paying policy is to calculate the **payout ratio**, which tells you what percentage of profit the company is distributing to its shareholders. The payout ratio is calculated by dividing cash dividends by profit. The payout ratio for Corus Entertainment Inc. (using "Net Income attributable to Shareholders") for the year ended August 31, 2014, is shown in Illustration 14-13.

▶ **ILLUSTRATION** **14-13**
Payout ratio

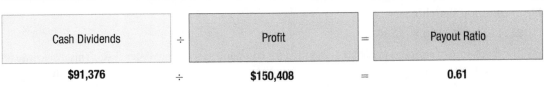

Cash Dividends	÷	Profit	=	Payout Ratio
$91,376	÷	**$150,408**	=	**0.61**

Corus's payout ratio is 0.61. This indicates that, for every dollar of profit earned during the fiscal year, the company has paid approximately $0.61 to the owners.

Corus's payout ratio indicates that slightly more than half of its profits are being distributed to shareholders and the remaining profits are being reinvested in the company to accomplish growth targets.

The payout ratio can also be expressed on a per share basis by dividing dividends per share by earnings per share. For Corus, the alternative calculation would be as shown in Illustration 14-14.

Cash Dividends per Share	÷	Earnings per Share	=	Payout Ratio
$1.06	÷	$1.77	=	0.60

▶ **ILLUSTRATION 14-14**
Alternative payout ratio calculation

Determining the payout ratio in this manner provides a slightly different payout ratio of 0.60 compared to Illustration 14-13 which was calculated as 0.61. The difference is due to rounding the earnings per share to two decimal places.

In general, more mature companies usually have a high payout ratio because growth is no longer a strategic objective. A low payout ratio can indicate that a company is retaining as much cash flow as possible for future growth. A steady payout ratio indicates that a company is confident about future earnings and its growth strategy. A payout ratio will provide some important information about a company but should be considered along with other important financial ratios and company information. Finally, payout ratios will vary between industries. For example, utilities have high payout ratios. Conclusions should only be drawn after comparing company-specific ratios with industry averages.

ACCOUNTING IN ACTION
ALL ABOUT YOU INSIGHT

© Sheriar Hirjikaka, 2012

Suppose you have some extra cash. Should you invest it in some shares of a public company or put it in a savings account and earn interest? Buying shares in a company is a greater risk than putting the cash in a savings account. Investing in a company's shares carries neither a promise that your investment will be returned to you nor a guarantee that your investment will earn income. However, investing in shares can often provide higher income than a savings account. Shareholders can earn income by receiving dividends or by selling the shares at a price higher than what they paid for them. Share prices are determined by the interaction of the buyers and the sellers in the market. Share prices can be influenced by both objective factors, such as a company's profits, and subjective factors, such as future share price expectations, including unverified rumours. Nevertheless, if a company prospers, the price of its common shares will typically rise in the long run. If the company doesn't prosper, or if external factors such as the economy are negative, the share price will likely decline.

Q   If you were thinking of investing in a company, where might you find information about the company's dividend policy, its profitability, and its share price?

BEFORE YOU GO ON...DO IT 6 ▶ Earnings per Share and Price-Earnings Ratio

Corral Limited, a publicly traded company, reported profit of $249,750 on its October 31 year-end income statement. The shareholders' equity section of its balance sheet reported 3,000, $2 noncumulative preferred shares and 50,000 common shares. At the beginning of the fiscal year, 40,000 had been issued, 15,000 more were issued on March 1, and 5,000 were repurchased on August 1. The preferred dividend was declared and paid during the year. The market price per share on October 31 was $40.

(a) Calculate Corral's earnings per share.
(b) Calculate Corral's price-earnings ratio.

(continued)

BEFORE YOU GO ON...DO IT Earnings per Share and Price-Earnings Ratio *(continued)*

Action Plan

- Subtract the preferred dividends from profit to determine the income available for common shareholders.
- Adjust the shares for the fraction of the year they were outstanding to determine the weighted average number of shares.
- Divide the income available for common shareholders by the weighted average number of shares to calculate the earnings per share.

Solution

(a) Preferred dividends: 3,000 preferred shares × $2 dividend per share = $6,000
Income available to common shareholders: $249,750 − $6,000 = $243,750
Weighted average number of common shares:

Time period	Actual number of common shares	Fraction of the year	Weighted average
November 1—February 28: beginning number of shares	40,000	$^4/_{12}$	13,333
March 1: issued shares	15,000		
March 1—July 31: actual number of shares	55,000	$^5/_{12}$	22,917
August 1: reacquired shares	−5,000		
August 1—October 31: actual number of shares	50,000	$^3/_{12}$	12,500
			48,750

Earnings per share: $\dfrac{\$243,750}{48,750} = \$5$

(b) Price-earnings ratio: $40 ÷ $5 = 8

Related exercise material: BE14–13, BE14–14, BE14–15, E14–11, E14–12, and E14–13.

Comparing IFRS and ASPE

Key Differences	International Financial Reporting Standards (IFRS)	Accounting Standards for Private Enterprises (ASPE)
Other comprehensive income and statement of comprehensive income	Required	Not required; only an income statement is required.
Statement of changes in shareholders' equity	Required	Changes in retained earnings presented in the statement of retained earnings. Changes to other shareholders' equity accounts presented in the notes.
EPS	Required	Not required

Demonstration Problem

On January 1, 2017, Magnolia Corporation, a public company, had the following shareholders' equity accounts:

Common shares, unlimited number authorized, 260,000 issued	$3,120,000
Retained earnings	3,200,000
Accumulated other comprehensive income	75,000

During the year, the following transactions occurred:

Jan. 18	Reacquired 10,000 common shares for $13 per share.
Apr. 10	Discovered that it had understated its cost of goods sold in 2016 by $50,000.
June 1	Announced a 2-for-1 stock split of the common shares. Immediately before the split, the share price was $13.50 per share.
June 30	Declared a $0.40 cash dividend to common shareholders of record on July 16, payable August 1.
Aug. 1	Paid the dividend declared on June 30.
Nov. 30	Reacquired 40,000 common shares for $5.50 per share.
Dec. 30	Declared a 5% stock dividend to common shareholders of record on January 15, distributable January 31. On December 30, the share price was $5 per share. On January 15, it was $5.50 per share, and on January 31, it was $6 per share.

In addition, Magnolia Corporation reported profit of $590,000 and a pre-tax loss on equity investments of $60,000, to be reported in other comprehensive income (loss).

The company has a 30% income tax rate.

Instructions

(a) Record the transactions.

(b) Prepare a statement of comprehensive income.

(c) Prepare a statement of changes in shareholders' equity.

(d) Prepare the shareholders' equity section of the balance sheet.

ACTION PLAN

- Keep a running total of the number of shares issued and total cost of shares.
- When shares are reacquired, reduce Common Shares by the average per share amount. If reacquiring for less than the average amount, the difference is credited to a contributed surplus account. If reacquiring for more than the average amount, the difference is first debited to any previous contributed surplus, then to Retained Earnings.
- Errors from prior periods are corrected, net of income tax, to the Retained Earnings account.
- Adjust the number of shares for the stock split, but make no journal entry.
- Make journal entries for dividends on the declaration and payment dates, but not on the record date.
- Apply the stock dividend percentage to the number of shares issued. Multiply the new shares to be issued by the shares' fair value at the date of declaration.
- If not prepared on an all-inclusive basis, the statement of comprehensive income starts with profit. Other comprehensive income (loss) is added to (deducted from) profit on a net-of-tax basis.
- Recall that the statement of changes in shareholders' equity explains the changes for the period in the beginning and ending balances of each shareholders' equity account.
- The balance sheet reports shareholders' equity at the end of the period. These numbers are the ending balances on the statement of changes in shareholders' equity.

SOLUTION TO DEMONSTRATION PROBLEM

(a)

Jan. 18	Common Shares [($3,120,000 ÷ 260,000) × 10,000]	120,000	
	Retained Earnings ($130,000 − $120,000)	10,000	
	Cash ($13 × 10,000)		130,000
	To record reacquisition of 10,000 common shares.		
Apr. 10	Retained Earnings ($50,000 − $15,000)	35,000	
	Income Tax Payable ($50,000 × 30%)	15,000	
	Merchandise Inventory		50,000
	To adjust for understatement of cost of goods sold in 2016.		
June 1	Memo entry only about 2-for-1 stock split. Now 500,000 [(260,000 − 10,000) × 2] common shares.		
30	Cash Dividend—Common	200,000	
	Dividend Payable		200,000
	To record cash dividend ($0.40 × 500,000).		
Aug. 1	Dividend Payable	200,000	
	Cash		200,000
	To record payment of cash dividend.		
Nov. 30	Common Shares [($3,000,000 ÷ 500,000) × 40,000]	240,000	
	Contributed Surplus—Reacquisition of Common Shares		20,000
	Cash ($5.50 × 40,000)		220,000
	Reacquired 40,000 common shares for $20,000 ($240,000 − $220,000) less than average.		

Common Shares	Number	Cost
Jan. 1, Balance	260,000	$3,120,000
Jan. 18 reacquisition	(10,000)	(120,000)
June 1 2-for-1 split	250,000	0
Balance Nov. 30	500,000	$3,000,000

Dec. 30	Stock Dividend (23,000 × $5)	115,000	
	Stock Dividend Distributable		115,000
	To record stock dividend to common shareholders. (460,000 × 5% = 23,000)		

Common Shares	Number	Cost
Balance Nov. 30	500,000	$3,000,000
Nov. 30 reacquisition	(40,000)	(240,000)
Balance Dec. 30	460,000	$2,760,000

(b)

MAGNOLIA CORPORATION
Statement of Comprehensive Income
Year Ended December 31, 2017

Profit	$590,000
Other comprehensive income (loss)	
Loss on equity investments, net of $18,000[1] of income tax savings	(42,000)[2]
Comprehensive income	$548,000

[1]$18,000 = $60,000 \times 30\%$; [2]$42,000 = $60,000 - $18,000

(c)

MAGNOLIA CORPORATION
Statement of Changes in Shareholders' Equity
Year Ended December 31, 2017

	Common shares	Stock dividends distributable	Contributed surplus— reacquisition of common shares	Retained earnings	Accumulated other comprehensive income	Total
Balance January 1, as previously reported	$3,120,000	$ 0	$ 0	$3,200,000	$75,000	$6,395,000
Correction of error in cost of goods sold, net of $15,000 income tax				(35,000)		(35,000)
Balance January 1, as restated	3,120,000	0	0	3,165,000	75,000	6,360,000
Reacquired shares	(360,000)		20,000	(10,000)		(350,000)
Stock dividend		115,000		(115,000)		0
Cash dividend				(200,000)		(200,000)
Comprehensive income				590,000	(42,000)	548,000
Balance, December 31	$2,760,000	$115,000	$20,000	$3,430,000	$33,000	$6,358,000

(d)

MAGNOLIA CORPORATION
Balance Sheet (partial)
December 31, 2017

Shareholders' equity	
Contributed capital	
Common shares, unlimited number authorized, 460,000 issued	$2,760,000
Common stock dividend distributable, 23,000 shares	115,000
Contributed surplus—reacquisition of common shares	20,000
Total contributed capital	2,895,000
Retained earnings	3,430,000
Accumulated other comprehensive income	33,000
Total shareholders' equity	$6,358,000

Summary of Learning Objectives

1. **Explain how to account for stock dividends and stock splits, and compare their financial impact.** Journal entries for stock dividends are required at the declaration and distribution dates. There is no journal entry for a stock split. Stock dividends reduce retained earnings and increase common shares, but have no impact on total shareholders' equity. Both stock dividends and stock splits increase the number of shares issued. Stock dividends and splits reduce the fair value of the shares, but have no impact on the company's financial position.

2. **Explain how to account for the reacquisition of shares.** When shares are reacquired, the average per share amount is debited to the Common Shares account. If the shares are reacquired at a price below the average per share amount, the difference is credited to a contributed surplus account. If the shares are reacquired at a price above the average per share amount, the difference is debited first to a contributed surplus account if a balance exists, and then to the Retained Earnings account.

3. **Prepare an income statement showing continuing and discontinued operations, and prepare a statement of comprehensive income.** Gains or losses on discontinued operations must be presented net of income tax after profit (or loss) from continuing operations. Companies following IFRS must prepare a statement of comprehensive income that reports all increases and decreases to shareholders' equity during a period except changes resulting from the sale or repurchase of shares and from the payment of dividends. The statement of comprehensive income can be prepared on an all-inclusive basis, or can start with profit or loss as shown on a separate income statement.

4. **Explain the different types of accounting changes and account for the correction of a prior period error.** A change in an accounting estimate is not an error and only the current and future periods are revised. A change in accounting policy, from the method used in the previous year, is allowed only when there is a change in GAAP or if it results in the financial statements providing more reliable and relevant information. These changes are applied retrospectively when possible. If an error in a prior year's profit is found after the temporary accounts have been closed and the statements have been issued, then beginning retained earnings is adjusted. This is shown in the financial statements as a correction to beginning retained earnings net of the related income tax impact.

5. **Prepare a statement of changes in shareholders' equity.** A statement of changes in shareholders' equity explains all of the changes in each of the shareholders' equity accounts, and in total, for the reporting period. This includes changes in contributed capital (Common Shares, Preferred Shares, and any other contributed surplus accounts), Retained Earnings, and Accumulated Other Comprehensive Income. The statement is required for companies reporting under IFRS.

6. **Explain earnings and dividend performance and calculate performance ratios.** Profitability measures that are used to analyze shareholders' equity include return on equity (discussed in Chapter 13), earnings per share, the price-earnings ratio, and the payout ratio. Earnings (loss) per share is calculated by dividing profit (loss) available to the common shareholders by the weighted average number of common shares and is reported only under IFRS. The price-earnings ratio is calculated by dividing the market price per share by the earnings per share. The payout ratio is calculated by dividing cash dividends by profit.

Glossary

Accumulated other comprehensive income   The cumulative amount of other comprehensive income and losses over the life of the company reported as a separate amount in shareholders' equity. (p. 740)

Basic earnings per share   The profit (or loss) earned by each common share. It is calculated by subtracting any preferred dividends declared from profit and dividing the result by the weighted average number of common shares. (p. 750)

Change in an accounting estimate   A change in an accounting estimate because of a change in circumstances or because new information about the estimate is available that indicates that the estimate needs to be changed. (p. 742)

Change in an accounting policy   The use of a generally accepted accounting policy in the current year that is different from the one used in the preceding year. (p. 742)

Component of an entity   A separate major line of business or geographic area of operations. (p. 737)

Comprehensive income   All changes in shareholders' equity during a period except for changes resulting from the sale or repurchase of shares, or from the payment of dividends. (p. 739)

Continuing operations   The revenues, expenses, and profit or loss generated from a company's ongoing activities. (p. 737)

Discontinued operations   A component of an enterprise that has been disposed of or is reclassified as "held for sale." (p. 737)

Distribution date   The date when stock dividends are distributed to shareholders. (p. 731)

Earnings per share (EPS)   The profit (or loss) earned by each common share. (p. 748)

Fully diluted earnings per share   Earnings per share adjusted for the maximum possible dilution that would occur if securities were converted, or changed, into common shares. (p. 750)

Intraperiod tax allocation   The procedure of associating income tax expense with the specific item that directly affects the income tax for the period. (p. 738)

Other comprehensive income (loss)   Gains and losses that are not included in profit but affect shareholders' equity. (p. 739)

Payout ratio   A ratio that measures the percentage of income distributed as cash dividends. It is calculated by dividing cash dividends by profit. (p. 750)

Price-earnings (PE) ratio   The ratio of the price of a common share to earnings per common share. (p. 750)

Prior period error   A material error made in a revenue or expense account in a prior year that misstated that year's profit. (p. 742)

Prospective application   An approach used for changes in accounting estimates that recognizes the effect of the change in the estimate in the current and future periods only. (p. 742)

Retrospective application   An approach used for changes in accounting policies that requires the new policy to be applied as if that policy had always been in use. (p. 742)

Retrospective restatement   An approach used when correcting prior period errors that requires the corrections be made to the

recognition, measurement, and disclosure of elements of the financial statements as if the error had never occurred. (p. 742)

Reverse stock split   A decrease in the number of shares issued. A 1-for-3 reverse stock split would reduce the amount of shares owned by a shareholder to one for every three shares owned before the split. (p. 732)

Statement of changes in shareholders' equity   A statement that reports all increases and decreases to shareholders' equity during a period. (p. 744)

Statement of comprehensive income   A statement that reports all items included in comprehensive income during a period. (p. 739)

Stock dividend   A pro rata distribution of the corporation's own shares to shareholders. (p. 730)

Stock split   The issue of additional shares to shareholders according to their percentage ownership. A 2-for-1 stock split means that two new shares are issued in exchange for one old share. No journal entries are required for a stock split. (p. 731)

Treasury shares   A corporation's own shares that have been reacquired and not yet retired or cancelled. They are held in "treasury" for later reissue or cancellation. (p. 734)

Weighted average number of common shares   The number of common shares issued during the year, with any shares purchased or issued during the year weighted by the fraction of the year that they have been outstanding. (p. 749)

▶ Self-Study Questions

Answers are at the end of the chapter.

(LO 1) K   1. Which of the following statements about stock dividends and stock splits is correct?
    (a) A stock dividend decreases total shareholders' equity; a stock split increases total shareholders' equity.
    (b) Both result in an increased percentage ownership for shareholders.
    (c) Both are recorded at the fair value of the shares on the declaration date.
    (d) Both result in no change in total shareholders' equity.

(LO 1) C   2. Rutger Inc. has retained earnings of $500,000 and total shareholders' equity of $2 million. It has 100,000 common shares issued, which are currently selling for $30 per share. If Rutger declares a 10% share dividend on its common shares:
    (a) net income will decrease by $300,000.
    (b) Retained Earnings will decrease by $300,000 and total shareholders' equity will increase by $300,000.
    (c) Retained Earnings will increase by $300,000 and total shareholders' equity will decrease by $300,000.
    (d) Retained Earnings will decrease by $300,000 and common shares will increase by $300,000.

(LO 2) C   3. A company will buy back its own shares to:
    (a) increase the share price.
    (b) decrease the share price.
    (c) increase the number of shares available for dividends.
    (d) save cash.

(LO 2) AP   4. Common shares are repurchased for $150,000 by a company with Contributed Surplus—Reacquisition of Shares $75,000; and Retained Earnings $750,000. Based on the average per share amount, the repurchased shares have a dollar amount of $125,000. The journal entry to record the repurchase would include a:
    (a) debit to Retained Earnings of $25,000.
    (b) credit to Contributed Surplus—Reacquisition of Shares of $25,000.
    (c) debit to Contributed Surplus—Reacquisition of Shares of $25,000.
    (d) debit to Common Shares of $150,000.

(LO 3) K   5. Discontinued operations:
    (a) are reported as part of operating expenses on the income statement.
    (b) are reported separately on the income statement as a nonrecurring item.
    (c) are never presented net of applicable income tax.
    (d) result in an entry to Retained Earnings directly.

(LO 4) K   6. Which of the following statements about accounting changes is true?
    (a) Changes in accounting estimates are accounted for prospectively.
    (b) Changes in accounting policies are accounted for retrospectively.
    (c) Error corrections are accounted for retrospectively.
    (d) All of the above are true.

(LO 4) K   7. A correction of a prior period error is reported:
(a) in the income statement.
(b) directly in the shareholders' equity section of the balance sheet.
(c) in either the statement of retained earnings or the statement of changes in shareholders' equity as an adjustment to the beginning balance of Retained Earnings.
(d) in either the statement of retained earnings or the statement of changes in shareholders' equity as an adjustment to the ending balance of Retained Earnings.

(LO 5) AP 8. Which of the following is **not** reported in a statement of changes in shareholders' equity?
(a) A reacquisition of share capital
(b) Accumulated other comprehensive income
(c) Stock dividends
(d) Fair value of common shares

(LO 6) AP 9. For the year ended May 31, 2017, Sonic Corporation reported profit of $42,000. At the beginning of the year, it had 10,000 common shares issued. On February 28, 2017, the company issued 8,000 common shares for cash. The market price per share was $66.50 on May 31, 2017. It had no preferred shares. What are Sonic Corporation's earnings per share and price-earnings ratios?
(a) $2.33 and 28 times
(b) $3.00 and 22 times
(c) $3.50 and 19 times
(d) $4.20 and 16 times

(LO 6) C 10. Bernard Dupuis is nearing retirement and would like to invest in shares that will give him a steady income. Bernard should choose shares with a high:
(a) earnings per share.
(b) price-earnings ratio.
(c) payout ratio.
(d) return on equity.

▶ Questions

(LO 1) K   1. What entries are made for stock dividends on common shares on (a) the declaration date, (b) the record date, and (c) the distribution date?

(LO 1) C   2. Freddy Investor says, "The shares I recently bought just declared a 2-for-1 stock split. Now I've doubled my investment!" Is Freddy correct—is he any better off after the stock split?

(LO 1) C   3. Contrast the effects of a cash dividend and stock dividend on a company's (a) assets, (b) liabilities, (c) share capital, (d) retained earnings, and (e) number of shares.

(LO 2) K   4. Why would a company repurchase some of its shares? Give some reasons.

(LO 2) C   5. Wilmor Inc. repurchases 1,000 of its own common shares. What effect does this transaction have on (a) total assets, (b) total liabilities, and (c) total shareholders' equity?

(LO 2) C   6. Describe how the Contributed Surplus—Reacquisition of Common Shares account is affected when shares are repurchased.

(LO 2) C   7. Camille Sox is preparing the journal entry for the reacquisition of common shares. She believes that the Common Shares account should be debited for the amount of cash paid for the shares no matter what the average per share amount is. Do you agree with her? If not, explain to Camille the correct way to account for the reacquisition.

(LO 3) C   8. Describe intraperiod income tax allocation and why it is important.

(LO 3) C   9. What are discontinued operations? Why is it important to report discontinued operations separately from profit or loss from continuing operations?

(LO 3) C 10. Explain the terms "comprehensive income," "other comprehensive income," and "accumulated other comprehensive income." Include in your explanation how and where they are reported in the financial statements.

(LO 3) C 11. Describe the two methods of preparing a statement of comprehensive income.

(LO 4) C 12. When is a company allowed to change an accounting policy? How should it be accounted for in the financial statements?

(LO 4) C 13. Under what circumstances will a company change an accounting estimate? How is it accounted for, and why is it not considered an error?

(LO 5) C 14. Identify the shareholders' equity accounts. For each account, provide examples of transactions that will increase and decrease the account identified.

(LO 5) K 15. What are the two components of comprehensive income?

(LO 6) C 16. Distinguish between basic earnings per share and fully diluted earnings per share.

(LO 6) C 17. When calculating EPS: (a) Why is profit available to the common shareholders not always the same as profit? (b) Why is the weighted average number of shares used instead of the number of shares issued at the end of the year?

(LO 6) C 18. If all other factors stay the same, indicate whether each of the following is generally considered favourable or unfavourable by a potential investor: (a) a decrease in return on equity, (b) an increase in earnings per share, (c) a decrease in the price-earnings ratio, and (d) an increase in the payout ratio.

▶ Brief Exercises

Record stock dividend and determine percentage ownership. (LO 1) AP

BE14–1 On March 1, Houseboat Ltd. had 400,000 common shares issued and the balance in its Common Shares account was $600,000. The company declared a 5% stock dividend to shareholders of record on March 14, to be distributed on March 31. The fair value per share was $5 on March 1, $4.85 on March 14, and $5.35 on March 31. Prepare the entries on the appropriate dates to record the stock dividend.

Analyze impact of stock dividend. (LO 1) AP

BE14–2 The shareholders' equity section of Ferndale Corporation's balance sheet consists of 225,000 common shares for $2 million, and retained earnings of $600,000. A 10% stock dividend is declared when the fair value per share is $12. Show the before-and-after effects of the dividend on (a) share capital, (b) retained earnings, (c) total shareholders' equity, and (d) the number of shares.

Compare cash dividend, stock dividend, and stock split. (LO 1) AP

BE14–3 Indicate whether each of the following transactions would increase (+), decrease (–), or have no effect (NE) on total assets, total liabilities, total shareholders' equity, and the number of shares:

Transaction	Assets	Liabilities	Shareholders' Equity	Number of Shares
(a) Declared a cash dividend.				
(b) Paid the cash dividend declared in part (a).				
(c) Declared a stock dividend.				
(d) Distributed the stock dividend declared in part (c).				
(e) Split stock 2 for 1.				

Record reacquisition of shares. (LO 2) AP

BE14–4 On December 31, 2016, Liquorice Treats Limited reported 40,000 common shares issued and a balance in the Common Shares account of $250,000. On April 5, 2017, it reacquired 8,000 of these shares. This is the first time Liquorice Treats has reacquired any of its shares. Record the reacquisition of the shares assuming the company paid (a) $45,000 and (b) $60,000 to reacquire the shares.

Calculate average per share amount; record reacquisition. (LO 2) AP

BE14–5 On February 7, 2017, Flathead Corp. had a balance of $315,000 in its Common Shares account and the total number of shares issued was 25,000. On February 8, 2017, Flathead paid $10,000 to reacquire 1,000 shares. On December 22, 2017, the company paid $28,000 to reacquire 2,000 shares. (a) Determine the average per share amount on February 7 and December 22, 2017. (b) Record the two transactions in which Flathead reacquired its shares.

Calculate income tax on continuing and discontinued operations. (LO 3) AP

BE14–6 Olivier Corporation reported the following pre-tax amounts for the year ended August 31, 2017: profit before income tax (on the company's continuing operations), $320,000; loss from operations of discontinued operations, $85,000; and gain on disposal of assets of discontinued operations, $60,000. Olivier is subject to a 20% income tax rate. Calculate (a) the income tax expense on continuing operations, and (b) any income tax expense or savings on each item of discontinued operations.

Prepare an income statement with discontinued operations. (LO 3) AP

BE14–7 Refer to the data given for Olivier Corporation in BE14–6. Assume that the profit before income tax of $320,000 is from $500,000 of revenue and $180,000 of operating expenses. Prepare an income statement.

Prepare statement of comprehensive income. (LO 3) AP

BE14–8 For the year ended December 31, 2017, Jet Set Airlines reported profit of $920,000 and a gain on an equity investment of $66,000, before income tax. This gain is other comprehensive income. Jet Set has a tax rate of 30%. Prepare a statement of comprehensive income.

Record correction of prior period error. (LO 4) AP

BE14–9 On March 1, 2017, Broadfoot Bakeries Inc. discovered that the cost of Land purchased in 2016 was erroneously recorded as rent expense. The cost of the Land was $5,000. The company's year end is December 31 and the income tax rate is 20%. Prepare the journal entry to correct this error.

Prepare a statement of retained earnings with correction of prior period error. (LO 4) AP

BE14–10 Broadfoot Bakeries Inc. reported retained earnings of $394,000 on December 31, 2016. For the year ended December 31, 2017, the company had profit of $128,000, and it declared and paid dividends of $44,000. Assuming the company reports under ASPE, and referring to the data for Broadfoot Bakeries in BE14–9, prepare a statement of retained earnings.

Determine missing amounts in shareholders' equity accounts. (LO 5) AP

BE14–11 Peninsula Supply Corporation provided the following schedule detailing the changes in the shareholders' equity accounts during 2016 and 2017. Determine the missing amounts.

	2017		2016	
	Number of Shares	Amount	Number of Shares	Amount
Common shares, unlimited authorized				
Balance, January 1	500,000	$ (b)	500,000	$600,000
Issued shares for cash	50,000	32,500		0
Reacquired shares	(25,000)	(c)		0
Balance, December 31	(a)	603,750	500,000	600,000
Contributed surplus—reacquisition of common shares				
Balance, January 1		15,000		15,000
Reacquired common shares		8,000		0
Balance, December 31		(d)		15,000
Retained earnings				
Balance, January 1		179,500		190,000
Profit (loss)		22,500		(h)
Common dividends—Cash		(e)		(30,000)
Balance, December 31		181,000		179,500
Accumulated other comprehensive income				
Balance, January 1		51,000		(i)
Other comprehensive income (loss)		(f)		(3,000)
Balance, December 31		68,000		51,000
Shareholders' equity, December 31		$ (g)		$ (j)

BE14–12 Refer to the data for Peninsula Supply Corporation presented in BE14–11. (a) Prepare the statement of changes in shareholders' equity for the year ended December 31, 2017. (b) Prepare the shareholders' equity section of the balance sheet at December 31, 2017.

Prepare a statement of changes in shareholders' equity and shareholders' equity section of a balance sheet. (LO 5) AP

BE14–13 Franklin Corporation had 20,000 common shares on January 1, 2017. On March 1, 5,000 shares were repurchased. On June 1 and September 30, 6,000 and 10,000 shares were issued, respectively. Calculate the weighted average number of shares.

Calculate weighted average number of shares. (LO 6) AP

BE14–14 Northlake Limited reports profit of $454,000 and its weighted average number of common shares is 220,000. Northlake also has 22,000, $2.50 preferred shares. Calculate earnings per share under each of the following independent assumptions:
(a) preferred shares are cumulative and the dividend was paid.
(b) preferred shares are cumulative and the dividend was not paid.
(c) preferred shares are noncumulative and the dividend was paid.
(d) preferred shares are noncumulative and the dividend was not paid.

Calculate earnings per share. (LO 6) AP

BE14–15 Highlink, Inc. reported earnings per share of $4 based on a profit after tax of $450,000. The company's common shares were selling at $24 per share. During the same year, the company declared and paid total cash dividends of $90,000. Calculate the price-earnings ratio and the payout ratio.

Calculate price-earnings and payout ratios. (LO 6) AP

▶ Exercises

E14–1 Smart Mart Inc. is considering one of three options: (1) paying a $0.40 cash dividend, (2) distributing a 5% stock dividend, or (3) effecting a 2-for-1 stock split. The current fair value is $14 per share.

Compare cash dividend, stock dividend, and stock split. (LO 1) AP

Instructions

In the chart below, indicate the financial impact on the financial statement items listed of each action under consideration.

*Cash divizion = 60.000 * 0.40 = 24000* (handwritten)

	Before Action	(1) After Cash Dividend	(2) After Stock Dividend	(3) After Stock Split
Total assets	$1,875,000	1851000	1875000	
Total liabilities	$ 75,000	775000	75000	
Common shares	1,200,000	1200000	1242000	
Retained earnings	600,000	576000	558000	
Total shareholders' equity	1,800,000	1776000	1800000	
Total liabilities and shareholders' equity	$1,875,000	1875000	1875000	12000
Number of common shares	60,000	60000	63000	

(handwritten: 3k shares)

Prepare correct entries for dividends and stock split. (LO 1) AP

E14-2 Before preparing financial statements for the current year, the chief accountant for Patel Ltd. provided the following information regarding the accounting for dividends and stock splits:

1. Patel has 20,000, $4 noncumulative preferred shares issued. It paid the preferred shareholders the quarterly dividend, and recorded it as a debit to Dividends Expense and a credit to Cash.
2. A 5% stock dividend (1,000 shares) was declared on the common shares when the fair value per share was $12. To record the declaration, Retained Earnings was debited and Dividends Payable was credited. The shares have not been issued yet.
3. The company declared a 2-for-1 stock split on its 20,000, $4 noncumulative preferred shares. The average per share amount of the preferred shares before the split was $70. The split was recorded as a debit to Retained Earnings of $1.4 million and a credit to Preferred Shares of $1.4 million.

Instructions

Determine if each of the above transactions was recorded correctly and, if not, prepare the correct entry.

Record issue and reacquisition of shares. (LO 2) AP

E14-3 Moosonee Ltd. had the following share transactions during its first year of operations:

Jan. 6   Issued 200,000 common shares for $1.50 per share. *200000 × 1.50 = 300k*
     12   Issued 50,000 common shares for $1.75 per share. *50k × 1.75 = 87500*
Mar. 17   Issued 1,000 preferred shares for $105 per share. *1k × 105 = 105k*
July 18   Issued 1 million common shares for $2 per share. *1M × 2 = 2M*
Nov. 17   Reacquired 200,000 common shares for $1.95 per share. *200k × 1.95*
Dec. 30   Reacquired 150,000 common shares for $1.80 per share.

Instructions

(a) Journalize the transactions.
(b) How many common shares remain at the end of the year?

Prepare a partial income statement showing discontinued operations presentation. (LO 3) AP

E14-4 Shrink Ltd. has profit from continuing operations of $320,000 for the year ended December 31, 2017. It also has the following before considering income tax: a net gain of $60,000 from the discontinuance of a component of the entity, which includes a $90,000 profit from the operation of the segment and a $30,000 loss on its disposal.

    Assume that the income tax rate on all items is 30%.

(handwritten: 90k × 30% → 27000 − 90k = 63000; 30k × 30% → 9000 − 30k = (21k); 42000 + 30k)

Instructions

Prepare a partial income statement, beginning with profit from continuing operations, using the all-inclusive format. (*Hint:* Use Illustration 14-4 as a presentation guide.)

Prepare income statement with discontinued items and statement of comprehensive income. (LO 3) AP

E14-5 Top Brands Limited reported the following selected information for the year ended March 31, 2017:

Advertising expense	$ 7,000	Interest expense	$ 5,500
Cash dividends—common	5,000	Loss on discontinued operations	18,000
Depreciation expense	3,000	Loss on equity investments	3,000
Fees earned	62,000	Rent revenue	34,000
Gain on disposal of equipment	1,500	Retained earnings, April 1, 2016	19,000
Income tax payable	6,600	Telephone expense	8,000

The company's income tax rate is 30%. The company reports gains and losses on its equity investments as other comprehensive income.

Instructions

Prepare an income statement and a separate statement of comprehensive income for Top Brands Limited.

E14-6   On July 9, 2017, Silver Fox Enterprises Inc. discovered it had recorded the $75,000 purchase of land as legal expense on November 8, 2016. The company had reported retained earnings of $573,500 at its previous year end, December 31, 2016.

During 2017, Silver Fox had profit of $193,000 and it declared and paid cash dividends of $216,000. Silver Fox has a 25% income tax rate.

Record correction of prior period error and prepare statement of retained earnings. (LO 4) AP

Instructions

(a) Prepare the journal entry to correct the error.
(b) Assuming the company reports under ASPE, prepare a statement of retained earnings.

E14-7   On January 1, 2017, Fyre Lite Corporation had retained earnings of $650,000. During the year, Fyre Lite had the following selected transactions:

Prepare a statement of retained earnings with correction of prior period error. (LO 1, 2, 3, 4) AP

1. Declared and paid cash dividends, $245,000.
2. Earned profit before income tax, $750,000.
3. Corrected a prior period error of $85,000, before income tax, which resulted in an understatement of profit in 2016.
4. Reacquired 25,000 common shares for $50,000 more than the original issue price. This was the first time the company had ever reacquired its own shares.
5. Completed a 3-for-1 stock split of the common shares.

Fyre Lite has a 25% income tax rate and reports under ASPE.

Instructions

Prepare a statement of retained earnings for the year ended December 31, 2017.

E14-8   Kettle Creek Corporation had the following transactions and events:

Indicate effects of transactions on shareholders' equity. (LO 1, 4, 5) AP

1. Declared a cash dividend.
2. Issued common shares for cash.
3. Completed a 2-for-1 stock split of the common shares.
4. Declared a stock dividend on the common shares.
5. Distributed the stock dividend declared in item 4.
6. Made a correction of a prior period error for an understatement of profit.
7. Repurchased common shares for less than their initial issue price.
8. Comprehensive income included profit and a gain reported as other comprehensive income.

Instructions

Indicate the effect(s) of each of the above items on the subdivisions of shareholders' equity. Present your answer in tabular form with the following columns. Use "I" for increase, "D" for decrease, and "NE" for no effect. Item 1 is given as an example.

Item	Contributed Capital		Retained Earnings	Accumulated Other Comprehensive Income	Total Shareholders' Equity
	Share Capital	Additional			
1.	NE	NE	D	NE	D

E14-9   On January 1, 2017, Marchelle Incorporated had an unlimited number of common shares authorized, 220,000 issued, and the balance in the Common Shares account was $2.2 million. The company reported a balance in Retained Earnings on this date of $850,000 and accumulated other comprehensive income of $27,000. During the year, the following occurred:

Prepare a statement of changes in shareholders' equity. (LO 1, 3, 5) AP

1. Issued 80,000 common shares at $15 per share on July 1.
2. Declared a 3-for-2 stock split on September 30 when the fair value was $19 per share.
3. Declared a 5% stock dividend on December 9 to common shareholders of record at December 30, distributable on January 16, 2018. At the declaration date, the fair value of the common shares was $22 per share.
4. Earned profit of $390,000 for the year.
5. Recognized a loss on equity investments of $38,000 before tax, which will be reported as other comprehensive income. The company's income tax rate is 25%.

Instructions

Prepare a statement of changes in shareholders' equity for the year ended December 31, 2017.

Prepare journal entries for shareholder transactions and prepare a statement of changes in shareholders' equity. (LO 2, 3, 5) AP

E14-10 Ruby Red Rental Corporation had the following balances in its shareholders' equity accounts at January 1, 2017:

Accumulated other comprehensive income (loss)	$ (25,000)
Contributed surplus—reacquisition of common shares	540,000
Retained earnings	1,500,000
Common shares (32,000 shares)	800,000

Ruby Red had the following transactions and events during 2017:

Feb. 2 Repurchased 1,000 shares for $44,500.
Apr. 17 Declared and paid cash dividends of $70,000.
Oct. 29 Issued 2,000 shares for $104,000 cash.
Dec. 31 Reported comprehensive income of $425,000, which included other comprehensive income of $40,000.

Instructions

(a) Prepare journal entries to record the transactions that took place during 2017.
(b) Prepare a statement of changes in shareholders' equity at December 31, 2017.
(c) Calculate the number of shares issued as at December 31, 2017.

Calculate earnings per share. (LO 6) AP

E14-11 Salmon Limited reported profit of $465,325 for its November 30, 2017, year end. Cash dividends of $90,000 on the common shares and $65,000 on the noncumulative preferred shares were declared and paid during the year. The following information is available regarding Salmon's common shares:

Dec. 1, 2016 The opening number of common shares was 60,000. 60k × 12/12 = 60 000
Feb. 28, 2017 Sold 10,000 common shares for $200,000 cash. 10k × 9/12 = 7500
May 31, 2017 Reacquired 5,000 common shares for $90,000 cash. (5000) × 6/12 = 2500
Nov. 1, 2017 Issued 15,000 common shares in exchange for land with a fair value of $310,000. 15k × 1/12 = 1250

Instructions

(a) Calculate the profit available to common shareholders. 465325 - 65 000 = 40325
(b) Calculate the weighted average number of common shares for the year. 60k + 7500 + 2500 + 1250 = 66250
(c) Calculate earnings per share for the year. 400325 ÷ 66 250 = $6.04

Calculate earnings per share. (LO 6) AP

E14-12 On December 31, 2016, Nettle Corporation had 5,000, $2 preferred shares and 80,000 common shares issued. During 2017, the company completed the following share transactions:

Apr. 1 Sold 10,000 common shares for $5,000 cash.
Sept. 30 Reacquired 5,000 common shares for $1,800 cash.

Nettle's profit in 2017 was $520,000.

Instructions

(a) Calculate the weighted average number of common shares for 2017.
(b) Calculate earnings per share under each of the following independent assumptions:
　1. Preferred shares are cumulative and dividends were
　　(i) declared.
　　(ii) not declared.
　2. Preferred shares are noncumulative and dividends were
　　(i) declared.
　　(ii) not declared.

Calculate ratios and comment. (LO 6) AN

E14-13 The following financial information is available for Longmire Lumber Ltd. as at December 31 (in thousands, except for per share amounts):

	2017	2016	2015
Profit	$1,978	$2,131	$2,663
Preferred share dividends (total)	$73	$43	$30
Weighted average number of common shares	÷ 502	500	501
Dividends per common share	$2.50	$2.25	$2.10
Market price per common share	$43.00	$49.75	$56.25

Instructions

(a) Calculate the earnings per share, price-earnings ratio, and payout ratio for the common shareholders for each of the three years.
(b) Using the information in part (a), comment on Longmire's earnings performance and dividend record.

▶ Problems: Set A

P14–1A   The condensed balance sheet of Laporte Corporation reports the following:

Compare impact of cash dividend, stock dividend, and stock split. (LO 1) AP

> **LAPORTE CORPORATION**
> Balance Sheet (partial)
> June 30, 2017
>
> | | |
> |---|---:|
> | Total assets | $12,000,000 |
> | | |
> | Liabilities and shareholders' equity | |
> | Total liabilities | $ 4,000,000 |
> | | |
> | Shareholders' equity | |
> | Common shares, unlimited number authorized, 400,000 issued | 2,000,000 |
> | Retained earnings | 6,000,000 |
> | Total shareholders' equity | 8,000,000 |
> | Total liabilities and shareholders' equity | $12,000,000 |

The market price of the common shares is currently $30 per share. Laporte wants to assess the impact of three possible alternatives on the corporation and its shareholders. The alternatives are:

1. Payment of a $1.50 per share cash dividend
2. Distribution of a 5% stock dividend
3. A 3-for-1 stock split

Instructions

(a) For each alternative, determine the impact on (1) assets, (2) liabilities, (3) common shares, (4) retained earnings, (5) total shareholders' equity, and (6) the number of shares.
(b) Assume a Laporte shareholder currently owns 1,000 common shares at a cost of $28,000. What is the impact of each alternative for the shareholder, assuming that the shares' market price changes proportionately with the alternative?

TAKING IT FURTHER   What are the advantages and disadvantages to the company of a stock split?

P14–2A   On December 31, 2016, LeBlanc Corporation had the following shareholders' equity accounts:

Record and post transactions; prepare shareholders' equity section. (LO 1, 2) AP

> **LEBLANC CORPORATION**
> Balance Sheet (partial)
> December 31, 2016
>
> | | |
> |---|---:|
> | Shareholders' equity | |
> | Common shares (unlimited number of shares authorized, | |
> | 90,000 issued) | $1,100,000 |
> | Retained earnings | 540,000 |
> | Total shareholders' equity | $1,640,000 |

During the year, the following transactions occurred:

Jan.	15	Declared a $1 per share cash dividend to shareholders of record on January 31, payable February 15.
July	1	Announced a 3-for-2 stock split. The market price per share on the date of the announcement was $15.
Dec.	15	Declared a 10% stock dividend to shareholders of record on December 30, distributable on January 15. On December 15, the market price of each share was $10; on December 30, $12; and on January 15, $11.
	31	Determined that profit before income tax for the year was $450,000. The company has a 30% income tax rate.

Instructions

(a) Journalize the transactions and closing entries.
(b) Create general ledger accounts and enter the beginning balances from the December 31, 2016, partial balance sheet. Post the entries in part (a) to the shareholders' equity accounts. (*Note:* Open additional shareholders' equity accounts as needed.)
(c) Prepare the shareholders' equity section of the balance sheet at December 31, 2017.

TAKING IT FURTHER   What are the advantages and disadvantages to investors when a company declares a stock dividend or a stock split?

Determine impact of reacquired shares.
(LO 2) AP

P14–3A   Advanced Technologies Inc. reported the following information related to its shareholders' equity on January 1:

Common shares, 1,000,000 authorized, 500,000 shares issued	$1,500,000
Contributed surplus—reacquisition of common shares	15,000
Retained earnings	720,000

During the year, the following transactions related to common shares occurred in the order listed:

1. Issued 35,000 shares at $4.20 per share.
2. Reacquired 10,000 shares at $3.00 per share.
3. Issued 5,000 shares at $4.50 per share.
4. Reacquired 18,000 shares at $4 per share.
5. Reacquired 75,000 shares at $3 per share.

Instructions

(a) Calculate the number of shares authorized and issued at the end of the year.
(b) Determine the ending balances in each of the following accounts: Common Shares, Contributed Surplus— Reacquisition of Common Shares, and Retained Earnings.

TAKING IT FURTHER   Why is it important to report the number of shares issued? The number authorized?

Record stock dividends, splits, and reacquisition of shares. Report balances in shareholders' equity.
(LO 1, 2) AP

P14–4A   The following shareholders' equity accounts are reported by Branch Inc. on January 1:

Common shares (unlimited authorized, 150,000 issued)	$2,400,000
Preferred shares ($4 cumulative, convertible, 100,000 authorized, 5,000 issued)	375,000
Contributed surplus—reacquisition of common shares	30,000
Retained earnings	1,275,000

The following selected transactions occurred during the year:

Feb.	11	Issued 50,000 common shares at $20 per share.
Mar.	2	Reacquired 20,000 common shares at $22 per share.
June	14	Split the common shares 2 for 1 when the common shares were trading at $30 per share.
July	25	Reacquired 500 preferred shares at $70 per share.
Sept.	16	Reacquired 50,000 common shares for $17 per share.
Oct.	27	Declared a 5% common stock dividend distributable on December 13 to shareholders of record on November 24. The fair value of the common shares on October 27 was $19 per share.
Dec.	13	Distributed the stock dividend declared on October 27. The fair value of the common shares on December 13 was $21 per share.

Instructions

(a) Prepare journal entries for the transactions.
(b) Show how each class of shares will be presented in the shareholders' equity section of the balance sheet at December 31.

TAKING IT FURTHER   Why is the Contributed Surplus account reported in shareholders' equity?

Prepare income statement and statement of comprehensive income.
(LO 3) AP

P14–5A   The ledger of Port Hope Corporation at November 30, 2017, contains the following summary data:

Cash dividends—common	$ 65,000	Operating expenses	$1,120,000
Cash dividends—preferred	25,000	Other comprehensive income—loss on	
Common shares	325,000	equity investments (before income tax)	83,000
Cost of goods sold	7,280,000	Rent revenue	48,000
Depreciation expense	355,000	Preferred shares ($5 noncumulative)	400,000
Sales	9,124,000	Retained earnings, December 1, 2016	755,000

Your analysis reveals the following additional information:

1. The company has a 25% income tax rate.
2. The communications devices division was discontinued on August 31. The profit from operations for the division up to that day was $20,000 before income tax. The division was sold at a loss of $75,000 before income tax.

3. There were 200,000 common and 5,000 preferred shares issued on December 1, 2016, with no changes during the year.

Instructions

(a) Prepare a multiple-step income statement for the year.

(b) Prepare a statement of comprehensive income as a separate statement.

TAKING IT FURTHER   Why are gains and losses from discontinued operations reported separately from continuing operations?

P14–6A   The ledger of Zug Limited at October 31, 2017, contains the following summary data:

Cash dividends—common	$ 120,000	Operating expenses	$929,000
Common shares	650,000	Interest expense	54,000
Depreciation expense	87,000	Retained earnings, November 1, 2016	575,000
Fees earned	1,476,000		

Correct error from prior period; prepare statement of retained earnings. (LO 2, 3, 4) AP

Your analysis reveals the following additional information:

1. The company has a 25% income tax rate.

2. On March 19, 2017, Zug discovered an error made in the previous fiscal year. A $57,000 payment of a note payable had been recorded as interest expense.

3. On April 10, 2017, common shares costing $75,000 were reacquired for $97,500. This is the first time the company has reacquired common shares.

Instructions

(a) Prepare a journal entry to correct the prior period error.

(b) Prepare the journal entry to record the reacquisition of common shares.

(c) Calculate profit for the year ended October 31, 2017.

(d) Prepare the statement of retained earnings for the company for the year ended October 31, 2017.

TAKING IT FURTHER   If an error from a previous period is found and corrected, why is it also important to restate the prior years' data shown for comparative purposes?

P14–7A   The post-closing trial balance of Jajoo Corporation at December 31, 2017, contains the following share-holders' equity accounts:

$5 noncumulative preferred shares (10,000 issued)	$1,100,000
Common shares (400,000 issued)	2,000,000
Retained earnings	3,146,000

Record and post transactions; prepare a statement of changes in shareholders' equity. (LO 2, 4, 5) AP

A review of the accounting records reveals the following:

1. The January 1, 2017, balance in Common Shares was $1,280,000 (320,000 shares), the balance in Contributed Surplus—Reacquisition of Common Shares was $30,000, and the balance in Retained Earnings was $2,443,500.

2. One of the company's shareholders needed cash for a personal expenditure. On January 15, the company agreed to reacquire 20,000 shares from this shareholder for $7 per share.

3. On July 1, the company corrected a prior period error that resulted in an increase to the Long-Term Investment account, as well as to the prior year's profit of $250,000 before income tax.

4. On October 1, 100,000 common shares were sold for $8 per share.

5. The preferred shareholders' dividend was declared and paid in 2017 for two quarters. Due to a cash shortage, the last two quarters' dividends were not declared or paid.

6. Profit for the year before income tax was $760,000. The company has a 25% income tax rate.

Instructions

(a) Open general ledger accounts for the shareholders' equity accounts listed in item (1) above and enter opening balances.

(b) Prepare journal entries to record transactions (2) to (5) and post to general ledger accounts.

(c) Prepare entries to close dividends and the Income Summary account and post.

(d) Prepare a statement of changes in shareholders' equity for the year.

TAKING IT FURTHER   Why is the prior period adjustment for the error in a prior year's profit recorded in the Retained Earnings account instead of being a correction to profit in the 2017 financial statements?

P14–8A   The adjusted trial balance for Pansy Paints Ltd. at December 31, 2017, is presented below. Pansy's income tax rate is 25% and journal entries for income tax expense have not yet been prepared. There were no common share transactions during the year.

Prepare financial statements. (LO 2, 3, 5) AP

PANSY PAINTS LTD.
Adjusted Trial Balance
December 31, 2017

	Debit	Credit
Accounts payable		$54,620
Accounts receivable	$35,430	
Accumulated depreciation—equipment		24,300
Accumulated depreciation—building		145,500
Accumulated other comprehensive income (loss)—January 1, 2017	0	
Advertising expense	7,860	
Building	425,000	
Cash	180,000	
Cash dividends—common	15,000	
Common shares (18,000 issued)		255,000
Contributed surplus—reacquisition of common shares		7,500
Cost of goods sold	412,000	
Depreciation expense	29,000	
Dividends payable		1,000
Equipment	95,000	
Gain on sale of equipment		850
Interest expense	4,650	
Income tax expense	0	
Income tax payable		0
Merchandise inventory	83,460	
Other comprehensive income—loss on equity investment (before income tax)	5,400	
Office expense	11,000	
Retained earnings—January 1, 2017		35,030
Sales		780,000
	$1,303,800	$1,303,800

Instructions

(a) Prepare a statement of comprehensive income using the all-inclusive format. (Ignore earnings per share.)
(b) Prepare a statement of changes in shareholders' equity.
(c) Prepare the shareholders' equity section of the balance sheet at December 31, 2017.

TAKING IT FURTHER Explain the two methods of preparing a statement of comprehensive income. Is one method better than the other?

Prepare a statement of changes in shareholders' equity. (LO 5) AP

P14–9A The shareholders' equity accounts of Tmao, Inc. at December 31, 2016, are as follows:

Preferred shares, $3 noncumulative, unlimited number authorized, 4,000 issued	$400,000
Common shares, unlimited number authorized, 160,000 issued	800,000
Retained earnings	450,000
Accumulated other comprehensive loss	(50,000)

Tmao has a 35% income tax rate. During the following fiscal year, ended December 31, 2017, the company had the following transactions and events:

Feb. 1 Repurchased 10,000 common shares for $40,000.
July 12 Announced a 2-for-1 preferred stock split. The market price of the preferred shares at the date of announcement was $150.
Dec. 1 Declared the annual cash dividend ($1.50 post-split) to the preferred shareholders of record on January 10, 2018, payable on January 31, 2018.
18 Declared a 10% stock dividend to common shareholders of record at December 20, distributable on January 12, 2018. The fair value of the common shares was $12 per share.
31 Determined that for 2017, profit before income tax was $350,000 and other comprehensive income, net of income tax expense of $35,000, was $65,000.

Instructions

Prepare a statement of changes in shareholders' equity for the year ended December 31, 2017.

TAKING IT FURTHER How does comprehensive income impact the shareholders' equity in the balance sheet? Is this the same for companies following ASPE?

P14–10A   The shareholders' equity accounts of Blue Bay Logistics Ltd. on April 1, 2016, the beginning of the   Calculate earnings per share.
fiscal year, are as follows: *(LO 6) AP*

$6 cumulative preferred shares (20,000 issued)	$1,800,000
Common shares (500,000 issued)	3,750,000
Retained earnings	1,550,000
Total shareholders' equity	$7,100,000

During the year, the following transactions occurred:

2016

June 1	Reacquired 12,000 common shares for $9 per share.
July 1	Issued 50,000 common shares for $10 per share.
Sept. 30	Reacquired 8,000 common shares for $9.50 per share.

2017

Jan. 31	Issued 60,000 common shares in exchange for land. The land's fair value was $600,000.
Mar. 31	Profit for the year ended March 31, 2017, was $973,600.

Instructions

(a) Calculate the weighted average number of common shares for the year.
(b) Assuming the preferred share dividends are one year in arrears, calculate the earnings per share if no preferred
    dividends are declared during the year.
(c) What is the total number of common shares issued on March 31, 2017?

TAKING IT FURTHER   Why is earnings per share an important measure for common shareholders but not for
preferred shareholders?

P14–11A   The following financial information (in millions except for per share amounts) is for two major corpo-   Calculate ratios and
rations for the three fiscal years ended December 31 as follows: comment. *(LO 6) AN*

Canadian Pacific Railway Limited	2014	2013	2012
Weighted average number of common shares	172.8	174.9	171.8
Profit	$ 1,476	$ 875	$ 484
Dividends	$ 241	$ 246	$ 232
Market price per share (December 31)	$223.75	$160.65	$100.90

Canadian National Railway Company	2014	2013	2012
Weighted average number of common shares	819.9	843.1	871.1
Profit	$3,167	$2,612	$2,680
Dividends	$ 818	$ 724	$ 652
Market price per share (December 31)	$80.02	$60.56	$90.33

Neither company has preferred shares issued.

Instructions

(a) Calculate earnings per share and the price-earnings and dividend payout ratios for each company for 2014,
    2013, and 2012. Comment on whether their ratios have improved or deteriorated.
(b) Compare Canadian Pacific's ratios with Canadian National's.

TAKING IT FURTHER   Why is the presentation of fully diluted earnings per share required under IFRS, given
that it is a hypothetical number?

P14–12A   Highlander Inc. reported the following selected information for the past three years (in millions,   Calculate and evaluate ratios
except for per share amounts):   with discontinued operations.
                                                                                                                          (LO 3, 6) AN

	2017	2016	2015
Net sales	$4,000	$3,100	$2,600
Average shareholders' equity	3,400	2,400	1,800
Preferred dividends	20	20	15
Profit from continuing operations	$1,160	$ 810	$ 570
Loss on disposal of discontinued operations	340		
Loss from discontinued operations	110	80	70
Profit	$ 710	$ 730	$ 500
Weighted average number of common shares	300	290	280
Market price per share	$45.50	$33.65	$44.80

Instructions

(a) Calculate Highlander's return on equity, earnings per share, and price-earnings ratios before and after discontinued operations for 2017, 2016, and 2015.
(b) Evaluate Highlander's performance over the past three years before and after discontinued operations.

TAKING IT FURTHER   Explain how reporting discontinued operations separately would affect your analysis of Highlander's performance.

▶ Problems: Set B

Compare impact of cash dividend, stock dividend, and stock split. (LO 1) AP

P14–1B   The condensed balance sheet of Erickson Corporation reports the following:

ERICKSON CORPORATION Balance Sheet (partial) January 31, 2017		
Total assets		$9,000,000
Liabilities and shareholders' equity		
Liabilities		$2,500,000
Shareholders' equity		
Common shares, unlimited number authorized, 500,000 issued	$3,000,000	
Retained earnings	3,500,000	6,500,000
Total liabilities and shareholders' equity		$9,000,000

The market price of the common shares is currently $30 per share. Erickson wants to assess the impact of three possible alternatives on the corporation and its shareholders. The alternatives are:

1. Payment of a $1.50 per share cash dividend
2. Distribution of a 5% stock dividend
3. A 2-for-1 stock split

Instructions

(a) For each alternative, determine the impact on (1) assets, (2) liabilities, (3) common shares, (4) retained earnings, (5) total shareholders' equity, and (6) the number of shares.
(b) Assume an Erickson shareholder currently owns 2,000 common shares at a cost of $50,000. What is the impact of each alternative for the shareholder, assuming that the market price of the shares changes proportionately with the alternative?

TAKING IT FURTHER   What is the purpose of a reverse stock split? When might a company take this action?

Record and post transactions; prepare shareholders' equity section. (LO 1) AP

P14–2B   On December 31, 2016, Asaad Corporation had the following shareholders' equity accounts:

ASAAD CORPORATION Balance Sheet (partial) December 31, 2016	
Shareholders' equity	
Common shares (unlimited number of shares authorized, 75,000 shares issued)	$1,700,000
Retained earnings	600,000
Total shareholders' equity	$2,300,000

During 2017, the following transactions occurred:

Feb. 1   Declared a $1 cash dividend to shareholders of record on February 15 and payable on March 1.
Apr. 1   Announced a 2-for-1 stock split. The market price per share was $36 on the date of the announcement.
Dec. 1   Declared a 5% stock dividend to shareholders of record on December 20, distributable on January 5. On December 1, the shares' market price was $16 per share; on December 20, it was $18 per share; and on January 5, it was $15 per share.
     31   Determined that profit before income tax for the year was $400,000. The company has a 25% income tax rate.

Instructions

(a) Journalize the transactions and closing entries.

(b Create general ledger accounts and enter the beginning balances from the December 31, 2016, partial balance sheet. Post the entries in part (a) to the shareholders' equity accounts. (*Note:* Open additional shareholders' equity accounts as needed.)

(c) Prepare the shareholders' equity section of the balance sheet at December 31, 2017.

TAKING IT FURTHER   Stock splits and stock dividends do not change the company's total assets. Given that, why does the share price change after a stock split or stock dividend?

P14–3B   The following is related to the shareholders' equity of Adanac Limited on January 1:

Determine impact of reacquired shares. (LO 2) AP

Common shares, 150,000 authorized, 14,000 shares issued	$490,000
Contributed surplus—reacquisition of common shares	12,000
Retained earnings	220,000

During the year, the following transactions related to common shares occurred in the order listed:

1. Reacquired 600 shares at $44 per share.
2. Issued 3,600 shares at $47 per share.
3. Issued 1,000 shares at $64.50 per share.

4. Reacquired 1,200 shares at $58 per share.
5. Reacquired 1,500 shares at $36 per share.

Instructions

(a) Calculate the number of shares authorized and issued at the end of the year.

(b) Determine the ending balances in each of the following accounts: Common Shares, Contributed Surplus—Reacquisition of Common Shares, and Retained Earnings.

TAKING IT FURTHER   One of the reasons a company might reacquire its own shares is to have shares available to fulfill employee stock compensation plans. What are some reasons a company would compensate employees with shares instead of cash bonuses?

P14–4B   The following shareholders' equity accounts are reported by Talty Inc. on January 1:

Record stock dividends, splits, and reacquisition of shares. Show impact of transactions on accounts. (LO 1, 2) AP

Common shares (unlimited authorized, 500,000 issued)	$4,000,000
Preferred shares ($9 noncumulative, convertible, 100,000 authorized, 4,000 issued)	600,000
Contributed surplus—reacquisition of common shares	2,000
Retained earnings	1,958,000

The following selected transactions occurred during the year:

Jan. 17	Issued 50,000 common shares at $10 per share.
Feb. 27	Reacquired 20,000 common shares at $12 per share.
Apr. 14	Split the common shares 2 for 1 when the common shares were trading at $20 per share.
June 25	Reacquired 500 preferred shares at $145 per share.
Aug. 16	Reacquired 100,000 common shares for $11 per share.
Oct. 17	Declared a 5% common stock dividend distributable on December 3 to shareholders of record on November 14. On October 17, the fair value of the common shares was $10.
Dec. 3	Distributed the stock dividend declared on October 17. On December 3, the fair value of the common shares was $12.50.

Instructions

(a) Prepare journal entries for the transactions.

(b) Show how each class of shares will be presented in the shareholders' equity section of the balance sheet at December 31.

TAKING IT FURTHER   Provide possible reasons why Talty split the common shares and issued a stock dividend.

P14–5B   The ledger of Coquitlam Corporation at December 31, 2017, contains the following summary data:

Prepare income statement and comprehensive income statement. (LO 3) AP

Cash dividends—common	$ 125,000	Other comprehensive income—gain on equity	
Cash dividends—preferred	55,000	investments (before income tax)	$ 47,000
Cost of goods sold	888,000	Other expenses	18,000
Sales	1,750,000	Retained earnings, January 1, 2017	642,000
Operating expenses	451,000		

Your analysis reveals the following additional information:

1. The company has a 25% income tax rate.
2. The ceramics division was discontinued on July 31. The loss from operations for the division up to that day was $150,000 before income tax. The division was sold at a pre-tax gain of $70,000 before income tax.
3. There were 200,000 common and 100,000 noncumulative preferred shares issued on December 31, 2016, with no changes during the year.

Instructions

(a) Prepare a multiple-step income statement for the year.

(b) Prepare a statement of comprehensive income as a separate statement.

TAKING IT FURTHER   What are the characteristics of a component of an entity? What information does profit (loss) from continuing operations provide to a user? What information does profit (loss) from discontinued operations provide to a user?

Correct error from prior period; prepare a statement of retained earnings.
(LO 2, 3, 4) AP

P14–6B   The ledger of Weather Vane Limited at September 30, 2017, contains the following summary data:

Cash dividends—common	$ 150,000	Operating expenses	$971,000
Common shares	750,000	Commission revenue	65,000
Depreciation expense	74,000	Retained earnings, October 1, 2016	845,000
Fees earned	1,647,000		

Your analysis reveals the following additional information:

1. The company has a 25% income tax rate.
2. On July 9, 2017, Weather Vane discovered an error made in the previous fiscal year. A $61,500 payment of a note payable had been recorded as interest expense.
3. On August 18, 2017, common shares costing $57,500 were reacquired for $90,000. This is the first time the company has reacquired common shares.

Instructions

(a) Prepare a journal entry to correct the prior period error.

(b) Prepare the journal entry to record the reacquisition of common shares.

(c) Calculate profit for the year ended September 30, 2017.

(d) Prepare the statement of retained earnings for the year ended September 30, 2017.

TAKING IT FURTHER   Why are other comprehensive income or loss amounts reported separately on the statement of comprehensive income?

Record and post transactions; prepare a statement of changes in shareholders' equity. (LO 2, 4, 5) AP

P14–7B   The post-closing trial balance of Michaud Corporation at December 31, 2017, contains the following shareholders' equity accounts:

$4 cumulative preferred shares (15,000 shares issued)	$ 850,000
Common shares (250,000 shares issued)	3,200,000
Contributed surplus—reacquisition of common shares	20,000
Retained earnings	1,418,000

A review of the accounting records reveals the following:

1. The January 1, 2017 opening balance in Common Shares was $3,210,000 (255,000 shares), Preferred Shares was $850,000 (15,000 shares), and the balance in Retained Earnings was $980,000.
2. On March 1, 20,000 common shares were sold for $15.50 per share.
3. One of the company's shareholders needed cash for personal reasons. On July 1, the company agreed to reacquire 25,000 shares from this shareholder for $12 per share.
4. On September 1, the company discovered a $60,000 error that overstated sales in 2016. All sales were made on account. The company has a 30% income tax rate.
5. The preferred shareholders' dividend was declared and paid in 2017 for three quarters. Due to a cash shortage, the last quarter's dividend was not paid.
6. Profit for the year before income tax was $750,000.

Instructions

(a) Open general ledger accounts for the shareholders' equity accounts listed in item (1) above and enter opening balances.

(b) Prepare journal entries to record transactions (2) to (5) and post to general ledger accounts.

(c) Prepare entries to close dividends and the Income Summary account and post.

(d) Prepare a statement of changes in shareholders' equity for the year.

TAKING IT FURTHER   If the amount of the error in sales in 2016 was instead as a result of a change in accounting policy from one revenue recognition policy to another, how would it be accounted for? Is it possible that a change in accounting policy can be accounted for similar to a change in accounting estimate? If so, under what circumstances would this be the case?

Prepare financial statements.
(LO 2, 3, 5) AP

P14–8B   The adjusted trial balance for Aster Automobiles Inc. at December 31, 2017, is presented below. Aster's income tax rate is 25% and journal entries for income tax expense have not yet been prepared. There were no common share transactions during the year.

ASTER AUTOMOBILES INC.
Adjusted Trial Balance
December 31, 2017

	Debit	Credit
Accounts payable		$44,620
Accounts receivable	$25,430	
Accumulated depreciation—equipment		14,300
Accumulated depreciation—building		95,500
Accumulated other comprehensive income (loss)—January 1, 2017	0	
Advertising expense	5,860	
Building	375,000	
Cash	170,000	
Cash dividends—common	5,000	
Common shares (10,000 shares issued)		245,000
Contributed surplus—reacquisition of common shares		5,500
Cost of goods sold	356,000	
Depreciation expense	19,000	
Dividends payable		900
Equipment	85,000	
Gain on sale of equipment		800
Interest expense	2,650	
Income tax expense	0	
Income tax payable		0
Merchandise inventory	73,460	
Other comprehensive income—loss on equity investment		
(before income tax)	3,400	
Office expense	9,000	
Retained earnings—January 1, 2017		53,180
Sales		670,000
	$1,129,800	$1,129,800

Instructions

(a) Prepare a statement of comprehensive income on an all-inclusive basis. (Ignore earnings per share.)
(b) Prepare a statement of changes in shareholders' equity for the year.
(c) Prepare the shareholders' equity section of the balance sheet at December 31, 2017.

TAKING IT FURTHER Why is it important to report the changes that took place in shareholders' equity during the year?

P14–9B The shareholders' equity accounts of Kanada Inc. at September 30, 2016, are as follows:

Preferred shares, $5 noncumulative, unlimited number authorized, 6,000 issued	$465,000
Common shares, unlimited number authorized, 25,000 issued	900,000
Retained earnings	540,000
Accumulated other comprehensive income	95,000

Prepare a statement of changes in shareholders' equity. (LO 5) AP

Kanada has a 30% income tax rate. During the following fiscal year, ended September 30, 2017, Kanada had the following transactions and events:

Mar. 14   Declared a 4% common stock dividend to shareholders of record at March 31, distributable on April 5. The fair value of the common shares was $35 per share on March 14, $37 on March 31, and $38 on April 5.
Aug. 1   Reacquired 2,000 common shares for $80,000.
     25   Announced a 2-for-1 common stock split. The market price of the common shares at the date of announcement was $62 per share.
     30   Determined that other comprehensive income for the year was $27,000 and profit was $325,000, both before income tax.
Sept.25   Declared the annual dividend payable to the preferred shareholders of record on October 5, payable on October 31.

Instructions

Prepare a statement of changes in shareholders' equity for the year ended September 30, 2017. (Round per share amounts to the nearest cent.)

TAKING IT FURTHER How does comprehensive income impact the shareholders' equity in the balance sheet? Is this the same for companies following ASPE?

Calculate earnings per share.
(LO 6) AP

P14–10B The shareholders' equity accounts of Gualtieri Inc. on August 1, 2016, the beginning of its fiscal year, are as follows:

$4 noncumulative preferred shares (25,000 issued)	$1,250,000
Common shares (350,000 issued)	3,750,000
Retained earnings	2,250,000
Total shareholders' equity	$7,250,000

During the year, the following transactions occurred:

Nov. 30 Issued 37,500 common shares for $12 per share.
Feb. 1 Reacquired 6,000 common shares for $10 per share.
Mar. 1 Issued 30,000 common shares in exchange for equipment. The equipment's fair value was $40,000.
July 31 Profit for the year ended July 31, 2017, was $1,022,800.

Instructions
(a) Calculate the weighted average number of common shares for the year.
(b) Calculate the earnings per share if no preferred share dividends are declared during the year.
(c) Calculate the earnings per share if the company declares a preferred share dividend of $60,000.
(d) What are the total common shares issued on July 31, 2017?

TAKING IT FURTHER Why is it important to use a weighted average number of shares in the earnings per share calculations? Why not just use the average number of shares during the year?

Calculate ratios and
comment. (LO 6) AN

P14–11B The following financial information (in millions except for market price per share) is for two major corporations for the two fiscal years ended December 31 as follows:

Husky Energy Inc.	2014	2013
Weighted average number of common shares	983.6	983.0
Profit	$1,258	$1,829
Dividends—common shareholders	$1,180	$1,180
Dividends—preferred shareholders	$13	$13
Market price per share (December 31)	$27.50	$33.70

Suncor Energy Inc.	2014	2013
Weighted average number of common shares	1,462	1,501
Profit	$2,699	$3,911
Dividend—common shareholders	$1,490	$1,095
Market price per share (December 31)	$36.90	$37.24

Suncor does not have preferred shares issued. Husky issued preferred shares in 2011.

Instructions
(a) Calculate earnings per share and the price-earnings and dividend payout ratios for each company for 2014 and 2013. Comment on whether their ratios have improved or deteriorated.
(b) Compare Husky's ratios with Suncor's.

TAKING IT FURTHER Why is the presentation of fully diluted earnings per share required under IFRS, given that it is a hypothetical number?

Calculate and evaluate ratios
with discontinued operations.
(LO 3, 6) AN

P14–12B All Care Inc. reported the following selected information for the past three years (in millions, except for per share amounts):

	2017	2016	2015
Sales and operating revenues	$20,300	$24,900	$23,800
Average shareholders' equity	3,400	2,400	1,900
Preferred dividends	80	80	60
Profit from continuing operations	$ 1,250	$ 1,130	$ 990
Loss on disposal of discontinued operations	620		
Loss from discontinued operations	200	150	180
Profit	$ 430	$ 980	$ 810
Weighted average number of common shares	450	470	460
Market price per share	$ 24.40	$ 19.88	$ 21.60

Instructions
(a) Calculate All Care's return on equity, earnings per share, and price-earnings ratios before and after discontinued operations for 2017, 2016, and 2015.
(b) Evaluate All Care's performance over the past three years before and after discontinued operations.

TAKING IT FURTHER How would reporting discontinued operations affect your analysis of All Care's performance?

CHAPTER 14: BROADENING YOUR PERSPECTIVE

▶ Financial Reporting and Analysis

Financial Reporting Problem

BYP14–1 Refer to the consolidated financial statements and accompanying notes for Corus Entertainment Inc. reproduced in Appendix A.

Instructions

(a) Did Corus report any of the following in fiscal 2014: (1) stock dividends or stock splits, (2) other comprehensive income, or (3) corrections of prior period errors?

(b) Did Corus repurchase any shares in fiscal 2014 or 2013? If so, how much cash did it spend to reacquire the shares?

(c) Basic EPS of $1.77 for 2014 was reported in the chapter in Illustration 14-11. How much was basic EPS for 2013? Did EPS improve or weaken in 2014?

(d) Did Corus report any fully diluted EPS in fiscal 2014 and 2013? If yes, what was the difference between these amounts and the basic EPS in each year?

(e) Corus's price-earnings ratio for 2014 was reported in the chapter in Illustration 14-12. The price-earnings ratio for 2013 was 13.2 times (based on a market value per share of $25.25 on August 30, 2013). Did the price-earnings ratio improve or weaken in 2014? Is your answer consistent with your findings in part (c)? Explain.

(f) Corus's payout ratio for 2014 was reported in the chapter in Illustration 14-13. Calculate its payout ratio for 2013. Explain what caused the difference between the two years.

Interpreting Financial Statements

BYP14–2 Potash Corporation of Saskatchewan Inc., known as PotashCorp, is the world's largest fertilizer enterprise by capacity and a leading supplier to three distinct market categories: agriculture, animal nutrition, and industrial chemicals. PotashCorp completed a share repurchase plan in 2014. Financial information for PotashCorp for the years ended December 31, 2014 and 2013, follows (in millions of U.S. dollars, except per share data):

	2014	2013
Profit for the year	$1,536	$1,785
Shareholders' equity at December 31	$8,792	$9,628
Cash dividends declared during the year	$1,164	$1,146
Number of shares outstanding (at year end)	830.2	856.1
Weighted average number of shares outstanding	838.1	864.6

Instructions

(a) Explain the different effects that a cash dividend, stock dividend, and stock split would have on PotashCorp's assets, liabilities, shareholders' equity, and the number of shares outstanding.

(b) What is the likely reason that PotashCorp has repurchased shares over the past two fiscal years?

(c) During the period of August 2013 and June 2014, PotashCorp instituted a share reacquisition plan. The company repurchased a total of 43.3 million shares over this period of time. In 2012, the market price per share was $40.48, in 2013 it was $35.02, and in 2014 it was $41.07. In 2012, the dividend declared per share was $0.70; in 2013, $1.33; and in 2014, $1.40. Comment on the impact the reacquisition may have had on the market price and dividends per share.

(d) Based on the following excerpt from the PotashCorp notes to the financial statements for 2014 on the share reacquisition, did the company pay more than the average per share amount or less than the average per share amount? Explain.

	2014	2013
Common shares repurchased for cancellation	29,200,892	14,145,100
Average price per share	$ 35.31	$ 31.46
Repurchase resulted in a reduction of:		
Share capital	$ 53	$ 25
Contributed surplus[1]	2	82
Retained earnings[1]	976	338
Total cost	$ 1,031	$ 445

[1] The excess of net cost over the book value of the shares.

(e) Calculate the return on shareholders' equity, earnings per share, and payout ratio for the shareholders for 2014 and 2013. Comment on the company's profitability. Shareholders' equity at December 31, 2012, was $9,912.

▶ Critical Thinking

Collaborative Learning Activity

Note to instructor: Additional instructions and material for this group activity can be found on the Instructor Resource Site and in *WileyPLUS.*

BYP14–3 In this group activity, you will complete a statement of changes in shareholders' equity and recreate the journal entries underlying those changes through your analysis of the incomplete information given.

Communication Activity

BYP14–4 Earnings per share is the most commonly cited financial ratio. Indeed, share prices rise and fall in reaction to a company's earnings per share. The price-earnings ratio is also published in many newspapers' stock market listings.

Instructions

Write a memo explaining why earnings per share and the price-earnings ratio are so important to investors. Explain how both ratios are calculated and how they relate to each other. Include in your memo an explanation of how to interpret a high or low price-earnings ratio. Also comment on why you think earnings per share is not required to be reported under ASPE.

"All About You" Activity

BYP14–5 In the "All About You" feature, we learned about investing in shares of a company. You have recently inherited $10,000 and you are considering investing in **Canadian Tire Corporation, Limited's** common shares and you want to learn more about the company.

Instructions

Go to Canadian Tire's website at http://corp.canadiantire.ca, click on "Investors," and then click on "Annual Reports" via "Financial Reporting," and select the "2014 Annual Report." (*Note:* If you are not able to find the annual report on the Canadian Tire site—if, for example, Canadian Tire's shares are no longer publicly traded, then it may remove previously published annual reports and financial statements from its website—it is always available on SEDAR. See part [g] of this problem for instructions on how to use SEDAR.)

(a) Go to page 7 of the 2014 annual report, "Company and industry overview." What are Canadian Tire's distinct sources of revenue? How might this information help you with your investment decision?

(b) Go to page 5 of the 2014 annual report, which shows the table of contents of the "Management's Discussion and Analysis" (MD&A). According to the table of contents, what information is included in Canadian Tire's MD&A? How might the MD&A help you with your investment decision?

(c) Go to page 13 of the 2014 annual report, "4.0 Historical Performance Highlights." What were the cash dividends per share declared in 2014 and 2013? How might this information be helpful with your investment decision?

(d) Go to page 64 of the 2014 annual report, "Consolidated Statements of Income." What was Canadian Tire's basic earnings per share at December 31, 2014?

(e) On the "Investors" page of Canadian Tire's website, click on "Shareholders." What information is provided in this section of Canadian Tire's website? Go to "Stock Information" and click on "Historical Stock Quote Lookup" for the security "CTC.A." What was Canadian Tire's share price at December 31, 2014?

(f) Calculate Canadian Tire's price-earnings ratio at December 31, 2014.

(g) Go to www.sedar.com and click on "English." Click on "Issuer Profiles." Under "Companies," click on "C" and then scroll down and click on "Canadian Tire Corporation, Limited." Which stock exchange is Canadian Tire listed on? What is Canadian Tire's stock symbol? Who are Canadian Tire's auditors?

(h) On the Canadian Tire page you found in part (g), click on "View This Company's Documents." What types of documents are provided on this site?

(i) Go to www.google.ca/finance and in the search field, type in Canadian Tire's stock symbol "CTC", press enter to access the Canadian Tire Corporation Limited financial analysis. Scroll down the page and click on "More from Reuters". On this page, click the tab "Financials." What is Canadian Tire's most recent price-earnings ratio? What is the most recent industry average price-earnings ratio? Comment on Canadian Tire's price-earnings ratio compared with the industry average.

Santé Smoothie Saga

(**Note:** This is a continuation of the Santé Smoothie Saga from Chapters 1 through 13.)

BYP14–6 Now that Natalie is a shareholder of the bakery and the smoothies are becoming a significant portion of the business revenues, Natalie and her parents have changed the name of the company to Santé Smoothies & Sweets Ltd.

Natalie is planning on completing college in April 2019. In the meantime, she tries to spend approximately 20 hours a week at Santé Smoothies & Sweets. She is developing an understanding of all of the business operations so she can step into her new position as administrator on May 1, 2019. There are challenges every day when operating a business and she is thrilled to be a part of the process. Janet and Brian are also excited to have Natalie on board and believe that Natalie's input has been instrumental in helping make some of their critical business decisions.

To ensure that Natalie does not consider other business opportunities and leave the business, Janet and Brian would like to provide Natalie with a greater ownership interest in Santé Smoothies & Sweets, Ltd. One option that is being discussed is the buyback of shares by Santé Smoothies & Sweets, Ltd. from Janet and Brian to enable Natalie to hold a one-third ownership interest in the bakery without having to purchase additional shares.

Recall that on April 1, 2018, Natalie purchased 10 shares of Santé Sweets Ltd. for $1,200 per share and that Brian and Janet each own 100 of the remaining 200 shares.

The shareholders' equity accounts of Santé Smoothies & Sweets, Ltd. are as follows:

Common shares	$ 12,200
Retained earnings	241,026

Janet and Brian are thinking that it might be best for all three of them to each own 10 shares of Santé Smoothies & Sweets, Ltd. They are confused, however, about the process of shares being reacquired and have come to you with the following questions:

1. If Santé Smoothies & Sweets, Ltd. reacquires the common shares we hold, how will a fair value for each common share reacquired be determined?

2. Natalie has recently purchased shares in Santé Smoothies & Sweets, Ltd. for $1,200 per share. Is this amount a fair value to use as a purchase price for reacquisition of the shares? Why or why not?

3. How much cash will Santé Smoothies & Sweets, Ltd. need to reacquire the shares that we hold if we assume a price of $1,200 per share?

4. Last year the business paid total dividends of $85,000. If our shares are reacquired, will Santé Smoothies & Sweets, Ltd. be able to pay a dividend next year? Do you think there will be enough in retained earnings to pay a dividend? Will the amount of the dividend we each receive change once Natalie owns a one-third interest in the company?

5. If we choose not to have the company reacquire our shares, then how can we ensure that Natalie stays on with us?

Instructions

(a) Answer Janet and Brian's questions.

(b) Prepare the journal entry to record the reacquisition of shares by Santé Smoothies & Sweets, Ltd. from Janet and Brian assuming that $1,200 per share is a fair value.

(c) Calculate the amount of share capital after the shares have been reacquired from Janet and Brian and the average per share amount.

ANSWERS TO CHAPTER QUESTIONS

ANSWERS TO ACCOUNTING IN ACTION INSIGHT QUESTIONS

Ethics Insight, p. 731

Q: Is there anything unethical about Ramsey's intentions or actions? Explain.

A: There is nothing unethical in issuing a stock dividend. However, the president's order to write a press release convincing the shareholders that the stock dividend is just as good as a cash dividend is unethical. A stock dividend is not a cash dividend and does not necessarily place the shareholder in the same position. A stock dividend is not paid in cash, it is "paid" in shares. This does provide a future potential opportunity to receive cash if the additional shares can be profitably sold.

Across the Organization, p. 733

Q: If a company announces a reverse stock split, is this considered a positive or negative sign about its future?

A: Although a company declares a reverse stock split because its share price is unacceptably low—and that is usually because a company is not doing well—the reverse split doesn't change whether or not the company can improve its performance in the future. A reverse stock split, similar to a normal stock split, doesn't change anything about the company, because the total value of the company remains the same. Therefore, it can be argued that a reverse split shouldn't be considered either positive or negative.

All About You, p. 751

Q: If you were thinking of investing in a company, where might you find information about the company's dividend policy, its profitability, and its share price?

A: The company website will usually provide the company's annual report, which includes information about the company's performance and future plans in the Management Discussion and Analysis. As well, the annual report will include the financial statements, which provide information about the company's profitability and dividend policy. Some company websites also provide information on the share price. Another source is www.sedar.com, an official website that publishes public company annual reports that are filed with the Canadian Securities Administrators. As well, there are independent financial websites that provide share price information and comparable financial ratio information. Investors can also subscribe to services to obtain financial research reports on companies.

ANSWERS TO SELF-STUDY QUESTIONS

1. d   2. d   3. a   4. c   5. b   6. d   7. c   8. d   9. c   10. c

15 NON-CURRENT LIABILITIES

CHAPTER PREVIEW ▶ While all companies have liabilities, excessive liabilities can be dangerous. In this chapter, we will explain the accounting for the major types of non-current liabilities reported on the balance sheet. Non-current liabilities are obligations that are expected to be paid more than one year in the future. These liabilities include bonds, instalment notes, and lease obligations.

FEATURE STORY ▶ A NEW LEASE ON AIRCRAFT ACCOUNTING

CALGARY, Alta.—Many companies choose to lease rather than buy major items of property, plant, and equipment, such as buildings and vehicles. Airlines will typically have a combination of leased and owned aircraft to fit their needs. With a fleet of over 120 aircraft, about one-third of which are leased, Calgary-based WestJet has significant lease obligations. Those lease obligations will likely continue to grow because the airline plans to have a fleet of up to 219 aircraft by 2027. Yet, are these long-term liabilities reflected on its statement of financial position?

As this text went to press, accounting standards required leases to be reported as one of two types: operating leases or finance leases. To be classified as a finance lease, certain criteria must be met: the company takes ownership of the asset or the company has the option to purchase the asset at a bargain price at the end of the lease term, the lease needs to be for a substantial period of the asset's estimated economic life, and the lease payments need to represent a substantial portion of the asset's fair value. In WestJet's case, its leased aircraft have not met the test for a finance lease because there is no bargain purchase option; the airline will not own the aircraft at the end of the lease's term; the leases range from 8 to 14 years, just a portion of the aircraft's economic lives; and the lease payments are only a portion of the aircraft's fair value.

For these reasons, WestJet has accounted for its aircraft leases as operating leases, reporting the aircraft rental expense—that is, the lease payments—on its statement of earnings. This means neither the planes themselves nor the related long-term debt is reported on its statement of financial position, but instead they are included in a lease commitment note in the financial statements. This practice of keeping certain liabilities off a company's balance sheet is called off–balance sheet financing. In its notes to the financial statements, WestJet has adjusted its debt to include off–balance sheet aircraft operating leases, which amounted to $1.4 billion in 2014.

WestJet's reporting practice may change, however, as changes to IFRS requiring all leases to be classified as finance leases have been proposed. The proposed changes would affect WestJet's reporting of its leased assets and liabilities. If leases are classified as finance leases, the airplanes would be reported as assets, with the corresponding liability.

Before the expected IFRS change, WestJet said that treating all aircraft leases as finance leases would make it easier for readers of financial statements to make comparisons among all airlines.

Sources: WestJet 2014 annual report; WestJet corporate website, www.westjet.com; Deloitte, "IFRS Project Highlights—Leases," April 2015.

Getty Images/Roberto Machado Noa

CHAPTER OUTLINE | LEARNING OBJECTIVES

The chapter is organized as follows:

1	Describe the characteristics of bonds.	**Bonds Payable** • Types of bonds • Bond issuance • Bond trading	**DO IT 1** Bond terminology
2	Calculate the price of a bond.	**Bond Pricing** • Discount or premium on bonds	**DO IT 2** Determining the issue price of a bond
3	Account for bond transactions.	**Accounting for Bond Issues** • Issuing bonds at face value • Issuing bonds at a discount • Issuing bonds at a premium • Issuing bonds at a discount versus at a premium • Bond interest accruals	**DO IT 3** Accrual and amortization of interest
4	Account for the retirement of bonds.	**Accounting for Bond Retirements** • Redeeming bonds at maturity • Redeeming bonds before maturity	**DO IT 4** Bond redemption
5	Account for instalment notes payable.	**Instalment Notes Payable** • Fixed principal payments • Blended payments • Current and non-current portions	**DO IT 5** Preparing an instalment schedule and recording note issuance
6	Account for leases.	**Lease Liabilities** • Operating leases • Finance leases	**DO IT 6** Lease liability
7	Explain and illustrate the methods for the presentation and analysis of non-current liabilities.	**Statement Presentation and Analysis** • Presentation • Analysis	**DO IT 7** Debt ratios

LEARNING OBJECTIVE 1

Describe the characteristics of bonds.

Bonds Payable

Alternative terminology Non-current liabilities are also referred to as *long-term liabilities.*

Non-current liabilities are obligations that a company expects to pay more than one year in the future. Common examples of non-current liabilities include bonds payable, instalment notes payable, and finance leases.

Just as people need money for long periods of time, so do companies. Sometimes, large corporations and governments need more money than the average bank can lend for certain types of projects, such as purchasing another company or constructing dams and power generating stations. One solution to raise money is to issue debt securities such as bonds. **Bonds** represent a promise to repay a specified amount in the future, along with a promise to pay periodic interest at a specified rate. Bonds may be issued to thousands of investors in small denominations (usually $1,000 or multiples of $1,000). In this way, thousands of investors each lend part of the funds needed.

For a corporation that wants long-term financing, issuing bonds offers some advantages over issuing and selling shares. As Illustration 15-1 shows, one reason to issue bonds is that they do not affect shareholder control. Because bondholders do not have voting rights, owners can raise capital with bonds and still maintain corporate control. In addition, bonds are attractive to corporations because the cost of bond interest is tax-deductible. Dividends do not provide the same tax benefit.

▶ILLUSTRATION **15-1**
Advantages of debt over equity financing

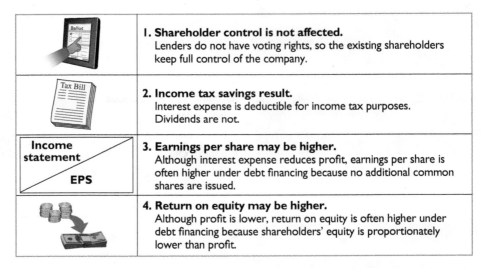

	1. Shareholder control is not affected. Lenders do not have voting rights, so the existing shareholders keep full control of the company.
	2. Income tax savings result. Interest expense is deductible for income tax purposes. Dividends are not.
	3. Earnings per share may be higher. Although interest expense reduces profit, earnings per share is often higher under debt financing because no additional common shares are issued.
	4. Return on equity may be higher. Although profit is lower, return on equity is often higher under debt financing because shareholders' equity is proportionately lower than profit.

To illustrate an advantage of bond financing, assume that Microsystems Inc. is considering two plans for financing the construction of a new $5-million plant. Plan A involves issuing 200,000 common shares at the current market price of $25 per share. Plan B involves issuing $5 million of 4% bonds at face value. Income before interest and taxes on the new plant will be $1.5 million. Income taxes are expected to be 30%. Microsystems currently has 100,000 common shares outstanding and shareholders' equity of $2,500,000. Illustration 15-2 shows the alternative effects on earnings per share and return on equity.

▶ILLUSTRATION **15-2**
Comparison of effects of issuing equity versus bonds

	Plan A: Issue Equity	Plan B: Issue Bonds
Profit before interest and income tax	$1,500,000	$1,500,000
Interest expense	0	200,000
Profit before income tax	1,500,000	1,300,000
Income tax expense	450,000	390,000
Profit	$1,050,000	$ 910,000
Number of shares	300,000	100,000
Earnings per share	$3.50	$9.10
Shareholders' equity	$8,550,000	$3,410,000
Return on equity	12%	27%

Profit is $140,000 ($1,050,000 − $910,000) lower with the long-term debt financing. However, when this profit is spread over 200,000 fewer shares, earnings per share jumps from $3.50 per share to $9.10 per share.

After seeing the effect of debt on earnings per share, one might ask why companies do not rely exclusively on debt financing rather than equity financing. The answer is that debt is riskier than equity because interest must be paid regularly each period and the principal of the debt must be paid at maturity. If a company is unable to pay its interest or principal, creditors could force the company to sell its assets to repay its liabilities. In contrast, if equity is issued, a company is not required to pay dividends or repay the shareholders' investment.

Even if doing so is riskier, most companies still choose to issue debt. They do this because money that is borrowed increases earnings per share and it also produces a higher return on equity for the shareholders. You may have heard the saying about "using other people's money to make money." In general, debt can increase the return on equity if the company can borrow at one rate and invest the borrowed money in company operations that earn a higher rate. Borrowing at one rate and investing at a different rate is known as **financial leverage**. Financial leverage is said to be "positive" if the rate of return is higher than the rate of borrowing. It is said to be "negative" if the rate of return is lower than the rate of borrowing.

As we can see in Illustration 15-2, Microsystems' return on equity increases from 12% in Plan A, where equity financing is used, to 27% in Plan B, where debt financing is used. Even though profit is lower under debt financing, there is much less equity to spread the profit across. If equity financing is used, shareholders' equity is $8,550,000. If debt financing is used, shareholders' equity is only $3,410,000.

ACCOUNTING IN ACTION
ALL ABOUT YOU INSIGHT

Getty Images/Yin Yang

Having enough cash to pay for education and living expenses while going to college or university is often a problem for students. One option is to use student loans. The federal, provincial, and territorial governments as well as private financial institutions all offer student loan programs.

Just like a business, a student can benefit from financial leverage, by borrowing for an education that will result in higher future earnings. Research shows that post-secondary graduates are more likely to be employed, and they earn more than those who do not continue their studies past high school. Over their working life, a college graduate will earn $394,000 more than a high school graduate, while a bachelor's degree holder will earn $745,800 more, according to the former Canada Millennium Scholarship Foundation.

While student loan programs offer interest-free financing while the student is in school, eventually they have to be paid. Just as with businesses, too much debt can result in graduates struggling to make their loan payments. With the average Canadian student graduating with around $27,000 in debt, paying it off quickly is a smart financial move.

Sources: Trevor Melanson, "Is Getting a Bachelor's Degree Still Worth It?," *Canadian Business,* April 24, 2014; Joseph Berger and Andrew Parkin, "The Value of a Degree: Education Employment and Earnings in Canada," *The Price of Knowledge: Access and Student Finance in Canada*, vol. 4, chapter 1, 2009.

Q What should you consider in your decision about how much is appropriate to borrow for your education?

TYPES OF BONDS

When an entity issues bonds, they may be assigned different features. The following is an explanation of the common features that may be assigned to bonds.

Secured and Unsecured Bonds

Secured bonds have specific assets pledged as **collateral** by the bond issuer. For example, a bond secured by real estate is called a **mortgage bond**. A bond secured by specific assets set aside to redeem (retire) the bonds is called a **sinking fund bond**.

Unsecured bonds (also called **debentures**) are issued against the general credit of the borrower. Companies with good credit ratings use these bonds extensively.

Convertible and Callable Bonds

Bonds that can be converted into common shares at the bondholder's option are **convertible bonds**. The conversion feature generally is attractive to bond buyers. Bonds that the issuing company can redeem (buy back) at a stated dollar amount prior to maturity are **callable bonds**, also known as **redeemable bonds**. A call feature is included in nearly all corporate bond issues.

BOND ISSUANCE

Bonds are similar to shares in that they are sold to, and purchased by, investors on organized securities exchanges. As previously stated, bonds are usually sold in small denominations ($1,000 or multiples of $1,000). As a result, bonds attract many investors.

Bond interest rates are linked to the bond's risk level. Normally, the higher the credit risk of the company issuing the bonds, the higher the interest rate of the bonds. For example, banks might pay 1% or 2% on a term deposit, because there is almost no risk. On the other hand, a corporate bond with a strong credit rating might pay 3% or 4%. A corporate bond with a lower credit rating will likely have to pay a higher rate because of the higher risk. Interest rates vary with risk, but they also vary with duration, the type of bond, the general state of the economy, and many other factors.

In a corporation, the board of directors must approve the bond issue. In authorizing the bond issue, the board of directors must state the number of bonds to be authorized (the total number of bonds the company is allowed to sell), the total face value, the contractual interest rate, and the maturity date. As happens with issues of share capital, the total number of bonds authorized is often more than the number of bonds the company plans to issue immediately. This is done intentionally to help ensure that the company will have the flexibility it needs to meet future cash requirements by selling more bonds.

The **face value** of the bonds is the amount that the company (known as the issuer) must pay at the **maturity date** (the date on which the final payment is due). The face value is also called the **par value** and **maturity value**. The **contractual interest rate** is the rate that is used to determine the amount of interest the borrower pays and the investor receives. The contractual interest rate is commonly known as the **coupon interest rate** or **stated interest rate**. Usually, the contractual rate is stated as an annual rate and interest is paid semi-annually. For example, if the contractual interest rate on a bond is 5% semi-annually, interest is paid twice a year at a rate of 2.5% (5% × $^{6}/_{12}$).

All of these details are included in a **bond certificate**, which is issued to investors to provide evidence of an investor's credit claim against the company. As shown in Illustration 15-3, a bond certificate provides the following information: name of the issuer, face value, contractual interest rate, and maturity date. Usually an investment company that specializes in selling securities sells the bonds for the issuing company.

ACCOUNTING IN ACTION
ETHICS INSIGHT

Some companies try to minimize the amount of debt reported on their balance sheet by not reporting certain types of commitments such as liabilities. This subject is of intense interest in the financial community. As an example, Lehman Brothers, a giant investment company in the United States, announced in September 2008 that it would file for bankruptcy protection after suffering huge losses in the mortgage market. In 2010, the bankruptcy examiner's report stated that Lehman's accounting had misled investors. One of the tricks that Lehman used was to temporarily transfer investment assets to a related company in exchange for cash. The company then used the cash to temporarily reduce its liabilities by paying off debt, thus making its balance sheet look better than it was. After the company's financial statements were published, it borrowed the cash again and took back the assets.

Q How could paying off debt and then immediately borrowing again, right after the financial statements are published, mislead investors?

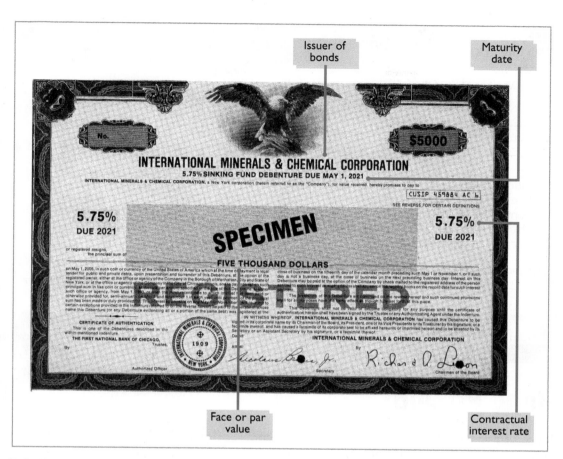

▶ILLUSTRATION **15-3**
Bond certificate

Issuer of bonds

Maturity date

Face or par value

Contractual interest rate

BOND TRADING

A corporation records the bond transactions when it issues (sells) or redeems (buys back) bonds.
When bondholders convert bonds into common shares, the corporation also records the bond transactions. However, corporate bonds, like share capital, may also be traded on an organized securities exchange. When bondholders sell their bond investments to other investors, the issuing firm receives no further money on the transaction, nor does it journalize the transaction (although it does keep records of the names of bondholders in some cases). Because bondholders can sell their bonds to other investors, they are able to convert their bonds into cash at any time by selling the bonds at the current market price. The following shows an example of bond prices and yields, which are published daily in the financial press.

Issuer	Coupon	Coupon Frequency	Maturity Date	Price	Yield
Bell CDA	6.100	S	2035-Mar-16	115.44	4.95

Bond prices are quoted as a percentage of the bonds' face value, which is usually $1,000. For example, if a bond was sold for 115.44, this means $1,154.40 ($1,000 × 115.44%) was the selling price, or **market value**, of each $1,000 bond. This yields a **market interest rate of 4.95%**. The **market interest rate** is the rate that investors demand for lending their money. Note these bonds are selling at a premium because the market interest rate is lower than the contractual interest rate. We will learn more about market interest rates and bond premiums in the next section.

Alternative terminology Market interest rate or yield is also referred to as the *effective rate*.

KEY BOND TERMINOLOGY

Face value The amount that the company (known as the issuer) must pay at the maturity date. The face value is also called the **par value** or **maturity value**.

Contractual interest rate The rate used to determine the amount of interest the borrower pays and the investor receives. Also commonly known as the **coupon interest rate** or **stated interest rate**.

Market interest rate The rate that investors demand for lending their money. Also known as the **effective rate**.

BEFORE YOU GO ON...DO IT   **1**   **Bond Terminology**

State whether each of the following statements is true or false.

_____ 1. A mortgage bond is an example of a secured bond.
_____ 2. Unsecured bonds are also known as debenture bonds.
_____ 3. The stated rate is the rate investors demand for lending funds.
_____ 4. The face value is the amount of principal the issuing company must pay at the maturity date.
_____ 5. The market price of a bond is equal to its maturity value.

Action Plan
- Review the types of bonds and the basic terms associated with bonds.

Solution
1. True. 2. True. 3. False. The stated rate is the contractual interest rate used to determine the amount of cash interest the borrower pays. 4. True. 5. False. The market price of a bond is the value at which it should sell in the marketplace. As a result, the selling price of the bond and its maturity value are often different.

Related exercise material: BE15-1 and E15-1.

LEARNING OBJECTIVE   **2**   Calculate the price of a bond.

Bond Pricing

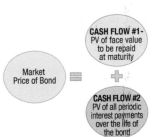

2017
$1 million

≠

2037
$1 million

Same dollars at different times are not equal.

Helpful hint The market price of a bond is the sum of the discounted future cash flows, which are (1) the amount to be repaid at maturity and (2) the periodic interest payments.

If you were an investor wanting to purchase a bond, how would you determine how much to pay? To be more specific, assume that Candlestick Inc. issues a zero-interest bond (pays no interest) with a face value of $1 million due in five years. For this bond, the only cash you receive is $1 million at the end of five years. Would you pay $1 million for this bond? We hope not! One million dollars received five years from now is not the same as $1 million received today.

The reason you should not pay $1 million relates to the **time value of money**. If you had $1 million today, you could invest it. From that investment, you would earn interest. At the end of five years, your investment would be worth much more than $1 million. If someone were to pay you $1 million five years from now, you would want to find out its equivalent today. In other words, you would want to determine how much must be invested today at current interest rates to have $1 million in five years. That amount—what must be invested today at a specific rate of interest over a specific amount of time—is called the **present value**.

The **present value (PV) of a bond is the price or market value at which it should sell in the marketplace.** This is determined by discounting the future cash flows of a bond. The future cash flows are as follows:

1. The face value (amount) of the bond to be repaid at maturity
2. The periodic interest payments at the stated interest rate over the life of the bond

To illustrate, assume that on January 1, 2017, Candlestick Inc. issues $1 million of 5% bonds due in five years, with interest payable semi-annually. The purchaser of the bonds would receive two cash inflows:

1. They will receive the principal of $1 million in five years (the bond's maturity).
2. They will also receive the periodic interest payments of 5% semi-annually (the contractual interest rate) over the five years the bonds are outstanding.

Interest is calculated as follows:

CASH FLOW #1
PV of face value to be repaid at maturity

Market Price of Bond = +

CASH FLOW #2
PV of all periodic interest payments over the life of the bond

Face Value of Bond	×	Annual Interest Rate	×	Time in Terms of One Year	=	Interest

Also recall that interest rates are stated in annual terms. Therefore, for Candlestick, the interest payments are as follows:

$$\$1,000,000 \times 5\% \times {}^{6}/_{12} \text{ months} = \$25,000$$

Illustration 15-4 shows the time diagram for both cash flows.

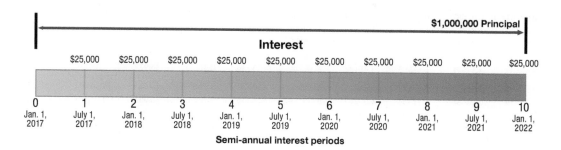

▸ILLUSTRATION 15-4
Time diagram of bond cash flows

Note that there is no interest payment on January 1, 2017—time period 0—because the bonds have not been outstanding for any period of time, so no interest has been incurred.

We will now calculate the present value of Candlestick's bonds. To do this, we will use the present value factors from the present value tables found here. Both tables are required to calculate the price of a bond. The PV-1 Table is used to calculate the present value of a future lump sum amount. The PV-2 table is used to determine the present value of a future stream of cash payments. Further explanation regarding these tables is presented in Appendix PV at the end of this book.

TABLE PV-1
PRESENT VALUE OF 1
$$PV = \frac{1}{(1 + i)^n}$$

(n) Periods	1.5%	2%	2.5%	3%	3.5%	4%	5%	6%	7%	8%	9%	10%
1	0.98522	0.98039	0.97561	0.97087	0.96618	0.96154	0.95238	0.94340	0.93458	0.92593	0.91743	0.90909
2	0.97066	0.96117	0.95181	0.94260	0.93351	0.92456	0.90703	0.89000	0.87344	0.85734	0.84168	0.82645
3	0.95632	0.94232	0.92860	0.91514	0.90194	0.88900	0.86384	0.83962	0.81630	0.79383	0.77218	0.75131
4	0.94218	0.92385	0.90595	0.88849	0.87144	0.85480	0.82270	0.79209	0.76290	0.73503	0.70843	0.68301
5	0.92826	0.90573	0.88385	0.86261	0.84197	0.82193	0.78353	0.74726	0.71299	0.68058	0.64993	0.62092
6	0.91454	0.88797	0.86230	0.83748	0.81350	0.79031	0.74622	0.70496	0.66634	0.63017	0.59627	0.56447
7	0.90103	0.87056	0.84127	0.81309	0.78599	0.75992	0.71068	0.66506	0.62275	0.58349	0.54703	0.51316
8	0.88771	0.85349	0.82075	0.78941	0.75941	0.73069	0.67684	0.62741	0.58201	0.54027	0.50187	0.46651
9	0.87459	0.83676	0.80073	0.76642	0.73373	0.70259	0.64461	0.59190	0.54393	0.50025	0.46043	0.42410
10	0.86167	0.82035	0.78120	0.74409	0.70892	0.67556	0.61391	0.55839	0.50835	0.46319	0.42241	0.38554
11	0.84893	0.80426	0.76214	0.72242	0.68495	0.64958	0.58468	0.52679	0.47509	0.42888	0.38753	0.35049
12	0.83639	0.78849	0.74356	0.70138	0.66178	0.62460	0.55684	0.49697	0.44401	0.39711	0.35553	0.31863
13	0.82403	0.77303	0.72542	0.68095	0.63940	0.60057	0.53032	0.46884	0.41496	0.36770	0.32618	0.28966
14	0.81185	0.75788	0.70773	0.66112	0.61778	0.57748	0.50507	0.44230	0.38782	0.34046	0.29925	0.26333
15	0.79985	0.74301	0.69047	0.64186	0.59689	0.55526	0.48102	0.41727	0.36245	0.31524	0.27454	0.23939
16	0.78803	0.72845	0.67362	0.62317	0.57671	0.53391	0.45811	0.39365	0.33873	0.29189	0.25187	0.21763
17	0.77639	0.71416	0.65720	0.60502	0.55720	0.51337	0.43630	0.37136	0.31657	0.27027	0.23107	0.19784
18	0.76491	0.70016	0.64117	0.58739	0.53836	0.49363	0.41552	0.35034	0.29586	0.25025	0.21199	0.17986
19	0.75361	0.68643	0.62553	0.57029	0.52016	0.47464	0.39573	0.33051	0.27651	0.23171	0.19449	0.16351
20	0.74247	0.67297	0.61027	0.55368	0.50257	0.45639	0.37689	0.31180	0.25842	0.21455	0.17843	0.14864

TABLE PV-2 **PRESENT VALUE OF AN ANNUITY OF 1** $PV = PMT\left(\dfrac{1 - (1 + i)^{-n}}{i}\right)$												

(n) Periods	1.5%	2%	2.5%	3%	3.5%	4%	5%	6%	7%	8%	9%	10%
1	0.98522	0.98039	0.97561	0.97087	0.96618	0.96154	0.95238	0.94340	0.93458	0.92593	0.91743	0.90909
2	1.95588	1.94156	1.92742	1.91347	1.89969	1.88609	1.85941	1.83339	1.80802	1.78326	1.75911	1.73554
3	2.91220	2.88388	2.85602	2.82861	2.80164	2.77509	2.72325	2.67301	2.62432	2.57710	2.53129	2.48685
4	3.85438	3.80773	3.76197	3.71710	3.67308	3.62990	3.54595	3.46511	3.38721	3.31213	3.23972	3.16987
5	4.78264	4.71346	4.64583	4.57971	4.51505	4.45182	4.32948	4.21236	4.10020	3.99271	3.88965	3.79079
6	5.69719	5.60143	5.50813	5.41719	5.32855	5.24214	5.07569	4.91732	4.76654	4.62288	4.48592	4.35526
7	6.59821	6.47199	6.34939	6.23028	6.11454	6.00205	5.78637	5.58238	5.38929	5.20637	5.03295	4.86842
8	7.48593	7.32548	7.17014	7.01969	6.87396	6.73274	6.46321	6.20979	5.97130	5.74664	5.53482	5.33493
9	8.36052	8.16224	7.97087	7.78611	7.60769	7.43533	7.10782	6.80169	6.51523	6.24689	5.99525	5.75902
10	9.22218	8.98259	8.75206	8.53020	8.31661	8.11090	7.72173	7.36009	7.02358	6.71008	6.41766	6.14457
11	10.07112	9.78685	9.51421	9.25262	9.00155	8.76048	8.30641	7.88687	7.49867	7.13896	6.80519	6.49506
12	10.90751	10.57534	10.25776	9.95400	9.66333	9.38507	8.86325	8.38384	7.94269	7.53608	7.16073	6.81369
13	11.73153	11.34837	10.98318	10.63496	10.30274	9.98565	9.39357	8.85268	8.35765	7.90378	7.48690	7.10336
14	12.54338	12.10625	11.69091	11.29607	10.92052	10.56312	9.89864	9.29498	8.74547	8.24424	7.78615	7.36669
15	13.34323	12.84926	12.38138	11.93794	11.51741	11.11839	10.37966	9.71225	9.10791	8.55948	8.06069	7.60608
16	14.13126	13.57771	13.05500	12.56110	12.09412	11.65230	10.83777	10.10590	9.44665	8.85137	8.31256	7.82371
17	14.90765	14.29187	13.71220	13.16612	12.65132	12.16567	11.27407	10.47726	9.76322	9.12164	8.54363	8.02155
18	15.67256	14.99203	14.35336	13.75351	13.18968	12.65930	11.68959	10.82760	10.05909	9.37189	8.75563	8.20141
19	16.42617	15.67846	14.97889	14.32380	13.70984	13.13394	12.08532	11.15812	10.33560	9.60360	8.95011	8.36492
20	17.16864	16.35143	15.58916	14.87747	14.21240	13.59033	12.46221	11.46992	10.59401	9.81815	9.12855	8.51356

STEP 1: Calculate the present value of the face value of the bond

In this case, determine the present value of the $1 million (face value) to be received in five years. To do this:

- Use Table PV-1 (the present value of $1) to determine the correct factor to use to calculate the present value of the face value, which is a single payment, paid at maturity. **The appropriate factor is found at the intersection of the number of periods (n) and the interest rate (i).**

  - **The number of periods (n) is the number of interest payments to be made over the life of the bond.** In the Candlestick example, interest is paid semi-annually over the five years to maturity. This means that there are 10 semi-annual interest periods.

$$n = 10 \text{ or } (5 \times 2)$$

  - **The interest rate (i), is stated for the year but it will be paid semi-annually.** Therefore, the 5% annual market interest rate means that there is a 2.5% semi-annual market rate.

$$[i = 2.5\% \text{ or } (5\% \times {}^{6}/_{12})]$$

- Using n = 10 and i = 2.5%, the factor where the two numbers intersect is **0.78120**.

Therefore, the present value of $1,000,000 (the face value) of the bond to be received in five years is

$$\$1,000,000 \times 0.78120 \ (n = 10, i = 2.5\%) = \mathbf{\$781,200}$$

STEP 2: Calculate the present value of the interest payments

In this case, determine the present value of the interest payments of $25,000 to be made semi-annually over the next 5 years:

- Use Table PV-2 (the present value of an annuity of 1) to calculate the present value of the interest. Again, the appropriate factor is found at the intersection of the number of periods (n) and the interest rate (i).
- The present value factor is found using the same number of periods (n) and interest rate (i) as is used to calculate the present value of the principal.
- For Candlestick, the present value factor to be used to calculate the present value of the interest payments for n = 10 and i = 2.5% is **8.7520**. (To avoid rounding issues in this illustration we will truncate this factor to four decimal places.)

Helpful hint The bonds' face value and contractual interest rate are *always* used to calculate the interest payment and the market interest rate is *always* used to determine the present value.

Therefore, the present value of $25,000 (interest payments) received for each of 10 periods

$$\$25,000 \times 8.7520 \ (n = 10, \ i = 2.5\%) = \mathbf{\$218,800}$$

Cash Flow #1–
$781,200

STEP 3: Add the results of step one and step two together:

Market price of bond	= Cash Flow #1	+ Cash Flow #2
$1,000,000	= $781,200	+ $218,800

Market
Price of Bond
$1,000,000

Cash Flow #2–
$218,800

Note that the bonds' face value and contractual interest rate are always used to calculate the interest payment. While the contractual interest rate is used to determine the interest payment, **the market interest rate is always used to determine the present value.** In the Candlestick example, the contractual rate and the market rate are the same. When these two rates are the same, the present value (market value) of the bonds equals the face value.

The present value can also be determined mathematically using a financial calculator or spreadsheet program. The same variables as described above are used. The inputs (variables) required to calculate present value are the **future value** (*FV*), which is the face amount to be paid at maturity; the market rate of interest per interest period (*i*); the number of interest periods (*n*); and the interest payment (*PMT*).

In the Candlestick example, the following variables would be used:

Future value (*FV*) = $1,000,000
Number of semi-annual interest periods (*n*) = 10 (5 years × 2)
Semi-annual interest rate (*i*) = 2.5% (5% × $^6/_{12}$)
Interest payments (*PMT*) = $25,000

The specific methodology and required settings differ among financial calculators, so it is important to read the manual before using yours to calculate present values. However, the inputs and the concepts are the same for all calculators. You should be aware that the present value amounts will most likely differ by a few dollars from those calculated using present value tables. This is because the factors in the present value tables are rounded to five decimal places.

DISCOUNT OR PREMIUM ON BONDS

The present value illustration above assumed that the market interest rate and the contractual interest rate paid on the bonds were the same. However, this is rarely the case because market interest rates change daily. They are influenced by the type of bond issued, the state of the economy, current industry conditions, and the company's performance. The market and contractual interest rates are often quite different. As a result, bonds sell below or above face value.

To illustrate, suppose that investors have one of two options: (1) purchase bonds that have just been issued with a contractual interest rate of 6%, or (2) purchase bonds issued at an earlier date with a lower contractual interest rate of 5%. If the bonds are of equal risk, investors will choose the 6% investment. To make the investments equal, investors will therefore demand a rate of interest higher than the 5% contractual interest rate provided in option 2. But investors cannot change the contractual interest rate. What they can do, instead, is pay less than the face value for the bonds. By paying less for the bonds, investors can effectively get the market interest rate of 6%. In these cases, bonds sell at a **discount**.

On the other hand, the market interest rate may be lower than the contractual interest rate. In that case, investors will have to pay more than the face value for the bonds. That is, if the market interest rate is 4% and the contractual interest rate is 5%, the issuer will require more funds from the investors. In these cases, bonds sell at a **premium**. The relationship between bond contractual interest rates and market interest rates, and the resultant selling price, is shown in Illustration 15-5.

Issuing bonds at an amount different from face value is quite common. From the time the bonds are authorized by the board of directors until they are issued, it is unlikely the interest rate will remain the same. By the time a company decides to issue the bonds, prints the bond certificates, and markets the bonds, it will be a coincidence if the market rate and the contractual rate are the same. Thus, the sale of bonds at a discount does not mean that the issuer's financial strength is questionable. Nor does the sale of bonds at a premium indicate superior financial strength. Also, the fluctuations in the market interest rate after the bonds are issued do not have an impact on the accounting for the bond issue.

▶ILLUSTRATION 15-5
Interest rates and bond prices

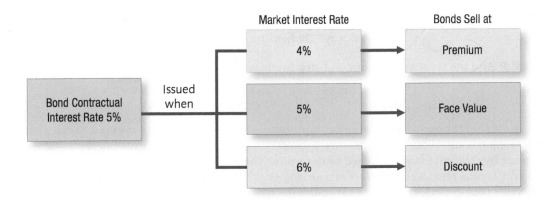

Action Plan

- Identify the key inputs required to determine present value, whether using tables or a financial calculator. Remember to double the number of periods and halve the annual interest rate when the interest is paid semi-annually.
- To calculate the present value (issue price), use the semi-annual market interest rate for (*i*). Use the face value of the bonds and the contractual interest rate to calculate the semi-annual interest payments (*PMT*). The interest payments, which recur periodically, are an annuity. The face value of the bonds is the (*FV*), which is a single sum.

BEFORE YOU GO ON...DO IT ② ▶ **Determining the Issue Price of a Bond**

On January 1, 2017, R & B Inc. issues $500,000 of 10-year, 4% bonds to yield a market interest rate of 5%. Interest is paid semi-annually on January 1 and July 1.

Using present value concepts, calculate the issue price of the bonds. Round all calculations to the nearest dollar. Recall that, when using a financial calculator, cash outflows should be reflected with a negative sign.

Solution

Key inputs: Future value (*FV*) = $500,000
Semi-annual market interest rate (*i*) = 2.5% (5% × 6/12)
Interest payment (*PMT*) = $10,000 ($500,000 × 4% × 6/12)
Number of semi-annual periods (*n*) = 20 (10 × 2)

Present value of $500,000 received in 20 periods	
$500,000 × 0.61027 (*n* = 20, *i* = 2.5)	$305,135
Present value of $10,000 received for each of 20 periods	
$10,000 × 15.58916 (*n* = 20, *i* = 2.5)	155,892
Present value (issue price)	$461,027

Related exercise material: BE15–2, BE15–3, E15–2, E15–3, and E15–4.

LEARNING OBJECTIVE ③ ▶ **Account for bond transactions.**

Accounting for Bond Issues

As previously stated, a corporation records bond transactions when it issues (sells) or redeems (buys back) bonds and when bondholders convert bonds into common shares. We will now look at accounting for bonds at face value, below face value (at a discount), or above face value (at a premium).

ISSUING BONDS AT FACE VALUE

To illustrate the accounting for bonds, let's continue the example discussed in the last section, where Candlestick Inc. issues 5-year, 5%, $1-million bonds on January 1, 2017, to yield a market interest rate of 5%. These bonds are issued at 100 (100% of face value). We calculated that the bonds' market value is equal to the face value.

When the bonds are sold, the incoming cash must be recorded as well as the related liability. Therefore, the entry to record the sale is as follows:

Jan. 1	Cash	1,000,000	
	Bonds Payable		1,000,000
	To record sale of bonds at face value.		

A = L + SE
+1,000,0000 +1,000,0000
↑ Cash flows: +1,000,0000

These bonds payable are reported at **amortized cost** in the non-current liabilities section of the balance sheet because the maturity date (January 1, 2022) is more than one year away. **Amortized cost is the face value of the bonds minus any unamortized discount or plus any unamortized premium.** In this example, because the bonds were issued at face value, the amortized cost is $1 million, the face value of the bonds.

Alternative terminology Amortized cost is also referred to as carrying value or carrying amount

Over the term (life) of the bonds, entries are required to record the bond interest. Interest is payable semi-annually on January 1 and July 1 on the bonds described above. As shown earlier, **the semi-annual interest payment is determined using the face value of the bonds and the contractual interest rate.** In the Candlestick bond example, the interest payment is $25,000 ($1,000,000 [face value] × 5% [contractual rate] × 6/12).

The **effective-interest method of amortization** is used to calculate **interest expense** so that the expense reflects the actual cost of borrowing. **The effective-interest method uses the market interest rate, at the date the bonds were issued, applied to the amortized cost of the bonds payable to determine interest expense.** On July 1, 2017, the first interest payment date, Candlestick will record interest expense of $25,000 ($1,000,000 [amortized cost] × 5% [market rate] × 6/12). In this example, the contractual interest rate is equal to the market rate, so the interest expense is equal to the interest payment. The entry for the interest payment, assuming no previous accrual of interest, is:

July 1	Interest Expense	25,000	
	Cash		25,000
	To record payment of bond interest.		

A = L + SE
−25,000 −25,000
↓ Cash flows: −25,000

At December 31, Candlestick's year end, an adjusting entry is needed to recognize the $25,000 of interest expense incurred since July 1. The entry is as follows:

Dec. 31	Interest Expense	25,000	
	Interest Payable		25,000
	To accrue bond interest.		

A = L + SE
+25,000 −25,000
Cash flows: no effect

Interest payable is classified as a current liability because it is scheduled for payment within the next year. (In fact, it is due the next day in this case.) When the interest is paid on January 1, 2018, Interest Payable is debited and Cash is credited for $25,000.

ISSUING BONDS AT A DISCOUNT

The previous example assumed that the contractual (stated) interest rate and the market (effective) interest rate paid on the bonds were the same. Recall that the **contractual interest rate** is the rate applied to the face (par) value to arrive at the interest paid in a year. The **market interest rate** is the rate investors demand for lending funds to the corporation. Also recall that the contractual interest rate and the market interest rate are often not the same, and therefore bonds sell above or below the face value. When a bond is sold for less than its face value, the difference between its face value and its selling price is called a **discount**.

To illustrate the issue of bonds at a discount, assume that on January 1, 2017, the Candlestick bonds are issued to yield a market interest rate of 6%. Investors will not be interested in buying the Candlestick bonds with a contractual rate of 5%, so the value of the bond will fall below its face value.

To determine the selling price of the bonds, we must determine the variables to input into a calculator or determine the appropriate present value factor per the present value tables. The factors are as follows:

Future value (FV) = $1,000,000
Number of semi-annual interest periods (n) = 10 (5 years × 2)
Semi-annual market interest rate (i) = 3% (6% annual market rate × $^{6}/_{12}$)
Interest payments (PMT) = $25,000 ($1,000,000 × 5% [contractual rate] × $^{6}/_{12}$)

Remember to always use the market interest rate to determine the present value factor (i) and the contractual interest rate to determine the interest payment. Using the present value tables in this chapter, we can determine that the bonds will sell for $957,345 (95.7345% of face value):

Present value of $1 million received in 10 periods	
$1,000,000 × 0.74409 ($n$ = 10, i = 3%)	$744,090
Present value of $25,000 received for each of 10 periods	
$25,000 × 8.53020 ($n$ = 10, i = 3%)	213,255
Present value (market price) of bonds	$957,345

The issue price of $957,345 results in a bond discount of $42,655 ($1,000,000 − $957,345). The entry to record the bond issue is as follows:

A	=	L	+	SE
+957,345		+957,345		

▲ Cash flows: +957,345

Jan. 1	Cash		957,345	
	Bonds Payable			957,345
	To record sale of bonds at a discount.			

You will recall that bonds payable are reported at amortized cost. At the date the bonds are issued, the issue price is equal to amortized cost. In this example, the issue cost of $957,345 is equal to the face value of $1 million less the unamortized discount of $42,655, which, by definition, is the amortized cost.

The issue of bonds below face value causes the total cost of borrowing to differ from the interest paid. That is, the issuing corporation must pay not only the contractual interest rate over the term of the bonds, but also the face value ($1,000,000) at maturity. Therefore, the difference between the issue price and the face value of the bonds—the discount—is an additional cost of borrowing. The company records this additional cost of borrowing as interest expense over the life of the bonds, as shown in Illustration 15-6.

▶ **ILLUSTRATION 15-6**
Total cost of borrowing—bonds issued at a discount

Bonds Issued at a Discount	
Semi-annual interest payments	
($25,000 × 10)	$250,000
Add: Bond discount	42,655
Total cost of borrowing	**$292,655**

Alternatively, we can calculate the total cost of borrowing as shown in Illustration 15-7.

▶ILLUSTRATION 15-7
Alternative calculation of total cost of borrowing for bonds sold at a discount

Bonds Issued at a Discount	
Principal at maturity	$1,000,000
Semi-annual interest payments	250,000
Cash to be paid to bondholders	1,250,000
Less cash received from bondholders	957,345
Total cost of borrowing	**$ 292,655**

The total cost of borrowing—the interest payments and bond discount—must be allocated to interest expense over the life of the bonds. The allocation of the bond discount over the life of the bonds is called **amortizing the discount**. The amortization of the discount **increases the amount of interest expense** reported each period. That is, after the company amortizes the discount, the amount of the interest expense it reports in a period will exceed the contractual amount. The effective-interest method is used to calculate the amortization of the bond discount (and premiums, which will be discussed in the next section) each period. As shown in Illustration 15-6, for the bonds issued by Candlestick Inc., total interest expense will exceed the contractual interest by $42,655 over the life of the bonds. As the discount is amortized, its balance declines. As a consequence, the bonds' amortized cost will increase, until at maturity the bonds' amortized cost equals their face amount. This is shown in Illustration 15-8.

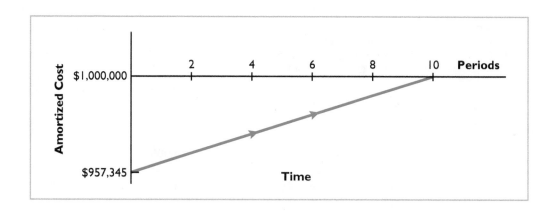

▶ILLUSTRATION 15-8
Amortization of bond discount

In order to amortize the discount, companies allocate the bond discount to interest expense in each period in which the bonds are outstanding. This results in **varying amounts** of amortization and interest expense per period but a **constant percentage rate**.

There are three steps required to calculate the interest expense and the amortization amount using the effective-interest method:

1. Calculate the **bond interest expense** by multiplying the bonds' amortized cost at the beginning of the interest period by the market interest rate.
2. Calculate the **bond interest paid** (or accrued) by multiplying the bonds' face value by the contractual interest rate.
3. Calculate the **amortization amount** by determining the difference between the amounts calculated in steps (1) and (2).

Using our Candlestick example, the company sold $1 million of 5-year, 5% semi-annual interest bonds. This resulted in a bond discount of $42,655. This discount is amortized every time an interest payment is made as follows:

1. **Bond interest expense** = the amortized cost of the bonds at the beginning of the period × the market interest rate

$$(\$957,345 \times 6\% \times {}^6\!/_{12}) = \$28,720$$

Helpful hint Note that the amount of periodic interest expense increases over the life of the bonds when the effective-interest method is used for bonds issued at a discount. The reason is that a constant percentage is applied to an increasing bond amortized cost to calculate interest expense. The amortized cost is increasing because of the amortization of the discount.

2. **Bond interest paid (or accrued)** = the bonds' face value $\times$ the contractual interest rate

$$(\$1,000,000 \times 5\% \times {}^{6}/_{12}) = \$25,000$$

3. **Amortization amount** = the difference between the interest expense and the interest paid

$$\$28,720 - \$25,000 = \$3,720$$

These steps are shown in Illustration 15-9.

▶ ILLUSTRATION 15-9
Calculation of .
amortization using the
effective-interest method

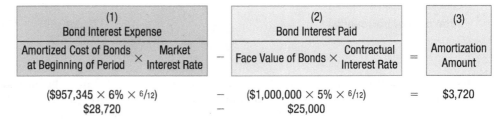

(1) Bond Interest Expense	(2) Bond Interest Paid	(3)
Amortized Cost of Bonds at Beginning of Period $\times$ Market Interest Rate	$-$ Face Value of Bonds $\times$ Contractual Interest Rate $=$	Amortization Amount

$$(\$957,345 \times 6\% \times {}^{6}/_{12}) \qquad - \qquad (\$1,000,000 \times 5\% \times {}^{6}/_{12}) \qquad = \qquad \$3,720$$
$$\$28,720 \qquad\qquad - \qquad\qquad \$25,000$$

▶ ILLUSTRATION 15-10
Bond discount
amortization schedule

Preparing a bond discount amortization schedule as shown in Illustration 15-10 facilitates the recording of interest expense and the discount amortization. (For simplicity, amounts have been rounded to the nearest dollar in this schedule.)

CANDLESTICK INC.
Bond Discount Amortization Schedule
Effective-Interest Method: Semi-Annual Interest Payments

Interest Periods	(A) Interest Payment ($1,000,000 × 5% × ⁶/₁₂)	(B) Interest Expense = Preceding Bond Amortized Cost × 6% × ⁶/₁₂	(C) Discount Amortization (B − A)	(D) Bond Amortized Cost + C
Issue Date				$ 957,345
1	$ 25,000	$28,720 (957,345 × 6% × ⁶/₁₂)	$ 3,720	961,065
2	25,000	28,832 (961,065 × 6% × ⁶/₁₂)	3,832	964,897
3	25,000	28,947 (964,897 × 6% × ⁶/₁₂)	3,947	968,844
4	25,000	29,065 (968,844 × 6% × ⁶/₁₂)	4,065	972,909
5	25,000	29,187 (972,909 × 6% × ⁶/₁₂)	4,187	977,096
6	25,000	29,313 (977,096 × 6% × ⁶/₁₂)	4,313	981,409
7	25,000	29,442 (981,409 × 6% × ⁶/₁₂)	4,442	985,851
8	25,000	29,576 (985,851 × 6% × ⁶/₁₂)	4,576	990,427
9	25,000	29,713 (990,427 × 6% × ⁶/₁₂)	4,713	995,140
10	25,000	29,860 (995,140 × 6% × ⁶/₁₂)[1]	4,860	1,000,000
	$250,000	$292,655	$42,655	

Column A remains constant because the face value of the bonds ($1,000,000) is multiplied by the semi-annual contract rate (5% × ⁶/₁₂) each period

Column B is calculated as the preceding bond amortized cost multiplied by the semi-annual market interest rate (6% × ⁶/₁₂)

Column C indicates the discount to be amortized each period

Column D increases each period until it equals face value at maturity

[1]$6 difference due to rounding

The amortization schedule is helpful in that the first three columns give the numbers for the journal entries for each period as follows:

- Column A provides the amount to credit Cash (or Interest Payable). Note that this column remains constant as the face value of the bonds ($1,000,000) and the semi-annual contractual interest rate (2.5%) are the same each period.
- Column B shows the debit to Interest Expense. It is calculated by multiplying the bond's amortized cost at the beginning of the period by the semi-annual market interest rate. Note that, while the

semi-annual market interest rate (3%) stays constant each interest period, the interest expense increases because the bond's amortized cost increases.

- Column C is the credit to Bonds Payable. It is the amortization of the bond discount, which is the difference between the interest expense and the interest payment. The amounts in this column increase throughout the amortization period because the interest expense increases. Notice that the total of this column—$42,655—is equal to the discount when the bond was issued on January 1, 2017.
- Column D is the bond's amortized cost. Note that the amortized cost of the bonds increases by the discount amortization amount each period until it reaches the face value of $1 million at the end of period 10 (January 1, 2022), when the discount is fully amortized. This is because Candlestick must repay $1 million at maturity even though it received only $957,345 from the sale of the bonds on January 1, 2017.

Based on the above, we record the interest expense, amortization of the discount, and payment of interest on the first interest payment date as follows:

July 1	Interest Expense ($957,345 × 6% × 6/12)	28,720	
	Cash ($1,000,000 × 5% × 6/12)		25,000
	Bonds Payable ($28,720 − $25,000)		3,720
	To record payment of bond interest and amortization of bond discount.		

A	=	L	+	SE
−25,000		+3,720		−28,720

↓ Cash flows: −25,000

Note that the amortization of the bond discount is recorded as an increase (credit) in the Bonds Payable account. Also note that, as previously explained, the interest expense includes both the interest payment ($25,000) and the bond discount amortization ($3,720). Remember that issuing a bond at a discount increases the cost of borrowing above the contractual interest rate.

At the second interest period, the bond's amortized cost is now the original price of the bond plus the amortized discount ($957,345 + $3,720) = $961,065. To calculate the interest expense for the second interest period, we multiply the amortized cost of the bonds by the market interest rate to arrive at $28,832 ($961,065 × 6% × 6/12). The interest payment is unchanged at $25,000. The amortization is $3,832, the difference between the interest expense and the interest paid ($28,832 − $25,000).

At Candlestick's year end, the following adjusting entry is made for the second interest period:

Dec. 31	Interest Expense ($961,065 × 6% × 6/12)	28,832	
	Interest Payable ($1,000,000 × 5% × 6/12)		25,000
	Bonds Payable ($28,832 − $25,000)		3,832
	To record accrual of bond interest and amortization of bond discount.		

A	=	L	+	SE
		+3,832		−28,832
		+25,000		

Cash flows: no effect

Note that Interest Payable is credited rather than Cash because the next interest payment date is January 1. On January 1, 2018, the Interest Payable account will be debited and the Cash account credited.

ISSUING BONDS AT A PREMIUM

Just as bonds may be sold at a discount, they may also be sold at a premium. This happens when the market rate of interest is **lower than** the contractual interest rate. Investors will have to pay more than face value for the bonds. That is, if the market rate of interest is 4% but the contractual interest rate on the bonds is 5%, the price of the bonds will be bid up. To illustrate the issue of bonds at a premium (above face value), assume instead that on January 1, 2017, Candlestick's 5-year, 5% bonds are issued to yield a market interest rate of 4%. Receiving a premium will result in a cost of borrowing of 4%.

Recall that to determine the selling price of the bonds we must determine the variables to input into a calculator or determine the appropriate present value factor per the present value tables. The variables used to determine the issue price of the bonds are:

Future value (FV) = $1,000,000
Number of semi-annual interest periods (n) = 10 (5 years $\times$ 2)
Semi-annual market interest rate (i) = 2% (4% annual market rate $\times$ $6/12$)
Semi-annual interest payments
(PMT) = $25,000 ($1,000,000 $\times$ 5% [contractual rate] $\times$ $6/12$)

Note that the only variable that has changed from the previous example is the market interest rate. **Remember to always use the market interest rate to determine the present value factor (i) and the contractual interest rate to determine the interest payment.** Using the present value tables in this chapter, we determine that the bonds will sell for $1,044,915 as follows:

Present value of $1 million received in 10 periods	
$1,000,000 $\times$ 0.82035 (n = 10, i = 2)	$ 820,350
Present value of $25,000 received for each of 10 periods	
$25,000 $\times$ 8.98259 (n = 10, i = 2)	224,565
Present value (market price) of bonds (104.4915% of face value)	$1,044,915

This issue price results in a premium of $44,915 ($1,044,915 – $1,000,000). The entry to record the sale would be as follows:

<table>
<tr><td>A = L + SE
+1,044,915 +1,044,915

↑Cash flows: +1,044,915</td><td>Jan. 1</td><td>Cash
    Bonds Payable
    To record sale of bonds at a premium.</td><td>1,044,915</td><td>
1,044,915</td></tr>
</table>

As previously stated, bonds are reported at amortized cost, which is equal to the issue price at the date the bonds are issued. In this example, the bonds' amortized cost is $1,044,915: the face value of the bonds of $1 million plus the unamortized premium of $44,915. The sale of bonds above face value causes the total cost of borrowing to be **less than the bond interest paid**. The reason: the borrower is not required to pay the bond premium at the maturity date of the bonds. Thus, the bond premium is considered to be **a reduction in the cost of borrowing** that reduces bond interest over the life of the bonds. Candlestick will repay only $1 million at maturity, even though it received $1,044,915 from the sale of the bonds. The calculation of the total cost of borrowing for bonds issued at a premium is shown in Illustration 15-11.

▶ **ILLUSTRATION 15-11**
Total cost of borrowing—bonds issued at a premium

Bonds Issued at a Premium	
Semi-annual interest payments	
($25,000 $\times$ 10)	$250,000
Less: Bond premium	44,915
Total cost of borrowing	**$205,085**

Alternatively, we can calculate the total cost of borrowing as shown in Illustration 15-12.

▶ **ILLUSTRATION 15-12**
Alternative calculation of total cost of borrowing for bonds sold at a premium

Bonds Issued at a Premium	
Principal at maturity	$1,000,000
Semi-annual interest payments	250,000
Cash to be paid to bondholders	1,250,000
Less: Cash received from bondholders	1,044,915
Total cost of borrowing	**$ 205,085**

The total cost of borrowing—the interest payments less the bond premium—must be allocated to interest expense over the life of the bonds. The allocation of the bond premium over the life of the bonds is called **amortizing the premium**. The amortization of the premium reduces the amount of interest expense that is recorded each period. That is, after the company amortizes the premium, the amount of interest expense it reports in a period will be less than the contractual amount. The same method—the effective-interest method—used to allocate bond discounts is also used to allocate bond premiums to interest expense. As the premium is amortized, its balance declines. As a consequence, the amortized cost of the bonds also decreases, until at maturity the amortized cost equals the bonds' face amount. As shown in Illustration 15-13, for the bonds issued by Candlestick, the total interest expense will be less than the contractual interest by $44,915 over the life of the bonds. As the premium is amortized, its balance decreases and as a consequence, the bonds' amortized cost also decreases until at maturity their amortized cost equals the face amount.

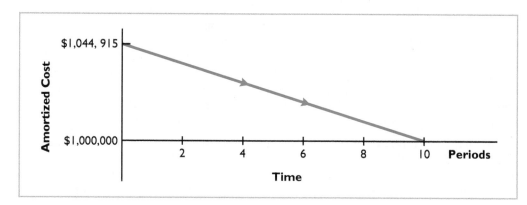

▶ILLUSTRATION 15-13
Amortization of bond premium

Continuing our example, assume Candlestick Inc. sells the bonds described above for $1,044,915. This would result in a bond premium of $44,915. Illustration 15-14 is a bond premium amortization

▶ILLUSTRATION 15-14
Bond premium amortization schedule

CANDLESTICK INC.
Bond Premium Amortization Schedule
Effective-Interest Method: Semi-Annual Interest Payments

Interest Periods	(A) Interest Payment ($1,000,000 × 5% × 6/12)	(B) Interest Expense = Preceding Bond Amortized Cost × 4% × 6/12	(C) Premium Amortization (A − B)	(D) Bond Amortized Cost − C
Issue Date				$1,044,915
1	$ 25,000	$20,898 (1,044,915 × 4% × 6/12)	$ 4,102	1,040,813
2	25,000	20,816 (1,040,813 × 4% × 6/12)	4,184	1,036,629
3	25,000	20,733 (1,036,629 × 4% × 6/12)	4,267	1,032,362
4	25,000	20,647 (1,032,362 × 4% × 6/12)	4,353	1,028,009
5	25,000	20,560 (1,028,009 × 4% × 6/12)	4,440	1,023,569
6	25,000	20,471 (1,023,569 × 4% × 6/12)	4,529	1,019,040
7	25,000	20,381 (1,019,040 × 4% × 6/12)	4,619	1,014,421
8	25,000	20,288 (1,014,421 × 4% × 6/12)	4,712	1,009,709
9	25,000	20,194 (1,009,709 × 4% × 6/12)	4,806	1,004,903
10	25,000	20,097 (1,004,903 × 4% × 6/12)[1]	4,903	1,000,000
	$250,000	$205,085	$44,915	

Column A   remains constant because the face value of the bonds ($1,000,000) is multiplied by the semi-annual contract rate (5% × 6/12) each period
Column B   is calculated as the preceding bond amortized cost multiplied by the semi-annual market interest rate (4% × 6/12)
Column C   indicates the premium to be amortized each period
Column D   decreases each period until it equals face value at maturity
[1]$1 difference due to rounding

schedule that demonstrates the amortization of this premium. This facilitates the recording of interest expense and the premium amortization. (For simplicity, amounts have been rounded to the nearest dollar in this schedule.)

Recall from Illustration 15-10 that columns A, B, and C in the amortization schedule give the numbers for each period's journal entries.

- Column A provides the amount to credit Cash (or Interest Payable). The amounts in this column stay the same because the face value of the bonds and the semi-annual contractual interest rate are the same each period.
- Column B shows the debit to Interest Expense. It is calculated by multiplying the bonds' amortized cost at the beginning of the period by the semi-annual market interest rate. Note that, while the semi-annual market interest rate (2%) stays constant each interest period, the interest expense decreases because the bond's amortized cost decreases.
- Column C is the debit to Bonds Payable. It is the difference between the interest payment and the interest expense. The amounts in this column increase throughout the amortization period because the interest expense decreases as the amortized cost of the bonds decreases. Notice that the total of this column—$44,915—is equal to the premium when the bond was issued on January 1, 2017.
- Column D is the bond's amortized cost. Note that the amortized cost of the bonds decreases by the premium amortization amount each period until it reaches the face value of $1 million at the end of period 10 (January 1, 2022). Note that even though Candlestick received $1,044,915 from the sale of the bonds on January 1, 2017, it is only required to pay $1 million at maturity.

Based on the above, for the first interest period, the interest expense is $20,898, calculated by multiplying the bonds' amortized cost by the market interest rate ($1,044,915 $\times$ 4% $\times$ $^6/_{12}$). The interest payment, $25,000, is the same as for the bonds issued at discount as it is calculated by multiplying the bonds' face value by the contractual interest rate ($1,000,000 $\times$ 5% $\times$ $^6/_{12}$). The premium amortization is then calculated as the difference between the interest paid and the interest expense ($25,000 $-$ $20,898 = $4,102).

The entry on the first interest payment date is as follows:

A	=	L	+	SE
−25,000		−4,102		−20,898

↓ Cash flows: −25,000

July 1	Interest Expense ($1,044,915 × 4% × $^6/_{12}$)	20,898	
	Bonds Payable ($25,000 − $20,898)	4,102	
	Cash ($1,000,000 × 5% × $^6/_{12}$)		25,000
	To record payment of bond interest and amortization of bond premium.		

Note that the amortization of the bond premium is recorded as a decrease (debit) in the Bonds Payable account, and that the interest expense is less than the interest payment. This reflects the reduced cost of borrowing.

For the second interest period, the bonds' amortized cost is now $1,040,813 ($1,044,915 $-$ $4,102). To calculate the interest expense for the second interest period, we multiply the amortized cost of the bonds by the market interest rate to arrive at $20,816 ($1,040,813 $\times$ 4% $\times$ $^6/_{12}$). The interest payment is unchanged at $25,000. As before, the amortization is the difference between the interest paid and the interest expense ($25,000 $-$ $20,816 = $4,184).

For the second interest period, at Candlestick's year end, the following adjusting entry is made:

A	=	L	+	SE
		−4,184		−20,816
		+25,000		

Cash flows: no effect

Dec. 31	Interest Expense ($1,040,813 × 4% × $^6/_{12}$)	20,816	
	Bonds Payable ($25,000 − $20,816)	4,184	
	Interest Payable ($1,000,000 × 5% × $^6/_{12}$)		25,000
	To record accrual of bond interest and amortization of bond premium.		

ISSUING BONDS AT A DISCOUNT VERSUS AT A PREMIUM

Illustration 15-15 summarizes some of the differences between issuing a bond at a discount and a premium under the effective-interest method of amortization.

	Bond Issued at a Discount	**Bond Issued at a Premium**
Market interest rate	Greater than the contractual interest rate	Less than the contractual interest rate
Periodic interest payment	Same each period	Same each period
Periodic interest expense	Greater than the interest payment	Less than the interest payment
	Increases each period	Decreases each period
Bond's amortized cost	Increases to face value at maturity	Decreases to face value at maturity

▶ILLUSTRATION 15-15
Comparison of the effects of issuing bonds at a discount or a premium

The effective-interest method is required for companies reporting under IFRS. Private companies reporting under ASPE can choose to use either the effective-interest method or other methods if they do not differ significantly from the effective-interest method. Because the use of the effective-interest method is prevalent, we focus on this method in this text.

ASPE

BOND INTEREST ACCRUALS

As we have seen, an adjusting entry is required to record the interest expense and the amortization of any premium or discount up to the year-end date. So far in our discussions, the year-end date has been the day before the payment date. However, how do we account for bond interest and amortization when the year-end falls on another day during the interest period?

To demonstrate, let's continue with the Candlestick Inc. case. Candlestick issues 5-year, 5%, $1-million bonds on January 1, 2017. Let's assume the bonds are issued at par (yield a market interest rate of 5%) and interest is payable semi-annually. However, instead of a December 31 year end, Candlestick has an April 30 year end.

On April 30, 2017, Candlestick will have to accrue the interest expense incurred for the four months the bond has been outstanding. Since no payment will be made on April 30, Candlestick will credit interest payable to record the liability incurred up to year end. Thus, Candlestick will record interest expense and interest payable of $16,667 ($1,000,000 × 5% × 4/12). The entry for the interest accrual is:

April 30	Interest Expense ($1,000,000 × 5% × 4/12)	16,667	
	Interest Payable		16,667
	To record accrual of bond interest.		

A = L + SE
+16,667 −16,667
Cash flows: no effect

Note that, like all adjusting journal entries, there is no impact on the Cash account. On July 1, when the interest payment is due, Candlestick must now record the interest payment with a credit to the Cash account. However, it only records the interest expense for the two months that have passed since year end. Also, as the interest payable recorded at year end is now being settled, the Interest Payable account will be debited. The entry is as follows:

July 1	Interest Expense ($1,000,000 × 5% × 2/12)	8,333	
	Interest Payable	16,667	
	Cash		25,000
	To record payment of bond interest.		

A = L + SE
−25,000 −16,667 −8,333
↓ Cash flows: 25,000

Now let's consider a bond sold at a discount. Assume Candlestick sold a 5-year, 5%, $1-million bond for $957,345 on January 1, 2017. Interest is payable semi-annually. This results in a discount of $42,655.

Candlestick has an April 30 year end. On April 30, an adjusting entry is required to record the interest expense. However, the discount must also be amortized at this time.

To determine the amounts to record for this adjusting entry, Candlestick can refer to the bond amortization schedule prepared for the first interest payment, as shown in Illustration 15-16. Recall that this table reflects time periods of six months.

▶ILLUSTRATION **15-16**
Bond discount
amortization schedule

	(A)	(B)	(C)	(D)
Interest Periods	Interest Payment ($1,000000 × 5% × $^6/_{12}$)	Interest Expense = Preceding Bond Amortized Cost × 6% × $^6/_{12}$	Discount Amortization (B − A)	Bond Amortized Cost + C
Issue Date				$957,345
1	$25,000	$28,720 ($957,345 × 6% × $^6/_{12}$)	$3,720	961,065

CANDLESTICK INC.
Bond Discount Amortization Schedule
Effective-Interest Method: Semi-Annual Interest Payments

Because we have an April 30 year end, Candlestick records interest expense for only a four-month period. In order to do this, the interest expense and the bond discount from the amortization table can be prorated for a four-month period. Therefore, the journal entry is as follows:

A	=	L	+	SE
		+16,667		−19,147
		+ 2,480		

Cash flows: no effect

Apr. 30	Interest Expense ($28,720 × $^4/_6$)	19,147	
	Interest Payable ($25,000 × $^4/_6$)		16,667
	Bonds Payable ($3,720 × $^4/_6$)		2,480
	To record accrued bond interest and amortization		
	of bond discount at year end.		

On July 1, when Candlestick actually makes the interest payment, it will record the interest expense and the amortization of the bond discount for the remaining two-month period. It will also remove the interest payable because with the payment this liability will be settled. The entry will be as follows:

A	=	L	+	SE
−25,000	=	−16,667		−9,573
		+ 1,240		

↓ Cash flows: 25,000

July 1	Interest Expense ($28,720 × $^2/_6$)	9,573	
	Interest Payable	16,667	
	Bonds Payable ($3,720 × $^2/_6$)		1,240
	Cash		25,000
	To record payment of bond interest and		
	amortization of bond discount.		

BEFORE YOU GO ON...DO IT **3** ▸ **Accrual and Amortization of Interest**

On January 1, 2017, R & B Inc. issues $500,000 of 10-year, 4% bonds to yield a market interest rate of 5%. This resulted in an issue price of $461,050. Interest is paid semi-annually on January 1 and July 1.

(a) Prepare an amortization schedule for the first four interest periods. Round all calculations to the nearest dollar.

(b) Assuming that R & B has a December 31 year-end, prepare the entry to record the accrual of interest and amortization of any bond discount or premium on December 31, 2017.

(c) Prepare the entry to record the payment of interest on January 1, 2018.

(d) Assuming that R & B Inc. has an April 30 year end, record the interest accrual at April 30, 2017, and the subsequent interest payment on July 1, 2017.

(continued)

BEFORE YOU GO ON...DO IT **3** ▷ **Accrual and Amortization of Interest** *(continued)*

Solution

(a)

R & B INC.
Bond Discount Amortization Schedule
Effective-Interest Method

Semi-Annual Interest Period	(A) Interest Payment ($500,000 × 4% × $^6/_{12}$)	(B) Interest Expense (D × 5% × $^6/_{12}$)	(C) Discount Amortization (B − A)	(D) Bond Amortized Cost + C
Jan. 1, 2017				$461,050
July 1, 2017	$10,000	$11,526	$1,526	462,576
Jan. 1, 2018	10,000	11,564	1,564	464,140
July 1, 2018	10,000	11,603	1,603	465,743
Jan. 1, 2019	10,000	11,643	1,643	467,386

(b) Dec. 31, 2017	Interest Expense	11,564	
	Bonds Payable		1,564
	Interest Payable		10,000
	To record accrual of interest and amortization of discount.		
(c) Jan. 1, 2018	Interest Payable	10,000	
	Cash		10,000
(d) April 30, 2017	Interest Expense ($11,526 × $^4/_6$)	7,684	
	Bonds Payable ($1,526 × $^4/_6$)		1,017
	Interest Payable		6,667
July 1, 2017	Interest Expense ($11,526 × $^2/_6$)	3,842	
	Interest Payable	6,667	
	Bonds Payable ($1,526 × $^2/_6$)		509
	Cash		10,000

Related exercise material: BE15–4, BE15–5, BE15–6, BE15–7, BE15–8, BE15–9, BE15–10, BE15–11, BE15–12, E15–5, E15–6, E15–7, E15–8, E15–9, E15–10, E15–11, and E5–12.

Action Plan

- Calculate the interest payment by multiplying the face value by the semi-annual contractual rate. Calculate the interest expense by multiplying the semi-annual market rate (half of the market or yield rate) by the amortized cost of the bonds payable.
- The amount of the discount (premium) amortization is the difference between the interest payment and the interest expense.
- The amortized cost of bonds issued at a discount increases by the amount of the discount amortization each interest period.
- Where the year end and bond interest payment do not coincide, an interest accrual is required. Use the amortization table and prorate the amounts for the time period outstanding.

LEARNING OBJECTIVE 4 ▷ **Account for the retirement of bonds.**

Accounting for Bond Retirements

Bonds may be retired either (1) when they mature, or (2) when the issuing corporation purchases them from the bondholders on the open market before they mature. Some bonds have special redemption provisions that allow them to be retired before they mature. As we learned earlier in this chapter, redeemable bonds can be retired at a stated dollar amount at the option of the company.

The retirement of bonds at and before maturity is explained in the following sections.

REDEEMING BONDS AT MATURITY

Regardless of the issue price of bonds, the amortized cost of the bonds at maturity will equal their face value. By the time the bonds mature, any discount or premium will be fully amortized.

Assuming that the interest for the last interest period has been paid and recorded, the entry to record the redemption of the Candlestick bonds at maturity, January 1, 2022, is as follows:

A = L + SE
−1,000,000 −1,000,000

↓ Cash flows: −1,000,000

Jan. 1	Bonds Payable	1,000,000	
	Cash		1,000,000
	To record redemption of bonds at maturity.		

Because the amortized cost of the bonds equals the face value at maturity, there is no gain or loss.

REDEEMING BONDS BEFORE MATURITY

Alternative terminology Redemption price is also referred to as the *call price.*

Why would a company want to have the option to retire its bonds early? If interest rates drop, it can be a good idea financially to retire the bond issue and replace it with a new bond issue at a lower interest rate. Or, a company may become financially able to repay its debt earlier than expected. When a company purchases non-redeemable bonds on the open market, it pays the going market price. If the bonds are redeemable, the company will pay the bondholders an amount that was specified at the time of issue, known as the **redemption price**. To make the bonds more attractive to investors, the redemption price is usually a few percentage points above the face value.

If the bonds are redeemed between semi-annual interest payment dates, it will be necessary to pay the required interest and record the related amortization of any premiums or discounts. To record the redemption of bonds, it is necessary to:

1. eliminate the amortized cost of the bonds (balance in Bonds Payable account),
2. record the cash paid, and
3. recognize the gain or loss on redemption.

Helpful hint If a bond is redeemed prior to its maturity date and its amortized cost exceeds its redemption price, this results in a gain.

A loss on redemption is recorded if the cash paid is more than the amortized cost of the bonds. There is a gain on redemption when the cash paid is less than the amortized cost of the bonds. This is shown in Illustration 15-17.

▶ **ILLUSTRATION 15-17**
Loss and gain on redemption of bonds

To illustrate, assume that Candlestick sells its bonds that were issued at a premium as described in the last section. It retires its bonds at 103 at the end of the fourth year (eighth period) after paying the semi-annual interest. The premium amortization schedule in Illustration 15-14 shows that the bonds' amortized cost at the redemption date (January 1, 2021) is $1,009,709. The entry to record the redemption on January 1, 2021 (end of the eighth interest period) is:

A = L + SE
−1,030,000 −1,009,709 −20,291

↓ Cash flows: −1,030,000

Jan. 1	Bonds Payable	1,009,709	
	Loss on Bond Redemption	20,291	
	Cash ($1,000,000 × 103%)		1,030,000
	To record redemption of bonds at 103.		

There is a loss on the bond redemption because Candlestick paid $1,030,000, which is $20,291 more to redeem the bonds than the amortized cost of the bonds of $1,009,709.

Losses and gains on bond redemption are reported separately in the income statement as other expenses or other revenues, similar to interest expense.

R & B Inc. issued $500,000, 10-year bonds at a discount. Prior to maturity, when the bonds' amortized cost is $496,000, the company redeems the bonds at 98. Prepare the entry to record the redemption of the bonds.

Solution

There is a gain on redemption. The cash paid, $490,000 ($500,000 × 98%), is less than the amortized cost of $496,000. The entry is:

Bonds Payable	496,000	
Gain on Bond Redemption		6,000
Cash		490,000
To record redemption of bonds at 98.		

Related exercise material: BE15–13, BE15–14, E15–13, and E15–14.

Action Plan
- To record the redemption, eliminate the amortized cost of the bonds, record the cash paid, and calculate and record the gain or loss (the difference between the cash paid and the amortized cost).

**LEARNING
OBJECTIVE** **Account for instalment notes payable.**

Instalment Notes Payable

The use of notes payable for non-current debt financing is quite common. **Non-current notes payable** are similar to short-term notes payable except that the term of the notes exceeds one year. While short-term notes are normally repayable in full at maturity, most non-current notes are repayable in a series of periodic payments and are referred to as **instalment notes**. These payments are known as **instalments** and are paid monthly, quarterly, semi-annually, or at another defined period.

Notes payable may have either a fixed interest rate or a floating interest rate. A **fixed interest rate** is constant for the entire term of the note. A **floating** (or **variable**) **interest rate** changes as market rates change. A floating interest rate is often based on the prime borrowing rate. Prime is the interest rate that banks charge their most creditworthy customers. This rate is usually increased by a specified percentage that matches the company's risk profile—in other words, it depends on how risky the company is judged to be.

A non-current note may be secured by a **mortgage** that pledges title to specific assets as security for a loan. Individuals widely use **mortgage notes payable** to purchase homes, and many small and some large companies use them to acquire plant assets. Unsecured notes are issued against the general credit of the borrower. There are no assets used as collateral.

As explained earlier, most non-current notes payable are paid in instalments. Each instalment payment consists of (1) interest on the unpaid balance of the loan, and (2) a reduction of loan principal. Payments generally take one of two forms: (1) fixed principal payments plus interest, or (2) blended principal and interest payments. Let's look at each of these payment patterns in more detail.

FIXED PRINCIPAL PAYMENTS

Instalment notes with fixed principal payments are repayable in **equal periodic amounts, plus interest**. To illustrate, assume that on January 1, 2017, Bélanger Ltée issues a $120,000, 5-year, 7% note payable to finance a new research laboratory. The entry to record the issue of the note payable is as follows:

Jan. 1	Cash	120,000	
	Notes Payable		120,000
	To record 5-year, 7% note payable.		

A	=	L	+	SE
+120,000		+120,000		

↑Cash flows: +120,000

The terms of the note provide for equal monthly instalment payments of $2,000 ($120,000 ÷ 60 monthly periods) on the first of each month, plus interest, based on an annual rate of 7%, on the outstanding principal balance. Monthly interest expense is calculated by multiplying the outstanding principal balance by the interest rate. The calculation of interest expense for notes payable is similar to that of bonds payable—both use the effective-interest method.

For the first payment date—February 1—interest expense is $700 ($120,000 $\times$ 7% $\times$ $^1/_{12}$). Since 7% is an annual interest rate, it must be adjusted for the monthly time period. The cash payment of $2,700 for the month of February is the sum of the instalment payment, $2,000, which is applied against the principal, plus the interest, $700.

The entry to record the first instalment payment on February 1 is as follows:

A	=	L	+	SE
−2,700		−2,000		−700

↓Cash flows: −2,700

Feb. 1	Interest Expense ($120,000 $\times$ 7% $\times$ $^1/_{12}$)	700	
	Notes Payable	2,000	
	Cash ($2,000 + $700)		2,700
	To record monthly payment on note.		

An instalment payment schedule is a useful tool to help organize this information and prepare journal entries. The instalment payment schedule for the first few months for Bélanger Ltée, rounded to the nearest dollar, is shown in Illustration 15-18.

▶ILLUSTRATION 15-18
Instalment payment schedule—fixed principal payments

	BÉLANGER LTÉE			
	Instalment Payment Schedule—Fixed Principal Payments			
Interest Period	**(A) Cash Payment (B + C)**	**(B) Interest Expense (D $\times$ 7% $\times$ $^1/_{12}$)**	**(C) Reduction of Principal ($120,000 ÷ 60)**	**(D) Principal Balance − C**
Jan. 1				$120,000
Feb. 1	$2,700	$700	$2,000	118,000
Mar. 1	2,688	688	2,000	116,000
Apr. 1	2,677	677	2,000	114,000

Column A, the cash payment, is the total of the instalment payment, $2,000 (Column C), plus the interest (Column B). The cash payment changes each period because the interest amount changes. Column B determines the interest expense, which decreases each period because the principal balance, on which interest is calculated, decreases. Column C is the portion of the payment that is applied against the principal. The monthly reduction of principal of $2,000 per month is constant each period in a "fixed principal payment" pattern. Column D is the principal balance, which decreases each period by the amount of the instalment payment (Column C).

In summary, with fixed principal payments, the interest decreases each period (as the principal decreases). The portion applied to the reduction of loan principal stays constant, but because of the decreasing interest, the total cash payment decreases.

BLENDED PAYMENTS

Instalment notes with blended payments are repayable in **equal periodic amounts that include the principal and the interest**. With blended payments, the amounts of interest and principal that are applied to the loan change with each payment. Specifically, as happens with fixed principal payments, the interest decreases each period (as the principal decreases). In contrast to fixed principal payments, however, the portion that is applied to the loan principal increases each period.

To illustrate, assume that instead of fixed principal payments, Bélanger Ltée repays its $120,000 note payable in blended payments of $2,376 each month. The blended payment is calculated using present value calculations as shown in Appendix PV. As with the fixed principal payments illustrated in the previous section, monthly interest expense is calculated by multiplying the outstanding principal balance by the interest rate. For the first payment date—February 1—interest expense is

$700 ($120,000 $\times$ 7% $\times$ $^{1}/_{12}$ months). The payment of $2,376 is fixed for each month, and includes interest and principal amounts, which will vary. In February, the principal balance will be reduced by $1,676, which is the difference between the payment of $2,376 and the interest amount of $700.

The entry to record the issue of the note payable is the same as in the previous section. The amounts in the journal entry to record the payment on February 1 change as follows:

Feb. 1	Interest Expense ($120,000 × 7% × $^{1}/_{12}$)	700	
	Notes Payable ($2,376 − $700)	1,676	
	Cash		2,376
	To record monthly payment on note.		

A	=	L	+	SE
−2,376		−1,676		−700

↓Cash flows: −2,376

An instalment payment schedule can also be prepared for blended principal and interest payments. Illustration 15-19 shows the instalment payment schedule for the first few months for Bélanger Ltée, rounded to the nearest dollar.

		BÉLANGER LTÉE		
		Instalment Payment Schedule—Blended Payments		
	(A)	(B)	(C)	(D)
		Interest Expense	Reduction of Principal	Principal
Interest Period	Cash Payment	(D × 7% × $^{1}/_{12}$)	(A − B)	Balance − C
Jan. 1				$120,000
Feb. 1	$2,376	$700	$1,676	118,324
Mar. 1	2,376	690	1,686	116,638
Apr. 1	2,376	680	1,696	114,942

▶ ILLUSTRATION 15-19
Instalment payment schedule—blended payments

Column A, the cash payment, is specified and is the same for each period. The amount of this cash payment can be calculated using present value techniques discussed earlier in the chapter and in Appendix PV to this textbook. Column B determines the interest expense, which decreases each period because the principal balance on which interest is calculated also decreases. Column C is the amount by which the principal is reduced. This is the difference between the cash payment of $2,376 (Column A) and the interest for the period (Column B). Consequently, this amount will increase each period. Column D is the principal balance, which decreases each period by an increasing amount; that is, by the reduction of the principal amount from Column C.

In summary, with blended payments, the interest decreases each period as the principal decreases. The cash payment stays constant, but because of the decreasing interest, the reduction of principal increases.

Illustration 15-20 summarizes the differences between instalment notes payable with fixed principal payments and blended principal payments.

Instalment Payment Pattern	Principal	Interest	Total Cash Payment
Fixed principal plus interest	Constant: Reduction of principal equal each period	Decreases: Interest expense decreases each period	Decreases: Total cash payment decreases each period
Blended principal and interest	Increases: Reduction of principal increases each period	Decreases: Interest expense decreases each period	Constant: Total cash payment equal each period

▶ ILLUSTRATION 15-20
Difference between instalment notes with fixed principal payments and blended principal payments

CURRENT AND NON-CURRENT PORTIONS

With both types of instalment notes payable, the reduction in principal for the next year must be reported as a current liability, and is normally called "Current portion of note payable." The remaining unpaid principal is classified as a non-current liability. No journal entry is necessary; it is simply a reclassification of amounts for the balance sheet. For example, consider the following fixed principal annual instalment payment schedule shown in Illustration 15-21.

▶ILLUSTRATION 15-21
Current and non-current portion of note payable

Interest Period	Cash Payment	Interest Expense	Reduction of Principal	Principal Balance
Issue Date				$50,000
2017	$13,500	$3,500	$10,000	40,000
2018	12,800	2,800	10,000	30,000
2019	12,100	2,100	10,000	20,000
2020	11,400	1,400	10,000	10,000
2021	10,700	700	10,000	0

If financial statements were being prepared at the end of 2018, the company would report $30,000 as its total liability for the bank loan, shown in green in the principal balance column. Of this, $10,000 ($30,000 − $20,000)—the amount to be repaid within the next year (2019), which is also highlighted in Illustration 15-21 in green—would be reported as a current liability. The company would report $20,000—the amount to be repaid beyond next year (2020 and 2021)—as a non-current liability. This amount is highlighted in blue in Illustration 15-21. Note that when the current portion ($10,000) and the non-current portion ($20,000) are added together, the amount should agree with the total amount owing at the end of 2018 ($30,000).

BEFORE YOU GO ON...DO IT	5	Preparing an Instalment Schedule and Recording Note Issuance

Action Plan

- For the instalment payment schedule, multiply the interest rate by the principal balance at the beginning of the period to determine the interest expense. Remember to adjust the interest rate to the semi-annual rate. The reduction of principal is the difference between the cash payment and the interest expense.
- Use the amortization table to record the semi-annual mortgage payments.
- Remember to separate the current and non-current portions of the note in the balance sheet. The current portion is the amount of principal that will be repaid in the next year (2019). The total of the current and non-current portions should equal the outstanding principal balance in the amortization table at December 31, 2018.

On December 31, 2017, Tian Inc. issued a $500,000, 15-year, 8% mortgage note payable. The terms provide for semi-annual blended payments of $28,915 on June 30 and December 31. (a) Prepare an instalment payment schedule for the first two years of the note (through to December 31, 2019). (b) Prepare the journal entries required to record the issue of the note on December 31, 2017, and the first two instalment payments. (c) Show the presentation of the liability on the balance sheet at December 31, 2018.

Solution

(a)

Interest Period	Cash Payment	Interest Expense	Reduction of Principal	Principal Balance
Dec. 31, 2017				$500,000
June 30, 2018	$28,915	$20,000	$ 8,915	491,085
Dec. 31, 2018	28,915	19,643	9,272	481,813
June 30, 2019	28,915	19,273	9,642	472,171
Dec. 31, 2019	28,915	18,887	10,028	462,143

(b)

Dec. 31, 2017	Cash	500,000	
	Mortgage Note Payable		500,000
	To record issue of 15-year, 8% mortgage note payable.		
June 30, 2018	Interest Expense ($500,000 × 8% × 6/12)	20,000	
	Mortgage Note Payable ($28,915 − $20,000)	8,915	
	Cash		28,915
	To record semi-annual payment on note.		
Dec. 31, 2018	Interest Expense ($491,085 × 8% × 6/12)	19,643	
	Mortgage Note Payable ($28,915 − $19,643)	9,272	
	Cash		28,915
	To record semi-annual payment on note.		

(continued)

BEFORE YOU GO ON...DO IT **Preparing an Instalment Schedule and Recording Note Issuance** *(continued)*

(c)

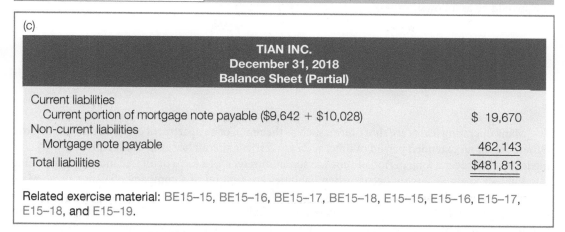

TIAN INC. December 31, 2018 Balance Sheet (Partial)	
Current liabilities	
Current portion of mortgage note payable ($9,642 + $10,028)	$ 19,670
Non-current liabilities	
Mortgage note payable	462,143
Total liabilities	$481,813

Related exercise material: BE15–15, BE15–16, BE15–17, BE15–18, E15–15, E15–16, E15–17, E15–18, and E15–19.

LEARNING OBJECTIVE **Account for leases.**

Lease Liabilities

A **lease** is a contractual arrangement between two parties. A party that owns an asset (the **lessor**) agrees to allow another party (the **lessee**) to use the specified property for a series of cash payments over an agreed period of time.

Currently for financial reporting purposes, leases are classified as either finance leases or operating leases. Whether a lease is a finance lease or an operating lease depends on the economic reality of the transaction rather than the legal form of the lease agreement. We will discuss these two types of leases in the next sections.

Illustration 15-22 summarizes the major difference between an operating and a finance lease.

> **ILLUSTRATION** **15-22**
> Types of leases

Helpful hint A finance lease situation is one that, although legally a rental, is in substance an instalment purchase by the lessee. Accounting standards require that substance over form be used in such a situation.

OPERATING LEASES

The rental of an apartment and the rental of a car are examples of **operating leases**. Under an operating lease, the lessee (or renter) obtains the temporary use of the property. Because the benefits and risks of ownership do not transfer, the lease (rental) payments are recorded as an expense by the lessee and as revenue by the lessor. For example, assume that a sales representative for Western Inc. leases a car from Thrifty car rental at the airport on July 17. Thrifty charges a total of $275. The entry by the lessee, Western Inc., would be as follows:

A	=	L	+	SE
−275				−275

↓Cash flows: −275

July 17	Car Rental Expense	275	
	Cash		275
	To record payment of lease rental charge.		

Many operating leases are short-term, such as the rental of an apartment or car as described above. Others are for an extended period of time, such as WestJet's aircraft leases in our feature story. Operating leases that cover a long period of time are sometimes seen as a form of off–balance sheet financing. **Off–balance sheet financing** occurs when liabilities are kept off of a company's balance sheet. Many people argue that, if an operating lease results in the long-term use of an asset and an unavoidable obligation, it should be recorded as an asset and a liability. To reduce these concerns, companies are required to report their operating lease obligations in detail in a note to the financial statements, which WestJet does. This allows analysts and other financial statement users to understand the impact of such leases on the entity's financial results.

To further address the concern about off–balance sheet financing, in early 2016 the International Accounting Standards Board issued a new lease standard effective for reporting periods on or after January 1, 2019. The new standard recognizes that, under any lease agreement, the lessee's right to use property meets the definition of an asset and the related obligation to make periodic rental payments meets the definition of a liability. Therefore, with few exceptions, in the future most leases will be accounted for by recording an asset and liability.

FINANCE LEASES

In a **finance lease** contract, substantially all of the benefits and risks of ownership of the leased property are transferred to the lessee. This gives the lessee control of the property. Because the definition of an asset is based on control (and not legal ownership), a finance lease is in substance the purchase of property using a lease to finance the purchase. Therefore, under a finance lease, both an asset and a liability are shown on the balance sheet. Under ASPE, a finance lease is called a **capital lease**.

Accountants must use professional judgement in deciding if a lease should be classified as a finance lease. Under IFRS, the lessee must classify the lease as a finance lease and record an asset and a lease liability if any of the following qualitative conditions exists.

1. **Transfer of ownership:** If the lease transfers ownership of the asset to the lessee during or at the end of the lease term, the leased asset and lease liability should be recorded on the lessee's books.
2. **Option to buy:** If the lessee has an option to purchase the asset during the lease term at a price that is much below its fair value (called a bargain purchase option), we can assume that the lessee will choose to use this option. Thus, the leased asset and lease liability should be recorded on the lessee's books.

3. **Lease term:** If the lease term is for the major part of the economic life of the leased property, the asset has effectively been purchased and should be recorded as an asset along with the lease liability by the lessee. Under IFRS, professional judgement is used to assess if the lease term is for the major part of the economic life. In comparison, under ASPE, a lease is classified as a capital lease if the lease term is equal to 75% or more of the economic life of the leased property.

4. **Purchase price:** If the present value of the lease payments amounts to substantially all of the fair value of the leased property, the lessee has essentially paid for the asset. As a result, the leased asset and lease liability should be recorded on the books of the lessee. Similar to condition 3, under IFRS, professional judgement is used, and under ASPE, a specific benchmark is used to assess if this condition is met. Under ASPE, if the present value of the lease payments is equal to or greater than 90% of the fair value of the leased property, then the lease is a capital lease.

5. **Specialized asset:** If the leased asset is of such a specialized nature that only the lessee can use it, the leased asset and lease liability should be recorded on the lessee's books. ASPE does not include this condition.

To illustrate, assume that Fortune Ltd., a public company using IFRS, decides to lease new equipment. The lease period is 10 years and the economic life of the leased equipment is estimated to be 14 years. The present value of the lease payments is $170,000 and the fair market value of the equipment is $200,000. There is no transfer of ownership during the lease term.

In this example, Fortune has essentially acquired the equipment. Conditions (3) and (4) listed above have both been met. First, the lease term is for the major part of the asset's economic life (10 years ÷ 14 years = 71.43%). Second, the present value of cash payments amounts to substantially all of the equipment's fair market value ($170,000 ÷ $200,000 = 85%). The present value of the cash payments in a finance lease is calculated in the same way that was explained earlier in the chapter for bond interest payments.

Note that, while two conditions were met in this case, only one condition has to be met for the lease to be treated as a finance lease. The entry to record the transaction is as follows:

Nov. 27	Leased Asset—Equipment	170,000	
	Lease Liability		170,000
	To record leased asset and lease liability.		

A   =   L   +   SE
+170,000   +170,000

Cash flows: no effect

The leased asset is reported in the balance sheet under property, plant, and equipment. The portion of the lease liability that is expected to be paid in the next year is reported as a current liability. The remainder is classified as a non-current liability.

After it is acquired, the leased asset is depreciated just as any other long-lived asset is. In addition, the lease payment is allocated between interest expense and the reduction of the principal balance of the lease liability, similar to what was shown earlier in the chapter for blended principal and interest payments on notes payable.

To summarize, for a finance lease, both an asset and a liability are reported on the balance sheet. Two expenses—depreciation expense related to the leased asset and interest expense related to the lease liability—are reported in the income statement. For an operating lease, no asset or liability is reported on the balance sheet. The only expense that is reported in the income statement is rental expense.

Action Plan

- Know the five qualitative conditions to distinguish between an operating and a finance lease under IFRS. A lease is considered to be a finance lease if any one of the following conditions is met: (1) there will be a transfer of ownership, (2) there is a bargain purchase option, (3) the lease term is for the major part of the economic life, (4) the present value of the lease payments amounts to substantially all of the fair value of the leased property, and (5) the asset is a specialized asset.
- Understand the impact of an operating and a finance lease on the income statement and balance sheet. With an operating lease, no asset or liability is recorded; with a finance lease, both an asset and a liability are recorded.

BEFORE YOU GO ON...DO IT ⑥ **Lease Liability**

Alert Company has the following two leasing options to acquire a new machine:

	Lease Option 1	Lease Option 2
Transfer of ownership	No	No
Bargain purchase option	No	No
Lease term	8 years	2 years
Estimated useful life	11 years	5 years
Fair market value	$20,000	$20,000
Present value of lease payments	$17,000	$9,000

Discuss how each lease option would affect Alert's financial statements assuming the company uses IFRS.

Solution

Lease option 1 would be recorded as a finance lease because the lease term is a major part of the economic life of the machinery (8 years ÷ 11 years = 72.7%). Because of this, an asset and a liability would be reported on the balance sheet. Depreciation expense and interest expense would be reported on the income statement.

Lease option 2 would be recorded as an operating lease because none of the five conditions of a finance lease have been met. There would be no impact on the balance sheet, but the lease payments would be reported as rental expense on the income statement.

Related exercise material: BE15–19, BE15–20, BE15–21, and E15–20.

Statement Presentation and Analysis

Companies report non-current liabilities in a separate section of the balance sheet immediately following current liabilities as shown below. Details of the non-current liabilities, such as interest rates, maturity dates, and assets pledged as collateral, are disclosed in the notes to the financial statements. This is so investors and creditors can understand the impact of such liabilities on a company's solvency (its ability to pay). We will look at the presentation and analysis of liabilities in the next sections.

PRESENTATION

The liabilities section of the balance sheet for Willow Company Ltd. is presented below.

WILLOW COMPANY LTD. Balance Sheet (partial) December 31, 2017	
Current Liabilities	
Accounts payable	$ 70,000
Bond interest payable	18,400
Current portion of mortgage note payable	55,520
Current portion of lease liability	113,220
Total current liabilities	257,140
Non-current liabilities	
Bonds payable, 4%, due in 2021	920,000
Mortgage note payable, 8%, due in 2025	444,480
Lease liability	526,780
Total non-current liabilities	1,891,260
Total liabilities	$2,148,400

Recall that the amount of debt maturing within 12 months of the balance sheet date should be reported under current liabilities Therefore, the principal payments for the next year on the notes payable and lease liabilities are reported in current liabilities and the remaining unpaid principal is classified in non-current liabilities. In the Willow example, the company has a mortgage note payable of $500,000 ($55,520 + $444,480); $55,520 will be paid in 2018 and the remaining amount of $444,480 classified in non-current liabilities will be paid off in instalments from 2019 to 2025. Similarly, the current portion of the lease liability ($113,220) is the principal payments on the leases that will be made in 2018 and the non-current lease liability ($526,780) is the principal amount that will be paid in 2019 and future years.

Note that Willow is reporting bond interest payable of $18,400 in current liabilities because the interest will be paid in 2018 and bonds payable of $920,000 in non-current liabilities because the bonds mature in 2021. Note that there is no current portion of bonds payable because the bonds are paid off in one lump sum at maturity.

ANALYSIS

Long-term creditors and investors are interested in solvency ratios, which measure a company's ability to repay its non-current liabilities and survive over a long period of time. They are particularly interested in a company's ability to pay interest when it is due and to repay its debt at maturity. Two examples of solvency ratios are debt to total assets and the interest coverage ratio. They are explained next.

Debt to Total Assets

Debt to total assets measures the percentage of the total assets that is financed by creditors rather than by shareholders. Financing provided by creditors is riskier than financing provided by shareholders, because debt must be repaid at specific points in time whether the company is doing well or not.

Illustration 15-23 shows how the debt to total assets ratio is calculated. Using data from Corus Entertainment's financial statements (dollars in thousands), the ratio is calculated by dividing total liabilities (both current and long-term) by total assets (dollars in thousands).

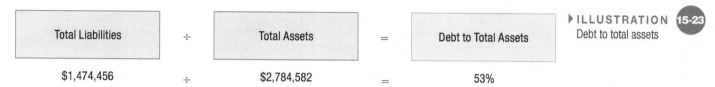

Total Liabilities	÷	Total Assets	=	Debt to Total Assets
$1,474,456	÷	$2,784,582	=	53%

▶ ILLUSTRATION 15-23
Debt to total assets

This means that 53% of Corus's assets are financed by creditors. The remainder, 47%, has been financed by shareholders. In general, the higher the percentage of debt to total assets, the greater the risk that the company may be unable to meet its maturing obligations.

Interest Coverage

The debt to total assets ratio must be interpreted in light of the company's ability to handle its debt. That is, a company might have a high debt to total assets ratio but still be able to easily pay its interest payments. Alternatively, a company may have a low debt to total assets ratio and struggle to cover its interest payments.

The **interest coverage ratio** indicates the company's ability to meet interest payments as they come due. It is calculated by dividing profit before interest expense and income tax expense by interest expense. The numerator is often abbreviated and called **EBIT**, which stands for "earnings before interest and tax." EBIT can be calculated by adding back interest expense and income tax expense to profit. Because these amounts were originally deducted to determine profit, adding them back has the effect of cancelling them.

Alternative terminology The interest coverage ratio is also commonly known as the times interest earned ratio.

Illustration 15-24 calculates interest coverage for Corus (dollars in thousands).

Profit + Interest Expense + Income Tax Expense (EBIT)	÷	Interest Expense	=	Interest Coverage
$156,169 + $48,320 + $53,433	÷	$48,320	=	5.3 times

▶ ILLUSTRATION 15-24
Interest coverage

With an interest coverage ratio of 5.3, Corus appears equipped to handle its interest payments.

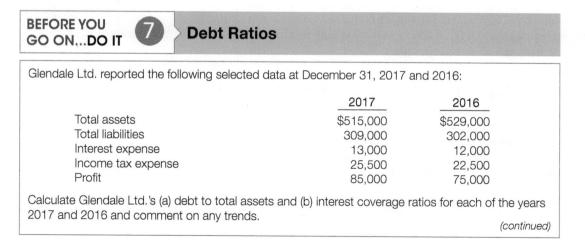

BEFORE YOU GO ON...DO IT　**7**　**Debt Ratios**

Glendale Ltd. reported the following selected data at December 31, 2017 and 2016:

	2017	2016
Total assets	$515,000	$529,000
Total liabilities	309,000	302,000
Interest expense	13,000	12,000
Income tax expense	25,500	22,500
Profit	85,000	75,000

Calculate Glendale Ltd.'s (a) debt to total assets and (b) interest coverage ratios for each of the years 2017 and 2016 and comment on any trends.

(continued)

Action Plan
- Divide the total liabilities by the total assets to calculate the debt to total assets ratio.
- Add the interest expense and income tax expense to profit to calculate earnings before interest and income tax.
- Divide the earnings before interest and income tax expense by the interest expense to calculate the interest coverage ratio.

> **BEFORE YOU GO ON...DO IT 7** > **Debt Ratios** *(continued)*

Solution

	2017	2016
(a) Debt to total assets	$309,000 ÷ $515,000 = 60%	$302,000 ÷ $529,000 = 57%
(b) Interest coverage	($85,000 + $25,500 + $13,000) ÷ $13,000 = 9.5 times	($75,000 + $22,500 + $12,000) ÷ $12,000 = 9.1 times

Glendale's debt to total assets increased in 2017 over 2016. In general, the higher the debt to total assets, the greater the risk that the company may be unable to meet its maturing obligations. The company's interest coverage ratio increased to 9.5 times. In general it is better to have a higher interest coverage ratio. Even though Glendale's debt to total assets increased, given the increase in interest coverage, the company seems well equipped to meet its interest payments.

Related exercise material: BE15–22, BE15–23, BE15–24, E15–21, and E15–22.

Comparing IFRS and ASPE

Key Differences	International Financial Reporting Standards (IFRS)	Accounting Standards for Private Enterprises (ASPE)
Bond discount and premium amortization	Must use the effective-interest method to amortize any bond discount or premium.	Normally will use the effective-interest method to amortize any bond discount or premium but permitted to use alternative methods if the results do not differ materially from the effective-interest method.
Leases: terminology	Non-operating leases are called "finance leases."	Non-operating leases are called "capital leases."
Leases: classification as finance/capital lease	• Professional judgement is used to assess whether the lease term is the major part of economic life or if the present value of the lease payments amounts to substantially the fair value of the leased property. • Lease of a specialized asset is a finance lease.	• Specific benchmarks are used when assessing lease term (75%) and the present value of the lease payments (90%). • Does not include the specialized asset condition.

Demonstration Problem 1

On January 1, 2017, Fallon Inc. issued $500,000 of 10-year, 7% bonds at 93.205 because the market interest rate was 8%. Interest is payable semi-annually on January 1 and July 1. Fallon's year end is June 30. On January 1, 2020, Fallon redeemed all of these bonds at 90 after making the semi-annual interest payment.

Instructions
(a) Using present value concepts, prove the issue price of the bonds of 93.205. Round all calculations to the nearest dollar.
(b) Prepare the journal entry to record the issue of the bonds on January 1, 2017.
(c) Prepare a bond discount amortization schedule for the first six interest periods.
(d) Prepare the journal entry to record the interest accrual on June 30.
(e) Show the presentation of the interest payable and the bonds payable on Fallon's balance sheet on June 30, 2017.
(f) Prepare the journal entry to record the payment of the interest on January 1, 2020, and the redemption of the bonds on January 1, 2020.

SOLUTION TO DEMONSTRATION PROBLEM 1

(a)

1. $500,000 × 93.205% $466,025
2. Key inputs:
   Future value $(FV) = \$500,000$
   Market interest rate $(i) = 4\%(8\% × {}^6/_{12})$
   Interest payment $(PMT) = \$17,500$ $(\$500,000 × 7\% × {}^6/_{12})$
   Number of semi-annual periods $(n) = 20$ $(10 × 2)$
   Present value of $500,000 received in 20 periods $228,195
   $500,000 × 0.45639 $(n = 20, i = 4\%)$
   Present value of $17,500 received for each of 20 periods   237,830
   $17,500 × 13.59033 $(n = 20, i = 4\%)$

   Present value (market price) of bonds $466,025

(b)

Jan. 1, 2017	Cash	466,025	
	Bonds Payable		466,025
	To record issue of 10-year, 7% bonds.		

(c)

FALLON INC.
Bond Discount Amortization Schedule
Effective-Interest Method

Semi-Annual Interest Period	(A) Interest Payment ($500,000 × 7% × ⁶/₁₂)	(B) Interest Expense (D × 8% × ⁶/₁₂)	(C) Discount Amortization (B − A)	(D) Bond Amortized Cost + C
Jan. 1, 2017				$466,025
July 1, 2017	$17,500	$18,641	$1,141	467,166
Jan. 1, 2018	17,500	18,687	1,187	468,353
July 1, 2018	17,500	18,734	1,234	469,587
Jan. 1, 2019	17,500	18,783	1,283	470,870
July 1, 2019	17,500	18,835	1,335	472,205
Jan. 1, 2020	17,500	18,888	1,388	473,593

(d)

June 30, 2017	Interest Expense	18,641	
	Bonds Payable		1,141
	Interest Payable		17,500
	To record accrual of semi-annual interest.		

(e)

FALLON INC.
Balance Sheet (partial)
June 30, 2017

Current liabilities
   Bond interest payable $17,500
Non-current liabilities
   Bonds payable $467,166

ACTION PLAN

- Calculate the proceeds using the stated percentage rate; multiply the face value by the issue price expressed as a percentage (e.g., 93.205%).
- Identify the key inputs required to determine present value, whether using tables or a financial calculator.
- Calculate the present value (issue price) using the semi-annual market interest rate for *(i)*. Use the face value of the bonds and the contractual interest rate to calculate the semi-annual interest payments. The face value of the bonds is the (FV), which is a single sum. The interest payments, which recur periodically, are an annuity. Don't forget to double the number of interest periods and halve the interest rate for semi-annual interest.
- If the proceeds are greater than the face value, the difference is a premium. If the proceeds are less than the face value, the difference is a discount.
- Debit cash and credit bonds payable for the amount the bonds were issued at.
- Calculate the interest expense by multiplying the semi-annual market rate by the amortized cost of the bonds payable.
- The amount of the discount (premium) amortization is the difference between the interest payment and the interest expense.
- Amortization of a bond discount increases interest expense; amortization of a bond premium decreases interest expense.
- To record the redemption: update any partial period interest and amortization if required, (1) eliminate the amortized cost of the bonds by removing the balance from the Bonds Payable account, (2) record the cash paid, and (3) calculate and record the gain or loss (the difference between the cash paid and the amortized cost).

Solution to Demonstration Problem 1 *continued*

(f)

Jan. 1, 2020	Interest Expense	18,888	
	Bonds Payable		1,388
	Cash		17,500
	To record payment of semi-annual interest.		
Jan. 1, 2020	Bonds Payable	473, 593	
	Cash ($500,000 × 90%)		450,000
	Gain on Redemption of Bonds		
	($473,593 − $450,000)		23,593
	To record redemption of bonds.		

Demonstration Problem 2

Note: This demonstration problem uses the same facts as those shown in the "Do It 5" problem at the end of the Instalment Notes Payable section, but the nature and amount of the payment are changed.

On December 31, 2017, Tian Inc. issued a $500,000, 15-year, 8% mortgage note payable. The terms provide for semi-annual fixed principal payments of $16,667 on June 30 and December 31. Tian's year end is December 31.

Instructions
Round your answers to the nearest dollar.
(a) Prepare an instalment payment schedule for the first two years of the note (through to December 31, 2019).
(b) Prepare the journal entries to record the issue of the note on December 31, 2017, and the first two instalment payments.
(c) Indicate the current and non-current amounts for the mortgage note payable at December 31, 2018.
(d) What is the difference between your results here using a fixed principal payment and the results shown using a blended payment for the same situation illustrated in the "Do It 5" problem at the end of the Instalment Notes Payable section?

ACTION PLAN

- Determine the amount of the fixed principal payment by dividing the principal borrowed ($500,000) by the number of periods (15 years × 2).
- Determine the interest expense for the mortgage by multiplying the semi-annual interest rate by the principal balance at the beginning of the period. The cash payment is the total of the principal payment and interest expense.
- Use the payment schedule to record the reduction of principal, the interest expense, and the cash payment.
- The current portion of the mortgage note payable is the amount of principal that will be repaid in the next year. The non-current portion is the remaining balance.

SOLUTION TO DEMONSTRATION PROBLEM 2

(a)

Semi-Annual Interest Period	Cash Payment	Interest Expense	Reduction of Principal	Principal Balance
Dec. 31, 2017 (Issue date)				$500,000
June 30, 2018	$36,667[1]	$20,000[2]	$16,667[3]	483,333[4]
Dec. 31, 2018	36,000	19,333	16,667	466,666
June 30, 2019	35,334	18,667	16,667	449,999
Dec. 31, 2019	34,667	18,000	16,667	433,332

[1]$20,000 + $16,667 = $36,667
[2]$500,000 × 8% × 6/12 = $20,000
[3]$500,000 ÷ 30 periods = $16,667
[4]$500,000 − $16,667 = $483,333

(b)

Dec. 31, 2017	Cash	500,000	
	Mortgage Note Payable		500,000
	To record issue of 15-year, 8% mortgage note payable.		
June 30, 2018	Interest Expense	20,000	
	Mortgage Note Payable	16,667	
	Cash		36,667
	To record semi-annual payment on note.		
Dec. 31, 2018	Interest Expense	19,333	
	Mortgage Note Payable	16,667	
	Cash		36,000
	To record semi-annual payment on note.		

(c) The current liability is $33,334 ($16,667 + $16,667).
The non-current liability is $433,332.
The total liability is $466,666, the balance at the end of the second period, December 31, 2018.

(d) In a blended payment situation, the cash payment stays constant. In a fixed principal payment situation, the reduction of the principal stays constant. In both situations, the same amount of principal is ultimately repaid over the same period of time—just in a different payment pattern.

▶ Summary of Learning Objectives

1. **Describe the characteristics of bonds.** Debt offers the following advantages over equity: (1) shareholder control is not affected, (2) income tax savings result, (3) earnings per share may be higher, and (4) return on equity may be higher. Bonds are a common form of non-current debt issued by entities. Bonds have many different features and may be secured, unsecured, convertible, and callable. The terms of the bond are set forth in the bond indenture, and a bond certificate provides the specific information about the bond itself.

2. **Calculate the price of a bond.** Because interest rates fluctuate, the market price of a bond may vary. Bond pricing is determined using time value of money concepts. To calculate the price of a bond, it is necessary to calculate the present value of the following two cash flows associated with the bond: (1) the present value of the interest payments over the life of the bond and (2) the present value of the principal to be repaid. This calculation may be done using either present value tables or a financial calculator.

3. **Account for bond transactions.** When bonds are issued, the Bonds Payable account is credited for the bonds' market value (present value). Bonds are issued at a discount if the market interest rate is higher than the contractual interest rate. Bonds are issued at a premium if the market interest rate is lower than the contractual interest rate.

Bond discounts and bond premiums are amortized to interest expense over the life of the bond using the effective-interest method of amortization. Amortization of the bond discount or premium is the difference between the interest paid and the interest expense. Interest paid is calculated by multiplying the face value of the bonds by the contractual interest rate. Interest expense is calculated by multiplying the amortized cost of the bonds at the beginning of the interest period by the market interest rate. The amortization of a bond discount increases interest expense. The amortization of a bond premium decreases interest expense.

4. **Account for the retirement of bonds.** When bonds are retired at maturity, Bonds Payable is debited and Cash is credited. There is no gain or loss at retirement. When bonds are redeemed before maturity, it is necessary to pay and record any unrecorded interest, (1) eliminate the amortized cost of the bonds at the redemption date, (2) record the cash paid, and (3) recognize any gain or loss on redemption.

5. **Account for instalment notes payable.** Instalment notes payable are repayable in a series of instalments. Each payment consists of (1) interest on the unpaid balance of the note, and (2) a reduction of the principal balance. These payments can be either (1) fixed principal plus interest payments or (2) blended principal and interest

payments. With fixed principal payments, the reduction in principal is constant but the cash payment and interest decrease each period (as the principal decreases). With blended payments, the cash payment is constant but the interest decreases and the principal reduction increases each period.

6. ***Account for leases.*** For an operating lease, lease (or rental) payments are recorded as an expense by the lessee (renter). For a finance or capital lease, the transaction is considered to be equivalent to a purchase of an asset. The lessee records the asset and the related obligation at the present value of the future lease payments. The income statement reflects both the interest expense and depreciation expense.

7. ***Explain and illustrate the methods for the presentation and analysis of non-current liabilities.*** The current portion of debt is the amount of the principal that must be paid within one year of the balance sheet date. This amount is reported as a current liability in the balance sheet, and the remaining portion of the principal is reported as a non-current liability. The nature of each liability should be described in the notes accompanying the financial statements. A company's long-term solvency may be analyzed by calculating two ratios. Debt to total assets indicates the proportion of company assets that is financed by debt. Interest coverage measures a company's ability to meet its interest payments as they come due.

Glossary

Amortized cost   The face value (principal amount) of the bonds less any unamortized discount or plus any unamortized premium. (p. 787)

Amortizing the discount   The allocation of the bond discount to interest expense over the life of the bonds. (p. 789)

Amortizing the premium   The allocation of the bond premium to interest expense over the life of the bonds. (p. 793)

Bond   A debt security that is traded on an organized securities exchange, is issued to investors, and has these properties: the principal amount will be repaid at a designated maturity date and periodic interest is paid (normally semi-annually) at a specified rate on the principal amount. (p. 778)

Bond certificate   A legal document indicating the name of the issuer, the face value of the bond, and other data such as the contractual interest rate and maturity date of the bond. (p. 780)

Callable bonds   Bonds that the issuing company can redeem (buy back) at a stated dollar amount prior to maturity. Also known as *redeemable bonds*. (p. 780)

Capital lease   A lease that transfers substantially all the benefits and risks of ownership to the lessee, so that the lease effectively results in a purchase of the asset under ASPE. Referred to a *finance lease* under IFRS. (p. 804)

Collateral   Assets pledged as security on a loan. (p. 779)

Contractual interest rate   The rate that determines the amount of interest the borrower pays and the investor receives. Also known as *coupon interest rate* and *stated interest rate*. (p. 780)

Convertible bonds   Bonds that can be converted into common shares at the bondholder's option. (p. 780)

Coupon interest rate   The rate that determines the amount of interest the borrower pays and the investor receives. Also known as *contractual interest rate* and *stated interest rate*. (p. 780)

Debentures   Bonds issued against the general credit of the borrower. Also known as *unsecured bonds*. (p. 780)

Debt to total assets   The ratio of total liabilities to total assets. Indicates the proportion of assets that is financed by debt. (p. 807)

Discount (on bonds payable)   The difference that results when bonds' selling price is less than their face value. This occurs when the market interest rate is greater than the contractual interest rate. (p. 785)

EBIT   Earnings before interest and tax, calculated as profit + interest expense + income tax expense. (p. 807)

Effective-interest method of amortization   A method of calculating interest expense and of amortizing a bond discount or bond premium that results in periodic interest expense equal to a constant percentage of the amortized cost of the bonds. (p. 787)

Face value   The amount of principal that the issuer must pay at the bond's maturity date. Also known as *maturity value* and *par value*. (p. 780)

Finance lease   A lease that transfers all the benefits and risks of ownership to the lessee, so that the lease effectively results in a purchase of the asset under IFRS. Also known as *capital lease* under ASPE. (p. 804)

Financial leverage   Borrowing at one rate and investing at a different rate. (p. 779)

Fixed interest rate   An interest rate that is constant (unchanged) over the term of the debt. (p. 799)

Floating (or variable) interest rate   An interest rate that changes over the term of the debt with fluctuating market rates. (p. 799)

Future value   An amount that will be paid in the future. In the case of bonds payable, it is the face amount of the bonds. (p. 785)

Instalment note   Normally a long-term note that is payable in a series of periodic payments. (p. 799)

Instalments   A series of periodic payments made to repay a note payable. (p. 799)

Interest coverage ratio   A measure of a company's ability to meet its interest obligations. It is calculated by dividing profit (earnings) before interest expense and income tax expense (EBIT) by interest expense. (p. 807)

Lease   A contractual arrangement between two parties where the party that owns an asset agrees to allow another party to use the specified property for a series of cash payments over an agreed period of time. (p. 803)

Lessee The renter of a property. (p. 803)

Lessor The owner of an asset for rent. (p. 803)

Market (effective) interest rate The rate that investors require for lending money to a company. (p. 781)

Market value (of the bond) The price that the bond trades at. (p. 781)

Maturity date The date on which the final payment on a debt security is due to be repaid by the issuer to the investor. (p. 780)

Maturity value The amount of principal that the issuer must pay at the bond's maturity date. Also known as *face value* and *par value*. (p. 780)

Mortgage bond A secured bond where real estate is provided as collateral. (p. 779)

Mortgage note payable An instalment note payable that pledges title to specific assets as security for a loan. (p. 799)

Non-current liability Obligation that is expected to be paid after one year or longer. (p. 778)

Off–balance sheet financing The intentional effort by a company to structure its financing arrangements to avoid showing liabilities on its books. (p. 804)

Operating lease A lease where the benefits and risks of ownership are not transferred to the lessee. (p. 803)

Par value The amount of principal that the issuer must pay at a bond's maturity date. Also known as *face value* and *maturity value*. (p. 780)

Premium (on bonds payable) The difference that results when bonds' selling price is greater than their face value. This occurs when the market interest rate is less than the contractual interest rate. (p. 785)

Present value The amount that must be invested today at a specified interest rate to have a certain amount in the future. (p. 782)

Redeemable bonds Bonds that the issuer can retire at a stated dollar amount before maturity. Also known as *callable bonds*. (p. 780)

Redemption price An amount that a company pays to buy back bonds that is specified at the time the bonds are issued. (p. 798)

Secured bonds Bonds with specific assets pledged as collateral by the bond issuer. (p. 779)

Sinking fund bonds Bonds secured by specific assets set aside to redeem (retire) the bonds. (p. 779)

Stated interest rate The rate that determines the amount of interest the borrower pays and the investor receives. Also known as *contractual interest rate* and *coupon interest rate*. (p. 780)

Unsecured bonds Bonds issued against the general credit of the borrower. Also known as *debentures*. (p. 780)

▶ Self-Study Questions

Answers are at the end of the chapter.

(LO 1) K **1.** The term used for bonds that are unsecured is:
(a) callable bonds.
(b) sinking fund bonds.
(c) debenture bonds.
(d) convertible bonds.

(LO 1) K **2.** The market interest rate:
(a) is the contractual interest rate used to determine the amount of cash interest paid by the borrower.
(b) is listed in the bond indenture.
(c) is the rate investors demand for lending funds.
(d) All of the above.

(LO 2) AP **3.** A 10-year bond is issued with semi-annual interest payments. The contractual rate of the bond is 4%, while the current market rate is 3%. The n and i factors to determine the price of the bond is:
(a) $n = 10$, $i = 2\%$
(b) $n = 20$, $i = 3\%$
(c) $n = 20$, $i = 2\%$
(d) $n = 20$, $i = 1.5\%$

(LO 2) K **4.** If bonds are issued at a discount, it indicates that:
(a) the contractual interest rate is higher than the market interest rate.
(b) the market interest rate is higher than the contractual interest rate.
(c) the contractual interest rate and the market interest rate are the same.
(d) the bonds are junk bonds.

(LO 2) K **5.** Communications Inc. issues $1 million of 10-, 4% bonds when the market rate of interest is Interest is paid semi-annually. Investors will
(a) not buy the bonds because the market of interest is higher than the contractual interest.
(b) buy the bonds for $1 million.
(c) buy the bonds for more than $1 m.
(d) buy the bonds for less than $1 m.

(LO 3) AP **6.** On January 1, Shears Corp. issues 0,000 of 5-year, 4% bonds at 101. The entry to rec the issue of the bonds is:
(a) debit to Cash for $400,000 a credit to Bonds Payable for $400,000.
(b) credit to Cash for $400,00 and debit to Bonds Payable for $400,000.
(c) credit to Cash for $404,0 and debit to Bonds Payable for $404,000.
(d) debit to Cash for $404,000 and credit to Bonds Payable for $404,000

(LO 3) K   7. When bonds are issued at a discount, the discount is amortized over the life of the bonds. The best reason for amortizing the bond discount is to:
     (a) reflect that the bond discount is considered an increase in the cost of borrowing.
     (b) decrease the amortized cost of the bond to its face value at maturity.
     (c) reflect that the bond discount is considered a reduction in the cost of borrowing.
     (d) ensure the bond payable is recorded at its fair value over the life of the bond.

(LO 4) AP   8. Gester Corporation redeems its $100,000 face value bonds at 105 on January 1, after the payment of semi-annual interest. The amortized cost of the bonds at the redemption date is $103,745. The entry to record the redemption will be:
     (a) a debit to Bonds Payable of $103,745 and a credit to Cash of $103,745.
     (b) a debit to Bonds Payable of $100,000, a debit to Loss on Bond Redemption of $3,745, and a credit to Cash of $103,745.
     (c) a debit to Bonds Payable of $103,745, a debit to Loss on Bond Redemption of $1,255, and a credit to Cash of $105,000.
     (d) a debit to Bonds Payable of $105,000 and a credit to Cash of $105,000.

(LO 5) AP   9. Zhang Inc. issues a $497,000, 3-year, 7% instalment note payable on January 1. The note will be paid in three annual blended payments of $189,383 each. What is the amount of interest expense that should be recognized by Zhang in the second year?
     (a) $21,533
     (b) $23,193
     (c) $23,968
     (d) $34,790

(LO 5) AP 10. Assume that the note issued by Zhang Inc. in question 9 above will be paid with fixed principal payments of $165,667 each. What is the amount of interest expense that should be recognized by Zhang in the second year?
     (a) $25,628
     (b) $23,193
     (c) $11,596
     (d) $34,790

(LO 6) C 11. The lease term for Lease A is equal to 74% of the estimated economic life of the leased property. The lease term for Lease B is equal to 45% of the estimated economic life of the leased property. Assuming the lessee reports under IFRS and no other conditions are met, how should the lessee classify these leases?

	Lease A	Lease B
(a)	Operating lease	Finance lease
(b)	Operating lease	Operating lease
(c)	Finance lease	Operating lease
(d)	Finance lease	Finance lease

(LO 7)AN 12. Which of the following situations would most likely indicate that a company's solvency has deteriorated?
     (a) Increasing debt to total assets and increasing interest coverage ratios
     (b) Decreasing debt to total assets and decreasing interest coverage ratios
     (c) Increasing debt to total assets and decreasing interest coverage ratios
     (d) Decreasing debt to total assets and increasing interest coverage ratios

Questions

(LO 1)   1. What is the difference between a current liability and a non-current liability? Give two examples of each type of liability.

(LO 1) C   2. Contrast the following types of bonds: (a) secured and unsecured, and (b) convertible and callable.

(LO 1) K   3. The following terms are important in issuing bonds: (a) face value, (b) contractual interest rate, (c) bond certificate. Explain each of these terms.

(LO 2) K   4. Describe the two major obligations incurred by a company when bonds are issued.

(LO 2) K   5. Explain how the price of a bond is determined.

(LO 2) C   6. Assume that Stoney Inc. sold bonds with a face value of $100,000 for $102,000. Was the market interest rate equal to, less than, or greater than the bonds' contractual interest rate? Explain.

(LO 3) K   7. Explain how the bond discount amortization is calculated using the effective-interest method when bonds are issued at a discount.

(LO 3) C   8. Windsor Corporation issues $500,000 of 9%, 5-year bonds on January 1, 2017, at 104. If Windsor uses the effective-interest method in amortizing the premium, will the annual interest expense increase or decrease over the life of the bonds? Explain.

(LO 4) AP   9. Which accounts are debited and which are credited if a bond issue originally sold at a premium is redeemed before maturity at 97 immediately following the payment of interest?

(LO 4) C 10. Why is there no gain or loss when bonds are redeemed at maturity, but there usually is a gain or loss when bonds are redeemed before maturity?

(LO 5) C   11. What is the difference between instalment notes payable with fixed principal payments and those with blended payments?

(LO 5) AP 12. Pavlina borrowed $15,000 from the bank and signed a 3-year, 6% instalment note payable with fixed annual principal payments. She wants to know how to calculate what the annual fixed principal payment will be. Explain.

(LO 5) AP 13. Bob Holowachuk, a friend of yours, recently purchased a home for $300,000. He paid $30,000 as a cash down payment and financed the remainder with a 20-year, 6% mortgage, payable in blended payments of $1,934 per month. At the end of the first month, Bob received a statement from the bank indicating that only $584 of the principal was paid during the month. At this rate, he calculated that it will take over 38 years to pay off the mortgage. Do you agree? Explain.

(LO 6) C   14. What is a lease? Distinguish between a finance lease and an operating lease.

(LO 6) C   15. What is off–balance sheet financing? Why are long-term operating leases considered to be a form of off–balance sheet financing?

(LO 6) C   16. Josh doesn't understand why leased property can be recorded as an asset when a company does not own the property. Explain this to Josh.

(LO 7) K   17. In addition to what is reported in the balance sheet for non-current liabilities, what information is provided in the notes to the financial statements?

(LO 7) K   18. How are the current and non-current portions of a mortgage note payable determined for presenting them in the liabilities section of the balance sheet?

(LO 7) K   19. Distinguish between liquidity and solvency. Mention two ratios that are used to measure each.

(LO 7) C   20. Huan Yue is wondering why the debt to total assets and interest coverage ratios are calculated. Answer her question and explain why the debt to total assets ratio should never be interpreted without also referring to the interest coverage ratio.

▶ Brief Exercises

BE15–1   State whether each of the following statements is true or false.

1. A disadvantage of issuing bonds is that it puts current shareholders at risk of losing full control of the company.
2. Financial leverage is when a company borrows at one rate and invests at a different rate.
3. Bonds, like shares, may be bought by investors on organized securities exchanges.
4. Convertible bonds are also known as callable bonds.
5. The market rate is the rate investors demand for lending funds.

Evaluate statements about bonds. (LO 1) C

BE15–2   Precision Inc. issued $900,000 of 10-year, 5% bonds on January 1, 2017. Interest is to be paid semi-annually. The market interest rate was 6%.

(a) What is the face value of the bond? When will this be paid?
(b) What interest rate will be used to determine the price of the bond?
(c) How many interest payments will be made over the life of the bond?
(d) What will the interest payments be every six months?

Determine present value factors (LO 2) AP

BE15–3   Carvel Corp. issued $500,000 of 10-year, 5% bonds with interest payable semi-annually. How much did Carvel receive from the sale of these bonds if the market interest rate was (a) 4%, (b) 5%, and (c) 6%?

Calculate present value of bond. (LO 2) AP

BE15–4   Rockwell Corporation issued $2 million of 5-year, 3% bonds dated January 1, 2017, at 100. Interest is payable annually on January 1 and July 1. Rockwell has a December 31 year end.

(a) Prepare the journal entry to record the sale of these bonds on January 1, 2017.
(b) Prepare the journal entry to record the first interest payment on July 1, 2017.
(c) Prepare the adjusting journal entry on December 31, 2017, to accrue the interest expense.

Record bond transactions for bonds at par. (LO 3) AP

BE15–5   Randle Inc. issues $300,000 of 10-year, 8% bonds at 98. Prepare the journal entry to record the sale of these bonds on March 1, 2017.

Prepare entry for bonds issued at a discount. (LO 3) AP

BE15–6   Price Company issues $400,000 of 20-year, 7% bonds at 101. Prepare the journal entry to record the sale of these bonds on June 1, 2017.

Prepare entry for bonds issued at a premium. (LO 3) AP

BE15–7   Frankum Company has issued three different bonds during 2017. Interest is payable annually on each of these bonds. Calculate the price of the bonds and prepare the journal entry to record each bond transaction at the date of issue.

Prepare entry for bonds issued. (LO 3) AP

(a) On January 1, 2017, Frankum issued 1,000, 8%, 5-year, $1,000 bonds dated January 1, 2017, at face value.
(b) On July 1, Frankum issued $900,000 of 9%, 5-year bonds dated July 1, 2017, at 102.
(c) On September 1, Frankum issued $400,000 of 7%, 5-year bonds dated September 1, 2017, at 98.

Use effective-interest method of bond amortization. (LO 3) AP

BE15–8   Presented below is the partial bond premium amortization schedule for Gomez Corp. Gomez uses the effective-interest method of amortization.

Interest Periods	Interest Payment	Interest Expense	Premium Amortization	Bond Amortized Cost
Issue date				$108,530
1	$4,000	$3,256	$744	107,786
2	4,000	3,234	766	107,020

(a) Prepare the journal entry to record the payment of interest and the premium amortization at the end of the first two periods.
(b) Explain why interest expense is less than interest paid.
(c) Explain why interest expense will decrease each period.

Complete amortization schedule and answer questions. (LO 3) AP

BE15–9   A partial bond amortization schedule for $2-million, 5-year bonds is presented below:

Semi-Annual Interest Period	Interest [2]	Interest [3]	[1] Amortization	Bond Amortized Cost
Issue Date				$1,912,479
Apr. 30	$40,000	$[4]	$7,812	1,920,291
Oct. 31	40,000	48,007	[5]	[6]

(a) Fill in the missing words or amounts for items [1] through [6].
(b) What is the bonds' face value?
(c) What is the bonds' contractual interest rate? The market interest rate?
(d) Prepare the journal entries for the first two interest payments.

Record bond interest using amortization schedule. (LO 3) AP

BE15–10   A partial bond amortization schedule for Chiasson Corp. is provided below. Chiasson has a December 31 year end.

Semi-Annual Interest Period	Interest Payment	Interest Expense	Amortization	Bond Amortized Cost
Jan. 1, 2017				$286,872
July 1, 2017	$6,000	$7,172	$1,172	288,044
Jan. 1, 2018	6,000	7,201	1,201	289,245
July 1, 2018	6,000	7,231	1,231	290,476

(a) Was the bond issued at a premium or discount?
(b) Record the interest payment on July 1, 2017.
(c) Record the adjusting entry on December 31, 2017.
(d) Record the interest payment on January 1, 2018.

Prepare amortization schedule. (LO 3) AP

BE15–11   Elsworth Ltd. issued $1 million of 5-year, 4% bonds dated May 1, 2017, for $1,046,110 when the market interest rate was 3%. Interest is paid semi-annually on May 1 and November 1. Prepare an amortization schedule for the first three interest payments.

Record bond interest using amortization schedule. (LO 3) AP

BE15–12   Villa Corporation issued $3 million of 7-year, 4% bonds dated January 1, 2017, for $2,661,118. The market interest rate when the bonds were issued was 6%. Interest is payable semi-annually on January 1 and July 1. Villa has a December 31 year end.

(a) Prepare an amortization schedule for the first three interest payments.
(b) Prepare the journal entry to record the first interest payment on July 1, 2017.
(c) Prepare the adjusting journal entry on December 31, 2017, to accrue the interest expense.
(d) Prepare the journal entry for the payment of interest on January 1, 2018.

Record redemption of bonds. (LO 4) AP

BE15–13   The balance sheet for Miley Consulting reports the following information on July 1, 2017.

Non-current liabilities
Bonds payable, 4%, due 2020 $940,000

The face value of these bonds is $1,000,000. Miley decides to redeem these bonds at 101 after paying annual interest. Prepare the journal entry to record the redemption on July 1, 2017.

Prepare entry for bond redemption. (LO 4) AP

BE15–14   Prater Corporation issued $400,000 of 10-year bonds at a discount. Prior to maturity, when the bonds' amortized cost was $390,000, the company redeemed the bonds at 97. Prepare the entry to record the redemption of the bonds.

BE15–15   You qualify for a $10,000 loan from the Canada Student Loans Program to help finance your education. Once you graduate, you start repaying this note payable at an interest rate of 4.8%. The monthly cash payment is $105.09, principal and interest, for 120 payments (10 years). Prepare an instalment payment schedule for the first four payments.

Prepare instalment payment schedule. (LO 5) AP

BE15–16   Eyre Inc. issues a $360,000, 10-year, 6% mortgage note payable on November 30, 2017, to obtain financing for a new building. The terms provide for monthly instalment payments. Prepare the journal entries to record the mortgage loan on November 30, 2017, and the first two payments on December 31, 2017, and January 31, 2018, assuming the payment is:

Record note transactions. (LO 5) AP

(a) a fixed principal payment of $3,000.
(b) a blended payment of $3,997.

BE15–17   The following instalment payment schedule is for an instalment note payable:

Calculate current and non-current portion of notes payable. (LO 5) AP

Interest Period	Cash Payment	Interest Expense	Reduction of Principal	Principal Balance
Jan. 1, 2017				$40,000
Jan. 1, 2018	$12,000	$2,000	$10,000	30,000
Jan. 1, 2019	11,500	1,500	10,000	20,000
Jan. 1, 2020	11,000	1,000	10,000	10,000
Jan. 1, 2021	10,500	500	10,000	0

(a) What are the non-current and current portions of the note at December 31, 2017?
(b) What are the non-current and current portions of the note at December 31, 2020?

BE15–18   Elbow Lake Corp. issues a $600,000, 4-year, 4% note payable on March 31, 2017. The terms provide for fixed principal payments annually of $150,000.

Record note transaction; show balance sheet presentation. (LO 5) AP

(a) Prepare the journal entries to record the note on March 31, 2017, and the first payment on March 31, 2018.
(b) Show the balance sheet presentation of the current and non-current liability related to the note as at March 31, 2018.

BE15–19   Prepare the journal entries that the lessee should make to record the following transactions.

Contrast accounting for an operating and capital lease. (LO 6) AP

1. The lessee makes a lease payment of $80,000 to the lessor for equipment in an operating lease transaction.
2. Imhoff Company leases equipment from Noble Construction, Inc. The present value of the lease payments is $700,000. The lease qualifies as a capital lease.

BE15–20   Pierre Paquin leases office space for $2,500 per month from Privateer Commercial Realty Ltd. The lease agreement is for five years. Prepare the journal entry to record the monthly lease payment by the lessee.

Record lease. (LO 6) AP

BE15–21   Chang Corp. leases new manufacturing equipment from Bracer Construction, Inc. The present value of the lease payments is $300,000 and the fair value is $320,000.

Record lease. (LO 6) AP

(a) Which company is the lessor and which company is the lessee?
(b) Prepare the journal entry to record the lease for the lessee.

BE15–22   Selected liability items for Waugh Corporation at December 31, 2017, follow. Prepare the liabilities section of Waugh's balance sheet.

Prepare liabilities section of balance sheet (LO 7) AP

Accounts payable	$ 48,000	Income tax payable	$ 8,000
Bonds payable, due 2028	1,035,000	Notes payable (net of current portion)	145,000
Current portion of notes payable	25,000	Interest payable	26,000
Current portion of lease liability	25,000	Total lease liability	75,000

BE15–23   Molson Coors Brewing Company reported the following selected data at December 31, 2014 (in U.S. $ millions):

Calculate solvency ratios. (LO 7) AP

Total assets	$13,996.3
Total liabilities	6,110.2
Interest expense	145.0
Income tax expense	69.0
Profit	513.5

Calculate the company's (a) debt to total assets and (b) interest coverage ratios.

▶ Exercises

Evaluate statements about bonds. (LO 1, 2) K

E15–1   Nick Bosch has prepared the following list of statements about bonds.

1. Bonds are a form of interest-bearing notes payable.
2. Secured bonds have specific assets of the issuer pledged as collateral for the bonds.
3. Secured bonds are also known as debenture bonds.
4. A conversion feature may be added to bonds to make them more attractive to bond buyers.
5. The rate used to determine the amount of cash interest the borrower pays is called the market interest rate.
6. Bond prices are usually quoted as a percentage of the face value of the bond.
7. The present value of a bond is the value at which it should sell in the marketplace.

Instructions

Identify each statement as true or false. If false, indicate how to correct the statement.

Calculate present value of bonds and record bond issuance. (LO 2, 3) AP

E15–2   Whittemore Corp. issued $500,000 of 3-year, 4% bonds on May 1, 2017. The market interest rate when the bonds were issued was 8%. Interest is payable quarterly.

Instructions

(a) What is the number of interest payments that will be made over the life of the bond?
(b) How much interest will be paid each period?
(c) Determine the price of the bond.
(d) Prepare the journal entry to record the issuance of the bond.

Calculate present value of bonds. (LO 2) AP

E15–3   Central College is about to issue $1 million of 10-year bonds that pay a 6% annual interest rate, with interest payable semi-annually.

Instructions

Calculate the issue price of these bonds if the market interest rate is:
(a) 5%.
(b) 6%.
(c) 7%.

Calculate present value of bonds and record bond issuance. (LO 2, 3) AP

E15–4   Laudie issued $400,000 of 5%, 5-year bonds on January 1, 2017. Interest is payable semi-annually.

Instructions

Calculate the price of the bond and prepare the journal entry to record the issuance of the bond assuming the market rate of interest is:

(a) 4%.
(b) 5%.
(c) 6%.

Record bond transactions. (LO 3) AP

E15–5   Lombard Company issued $400,000 of 8%, 10-year bonds on January 1, 2017, at face value. Interest is payable annually on January 1, 2018.

Instructions

Prepare the journal entries to record the following events:

(a) the issuance of the bonds.
(b) the accrual of interest on December 31, 2017.
(c) the payment of interest on January 1, 2018.
(d) Assuming Lombard has a September 30 year end, prepare the adjusting journal entry needed on September 30, 2017, and prepare the journal entry to record the interest payment on January 1, 2018, assuming reversing entries have not been used.

Record bond transactions. (LO 3) AP

E15–6   On September 1, 2017, Praise Corporation issued $600,000 of 10-year, 3% bonds at 96. Interest is payable semi-annually on September 1 and March 1. Praise's fiscal year end is February 28.

Instructions

(a) Is the market rate of interest higher or lower than 3%? Explain.
(b) Record the issue of the bonds on September 1, 2017.
(c) Record the accrual of interest on February 28, 2018, assuming the semi-annual amortization amount for this interest period is $1,014.
(d) Record the payment of interest on March 1, 2018.

Record bond transactions. (LO 3) AP

E15–7   On July 31, 2017, Mooney Inc. issued $500,000 of 5-year, 4% bonds at 102. Interest is payable semi-annually on July 31 and January 31. Mooney's fiscal year end is January 31.

Instructions

(a) Is the market rate of interest higher or lower than 4%? Explain.
(b) Record the issue of the bonds on July 31, 2017.
(c) Record the payment of interest on January 31, 2018, assuming the semi-annual amortization amount for this interest period is $923.

E15-8   Bight Corporation issued $400,000 of 5-year bonds on April 1, 2016. Interest is paid semi-annually on April 1 and October 1. Below is a partial amortization schedule for the first few years of the bond issue.

Answer questions about amortization schedule.
(LO 3) AP

Semi-Annual Interest Period	Interest Payment	Interest Expense	Amortization	Bond Amortized Cost
Apr. 1, 2016				$418,444
Oct. 1, 2016	$8,000	$6,277	$1,723	416,721
Apr. 1, 2017	8,000	6,251	1,749	414,972
Oct. 1, 2017	8,000	6,225	1,775	413,197
Apr. 1, 2018	8,000	6,198	1,802	411,395
Oct. 1, 2018	8,000	6,171	1,829	409,566
Apr. 1, 2019	8,000	6,143	1,857	407,709

Instructions

(a) Were the bonds issued at a discount or at a premium?
(b) What is the bonds' face value?
(c) What will the bonds' amortized cost be at the maturity date?
(d) What will be the total interest payment over the five-year life of the bonds? Total interest expense?
(e) Prepare the journal entry to record the issuance of the bond.
(f) Prepare the journal entry for the first interest payment.
(g) Prepare the adjusting journal entry on December 31, 2016, assuming this is Bight's year end.
(h) Prepare the journal entry for the payment of interest on April 1, 2017. Assume no reversing entries have been used.

E15-9   Messer Company issued $600,000 of 8%, 7-year bonds on January 1, 2017. The bonds pay interest annually.

Calculate bond issue and prepare amortization schedule of a bond premium.
(LO 3) AP

Instructions

(a) Assuming the market interest rate on January 1, 2017, was 7%, calculate the bond's issue price.
(b) Prepare an effective interest amortization table for this bond.

E15-10   Korman Company issued $800,000 of 7%, 7-year bonds on January 1, 2017. The bonds pay interest annually.

Calculate bond issue and prepare amortization schedule of a bond discount.
(LO 3) AP

Instructions

(a) Assuming the market interest rate on January 1, 2017, was 8%, calculate the bond's issue price.
(b) Prepare an effective interest amortization table for this bond.

E15-11   Western Inc. issues $800,000 of 5-year, 6% bonds on January 1, 2017. The bonds pay interest annually.

Calculate and record bond transactions (LO 3) AP

Instructions

(a) Calculate the issue price of the bonds using a market rate of 5% and record the bond issue.
(b) Prepare an effective interest amortization table for the bonds.
(c) Prepare the journal entries to record the first three interest payments.
(d) Assuming Western has an October 31 year end, prepare the adjusting entry for interest on October 31, 2017.

E15-12   Amlani Company issues $500,000 of 5-year, 7% bonds on January 1, 2017. Interest is paid annually.

Prepare entries for bonds issued at a discount.
(LO 3) AP

Instructions

(a) Assuming the market interest rate was 9% on the date of issue, record the issue of the bonds.
(b) Prepare an effective interest amortization table for the bonds.
(c) Prepare the journal entries to record the first three interest payments.
(d) Assuming Amlani has an October 31 year end, record the adjusting entry for interest on October 31, 2017.

Prepare entries for bond redemption. (LO 4) AP

E15–13 Two independent situations follow:

1. Longbine Corporation redeemed $130,000 face value, 12% bonds on June 30, 2017, at 102. The bonds' amortized cost at the redemption date was $117,500. The bonds pay annual interest, and the interest payment due on June 30, 2017, has been made and recorded.
2. Tastove Inc. redeemed $150,000 face value, 12.5% bonds on June 30, 2017, at 98. The bonds' amortized cost at the redemption date was $151,000. The bonds pay annual interest, and the interest payment due on June 30, 2017, has been made and recorded.

Instructions

For each situation above, prepare the appropriate journal entry for the redemption of the bonds.

Prepare bond interest and bond redemption entries. (LO 3, 4) AP

E15–14 On January 1, 2017, Chilton Ltd. issued $500,000 of 5%, 5-year bonds. The bonds were issued to yield a market interest rate of 6%. Chilton's year end is December 31. On January 1, 2019, immediately after making and recording the semi-annual interest payment, Chilton redeemed the bonds. A partial bond amortization schedule is presented below.

Semi-Annual Interest Period	Interest Payment	Interest Expense	Amortization	Bond Amortized Cost
Jan. 1, 2017				$478,674
July 1, 2017	$12,500	$14,360	$1,860	480,534
Jan. 1, 2018	12,500	14,416	1,916	482,450
July 1, 2018	12,500	14,474	1,974	484,424
Jan. 1, 2019	12,500	14,533	2,033	486,457

Instructions

(a) Prepare the journal entry to record the payment of interest on July 1, 2017.
(b) Prepare the journal entry to accrue the interest expense on December 31, 2017.
(c) Prepare the journal entry to record the payment of interest on January 1, 2018.
(d) Prepare the journal entry to record the redemption of the bonds assuming they were redeemed at 100 on January 1, 2019.
(e) Prepare the journal entry to record the redemption of the bonds assuming they were redeemed at 96.

Record mortgage note payable. (LO 5) AP

E15–15 Cove Resort Corp. issued a 20-year, 7%, $240,000 mortgage note payable to finance the construction of a new building on December 31, 2017. The terms provide for semi-annual instalment payments on June 30 and December 31.

Instructions

Prepare the journal entries to record the mortgage note payable and the first two instalment payments assuming the payment is:

(a) a fixed principal payment of $6,000.
(b) a blended payment of $11,239.

Analyze instalment payment schedule and identify current and non-current portions. (LO 5) AP

E15–16 The following instalment payment schedule is for an instalment note payable:

Interest Period	Cash Payment	Interest Expense	Reduction of Principal	Principal Balance
Jan. 1, 2017				$100,000
Jan. 1, 2018	$23,097	$5,000	$18,097	81,903
Jan. 1, 2019	23,097	4,095	19,002	62,901
Jan. 1, 2020	23,097	3,145	19,952	42,949
Jan. 1, 2021	23,097	2,147	20,950	21,999
Jan. 1, 2022	23,097	1,100	21,999	0

Instructions

(a) Is this a fixed principal or blended payment schedule?
(b) What is the interest rate on the note?
(c) Prepare the journal entry to record the first instalment payment.
(d) What are the non-current and current portions of the note at December 31, 2018?

E15–17   The following instalment payment schedule is for an instalment note payable:

Interest Period	Cash Payment	Interest Expense	Reduction of Principal	Principal Balance
Jan. 1, 2017				$174,000
July 1, 2017	$28,710	$6,960	$21,750	152,250
Jan. 1, 2018	27,840	6,090	21,750	130,500
July 1, 2018	26,970	5,220	21,750	108,750
Jan. 1, 2019	26,100	4,350	21,750	87,000

Instructions

(a) Is this a fixed principal or blended payment schedule?
(b) What is the interest rate on the note?
(c) What is the maturity date on the note?
(d) Prepare the journal entry to record the first instalment payment.
(e) What are the non-current and current portions of the note after the second payment?

Analyze instalment payment schedule and identify current and non-current portions. (LO 5) AP

E15–18   On January 1, 2017, Wolstenholme Corp. borrows $18,000 by signing a 3-year, 7% note payable. The note is repayable in three annual blended payments of $6,859 on December 31 of each year.

Instructions

(a) Prepare an instalment payment schedule for the note.
(b) Prepare journal entries to record the note and the first instalment payment.
(c) What amounts would be reported as current and non-current in the liabilities section of Wolstenholme's balance sheet at December 31, 2017?

Prepare instalment payment schedule and record note payable. Identify balance sheet presentation. (LO 5) AP

E15–19   On January 1, 2017, Jarvis Corp. borrows $8,400 by signing a 3-year, 3% note payable. The note is repayable in three annual fixed principal payments on December 31 of each year.

Instructions

(a) Calculate the annual principal payment.
(b) Prepare an instalment payment schedule for the note.
(c) Prepare journal entries to record the note and the first instalment payment.
(d) What amounts would be reported as current and non-current in the liabilities section of Jarvis' balance sheet at December 31, 2017?

Prepare instalment payment schedule and record note payable. Identify balance sheet presentation. (LO 5) AP

E15–20   Two independent situations follow:

1. Ready Car Rental leased a car to Dumfries Company for one year. Terms of the lease agreement call for monthly payments of $750, beginning on May 21, 2017.
2. On January 1, 2017, InSynch Ltd. entered into an agreement to lease 60 computers from HiTech Electronics. The terms of the lease agreement require three annual payments of $43,737 (including 5.5% interest), beginning on December 31, 2017. The present value of the three payments is $118,000 and the market value of the computers is $120,000.

Instructions

(a) What kind of lease—operating or finance—should be recorded in each of the above situations? Explain your rationale.
(b) Prepare the journal entry, if any, that each company must make to record the lease agreement.

Analyze and record leases. (LO 6) AP

E15–21   Dollarama reported the following selected data (in millions):

	2015	2014
Total assets	$1,700.8	$1.566.8
Total liabilities	960.3	702.6
Profit	295.4	250.0
Income tax expense	107.1	92.7
Interest expense	19.9	11.6

Instructions

(a) Calculate the debt to total assets and interest coverage ratios for 2015 and 2014. Did Dollarama's solvency improve, worsen, or remain unchanged in 2015?
(b) The notes to Dollarama's financial statements show that the company has future operating lease commitments totalling $926.6 million. What is the significance of these unrecorded obligations when analyzing Dollarama's solvency?

Analyze solvency. (LO 7) AP

Prepare non-current
liabilities section of balance
sheet. (LO 7) AP

E15–22 The adjusted trial balance for Ray Corporation at July 31, 2017, the corporation's fiscal year end, contained the following:

Accounts payable	$ 96,000	Note payable	$140,000
Accounts receivable	112,000	Lease liability	65,000
Bonds payable, due 2021	205,000	Note receivable, due December 2017	35,000
Interest payable	5,000	Unearned revenue	10,000

Of the lease liability amount, $16,250 is due within the next year. Total payments on the note payable in the fiscal year 2018 will be $27,000: $7,000 is for interest and $20,000 for principal repayments.

Instructions

(a) Prepare the non-current liabilities section of the balance sheet as at July 31, 2017.

(b) Some of the accounts above belong in the balance sheet but not in its non-current liabilities section. What is the correct classification for them?

▶ Problems: Set A

Prepare entries to record
issuance of bonds at par
and interest accrual, and show
balance sheet presentation.
(LO 1, 2, 3, 7) AP

P15–1A On May 1, 2017, Herron Corp. issued $600,000 of 9%, 5-year unsecured bonds at face value. The bonds were dated May 1, 2017, and pay interest annually on May 1. Financial statements are prepared annually on December 31.

Instructions

(a) Is this a debenture bond? Why or why not?

(b) Prepare the journal entry to record the issuance of the bonds.

(c) Prepare the adjusting entry to record the accrual of interest on December 31, 2017.

(d) Show the balance sheet presentation at December 31, 2017.

(e) Prepare the journal entry to record the payment of interest on May 1, 2018, assuming Herron does not use reversing entries.

(f) Prepare the adjusting entry to record the accrual of interest on December 31, 2018.

<u>TAKING IT FURTHER</u> As a source of long-term financing, what are the major advantages of issuing debt instead of issuing shares? What are the disadvantages?

Fill in missing amounts in
amortization schedule, record
bond transactions, and show
balance sheet presentation.
(LO 2, 3, 7) AP

P15–2A On January 1, 2017, Global Satellites issued $1.4-million, 10-year bonds. The bonds pay semi-annual interest on July 1 and January 1, and Global has a December 31 year end. A partial bond amortization schedule is presented below:

Semi-Annual Interest Period	Interest Payment	Interest Expense	Amortization	Bond Amortized Cost
Jan. 1, 2017				$1,300,514
July 1, 2017	$[1]	$[2]	$3,518	1,304,032
Jan. 1, 2018	42,000	45,641	3,641	1,307,673
July 1, 2018	42,000	45,769	[3]	1,311,442
Jan. 1, 2019	42,000	45,900	[4]	[5]
July 1, 2019	42,000	46,037	4,037	1,319,379
Jan. 1, 2020	42,000	46,178	4,178	1,323,557

Instructions

(a) Were the bonds issued at a premium or a discount?

(b) What is the face value of the bonds?

(c) What is the contractual rate of interest?

(d) Fill in the missing amounts for items [1] through [5].

(e) What was the market interest rate when the bonds were issued?

(f) Record the issue of the bonds on January 1, 2017.

(g) Record the interest payment on July 1, 2017.

(h) Record the accrual of interest on December 31, 2017.

(i) What amounts would be reported as current and non-current in the liabilities section of Global's December 31, 2017, balance sheet?

<u>TAKING IT FURTHER</u> Why would Global's board of directors not have set the contractual interest rate at the market interest rate on the date of issue when it authorized the bond issue?

P15–3A   Paris Products Ltd. issued $3 million of 5%, 5-year bonds on January 1, 2017. The bonds were dated January 1 and pay interest annually. There is no collateral secured against the bonds and Paris Products may buy back the bonds at any time. The market interest rate was 6% for these bonds. Paris has a calendar year end.

Describe the features of a bond, calculate the price of a bond, and record bond transactions. (LO 1, 2, 3) AP

Instructions

(a) Describe the features of these bonds.
(b) Calculate the price of the bonds and record the bond issue.
(c) Prepare an effective interest amortization table for these bonds. Round amounts to the nearest dollar.
(d) Record any required adjusting entries and subsequent payment for the first three interest payments assuming reversing entries have not been used.

TAKING IT FURTHER   Explain the difference between a contractual interest rate and market interest rate. Explain why one rate changes over the term of the bonds and the other stays the same.

P15–4A   Colton Cars Co. issued $1.8 million of 5%, 5-year bonds on January 1, 2017. The bonds were dated January 1 and pay interest annually. The bonds are secured with real estate holdings and the bondholder has the option to convert the bonds into common shares. The market interest rate was 4% for these bonds. Coulton has a calendar year end.

Describe the features of a bond, calculate the price of a bond, and record bond transactions. (LO 1, 2, 3) AP

Instructions

(a) Describe the features of these bonds.
(b) Calculate the price of the bonds and record the bond issue.
(c) Prepare an effective interest amortization table for these bonds. Round amounts to the nearest dollar.
(d) Journalize the first three interest payments assuming reversing entries have been used.

TAKING IT FURTHER   Landon Colton, the owner of Colton Cars Co., wants to know why a board of directors doesn't set the contractual interest rate at the market interest rate on the date of issue when it authorizes a bond issue. He argues that, if the contractual interest rate was set at the market rate, then companies would not have to issue bonds at a premium or discount. Explain this to Landon.

P15–5A   On May 1, 2017, MEM Corp. issued $900,000 of 5-year, 7% bonds at 98. The bonds pay interest annually on May 1. MEM's year end is April 30.

Calculate effective rate using Excel or a financial calculator and record bond transactions. (LO 2, 3, 4) AP

Instructions

(a) Record the issue of the bonds on May 1, 2017.
(b) Calculate the effective rate of the bonds using Excel or a financial calculator.
(c) Prepare an effective interest amortization table for this bond.
(d) Record the accrual of interest at April 30, 2018.
(e) Record the interest payment on May 1, 2018.
(f) Assuming instead that MEM has a December 31, 2017, year end, prepare the adjusting entry relating to these bonds and the subsequent interest payment on May 1, 2018.
(g) Assume that on May 1, 2018, after payment of the interest, MEM redeems all of the bonds at 104. Record the redemption of the bonds.

TAKING IT FURTHER   Why would MEM elect to redeem the bonds early?

P15–6A   On July 1, 2017, Webhancer Corp. issued $4 million of 10-year, 5% bonds at $4,327,029. This price resulted in a 4% market interest rate on the bonds. The bonds pay semi-annual interest on July 1 and January 1, and Webhancer has a December 31 year end.

Record bond transactions. (LO 2, 3, 4) AP

Instructions

(a) Record the issue of the bonds on July 1, 2017.   Cash = 4327029 → Bon payable
(b) Prepare an effective interest amortization table for the first five interest payments for these bonds. Round amounts to the nearest dollar.
(c) Record the accrual of interest at December 31, 2017, and the subsequent payment on January 1, 2018.
(d) Assuming instead that Webhancer has an August 31 year end, prepare the adjusting entry related to these bonds on August 31, 2017, as well as the subsequent interest payment on January 1, 2018.

Jan 1 – In Pay = 100.00 Cash 100k
Bond pay, Int payable
Dec 31 Int Exp, Bond pay, Int payable
Int Exp (100,000 × 2/6) In pay (4M×2.5%)
Bond Cx × 2/6 × 2/6)

TAKING IT FURTHER   Assuming that the bonds were issued at a market interest rate of 6%, calculate the issue price of the bonds.   (4M × 0.55368) + (4M × 2.5% × 15.58916)

Record bond transactions including bond redemption; show balance sheet presentation. (LO 2, 3, 4, 7) AP

P15–7A   On January 1, 2017, Alberta Hydro Ltd. issued bonds with a maturity value of $8 million when the market rate of interest was 4%. The bonds have a coupon (contractual) interest rate of 5% and mature on January 1, 2027. Interest on the bonds is payable semi-annually on July 1 and January 1 of each year. The company's year end is December 31.

Instructions

(a) Calculate the issue price of the bonds.

(b) Prepare a bond amortization schedule from the date of issue up to and including January 1, 2019.

(c) Prepare all of the required journal entries related to the bonds that Alberta Hydro will record during 2017, including any adjusting journal entries at December 31, 2017.

(d) What amounts would be reported as current and non-current in the liabilities section of Alberta Hydro's December 31, 2017, balance sheet?

(e) Record the payment of interest on January 1, 2018.

(f) The bonds were redeemed on January 1, 2019 (after the interest had been paid and recorded) at 102. Prepare the journal entry for the redemption of the bonds.

(g) Assume instead that the bonds were not redeemed on January 1, 2019. Record the entry for the repayment of the bonds on January 1, 2027.

(h) What will be the total interest payment over the 10-year life of the bonds? What will be the total interest expense over the 10-year life of the bonds?

TAKING IT FURTHER   Explain why the total interest payment over the 10-year life of the bonds is equal to or different than the total interest expense over the 10-year life of the bonds.

Prepare entries to record issuance of bonds, balance sheet presentation, and bond redemption. (LO 3, 4, 7) AP

P15–8A   Kershaw Electric sold $6 million of 10%, 10-year bonds on January 1, 2017. The bonds were dated January 1, 2017, and paid interest on January 1. The bonds were sold at 98.

Instructions

(a) Prepare the journal entry to record the issuance of the bonds on January 1, 2017.

(b) Assume that at December 31, 2017, $8,000 of the discount has been amortized. Show the balance sheet presentation of the non-current liability at December 31, 2017.

(c) Assume that on January 1, 2019, when the bonds' amortized cost was $5,896,000, the company redeemed the bonds at 102. Record the redemption of the bonds assuming that interest for the period had already been paid.

TAKING IT FURTHER   How will the total cost of borrowing be affected if a bond is sold (a) at a discount and (b) at a premium?

Prepare instalment payment schedule, record note transactions, and show balance sheet presentation. (LO 5, 7) AP

P15–9A   A local company has just approached a venture capitalist for financing to develop a ski hill. On April 1, 2017, the venture capitalist lent the company $1 million at an interest rate of 5%. The loan is repayable over four years in fixed principal payments. The first payment is due March 31, 2018. The ski hill operator's year end will be December 31.

Instructions

(a) Record the issue of the note payable on April 1, 2017.

(b) Calculate the amount of the fixed principal payment.

(c) Prepare an instalment payment schedule.

(d) Record the accrual of interest on December 31, 2017, and the instalment payment on March 31, 2018.

(e) What amounts would be reported as current and non-current in the liabilities section of the company's December 31, 2017, balance sheet?

(f) Record the accrual of interest on December 31, 2018, and the instalment payment on March 31, 2019.

TAKING IT FURTHER   Explain how the interest expense and reduction of the note payable would change in parts (b) and (c) if the note had been repayable in blended payments of $282,012, rather than in fixed principal payments.

Record note transactions. (LO 5) AP

P15–10A   Olsen Well Services Ltd. purchased equipment for $905,000 on September 30, 2017. The equipment was purchased with a $137,000 cash down payment and through the issue of a $768,000, 5-year, 3.6% mortgage note payable for the balance. The terms provide for the mortgage to be repaid in monthly blended payments of $14,006 starting on October 31.

Instructions

(a) Record the issue of the note payable on September 30.

(b) Record the first two instalment payments on October 31 and November 30. Round amounts to the nearest dollar.

(c) Repeat part (b) assuming that the terms provided for monthly fixed principal payments of $12,800, rather than blended payments of $14,006.

TAKING IT FURTHER   If the instalments are fixed principal payments of $12,800, will the interest expense over the life of the note be greater than, the same as, or less than if the instalments are a blended payment of $14,006? Explain.

P15–11A   Kinyae Electronics issues a $600,000, 10-year, 9% mortgage note payable on December 31, 2017, to help finance a plant expansion. The terms of the note provide for semi-annual blended payments of $46,126. Payments are due on June 30 and December 31.

Instructions

(a) Prepare an instalment payment schedule for the first two years. Round all calculations to the nearest dollar.
(b) Record the issue of the mortgage note payable on December 31, 2017.
(c) Show how the mortgage liability should be reported on the balance sheet at December 31, 2017. (*Hint:* Remember to report any current portion separately from the non-current liability.)
(d) Record the first two instalment payments on June 30, 2018, and December 31, 2018.

Prepare instalment payment schedule and record note transactions. Show balance sheet presentation. (LO 5) AP

TAKING IT FURTHER   Indicate the advantages and disadvantages of making fixed principal payments versus blended payments.

P15–12A   Three different lease transactions are presented below for Manitoba Enterprises, a public company. Assume that all lease transactions start on January 1, 2017. Manitoba does not receive title to the properties, either during the lease term or at the end of it. The yearly rental for each of the leases is paid on January 1 starting on January 1, 2017.

Analyze lease situations. Discuss financial statement presentation. (LO 6) AP

	Manufacturing Equipment	Vehicles	Office Equipment
Lease term	5 years	6 years	3 years
Estimated economic life	15 years	7 years	6 years
Yearly rental payment	$14,000	$14,981	$ 3,900
Fair market value of leased asset	$98,000	$85,000	$17,500
Present value of lease rental payments	$55,000	$74,800	$ 9,500

Instructions

(a) Which of the above leases are operating leases and which are finance leases? Explain.
(b) How should the lease transaction for each of the above assets be recorded on January 1, 2017?
(c) Describe how the lease transaction would be reported on the 2017 income statement and balance sheet for each of the above assets.

TAKING IT FURTHER   For each of the leases, prepare any required adjusting journal entries on December 31, 2017. Assume that Manitoba Enterprises would pay 8% interest if it borrowed cash and purchased the equipment instead of leasing it.

P15–13A   Loblaw Companies Limited reported the following selected information (in millions):

Calculate and analyze solvency ratios. (LO 7) AN

	Jan. 3, 2015	Dec. 28, 2013
Total assets	$33,684	$20,741
Total liabilities	20,897	13,741
Interest expense	466	287
Income tax expense	25	226
Profit	53	627

Instructions

(a) Calculate Loblaw's debt to total assets and interest coverage ratios for each year.
(b) Based on the ratios calculated in part (a), what conclusions can you make about Loblaw's solvency?

TAKING IT FURTHER   Explain the impact that an operating lease has on a company's solvency ratios.

P15–14A   The adjusted trial balance for Sykes Ltd. at October 31, 2017, contained the following:

Prepare liabilities section of balance sheet and analyze leverage. (LO 7) AP

Accounts payable	$ 57,000	Income tax payable	$ 5,900
Accounts receivable	98,000	Note payable	230,211
Allowance for doubtful accounts	4,900	Interest expense	53,330
Bonds payable, due 2020	500,000	Lease liability	40,243
Interest payable	15,000	Note receivable, due December 2018	35,000
Income tax expense	11,800	Unearned revenue	10,000

Of the lease liability amount, $26,430 is due within the next year. Total payments on the note payable in the next 12 months will be $20,800, of which $11,125 is for interest. Sykes reported profit for the year ended October 31, 2017, of $36,000. Total assets are $2,044,147.

Instructions

(a) Prepare the liabilities section of the balance sheet.
(b) Calculate Sykes's debt to total assets and interest coverage ratios for the year ended October 31, 2017.
(c) Based on the ratios calculated in part (b), what conclusions can you make about Sykes's solvency?

TAKING IT FURTHER What other information would help in the analysis of the company's solvency?

▶ Problems: Set B

Prepare entries to record issuance of bonds at par and interest accrual, and show balance sheet presentation.
(LO 1, 2, 3, 7) AP

P15–1B On March 1, 2017, Jade Corp. issued $200,000 of 7%, 5-year unsecured bonds at face value. The bonds were dated March 1, 2017, and pay interest semi-annually on March 1 and September 1. Financial statements are prepared annually on June 30.

Instructions

(a) Is this a debenture bond? Why or why not?
(b) Prepare the journal entry to record the issuance of the bonds.
(c) Prepare the adjusting entry to record the accrual of interest on June 30, 2017. Round amounts to the nearest dollar.
(d) Show the balance sheet presentation at June 30, 2017.
(e) Prepare the journal entry to record the payment of interest on September 1, 2017, assuming Jade does not use reversing entries.
(f) Prepare the journal entry to record the payment of interest on March 1, 2018.

TAKING IT FURTHER As a source of long-term financing, what are the major advantages of issuing debt instead of issuing shares? What are the disadvantages?

Fill in missing amounts in amortization schedule, record bond transactions, and show balance sheet presentation.
(LO 2, 3, 7) AP

P15–2B On January 1, 2017, Ponasis Corporation issued $2.5-million, 10-year bonds. The bonds pay semi-annual interest on July 1 and January 1, and Ponasis has a December 31 year end. Presented below is a partial amortization schedule.

Semi-Annual Interest Period	Interest Payment	Interest Expense	Amortization	Bond Amortized Cost
Jan. 1, 2017				$[1]
July 1, 2017	$62,500	$[2]	$8,412	2,695,981
Jan. 1, 2018	[3]	53,920	8,580	2,687,401
July 1, 2018	62,500	53,748	8,752	2,678,649
Jan. 1, 2019	62,500	53,573	[4]	[5]
July 1, 2019	62,500	53,394	9,106	2,660,616
Jan. 1, 2020	62,500	53,212	9,288	2,651,328

Instructions

(a) Were the bonds issued at a discount or a premium?
(b) What is the face value of the bonds?
(c) What is the contractual rate of interest?
(d) Fill in the missing amounts for items [1] through [5].
(e) What was the market interest rate when the bonds were issued?
(f) Record the issue of the bonds on January 1, 2017.
(g) Record the interest payment on July 1, 2017.
(h) Record the accrual of interest on December 31, 2017.
(i) What amounts would be reported as current and non-current in the liabilities section of Ponasis's December 31, 2017, balance sheet?

TAKING IT FURTHER Why would Ponasis's board of directors not have set the contractual interest rate at the market interest rate on the date of issue when it authorized the bond issue?

P15–3B   Universal Corporation issued $2 million of 5%, 10-year bonds on January 1, 2017. The bonds were dated January 1 and pay interest annually. There is no collateral secured against the bonds and Universal may buy back the bonds at any time. The market interest rate was 4% for these bonds. Universal has a calendar year end.

Describe the features of a bond, calculate the price of a bond, and record bond transactions. (LO 1, 2, 3) AP

Instructions

(a) Describe the features of these bonds.
(b) Calculate the price of the bonds and record the bond issue.
(c) Prepare an effective interest amortization table for these bonds for the first five years. Round amounts to the nearest dollar.
(d) Record any required adjusting entries and subsequent payment for the first three interest payments assuming reversing entries have not been used.

TAKING IT FURTHER   Geoff doesn't understand why the interest expense recorded is higher than the cash paid for interest when bonds are issued at a discount and why the interest expense is lower than the cash paid when bonds are issued at a premium. Explain this to Geoff.

P15–4B   Glover Corporation issued $3.5 million of 6%, 5-year bonds on January 1, 2017. The bonds were dated January 1 and pay interest annually. Glover has a December 31 year end. The bonds are secured with real estate holdings and the bondholder has the option to convert the bonds into common shares. The market interest rate was 7% for these bonds.

Describe the features of a bond, calculate the price of a bond, and record bond transactions. (LO 1, 2, 3) AP

Instructions

(a) Describe the features of these bonds.
(b) Calculate the price of the bonds and record the bond issue.
(c) Prepare an effective interest amortization table for these bonds. Round amounts to the nearest dollar.
(d) Journalize the first three interest payments assuming reversing entries have been used.

TAKING IT FURTHER   Why would a bondholder request to have their bonds converted into common shares?

P15–5B   On October 1, 2017, PFQ Corp. issued $800,000 of 10-year, 5% bonds at 98. The bonds pay interest annually on October 1. PFQ's year end is September 30.

Calculate effective rate using Excel or a financial calculator and record bond transactions. (LO 2, 3, 4, 7) AP

Instructions

(a) Record the issue of the bonds on October 1, 2017.
(b) Calculate the effective rate using Excel or a financial calculator.
(c) Prepare an effective interest amortization table for these bonds up to and including October 1, 2020.
(d) Record the accrual of interest at September 30, 2018.
(e) Record the interest payment on October 1, 2018.
(f) Assuming instead that PFQ Corp. has a December 31 year end, prepare the adjusting entry related to these bonds on December 31, 2017, as well as the subsequent interest payment on October 1, 2018.
(g) Assume that on October 1, 2018, after payment of the interest, PFQ redeems all of the bonds at 97. Record the redemption of the bonds.

TAKING IT FURTHER   Why would PFQ elect to redeem the bonds before they reach maturity?

P15–6B   On July 1, 2017, Waubonsee Ltd. issued $3.2 million of 10-year, 6% bonds at $3,449,427. This price resulted in a market interest rate of 5%. The bonds pay semi-annual interest on July 1 and January 1, and Waubonsee has a December 31 year end.

Record bond transactions. (LO 2, 3, 4) AP

Instructions

(a) Record the issue of the bonds on July 1, 2017.
(b) Prepare an effective interest amortization table for the first five interest payments for these bonds. Round amounts to the nearest dollar.
(c) Record the accrual of interest at December 31, 2017, and the payment on January 1, 2018.
(d) Assuming Waubonsee Ltd. has an October 31 year end, prepare the adjusting entry related to these bonds on October 31, 2017, as well as the subsequent interest payment on January 1, 2018.
(e) Assume that on January 1, 2018, after payment of the interest, Waubonsee Ltd. redeems all of the bonds at 102. Record the redemption of the bonds.

TAKING IT FURTHER   Assuming that the bonds were issued at a market interest rate of 8%, calculate the issue price of the bonds.

P15–7B   On January 1, 2017, Vision Inc. issued bonds with a maturity value of $5 million when the market rate of interest was 5%. The bonds have a coupon (contractual) interest rate of 4% and mature on January 1, 2022. Interest on the bonds is payable semi-annually on July 1 and January 1 of each year. The company's year end is December 31.

Record bond transactions including bond redemption; show balance sheet presentation. (LO 2, 3, 4, 7) AP

Instructions

(a) Calculate the bonds' issue price.

(b) Prepare a bond amortization schedule from the date of issue up to and including January 1, 2019.

(c) Prepare all of the required journal entries related to the bonds that Vision Inc. will record during 2017, including any adjusting journal entries at December 31, 2017.

(d) What amounts would be reported as current and non-current in the liabilities section of Vision's December 31, 2017, balance sheet?

(e) Record the payment of interest on January 1, 2018.

(f) The bonds were redeemed on January 1, 2019 (after the interest had been paid and recorded) at 98. Prepare the journal entry for the redemption of the bonds.

(g) Assume instead that the bonds were not redeemed on January 1, 2019. Record the entry for the repayment of the bonds on January 1, 2022.

(h) What will be the total interest payment over the five-year life of the bonds? What will be the total interest expense over the five-year life of the bonds?

TAKING IT FURTHER Explain why the total interest payment over the five-year life of the bonds is equal to or different than the total interest expense over the five-year life of the bonds.

Prepare entries to record issuance of bonds, balance sheet presentation, and bond redemption. (LO 3, 4, 7) AP

P15–8B Lopez Co. sold $600,000 of 9%, 10-year bonds on January 1, 2017. The bonds were dated January 1, and interest is paid on January 1 and July 1. The bonds were sold at 105.

Instructions

(a) Prepare the journal entry to record the issuance of the bonds on January 1, 2017.

(b) Assume that at December 31, 2017, $2,000 of the premium has been amortized. Show the balance sheet presentation of accrued interest and the bond liability at December 31, 2017.

(c) Assume that on January 1, 2019, when the bonds' amortized cost was $624,000, the company redeemed the bonds at 105. Record the redemption of the bonds assuming that interest for the period has already been paid.

TAKING IT FURTHER Why would the bond redemption result in a gain or a loss to Lopez Co.?

Prepare instalment payment schedule, record note transactions, and show balance sheet presentation. (LO 5, 7) AP

P15–9B Peter Furlong has just approached a venture capitalist for financing for his sailing school. The lenders are willing to lend Peter $120,000 in exchange for a note payable at a high-risk interest rate of 7%. The note is payable over three years in blended payments of $22,520. Payments are made semi-annually on October 31 and April 30. Peter receives the $120,000 on May 1, 2017, the first day of his fiscal year.

Instructions

(a) Record the issue of the note payable on May 1.

(b) Prepare an instalment payment schedule.

(c) Record the first two instalment payments on October 31 and April 30.

(d) What amounts would be reported as current and non-current in the liabilities section of the company's April 30, 2018, balance sheet?

(e) If the note had been repayable in fixed principal payments, rather than in blended payments, calculate how much the cash payments would have been on October 31 and April 30.

TAKING IT FURTHER Indicate which instalment payment method (blended or fixed) results in the larger principal repayment on April 30, 2020 (the date of the last payment). Explain.

Record note transactions. (LO 5) AP

P15–10B Solar Power Corporation purchased equipment for $900,000 on September 30, 2017. The equipment was purchased with a $150,000 down payment and the issue of a $750,000, 3-year, 3.6% mortgage note payable for the balance. The terms provide for quarterly blended payments of $66,216 starting on December 31. Solar Power's year end is December 31.

Instructions

(a) Record the purchase of equipment on September 30, 2017.

(b) Record the first two instalment payments on December 31, 2017, and March 31, 2018.

(c) Repeat part (b) assuming that the terms provided for quarterly fixed principal payments of $62,500, rather than blended payments of $66,216.

TAKING IT FURTHER What will be the total interest expense over the life of the note if blended payments of $66,216 are made on a quarterly basis over three years?

P15–11B Elite Electronics issues a $450,000, 10-year, 7.5% mortgage note payable on December 31, 2017. The terms of the note provide for semi-annual fixed principal payments of $22,500, plus interest, on June 30 and December 31. Elite Electronics' year end is December 31.

Prepare instalment payment schedule and record note transactions. Show balance sheet presentation. (LO 5, 7) AP

Instructions

(a) Prepare an instalment payment schedule for the first two years. Round all calculations to the nearest dollar.

(b) Record the issue of the mortgage note payable on December 31, 2017.

(c) Show how the mortgage liability should be reported on the balance sheet at December 31, 2018. (*Hint:* Remember to report any current portion separately from the non-current liability.)

(d) Record the first two instalment payments on June 30, 2018, and December 31, 2018.

TAKING IT FURTHER If the semi-annual payments were blended, would the amount of cash paid on a semi-annual basis be greater than, equal to, or less than the fixed principal payments made for the first two instalments? For the last instalment?

P15–12B Presented below are three different lease transactions that occurred for Klippert Inc., a public company. Assume that all lease contracts start on January 1, 2017. Klippert does not receive title to any of the properties, either during the lease term or at the end of it. Annual lease payments are made on January 1 of each year starting on January 1, 2017.

Analyze lease situations. Discuss financial statement presentation. (LO 6) AP

	Manufacturing Equipment	Office Equipment	Vehicles
Annual lease rental payment	$13,260	$4,092	$13,929
Lease term	5 years	3 years	6 years
Estimated economic life	15 years	6 years	7 years
Fair market value of leased asset	$90,540	$18,760	$91,000
Present value of lease rental payments	$54,690	$10,040	$75,379

Instructions

(a) Which of the leases above are operating leases and which are finance leases? Explain.

(b) How should the lease transaction for each of the above assets be recorded on January 1, 2017?

(c) Describe how the lease transaction would be reported on the income statement and balance sheet for each of the above assets for 2017.

TAKING IT FURTHER For each of the leases, prepare any required adjusting journal entries on December 31, 2017. Assume that Klippert Inc. would pay 7% interest if it borrowed cash and purchased the equipment instead of leasing the equipment.

P15–13B Suncor Energy Inc. reported the following selected information (in millions):

Calculate and analyze solvency ratios. (LO 7) AN

	2014	2013
Total assets	$79,671	$78,315
Total liabilities	38,068	37,135
Interest expense	1,429	1,162
Income tax expense	1,891	2,465
Profit	2,699	3,911

Instructions

(a) Calculate Suncor Energy's debt to total assets and interest coverage ratios for each year.

(b) Based on the ratios calculated in part (a), what conclusions can you make about Suncor's solvency?

TAKING IT FURTHER Suncor Energy Inc. had total operating lease, rent, and other commitments that required annual payments of $600 million at the end of 2014. Explain the impact that an operating lease has on a company's solvency ratios. Does this information change any of your conclusions in part (b)?

P15–14B The adjusted trial balance for Carey Corporation at December 31, 2017, contained the following:

Prepare liabilities section of balance sheet and analyze leverage. (LO 7) AP

Accounts payable	$ 76,000	Income tax payable	$ 37,176
Accounts receivable	89,000	Note payable	158,666
Allowance for doubtful accounts	4,450	Interest expense	49,568
Bonds payable, due 2022	1,000,000	Lease liability	99,869
Interest payable	30,000	Note receivable, due December 2019	65,000
Income tax expense	74,353	Unearned revenue	25,000

Of the lease liability amount, $22,800 is due within the next year. Total payments on the instalment note payable in 2018 will be $24,400, of which $7,480 is for interest. Total assets are $2,594,031 and profit is $173,500.

Instructions

(a) Prepare the liabilities section of the balance sheet.
(b) Calculate Carey's debt to total assets and interest coverage ratios for the year ended December 31, 2017.
(c) Based on the ratios calculated in part (b), what conclusions can you make about Carey's solvency?

<u>TAKING IT FURTHER</u>   Are long-term creditors more concerned with solvency or liquidity? Explain.

CHAPTER 15: BROADENING YOUR PERSPECTIVE

▶ Financial Reporting and Analysis

Financial Reporting Problem

BYP15–1   Refer to the consolidated financial statements and notes of Corus Entertainment Ltd. in Appendix A.

Instructions

(a) Referring to Note 13, what was the long-term debt reported by Corus on August 31, 2014, and August 31, 2013? By how much has Corus's total debt increased (decreased) since August 31, 2013?
(b) Determine whether Corus redeemed any long-term liabilities during the fiscal year ended August 31, 2014.
(c) Corus's debt to total assets and interest coverage ratios for fiscal 2014 were calculated in Illustrations 15-23 and 15-24, respectively, in the chapter. Calculate these ratios for fiscal 2013. Comment on whether Corus's solvency improved or worsened since 2013.

Interpreting Financial Statements

BYP15–2   Gap Inc. and lululemon athletica inc. are specialty clothing merchandisers. Here are recent financial data for the companies:

	Gap Inc. (in millions of U.S. dollars)	lululemon athletica (in millions of U.S. dollars)
Balance sheet data	January 31, 2015	February 1, 2015
Total assets	$7,690	$1,296
Total liabilities	2,473	207
	Year ended	Year ended
Income statement data	January 31, 2015	February 1, 2015
Interest expense	$ 75	$ 14
Income tax expense	751	114
Profit	1,262	239

Instructions

(a) Calculate the debt to total assets and interest coverage ratios for Gap and lululemon.
(b) Discuss the solvency of each company compared with the other.

(c) The notes to the financial statements for Gap and lululemon indicate that the companies have significant operating lease commitments. Discuss the implications of these operating leases for each company's solvency.

▶ Critical Thinking

Collaborative Learning Activity

Note to instructor: Additional instructions and material for this group activity can be found on the Instructor Resource Site and in *WileyPLUS*.

BYP15–3   In this group activity, you will analyze and compare three financing alternatives for the purchase of a new vehicle. Your instructor will evaluate your group on your analysis as well as your rationale for selecting one of the alternatives. A lease option will be introduced at the end of the activity.

Communication Activity

BYP15–4   Sam Masasi, president of Masasi Corporation, is considering the issuance of bonds to finance an expansion of his business. He has asked you to (1) discuss the advantages of bonds over common share financing, (2) discuss the disadvantages of bonds over common share financing, (3) indicate the types of bonds he might issue, and (4) explain the issuing procedures used in bond transactions.

Instructions

Write a memo to the president, answering his request.

"All About You" Activity

BYP15–5   As indicated in the "All About You" feature in this chapter, a student can benefit from financial leverage by borrowing to pay for an education. However, too much leverage can result in graduates struggling to make their loan payments. With most government student loan programs, you have at least six months' grace after your post-secondary education before you have to start paying back your loan. If you take advantage of the grace period, the maximum number of monthly payments is 114; however, you may request an extended amortization period of up to 174 months by revising the terms of your loan agreement.

Instructions

Go to www.canlearn.ca to answer the following questions regarding monthly payments and the total interest payable on student loans. On the website, click on "Online Tools" and click on the link "Loan Repayment Estimator."

(a) Under Option 1 in the Loan Repayment Estimator, enter the loan amount of $20,000 and assume that you take advantage of the grace period and the grace period interest is included in your loan balance. Also assume a fixed interest rate and 114 months of repayment.
1. What is the amount of each monthly payment?
2. How much interest is payable over the 114 months?

(b) Under Option 1 in the Loan Repayment Estimator, enter the amount of $20,000 and assume that you take advantage of the grace period and the grace period interest is included in your loan balance. Also assume a fixed interest rate and 174 months of repayment.
1. What is the amount of each monthly payment?
2. How much interest is payable over the 174 months?

(c) Which student loan repayment term is the better option?

Santé Smoothie Saga

(*Note:* This is a continuation of the Santé Smoothie Saga from Chapters 1 through 14.)

BYP15–6   Janet, Brian, and Natalie have recently negotiated a contract to provide all natural granola bars on a weekly basis to a number of coffee shops in their area. As a result of the anticipated demand for the bars, they are making plans to purchase an additional commercial oven. The cost of this oven is estimated at $25,000, and the company already has $4,000 set aside for the purchase. Janet, Brian, and Natalie have met with their bank manager. She is willing to lend Santé Smoothies and Sweets Ltd. $21,000 on May 1, 2018, for a period of three years at a 4% interest rate.

The bank manager has set out the following two payment alternatives:

Alternative 1: The terms provide for fixed principal payments of $3,500 plus interest on May 1 and November 1 of each year.

Alternative 2: The terms provide for blended payments of $3,749 on May 1 and November 1 of each year.

Janet, Brian, and Natalie ask you to help them decide which alternative is better for them.

Instructions

(a) Prepare instalment payment schedules for each of the alternatives for the full term of the loan.
(b) Prepare the journal entry for the purchase of the oven and the issue of the note payable on May 1, 2018.
(c) Prepare the journal entries for the first two instalment payments under each alternative. Assume that reversing entries have been recorded on year-end accruals of interest.
(d) Determine the current portion of the note payable and the non-current portion of the note payable as at May 31, 2019, the company's year end, under each alternative.
(e) Prepare the adjusting journal entries required at May 31, 2019, the company's year end, under each alternative. Round amounts to the nearest dollar.
(f) Which payment alternative do you recommend? Why?

ANSWERS TO CHAPTER QUESTIONS

ANSWERS TO ACCOUNTING IN ACTION INSIGHT QUESTIONS

All About You p. 779

Q: What should you consider in your decision about how much is appropriate to borrow for your education?
A: You should consider the cost of tuition and books; living expenses; other sources of cash, such as parents, part-time job, and scholarships and grants; expected income upon graduation; living expenses and other financial commitments after graduation; and expected interest rates and payment schedule on the student loan.

Ethics Insight, p. 780

Q: How could paying off debt and then immediately borrowing again, right after the financial statements are published, mislead investors?

A: Paying debt off and then immediately borrowing again, right after the financial statements are published, has the sole purpose of manipulating the financial position of the company as at the balance sheet date. Paying the debt off immediately before issuing financial statements gave investors an incorrect representation of the true liquidity and solvency position of Lehman Brothers. In turn, the investors may have made inappropriate investment decisions. The manipulated balance sheet does not faithfully represent the economic events of Lehman Brothers.

Management should be ethically obligated to ensure that the company's financial statements accurately reflect the true financial position of the company so that investors (shareholders) can make informed decisions.

ANSWERS TO SELF-STUDY QUESTIONS

1. c   2. c   3. d   4. b   5. d   6. d   7. a   8. c   9. c   10. b   11. c   12. c

16 INVESTMENTS

CHAPTER PREVIEW   Investments can include debt and equity, and can be made by individuals or corporations. As indicated in our feature story on Agrium, investments are made to generate investment income or for strategic purposes. They can be held for a short or long period of time. The way in which a company accounts for its investments is determined by the nature and purpose of the investment. This chapter refers to the standards in IFRS 9 *Financial Instruments*. IFRS 9 replaces IAS 39, which was still being used at the time of writing. IFRS 9 must be adopted for annual financial reporting beginning January 1, 2018, but the standard has been adopted early by some companies. To ensure clarity, we have not included a comparison of IFRS 9 and IAS 39.

FEATURE STORY

GROWING AN AGRICULTURAL BUSINESS THROUGH STRATEGIC INVESTMENTS

CALGARY, Alta.—Like all large organizations, Agrium Inc. makes investments to earn money on its extra cash or to help grow the business. Another type of investment, strategic investments, involves buying all or part of another company, such as a competitor or supplier.

In the case of Agrium, a leading global producer, marketer, and retailer of agricultural products such as fertilizers, strategic investments are key. In 2014, it completed the integration of the retail business of a competitor, Viterra Inc. Agrium acquired about 210 Viterra stores across Western Canada and 13 in Australia for approximately C$300 million. The deal gave Agrium a chain of 270 stores, making it the largest crop input business on the prairies. "Viterra's assets are an excellent strategic fit for Agrium and we are pleased to have finalized this highly accretive acquisition. Much of the success of this acquisition can be attributed to our integrated strategy. It gave us first access to the opportunity, allowed us to optimize the value of specific divested assets and to maximize potential synergies," said Mike Wilson, who was President and CEO of Agrium at the time.

When Agrium announced the deal in 2013, it said it expected that the Viterra stores would contribute between C$75 million and C$90 million per year of earnings before interest, taxes, depreciation, and amortization. Agrium also expected that the Viterra stores would save the company between C$15 million and C$20 million a year by reducing inefficiencies.

Because Agrium acquired 100% of Viterra's retail assets, those assets became part of Agrium and are not reported separately in its financial statements. Agrium does own portions of other companies, however, and those strategic investments are reported separately, as "associates and joint ventures." Associates are generally those companies in which the investor company owns between 20% and 50% of the common shares. In Agrium's case, its main associate is a manufacturer and distributor of crop nutrients in Egypt, of which Agrium owns 26%. Its main joint venture is a 50% stake in a manufacturer and distributor of crop nutrients in Argentina.

Agrium reported an amount of "investments in associates and joint ventures" of US$576 million in 2014 on its consolidated balance sheets. In 2014, Agrium's investments in its associates and joint ventures lost money, and Agrium reported a "share of comprehensive loss of associates and joint ventures" of US$4 million on its consolidated statements of comprehensive income.

Strategic investments allow companies like Agrium to own a bigger market share and diversify into new products and services to better serve existing customers.

Sources: Sean Pratt, "Agrium Top Input Retailer with 270 Prairie Outlets," *The Western Producer*, October 10, 2013; "Agrium Completes Acquisition of Viterra Retail Assets," Agrium Inc. news release, October 1, 2013; Agrium Inc. 2014 annual report.

© Larry McDougal/CP Images

The chapter is organized as follows:

Classifying Investments

Corporations generally purchase **debt instruments** (term deposits, treasury bills, bonds, or similar items that can be bought and sold) and **equity instruments** (preferred and common shares of another company) for one of two reasons. They either purchase an instrument as

1. a **non-strategic investment** to generate investment income, or
2. a **strategic investment** with the intention of establishing and maintaining a long-term operating relationship with another company.

> Helpful hint   Debt and equity instruments are also referred to as *debt and equity securities* and these terms will be used interchangeably throughout the chapter.

NON-STRATEGIC INVESTMENTS

There are several reasons for a company to purchase debt or equity **securities** of another company as a non-strategic investment. A corporation may have excess cash that it does not immediately need. For example, many companies experience seasonal fluctuations in sales. A marina in Dartmouth, Nova Scotia, has more sales in the spring and summer than in the fall and winter. The reverse is true for a ski shop in Whistler, British Columbia. Thus, at the end of an operating cycle, many companies have cash on hand that is temporarily idle until the start of another operating cycle. These companies may invest the excess funds to earn, through interest and dividends, a greater return than they would get by just keeping the money in the bank. Illustration 16-1 shows the role that temporary investments play in the operating cycle.

▶ **ILLUSTRATION 16-1**
Temporary investments and operating cycle

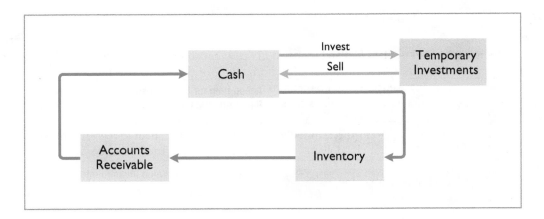

When investing excess cash for short periods of time, corporations invest in debt securities—usually money-market instruments, which are low risk and highly liquid. **Money-market instruments** include money-market funds, term deposits, and treasury bills. It is not wise to invest short-term excess cash in equity securities, because share prices can drop suddenly and dramatically. If a company does invest in shares and the price of the shares falls, when the company needs cash again within a short period, it will be forced to sell the shares at a loss. Money-market instruments do not change in fair value. Their value comes from the interest they generate.

Some companies will choose to invest cash in debt securities (such as bonds) over a longer term to generate investment income. The objective is to generate a steady source of interest income. Investment income can also be generated by investing in equity securities (such as common shares of another company). An investment in equity securities will generate dividend income, but as mentioned above, equity securities can be a riskier investment when market prices of shares fluctuate. Preferred shares are sometimes a safer equity investment and are usually purchased for dividend purposes, but both common and preferred shares can and do pay dividends.

Companies also invest in debt and equity securities hoping that they can sell them at a higher price than they originally paid for them. They speculate that the investment will increase in value and result in a gain when it is sold. Some companies, such as financial institutions, are in the business of actively buying and selling securities in the hope of generating investment income from price fluctuations. Debt and equity securities that are purchased for the purpose of reselling in the short term at a gain are called **held-for-trading investments**.

Alternative terminology Held-for-trading investments are also referred to as *trading investments*.

Still other companies will purchase investments to generate dividend income and also with the intention to sell at a gain. These investments have a dual purpose.

Illustration 16-2 summarizes the reasons that companies purchase investments in debt and equity securities.

▶ **ILLUSTRATION 16-2**
Why businesses invest

Reason	Typical Investment	Types of Investments
To house excess cash until needed	Low-risk, highly liquid, short-term securities such as money-market funds	Non-Strategic
To generate earnings *I need 1,000 treasury bills by tonight*	Debt securities (bonds) and equity securities (common and preferred shares)	Non-Strategic
To meet strategic goals	Shares in companies in a related industry or in an unrelated industry that the company wishes to enter	Strategic

Investments should be classified and reported in the financial statements in such a way as to provide users of financial statements with relevant information for decisions. This includes information that allows financial statement users to predict a company's future cash flows.

Generally a non-strategic investment is classified and reported based on the purpose of the investment and on whether it is debt or equity. The classification of an investment also determines how the investment is valued both at the time it is initially recognized and subsequent to recognition. Valuation is the process used to determine the dollar amount that an element of the financial statements will be reported at.

Illustration 16-3 shows how companies reporting under IFRS classify and value non-strategic investments.

▶ **ILLUSTRATION 16-3**
Classification and reporting of non-strategic investments under IFRS

Type of Instrument	Purpose	Balance Sheet Classification and Valuation	
Short-term debt instruments	Held to earn interest income	Current assets	Amortized cost
Long-term debt instruments	Held to earn interest income	Non-current assets	Amortized cost
Short- or long-term debt instruments	Held for trading purposes	Current assets	Fair value
Equity instruments	Held for trading purposes	Current assets	Fair value
Equity instruments	Other purpose: short-term	Current assets	Fair value
Equity instruments	Other purpose: long-term	Non-current assets	Fair value

Notice that there are essentially two valuation methods for investments under IFRS: (1) amortized cost and (2) fair value. ASPE uses both of these methods also. The main difference between IFRS and ASPE lies in the criteria that must be fulfilled for each category of investment. We will discuss the criteria in the sections that follow.

Note that the purpose of the investment is the most important factor in determining the balance sheet classification and valuation. The type of instrument does have an impact, as shown above, but the main consideration is why management purchases the investment.

STRATEGIC INVESTMENTS

While either debt or equity securities can be purchased as a non-strategic investment, only equity securities (normally common shares) can be purchased as a strategic investment. Only equity securities give the investor the right to vote at shareholders' meetings. Thus only investments in equity securities can result in influence or control over another company.

Companies make strategic investments for different reasons. A company may make a strategic investment to become part of a different industry when it buys some or all of the common shares of another company in a related or new industry or it may invest in a company in the same industry to expand its operations or eliminate some of the competition. For example, Corus Entertainment Inc. began operations in 1999 and grew quickly through a series of key acquisitions of other companies such as CMT Canada, YTV, and Treehouse. In its 2014 annual report, Corus stated its purpose for strategic investments: "We saw the value of owning content early." Corus's business model was to grow the company through strategic investments and it is now one of Canada's leading entertainment companies.

The percentage of ownership or the degree of influence determines how a strategic investment is reported. The reporting of strategic investments will be discussed later in the chapter. Note also that, while non-strategic investments can be either short- or long-term, strategic investments can only be long-term.

ACCOUNTING IN ACTION
BUSINESS INSIGHT

On August 26, 2014, Burger King Corporation announced the launch of Restaurant Brands International, a merger of Burger King Corporation and Canada's iconic coffee chain, Tim Hortons. The new company will be the third-largest quick-service restaurant company in the world, with estimated annual sales of US$23 billion and 18,000 restaurants in 100 countries. 3G Capital, an investment company specializing in providing long-term value and maximizing the potential of brands, currently owns 51% of the new company. In a news release to announce the deal, Alex Behring, Executive Chairman of

Burger King and Managing Partner of 3G Capital, said "Our combined size, international footprint and industry-leading growth trajectory will deliver superb value and opportunity for both Burger King and Tim Hortons shareholders." Marc Caira, President and CEO of Tim Hortons, said "this transaction will enable us to move more quickly and efficiently to bring Tim Hortons iconic Canadian brand to a new global customer base."

Source: "World's Third Largest Quick Service Restaurant Company Launched with Two Iconic and Independent Brands: Tim Hortons and Burger King," corporate news release, August 26, 2014.

© Jake Wright/CP Images

 Is this a strategic or non-strategic investment for 3G Capital? How will 3G Capital benefit from this investment?

> **Reporting of Strategic and Non-Strategic Investments**

ABC Corp., a public company reporting under IFRS, made the following investments during the year.

1. Purchased a bond with the intent to resell at a gain.
2. Purchased bonds to earn interest income.
3. Purchased common shares of a company, to be sold if the share price increases.
4. Purchased a treasury bill that will mature in three months to earn interest during the normal seasonal slowdown.
5. Purchased 100% of the common shares of ABC's major competitor.

(a) For each investment, indicate if it is a strategic investment or a non-strategic investment.
(b) For each non-strategic investment, indicate if it should be reported at amortized cost or fair value.

Solution

(a)   (b)

1. Non-strategic   Fair value
2. Non-strategic   Amortized cost
3. Non-strategic   Fair value
4. Non-strategic   Amortized cost
5. Strategic   Not applicable

Related exercise material: BE16–1, BE16–2, E16–1, and E16–2.

Action Plan
- Non-strategic investments are purchased to earn investment income.
- Strategic investments are purchased with the intention of establishing a long-term relationship with the company.

**LEARNING
OBJECTIVE 2** > **Demonstrate the accounting for debt investments that are reported at amortized cost.**

Accounting for Debt Investments Reported at Amortized Cost

An amortized cost (AC) investment under IFRS is one that meets the following two criteria:

1. A company intends to hold and manage the investment with the objective of collecting contractual cash flows.
2. The investment has contractual terms that give rise to cash flows that are solely principal and interest payments.

An investment in a debt security meets these two criteria when management purchases it with the express purpose of holding it and earning interest. Under ASPE, amortized cost is a "catch-all" category, in that it is used for any investment in debt securities that is not designated as a fair value investment by management. This is the only criterion in ASPE.

In this section, we will demonstrate how to account for an investment categorized as amortized cost. You will recall from Chapter 15 that amortized cost is equal to:

Maturity value
Less: unamortized discount or Plus: unamortized premium
= Amortized cost of debt investment

Alternative terminology Amortized cost of debt investment is also sometimes referred to as carrying value or carrying amount.

Also recall that under IFRS, the effective-interest method is used to amortize any discount or premium and record interest expense on bonds payable. This method is also used to record interest revenue and amortize any premiums or discounts on debt investments reported at amortized cost. Under ASPE, the effective-interest method can be used, but other methods are permitted.

Debt investments that are valued at amortized cost can include both short-term and long-term debt investments. **Short-term debt investments** are instruments that will mature within 12 months of the balance sheet date. **Long-term debt investments** are instruments with a maturity of longer than 12 months after the balance sheet date. Regardless of the term of the debt, the accounting for all debt instruments reported at amortized cost has some basic similarities. Entries are required to record the following.

1. **The acquisition:** Debt investments are recorded at the purchase price paid for the investment.
2. **Interest revenue and amortization of any discount or premium:** Interest revenue is recognized as it accrues and any discount or premium is amortized using the effective-interest method. The investment is reported at amortized cost on the balance sheet.
3. **The sale or disposition at maturity:** When the investment matures or is sold, the cash received is recorded and its carrying value (amortized cost) is eliminated. If the instrument is sold before maturity, a gain is recorded if the cash received is greater than the amortized cost of the investment and a loss is recorded if the cash received is less than the amortized cost.

You will recall that debt investments include money-market instruments as well as bonds, and a large variety of other debt securities. The following sections illustrate accounting for debt investments at amortized cost for both money-market instruments and bonds.

MONEY-MARKET INSTRUMENTS

As we have learned, money-market instruments are reasonably safe investments that allow a company to earn a higher interest rate than it can normally earn on a regular bank account balance. Examples of money-market instruments are term deposits, treasury bills, and money-market funds. This section looks at the accounting for treasury bills.

Government of Canada treasury bills are short-term debt instruments issued by the federal government. These instruments are a safe investment and have a wide variety of maturity dates up to a maximum of one year. Treasury bills are purchased at an amount less than the maturity value. The difference between purchase price and value at maturity, or date sold, is the interest earned on the investment. Treasury bills may be quickly converted to cash before their maturity date because there is a well-established resale market.

Recording Acquisitions of Treasury Bills

Treasury bills are recorded at their purchase price. For example, assume that on October 1, 2017, Sulphur Research Limited purchases a $10,000, 150-day treasury bill for $9,756. The treasury bills are trading at a market interest rate of 6% annually. The entry to record the investment is as follows:

A = L + SE			
+9,756			
−9,756			

↓ Cash flows: −9,756

Oct. 1	Short-Term Investment at AC—Treasury Bill	9,756	
	Cash		9,756
	To record purchase of 150-day treasury bill at 6%.		

Note that the treasury bill is recorded at the purchase price on October 1. The treasury bill was purchased at a discount of $244, the difference between face value ($10,000) and the purchase price ($9,756). Investments in treasury bills are reported as current assets on the balance sheet. As we learned in Chapter 7, investments in treasury bills of less than 90 days are usually classified as cash equivalents.

Recording Interest Revenue and Amortizing the Discount

Interest revenue is calculated by multiplying the market interest rate by the investment's carrying value (amortized cost). The discount is amortized over the term of the treasury bill using the effective-interest method. Because interest revenue is not received in cash during the term of the treasury bill, the discount amortization is equal to interest revenue.

Sulphur Research Limited's year end is December 31, so interest revenue of $146 is accrued for the months of October, November, and December ($9,756 × 6% × $^{3}/_{12}$ rounded to the nearest dollar). The adjusting journal entry on December 31 follows:

Dec. 31	Short-Term Investment at AC—Treasury Bill	146	
	Interest Revenue		146
	To accrue interest revenue and amortize discount		
	on a 150-day treasury bill.		

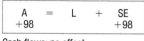

A = L + SE
+146   +146

Cash flows: no effect

Note that the debit to the treasury bill investment account increases the amortized cost of the investment by reducing the discount to $98 ($244 − $146). The treasury bill is reported on the December 31 balance sheet at its amortized cost of $9,902 ($9,756 + $146). Interest revenue is reported under other revenues in the income statement.

Recording the Maturity of Treasury Bills

On February 28, 2018, when the treasury bill matures, it is necessary to (1) update the interest and amortize the discount for the latest period, and (2) record the receipt of cash and remove the treasury bill investment account. The interest revenue of $98 is for the months of January and February and is equal to the difference between the face value ($10,000) and the amortized cost ($9,902). The entry to record the interest revenue and amortize the remaining discount is as follows:

Feb. 28	Short-Term Investment at AC—Treasury Bill	98	
	Interest Revenue		98
	To accrue interest revenue and amortize discount		
	on a 150-day treasury bill.		

A = L + SE
+98   +98

Cash flows: no effect

Note that the amortized cost of the treasury bill is now $10,000 ($9,902 + $98), equal to its face value. The entry to record the receipt of cash and eliminate the treasury bill is as follows:

Feb. 28	Cash	10,000	
	Short-Term Investment at AC—Treasury Bill		10,000
	To record the receipt of cash and eliminate the treasury bill		
	investment account.		

A = L + SE
+10,000
−10,000

↑Cash flows: +10,000

BONDS

Bonds were discussed in Chapter 15 from the liability side; that is, from the issuer's perspective. Corporations, governments, and universities issue bonds that are then purchased by investors. The issuer of the bonds is known as the **investee**. The purchaser of the bonds, or the bondholder, is known as the **investor**. The investor's accounting for bonds reported at amortized cost is the mirror image of the accounting from the issuer's perspective and is illustrated below.

To illustrate the investor's accounting, assume that Lionheart Properties Inc. acquires Doan Inc.'s $50,000, 5-year, 6% bonds on January 1, 2017. The bonds pay interest on January 1 and July 1 each year. The bonds were issued to yield 8%. In Appendix PV, we demonstrate a variety of ways to determine present value. Recall that the price of a bond will be equal to the present value of future cash flows. In this chapter, we will calculate the price of a bond using a financial calculator. Note that the present value of a bond investment can also be determined using the present value tables in Appendix PV.

Recording Acquisition of Bonds

At acquisition, the investment in bonds is recorded at the purchase price. Recall from Chapter 15 that bonds will sell at a discount (purchase price is below face value) if the market interest rate is higher than the contract rate of 6%. Bonds are sold at a premium (purchase price is above face value) if the market interest rate is lower than the contract rate of 6%.

The Doan Inc. bonds will be issued at a discount because the market interest rate is higher than the contract rate. Using a financial calculator, Lionheart Properties Inc. will calculate the price of the bond using an interest rate per semi-annual payment period of 4% (8% × $^{6}/_{12}$), number of periods of 10 (5 years × 2 payments per year), payment of $1,500 ($50,000 × 6% × $^{6}/_{12}$) and a future value of $50,000. The present value of the bond using these inputs is $45,945 (result rounded to nearest dollar) as demonstrated below:

Enter:	4	10	1,500	50,000			Result
Press:	I/Y	N	PMT	FV	CPT	PV	(45,945)

Lionheart Properties will record the purchase of the bond as follows:

A	=	L	+	SE
+45,945				
−45,945				

↓ Cash flows: −45,945

Jan. 1, 2017	Long-Term Investments at AC—Bonds, Doan Inc.	45,945	
	Cash		45,945
	To record purchase of Doan Inc. 5-year, 6% bonds to earn interest.		

Given that the bonds are being held to earn interest revenue and not to trade, and the term of the bonds is five years, the bonds will be reported in non-current assets on the balance sheet.

As you go through this illustration of accounting for bonds at amortized cost from the investor's perspective, you may want to refer to the section on "Issuing Bonds at a Discount" in Chapter 15 to see the similarities and differences in the accounting for bonds between the investor and investee.

Recording Interest Revenue and Amortizing the Discount or Premium

When bonds are reported at amortized cost, any premium or discount recorded in the investment account is amortized to interest revenue over the remaining term of the bonds. If there is a bond premium, interest revenue is reduced by the amortization amount. If there is a bond discount, interest revenue is increased by the amortization amount. Recall from earlier in the chapter that, like the issuer of the bonds, **the investor uses the effective-interest method of amortization**.

Continuing with the Lionheart Properties example, after the entry to recognize the purchase of the bond, the balance in the long-term investment account is $45,945. This bond was sold at a discount of $4,055 ($50,000 face value – $45,945 purchase price). Using this information, we can prepare a partial amortization schedule similar to those prepared in Chapter 15, only from the perspective of the investor. Note that column (A) is labelled interest received and not interest paid and column (B) is labelled interest revenue, not interest expense. Illustration 16-4 shows the amortization schedule for the first six interest payment periods.

▶ ILLUSTRATION **16-4**
Partial bond amortization schedule—effective-interest method

LIONHEART PROPERTIES INC.
Bond Amortization Schedule
Effective-Interest Method Amortization—Semi-Annual Interest Payments

	(A)	(B)	(C)	(D)
Interest Periods	Interest Received ($50,000 × 6% × 6/12)	Interest Revenue (Preceding Bond Carrying Value × 8% × 6/12)	Discount Amortization (B) − (A)	Bond Carrying Value (Preceding Bond Carrying Value + (C))
				$45,945
July 1, 2017	$1,500	$1,838	$338	46,283
Jan. 1, 2018	1,500	1,851	351	46,634
July 1, 2018	1,500	1,865	365	46,999
Jan. 1, 2019	1,500	1,880	380	47,379
July 1, 2019	1,500	1,895	395	47,774
Jan. 1, 2020	1,500	1,911	411	48,185

Recall that the bonds pay semi-annual interest payments on July 1 and January 1 each year. The regular **cash** interest payment will be $1,500 ($50,000 $\times$ 6% $\times$ $^6/_{12}$). Using the effective-interest method, interest **revenue** is calculated by multiplying the amortized cost (carrying value) of the investment by the semi-annual market interest rate. On July 1, 2017, Lionheart will record $1,838 interest revenue ($45,945 $\times$ 4%). The amortization of the discount is the difference between the cash interest received and the interest revenue or $338 ($1,838 − $1,500).

The entry to record the receipt of the interest and amortization of the discount on **July 1, 2017** (from the amortization schedule in Illustration 16-4) is as follows:

July 1, 2017	Cash	1,500	
	Long-Term Investments at AC—Bonds, Doan Inc.	338	
	Interest Revenue		1,838
	To record receipt of interest on Doan Inc. 5-year, 6% bonds.		

A	=	L	+	SE
+1,500				+1,838
+338				

↑Cash flows: +1,500

Assume that Lionheart Properties has a December 31 year end. The entry to record accrued interest revenue on **December 31, 2017** (interest period #2 on the schedule in Illustration 16-4) is as follows:

Dec. 31, 2017	Interest Receivable	1,500	
	Long-Term Investments at AC—Bonds, Doan Inc.	351	
	Interest Revenue		1,851
	To record accrual of interest on Doan Inc. 5-year, 6% bonds.		

A	=	L	+	SE
+1,500				+1,851
+351				

Cash flows: no effect

On **January 1, 2018**, the cash interest is received and the following entry is made:

Jan. 1, 2018	Cash	1,500	
	Interest Receivable		1,500
	To record receipt of interest on Doan Inc. 5-year, 6% bonds.		

A	=	L	+	SE
+1,500				
−1,500				

↑Cash flows: +1,500

Illustration 16-5 compares the recording of the bonds as an investment for Lionheart Properties Inc. (the investor) and as a liability for Doan Inc. (the investee) for the bond issue and first interest payment date.

▶ ILLUSTRATION **16-5**
Comparison of bond investment and liability— effective-interest method

LIONHEART PROPERTIES INC. (INVESTOR)		
Jan. 1	Long-Term Investments at AC—Bonds, Doan Inc. 45,945	
	Cash	45,945
July 1	Cash 1,500	
	Long-Term Investments at AC—Bonds, Doan Inc. 338	
	Interest Revenue	1,838

DOAN INC. (INVESTEE)		
Jan. 1	Cash 45,945	
	Bonds Payable	45,945
July 1	Interest Expense 1,838	
	Bonds Payable	338
	Cash	1,500

Note that on January 1, 2017, Lionheart recorded a non-current asset, and Doan recorded a non-current liability. On July 1, 2017, Lionheart recorded interest revenue and Doan recorded interest expense.

© Jane0606/Shutterstock

It is often stated that bond investments are safer than stock investments. After all, with an investment in bonds, you are guaranteed return of principal and interest payments over the life of the bonds. However, here are some other factors you may want to consider if you want to invest in bonds issued by corporations or governments:

- Overall economic fears can drive down the yields of corporate bonds. For example, in the third quarter of 2015, the value of Canadian corporate bonds fell an average of 1.1% because of a sluggish economy, particularly due to the fall in prices of oil and other commodities.
- In 2013, the value of bonds in the United States fell by 2% due to interest rate risk. That is, when interest rates rise, it makes the yields paid on existing bonds less attractive. As a result, the price of the existing bond you are holding falls.
- While interest rates are currently low, it is likely that they will increase in the future. If you hold bonds, there is a real possibility that the value of your bonds will be reduced.
- The longer the time frame of the bond, the higher yields it will pay, because a longer time frame is riskier—no one knows what might happen far into the future—and investors want to be rewarded for taking on that risk. For example, in early 2016, Government of Canada two-year bonds had a yield of 1.25%, while 10-year bonds were paying 2.25%.

- Credit risk also must be considered. Credit risk means that a company may not be able to pay back what it borrowed. Former bondholders in companies like General Motors, United Airlines, and Eastman Kodak saw their bond values drop substantially when these companies declared bankruptcy. The higher the risk a company will default, the higher its bond yield will be.

An advantage of investing in a bond over stock is that if you hold a bond to maturity, you will receive your principal and also interest payments over the life of the bond. But if you have to sell your bond investment before maturity, you may be facing a roller coaster regarding its value.

There are also advantages to corporations to issuing bonds versus issuing shares. For example, issuing bonds does not dilute the ownership in the corporation the way issuing more shares does. That means that any increase in a corporation's assets remain in shareholders' equity for existing shareholders. Bondholders are only entitled to earn interest, and not receive dividends or have a say in how a corporation is run, the way shareholders do.

Sources: Bank of Canada, "Canadian Bond Yields: 10-Year Lookup," www.bankofcanada. ca/rates/interest-rates/lookup-bond-yields/, accessed February 17, 2016; Allison McNeely, Bloomberg News, "Canada's Corporate Bonds Are Worst Among Peers with Room to Drop," *The Globe and Mail*, September 30, 2015; Rob Carrick, "Got a Defined Benefit Plan? Lighten Up on Bonds," *The Globe and Mail*, September 5, 2014; Bryan Borzykowski, "Corporate Bonds and Government Bonds for Safe Investments," CanadianLiving.com, October 10, 2011.

Q As an investor, what are the advantages and disadvantages of bond investments?

Recording the Maturity of Bonds

Regardless of the bonds' purchase price, amortized cost at maturity will equal face value. By the time the bonds mature, any discount or premium will be fully amortized. Assuming that the interest for the last interest period has been received and recorded, the entry to record the receipt of cash for the Doan Inc. bonds at maturity, January 1, 2022, is as follows:

A	=	L	+	SE
+50,000				
−50,000				

Cash flows: +50,000

Jan. 1	Cash	50,000	
	Long-Term Investments at AC—Bonds, Doan Inc.		50,000
	To record maturity of Doan Inc. 5-year, 6% bonds.		

Because the amortized cost of the bonds equals the face value at maturity, there is no gain or loss.

Recording the Sale of Bonds Before Maturity

Although a company may purchase bonds to earn interest revenue, it may have to sell the bonds before maturity if it needs the cash, or the company may choose to sell the bonds because interest rates have increased and it can earn a higher return by investing in other securities.

When a bond is sold before its maturity date, the following entries are required:

1. Update the investment account for any unrecorded interest revenue and the amortization of the discount or premium.
2. Record the sale of the bond.
   (a) Record the cash received.
   (b) Remove the amortized cost of the bond investment from the accounting records.
   (c) Record any gain or loss on the sale. Illustration 16-6 shows how a gain or loss is determined.

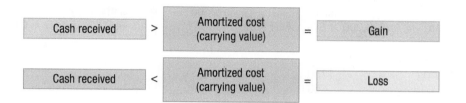

▶ ILLUSTRATION 16-6
Gain and loss on sale of debt investment valued at amortized cost

To illustrate, assume Lionheart sells its investment in the Doan Inc. bonds on January 1, 2020, for $49,500. The amortized cost of the bonds on January 1, 2020 (interest period #6 on the amortization schedule in Illustration 16-4) is $48,185. Assuming that interest revenue was correctly accrued on December 31, 2019, and interest received was correctly recorded on January 1, 2020, the only remaining entry required is to record the sale of the bonds as follows:

Jan. 1, 2020	Cash	49,500	
	Long-Term Investments at AC—Bonds, Doan Inc.		48,185
	Gain on Sale of Bond Investments		1,315
	To record sale of Doan Inc. 5-year, 6% bonds.		

A = L + SE
+49,500   +1,315
−48,185

↑Cash flows: +49,500

A gain is recognized on the sale of the bonds because the bonds were sold at a price ($49,500) that was greater than the amortized cost ($48,185). Conversely, a loss on the sale would be recognized if the bonds were sold at a price that was less than the amortized cost of the bonds. Losses and gains on sale are reported in other expenses or other revenues, respectively.

BEFORE YOU GO ON...DO IT   **Bond Amortization**

During 2017, Chai Corporation had the following transactions for debt investments purchased to earn interest:

Jan. 1   Purchased 10-year, 5% Jarvis Corp. bonds with a face value of $30,000 for $27,768. The market interest rate is 6%. Interest is payable semi-annually on July 1 and January 1.

Apr. 1   Purchased a $20,000, 120-day treasury bill for $19,600.

July 1   Received semi-annual interest on the investment in the Jarvis bonds.

     30   Received cash for the maturity of the treasury bill.

(a) Prepare a bond amortization schedule for the first three interest periods for Chai's investment in the Jarvis bonds. Chai Corporation uses the effective-interest method to amortize any discounts or premiums on bond investments.
(b) Record the above transactions for Chai Corporation.
(c) Prepare the adjusting entry for the accrual of interest on December 31, Chai's year end.

(continued)

Action Plan
• To create the amortization schedule, calculate the cash interest received by multiplying the face value of the bonds by the semi-annual contractual interest rate. Calculate the interest revenue by multiplying the amortized cost of the bonds by the semi-annual market interest rate.

Action Plan (continued)

- In the amortization schedule the amount of the discount (premium) amortization is the difference between the interest received and the interest revenue. The amortized cost of the bonds purchased increases by the amount of the discount amortization and decreases by the amount of the premium amortization.
- When investments are purchased, they are recorded at their purchase price.
- Interest revenue is recorded as it accrues.
- The investments are reported at amortized cost on the balance sheet; therefore, premiums and discounts on these investments are amortized when interest revenue is recognized. Use the amortization schedule to record the interest revenue on the bonds.
- When the investments mature, the cash received is recorded and the investment account is eliminated.

BEFORE YOU GO ON...DO IT **2**   **Bond Amortization** (continued)

Solution

(a)

		(A)	(B)	(C)	(D)
	Interest Period	Interest Received ($30,000 × 5% × $^6/_{12}$)	Interest Revenue (D × 6% × $^6/_{12}$)	Discount Amortization (B − A)	Bond Amortized Cost (D + C)
Purchase Jan. 1, 2017					$27,768
(1) July 1, 2017		$750	$833	$83	27,851
(2) Jan. 1, 2018		750	836	86	27,937
(3) July 1, 2018		750	838	88	28,025
(4) Jan. 1, 2019		750	841	91	28,116

Bond Discount Amortization Schedule — Investor — Effective-Interest Method

(b)

Date	Account	Debit	Credit
Jan. 1	Long-Term Investments at AC—Bonds, Jarvis Corp.	27,768	
	Cash		27,768
	To record purchase of Jarvis 10-year, 5% bonds.		
Apr. 1	Short-Term Investment at AC—Treasury Bill	19,600	
	Cash		19,600
	To record purchase of a 120-day treasury bill.		
July 1	Cash	750	
	Long-Term Investments at AC—Bonds, Jarvis Corp.	83	
	Interest Revenue		833
	To record interest received on Jarvis 10-year, 5% bonds.		
July 30	Short-Term Investment at AC—Treasury Bill	400	
	Interest Revenue		400
	To record interest revenue on a 120-day treasury bill.		
	Cash	20,000	
	Short-Term Investment at AC—Treasury Bill		20,000
	To record maturity of a 120-day treasury bill.		
(c) Dec. 31	Interest Receivable	750	
	Long-Term Investments at AC—Bonds, Jarvis Corp.	86	
	Interest Revenue		836
	To accrue semi-annual interest on Jarvis 10-year, 5% bonds.		

Related exercise material: BE16–3, BE16–4, BE16–5, E16–3, E16–4, E16–5, and E16–6.

LEARNING OBJECTIVE 3   Demonstrate the accounting for fair value investments.

Accounting for Fair Value Investments

Alternative terminology Another common term for fair value is *market value*.

Illustration 16-3 showed that debt and equity investments purchased principally for resale are reported at fair value. Recall from Chapter 1 that **fair value** is generally the amount an asset could be sold for in a market. Debt and equity investments that are purchased for resale and traded on public markets will have a readily determinable fair value, which is the quoted market price of the investment. When these investments are accounted for using fair value, at the end of each reporting period, the fair value is determined and the investment account is adjusted to reflect that fair value.

IFRS defines two sub-categories of fair value valuation methods as follows:

1. **Fair value through profit or loss (FVTPL)** investments are any investments in debt or equity securities that do not meet the criteria established for amortized cost investments and have not been designated by management as fair value through other comprehensive income (discussed next). The FVTPL category requires fair value adjustments to be recorded as gains or losses on the statement of comprehensive income and for them to be included in the determination of either profit or loss for a company.

2. **Fair value through other comprehensive income (FVTOCI)** investments are any equity securities designated by management to this category. The FVTOCI category requires fair value adjustments to be recorded as gains or losses in the other comprehensive income portion of the statement of comprehensive income. We first introduced other comprehensive income in Chapter 14.

Notice that FVTPL is essentially a catch-all category for accounting and reporting purposes under IFRS. In other words, if an investment does not qualify as amortized cost or FVTOCI, it is automatically considered to be FVTPL.

Under ASPE, the guidance is somewhat different. ASPE requires that any **equity** security investment that is traded on an active market (such as the TSX) be valued using FVTPL, but management can also designate any investment in debt or equity as FVTPL. There is no such category as FVTOCI in ASPE and the catch-all category is either amortized cost or simply cost.

In accounting for investments held for resale and reported at FVTPL or FVTOCI, entries are required to record the following.

1. **The acquisition:** Held for resale investments are recorded at their fair value on the date of purchase.

2. **Interest and dividend revenue:** Interest revenue is recognized as it accrues and dividend revenue is recognized when the company receives the cash dividend or becomes entitled to the cash dividend. You will recall from Chapter 13 that an investor will be entitled to receive a dividend from the company paying dividends (investee) if the investor holds the shares on the date of record.

3. **Fair value adjustments:** Because trading investments are reported at fair value on the balance sheet, accounting entries are required to adjust the investment's carrying value for any increases or decreases in its fair value. This is referred to as a **fair value adjustment**. Recall that the carrying value of an asset or liability is the balance reported on the balance sheet. A gain is recorded if the fair value is higher than the carrying value and a loss is recorded if the fair value is less than the carrying value. This is shown in Illustration 16-7.

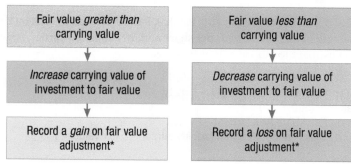

*Gains and losses on fair value adjustments for FVTPL investments are reported in the income statement; for FVTOCI investments, they are reported in other comprehensive income.

▶ **ILLUSTRATION 16-7**
Recording gains and losses on fair value adjustments

4. **The sale of the investment:** When the investment is sold, the cash received is recorded, the investment account is eliminated, and a gain or loss is recorded. Like investments reported at amortized cost, the gain or loss is equal to the difference between the cash received and the carrying value of the investment.

FAIR VALUE THROUGH PROFIT OR LOSS

The following section illustrates how to account for two common types of FVTPL investments: common shares (equity investments) and bonds (debt investments).

EQUITY INVESTMENTS—COMMON SHARES

Recording Acquisitions of Common Shares

When an equity instrument is purchased for resale, the investment is recorded at fair value, which is equal to the price the shares are trading at on the date of purchase. Assume, for example, that on July 1, 2017, Demetri Corporation purchased 500 common shares of Perchak Ltd. at $30 per share. Demetri Corporation purchased the shares for resale.

The entry to record the equity investment is as follows:

```
A    =   L   +   SE
+15,000
-15,000
↓Cash flows: -15,000
```

July 1	Short-Term Investments at FVTPL—Equity, Perchak Ltd.	15,000	
	Cash (500 × $30)		15,000
	To record purchase of 500 Perchak Ltd. common shares.		

This investment was purchased with the intention of selling it at a profit within one year. It will be reported as a current asset on the balance sheet.

Recording Dividend Revenue

During the time the shares are held, entries are required for any cash dividends that are received. If a $2 per share dividend is received by Demetri on December 1, the entry is as follows:

```
A    =   L   +   SE
+1,000          +1,000
↑Cash flows: +1,000
```

Dec. 1	Cash (500 × $2)	1,000	
	Dividend Revenue		1,000
	To record receipt of cash dividend from Perchak Ltd.		

Dividend revenue is reported under other revenues in the income statement.

Recording Fair Value Adjustments of Shares at the Balance Sheet Date

On December 31, 2017, Demetri's fiscal year end, Perchak Ltd.'s shares are trading on the stock exchange at $33. This is an increase of $3 ($33 − $30) per share and, as explained earlier, results in a gain. The entry to record the adjustment to fair value is as follows:

```
A    =   L   +   SE
+1,500          +1,500
Cash flows: no effect
```

Dec. 31	Short-Term Investments at FVTPL—Equity, Perchak Ltd. (500 × $3)	1,500	
	Gain on Fair Value Adjustment—FVTPL		1,500
	To record adjustment of Perchak Ltd. investment to fair value.		

The investment in Perchak common shares will be reported on the balance sheet at its fair value of $16,500 ($15,000 + $1,500), which is the new carrying value of the investment. The gain on fair value adjustment—FVTPL is reported under other revenues in the income statement. Note that the common shares are still owned by Demetri; no sale has taken place yet.

Recording Sales of Shares

When shares are sold, the difference between the proceeds from the sale and the carrying value of the shares is recognized as a gain or loss. Assume that Demetri receives proceeds of $17,000 on the sale of its

Perchak common shares on October 10, 2018. Because the shares' carrying value is $16,500 ($15,000 + $1,500), there is a gain of $500 ($17,000 − $16,500). The entry to record the sale is as follows:

Oct. 10	Cash	17,000	
	Short-Term Investments at FVTPL—Equity,		
	Perchak Ltd.		16,500
	Gain on Sale of FVTPL Investments ($17,000 − $16,500)		500
	To record sale of Perchak Ltd. common shares.		

A	=	L	+	SE
+17,000				+500
−16,500				

↑Cash flows: +17,000

This gain is reported under other revenue in the income statement.

DEBT INVESTMENTS—BONDS

Recording Acquisitions of Bonds

The following example illustrates the accounting for bonds purchased for resale. At acquisition, an investment in bonds held for resale is recorded at their fair value, which is equal to the price paid to purchase the bonds on the date of purchase. Assume Maibee Corporation acquires $100,000 face value of PEL Inc. 10-year, 6% bonds on January 1, 2017, at par value. Maibee Corporation purchased the bonds for resale. The entry to record the investment is as follows:

Jan. 1	Short-Term Investments at FVTPL—Bonds, PEL Inc.	100,000	
	Cash		100,000
	To record purchase of PEL Inc. bonds for the purpose		
	of resale.		

A	=	L	+	SE
+100,000				
−100,000				

↓Cash flows: −100,000

Recording Interest Revenue

The PEL Inc. bonds pay interest of $3,000 ($100,000 × 6% × $^{6}/_{12}$) semi-annually on July 1 and January 1. The following entry records the receipt of interest on July 1, 2017:

July 1	Cash	3,000	
	Interest Revenue		3,000
	To record receipt of interest on PEL Inc. bonds.		

| A | = | L | + | SE |
| +3,000 | | | | +3,000 |

↑Cash flows: +3,000

Note that, because the bonds were purchased at par value—that is, there was no premium or discount—cash interest received will be equal to interest revenue. If the bonds were purchased at an amount other than par, the premium or discount would be amortized using the effective-interest method as demonstrated earlier in the chapter.

Assuming Maibee's year end is December 31, 2017, an entry is required to accrue interest revenue for the interest earned. The following entry records the accrual of interest on December 31:

Dec. 31	Interest Receivable	3,000	
	Interest Revenue		3,000
	To record accrual of interest on PEL Inc. bonds.		

| A | = | L | + | SE |
| +3,000 | | | | +3,000 |

Cash flows: no effect

Note that on January 1, 2018, when the interest payment is received from PEL, interest receivable will be credited.

Recording Fair Value Adjustments of Bonds at the Balance Sheet Date

You will recall from Chapter 15 that bonds trade on the public market at prices that reflect the current market interest rate. If the market interest rate changes after a company purchases bonds, the bonds' fair value will be different from their purchase price. If the market interest rate increases above the stated rate on the bond, the bonds' fair value will decrease. If the market interest rate decreases below the stated rate on the bond, the bonds' fair value will increase. Assume that on December 31, 2017, Maibee's year end, the market interest rate increased above the 6% stated rate on the PEL bonds. The bonds are now trading at 99 (99% of their face value, or $99,000). The entry to record the adjustment to fair value is as follows:

A	=	L	+	SE
−1,000				−1,000

Cash flows: no effect

Dec. 31	Loss on Fair Value Adjustment—FVTPL ($100,000 − $99,000)	1,000	
	Short-Term Investments at FVTPL—Bonds, PEL Inc.		1,000
	To record adjustment of PEL Inc. bonds to fair value.		

The investment in PEL Inc.'s bonds will be reported on the balance sheet in current assets at its fair value of $99,000, which is the new carrying value of the bonds. The loss on fair value adjustment—FVTPL is reported under other expenses in the income statement.

Note that a fair value adjustment does not affect any premium or discount amortization of a bond. Amortization of the premium or discount is based on the original purchase price of the bond for as long as the investor owns the bonds. You will learn more about fair value adjustments of bond investment with a premium or discount in intermediate accounting courses.

Recording Sales of Bonds

When the bonds are sold, two entries are required.

1. Record any accrued interest revenue up to the date of sale.
2. Record the sale of the bond.
   (a) Record cash proceeds received.
   (b) Remove the bond investment from the accounting records.
   (c) Record any gain or loss on the sale. Gain or loss is calculated in the usual manner: it is the difference between the proceeds received and the carrying value of the investment.

Assume, for example, that on July 1, 2018, interest rates in the market decrease and Maibee Corporation sells the PEL Inc. investment for $101,500, after receiving (and recording) the interest. Because the bonds' carrying value is $99,000, a gain of $2,500 is recorded. The entry to record the sale is as follows:

A	=	L	+	SE
+101,500				+2,500
−99,000				

↑Cash flows: +101,500

July 1	Cash	101,500	
	Gain on Sale of FVTPL Investments ($101,500 − $99,000)		2,500
	Short-Term Investments at FVTPL—Bonds, PEL Inc.		99,000
	To record sale of PEL Inc. bonds.		

The gain on the sale of the bonds is reported as other revenues in the income statement.

FAIR VALUE THROUGH OTHER COMPREHENSIVE INCOME

As mentioned previously, IFRS has two sub-categories for fair value investments. The first, FVTPL, was discussed in the previous section. Here we will demonstrate FVTOCI. The accounting for FVTOCI investments is very similar to that of FVTPL. The differences arise in relation to:

- accounting for fair value adjustments at the balance sheet date, and
- accounting for the sale of the investment.

Recall that an FVTOCI investment can be any investment in an equity security designated by management as an FVTOCI investment. In other words, management may choose to designate an investment in this way because the gains and losses arising from fair value adjustments may not be relevant information to users when assessing a company's economic performance. Therefore, these gains and losses will be excluded from profit or loss but will be reported in other comprehensive income. You will recall from Chapter 14 that companies reporting under ASPE do not report comprehensive income; therefore, FVTOCI is not an option that managers can choose when reporting under ASPE.

The entries for an investment in common shares where gains or losses on fair value adjustments are reported in other comprehensive income (OCI) are illustrated with the following example.

Recording Acquisitions of Shares

Assume that Cooke Ltd. purchases 5,000 common shares of Depres Company for $20 per share on October 1, 2017. Cooke Ltd. has elected to designate the investment as FVTOCI. The entry to record the acquisition is as follows:

Oct. 1	Long-Term Investments at FVTOCI—Equity, Depres Co. Cash (5,000 × $20) To record purchase of 5,000 Depres common shares.	100,000	100,000

```
A      =   L   +   SE
+100,000
-100,000
↓Cash flows: -100,000
```

Note that FVTOCI investments will generally be classified as non-current and will be reported on the balance sheet with other long-term investments.

Recording Dividend Revenue

Assume that on November 1, 2017, Depres pays a dividend of $3 per share. The entry to record the dividend revenue is as follows:

Nov. 1	Cash (5,000 × $3) Dividend Revenue To record receipt of cash dividend from Depres Co.	15,000	15,000

```
A      =   L   +   SE
+15,000            +15,000
↑Cash flows: +15,000
```

Note that the first two entries in the FVTOCI valuation method are the same as the first two entries in FVTPL valuation.

Recording the Fair Value Adjustment at Balance Sheet Date

Assume that on December 31, 2017, Cooke Ltd.'s year end, Depres common shares are trading at $22, an increase of $2 per share since the shares were purchased on October 1. The entry to record the change in fair value is as follows:

Dec. 31	Long-Term Investments at FVTOCI—Equity, Depres Co. (5,000 × $2) OCI—Gain on Fair Value Adjustment To record adjustment of Depres Co. investment to fair value.	10,000	10,000

```
A      =   L   +   SE
+10,000           +10,000
Cash flows: no effect
```

Recall from Chapter 14 that gains and losses included in other comprehensive income are reported net of tax. Assuming a 30% tax rate, $7,000 ($10,000 − [$10,000 × 30%]) will be reported as other comprehensive income on the statement of comprehensive income. As a result, Accumulated Other Comprehensive Income will be increased by the fair value adjustment of $7,000. You will recall from Chapter 14 that accumulated other comprehensive income is reported in shareholders' equity.

Recording Sales of Shares

When FVTOCI equity investments are sold, the difference between the proceeds from the sale and the carrying value of the investment is recognized as a gain or loss and reported in other comprehensive income. Assume that Cooke receives proceeds of $111,000 on the sale of its Depres common shares on October 10, 2018. Because the shares' carrying value is $110,000, there is a gain of $1,000 ($111,000 − $110,000). The entry to record the sale is made in the usual manner with a gain recorded in other comprehensive income as follows:

A	=	L	+	SE
+111,000				+1,000
−110,000				

↑ Cash flows: +111,000

Oct. 10	Cash	111,000	
	Long-Term Investments at FVTOCI—Equity, Depres Co.		110,000
	OCI—Gain on Sale of FVTOCI Investments ($11,000 – $10,000)		1,000
	To record sale of Depres Co. common shares.		

OCI—Gain on Sale of FVTOCI Investments would subsequently be closed to Accumulated Other Comprehensive Income during the closing process at year end.

At this point, an additional journal entry would be made to transfer the accumulated gains and losses on this investment from Accumulated Other Comprehensive Income (AOCI) to Retained Earnings because all of the gains and losses have been realized. Note that at no point do the gains and losses from FVTOCI investments enter into the calculation of profit or loss, but once sold, all gains and losses can be recorded in retained earnings.

ACCOUNTING IN ACTION
ETHICS INSIGHT

© Henrik Jonsson/istockphoto

Kreiter Financial Services Limited, a public company, purchased a large portfolio of debt and equity investments during 2017. The portfolio's total fair value at December 31, 2017, is greater than its total cost. Some securities have increased in value and others have decreased. Vicki Lemke, the financial vice-president, and Ula Greenwood, the controller, are busy classifying the securities in the portfolio for the first time.

Lemke suggests classifying the securities as follows:

1. Securities that have increased in value as investments at fair value through profit or loss.

2. Equity securities that have decreased in value as investments at fair value through other comprehensive income.

3. Debt securities that have decreased in value as amortized cost.

Greenwood disagrees. She says that they should follow the GAAP recommendations on how investments should be classified.

 Q What will be the effect on profit if the investments are reported as Lemke suggests? Be specific. Is there anything unethical in what Lemke proposes?

BEFORE YOU
GO ON...DO IT   **Accounting for Investments in Common Shares
and Bonds at Fair Value**

During 2017, Lang Corporation had the following transactions:

Jan.	2	Purchased an investment in Utility Corp. $20,000, five-year, 4% bonds at par for the purpose of resale.
Mar.	1	Purchased 5,000 common shares of Park Ave. for $10 each, which management designated as an FVTOCI investment.
July	1	Received semi-annual interest on the Utility Corp. bonds.
	2	Sold half of the Utility Corp. bonds for $10,500.
Sept.	1	Purchased 1,000 common shares of Electric Ltd. for $15 per share to be held for resale.
Nov.	1	Received a $2 dividend on the Electric Ltd. shares.
Dec.	31	The remaining Utility Corp. bonds' fair value was $9,750. The Electric Ltd. common shares were trading at $14 per share and the Park Ave. common shares were trading at $12 per share.

(a) Record the above transactions.
(b) Prepare the required adjusting journal entries at December 31, Lang's financial year end.
(c) Show how the investments would be reported in the balance sheet.
(d) Show how the interest revenue, dividend revenue, and gains and losses will be reported on the statement of comprehensive income.
(e) Assume that on January 15, 2018, Lang sells the Electric Ltd. shares for $13.50 per share. Record the sale of the shares.

Solution

(a)

Jan.	2	Short-Term Investments at FVTPL—Bonds, Utility Corp.	20,000	
		Cash		20,000
		To record purchase of Utility Corp. bonds.		
Mar.	1	Long-Term Investments at FVTOCI—Equity, Park Ave.	50,000	
		Cash		50,000
		To record purchase of Park Ave. common shares.		
July	1	Cash	400	
		Interest Revenue		400
		To record receipt of interest from Utility Corp.		
	2	Cash	10,500	
		Short-Term Investments at FVTPL—Bonds, Utility Corp.		10,000
		Gain on Sale of FVTPL Investments		500
		To record sale of half of Utility Corp. bonds.		
Sept.	1	Short-Term Investments at FVTPL—Equity, Electric Ltd.	15,000	
		Cash		15,000
		To record purchase of Electric Ltd. common shares.		
Nov.	1	Cash	2,000	
		Dividend Revenue		2,000
		To record dividends received from Electric Corp. (1,000 × $2).		

(b)

Dec.	31	Interest Receivable ($10,000 × 4% × 6/12)	200	
		Interest Revenue		200
		To accrue semi-annual interest on Utility Corp. bonds.		
	31	Loss on Fair Value Adjustment—FVTPL	250	
		Short-Term Investments at FVTPL—Bonds, Utility Corp.		250
		To record fair value adjustment on Utility Corp. bonds ($10,000 − $9,750).		
	31	Long-Term Investments at FVTOCI—Equity, Park Ave.	10,000	
		OCI—Gain on Fair Value Adjustment		10,000
		To record fair value adjustment on Park Ave. investment [5,000 × ($12 − $10)].		

Action Plan
- Record the interest revenue on the bond.
- When the bonds are sold, the difference between the bonds' carrying value and the proceeds is reported as a gain or loss.
- Record the interest accrued on the bonds held for the period July 2 to December 31.
- Fair value adjustments are the difference between the investments' carrying value and fair value.
- When the shares are sold, the difference between the shares' carrying value and the proceeds is reported as a gain or loss.

(continued)

BEFORE YOU GO ON...DO IT > Accounting for Shares and Bonds (continued)

Dec. 31	Loss on Fair Value Adjustment—FVTPL	1,000	
	Short-Term Investments at FVTPL—Equity, Electric Ltd.		1,000
	To record fair value adjustment on Electric Ltd.		
	investment [1,000 × ($15 − $14)].		

(c) The investments will be reported in current assets on the balance sheet.

(d) On the statement of comprehensive income, interest revenue, dividend revenue and gain on sale of Utility Corp. bonds will be reported in other revenues. Losses from fair value adjustments for FVTPL investments will be reported in other expenses. The investments in Electric Ltd. and Utility Ltd. will be reported as current assets on the balance sheet and the investment in Park Ave. will be reported as a non-current asset.

(e)

Jan. 15	Cash (1,000 × $13.50)	13,500	
	Loss on Sale of FVTPL Investments ($14,000 − $13,500)	500	
	Short-Term Investments at FVTPL—Equity, Electric Ltd.		14,000
	To record sale of Electric Ltd. common shares.		

Related exercise material: BE16–6, BE16–7, BE16–8, BE16–9, BE16–10, E16–7, E16–8, and E16–9.

LEARNING OBJECTIVE **4** > Explain how to account for strategic investments and demonstrate the accounting for strategic investments with significant influence.

Accounting for Strategic Investments

Recall from the start of the chapter that strategic investments are always long-term investments in equity securities. The accounting for strategic investments is based on how much influence the investor has over the operating and financial affairs of the issuing corporation (the investee). The degree of influence depends primarily on the percentage of common shares owned by the investor. Illustration 16-8 shows the general accounting guidelines for the levels of influence.

▶ ILLUSTRATION 16-8

Financial reporting guidelines for strategic investments

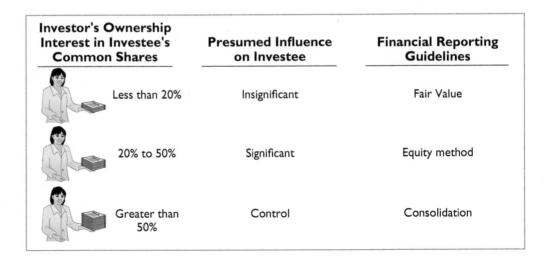

Investor's Ownership Interest in Investee's Common Shares	Presumed Influence on Investee	Financial Reporting Guidelines
Less than 20%	Insignificant	Fair Value
20% to 50%	Significant	Equity method
Greater than 50%	Control	Consolidation

An investor company that owns less than 20% of the common shares of another company is generally presumed not to have significant influence over the decisions of the investee company. Under IFRS, a long-term equity investment where there is no significant influence is reported at either FVTPL or FVTOCI, as discussed in the previous section. Under ASPE, the investment would be reported at fair value if there is a quoted market price for the shares and at cost if there is no quoted market price.

A company may invest in equity securities to maintain a long-term operating relationship. **When an investor owns 20% to 50% of the common shares of another company, the investor is generally presumed to have a significant influence over the investee's decisions.** Significant influence is the ability to participate in the investee's operating and financial policy decisions. When an investee can be significantly influenced, it is known as an **associate** and the investor uses the equity method to account for the investment.

The influence that an investor is assumed to have may be weakened by other factors. For example, an investor that acquires a 25% interest as the result of a "hostile" takeover may not have significant influence over the investee. Among the questions that should be answered to determine an investor's influence are:

1. Does the investor have representation on the investee's board of directors?
2. Does the investor participate in the investee's policy-making process?
3. Are there material transactions between the investor and investee?
4. Are the common shares that are held by other shareholders concentrated among a few investors or dispersed among many?

In other words, companies are required to use judgement when determining if significant influence exists instead of blindly following the guidelines. If circumstances exist that indicate the investor does not have significant influence, regardless of the amount owned, the investment is reported at fair value. The exception, as noted above, is that when the company is reporting under ASPE, the investment would be reported at cost if there were no quoted market price for the shares.

Typically, when an investor owns more than 50% of a corporation's common shares, it has more than significant influence—it has control. Control is the power to direct the operating and financial activities of the investee. Like significant influence, professional judgement is required to determine if there is control. If the investor has control over an investee, it is known as the **parent company** and the investee is known as the **subsidiary company**. Even though the investee is a separate legal entity, it is part of a group of corporations controlled by the parent. In order to show the users of the parent's financial statements the full extent of the group's operations, the financial statements of all the companies within the group are combined, resulting in **consolidated financial statements**. The process of preparing consolidated financial statements is beyond the scope of an introductory accounting course and is addressed in advanced accounting courses.

EQUITY METHOD

As noted earlier, when an investor company has significant influence over the investee (which is known as an associate), the equity method is used to account for the investment.

Under the **equity method**, an investor would make the following entries to record an investment in an associate:

1. **Record the acquisition of shares:** The investor will initially record the acquisition at what it cost the investor to purchase the shares. This treatment is similar to equity securities purchased for the purpose of resale, discussed in the previous section. But because the acquisition is strategic, the investment will be recognized in a non-current asset account called Investment in Associate.
2. **Record its share of the associate's profit (loss):** Annually the investor will increase (debit) the investment account and increase (credit) an income account for the investor's share of the associate's profit. Conversely, when the associate has a loss, the investor increases (debits) a loss account and decreases (credits) the investment account for its share of the associate's loss.
3. **Record the dividends received:** The investor will decrease (credit) the investment account when dividends are received. The investment account is reduced for dividends received because the associate's net assets are decreased when a dividend is paid.

Recall that in Chapter 13, we learned that retained earnings in a corporation is increased for profit and decreased for a loss and decreased when dividend payments are made. In its simplest form, the equity method requires that the investment reported by the investor reflect approximately the **investor's share** of the associate's retained earnings. Therefore, the investment account is also increased for profit and decreased for loss and dividend payments.

The following example demonstrates the equity method.

Recording Acquisitions of Shares

Assume that Milar Corporation (the investor) acquires 30% of the common shares of Beck Corporation (the associate) for $120,000 on January 1, 2017, and that Milar has significant influence over Beck. The entry to record the investment is:

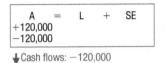

	A	=	L	+	SE
	+120,000				
	−120,000				

↓Cash flows: −120,000

Jan. 1	Investment in Associate—Beck Corporation	120,000	
	Cash		120,000
	To record purchase of 30% of Beck Corp. common shares.		

Recording Share of Associate's Profit or Loss

For the year ended December 31, 2017, Beck reports profit of $100,000. Milar records its share of 30% of Beck's profit in an account called Income from Investment in Associate (similar to a revenue/gain account), which is $30,000 ($100,000 × 30%). The entry is as follows:

	A	=	L	+	SE
	+30,000				+30,000

Cash flows: no effect

Dec. 31	Investment in Associate—Beck Corporation	30,000	
	Income from Investment in Associate		30,000
	To record 30% share of Beck Corp.'s profit.		

Recording Dividends Received

In December 2017, Beck declares and pays a total dividend of $40,000. Milar records its share of the dividend, $12,000 ($40,000 × 30%). The entry is as follows:

	A	=	L	+	SE
	+12,000				
	−12,000				

↑Cash flows: +12,000

Dec. 31	Cash	12,000	
	Investment in Associate—Beck Corporation		12,000
	To record dividends received from Beck Corp.		

After the transactions for the year have been posted, the investment and income accounts will show the following:

Investment in Associate—Beck Corporation				Income from Investment in Associate		
Jan. 1	120,000				Dec. 31	30,000
Dec. 31	30,000	Dec. 31	12,000			
Dec. 31	Bal. 138,000					

During the year, the investment account has increased by $18,000 ($138,000 − $120,000). This $18,000 is Milar's 30% equity in the $60,000 increase in Beck's retained earnings ($100,000 − $40,000). In addition, Milar will report $30,000 of income from its investment, which is 30% of Beck's profit of $100,000.

COST METHOD

Companies reporting under ASPE can choose to use either the equity method or the cost method to account for investments in associates. The cost method can also be used for non-strategic investments under ASPE when no quoted market price is available. Under the cost method, the investment is initially recorded at cost and is not subsequently adjusted until sold. Dividend revenue is reported in profit. The investment is reported at cost on the balance sheet in non-current assets.

Recording Acquisitions of Shares

Assume that Passera Corporation (the investor) reports under ASPE and on July 1, 2017, it acquires 1,000 common shares of Beale Corporation (the investee) at $40 per share. Beale Corporation is also a private company and there is no quoted market price for its shares. Passera Corporation has significant influence over Beale Corporation. The cost method will be used to account for the investment. The entry to record the investment is:

July 1	Investment in Associate—Beale Corporation	40,000	
	Cash		40,000
	To record purchase of Beale common shares.		

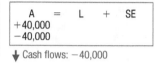

A = L + SE
+40,000
−40,000

↓ Cash flows: −40,000

The investment will be reported in Passera Corporation's balance sheet in non-current assets.

Recording Dividend Revenue

When using the cost method to account for a strategic investment, dividend revenue is recorded when the investee declares cash dividends. On October 1, Beale declares and pays a $2 per share dividend. The entry to record the dividend is:

Oct. 1	Cash (1,000 × $2)	2,000	
	Dividend Revenue		2,000
	To record receipt of cash dividend from Beale Corporation.		

A = L + SE
+2,000   +2,000

↑ Cash flows: +2,000

Dividend revenue is reported as other revenue in the income statement.

When using the cost method, no journal entry is required to record the investor's share of the investee's earnings, which makes the accounting for an associate under ASPE less complex and costly.

BEFORE YOU GO ON...DO IT   **④**   **Cost and Equity Methods**

CJW Inc., a public company, made the following investment during 2017:

Acquired 20% of the 400,000 common shares of Stillwater Corp. for $6 per share on January 2, 2017. On August 30, 2017, Stillwater paid a $0.10 per share dividend. On December 31, 2017, Stillwater reported profit of $244,000 for the year. Assume CJW has significant influence over Stillwater.

(a) Prepare all necessary journal entries for CJW Inc. for 2017.
(b) Determine the balance in the investment account on December 31, 2017, after all entries are posted.
(c) Assume that CJW Inc. is a private company and follows ASPE. Prepare the journal entries CJW would make for the investment in Stillwater Corp. if it uses the cost method.
(d) Determine the balance in the investment account on December 31, 2017, assuming the facts in part (c).

(continued)

BEFORE YOU GO ON...DO IT Cost and Equity Methods *(continued)*

Action Plan

- Use the equity method for ownership when there is significant influence (normally ownership of 20% or more of the common shares of another corporation).
- Under the equity method, recognize income from investment in associate when the associate declares a profit. The distribution of dividends is not income; rather, it reduces the equity investment.
- Use the cost method to account for an investment in an associate under ASPE if there is no quoted market price.

Solution

(a) Number of shares of Stillwater Corp. purchased = 80,000 (400,000 x 20%)

Jan.	2	Investment in Associate—Stillwater Corp.	480,000	
		Cash (80,000 × $6)		480,000
		To record purchase of 80,000 Stillwater Corp. common shares.		
Aug.	30	Cash	8,000	
		Investment in Associate—Stillwater Corp.		8,000
		To record receipt of cash dividend from Stillwater Corp. ($0.10 × 80,000).		
Dec.	31	Investment in Associate—Stillwater Corp.	48,800	
		Income from Investment in Associate		48,800
		To record 20% share of Stillwater Corp.'s profit. ($244,000 × 20%).		

(b) The balance in the Investment in Associate—Stillwater Corp. account is $520,800, determined as follows:

Investment in Associate—Stillwater Corp.

Jan. 2	480,000	Aug. 30		8,000
Dec. 31	48,800			
Dec. 31	Bal. 520,800			

(c)

Jan.	2	Investment in Associate—Stillwater Corp.	480,000	
		Cash (80,000 × $6)		480,000
		To record purchase of 80,000 Stillwater Corp. common shares.		
Aug.	30	Cash	8,000	
		Dividend Revenue		8,000
		To record receipt of cash dividend from Stillwater Corp. ($0.10 × 80,000).		

(d) The balance in the long-term investment account when CJW uses the cost method is $480,000, the original cost of the investment. When using the cost method under ASPE, no adjustments are made to the investment account for the investor's share of the investee's profits and dividends are recorded as revenue when received.

Related exercise material: BE16–11, BE16–12, BE16–13, and E16–11.

LEARNING OBJECTIVE 5 Explain how investments are reported in the financial statements.

Reporting of Investments

This section reviews the presentation of investments in the balance sheet, income statement, and statement of comprehensive income.

BALANCE SHEET

Recall that under IFRS, non-strategic debt and equity investments are categorized as one of the following:

1. Amortized cost
2. Fair value through profit or loss
3. Fair value through other comprehensive income

These categories indicate how an asset is accounted for and valued on the balance sheet. Investments must also be classified on the balance sheet as either current or non-current. How do we know when an investment is current? An investment asset is classified as current when:

- It is expected to be sold or otherwise realized within the entity's normal operating cycle or within 12 months from the balance sheet date.
- It is held primarily for trading purposes.
- It is a cash equivalent. Recall from Chapter 7 that cash equivalents are short-term, highly liquid (easily sold) investments that are not subject to significant risk of changes in value, such as term deposits, treasury bills, and guaranteed investment certificates.

Any investment that is not classified as current according to the criteria listed above is classified as non-current.

Investments Classified as Current Assets

In most cases, money-market investments and FVTPL investments—specifically those held for trading purposes—will be classified as current assets. Recall that FVTPL investments can be either debt or equity securities. However, amortized cost and FVTOCI investments can also be classified as current if they mature within 12 months of the balance sheet date or management intends to sell the investment within 12 months of the balance sheet date.

Illustration 16-9 shows one possible presentation for investments classified as current assets on the balance sheet for Nanoview Corporation.

NANOVIEW CORPORATION Balance Sheet (partial) December 31, 2017	
Assets	
Current assets	
Cash and cash equivalents	$ 28,000
Short-term investments at fair value through profit or loss—equity	143,000
Accounts receivable	15,000
Prepaid expenses	5,440
Notes receivable	34,200

▶ILLUSTRATION 16-9
Presentation of investments classified as current

Investments Classified as Non-Current Assets

Long-term debt instruments, such as bonds, that are held to earn interest income are classified as non-current assets until they are about to mature. Any portion that is expected to mature within the year is classified as a current asset. In addition, all equity securities that are purchased for strategic purposes are classified as non-current assets.

Illustration 16-10 shows one possible presentation for investments classified as non-current assets on the balance sheet of Nanoview Corporation.

NANOVIEW CORPORATION Balance Sheet (partial) December 31, 2017	
Assets	
Non-current assets	
Long-term investments at amortized cost—bonds	$40,500
Long-term investment at fair value through other comprehensive income—equity	17,480
Investment in associate	39,460
Property, plant, and equipment	20,077
Intangible assets	67,837

▶ILLUSTRATION 16-10
Presentation of investments classified as non-current

Separate disclosure is required for long-term investments reported at fair value, at cost, and at amortized cost, and for investments accounted for using the equity method. In addition, for equity investments reported at fair value, those investments where gains and losses are reported in other comprehensive income and those where gains and losses are reported in the income statement should be separately disclosed.

INCOME STATEMENT AND STATEMENT OF COMPREHENSIVE INCOME

This chapter has shown that companies can earn different types of income on investments, including (1) interest revenue, (2) dividend revenue, (3) gains or losses on fair value adjustments, (4) gains or losses on sale of the investment, and (5) equity income from a strategic investment with significant influence. Most of these items are included in profit in the non-operating section of the income statement. But you will recall that a company reporting under IFRS may elect to categorize and value an investment as fair value through other comprehensive income, in which case gains and losses related to these instruments will be reported in other comprehensive income. This is summarized in Illustration 16-11.

Illustration 16-11 shows one possible presentation for revenue, gains, and losses on the income statement and statement of comprehensive income of Nanoview Corporation. Nanoview uses a separate format for the income statement and the statement of comprehensive income.

▶ ILLUSTRATION 16-11
Presentation of investment revenue and gains and losses

NANOVIEW CORPORATION Income Statement Year Ended December 31, 2017		
Revenue		$460,170
Operating expenses		
Depreciation expense	$ 32,220	
Insurance expense	9,120	
Employee wages and benefits expense	184,990	
Total expenses		226,330
Profit from operations		233,840
Other revenues (expenses)		
Interest expense	(3,120)	
Dividend revenue	2,880	
Interest revenue	8,640	
Net gains on investments	15,210	
Income from investment in associate	8,660	32,270
Profit before income tax		266,110
Income tax		53,220
Profit		$212,890

NANOVIEW CORPORATION Statement of Comprehensive Income Year Ended December 31, 2017	
Profit	$212,890
Other comprehensive income	
Net change in fair value of investments through other comprehensive income (net of tax)	(9,400)
Total comprehensive income	$203,490

The example above shows a practical presentation of the statement of comprehensive income. Note that the various sources of revenue from investments, such as dividend revenue and interest revenue, can be combined and reported simply as "Investment revenue." Similarly, gains and losses on fair value adjustments for FVTPL investments and gains and losses on the sale of investments can be combined and presented as one amount on the statement: "Net gains (losses) on investments." IFRS requires that interest revenue and details about fair value changes be disclosed separately. This is normally done in the notes to the financial statements. ASPE follows much of the same guidelines for the presentation of revenue, gains, and losses on the income statement but requires fewer details to be presented. Of course, on an income statement prepared under ASPE, other comprehensive income is not reported.

SUMMARY OF INVESTMENTS

Illustration 16-12 provides a summary of investment categories and valuation requirements.

▶ ILLUSTRATION 16-12
Summary of investment categories and valuation requirements

Investment Category	Category Criteria	Examples	Valuation Method—IFRS	Valuation Method—ASPE
Non-strategic Investments				
Amortized Cost	A debt security held to earn interest income	• Money-market instruments • Bonds	Amortized cost using the effective-interest method	Amortized cost using the effective interest method or other permitted methods.
Fair Value Through Profit or Loss (FVTPL)	Any investment in debt or equity that is not an amortized cost or FVTOCI investment, including those investments held for trading purposes	• Common shares of another company • Bonds issued by another company	Fair value; gains and losses included in profit or loss	Fair value; gains and losses included in profit or loss if the security is actively traded on an organized exchange
Fair Value Through Other Comprehensive Income (FVTOCI)	Any equity investment that is designated by management to this category that is not held for trading purposes	• Common shares of another company	Fair value; gains and losses included in other comprehensive income	N/A
Strategic Investments				
Associate	Strategic investment with significant influence	20% – 50% ownership in the common shares of another company	Equity	FVTPL if quoted market price available or cost if no quoted market price available or equity method
Subsidiary	Strategic investment with control	Greater than 50% ownership in the common shares of another company	Consolidation	FVTPL if quoted market price available or equity or consolidation

---

ACCOUNTING IN ACTION
ALL ABOUT YOU INSIGHT

© istockphoto.com/Maria Toutoudaki

Canadians need to save for many different things over their lifetimes. To reduce taxes on savings and help individuals achieve their goals, the Canadian government introduced a new investment vehicle, the tax-free savings account (TFSA), starting in 2009. Canadians aged 18 and older can contribute every year to a TFSA. The maximum annual amount was proposed to be $5,500 starting January 1, 2016, and would be subject to indexation. Investment income on the TFSA is not taxable. If an individual is not able to contribute the allowed $5,500 per year, they are able to carry forward any unused contribution to future years. Funds can be withdrawn from the TFSA at any time and for any purpose. The amount withdrawn can be put back in the TFSA at a later date. Canadians from all income levels can participate.

Source: Canada Revenue Agency, "The Tax-Free Savings Account," http://www.cra-arc. gc.ca/tx/ndvdls/tpcs/tfsa-celi/menu-eng.html.

Q Is it beneficial for you, while you are a student, to invest in a TFSA even though you may not have taxable income? Would you classify your investment in a TFSA as a long-term or short-term investment?

Zaboschuk Corporation, a public company, has the following asset account balances at December 31, 2017. Prepare the assets section of Zaboschuk's balance sheet at December 31.

Accounts receivable	$ 84,000
Accumulated depreciation—buildings	200,000
Accumulated depreciation—equipment	54,000
Allowance for doubtful accounts	4,000
Buildings	800,000
Cash	21,000
Equipment	180,000
Goodwill	170,000
Inventory	130,000
Investment in associates	150,000
Land	200,000
Long-term investments at AC—bonds	50,000
Long-term investments at FVTOCI—equity	90,000
Prepaid insurance	23,000
Short-term investment at AC—treasury bill (maturity 120 days)	15,000
Short-term investments at FVTPL—equity	65,000

Action Plan

- Organize each asset account into its proper classification: current assets; long-term investments; property, plant, and equipment; and intangible assets.
- Remember that contra asset accounts reduce the related account balance.

Solution

ZABOSCHUK CORPORATION
Balance Sheet (partial)
December 31, 2017

Assets

Current assets			
Cash			$ 21,000
Short-term investment at amortized cost—treasury bill			15,000
Short-term investments at fair value through profit or loss—equity			65,000
Accounts receivable		$ 84,000	
Less: Allowance for doubtful accounts		4,000	80,000
Inventory			130,000
Prepaid insurance			23,000
Total current assets			334,000
Non-current assets			
Long-Term Investments			
Long-term investments at fair value through other comprehensive income—equity			90,000
Long-term investments at amortized cost—bonds			50,000
Investment in associates			150,000
Total long-term investments			290,000
Property, plant, and equipment			
Land		$200,000	
Buildings	$800,000		
Less: Accumulated depreciation	200,000	600,000	
Equipment	$180,000		
Less: Accumulated depreciation	54,000	126,000	
Total property, plant, and equipment			926,000
Goodwill			170,000
Total assets			$1,720,000

Related exercise material: BE16–14, BE16–15, BE16–16, E16–10, E16–12, E16–13, and E16–14.

Comparing IFRS and ASPE

Key Differences	International Financial Reporting Standards (IFRS)	Accounting Standards for Private Enterprises (ASPE)
A debt security held to earn interest income	Amortized cost using the effective interest method to amortize any discount or premium.	Amortized cost using either the effective-interest method but permitted to use alternative methods to amortize any discount or premium.
Debt and equity securities held for trading	Use fair value through profit or loss if investment does not meet the criteria for amortized cost or FVTOCI.	Use fair value through profit or loss if quoted market price is available. Use cost or amortized cost if quoted market price is not available.
Equity securities not primarily held for trading	Management can elect to use fair value through other comprehensive income; otherwise, use fair value through profit or loss.	Use fair value through profit or loss if quoted market price is available. Use cost if quoted market price is not available.
Strategic investment—significant influence	Must use equity method.	May use equity method, or fair value through profit or loss if quoted market price is available, or cost if quoted market price is not available.
Strategic investment—control	Must use consolidation.	May use fair value through profit or loss if quoted market price is available, or equity method or consolidation.

Demonstration Problem

In its first year of operations, which ended December 31, 2017, Northstar Finance Corporation, a public company, had the following selected transactions.

Jan.   1   Purchased 25% of the common shares of Southview Finance Ltd. for $125,000. Northstar has significant influence over Southview's operations.

Mar. 14   Purchased a $10,000 treasury bill for $9,950.

May   5   Purchased 15% of the common shares of Eastgate Financial Co. for $28,000. Northstar elected to categorize the investment as FVTOCI.

June 1   Purchased 600 Sanburg Inc. common shares for trading purposes at $24.50 per share.

   29   Received $10,000 from the matured treasury bill.

July   1   Purchased $100,000 of Lower Corporation 10-year, 5% bonds for $92,561 to earn interest. The market interest rate is 6%. Interest is paid semi-annually, on July 1 and January 1.

   1   Purchased 800 Cey Corporation common shares for trading purposes at $33.75 per share.

Sept. 1   Received a $1 per share cash dividend from Cey Corporation.

Oct.   8   Received dividends of $5,000 from Southview Finance Ltd.

Nov. 1   Sold 200 Sanburg common shares for $26.25 per share.

Dec. 15   Received a $0.50 per share cash dividend on Sanburg common shares.

   31   The market prices per share were $25 for Sanburg and $30 for Cey.

   31   Accrued interest revenue on the Lower Corporation bonds.

   31   The market price of the Eastgate common shares was $26,000.

   31   Southview reported profit of $90,000 for the year ended December 31, 2017.

   31   Northstar reported profit from operations of $250,000 for the year ended December 31, 2017. Northstar's income tax rate is 30%.

Instructions
(a) Record the transactions.
(b) Prepare the adjusting entries at December 31 to report the securities at their fair value.
(c) Prepare a statement of comprehensive income starting with profit from operations.
(d) Show the presentation of the investment accounts and accumulated other comprehensive income in the balance sheet.

ACTION PLAN

- Keep a running balance of the number of shares purchased and sold.
- Calculate the gain or loss on sale by subtracting the securities' carrying value from the proceeds.
- Determine the adjustment to fair value based on the difference between the securities' total cost and total fair value.
- Calculate the interest revenue on the bonds using the effective-interest method. Multiply the carrying value of the bonds by the semi-annual market interest rate. Calculate the interest receivable by multiplying the face value of the bonds by the semi-annual contractual rate. Increase the investment in bonds by the difference between the interest receivable and the interest revenue.
- Determine the equity method income from investment in associate by multiplying the associate's profit by the percentage of the common shares the investor company owns.
- Determine the profit before income tax by adding the other revenues and expenses to profit from operations.

SOLUTION TO DEMONSTRATION PROBLEM

(a)

Jan.	1	Investment in Associate—Southview Finance	125,000	
		Cash		125,000
		To record purchase of significant influence investment in Southview.		
Mar.	14	Short-Term Investment at AC—Treasury Bill	9,950	
		Cash		9,950
		To record purchase of treasury bill.		
May	5	Long-Term Investments at FVTOCI—Equity, Eastgate Financial Co.	28,000	
		Cash		28,000
		To record purchase of Eastgate Financial common shares.		
June	1	Short-Term Investments at FVTPL—Equity, Sanburg Inc.	14,700	
		Cash (600 × $24.50)		14,700
		To record purchase of 600 Sanburg Inc. common shares.		
	29	Short-Term Investment at AC—Treasury Bill	50	
		Interest Revenue		50
		Cash	10,000	
		Short-Term Investment at AC—Treasury Bill		10,000
		To record maturity of treasury bill.		
July	1	Long-Term Investments at AC—Bonds, Lower Corporation	92,561	
		Cash		92,561
		To record purchase of Lower Corporation 10-year, 5% bonds.		
	1	Short-Term Investments at FVTPL—Equity, Cey Corp.	27,000	
		Cash (800 × $33.75)		27,000
		To record purchase of 800 Cey common shares.		

- Calculate income tax expense by multiplying profit before income tax by the tax rate.
- Calculate the other comprehensive income reported in the comprehensive income statement by deducting the income tax on the fair value adjustment from the fair value adjustment.
- Calculate the accumulated other comprehensive income by adding the opening balance (zero in the first year of operations) and the fair value adjustment net of tax.

Date		Debit	Credit
Sept. 1	Cash (800 × $1)	800	
	Dividend Revenue		800
	To record receipt of $1 per share dividend from Cey Corp.		
Oct. 8	Cash	5,000	
	Investment in Associate—Southview Finance		5,000
	To record receipt of dividends from Southview Finance Co.		
Nov. 1	Cash (200 × $26.25)	5,250	
	Short-Term Investments at FVTPL—Equity, Sanburg Inc.		
	[(200 ÷ 600) × $14,700)]		4,900
	Gain on Sale of FVTPL Investments		350
	To record sale of 200 Sanburg Inc. common shares.		
Dec. 15	Cash [(600 − 200) × $0.50]	200	
	Dividend Revenue		200
	To record receipt of $0.50 per share dividend from Sanburg Inc.		

(b)

Short-term Investments	Cost	Fair Value	Gain (Loss) on Fair Value Adjustment
Sanburg common shares (400)	$ 9,800	$10,000	$ 200
Cey common shares (800)	27,000	24,000	(3,000)
Total	$36,800	$34,000	$(2,800)

Date		Debit	Credit
Dec. 31	Loss on Fair Value Adjustment—FVTPL	2,800	
	Short-Term Investments at FVTPL—Equity, Sanburg Inc.	200	
	Short-Term Investments at FVTPL—Equity, Cey		3,000
	To record fair value adjustment on FVTPL investments.		
31	Interest Receivable ($100,000 × 5% × $^6/_{12}$)	2,500	
	Long-Term Investments at AC—Bonds, Lower Corporation	277	
	Interest Revenue ($92,561 × 6% × $^6/_{12}$)		2,777
	To record the accrual of interest on the Lower Corporation 10-year, 5% bonds.		
31	OCI—Loss on Fair Value Adjustment ($28,000 − $26,000)	2,000	
	Long-Term Investments at FVTOCI—Equity, Eastgate Financial Co.		2,000
	To record fair value adjustment on Eastgate Financial investment.		
31	Investment in Associate—Southview Finance ($90,000 × 25%)	22,500	
	Income from Investment in Associate		22,500
	To record 25% share of Southview Finance Co.'s profit.		

(c)

NORTHSTAR FINANCE CORPORATION Statement of Comprehensive Income (partial) Year Ended December 31, 2017	
Profit from operations	$250,000
Other revenues and expenses	
Other revenue	
Income from investment in associate	22,500
Interest revenue ($2,777 + $50)	2,827
Dividend revenue ($800 + $200)	1,000
Gain on sale of fair value through profit or loss investments	350
	26,677
Other expenses	
Loss on fair value adjustment—fair value through profit or loss	2,800
Total other revenues and expenses	23,877
Profit before income tax	273,877
Income tax ($273,877 × 30%)	82,163
Profit	191,714
Other comprehensive income (loss)	
Loss on fair value adjustment, net of $600 income tax	1,400
($2,000 – [$2,000 × 30%])	
Comprehensive income	$190,314

(d)

NORTHSTAR FINANCE CORPORATION Balance Sheet (partial) December 31, 2017	
Assets	
Current assets	
Short-term investments at fair value through profit or loss	$ 34,000
Non-current assets	
Long-term investments at amortized cost ($92,561 + $277)	92,838
Long-term investments at fair value through other comprehensive income ($28,000 – $2,000)	26,000
Investment in associate ($125,000 + $22,500 – $5,000)	142,500
Total non-current assets	261,338
Liabilities and Shareholders' Equity	
Shareholders' equity	
Accumulated other comprehensive income (loss)	(1,400)

▶ Summary of Learning Objectives

1. *Identify reasons to invest, and classify investments.* Companies purchase debt and equity securities of other companies for two main reasons: (1) for non-strategic reasons as a source of investment income, and (2) for strategic reasons, such as gaining control of a competitor, influencing strategic alliances, or moving into a new line of business.

Non-strategic investments are debt and equity securities that are purchased for purposes of earning interest or dividend revenue or of selling them in the short term at a gain. Investments purchased for selling in the short term are called trading investments and are reported at fair value. Debt investments reported at amortized cost may be short-term or long-term. Strategic investments are always investments in equity securities and are classified as long-term investments.

2. ***Demonstrate the accounting for debt investments that are reported at amortized cost.*** Companies reporting under IFRS report debt investments purchased for the purposes of earning interest income at amortized cost. Companies reporting under ASPE may report all investments in debt instruments at amortized cost or at fair value if a fair value can be reliably determined. Debt investments include money-market instruments, bonds, and similar items. Entries are required to record the (1) acquisition, (2) interest revenue, and (3) maturity or sale. Interest revenue is recognized as it accrues and any discount or premium is amortized using the effective-interest method under IFRS. Companies reporting under ASPE will use the effective-interest method but are permitted to use other methods.

3. ***Demonstrate the accounting for fair value investments.*** Under IFRS, debt and equity investments held for trading purposes and investments that do not meet the criteria for amortized cost or fair value through other comprehensive income are reported at fair value through profit or loss. Fair value through profit or loss is a "catch-all" category for investments. When using this valuation method, adjustments to the fair value of assets are included in the calculation of profit or loss on the income statement or statement of comprehensive income. Certain investments in equity may be categorized as fair value through other comprehensive income and are reported at fair value each reporting period. However, gains or losses from fair value adjustments are included in other comprehensive income on the statement of comprehensive income. Under ASPE, any investment that has a quoted market price may be accounted for using fair value through profit or loss; otherwise, cost or amortized cost is used. An equity investment may be in either preferred or common shares of another corporation. Entries are required to record the (1) acquisition, (2) investment revenue, (3) fair value adjustments, and (4) sale.

4. ***Explain how to account for strategic investments and demonstrate the accounting for strategic investments with significant influence.*** Strategic investments are long-term investments in common shares of another company. The accounting for strategic investments is based on how much influence the investor has over the operating and financial affairs of the issuing corporation (the investee). The investor company is usually considered not to have significant influence over the investee company when it owns less than 20% of the investee. In this case, the investor company reports the investment in the investee company at either fair value through profit or loss or, under IFRS, fair value through other comprehensive income.

When there is significant influence (ownership is usually 20% or more), the investee is called an associate. The equity method is used to account for investments with significant influence. The equity method records investment revenue when profit is reported by the associate and increases the investor's investment account accordingly. Dividends that are received reduce the value of the investment account. Under ASPE, companies can elect to report investments with significant influence at fair value if there is a quoted market price or using the equity method. In the absence of a quoted market price, the investment may be reported at cost.

When a company controls the common shares of another company (that is, its ownership is usually greater than 50%), consolidation is required and consolidated financial statements are prepared.

5. ***Explain how investments are reported in the financial statements.*** Investments held for trading purposes and categorized as fair value through profit or loss are presented in the current assets section of the balance sheet. This includes equity investments and short- and long-term debt investments as long as they have been purchased with the intent to resell. Debt investments reported at amortized cost, maturing within 12 months of the balance sheet date, are also reported in current assets. Debt instruments reported at amortized cost with maturity dates of longer than 12 months from the date of the balance sheet and equity investments that are purchased for strategic purposes are reported in long-term investments. Gains and losses resulting from investments categorized as fair value through profit or loss are reported in the income statement and are presented in other revenues or other expenses. Gains and losses resulting from equity investments categorized as fair value through other comprehensive income are reported in other comprehensive income, then closed to accumulated other comprehensive income in the shareholders' equity section of the balance sheet.

▶ Glossary

Associate An investee in which the investor has significant influence. (p. 853)

Consolidated financial statements Financial statements that combine the parent company's financial statements with the financial statements of the companies that are controlled by the parent. (p. 853)

Debt instruments Debt obligations such as money-market instruments, bonds, or similar items that can be bought and sold. Also called *debt securities*. (p. 834)

Equity instruments An ownership interest in a corporation such as preferred and common shares. Also called *equity securities*. (p. 834)

Equity method   An accounting method in which the investment in common shares is initially recorded at cost. The investment account is then adjusted annually to show the investor's equity in the associate (investee). (p. 853)

Fair value   The amount an investment can be sold for in the market. Typically this will be the quoted market price in a public market. (p. 845)

Fair value adjustment   An accounting entry to adjust the carrying value of an investment for any increases or decreases in its fair value. (p. 845)

Fair value through other comprehensive income (FVTOCI) Investment classification made by management for an investment in equity securities. Fair value adjustments for these investments are reported as gains and losses in the other comprehensive income portion of the statement comprehensive income. (p. 845)

Fair value through profit or loss (FVTPL)   Investment classification for any investments in debt or equity securities that do not meet the criteria established for amortized cost investments and have not been designated by management as fair value through other comprehensive income. Fair value adjustments are reported as gains and losses on the income statement and are therefore included in the determination of either a profit or loss for a company. (p. 845)

Held-for-trading investments   Debt or equity securities that are bought and held for sale in the near term, mainly to generate earnings from short-term price differences. Also known as *trading investments*. (p. 835)

Investee   The corporation that issues (sells) the debt or equity securities that investors purchase. (p. 839)

Investor   The corporation that buys (owns) the debt or equity securities issued by another company. (p. 839)

Long-term debt instruments   Debt instruments with a maturity of longer than 12 months after the balance sheet date. (p. 838)

Money-market instruments   Short-term debt instruments that are low risk and highly liquid, such as money-market funds, term deposits, and treasury bills. (p. 834)

Non-strategic investment   An investment that is purchased mainly to generate investment income. (p. 834)

Parent company   A company that controls, or owns more than 50% of the common shares of, another company. (p. 853)

Securities   Debt or equity instruments that a company may invest in. (p. 834)

Short-term debt instruments   Debt instruments that mature within 12 months of the balance sheet date. (p. 838)

Strategic investment   An investment in equity securities that is purchased to maintain a long-term operating relationship with another company. (p. 834)

Subsidiary company   A company whose common shares are controlled by another company. Usually, more than 50% of its common shares are owned by the other company. (p. 853)

▶ Self-Study Questions
Answers are at the end of the chapter.

(LO 1) K   1. Under IFRS, the most important factor for determining the classification and valuation of a non-strategic investment is:
    (a) whether the investment is in a debt instrument or an equity instrument.
    (b) whether the investment is in a private or public corporation.
    (c) whether the investment is a long-term or current investment.
    (d) the purpose of the investment.

(LO 1) K   2. The most significant difference between a held-for-trading investment and a strategic investment is:
    (a) held-for-trading investments may earn dividend income, whereas strategic investments may not.
    (b) equity instruments purchased for trading purposes are more likely to be listed on a public stock exchange.
    (c) strategic investments are usually investments in private corporations, whereas held-for-trading investments are not.
    (d) a held-for-trading investment is purchased for resale in the near future at a gain and a strategic investment is purchased to have a long-term operating relationship between the companies.

(LO 2) K   3. Which of the following statements is false?
    (a) Debt instruments purchased to earn interest are reported at amortized cost.

    (b) Debt instruments purchased by a company reporting under IFRS must be reported at fair value.
    (c) Debt instruments include term deposits, treasury bills, money-market funds, and bonds.
    (d) Under IFRS, the discount or premium on bonds reported at amortized cost is amortized using the effective-interest method.

(LO 2) AP   4. The accounting entry to record the accrual of interest on a treasury bill is:
    (a) debit Interest Revenue and credit Short-Term Investment—Treasury Bill.
    (b) debit Interest Revenue and credit Cash.
    (c) debit Short-Term Investment—Treasury Bill and credit Interest Revenue.
    (d) debit Cash and credit Short-Term Investment—Treasury Bill.

(LO 3, 4) K   5. Which securities are valued at fair value in public companies?
    (a) Short-term investment in debt instrument held to earn interest
    (b) Long-term investment in 25% of the common shares of an associate
    (c) Long-term investment in bonds held to earn interest
    (d) Investments in debt or equity securities held for trading purposes

(LO 3) AP 6. During 2017, Boscha Ltd. purchased common shares in International Inc. for $240,000 categorized as FVTPL. At December 31, the fair value of the shares is $225,000. The journal entry to adjust the investment at year end is:

(a) Loss on Fair Value Adjustment—

FVTPL	15,000	
Short-Term Investments at FVTPL—Equity, International Inc.		15,000

(b) Short-Term Investments at FVTPL—Equity, International

Inc.	15,000	
Gain on Fair Value Adjustment—FVTPL		15,000

(c) OCI—Loss on Fair Value

Adjustment	15,000	
Short-Term Investments at FVTPL—Equity, International Inc.		15,000

(d) No journal entry is required because losses are not recorded until the investment is sold.

(LO 4) K 7. The equity method of accounting for an investment in common shares is normally used when the investor owns:
(a) less than 20% of the investee's common shares.
(b) 20% or more of the investee's common shares.
(c) 20% or more of the investee's preferred shares.
(d) more than 50% of the investee's common shares.

(LO 4) AP 8. The Big K Ranch owns 20% of the Little L Ranch's common shares. The Little L Ranch reported profit of $150,000 and paid dividends of $40,000 this year. How much investment revenue would the Big K Ranch report if it used the equity method?
(a) $22,000
(b) $30,000
(c) $110,000
(d) $8,000

(LO 5) K 9. Which of the following investment reporting requirements is true?
(a) All investments in debt securities are classified as current assets.

(b) Strategic investments of 20% or more of the investee's common shares are reported as non-current assets.
(c) All gains and losses on fair value adjustments must be reported in profit.
(d) Equity investments are always classified as current assets.

(LO 3, 5) AP 10. During 2017, Voser Ltd. purchased 100,000 common shares of Canadian Corp. for $325,000 when the shares were trading at $3.25 per share. The shares are held for trading purposes. On September 30, Voser received $15,000 of dividends from Canadian Corp. At December 31, the shares were trading at $3.50 per share. Voser Ltd. would report the following in its December 31 financial statements:
(a) Short-term investments at FVTPL—Equity, Canadian Corp. in the amount of $325,000 in current assets on the balance sheet, investment revenue—dividends of $15,000 in other revenues in the income statement, and a $25,000 gain on fair value adjustment—FVTPL in other revenues in the income statement
(b) Short-term investments at FVTPL—Equity, Canadian Corp. in the amount of $350,000 in current assets on the balance sheet, dividends of $15,000 as a deduction from retained earnings, and a $25,000 gain on fair value adjustment—FVTPL in other revenues in the income statement
(c) Short-term investments at FVTPL—Equity, Canadian Corp. in the amount of $350,000 in current assets on the balance sheet, investment revenue—dividends of $15,000 in other revenues in the income statement, and a $25,000 gain on fair value adjustment—FVTPL in other revenues in the income statement
(d) Short-term investments at FVTOCI—Equity, Canadian Corp. in the amount of $350,000 in current assets on the balance sheet, investment revenue—dividend of $15,000 in other revenues in the income statement, and a $25,000 gain on fair value adjustment—FVTPL in other comprehensive income

Questions

(LO 1) K 1. Why might a corporation purchase debt or equity securities of another company?

(LO 1) C 2. What are the differences between non-strategic and strategic investments?

(LO 1) C 3. On November 15, 2017, Uram Mining Ltd. announced that it will be purchasing a 32% share in the newly incorporated White Shell Supplies Company. Uram Mining Ltd. owns and operates a mining operation focused on uranium extraction. White Shell Supplies is located in Northern

Saskatchewan and manufactures parts and supplies for mining equipment. Is this a non-strategic investment or a strategic investment by Uram Mining Ltd.? Explain.

(LO 1) C 4. What is a fair value measurement? How is fair value established for investments?

(LO 2) K 5. When is it appropriate to report an investment in bonds at amortized cost?

(LO 2) C 6. In what ways does reporting investments held to earn interest at amortized cost provide users of financial statements with relevant information?

(LO 2) C   7. Under what circumstances would an investor record a gain on the sale of a bond investment? When would a loss on the sale of a bond investment be recorded?

(LO 3) K   8. What are the differences between the fair value through profit or loss and fair value through other comprehensive income investment categories?

(LO 3) K   9. When are investments in debt and equity securities classified as fair value through profit or loss?

(LO 3) C   10. Why would management designate an investment in equity securities as fair value through other comprehensive income?

(LO 3) C.   11. Theo Wingert has asked for your assistance regarding the accounting and reporting of an investment. "My boss told me this was to be a fair value through other comprehensive income investment and I am not sure what to do next." Explain to Theo what journal entries are required to account for this investment.

(LO 4) C   12. What evidence indicates that an investor has significant influence over an investee? What evidence suggests control? Explain and be sure to include all relevant factors involved.

(LO 4) C   13. You have been assigned the task of training a summer student for your company. The student is required to account for an investment in an associate. Provide the student with instructions. Include an explanation of what an investment in associate means and the required journal entries each year.

(LO 3, 4) 14. Refer to question #13. After you explain the appropriate accounting to the student, she comes to you with questions. She is confused about the equity method. Explain how the equity method of accounting for investments is different from other investment valuations. What information will the equity method provide for a user of the financial statements?

(LO 4) C   15. Identify what is included in the carrying value of a strategic investment using the (a) equity method, and (b) cost method.

(LO 4) K   16. When is an investee referred to as an associate? When is an investee referred to as a subsidiary?

(LO 5) K   17. In the chapter, we discussed five categories of investments. Describe each category and include the valuation method used for both IFRS and ASPE.

(LO 5) K   18. Identify the proper statement presentation of the following investments: (a) investments held for trading purposes, (b) short-term debt investments purchased to earn interest, (c) debt investments purchased to earn interest with maturities longer than 12 months, and (d) strategic investments accounted for using the equity method.

(LO 5) C   19. When may a company report gains or losses on fair value adjustments through other comprehensive income? Why might a company choose to report these gains and losses in other comprehensive income?

▶ Brief Exercises

Identify terminology.
(LO 1) K

BE16–1   The following terms were introduced in this chapter:

1. Strategic investments
2. Non-strategic investments
3. Short-term investments at fair value through profit or loss (FVTPL)
4. Long-term investments at amortized cost (AC)

Match each term with the following definitions:

(a) _____ Debt securities that are held to earn interest income
(b) _____ Investments purchased to influence or control another company
(c) _____ Debt or equity securities that are bought and held for sale in the near term at a profit
(d) _____ Investments purchased mainly to generate investment income

Classify investments.
(LO 1) C

BE16–2   For each of the following investments, identify the (a) reason for the investment (non-strategic or strategic), (b) balance sheet classification (current or non-current asset), and (c) valuation reported on the balance sheet. Assume that the investor is a public company. The first one has been done for you as an example.

Investment	(a) Reason	(b) Classification	(c) Valuation
1. 120-day treasury bill	Non-strategic	Current asset	Amortized cost
2. Common shares purchased by a bank for resale in the near future at a gain			
3. 15% of the common shares of a public company designated as FVTOCI			
4. Five-year bonds purchased by a company to hold and earn interest			
5. 10-year bonds purchased to sell in the near future at a gain			

BE16–3   On December 2, 2017, Nudesign Furniture Ltd. purchased a $150,000, Canadian government 120-day treasury bill for $148,900. On December 31, $275 of interest had accrued on the treasury bill. On April 1, 2018, the treasury bill matured. Prepare the journal entries to record the (a) purchase of the treasury bill; (b) accrual of interest on December 31, 2017; and (c) receipt of cash on April 1, 2018.

Account for debt investment reported at amortized cost. (LO 2) AP

BE16–4   On January 1, 2017, Chan Ltd., a public company, purchased $600,000 of five-year, 4% bonds at par from Pullen Corporation. Interest is received semi-annually on July 1 and January 1. Chan purchased the bonds to earn interest. At December 31, 2017, the bonds were trading at 101. Prepare the journal entries to record (a) the purchase of the bonds on January 1, (b) the receipt of interest on July 1, and (c) any adjusting entries required at December 31.

Account for debt investment reported at amortized cost—effective-interest method. (LO 2) AP

BE16–5   Strand Corp. purchased $300,000 of five-year, 4% Hydrocor bonds at 99 on June 30, 2017. Strand Corp. purchased the bonds to earn interest. Interest is paid semi-annually each June 30 and December 31. The semi-annual amortization amount for the first interest period is $273 determined using the effective-interest method. At December 31, 2017, the bonds were trading at 98. Prepare the required journal entries on June 30 and December 31, 2017.

Account for debt investment reported at amortized cost—effective-interest method. (LO 2) AP

BE16–6   On July 1, 2017, Moon Corporation, a private company, purchased $400,000 of six-year, 6% Star Corporation bonds for $420,000. The bonds pay interest each June 30. The bonds were purchased to earn interest and the market interest rate at the time of purchase was 5%. The company uses the effective-interest method to amortize any premium or discount on debt security investments. Prepare the required journal entries on July 1 and December 31, 2017, and June 30, 2018.

Account for debt investment reported at amortized cost—effective-interest method. (LO 3) AP

BE16–7   Using the data presented in BE16–5, assume Strand Corp. is a public company and that it purchased Hydrocor's bonds for trading purposes. Prepare the journal entries to record (a) the purchase of the bonds on June 30, 2017; (b) the receipt of the first interest payment on December 31, 2017; and (c) any required adjusting journal entries on December 31, 2017.

Account for fair value through profit or loss investment. (LO 3) AP

BE16–8   On August 1, McLain Finance Inc. buys 3,000 Datawave common shares for trading purposes for $114,000 cash. On October 15, McLain receives a cash dividend of $2.75 per share from Datawave. On December 1, McLain sells the shares for $120,000 cash. Prepare the journal entries to record the (a) purchase of the shares, (b) receipt of the dividend, and (c) sale of the shares.

Account for sale of fair value through profit or loss investment. (LO 3) AP

BE16–9   On April 1, 2017, Perfect Plastics Company purchased 40,000 common shares in Ecotown Ltd. for $15 per share. Management has designated the investment as FVTOCI. On December 5, Ecotown paid dividends of $0.10 per share and its shares were trading at $17 per share on December 31. Prepare the required entries to record the purchase, dividends, and year-end adjusting journal entry (if any) for this investment.

Account for fair value through other comprehensive income investment. (LO 3) AP

BE16–10   Using the data presented in BE16–9, assume that the investment in Ecotown's common shares is sold on January 15, 2018, for $690,000. Prepare the journal entry to record the sale of the investment.

Account for sale of fair value through other comprehensive income investment. (LO 3) AP

BE16–11   On January 1, Poitras Ltée, a public company, purchases 20% of Hook Corporation's common shares for $250,000 for strategic purposes. For the year ended December 31, Hook reports profit of $220,000 and pays a $15,000 cash dividend. The fair value of Poitras's investment in Hook at December 31 is $270,000. Prepare journal entries required assuming Poitras has significant influence over Hook.

Account for strategic investment—equity method. (LO 4) AP

BE16–12   On January 1, 2017, McAdam Ltd., a private company reporting under ASPE, purchased 25% of the common shares of Tomecek Corporation for $175,000. Tomecek reported profit of $85,000 for 2017 and paid dividends of $12,000 on December 31, 2017. McAdam's year end is December 31. Assuming that there is not a quoted market price for Tomecek's shares, and that McAdam elects to report investments with significant influence using the cost method, prepare the required journal entries.

Account for strategic investment at cost. (LO 4) AP

BE16–13   Wren Inc., a public company, owns 20% of Dong Ltd.'s common shares for strategic purposes. The investment's carrying value at January 1, 2017, is $300,000. During the year, Dong reported profit of $250,000 and paid a dividend of $20,000. The investment's fair value on December 31, 2017, Wren's year end, is $315,000.

Compare impact of reporting strategic investment at cost and using the equity method. (LO 4) AP

(a) Assuming Wren has significant influence over Dong, indicate the amount reported on the balance sheet for the investment at December 31 and the amount of investment income reported in the income statement.

(b) Assume instead that Wren is a private company and reports the investment using cost. Indicate the amount reported on the balance sheet for the investment at December 31 and the amount of investment income reported in the income statement.

Prepare statement of comprehensive income. (LO 5) AP

BE16–14   Atwater Corporation, a public corporation, reported a gain on fair value adjustment of $46,000 net of tax on an investment reported at fair value through other comprehensive income, and a loss on fair value adjustment of $50,000 before tax on an investment held for trading purposes for the year ended April 30, 2017. The company's profit before other revenues and expenses was $650,000 and it has a 35% income tax rate. Prepare a partial, all-inclusive statement of comprehensive income beginning with profit from operations.

Classify accounts. (LO 5) AP

BE16–15   Indicate on which financial statement (that is, balance sheet, income statement, or statement of comprehensive income) each of the following accounts would be reported if the investor is a public company. The company presents the statement of comprehensive income separately from the income statement. Also give the appropriate financial statement classification (e.g., current assets, non-current assets, other revenue, other comprehensive income).

Account	Financial Statement	Classification
Short-term investments at FVTPL—bonds		
Dividend revenue		
Investment in associate		
Long-term investments at AC—bonds		
Gain on sale of FVTPL investments		
Other comprehensive income—gain on fair value adjustment		
Loss on fair value adjustment—FVTPL		
Interest revenue		

Report investments in balance sheet. (LO 5) AP

BE16–16   Sabre Corporation, a public company, has the following investments at November 30, 2017:

1. Investments held for trading purposes: common shares of National Bank, carrying value $25,000, fair value $26,000, and five-year, 5% bonds of Turbo Corp., carrying value $50,000, fair value $48,000
2. FVTOCI investment: 25% of the common shares of Sword Corp., carrying value $108,000, fair value $105,000
3. Strategic investment: common shares of Epee Inc. (30% ownership), cost $210,000, equity method balance $250,000
4. Debt investment purchased to earn interest: bonds of Ghoti Ltd. maturing in four years, amortized cost $150,000, fair value $175,000
5. Debt investment purchased to earn interest: Canadian government 120-day treasury bill, purchased at $25,000, $125 interest accrued to November 30, 2017

Show how the investments would be reported in the assets section of the balance sheet.

▶ Exercises

Distinguish between non-strategic and strategic investments. (LO 1) C

E16–1   Awisse Telecommunications Ltd. has several investments in debt and equity securities of other companies.

1. 15% of the common shares of Lewis Telecommunications Inc., with the intent of purchasing at least 10% more of the common shares and requesting a seat on Lewis's board of directors.
2. 100% of the 15-year bonds issued by Li Internet Ltd., intended to be held for 15 years to earn interest.
3. 95% of the common shares of Barlow Internet Services Inc.
4. 120-day treasury bill.
5. 10% of the common shares of Talk to Us Ltd., to be sold if the share price increases.

Instructions

Indicate whether each of the above investments is a non-strategic or strategic investment and explain why.

Classify investments. (LO 1) C

E16–2   Kroshka Holdings Corporation has several investments in the debt and equity securities of other companies:

1. 10-year BCE bonds, purchased to earn interest.
2. 10-year GE bonds, intended to be sold if interest rates go down.
3. One-year Government of Canada bonds, purchased to earn interest.
4. 180-day treasury bill, intended to be held to earn interest.

5. Bank of Montreal preferred shares, purchased to sell in the near term at a profit.
6. Loblaw common shares, purchased to sell in the near term at a profit.
7. 60% of the common shares of Pizzutto Holdings Corporation, a major competitor of Kroshka Holdings.
8. 22% of the common shares of Kesha Inc., one of Kroshka Holdings' suppliers.

Instructions

(a) Indicate whether each of the above investments is a non-strategic or strategic investment.
(b) Indicate whether each of the above investments would be classified as a current asset or non-current asset in Kroshka Holdings' balance sheet.
(c) For each investment that you classified as non-strategic, indicate the value the investment will be reported at in the balance sheet assuming that Kroshka is a public company.

E16–3   Stevens Corporation, during the year ended October 31, 2017, had the following transactions for money-market instruments purchased to earn interest:

Record debt investments reported at amortized cost. (LO 2) AP

Jan. 2   Purchased a 120-day, $40,000 treasury bill maturing on May 1 for $39,760.
May 1   The treasury bill matured.
Aug. 1   Invested $65,000 in a money-market fund.
    31   Received notification that $163 of interest had been earned and added to the fund.
Sept. 30   Received notification that $163 of interest had been earned and added to the fund.
Oct. 1   Purchased a 90-day, 2.4%, $30,000 treasury bill for $29,821.
    15   Cashed the money-market fund and received $65,408.

Instructions

(a) Prepare the journal entries to record the above transactions.
(b) Prepare any required adjusting journal entries at October 31.

E16–4   On July 1, 2017, Imperial Inc., a public company, purchased $500,000 of Acme Corp. 10-year, 4% bonds for $461,000 to earn interest. The bonds had a market interest rate of 5%. The bonds pay interest semi-annually on January 1 and July 1. Imperial Inc. has a December 31 year end. At December 31, 2017, the bonds are trading at 96.

Record debt investment reported at amortized cost and bond liability. (LO 2) AP

Instructions

(a) Assuming Imperial Inc. purchased the bonds from Acme Corp., record the journal entries required on July 1 for (1) Imperial Inc., and (2) Acme Corp.
(b) Record any adjusting journal entries that are required at December 31 for (1) Imperial Inc., and (2) Acme Corp.
(c) Record the receipt and payment of the first interest payment on January 1, 2018, for (1) Imperial Inc., and (2) Acme Corp.

E16–5   On April 1, 2017, Bight Corporation issued $400,000, ~~Face Value~~ five-year bonds. On this date, Shoreline Corporation purchased the bonds from Bight to earn interest. Interest is received semi-annually on April 1 and October 1 and Shoreline's year end is March 31. Below is a partial amortization schedule for the first three interest periods of the bond issue.

Use a bond amortization schedule to record debt investment transactions at amortized cost. (LO 2) AP

Semi-Annual Interest Period	Interest Received	Interest Revenue	Amortization	Bond Amortized Cost
April 1, 2017				$418,444
October 1, 2017	$8,000	$6,277	$1,723	416,721
April 1, 2018	8,000	6,251	1,749	414,972
October 1, 2018	8,000	6,225	1,775	413,197

Instructions

(a) Were the bonds purchased at a discount or at a premium?   *premium becoz paid more than FV =400 000*
(b) What is the face value of the bonds?   *400,000*
(c) What will the bonds' amortized cost be at the maturity date?   *400,000 becoz the idea is to get the FV back at the En*
(d) What is the bonds' contractual interest rate? The market interest rate?   *① 8K ÷ 400k = 2% ·an = 9%×2 4%   ② 6,277 ÷ 418,444 = 1.5% Semi ·an 1.5 × 2 = 3%*
(e) Prepare the journal entries to record the purchase of the bonds; the receipt of interest on October 1, 2017; the accrual of interest on March 31, 2018; and the receipt of interest on April 1, 2018.

E16–6   The following transactions relate to Portland Cement Ltd.'s investment in the debt securities of Widget Makers Inc. during 2017 and 2018. Portland is a public company and purchased the investment to earn interest income.

Account for debt investments at amortized cost. (LO 2) AP

2017

Jan. 1   Purchased $120,000 of Widget Makers Inc. eight-year, 7% bonds for $135,666, to yield a market interest rate of 5%. Interest is payable semi-annually on July 1 and January 1.

July 1   Received semi-annual interest on Widget Makers' bonds.

Dec. 31   Accrued interest at Portland's year end.

2018

Jan. 1   Recorded receipt of interest payment from bonds.

July 1   Recorded receipt of interest payment from bonds.

2   Sold the bonds on the open market for $131,000.

Instructions

(a) Record the above transactions. (Round all amounts to the nearest dollar.)

(b) What is the balance in the investment account on December 31, 2017?

Record debt investment held for trading purposes. (LO 3) AP

E16–7   On August 1, 2017, Chen Corporation, a public company, purchased $100,000 of Alaska Ltd. five-year, 7% bonds at par. The bonds were purchased for trading purposes and pay interest semi-annually on January 31 and July 31 of each year. On December 31, 2017, Chen's year end, the bonds' fair value was $101,000. The bonds were sold on February 1, 2018, for $102,000.

Instructions

(a) Record the purchase of the bonds on August 1, 2017.

(b) Record any adjusting journal entries that are required at December 31, 2017.

(c) Indicate how the investment is presented on Chen Corporation's December 31, 2017, balance sheet.

(d) Record the receipt of the first interest payment on January 31, 2018.

(e) Record the sale of the bonds on February 1, 2018.

Record debt and equity trading investments. (LO 3) AP

E16–8   Following is information for Marcel Ltée's investments held for trading. Marcel is a public company and has a December 31 year end.

2017

Sept. 28   Purchased 3,500 shares of Cygman Limited for $40 per share.

Oct. 1   Purchased $300,000 of Rauk Inc. 4% bonds at face value. The bonds pay interest semi-annually on April 1 and October 1.

Nov. 12   Sold 1,900 Cygman shares for $42 per share.

Dec. 1   Received $1.50 per share dividend from Cygman.

31   Cygman shares were trading at $38 per share and the Rauk bonds were trading at 101.

2018

Mar. 31   Sold the remaining Cygman shares for $40 per share.

Apr. 1   Received interest on the Rauk bonds.

Oct. 1   Received interest on the Rauk bonds.

Dec. 31   Rauk bonds were trading at 102.

Instructions

Record the above transactions, including any required adjusting entries, for 2017 and 2018.

Determine equity investment at fair value through profit or loss transactions. (LO 3) AP

E16–9   The following was reported by Church Financial in its December 31, 2017, financial statements:

Short-term investments at FVTPL—equity, December 31, 2016	$11,000
Short-term investments at FVTPL—equity, December 31, 2017	15,000
Gain on fair value adjustment—FVTPL	2,500
Loss on sale of FVTPL investments	3,000

The carrying value of the investments sold was $4,000.

Instructions

(a) What is the cash amount received on the sale of the investment?

(b) Prepare the journal entries that were recorded by Church to record the sale of the investment and the gain on fair value adjustment at December 31, 2017.

(c) Post the journal entries to the Short-Term Investments at FVTPL—Equity T account.

(d) Calculate the amount of investments purchased in 2017. Prepare the entry to record the purchase.

Record adjusting entry for fair value investments, show statement presentation, and record sale. (LO 3, 5) AP

E16–10   At December 31, 2017, the trading investments for Yanik Inc., are as follows:

Security	Investment Category	Carrying Value	Fair Value
Co. A common shares	FVTPL	$18,500	$16,000
Co. B preferred shares	FVTPL	12,500	14,000
Co. C common shares	FVTOCI	23,000	19,000
Total		$54,000	$49,000

Instructions

(a) Prepare the adjusting entries required at December 31 to report the above investments at fair value.

(b) Show the financial statement presentation of the investments and the gains and losses on fair value adjustments at December 31, 2017. (Ignore income tax.)

(c) Assuming that on March 20, 2018, Yanik sold Co. B preferred shares for $13,500, prepare the journal entry to record this transaction.

E16–11   Visage Cosmetics, a public company, acquires 40% of Image Fashion Inc.'s 30,000 common shares for $18 per share on January 2, 2017. On June 15, Image Fashion pays a cash dividend of $30,000. On December 31, Image Fashion reports profit of $380,000 for the year. At December 31, Image Fashion shares are trading at $22 per share.

Record strategic equity investments. (LO 4) AP

Instructions

(a) Prepare the required journal entries to record the Image Fashion Inc. investment assuming significant influence exists.

(b) Determine the balance in the investment account on December 31, 2017, Visage Cosmetics' year end.

E16–12   On January 1, 2017, Studio27 Ltd., a private company, buys 25% of Sugar Maple Candy Company's 200,000 common shares for $480,000. On December 31, 2017, Sugar Maple pays a $35,000 cash dividend and reports profit of $280,000. At December 31, 2017, Sugar Maple's shares are trading at $12.50 per share. Both companies have a December 31 year end. Studio27 is able to appoint one board member to Sugar Maple's board of directors and this person has been influential in directing the operations of the company.

Record strategic equity investment; determine balance sheet presentation. (LO 4, 5) AP

Instructions

(a) Record the above transactions assuming Studio27 uses the equity method to report its investment in Sugar Maple Candy Company.

(b) Determine the amounts to be reported on Studio27's balance sheet and income statement for its investment in Sugar Maple at December 31, 2017.

(c) Repeat parts (a) and (b) assuming Studio27 elects to use the cost method for significant influence investments.

E16–13   You are provided with the following balance sheet accounts of New Bay Inc., a public company, as at December 31, 2017:

Prepare balance sheet. (LO 5) AP

Accounts payable	$ 35,000
Accounts receivable	60,000
Accumulated depreciation—equipment	40,000
Accumulated other comprehensive income	2,000
Allowance for doubtful accounts	10,000
Bonds payable, 8%, due 2019	268,000
Cash	22,000
Common shares, 10,000, no par value unlimited authorized, 10,000 issued	100,000
Equipment	66,000
Interest payable	18,000
Interest receivable	1,500
Investment in associate	55,000
Long-term investments at AC—bonds, Aliant Inc. (mature January 1, 2021)	180,000
Long-term investments at FVTOCI—equity	25,000
Note receivable, 5%, due April 21, 2020	60,000
Retained earnings	45,000
Short-term investments at FVTPL—equity	48,500

Instructions

Prepare New Bay's classified balance sheet at December 31, 2017. Assume any investments reported at fair value through other comprehensive income are long-term.

E16–14   You are provided with the following income accounts of Oakridge Ltd. for the year ended December 31, 2017. Oakridge reported profit from operations of $125,000 for the year ended December 31, 2017. Oakridge's income tax rate is 30%.

Prepare statement of comprehensive income. (LO 5) AP

Interest revenue	$5,000
Gain on sale of FVTPL investments	1,500
OCI—gain on fair value adjustment	3,000
Loss on fair value adjustment—FVTPL	7,500
Interest expense	8,000

Instructions

(a) Does Oakridge use ASPE or IFRS? Explain.
(b) Prepare an all-inclusive statement of comprehensive income starting with profit from operations.

▶ Problems: Set A

Record debt investments; show statement presentation. (LO 2, 5) AP

P16–1A   Liu Corporation had the following transactions in debt instruments purchased to earn interest during the year ended December 31, 2017:

Jan.	1	Purchased a 180-day (six-month) Government of Canada treasury bill for $98,039.
June	30	Received $100,000 cash when the treasury bill matured.
July	5	Purchased a money-market fund for $25,000.
Oct.	1	Cashed in the money-market fund, receiving $25,185.
	1	Purchased a six-month, 3%, term deposit for $75,000.
Dec.	31	Accrued semi-annual interest on the term deposit.

Instructions

(a) Record the transactions.
(b) Show the financial statement presentation of the investment at December 31 and any related accounts.

TAKING IT FURTHER   What was the annual rate of interest earned on the treasury bill?

Record debt investment at amortized cost; show statement presentation. (LO 2, 3, 5) AP

P16–2A   On January 1, 2017, Morrison Inc., a public company, purchased $600,000 of Pearl Corporation's five-year, 4% bonds for $627,660 when the market interest rate was 3%. Interest is received semi-annually on July 1 and January 1. Morrison's year end is December 31. Morrison intends to hold Pearl's bonds until January 1, 2022, the date the bonds mature. The bonds' fair value on December 31, 2017, was $620,000.

Instructions

(a) Record the purchase of the bonds on January 1, 2017.
(b) Prepare the entry to record the receipt of interest on July 1, 2017.
(c) Prepare the adjusting entry required at December 31, 2017.
(d) Show the financial presentation of the bonds for Morrison on December 31, 2017.
(e) Prepare the entry to record the receipt of interest on January 1, 2018.
(f) Prepare the entry to record the receipt on maturity of the bonds on January 1, 2022. Assume the entry to record the last interest payment has been recorded.
(g) How would your answers to parts (a) through (c) change if the bonds were purchased for the purpose of trading?

TAKING IT FURTHER   What was the market interest rate on December 31, 2017, when the bonds' fair value was $620,000? (*Hint*: How many interest periods are left after January 1, 2018?)

Record debt investment at amortized cost, prepare bond amortization schedule, and record liability; show statement presentation. (LO 2, 5) AP

P16–3A   On January 1, 2017, Power Ltd. issued bonds with a maturity value of $5 million for $4,797,000, when the market rate of interest was 8%. The bonds have a contractual interest rate of 7% and mature on January 1, 2022. Interest on the bonds is payable semi-annually on July 1 and January 1 of each year. On January 1, 2017, Finance Company, a public company, purchased Power Ltd. bonds with a maturity value of $1 million to earn interest. On December 31, 2017, the bonds were trading at 98. Both companies' year end is December 31.

Instructions

(a) What amount did Finance Company pay for Power Ltd.'s bonds?
(b) Prepare the journal entry for Finance Company (investor) on January 1, 2017.
(c) Prepare a bond amortization schedule for Finance Company for the first four interest periods.
(d) Prepare the journal entries for Finance Company to record (1) the receipt of interest on July 1, 2017; (2) the accrual of interest on December 31, 2017; and (3) the receipt of interest on January 1, 2018.
(e) Show how the bonds and related income statement accounts would be presented in Finance Company's financial statements for the year ended December 31, 2017.
(f) Prepare the journal entry for Power Ltd. (investee) on January 1, 2017.
(g) Prepare the journal entries for Power Ltd. to record (1) the payment of interest on July 1, 2017; (2) the accrual of interest expense on December 31, 2017; and (3) the payment of interest on January 1, 2018.
(h) Show how the bonds and related income statement accounts would be presented in Power Ltd.'s financial statements for the year ended December 31, 2017.

TAKING IT FURTHER   Calculate the total cash inflow from the bonds if Finance Company holds the Power Ltd. bonds until maturity.

P16–4A   During the year ended December 31, 2017, Rakai Corporation, a public company, had the following transactions related to investments held for trading purposes:

Feb. 1   Purchased 575 IBF common shares for $25,300.
Mar. 1   Purchased 1,500 Raimundo common shares for $48,000.
Apr. 1   Purchased $200,000 of CRT 3% bonds at par. Interest is payable semi-annually on April 1 and October 1.
July 1   Received a cash dividend of $1.50 per share on the IBF common shares.
Aug. 1   Sold 250 IBF common shares at $48 per share.
Oct. 1   Received the semi-annual interest on the CRT bonds.
      1   Sold the CRT bonds for $205,000.
Dec. 31   The fair values of the IBF and Raimundo common shares were $50 and $28 per share, respectively.

Record equity and debt investments categorized as fair value through profit or loss; show statement presentation. (LO 3, 5) AP

Instructions

(a) Record the transactions and any required year-end adjusting entries.
(b) Show the financial statement presentation of the investments and any related accounts in the financial statements for the year ended December 31, 2017.

TAKING IT FURTHER   If Rakai Corporation anticipated that it would need the cash that was used to invest in the investments in the near future, should the company have invested in equity securities? What would you recommend to the company?

P16–5A   During 2016, Financial Holdings, a public company, purchased equity securities for trading purposes. At December 31, 2016, the securities for Financial Holdings were as follows:

Record equity investments; show statement presentation. (LO 3, 5) AP

Security	Quantity	Cost	Market Value
Sabo common shares	1,000	$15,000	$13,500
PYK $1.50 preferred shares	2,000	24,000	24,500
Total		$39,000	$38,000

The following transactions with respect to Financial Holdings' investments occurred during 2017:

Jan. 15   Purchased 1,500 common shares of Hazmi for $15.00 per share. The shares are designated as fair value through other comprehensive income.
Mar. 20   Received dividends on the PYK preferred shares of $1.50 per share.
June 15   Sold 750 of the Sabo common shares for $15.75 per share.
Aug.   5   Received dividends on the Sabo common shares of $2.50 per share.
Oct. 15   Received an additional 1,500 common shares of Hazmi as a result of a 2-for-1 stock split. *No Entry b'coz no $ to value the only thing that ∆ is # Share & cost/share*

At December 31, 2017, the securities held by Financial Holdings were trading on the TSX at the following prices:

Security	Price
Sabo common shares	$16.00
PYK $1.50 preferred shares	13.75
Hazmi common shares	7.00

Instructions

(a) Show how the securities would be reported on Financial Holdings' December 31, 2016, balance sheet.
(b) Record Financial Holdings' 2017 transactions and any required adjusting journal entries at December 31, 2017.
(c) Show how the investment income, gains, and losses would be reported on the statement of comprehensive income for the year ended December 31, 2017. (Ignore income tax)

TAKING IT FURTHER   Calculate the total profit/loss (over the life of the investment) that Financial Holdings made on the 750 Sabo common shares sold on June 15, 2017, and calculate the percentage return on the investment.

Identify impact
of investments on
financial statements.
(LO 2, 3, 4, 5) AP

P16-6A Corded Industries Ltd., a public company, reported the following on its November 30, 2016, balance sheet.

Long-term investments at fair value through other comprehensive income—equity, Cedarshakes Ltd. (10,000 shares)	$136,000
Short-term investments at fair value through profit or loss	
Johnny's Bakery Ltd. (14,000 shares)	18,000
Sally's Tea Ltd., $50,000 par value, 10% bonds, due December 31, 2019 (originally purchased at par)	54,000
Long-term investments at amortized cost	
120-day treasury bill	20,000
Investment in associate, Diane's Cosmetics Inc. (35,000 shares) (accounted for using the equity method)	425,000

The following transactions took place during 2017:

1. Dividends were received from Cedarshakes Ltd.
2. Interest was received on the treasury bill.
3. The treasury bill was cashed with no additional interest received.
4. Interest was received on the Sally's Tea bonds.
5. Dividends were received from Johnny's Bakery Ltd.
6. Dividends were received from Diane's Cosmetics.
7. Sold 7,000 common shares of Johnny's Bakery at a gain.
8. Sold 3,000 common shares of Cedarshakes at a loss.
9. Received the financial statements of Diane's Cosmetics reporting a profit for the year.
10. Received the financial statements for Cedarshakes Ltd. reporting a loss for the year.
11. The fair value of the remaining Cedarshakes shares was greater than the carrying value at year end.
12. The fair value of the remaining shares of Johnny's Bakery was less than the carrying value at year end.
13. The fair value of the Sally's Tea bonds was greater than the carrying value at year end.
14. The fair value of Diane's Cosmetics was greater than the carrying value at year end.

Instructions

Using the following table format, indicate whether each of the above transactions would result in an increase (+), a decrease (−), or no effect (NE) in each category. The first one has been done for you as an example.

	Balance Sheet		Income Statement			Statement of Comprehensive Income
Assets	Liabilities	Shareholders' Equity	Revenues and Gains	Expenses and Losses	Profit	Other Comprehensive Income
1. +	NE	+	+	NE	+	NE

TAKING IT FURTHER Assume instead that Corded Industries is a private company. How would your response to the question differ if the company reported under ASPE?

Analyze investment and
compare fair value, equity
method, and cost method.
(LO 3, 4) AN

P16-7A Sandhu Ltd. has 400,000 common shares authorized and 120,000 shares issued on December 31, 2016. On January 2, 2017, Kang Inc., which reports under IFRS, purchased shares of Sandhu for $40 per share on the stock market from another investor. Kang intends to hold these shares as a long-term investment and initially categorizes it as FVTOCI.

Kang's accountant prepared a trial balance as at December 31, 2017, under the assumption that the investment is valued at FVTOCI. Under this assumption, the trial balance included the following accounts and amounts related to the Sandhu investment:

Long-term investments at FVTOCI—equity, Sandhu Ltd.	$1,320,000
Dividend revenue	90,000
OCI—gain on fair value adjustment	120,000

Instructions

(a) How many shares of Sandhu did Kang purchase on January 2? (*Hint:* Subtract the OCI—gain on fair value adjustment from the investment account.)

(b) What percentage of Sandhu does Kang own?

(c) What was the amount of the cash dividend per share that Kang received from Sandhu in 2017?

(d) What was the fair value per share of Sandhu shares at December 31, 2017?

(e) Assume that, after closely examining the situation, Kang's auditors determine that Kang does have significant influence over Sandhu. Accordingly, the investment account is adjusted to $1.4 million at December 31, 2017. What was the profit reported by Sandhu for the year ended December 31, 2017?

(f) Assuming that Kang does have significant influence over Sandhu, what amount will Kang report on its income statement for 2017 with regard to this investment?

(g) How would your answer to part (f) change if Kang reported under ASPE and chose to use the cost method to account for its investment in Sandhu because the shares did not have a quoted market price?

TAKING IT FURTHER   What are the potential advantages to a company of having significant influence over another company? Explain.

P16–8A   On January 1, 2017, Neitzche Company, a public company, purchased 35% of the common shares of Triple Titanium Inc. for $525,000. The remaining shares (65%) are held by the family members of the company's founder. Neitzche considers this a strategic investment and a critical step into developing consumer markets. Triple Titanium is currently a supplier to Neitzche. Neitzche placed two members on the 10-person board of directors of Triple Titanium and the two members believe they have been influential on the board through the year. Neitzche and Triple Titanium both have December 31 year ends.

Assess strategic investments; record investment using equity method. Show statement presentation. (LO 4, 5) AP

During 2017, Triple Titanium reported profit of $300,000 and paid total dividends of $65,000.

Instructions

(a) Refer to the facts in the question. Does Neitzche have significant influence over Triple Titanium?

(b) Prepare the following journal entries for Neitzche, assuming significant influence does exist.

  1. The acquisition of the investment

  2. Investment revenue and receipt of dividends related to the investment

(c) During 2018, Triple Titanium reports profit of $240,000 and pays total dividends of $80,000. Prepare the required journal entries related to these transactions on Neitzche's books.

(d) Determine the balance in the investment account on December 31, 2017, and December 31, 2018.

(e) Show how the investment account and related revenue accounts would be reported on the financial statements for December 31, 2017.

TAKING IT FURTHER   If Neitzche purchases an additional 30% of the common shares of Triple Titanium, how would your answer to part (a) change?

P16–9A   Silver Lining Corporation, a public company, is a large silver producer. Selected condensed information (in millions) for Silver Lining Corporation follows for the year ended September 30, 2017:

Prepare income statement and statement of comprehensive income. (LO 5) AP

Cost of sales	$2,214
Loss from investment in associate	6
Silver sales	3,350
Income tax expense	60
Interest expense	7
Interest revenue	38
Operating expenses	639
Dividend revenue	6
Loss on fair value adjustments—FVTPL	27
OCI—gain on fair value adjustments (net of taxes of $5)	12

Instructions

(a) Prepare an income statement and a separate statement of comprehensive income for the year ended September 30, 2017.

(b) Silver Lining Corporation had an opening balance in its Accumulated Other Comprehensive Income account of $49 million. What is the ending balance it would report in the shareholders' equity section of its balance sheet at September 30, 2017?

TAKING IT FURTHER   If a company has purchased common shares of another company and designated them FVTOCI, IFRS generally does not allow the investor to reclassify the investment as FVTPL. Why do standard setters want to prevent companies from reclassifying investments?

Prepare statement of comprehensive income and balance sheet. (LO 5) AP

P16–10A Presented in alphabetical order, the following data are from the accounting records of Stinson Corporation, a public company, at April 30, 2017:

Accounts payable	$ 65,000
Accounts receivable	48,000
Accumulated depreciation—equipment	72,000
Accumulated other comprehensive income	18,000
Bonds payable, due 2021	150,000
Cash	100,480
Common shares (no par value, unlimited authorized, 200,000 issued)	300,000
Depreciation expense	27,500
Dividend revenue	11,000
Equipment	275,000
Gain on fair value adjustments—FVTPL	1,500
Gain on sale of FVTPL investments	3,000
Income tax expense	82,860
Income tax payable	25,000
Interest expense	7,500
Interest receivable	1,680
Interest revenue	3,360
Investment in associate	170,000
Long-term investments at AC—bonds due 2019	24,000
Long-term investments at FVTOCI—equity	220,000
Loss on fair value adjustment—FVTPL	1,500
OCI—loss on fair value adjustment, net of $3,600 tax	12,000
Rent expense	79,000
Retained earnings	161,660
Salaries expense	235,000
Service revenue	550,000
Short-term investments at FVTPL—bonds	61,000
Short-term investments at FVTPL—equity	15,000

Instructions

Prepare a statement of comprehensive income and balance sheet at April 30, 2017.

TAKING IT FURTHER Calculate return on equity for Stinson Corporation on April 30, 2017. Total shareholders' equity on April 30, 2016, was $510,400. Comment on Stinson's operating performance assuming that the industry average return on equity is 18%.

▶ Problems: Set B

Record debt investments; show statement presentation. (LO 2, 5) AP

P16–1B Lannan Corp. had the following debt instrument transactions during the year ended December 31, 2017. The debt instruments were purchased to earn interest.

Feb.	1	Purchased six-month term deposit for $50,000.
Aug.	1	Term deposit matured and $51,250 cash was received.
	1	Purchased a money-market fund for $55,000.
Dec.	1	Cashed in money-market fund and received $55,735 cash.
	1	Purchased a 90-day (three-month) treasury bill for $99,260.
	31	The treasury bill's value with accrued interest was $99,508.

Instructions

(a) Record the transactions.

(b) Show the financial statement presentation of the debt investments and any related accounts at December 31.

TAKING IT FURTHER What was the annual rate of interest on the term deposit that Lannan Corp. purchased on February 1, 2017?

P16–2B On July 1, 2017, Givarz Corporation, a public company, purchased $300,000 of Schuett Corp. 10-year, 3% bonds at 91.8 when the market rate of interest was 4%. Interest is received semi-annually on July 1 and January 1. Givarz's year end is December 31. Givarz intends to hold the bonds until July 1, 2027, the date the bonds mature. The bonds were trading at 96 on December 31, 2017.

Record debt investments; show statement presentation. (LO 2, 3, 5) AP

Instructions

(a) Record the purchase of the bonds on July 1, 2017.
(b) Prepare the adjusting entry required at December 31, 2017.
(c) Show the financial presentation of the investment in Schuett Corp.'s bonds on December 31, 2017.
(d) Prepare the entry to record the receipt of interest on January 1, 2018.
(e) Prepare the entry to record the receipt of interest on July 1, 2018.
(f) Prepare the entry to record the receipt on maturity of the bonds on July 1, 2027. Assume the entry to record the last interest payment has been recorded.
(g) How would your answers to parts (a) and (b) change if the bonds were purchased for the purpose of trading?

TAKING IT FURTHER What was the market interest rate on December 31, 2017, when the bonds were trading at 96? (*Hint*: How many interest periods are left after December 31, 2017?)

P16–3B On January 1, 2017, Surge Ltd. issued bonds with a maturity value of $6 million at 104 when the market rate of interest was 4.5%. The bonds have a contractual interest rate of 5% and mature on January 1, 2027. Interest on the bonds is payable semi-annually on July 1 and January 1 of each year. On January 1, 2017, Treasury Ltd., a private company, purchased Surge Ltd. bonds with a maturity value of $2 million to earn interest. Treasury Ltd. will account for the investment at amortized cost using the effective-interest method to amortize the premium or discount. On December 31, 2017, the bonds were trading at 103. Both companies' year end is December 31.

Record debt investment at amortized cost, prepare bond amortization schedule, and record liability; show statement presentation. (LO 3, 5) AP

Instructions

(a) What amount did Treasury Ltd. pay for Surge Ltd.'s bonds?
(b) Prepare the journal entry for Treasury Ltd. (investor) on January 1, 2017.
(c) Prepare a bond amortization schedule for Treasury Ltd. for the first four interest periods.
(d) Prepare the journal entries for Treasury Ltd. to record the receipt of interest on July 1, 2017, the accrual of interest on December 31, 2017, and the receipt of interest on January 1, 2018. Show how the bonds and related income statement accounts would be presented in Treasury Ltd.'s financial statements for the year ended December 31, 2017.
(e) Prepare the journal entry for Surge Ltd. (investee) on January 1, 2017.
(f) Prepare the journal entries for Surge Ltd. to record the payment of interest on July 1, 2017; the accrual of interest on December 31, 2017; and the payment of interest on January 1, 2018, assuming the company uses the effective-interest method to amortize any premium or discount.
(g) Show how the bonds and related income statement accounts would be presented in Surge Ltd.'s financial statements for the year ended December 31, 2017.

TAKING IT FURTHER Did the market interest rate on the bonds increase or decrease between January 1, 2017, and December 31, 2017? Will Treasury Ltd. want the market interest rate on the bonds to increase or decrease if it holds the bonds to earn interest? Explain.

P16–4B During the year ended December 31, 2017, Mead Investment Corporation, a public company, had the following transactions related to investments held for trading:

Record debt and equity investments categorized at fair value through profit or loss; show statement presentation. (LO 3, 5) AP

Feb.	1	Purchased 2,400 Lemelin common shares for $63,600.
Mar.	1	Purchased 600 RSD common shares for $7,500.
Apr.	1	Purchased $100,000 of MRT 4% bonds at par. Interest is payable semi-annually on April 1 and October 1.
July	1	Received a cash dividend of $2 per share on the Lemelin common shares.
Aug.	1	Sold 1,600 Lemelin common shares at $25 per share.
Oct.	1	Received the semi-annual interest on the MRT bonds.
	2	Sold the MRT bonds for 101.
Dec.	31	The fair values of the Lemelin and RSD common shares were $28 and $14 per share, respectively.

Instructions

(a) Record the transactions and any required year-end adjusting entries.
(b) Show the financial statement presentation of the trading investments and any related accounts in Mead's financial statements for the year ended December 31, 2017.

TAKING IT FURTHER   When Mead invested in the MRT bonds, was it anticipating that the market interest rate would go up or down? Explain.

Record equity trading investments; show statement presentation. (LO 3, 5) AP

P16–5B   During 2016, Commercial Inc. purchased equity securities held for trading purposes. At December 31, 2016, the securities for Commercial Inc. were as follows:

Security	Quantity	Cost	Market Value
Fahim common shares	1,500	$36,000	$39,000
PLJ common shares	2,000	14,000	16,500
Total		$50,000	$55,500

The following transactions with respect to Commercial Inc.'s investments occurred during 2017:

Apr. 15   Sold 1,250 of the Fahim common shares for $27.00 per share.
June 15   Purchased an additional 1,000 of Fahim common shares for $27.50 per share.
July 31   Purchased 4,000 common shares of Hopeful Industries Ltd. at $4 per share. The investment will be reported using fair value through other comprehensive income.
Aug. 5   Received dividends on the PLJ common shares of $2.50 per share.
Oct. 15   Received an additional 4,000 common shares of Hopeful Industries Ltd. as a result of a 2-for-1 stock split.

At December 31, 2017, the securities held by Commercial Inc. were trading on the TSX at the following prices:

Security	Price
Fahim common shares	$30.00
PLJ common shares	6.00
Hopeful Industries common shares	1.60

Instructions
(a) Show how the securities would be reported on Commercial Inc.'s December 31, 2016, balance sheet.
(b) Record Commercial Inc.'s 2017 transactions and any required adjusting journal entries at December 31, 2017.
(c) Show how investment income, gains, and losses would be reported on the statement of comprehensive income for the year ended December 31, 2017. (Ignore income tax.)

TAKING IT FURTHER   Why might the Hopeful Industries common shares be reported at FVTOCI instead of FVTPL like the other securities?

Identify impact of investments on financial statements. (LO 2, 3, 4, 5) AP

P16–6B   Pepper Corporation, a public company, reported the following on its July 31, 2016, balance sheet.

Long-term investments at fair value through other comprehensive income	
Hegal Ltd. (5,000 common shares)	$36,000
Baudillard Company (8,000 common shares)	18,000
Short-term investments at fair value through profit or loss	
Locke Systems Ltd., $70,000 par value, 4% bonds, due	
June 30, 2021 (originally purchased at par)	68,000
Truman Manufacturing Co. (6,000 common shares)	14,000
Long-term investments at amortized cost	
Aquinas Filtering Corp., $100,000, 5% bonds, due June 1,	
2018, interest payments annually	
(originally purchased at 98)	99,000
Investment in associate, Lincoln Corporation (3,000 common shares)	25,000

The following transactions took place during 2017:

1. Dividends were received from Hegal Ltd.
2. Sold the Locke Systems bonds at a loss.
3. Dividends were received from Lincoln Corporation.
4. Annual interest payment was received from Aquinas Filtering.

5. Dividends were received from Baudillard.
6. Paid dividends to shareholders of Pepper Corporation.
7. Sold the 1,500 Hegal common shares at a loss.
8. Received the financial statements from Lincoln Corporation reporting a profit for the year.
9. Purchased 4,000 additional shares of Baudillard Company.
10. Accrued interest on the Aquinas bonds at year end.
11. Received the financial statements from Aquinas Filtering Corp. reporting a profit for the year.
12. The fair value of Baudillard Company's shares was greater than the carrying value at year end.
13. The fair value of the Aquinas Filtering bonds was less than the carrying value at year end.
14. The fair value of Truman Manufacturing's shares was greater than the carrying value.
15. The fair value of the remaining Hegal common shares was less than the carrying value at year end.

Instructions

Using the following table format, indicate whether each of the above transactions would result in an increase (+), a decrease (−), or no effect (NE) in each category. The first one has been done for you as an example.

Balance Sheet			Income Statement			Statement of Comprehensive Income
Assets	Liabilities	Shareholders' Equity	Revenues and gains	Expenses and losses	Profit	Other Comprehensive Income
+	NE	+	+	NE	+	NE

TAKING IT FURTHER   Assume instead that Pepper Corporation is a private company. How would your response to the question differ if the company reported under ASPE? What choices would the company have for reporting the investment in an associate?

P16–7B   On January 2, 2017, Hadley Inc., which reports under IFRS, purchased shares of Letourneau Corp. for $10 a share. Hadley intends to hold these shares as a long-term investment. During 2017, Letourneau reported profit of $1 million and paid cash dividends of $200,000. The investment's fair value at December 31, 2017, was $970,000.

Analyze investment and compare fair value, equity method, and cost method. (LO 3, 4) AN

Hadley's accountant prepared a trial balance as at December 31, 2017, under the assumption that Hadley could exercise significant influence over Letourneau. The trial balance included the following:

Investment in associate	$960,000
~~Less~~ Income from investment in associate	200,000

Instructions

(a) What percentage of Letourneau's shares does Hadley own? (*Hint*: The ownership percentage can be determined using the share of profit from associate.) $250000 \div 1M = 20\%$
(b) What was the amount of cash dividend that Hadley received from Letourneau? $200.000 \times 20\% = 40,000$
(c) How many Letourneau shares did Hadley purchase on January 2?
(d) Assume that, after closely examining the situation, Hadley's auditors determine that Hadley does not have significant influence over Letourneau. What amount should be reported on Hadley's balance sheet at December 31, 2017, assuming that Hadley chooses to designate the investment as FVTOCI? What will be reported in Hadley's statement of comprehensive income for the year ended December 31, 2017? The company's tax rate is 20%.
(e) How would your answer to part (d) change if Hadley reported under ASPE and Letourneau's shares did not have a quoted market price?

TAKING IT FURTHER   What factors should be considered when determining whether a company has significant influence over another company? Could a company have significant influence over another company if it owned 19% of the common shares of the investee? Explain.

P16–8B   On March 1, 2017, Carnegie Inc., a public company, purchased 15% of the common shares of Aquinas Auto Inc. for $225,000. The remaining shares (85%) are widely dispersed. Carnegie Inc. considers this a strategic investment and a critical step into a developing consumer market. Carnegie has placed two members on the eight-person board of directors of Aquinas and the two members believe they have been influential on the board through the year. Carnegie and Aquinas both have a December 31 year end.

Record strategic equity investments, using fair value, cost, and equity methods. Show statement presentation. (LO 4, 5) AP

During 2017, Aquinas Auto reported profit of $150,000 and paid total dividends of $35,000.

Instructions

(a) Refer to the facts in the question. Does Carnegie have significant influence over Aquinas Auto?

(b) Prepare the following journal entries for Carnegie assuming significant influence does exist.
   1. The acquisition of the investment
   2. Investment revenue and receipt of dividends related to the investment

(c) During 2018, Aquinas reports profit of $325,000 and pays total dividends of $45,000. Prepare the required journal entries related to these transactions on Carnegie's books.

(d) Determine the balance in the investment account on December 31, 2017, and December 31, 2018.

(e) Show how the investment account and related revenue accounts would be reported on the financial statements for December 31, 2017.

TAKING IT FURTHER   In the question, Carnegie asserts that the investment in Aquinas is a strategic decision to help enter a new consumer market. How will owning a portion of Aquinas help Carnegie in this regard?

Prepare income statement and statement of comprehensive income. (LO 5) AP

P16–9B   Selected condensed information (in millions) for Investments R Us Company, a public company, follows for the year ended November 30, 2017.

Income from investment in associate	$ 4
Gain on fair value adjustments—FVTPL	2
Gain on sale of land	26
Income tax expense	781
Interest expense	299
Interest revenue	6
Dividend revenue	3
Operating expenses	4,616
Loss on sale of FVTPL investments	194
OCI—loss on fair value adjustment (net of tax)	68
Other expenses	21
Revenues	7,240

Instructions

(a) Prepare an income statement and separate statement of comprehensive income for the year ended November 30, 2017.

(b) Investments R Us Company had an opening balance in its Accumulated Other Comprehensive Loss account of $150 million. What is the ending balance it would report in the shareholders' equity section of its balance sheet at November 30, 2017?

TAKING IT FURTHER   Explain why a company may want to report gains and losses on fair value adjustments for its investments in other comprehensive income instead of including them in profit.

Prepare statement of comprehensive income and balance sheet. (LO 5) AP

P16–10B   Presented in alphabetical order, the following data are from the accounting records of Vladimir Corporation at December 31, 2017:

Accounts payable	$ 85,000
Accounts receivable	68,000
Accumulated depreciation—equipment	92,000
Accumulated other comprehensive income, January 1, 2017	28,000
Allowance for doubtful accounts	4,000
Bonds payable 4%, due January 1, 2022	250,000
Cash	150,000
Common shares (no par value, unlimited authorized, 200,000 issued)	250,000
Depreciation expense	28,000
Dividend revenue	9,000
Equipment	288,000
Gain on fair value adjustment—FVTPL	2,600
Gain on sale of FVTPL investments	2,500
Income from investment in associate	31,000
Income tax expense	79,290
Income tax payable	16,000
Interest expense	12,500
Interest payable	5,000

Interest revenue	$ 3,300
Investment in associate	215,000
Long-term investments at AC—bonds due 2019	36,000
Long-term investments at FVTOCI—equity	185,000
Loss on fair value adjustment—FVTPL, common shares	1,500
Notes receivable—due 2020	75,000
Other comprehensive income—gain on fair value adjustment, net of $3,600 tax	12,000
Rent expense	45,000
Retained earnings, December 31, 2017	394,500
Salaries expense	335,000
Service revenue	651,000
Short-term investments at FVTPL—bonds	82,500
Short-term investments at FVTPL—equity	37,000

Instructions

Prepare a statement of comprehensive income and balance sheet at December 31, 2017.

TAKING IT FURTHER   Calculate the return on equity for Vladimir Corporation on December 31, 2017. Total shareholders' equity on December 31, 2016, was $605,100. Comment on Vladimir's performance assuming that the industry average is 36%.

▶ Cumulative Coverage—Chapters 13 to 16

Plankton Corporation's trial balance at December 31, 2017, is presented below:

PLANKTON CORPORATION
Trial Balance
December 31, 2017

	Debit	Credit
Cash	$ 48,000	
Accounts receivable	51,000	
Allowance for doubtful accounts		$ 2,500
Merchandise inventory	22,700	
Investment in associate	85,000	
Long-term investment at FVTOCI—equity	30,000	
Land	90,000	
Building	200,000	
Accumulated depreciation—building		40,000
Equipment	40,000	
Accumulated depreciation—equipment		15,000
Accounts payable		18,775
Income tax payable		4,500
Bonds payable (6%, due January 1, 2022)		126,025
Common shares, unlimited number of no par value shares authorized, 100,000 issued		100,000
Retained earnings		110,775
Accumulated other comprehensive income		5,000
Sales		750,000
Cost of goods sold	370,000	
Operating expenses	180,000	
Interest revenue		375
Interest expense	6,250	
Income tax expense	50,000	
Total	$1,172,950	$1,172,950

All transactions and adjustments for 2017 have been recorded and reported in the trial balance except for the items described below.

Jan.	7	Issued 1,000 preferred shares for $25,000. In total, 100,000, $2, noncumulative, convertible, preferred shares are authorized. Each preferred share is convertible into five common shares.
Mar.	16	Purchased 800 common shares of Osborne Inc., to be held for trading purposes, for $24 per share.
July	1	Purchased $100,000 Solar Inc. 10-year, 5% bonds at 108.2, when the market interest rate was 4%. Interest is received semi-annually on July 1 and January 1. Plankton purchased the bonds to earn interest.
Aug.	2	Sold the Osborne common shares for $25 per share.
	5	Invested $20,000 in a money-market fund.
Sept.	25	Five hundred of the preferred shares issued on January 7 were converted into common shares.
Oct.	24	Cashed in the money-market fund, receiving $20,000 plus $200 interest.
Nov.	30	Obtained a $50,000 bank loan by issuing a three-year, 6% note payable. Plankton is required to make equal blended payments of $1,521 at the end of each month. The first payment was made on December 31. Note that at December 31, $15,757 of the note payable is due within the next year.
Dec.	1	Declared the annual dividend on the preferred shares on December 1 to shareholders of record on December 23, payable on January 15.
	31	Plankton owns 40% of RES. RES earned $20,000 and paid dividends of $1,200 in 2017. The fair value of the RES investment was $98,000.
	31	Semi-annual interest is receivable on the Solar Inc. bonds on January 1, 2018. The bonds were trading at 106 on December 31, 2017.
	31	The annual interest is due on the bonds payable on January 1, 2018. The par value of the bonds is $130,000 and the bonds were issued when the market interest rate was 7%.
	31	The fair value of the long-term investment at FVTOCI—equity was $28,000. Ignore income tax calculation.

Instructions

(a) Record the transactions.

(b) Prepare an updated trial balance at December 31, 2017, that includes these transactions.

(c) Using the income statement accounts in the trial balance, calculate income before income tax. Assuming Plankton has a 27% income tax rate, prepare the journal entry to adjust income taxes for the year. Note that Plankton has recorded $50,000 of income tax expense for the year to date. Update the trial balance for this additional entry. For the purposes of this question, ignore the income tax relating to other comprehensive income.

(d) Prepare the following financial statements for Plankton: (1) income statement, (2) statement of comprehensive income, (3) statement of changes in shareholders' equity, and (4) balance sheet. For the purposes of this question, ignore the income tax on other comprehensive income and accumulated other comprehensive income.

(e) Assuming instead that Plankton purchased the Solar Inc. bonds for trading purposes, describe how the investment and related income should be valued and reported in Plankton's financial statements.

(f) For each of Plankton's investments, explain how the valuation and reporting of the investment and related income accounts might differ if Plankton were a private company reporting under ASPE.

CHAPTER 16: BROADENING YOUR PERSPECTIVE

▶ Financial Reporting and Analysis

Financial Reporting Problem

BYP16-1 Refer to the financial statements and accompanying notes for Corus Entertainment Inc. presented in Appendix A. Corus purchases mainly strategic investments as part of its strategy for continued growth. On the consolidated statements of financial position (another term for balance sheet), the company reports "Investments and intangibles" on August 31, 2014, of $47,630,000.

Instructions

(a) Locate Note 19, which details other expenses (income), in the notes to the financial statements and list Corus's strategic investments. Determine the total profit or loss from investment in associates. (Corus refers to this as "Equity loss of investees.")

(b) Locate Note 5 in the notes to the financial statements. What is the total investment amount in associates on August 31, 2014? List the companies that Corus has significant influence over.

(c) Refer to Note 3—*Determination of fair value*. Corus reports information on how it determines fair value and refers to the three levels of the fair value hierarchy. Describe the levels of the hierarchy. Using each level in the hierarchy, discuss how you would determine a fair value for an investment in common shares.

Interpreting Financial Statements

BYP16-2   Royal Bank of Canada is one of the largest banks in Canada. According to its 2014 annual report, it had approximately 78,000 employees serving 16 million customers throughout the world. The bank's business largely involves borrowing money and lending it to others, but at any given time it will have a large amount of money invested in securities when that money is not out on loan. It also acts as an investment dealer, buying investments from one client and selling them to another. The company reported the following information in its 2014 financial statements (in millions of dollars):

	2014	2013
Short-term investments at FVTPL		
Debt instruments	$100,229	$ 98,834
Equity instruments	51,151	45,189
	$151,380	$144,023

Instructions

(a) In your opinion, why does the Royal Bank have a higher percentage of its investments held for trading purposes in debt instruments than in equity instruments?

(b) How will the debt instruments be valued on the Royal Bank's balance sheet?

(c) The Royal Bank also reported other investments at fair value through other comprehensive income. What are the advantages of reporting gains and losses in other comprehensive income instead of profit? What are the disadvantages?

▶ Critical Thinking

Collaborative Learning Activity

Note to instructor: Additional instructions and material for this group activity can be found on the Instructor Resource Site and in *WileyPLUS*.

BYP16-3   In this group activity, you will compare the accounting for bonds payable with two types of bond investments: long-term investment in bonds, and held-for-trading investment in bonds. By comparing and contrasting the accounting treatments, you will use your previous knowledge about bonds payable to get a better understanding of the accounting for investments.

Communication Activity

BYP16-4   Under International Financial Reporting Standards, investments in debt instruments are reported at either amortized cost or fair value through profit or loss. The president of Lunn Financial Enterprises does not understand why there are two methods and wonders why all debt investments are not reported at amortized cost.

Instructions

Write a memo to the president of Lunn Financial Enterprises, explaining when it is appropriate to report debt investments at amortized cost and when it is appropriate to report debt investments at fair value through profit or loss. Discuss in your memo why reporting different debt investments using different methods gives better information for investors and creditors to evaluate the performance of the company's investment portfolio.

"All About You" Activity

BYP16-5   As indicated in the "All About You" feature in this chapter, any Canadian aged 18 or older can save up to $5,500 every year in a tax-free savings account (TFSA). TFSA savings can be used for any purpose, including for a vacation, to buy a car, or to start a small business. The goal of TFSAs is to allow Canadians to save more and achieve their goals quicker.

Instructions

(a) Do a search on TFSAs and RRSPs. What are the similarities and differences between the two savings options?

(b) Go to www.cra-arc.gc.ca/tfsa/ and click on the link "Types of investments." Note that the government allows a variety of investment options, including equity securities listed on a stock exchange and bonds. What types of investment income will you earn on equity securities? Bonds? What might be the benefits of investing in equity securities? The risks?

(c) All of the banks in Canada provide a TFSA calculator where you can determine the amount of tax savings from a contribution. Do a search for "TFSA calculator" and choose a banking website of your choice. Assume the following information.

1. Your income range for
    income tax purposes: $10,000 − $39,999
2. Monthly contribution in a TFSA: $200
3. Rate of return: 6%
4. Term of investment: 20 years

How much more will you save in a TFSA than in a taxable savings account? If you are using a TSFA calculator that requires a single amount instead of a range, use the amount at the high end of the ranges given.

(d) Assume the same as in part (c) except assume that your income range for income tax purposes is $40,000 to $79,999. How much more will you save in a TFSA than in a taxable account?

Santé Smoothie Saga

(*Note:* This is a continuation of the Santé Smoothie Saga from Chapters 1 through 15.)

BYP16-6   It is now the end of January 2019 and Santé Smoothies & Sweets Ltd. has been so successful, it has an amount of excess cash and would like to invest it. The Koebels also wish to expand their operation by diversifying into a deli business. They feel that there are many synergies between baked goods, smoothies, and made-to-order sandwiches and deli meats.

The family decides to make the following investments:

1) 200 common shares of Loblaw Companies Limited	$13,718
2) 400 common shares of WestJet Airlines Ltd.	11,650
3) 1,000 common shares of Nouveau Delight Ltd.	30,000
4) $20,000 Bell Canada 4-year, 5% corporate bonds*	21,487

*pay annual interest on February 1, issued to yield 3%

Nouveau Delight Ltd. is a privately owned specialty deli operation that has several locations throughout the city. It offers a variety of all-natural deli meats, gluten-free paninis, and made-to-order sandwiches and salads. Janet, Brian, and Natalie were approached by Ken Thornton, who is a shareholder of Nouveau Delight Ltd. Ken wants to retire and would like to sell his 1,000 shares in Nouveau Delight, which represent 20% of all shares issued. Nouveau is currently operated by Ken's twin daughters, who each own 40% of the common shares.

The business has been operating for approximately five years, and in the past two years, Ken has lost interest and left the day-to-day operations to his daughters. Both daughters at times find the work at the deli overwhelming. They would like to have a third shareholder involved to take over some of the responsibilities of running a small business. Both feel that Janet, Brian, and Natalie are entrepreneurial in spirit and that their expertise would be a welcome addition to the business operation.

Ken has met with Janet, Brian, and Natalie to discuss the business operation. All have concluded that there would be many advantages for Santé Smoothies & Sweets Ltd. to acquire an interest in Nouveau Delight. One of the major advantages would be the sale of organic baked goods and smoothies at the delis.

Natalie has come to you with a few questions about these investments:

1. We are unsure about how much influence we will have in the decision-making process for Nouveau Delight. Would the amount of influence we have affect how we account for this investment? (Recall that Santé Smoothies & Sweets Ltd. reports under ASPE.)
2. How do we record these investments in the accounting records? (Be sure to discuss the importance of classifying the investments—strategic, passive, and fair value through profit or loss, fair value through other comprehensive income, or amortized cost.)

Instructions

(a) Answer Natalie's questions.
(b) What other information would you likely obtain before you recommend whether the investment in the deli should be accounted for using the equity method?
(c) Explain to Janet, Brian, and Natalie some of the differences in accounting for this investment on Santé Smoothies & Sweets Ltd.'s balance sheet if the cost method were chosen instead of the equity method.
(d) Prepare the journal entries required to record all the investments. (Assume they were purchased on February 1, 2019.)
(e) On May 31, 2019, the market value per share of the Loblaw's shares is $72.15; that of the WestJet shares is $25.50 per share. Prepare any journal entries required to adjust the investments at the year end and accrue any interest revenue. Assume Santé Smoothies & Sweets Ltd. chooses to use the cost method to record the investment in the deli.

ANSWERS TO CHAPTER QUESTIONS

ANSWERS TO ACCOUNTING IN ACTION INSIGHT QUESTIONS

Business Insight, p. 836

Q: Is this a strategic or non-strategic investment for 3G Capital? How will 3G Capital benefit from this investment?

A: Given that 3G Capital owns 51% of the company, this is a strategic investment on its behalf, mainly because it has control.

3G will benefit from this investment by increasing its consolidated sales revenues and having opportunities to enter additional global markets. But 3G is an investment company, so its goal is to invest in companies and grow its brand and sales. It will likely at some point sell either all of its investment or a portion at a gain. Of course, there are risks involved in this venture. The strategic and growth opportunities are clear for both 3G and the shareholders who own the remaining shares in the company. However, competition in this industry is strong, and both Burger King and Tim Hortons will have to ensure that they continue to maintain brand loyalty in their home markets by delivering consistent service and products. In order to compete on the world stage, companies need the capital and resources to expose their brand to a large number of consumers. In the quick-service restaurant industry, major players such as McDonald's have captured a major market share globally. The creation of a new company with two iconic brands will allow greater exposure for both Tim Hortons and Burger King, each relying on the strength of the other to enter into marketplaces it has yet been unable to penetrate.

Business Insight, p. 842

Q: As an investor, what are the advantages and disadvantages of bond investments?

A: From the investor's point of view, the advantage of a bond investment is that the investor will receive regular interest payments over the term of the bond and the principal will be returned at the end of the bond term. A bond investment offers lower risk in that the principal amount is not generally at risk;

after all, the investor is in a similar position as any other lender. The disadvantage of a bond investment in our current economy is related to interest rate fluctuations and the risk of a company's failure. If an investor chooses to sell the bond before the maturity or is forced to sell, interest rate risk may mean that the investor does not receive the original principal invested back. If the bond investment is not secured, the investor is risking the entire principal and interest payments should a company fail.

Ethics Insight, p. 850

Q: What will be the effect on profit if the investments are reported as Lemke suggests? Be specific. Is there anything unethical in what Lemke proposes?

A: By classifying the securities that have increased in fair value as fair value through profit and loss, the company would show the gains on the fair value adjustment of these securities on its income statement and increase profit. Losses would not be reported on the income statement if the company chooses not to classify investments that have decreased in value as fair value through profit and loss. In this case, equity securities that have decreased in value are going to be classified as fair value through other comprehensive income, meaning any fair value losses will be reported outside of profit. Debt securities that are classified as amortized cost are not adjusted to fair value for reporting purposes; therefore, decreases in value for these securities will not affect profit until they are ultimately sold.

What Lemke proposes is unethical since it is knowingly not in accordance with IFRS. It is the company's intention with respect to its investment securities and not their potential effects on earnings that should determine how they are classified. The qualitative characteristic of faithful representation is not met if the investments are classified based on performance. The classification is meant to reflect the purpose of each investment for both balance sheet and income statement presentation. Classification based on performance also violates neutrality because it factors in a bias to attain a predetermined result. Stakeholders that could be adversely affected are the company's officers and directors, the independent auditors, the shareholders, and prospective investors.

All About You, p. 859

Q: Is it beneficial for you, while you are a student, to invest in a TFSA even though you may not have taxable income? Would you classify your investment in a TFSA as a long-term or short-term investment?

A: Yes, provided you have cash that you do not need in the short term, it is beneficial for you to contribute to a TFSA. Investments earn investment income. By contributing to a TFSA sooner rather than later, you will be able to protect more investment income from being taxed. The investment in a TFSA will be a long-term investment.

ANSWERS TO SELF-STUDY QUESTIONS

1. d   2. d   3. b   4. c   5. d   6. a   7. b   8. b   9. b   10. c

17

THE CASH FLOW STATEMENT

CHAPTER PREVIEW The ability of a business to survive is linked to its ability to generate cash. So how do companies generate cash? How do they use cash? Where can financial statement users get this information? This chapter, which presents the cash flow statement, will answer these and similar questions.

FEATURE STORY ▸ GOING WITH THE CASH FLOW

LUNENBURG, N.S.—When you don't have much money in your wallet, you might joke that you have a "cash flow problem." But to a business, cash flow is no laughing matter. If it's taking too long to collect money owed by customers, while its suppliers are demanding to be paid for items it purchased, a business might have a negative cash flow that could cause it to go bankrupt. Companies and their investors keep a close eye on the inflow and outflow of cash, which is recorded on the cash flow statement.

Let's look at High Liner Foods' cash flow statement as an example. High Liner, through its predecessor companies, has been in the seafood business in Lunenburg since 1899. It is the leading North American processor and marketer of processed frozen seafood, selling products to retailers and restaurants under brand names such as High Liner, Fisher Boy, and Sea Cuisine. Its cash flow statement, which it calls the consolidated statement of cash flows, shows the amounts of cash either provided by or used in the business in three main areas of activity: operating activities, financing activities, and investing activities.

High Liner's operating activities include net income from sales of its frozen seafood products such as fish sticks, shrimp, and scallops, along with interest and income taxes paid. In its 2014 annual report, the consolidated statement of cash flows shows that, for the 53-week period ending January 3, 2015, High Liner generated a net cash flow from operating activities of $22.2 million (all amounts are in U.S. dollars).

Next, High Liner's cash flow statement reports the amount of cash provided by or used in financing activities, which are activities used to finance the business. This included the repayment of lease obligations (for leases on things such as cold storage facilities and some of its processing plants), the payment of dividends on common shares, and proceeds from long-term debt. In its 2014 annual report, the company had net cash flows provided by financing activities of $18.2 million.

Finally, High Liner's cash flow statement shows net cash flows provided by or used in investing activities, which include investments in financial markets or capital assets. For High Liner, its 2014 investing activities included the purchase of property, plant, and equipment, and the acquisition of a new business—Atlantic Trading Company LLC, a large importer of frozen Atlantic salmon into the United States—for an estimated purchase price of $17.9 million. For 2014, High Liner had net cash flows used by investing activities of $40.3 million.

The total of cash flows provided by operating and investing activities of $22.2 million plus $18.2 million, respectively, minus cash flows used by investing activities of $40.3 million meant that High Liner generated $0.1 million of cash in fiscal 2014.

Sources: High Liner Foods' corporate website, www.highlinerfoods.com/; High Liner Foods' 2014 annual report.

CHAPTER OUTLINE

LEARNING OBJECTIVES

1	**Discuss the usefulness, content, and format of the cash flow statement.**	**Reporting of Cash Flows** • Usefulness of the cash flow statement • Content of the cash flow statement	**DO IT 1** Classification of cash flows
2	**Prepare a cash flow statement using the indirect method.**	**Preparation of the Cash Flow Statement** • Indirect method	**DO IT 2a** Cash from operating activities **DO IT 2b** Cash from investing and financing activities **DO IT 2c** Indirect method
3	**Prepare the operating section of the cash flow statement using the direct method.**	• Direct method	**DO IT 3** Direct method
4	**Analyze the cash flow statement.**	**Using the Information in the Financial Statements** • Free cash flow	**DO IT 4** Free cash flow

Reporting of Cash Flows

The financial statements we have studied so far present only partial information about a company's cash flows (cash receipts and cash payments). For example, when comparing year-over-year changes of balance sheet accounts such as property, plant, and equipment, we may be able to determine that asset additions were made during the year, but we cannot determine how these additions were paid for. Likewise, the income statement presents profit, but it does not indicate the amount of cash generated by operations. Yet this is useful information to financial statement users. Therefore, financial statements include the cash flow statement, which provides a detailed summary of where cash came from and how it was used.

USEFULNESS OF THE CASH FLOW STATEMENT

Alternative terminology Under IFRS, the cash flow statement is commonly referred to as the *statement of cash flows*.

The **cash flow statement** reports cash receipts, cash payments, and the net change in cash for the entity. The information in the statement of cash flows helps investors, creditors, and other interested parties understand what is happening to a company's most liquid resource—its cash. The benefits of cash flow statements are that they present the sources and uses of cash, so users are better able to assess the following:

1. **The entity's ability to generate future cash flows.** By examining relationships between items in the cash flow statement, investors can better predict the amounts, timing, and uncertainty of future cash flows than they can from accrual accounting data.
2. **The entity's ability to pay dividends and meet obligations.** If a company does not have adequate cash, it cannot pay employees, settle debts, or pay dividends. Employees, creditors, and shareholders should be particularly interested in this statement because it alone shows the flows of cash in a business.
3. **The cash investing and financing transactions during the period.** By examining a company's investing and financing transactions, financial statement users can better understand why assets and liabilities changed during the period.
4. **The reasons for the difference between profit and net cash provided (used) by operating activities.** Profit provides information on the success or failure of a business. However, some financial statement users are critical of accrual-basis profit because it requires many estimates. As a result, users often challenge the reliability of the profit number. Such is not the case with cash. Users of the cash flow statement want to understand the reasons for the difference between profit and net cash provided by operating activities. They can then assess for themselves the interpretation of the profit number.

CONTENT OF THE CASH FLOW STATEMENT

ETHICS NOTE
Though we discourage reliance on cash flows to the exclusion of accrual accounting, comparing net cash provided by operating activities with profit can reveal important information about the "quality" of reported profit. Such a comparison can reveal the extent to which profit provides a good measure of actual performance.

Before we can start preparing the cash flow statement, we must first understand what it includes and why. We will begin by reviewing the definition of cash used in the cash flow statement and then we will discuss how cash receipts and payments are classified within the statement.

Definition of Cash

The cash flow statement is often prepared using "cash and cash equivalents" as its basis. You will recall from Chapter 7 that cash consists of cash on hand (coins, paper currency, and cheques) and money on deposit at a bank less any bank overdrafts. Cash equivalents are short-term, highly liquid debt investments that are readily convertible to known amounts of cash. Because of the varying definitions of "cash" that can be used in this statement, companies must clearly define cash as it is used in their particular statement.

Classification of Cash Flows

Now that we have defined cash, let's consider how it is portrayed in the cash flow statement. The cash flow statement classifies cash receipts and cash payments into three types of activities: (1) operating, (2) investing, and (3) financing activities. The transactions and other events for each kind of activity are as follows:

1. **Operating activities** include the cash effects of transactions that create revenues and expenses. Thus, operating activities generally relate to the day-to-day operations of the business that impact profit. As we saw in the High Liner Foods opening story, operating activities include such things as sales, leading to profit.
2. **Investing activities** generally affect non-current asset accounts and include:
   (a) buying and selling of long-lived assets,
   (b) buying and selling of long-term debt or equity investments, and
   (c) lending money and collecting the loans.
3. **Financing activities** generally affect non-current liability and shareholders' equity accounts and include:
   (a) obtaining cash from issuing debt and repaying the amounts borrowed,
   (b) obtaining cash from shareholders, and
   (c) paying shareholders dividends.

Illustration 17-1 lists typical cash receipts (inflows) and cash payments (outflows) in each of the three classifications.

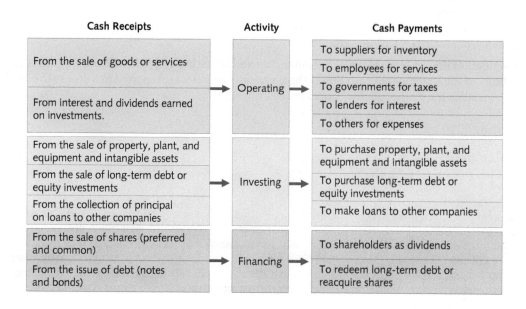

▶ILLUSTRATION 17-1
Cash receipts and payments classified by activity

While the above illustration shows how cash receipts and payments are categorized in the cash flow statement, the following general guidelines will help to prepare the cash flow statement:

1. Operating activities involve income statement accounts and changes in the current assets and liabilities of the balance sheet.
2. Investing activities involve cash flows from changes in investments and long-term assets.
3. Financing activities involve cash outflows resulting from changes in long-term liability and shareholders' equity items.

These activities are shown in Illustration 17-2.

Note that these are general guidelines and there are exceptions. For example, the receipt of investment revenue (interest and dividends) may be classified as operating or investing activities, depending on the financial reporting framework of the entity.

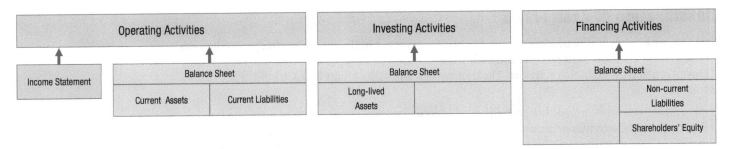

▶ ILLUSTRATION 17-2
Operating, investing,
and financing activities

For example, the reporting of interest and dividends is different for entities reporting under IFRS and ASPE. Companies reporting under IFRS have a choice as to where to classify interest and dividends: they may be classified as either an operating or an investing activity. Interest and dividends paid may also be classified as either an operating or a financing activity. Once the choice is made, it must be applied consistently.

Private companies reporting under ASPE must classify interest (received and paid) and dividends received as operating activities. Under ASPE, dividends paid are classified as financing activities.

Significant Noncash Activities

Not all of a company's significant investing and financing activities involve cash. The following are examples of significant noncash activities:

1. Issue of debt to purchase assets
2. Issue of common shares to purchase assets
3. Conversion of debt or preferred shares to common shares
4. Exchange of property, plant, and equipment

Companies do not report significant financing and investing activities that do not affect cash in the body of the statement of cash flows. These noncash activities are reported in a note to the financial statements to satisfy the full disclosure concept.

ACCOUNTING IN ACTION
ALL ABOUT YOU INSIGHT

Similar to a business, you need to consider your cash situation. How much can you afford to spend, and what are your sources of cash? For many Canadians, using a credit card to easily access cash means they spend more than they can afford. At the end of 2014, the average Canadian's consumer debt load, excluding mortgages, rose 2.9% from the year before to $20,967, driven mainly by credit cards. In 2015, 1 in 4 Canadians said in a BMO survey that they pay off their credit card bill every month using all their available funds, and then go into debt to pay for other things. The same number of respondents said that they see their credit card as another source of spending money. Credit Canada, a non-profit credit counselling agency that helps consumers get out of debt, recommends that Canadians pay off their credit card bills in full every month and not just make the minimum payment. It notes that carrying a $5,000 balance for a year at a typical credit card interest rate of around 20% would cost nearly $1,200 in interest.

Sources: Roma Luciw, "Canadians Take on Even More Debt, Says New Report Calling for Vigilance," *The Globe and Mail*, March 3, 2015; Garry Marr, "Why Slipping on Your Credit Card Payments Is About to Cost You Bigger Bucks," *Financial Post*, February 20, 2015; Heather Loney, "Nearly Half of Canadians Have Credit Card Debt, Report Shows," Globalnews.ca, February 10, 2015.

Q Is it appropriate to use your credit card to pay for your operating activities such as your groceries, clothes, and entertainment? Is it appropriate to use your credit card to finance your investment activities such as tuition or, if you have a large enough limit, a car?

Format of the Cash Flow Statement

The cash flow statement presents the results of the operating, investing, and financing activities plus significant noncash investing and financing activities. Illustration 17-3 shows a widely used form of the statement of cash flows.

COMPANY NAME **Statement of Cash Flows** **For the Period Covered**		
Cash flows from operating activities		
(List of individual inflows and outflows)	<u>XX</u>	
Net cash provided (used) by operating activities		XXX
Cash flows from investing activities		
(List of individual inflows and outflows)	<u>XX</u>	
Net cash provided (used) by investing activities		XXX
Cash flows from financing activities		
(List of individual inflows and outflows)	<u>XX</u>	
Net cash provided (used) by financing activities		<u>XXX</u>
Net increase (decrease) in cash		XXX
Cash at beginning of period		<u>XXX</u>
Cash at end of period		<u>XXX</u> ←
Noncash investing and financing activities		
(List of individual noncash transactions)		<u>XXX</u>

▶ILLUSTRATION 17-3
Format of statement of cash flows

> Must agree to the cash balance per the balance sheet

Note that the cash flow statement covers a period of time and therefore the heading refers to "For the year ended." The operating activities section is always presented first. This is followed by the investing activities and financing activities sections. A subtotal is calculated for each of the sections (operating, investing, and financing) to determine the net increase or decrease in cash from each activity. **Any significant noncash investing and financing activities are reported in a note to the financial statements.** The subtotals for the three activities are determined to identify whether there was a net increase or decrease in cash for the period. This subtotal is then added to the beginning-of-period cash balance to obtain the end-of-period cash balance. **The end-of-period cash balance must agree with the cash balance reported on the balance sheet.**

The cash flow statement may be prepared using one of two methods: the indirect or the direct method. This difference affects the operating section of the cash flow statement only. Note that **both methods arrive at the same amount but they differ in how they arrive at the amount for net cash provided by operating activities**. The **indirect method** adjusts profit for items that do not affect cash. A great majority of companies use this method. Companies favour the indirect method for two reasons: (1) it is easier and less costly to prepare, and (2) it focuses on the differences between profit and net cash flow from operating activities. The **direct method** shows operating cash receipts and payments. It is prepared by adjusting each item in the income statement from the accrual basis to the cash basis. Standard setters prefer the direct method but allow the use of either method.

In the next section we will prepare a cash flow statement using the indirect method. After that section, we will prepare the operating section of the cash flow statement using the direct method.

Helpful hint Whether the indirect or direct method (described in the "Direct Method" section below) is used, net cash provided (used) by operating activities will be the same.

Action Plan

- Identify the three types of activities that are used to report all cash inflows and outflows.
- Report as operating activities the cash effects of transactions that create revenues and expenses, and that are included when profit is determined.
- Report as investing activities transactions to (a) acquire and dispose of long-term investments and long-lived assets, and (b) lend money and collect loans.
- Report as financing activities transactions to (a) obtain cash by issuing debt and repaying the amounts borrowed, and (b) obtain cash from shareholders and pay them dividends.

BEFORE YOU GO ON...DO IT **Classification of Cash Flows**

Carrier Transport Ltd. had the following transactions:

1. Issued common shares for cash.
2. Sold a long-term equity investment.
3. Purchased a truck. Made a cash down payment and financed the remainder with a note payable.
4. Paid for inventory purchases.
5. Collected cash for services provided.
6. Paid the blended monthly mortgage payment (interest and principal) on the note payable.

Classify each of these transactions by type of cash flow activity. Indicate whether the transaction would be reported as a cash inflow or cash outflow.

Solution

1. Financing activity; cash inflow
2. Investing activity; cash inflow
3. Investing activity; cash outflow for down payment. The remainder is a noncash investing (truck) and financing (note payable) activity.
4. Operating activity; cash outflow
5. Operating activity; cash inflow
6. Operating activity; cash outflow for the interest portion of the payment. Financing activity; cash outflow for the principal portion of the payment.

Related exercise material: BE17–1, BE17–2, E17–1, E17–2, and E17–3.

LEARNING OBJECTIVE **Prepare a cash flow statement using the indirect method.**

Preparation of the Cash Flow Statement

Now that we understand the content and format of a cash flow statement, where do we find the information to prepare it? We could examine the cash account in the general ledger and sort each cash receipt and payment into the different types of operating activities, investing activities, or financing activities shown in Illustration 17-1. But this is not practical or necessary. Instead, we prepare the cash flow by examining the changes in all of the other accounts.

The information to prepare the cash flow statement usually comes from three sources:

1. The **comparative balance sheet** shows the balances at the beginning and end of the period for each asset, liability, and shareholders' equity item. This information is used to determine the changes in each asset, liability, and shareholders' equity item during that period.
2. The **income statement** helps us determine the amount of cash provided or used by operating activities during the period.
3. **Additional information** includes transaction data that are needed to determine how cash was provided or used during the period.

The four steps to preparing the cash flow statement from these data sources are shown in Illustration 17-4.

Buying and selling goods

Step 1: Prepare operating activities section.
Determine the net cash provided (used) by operating activities by converting profit from an accrual basis to a cash basis. To do this, analyze the current year's income statement, relevant current asset and current liability accounts from the comparative balance sheets, and selected information.

Investing

Step 2: Prepare investing activities section.
Determine the net cash provided (used) by investing activities by analyzing changes in non-current asset accounts from the comparative balance sheets, and selected information.

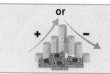

Financing

Step 3: Prepare financing activities section.
Determine the net cash provided (used) by financing activities by analyzing changes in non-current liability and equity accounts from the comparative balance sheets, and selected information.

or

Step 4: Complete the cash flow statement.
Determine the net increase (decrease) in cash. Compare the net change in cash reported on the statement of cash flows with the change in cash reported on the balance sheet to make sure the amounts agree.

▶ILLUSTRATION
Steps in preparing the cash flow statement

INDIRECT METHOD

To explain and illustrate the preparation of a cash flow statement using the indirect method, we will use financial information from Computer Services Corporation. Illustration 17-5 presents Computer Services' comparative balance sheets, its current-year income statement, and related financial information.

COMPUTER SERVICES CORPORATION Balance Sheet December 31			
Assets	**2017**	**2016**	**Increase (Decrease)**
Current assets			
Cash	$ 55,000	$ 33,000	$ 22,000
Accounts receivable	20,000	30,000	(10,000)
Inventory	15,000	10,000	5,000
Prepaid expenses	5,000	1,000	4,000
Property, plant, and equipment			
Land	130,000	20,000	110,000
Building	160,000	40,000	120,000
Accumulated depreciation—building	(11,000)	(5,000)	6,000
Equipment	27,000	10,000	17,000
Accumulated depreciation—equipment	(3,000)	(1,000)	2,000
Total assets	$398,000	$138,000	
Liabilities and Shareholders' Equity			
Current liabilities			
Accounts payable	$ 28,000	$ 12,000	$ 16,000
Income tax payable	6,000	8,000	(2,000)
Non-current liabilities			
Bonds payable	130,000	20,000	110,000
Shareholders' equity			
Common shares	70,000	50,000	20,000
Retained earnings	164,000	48,000	116,000
Total liabilities and shareholders' equity	$398,000	$138,000	

▶ILLUSTRATION 17-5
Computer Services' financial information

(continued)

▶ILLUSTRATION 17-5
(continued)

COMPUTER SERVICES CORPORATION		
Income Statement		
Year Ended December 31, 2017		
Sales revenue		$507,000
Cost of goods sold		150,000
Gross profit		357,000
Operating expenses	$111,000	
Depreciation expense	9,000	
Loss on sale of equipment	3,000	123,000
Profit from operations		234,000
Other expenses		
Interest expense		42,000
Profit before income tax		192,000
Income tax expense		47,000
Profit		$145,000

Additional information for 2017:

1. A $29,000 cash dividend was paid.
2. Land was acquired by issuing $110,000 of long-term bonds.
3. Equipment costing $25,000 was purchased for cash.
4. Equipment with a carrying amount of $7,000 (cost of $8,000, less accumulated depreciation of $1,000) was sold for $4,000 cash.
5. Depreciation expense consists of $6,000 for the building and $3,000 for equipment.

We will now apply the four steps using the above information for Computer Services Corporation. In the following sections, we will review the journal entries to record transactions and analyze T accounts for balance sheet accounts in order to help you understand the preparation of the cash flow statement.

Step 1: Operating Activities

Determine the Net Cash Provided (Used) by Operating Activities by Converting Profit from an Accrual Basis to a Cash Basis

In order to perform this step and determine the cash provided (used) by operating activities, profit must be converted from an accrual basis to a cash basis. Why is this necessary? Recall that under generally accepted accounting principles, companies use the accrual basis of accounting. This basis requires that companies record revenue when it is earned, not when the cash is collected. Similarly, expenses are recorded even if they have not yet been paid, and some expenses, such as depreciation, are never paid in cash at all. For these reasons, under the accrual basis of accounting, profit is not the same as net cash. Therefore, companies must adjust profit to convert certain items to the cash basis.

To adjust profit to a cash basis, the indirect method starts with profit and converts it to net cash provided by operating activities. The starting point is to identify any noncash items such as depreciation expense and adjust profit appropriately. Illustration 17-6 shows some of the types of adjustments that are made to adjust accrual-based profit but that do not affect cash. The first two types of adjustments are found on the income statement. The last type of adjustment—changes to current asset and current liability accounts—is found on the balance sheet.

▶ILLUSTRATION 17-6
Three types of adjustments to convert profit to net cash provided by operating activities

Profit	+/−	Adjustments	=	Net Cash Provided/Used by Operating Activities

- Add back noncash expenses, such as depreciation expense and amortization expense.
- Deduct gains and add losses that resulted from investing and financing activities.
- Analyze changes to noncash current asset and current liability accounts.

Depreciation Expense. Computer Services' income statement reports depreciation expense of $9,000. Although depreciation expense reduces profit, it does not reduce cash. To illustrate this, let's look at the journal entry posted by Computer Services to record the depreciation expense of $9,000. This was recorded as follows:

Depreciation Expense	9,000	
Accumulated Depreciation—Building		6,000
Accumulated Depreciation—Equipment		3,000

Helpful hint Depreciation is similar to any other expense in that it reduces profit. It differs in that it does not involve a current cash outflow. That is why it must be added back to profit to arrive at net cash provided by operating activities.

A	=	L	+	SE
−6,000				−9,000
−3,000				

Cash flows: no effect

Note that the depreciation entry has no impact on cash. In other words, depreciation is a noncash item. The company must add it back to profit to arrive at the net cash provided by operating activities. A partial operating activities section of the cash flow statement for Computer Services is shown below, with the addition of the noncash expense to profit highlighted in green.

Operating activities	
Profit	$145,000
Adjustments to reconcile profit to net cash provided (used) by operating activities:	
Depreciation expense	9,000

Gains and Losses. We previously stated that the cash received from the sale of long-lived assets should be reported in the investing activities section of the cash flow statement. However, such gains and losses are initially recorded on the income statement and included in the determination of profit. Therefore, when preparing the cash flow statement, we must remove from profit all gains or losses from the sale of long-lived assets and adjust them so they are reported under investing activities.

Why is this necessary? Perhaps it will help if we review the accounting for the sale of a long-lived asset. The sale of a long-lived asset is recorded by:

Helpful hint Gains are deducted from and losses are added to profit in the indirect method. These items affect profit but they are not cash items. The cash inflow or outflow on the purchase or sale of assets is reflected by the cash paid or the cash proceeds, reported in the investing section of the cash flow statement.

1. recognizing the cash received,
2. removing the asset and accumulated depreciation account from the books, and
3. recognizing any gain or loss on the sale.

To illustrate, recall that Computer Services' income statement reported a $3,000 loss on the sale of equipment. With the additional information provided in Illustration 17-5, we can reconstruct the journal entry to record the sale of equipment:

Cash	4,000	
Accumulated Depreciation—Equipment	1,000	
Loss on Sale of Equipment	3,000	
Equipment		8,000

A	=	L	+	SE
+4,000				−3,000
+1,000				
−8,000				

↑Cash flows: +4,000

Note that $4,000 is the cash received on the sale of the equipment. The $4,000 of cash that is received is not considered part of operating activities; rather, it is part of investing activities. Selling long-lived assets is not part of a company's primary activities so this does not belong in the operating activities section of the cash flow statement. Also note that the $3,000 loss on the sale of the equipment does not reflect the actual cash received on the disposal of the equipment. Logically, then, to calculate the net cash provided (used) by operating activities, we have to eliminate the gain or loss on the sale of an asset from profit.

To eliminate the $3,000 loss on the sale of equipment, we have to add it back to profit to arrive at net cash provided (used) by operating activities. Adding back the loss cancels the original deduction. This is illustrated in the following partial cash flow statement for Computer Services:

Operating activities	
Profit	$145,000
Adjustments to reconcile profit to net cash provided (used) by operating activities:	
Depreciation expense	9,000
Loss on sale of equipment	3,000

If a gain on sale occurs rather than a loss, the gain is deducted from profit in order to determine net cash provided (used) by operating activities. **For both a gain and a loss, the actual amount of cash received from the sale of the asset is reported in the investing activities section of the cash flow statement.**

Note that gains and losses may also arise if an entity holds investments. These may be either realized or unrealized gains and losses. Recall that such gains and losses are reported on the income statement, and therefore they are included in the determination of profit. As demonstrated above using long-lived assets, gains and losses are noncash items that require adjustment in the operating section of the cash flow statement to cancel the original profit impact. This is necessary to determine the net cash from operating activities.

Changes in Noncash Current Asset and Current Liability Accounts. In addition to the noncash expenses and gains and losses discussed in the previous sections, there are other reasons why profit is not the same amount as cash from operations. Recall that accrual-basis accounting means revenues are recorded in the period earned and expenses are recorded in the period incurred. For example, the Accounts Receivable account reflects amounts owed to the company for sales that have been made but for which the cash has not yet been received. Prepaid Insurance reflects insurance that has been paid for but has not yet expired (and therefore has not been expensed). Similarly, Salaries Payable reflects salaries expense that has been incurred but has not been paid.

As a result, companies need to adjust profit for these accruals and prepayments to determine net cash provided by operating activities. Thus, they must analyze the change in each current asset and current liability account to determine its impact on profit and cash.

Changes in Noncash Current Assets. The adjustments to profit that are required for changes in noncash current asset accounts to arrive at net cash provided (used) by operating activities are shown in Illustration 17-7.

▶ **ILLUSTRATION** **17-7**
Adjustments to profit for changes in noncash current asset accounts

Increase in noncash current assets	Deduct
Decrease in noncash current assets	Add

We will illustrate these adjustments by analyzing the changes in Computer Services' current asset accounts and related journal entries.

Changes in Accounts Receivable. Illustration 17-5 indicated that Computer Services had $507,000 in sales revenue reported on its income statement. Assuming all sales are on account, the entry to record sales is (in summary for the year):

A	=	L	+	SE
+507,000				+507,000

Cash flows: no effect

Accounts Receivable	**507,000**	
Sales Revenue		507,000

While sales for the year were $507,000, did cash also increase by the same amount? To answer this question, we need to analyze Computer Services' Accounts Receivable account. Accounts Receivable increases when a sale is made and decreases when cash is collected, as demonstrated below:

Accounts Receivable	
Opening balance + Sales on account	– Cash receipts
Ending balance	

We know Computer Services started the year with a balance of $30,000 in Accounts Receivable and ended with $20,000. We can see that its Accounts Receivable account decreased by $10,000 ($30,000 – $20,000) during the period. This means the company collected $10,000 of cash more than it had sales in the period. From the journal entry, we know that sales were $507,000. Using the information provided, we can analyse the Accounts Receivable account and determine the cash receipts:

Accounts Receivable			
Jan. 1 Balance	30,000		
Sales revenue	507,000	Receipts from customers	517,000
Dec. 31 Balance	20,000		

$10,000 net decrease

Cash receipts were $517,000 ($30,000 + $507,000 − $20,000). The $517,000 of cash receipts is $10,000 ($517,000 − $507,000) larger than sales revenue, the same amount the Accounts Receivable decreased ($10,000) during the year. Therefore, when accounts receivable decrease during the year, revenues on an accrual basis are lower than revenues on a cash basis. In other words, more cash was collected during the period than was recorded as revenue. We add the amount of the decrease in Accounts Receivable ($10,000) to profit to arrive at the net cash provided from operating activities. This is illustrated in the following partial cash flow statement for Computer Services:

Operating activities	
Profit	$145,000
Adjustments to reconcile profit to net cash provided (used) by operating activities:	
Depreciation expense	9,000
Loss on sale of equipment	3,000
Decrease in accounts receivable	10,000

Using the same logic, this means that, when the Accounts Receivable balance increases during the year, revenues on an accrual basis are higher than cash receipts. Therefore, the amount of the increase in Accounts Receivable is deducted from profit to arrive at net cash provided (used) by operating activities.

Changes in Inventory. Computer Services reported cost of goods sold of $150,000 in its income statement. As demonstrated in the journal entry below, when the cost of goods sold is recorded, the Inventory account is credited.

Helpful hint If accounts receivable increase, deduct the increase from profit in the operating section of the cash flow statement. If accounts receivable decrease, add the decrease to profit in the operating section of the cash flow statement.

Cost of Goods Sold	150,000	
Inventory		150,000

A	=	L	+	SE
−150,000				−150,000

Cash flows: no effect

Cost of goods sold decreased profit by $150,000, but how much cash was used to purchase inventory during the period? To answer this question, we need to analyze the Inventory account. The Inventory account decreases when inventory is sold and increases when inventory is purchased, as noted below:

Inventory	
Opening balance	
+ Purchase of inventory	− Sale of inventory
Ending balance	

The T account below indicates that Computer Services started the year with a balance of $10,000 in the Inventory account and ended with $15,000. Using these amounts and the $150,000 of cost of goods sold from above journal entry, we can analyze the Inventory account to determine the cost of goods purchased as follows:

Inventory			
Jan. 1 Balance	10,000		
Purchases	155,000	Cost of goods sold	150,000
Dec. 31 Balance	15,000		

$5,000 net increase

The cost of goods purchased during the period is $155,000 ($150,000 − $10,000 + $15,000), which is $5,000 ($155,000 − $150,000) greater than the cost of goods sold. Note that this difference is equal to the increase in the Inventory account during the period ($15,000 − $10,000). When the Inventory account increases, more inventory was purchased during the period than the amount sold. Because the cost of goods sold of $150,000 has already been deducted on the income statement, we simply deduct the $5,000 increase in inventory on the cash flow statement. This deduction is illustrated in the partial cash flow statement for Computer Services (Illustration 17-9) presented at the end of this section.

Following the same logic, if inventory had decreased, this would mean that the cost of goods purchased was less than the cost of goods sold and we would add the decrease back to profit.

This adjustment does not completely convert cost of goods sold to cash paid for inventory. The analysis of accounts payable—shown later—completes the calculation of payments made to suppliers by converting the cost of goods purchased from an accrual basis to a cash basis.

Changes in Prepaid Expenses. Computer Services reported $111,000 of operating expenses in its income statement. This reflects the amount of operating expenses used during the period. Again, it does not reflect the amount of cash paid for operating expenses. To determine the cash paid, we need to analyze the Prepaid Expenses account. This account increases when a prepayment is made and decreases when an expense is recorded in the income statement as shown below.

Prepaid Assets	
Opening balance + Prepayments made	− Prepayments expensed (used)
Ending balance	

To help us determine the cash paid for operating expenses, we can assume that the following summary journal entry was made to record the operating expenses:

A = L + SE	Operating Expenses
−111,000	Prepaid Expenses

	111,000	
		111,000

A = L + SE
−111,000   −111,000

Cash flows: no effect

Computer Services started the year with a balance of $1,000 in the Prepaid Expenses account and ended with $5,000. Using these amounts and the operating expenses of $111,000 recorded in the above journal entry, we can analyze the Prepaid Expenses account to determine the cash paid for operating expenses as follows:

Prepaid Expenses			
Jan. 1 Balance	1,000		
Payments for expenses	(115,000)	Operating expenses	111,000
Dec. 31 Balance	5,000		

$4,000 net increase

The cash paid for operating expenses is $115,000 ($111,000 − $1,000 + $5,000), which is $4,000 ($115,000 − $111,000) more than the operating expenses reported in the income statement. Note that this difference is equal to the increase in Prepaid Expenses during the period

($5,000 − $1,000). When prepaid expenses increase, cash paid for expenses is higher than the expenses reported in the income statement on an accrual basis. In other words, cash payments were made in the current period, but the expenses will not be recorded in the income statement until future periods. Because operating expenses of $111,000 have already been deducted on the income statement, we simply deduct the $4,000 increase in prepaid expenses on the cash flow statement to convert profit to net cash provided (used) by operating activities. This deduction is illustrated in the partial cash flow statement for Computer Services (Illustration 17-9) presented at the end of this section.

Following the same logic, if prepaid expenses decreased during the period, this would mean that the cash paid for expenses was less than the operating expenses recorded in the income statement. We would then add the decrease back to profit when calculating cash provided (used) by operating activities.

If Computer Services had any accrued expenses payable, such as Salaries Payable, these would also have to be considered before we could completely determine the amount of cash paid for operating expenses. We will look at changes in current liability accounts in the next section.

Changes in Current Liabilities. The adjustments to profit that are required for changes in noncash current liability accounts to arrive at net cash provided (used) by operating activities are shown in Illustration 17-8.

Helpful hint If prepaid items increase, deduct the increase from profit in the operating section of the cash flow statement. If prepaid items decrease, add the decrease to profit in the operating section of the cash flow statement.

Increase in noncash current liabilities	Add
Decrease in noncash current liabilities	Deduct

▶ **ILLUSTRATION** **17-8**
Adjustments to profit for changes in noncash current liability accounts

We will illustrate these adjustments by analyzing the changes in Computer Services' current liability accounts: Accounts Payable and Income Tax Payable.

Changes in Accounts Payable. In some companies, the Accounts Payable account is used only to record purchases of inventory on account. Other accounts are used to record other credit purchases and accrued expenses such as salaries payable. For simplicity, in this chapter we assume only inventory purchases are recorded in the accounts payable account.

You will recall that we determined, in the analysis of Computer Services' Inventory account earlier, that the cost of goods purchased was $155,000. Assuming all of the purchases were on account, the entry to record the purchases is (in summary):

Inventory	155,000
Accounts Payable	**155,000**

A	=	L	+	SE
+155,000		+155,000		

Cash flows: no effect

The amount of inventory purchased was $155,000, but what amount of cash was paid to suppliers for goods purchased? We can answer this question by analyzing the Accounts Payable account. Accounts Payable increases by the cost of goods purchased and decreases by cash paid to suppliers.

Accounts Payable	
	Opening balance
− Cash payments to suppliers	+ Purchases on account
	Ending balance

Illustration 17-5 indicates that Computer Services started the year with a balance of $12,000 in Accounts Payable and ended with $28,000. Using these amounts and the accounts payable of $155,000 recorded in the above journal entry, we analyze the Accounts Payable account to determine the cash paid for inventory as follows:

Accounts Payable				
		Jan. 1	Balance	12,000
Payments to suppliers	139,000		Purchases	155,000
		Dec. 31	Balance	28,000

$16,000 net increase

The cash paid to suppliers for inventory is $139,000 ($12,000 + $155,000 − $28,000), which is $16,000 ($155,000 − $139,000) less than the cost of goods purchased. Note that this difference is equal to the increase in Accounts Payable during the period ($28,000 − $12,000). When the balance in the Accounts Payable account increases, the company has received more goods than it actually paid for. Because cost of goods sold of $150,000 has already been deducted on the income statement and we have also deducted the $5,000 increase in inventory to adjust for the cost of goods purchased, we simply add the $16,000 increase in accounts payable on the cash flow statement to convert profit to net cash provided (used) by operating activities. This deduction is illustrated in the partial cash flow statement for Computer Services (Illustration 17-9) presented at the end of this section.

Similarly, if the Accounts Payable account decreased, it would mean that the cash paid to suppliers was more than the purchases and this decrease would be deducted from profit.

Note that the conversion of the cost of goods sold on the income statement to the cash paid for goods purchased involves two steps.

1. The change in the Inventory account adjusts the cost of goods sold to the cost of goods purchased.
2. The change in the Accounts Payable account adjusts the cost of goods purchased to the payments to suppliers.

> **Helpful hint** If accounts payable increase, add the increase to profit in the operating section of the cash flow statement. If accounts payable decrease, deduct the decrease from profit in the operating section of the cash flow statement.

These changes for Computer Services are summarized as follows:

Cost of goods sold	$150,000
Add: Increase in inventory	5,000
Cost of goods purchased	155,000
Less: Increase in accounts payable	16,000
Cash payments to suppliers	$139,000

Changes in Income Tax Payable. Computer Services reported $47,000 in income tax expense on the income statement. The journal entry to record the income tax expense is as follows:

A	=	L	+	SE
		+47,000		−47,000

Cash flows: no effect

Income Tax Expense	47,000	
Income Tax Payable		**47,000**

We can see that profit was decreased by income tax expense of $47,000, but how much cash was paid for income tax? To answer this question, we need to analyze Computer Services' Income Tax Payable account. The Income Tax Payable account increases when income tax expense is recorded and decreases when income tax is paid.

Income Tax Payable	
	Opening balance
− Income tax paid	+ Income tax expense
	Ending balance

Computer Services started the year with a balance of $8,000 in Income Tax Payable and ended with $6,000. Using these amounts and the income tax expense of $47,000 recorded in the above journal entry, we analyze the Income Tax Payable account to determine the cash paid for income tax as follows:

Income Tax Payable			
	Jan. 1	Balance	8,000
Payments for Income tax 49,000		Income tax expense	47,000
	Dec. 31	Balance	6,000

} $2,000 net decrease

The cash paid for income tax is $49,000 ($8,000 + $47,000 − $6,000), which is $2,000 ($49,000 − $47,000) more than the income tax expense. Note that this difference is equal to the decrease in income tax payable during the period ($8,000 − $6,000). When the Income Tax Payable account decreases, it means that more income tax was paid than the recorded income tax expense in the income statement. Because income tax expense of $47,000 has already been deducted on the income statement, we simply deduct the $2,000 decrease in income tax payable on the cash flow statement to convert profit to net cash provided (used) by operating activities. This deduction is illustrated in the partial cash flow statement for Computer Services (Illustration 17-9) presented at the end of this section.

If Computer Services had other accrued expenses payable, they would be analyzed similarly to the Income Tax Payable account.

The partial cash flow statement that follows in Illustration 17-9 shows the impact on operating activities of the changes in current asset and current liability accounts. (The changes are highlighted in green.) It also shows the adjustments that were described earlier for noncash expenses and gains and losses. The operating activities section of the cash flow statement is now complete.

Helpful hint If taxes payable increase, add the increase to profit in the operating section of the cash flow statement. If taxes payable decrease, deduct the decrease from profit in the operating section of the cash flow statement.

COMPUTER SERVICES CORPORATION Cash Flow Statement (partial) Year Ended December 31, 2017		
Operating activities		
Profit		$145,000
Adjustments to reconcile profit to net cash provided (used) by operating activities:		
Depreciation expense	$ 9,000	
Loss on sale of equipment	3,000	
Decrease in accounts receivable	10,000	
Increase in inventory	(5,000)	
Increase in prepaid expenses	(4,000)	
Increase in accounts payable	16,000	
Decrease in income tax payable	(2,000)	27,000
Net cash provided by operating activities		172,000

▶ILLUSTRATION 17-9
Net cash provided by operating activities—indirect method

Note that **if current assets increase, deduct the amount of the increase from profit. Conversely, if current assets decrease, add the decrease to profit.** The opposite is true of current liabilities. **If current liabilities increase, add the increase to profit. However, if current liabilities decrease, deduct the decrease from profit.** In summary, Computer Services earned a profit of $145,000 and the profit-generating activities generated cash of $172,000 during the year.

New businesses need cash to expand, but where does this cash come from? One possible source is by selling shares to investors through an Initial Public Offering (IPO). Most recently, there has been renewed interest in the Canadian tech industry as more IPOs are being reported. In 2014, the Canadian technology sector had three initial public offerings worth $193 million, compared with 12 IPOs worth $1.4 billion in 2006. This was demonstrated in May 2015 when Shopify, an e-commerce platform for small and medium-sized businesses, raised over $100 million in its initial public offering. This has led to speculation that other Canadian tech companies such as Hootsuite, D2L Corp. (formerly Desire2Learn), and BuildDirect, may follow suit and issue shares to the public over the next few years. While some fear this is reminiscent of the tech bubble, the sentiment is that Canadian tech companies that do hit the public markets are uniquely positioned to succeed, as these companies are mature and have learned to perform with few resources.

Sources: Euan Rocha and Alastair Sharp, "Hootsuite Says Could Go Public Sooner after Shopify IPO Success," Reuters, May 21, 2015; Shopify Inc., Prospectus filed with the U.S. Securities and Exchange Commission, 2015; Shira Ovide, "Tech Firms' Cash Hoards Cool Fears of a Meltdown," *Wall Street Journal*, May 14, 2014; John Talik, "Canada IPO Market Trades Commodities for Tech as Valuations Climb," Reuters, March 5, 2015; John Gray "Cashing in on Canada's Hot IPO Tech Market," BNN, June 9, 2015.

Q What implications does a company's ability to raise cash have for its growth and survival?

Summary of Conversion to Net Cash Provided (Used) by Operating Activities—Indirect Method. As shown in Illustration 17-9, the cash flow statement prepared by the indirect method starts with profit. Profit is then adjusted to arrive at net cash provided (used) by operating activities. Adjustments to profit that are typically required are summarized as follows:

Noncash expenses	Depreciation expense	Add
	Amortization expense (intangible assets)	Add
Gains and losses	Gain on sale of asset	Deduct
	Loss on sale of asset	Add
Changes in noncash current asset and current liability accounts	Increase in current asset account	Deduct
	Decrease in current asset account	Add
	Increase in current liability account	Add
	Decrease in current liability account	Deduct

BEFORE YOU GO ON...DO IT **2a** **Cash from Operating Activities**

Selected financial information follows for Reynolds Ltd. at December 31. Prepare the operating activities section of the cash flow statement using the indirect method.

	2017	2016	Increase (Decrease)
Current assets			
Cash	$54,000	$37,000	$17,000
Accounts receivable	68,000	26,000	42,000
Inventory	54,000	10,000	44,000
Prepaid expenses	4,000	6,000	(2,000)
Current liabilities			
Accounts payable	23,000	50,000	(27,000)
Accrued expenses payable	10,000	0	10,000

(continued)

BEFORE YOU GO ON...DO IT ②a ❯ **Cash from Operating Activities** *(continued)*

REYNOLDS LTD.
Income Statement
Year Ended December 31, 2017

Sales revenue		$890,000
Cost of goods sold		465,000
Gross profit		425,000
Operating expenses	$188,000	
Depreciation expense	33,000	
Loss on sale of equipment	2,000	223,000
Profit from operations		202,000
Other expenses		
Interest expense		12,000
Profit before income tax		190,000
Income tax expense		65,000
Profit		$125,000

Solution

REYNOLDS LTD.
Cash Flow Statement (partial)
Year Ended December 31, 2017

Operating activities		
Profit		$125,000
Adjustments to reconcile profit to net cash		
provided (used) by operating activities:		
Depreciation expense	$33,000	
Loss on sale of equipment	2,000	
Increase in accounts receivable	(42,000)	
Increase in inventories	(44,000)	
Decrease in prepaid expenses	2,000	
Decrease in accounts payable	(27,000)	
Increase in accrued expenses payable	10,000	(66,000)
Net cash provided by operating activities		59,000

Related exercise material: BE17–3, BE17–4, BE17–5, BE17–6, BE17–7, E17–4, E17–5, and E17–6.

Action Plan

- Start with profit reported on the income statement to determine the net cash provided (used) by operating activities.
- Examine the income statement: Add noncash expenses and deduct noncash revenues. Add losses and deduct gains.
- Analyze the current assets and current liabilities in the balance sheet. Add decreases in related noncash current asset accounts and increases in related noncash liability accounts. Deduct increases in related noncash current asset accounts and decreases in related noncash liability accounts.

Step 2: Investing Activities

Determine the Net Cash Provided (Used) by Investing Activities by Analyzing Changes in Long-Term Asset Accounts

Regardless of whether the indirect or direct method is used to calculate operating activities, investing and financing activities are measured and reported in the same way. While there are exceptions, for the most part investing activities affect long-term asset accounts, such as long-term investments; property, plant, and equipment; and intangible assets.

To determine the investing activities, again we must examine the balance sheet and additional information in Illustration 17-5. The change in each long-term asset account is analyzed to determine what effect, if any, it had on cash. Computer Services has no investments or notes receivable Note that if Computer Services had purchased investments during the year, the cash paid would be reported as a cash outflow, while the cash proceeds on investments sold would be reported as a cash inflow. Let's now consider Computer Services' three long-term asset accounts that must be analyzed: Land, Building, and Equipment.

Land. Land increased by $110,000 during the year, as reported in Computer Services' balance sheet. The additional information in Illustration 17-5 states that this land was purchased by issuing long-term bonds. The journal entry to record the purchase of the land is as follows:

A = L + SE
+110,000 +110,000

Cash flows: no effect

Land	110,000	
Bonds Payable		110,000

As shown in the journal entry, issuing bonds for land has no effect on cash and is not reported in the cash flow statement. It is, however, a significant noncash investing and financing activity that must be disclosed in a note to the statement.

Building. The Building account increased by $120,000 during the year. What caused this increase? No additional information has been given for this change. Whenever unexplained differences in accounts occur, we assume the transaction was for cash. That is, we would assume the entry to record the acquisition or expansion of the building is as follows:

A = L + SE
+120,000
−120,000

↓ Cash flows: −120,000

Building	120,000	
Cash		120,000

The cash outflow for the purchase of the building of $120,000 is a use of cash and it is deducted as an investing activity in the cash flow statement.

Now let's look at the the Accumulated Depreciation—Building account. It increased by $6,000 during the year:

Accumulated Depreciation — Building			
	Jan. 1	Balance	5,000
		Depreciation expense	6,000
	Dec. 31	Balance	11,000

$6,000 net increase {

As explained in the additional information in Illustration 17-5, this increase resulted from the depreciation expense reported on the income statement for the building. The journal entry to record the depreciation expense is as follows:

A = L + SE
−6,000 −6,000

Cash flows: no effect

Depreciation Expense	6,000	
Accumulated Depreciation—Building		6,000

As the journal entry shows, depreciation expense is a noncash charge and does not affect the cash flow statement.

Equipment. The Computer Services' Equipment account increased by $17,000. The additional information in Illustration 17-5 explains that this was a net increase resulting from two different transactions: (1) a purchase of equipment for $25,000 cash, and (2) a sale of equipment with a carrying amount of $7,000 (cost of $8,000, less accumulated depreciation of $1,000) for $4,000 cash. Let's consider the equipment purchase first. The journal entry to record the purchase of equipment is as follows:

A = L + SE
+25,000
−25,000

↓ Cash flows: −25,000

Equipment	25,000	
Cash		25,000

Based on the journal entry above, we can see the purchase of the equipment is a use of cash and therefore it is deducted as a $25,000 cash outflow in the investing section of the cash flow statement.

Now, let's analyze the sale of the equipment. The journal entry to record the sale of the equipment is as follows:

Cash	4,000	
Accumulated Depreciation—Equipment	1,000	
Loss on Sale of Equipment	3,000	
Equipment		8,000

A	=	L	+	SE
+4,000				−3,000
−1,000				
−8,000				

↑Cash flows: +4,000

Note that, for the sale of the equipment, it is the cash proceeds that are reported on the cash flow statement, not the cost of the equipment sold. Therefore the $4,000 cash proceeds from the sale of the equipment is reported as a cash inflow in the investing section of the cash flow statement.

The T account below summarizes the changes in the Equipment account during the year:

Equipment			
Jan. 1 Balance	10,000		
Purchase of equipment	25,000	Cost of equipment sold	8,000
Dec. 31 Balance	27,000		

$17,000 net increase

Note that each transaction, both the purchase and the sale, must be reported separately on the cash flow statement. It is not correct to report the net change in a long-term balance sheet account as simply an increase or decrease in that account.

Also note, in the above example, you were given additional information about both the purchase and the sale of equipment. **Often, in analyzing accounts, you will be given just one piece of information and are expected to deduce the missing information.**

Using the equipment example above, we know the beginning account balance is $10,000 and the ending account balance is $27,000. Therefore, the Equipment account increased by $17,000, but was $17,000 of equipment purchased? No; during the year, equipment was both purchased and sold, resulting in an overall net increase of $17,000 in the account. This is because the Equipment account increases as assets are purchased and decreases as equipment is disposed of (by sale or obsolescence) as follows:

Equipment	
Opening balance	
+ Cost of assets purchased	− Cost of assets sold
Ending balance	

Given the above T account, if we are provided with only one piece of information, we can analyze the Equipment account to determine the unknown amount. Assume, we know only the cost of the equipment sold ($8,000) so we need to determine the cost of the equipment purchased as follows:

Equipment			
Opening balance	10,000		
Cost of assets purchased	?	8,000	Cost of equipment sold
Ending balance	27,000		

With the information provided, we can determine the cost of the assets purchased as $25,000 ($10,000 + cost of assets purchased − $8,000 = $27,000).

Accumulated Depreciation. Recall, that when a long lived asset is sold or disposed, the related accumulated depreciation must also be removed from the books. Therefore, let's now turn to the related accumulated depreciation account. Reviewing the comparative balance sheet for Computer Services, we can see that accumulated depreciation for equipment increased by $2,000. However this change does not represent the depreciation expense for the year. The additional information in Illustration 17-5 told us that there was $3,000 of depreciation expense for the equipment and that the equipment sold had $1,000 of accumulated depreciation.

The journal entry to record the depreciation expense is as follows:

A	=	L	+	SE	
−3,000				−3,000	

Cash flows: no effect

Depreciation Expense	3,000	
Accumulated Depreciation—Equipment		3,000

This journal entry, combined with the journal entry shown earlier for the sale of the equipment, helps us understand the changes to the Accumulated Depreciation account.

The T account below for Accumulated Depreciation—Equipment shows that these two items explain the overall net increase of $2,000.

$2,000 net increase {

Accumulated Depreciation—Equipment				
		Jan. 1 Balance	1,000
Sale of equipment	1,000	Depreciation expense	3,000
		Dec. 31 Balance	3,000

Now let's assume the accumulated depreciation for the equipment was not provided in the additional information. We would have to perform an account analysis to determine this amount. Note that accumulated depreciation changes when depreciation expense is recorded and when assets are sold or disposed of as demonstrated in the T-account below:

Accumulated Depreciation	
	Opening balance
− Accumulated depreciation on assets sold or disposed of	+ Depreciation expense
	Ending balance

Using this information, we can analyze the accumulated depreciation account. From the balance sheet information, we know we started the year with $1,000 and ended the year with $3,000. Since the depreciation expense was $3,000, the accumulated depreciation removed from the books must have been $1,000 ($1,000 + $3,000 − accumulated depreciation on equipment sold = $3,000).

We can see the sale of the equipment affects one account on Computer Services' income statement (Loss on Sale of Equipment) and three accounts on its balance sheet (Cash, Equipment, and Accumulated Depreciation). In the cash flow statement, it is important to report the effects of this sale in one place: the investing activities section. The overall result is that the sale of the equipment ends up having no effect on the operating activities section of the cash flow statement. Instead, the cash proceeds received from the sale of the equipment are shown fully in the investing activities section.

The investing activities section of Computer Services' cash flow statement is shown in Illustration 17-10 and reports the changes in the three accounts: Land, Building, and Equipment.

Helpful hint Note that in the investing activities section, positive numbers indicate cash inflows (receipts) and negative numbers indicate cash outflows (payments).

▶ ILLUSTRATION 17-10
Net cash used by investing activities

COMPUTER SERVICES CORPORATION Cash Flow Statement (partial) Year Ended December 31, 2017		
Investing activities		
Purchase of building	$(120,000)	
Purchase of equipment	(25,000)	
Sale of equipment	4,000	
Net cash used by investing activities		$(141,000)
Note x: Significant noncash investing and financing activities:		
Issue of bonds to purchase land		$110,000

Step 3: Financing Activities

Determine the Net Cash Provided (Used) by Financing Activities by Analyzing Changes in Long-Term Liability and Equity Accounts

The third step in preparing a cash flow statement is to analyze the changes in long-term liability and equity accounts. If short-term notes payable are issued for lending purposes, they should be reported in the financing activities section. Computer Services has no notes payable but has one long-term liability account, Bonds Payable, and two shareholders' equity accounts, Common Shares and Retained Earnings.

Bonds Payable. Bonds Payable increased by $110,000. As indicated earlier, land was acquired from the issue of these bonds. This noncash transaction is reported as a note to the cash flow statement because it is a significant financing activity.

Common Shares. Computer Services' Common Shares account increased by $20,000. Because there is no additional information about any reacquisition of shares, we assume that this change is due entirely to the issue of additional common shares for cash. The entry to record the issue of common shares is as follows:

Cash	20,000	
Common Shares		20,000

A	=	L	+	SE
+20,000				+20,000

↑Cash flows: +20,000

This cash inflow is reported in the financing activities section of the cash flow statement. If the company had also reacquired shares, the amount of cash paid to reacquire the common shares would be reported as a cash outflow in the financing section.

Retained Earnings. Retained Earnings increased by $116,000 during the year, but what caused this increase? Were there any non-operating cash transactions that changed retained earnings? We know Computer Services reported profit of $145,000 for the year, but did it pay dividends? To determine this, we need to analyze the Retained Earnings account. The journal entry to record profit in the Retained Earnings account is as follows:

Income Summary	145,000	
Retained Earnings		145,000

A	=	L	+	SE
				−145,000
				+145,000

Cash flows: no effect

We know that profit increases retained earnings and the declaration of dividends and drawings decrease retained earnings, as shown below:

Retained Earnings	
	Opening balance
− Declared dividends/ drawings	+ profit
	Ending balance

From the balance sheet, we can see Computer Services started the year with $48,000 in its Retained Earnings account and ended the year with $164,000. Using these amounts and the profit recorded in the journal entry above, we can perform an account analysis to determine if there were dividends declared.

Retained Earnings		
	48,000	Opening balance
Dividends declared ($29,000)	145,000	Profit
	164,000	Ending balance

Therefore, the dividends declared is determined to be $29,000 ($48,000 + $145,000 − dividends declared = $164,000).

Note that the Retained Earnings account above only reports the dividends declared. This amount must be adjusted to determine the dividends paid, if there is any change in the balance of the Dividends Payable account reported in the current liabilities section of the balance sheet. The relationship among cash payments for dividends, dividends declared, and changes in dividends payable is shown in Illustration 17-11.

▶ **ILLUSTRATION 17-11**
Formula to calculate dividends paid in cash

Cash payments for dividends	=	Dividends declared	{ + Decrease in dividends payable or − Increase in dividends payable

Helpful hint Note that, in the financing activities section, positive numbers indicate cash inflows (receipts) and negative numbers indicate cash outflows (payments).

The additional information in Illustration 17-5 indicates that Computer Services paid a cash dividend of $29,000. In this example, the dividends declared are equal to the dividends paid. The cash dividend paid is reported as a cash outflow in the financing activities section of the cash flow statement.

The financing activities section of Computer Services' cash flow statement is shown in Illustration 17-12 and reports the issue of common shares and payment of a dividend. The information on the significant noncash financing activity of bonds being issued to purchase land has already been illustrated and is not included here.

▶ **ILLUSTRATION 17-12**
Net cash used by financing activities

COMPUTER SERVICES CORPORATION
Cash Flow Statement (partial)
Year Ended December 31, 2017

Financing activities		
Issue of common shares	$20,000	
Payment of cash dividend	(29,000)	
Net cash used by financing activities		$(9,000)

BEFORE YOU GO ON...DO IT 2b ▷ **Cash from Investing and Financing Activities**

Western Corporation reported an opening balance of $146,000 and an ending balance of $135,000 in its Equipment account and an opening balance of $47,000 and an ending balance of $62,000 in its Accumulated Depreciation—Equipment account. During the year, it sold equipment with a cost of $21,000 for cash at a gain on the sale of $1,000. It also purchased equipment for cash. It recorded depreciation expense of $31,000. Analyze the Equipment and Accumulated Depreciation accounts to calculate (a) the cash received from the sale of the equipment, and (b) the cash paid for equipment.

Action Plan
• Prepare a T account for Accumulated Depreciation—Equipment and enter the beginning and ending balances and the depreciation expense. Recall that depreciation expense increases accumulated depreciation. Use this information to calculate the accumulated depreciation of the equipment sold during the year.

Solution

(a) Determine the accumulated depreciation on the equipment sold:

Accumulated Depreciation – Equipment

Sale of equipment ?	47,000	Opening balance
	31,000	Depreciation expense for the period
	62,000	Ending balance

Accumulated depreciation on equipment sold = $47,000 (opening accumulated depreciation balance) + $31,000 (depreciation expense) − $62,000 (ending accumulated depreciation balance) = $16,000
So accumulated depreciation on the equipment sold = $16,000

(continued)

| BEFORE YOU GO ON...DO IT | Cash from Investing and Financing Activities *(continued)* |

Next, determine the cash proceeds on the equipment sold:

Original cost of equipment	$21,000
Less: Accumulated depreciation	(16,000) (from above)
Carrying amount	5,000
Cash proceeds	?
Gain on sale of equipment	$ 1,000

Because there was a gain on the sale of the equipment, the proceeds were greater than the carrying amount. Therefore, proceeds were $6,000 ($1,000 + $5,000).

(b)

Equipment

Opening balance	146,000		
Equipment purchased	?	21,000	Disposed
Ending balance	135,000		

Cost of equipment purchased = $146,000 (opening equipment balance) − $21,000 (cost of equipment sold) − $135,000 (ending equipment balance) = $10,000

Therefore, $10,000 of equipment was purchased.

Related exercise material: BE17–8, BE17–9, BE17–10, BE17–11, BE17-12, E17–7, and E17–8.

- Calculate the carrying amount of the equipment sold. Remember that the carrying amount is equal to the cost of the equipment sold less the accumulated depreciation on the equipment sold.
- Calculate the cash proceeds on the sale of the equipment. Because there is a gain on the sale, the equipment sold for more than its carrying amount. Therefore, add the gain on sale to the carrying amount to determine the cash proceeds.
- Prepare a T account for Equipment and record the beginning and ending balances and the cost of the equipment sold. Use this information to calculate the cost of the equipment purchased.

Step 4: The Cash Flow Statement

Prepare the Cash Flow Statement and Determine the Net Increase (Decrease) in Cash

The final step is to calculate the overall net increase or decrease in cash for the year by adding cash provided or used in each of the three sections of the cash flow statement. Computer Services' net increase in cash of $22,000 is calculated as follows:

Net cash provided by operating activities	$172,000
Net cash used by investing activities	(141,000)
Net cash used by financing activities	(9,000)
Net increase in cash	$ 22,000

The $22,000 net increase in cash is then added to cash at the beginning of the year of $33,000 to equal $55,000 of cash at the end of the year. This number is compared with the cash account balance in the year-end balance sheet, which also shows that cash is $55,000 at the end of the year. This is known as proving the cash balance. If cash at the end of the year on the cash flow statement is not equal to cash on the balance sheet, there is an error in the cash flow statement, which will need to be found and corrected.

Using this information and the partial cash flow statements shown in Illustrations 17-9, 17-10, and 17-12, we can now present a complete cash flow statement for Computer Services Corporation using the indirect method of preparing the operating activities section in Illustration 17-13.

▶ ILLUSTRATION 17-13
Cash flow statement—
indirect method

COMPUTER SERVICES CORPORATION
Cash Flow Statement
Year Ended December 31, 2017

Operating activities		
Profit		$145,000
Adjustments to reconcile profit to net cash		
provided (used) by operating activities:		
Depreciation expense	$ 9,000	
Loss on sale of equipment	3,000	
Decrease in accounts receivable	10,000	
Increase in inventory	(5,000)	
Increase in prepaid expenses	(4,000)	
Increase in accounts payable	16,000	
Decrease in income tax payable	(2,000)	27,000
Net cash provided by operating activities		172,000
Investing activities		
Purchase of building	$(120,000)	
Purchase of equipment	(25,000)	
Sale of equipment	4,000	
Net cash used by investing activities		(141,000)
Financing activities		
Issue of common shares	$ 20,000	
Payment of cash dividend	(29,000)	
Net cash used by financing activities		(9,000)
Net increase in cash		22,000
Cash, January 1		33,000
Cash, December 31		$ 55,000

Note x: Significant noncash investing and financing activities:
Issue of bonds to purchase land $110,000

BEFORE YOU GO ON...DO IT **2c** ▷ **Indirect Method**

Selected information follows for Reynolds Ltd. at December 31. Prepare a cash flow statement using the indirect method.

	2017	2016	Increase (Decrease)
Cash	$ 54,000	$ 37,000	$ 17,000
Property, plant, and equipment			
Land	45,000	70,000	(25,000)
Buildings	200,000	200,000	0
Accumulated depreciation—buildings	(21,000)	(11,000)	10,000
Equipment	193,000	68,000	125,000
Accumulated depreciation—equipment	(28,000)	(10,000)	18,000
Long-term liabilities and shareholders' equity			
Bonds payable	110,000	150,000	(40,000)
Common shares	220,000	60,000	160,000
Retained earnings	206,000	136,000	70,000

Additional information:

1. Cash provided from operating activities was $59,000.
2. Equipment was bought for cash. Equipment with a cost of $41,000 and a carrying amount of $36,000 was sold at a loss of $2,000.
3. Bonds of $40,000 were redeemed at their face value for cash.
4. Profit was $125,000 and a cash dividend was paid.

(continued)

BEFORE YOU GO ON...DO IT **Indirect Method** *(continued)*

Solution

REYNOLDS LTD.		
Cash Flow Statement		
Year Ended December 31, 2017		

Operating activities		
Net cash provided by operating activities		$ 59,000
Investing activities		
Sale of land	$ 25,000	
Sale of equipment	34,000[1]	
Purchase of equipment	(166,000)[2]	
Net cash used by investing activities		(107,000)
Financing activities		
Redemption of bonds	$ (40,000)	
Issue of common shares	160,000	
Payment of dividends	(55,000)[3]	
Net cash provided by financing activities		65,000
Net increase in cash		17,000
Cash, January 1		37,000
Cash, December 31		$ 54,000

[1]Sale of equipment: $36,000 (carrying amount) − $2,000 (loss) = $34,000
[2]Purchase of equipment: $68,000 (opening Equipment balance) − $41,000 (cost of equipment sold) − $193,000 (ending Equipment balance) = $166,000 (purchase of equipment)
[3]Payment of dividends: $136,000 (opening Retained Earnings) + $125,000 (profit) − $206,000 (ending Retained Earnings) = $55,000 (Dividends)

Related exercise material: E17-9, E17–11, and E17–18.

Action Plan

- Determine the net cash provided (used) by investing activities. Investing activities generally relate to changes in long-term asset accounts.
- Determine the net cash provided (used) by financing activities. Financing activities generally relate to changes in long-term liability and shareholders' equity accounts.
- Determine the net increase (decrease) in cash and add it to the beginning-of-period cash. Verify that this amount agrees with the end-of-period cash balance reported on the balance sheet.

LEARNING OBJECTIVE		**Prepare the operating section of the cash flow statement using the direct method.**

DIRECT METHOD

As mentioned earlier in the chapter, the operating section of the cash flow statement can be prepared using either the indirect or direct method. By reporting cash receipts and payments, the direct method provides information that is useful to investors and creditors in predicting future cash flows that is not available under the indirect method.

The difference between the cash receipts and cash payments is the net cash provided (used) by operating activities. These relationships are shown in Illustration 17-14.

Under the direct method, net cash provided (used) by operating activities is calculated by adjusting each individual revenue and expense item in the income statement from the accrual basis to the cash basis. We will start by determining cash receipts.

Helpful hint In the indirect method, profit is adjusted to determine cash provided (used) by operating activities. In the direct method, each revenue and expense is adjusted to determine cash receipts and cash payments for operating activities.

Cash Receipts

Computer Services has only one source of cash receipts: its customers.

Cash Receipts from Customers. The income statement for Computer Services reported sales revenue from customers of $507,000. How much of that was cash receipts? To answer that, a company considers the change in accounts receivable during the year. When accounts receivable increase during the year, revenues on an accrual basis are higher than cash receipts from customers. Operations lead to revenues, but not all of those revenues result in cash receipts. To determine the amount of cash receipts, a company deducts the increase in accounts receivable from sales revenue.

▶ **ILLUSTRATION 17-14**
Major classes of operating cash receipts and payments

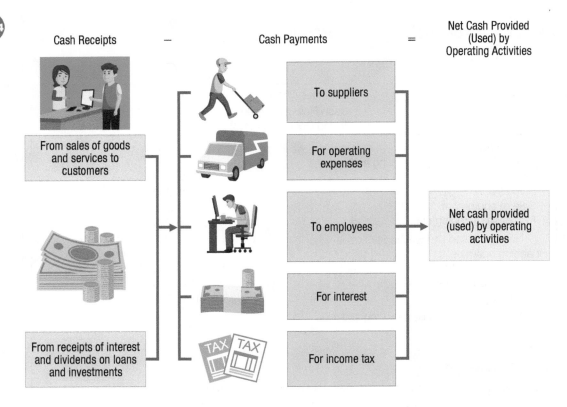

On the other hand, there may be a decrease in accounts receivable. That would occur if cash receipts from customers exceeded sales revenue. In that case, a company adds the decrease in accounts receivable to sales revenue. For Computer Services, accounts receivable decreased by $10,000. Thus, cash receipts from customers were $517,000, calculated as shown in Illustration 17-15.

▶ **ILLUSTRATION 17-15**
Calculation of cash receipts from customers

Sales revenue	$507,000
Add: Decrease in accounts receivable	10,000
Cash receipts from customers	**$517,000**

Helpful hint The T account shows that sales revenue plus decrease in accounts receivable equals cash receipts.

Computer Services can also determine the cash receipts from customers by analyzing the Accounts Receivable account as shown in Illustration 17-16.

▶ **ILLUSTRATION 17-16**
Analysis of Accounts Receivable

Accounts Receivable			
Jan. 1 Balance	30,000	Receipts from customers	517,000
Sales revenue	507,000		
Dec. 31 Balance	20,000		

Illustration 17-17 shows the relationships among cash receipts from customers, sales revenue, and changes in accounts receivable.

▶ **ILLUSTRATION 17-17**
Formula to calculate cash receipts from customers—direct method

Cash Receipts from Customers	=	Sales Revenue	{	+ Decrease in Accounts Receivable
				or
				− Increase in Accounts Receivable

Cash Receipts from Interest and Dividends. Computer Services does not have cash receipts from any source other than customers. If an income statement reports other revenues, such as interest and/or dividend revenue, these amounts must be adjusted for any accrued amounts receivable to determine the actual cash receipts. Decreases in accrued receivable accounts would be added to accrual-based revenues.

Cash Payments

Computer Services has many sources of cash payments: to suppliers and for operating expenses, interest, and income taxes. We will analyze each of these in the next sections.

Cash Payments to Suppliers. Computer Services reported cost of goods sold of $150,000 on its income statement. But how much cash was paid to suppliers? To answer that, we must first find purchases for the year. To find purchases, a company adjusts cost of goods sold for the change in inventory. When inventory increases during the year, purchases for the year have exceeded cost of goods sold. As a result, to determine the amount of purchases, a company adds the increase in inventory to cost of goods sold.

In 2017, Computer Services' inventory increased by $5,000. It calculates purchases as shown in Illustration 17-18.

Cost of goods sold	$150,000
Add: Increase in inventory	5,000
Purchases	$155,000

▶ ILLUSTRATION **17-18**
Calculation of purchases

Computer Services can also determine purchases from an analysis of the Inventory account, as shown in Illustration 17-19.

Inventory				
Jan. 1 Balance		10,000	Cost of goods sold	150,000
Purchases		155,000		
Dec. 31 Balance		15,000		

▶ ILLUSTRATION **17-19**
Analysis of Inventory account

After calculating purchases, a company can determine cash payments to suppliers. This is done by adjusting purchases for the change in accounts payable. When accounts payable increase during the year, purchases on an accrual basis are higher than they are on a cash basis. As a result, to determine cash payments to suppliers, a company deducts the increase in accounts payable from purchases.

On the other hand, if cash payments to suppliers exceed purchases, there will be a decrease in accounts payable. In that case, a company adds the decrease in accounts payable to purchases. For Computer Services, cash payments to suppliers were $139,000, calculated as shown in Illustration 17-20.

Purchases	$155,000
Deduct: Increase in accounts payable	16,000
Cash payments to suppliers	$139,000

▶ ILLUSTRATION **17-20**
Calculation of cash payments to suppliers

Computer Services also can determine cash payments to suppliers from an analysis of the Accounts Payable account, as shown in Illustrations 17-21 and 17-22.

Accounts Payable					
Payments to suppliers		139,000	Jan. 1	Balance	12,000
				Purchases	155,000
			Dec. 31	Balance	28,000

▶ ILLUSTRATION **17-21**
Analysis of Accounts Payable

▶ **ILLUSTRATION** 17-22
Formula to calculate cash payments to suppliers—direct method

Illustration 17-22 shows the relationships among cash payments to suppliers, cost of goods sold, changes in inventory, and changes in Accounts Payable.

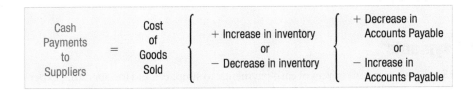

Cash Payments for Operating Expenses. Computer Services reported $111,000 of operating expenses in its income statement. This means that profit decreased by $111,000, but what was the amount of cash paid for operating expenses? To answer that, we need to adjust this amount for any changes in prepaid expenses and accrued expenses payable. For example, if prepaid expenses increased during the year, cash paid for operating expenses is higher than operating expenses reported on the income statement. To convert operating expenses to cash payments for operating expenses, a company adds the increase in prepaid expenses to operating expenses. On the other hand, if prepaid expenses decrease during the year, it deducts the decrease from operating expenses.

Companies must also adjust operating expenses for changes in accrued expenses payable. When accrued expenses payable increase during the year, operating expenses on an accrual basis are higher than they are on a cash basis. As a result, to determine cash payments for operating expenses, a company deducts an increase in accrued expenses payable from operating expenses. On the other hand, a company adds a decrease in accrued expenses payable to operating expenses because cash payments exceed operating expenses. Computer Services' cash payments for operating expenses were $115,000, calculated as shown in Illustration 17-23.

▶ **ILLUSTRATION** 17-23
Calculation of cash payments for operating expenses

Operating expenses	$111,000
Add: Increase in prepaid expenses	4,000
Cash payments for operating expenses	**$115,000**

Illustration 17-24 shows the relationships among cash payments for operating expenses, changes in prepaid expenses, and changes in accrued expenses payable.

▶ **ILLUSTRATION** 17-24
Formula to calculate cash payments for operating expenses—direct method

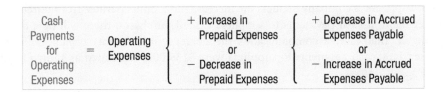

You may be wondering how depreciation is treated under the direct method. **Depreciation expense is not shown on a statement of cash flows under the direct method because it is a noncash charge.** However, if the amount for operating expenses includes depreciation expense, operating expenses must be reduced by the amount of depreciation to determine cash payments for operating expenses.

Likewise, recall that Computer Services incurred a loss on the disposal of equipment of $3,000. This is also a noncash charge—it reduces profit, but it does not reduce cash. **Thus, the loss on disposal of equipment is not shown on the statement of cash flows under the direct method.**

Other charges to expense that do not require the use of cash, such as the amortization of intangible assets, depletion expense, and bad debt expense, are treated in the same manner as depreciation.

Cash Payments to Employees. Companies may report payments to employees separately from operating expenses. To determine payments to employees, you would have to know the salary expense amount on the income statement and any salaries payable on the comparative balance sheets. Cash payments to employees, reported on the cash flow statement, would equal the salary expense, plus any decrease (or less any increase) during the period in salaries payable.

Cash Payments for Interest. Computer Services reported interest expense of $42,000 on the income statement. Because the balance sheet did not include an accrual for interest payable for 2016 or 2017, the amount reported as expense is the same as the amount of interest paid.

If the comparative balance sheets reported interest payable, cash payments for interest would be calculated by adding a decrease in interest payable to interest expense or deducting an increase in interest payable to interest expense.

Cash Payments for Income Taxes. Computer Services reported income tax expense of $47,000 on the income statement. Income tax payable, however, decreased by $2,000. This decrease means that income taxes paid were more than income taxes reported in the income statement. Cash payments for income taxes were therefore $49,000, as shown in Illustration 17-25.

Income tax expense	$47,000
Add: Decrease in income tax payable	2,000
Cash payments for income taxes	**$49,000**

▶ **ILLUSTRATION 17-25**
Calculation of cash payments for income taxes

Computer Services can also determine cash payments for income taxes from an analysis of the Income Tax Payable account, as shown in Illustration 17-26.

Income Tax Payable

Cash payments for income taxes	49,000	Jan. 1	Balance	8,000
			Income tax expense	47,000
		Dec. 31	Balance	6,000

▶ **ILLUSTRATION 17-26**
Analysis of Income Tax Payable account

Illustration 17-27 shows the relationships among cash payments for income taxes, income tax expense, and changes in income tax payable.

$$\text{Cash Payments for Income Taxes} = \text{Income Tax Expense} \left\{ \begin{array}{l} + \text{ Decrease in Income Tax Payable} \\ \text{or} \\ - \text{ Increase in Income Tax Payable} \end{array} \right.$$

▶ **ILLUSTRATION 17-27**
Formula to calculate cash payments for income taxes

Helpful hint Note that in the operating activities section, positive numbers indicate cash inflows (receipts) and negative numbers indicate cash outflows (payments). As well, whether the direct or indirect method is used, net cash provided (used) by operating activities will be the same.

All of the revenues and expenses in the Computer Services income statement have now been adjusted to a cash basis. This information is put together in Illustration 17-28, which shows the operating activities section of the cash flow statement using the direct method.

▶ **ILLUSTRATION 17-28**
Net cash provided by operating activities—direct method

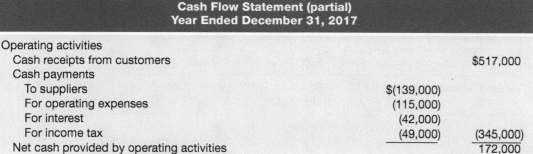

COMPUTER SERVICES CORPORATION
Cash Flow Statement (partial)
Year Ended December 31, 2017

Operating activities		
Cash receipts from customers		$517,000
Cash payments		
To suppliers	$(139,000)	
For operating expenses	(115,000)	
For interest	(42,000)	
For income tax	(49,000)	(345,000)
Net cash provided by operating activities		172,000

BEFORE YOU GO ON...DO IT   3   Direct Method

Action Plan

- Determine the net cash provided (used) by operating activities by adjusting each revenue and expense item for changes in the related current asset and current liability account.
- To adjust revenues for changes in related current asset and current liability accounts, add decreases in current asset accounts and increases in current liability accounts. Deduct increases in current asset accounts and decreases in current liability accounts.
- To adjust expenses for changes in related current asset and current liability accounts, add increases in current asset accounts and decreases in current liability accounts. Deduct decreases in current asset accounts and increases in current liability accounts.
- Assume that the accounts payable relate to suppliers and that the accrued expenses payable relate to operating expenses.
- Report cash receipts and cash payments by major sources and uses: cash receipts from customers and cash payments to suppliers, for operating expenses, to employees, for interest, and for income taxes

Selected financial information follows for Reynolds Ltd. at December 31. Prepare the operating activities section of the cash flow statement using the direct method.

	2017	2016	Increase (Decrease)
Current assets			
Cash	$54,000	$37,000	$17,000
Accounts receivable	68,000	26,000	42,000
Inventory	54,000	10,000	44,000
Prepaid expenses	4,000	6,000	(2,000)
Current liabilities			
Accounts payable	23,000	50,000	(27,000)
Accrued expenses payable	10,000	0	10,000

REYNOLDS LTD.
Income Statement
Year Ended December 31, 2017

Sales revenue		$890,000
Cost of goods sold		465,000
Gross profit		425,000
Operating expenses	$188,000	
Depreciation expense	33,000	
Loss on sale of equipment	2,000	223,000
Profit from operations		202,000
Other expenses		
Interest expense		12,000
Profit before income tax		190,000
Income tax expense		65,000
Profit		$125,000

Solution

REYNOLDS LTD.
Cash Flow Statement (partial)
Year Ended December 31, 2017

Operating activities		
Cash receipts from customers		$848,000[1]
Cash payments		
To suppliers	$(536,000)[2]	
For operating expenses	(176,000)[3]	
For interest	(12,000)	
For income tax	(65,000)	(789,000)
Net cash provided by operating activities		59,000

Calculations:

[1] Cash receipts from customers: $890,000 − $42,000 = $848,000
[2] Payments to suppliers: $465,000 + $44,000 + $27,000 = $536,000
[3] Payments for operating expenses: $188,000 − $2,000 − $10,000 = $176,000

Related exercise material: BE17–13, BE17–14, BE17–15, BE17–16, BE17–17, BE17–18, E17–12, E17–13, E17–14, E17–15, E17–16, and E17–17.

Using the Information in the Financial Statements

The cash flow statement gives information about a company's financial health that cannot be found in the other financial statements. None of the other financial statements give enough information for decision-making by themselves. The income statement; statements of comprehensive income, retained earnings, and changes in shareholders' equity; and the balance sheet must be read along with the cash flow statement in order to fully understand a company's financial situation.

For example, the income statement might show a profitable company. However, a rapidly growing company might also find it difficult to pay its current liabilities because its cash is being used to finance its growth. Both successful and unsuccessful companies can have problems with cash flow. The sustainability of a business is linked to its ability to generate cash. Most entities consider cash flows generated from operations as a key indicator of the company's health.

Consider the condensed income and cash flow data shown below for three different companies, each operating in the same industry.

	Company A	Company B	Company C
Profit (loss)	$ 75,000	$ 25,000	$(50,000)
Cash provided (used) by operating activities	$100,000	$(25,000)	$(25,000)
Cash provided (used) by investing activities	(50,000)	(25,000)	35,000
Cash provided (used) by financing activities	(25,000)	75,000	15,000
Net increase in cash	$ 25,000	$ 25,000	$ 25,000

In this example, we have assumed that each company has the same change in cash, an increase of $25,000. However, the increase in cash is generated differently by each company.

Company A reports profit of $75,000 and a positive cash flow from operating activities of $100,000. How can Company A's cash provided by operating activities be higher than its profit? This could occur in any of these three situations, if it has:

1. noncash expenses such as depreciation,
2. reduced current assets such as receivables or inventory, or
3. increased current liabilities such as accounts payable.

Depending on which of the situations created Company A's higher cash flow from operating activities, there could be different implications. For example, if receivables are lower, this could be because the company is collecting them faster. If so, this is a good thing. Alternatively, receivables could have decreased because sales decreased. This is not good, and has implications for future profitability.

For now, we know that Company A's operating activities produced a positive cash flow of $100,000, which allowed it to invest $50,000 in its long-lived assets and repay $25,000 of its debt and/or pay dividends. Based only on this information, Company A appears to be in a strong financial position.

Company B also produced a positive profit, but used up $25,000 of cash in its operating activities. How could Company B's profit result in a negative operating cash flow? Company B may be in the early stages of its development. It may have quickly increased receivables and inventories. It ended up with the same increase in the cash balance as Company A only because it borrowed money. If Company B is indeed a new and rapidly growing company, this is fine. If not, this type of cash flow pattern would not be sustainable in the long run.

Assuming Company B is a start-up company, its cash flow figures appear to be reasonable. For example, early in its operations, during its growth stage, a company would be expected to generate a small amount of profit (or a loss) and negative cash from its operating activities. It will likely also be spending large amounts to purchase productive assets, and will finance these purchases by issuing debt or equity securities. Thus, during its early years, cash from operating and investing activities will likely be negative, while cash from financing activities will be positive.

Company C, which reported both a loss and a negative cash flow from operating activities, is able to produce a positive change in cash only by selling long-lived assets and borrowing additional debt. A company that generates cash mainly from investing activities is usually in a downsizing or restructuring situation. This is fine if the assets being disposed of are unnecessary or unprofitable. However, if the company is in a position where it must sell off income-producing assets to generate cash, then this will affect future revenue and profitability.

As you can see from the above example, analyzing cash flows from different activities along with the information in the other financial statements can provide significant information about a company's overall financial health and activities.

FREE CASH FLOW

Another way of evaluating cash flows is to determine how much discretionary cash flow a company has—in other words, how much cash it has available to expand, repay debt, pay dividends, or do whatever it best determines. This discretionary cash flow is a measure of solvency known as "free cash flow."

Free cash flow describes the cash remaining from operating activities after making cash outlays for capital expenditures. Using net cash provided by operating activities as a proxy for free cash flow is not enough because it does not take into account the fact that a company must invest in new assets, such as property, plant, and equipment, to maintain its current level of operations. However, the cash flow statement rarely separates investing activities into those required for maintenance and those used for expansion. So we are often forced to use the net cash used by investing activities rather than capital expenditures incurred to maintain productive capacity when calculating free cash flow.

To calculate free cash flow, the net cash used for investing activities is deducted from the net cash provided by operating activities. Illustration 17-29 uses data from Corus's cash flow statement (in thousands) to illustrate the calculation of free cash flow.

▶ILLUSTRATION **17-29**
Free cash flow

Cash Provided (Used) by Operating Activities	−	Cash Used (Provided) by Investing Activities	=	Free Cash Flow
$194,477	−	$526,246	=	−$331,769

Corus has negative free cash flow of $331,769 thousand. The cash Corus produced from operating activities was less than the amount needed to cover its current year's investing activities. Some of the significant investments include, $497,393 spent to invest in expansion and $11,976 spent to either maintain its existing productive capacity, to expand, or for both purposes.

ACCOUNTING IN ACTION
ETHICS INSIGHT

Radu Razvan/iStockphoto

While investors tend to view the cash flow statement as a true picture of a company's financial situation, some advisors say it can be manipulated to make things look better. Among other things, management can misclassify cash into operating, investing, and financing activities. That is what allegedly happened with Sino-Forest Corp., a Chinese-based forestry company with an office in Canada. When the company acquired timber in China, it recorded the purchases on the cash flow statement as cash used in investing activities. After selling the timber, Sino-Forest treated the sales revenue as cash provided by operating

activities. As a result, the cash flow statement showed cash inflow from the sale of timber in its operating activities and cash outflow for the purchase of the timber in its investing activities—allegedly overstating cash from operations by excluding the cost of timber sold. Most companies record such purchases as an outflow of cash from operating activities. In 2012, Sino-Forest sought bankruptcy protection and put itself up for sale. In late 2014, the Ontario Securities Commission held a hearing into allegations that Sino-Forest had committed fraud, which the company denied. At the time of writing, the hearing outcome had not been announced.

Sources: Janet McFarland and Jeff Gray, "Sino-Forest Fraud Result of 'Deceitful Conduct' by Management, Hearing Told," *The Globe and Mail*, September 2, 2014; Jeff Gray and Andy Hoffman, "Report Alleges Possibility Sino-Forest 'An Accounting Fiction,'" *The Globe and Mail*, July 18, 2012; Charmaine Noronha, "Timber Company Sino-Forest Files for Bankruptcy in Ontario Court," Associated Press, *The China Post*, April 1, 2012; Al Rosen and Mark Rosen, "Don't Be Suckered by Cash Flow Statements," Advisor.ca, August 1, 2011.

 Q Why would management of a company want to overstate cash flow from operating activities?

BEFORE YOU GO ON...DO IT 4 **Free Cash Flow**

Speyside Inc. reported the following information:

	2017	2016
Profit (loss)	$50,000	$(5,000)
Cash provided (used) by operating activities	25,000	(10,000)
Cash provided (used) by investing activities	(10,000)	(70,000)
Cash provided (used) by financing activities	(8,000)	100,000

Calculate free cash flow for each of the years and comment on Speyside's stage of development in 2017 and 2016.

Solution

	2017	2016
Free cash flow	$15,000 = $25,000 − $10,000	$(80,000) = $(10,000) + $(70,000)

Speyside had negative free cash flow in 2016 and its cash was provided through its financing activities, indicating the company may have been in the start-up phase of its development. In 2017, the company had positive free cash flow and was profitable, indicating that the company was able to start generating profit and cash from its operations, continue to invest, and have cash available to reduce financing or pay dividends.

Related exercise material: BE17–19, BE17-20, E17–19, and E17–20.

Action Plan
- Calculate the free cash flow by deducting cash provided (used) by investing activities from cash provided (used) by operating activities.

Comparing IFRS and ASPE

Key Differences	International Financial Reporting Standards (IFRS)	Accounting Standards for Private Enterprises (ASPE)
Classification of interest and dividends	Interest and dividends received may be classified as operating or investing activities.	Interest and dividends received are classified as operating activities.
	Interest and dividends paid may be classified as operating or financing activities.	Interest paid is classified as an operating activity. Dividends paid are classified as a financing activity.
	Once the choice is made, it must be applied consistently.	

Demonstration Problem

The income statement for the year ended December 31, 2017, for Kosinski Manufacturing Ltd. contains the following condensed information:

KOSINSKI MANUFACTURING LTD. Income Statement Year Ended December 31, 2017		
Sales		$6,583,000
Cost of goods sold		3,572,000
Gross profit		3,011,000
Operating expenses	$2,289,000	
Gain on sale of equipment	(24,000)	2,265,000
Profit from operations		746,000
Other expenses		
Interest expense		85,000
Profit before income tax		661,000
Income tax expense		298,000
Profit		$ 363,000

Kosinski's comparative balance sheet at December 31 contained the following account balances:

	2017	2016
Cash	$ 204,500	$ 180,000
Accounts receivable	775,000	610,000
Inventory	834,000	917,000
Prepaid expenses	29,000	25,000
Equipment	6,906,000	7,065,000
Accumulated depreciation—equipment	(2,497,000)	(2,355,000)
Total assets	$6,251,500	$6,442,000
Accounts payable	$ 517,000	$ 601,000
Interest payable	6,000	0
Income taxes payable	24,500	20,000
Dividends payable	5,000	10,000
Long-term notes payable	1,500,000	2,000,000
Common shares	3,075,000	3,000,000
Retained earnings	1,124,000	811,000
Total liabilities and shareholders' equity	$6,251,500	$6,442,000

Additional information:

1. Operating expenses include depreciation expense of $880,000.
2. Accounts payable relate to the purchase of inventory.
3. Equipment that cost $984,000 was sold at a gain of $24,000.
4. New equipment was purchased during the year for $825,000.
5. Dividends declared in 2017 totalled $50,000.
6. Common shares were sold for $75,000 cash.

Instructions
Prepare the cash flow statement using either (a) the indirect method or (b) the direct method, as assigned by your instructor.

SOLUTION TO DEMONSTRATION PROBLEM

(a) Indirect method

KOSINSKI MANUFACTURING LTD.
Cash Flow Statement
Year Ended December 31, 2017

Operating activities		
Profit		$ 363,000
Adjustments to reconcile profit to net cash		
provided by operating activities:		
Depreciation expense	$ 880,000	
Gain on sale of equipment	(24,000)	
Increase in accounts receivable	(165,000)	
Decrease in inventory	83,000	
Increase in prepaid expenses	(4,000)	
Decrease in accounts payable	(84,000)	
Increase in interest payable	6,000	
Increase in income taxes payable	4,500	696,500
Net cash provided by operating activities		1,059,500
Investing activities		
Sale of equipment	270,000	
Purchase of equipment	(825,000)	
Net cash used by investing activities		(555,000)
Financing activities		
Repayment of notes payable ($2,000,000 − $1,500,000)	(500,000)	
Issue of common shares	75,000	
Payment of cash dividends ($50,000 + $10,000 − $5,000)	(55,000)	
Net cash used by financing activities		(480,000)
Net increase in cash		24,500
Cash, January 1		180,000
Cash, December 31		$ 204,500

Calculations:

Accumulated depreciation on machinery sold: $2,355,000 (accumulated depreciation beginning) + $880,000 (depreciation expense) − $2,497,000 (accumulated depreciation ending) = $738,000

Carrying amount of machinery sold: $984,000 (cost of equipment sold) − $738,000 (accumulated depreciation) = $246,000

Proceeds on sale: $246,000 (carrying amount) + $24,000 (gain) = $270,000

(b) Direct method

KOSINSKI MANUFACTURING LTD.
Cash Flow Statement
Year Ended December 31, 2017

Operating activities		
Cash receipts from customers		$6,418,000[1]
Cash payments		
To suppliers	$(3,573,000)[2]	
For operating expenses	(1,413,000)[3]	
For interest	(79,000)[4]	
For income tax	(293,500)[5]	(5,358,500)
Net cash provided by operating activities		1,059,500

ACTION PLAN

- Determine the net cash provided (used) by operating activities. Operating activities generally relate to revenues and expenses shown on the income statement, which are affected by changes in related noncash current assets and current liabilities in the balance sheet, and noncash items in the income statement. In the indirect method, convert profit from an accrual basis to a cash basis. In the direct method, convert each revenue and expense from an accrual basis to a cash basis.
- Determine the net cash provided (used) by investing activities. Investing activities generally relate to changes in long-term assets.
- Determine the proceeds on sale of equipment by analyzing the Accumulated Depreciation account to determine the accumulated depreciation on the asset sold. Then calculate the carrying amount, which is then added to the gain to determine proceeds.
- Determine the net cash provided (used) by financing activities. Financing activities generally relate to changes in long-term liability and shareholders' equity accounts.
- Dividends paid are equal to dividends declared plus a decrease in dividends payable or minus an increase in dividends payable.
- Determine the net increase (decrease) in cash and add it to the beginning-of-period cash balance. Verify that this amount agrees with the end-of-period cash balance reported on the balance sheet.
- Note the similarities and differences between the indirect and direct methods: both methods report the same total amount of cash provided (used) by operating activities but report different detail in this section. The information in the investing and financing sections is the same in both methods.

Investing activities		
Sale of machinery	270,000	
Purchase of machinery	(825,000)	
Net cash used by investing activities		(555,000)
Financing activities		
Repayment of note payable	(500,000)	
Issue of common shares	75,000	
Payment of cash dividends	(55,000)	
Net cash used by financing activities		(480,000)
Net increase in cash		24,500
Cash, January		180,000
Cash, December 31		$ 204,500

Calculations:
[1]Cash receipts from customers: $6,583,000 (sales) − $165,000 = $6,418,000
[2]$3,572,000 − $83,000 + $84,000 = $3,573,000
[3]$2,289,000 − $880,000 + $4,000 = $1,413,000
[4]$85,000 − $6,000 = $79,000
[5]$298,000 − $4,500 = $293,500

▶ Summary of Learning Objectives

1. **Discuss the usefulness, content, and format of the cash flow statement.** The cash flow statement gives information about the cash receipts and cash payments resulting from a company's operating, investing, and financing activities during the period.

     In general, operating activities include the cash effects of transactions that affect profit. Investing activities generally include cash flows resulting from changes in long-term asset items. Financing activities generally include cash flows resulting from changes in long-term liability and shareholders' equity items.

2. **Prepare a cash flow statement using the indirect method.** There are four steps to prepare a cash flow statement: (1) Determine the net cash provided (used) by operating activities. In the indirect method, this is done by converting profit from an accrual basis to a cash basis. (2) Analyze the changes in long-term asset accounts and record them as investing activities, or as significant noncash transactions. (3) Analyze the changes in long-term liability and equity accounts and record them as financing activities, or as significant noncash transactions. (4) Prepare the cash flow statement and determine the net increase or decrease in cash.

3. **Prepare the operating section of the cash flow statement using the direct method.** The operating section of the cash flow statement can be prepared using the direct method. The direct method is generally preferred by investors because it provides more detailed information as to the sources and uses of cash. While this method also converts profit from an accrual to a cash basis, it reports the cash receipts from customers, cash receipts from interest, dividends, and loans, as well as cash payments to suppliers, employees, interest, taxes, and operating expenses.

4. **Analyze the cash flow statement.** The cash flow statement must be read along with the other financial statements in order to adequately assess a company's financial position. In addition, it is important to understand how the net change in cash is affected by each type of activity—operating, investing, and financing—especially when different companies are being compared. Free cash flow is a measure of solvency: it indicates how much of the cash that was generated from operating activities during the current year is available after making necessary payments for capital expenditures. It is calculated by subtracting the cash used by investing activities from the cash provided by operating activities.

▶ Glossary

Cash flow statement   A financial statement that gives information about a company's cash receipts and cash payments during a period and classifies them as operating, investing, and financing activities. (p. 890)

Direct method   A method of determining the net cash provided (used) by operating activities by adjusting each item in the income statement from the accrual basis to the cash basis. (p. 893)

Financing activities   Cash flow activities from long-term liability and equity accounts. These include (a) obtaining cash by issuing debt and repaying the amounts borrowed, and (b) obtaining cash from shareholders and providing them with a return on their investment. (p. 891)

Free cash flow   Cash provided by operating activities less cash used by investing activities. (p. 920)

Indirect method   A method of preparing a cash flow statement in which profit is adjusted for items that did not affect cash, to determine net cash provided (used) by operating activities. (p. 893)

Investing activities   Cash flow activities from long-term asset accounts. These include (a) acquiring and disposing of investments and long-lived assets, and (b) lending money and collecting on those loans. (p. 891)

Operating activities   Cash flow activities that include the cash effects of transactions that create revenues and expenses, and thus affect profit. (p. 891)

▶ Self-Study Questions
Answers are at the end of the chapter.

(LO 1) K   1. The statement of cash flows classifies cash receipts and cash payments by these activities:
(a) operating and non-operating.
(b) investing, financing, and operating.
(c) financing, operating, and non-operating.
(d) investing, financing, and non-operating.

(LO 1) C   2. Which of the following is an example of a cash flow from an operating activity?
(a) A payment of cash for income tax
(b) A receipt of cash from the sale of common shares
(c) A payment of cash for the purchase of equipment used in operations
(d) A receipt of cash from the issue of a mortgage payable

(LO 1) C   3. Which of the following is an example of a cash flow from an investing activity?
(a) A receipt of cash from the issue of bonds
(b) A payment of cash to purchase common shares
(c) A receipt of cash from the sale of equipment
(d) The acquisition of land by issuing bonds

(LO 2) AP   4. A company had profit of $215,000. Depreciation expense is $27,000. During the year, Accounts Receivable increased by $25,000. Accounts Payable decreased by $2,000. Net cash provided by operating activities is:
(a) $213,000.
(b) $215,000.
(c) $267,000.
(d) $265,000.

(LO 2) C   5. It is necessary to make an adjustment for the gain or loss on a sale of a long-lived asset to determine cash provided (used) by operating activities under the indirect method because
(a) the sale of a long-lived asset is a financing activity, not an operating activity.
(b) the gain or loss is generally not recorded in the same period that cash is received from the sale of the long-lived asset.
(c) the gain or loss on the sale of a long-lived asset is the result of incorrectly recording depreciation expense over the life of the asset.
(d) the gain or loss is not equal to the cash proceeds received on the sale.

(LO 2) AP   6. Retained earnings were $197,000 at the beginning of the year and $386,500 at the end of the year. Profit was $200,000. Dividends payable were $2,000 at the beginning of the year and $2,500 at the end of the year. What amount should be reported in the financing activities section of the cash flow statement for dividend payments?
(a) $500
(b) $10,000
(c) $10,500
(d) $11,000

(LO 2) AP   7. The acquisition of land by issuing common shares is
(a) reported in the cash flow statement as both an investing and a financing transaction.
(b) a noncash transaction and would be reported in the cash flow statement only if using the indirect method.
(c) reported in the cash flow statement only if the statement is prepared using the direct method.
(d) an investing and financing transaction that is not reported in the cash flow statement because it is a noncash transaction.

(LO 3) AP   8. The beginning balance in Accounts Receivable is $44,000. The ending balance is $42,000. Sales during the period are $149,000. Cash receipts from customers are:
(a) $151,000.
(b) $149,000.
(c) $147,000.
(d) $107,000.

(LO 3) K   9. Which of the following items is reported on a statement of cash flows prepared by the direct method?
(a) Loss on disposal of building
(b) Increase in accounts receivable
(c) Depreciation expense
(d) Cash payments to suppliers

(LO 4) K   10. Free cash flow gives an indication of a company's ability to generate:
(a) sales.
(b) profit.
(c) cash for discretionary uses.
(d) cash for investments.

▶ Questions

(LO 1) C   1. What is a cash flow statement and how is it useful to investors and creditors?

(LO 1) K   2. How is cash generally defined for purposes of the cash flow statement?

(LO 1) C   3. Identify, and describe the differences among, the three types of activities reported in the cash flow statement. Give an example of each.

(LO 1) K   4. What are the general guidelines in terms of the classification of income statement and balance sheet items to operating, investing, and financing activities? Give an example of an exception to these guidelines.

(LO 2) C   5. What information is used in preparing the cash flow statement?

(LO 2) C   6. Explain why the increase or decrease in cash is not equal to the profit or loss reported in the income statement. How can a company's cash balance decrease when the company has earned profit? Conversely, how can cash increase when a company has incurred a loss?

(LO 2) C   7. Explain why increases in noncash current asset account balances are deducted from profit and increases in noncash current liability account balances are added to profit when determining cash provided (used) by operating activities using the indirect method.

(LO 2) C   8. Fresh Foods Inc. uses the indirect method to report cash provided from operating activities. Vijaya, the company president, argues, "Depreciation should not be reported as a cash inflow in the operating section of the cash flow statement, because it is not a cash flow." Is Vijaya correct? Explain why or why not.

(LO 2) C   9. Gail doesn't understand why losses are added and gains are deducted from profit when calculating cash provided (used) by operating activities in the indirect method. She argues that losses must be deducted and gains added because they are on the income statement. Explain to Gail why she is wrong.

(LO 3) C   10. Environmental Equipment Ltd. reported $500,000 of sales on its income statement and $475,000 of cash collected from customers on its cash flow statement. Provide reasons why cash collected from customers is not equal to the sales reported in the income statement.

(LO 3) C   11. Under the direct method, why is depreciation expense not reported in the operating activities section?

(LO 3) C   12. Contrast the advantages and disadvantages of the direct and indirect methods of preparing the cash flow statement. Are both methods acceptable? Which method is preferred by standard setters? Which method is more popular? Why?

(LO 2) C   13. Explain how the sale of equipment at a gain is reported on a cash flow statement. Do the same for the sale of equipment at a loss.

(LO 2) C   14. If a company reported cash dividends of $80,000 in its statement of changes in shareholders' equity, would this amount also be reported as a cash outflow in the cash flow statement? Explain why or why not.

(LO 4) C   15. In general, should a financially healthy, growing company be providing or using cash in each of the three activities in the cash flow statement? Explain why this would normally be expected.

(LO 4) C   16. How is it possible for a company to report positive net cash from operating activities but have a negative free cash flow?

▶ Brief Exercises

Indicate impact of transactions on cash. (LO 1) AP

BE17–1 For each of the following transactions, indicate whether it will increase (+), decrease (−), or have no effect (NE) on a company's cash flows:

(a) _____ Repayment of a mortgage payable

(b) _____ Sale of land for cash at a loss

(c) _____ Reacquisition of common shares

(d) _____ Purchase of equipment

(e) _____ Acquisition of equipment by an issue of common shares

(f) _____ Issuing preferred shares for cash

(g) _____ Collection of accounts receivable

(h) _____ Recording depreciation expense

(i) _____ Declaring cash dividends

Classify transactions by activity. (LO 1) C

BE17–2 Classify each of the transactions listed in BE17–1 as an operating (O), investing (I), financing (F), or significant noncash investing and financing activity (NC). If a transaction does not belong in any of these classifications, explain why.

Indicate impact on cash from operating activities—indirect method. (LO 2) AP

BE17–3 Indicate whether each of the following transactions would be added to (+) or subtracted from (−) profit in determining the cash provided (used) by operating activities using the indirect method:

(a) _____ Depreciation expense

(b) _____ Increase in accounts receivable

(c) _____ Decrease in inventory

(d) _____ Decrease in accounts payable

(e) _____ Increase in income tax payable

(f) _____ Loss on sale of equipment

(g) _____ Impairment loss for goodwill

(h) _____ Decrease in prepaid insurance

BE17-4   Diamond Ltd. reported profit of $850,000 for the year ended November 30, 2017. Depreciation expense for the year was $175,000, Accounts Receivable increased by $80,000, Prepaid Expenses decreased by $35,000, and Accounts Payable increased by $170,000. Calculate the net cash provided (used) by operating activities using the indirect method.

Calculate cash from operating activities—indirect method. (LO 2) AP

BE17-5   The comparative balance sheets for Montalvo Company show these changes in noncash current asset accounts: Accounts Receivable decreased $80,000, Prepaid Expenses increased $28,000, and Inventory increased $30,000. Calculate net cash provided by operating activities using the indirect method assuming that profit is $300,000 for the year ended May 31, 2017.

Calculate cash from operating activities—indirect method. (LO 2) AP

BE17-6   The comparative balance sheets for Chas Company show these changes in noncash current accounts: Accounts Receivable increased $35,500, Prepaid Expenses decreased $12,800, and Inventory decreased $22,500. Accounts Payable increased $16,000. Calculate net cash provided by operating activities using the indirect method assuming that profit is $300,000 for the year ended June 30, 2017. Depreciation expense for the year was $32,000 and the company incurred a gain on sale of equipment of $25,000.

Calculate cash from operating activities—indirect method. (LO 2) AP

BE17-7   Mirzaei Ltd. reported the following information in its balance sheet and income statement for the year ended March 31, 2017:

Calculate cash from operating activities—indirect method. (LO 2) AP

	2017	2016
Accounts receivable	$60,000	$40,000
Inventory	63,000	70,000
Prepaid expenses	4,000	2,000
Accounts payable	35,000	40,000
Income tax payable	16,000	10,000
Depreciation expense	50,000	
Gain on sale of equipment	45,200	
Profit	330,000	

Calculate the net cash provided (used) by operating actitvities using the indirect method.

BE17-8   The T accounts for equipment and the related accumulated depreciation for Trevis Corporation are as follows:

Determine cash received from sale of equipment. (LO 2) AP

Equipment				Accumulated Depreciation—Equipment			
Beg. bal.	80,000					Beg. bal.	44,500
Purchases	41,600	Disposals	24,000	Disposals	5,500	Depreciation	12,000
End. bal.	97,600					End. bal.	51,000

In addition, Trevis's income statement reported a loss on the sale of equipment of $1,500. What will be reported on the cash flow statement with regard to the sale of equipment if Trevis uses the indirect method?

BE17-9   The Retained Earnings account for Luo Company at the end of 2017 is shown here:

Determine dividends declared. (LO 2) AP

Retained Earnings			
Cash Dividends Paid?		Opening balance	27,500
		Profit	43,400
		Ending balance	63,200

What amount was reported on the cash flow statement as "cash dividends paid" assuming there was no balance at the beginning or end of the year in the Dividends Payable account.

BE17-10   Selected information follows for Cathrea Select Corporation at December 31:

Prepare the investing activities section of the cash flow statement. (LO 2) AP

	2017	2016
Land	$ 95,000	$180,000
Buildings	250,000	250,000
Accumulated depreciation—buildings	(55,000)	(45,000)
Equipment	237,000	148,000
Accumulated depreciation—equipment	(86,000)	(78,000)

Additional information:

1. Land was sold for cash at a gain of $35,000.
2. Equipment was bought for cash.

Prepare the investing activities section of the cash flow statement.

Determine dividends paid.
(LO 2) AP

BE17–11 The following was reported in Sanaz Ltd.'s 2017 financial statements:

	2017	2016
Dividends payable	$ 24,000	$ 20,000
Retained earnings	261,000	114,000
Profit	197,000	

Calculate cash payments for dividends.

Prepare the financing activities section of the cash flow statement. (LO 2) AP

BE17–12 Selected information follows for Cathrea Select Corporation at December 31:

	2017	2016
Bonds payable	$995,000	$995,000
Mortgage notes payable	475,000	200,000
Common shares	55,000	45,000
Retained earnings	165,000	85,000

Additional information:

1. Principal payments on the mortgage payable were $25,000.
2. A building was purchased for $500,000 by paying $200,000 cash and signing a mortgage note payable for the balance.
3. Profit for the year was $145,000.

Assuming the company reports under ASPE and all dividends have been paid, prepare the financing activities section of the cash flow statement.

Calculate cash received from customers—direct method.
(LO 3) AP

BE17–13 Westcoast Corporation reported the following in its December 31, 2017, financial statements.

	2017	2016
Accounts receivable balance, December 31	$123,850	$137,500
Sales revenue	640,000	

Calculate the cash receipts from customers.

Calculate cash payments to suppliers—direct method.
(LO 3) AP

BE17–14 Winter Sportswear Inc. reported the following in its December 31, 2017, financial statements.

	2017	2016
Inventory	$55,600	$50,000
Accounts payable	62,200	55,000
Cost of goods sold	89,500	

Calculate (a) the cost of goods purchased, and (b) cash payments to suppliers.

Calculate cash payments for operating expenses—direct method. (LO 3) AP

BE17–15 Linus Corporation reported the following in its March 31, 2017, financial statements.

	2017	2016
Prepaid expenses	$ 23,400	$12,500
Accrued expenses payable	14,900	8,500
Operating expenses	100,000	

Calculate the cash payments for operating expenses.

Calculate cash payments to employees—direct method.
(LO 3) AP

BE17–16 ICE Inc. reported the following in its December 31, 2017, financial statements.

	2017	2016
Salaries payable	$ 2,500	$4,000
Salaries expense	188,000	

Calculate the cash payments to employees.

Calculate cash payments for income tax—direct method.
(LO 3) AP

BE17–17 Home Grocery Corporation reported the following in its 2017 financial statements.

	2017	2016
Income tax payable	$17,000	$8,000
Income tax expense	90,000	

Calculate the cash payments for income tax.

BE17–18   Angus Meat Corporation reported the following information for the year ended December 31:

Calculate cash from operating activities—direct method. (LO 3) AP

Balance sheet accounts:	2017	2016		Income statement accounts:	2017
Accounts receivable	$85,000	$60,000		Sales	$375,000
Inventory	62,000	55,000		Gain on sale of land	15,000
Prepaid expenses	5,000	9,000		Cost of goods sold	150,000
Accounts payable	35,000	42,000		Operating expenses	75,000
Income tax payable	14,000	9,000		Depreciation expense	20,000
				Income tax expense	50,000

Calculate the net cash provided (used) by operating activities using the direct method.

BE17–19   Hill Corporation reported net cash provided by operating activities of $360,000, net cash used by investing activities of $250,000 (including cash spent for capital assets of $200,000), and net cash provided by financing activities of $70,000. Dividends of $140,000 were paid. Calculate free cash flow.

Calculate free cash flow. (LO 4) AP

BE17–20   Two companies reported the following information:

Use cash flows to identify new company. (LO 4) AN

	Company A	Company B
Profit (loss)	$ (5,000)	$100,000
Cash provided (used) by operating activities	(10,000)	50,000
Cash provided (used) by investing activities	(70,000)	30,000
Cash provided (used) by financing activities	120,000	(100,000)

(a) Calculate free cash flow for each company.
(b) Which company is more likely to be in the early stages of its development? Explain.

▶ Exercises

E17–1   An analysis of the comparative balance sheet, the current year's income statement, and the general ledger accounts of Wellman Corp. uncovered the following items. Assume all items involve cash unless there is information to the contrary. Assume Wellman uses ASPE to prepare its financial statements.

Classify transactions. (LO 1) AP

1. Payment of interest on notes payable
2. Exchange of land for patent
3. Sale of building
4. Payment of dividends
5. Depreciation
6. Receipt of dividends on investment
7. Receipt of interest on notes receivable
8. Issuance of common shares
9. Amortization of patent
10. Issuance of Wellman bonds at par for land
11. Purchase of land
12. Conversion of bonds into common shares
13. Sale of land at a loss
14. Sale of Wellman bonds

Instructions

Indicate how each item should be classified in the cash flow statement using these four major classifications: operating activity (indirect method), investing activity, financing activity, and significant noncash investing and financing activity.

E17–2   Eng Corporation, a private corporation reporting under ASPE, had the following transactions:

Classify transactions. (LO 1) AP

Transaction	(a) Classification	(b) Cash Inflow or Outflow
1. Sold inventory for $1,000 cash.	O	+$1,000
2. Purchased a machine for $30,000. Made a $5,000 down payment and issued a long-term note for the remainder.		
3. Issued common shares for $50,000.		
4. Collected $16,000 of accounts receivable.		
5. Paid a $25,000 cash dividend.		
6. Sold a long-term equity investment with a carrying value of $15,000 for $10,000.		
7. Sold $200,000 worth of bonds at par.		
8. Paid $18,000 on accounts payable.		
9. Purchased inventory for $28,000 on account.		
10. Purchased a long-term investment in bonds for $100,000.		
11. Sold equipment with a carrying amount of $16,000 for $13,000.		
12. Paid $12,000 interest expense on long-term notes payable.		

Instructions

Complete the above table for each of the following requirements. The first one has been done for you as an example.

(a) Classify each transaction as an operating activity (O), investing activity (I), financing activity (F), or noncash transaction (NC).

(b) Specify whether the transaction represents a cash inflow (+), cash outflow (−), or has no effect (NE) on cash, and the amount of the cash flow.

Prepare journal entry and determine effect on cash flows. (LO 2) AP

E17–3 Crabtree Corporation had the following transactions.

1. Sold land (cost $12,000) for $15,000.
2. Issued common shares for $20,000.
3. Recorded depreciation on buildings for $17,000.
4. Paid salaries of $9,000.
5. Issued 1,000 common shares in exchange for equipment with market value of $8,000.
6. Sold equipment (cost $10,000, accumulated depreciation $7,000) for $1,200.

Instructions

For each transaction above, (a) prepare the journal entry, and (b) indicate how it would affect the statement of cash flows using the indirect method.

Prepare operating activities section—indirect method. (LO 2) AP

E17–4 Pesci Ltd. is a private company reporting under ASPE. Its income statement and changes in current assets and current liabilities for the year are reported below:

PESCI LTD. Income Statement Year Ended November 30, 2017		
Sales		$948,000
Cost of goods sold		490,000
Gross profit		458,000
Operating expenses	$310,000	
Depreciation expense	50,000	
Gain on sale of equipment	(10,000)	350,000
Profit before income tax		108,000
Income tax expense		30,000
Profit		$ 78,000
Changes in current assets and current liabilities were as follows:		
Accounts receivable	$36,000	decrease
Inventory	19,000	increase
Prepaid expenses	2,000	increase
Accounts payable	12,000	decrease
Dividends payable	5,000	decrease
Income taxes payable	4,000	decrease

Instructions

Prepare the operating activities section of the cash flow statement using the indirect method.

Prepare operating activities section—indirect method. (LO 2) AP

E17–5 The current sections of Scooters Rentals balance sheets at December 31, 2017 and 2016, are presented here. Scooters' profit for 2017 was $153,000. Depreciation expense was $24,000.

	2017	2016
Current assets		
Cash	$105,000	$ 99,000
Accounts receivable	110,000	89,000
Inventory	158,000	172,000
Prepaid expenses	27,000	22,000
Total current assets	$400,000	$382,000

	2017	2016
Current liabilities		
Accrued expenses payable	$ 15,000	$ 5,000
Accounts payable	85,000	92,000
Total current liabilities	$100,000	$ 97,000

Instructions

Prepare the net cash provided by operating activities section of the company's statement of cash flows for the year ended December 31, 2017, using the indirect method.

E17–6 The current assets and liabilities sections of the comparative balance sheet of Charron Inc., a private company reporting under ASPE, at October 31 are presented below, along with the income statement:

Prepare operating activities section—indirect method. (LO 2) AP

CHARRON INC.
Comparative Balance Sheet Accounts

	2017	2016
Cash	$99,000	$105,000
Accounts receivable	64,000	41,000
Inventory	32,500	46,000
Prepaid expenses	7,500	5,800
Accounts payable	43,000	36,000
Accrued expenses payable	5,000	8,000
Dividends payable	24,000	17,000
Income taxes payable	6,800	11,800

CHARRON INC.
Income Statement
Year Ended October 31, 2017

Sales		$625,000
Cost of goods sold		390,000
Gross profit		235,000
Operating expenses	$88,000	
Depreciation expense	23,000	
Loss on sale of equipment	8,000	119,000
Profit before income taxes		116,000
Income taxes		29,000
Profit		$ 87,000

Instructions

Prepare the operating activities section of the cash flow statement using the indirect method.

E17–7 The three accounts shown below appear in the general ledger of Halo Corp. during 2017.

Determine investing and financing activities. (LO 2) AP

Equipment

Date	Debit	Credit	Balance
Jan. 1 Balance			160,000
July 31 Purchase of equipment	70,000		230,000
Nov. 10 Cost of equipment sold		49,000	181,000

Accumulated Depreciation—Equipment

Date	Debit	Credit	Balance
Jan. 1 Balance			71,000
Nov. 10 Accumulated depreciation on equipment sold	30,000		41,000
Dec. 31 Depreciation for year		28,000	69,000

Retained Earnings

Date	Debit	Credit	Balance
Jan. 1 Balance			105,000
Aug. 23 Dividends (cash)	14,000		91,000
Dec. 31 Profit		77,000	168,000

Instructions

From the postings in the accounts, indicate how the information is reported on a cash flow statement using the indirect method. The loss on disposal of equipment was $7,000.

Determine investing and financing activities. (LO 2) AP

E17-8 Dupré Corp. is a private company reporting under ASPE. The following selected accounts are from the general ledger for the year ended December 31, 2017:

Equipment					Accumulated Depreciation—Equipment			
Jan. 1	260,000						Jan. 1	117,000
July 31	65,000	Nov. 10	46,000		Nov. 10	38,000		
							Dec. 31	33,000
Dec. 31	279,000						Dec. 31	112,000

Retained Earnings				
		Jan. 1	130,000
Aug. 23	8,000	Dec. 31	84,000
		Dec. 31	206,000

Additional information:

July 31   Equipment was purchased for cash.
Aug. 23   A cash dividend was paid.
Nov. 10   A loss of $3,000 was incurred on the sale of equipment.
Dec. 31   Depreciation expense was recorded for the year.
Dec. 31   Closing entries were recorded.

Instructions

From the postings in the above accounts and additional information provided, indicate what information would be reported in the investing and/or financing activities sections of the cash flow statement.

Prepare statement of cash flows—indirect method. (LO 2) AP

E17-9 Lu Corporation's comparative balance sheet is presented below.

LU CORPORATION		
Balance Sheet		
December 31		
	2017	2016
Cash	$ 14,300	$ 10,700
Accounts receivable	21,200	23,400
Land	20,000	26,000
Buildings	70,000	70,000
Accumulated depreciation—buildings	(15,000)	(10,000)
Total	$110,500	$120,100
Accounts payable	$ 12,370	$ 31,100
Common shares	75,000	69,000
Retained earnings	23,130	20,000
Total	$110,500	$120,100

Additional information:

1. Profit was $22,630. Dividends declared and paid were $19,500.
2. No noncash investing and financing activities occurred during 2017.
3. The land was sold for cash of $4,900 resulting in a loss of $1,100 on the sale of the land.

Instructions

Prepare a cash flow statement for 2017 using the indirect method. Lu Corporation reports under ASPE.

Determine investing and financing activities. (LO 2) AP

E17-10 Preferred Homes Ltd., a private company reporting under ASPE, reported the following for the year ended September 30, 2017:

	2017	2016
Land	$300,000	$200,000
Building	350,000	350,000
Equipment	139,000	125,000
Accumulated depreciation	65,000	55,000
Dividends payable	10,000	20,000
Mortgage note payable	110,000	50,000
Common shares	235,000	150,000
Retained earnings	220,000	80,000
Depreciation expense	15,000	
Gain on equipment sold	2,000	
Profit	210,000	

Additional information:

1. Equipment was purchased for $20,000.
2. Land was purchased for $35,000 cash and a mortgage note payable was issued.
3. Common shares were issued for $85,000 cash.

Instructions

Prepare the investing and financing activities sections of the cash flow statement and any required note disclosure. (*Hint:* Use T accounts to help you calculate the cash flows.)

E17–11 Savary Limited is a private company reporting under ASPE. Its comparative balance sheet at December 31 is as follows:

Prepare cash flow statement—indirect method. (LO 2) AP

SAVARY LIMITED Balance Sheet December 31		
Assets	**2017**	**2016**
Cash	$ 114,000	$ 85,000
Accounts receivable	750,000	600,000
Inventory	500,000	330,000
Prepaid insurance	18,000	25,000
Equipment and vehicles	1,250,000	1,000,000
Accumulated depreciation	(350,000)	(280,000)
Total assets	$2,282,000	$1,760,000
Liabilities and Shareholders' Equity		
Accounts payable	$ 226,000	$ 200,000
Salaries payable	30,000	40,000
Interest payable	26,000	20,000
Notes payable	500,000	350,000
Common shares	600,000	400,000
Retained earnings	900,000	750,000
Total liabilities and shareholders' equity	$2,282,000	$1,760,000

Additional information:

1. Profit for 2017 was $200,000.
2. Equipment was purchased during the year. No equipment was sold.
3. Cash dividends were paid to the common shareholders during the year.

Instructions

Prepare the cash flow statement using the indirect method.

E17–12 Macgregor Company completed its first year of operations on December 31, 2017. Its initial income statement showed that Macgregor had revenues of $192,000 and operating expenses of $78,000. Accounts receivable and accounts payable at year end were $60,000 and $23,000, respectively. Assume that accounts payable related to operating expenses. Ignore income taxes.

Calculate cash payments—direct method. (LO 3) AP

Instructions

Calculate net cash provided by operating activities using the direct method.

Prepare cash flow statement—direct method. (LO 3) AP

E17–13   The accounting records of Flypaper Airlines Inc. reveal the following transactions and events for the year ended March 31, 2017:

Payment of interest	$ 8,000	Common shares issued in exchange for land	$ 35,000
Cash sales	53,000	Payment of salaries	51,000
Receipt of dividend revenue	14,000	Depreciation expense	16,000
Payment of income tax	7,500	Proceeds from sale of aircraft	212,000
Profit	38,000	Purchase of equipment for cash	22,000
Payment of accounts payable	110,000	Loss on sale of aircraft	3,000
Payment for land	174,000	Payment of dividends	14,000
Collection of accounts receivable	201,000	Payment of operating expenses	28,000

Additional information:

Flypaper Airlines' cash on April 1, 2016, was $35,000.

Instructions

Assuming Flypaper reports under ASPE, prepare a cash flow statement using the direct method.

Calculate net cash provided by operating activities using the direct method. (LO 3) AP

E17–14   Using the data presented for Pesci Ltd. in E17–4, prepare the operating activities section of the cash flow statement using the direct method.

Calculate operating cash flows—direct method. (LO 3) AP

E17–15   The following information is taken from the general ledger of Robin Limited:

1. Sales revenue	$275,000
Accounts receivable, January 1	22,900
Accounts receivable, December 31	37,000
2. Cost of goods sold	$110,000
Inventory, January 1	9,200
Inventory, December 31	5,900
Accounts payable, January 1	8,600
Accounts payable, December 31	6,900
3. Operating expenses	$ 70,000
Depreciation expense (included in operating expenses)	20,000
Prepaid expenses, January 1	3,000
Prepaid expenses, December 31	5,500
Accrued expenses payable, January 1	6,500
Accrued expenses payable, December 31	4,500
4. Interest expense	$ 18,000
Interest payable, January 1	4,000
Interest payable, December 31	4,000
Notes payable, January 1	397,000
Notes payable, December 31	397,000

Instructions

Using the direct method, calculate:

(a) cash receipts from customers
(b) cash payments to suppliers

(c) cash payments for operating expenses
(d) cash payments for interest expense

Prepare operating activities section—direct method. (LO 3) AP

E17–16   McTavish Ltd. completed its first year of operations on September 30, 2017. McTavish reported the following information at September 30, 2017:

McTAVISH LTD.	
Selected balance sheet account balances at September 30, 2017	
Accounts receivable	$23,000
Prepaid expenses	3,100
Accrued expenses payable	10,500
Interest payable	500
Dividends payable	3,800
Income taxes payable	9,800

```
                        McTAVISH LTD.
                      Income Statement
                Year Ended September 30, 2017

Service revenue                                      $285,000
Operating expenses                       $122,000
Depreciation expense                       12,300
Gain on sale of equipment                  (5,750)    128,550
                                                     _____
Profit from operations                                156,450
Interest expense                                        4,000
                                                     _____
Profit before income tax                              152,450
Income tax expense                                     38,500
                                                     _____
Profit                                               $113,950
                                                     ========
```

Instructions

Assuming that McTavish reports under ASPE, prepare the operating section of a cash flow statement using the direct method.

E17-17 The income statement and account balances for Charron Inc. are presented in E17-6.

Instructions

Prepare the cash flow statement using the direct method.

Prepare cash flow statement—direct method. (LO 3) AP

E17-18 The comparative balance sheet for Storm Adventures Ltd., a private company reporting under ASPE, follows:

Prepare cash flow statement—indirect and direct methods. (LO 2, 3) AP

STORM ADVENTURES LTD. Balance Sheet December 31		
Assets	2017	2016
Cash	$ 43,000	$ 12,600
Accounts receivable	76,000	85,000
Inventory	160,000	172,000
Prepaid expenses	12,000	5,000
Land	50,000	75,000
Equipment	270,000	190,000
Accumulated depreciation	(90,000)	(40,000)
Total assets	$521,000	$499,600
Liabilities and Shareholders' Equity		
Accounts payable	$ 43,000	$ 38,000
Dividends payable	7,500	5,000
Income taxes payable	2,500	6,000
Bonds payable	120,000	180,000
Common shares	207,000	167,000
Retained earnings	141,000	103,600
Total liabilities and shareholders' equity	$521,000	$499,600

Additional information:

1. Profit for 2017 was $69,900.
2. Bonds payable of $60,000 were retired at maturity.
3. Common shares were issued for $40,000.
4. Land was sold at a loss of $10,000.
5. No equipment was sold during 2017.
6. Net sales for the year were $678,000.
7. Cost of goods sold for the year was $439,800.
8. Operating expenses (not including depreciation expense) were $80,000.
9. Interest expense was $5,000.
10. Income tax expense was $23,300.

Instructions

Prepare a cash flow statement using either (a) the indirect method or (b) the direct method, as assigned by your instructor.

Compare cash flows for two companies. (LO 4) AN

E17–19   Condensed cash flow statements are as follows for two companies operating in the same industry:

	Company A	Company B
Cash provided (used) by operating activities	$200,000	$(180,000)
Cash provided (used) by investing activities	(20,000)	(20,000)
Cash provided (used) by financing activities	(60,000)	320,000
Increase in cash	120,000	120,000
Cash, beginning of period	30,000	30,000
Cash, end of period	$150,000	$ 150,000

Instructions

Which company is in a better financial position? Explain why.

Calculate and discuss free cash flow. (LO 4) AN

E17–20   Selected information for a recent year follows for **Bank of Montreal** and **Scotiabank** (in millions):

	Bank of Montreal	Scotiabank
Profit	$ 4,333	$ 7,298
Cash provided (used) by operating activities	(2,927)	4,944
Cash provided (used) by investing activities	3,293	(586)
Cash provided (used) by financing activities	(465)	(4,186)

Instructions

(a) Calculate the increase or decrease in cash for each company.
(b) Calculate the free cash flow for each company.
(c) Which company appears to be in a stronger financial position? Explain.
(d) In what way might a bank's free cash flow be different from the free cash flow of a manufacturing company?

▶ Problems: Set A

Classify transactions by activity. Indicate impact on cash and profit. (LO 1) AP

P17–1A   You are provided with the following transactions that took place during a recent fiscal year:

Transaction	(a) Classification	(b) Cash
1. Paid telephone bill for the month.	O	–
2. Sold equipment for cash, at a loss.		
3. Sold an investment, at a gain.		
4. Acquired a building by paying 10% in cash and signing a mortgage payable for the balance.		
5. Made principal repayments on the mortgage.		
6. Paid interest on the mortgage.		
7. Sold inventory on account, at a price greater than cost.		
8. Paid wages owing (previously accrued) to employees.		
9. Declared and paid a cash dividend to common shareholders.		
10. Paid rent in advance.		
11. Sold inventory for cash, at a price greater than cost.		
12. Wrote down the value of inventory to net realizable value, which was lower than cost.		
13. Received semi-annual bond interest.		
14. Received dividends on an investment in associate.		
15. Issued common shares.		
16. Paid a cash dividend to common shareholders.		
17. Collected cash from customers on account.		
18. Collected service revenue in advance.		

Instructions

Assuming the company is reporting under IFRS, complete the above table for each of the following requirements. The first one has been done for you as an example.

(a) Classify each transaction as an operating activity (O), an investing activity (I), a financing activity (F), or a noncash transaction (NC) on the cash flow statement. If there is a choice of how a transaction is classified, indicate the alternative classifications.

(b) Specify whether the transaction will increase (+), decrease (−), or have no effect (NE) on cash reported on the balance sheet.

TAKING IT FURTHER   Explain how an operating activity can increase cash but not increase profit.

P17–2A   Molloy Ltd. reported the following for the fiscal year 2017:

Prepare operating activities
section—indirect and direct
methods. (LO 2, 3) AP

MOLLOY LTD. Income Statement Year Ended September 30, 2017		
Sales		$580,000
Cost of goods sold		340,000
Gross profit		240,000
Operating expenses	$ 96,000	
Depreciation expense	25,000	
Gain on sale of land	(35,000)	86,000
Profit before income tax		154,000
Income tax expense		38,000
Profit		$116,000

Additional information:

1. Accounts receivable decreased by $15,000 during the year.
2. Inventory increased by $7,000 during the year.
3. Prepaid expenses decreased by $5,000 during the year.

4. Accounts payable to suppliers increased by $10,000 during the year.
5. Accrued expenses payable increased by $4,000 during the year.
6. Income tax payable decreased by $6,000 during the year.

Instructions

Prepare the operating activities section of the cash flow statement using either (a) the indirect method or (b) the direct method, as assigned by your instructor.

TAKING IT FURTHER   In what circumstances will the direct method result in a different amount of cash provided (used) by operations than the indirect method?

P17–3A   The income statement of Hanalei International Inc. contained the following condensed information:

Prepare operating activities
section—indirect and direct
methods. (LO 2, 3) AP

HANALEI INTERNATIONAL INC. Income Statement Year Ended December 31, 2017		
Service revenue		$480,000
Operating expenses	$245,000	
Depreciation expense	35,000	
Loss on sale of equipment	25,000	305,000
Profit from operations		175,000
Other revenues and expenses		
Interest expense		10,000
Profit before income taxes		165,000
Income tax expense		41,250
Profit		$123,750

Hanalei's balance sheet contained the following comparative data at December 31:

	2017	2016
Accounts receivable	$52,000	$40,000
Prepaid insurance	5,000	8,000
Accounts payable	30,000	41,000
Interest payable	2,000	1,250
Income tax payable	3,000	4,500
Unearned revenue	12,000	8,000

Additional information: Accounts payable relate to operating expenses.

Instructions

Assuming Hanalei reports under ASPE, prepare the operating activities section of the cash flow statement using either (a) the indirect method or (b) the direct method, as assigned by your instructor.

TAKING IT FURTHER   What are the advantages and disadvantages of the direct method of determining cash provided (used) by operating activities?

Calculate cash flows for investing and financing activities. (LO 2) AP

P17–4A   Trudeau Inc. is a private company reporting under ASPE. The following selected account balances were reported in Trudeau Inc's financial statements at year end:

	2017	2016
Cash	$ 22,125	$ 10,000
Buildings	850,000	750,000
Equipment	393,000	340,000
Land	100,000	60,000
Accumulated depreciation—buildings	307,500	300,000
Accumulated depreciation—equipment	124,000	94,000
Dividends payable	6,250	2,500
Mortgage payable	545,000	585,000
Notes payable	340,000	310,000
Common shares: 46,000 shares in 2017; 40,000 in 2016	807,000	685,000
Retained earnings	200,000	100,000
Cash dividends declared	25,000	10,000
Depreciation expense—buildings	25,000	42,500
Depreciation expense—equipment	49,125	27,000
Gain on sale of equipment	1,000	0
Loss on sale of building	10,000	0
Interest expense	48,250	44,750

Additional information:

1. Purchased $75,000 of equipment for $10,000 cash and a note payable for the remainder.
2. Equipment was also sold during the year.
3. Sold a building that originally cost $50,000.
4. Used cash to purchase land and a building.
5. Mortgage payments and notes payable payments included interest and principal amounts.
6. Common shares were issued for cash.

Instructions

(a) Determine the amount of any cash inflows or outflows related to investing activities in 2017. (*Hint:* Use T accounts to calculate the cash flows.)
(b) What was the amount of profit reported by Trudeau Inc. in 2017?
(c) Determine the amount of any cash inflows or outflows related to financing activities in 2017. (*Hint:* Use T accounts to calculate the cash flows.)
(d) Identify and determine the amount of any noncash financing activities in 2017.
(e) Calculate the cash operating activities. (*Hint:* Using the cash balances provided, calculate increase or decrease in cash first.)

TAKING IT FURTHER   Is it unfavourable for a company to have a net cash outflow from investing activities?

Prepare a cash flow statement—indirect method—and calculate free cash flow. (LO 2, 4) AP

P17–5A   The following are the financial statements of Gil Company.

GIL COMPANY
Balance Sheet
December 31

Assets	2017	2016
Cash	$ 38,000	$ 20,000
Accounts receivable	30,000	14,000
Inventory	27,000	20,000
Equipment	60,000	78,000
Accumulated depreciation—equipment	(29,000)	(24,000)
Total	$126,000	$108,000

Liabilities and Shareholders' Equity		
Accounts payable	$ 24,000	$ 15,000
Income taxes payable	7,000	8,000
Notes payable	27,000	33,000
Common shares	18,000	14,000
Retained earnings	50,000	38,000
Total	$126,000	$108,000

GIL COMPANY
Income Statement
For the Year Ended December 31, 2017

Sales		$242,000
Cost of goods sold		175,000
Gross profit		67,000
Operating expenses		24,000
Income from operations		43,000
Interest expense		3,000
Income before income taxes		40,000
Income tax expense		8,000
Profit		$ 32,000

Additional information:

1. Dividends declared and paid were $20,000. Gil reports under ASPE.
2. During the year, equipment was sold for $8,500 cash. This equipment cost $18,000 originally and had a carrying value of $8,500 at the time of sale.
3. All depreciation expense, $14,500, is in the operating expenses.
4. All sales and purchases are on account.

Instructions

(a) Prepare a statement of cash flows using the indirect method.
(b) Calculate free cash flow.

TAKING IT FURTHER Gil Company had a positive cash balance at the beginning and end of 2017. Given that, is it possible that the company could have had a negative cash balance at one or more points during the year? Explain.

P17–6A   Strong Shoes' comparative balance sheet is presented below. Strong reports under ASPE.

Prepare a cash flow statement—indirect method—and calculate free cash flow. (LO 2, 4) AP

STRONG SHOES
Balance Sheet
December 31

	2017	2016
Cash	$ 28,200	$ 17,700
Accounts receivable	24,200	22,300
Long-term investments	23,000	16,000
Equipment	60,000	70,000
Accumulated depreciation—equipment	(14,000)	(10,000)
Total	$121,400	$116,000
Accounts payable	$ 19,600	$ 11,100
Notes payable	10,000	30,000
Common shares	60,000	45,000
Retained earnings	31,800	29,900
Total	$121,400	$116,000

Additional information:

1. Profit was $28,300. Dividends declared and paid were $26,400.
2. Equipment that cost $10,000 and had accumulated depreciation of $1,200 was sold for $4,300.
3. All other changes in non-current account balances had a direct effect on cash flows, except the change in accumulated depreciation.

Instructions

(a) Prepare a statement of cash flows for 2017 using the indirect method.
(b) Calculate free cash flow.

TAKING IT FURTHER   Strong Shoes is considering changing its method of reporting operating activities from the indirect method to the direct method. Why would the company want to do this? How would this affect the net cash provided (used) by operating activities? Explain.

Prepare a cash flow statement—indirect method. (LO 2) AP

P17–7A   Coyote Ltd., a private company reporting under ASPE, reported the following for the years ended May 31, 2017 and 2016.

COYOTE LTD. Balance Sheet May 31		
Assets	2017	2016
Cash	$ 12,600	$ 43,000
Accounts receivable	85,000	76,000
Inventory	172,000	160,000
Prepaid expenses	5,000	7,500
Land	125,000	75,000
Equipment	325,000	190,000
Accumulated depreciation	(68,250)	(40,000)
Total assets	$656,350	$511,500
Liabilities and Shareholders' Equity		
Accounts payable	$ 43,000	$ 38,000
Dividends payable	7,500	5,000
Income taxes payable	2,500	6,000
Mortgage payable	125,000	80,000
Common shares	217,000	167,000
Retained earnings	261,350	215,500
Total liabilities and shareholders' equity	$656,350	$511,500

Additional information:

1. Profit for 2017 was $108,000.
2. Common shares were issued for $50,000.
3. Land with a cost of $50,000 was sold at a loss of $20,000.
4. Purchased land with a cost of $100,000 with a $55,000 down payment and financed the remainder with a mortgage note payable.
5. No equipment was sold during 2017.

Instructions

Prepare a cash flow statement for the year using the indirect method.

TAKING IT FURTHER   Is it unfavourable for a company to have a net cash outflow from financing activities?

Prepare cash flow statement—direct method. (LO 3) AP

P17–8A   Refer to the information presented for Coyote Ltd. in P17–7A.

Additional information:

1. Net sales for the year were $673,250.
2. Cost of goods sold for the year was $403,950.
3. Operating expenses, including depreciation expense, were $100,300.
4. Interest expense was $5,000.
5. Income tax expense was $36,000.
6. Accounts payable is used for merchandise purchases.

Instructions

Prepare a cash flow statement for the year using the direct method.

TAKING IT FURTHER Indicate what transactions might be classified differently if the company were reporting under IFRS instead of ASPE.

P17–9A Condensed financial data follow for E-Perform Ltd. E- Perform reports under ASPE.

Prepare cash flow statement—indirect method and direct method. (LO 2, 3) AP

E-PERFORM LTD.
Balance Sheet
December 31

Assets	2017	2016
Cash	$ 97,800	$ 48,400
Accounts receivable	75,800	43,000
Inventory	122,500	92,850
Prepaid expenses	38,400	26,000
Long-term investments	128,000	114,000
Property, plant, and equipment	270,000	242,500
Accumulated depreciation	(50,000)	(52,000)
Total assets	$682,500	$514,750

Liabilities and Shareholders' Equity		
Accounts payable	$ 93,000	$ 77,300
Accrued expenses payable	11,500	7,000
Notes payable	110,000	150,000
Common shares	234,000	175,000
Retained earnings	234,000	105,450
Total liabilities and shareholders' equity	$682,500	$514,750

E-PERFORM LTD.
Income Statement
Year Ended December 31, 2017

Sales		$492,780
Cost of goods sold		185,460
Gross profit		307,320
Operating expenses	$62,410	
Depreciation expense	46,500	
Loss on sale of equipment	7,500	116,410
Profit from operations		190,910
Other expenses		
Interest expense		4,730
Profit before income tax		186,180
Income tax expense		45,000
Profit		$141,180

Additional information:

1. New equipment costing $85,000 was purchased for $25,000 cash and a $60,000 note payable.
2. Equipment with an original cost of $57,500 was sold at a loss of $7,500.
3. Notes payable matured during the year and were repaid.
4. A long-term investment was acquired for cash.

Instructions

(a) Prepare a cash flow statement for the year using the indirect method.
(b) Prepare the operating section of the cash flow statement using the direct method assuming that accounts payable relate only to merchandise creditors and that accrued expenses payable and prepaid expenses relate to operating expenses.

TAKING IT FURTHER   E-Perform Ltd.'s cash balance more than doubled in 2017. Briefly explain what caused this, using the cash flow statement.

Prepare cash flow statement—
indirect method and direct
method. (LO 2, 3) AP

P17–10A   The financial statements of Wetaskiwin Ltd., a private company reporting under ASPE, follow:

WETASKIWIN LTD.
Balance Sheet
December 31

Assets	2017	2016
Cash	$ 9,000	$ 10,000
Short-term notes receivable	14,000	23,000
Accounts receivable	28,000	14,000
Inventory	29,000	25,000
Property, plant, and equipment	73,000	78,000
Accumulated depreciation	(30,000)	(24,000)
Total assets	$123,000	$126,000

Liabilities and Shareholders' Equity		
Accounts payable	$ 25,000	$ 43,000
Income tax payable	3,000	20,000
Notes payable	15,000	10,000
Common shares	25,000	25,000
Retained earnings	55,000	28,000
Total liabilities and shareholders' equity	$123,000	$126,000

WETASKIWIN LTD.
Income Statement
Year Ended December 31, 2017

Sales		$286,000
Cost of goods sold		194,000
Gross profit		92,000
Operating expenses	$38,000	
Loss on sale of equipment	2,000	40,000
Profit from operations		52,000
Other revenues and expenses		
Interest revenue	$(1,000)	
Interest expense	2,000	1,000
Profit before income tax		51,000
Income tax expense		15,000
Profit		$ 36,000

Additional information:

1. Short-term notes receivable are from loans to other companies. During the year, the company collected the outstanding balance at December 31, 2016, and made new loans in the amount of $14,000.
2. Equipment was sold during the year. This equipment cost $15,000 originally and had a carrying amount of $10,000 at the time of sale.
3. Equipment costing $10,000 was purchased in exchange for a $10,000 note payable.
4. Depreciation expense is included in operating expenses.
5. Accounts receivable are from the sale of merchandise on credit.
6. Accounts payable relate to the purchase of merchandise on credit.

Instructions

(a) Prepare a cash flow statement for the year using the indirect method.
(b) Prepare the operating section of the cash flow statement using the direct method.

TAKING IT FURTHER   Wetaskiwin Ltd. had a relatively small change in its cash balance in 2017; cash decreased by only $1,000. Is it still necessary or important to prepare a cash flow statement? Explain.

P17–11A   Presented below is the comparative balance sheet for Diatessaron Inc., a private company reporting under ASPE, at December 31, 2017 and 2016:

Prepare cash flow statement—indirect method. (LO 2) AP

DIATESSARON INC.
Balance Sheet
December 31

Assets	2017	2016
Cash	$ 67,000	$ 98,000
Accounts receivable	101,000	75,000
Inventory	205,000	155,500
Long-term investment	101,500	0
Property, plant, and equipment	535,000	460,000
Less: Accumulated depreciation	(162,500)	(140,000)
	$847,000	$648,500
Liabilities and Shareholders' Equity		
Accounts payable	$ 57,500	$ 47,000
Dividends payable	6,000	0
Income tax payable	14,000	15,000
Long-term notes payable	25,000	0
Common shares	630,000	525,000
Retained earnings	114,500	61,500
	$847,000	$648,500

DIATESSARON INC.
Income Statement
Year Ended December 31, 2017

Sales		$663,000
Cost of goods sold		432,000
Gross profit		231,000
Operating expenses	$147,500	
Loss on sale of equipment	3,000	150,500
Profit from operations		80,500
Interest expense	3,000	
Interest revenue	(4,500)	(1,500)
Profit before income tax		82,000
Income tax expense		14,000
Profit		$ 68,000

Additional information:

1. Cash dividends of $15,000 were declared.
2. A long-term investment was acquired for cash at a cost of $101,500.
3. Depreciation expense is included in the operating expenses.
4. The company issued 10,500 common shares for cash on March 2, 2017. The fair value of the shares was $10 per share. The proceeds were used to purchase additional equipment.
5. Equipment that originally cost $30,000 was sold during the year for cash. The equipment had a carrying value of $9,000 at the time of sale.
6. The company issued a note payable for $28,000 and repaid $3,000 by year end.

Instructions

Prepare a cash flow statement for the year using the indirect method.

TAKING IT FURTHER   Is it necessary to show both the proceeds from issuing a new note payable and the partial repayment of notes payable? Or is it sufficient to simply show the net increase or decrease in notes payable, as is done with accounts payable? Explain.

P17–12A   Refer to the information presented for Diatessaron Inc. in P17–11A.

Prepare cash flow statement—direct method. (LO 3) AP

Additional information:

1. All purchases of inventory are on credit.
2. Accounts Payable is used only to record purchases of inventory.

Instructions

Prepare a cash flow statement for the year using the direct method.

TAKING IT FURTHER Why is it necessary to know that Accounts Payable is used for purchases of inventory when using the direct method, but not the indirect method?

Calculate free cash flow and evaluate cash. (LO 4) AN

P17–13A Selected information (in US$ millions) for two close competitors, Potash Corporation of Saskatchewan Inc. and Agrium Inc., follows for the year ended December 31, 2014:

	Potash	Agrium
Profit	$ 1,536	$ 720
Cash provided by operating activities	2,614	1,312
Cash used by investing activities	(1,160)	(2,068)
Cash provided (used) by financing activities	(1,867)	856
Cash and cash equivalents, end of period	215	848
Dividends paid	(1,141)	(848)

Instructions

(a) Calculate the free cash flow for each company.
(b) Which company appears to be in a stronger financial position?

TAKING IT FURTHER By comparing the companies' cash flows, can you tell which company is likely in a growth stage? Explain.

▶ Problems: Set B

Classify transactions by activity. Indicate impact on cash and profit. (LO 1) AP

P17–1B You are provided with the following transactions that took place during a recent fiscal year:

Transaction	(a) Classification	(b) Cash
1. Paid telephone bill for the month.	O	–
2. Sold land for cash, at a gain.	____	____
3. Acquired land by issuing common shares.	____	____
4. Paid a cash dividend to preferred shareholders.	____	____
5. Performed services for cash.	____	____
6. Performed services on account.	____	____
7. Purchased inventory for cash.	____	____
8. Purchased inventory on account.	____	____
9. Paid income tax.	____	____
10. Made principal repayment on a trade note payable.	____	____
11. Paid semi-annual bond interest.	____	____
12. Received rent from a tenant in advance.	____	____
13. Recorded depreciation expense.	____	____
14. Reacquired common shares at a price greater than the average cost of the shares.	____	____
15. Issued preferred shares for cash.	____	____
16. Collected cash from customers on account.	____	____
17. Issued a note payable.	____	____
18. Paid insurance for the month.	____	____

Instructions

Assuming the company is reporting under IFRS, complete the above table for each of the following requirements, assuming none of the transactions were previously accrued. The first one has been done for you as an example.

(a) Classify each transaction as an operating activity (O), an investing activity (I), a financing activity (F), or a noncash transaction (NC) on the cash flow statement. If there is choice in how a transaction is classified, indicate the alternative classifications.

(b) Specify whether the transaction will increase (+), decrease (−), or have no effect (NE) on cash reported on the balance sheet.

<u>TAKING IT FURTHER</u>   Explain how an operating activity can decrease cash but not decrease profit.

P17–2B   Lui Inc. reported the following for the fiscal year 2017:

Prepare operating activities section—indirect and direct methods. (LO 2, 3) AP

LUI INC. Income Statement Year Ended December 31, 2017		
Sales		$820,000
Cost of goods sold		492,000
Gross profit		328,000
Operating expenses	$162,000	
Depreciation expense	28,500	
Loss on sale of equipment	9,500	200,000
Profit from operations		128,000
Other expenses		
Interest expense		7,500
Profit before income taxes		120,500
Income tax expense		30,000
Profit		$ 90,500

Additional information:

1. Accounts receivable decreased by $21,000 during the year.
2. Inventory increased by $32,000 during the year.
3. Prepaid expenses decreased by $7,000 during the year.
4. Accounts payable to suppliers decreased by $5,000 during the year.
5. Accrued expenses payable increased by $8,500 during the year.
6. Interest payable increased by $3,500 during the year.
7. Income tax payable decreased by $6,500 during the year.

Instructions

Assuming the company reports under ASPE, prepare the operating activities section of the cash flow statement using either (a) the indirect method or (b) the direct method, as assigned by your instructor.

<u>TAKING IT FURTHER</u>   Will the amount of cash provided (used) by operations always be the same amount if it is determined by using the direct method or the indirect method? Explain.

P17–3B   Sable Island Ltd. is a private company reporting under ASPE. Its income statement contained the following condensed information:

Prepare operating activities section—indirect and direct methods. (LO 2, 3) AP

SABLE ISLAND LTD. Income Statement Year Ended December 31, 2017		
Fees earned		$900,000
Operating expenses	$642,000	
Depreciation expense	50,000	
Gain on sale of equipment	(23,000)	669,000
Profit from operations		231,000
Other expenses		
Interest expense		5,000
Profit before income tax		226,000
Income tax expense		56,500
Profit		$169,500

Sable Island's balance sheet contained the following comparative data at December 31:

	2017	2016
Accounts receivable	$48,000	$56,000
Prepaid expenses	14,000	11,500
Accounts payable	41,000	36,000
Income tax payable	4,000	9,250
Interest payable	1,000	550
Unearned revenue	13,750	10,000

Additional information: Accounts payable relate to operating expenses.

Instructions

Prepare the operating activities section of the cash flow statement using either (a) the indirect method or (b) the direct method, as assigned by your instructor.

TAKING IT FURTHER   What are the advantages and disadvantages of the indirect method of determining cash provided (used) by operating activities?

Calculate cash flows for investing and financing activities. (LO 2) AP

P17–4B   Bird Corp., a private company reporting under ASPE, reported the following in its financial statements:

	2017	2016
Cash	$ 21,000	$ 5,000
Accumulated depreciation—building	578,750	600,000
Accumulated depreciation—equipment	218,000	192,000
Depreciation expense—building	31,250	30,000
Depreciation expense—equipment	48,000	45,000
Building	1,310,000	1,250,000
Equipment	492,000	480,000
Land	250,000	200,000
Notes payable	214,000	216,000
Mortgage payable	335,000	350,000
Preferred shares: 7,000 shares in 2017; 5,000 in 2016	175,000	125,000
Common shares: 8,000 shares in 2017; 10,000 in 2016	123,200	154,000
Contributed surplus—reacquisition of common shares	1,500	0
Cash dividends—preferred	6,250	6,250
Retained earnings	300,000	240,000
Interest expense	23,000	28,000
Loss on sale of equipment	5,000	0
Gain on sale of building	18,000	0

Additional information:

1. Purchased land for $50,000 and building for $130,000 by making a $25,000 down payment and financing the remainder with a note payable.
2. A building was sold during the year.
3. Cash was used to purchase equipment.
4. Equipment with an original cost of $28,000 was sold during the year.
5. Mortgage payable and notes payable payments included interest and principal amounts.
6. The company paid $157,000 of notes payable that matured during the year.
7. The company reacquired 2,000 common shares in 2017, with an average cost of $30,800.
8. Preferred shares were sold for cash.

Instructions

(a) Determine the amount of any cash inflows or outflows related to investing activities in 2017. (*Hint:* Use T accounts to calculate the cash flows.)
(b) What was the amount of profit reported by Bird Corp. in 2017?
(c) Determine the amount of any cash inflows or outflows related to financing activities in 2017. (*Hint:* Use T accounts to calculate the cash flows.)

(d) Identify and determine the amount of any noncash financing activities in 2017.
(e) Calculate the cash from net cash provided (used) by operating activities. (*Hint:* Using the cash balances provided, calculate increase or decrease in cash first.)

TAKING IT FURTHER   Is it favourable for a company to have a net cash inflow from investing activities?

P17–5B   Presented below are the financial statements of Gaudette Company.

Prepare a cash flow statement—indirect method—and calculate free cash flow. (LO 2, 4) AP

GAUDETTE COMPANY
Balance Sheet
December 31

Assets	2017	2016
Cash	$ 28,000	$ 33,000
Accounts receivable	23,000	14,000
Inventory	41,000	25,000
Equipment	70,000	78,000
Accumulated depreciation—equipment	(27,000)	(24,000)
Total	$135,000	$126,000

Liabilities and Shareholders' Equity		
Accounts payable	$ 31,000	$ 43,000
Income taxes payable	26,000	20,000
Notes payable	20,000	10,000
Common shares	25,000	25,000
Retained earnings	33,000	28,000
Total	$135,000	$126,000

GAUDETTE COMPANY
Income Statement
For the Year Ended December 31, 2017

Sales		$286,000
Cost of goods sold		194,000
Gross profit		92,000
Selling expenses	$28,000	
Administrative expenses	9,000	37,000
Profit from operations		55,000
Interest expense		7,000
Profit before income taxes		48,000
Income tax expense		10,000
Profit		$ 38,000

Additional information:

1. Dividends of $33,000 were declared and paid. Gaudette reports under ASPE.
2. During the year, equipment was sold for $10,000 cash. This equipment cost $13,000 originally and had a carrying value of $10,000 at the time of sale.
3. All depreciation expense, $6,000, is in the selling expense category.
4. All sales and purchases are on account.
5. Additional equipment was purchased for $5,000 cash.

Instructions

(a) Prepare a statement of cash flows using the indirect method.
(b) Calculate free cash flow.

TAKING IT FURTHER Gaudette Company had a positive cash balance at the beginning and end of 2017. Given that, is it possible that the company could have had a negative cash balance at one or more points during the year? Explain.

Prepare a cash flow statement—indirect method—and calculate free cash flow. (LO 2, 4) AP

P17–6B Condensed financial data of Wanwright Company are shown below. Wanwright reports under ASPE.

WANWRIGHT COMPANY		
Balance Sheet		
December 31		
Assets	2017	2016
Cash	$ 92,700	$ 33,400
Accounts receivable	70,800	37,000
Inventory	131,900	102,650
Investments	84,500	107,000
Plant assets	310,000	205,000
Accumulated depreciation	(49,500)	(40,000)
Total	$640,400	$445,050
Liabilities and Shareholders' Equity		
Accounts payable	$ 62,700	$ 48,280
Salaries payable	15,100	18,830
Notes payable	140,000	70,000
Common shares	250,000	200,000
Retained earnings	172,600	107,940
Total	$640,400	$445,050

WANWRIGHT COMPANY	
Income Statement	
For the Year Ended December 31, 2017	
Sales	$297,500
Gain on sale of plant assets	5,000
	302,500
Less:	
Cost of goods sold	119,460
Operating expenses	14,670
Depreciation expense	35,500
Income taxes	27,270
Interest expense	2,940
Total expenses	199,840
Profit	$102,660

Additional information:

1. New plant assets costing $141,000 were purchased for cash during the year.
2. Investments were sold at cost.
3. Plant assets costing $36,000 were sold for $15,000, resulting in a gain of $5,000.
4. A cash dividend of $38,000 was declared and paid during the year.

Instructions

(a) Prepare a statement of cash flows using the indirect method.
(b) Calculate the free cash flow.

TAKING IT FURTHER If a company has a loss, does that mean that there has also been a net reduction in cash from operating activities? Explain.

Prepare a cash flow statement—indirect method. (LO 2) AP

P17–7B King Corp., a private company reporting under ASPE, reported the following for the years ended July 31, 2017 and 2016:

KING CORP.
Balance Sheet
July 31

Assets	2017	2016
Cash	$ 24,200	$ 11,000
Accounts receivable	106,000	92,000
Inventory	202,000	190,000
Prepaid expenses	7,500	6,000
Note receivable	40,000	5,000
Land	145,000	105,000
Equipment	225,000	170,000
Accumulated depreciation	(81,000)	(35,000)
Total assets	$668,700	$544,000
Liabilities and Shareholders' Equity		
Accounts payable	$ 33,000	$ 42,000
Salaries payable	6,500	3,800
Income taxes payable	6,000	1,500
Mortgage note payable	65,000	80,000
Common shares	185,000	150,000
Retained earnings	373,200	266,700
Total liabilities and shareholders' equity	$668,700	$544,000

Additional information:

1. Profit for 2017 was $106,500.
2. Common shares were issued for $35,000.
3. Land with a cost of $60,000 was sold at a gain of $30,000; $55,000 cash was received and a note receivable was issued for the remainder.
4. Purchased land with a cost of $100,000 with cash.
5. Equipment with a cost of $25,000 and carrying value of $20,000 was sold for $14,000 cash.
6. Equipment was purchased with cash.

Instructions

Prepare a cash flow statement for the year using the indirect method.

TAKING IT FURTHER   Is it favourable for a company to have a net cash inflow from financing activities?

P17–8B   Refer to the information presented for King Corp. in P17–7B.

Additional information:

1. Net sales for the year were $927,250.
2. Cost of goods sold for the year was $552,750.
3. Operating expenses, including depreciation expense, were $241,000.
4. Interest revenue was $3,500.
5. Interest expense was $6,500.
6. Income tax expense was $48,000.
7. Accounts payable relate to merchandise purchases and accrued expenses payable relate to operating expenses.

Prepare a cash flow statement—direct method. (LO 3) AP

Instructions

Prepare a cash flow statement for the year using the direct method.

TAKING IT FURTHER   Indicate what transactions might be classified differently if the company were reporting under IFRS instead of ASPE.

P17–9B   Presented below are the comparative balance sheets and income statement for Wayfarer Inc., a private company reporting under ASPE.

Prepare cash flow statement— indirect method and direct method. (LO 2, 3) AP

WAYFARER INC.
Balance Sheet
December 31

Assets	2017	2016
Cash	$ 120,600	$ 176,400
Accounts receivable	181,800	135,000
Inventory	369,000	257,400
Long-term investment	176,400	0
Property, plant, and equipment	1,008,000	828,000
Accumulated depreciation	(292,500)	(252,000)
	$1,563,300	$1,144,800
Liabilities and Shareholders' Equity		
Accounts payable	$ 157,500	$ 117,000
Dividends payable	10,800	0
Income tax payable	25,200	28,800
Long-term notes payable	81,000	0
Common shares	1,170,000	945,000
Retained earnings	118,800	54,000
	$1,563,300	$1,144,800

WAYFARER INC.
Income Statement
Year Ended December 31, 2017

Sales		$1,137,600
Cost of goods sold		772,200
Gross profit		365,400
Operating expenses	$265,500	
Loss on sale of equipment	3,600	269,100
Profit from operations		96,300
Interest expense	5,400	
Interest revenue	(9,900)	(4,500)
Profit before income tax		100,800
Income tax expense		25,200
Profit		$ 75,600

Additional information:

1. Cash dividends of $10,800 were declared on December 30, 2017, payable on January 15, 2018.
2. A long-term investment was acquired for cash at a cost of $176,400.
3. Depreciation expense is included in the operating expenses.
4. The company issued 22,500 common shares for cash on March 2, 2017. The fair value of the shares was $10 per share. The shares were used to purchase additional equipment.
5. Equipment that originally cost $45,000 was sold during the year for cash. The equipment had a net book value of $16,200 at the time of sale.
6. The company issued a note payable for $90,000 and repaid $9,000 of it by year end.
7. Accounts Payable is used for merchandise purchases.
8. Accounts receivable relate to merchandise sales.

Instructions

(a) Prepare a cash flow statement for the year using the indirect method.
(b) Prepare the operating section of the cash flow statement using the direct method.

TAKING IT FURTHER   Wayfarer Inc.'s cash balance decreased by $55,800 in 2017. Briefly explain what caused this, using the cash flow statement. Should management be concerned about this decrease? Explain.

P17–10B   Condensed financial data follow for Galenti Inc. Galenti is a private company reporting under ASPE.

Prepare cash flow statement—direct method and indirect method. (LO 2, 3) AP

GALENTI INC.
Balance Sheet
December 31

Assets	2017	2016
Cash	$102,700	$ 47,250
Short-term investments	94,500	107,000
Accounts receivable	80,800	37,000
Inventory	111,900	102,650
Prepaid expenses	10,000	16,000
Property, plant, and equipment	290,000	205,000
Accumulated depreciation	(49,500)	(40,000)
Total assets	$640,400	$474,900
Liabilities and Shareholders' Equity		
Accounts payable	$ 62,700	$ 54,280
Accrued expenses payable	12,100	18,830
Notes payable	140,000	80,000
Common shares	250,000	200,000
Retained earnings	175,600	121,790
Total liabilities and shareholders' equity	$640,400	$474,900

GALENTI INC.
Income Statement
Year Ended December 31, 2017

Revenues		
Sales		$307,500
Gain on sale of equipment		8,750
		316,250
Expenses		
Cost of goods sold	$99,460	
Operating expenses	24,670	
Depreciation expense	58,700	
Interest expense	2,940	
Loss on sale of short-term investments	7,500	193,270
Profit before income tax		122,980
Income tax expense		32,670
Profit		$ 90,310

Additional information:

1. Short-term investments (reported at cost) were sold for $15,000, resulting in a loss of $7,500. Investments were also purchased during the year.
2. New equipment costing $141,000 was purchased for $71,000 cash and a $70,000 note payable.
3. Equipment with an original cost of $56,000 was sold, resulting in a gain of $8,750.
4. Notes payable that matured during the year were paid in cash.
5. Accounts Payable is used for merchandise purchases.
6. Prepaid expenses and accrued expenses payable relate to operating expenses.
7. Accounts receivable relate to merchandise sales.

Instructions

(a) Prepare a cash flow statement for the year using the indirect method.
(b) Prepare the operating section of the cash flow statement using the direct method.

TAKING IT FURTHER   Galenti had a large cash balance (of $102,700) at December 31, 2017. What recommendations with respect to cash management might you make to Galenti's management? Explain.

Prepare cash flow statement—
indirect method. (LO 2) AP

P17–11B   The financial statements of Milk River Ltd. follow:

MILK RIVER LTD.
Balance Sheet
December 31

Assets	2017	2016
Cash	$ 13,000	$ 5,000
Accounts receivable	32,000	24,000
Inventory	33,000	20,000
Property, plant, and equipment	90,000	78,000
Accumulated depreciation	(30,000)	(24,000)
Goodwill	5,000	16,000
Total assets	$143,000	$119,000
Liabilities and Shareholders' Equity		
Accounts payable	$ 18,000	$ 15,000
Income taxes payable	2,000	4,000
Notes payable	42,000	52,750
Common shares	18,000	14,000
Retained earnings	63,000	33,250
Total liabilities and shareholders' equity	$143,000	$119,000

MILK RIVER LTD.
Income Statement
Year Ended December 31, 2017

Sales		$256,000
Cost of goods sold		140,000
Gross profit		116,000
Operating expenses	$64,000	
Gain on sale of equipment	(2,000)	
Impairment loss on goodwill	11,000	73,000
Profit from operations		43,000
Other revenues and expenses		
Interest expense		4,000
Profit before income tax		39,000
Income tax expense		9,250
Profit		$ 29,750

Additional information:

1. Equipment costing $24,000 was purchased with an $8,000 down payment and the remainder was financed with a note payable.
2. During the year, equipment was sold for $10,500 cash. This equipment had cost $12,000 originally and had a carrying amount of $8,500 at the time of sale.
3. All depreciation expenses are in the operating expenses category.
4. Notes payable were also repaid during the year.

Instructions

Prepare a cash flow statement for the year using the indirect method.

TAKING IT FURTHER   If equipment was both purchased and sold during the year, is it important to show both of these transactions? Or is it sufficient to show only the net increase or decrease in equipment, similar to how increases and decreases in inventory are shown?

Prepare cash flow statement—
direct method. (LO 3) AP

P17–12B   Refer to the information presented for Milk River Ltd. in P17–11B. Further analysis reveals that accounts payable relate to purchases of merchandise inventory.

Instructions

Prepare a cash flow statement for the year using the direct method.

TAKING IT FURTHER Explain why it is important to know if the company paid cash or financed the purchase of equipment and how this is shown on the cash flow statement.

P17–13B Selected information for two competitors, **The Gap Inc.** and **lululemon athletica inc.**, follows:

Calculate free cash flow and evaluate cash. (LO 3) AN

	The Gap (in US$ millions) for the year ended January 31, 2015	lululemon (in US$ millions, for the year ended February 1, 2015)
Profit	$ 1,262	$ 239
Cash provided by operating activities	2,129	314
Cash used by investing activities	(596)	(120)
Cash used by financing activities	(1,507)	(149)
Cash and cash equivalents, end of period	1,515	664

Instructions

(a) Calculate the free cash flow for each company.
(b) Which company appears to be in a stronger financial position?

TAKING IT FURTHER By comparing the companies' cash flows, can you tell which company may be in a growth stage? Explain.

CHAPTER 17: BROADENING YOUR PERSPECTIVE

▶ Financial Reporting and Analysis

Financial Reporting Problem

BYP17–1 Refer to the consolidated financial statements for **Corus Entertainment Inc.**, which are reproduced in Appendix A at the end of the textbook.

Instructions

(a) How does Corus define "cash" for the purpose of its cash flow statement?
(b) What was the increase or decrease in cash for the year ended August 31, 2014?
(c) What were the significant investing activities reported in Corus's 2014 cash flow statement?
(d) What were the significant financing activities reported in Corus's 2014 cash flow statement?
(e) Did Corus report any significant noncash investing and financing activities in 2014?

Interpreting Financial Statements

BYP17–2 **Andrew Peller Limited** is a leading producer and marketer of wines in Canada, with wineries in British Columbia, Ontario, and Nova Scotia. The company's March 31, 2014, balance sheet reported current assets of $146.1 million and current liabilities of $101.6 million, including bank indebtedness (negative cash balance) of $54.4 million. Andrew Peller Limited reported a profit for fiscal 2014 of $14.0 million. The company reported on its cash flow statement for 2014 that it generated $25.0 million of cash from operating activities. The company used $11.1 million in investing activities, primarily for the purchase of property, equipment, and vines. The company's financing activities used $13.9 million cash. The company paid dividends in the amount of $5.4 million during 2014.

Instructions

(a) What was Andrew Peller Limited's increase or decrease in cash during the year?
(b) Do you believe that Andrew Peller Limited's creditors should be worried about its lack of cash? Explain why or why not.
(c) How is it possible for a company to report a profit of $14.0 million and generate $25.0 million of cash from its operating activities?
(d) Calculate Andrew Peller Limited's free cash flow for fiscal 2014. Explain what this free cash flow means.

▶ Critical Thinking

Collaborative Learning Activity

Note to instructor: Additional instructions and handout material for this group activity can be found on the Instructor Resource Site and in *WileyPLUS*.

BYP17–3 In this group activity, you will be given a balance sheet at the beginning of the year, the income statement and cash flow statement for the year, and additional data. Using that information, you will prepare the year-end balance sheet.

Communication Activity

BYP17–4 Many investors today prefer the cash flow statement over the income statement. They believe that cash-based data are a better measure of performance than accrual-based data because the estimates and judgements that are required for accrual accounting allow management too much discretion to manipulate the results.

Instructions

Write a brief memo explaining whether or not it is harder for management to manipulate income using cash-based data than accrual-based data. In your answer, say which financial statement, in your opinion, is the best measure of a company's performance, and explain why.

"All About You" Activity

BYP17–5   It is common to read news reports that many Canadians have big debt loads and negative cash flows. Assume you are a student enrolled in your second year of university and have just learned about the importance of managing cash flows and how to prepare a cash flow statement. You want to use your knowledge to prepare a cash budget for the upcoming year, September 1, 2017, to August 31, 2018. To help you prepare next year's cash budget, you have prepared a cash flow statement for the past year, September 1, 2016, to August 31, 2017.

MY CASH FLOW STATEMENT
Year Ended August 31, 2017

Operating Activities	
Cash received from summer job	$ 8,000
Cash contribution from parents	3,600
Cash paid for rent, utilities, cable, Internet	(4,000)
Cash paid for groceries	(3,200)
Cash paid for clothes	(3,000)
Cash paid for gas, insurance, parking	(4,420)
Cash paid for miscellaneous	(500)
Cash paid for interest on credit card	(180)
Cash used in operating activities	(3,700)
Investing Activities	
Tuition and books	(7,000)
Laptop and printer	(1,200)
Cash used in investing activities	(8,200)
Financing Activities	
Student loan	7,500
Loan from parents	1,500
Purchases on credit card	1,000
Cash provided from financing activities	10,000
Decrease in cash	(1,900)
Cash, September 1, 2016	4,000
Cash, August 31, 2017	$ 2,100

Instructions

(a) Comment on your cash position on August 31, 2017, compared with September 1, 2016.

(b) Prepare a cash flow forecast for September 1, 2017, to August 31, 2018, based on the following estimates and assumptions:
   1. Tuition and books $7,500
   2. Student loan $7,500
   3. Your parents will contribute $4,000 toward your rent, utilities, cable, and Internet. You will not have to pay your parents back for this contribution.
   4. Rent, utilities, cable, and Internet $4,000
   5. Groceries $3,600
   6. Gas, insurance, and parking $4,600
   7. Clothes $3,000
   8. Miscellaneous $500
   9. You plan to pay off the amount owed on your credit card right away.
   10. Your parents will lend you an additional $1,500 if you need it.
   11. You are pretty sure that you will be rehired by the same company next summer; however, you do not think you will get a raise in pay.

(c) What is the amount of cash you forecast you will have at August 31, 2018?

(d) Will you need to borrow the additional $1,500 from your parents?

(e) Will you be able to pay off the $1,000 owed on your credit card? Should you try to do so?

(f) What actions may you be able to take to improve your cash flow?

 *Santé Smoothie Saga*

BYP17–6   (*Note:* This is a continuation of the Santé Smoothie Saga from Chapters 1 through 16.)

Santé Smoothie & Sweets Ltd. has been providing all natural granola bars to Coffee Beans Ltd., a private company, on a weekly basis over the past two years. Coffee Beans, thrilled with the quality of goods and service it is receiving from Santé has approached the Koebels to join its team. Coffee Beans is expanding and hopes that the Koebels would consider the sale of Santé Smoothie & Sweets Ltd.

shares to Coffee Beans. In exchange, Janet, Brian, and Natalie would then become both shareholders and employees of Coffee Beans Ltd.

Janet, Brian, and Natalie have worked hard to achieve the success that Santé Smoothie & Sweets has achieved. They are reluctant to join another team unless they can be reasonably assured that there will be future growth in the business they are investing in. Selected information for Santé Smoothie & Sweets and Coffee Beans follows:

	Santé Smoothie & Sweets Ltd. Year Ended May 31, 2018	Coffee Beans Ltd. Year Ended December 31, 2017	Coffee Beans Ltd. Year Ended December 31, 2016
Profit	$ 199,629	$ 1,465,466	$ 1,259,966
Net cash provided by operating activities	$ 235,279	$ 1,137,650	$ 2,324,547
Net cash used by investing activities	(157,833)	(4,545,728)	(3,036,676)
Net cash (used) provided by financing activities	(37,071)	7,406,647	955,201
Cash, end of year	199,443	4,469,552	470,983
Current liabilities	31,121	5,190,005	5,046,240
Total liabilities	81,551	10,398,638	7,076,968
Dividends paid	120,000	0	0

Instructions

(a) Calculate the net increase in cash and the amount of cash at the beginning of the year that would have been included on the statement of cash flows for each company.

(b) Calculate free cash flow for each company.

(c) Compare the provision and use of cash in each of the three activities—operating, investing, and financing—by each company.

(d) Based on information provided in parts (a) and (b), identify why Coffee Beans is pursuing an investment in Santé Smoothie & Sweets Ltd.

(e) Based on information provided in parts (a) and (b), identify for the Koebels some of the issues they should consider and additional information they would require before making the decision to sell their shares and/or be employed by Coffee Beans Ltd.

ANSWERS TO CHAPTER QUESTIONS

ANSWERS TO ACCOUNTING IN ACTION INSIGHT QUESTIONS

All About You, p. 892

Q: Is it appropriate to use your credit card to pay for your operating activities such as your groceries, clothes, and entertainment? Is it appropriate to use your credit card to finance your investment activities such as tuition or, if you have a large enough limit, a car?

A: Credit cards should never be used for a long-term financing activity because of the high interest rates charged by credit card companies. They can be effectively used for short-term operating activities such as paying for your groceries, clothes, and entertainment, provided that you are able to pay off the full amount of your credit card balance when the payment is due and avoid any interest charges. And credit cards should only be used for long-term investing activities if you will have enough cash to pay off the credit card bill before its due date and avoid interest charges. Long-term investment activities should be financed with long-term financing, if you do not have the cash to pay off the credit card bill before its due date. If you are buying a car or financing your education, you need either a long-term bank loan or a student loan where your payment schedule will match your long-term use of that car or education.

Across the Organization, p. 904

Q: What implications does a company's ability to raise cash have for its growth and survival?

A: All companies must have the ability to pay employees and suppliers as amounts come due and to respond quickly to changes in economic conditions in order to survive. Having access to adequate amounts of cash increases a company's financial flexibility. A company with the ability to raise cash should be in a better position to survive because it can generate cash to survive economic downturns. Also, a company that can generate cash is able to raise money to invest in its future growth.

Ethics Insight, p. 920

Q: Why would management of a company want to overstate cash flow from operating activities?

A: The ability to generate cash flows from operating activities is critical to a company's ability to survive and expand. A company must generate cash flows from its operations to pay off debt, pay dividends, and invest in new assets that will allow the company to grow. Generally, investors and creditors will be more willing to invest or lend to companies that report higher cash flows from operating activities.

ANSWERS TO SELF-STUDY QUESTIONS

1. b   2. a   3. c   4. b   5. d   6. b   7. d   8. a   9. d   10. c

18 FINANCIAL STATEMENT ANALYSIS

CHAPTER PREVIEW ▶ An important lesson can be learned from our feature story. Effective use of information is the key to decision-making. The purpose of this chapter is to introduce the tools used in financial statement analysis to help users evaluate, and make decisions about, a company's financial performance and position.

We will use three common tools of analysis—horizontal, vertical, and ratio—to analyze the financial statements of a hypothetical publicly traded small chain of stores called National Tire Ltd. We will then compare this analysis with Canadian Tire, a publicly traded national chain of stores that would be one of National Tire's competitors. We will conclude our discussion with some of the limiting factors users should be aware of in their analysis of financial information.

FEATURE STORY ▶ CORUS ENTERTAINS INVESTORS

TORONTO, Ont.—When investors are shopping for shares to buy, they will look at obvious things such as historic share price and dividend payouts. But they will also delve deeper into a company's financial statements and analyze its performance year over year and against its competitors.

Anyone considering buying shares in our feature company, Corus Entertainment Inc., would be smart to look at ratios measuring its liquidity (ability to pay short-term obligations), solvency (ability to survive in the long term), and profitability (operating success in a specific period). It's one thing to know how a company's share price and dividend payout have changed over time; it's another thing to try to predict how well the company will do in the future. That's where ratio analysis comes in.

Like all publicly traded companies, Corus is followed by financial analysts working at banks and other organizations who use ratios to determine whether to recommend to customers to buy, hold, or sell its shares. Analysts following Corus use ratios such as return on assets and return on equity to evaluate profitability.

One of the most common ratios that analysts use to assess a company's profitability is the payout ratio—the percentage of profit distributed as cash dividends to shareholders. Investors wanting a steady income from their investments will be looking to buy and hold shares that pay regular, attractive dividends. In fact, on Corus's investor relations section on its website, the most prominent feature is a chart showing the company's annual dividend payout history. After Corus

released its financial statements for the quarter ended May 2015, an analyst with TD Securities, Vince Valentini, estimated the firm's future payout ratio. Assuming an annual 5% dividend increase, Mr. Valentini estimated that Corus would have a payout ratio of 62% in 2016 and 71% in 2017. "This leads us to conclude that the risk/reward is favourable at current levels for long-term value investors," he said in recommending that clients buy Corus shares.

Mature companies such as Corus tend to pay out a higher portion of their profit as dividends than younger companies in growth mode, which tend to reinvest more of their profit in the business. Investors looking for steady dividends would likely want to invest in mature companies; others are willing to wait for growing companies to possibly pay off higher returns once they've stabilized.

These ratios don't appear in a company's financial statements. Instead, analysts and investors take the relevant numbers from the financial statements and make their own calculations. Companies like Corus know that they'll be subject to financial analysis and will be compared with other companies in the industry and the economy as a whole, and so they try to provide value to shareholders.

Sources: D. Milstead, "Don't Tune Out This Nearly 9% Dividend Yielding Stock Just Yet," *Globe and Mail*, August 21, 2015; "CJR.B Key Statistics—Corus Entertainment Inc. Cl B NV Financial Ratios," MarketWatch.com, accessed November 4, 2015; Corus Entertainment corporate website, www.corusent.com.

Filipe Frazao/Shutterstock

CHAPTER OUTLINE

LEARNING OBJECTIVES

The chapter is organized as follows:

1   **Identify the need for, and tools of, financial statement analysis.**

Basics of Financial Statement Analysis
- Comparative analysis
- Tools of analysis

DO IT 1

Basis of comparison and analytical tools

---

2   **Explain and apply horizontal analysis.**

Horizontal Analysis
- Balance sheet
- Income statement

DO IT 2

Horizontal analysis

---

3   **Explain and apply vertical analysis.**

Vertical Analysis
- Balance sheet
- Income statement

DO IT 3

Vertical analysis

---

4   **Identify and use ratios to analyze liquidity.**

Ratio Analysis
- Liquidity ratios

DO IT 4

Liquidity ratios

---

5   **Identify and use ratios to analyze solvency.**

- Solvency ratios

DO IT 5

Solvency ratios

---

6   **Identify and use ratios to analyze profitability.**

- Profitability ratios

DO IT 6

Profitability ratios

---

7   **Recognize the limitations of financial statement analysis.**

Limitations of Financial Statement Analysis
- Alternative accounting policies
- Comprehensive income
- Quality of information
- Economic factors

DO IT 7

Comprehensive income

Basics of Financial Statement Analysis

Analyzing financial statements involves evaluating three characteristics: a company's liquidity, solvency, and profitability. We learned in Chapters 1 and 11 that the objective of financial reporting is to provide investors and creditors with information useful for decision-making. For example, a short-term creditor, such as a supplier or banker, is primarily interested in liquidity: the ability of a borrower to pay obligations when they come due. This is extremely important in evaluating the safety of a loan. Conversely, a long-term creditor, such as a banker or bondholder, looks to profitability and solvency measures. These measures indicate the company's ability to survive over a long period of time. Similarly, investors look at a company's profitability and solvency to assess the likelihood of dividends and the growth potential of the share price. Creditors are also often interested in profitability, because a company's profit, or lack of it, can affect its ability to obtain financing.

COMPARATIVE ANALYSIS

To analyze financial statements in a meaningful way, the users of financial information must make comparisons with other financial statement data. Although every item reported in a financial statement has significance, it has limited value on its own. When Canadian Tire reported trade and other receivables of $880.2 million on its fiscal 2014 balance sheet, we know that the company had that amount of receivables at year end. However, we do not know if that is an increase or decrease compared with past years, or if Canadian Tire is collecting its receivables on a timely basis. To get this information, the amount of receivables must be compared with other financial statement data.

To make financial analysis useful, you must compare one financial statement item with a related financial statement item or items. Comparisons can be made on several different bases, including the following:

1. **Intracompany basis.** This basis compares an item or financial relationship within a company in the current year with one or more prior years. Intracompany comparisons are useful for identifying changes in financial relationships and discovering trends.
2. **Intercompany basis.** This basis compares an item or financial relationship of one company with the same item or relationship in one or more competing companies. Intercompany comparisons are useful for understanding a company's competitive position.

In some circumstances, a third basis of comparison, an industry basis, is also performed. This basis compares an item or financial relationship of a company with industry averages. However, for a company like Canadian Tire, determining which industry it is actually in can be problematic because it sells much more than tires. Canadian Tire sells a wide range of home, tools, leisure, and automotive products in its retail stores, in addition to apparel, sporting goods, gasoline, and financial services in some of its other businesses. Consequently, comparison with industry averages for diversified companies such as Canadian Tire has less relevance than intra- and intercompany comparisons.

TOOLS OF ANALYSIS

We use various tools to evaluate the significance of financial statement data for decision-making. Three commonly used tools are:

1. **Horizontal analysis** compares data, such as line items in a company's financial statements, by expressing them as dollar or percentage increases and decreases over two or more years (periods).
2. **Vertical analysis** compares data by expressing each item in a financial statement as a percentage of a base amount within the same financial statement and year (period).

3. **Ratio analysis** expresses the relationship between selected items of financial statement data within the same year (period).

Horizontal analysis helps identify changes and trends over time. For example, Canadian Tire could compare its trade and other receivables balance over the past five years to determine whether it has increased or decreased over that period. Horizontal analysis is mainly used for analysis of financial data *within* a company.

Vertical analysis focuses on the relationships between items on the same financial statement. Vertical analysis may be used for both intracompany and intercompany comparisons. For example, in an intracompany comparison, Canadian Tire could compare its trade and other receivables with its total assets to determine the relative proportion of its receivables. In an intercompany comparison, it could compare this percentage relationship with that of one of its competitors.

Vertical percentages can also be compared across time. Canadian Tire can compare its trade and other receivables as a percentage of its total assets for the current year with that of prior years (intracompany), and it can compare this percentage with that of its competitors (intercompany).

Ratio analysis helps us understand the relationship among selected items presented in one or more financial statements. For example, horizontal analysis can determine whether Canadian Tire's receivables have increased or decreased over time and vertical analysis can determine the proportion that Canadian Tire's receivables constitute of its total assets. However, only ratio analysis can relate receivables to revenues by calculating the receivables turnover ratio to determine how effectively the company is collecting its receivables. Ratio analysis is also used in both intracompany and intercompany comparisons. Canadian Tire can compare its receivables turnover ratio for the current year with that of prior years (intracompany), and can compare this ratio with that of its competitors (intercompany).

While horizontal and vertical analysis are being introduced in this chapter, you should already have some familiarity with ratio analysis, which was introduced in past chapters. In the following sections, we will explain and illustrate each of the three types of analysis: horizontal, vertical, and ratio.

BEFORE YOU GO ON...DO IT **Basis of Comparison and Analytical Tools**

Identify the appropriate basis of comparison and tool of analysis for each of the following financial situations.

	Basis of Comparison	Tool of Analysis
1. Analysis of a company's operating expenses over a 10-year period		
2. Comparison of a company's cost of goods sold with its net sales for the current period		
3. Comparison of a company's profit versus its net sales (profit margin) for the current period with that of a competitor		

Solution

Basis of Comparison	Tool of Analysis
1. Intracompany	Horizontal
2. Intracompany	Vertical
3. Intercompany	Ratio

Related exercise material: BE18–1 and BE18–2.

Action Plan

- Recall that the two bases of comparison are intracompany and intercompany. "Intra" means within and "inter" means between.
- Recall that there are three tools of analysis: horizontal, vertical, and ratio.

Horizontal Analysis

Horizontal analysis, also called **trend analysis**, is a technique for comparing a series of financial statement data over a period of time. The term "horizontal analysis" means that we view financial statement data from left to right (or right to left) across time.

The purpose of horizontal analysis is to determine the increase or decrease that has taken place over time. This change may be expressed as either a dollar amount or a percentage. For example, total revenue figures and horizontal analysis percentages for Canadian Tire for the most recent three-year period are shown in Illustration 18-1.

▶ILLUSTRATION **18-1**
Horizontal analysis for
Canadian Tire's revenue

CANADIAN TIRE CORPORATION, LIMITED Year Ended December 31 (in millions)			
	2014	**2013**	**2012**
Revenue	$12,462.9	$11,785.6	$11,427.2
% of base-year (2012) amount	109.1%	103.1%	100.0%
% change between years	5.7%	3.1%	

If we assume that 2012 is the base year, we can express revenue as a **percentage of the base-year amount**. This is calculated by dividing the amount for the specific year (or period) we are analyzing by the base-year (or period) amount, as shown in Illustration 18-2.

▶ILLUSTRATION **18-2**
Horizontal percent of
base year formula

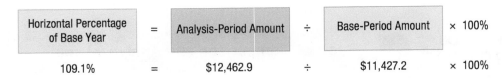

Horizontal Percentage of Base Year	=	Analysis-Period Amount	÷	Base-Period Amount	× 100%
109.1%	=	$12,462.9	÷	$11,427.2	× 100%

We can determine that Canadian Tire's total revenue in 2014 is 109.1% of the total revenue in 2012 by dividing $12,462.9 million by $11,427.2 million. In other words, revenue in 2014 was 9.1% greater than revenue two years earlier, in 2012. From this analysis, shown in the second row of Illustration 18-1, we can see Canadian Tire's revenue trend. Revenue has increased each year.

We can also use horizontal analysis to measure the percentage change between any two periods of time. This is known as a **horizontal percentage change for period**. It is calculated by dividing the dollar amount of the change between the specific year (or period) under analysis and the prior year (or period) by the prior-year (or period) amount, as shown in Illustration 18-3.

▶ILLUSTRATION **18-3**
Horizontal percentage
change for period formula

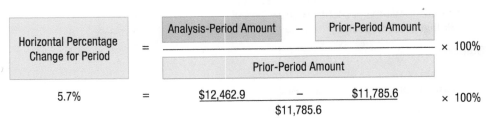

$$\text{Horizontal Percentage Change for Period} = \frac{\text{Analysis-Period Amount} - \text{Prior-Period Amount}}{\text{Prior-Period Amount}} \times 100\%$$

$$5.7\% = \frac{\$12,462.9 - \$11,785.6}{\$11,785.6} \times 100\%$$

For example, we can determine that Canadian Tire's revenue increased by $677.3 million ($12,462.9 million – $11,785.6 million) between 2013 and 2014. This increase can then be expressed as a percentage, 5.7%, by dividing the amount of the change between the two years, $677.3 million, by the amount in the prior year, $11,785.6 million. That is, in 2014, revenue increased by 5.7% compared with 2013. The horizontal percentage change for the period in Canadian Tire's revenue between each of the last three years (i.e., between 2014 and 2013, and between 2013 and 2012) is presented in the last row of Illustration 18-1.

BALANCE SHEET

To further illustrate horizontal analysis, we will use the hypothetical financial statements of National Tire Ltd. Its two-year condensed balance sheet, which shows dollar amount and percentage changes for a period, is presented in Illustration 18-4.

NATIONAL TIRE LTD. Balance Sheet December 31				
			Increase (Decrease)	
Assets	**2014**	**2013**	**Amount**	**Percentage**
Current assets				
Cash	$ 50,000	$ 55,000	$ (5,000)	(9.1)%
Short-term investments	20,000	35,000	(15,000)	(42.9)%
Accounts receivable	72,500	50,000	22,500	45.0%
Inventory	372,500	340,000	32,500	9.6%
Prepaid expenses	30,000	20,000	10,000	50.0%
Total current assets	545,000	500,000	45,000	9.0%
Property, plant, and equipment	400,000	450,000	(50,000)	(11.1)%
Intangible assets	55,000	65,000	(10,000)	(15.4)%
Total assets	$1,000,000	$1,015,000	$(15,000)	(1.5)%
Liabilities and Shareholders' Equity				
Liabilities				
Current liabilities	$ 337,700	$ 333,500	$ 4,200	1.3%
Non-current liabilities	400,000	475,000	(75,000)	(15.8)%
Total liabilities	737,700	808,500	(70,800)	(8.8)%
Shareholders' equity				
Common shares (300,000 shares issued)	110,000	110,000	0	0.0%
Retained earnings	152,300	96,500	55,800	57.8%
Total shareholders' equity	262,300	206,500	55,800	27.0%
Total liabilities and shareholders' equity	$1,000,000	$1,015,000	$(15,000)	(1.5)%

▶ ILLUSTRATION **18-4**
Horizontal analysis of balance sheet—percentage change for period

The horizontal percentages in Illustration 18-4 are an example of a percentage change for a period, and not a percentage of base year. It makes sense to calculate the percentage change for a period in this illustration because only two periods are under analysis. Note that, in a horizontal analysis, while the amount column of the increase or decrease is additive (e.g., the decrease in total liabilities of $70,800 is equal to +$4,200 − $75,000), the percentage column is not additive (8.8% is not equal to +1.3% − 15.8%).

The horizontal analysis of National Tire's comparative balance sheet shows that several changes have occurred between 2014 and 2013. In the current assets section, short-term investments decreased by $15,000, or 42.9%. This may be due to a decline in the fair value of the investments or the result of a sale of some of the investments. The accounts receivable increased by $22,500, or 45%. We will look at the income statement in the next section to determine whether sales increased by the same proportion as receivables. If not, this may indicate that the receivables are slow-moving.

Inventory increased by a larger dollar amount, $32,500, than did accounts receivable but not by as large a percentage: 9.6% for inventory compared with 45% for accounts receivable. Inventory may have changed because of increased sales; we will investigate this further when we analyze the income statement. Prepaid expenses increased by 50% in 2014. One has to be careful in interpreting percentage

Helpful hint The formula for the horizontal dollar change for a year is: Analysis year − prior year. The horizontal percentage change for a period formula is: (Analysis year − prior year) ÷ prior year.

changes like this. Because it is a proportionately large change ($10,000) on a small amount ($20,000), the percentage change is not as meaningful as it first appears.

The carrying amounts of both property, plant, and equipment and intangible assets decreased in 2014. This means that the company is disposing of more long-lived assets than it is acquiring (or that its depreciation and amortization exceed the acquisition of new assets). Overall, total assets decreased by $15,000, or 1.5%, from 2013 to 2014.

Current liabilities increased by 1.3%. Changes in current assets and current liabilities usually move in the same direction; that is, normally both will increase or both will decrease. In this case, both have risen, although current assets have increased more than current liabilities. This is better than the inverse: current liabilities increasing more than current assets.

Non-current liabilities decreased by $75,000, or 15.8%, in 2014. Retained earnings in the shareholders' equity section of the balance sheet increased significantly in 2014, by 57.8%. This suggests that National Tire Ltd. is financing its business by retaining profit, rather than by adding to its debt.

INCOME STATEMENT

Illustration 18-5 presents a horizontal analysis of National Tire's condensed income statement for the years 2013 and 2014.

▶ **ILLUSTRATION 18-5**
Horizontal analysis of income statement—percentage change for period

NATIONAL TIRE LTD. Income Statement Years Ended December 31				
			Increase (Decrease)	
	2014	**2013**	**Amount**	**Percentage**
Sales	$2,095,000	$1,960,000	$135,000	6.9%
Sales returns and allowances	98,000	123,000	(25,000)	(20.3)%
Net sales	1,997,000	1,837,000	160,000	8.7%
Cost of goods sold	1,381,000	1,240,000	141,000	11.4%
Gross profit	616,000	597,000	19,000	3.2%
Operating expenses	457,000	440,000	17,000	3.9%
Profit from operations	159,000	157,000	2,000	1.3%
Other expenses				
Interest expense	27,000	29,500	(2,500)	(8.5)%
Loss on fair value adjustment on short-term investments	15,000	0	15,000	n/a
Profit before income tax	117,000	127,500	(10,500)	(8.2)%
Income tax expense	23,400	25,500	(2,100)	(8.2)%
Profit	$ 93,600	$ 102,000	$ (8,400)	(8.2)%

Horizontal analysis of the income statement, illustrating dollar amounts and percentage changes for the period, shows that net sales increased by 8.7%. Sales do not appear to have increased at the same rate as receivables, which we can see from Illustration 18-4 increased by 45%. Later in the chapter, we will look at the receivables turnover ratio in the ratio analysis section to determine whether receivables are being collected more slowly or not. However, we must be cautious in over-interpreting this increase. This type of business relies a lot on cash sales, not credit sales.

To continue with our horizontal analysis of the income statement, we can observe that similar to net sales, cost of goods sold also increased. However, it is interesting to note that, while cost of goods sold increased by 11.4%, net sales only increased by 8.7%. This is not a sustainable situation over the long run and the relationship between pricing and costs will need to be carefully monitored. Also, while the cost of goods sold increased by 11.4%, we can see from Illustration 18-4 that inventory increased by 9.6%. Therefore, the cost of goods sold increased not only at a faster rate than sales, but also at a faster rate than inventory. We will look at the inventory turnover ratio later in the chapter to determine whether these increases are reasonable.

The net result of the changes in net sales and cost of goods sold is an increase in gross profit of 3.2%. Operating expenses outpaced this percentage increase at 3.9%. Normally, management tries to control operating expenses wherever possible, so we would hope to see operating expenses decrease or at least increase at a lower rate than gross profit.

Other expenses increased, primarily because of the loss on fair value adjustment relating to the short-term investments at fair value through profit and loss. Note that profit declined by the same amount as profit before income tax, 8.2%. This indicates that although income tax expense declined in 2014, its decline was proportionate to profit before income tax in each year. (That is, income tax expense is unchanged at 20% of profit before income tax in each year.)

A horizontal analysis of the percent changes between periods is pretty straightforward and is quite useful. But complications can occur in making the calculations. If an item has a small value in a base year and a large value in the next year, the percentage change may not be meaningful. In addition, if a negative amount appears in the base and there is a positive amount the following year, or vice versa, no percentage change can be calculated. Lastly, if an item has no value in a base year and a value in the next year, no percentage change can be calculated. We have not included a horizontal analysis of National Tire's statement of changes in shareholders' equity or cash flow statement. A horizontal analysis of these statements is not as useful because these statements give details about the changes between two periods. The value of these statements comes from the analysis of the changes during the year, and not from percentage comparisons of these changes against a base amount.

BEFORE YOU GO ON...DO IT **2** ▸ **Horizontal Analysis**

Selected, condensed information (in thousands) from Bubba Ltd.'s income statements follows:

	2017	2016	2015	2014
Net sales	$8,646	$9,468	$6,294	$5,035
Cost of goods sold	6,746	7,322	5,217	4,099
Gross profit	1,900	2,146	1,077	936
Operating expenses	1,396	1,504	948	641
Profit from operations	504	642	129	295
Income tax expense	76	96	19	44
Profit	$ 428	$ 546	$ 110	$ 251

(a) Using horizontal analysis, calculate the horizontal percentage of base year for 2014 to 2017, assuming that 2014 is the base year.

(b) Using horizontal analysis, calculate the percentage change between each of the following sets of years: 2017 and 2016, 2016 and 2015, and 2015 and 2014.

Solution

(a) Horizontal percentage of base-year amount

	2017	2016	2015	2014
Net sales	171.7%	188.0%	125.0%	100.0%
Cost of goods sold	164.6%	178.6%	127.3%	100.0%
Gross profit	203.0%	229.3%	115.1%	100.0%
Operating expenses	217.8%	234.6%	147.9%	100.0%
Profit from operations	170.8%	217.6%	43.7%	100.0%
Income tax expense	172.7%	218.2%	43.2%	100.0%
Profit	170.5%	217.5%	43.8%	100.0%

(b) Horizontal percentage change for year

	2017 to 2016	2016 to 2015	2015 to 2014
Net sales	(8.7)%	50.4%	25.0%
Cost of goods sold	(7.9)%	40.3%	27.3%
Gross profit	(11.5)%	99.3%	15.1%
Operating expenses	(7.2)%	58.6%	47.9%
Profit from operations	(21.5)%	397.7%	(56.3)%
Income tax expense	(20.8)%	405.3%	(56.8)%
Profit	(21.6)%	396.4%	(56.2)%

Related exercise material: BE18–3, BE18–4, BE18–5, E18–1, and E18–2.

Action Plan

- Horizontal percentage of base year: Set the base-year (2014) dollar amounts at 100%. Express each subsequent year's amount as a percentage of the base-year amount by dividing the dollar amount for the year under analysis by the base-year amount and multiplying by 100%.
- Horizontal percentage change for year: Find the percentage change between two years by dividing the dollar amount of the change between the current year and the prior year by the prior-year amount.

Vertical Analysis

Vertical analysis, also called **common size analysis**, is a technique for comparing an amount in a company's financial statements with a total (base) amount within the same financial statement. The term "vertical analysis" means that we view financial statement data from up to down (or down to up) within the same period of time.

Note that, while horizontal analysis compares data across more than one year, vertical analysis compares data within the same year. **Each financial statement item is expressed as a percentage of a base amount.** Therefore, it is calculated by dividing the financial statement amount under analysis by the relevant base amount for that particular financial statement, as shown in Illustration 18-6.

▷ ILLUSTRATION 18-6
Vertical analysis formula—percent of base amount

Vertical Analysis	=	Analysis Amount	÷	Base Amount	× 100%

The base amount commonly used for the balance sheet is **total assets**. The base amount for the income statement is usually **revenues** for a service company and **net sales** for a merchandising company.

BALANCE SHEET

We will illustrate vertical analysis by using National Tire's balance sheet and considering a two-year intracompany comparison.

Intracompany Comparison

Illustration 18-7 shows a vertical analysis of National Tire's comparative balance sheet. It is called an intracompany comparison because it analyzes information within the company. As was mentioned above, this analysis uses **total assets** as the base amount. Note that **total liabilities and shareholders' equity** equals total assets, so the same base amount (e.g., total assets) can be used for both assets as well as liabilities and shareholders' equity items.

▷ ILLUSTRATION 18-7
Vertical analysis of balance sheet—percent of base amount

NATIONAL TIRE LTD.
Balance Sheet
December 31

	2014		2013	
Assets	Amount	Percentage	Amount	Percentage
Current assets				
Cash	$ 50,000	5.0%	$ 55,000	5.4%
Short-term investments	20,000	2.0%	35,000	3.5%
Accounts receivable	72,500	7.2%	50,000	4.9%
Inventory	372,500	37.3%	340,000	33.5%
Prepaid expenses	30,000	3.0%	20,000	2.0%
Total current assets	545,000	54.5%	500,000	49.3%
Property, plant, and equipment	400,000	40.0%	450,000	44.3%
Intangible assets	55,000	5.5%	65,000	6.4%
Total assets	$1,000,000	100.0%	$1,015,000	100.0%

Liabilities and Shareholders' Equity				
Liabilities				
Current liabilities	$ 337,700	33.8%	$ 333,500	32.9%
Non-current liabilities	400,000	40.0%	475,000	46.8%
Total liabilities	737,700	73.8%	808,500	79.7%
Shareholders' equity				
Common shares (300,000 shares issued)	110,000	11.0%	110,000	10.8%
Retained earnings	152,300	15.2%	96,500	9.5%
Total shareholders' equity	262,300	26.2%	206,500	20.3%
Total liabilities and shareholders' equity	$1,000,000	100.0%	$1,015,000	100.0%

Vertical analysis shows the size of each item in the balance sheet compared with a base amount for each of 2014 and 2013. In addition to reviewing the respective proportion of each item in the balance sheet within a specific year, vertical analysis can also be used to compare changes in the individual asset, liability, and shareholders' equity items between years.

For example, we can see that current assets increased from 49.3% of total assets in 2013 to 54.5% of total assets in 2014. We can also see that the biggest change was in inventory, which increased from 33.5% of total assets in 2013 to 37.3% in 2014. This is contrary to what we first observed in Illustration 18-4, where it appeared that prepaid expenses had the greatest percentage increase in the current assets category. In Illustration 18-7, prepaid expenses increased by only one percentage point of total assets, from 2% in 2013 to 3% in 2014. You will recall our earlier words of caution about interpreting such a large percentage change (the 50% horizontal percentage change for period) as was presented for prepaid expenses in Illustration 18-4.

The carrying amounts of property, plant, and equipment and intangible assets decreased in absolute dollar amounts, as we saw in Illustration 18-4, and also decreased as relative percentages of total assets, as shown in Illustration 18-7. Property, plant, and equipment decreased from 44.3% in 2013 to 40.0% in 2014 and intangible assets decreased from 6.4% in 2013 to 5.5% in 2014.

Non-current liabilities decreased from 46.8% to 40.0%, while retained earnings increased from 9.5% to 15.2% of total liabilities and shareholders' equity between 2013 and 2014. These results reinforce the earlier observation that National Tire is financing its growth by retaining profit, rather than by issuing additional debt.

Note that National Tire has only one class of share capital—common shares—issued. Its common shares didn't actually change between 2013 and 2014, yet common shares are a different percentage of total assets in each year (10.8% in 2013 and 11.0% in 2014). This is because the base (total assets) has changed in each year while the amount of common shares has not.

Intercompany Comparison

The above vertical analysis illustrated an intracompany comparison—we compared changes in National Tire's balance sheet between 2013 and 2014. We can also use vertical analysis to compare companies in an intercompany comparison. This is a particularly helpful technique when companies are of different sizes.

For example, National Tire's main (hypothetical) competitor is Canadian Tire. Using vertical analysis, the condensed balance sheet (or the income statement) of the small retail company National Tire can be more meaningfully compared with the balance sheet (or income statement) of the giant retailer Canadian Tire, as shown in Illustration 18-8.

▶ILLUSTRATION 18-8
Intercompany balance
sheet comparison—vertical
analysis

BALANCE SHEET (in thousands)					
		National Tire December 31, 2014		Canadian Tire January 3, 2015	
Assets		Amount (in thousands)	Percentage	Amount (in millions)	Percentage
Current assets		$ 545.0	54.5%	$ 8,510.2	58.5%
Long-term receivables and other assets		0.0	0.0%	872.2	6.0%
Long-term investments		0.0	0.0%	176.0	1.2%
Property, plant, and equipment		400.0	40.0%	3,743.1	25.7%
Intangible assets		55.0	5.5%	1,251.7	8.6%
Total assets		$1,000.0	100.0%	$14,553.2	100.0%
Liabilities and Shareholders' Equity					
Liabilities					
Current liabilities		$ 337.7	33.8%	$ 4,578.8	31.5%
Non-current liabilities		400.0	40.0%	4,343.6	29.8%
Total liabilities		737.7	73.8%	8,922.4	61.3%
Shareholders' equity					
Share capital		110.0	11.0%	698.4	4.8%
Retained earnings		152.3	15.2%	4,075.1	28.0%
Accumulated other comprehensive income		0.0	0.0%	82.0	0.6%
Non-controlling interest		0.0	0.0%	775.3	5.3%
Total shareholders' equity		262.3	26.2%	5,630.8	38.7%
Total liabilities and shareholders' equity		$1,000.0	100.0%	$14,553.2	100.0%

Helpful hint The formula for
calculating these balance sheet
percentages for vertical analysis is:
$\dfrac{\text{Each item on B/S}}{\text{Total assets}} \times 100\%$

Canadian Tire's total assets are 14,553 times greater than the total assets of the much smaller National Tire. Vertical analysis helps eliminate this difference in size. For example, although National Tire has fewer dollars of property, plant, and equipment compared with Canadian Tire ($400,000 compared with $3,743 million), using percentages, its proportion of property, plant, and equipment is much larger (40.0% compared with 25.7%).

Although National Tire has fewer dollars of debt than Canadian Tire ($737.7 thousand compared with $8,922.4 million), it has a higher debt percentage than does Canadian Tire (73.8% compared with 61.3%). This is not surprising given that National Tire, as a much smaller company, may not have the same access to equity financing as does Canadian Tire. Alternatively, it may have deliberately chosen to finance its operations with proportionately more debt than equity than Canadian Tire. Regardless of the rationale, the company does have a lower equity base than Canadian Tire (26.2% compared with 38.7%).

INCOME STATEMENT

We now illustrate an intracompany comparison using vertical analysis of National Tire's income statement. A vertical analysis of the percentage of the base amount for each of 2013 and 2014 is shown in Illustration 18-9, with **net sales** used as the base amount.

NATIONAL TIRE LTD. Income Statement Years Ended December 31				
	2014		**2013**	
	Amount	**Percentage**	**Amount**	**Percentage**
Sales	$2,095,000	104.9%	$1,960,000	106.7%
Sales returns and allowances	98,000	4.9%	123,000	6.7%
Net sales	1,997,000	100.0%	1,837,000	100.0%
Cost of goods sold	1,381,000	69.2%	1,240,000	67.5%
Gross profit	616,000	30.8%	597,000	32.5%
Operating expenses	457,000	22.9%	440,000	24.0%
Profit from operations	159,000	7.9%	157,000	8.5%
Other expenses				
Interest expense	27,000	1.3%	29,500	1.6%
Loss on fair value adjustment on short-term investments	15,000	0.7%	0	0.0%
Profit before income tax	117,000	5.9%	127,500	6.9%
Income tax expense	23,400	1.2%	25,500	1.3%
Profit	$ 93,600	4.7%	$ 102,000	5.6%

▶ILLUSTRATION 18-9
Vertical analysis of
income statement percent
of base amount

We can see that the cost of goods sold as a percentage of net sales increased by 1.7 percentage points (from 67.5% to 69.2%) between 2013 and 2014. Operating expenses declined as a percentage of net sales by 1.1 percentage points (from 24.0% to 22.9%). As a result, profit from operations did not change substantially between 2013 and 2014: it declined by 0.6 percentage points (from 8.5% to 7.9%). Profit before income tax declined between 2013 and 2014 from 6.9% to 5.9%. Profit declined as well as a percentage of net sales from 2013 to 2014: it decreased by 0.9 percentage points. Although we saw National Tire's profit decrease by 8.2% between 2013 and 2014 in Illustration 18-5, its profitability is relatively unchanged (less than 1%) compared with net sales.

Vertical analysis can also be applied to intercompany comparisons of the income statement, similar to our comparison of National Tire and Canadian Tire in the balance sheet section above, although we have not chosen to do so here.

Helpful hint The formula for calculating the income statement percentages for vertical analysis is:
$$\frac{\text{Each item on I/S}}{\text{Net sales}} \times 100\%$$

BEFORE YOU GO ON...DO IT **Vertical Analysis**

Selected, condensed information (in thousands) from Bubba Ltd.'s income statements follows:

	2017	2016	2015	2014
Net sales	$8,646	$9,468	$6,294	$5,035
Cost of goods sold	6,746	7,322	5,217	4,099
Gross profit	1,900	2,146	1,077	936
Operating expenses	1,396	1,504	948	641
Profit from operations	504	642	129	295
Income tax expense	76	96	19	44
Profit	$ 428	$ 546	$ 110	$ 251

Using vertical analysis, calculate the percentage of the base amount for each year.

(continued)

Action Plan

- Vertical analysis: Find the relative percentage by dividing the specific income statement amount by the base amount (net sales) for each year and multiply by 100%.

Solution

	2017	2016	2015	2014
Net sales	100%	100%	100%	100%
Cost of goods sold	78%	77%	83%	81%
Gross profit	22%	23%	17%	19%
Operating expenses	16%	16%	15%	13%
Profit from operations	6%	7%	2%	6%
Income tax expense	1%	1%	0%	1%
Profit	5%	6%	2%	5%

Related exercise material: BE18–6, BE18–7, E18–3, E18–4, and E18–5.

Ratio Analysis

Ratio analysis expresses the relationships between selected financial statement items and is the most widely used tool of financial analysis. Ratios are generally classified into three types:

1. **Liquidity ratios.** These measure a company's short-term ability to pay its maturing obligations and to meet unexpected needs for cash.
2. **Solvency ratios.** These measure a company's ability to survive over a long period of time.
3. **Profitability ratios.** These measure a company's operating success for a specific period of time.

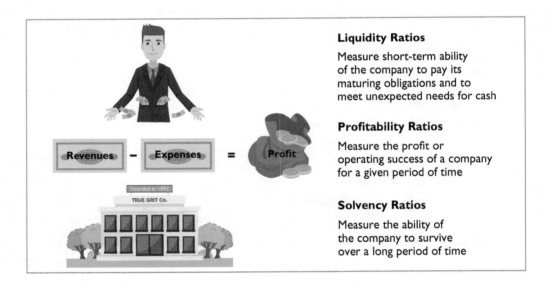

Liquidity Ratios

Measure short-term ability of the company to pay its maturing obligations and to meet unexpected needs for cash

Profitability Ratios

Measure the profit or operating success of a company for a given period of time

Solvency Ratios

Measure the ability of the company to survive over a long period of time

    In earlier chapters, we presented liquidity, solvency, and profitability ratios for evaluating a company's financial condition. In this section, we provide an example of a comprehensive financial analysis using these ratios. This analysis uses two bases for comparisons: (1) intracompany, comparing two years of data (2013 and 2014) for National Tire, and (2) intercompany, comparing National Tire with Canadian Tire, its main competitor, for the year ended December 31, 2014.

    You will recall that National Tire's balance sheet was presented in Illustration 18-4 and its income statement in Illustration 18-5. We will use these two financial statements to calculate National Tire's ratios in the next three sections. You can use these data to review the calculations to make sure you understand where the numbers came from. Detailed calculations are not shown for the ratios presented for National Tire Ltd. for 2013 or for Canadian Tire for 2014.

LEARNING OBJECTIVE	4	Identify and use ratios to analyze liquidity.

LIQUIDITY RATIOS

Liquidity ratios measure a company's short-term ability to pay its maturing obligations and to meet unexpected needs for cash. Short-term creditors, such as suppliers and bankers, are particularly interested in assessing liquidity. Liquidity ratios include the current ratio, the acid-test ratio, receivables turnover, collection period, inventory turnover, days sales in inventory, and the operating cycle.

Current Ratio

The current ratio is a widely used measure of a company's liquidity and short-term debt-paying ability. The ratio is calculated by dividing current assets by current liabilities. The 2014 and 2013 current ratios for National Tire (intracompany basis of comparison) and 2014 current ratio for Canadian Tire (intercompany basis of comparison) are shown below.

$$\text{Current ratio} = \frac{\text{Current assets}}{\text{Current liabilities}}$$

National Tire **2014**	National Tire **2013** = 1.5:1	Intracompany
$\dfrac{\$545,000}{\$337,700} = 1.6:1$	Canadian Tire **2014** = 1.9:1	Intercompany

What does the ratio actually mean? The 2014 ratio of 1.6:1 means that for every dollar of current liabilities, National Tire has $1.60 of current assets. National Tire's current ratio increased slightly between 2013 and 2014. Although its 2014 ratio is lower than Canadian Tire's current ratio of 1.9:1, National Tire appears to have more than enough current assets to pay its current liabilities.

$$\text{Current ratio} = \frac{\text{Current assets}}{\text{Current liabilities}}$$

ACCOUNTING IN ACTION
BUSINESS INSIGHT

The apparent simplicity of the current ratio can have real-world limitations because adding equal amounts to both the numerator and the denominator causes the ratio to decrease if the ratio is greater than 1:1.

Assume, for example, that a company has $2 million of current assets and $1 million of current liabilities. Thus, its current ratio is 2:1. If the company purchases $1 million of inventory on account, it will have $3 million of current assets and $2 million of current liabilities. Its current ratio therefore decreases to 1.5:1. If, instead, the company pays off $500,000 of its current liabilities, it will have $1.5 million of current assets and $500,000 of current liabilities. Its current ratio then increases to 3:1. Thus, any trend analysis should be done with care because the ratio is susceptible to quick changes and is easily influenced by management.

iunewind/iStockphoto

 How might management influence a company's current ratio?

Acid-Test Ratio

The current ratio is only one measure of liquidity. It does not consider the composition of the current assets. For example, a strong current ratio may not reveal the fact that a portion of the current assets may be tied up in slow-moving inventory or prepayments, which are much harder to convert into cash. Therefore, the acid-test ratio differs from the current ratio by excluding assets that are less liquid, such as inventory, which takes longer to be converted to cash. For merchandising companies, inventory must be sold before any accounts receivable or cash can be created.

The current assets for National Tire are presented below. The acid-test ratio is calculated by dividing the sum of cash, short-term investments, and receivables by current liabilities.

NATIONAL TIRE LTD. Balance Sheet December 31		
Assets	**2014**	**2013**
Current assets		
Cash	**$ 50,000**	**$ 55,000**
Short-term investments	**20,000**	**35,000**
Accounts receivable	**72,500**	**50,000**
Inventory	372,500	340,000
Prepaid expenses	30,000	20,000
Total current assets	545,000	500,000

The 2014 and 2013 acid-test ratios for National Tire and 2014 acid-test ratio for Canadian Tire are shown below.

Acid-test ratio = $\dfrac{\text{Cash + Short-term investments + Receivables}}{\text{Current liabilities}}$		
National Tire **2014** $\dfrac{\$50,000 + \$20,000 + \$72,500}{\$337,700} = 0.4{:}1$	National Tire **2013** = 0.4:1	Intracompany
	Canadian Tire **2014** = 0.4:1	Intercompany

Acid-test ratio =
Cash + Short-term investments
+ Receivables
Current liabilities

What does the ratio actually mean? The 2014 ratio of 0.4:1 means that for every dollar of current liabilities, National Tire has $0.40 of highly liquid current assets. The company's acid-test ratio is unchanged from 2013. However, it is much lower than its current ratio of 1.6:1. This indicates National Tire may have a large balance in its inventory and/or prepaid accounts. In addition, given that the current ratio increased and the acid-test ratio did not change in 2014, inventory and/or prepaid expenses likely increased. We will investigate the liquidity of both companies' inventory shortly, because this is the more significant account of the two.

National Tire's acid-test ratio is the same as Canadian Tire's. This is interesting given that its current ratio was lower. National Tire has a higher proportion of liquid assets (cash, short-term investments, and receivables) compared with its current liabilities than does Canadian Tire.

Receivables Turnover

Helpful hint To calculate an average balance sheet amount such as accounts receivable, add together the balance at the beginning of the year (which is the same as the balance at the end of the prior year) and the balance at the end of the year and divide the sum by 2.

We can measure liquidity by how quickly a company can convert certain assets to cash. How liquid, for example, are the accounts receivable? The ratio used to assess this is the accounts receivable turnover. This ratio measures the number of times, on average, that receivables are collected during the period. This ratio is calculated by dividing net credit sales (net sales less cash sales) by the average gross accounts receivable. Average accounts receivable can be calculated by adding the beginning and ending balances of the accounts receivable together and dividing by two.

Why do we use the balance sheet average? Because the income statement figures are for a period of time (i.e., a year) and the balance sheet figures are for a point in time—without averaging, we are not comparing similar items. Comparisons of end-of-period figures with end-of-period figures, or period figures with period figures, do not require averaging, as we saw in the current ratio and acid-test ratio calculated above.

Assuming that all sales are credit sales and that there is no allowance for doubtful accounts, the 2014 and 2013 receivables turnover figures for National Tire and 2014 receivables turnover ratio for Canadian Tire are shown below.

$$\text{Receivables turnover} = \frac{\text{Net credit sales}}{\text{Average gross accounts receivable}}$$		
National Tire **2014** $$\frac{\$1,997,000}{(\$72,500 + \$50,000) \div 2} = 32.6 \text{ times}$$	National Tire **2013** = 38.7 times	Intracompany
	Canadian Tire **2014** = 15.2 times	Intercompany

National Tire's receivables turn over (i.e., they are collected) 32.6 times a year. In general, the faster the receivables turn over, the better and more reliable the current ratio is for assessing liquidity.

> Receivables turnover =
> $$\frac{\text{Net credit sales}}{\text{Average gross accounts receivable}}$$

Although National Tire's receivables turnover declined (worsened) from 38.7 times in 2013 to 32.6 times in 2014, it is still much higher than Canadian Tire's receivables turnover of 15.2 times a year. Why is National Tire's receivables turnover so much higher than that of Canadian Tire? National Tire likely has fewer sales on account and therefore fewer receivables. More of its sales are for cash. Canadian Tire, on the other hand, has receivables from its franchise stores and company credit card, which may take longer to collect.

It is important to be careful in interpreting this ratio. We assumed that all sales were credit sales, when in fact, this is not a reasonable assumption. Companies do not disclose their credit and cash sales separately. However, intracompany and intercompany comparisons can still be made, because the same assumption—all sales were credit sales—was applied to Canadian Tire's data.

A popular variation of the receivables turnover is to convert it into a collection period stated in days. This is calculated by dividing the receivables turnover into the number of days in a year (365 days). National Tire's collection period for 2014 and 2013 and Canadian Tire's collection period for 2014 are shown below.

$$\text{Collection period} = \frac{\text{Days in year}}{\text{Receivables turnover}}$$		
National Tire **2014** $$\frac{365 \text{ days}}{32.6} = 11 \text{ days}$$	National Tire **2013** = 9 days	Intracompany
	Canadian Tire **2014** = 24 days	Intercompany

The effectiveness of a company's credit and collection policies is much easier to interpret using the collection period, rather than the receivables turnover ratio. National Tire's receivables were collected every 11 days in 2014. Although weaker than in 2013, they are still being collected faster than those of Canadian Tire. In addition, this collection period is well under the normal 30-day payment period. The general rule is that the actual days to collect should not be more than the number of credit days the company provides its customers (the time allowed for payment). Even Canadian Tire's higher collection period of 24 days is still a reasonable one. So, despite earlier concerns, receivables management appears to be in good shape for both companies.

> Collection period =
> $$\frac{\text{Days in year}}{\text{Receivables turnover}}$$

Inventory Turnover

Inventory turnover measures the average number of times that the inventory is sold during the period. Its purpose is to measure the liquidity of the inventory. The inventory turnover is calculated by dividing the cost of goods sold by the average inventory.

National Tire's 2014 and 2013 inventory turnover figures and the 2014 inventory turnover ratio for Canadian Tire are shown below.

$\text{Inventory turnover} = \dfrac{\text{Cost of goods sold}}{\text{Average inventory}}$		
National Tire **2014** $$\dfrac{\$1,381,000}{(\$372,500 + \$340,000) \div 2} = 3.9 \text{ times}$$	National Tire **2013** = 3.9 times	Intracompany
	Canadian Tire **2014** = 5.4 times	Intercompany

Inventory turnover =
$\dfrac{\text{Cost of goods sold}}{\text{Average inventory}}$

National Tire turns over (sells) its entire inventory 3.9 times a year. Its inventory turnover was unchanged between 2013 and 2014. National Tire's turnover ratio of 3.9 times is low compared with that of Canadian Tire's turnover of 5.4 times.

Generally, the faster that inventory is sold, the less cash there is tied up in inventory and the less chance there is of inventory becoming obsolete. In addition, the higher the inventory turnover, the more reliable the current ratio is for assessing liquidity. We made this same statement earlier in this chapter with respect to the receivables turnover ratio. That is, if the receivables and inventory turnover ratios are declining, the current ratio may increase simply because higher balances of receivables and inventory are included in current assets. In such cases, the turnover ratios are more relevant than the current ratio as measures of liquidity.

A variant of inventory turnover is the days sales in inventory. This is calculated by dividing the inventory turnover into the number of days in a year (365 days). National Tire's days sales in inventory for 2014 and 2013 and the 2014 days sales in inventory for Canadian Tire are shown below.

$\text{Days sales in inventory} = \dfrac{\text{Days in year}}{\text{Inventory turnover}}$		
National Tire **2014** $$\dfrac{365 \text{ days}}{3.9} = 94 \text{ days}$$	National Tire **2013** = 94 days	Intracompany
	Canadian Tire **2014** = 68 days	Intercompany

Days sales in inventory =
$\dfrac{\text{Days in year}}{\text{Inventory turnover}}$

National Tire's inventory turnover of 3.9 times divided into 365 days is approximately 94 days. In other words, National Tire has 94 days' (more than three months') worth of inventory on hand. This is relatively slow compared with Canadian Tire's 68 days.

It is important to use judgement in interpreting both the inventory turnover and days sales in inventory ratios. Remember that National Tire is composed of a few stores throughout the country, while Canadian Tire has more than 1,700 stores across the nation. Canadian Tire is large enough to take advantage of just-in-time and other computerized inventory management techniques, whereas National Tire likely does not have such sophisticated inventory options.

Nonetheless, National Tire must keep a close eye on its inventory. It runs the risk of being left with unsellable inventory, not to mention the additional costs of financing and carrying this inventory over a longer period of time.

Operating Cycle

Alternative terminology The *operating cycle* is also known as the *cash conversion cycle.*

The operating cycle measures the average time it takes to purchase inventory, sell it on account, and collect the cash from customers. It is calculated by adding the days sales in inventory and the collection period together. The 2014 and 2013 operating cycle figures for National Tire and 2014 operating cycle for Canadian Tire are shown below.

Operating cycle = Days sales in inventory + Collection period		
National Tire **2014** 94 days + 11 days = 105 days	National Tire **2013** = 103 days	Intracompany
	Canadian Tire **2014** = 92 days	Intercompany

In 2014, it took National Tire an average of 105 days (more than three months) from the time it purchased its inventory to sell it on account and collect the cash. This was two days slower than its operating cycle in 2013. Canadian Tire's operating cycle was much faster (shorter) than National Tire's in 2014.

Operating cycle = Days sales in inventory + Collection period

Liquidity Conclusion

Illustration 18-10 summarizes the intracompany liquidity ratios for National Tire.

NATIONAL TIRE LTD.			
Liquidity Ratio	**2014**	**2013**	**Comparison**
Current ratio	1.6:1	1.5:1	Better
Acid-test ratio	0.4:1	0.4:1	No change
Receivables turnover	32.6 times	38.7 times	Worse
Collection period	11 days	9 days	Worse
Inventory turnover	3.9 times	3.9 times	No change
Days sales in inventory	94 days	94 days	No change
Operating cycle	105 days	103 days	Worse

▶ ILLUSTRATION 18-10
Intracompany comparison of liquidity ratios

In an intracompany comparison for the years 2014 and 2013, as shown in Illustration 18-10, National Tire's current ratio increased slightly while its acid-test and inventory turnover ratios remained unchanged from 2013 to 2014. Although its receivables turnover ratio declined, it is still a strong result, and well within the normal collection period. And while its inventory turnover ratio did not change between 2013 and 2014, it is taking a long time to sell its inventory, which could be problematic in future. Because National Tire's receivables turnover ratio declined, its operating cycle—composed of both receivables and inventory—also declined in 2014.

In an intercompany comparison for 2014, as shown in Illustration 18-11, National Tire's overall liquidity is worse than those of Canadian Tire. While its receivables turnover and collection period are better than those of Canadian Tire, this is not as significant a factor in assessing its liquidity as is the management of its inventory. National Tire's inventory turnover, days sales in inventory, and resulting operating cycle are worse than those of Canadian Tire.

Liquidity Ratio	**National Tire**	**Canadian Tire**	**Comparison**
Current ratio	1.6:1	1.9:1	Worse
Acid-test ratio	0.4:1	0.4:1	Equal
Receivables turnover	32.6 times	15.2 times	Better
Collection period	11 days	24 days	Better
Inventory turnover	3.9 times	5.4 times	Worse
Days sales in inventory	94 days	68 days	Worse
Operating cycle	105 days	92 days	Worse

▶ ILLUSTRATION 18-11
Intercompany comparison of liquidity ratios

Summary of Liquidity Ratios

Illustration 18-12 summarizes the liquidity ratios we have used in this chapter, and throughout the textbook. In addition to the ratio formula and purpose, the desired direction (higher or lower) of the result is included.

Liquidity Ratio	Formula	What It Measures	Desired Result
Current	$\dfrac{\text{Current assets}}{\text{Current liabilities}}$	Short-term debt-paying ability	Higher
Acid-test	$\dfrac{\text{Cash + Short-term investments + Accounts receivable}}{\text{Current liabilities}}$	Immediate short-term debt-paying ability	Higher
Receivables turnover	$\dfrac{\text{Net credit sales}}{\text{Average gross accounts receivable}}$	Liquidity of receivables	Higher
Collection period	$\dfrac{\text{Days in year}}{\text{Receivables turnover}}$	Number of days receivables are outstanding	Lower
Inventory turnover	$\dfrac{\text{Cost of goods sold}}{\text{Average inventory}}$	Liquidity of inventory	Higher
Days sales in inventory	$\dfrac{\text{Days in year}}{\text{Inventory turnover}}$	Number of days inventory is on hand	Lower
Operating cycle	Days sales in inventory + Collection period	Number of days to purchase inventory, sell it on account, and collect the cash.	Lower

▶ **ILLUSTRATION** **18-12**
Liquidity ratios

To summarize, a higher result is generally considered to be better for the current, acid-test, receivables turnover, and inventory turnover ratios. For the collection period and days sales in inventory as well as the operating cycle, a lower result is better. That is, you want to take fewer days to collect receivables and have fewer days of inventory on hand—a shorter operating cycle—than the opposite situation.

Of course, there are exceptions. A current ratio can be artificially high at times because of higher balances of receivables and inventory included in current assets that are the result of slow-moving inventory or uncollectible receivables. This is why it is important never to conclude an assessment of liquidity based on only one ratio. In the case of the current ratio, it should always be interpreted along with the acid-test, receivables turnover, and inventory turnover ratios. Likewise, the acid-test ratio should always be interpreted along with the receivables turnover ratio.

BEFORE YOU GO ON...DO IT ④ **Liquidity Ratios**

The following liquidity ratios are available for two fast food companies:

	Henny Penny	Chicken Licken
Current ratio	1.3:1	1.5:1
Acid-test ratio	1.0:1	0.8:1
Receivables turnover	52 times	73 times
Inventory turnover	40 times	26 times

(a) Calculate the collection period, days sales in inventory, and operating cycle for each company.
(b) Indicate which company—Henny Penny or Chicken Licken—has the better result for each of the ratios provided above, in addition to the ratios you calculated in part (a).
(c) Overall, which of the two companies is more liquid? Explain.

Solution

(a)

	Henny Penny	Chicken Licken
Collection period	365 ÷ 52 = 7 days	365 ÷ 73 = 5 days
Days sales in inventory	365 ÷ 40 times = 9 days	365 ÷ 26 = 14 days
Operating cycle	7 + 9 = 16 days	5 + 14 = 19 days

(continued)

BEFORE YOU GO ON...DO IT ④ **Liquidity Ratios** (continued)

(b)

	Henny Penny	Chicken Licken	Comparison
Current ratio	1.3:1	1.5:1	Chicken Licken
Acid-test ratio	1.0:1	0.8:1	Henny Penny
Receivables turnover	52 times	73 times	Chicken Licken
Inventory turnover	40 times	26 times	Henny Penny
Collection period	7 days	5 days	Chicken Licken
Days sales in inventory	9 days	14 days	Henny Penny
Operating cycle	16 days	19 days	Henny Penny

(c) Henny Penny is the more liquid of the two companies. Although its receivables turnover is not as strong as that of Chicken Licken (52 times compared with 73 times), the collection period is still only 7 days, which is an excellent collection period by any standard. Of course, you wouldn't expect a fast food business to have many receivables anyway.

Henny Penny's inventory turnover, which is more important for a fast food business, is stronger than that of Chicken Licken. This slower inventory turnover may be artificially making Chicken Licken's current ratio look better than that of Henny Penny. This hunch is proven by the fact that although Chicken Licken has the (apparently) better current ratio, Henny Penny has the better acid-test ratio, which excludes the effect of inventory. In addition, Henny Penny has the better operating cycle of the two companies.

Related exercise material: BE18–8, BE18–9, BE18–10, BE18–11, E18–6, E18–7, E18–8, and E18–9.

Action Plan

- Review the formula for each ratio so you understand how it is calculated and how to interpret it.
- Remember that for liquidity ratios, a higher result is usually better except for the collection period, days sales in inventory, and operating cycle ratios.
- Review the impact of the receivables and inventory turnover ratios on the current ratio before concluding your analysis.
- Consider any industry factors that may affect your analysis.

LEARNING OBJECTIVE ⑤ Identify and use ratios to analyze solvency.

SOLVENCY RATIOS

Solvency ratios measure a company's ability to survive over a long period of time. Long-term creditors are interested in a company's long-term solvency, particularly its ability to pay interest as it comes due and to repay debt due at maturity. Solvency ratios include debt to total assets, interest coverage, and free cash flow.

Debt to Total Assets

Debt to total assets measures the percentage of the total assets that is provided by creditors. It is calculated by dividing total liabilities (both current and long-term) by total assets. The higher the percentage of debt to total assets, the greater the risk that the company may not be able to meet its maturing obligations. The lower the debt to total assets ratio, the more net assets there are to repay creditors if the company becomes insolvent. So, from a lender's point of view, a low ratio of debt to total assets is desirable.

National Tire's 2014 and 2013 debt to total assets ratios and the 2014 debt to total assets ratio for Canadian Tire are shown below.

Debt to total assets = $\dfrac{\text{Total liabilities}}{\text{Total assets}}$		
National Tire **2014** $\dfrac{\$737,700}{\$1,000,000} = 73.8\%$	National Tire **2013** = 79.7%	Intracompany
	Canadian Tire **2014** = 61.3%	Intercompany

A ratio of 73.8% means that creditors have provided 73.8% of National Tire's total assets. Although its ratio declined (improved) in 2014, National Tire's debt to total assets ratio is higher (worse) than Canadian Tire's ratio of 61.3%.

Debt to total assets =
$\dfrac{\text{Total liabilities}}{\text{Total assets}}$

Although National Tire has a high debt position, a more relevant calculation is whether or not it can afford this level of debt. The debt to total assets ratio should never be interpreted without also looking at the interest coverage ratio, discussed in the next section. A company may have a low debt to total assets ratio but be unable to cover its interest obligations. Alternatively, a company may have a high debt to total assets ratio but be easily able to cover its interest.

ACCOUNTING IN ACTION
ETHICS INSIGHT

Sabra Surkis, president of Surkis Industries, wants to issue a news release to improve her company's image and boost its share price, which has been gradually falling. As controller, you have been asked to provide a list of financial ratios along with some other operating statistics from Surkis Industries' first-quarter operations.

Two days after you provide the ratios and data requested, Carol Dunn, the public relations director of Surkis, asks you to review the financial and operating data contained in the news release written by the president and edited by Carol. In the news release, the president highlights the sales increase of 5.2% over last year's first quarter and the positive change in the current ratio from 1.1:1 last year to 1.5:1 this year. She also emphasizes that production was up 10.1% over the prior year's first quarter.

You note that the release contains only positive or improved ratios, and none of the negative or weakened ratios. For instance, there is no mention that the debt to total assets ratio has increased from 35.1% to 44.9%. Nor is it mentioned that the operating cycle has increased by 19%. There is also no indication that the reported profit for the quarter would have been a loss if the estimated lives of Surkis's machinery had not been increased by 20%.

Q Should you as controller remain silent? Does Carol have any responsibility?

Interest Coverage

The interest coverage ratio gives an indication of the company's ability to make its interest payments as they come due. It is calculated by dividing profit before interest expense and income tax expense by interest expense. Note that the interest coverage ratio uses profit before interest expense and income tax expense. This is often abbreviated as EBIT, which stands for earnings before interest and tax. The term "earnings" is used instead of "profit" in this phrase—both are commonly used and mean the same thing. EBIT represents the amount that is considered to be available to cover interest.

The 2014 and 2013 interest coverage ratios for National Tire and 2014 interest coverage ratio for Canadian Tire are shown below.

Interest coverage = $\dfrac{\text{Profit} + \text{Interest expense} + \text{Income tax expense}}{\text{Interest expense}}$		
National Tire **2014** $\dfrac{\$93,600 + \$27,000 + \$23,400}{\$27,000} = 5.3 \text{ times}$	National Tire **2013** = 5.3 times	Intracompany
	Canadian Tire **2014** = 9.1 times	Intercompany

Interest coverage =
$\dfrac{\text{Profit} + \text{Interest expense} + \text{Income tax expense}}{\text{Interest expense}}$

Despite National Tire's high debt to total assets ratio, it is able to cover its interest payments. Its profit before interest and income tax was 5.3 times the amount needed for interest expense in 2014 and 2013. National Tire's interest coverage remained unchanged in 2014, despite the improvement in its debt to total assets ratio. National Tire's interest coverage ratio is worse than Canadian Tire's coverage ratio of 9.1 times. Nonetheless, both companies are well equipped to handle their interest payments, with coverage ratios in excess of 5 times.

Free Cash Flow

One indication of a company's solvency, as well as of its ability to expand operations, repay debt, or pay dividends, is the amount of excess cash it generates after paying to maintain its current productive capacity. This amount is referred to as free cash flow.

National Tire's cash flow statement was not included in the illustrations shown earlier in the chapter. For your information and for the purpose of the calculation below, its cash provided by operating activities for the year ended December 31, 2014, was $110,000 and its cash used by investing activities was $40,000 for the same period.

The 2014 and 2013 free cash flow amounts for National Tire and 2014 free cash flow for Canadian Tire are shown below.

Free cash flow = Cash provided (used) by operating activities − Cash used (provided) by investing activities		
National Tire **2014**	National Tire **2013** = $100,000	Intracompany
$110,000 − $40,000 = $70,000	Canadian Tire **2014** = $(14.7) million	Intercompany

National Tire has $70,000 of "free" cash to invest in additional property, plant, and equipment; repay debt; and/or pay dividends. This is less than the $100,000 it had available in 2013. Canadian Tire reported a negative amount of free cash in 2014. This means it used $14.7 million more in investing activities than the cash generated from operating activities. However, as noted earlier, it is hard to make a meaningful comparison of absolute dollar amounts for two companies of such different sizes.

> Free Cash Flow =
> Cash provided (used) by
> operating activities − Cash
> used (provided) by investing
> activities.

Solvency Conclusion

In an intracompany comparison for the years 2014 and 2013, as shown in Illustration 18-13, National Tire's solvency generally improved in 2014, as its debt to total assets ratio improved and its interest coverage ratio remained unchanged. Its free cash flow declined.

NATIONAL TIRE LTD.			
Solvency Ratio	**2014**	**2013**	**Comparison**
Debt to total assets	73.8%	79.7%	Better
Interest coverage	5.3 times	5.3 times	No change
Free cash flow	$70,000	$100,000	Worse

▶ ILLUSTRATION 18-13
Intracompany
comparison of solvency ratios

Despite an improvement in solvency within National Tire, an intercompany comparison, as shown in Illustration 18-14, indicates its solvency was generally worse than that of Canadian Tire in 2014. It has a lower interest coverage ratio and it has a much larger proportion of debt to assets, but it has a better free cash flow.

Solvency Ratio	**National Tire**	**Canadian Tire**	**Comparison**
Debt to total assets	73.8%	61.3%	Worse
Interest coverage	5.3 times	9.1 times	Worse
Free cash flow	$70,000	$(14.7) million	Better

▶ ILLUSTRATION 18-14
Intercompany
comparison of solvency ratios

It is important to distinguish between National Tire and Canadian Tire in this analysis, because they are very different types of companies. National Tire, as a small company, relies mainly on debt for its financing and has to generate enough profit to cover its interest payments. In contrast, Canadian Tire, a large national company, relies more on equity for its financing needs.

Summary of Solvency Ratios

▶ ILLUSTRATION 18-15
Solvency ratios

Illustration 18-15 summarizes the solvency ratios we have used in this chapter, and throughout the textbook.

Solvency Ratio	Formula	What It Measures	Desired Result
Debt to total assets	$\dfrac{\text{Total liabilities}}{\text{Total assets}}$	Percentage of total assets provided by creditors	Lower
Interest coverage	$\dfrac{\text{Profit + Interest expense + Income tax expense (EBIT)}}{\text{Income expense}}$	Ability to meet interest payments	Higher
Free cash flow	Cash provided (used) by operating activities − Cash used (provided) by investing activities	Cash generated from operating activities that management can use after paying capital expenditures	Higher

For the debt to total assets ratio, a lower result is generally better. Having less debt reduces a company's dependence on debt financing and offers more flexibility for future financing alternatives. For the interest coverage ratio and free cash flow measure, a higher result is better.

It is important to interpret the debt to total assets and interest coverage ratios together. For example, a company may have a high debt to total assets ratio and a high interest coverage ratio, which indicates that it is able to handle a high level of debt. Or, it may have a low debt to total assets ratio and a low interest coverage ratio, indicating it has difficulty in paying its interest even for a low amount of debt. Consequently, you should always interpret a company's solvency after considering the interrelationship of these two ratios.

BEFORE YOU GO ON...DO IT **5** **Solvency Ratios**

Selected information from the financial statements of Home Affairs Corporation follows:

	2017	2016
Total assets	$1,000,000	$1,015,000
Total liabilities	737,700	809,000
Interest expense	32,000	32,500
Income tax expense	48,400	50,500
Profit	193,600	202,000

(a) Calculate the debt to total assets and interest coverage ratios for each year.
(b) Indicate whether each of the ratios you calculated in part (a) has improved or deteriorated in 2017, compared with 2016.
(c) Overall, has Home Affairs' solvency improved or deteriorated in 2017?

Action Plan

- Review the formula for each ratio so you understand how it is calculated and how to interpret it.
- The debt to total assets ratio should always be interpreted together with the interest coverage ratio.
- Remember that for debt to total assets, a lower result is better. For other solvency ratios, a higher result is better.

Solution

(a) and (b)

	(a)		(b)
	2017	2016	Comparison
Debt to total assets	$\dfrac{\$737,700}{\$1,000,000} = 73.8\%$	$\dfrac{\$809,000}{\$1,015,000} = 79.7\%$	Better
Interest coverage	$\dfrac{\$193,600 + \$32,000 + \$48,400}{\$32,000}$	$\dfrac{\$202,000 + \$32,500 + \$50,500}{\$32,500}$	
	= 8.6 times	= 8.8 times	Worse

(c) Overall, Home Affairs' solvency has improved in 2017. The debt to total assets ratio has declined (improved) in 2017. While the interest coverage ratio declined (deteriorated) marginally between 2017 and 2016, the company still has a strong coverage ratio at 8.6 times. Taken together, this leads us to conclude that overall solvency has improved.

Related exercise material: BE18–12, BE18–13, BE18–14, E18–10, and E18–11.

PROFITABILITY RATIOS

Profitability ratios measure a company's operating success for a specific period of time. A company's profit, or lack of it, affects its ability to obtain debt and equity financing, its liquidity position, and its growth. Investors and creditors are therefore interested in evaluating profitability. Profitability ratios include the gross profit margin, profit margin, asset turnover, return on assets, return on equity, earnings per share, price-earnings, and payout ratios.

Gross Profit Margin

The gross profit margin is determined by dividing gross profit (net sales less cost of goods sold) by net sales. This ratio indicates the percent of gross profit a company generates for each dollar of sales. Gross profit margins should be watched closely over time. If the gross profit margin is too high, the company may lose sales if its pricing is not competitive. If the gross profit margin is too low, the company may not have enough margin to cover its expenses.

National Tire's gross profit margin figures for 2014 and 2013 and Canadian Tire's gross profit margin for 2014 are shown below.

Gross profit margin = $\dfrac{\text{Gross profit}}{\text{Net sales}}$		
National Tire **2014** $\dfrac{\$616,000}{\$1,997,000} = 30.8\%$	National Tire **2013** = 32.5%	Intracompany
	Canadian Tire **2014** = 32.5%	Intercompany

National Tire's gross profit margin for 2014 means that 30.8 cents of each dollar of its sales that year went to cover operating and other expenses and generate a profit. National Tire's gross profit margin declined slightly, from 32.5% in 2013 to 30.8% in 2014.

National Tire's gross profit margin is slightly lower than Canadian Tire's. This could be the result of several factors. It may be that National Tire sells a different mix of merchandise than does Canadian Tire. In addition, National Tire's product costs may be higher in general.

Gross profit margin = $\dfrac{\text{Gross profit}}{\text{Net sales}}$

Profit Margin

Profit margin is a measure of the percentage of each dollar of sales that results in profit. It is calculated by dividing profit by net sales. National Tire's 2014 and 2013 profit margin figures and Canadian Tire's 2014 profit margin are shown below.

Profit margin = $\dfrac{\text{Profit}}{\text{Net sales}}$		
National Tire **2014** $\dfrac{\$93,600}{\$1,997,000} = 4.7\%$	National Tire **2013** = 5.6%	Intracompany
	Canadian Tire **2014** = 5.1%	Intercompany

National Tire's profit margin declined between 2013 and 2014, at 4.7% of net sales, primarily because of the loss relating to the fair value adjustment on its short-term investments. The profit margin has declined below that of Canadian Tire.

High-volume (high inventory turnover) businesses, such as grocery stores (Safeway or Sobeys) and discount stores (Walmart), generally experience low profit margins. In contrast, low-volume

Profit margin = $\dfrac{\text{Profit}}{\text{Net sales}}$

businesses, such as jewellery stores (Maison Birks) or airplane manufacturers (Boeing Co.), have higher profit margins.

Asset Turnover

Asset turnover measures how efficiently a company uses its assets to generate sales. It is determined by dividing net sales by average total assets. The resulting number shows the dollars of sales produced by each dollar of assets.

The 2014 and 2013 asset turnover ratios for National Tire and 2014 asset turnover ratio for Canadian Tire are shown below.

Asset turnover $= \dfrac{\text{Net sales}}{\text{Average total assets}}$		
National Tire **2014** $\dfrac{\$1,997,000}{(\$1,000,000 + \$1,015,000) \div 2} = 2.0 \text{ times}$	National Tire **2013** $= 1.7$ times	Intracompany
	Canadian Tire **2014** $= 0.9$ times	Intercompany

Asset turnover $=$ $\dfrac{\text{Net sales}}{\text{Average total assets}}$

In 2014, National Tire generated $2 of sales for each dollar it had invested in assets. This ratio improved from 2013, when its asset turnover was 1.7 times, or $1.70 of sales for each dollar of assets. Its 2014 asset turnover is also much higher than that of Canadian Tire. Its assets may be newer and more efficient than Canadian Tire's.

Return on Assets

An overall measure of profitability is return on assets. This ratio is calculated by dividing profit by average total assets. National Tire's return on assets figures for 2014 and 2013 and Canadian Tire's return on assets for 2014 are shown below.

Return on assets $= \dfrac{\text{Profit}}{\text{Average total assets}}$		
National Tire **2014** $\dfrac{\$93,600}{(\$1,000,000 + \$1,015,000) \div 2} = 9.3\%$	National Tire **2013** $= 9.7\%$	Intracompany
	Canadian Tire **2014** $= 4.5\%$	Intercompany

Return on assets $=$ $\dfrac{\text{Profit}}{\text{Average total assets}}$

National Tire's return on assets declined (worsened) from 2013 to 2014. Still, its 2014 return of 9.3% is more than double that of Canadian Tire. Although the percentage is high, it must be analyzed in perspective. National Tire's assets have been decreasing and profit is being compared with a relatively small asset base. Consequently, it results in a higher percentage proportionately.

Return on Equity

Alternative terminology *Return on equity* is also known as *return on investment.*

A popular measure of profitability is the return on equity ratio. This ratio shows how many dollars of profit were earned for each dollar invested by the shareholders. It is calculated by dividing profit by average total shareholders' equity.

Although we calculate this ratio using total shareholders' equity below, it can also be calculated using only the common shareholders' equity if there is more than one class of shares. In such cases, the numerator, profit, is reduced by any preferred dividends to determine the profit available for common shareholders. The denominator, average total shareholders' equity, is reduced by any share capital belonging to the preferred shareholders to determine average common shareholders' equity. You will recall that National Tire Ltd. has only one class of share capital—common shares—so it has no preferred shares or preferred dividends.

The return on equity figures for National Tire for 2014 and 2013 and return on equity for Canadian Tire for 2014 are shown below.

Return on equity = $\dfrac{\text{Profit}}{\text{Average shareholders' equity}}$		
National Tire **2014** $\dfrac{\$93,600}{(\$262,300 + \$206,500) \div 2} = 39.9\%$	National Tire **2013** = 50.9%	Intracompany
	Canadian Tire **2014** = 11.5%	Intercompany

Although it declined (worsened) in 2014, National Tire's return on equity is unusually high at 39.9%. The return on equity figure for Canadian Tire is much lower at 11.5%.

Note that National Tire's 2014 return on equity of 39.9% is much higher than its return on assets of 9.3%. The reason is that National Tire has made effective use of financial leverage. **Financial leverage** is when an entity borrows at one rate and invests at a different rate. Financial leverage is said to be positive if a company is able to earn a higher return on equity by using borrowed money in its operations than it has to pay on the borrowed money. Use of financial leverage has enabled National Tire to use money supplied by creditors to increase its return to the shareholders. Recall that National Tire has proportionately more debt than Canadian Tire. Given that it is able to create positive financial leverage on its borrowings, it is not surprising that National Tire's return on equity is higher than Canadian Tire's.

> Return on equity = $\dfrac{\text{Profit}}{\text{Average shareholders' equity}}$

Earnings per Share (EPS)

Earnings per share is a measure of the profit earned on each common share. Shareholders usually think in terms of the number of shares they own or plan to buy or sell. Reducing profit to a per-share basis gives a useful measure of profitability. This measure is widely used and reported. Because of the importance of the earnings per share ratio, publicly traded companies are required to present it directly on the income statement. As we mentioned earlier in this textbook, private companies using ASPE are not required to report earnings per share.

Earnings per share is calculated by dividing the profit available to common shareholders (profit less preferred dividends) by the weighted average number of common shares. National Tire's profit was reported in Illustration 18-5 and its number of common shares was reported in Illustration 18-4. You will recall that National Tire does not have any preferred shares, so there are no preferred dividends to consider in this calculation. There has been no change in the number of common shares over the past three years; consequently, the weighted average number of shares is the same as the issued number—300,000.

The earnings per share figures for National Tire for 2014 and 2013 and earnings per share for Canadian Tire for 2014 are shown below.

Earnings per share = $\dfrac{\text{Profit} - \text{Preferred dividends}}{\text{Weighted average number of common shares}}$		
National Tire **2014** $\dfrac{\$93,600 - \$0}{300,000} = \$0.31$	National Tire **2013** = \$0.34	Intracompany
	Canadian Tire **2014** = \$7.65	Intercompany

National Tire's earnings per share declined by $0.03 per share ($0.34 to $0.31) in 2014. Comparisons with Canadian Tire are not meaningful, because of the large differences in the number of shares issued by companies for different purposes. The only meaningful EPS comparison is an intracompany one.

> Earnings per share =
> $\dfrac{\text{Profit} - \text{Preferred dividends}}{\text{Weighted average number of common shares}}$

Price-Earnings (PE) Ratio

The price-earnings (PE) ratio is an often-quoted measure of the ratio of the market price of each common share to the earnings per share. The price-earnings ratio reflects investors' assessments of a company's future profitability. It is calculated by dividing the market price per share by earnings per share. The current market price of National Tire's shares is $1.40/share. Earnings per share was calculated above.

The price-earnings ratios for National Tire for 2014 and 2013 and the price-earnings ratio for Canadian Tire for 2014 are shown below.

Price-earnings ratio $= \dfrac{\text{Market price per share}}{\text{Earnings per share}}$		
National Tire **2014** $\dfrac{\$1.40}{\$0.31} = 4.5 \text{ times}$	National Tire **2013** = 3.5 times	Intracompany
	Canadian Tire **2014** = 16 times	Intercompany

Price-earnings ratio = $\dfrac{\text{Market price per share}}{\text{Earnings per share}}$

In 2014, National Tire's shares were valued at 4.5 times its earnings. The earnings per share, although declining, is still strong and the price of the shares has increased, indicating investors believe the company has expectations of future increases in profitability. Canadian Tire's 2014 price-earnings ratio is 16 times, which is much higher than National Tire's ratio of 4.5 times.

In general, a higher price-earnings ratio means that investors favour the company. They are willing to pay more for the shares because they believe the company has good prospects for long-term growth and profit in the future.

Payout Ratio

The payout ratio measures the percentage of profit distributed as cash dividends. It is calculated by dividing cash dividends by profit. National Tire paid $37,800 in dividends in 2014. Its profit was reported earlier in Illustration 18-5.

The 2014 and 2013 payout ratios for National Tire and 2014 payout ratio for Canadian Tire are shown below.

Payout ratio $= \dfrac{\text{Cash dividends}}{\text{Profit}}$		
National Tire **2014** $\dfrac{\$37,800}{\$93,600} = 40.4\%$	National Tire **2013** = 35.3%	Intracompany
	Canadian Tire **2014** = 25.5%	Intercompany

Payout ratio = $\dfrac{\text{Cash dividends}}{\text{Profit}}$

National Tire's 2014 payout ratio of 40.4% increased over its 2013 payout ratio and is significantly higher than the payout ratio of Canadian Tire. Many companies with stable earnings have high payout ratios. Companies that are expanding rapidly normally have low, or zero, payout ratios.

Profitability Conclusion

In an intracompany comparison, as shown in Illustration 18-16, National Tire's overall profitability declined between 2013 and 2014. All of its profitability measures declined except for its asset turnover, price-earnings, and payout ratios.

▶ ILLUSTRATION 18-16
Intracompany comparison of profitability ratios

NATIONAL TIRE LTD.			
Profitability Ratio	**2014**	**2013**	**Comparison**
Gross profit margin	30.8%	32.5%	Worse
Profit margin	4.7%	5.6%	Worse
Asset turnover	2.0 times	1.7 times	Better
Return on assets	9.3%	9.7%	Worse
Return on equity	39.9%	50.9%	Worse
Earnings per share	$0.31	$0.34	Worse
Price-earnings ratio	4.5 times	3.5 times	Better
Payout ratio	40.4%	35.3%	Better

In an intercompany comparison, as shown in Illustration 18-17, National Tire's overall profitability is better than that of Canadian Tire on all but three measures. Despite its lower profitability performance, investors are favouring Canadian Tire rather than National Tire, as evidenced by the price-earnings ratio.

Profitability Ratio	National Tire	Canadian Tire	Comparison
Gross profit margin	30.8%	32.5%	Worse
Profit margin	4.7%	5.1%	Worse
Asset turnover	2.0 times	0.9 times	Better
Return on assets	9.3%	4.5%	Better
Return on equity	39.9%	11.5%	Better
Earnings per share	$0.31	$7.65	n/a
Price-earnings ratio	4.5 times	16.0 times	Worse
Payout ratio	40.4%	25.5%	Better

▶ ILLUSTRATION 18-17

Intercompany comparison of profitability ratios

Summary of Profitability Ratios

Illustration 18-18 summarizes the profitability ratios we have used in this chapter, and throughout the textbook.

▶ ILLUSTRATION 18-18

Profitability ratios

Profitability Ratio	Formula	What It Measures	Desired Result
Gross profit margin	$$\frac{\text{Gross profit}}{\text{Net sales}}$$	Margin between selling price and cost of goods sold.	Higher
Profit margin	$$\frac{\text{Profit}}{\text{Net sales}}$$	Amount of profit generated by each dollar of sales.	Higher
Asset turnover	$$\frac{\text{Net sales}}{\text{Average total assets}}$$	How efficiently assets are used to generate sales.	Higher
Return on assets	$$\frac{\text{Profit}}{\text{Average total assets}}$$	Overall profitability of assets.	Higher
Return on equity	$$\frac{\text{Profit}}{\text{Average shareholders' equity}}$$	Profitability of shareholders' investment.	Higher
Earnings per share	$$\frac{\text{Profit} - \text{Preferred dividends}}{\text{Weighted average number of common shares}}$$	Amount of profit earned on each common share.	Higher
Price-earnings	$$\frac{\text{Market price per share}}{\text{Earnings per share}}$$	Relationship between market price per share and earnings per share.	Higher
Payout	$$\frac{\text{Cash dividends}}{\text{Profit}}$$	Percentage of profit distributed as cash dividends.	Higher

For the profitability ratios shown in Illustration 18-18, a higher result is generally considered to be better. However, there are some user-related considerations with respect to the price-earnings and payout ratios that must be understood. A higher price-earnings ratio generally means that investors favour that company and have high expectations of future profitability. However, some investors avoid shares with high PE ratios in the belief that they are overpriced, so not everyone prefers a high PE ratio.

Investors interested in purchasing a company's shares for income purposes (in the form of a dividend) are interested in companies with a high payout ratio. Investors more interested in purchasing a company's shares for growth purposes (for the share price's appreciation) are interested in a low payout ratio. They would prefer to see the company retain its profit rather than pay it out.

We have shown liquidity, solvency, and profitability ratios in separate sections in this chapter. However, it is important to recognize that financial statement analysis should not focus on one section in isolation from the others. Liquidity, solvency, and profitability are closely interrelated in most companies. For example, a company's profitability is affected by the availability of financing and short-term liquidity. Similarly, a company's solvency not only requires satisfactory liquidity but is also affected by its profitability.

It is also important to recognize that the ratios shown in Illustrations 18-12, 18-15, and 18-18 are only examples of commonly used ratios. You will find more examples as you learn more about financial analysis.

ACCOUNTING IN ACTION
ALL ABOUT YOU INSIGHT

The Washington Post/Getty Images

More Canadians are investing in the stock market largely because of the ease of trading stocks on-line. Traders range from students like you tracking their investments to seniors making adjustments to their retirement savings. Everybody wants to buy and sell stocks at just the right time. How do investors predict what stock prices will do and when to buy and sell stock?

Two early pioneers in providing investment advice to the masses were Tom and David Gardner, brothers who created an on-line investor service called The Motley Fool. Tom and David view themselves as twenty-first-century "fools," revealing the "truths" of the stock markets to small investors. Its website offters Fool followers stock quotes, company research reports, personal finance information, news, on-line seminars, podcasts, and message boards. The Motley Fool has grown substantially since its inception in 1993, offering even the most inexperienced investor the basic advice needed to master his or her own financial affairs.

Critics of on-line investor services, and in particular message boards, contend that they can exacerbate the rumour mill. They suggest that, because of the excitement created by some message board postings, share prices can get bid up to unreasonable levels. One potentially troubling aspect of message boards is that participants on a board rarely give their real identities—instead using aliases. Consequently, there is little to stop people from putting misinformation on the board to influence a share's price in the direction they desire.

Sources: Motley Fool website, www.fool.com; Don E. Giacomino and Michael D. Akers, "Examining an Online Investment Research Service: The Motley Fool," *Journal of Business and Economics Research*, volume 9, number 1, January 2011; Stacy Forster, "Motley Fool to 'Educate, Amuse, Enrich'...and Advise Investors," *The Wall Street Journal Online*, September 6, 2001.

Q Suppose you are thinking about investing in shares of Apple Inc. You scanned a variety of investor websites and found messages posted by two different investors. One says it's time to buy Apple shares; the other says it isn't. How should you decide whether to buy the shares or not?

BEFORE YOU GO ON...DO IT **6**   **Profitability Ratios**

Selected information from the financial statements of two competitor companies follows:

	Papat Corporation	Bearton Limited
Total assets, beginning of year	$388,000	$372,000
Total assets, end of year	434,000	536,000
Total shareholders' equity, beginning of year	269,000	296,000
Total shareholders' equity, end of year	294,000	344,000
Net sales	660,000	780,000
Gross profit	175,000	248,000
Profit	68,000	105,000

(a) For each company, calculate the following ratios: gross profit margin, profit margin, asset turnover, return on assets, and return on equity.

(b) Indicate which company—Papat or Bearton—has the better result for each of the ratios you calculated in part (a).

(c) Overall, which of the two companies is more profitable? Explain.

(continued)

BEFORE YOU GO ON...DO IT **6** ▷ **Profitability Ratios** *(continued)*

Solution

(a)

	Papat	Bearton
Gross profit margin	$\dfrac{\$175,000}{\$660,000} = 26.5\%$	$\dfrac{\$248,000}{\$780,000} = 31.8\%$
Profit margin	$\dfrac{\$68,000}{\$660,000} = 10.3\%$	$\dfrac{\$105,000}{\$780,000} = 13.5\%$
Asset turnover	$\dfrac{\$660,000}{(\$388,000 + \$434,000) \div 2} = 1.6$ times	$\dfrac{\$780,000}{(\$372,000 + \$536,000) \div 2} = 1.7$ times
Return on assets	$\dfrac{\$68,000}{(\$388,000 + \$434,000) \div 2} = 16.5\%$	$\dfrac{\$105,000}{(\$372,000 + \$536,000) \div 2} = 23.1\%$
Return on equity	$\dfrac{\$68,000}{(\$269,000 + \$294,000) \div 2} = 24.2\%$	$\dfrac{\$105,000}{(\$296,000 + \$344,000) \div 2} = 32.8\%$

(b)

	Papat	Bearton	Comparison
Gross profit margin	26.5%	31.8%	Bearton
Profit margin	10.3%	13.5%	Bearton
Asset turnover	1.6 times	1.7 times	Bearton
Return on assets	16.5%	23.1%	Bearton
Return on equity	24.2%	32.8%	Bearton

(c) Bearton Limited is more profitable than Papat Corporation on all profitability ratios.

Related exercise material: BE18–15, BE18–16, BE18–17, BE18–18, E18–12, E18–13, **and** E18–14.

Action Plan

- Review the formula for each ratio so you understand how it is calculated and how to interpret it.
- Don't forget to average the balance sheet figures [(beginning of period + end of period) ÷ 2] when comparing them with a period figure (e.g., net sales and profit).
- Remember that for profitability ratios, a higher result is usually better.

Illustration 18-19 is a summary of all the liquidity, solvency, and profitability ratios.

Liquidity Ratios	Formulas
Current ratio	$\dfrac{\text{Current assets}}{\text{Current liabilities}}$
Acid-test ratio	$\dfrac{\text{Cash + Short-term investments + Accounts receivable}}{\text{Current liabilities}}$
Receivables turnover	$\dfrac{\text{Net credit sales}}{\text{Average gross accounts receivable}}$
Collection period	$\dfrac{\text{Days in year}}{\text{Receivables turnover}}$
Inventory turnover	$\dfrac{\text{Cost of goods sold}}{\text{Average inventory}}$
Days sales in inventory	$\dfrac{\text{Days in year}}{\text{Inventory turnover}}$
Operating cycle	Days sales in inventory + Collection period
Solvency Ratios	
Debt to total assets	$\dfrac{\text{Total liabilities}}{\text{Total assets}}$
Interest coverage	$\dfrac{\text{Profit + Interest expense + Income tax expense (EBIT)}}{\text{Interest expense}}$
Free cash flow	Cash provided (used) by operating activities − Cash used (provided) by investing activities

▶ **ILLUSTRATION** **18-19**
Ratio formulas—A Summary

(continued)

▶ ILLUSTRATION 18-19
Ratio formulas–A
Summary (*continued*)

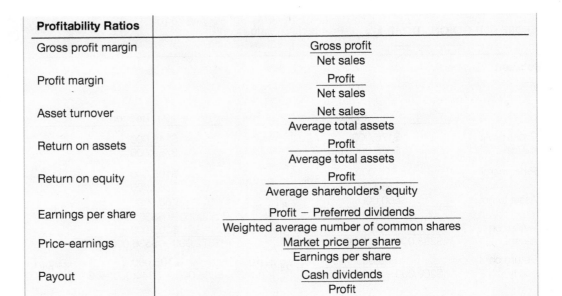

Profitability Ratios	
Gross profit margin	$\dfrac{\text{Gross profit}}{\text{Net sales}}$
Profit margin	$\dfrac{\text{Profit}}{\text{Net sales}}$
Asset turnover	$\dfrac{\text{Net sales}}{\text{Average total assets}}$
Return on assets	$\dfrac{\text{Profit}}{\text{Average total assets}}$
Return on equity	$\dfrac{\text{Profit}}{\text{Average shareholders' equity}}$
Earnings per share	$\dfrac{\text{Profit} - \text{Preferred dividends}}{\text{Weighted average number of common shares}}$
Price-earnings	$\dfrac{\text{Market price per share}}{\text{Earnings per share}}$
Payout	$\dfrac{\text{Cash dividends}}{\text{Profit}}$

LEARNING OBJECTIVE 7

Recognize the limitations of financial statement analysis.

Limitations of Financial Statement Analysis

Business decisions are frequently made by using one or more of the analytical tools illustrated in this chapter. But you should be aware of the limitations of these tools and of the financial statements they are based on.

ALTERNATIVE ACCOUNTING POLICIES

There are a wide variety of different accounting policies and practices that companies can use. For example, companies may use different inventory cost determination methods (specific identification, FIFO, or average) or different depreciation methods (straight-line, diminishing-balance, or units-of-production) depending on the pattern of the revenues (economic benefits) their assets produce. Different methods can result in different financial positions and performance, which will reduce comparability.

For example, Canadian Tire uses the diminishing-balance method of depreciation for much of its property, plant, and equipment. National Tire uses the straight-line method of depreciation. Consequently, profit and total assets could be different—depending on the amount of property, plant, and equipment and at what point in its useful life it is—simply because of the use of different depreciation methods. This would affect a number of solvency and profitability ratios.

Recall, however, that although depreciation expense and the carrying amount of property, plant, and equipment may be different in one or more periods because of the choice of depreciation methods, in total, over the life of the assets, there is no difference. We call differences created from alternative accounting policies "artificial" or timing differences. Although it is possible to detect differences in accounting policies by reading the notes to the financial statements, adjusting the financial data to compensate for the use of different policies can be difficult for the average user. In real life, analysts spend a great deal of time adjusting financial statement data for these types of differences in order to improve the comparability of the ratios.

Intercompany comparability may also be hindered by differing accounting policy options available for private companies. While National Tire is a publicly traded company using IFRS, it may have competitors that are private companies. You will recall that private companies have the choice of adopting IFRS or Accounting Standards for Private Enterprises. If a private company has chosen not to adopt IFRS, which is the most likely scenario, further complications can arise in trying to compare a private company with a public company for certain accounting policies.

Intracompany comparability can be affected by the use of different accounting policies over different periods of time. An entity may change its accounting policy if a change provides users with better information or a new accounting standard has been issued. When there is a change in accounting policy, balances may need to be restated for comparability purposes. However, not all years for which financial statements have been issued need to be restated. Consequently, comparing ratios when accounting policies have changed may result in misleading trends.

COMPREHENSIVE INCOME

Most financial analysis ratios exclude other comprehensive income. For example, profitability ratios generally use data from the income statement and not the statement of comprehensive income, which includes both profit and other comprehensive income. In fact, there are no standard ratio formulas incorporating comprehensive income.

However, where other comprehensive income is significant, and depending on the source of the income, some analysts will adjust profitability ratios to incorporate the effect of total comprehensive income. Of course, you will recall from past chapters that private companies following ASPE do not report comprehensive income, so this limitation would apply only to public and private companies following IFRS.

QUALITY OF INFORMATION

In evaluating a company's financial performance, the quality of the information provided is extremely important. A company that has high-quality information that is complete and transparent will not confuse or mislead users of the financial statements. Financial statements for companies like Canadian Tire, with full and transparent disclosure practices, have a high quality of information value. Other companies may limit the information they disclose. In such cases, the quality of the information will decrease.

Fortunately, the chief executive officer and chief financial officer of a publicly traded company must ensure, and personally declare, that the reported financial information is accurate, relevant, and understandable. In addition, audit committees are held responsible for reviewing the quality of the underlying estimates, accounting policies, and judgements involved in the preparation of the financial statements.

A strong corporate governance process, including an active board of directors and audit committee, is essential to ensuring the quality of information. Canadian Tire has received many commendations for past financial statements.

ECONOMIC FACTORS

You cannot properly interpret a financial analysis without also considering the economic circumstances in which a company operates. Economic measures, such as the rate of interest, unemployment, and changes in demand and supply, can have a significant impact on a company's performance.

During slow economic times, horizontal analyses and ratios compared across years can lose much of their relevance. When losses result in negative numbers, it is difficult to calculate percentages and ratios, much less interpret them. In such times, vertical analyses may be more useful. If a company has losses, they must be assessed based on the factors driving the loss in the current period. Less attention should be paid to comparing the losses with results from prior periods.

One must use this information, along with non-financial information, to try to assess what changes relate to the economic situation and what changes relate to factors that management can, or should be able to, control. For example, have operating expenses increased faster than revenues? Why? Are consumers not spending? Are prices too high? Have expenses not been adequately controlled or adjusted for the current marketplace? Particular attention must be paid to the company's results compared with those of its competitors.

BEFORE YOU GO ON...DO IT 7 › **Comprehensive Income**

The Royal Bank of Canada reported the following selected information (in millions) for the year ended October 31, 2014:

Total revenue	$34,108
Profit	9,004
Other comprehensive income	915
Total comprehensive income	9,919

(a) Calculate the profit margin using (1) profit as the numerator, and (2) total comprehensive income as the numerator.

(b) Should other comprehensive income be considered a significant factor in the analysis of the Royal Bank's profitability?

Solution

(a)

($ in millions)	(1)	(2)
Profit margin	$9,004 ÷ $34,108 = 26.4\%$	$9,919 ÷ $34,108 = 29.1\%$

(b) The two ratios differ by 10.2% [(29.1% − 26.4%) ÷ 26.4%]. The inclusion of other comprehensive income in the calculation of the profitability ratios is likely significant enough to make a difference in a user's decision-making.

Related exercise material: BE18–22 and E18–19.

Action Plan

- Recall the formula for profit margin: Profit ÷ Net sales (or Revenue). Substitute total comprehensive income instead of profit to determine the impact of other comprehensive income on profitability.
- To determine the significance of other comprehensive income, compare the ratios with and without other comprehensive income and assess whether the change in the ratio is significant enough to affect decision-making.

Comparing IFRS and ASPE

Key Differences	International Financial Reporting Standards (IFRS)	Accounting Standards for Private Enterprises (ASPE)
Earnings per share	Must be calculated and reported on the face of the income statement or statement of comprehensive income.	Earnings per share is not required to be reported.
Differences in accounting policy	Depending on the extent and significance of differences in accounting policies, comparisons may be difficult if a publicly traded company is compared with a private company using ASPE.	Depending on the extent and significance of differences in accounting policies, comparisons may be difficult if a private company using ASPE is compared with a public or private company using IFRS.
Comprehensive income	If other comprehensive income is significant, selected profitability ratios should be recalculated using total comprehensive income rather than profit.	Comprehensive income is not reported.

Demonstration Problem

Selected liquidity, solvency, and profitability ratios follow for two companies for a recent year:

	Kicking Horse	La Biche
Liquidity		
Current ratio	2.2:1	1.8:1
Collection period	28 days	20 days
Days sales in inventory	66 days	58 days
Solvency		
Debt to total assets	44.2%	44.4%
Interest coverage	9.1 times	10.2 times
Profitability		
Gross profit margin	37.1%	39.5%
Profit margin	8.8%	16.3%
Asset turnover	0.1 times	0.1 times
Return on assets	0.9%	1.6%
Return on equity	1.6%	2.9%

Instructions

(a) For each of the above ratios, identify which company, Kicking Horse (KH) or La Biche (LB), has the stronger result.
(b) Which company is more liquid? Explain.
(c) Which company is more solvent? Explain.
(d) Which company is more profitable? Explain.

ACTION PLAN

- Remember that for liquidity ratios, a higher result is usually better unless a ratio is the inverse of an original ratio (e.g., collection period, which uses the receivables turnover ratio in the denominator), in which case a lower result is better.
- The current ratio should always be interpreted together with the receivables turnover/collection period and inventory turnover/days sales in inventory ratios to ensure that the current ratio has not been artificially inflated by slow-moving receivables or inventory.
- The debt to total assets ratio, for which a lower result is usually better, should always be interpreted together with the interest coverage ratio, for which a higher result is usually better.
- Remember that for profitability ratios, a higher result is usually better.

SOLUTION TO DEMONSTRATION PROBLEM

(a)

	Stronger Result		Stronger Result
Current ratio	KH	Gross profit margin	LB
Collection period	LB	Profit margin	LB
Days sales in inventory	LB	Asset turnover	No difference
Debt to total assets	KH	Return on assets	LB
Interest coverage	LB	Return on equity	LB

(b) La Biche is more liquid than Kicking Horse. Although Kicking Horse appears to have a stronger current ratio than La Biche, it is slower at collecting its receivables and selling its inventory. Regardless, both companies still have good collection periods (less than 30 days). Still, La Biche's operating cycle is only 78 days (20 + 58) compared with Kicking Horse's 94 days (28 + 66).

(c) La Biche is more solvent than Kicking Horse. Although its debt to total assets ratio is marginally higher (worse) than that of Kicking Horse, its interest coverage ratio is also higher (better), indicating its ability to handle its debt.

(d) La Biche is more profitable than Kicking Horse on all profitability measures except for asset turnover, which is the same for both companies.

▶ Summary of Learning Objectives

1. **Identify the need for, and tools of, financial statement analysis.** Users of financial statements make comparisons in order to evaluate a company's past, current, and future performance and position. There are two commonly used bases of comparison: intracompany (within a company) and intercompany (between companies). The tools of financial analysis include horizontal, vertical, and ratio analysis.

2. *Explain and apply horizontal analysis.* Horizontal analysis is a technique for evaluating a series of data, such as line items in a company's financial statements, by expressing them as dollar or percentage increases or decreases over two or more periods of time. The horizontal percent of a base year is calculated by dividing the amount for the specific period under analysis by a base-period amount multiplied by 100%. This percentage calculation normally covers multiple periods. The horizontal percentage change for a period is calculated by dividing the dollar amount of the change between the specific period under analysis and the prior period by the prior-period amount multiplied by 100%. This percentage calculation normally covers two periods only.

3. *Explain and apply vertical analysis.* Vertical analysis is a technique for evaluating data within one period by expressing each item in a financial statement as a percentage of a relevant total (base amount) in the same financial statement. The vertical percentage is calculated by dividing the financial statement amount under analysis by the base amount multiplied by 100% for that particular financial statement, which is usually total assets for the balance sheet and revenues or net sales for the income statement.

4. *Identify and use ratios to analyze liquidity.* Liquidity ratios include the current ratio, acid-test ratio, receivables turnover, collection period, inventory turnover, days sales in inventory, and operating cycle. The formula, purpose, and desired result for each liquidity ratio are presented in Illustration 18-12.

5. *Identify and use ratios to analyze solvency.* Solvency ratios include debt to total assets, interest coverage, and free cash flow. The formula, purpose, and desired result for each solvency ratio are presented in Illustration 18-15.

6. *Identify and use ratios to analyze profitability.* Profitability ratios include the gross profit margin, profit margin, asset turnover, return on assets, return on equity, earnings per share, price-earnings, and payout ratios. The formula, purpose, and desired result for each profitability ratio are presented in Illustration 18-18.

7. *Recognize the limitations of financial statement analysis.* The usefulness of analytical tools can be limited by (1) the use of alternative accounting policies, (2) significant amounts of other comprehensive income, (3) the quality of the information provided, and (4) economic factors.

▶ Glossary

Horizontal analysis   A technique for evaluating a series of financial statement data over multiple periods of time to determine the percentage increase or decrease that has taken place. Also known as trend analysis. (p. 958)

Horizontal percentage change for period   A percentage measuring the change from one period to the next period. It is calculated by dividing the dollar amount of the change between the specific period under analysis and the prior period by the prior-period amount. (p. 960)

Liquidity ratios   Measures of a company's short-term ability to pay its maturing obligations and to meet unexpected needs for cash. (p. 968)

Percentage of the base-year amount   A percentage measuring the change since a base period. It is calculated by dividing the amount for the specific period under analysis by the base-period amount multiplied by 100%. (p. 960)

Profitability ratios   Measures of a company's operating success for a specific period of time. (p. 968)

Ratio analysis   A technique for evaluating financial statements that expresses the relationship between selected financial statement data. (p. 959)

Solvency ratios   Measures of a company's ability to survive over a long period of time. (p. 968)

Trend analysis   A technique for evaluating a series of financial statement data over multiple periods of time to determine the percentage increase or decrease that has taken place. Also known as horizontal analysis. (p. 960)

Vertical analysis   A technique for evaluating financial statement data within a period. Each item in a financial statement is expressed as a percentage of a total or base amount. Total assets is usually the base amount used in the balance sheet; total revenues or net sales in the income statement. Also known as common size analysis. (p. 958)

▶ Self-Study Questions
Answers are at the end of the chapter.

(LO 1) K 1. A comparison of operating expenses for a company over a five-year period is an example of which of the following comparative bases and analysis tools?
(a) Intracompany, horizontal analysis
(b) Intracompany, vertical analysis
(c) Intercompany, horizontal analysis
(d) Intercompany, vertical analysis

(LO 2) AP 2. Rankin Corporation reported net sales of $300,000, $330,000, and $360,000 in the years 2015, 2016, and 2017, respectively. If 2015 is the base year, what is the horizontal percent of base year for 2017?
(a) 83%   (c) 110%
(b) 92%   (d) 120%

(LO 2) AP 3. As indicated in Question 2 above, Rankin Corporation reported net sales of $300,000, $330,000, and $360,000 in the years 2015, 2016, and 2017, respectively. What is the horizontal percentage change for 2016 to 2017?
(a) 109% from 2016 to 2017

(b) 120% from 2016 to 2017

(c) 9% from 2016 to 2017

(d) 20% from 2016 to 2017

(LO 3) C   4. The following schedule shows what type of analysis?

	2017		2016	
	Amount	Percentage	Amount	Percentage
Current assets	$200,000	25%	$175,000	21%
Property, plant, and equipment	600,000	75%	650,000	79%
Total assets	$800,000	100%	$825,000	100%

(a) Horizontal analysis   (c) Vertical analysis

(b) Ratio analysis   (d) Intercompany comparison

(LO 3) K   5. In a vertical analysis, the base amount for depreciation expense is generally:

(a) net sales.

(b) depreciation expense in a previous year.

(c) total assets.

(d) total property, plant, and equipment.

Use the following selected financial data to answer items 6 to 8. Round all ratios to one decimal spot. Calculations involving days should be rounded to the nearest day.

	2017	2016
Accounts receivable	$ 45,000	$ 41,000
Inventory	34,000	28,000
Total shareholders' equity	572,000	438,000
Net credit sales	684,000	597,000
Cost of goods sold	450,000	398,000
Interest expense	14,000	12,000
Income tax expense	22,000	18,000
Profit	134,000	90,000

(LO 4) AP   6. What is the days sales in inventory for 2017?

(a) 28 days   (c) 21 days

(b) 25 days   (d) 32 days

(LO 5) AP   7. What is the interest coverage ratio for 2017?

(a) 7.3 times   (c) 11.2 times

(b) 10.6 times   (d) 12.1 times

(LO 6) AP   8. What is the return on equity for 2017?

(a) 22.2%   (c) 26.5%

(b) 23.4%   (d) 135.4%

(LO 4, 5, 6) AN   9. Which of the following changes in ratios are *both* indicative of an improvement in a company's financial situation?

(a) Increasing debt to total assets and interest coverage ratios

(b) Increasing current ratio and increasing days sales in inventory

(c) Decreasing asset turnover and return on equity ratios

(d) Decreasing collection period and increasing gross profit margin

(LO 7) C   10. Which of the following situations most likely indicates that a financial analysis should be interpreted with caution?

(a) Different inventory cost formulas are being used by competing companies with similar inventory.

(b) A company had no other comprehensive income.

(c) The economy is stable.

(d) The quality of information is high.

▶ Questions

(LO 1) K   1. Are short-term creditors, long-term creditors, and shareholders interested primarily in the same characteristics of a company? Explain.

(LO 1) K   2. What are the differences between the two bases of comparison: (a) intracompany and (b) intercompany?

(LO 1) C   3. Identify and describe the three commonly used tools of analysis.

(LO 2) K   4. Explain how the percentage change for a base year and the percentage change for a period are calculated in horizontal analysis.

(LO 2, 3) C   5. Horizontal analysis and vertical analysis are two different tools used in financial statement analysis. Explain how they are similar, and how they differ.

(LO 3) K   6. What base amount is usually assigned a 100% value in a vertical analysis of (a) the balance sheet and (b) the income statement?

(LO 3) C   7. Can vertical analysis be used to compare two companies of different sizes, such as Walmart, the world's

largest retailer, and Amazon.com, the ninth-largest retailer in the world? Explain.

(LO 4) K   8. (a) What do liquidity ratios measure? (b) What types of users would be most interested in liquidity ratios?

(LO 4) AN   9. A high current ratio does not always indicate that a company has a strong liquidity position. Explain why this may be the case.

(LO 4) K   10. What is the difference between the current ratio and the acid-test ratio?

(LO 4) C   11. Identify for which liquidity ratios a lower result might be better, and explain why.

(LO 5) K   12. (a) What do solvency ratios measure? (b) What types of users would be most interested in solvency ratios?

(LO 5) C   13. Wong Ltd. reported a debt to total assets ratio of 37% and an interest coverage ratio of 3 times in the current year. Its nearest competitor has a debt to total assets ratio of 39% and an interest coverage ratio of 2.5 times. Is Wong's solvency better or worse than that of its competitor?

(LO 5) C 14. Identify for which solvency ratios a lower result might be better, and explain why.

(LO 6) K 15. (a) What do profitability ratios measure? (b) What types of users would be most interested in profitability ratios?

(LO 6) K 16. The price earnings of General Motors (automaker) was 12, and the price earnings of Microsoft (computer software) was 38. Which company did the stock market favour? Explain.

(LO 4, 5, 6) C 17. Name the ratio(s) that should be used to help answer each of the following questions.
(a) How efficient is a company at using its assets to produce sales?
(b) What is the company's ability to pay its obligations immediately without selling inventory?
(c) How long does it take to purchase inventory, sell it on account, and collect the cash?

(d) How many dollars of profit were earned for each dollar invested by the shareholders?
(e) How able is a company to pay interest charges as they come due?

(LO 7) C 18. Identify and briefly explain the limitations of financial statement analysis.

(LO 7) AN 19. McCain Foods and Cavendish Farms are both private companies in the food-processing industry. McCain Foods uses IFRS and Cavendish Farms uses ASPE. What impact might these differing standards have when comparing ratios of these two companies?

(LO 7) C 20. Explain what other comprehensive income is and when it should be considered in comparing ratios from one company to another.

▶ Brief Exercises

Match terms with descriptions. (LO 1) K

BE18–1 Match each of the following terms with the most appropriate description.

Terms	Description
_____ 1. Intracompany	(a) An analysis tool that expresses relationships among selected items of financial statement data
_____ 2. Intercompany	(b) An analysis tool that evaluates data by expressing an item in a financial statement as a percentage of a total or base amount within the same financial statement
_____ 3. Horizontal analysis	(c) Comparisons made between companies
_____ 4. Vertical analysis	(d) An analysis tool that evaluates data by calculating and comparing the percentage increase or decrease of an item in a financial statement over multiple periods of time
_____ 5. Ratio analysis	(e) Comparisons made within a company

Identify comparisons and tools. (LO 1) C

BE18–2 Identify the appropriate basis of comparison—intracompany or intercompany—and better tool of analysis—horizontal or vertical—to use for each of the following financial situations.

	Basis of Comparison	Tool of Analysis
(a) Analysis of a company's dividend history		
(b) Comparison of different-sized companies		
(c) Comparison of gross profit to net sales among competitors		
(d) Calculation of a company's sales growth over time		

Prepare horizontal analysis. (LO 2) AP

BE18–3 Comparative data (in thousands) from the balance sheet of Winisk Ltd. are shown below. Using horizontal analysis, calculate the percent of base year, assuming 2014 is the base year.

	2017	2016	2015	2014
Cash	$ 24	$ 45	$ 30	$ 20
Accounts receivable	268	227	197	150
Inventory	499	481	395	325
Prepaid expenses	22	0	10	22
Total current assets	$813	$753	$632	$517

Prepare horizontal analysis. (LO 2) AP

BE18–4 Refer to BE18–3. Using horizontal analysis, calculate the percentage change for each year.

BE18–5 Windmill Ltd. reported the following financial results:

Profit was $500,000 in 2016, $450,000 in 2017, and $522,000 in 2018. Calculate the horizontal percentage change from (a) 2016 to 2017 and (b) 2017 to 2018. (c) Are the changes an increase or a decrease?

Calculate horizontal percentage of change.
(LO 2) AP

BE18–6 Comparative data from the balance sheet of Rioux Ltd. are shown below. Using vertical analysis, calculate the percentage of the base amount for each year.

Prepare vertical analyses.
(LO 3) AP

	2017	2016	2015
Current assets	$1,530,000	$1,175,000	$1,225,000
Property, plant, and equipment	3,130,000	2,800,000	2,850,000
Goodwill	10,000	90,000	0
Total assets	$4,670,000	$4,065,000	$4,075,000

BE18–7 Selected data (in thousands) from the income statement of JTI Inc. are shown below. Perform a vertical analysis and calculate the percentage of the base amount for the current year.

Prepare vertical analysis.
(LO 3) AP

Net sales	$1,934
Cost of goods sold	1,612
Gross profit	322
Operating expenses	218
Profit before income tax	104
Income tax expense	31
Profit	$ 73

BE18–8 For each of the following liquidity ratios, indicate whether the change would be viewed as an improvement or deterioration:

Compare liquidity ratios.
(LO 4) C

(a) A decrease in the receivables turnover
(b) A decrease in the collection period
(c) An increase in the days sales in inventory

(d) An increase in the inventory turnover
(e) A decrease in the acid-test ratio
(f) An increase in the operating cycle

BE18–9 Selected condensed data taken from a recent balance sheet of Underwood Inc. are as follows.

Calculate and evaluate current and acid-test ratios.
(LO 4) AN

UNDERWOOD INC.
Balance Sheet (partial)

Cash	$ 8,041,000
Short-term investments	4,947,000
Accounts receivable	6,545,000
Inventory	20,814,000
Prepaid assets	571,000
Total current assets	$40,918,000
Total current liabilities	$18,644,000

(a) Calculate the (1) current ratio and (2) acid-test ratio.
(b) What conclusions concerning Underwood's liquidity can be drawn?

BE18–10 The following data are taken from the financial statements of Rai Company.

Evaluate collection of accounts receivable.
(LO 4) AP

	2017	2016
Accounts receivable, end of year	$ 550,000	$ 520,000
Net credit sales	3,960,000	3,100,000

Terms for all sales are 1/10, n/60.

(a) Calculate for each year (1) the receivables turnover and (2) the collection period. At the end of 2015, accounts receivable was $480,000.
(b) What conclusions about the management of accounts receivable can be drawn?

Evaluate management of
inventory. (LO 4) AP

BE18–11   The following data are from the income statements of Haskin Company.

	2017	2016
Sales revenue	$6,420,000	$6,240,000
Beginning inventory	940,000	860,000
Purchases	4,340,000	4,661,000
Ending inventory	1,020,000	940,000

(a) Calculate for each year (1) the inventory turnover and (2) the days sales in inventory.

(b) What conclusions concerning the management of the inventory can be drawn?

Compare solvency ratios.
(LO 5) C

BE18–12   For each of the following solvency ratios, indicate whether the change would be viewed as an improvement or deterioration:

(a) A decrease in debt to total assets

(b) A decrease in interest coverage

(c) An increase in free cash flow

(d) A decrease in debt to total assets combined with an increase in interest coverage

Calculate solvency ratios.
(LO 5) AP

BE18–13   Dollarama Inc. reported the following selected financial data (in thousands) for a recent year:

Interest expense	$ 19,956
Income tax expense	107,195
Profit	295,410
Total assets	1,700,838
Total liabilities	960,358
Cash provided by operating activities	355,872
Cash used by investing activities	84,244

Calculate the following ratios: (a) debt to total assets, (b) interest coverage, and (c) free cash flow.

Evaluate solvency.
(LO 5) AN

BE18–14   The Culleye Corporation reported the following solvency ratios:

	2017	2016
Debt to total assets	56.0%	52.8%
Interest coverage	5.1 times	3.3 times

(a) Identify if each of the above solvency ratios is better or worse in 2017 compared with 2016.

(b) Has Culleye's overall solvency position improved or deteriorated in 2017? Explain.

Compare profitability ratios.
(LO 6) C

BE18–15   For each of the following profitability ratios, indicate whether the change would be viewed as an improvement or deterioration:

(a) An increase in the gross profit margin

(b) A decrease in asset turnover

(c) An increase in return on equity

(d) A decrease in earnings per share

(e) A decrease in the profit margin

Calculate profitability ratios.
(LO 6) AP

BE18–16   Loblaw Companies Limited reported the following items in its consolidated statement of earnings (in millions of dollars) for 2014 and 2013.

	2014	2013
Revenue	$42,611	$32,371
Cost of goods sold	32,063	24,701
Net earnings	53	627

(a) Calculate the (1) gross profit margin and (2) profit margin.

(b) What conclusions concerning the gross profit and profit margin can be drawn?

Calculate profitability ratios.
(LO 6) AP

BE18–17   Selected comparative statement data for Bluesky Company are presented below. All balance sheet data are as at December 31.

	2017	2016
Net sales	$750,000	$720,000
Profit	60,000	42,000
Total assets	600,000	500,000
Total common shareholders' equity	450,000	310,000

Calculate for 2017 the following: (a) asset turnover, (b) return on assets, and (c) return on equity.

BE18–18   Recently, the price-earnings ratio of Apple was 16 times and the price-earnings ratio of Chevron was 12 times. The payout ratio of each company was 28.0% and 38.6%, respectively. Which company's shares would you purchase for growth? For income? Explain.

Evaluate investor ratios. (LO 6) AN

BE18–19   (a) Indicate whether each of the following ratios is a liquidity (L) ratio, a solvency (S) ratio, or a profitability (P) ratio. (b) Indicate whether a higher or lower result is normally desirable.

Classify ratios. (LO 4, 5, 6) K

(a)	(b)		(a)	(b)	
___	___	Acid-test ratio	___	___	Interest coverage
___	___	Asset turnover	___	___	Inventory turnover
___	___	Collection period	___	___	Operating cycle
___	___	Debt to total assets	___	___	Profit margin
___	___	Gross profit margin	___	___	Return on equity

BE18–20   Name the ratio(s) that should be used to help answer each of the following questions.

Interpreting ratios. (LO 4, 5, 6) C

(a) How efficient is a company at using its assets to produce sales?
(b) What is the company's ability to pay its obligations immediately without selling inventory?
(c) How long does it take to purchase inventory, sell it on account, and collect the cash?
(d) How many dollars of profit were earned for each dollar invested by the shareholders?
(e) How able is a company to pay interest charges as they come due?

BE18–21   Selected comparative information (in thousands) is available for Halpenny Corporation.

Calculate averages. (LO 4, 6) AP

	2017	2016	2015
Accounts receivable	$ 1,090	$ 965	$ 880
Total assets	27,510	26,760	23,815
Total shareholders' equity	12,830	12,575	10,930

Halpenny wishes to calculate ratios for 2017 and 2016. (a) Calculate the average amounts to be used for accounts receivable, total assets, and total shareholders' equity in a ratio calculation in (1) 2017 and (2) 2016. (b) Identify for which ratio each of the above average amounts would be used. (c) Why are averages used in certain ratio calculations and not in others?

BE18–22   Stirling Corporation and Bute Inc. have similar types of inventory. At the end of the current year, Stirling reported an average inventory amount of $10,000, calculated using the FIFO cost formula. Bute reported an average inventory amount of $12,000, calculated using the average cost formula. Stirling reported cost of goods sold of $200,000, while Bute reported cost of goods sold of $180,000. Inventory prices have been falling during the current year. (a) Calculate the inventory turnover ratio for each company. (b) How might the fact that Stirling and Bute use different inventory cost formulas affect your comparison of the inventory turnover ratio between the two companies?

Evaluate impact of alternative cost formulas on inventory turnover. (LO 4, 7) AN

▶ Exercises

E18–1   Comparative data from the balance sheet of Dressaire Inc. are shown below.

Prepare horizontal analysis. (LO 2) AP

	2017	2016	2015
Current assets	$120,000	$ 80,000	$100,000
Non-current assets	400,000	350,000	300,000
Current liabilities	90,000	70,000	65,000
Non-current liabilities	145,000	125,000	150,000
Common shares	150,000	115,000	100,000
Retained earnings	135,000	120,000	85,000

Instructions

(a) Perform a horizontal percent of base year analysis using 2015 as the base year.
(b) Calculate the horizontal percentage change for each year.

Determine change in profit.
(LO 2) AN

E18–2   Selected horizontal percentages of the base year amount information for Coastal Ltd.'s income statement are shown below.

	2017	2016	2015
Net sales	101%	110%	100%
Cost of goods sold	100%	111%	100%
Operating expenses	99%	112%	100%
Income tax expense	106%	105%	100%

Instructions

Based on the above horizontal percentages, did Coastal's profit increase, decrease, or remain unchanged over the three-year period? Explain.

Prepare vertical analysis.
(LO 3) AP

E18–3   Comparative data from the income statement of Fleetwood Corporation are shown below.

	2017	2016
Net sales	$800,000	$600,000
Cost of goods sold	550,000	375,000
Gross profit	250,000	225,000
Operating expenses	175,000	125,000
Profit before income tax	75,000	100,000
Income tax expense	18,750	25,000
Profit	$ 56,250	$ 75,000

Instructions

Prepare a vertical analysis for Fleetwood Corporation.

Prepare horizontal and vertical analyses and identify changes. (LO 2, 3) AN

E18–4   Comparative data from the balance sheet of **BlackBerry Limited** are shown below.

BLACKBERRY LIMITED Consolidated Balance Sheet February 28, 2015, and March 1, 2014 (in U.S. millions)		
Assets	Feb. 28, 2015	Mar. 1, 2014
Current assets	$4,167	$4,848
Non-current assets	2,382	2,704
Total assets	$6,549	$7,552
Liabilities and Shareholders' Equity		
Current liabilities	$1,363	$2,268
Non-current liabilities	1,755	1,659
Total liabilities	3,118	3,927
Shareholders' equity	3,431	3,625
Total liabilities and shareholders' equity	$6,549	$7,552

Instructions

(a) Using horizontal analysis, calculate the percentage change between 2014 and 2015.
(b) Using vertical analysis, calculate the percentage of the base amount for each year.
(c) Based on your calculations in parts (a) and (b), identify any significant changes from 2014 to 2015.

Determine change in profit.
(LO 3) AN

E18–5   Selected vertical percentages of the base amount from Waubon Corp.'s vertically analyzed income statement are shown below.

	2017	2016	2015
Net sales	100.0%	100.0%	100.0%
Cost of goods sold	59.4%	60.5%	60.0%
Operating expenses	19.6%	20.4%	20.0%
Income tax expense	4.2%	3.8%	4.0%

Instructions

Based on the above vertical percentages, did Waubon's profit as a percentage of sales increase, decrease, or remain unchanged over the three-year period? Explain.

E18–6   Selected financial data for Shumway Ltd. are shown below.

Calculate liquidity ratios and evaluate liquidity. (LO 4) AN

	2017	2016	2015
Net sales	$6,420,000	$6,240,000	$5,430,000
Cost of goods sold	4,540,000	4,550,000	3,950,000
Accounts receivable (gross)	850,000	750,000	650,000
Inventory	1,020,000	980,000	840,000

Instructions

(a) Calculate for each of 2017 and 2016 the following ratios:
   1. Receivables turnover   4. Days sales in inventory
   2. Collection period   5. Operating cycle
   3. Inventory turnover

(b) Based on the ratios calculated in part (a), what conclusion(s) can be drawn about the management of the receivables and inventory?

E18–7   Big Game Inc. operates gaming stores across the country. Selected comparative financial statement data are shown below.

Calculate and compare liquidity ratios. (LO 4) AP

BIG GAME INC. Balance Sheet (partial) December 31 (in millions)			
	2017	2016	2015
Current assets			
Cash	$ 795	$ 91	$ 60
Short-term investments	55	60	40
Accounts receivable	676	586	496
Inventory	898	525	575
Prepaid expenses	41	52	29
Total current assets	$2,465	$1,314	$1,200
Total current liabilities	$1,890	$ 825	$ 750

Additional information:

(in millions)	2017	2016
Net credit sales	$8,258	$3,940
Cost of goods sold	5,328	2,650

Instructions

(a) Calculate the following liquidity ratios for 2017 and 2016.
   1. Current ratio   5. Inventory turnover
   2. Acid-test ratio   6. Days sales in inventory
   3. Receivables turnover   7. Operating cycle
   4. Collection period

(b) Indicate whether each of the liquidity ratios calculated in part (a) is better or worse in 2017.

E18–8   The following selected ratios are available for Pampered Pets Inc.:

Evaluate liquidity. (LO 4) AN

	2017	2016	2015
Current ratio	2.6:1	1.4:1	2.1:1
Acid-test ratio	0.8:1	0.6:1	0.7:1
Receivables turnover	6.7 times	7.4 times	8.2 times
Inventory turnover	7.5 times	8.7 times	9.9 times
Operating cycle	103 days	91 days	81 days

Instructions

(a) Has the company's collection of its receivables improved or weakened over the past three years?
(b) Is the company selling its inventory faster or slower than in past years?
(c) Overall, has the company's liquidity improved or weakened over the past three years? Explain.

E18–9   Hakim Inc. reported a current ratio of 1.5:1 in the current year, which is higher than last year's current ratio of 1.3:1. It also reported an acid-test ratio of 1:1, which is higher than last year's acid-test ratio of 0.6:1; receivables

Evaluate liquidity. (LO 4) AN

turnover of 8 times, which is less than last year's receivables turnover of 9 times; and an inventory turnover of 6 times, which is less than last year's inventory turnover of 7 times. Is Hakim's liquidity improving or deteriorating? Explain.

Calculate and compare solvency ratios. (LO 5) AP

E18-10   The following selected information (in thousands) is available for Osborne Inc.:

	2017	2016
Total assets	$3,886	$3,708
Total liabilities	2,177	1,959
Interest expense	27	17
Income tax expense	174	152
Profit	406	375
Cash provided by operating activities	925	580
Cash used by investing activities	475	300

Instructions

(a) Calculate the following solvency ratios of Osborne Inc. for 2017 and 2016.
   1. Debt to total assets
   2. Free cash flow
   3. Interest coverage
(b) Indicate whether each of the solvency ratios calculated in part (a) is better or worse in 2017.

Evaluate solvency. (LO 5) AN

E18-11   The following selected ratios are available for Ice Inc.:

	2017	2016	2015
Debt to total assets	40%	45%	50%
Interest coverage	1.0 times	1.5 times	2.0 times

Instructions

(a) Has the debt to total assets improved or weakened over the past three years?
(b) Has the interest coverage improved or weakened over the past three years?
(c) Overall, has the company's solvency improved or weakened over the past three years?

Calculate profitability ratios. (LO 6) AP

E18-12   Selected comparative statement data for Slaymaker Products are presented below. All balance sheet data are as at December 31.

	2017	2016
Net sales	$750,000	$720,000
Cost of goods sold	480,000	440,000
Interest expense	7,000	5,000
Profit	60,000	42,000
Accounts receivable	120,000	100,000
Inventory	85,000	75,000
Total assets	600,000	500,000
Total shareholders' equity	450,000	310,000

Instructions

Calculate the following ratios for 2017.
(a) Gross profit margin   (d) Return on assets
(b) Profit margin   (e) Return on shareholders' equity
(c) Asset turnover

Calculate and compare profitability ratios. (LO 6) AP

E18-13   The following selected information is for Xtreme Corporation:

	2017	2016	2015
Total assets	$350,000	$275,000	$274,467
Total shareholders' equity	133,500	100,000	50,000
Net sales	500,000	400,000	300,000
Cost of goods sold	375,000	290,000	180,000
Profit	33,500	30,000	20,000

Instructions

(a) Calculate the gross profit margin, profit margin, asset turnover, return on assets, and return on equity ratios for 2017 and 2016.
(b) Indicate whether each of the profitability ratios calculated in part (a) is better or worse in 2017.

E18–14   Potash Corporation of Saskatchewan Inc. and Agrium Inc. reported the following investor-related information recently:

Evaluate profitability.
(LO 6) AN

	Potash	Agrium
Earnings per share	$1.83	$5.51
Payout ratio	74.3%	59.7%
Price-earnings ratio	22.4 times	20.0 times
Gross profit margin	37.2%	22.1%
Profit margin	21.6%	4.5%
Return on equity	8.3%	10.7%

Instructions

(a) Based on the above information, can you tell which company is more profitable?
(b) Which company do investors favour?
(c) Which company would investors most likely purchase shares in for dividend income?

E18–15   The following is a selected list of ratios comparing Long Inc. and Circular Corporation for a recent year:

Classify and compare ratios.
(LO 1, 4, 5, 6) C

	Long	Circular	(a)	(b)
Acid-test ratio	1.1:1	0.8:1		
Asset turnover	1.7 times	1.6 times		
Current ratio	1.3:1	1.6:1		
Debt to total assets	30.1%	40.6%		
Gross profit margin	38.7%	38.6%		
Interest coverage	5.6 times	2.3 times		
Inventory turnover	5.8 times	5.1 times		
Operating cycle	119 days	134 days		
Profit margin	10.4%	8.5%		
Receivables turnover	6.5 times	5.9 times		
Return on assets	17.2%	13.7%		
Return on equity	24.8%	28.2%		

Instructions

(a) Classify each of the above ratios as a liquidity (L), solvency (S), or profitability (P) ratio.
(b) For each of the above ratios, indicate whether Long's ratio is better (B) or worse (W) than that reported by Circular.
(c) Identify whether the comparison done in part (b) is an intracompany comparison or an intercompany comparison.

E18–16   Selected comparative financial data (in thousands, except for share price) for Cineplex Inc. are shown below.

Calculate ratios
(LO 4, 5, 6) AN

	2014	2013
Revenue	$1,234,716	$1,171,267
Interest expense	21,948	10,743
Income tax expense	21,144	32,977
Profit	76,271	83,557
Total current assets	151,909	159,103
Total assets	1,609,416	1,591,378
Total current liabilities	335,930	319,094
Total liabilities	877,567	843,106
Total shareholders' equity	731,849	748,272
Cash provided by operating activities	180,258	224,648
Cash used by investing activities	106,712	297,225
Market price per share	44.83	44.06
Weighted average number of common shares	62,973	62,816

Instructions

(a) Calculate the following ratios for 2014:

1. Asset turnover	6. Interest coverage
2. Current ratio	7. Price-earnings ratio
3. Debt to total assets	8. Profit margin
4. Earnings per share	9. Return on assets
5. Free cash flow	10. Return on equity

(b) Indicate whether each of the above ratios is a measure of liquidity (L), solvency (S), or profitability (P).

Calculate ratios.
(LO 4, 5, 6) AP

E18–17 Rinker Corporation's comparative balance sheet is presented below.

RINKER CORPORATION
Balance Sheet
December 31

	2017	2016
Cash	$ 5,300	$ 3,700
Accounts receivable	21,200	23,400
Inventory	9,000	7,000
Land	20,000	26,000
Buildings	70,000	70,000
Accumulated depreciation—buildings	(15,000)	(10,000)
Total	$110,500	$120,100
Accounts payable	$ 10,370	$ 31,100
Common shares	75,000	69,000
Retained earnings	25,130	20,000
Total	$110,500	$120,100

Rinker's 2017 income statement included net sales of $120,000, cost of goods sold of $70,000, and profit of $14,000.

Instructions

Calculate the following ratios for 2017.
(a) Current ratio
(b) Acid-test ratio
(c) Receivables turnover
(d) Collection period
(e) Inventory turnover
(f) Days sales in inventory

(g) Profit margin
(h) Asset turnover
(i) Return on assets
(j) Return on equity
(k) Debt to total assets

Calculate missing information. (LO 4, 5, 6) AN

E18–18 Presented below is an incomplete balance sheet for Main River Corp.

MAIN RIVER CORP.
Balance Sheet
December 31, 2017

Assets	
Current assets	
Cash	$ 20,000
Accounts receivable	(a)
Inventory	(b)
Total current assets	365,000
Non-current assets	435,000
Total assets	$ (c)
Liabilities and Shareholders' Equity	
Current liabilities	$ (d)
Non-current liabilities	(e)
Total liabilities	(f)
Shareholders' equity	(g)
Total liabilities and shareholders' equity	$ (h)

Additional information:

1. Assume average balances equal ending balances for the purpose of this exercise.
2. The receivables turnover ratio is 13 times and net credit sales are $1,950,000.
3. The inventory turnover ratio is 6.5 times and cost of goods sold is $1,267,500.
4. The current ratio is 2:1.
5. The debt to total assets ratio is 70%.

Instructions

Calculate the missing information using the ratios. (*Hint:* Start with one ratio and get as much information as possible from it before trying another ratio. You may not be able to calculate the missing amounts in the same sequence as they are presented above.)

E18–19   A company reported the following selected information (in thousands):

Determine impact of other comprehensive income on profitability. (LO 6, 7) AN

	2017	2016	2015
Profit	$933	$ 867	$1,321
Other comprehensive income (loss)	(117)	793	(2,658)
Total comprehensive income (loss)	816	1,660	(1,337)

Instructions

Explain whether other comprehensive income would affect your analysis of this company's profitability, and if so how.

▶ Problems: Set A

P18–1A   The following condensed financial information is available for WestJet Airlines:

Prepare horizontal analysis and identify changes. (LO 2, 7) AN

WESTJET AIRLINES LTD.
Consolidated Statement of Earnings
Year Ended December 31 (in millions)

	2014	2013	2012	2011
Revenue	$3,976	$3,662	$3,427	$3,072
Operating expenses	3,501	3,263	3,052	2,815
Profit from operations	475	399	375	257
Other expenses	85	27	35	49
Profit before income taxes	390	372	340	208
Income tax expense	106	103	98	59
Profit	$ 284	$ 269	$ 242	$ 149

WESTJET AIRLINES LTD.
Balance Sheet
December 31 (in thousands)

Assets	2014	2013	2012	2011
Current assets	$1,730	$1,526	$1,635	$1,425
Non-current assets	2,916	2,617	2,112	2,049
Total assets	$4,646	$4,143	$3,747	$3,474
Liabilities and Shareholders' Equity				
Current liabilities	$1,338	$1,406	$1,188	$ 942
Non-current liabilities	1,531	1,147	1,087	1,162
Total liabilities	2,869	2,553	2,275	2,104
Shareholders' equity	1,777	1,590	1,472	1,370
Total liabilities and shareholders' equity	$4,646	$4,143	$3,747	$3,474

Instructions

(a) Perform a horizontal percent of base year analysis of WestJet's income statement and balance sheet, assuming 2011 is the base year.

(b) Using the analyses you prepared in part (a), identify any significant changes between 2011 and 2014.

(c) Which do you think would be more useful—percent of the base-year amount or calculating the percentage change between periods—to analyze WestJet between 2011 and 2014? Explain.

TAKING IT FURTHER   WestJet's financial information presented was prepared using IFRS. Prior to 2009, WestJet prepared its financial statements using the version of Canadian GAAP in place before IFRS was required. How would these differing standards affect your interpretation of WestJet's historical performance?

P18–2A   Comparative income statement data for Chen Inc. and Chuan Ltd., two competitors, are shown below for the year ended December 31, 2017.

Prepare vertical analysis, calculate profitability ratios, and compare. (LO 1, 3, 6) AN

	Chen	Chuan
Net sales	$1,849,035	$539,038
Cost of goods sold	1,060,490	338,006
Gross profit	788,545	201,032
Operating expenses	502,275	89,000
Profit from operations	286,270	112,032
Interest expense	6,800	1,252
Profit before income tax	279,470	110,780
Income tax expense	83,841	27,695
Profit	$ 195,629	$ 83,085
Additional information:		
Average total assets	$ 894,750	$251,313
Average total shareholders' equity	724,430	186,238

Instructions

(a) Using vertical analysis, calculate the percentage of the base amount of the income statement for each company.

(b) Calculate the gross profit margin, profit margin, asset turnover, return on assets, and return on equity ratios for 2017 for each company.

(c) Using the information calculated in parts (a) and (b), compare the profitability of each company.

(d) Is your comparison in part (c) an intracompany comparison or an intercompany comparison? Explain.

TAKING IT FURTHER How is your assessment of profitability affected by the differing sizes of the two companies, if at all? Explain.

Interpret horizontal and
vertical analysis.
(LO 2, 3, 7) AN

P18–3A Horizontal and vertical analysis of the income statement for a retail company selling ladies clothing is shown below.

TARA CORPORATION
Horizontal Income Statement
Year Ended January 31

	2017	2016	2015	2014
Net sales	140.0%	111.0%	114.0%	100.0%
Cost of goods sold	148.3%	113.3%	116.7%	100.0%
Gross profit	127.5%	107.5%	110.0%	100.0%
Operating expenses	171.4%	133.1%	126.9%	100.0%
Profit from operations	93.3%	87.6%	96.9%	100.0%
Other revenues and expenses				
Interest expense	40.0%	60.0%	80.0%	100.0%
Other revenue	240.0%	140.0%	200.0%	100.0%
Profit before income tax	140.0%	110.8%	113.8%	100.0%
Income tax expense	160.0%	116.0%	124.0%	100.0%
Profit	135.2%	109.5%	111.4%	100.0%

TARA CORPORATION
Vertical Income Statement
Year Ended January 31

	2017	2016	2015	2014
Net sales	100.0%	100.0%	100.0%	100.0%
Cost of goods sold	63.6%	61.2%	61.4%	60.0%
Gross profit	36.4%	38.8%	38.6%	40.0%
Operating expenses	21.4%	21.0%	19.5%	17.5%
Profit from operations	15.0%	17.8%	19.1%	22.5%
Other revenues and expenses				
Interest expense	(2.9)%	(5.4)%	(7.0)%	(10.0)%
Other revenue	0.9%	0.6%	0.9%	0.5%
Profit before income tax	13.0%	13.0%	13.0%	13.0%
Income tax expense	2.9%	2.6%	2.7%	2.5%
Profit	10.1%	10.4%	10.3%	10.5%

Instructions

(a) How effectively has the company controlled its cost of goods sold and operating expenses over the four-year period?

(b) Identify any other income statement components that have significantly changed over the four-year period for the company.

(c) Identify any additional information that might be helpful to you in your analysis of this company over the four-year period.

TAKING IT FURTHER   Explain how a horizontal analysis is affected if an account (a) has no value in a base year and a value in the next year, or (b) has a negative value in the base year and a positive value in the next year.

P18–4A   The comparative statements of Pristine Interiors Ltd. are presented as follows:

Calculate ratios. (LO 4, 5, 6) AP

PRISTINE INTERIORS LTD. Income Statement For the Year Ended December 31		
	2017	2016
Net sales	$2,055,750	$1,818,500
Cost of goods sold	1,169,000	1,011,500
Gross profit	886,750	807,000
Selling and administrative expenses	510,000	499,000
Income from operations	376,750	308,000
Other expenses and losses		
Interest expense	17,500	18,000
Income before income taxes	359,250	290,000
Income tax expense	107,775	87,000
Profit	$ 251,475	$ 203,000

PRISTINE INTERIORS LTD. Balance Sheet December 31			
Assets	2017	2016	2015
Current assets			
Cash	$ 87,250	$129,100	$114,200
Accounts receivable	181,600	107,800	102,800
Inventory	216,800	133,000	115,500
Total current assets	485,650	369,900	332,500
Property, plant, and equipment (net)	650,700	600,300	520,300
Total assets	$1,136,350	$970,200	$852,800
Liabilities and Shareholders' Equity			
Current liabilities			
Accounts payable	$ 283,175	$165,000	$145,400
Income taxes payable	45,000	43,500	42,000
Total current liabilities	328,175	208,500	187,400
Bonds payable	190,000	195,000	200,000
Total liabilities	518,175	403,500	387,400
Shareholders' equity			
Common shares	280,000	280,000	300,000
Retained earnings	338,175	286,700	165,400
Total shareholders' equity	618,175	566,700	465,400
Total liabilities and shareholders' equity	$1,136,350	$970,200	$852,800

Additional information:

1. All sales were on account.
2. Weighted-average common shares in 2017 were 57,000 and in 2016 were 55,000.

Instructions

(a) Calculate the following ratios for 2017 and 2016.

1. Gross profit margin	8. Return on common shareholders' equity
2. Profit margin	9. Return on assets
3. Earnings per share	10. Current ratio
4. Receivables turnover	11. Acid-test ratio
5. Collection period	12. Asset turnover
6. Inventory turnover	13. Debt to total assets
7. Days sales in inventory	

(b) Indicate whether each ratio has improved or deteriorated.

TAKING IT FURTHER   Calculate the operating cycle of Pristine Interiors for 2017 and compare the results to its nearest competitor, which has an operating cycle of 75 days. Does Pristine Interiors have a liquidity problem?

Calculate and evaluate ratios.
(LO 1, 4, 5, 6) AN

P18–5A   Condensed balance sheet and income statement data for Landwehr Corporation appear below:

LANDWEHR CORPORATION
Balance Sheet
December 31

	2017	2016	2015
Cash	$ 25,000	$ 20,000	$ 18,000
Accounts receivable	50,000	45,000	48,000
Other current assets	90,000	95,000	64,000
Property, plant, and equipment (net)	475,000	440,000	403,000
	$640,000	$600,000	$533,000
Current liabilities	$ 75,000	$ 80,000	$ 70,000
Long-term debt	80,000	85,000	50,000
Common shares	340,000	310,000	300,000
Retained earnings	145,000	125,000	113,000
	$640,000	$600,000	$533,000

LANDWEHR CORPORATION
Income Statement
For the Year Ended December 31

	2017	2016
Sales revenue	$740,000	$700,000
Less: Sales returns and allowances	40,000	50,000
Net sales	700,000	650,000
Cost of goods sold	420,000	400,000
Gross profit	280,000	250,000
Operating expenses (including income taxes)	235,000	220,000
Profit	$ 45,000	$ 30,000

Additional information:

1. The market price of Landwehr's common shares was $4.00, $5.00, and $8.00 for 2015, 2016, and 2017, respectively.
2. All dividends were paid in cash.
3. Weighted-average common shares were 32,000 in 2017 and 31,000 in 2016.

Instructions

(a) Calculate the following ratios for 2016 and 2017.

1. Profit margin	5. Payout ratio
2. Asset turnover	6. Debt to total assets
3. Earnings per share	7. Gross profit margin
4. Price-earnings ratio	

(b) Based on the ratios calculated, discuss briefly the improvement or lack thereof in Landwehr Corporation's financial position and operating results from 2016 to 2017.

TAKING IT FURTHER   Roberto Landwehr is puzzled. He believes the profit margin of Landwehr is an indication the company is doing well. Julie Beck, his accountant, says that more information is needed to determine the firm's financial well-being. Who is correct? Why?

P18–6A   Comparative financial statements for The Cable Company Ltd. are shown below.

Calculate ratios.
(LO 4, 5, 6) AP

THE CABLE COMPANY LTD.
Income Statement
Year Ended December 31

	2017	2016
Net sales	$1,948,500	$1,700,500
Cost of goods sold	1,025,500	946,000
Gross profit	923,000	754,500
Operating expenses	516,000	449,000
Profit from operations	407,000	305,500
Interest expense	28,000	19,000
Profit before income tax	379,000	286,500
Income tax expense	113,700	86,000
Profit	$ 265,300	$ 200,500

THE CABLE COMPANY LTD.
Balance Sheet
December 31

Assets	2017	2016
Current assets		
Cash	$ 68,100	$ 64,200
Accounts receivable	107,800	102,800
Inventory	143,000	115,500
Total current assets	318,900	282,500
Property, plant, and equipment	679,300	570,300
Total assets	$998,200	$852,800
Liabilities and Shareholders' Equity		
Current liabilities		
Accounts payable	$155,000	$125,400
Income tax payable	43,500	42,000
Current portion of mortgage payable	10,000	20,000
Total current liabilities	208,500	187,400
Mortgage payable	104,000	200,000
Total liabilities	312,500	387,400
Shareholders' equity		
Common shares (56,000 issued in 2017; 60,000 in 2016)	168,000	180,000
Retained earnings	517,700	285,400
Total shareholders' equity	685,700	465,400
Total liabilities and shareholders' equity	$998,200	$852,800

Additional information:

1. All sales were on account.
2. The allowance for doubtful accounts was $5,400 in 2017 and $5,100 in 2016.
3. On July 1, 2017, 4,000 shares were reacquired for $10 per share and cancelled.
4. In 2017, $5,000 of dividends were paid to the common shareholders.
5. Cash provided by operating activities was $316,200.
6. Cash used by investing activities was $161,300.

Instructions

Calculate all possible liquidity, solvency, and profitability ratios for 2017.

TAKING IT FURTHER   Based on the ratios you have calculated for 2017, can you determine whether The Cable Company's liquidity, solvency, and profitability are strong or weak? If not, what additional information would you require?

Calculate and evaluate ratios.
(LO 1, 4, 5, 6) AN

P18–7A   Comparative financial statements for Click and Clack Ltd. are shown below.

CLICK AND CLACK LTD.
Income Statement
Year Ended December 31

	2017	2016
Net sales	$900,000	$840,000
Cost of goods sold	625,000	575,000
Gross profit	275,000	265,000
Operating expenses	164,000	160,000
Profit from operations	111,000	105,000
Other revenues and expenses		
Interest expense	35,000	20,000
Profit before income tax	76,000	85,000
Income tax expense	18,750	20,000
Profit	$ 57,250	$ 65,000

CLICK AND CLACK LTD.
Balance Sheet
December 31

Assets	2017	2016	2015
Cash	$ 95,000	$ 85,000	$ 10,000
Accounts receivable	114,000	110,000	108,000
Inventories	130,000	125,000	97,000
Prepaid expenses	25,000	23,000	115,000
Land, buildings, and equipment	390,000	305,000	300,000
Total assets	$754,000	$648,000	$630,000
Liabilities and Shareholders' Equity			
Liabilities			
Notes payable	$110,000	$100,000	$100,000
Accounts payable	45,000	42,000	60,000
Accrued liabilities	32,000	40,000	30,000
Bonds payable, due 2020	190,000	150,000	181,000
Total liabilities	377,000	332,000	371,000
Shareholders' equity			
Common shares (20,000 issued)	200,000	200,000	200,000
Retained earnings	177,000	116,000	59,000
Total shareholders' equity	377,000	316,000	259,000
Total liabilities and shareholders' equity	$754,000	$648,000	$630,000

Additional information:

1. Seventy-five percent of the sales were on account.
2. The allowance for doubtful accounts was $4,000 in 2017, $5,000 in 2016, and $3,000 in 2015.
3. In 2017 and 2016, dividends of $3,000 and $8,000, respectively, were paid to the common shareholders.
4. Cash provided by operating activities was $103,500 in 2017 and $129,000 in 2016.
5. Cash used by investing activities was $115,500 in 2017 and $35,000 in 2016.

Instructions

(a) Calculate all possible liquidity, solvency, and profitability ratios for 2017 and 2016.
(b) Identify whether the change in each ratio from 2016 to 2017 calculated in part (a) was favourable (F), unfavourable (U), or no change (NC).
(c) Explain whether overall (1) liquidity, (2) solvency, and (3) profitability improved, deteriorated, or remained the same between 2016 and 2017.

TAKING IT FURTHER   Does this problem employ an intracompany comparison or an intercompany comparison? Which do you think is more useful?

P18–8A   Selected financial data for Big Rock Brewery Inc. and Brick Brewing Co. Ltd. are presented below.

Calculate and evaluate ratios.
(LO 4, 5, 6, 7) AN

	Big Rock Brewery Inc. (in $ thousands)	Brick Brewing Co. Ltd. (in $ thousands)
Statement of Comprehensive Income (Loss)		
Total revenue	$36,755	$36,333
Cost of sales	18,930	26,136
Gross profit	17,825	10,197
Operating expenses	17,110	8,076
Profit from operations	715	2,121
Interest expense (revenue)	(36)	535
Other expenses	153	–
Other non-operating income	351	436
Profit before income tax	949	2,022
Income tax expense	325	627
Profit	$ 624	$ 1,395
Balance Sheet		
Current assets	$ 9,680	$10,838
Non-current assets	38,487	34,096
Total assets	$48,167	$44,934
Current liabilities	$ 4,958	$ 6,335
Non-current liabilities	4,766	4,217
Total liabilities	9,724	10,552
Shareholders' equity	38,443	34,382
Total liabilities and shareholders' equity	$48,167	$44,934

Additional information:		
Average accounts receivable	$ 1,413	$ 6,179
Average inventories	3,398	3,676
Average total assets	45,412	45,651
Average total shareholders' equity	34,200	33,447

Instructions

(a) For each company, calculate the following ratios:

1. Current ratio	7. Gross profit margin
2. Receivables turnover	8. Profit margin
3. Inventory turnover	9. Asset turnover
4. Operating cycle	10. Return on assets
5. Debt to total assets	11. Return on equity
6. Interest coverage	

(b) Compare the liquidity, solvency, and profitability of the two companies.

TAKING IT FURTHER   How would other comprehensive loss factor into your analysis above?

P18–9A   Selected ratios for two companies operating in the office supply industry follow.

Evaluate ratios.
(LO 4, 5, 6) AN

Ratio	Fournitures Ltée	Supplies Unlimited
Acid-test ratio	1.0:1	0.8:1
Asset turnover	2.6 times	2.2 times
Current ratio	1.7:1	2.8:1
Debt to total assets	35.0%	30.3%
Gross profit margin	23.9%	35.4%
Interest coverage	4.2 times	6.6 times
Inventory turnover	6.0 times	3.1 times
Operating cycle	92 days	158 days
Price-earnings ratio	19.0 times	15.2 times
Profit margin	5.6%	4.1%
Receivables turnover	11.8 times	9.1 times
Return on assets	14.6%	9.0%
Return on equity	19.8%	12.5%

Instructions

(a) Both companies offer their customers credit terms of net 30 days. Indicate the ratio(s) that should be used to assess how well the accounts receivable are managed. Which company appears to be managing its accounts receivable better?

(b) Indicate the ratio(s) that should be used to assess inventory management. Which company appears to be managing its inventory better?

(c) Supplies Unlimited's current ratio is higher than Fourniture's. Identify two possible reasons for this.

(d) Which company is more solvent? Identify the ratio(s) that should be used to determine this and defend your choice.

(e) You notice that Fourniture's gross profit margin is significantly less than Supplies Unlimited's but its profit margin is higher. Identify two possible reasons for this.

(f) Which company do investors appear to believe has greater prospects for future profitability? Indicate the ratio(s) you used to reach this conclusion and explain your reasoning.

TAKING IT FURTHER   Which company is using leverage more effectively? Explain.

Evaluate ratios.
(LO 4, 5, 6) AN

P18–10A   The following ratios are available for beverage competitors **DAVIDsTEA Inc.** and **Starbucks Corporation** for a recent year:

	DAVIDsTEA Inc.	Starbucks Corporation
Liquidity		
Current ratio	2.0:1	1.4.1:1
Acid-test ratio	1.12:1	0.81:1
Receivables turnover	82.4 times	27.6 times
Inventory turnover	5.4 times	6.3 times
Operating cycle	72 days	71 days
Solvency		
Debt to total assets	100%	51%
Interest coverage	3.6 times	50.3 times
Profitability		
Gross profit margin	54.8%	58.3%
Profit margin	4.5%	12.6%
Asset turnover	2.0 times	1.5 times
Return on assets	9.2%	18.6%

Instructions

(a) Which company is more liquid? Explain.

(b) Which company is more solvent? Explain.

(c) Which company is more profitable? Explain.

TAKING IT FURTHER   The price-earnings ratio for DAVIDsTEA is 54.8 times, compared with Starbucks' price-earnings ratio of 27.4 times. Which company do investors favour? Is your answer consistent with your analysis of the two companies' profitability in part (c)?

Calculate missing information.
(LO 4, 5, 6) AN

P18–11A   Presented here are an incomplete income statement and balance sheet for Schwenke Corporation.

SCHWENKE CORPORATION
Income Statement
Year Ended December 31, 2017

Net sales	$ (a)
Cost of goods sold	(b)
Gross profit	(c)
Operating expenses	333,750
Profit from operations	(d)
Interest expense	10,500
Profit before income taxes	(e)
Income tax expense	(f)
Profit	$124,600

```
                    SCHWENKE CORPORATION
                         Balance Sheet
                       December 31, 2017

   Assets
   Current assets
      Cash                                        $    7,500
      Accounts receivable                              (g)
      Inventory                                        (h)
                                                  _____
         Total current assets                          (i)
   Property, plant, and equipment                      (j)
                                                  _____
      Total assets                                $    (k)
                                                  ===========
   Liabilities
      Current liabilities                         $    (l)
      Non-current liabilities                       120,000
                                                  _____
         Total liabilities                             (m)

   Shareholders' Equity
      Common shares                                  250,000
      Retained earnings                              400,000
                                                  _____
         Total shareholders' equity                  650,000
                                                  _____
      Total liabilities and shareholders' equity  $    (n)
                                                  ===========
```

Additional information:

1. The gross profit margin is 40%.
2. The income tax rate is 20%.
3. The inventory turnover is 8 times.

4. The current ratio is 3:1.
5. The asset turnover is 1.5 times.

Instructions

Calculate the missing information using the ratios. Use ending balances instead of average balances, where averages are required for ratio calculations. Show your calculations.

TAKING IT FURTHER   Why is it not possible to calculate the missing amounts in the same sequence (i.e., (a), (b), (c), etc.) that they are presented above?

▶ Problems: Set B

P18–1B   The following condensed financial information is available for **lululemon athletica inc.**

Prepare horizontal analysis and identify changes.
(LO 2, 7) AN

```
                          lululemon athletica inc.
                             Income Statement
                       Fiscal Year Ended (in millions)
```

	2015	2014	2013	2012
Revenue	$1,797	$1,591	$1,370	$1,000
Operating expenses	883	751	608	431
Profit from operations	914	840	762	569
Other expenses	531	443	381	279
Profit before income taxes	383	397	381	290
Income tax expense	144	117	110	105
Profit	$ 239	$ 280	$ 271	$ 185

lululemon athletica inc. Balance Sheet (in millions)				

Assets	Feb. 1, 2015	Feb. 2, 2014	Feb. 3, 2013	Jan. 29, 2012
Current assets	$ 951	$ 945	$ 787	$527
Non-current assets	345	307	264	208
Total assets	$1,296	$1,252	$1,051	$735
Liabilities and Shareholders' Equity				
Current liabilities	$ 160	$ 116	$ 133	$103
Non-current liabilities	47	39	31	25
Total liabilities	207	155	164	128
Shareholders' equity	1,089	1,097	887	607
Total liabilities and shareholders' equity	$1,296	$1,252	$1,051	$735

Instructions

(a) Perform a horizontal percent of base year analysis of lululemon's income statement and balance sheet, assuming 2012 is the base year.
(b) Using the analyses you prepared in part (a), identify any significant changes between 2012 and 2015.
(c) Which do you think would be more useful—a percent of base year amount or calculating the percentage change between periods—to analyze lululemon between 2012 and 2015? Explain.

TAKING IT FURTHER   If the operating expenses for lululemon are increasing at a faster rate than revenues, what are some of the things lululemon should consider to turn this trend around?

Prepare vertical analysis, calculate profitability ratios, and compare. (LO 1, 3, 6) AN

P18–2B   Comparative income statement data for Manitou Ltd. and Muskoka Ltd., two competitors, are shown below for the year ended June 30, 2017.

	Manitou	Muskoka
Net sales	$360,000	$1,400,000
Cost of goods sold	200,000	720,000
Gross profit	160,000	680,000
Operating expenses	60,000	272,000
Profit from operations	100,000	408,000
Rental income	12,000	24,000
Profit before income tax	112,000	432,000
Income tax expense	22,400	95,040
Profit	$ 89,600	$ 336,960
Additional information:		
Average total assets	$457,500	$1,725,000
Average total shareholders' equity	204,800	743,480

Instructions

(a) Using vertical analysis, calculate the percentage of the base amount of the income statement for each company.
(b) Calculate the gross profit margin, profit margin, asset turnover, return on assets, and return on equity ratios for 2017 for each company.
(c) Using the information calculated in parts (a) and (b), compare the profitability of each company.
(d) Is your comparison in part (c) an intracompany comparison or an intercompany comparison? Explain.

TAKING IT FURTHER   How is your assessment of profitability affected by the differing sizes of the two companies, if at all? Explain.

P18–3B   A horizontal and vertical analysis of the income statement for a service company providing consulting services is shown below.

Interpret horizontal and vertical analysis.
(LO 2, 3, 7) AP

COMFORT CORPORATION
Horizontal Income Statement
Year Ended January 31

	2017	2016	2015	2014
Revenue	120.0%	110.0%	114.0%	100.0%
Operating expenses	118.6%	111.4%	114.3%	100.0%
Profit from operations	123.3%	106.7%	113.3%	100.0%
Other revenues and expenses				
Interest expense	40.0%	60.0%	80.0%	100.0%
Other revenue	240.0%	140.0%	200.0%	100.0%
Profit before income tax	166.8%	130.2%	131.7%	100.0%
Income tax expense	166.8%	130.2%	131.7%	100.0%
Profit	166.8%	130.2%	131.7%	100.0%

COMFORT CORPORATION
Vertical Income Statement
Year Ended January 31

	2017	2016	2015	2014
Revenue	100.0%	100.0%	100.0%	100.0%
Operating expenses	69.2%	70.9%	70.2%	70.0%
Profit from operations	30.8%	29.1%	29.8%	30.0%
Other revenues and expenses				
Interest expense	(3.3)%	(5.4)%	(7.0)%	(10.0)%
Other revenue	1.0%	0.6%	0.9%	0.5%
Profit before income tax	28.5%	24.3%	23.7%	20.5%
Income tax expense	5.7%	4.9%	4.8%	4.1%
Profit	22.8%	19.4%	18.9%	16.4%

Instructions

(a) How effectively has the company controlled its operating expenses over the four-year period?
(b) Identify any other income statement components that have significantly changed over the four-year period for the company.
(c) Identify any additional information that might be helpful to you in your analysis of this company over the four-year period.

TAKING IT FURTHER   Shopify became a public corporation in May 2015. Can a meaningful horizontal and vertical analysis be prepared for its first full year of operations as a public company, the year ended December 31, 2015? Explain.

P18–4B   The comparative statements of Andy's Art Company are presented below.

Calculate ratios.
(LO 4, 5, 6) AP

ANDY'S ART COMPANY
Income Statement
For the Year Ended December 31

	2017	2016
Net sales	$2,153,650	$1,828,500
Cost of goods sold	1,119,900	1,010,500
Gross profit	1,033,750	818,000
Selling and administrative expense	750,000	516,000
Income from operations	283,750	302,000
Interest expense	20,000	18,000
Income before income taxes	263,750	284,000
Income tax expense	60,665	85,000
Profit	$ 203,085	$ 199,000

```
                          ANDY'S ART COMPANY
                             Balance Sheet
                             December 31
```

Assets	2017	2016	2015
Current assets			
Cash	$ 123,050	$129,100	$114,200
Accounts receivable (net)	142,600	122,800	102,800
Inventory	170,000	113,000	115,500
Total current assets	435,650	364,900	332,500
Property, plant, and equipment (net)	605,300	605,300	520,300
Total assets	$1,040,950	$970,200	$852,800
Liabilities and Shareholders' Equity			
Current liabilities			
Accounts payable	$ 165,000	$160,000	$145,400
Income taxes payable	46,250	43,500	42,000
Total current liabilities	211,250	203,500	187,400
Bonds payable	220,000	210,000	200,000
Total liabilities	431,250	413,500	387,400
Shareholders' equity			
Common shares	280,000	280,000	300,000
Retained earnings	329,700	276,700	165,400
Total shareholders' equity	609,700	556,700	465,400
Total liabilities and shareholders' equity	$1,040,950	$970,200	$852,800

Additional information:

1. All sales were on account.   2. Weighted-average common shares for both years was 57,000.

Instructions

Calculate the following ratios for 2017 and 2016. Indicate whether each ratio has improved or deteriorated.

(a) Gross profit margin
(b) Profit margin
(c) Earnings per share
(d) Receivables turnover
(e) Collection period
(f) Inventory turnover
(g) Days sales in inventory

(h) Return on common shareholders' equity
(i) Return on assets
(j) Current ratio
(k) Acid-test ratio
(l) Asset turnover
(m) Debt to total assets

TAKING IT FURTHER   Calculate the operating cycle for Andy's Arts and compare it to its nearest competitor, which has an operating cycle of 60 days. Does Andy's Arts have a liquidity problem?

Calculate and evaluate ratios.
(LO 1, 4, 5, 6) AN

P18–5B   Condensed balance sheet and income statement data for Lauer Corporation appear below.

```
                          LAUER CORPORATION
                             Balance Sheet
                             December 31
```

	2017	2016	2015
Cash	$ 25,000	$ 20,000	$ 18,000
Accounts receivable	50,000	45,000	48,000
Other current assets	90,000	95,000	64,000
Property, plant, and equipment (net)	475,000	440,000	403,000
	$640,000	$600,000	$533,000
Current liabilities	$ 65,000	$ 80,000	$ 70,000
Mortgage payable	80,000	85,000	50,000
Common shares	350,000	310,000	300,000
Retained earnings	145,000	125,000	113,000
	$640,000	$600,000	$533,000

LAUER CORPORATION
Income Statement
For the Year Ended December 31

	2017	2016
Sales revenue	$750,000	$710,000
Less: Sales returns and allowances	40,000	50,000
Net sales	710,000	660,000
Cost of goods sold	420,000	400,000
Gross profit	290,000	260,000
Operating expenses (including income taxes)	235,000	220,000
Profit	$ 55,000	$ 40,000

Additional information:

1. The market price of Lauer's common shares was $4.00, $5.00, and $8.00 for 2015, 2016, and 2017, respectively.
2. All dividends were paid in cash.
3. Weighted-average common shares were 32,000 in 2017 and 31,000 in 2016.

Instructions

(a) Calculate the following ratios for 2016 and 2017.

   1. Gross profit margin   5. Payout ratio
   2. Asset turnover   6. Debt to total assets
   3. Earnings per share   7. Profit margin
   4. Price-earnings ratio

(b) Based on the ratios calculated, discuss briefly the improvement or lack thereof in Lauer Corporation's financial position and operating results from 2016 to 2017.

TAKING IT FURTHER   Mr. Lauer is puzzled. He believes the profit margin of Lauer Corporation is an indication the company is doing well. Brittany Qi, his accountant, says that more information is needed to determine the firm's financial well-being. Who is correct? Why?

P18–6B   Comparative financial statements for The Rose Packing Corporation are shown below.

Calculate ratios.
(LO 4, 5, 6) AP

THE ROSE PACKING CORPORATION
Income Statement
Year Ended December 31

	2017	2016
Net sales	$790,000	$624,000
Cost of goods sold	540,000	405,600
Gross profit	250,000	218,400
Operating expenses	153,880	149,760
Profit from operations	96,120	68,640
Interest expense	3,200	1,200
Loss on sale of equipment	6,720	6,000
Profit before income tax	86,200	61,440
Income tax expense	12,930	9,216
Profit	$ 73,270	$ 52,224

THE ROSE PACKING CORPORATION
Balance Sheet
December 31

Assets	2017	2016
Current assets		
Cash	$ 49,380	$ 44,600
Accounts receivable	104,720	93,800
Inventory	96,400	74,000
Total current assets	250,500	212,400
Property, plant, and equipment	465,300	459,600
Total assets	$715,800	$672,000
Liabilities and Shareholders' Equity		
Current liabilities		
Accounts payable	$164,850	$130,000
Income tax payable	2,500	4,000
Other payables and accruals	12,800	22,000
Total current liabilities	180,150	156,000
Bonds payable	90,000	120,000
Total liabilities	270,150	276,000
Shareholders' equity		
Common shares (15,000 issued)	150,000	150,000
Retained earnings	295,650	246,000
Total shareholders' equity	445,650	396,000
Total liabilities and shareholders' equity	$715,800	$672,000

Additional information:

1. All sales were on account.
2. The allowance for doubtful accounts was $5,500 in 2017 and $4,500 in 2016.
3. In 2017, $23,620 of dividends were paid to the common shareholders.
4. Cash provided by operating activities was $116,780.
5. Cash used by investing activities was $51,660.

Instructions

Calculate all possible liquidity, solvency, and profitability ratios for 2017.

TAKING IT FURTHER Based on the ratios you have calculated for 2017, can you determine whether Rose Packing's liquidity, solvency, and profitability are strong or weak? If not, what additional information would you require?

Calculate and evaluate ratios. **P18-7B** Comparative financial statements for Track Ltd. are shown below.
(LO 1, 4, 5, 6) AN

TRACK LTD.
Income Statement
Year Ended December 31

	2017	2016
Net sales	$1,000,000	$940,000
Cost of goods sold	650,000	635,000
Gross profit	350,000	305,000
Operating expenses	200,000	180,000
Profit from operations	150,000	125,000
Interest expense (net)	35,000	35,000
Profit before income taxes	115,000	90,000
Income tax expense	17,250	13,500
Profit	$ 97,750	$ 76,500

TRACK LTD. Balance Sheet December 31			
Assets	2017	2016	2015
Cash	$ 50,000	$ 42,000	$ 33,000
Accounts receivable	100,000	87,000	77,000
Inventories	240,000	200,000	150,000
Prepaid expenses	25,000	31,000	30,000
Long-term debt investments	180,000	100,000	50,000
Land	75,000	75,000	75,000
Building and equipment	570,000	600,000	660,000
Total assets	$1,240,000	$1,135,000	$1,075,000
Liabilities and Shareholders' Equity			
Liabilities			
Notes payable	$ 125,000	$ 125,000	$ 125,000
Accounts payable	160,750	140,000	71,000
Accrued liabilities	52,000	50,000	20,000
Bonds payable, due 2020	100,000	100,000	200,000
Total liabilities	437,750	415,000	416,000
Shareholders' equity			
Preferred shares	200,000	200,000	200,000
Common shares (100,000 issued)	300,000	300,000	300,000
Retained earnings	302,250	220,000	159,000
Total shareholders' equity	802,250	720,000	659,000
Total liabilities and shareholders' equity	$1,240,000	$1,135,000	$1,075,000

Additional information:

1. All sales were on account.
2. The allowance for doubtful accounts was $5,000 in 2017, $4,000 in 2016, and $3,000 in 2015.
3. In each of 2017 and 2016, $15,500 of dividends were paid to the common shareholders.
4. Cash provided by operating activities was $133,500 in 2017 and $180,500 in 2016.
5. Cash used by investing activities was $110,000 in 2017 and $56,000 in 2016.

Instructions

(a) Calculate all possible liquidity, solvency, and profitability ratios for 2017 and 2016.
(b) Identify whether the change in each ratio from 2016 to 2017 calculated in part (a) was favourable (F), unfavourable (U), or no change (NC).
(c) Explain whether overall (1) liquidity, (2) solvency, and (3) profitability improved, deteriorated, or remained the same between 2016 and 2017.

TAKING IT FURTHER   Does this problem use an intracompany comparison or an intercompany comparison? Which do you think is more useful?

P18–8B   Early in 2014, Nordstrom, Inc. began opening stores across Canada to compete against Hudson's Bay   Calculate and evaluate ratios.
Company and other higher-end retailers. Selected financial data (in millions) for the two companies are presented   (LO 4, 5, 6, 7) AN
here.

	Hudson's Bay (C$) Jan. 31, 2015	Nordstrom (US$) Jan. 31, 2015
Statement of Comprehensive Income		
Total revenue	$8,169	$13,506
Cost of sales	4,893	8,406
Gross profit	3,276	5,100
Operating expenses	3,103	3,777
Profit from operations	173	1,323
Interest expense (revenue)	262	138
Other non-operating income	308	
Profit before income tax	219	1,185
Income tax expense (benefit)	(19)	465
Profit	$ 238	$ 720
Balance Sheet		
Current assets	$2,829	$ 5,224
Non-current assets	6,243	4,021
Total assets	$9,072	$ 9,245
Current liabilities	$2,144	$ 2,800
Non-current liabilities	4,436	4,005
Total liabilities	6,580	6,805
Shareholders' equity	2,492	2,440
Total liabilities and shareholders' equity	$9,072	$ 9,245

Additional information:

Average accounts receivable	$ 281	$ 2,242
Average inventories	2,199	1,632
Average total assets	8,507	8,910
Average total shareholders' equity	2,268	2,260

Instructions

(a) For each company, calculate the following ratios:

1. Current ratio	7. Gross profit margin
2. Receivables turnover	8. Profit margin
3. Inventory turnover	9. Asset turnover
4. Operating cycle	10. Return on assets
5. Debt to total assets	11. Return on equity
6. Interest coverage	

(b) Compare the liquidity, solvency, and profitability of the two companies.

TAKING IT FURTHER If the entities presented other comprehensive loss, should it be factored into your analysis above?

Evaluate ratios.
(LO 4, 5, 6) AN

P18–9B Selected ratios for two companies operating in the beverage industry follow.

Ratio	Refresh Ltd.	Flavour Corp.
Acid-test ratio	0:6:1	0:8:1
Asset turnover	1.0 times	1.0 times
Current ratio	2.2:1	1.6:1
Debt to total assets	56.0%	72.0%
Gross profit margin	73.8%	60.0%
Interest coverage	12.3 times	6.9 times
Inventory turnover	5.8 times	9.9 times
Operating cycle	98 days	74 days
Price-earnings ratio	20.3 times	14.3 times
Profit margin	9.3%	10.2%
Receivables turnover	10.4 times	9.8 times
Return on assets	11.2%	10.1%
Return on equity	25.7%	29.8%

Instructions

(a) Both companies offer their customers credit terms of net 30 days. Indicate the ratio(s) that should be used to assess how well the accounts receivable are managed. Which company appears to be managing its accounts receivable better?

(b) Indicate the ratio(s) that should be used to assess inventory management. Which company appears to be managing its inventory better?

(c) Refresh's current ratio is higher than Flavour's. Identify two possible reasons for this.

(d) Which company is more solvent? Identify the ratio(s) that should be used to determine this and defend your choice.

(e) You notice that Refresh's gross profit margin is significantly more than Flavour's but its profit margin is lower. Identify two possible reasons for this.

(f) Which company do investors appear to believe has greater prospects for future profitability? Indicate the ratio(s) you used to reach this conclusion and explain your reasoning.

TAKING IT FURTHER   Which company is using leverage more effectively? Explain.

P18–10B   The following ratios are available for Rogers Communications Inc. and Shaw Communications Inc. for a recent year:

Evaluate ratios.
(LO 4, 5, 6) AN

Liquidity	Rogers	Shaw
Current ratio	0.48:1	0.95:1
Acid-test ratio	0.36:1	0.81:1
Receivables turnover	8.3 times	10.7 times
Solvency		
Debt to total assets	79.3%	63.7%
Interest coverage	3.3 times	5.5 times
Profitability		
Profit margin	10.4%	16.9%
Asset turnover	0.5 times	0.4 times
Return on assets	5.4%	6.8%
Return on equity	26.4%	19.0%

Instructions

(a) Which company is more liquid? Explain.

(b) Which company is more solvent? Explain.

(c) Which company is more profitable? Explain.

TAKING IT FURTHER   Rogers' price-earnings ratio is 17.4 times, compared with Shaw's price-earnings ratio of 13.7 times. Which company do investors favour? Is your answer consistent with your analysis of the two companies' profitability in part (c)?

P18–11B   Presented here are an incomplete income statement and balance sheet for Vieux Corporation.

Calculate missing information.
(LO 4, 5, 6) AN

VIEUX CORPORATION Income Statement Year Ended December 31, 2017	
Net sales	$11,000,000
Cost of goods sold	(a)
Gross profit	(b)
Operating expenses	1,600,000
Profit from operations	(c)
Interest expense	(d)
Profit before income taxes	(e)
Income tax expense	707,000
Profit	$ (f)

VIEUX CORPORATION Balance Sheet December 31, 2017	
Assets	
Current assets	
Cash	$ (g)
Accounts receivable	(h)
Inventory	(i)
Total current assets	(j)
Long-term investments	430,000
Property, plant, and equipment	4,420,000
Total assets	$ (k)
Liabilities	
Current liabilities	$ (l)
Non-current liabilities	(m)
Total liabilities	(n)
Shareholders' equity	
Common shares	1,500,000
Retained earnings	1,900,000
Total shareholders' equity	3,400,000
Total liabilities and shareholders' equity	$ (o)

Additional information:

1. The gross profit margin is 40%.
2. The profit margin is 15%.
3. The receivables turnover is 10 times and all sales are on account.
4. The inventory turnover is 8 times.
5. The current ratio is 2:1.
6. The return on assets is 22%.

Instructions

Calculate the missing information using the ratios. Use ending balances instead of average balances, where averages are required for ratio calculations. Show your calculations.

TAKING IT FURTHER Why is it not possible to calculate the missing amounts in the same sequence (i.e., (a), (b), (c), etc.) that they are presented above?

CHAPTER 18: BROADENING YOUR PERSPECTIVE

▶ Financial Reporting and Analysis

Financial Reporting Problem

BYP18–1 The financial statements of Corus Entertainment are shown in Appendix A at the end of this textbook.

Instructions

(a) Using vertical analysis, calculate the vertical percentage of a base amount for Corus's balance sheets and income statements for 2014 and 2013.
(b) Identify any significant items or trends you observe from your vertical analysis in part (a).

Interpreting Financial Statements

BYP18–2 Selected financial ratios for Canadian National Railway (CN) and Canadian Pacific Railway (CP) are presented here for a recent year.

	CN	CP
Liquidity		
Current ratio	0.94:1	0.91:1
Acid-test ratio	0.7:1	0.7:1
Receivables turnover	13.9 times	10.3 times
Solvency		
Debt to total assets	58.0%	66.3%
Interest coverage	12.7 times	8.2 times
Free cash flow	$2,084 million	$2,200 million
Profitability		
Profit margin	26.1%	22.3%
Asset turnover	0.4 times	0.4 times
Return on assets	10.2%	8.8%
Return on equity	24.0%	23.2%

Instructions

(a) Comment on the relative liquidity of the two companies.
(b) Comment on the relative solvency of the two companies.
(c) Comment on the relative profitability of the two companies.

▶ Critical Thinking

Collaborative Learning Activity

Note to instructor: Additional instructions and material for this group activity can be found on the Instructor Resource Site and in *WileyPLUS.*

BYP18–3 In this group activity, you will analyze two companies on an intracompany, intercompany, and industry basis. Based on your analysis, you will recommend which company is a better investment. Your instructor will evaluate the groups based on their analysis and rationale for their recommendation.

Communication Activity

BYP18–4 You are a new member of the audit committee and board of directors of EasyMix Cement Inc. EasyMix was a private company using ASPE until last year, when it became a publicly traded company using IFRS. You are about to attend your first meeting of the audit committee, at which the year-end financial results, including key ratios, will be presented.

Instructions

Identify any of the limitations of financial statement analysis that you believe may apply to EasyMix. Prioritize your list and prepare questions that you should raise at the audit committee meeting to help you better understand the financial results and ratios presented.

"All About You" Activity

BYP18–5 In the "All About You" feature, you learned that there are on-line investment services that provide advice to investors. These services offer stock quotes, company research reports, personal finance information, news, on-line seminars, podcasts, and message boards. However, it is also important that as an investor you differentiate good information from bad information. Reading the financial statements and preparing a ratio analysis is one step in evaluating an investment. You have recently inherited $10,000 cash and you are considering investing in Canadian Tire Corporation, Limited's shares.

Instructions

Go to Canadian Tire's website at http://corp.canadiantire.ca and click on "Investors" then click on "Financial Reporting", followed by "Annual Disclosures" and go to the 2013 annual report.

(a) Included in the annual report is Management's Discussion and Analysis (MD&A), which provides highlights of the company's operations, explanations for changes in the company's financial position, and strategic plans for the future. How might the MD&A provide useful information in your evaluation of the financial statement ratios?

(b) On the "Investors" section of Canadian Tire's website, click on "Shareholders" and then click "Historical Stock Quote." What were Canadian Tire's shares closing price on the following dates?
   1. January 2, 2015
   2. December 28, 2013

(c) Calculate the following ratios for the 2013 fiscal year. Compare these with the 2014 ratios shown in the Ratio Analysis section of the chapter for Canadian Tire and reproduced in parentheses after each ratio below. For each 2014 ratio, has it improved or deteriorated from 2013?
   1. Current ratio (1.9:1)
   2. Inventory turnover (5.4 times)

3. Debt to total assets (61.3%)
4. Interest coverage (9.1 times)
5. Gross profit margin (32.5%)
6. Profit margin (5.1%)
7. Return on assets (4.5%)
8. Return on equity (11.5%)
9. Price-earnings ratio (16.0 times) (Use basic EPS)
10. Payout ratio (25.5%)

(d) Under "Shareholders," click on "Stock Information" and select all under the Stock Chart. Comment on the changes in the price of Canadian Tire's shares over the five years.

(e) Based on your brief analysis of Canadian Tire's ratios and share prices, do you think buying Canadian Tire's shares is a good investment for you? Explain.

(f) If you are investing in the stock market, will you rely solely on your analysis of the financial statements? The history of Canadian Tire's share price? Or do you think you might rely on both your financial statement analysis and the history of the share price? Explain.

(g) In the "All About You" feature, we learned that critics of message boards on investment services' sites say that message boards can intensify the rumour mill. Do you think that you should ignore message boards when making investment decisions? Explain.

 Santé Smoothie Saga

(**Note:** This is a continuation of the Santé Smoothie Saga from Chapters 1 through 17.)

BYP18–6 The Koebels have considered the offer extended by Coffee Beans Ltd. (see Chapter 17) and have turned it down. Instead, Brian, Janet, and Natalie have decided to continue operating Santé Smoothies & Sweets Ltd. and to expand the business.

Santé Smoothies & Sweets Ltd. once again has excess cash for its expansion but needs time to organize it. In the meantime, the cash could be invested. The Koebels have been approached by a family friend who works in the investment industry. This family friend has made a strong recommendation to buy shares in Okanagan Fruit & Vegetable Corp., a public company. Because Janet, Brian, and Natalie produce and sell fresh fruit and vegetable smoothies, they believe that investing in a public company that produces and distributes fruits and vegetables could be a good investment. The investment in Okanagan Fruit & Vegetable Corp. could provide a significant return on a short-term basis while the Koebels organize for the expansion.

In order to assess this investment, Natalie has calculated several ratios for both Okanagan Fruit & Vegetable Corp. and Santé Smoothies & Sweets Ltd. as follows:

Ratio	Okanagan Fruit & Vegetable Corp. Year Ended December 31, 2018	Okanagan Fruit & Vegetable Corp. Year Ended December 31, 2017	Santé Smoothies & Sweets Ltd. Year Ended May 31, 2018
Current ratio	1.0:1	1.1:1	8.4:1
Receivables turnover	15.6 times	18.5 times	47.8 times
Inventory turnover	21.4 times	22.6 times	7.6 times
Debt to total assets	31%	30%	13%
Interest Coverage	61 times	31 times	65 times
Return on common shareholders' equity	7.8%	8.1%	36.9%
Return on total assets	5.4%	5.7%	32.0%
Gross profit margin	19.5%	21.0%	75.3%
Profit margin	3.3%	3.9%	22.1%
Dividend payout	32.0%	9.8%	60.0%
Price-earnings ratio	24 times	19 times	n/a

Instructions

(a) Which company is more liquid? Explain.
(b) Which company is more solvent? Explain.
(c) Which company is more profitable? Explain.
(d) Are Okanagan's ratios improving? Explain.

(e) Overall, why do you think that ratios of Santé are stronger than those of Okanagan Fruit & Vegetable Corp.?

(f) What other considerations must the Koebels keep in mind before making an investment in any public company?

ANSWERS TO CHAPTER QUESTIONS

ANSWERS TO ACCOUNTING IN ACTION INSIGHT QUESTIONS

Business Insight, p. 969

Q: How might management influence a company's current ratio?

A: Management can affect the current ratio by speeding up or withholding payments on accounts payable just before the balance sheet date. Management can alter the cash balance by increasing or decreasing long-term assets or long-term debt, or by issuing or purchasing common shares.

Ethics Insight, p. 976

Q: Should you as controller remain silent? Does Carol have any responsibility?

A: The president's press release is incomplete, and to that extent the information is not fully disclosed, transparent, or of high quality and could be perceived as unethical.

    As controller, you should at least inform Carol, the public relations director, about the biased content of the release. She should be aware that the information she is about to release, while factually accurate, is incomplete. Both the controller and the public relations director (if she agrees) have the responsibility to inform the president of the bias of the about-to-be-released information.

All About You, p. 984

Q: Suppose you are thinking about investing in shares of **Apple Inc.** You scanned a variety of investor websites and found messages posted by two different investors. One says it's time to buy Apple shares; the other says it isn't. How should you decide whether to buy the shares or not?

A: Before purchasing any shares, you must ensure that you can differentiate the good information from the bad and don't get carried away by rumours. You should read the company's financial statements and calculate and review any relevant ratios (e.g., liquidity, solvency, profitability). You should also consider non-financial factors (e.g., the economy) in your decision.

ANSWERS TO SELF-STUDY QUESTIONS

1. a   2. d   3. c   4. c   5. a   6. b   7. d   8. c   9. d   10. a

SPECIMEN FINANCIAL STATEMENTS

Corus Entertainment

In this appendix, we illustrate current financial reporting with a comprehensive set of corporate financial statements that are prepared in accordance with generally accepted accounting principles (IFRS). We are grateful for permission to use the actual financial statements of Corus Entertainment—one of Canada's foremost integrated media and entertainment companies.

Corus's financial statement package features consolidated statements of financial position, consolidated statements of income and comprehensive income, consolidated statements of changes in shareholders' equity, consolidated statements of cash flows, and notes to the financial statements. The financial statements are preceded by two reports: a statement of management's responsibility for financial reporting and the independent auditors' report.

We encourage students to use these financial statements in conjunction with relevant material in the textbook. As well, these statements can be used to solve the Financial Reporting Problem in the Broadening Your Perspective section of the end-of-chapter material.

Annual reports, including the financial statements, are reviewed in detail in *WileyPLUS* and on the companion website to this textbook.

MANAGEMENT'S RESPONSIBILITY FOR FINANCIAL REPORTING

The accompanying consolidated financial statements of Corus Entertainment Inc. ("Corus") and all the information in this Annual Report are the responsibility of management and have been approved by the Board of Directors (the "Board").

The consolidated financial statements have been prepared by management in accordance with International Financial Reporting Standards. When alternative accounting methods exist, management has chosen those it deems most appropriate in the circumstances. Financial statements are not precise since they include certain amounts based on estimates and judgments. Management has determined such amounts on a reasonable basis in order to ensure that the consolidated financial statements are presented fairly in all material respects. Management has prepared the financial information presented elsewhere in this Annual Report and has ensured that it is consistent with the consolidated financial statements.

Corus maintains systems of internal accounting and administrative controls of high quality, consistent with reasonable cost. Such systems are designed to provide reasonable assurance that the financial information is relevant, reliable and accurate, and that the Company's assets are appropriately accounted for and adequately safeguarded. During the past year, management has maintained the operating effectiveness of internal control over external financial reporting. As at August 31, 2014, the Company's Chief Executive Officer and Chief Financial Officer evaluated, or caused an evaluation of under their direct supervision, the design and operation of the Company's internal controls over financial reporting (as defined in National Instrument 52-109, Certification of Disclosure in Issuers' Annual and Interim Filings) and, based on that assessment, determined that the Company's internal controls over financial reporting were appropriately designed and operating effectively.

The Board is responsible for ensuring that management fulfills its responsibilities for financial reporting, and is ultimately responsible for reviewing and approving the consolidated financial statements. The Board carries out this responsibility through its Audit Committee (the "Committee").

The Committee is appointed by the Board, and all of its members are independent unrelated directors. The Committee meets periodically with management, as well as with the internal and external auditors, to discuss internal controls over the financial reporting process, auditing matters and financial reporting items, to satisfy itself that each party is properly discharging its responsibilities, and to review the Annual Report, the consolidated financial statements and the external auditors' report. The Committee reports its findings to the Board for consideration when approving the consolidated financial statements for issuance to the shareholders. The Committee also considers, for review by the Board and approval by the shareholders, the engagement or re-appointment of the external auditors.

The consolidated financial statements have been audited by Ernst & Young LLP, the external auditors on behalf of the shareholders. Ernst & Young LLP has full and free access to the Committee.

John M. Cassaday
President and
Chief Executive Officer

Thomas C. Peddie FCPA, FCA
Executive Vice President
and Chief Financial Officer

INDEPENDENT AUDITORS' REPORT

TO THE SHAREHOLDERS OF CORUS ENTERTAINMENT INC.

We have audited the accompanying consolidated financial statements of **Corus Entertainment Inc.**, which comprise the consolidated statements of financial position as at August 31, 2014 and 2013, and the consolidated statements of income and comprehensive income, changes in equity and cash flows for the years then ended, and a summary of significant accounting policies and other explanatory information.

MANAGEMENT'S RESPONSIBILITY FOR THE CONSOLIDATED FINANCIAL STATEMENTS

Management is responsible for the preparation and fair presentation of these consolidated financial statements in accordance with International Financial Reporting Standards, and for such internal control as management determines is necessary to enable the preparation of consolidated financial statements that are free from material misstatement, whether due to fraud or error.

AUDITORS' RESPONSIBILITY

Our responsibility is to express an opinion on these consolidated financial statements based on our audits. We conducted our audits in accordance with Canadian generally accepted auditing standards. Those standards require that we comply with ethical requirements and plan and perform the audit to obtain reasonable assurance about whether the consolidated financial statements are free from material misstatement.

An audit involves performing procedures to obtain audit evidence about the amounts and disclosures in the consolidated financial statements. The procedures selected depend on the auditors' judgment, including the assessment of the risks of material misstatement of the consolidated financial statements, whether due to fraud or error. In making those risk assessments, the auditors consider internal control relevant to the entity's preparation and fair presentation of the consolidated financial statements in order to design audit procedures that are appropriate in the circumstances, but not for the purpose of expressing an opinion on the effectiveness of the entity's internal control. An audit also includes evaluating the appropriateness of accounting policies used and the reasonableness of accounting estimates made by management, as well as evaluating the overall presentation of the consolidated financial statements.

We believe that the audit evidence we have obtained in our audits is sufficient and appropriate to provide a basis for our audit opinion.

OPINION

In our opinion, the consolidated financial statements present fairly, in all material respects, the financial position of **Corus Entertainment Inc**. as at August 31, 2014 and 2013, and its financial performance and its cash flows for the years then ended in accordance with International Financial Reporting Standards.

Ernst & Young LLP

Toronto, Canada,
November 7, 2014

Chartered Professional Accountants
Licensed Public Accountants

CONSOLIDATED STATEMENTS OF FINANCIAL POSITION

	As at August 31,	As at August 31,	As at September 1,
(in thousands of Canadian dollars)	**2014**	2013	2012
ASSETS			
Current			
Cash and cash equivalents	**11,585**	81,266	19,198
Accounts receivable (notes 4 and 23)	**183,009**	164,302	163,345
Promissory note receivable (note 26)	**—**	47,759	—
Income taxes recoverable	**9,768**	351	9,542
Prepaid expenses and other	**13,032**	16,392	12,619
Total current assets	**217,394**	310,070	204,704
Tax credits receivable	**29,044**	41,564	43,865
Investments and intangibles (note 5)	**47,630**	42,975	42,390
Investment in joint ventures (note 26)	**—**	125,931	121,704
Property, plant and equipment (note 6)	**143,618**	151,192	163,280
Program and film rights (note 7)	**330,437**	232,587	229,306
Film investments (note 8)	**63,455**	62,274	67,847
Broadcast licenses (note 9)	**979,984**	515,036	520,770
Goodwill (note 9)	**934,859**	646,045	646,045
Deferred tax assets (note 20)	**38,161**	39,463	28,327
	2,784,582	2,167,137	2,068,238
LIABILITIES AND SHAREHOLDERS' EQUITY			
Current			
Accounts payable and accrued liabilities (note 11)	**170,411**	164,443	177,367
Income taxes payable (note 20)	**—**	—	1,303
Provisions (note 12)	**5,314**	3,941	2,322
Total current liabilities	**175,725**	168,384	180,992
Long-term debt (note 13)	**874,251**	538,966	518,258
Other long-term liabilities (note 14)	**171,793**	93,241	87,588
Deferred tax liabilities (note 20)	**252,687**	145,713	145,310
Total liabilities	**1,474,456**	946,304	932,148
SHAREHOLDERS' EQUITY			
Share capital (note 15)	**967,330**	937,183	910,005
Contributed surplus	**8,385**	7,221	7,835
Retained earnings	**313,361**	256,517	198,445
Accumulated other comprehensive income (loss) (note 16)	**3,767**	1,653	(812)
Total equity attributable to shareholders	**1,292,843**	1,202,574	1,115,473
Equity attributable to non-controlling interest	**17,283**	18,259	20,617
Total shareholders' equity	**1,310,126**	1,220,833	1,136,090
	2,784,582	2,167,137	2,068,238

Commitments, contingencies and guarantees (notes 13 and 27)
See accompanying notes

CONSOLIDATED STATEMENTS OF INCOME AND COMPREHENSIVE INCOME

For the years ended August 31,

(in thousands of Canadian dollars, except per share amounts)	2014	2013
Revenues	833,016	751,536
Direct cost of sales, general and administrative expenses (*note 17*)	543,378	500,562
Depreciation and amortization (*notes 5 and 6*)	24,068	26,812
Interest expense (*note 18*)	48,320	44,795
Broadcast license and goodwill impairment (*notes 9 and 10*)	83,000	5,734
Debt refinancing (*note 13*)	—	25,033
Business acquisition, integration and restructuring costs (*notes 12 and 26*)	46,792	7,343
Gain on acquisition (*note 26*)	(127,884)	—
Gain on sale of associated company (*note 26*)	—	(55,394)
Other expense (income), net (*note 19*)	5,740	(3,560)
Income before income taxes	209,602	200,211
Income tax expense (*note 20*)	53,433	34,462
Net income for the period	**156,169**	165,749
Net income attributable to:		
Shareholders	150,408	159,895
Non-controlling interest	5,761	5,854
	156,169	165,749
Earnings per share attributable to shareholders:		
Basic	$ 1.77	$ 1.91
Diluted	$ 1.76	$ 1.90
Net income for the period	156,169	165,749
Other comprehensive income (loss), net of tax: (*note 16*)		
Items that may be reclassified subsequently to net income:		
Unrealized foreign currency translation adjustment	1,720	2,333
Unrealized change in fair value of available-for-sale investments	446	132
Unrealized change in fair value of cash flow hedges	(52)	—
Actuarial (loss) gain on employee future benefits	(2,188)	616
	(74)	3,081
Comprehensive income for the period	156,095	168,830
Comprehensive income attributable to:		
Shareholders	150,334	162,976
Non-controlling interest	5,761	5,854
	156,095	168,830

See accompanying notes

CONSOLIDATED STATEMENTS OF CHANGES IN SHAREHOLDERS' EQUITY

(in thousands of Canadian dollars)	Share capital (*note 15*)	Contributed surplus	Retained earnings	Accumulated other comprehensive income (loss) (*note 16*)	Total equity attributable to shareholders	Non-controlling interest	Total shareholders' equity
At August 31, 2013	937,183	7,221	256,517	1,653	1,202,574	18,259	1,220,833
Comprehensive income (loss)	—	—	150,408	(74)	150,334	5,761	156,095
Actuarial loss transfer	—	—	(2,188)	2,188	—	—	—
Dividends declared	—	—	(91,376)	—	(91,376)	(6,737)	(98,113)
Issuance of shares under stock option plan	5,465	(862)	—	—	4,603	—	4,603
Issuance of shares under dividend reinvestment plan	24,682	—	—	—	24,682	—	24,682
Share-based compensation expense	—	2,026	—	—	2,026	—	2,026
At August 31, 2014	**967,330**	**8,385**	**313,361**	**3,767**	**1,292,843**	**17,283**	**1,310,126**
At August 31, 2012	910,005	7,835	198,445	(812)	1,115,473	20,617	1,136,090
Comprehensive income	—	—	159,895	3,081	162,976	5,854	168,830
Actuarial gain transfer	—	—	616	(616)	—	—	—
Dividends declared	—	—	(84,452)	—	(84,452)	(6,331)	(90,783)
Issuance of shares under stock option plan	1,155	(2,200)	—	—	(1,045)	—	(1,045)
Issuance of shares under dividend reinvestment plan	26,731	—	—	—	26,731	—	26,731
Shares repurchased	(708)	—	(756)	—	(1,464)	—	(1,464)
Share-based compensation expense	—	1,586	—	—	1,586	—	1,586
Acquisition of non-controlling interest (*note 26*)	—	—	(17,231)	—	(17,231)	(1,881)	(19,112)
At August 31, 2013	937,183	7,221	256,517	1,653	1,202,574	18,259	1,220,833

See accompanying notes

CONSOLIDATED STATEMENTS OF CASH FLOWS

For the years ended August 31,

(in thousands of Canadian dollars)	2014	2013
OPERATING ACTIVITIES		
Net income for the period	156,169	165,749
Add (deduct) non-cash items:		
Depreciation and amortization (notes 5 and 6)	24,068	26,812
Broadcast license and goodwill impairment (notes 9 and 10)	83,000	5,734
Amortization of program and film rights (notes 7 and 17)	207,639	168,883
Amortization of film investments (notes 8 and 17)	19,808	25,759
Deferred income taxes (note 20)	5,638	(11,332)
Increase in purchase price obligation (note 26)	3,336	—
Investment impairments (notes 5, 8 and 19)	—	7,121
Share-based compensation expense (note 15)	2,026	1,586
Imputed interest (note 18)	14,698	10,279
Tangible benefit obligation (note 26)	31,916	—
Debt refinancing (note 13)	—	25,033
Gain on sale of associated company (note 26)	—	(55,394)
Gain on acquisition (note 26)	(127,884)	—
Other	2,402	(14,393)
Net change in non-cash working capital balances related to operations (note 24)	22,945	6,768
Payment of program and film rights	(225,935)	(159,802)
Net additions to film investments	(25,349)	(46,074)
Cash provided by operating activities	**194,477**	156,729
INVESTING ACTIVITIES		
Additions to property, plant and equipment (note 6)	(11,976)	(13,029)
Business combinations (note 26)	(497,393)	—
Dividends from investment in joint ventures (note 3)	—	10,866
Net cash flows for investments and intangibles	(11,493)	(10,855)
Other	(5,384)	(652)
Cash used in investing activities	**(526,246)**	(13,670)
FINANCING ACTIVITIES		
Increase (decrease) in bank loans	333,243	(29,925)
Issuance of notes (note 13)	—	550,000
Redemption of notes (note 13)	—	(500,000)
Financing fees (note 13)	(587)	(26,732)
Issuance of shares under stock option plan	4,603	884
Shares repurchased (note 15)	—	(1,464)
Dividends paid	(65,474)	(56,696)
Dividends paid to non-controlling interest	(6,737)	(6,331)
Other	(2,960)	(10,727)
Cash provided by (used in) financing activities	**262,088**	(80,991)
Net change in cash and cash equivalents during the year	(69,681)	62,068
Cash and cash equivalents, beginning of the year	81,266	19,198
Cash and cash equivalents, end of the year	**11,585**	81,266

Supplemental cash flow disclosures (note 24)
See accompanying notes

NOTES TO CONSOLIDATED FINANCIAL STATEMENTS

(in thousands of Canadian dollars, except per share information)

1. CORPORATE INFORMATION

Corus Entertainment Inc. (the "Company" or "Corus") is a diversified Canadian communications and entertainment company. The Company is incorporated under the *Canada Business Corporations Act* and its Class B Non-Voting Shares are listed on the Toronto Stock Exchange (the "TSX") under the symbol CJR.B.

The Company's registered office is at 1500, 850 – 2nd Street SW, Calgary, Alberta, T2P 0R8. The Company's executive office is at Corus Quay, 25 Dockside Drive, Toronto, Ontario, M5A 0B5.

These consolidated financial statements include the accounts of the Company and all its subsidiaries and joint ventures. The Company's principal business activities are: the operation of radio stations; the operation of specialty, pay and conventional television networks; and the Corus content business which consists of the production and distribution of films and television programs, merchandise licensing, publishing and the production and distribution of animation software.

2. BASIS OF PREPARATION AND STATEMENT OF COMPLIANCE

These consolidated financial statements have been prepared in accordance with International Financial Reporting Standards ("IFRS") as issued by the International Accounting Standards Board ("IASB"). These consolidated financial statements have been prepared using the accounting policies in note 3.

These consolidated financial statements have been authorized for use in accordance with a resolution from the Board of Directors on October 23, 2014.

3. SIGNIFICANT ACCOUNTING POLICIES

BASIS OF PRESENTATION

The consolidated financial statements have been prepared on a cost basis, except for derivative financial instruments and available-for-sale financial assets, which have been measured at fair value. The consolidated financial statements are presented in Canadian dollars, which is also the Company's functional currency and all values are rounded to the nearest thousand, except where otherwise noted. Each entity consolidated by the Company determines its own functional currency based on the primary economic environment in which the entity operates.

BASIS OF CONSOLIDATION

Subsidiaries

The consolidated financial statements comprise the financial statements of the Company and its subsidiaries, which are the entities over which the Company has control. Control exists when the entity is exposed, or has rights, to variable returns from its involvement with the entity and has the ability to affect those returns through its power over the entity. The non-controlling interest component of the Company's subsidiaries is included in equity.

Subsidiaries are fully consolidated from the date of acquisition, being the date on which the Company obtains control, and continue to be consolidated until the date when such control ceases. The determination of control is assessed either through share ownership and/or control of the subsidiaries board of directors, which may require significant judgment.

The financial statements of the Company's subsidiaries are prepared for the same reporting period as the Company, using consistent accounting policies. All intra-company balances, transactions, unrealized gains and losses resulting from intra-company transactions and dividends are eliminated in full.

Associates and joint arrangements

Associates are entities over which the Company has significant influence. Significant influence is the power to participate in the financial and operating policy decisions of the investee but is not control or joint control over those policies.

A joint venture is a type of joint arrangement in which the parties that have joint control of the arrangement have rights to the net assets of the joint venture. Joint control is the contractually agreed sharing of control of an arrangement, which exists only when decisions about the relevant activities require unanimous consent of the parties sharing control.

The considerations made in determining joint control or significant influence are similar to those necessary to determine control over subsidiaries. The Company accounts for investments in associates and joint ventures using the equity method.

Investments in associates and joint ventures accounted for using the equity method are originally recognized at cost. Under the equity method, the investment in the associate or joint venture is carried on the consolidated statements of financial position at cost plus post-acquisition changes in the Company's share of income and other comprehensive income ("OCI"), less distributions of the investee. Goodwill on the acquisition of the associates and joint ventures is included in the cost of the investments and is neither amortized nor assessed for impairment separately.

The financial statements of the Company's equity-accounted for investments are prepared for the same reporting period as the Company. Where necessary, adjustments are made to bring the accounting policies in line with those of the Company. All intra-company unrealized gains resulting from intra-company transactions and dividends are eliminated against the investment to the extent of the Company's interest in the associate. Unrealized losses are eliminated in the same way as unrealized gains, but only to the extent that there is no evidence of impairment.

After the application of the equity method, the Company determines at each reporting date whether there is any objective evidence that the investment in the associate or joint venture is impaired and consequently, whether it is necessary to recognize an additional impairment loss on the Company's investment in its associate or joint venture. If this is the case, the Company calculates the amount of impairment as the difference between the recoverable amount of the associate and its carrying value and recognizes the amount in the consolidated statements of income and comprehensive income.

BUSINESS COMBINATIONS

Business combinations are accounted for using the acquisition method of accounting, which requires the Company to identify and attribute values and estimated lives to the intangible assets acquired based on their estimated fair value. These determinations involve significant estimates and assumptions regarding cash flow projections, economic risk and weighted average cost of capital. The cost of an acquisition is measured as the aggregate of the consideration transferred, measured at acquisition-date fair value and the amount of any non-controlling interest in the acquiree.

For each business combination, the acquirer measures the non-controlling interest in the acquiree either at fair value or at the proportionate share of the acquiree's identifiable net assets. Acquisition costs incurred are expensed and included in business acquisition, integration and restructuring costs.

When the Company acquires a business, it assesses the financial assets and liabilities assumed for appropriate classification and designation in accordance with the contractual terms, economic circumstances and pertinent conditions as at the acquisition date. This includes the separation of embedded derivatives in host contracts by the acquiree.

If the business combination is achieved in stages, the acquisition date fair value of the acquirer's previously held equity interest in the acquiree is remeasured to fair value at the acquisition date through profit or loss.

Any contingent consideration to be transferred by the acquirer will be recognized at fair value at the acquisition date. Subsequent changes to the fair value of the contingent consideration which is deemed to be a financial asset or liability will be recognized in accordance with International Accounting Standard ("IAS") 39 - *Financial Instruments: Recognition and Measurement* either in profit or loss or as a change to OCI. If the contingent consideration is classified as equity, it should not be remeasured until it is finally settled within equity.

REVENUE RECOGNITION

Advertising revenues are recognized in the period in which the advertising is aired under broadcast contracts and collection is reasonably assured.

Subscriber fee revenues are recognized monthly based on estimated subscriber levels for the period-end, which are based on the preceding month's actual subscribers as submitted by the broadcast distribution undertakings.

PROGRAM RIGHTS

Program rights represent contract rights acquired from third parties to broadcast television programs, feature films and radio programs. The assets and liabilities related to these rights are recorded when the Company controls the asset, the expected future economic benefits are probable and the cost is reliably measurable. The Company generally considers these criteria to be met and records the assets and liabilities when the license period has begun, the program material is accepted by the Company and the material is available for airing. Long-term liabilities related to these rights are recorded at the net present value of future cash flows, using an appropriate discount rate. These costs are amortized over the contracted exhibition period as the programs or feature films are aired. Program and film rights are carried at cost less accumulated amortization. At each reporting date, the Company assesses its program rights for indicators of impairment and, if any exist, the Company estimates the asset's or cash generating unit's ("CGUs") recoverable amount.

The amortization period and the amortization method for program rights are reviewed at least at the end of each reporting period. Changes in the expected useful life or the expected pattern of consumption of future economic benefits embodied in the assets are accounted for by changing the amortization period or method, as appropriate, and are treated as changes in accounting estimates. Amortization of program rights is included in direct cost of sales, general and administrative expenses and has been disclosed separately in the consolidated statements of cash flows.

FILM INVESTMENTS

Film investments represent the costs of projects in development, projects in process, the unamortized costs of proprietary films and television programs that have been produced by the Company or for which the Company has acquired distribution rights, and third-party-produced equity film investments. Such costs include development and production expenditures and attributed studio and other costs that are expected to benefit future periods. Costs are capitalized upon project greenlight for produced and acquired films and television programs.

The individual-film-forecast-computation method is used to determine amortization. Under this method, capitalized costs and the estimated total costs of participations and residuals, net of anticipated federal and provincial program contributions, production tax credits and coproducers' share of production costs, are charged to amortization expense on a series or program basis in the same ratio that current period actual revenues (numerator) bears to estimated remaining unrecognized future revenues as of the beginning of the current fiscal year (denominator). Future revenues are projected for periods generally not exceeding 10 years from the date of delivery or acquisition. For episodic television series, future revenues include estimates of revenues over a period generally not exceeding 10 years from the date of delivery of the first episode or, if still in production, five years from the date of delivery of the most recent episode, if later. Future revenues are based on historical sales performance for the genre of series or program, the number of episodes produced and the availability of rights in each territory. Estimates of future revenues can change significantly due to the level of market acceptance of film and television products. Accordingly, revenue estimates are reviewed periodically and amortization is adjusted prospectively. In addition, if revenue estimates change significantly with respect to a film or television program, the Company may be required to write down all or a portion of the unamortized costs of such film or television program, therefore impacting direct cost of sales, general and administrative expenses and profitability.

Projects in process represent the accumulated costs of television series or feature films currently in production.

Completed project and distribution rights are stated at the lower of unamortized cost and recoverable amount as determined on a series or program basis. Revenue and cost forecasts for each production are evaluated at each reporting date in connection with a comprehensive review of the Company's film investments, on a title-by-title basis. When an event or change in circumstances indicates that the recoverable amount of a film is less than its unamortized cost, the carrying value is compared to the recoverable amount and if the carrying value is higher, the carrying value is written down to the recoverable amount. The recoverable amount of the film is determined using management's estimates of future revenues under a discounted cash flow approach.

Third-party-produced equity film investments are carried at fair value. Cash received from an investment is recorded as a reduction of such investment on the consolidated statements of financial position and the Company records income on the consolidated statements of income and comprehensive income only when the investment is fully recouped.

The Company's revenues related to production and distribution revenues from the distribution and licensing of film rights; royalties from merchandise licensing, publishing and music contracts; sale of licenses, customer support, training and consulting related to the animation software business; revenues from customer support; and sale of books are recognized when the significant risks and rewards of ownership have transferred to the buyer; the amount of revenue can be measured reliably; it is probable that the economic benefits associated with the transaction will flow to the entity; the stage of completion of the transaction at the end of the reporting period can be measured reliably; the costs incurred for the transaction and the costs to complete the transaction can be measured reliably; and the Company does not retain either continuing managerial involvement or effective control.

Customer advances on contracts are recorded as unearned revenue until all of the foregoing revenue recognition conditions have been met.

Non-refundable advances, whether recoupable or non-recoupable, on royalties are recognized when the license period has commenced and collection is reasonably assured, unless there are future performance obligations associated with the royalty advance for which, in that case, revenue recognition is deferred and recognized when the performance obligations are discharged. Refundable advances are deferred and recognized as revenue as the performance obligations are discharged.

CASH AND CASH EQUIVALENTS

Cash and cash equivalents include cash and short-term deposits with maturities of less than three months at the date of purchase. Cash that is held in escrow, or otherwise restricted from use, is excluded from current assets and is reported separately from cash and cash equivalents.

PROPERTY, PLANT AND EQUIPMENT

Property, plant and equipment are stated at cost, net of accumulated depreciation and/or accumulated impairment losses, if any. Such cost includes the cost of replacing part of the property, plant and equipment, and borrowing costs for long-term construction projects if the recognition criteria are met. When significant parts of property, plant and equipment are required to be replaced at intervals, the Company recognizes such parts as individual assets with specific useful lives and depreciation, respectively. Repair and maintenance costs are recognized in the consolidated statements of income and comprehensive income as incurred.

Depreciation is recorded on a straight-line basis over the estimated useful lives of the assets as follows:

Land and assets not available for use	Not depreciated
Equipment	
Broadcasting	5 - 10 years
Computer	3 - 5 years
Leasehold improvements	Lease term
Buildings	
Structure	20 - 30 years
Components	10 - 20 years
Furniture and fixtures	7 years
Other	4 - 10 years

An item of property, plant and equipment and any significant part initially recognized are derecognized upon disposal or when no future economic benefits are expected from their use or disposal. Any gain or loss arising on derecognition of the asset (calculated as the difference between the net disposal proceeds and the carrying amount of the asset) is included in the consolidated statements of income and comprehensive income when the asset is derecognized.

The assets' residual values, useful lives and methods of depreciation are reviewed at least annually and the depreciation charge is adjusted prospectively, if appropriate.

BORROWING COSTS

Borrowing costs consist of interest and other costs that an entity incurs in connection with the borrowing of funds. Borrowing costs directly attributable to the acquisition, construction or production of an asset that necessarily takes a substantial period of time to get ready for its intended use or sale are capitalized as part of the cost of the asset. All other borrowing costs are expensed in the period they are incurred.

Amortization of film investments is included in direct cost of sales, general and administrative expenses and has been disclosed separately in the consolidated statements of cash flows.

GOODWILL AND INTANGIBLE ASSETS

Intangible assets acquired separately are measured on initial recognition at cost. Intangible assets acquired in a business combination are measured at fair value as at the date of acquisition. Following initial recognition, intangible assets are carried at cost less accumulated amortization and accumulated impairment charges, if any. Internally generated intangible assets such as goodwill, brands and customer lists, excluding capitalized program and film development costs, are not capitalized and expenditures are reflected in the consolidated statements of income and comprehensive income in the year in which the expenditure is incurred.

Intangible assets are recognized separately from goodwill when they are separable or arise from contractual or other legal rights and their fair value can be measured reliably. The useful lives of intangible assets are assessed as either finite or indefinite.

Intangible assets with finite lives are amortized over their useful economic lives and assessed for impairment whenever there is an indication that the intangible assets may be impaired. The amortization period and the amortization method for intangible assets with finite useful lives are reviewed at least at the end of each reporting period. Changes in the expected useful life or the expected pattern of consumption of future economic benefits embodied in the assets are accounted for by changing the amortization period or method, as appropriate, and are treated as changes in accounting estimates. The amortization expense on intangible assets with finite lives is recognized in the consolidated statements of income and comprehensive income in the expense category, consistent with the function of the intangible assets.

Amortization is recorded on a straight-line basis over the estimated useful life of the asset as follows:

Brand names, trade marks and digital rights	Agreement term
Software, patents and customer lists	3 - 5 years

Intangible assets with indefinite useful lives are not amortized. Broadcast licenses are considered to have an indefinite life based on management's intent and ability to renew the licenses without significant cost and without material modification of the existing terms and conditions of the license. The assessment of indefinite life is reviewed annually to determine whether the indefinite life continues to be supportable. If not, the change in useful life from indefinite to finite is made on a prospective basis.

Goodwill is initially measured at cost, being the excess of the aggregate of the consideration transferred and the amount recognized for non-controlling interest over the net identifiable assets acquired and liabilities assumed. If this consideration is lower than the fair value of the net identifiable assets of the subsidiary acquired, the difference is recognized in profit or loss.

After initial recognition, goodwill is measured at cost less any accumulated impairment losses. For the purpose of impairment testing, goodwill acquired in a business combination is, from the acquisition date, allocated to a CGU or group of CGUs that are expected to benefit from the synergies of the combination, irrespective of whether other assets or liabilities of the acquiree are assigned to those units. The group of CGUs is not larger than the level at which management monitors goodwill or the Company's operating segments.

Where goodwill forms part of a CGU and part of the operation within that unit is disposed of, the goodwill associated with the operation disposed of is included in the carrying amount of the operation when determining the gain or loss on disposal of the operation. Goodwill disposed of in this circumstance is measured based on the relative fair value of the operation disposed of and the portion of the CGU retained.

Broadcast licenses and goodwill are tested for impairment annually or more frequently if events or circumstances indicate that they may be impaired. The Company completes its annual testing during the fourth quarter each year.

Broadcast licenses by themselves do not generate cash inflows and therefore, when assessing these assets for impairment, the Company looks to the CGU to which the asset belongs. The identification of CGUs involves judgment and is based on how senior management monitors operations; however, the lowest aggregations of assets that generate largely independent cash inflows represent CGUs for broadcast license impairment testing.

CGUs for broadcast license impairment testing
For the Television segment, the Company has determined that there are two CGUs: (1) specialty and pay television networks that are operated and managed directly by the Company; and (2) other, as these are the levels at which independent cash inflows have been identified.

For the Radio segment, the Company has determined that the CGU is a radio cluster whereby a cluster represents a geographic area, generally a city, where radio stations are combined for the purpose of managing performance. These clusters are managed as a single asset by a general manager and overhead costs are allocated amongst the cluster and have independent cash inflows at the cluster level.

Groups of CGUs for goodwill impairment testing
For purposes of impairment testing of goodwill, the Company has grouped the CGUs within the Television and Radio operating segments and is performing the test at the operating segment level. This is the lowest level at which management monitors goodwill for internal management purposes.

Gains or losses arising from derecognition of an intangible asset are measured as the difference between the net disposal proceeds and the carrying amount of the asset and are recognized in the consolidated statements of income and comprehensive income when the asset is derecognized.

INCOME TAXES

Tax expense comprises current and deferred income taxes. Tax expense is recognized in the consolidated statements of income, unless it relates to items recognized outside the consolidated statements of income. Tax expense relating to items recognized outside of the consolidated statements of income is recognized in correlation to the underlying transaction in either OCI or equity.

PROVISIONS

Provisions are recognized if the Company has a present legal or constructive obligation as a result of past events, if it is probable that an outflow of resources will be required to settle the obligation, and a reliable estimate can be made of the amount of the obligation.

The amount recognized as a provision is the best estimate of the consideration required to settle the present obligation as of the date of the consolidated statements of financial position, taking into account the risks and uncertainties surrounding the obligation. In some situations, external advice may be obtained to assist with the estimates.

Provisions are discounted and measured at the present value of the expenditure expected to be required to settle the obligation, using an after-tax discount rate that reflects the current market assessments of the time value of money and the risks specific to the obligation. The increase in the provision due to the passage of time is recognized as interest expense. Future information could change the estimates and thus impact the Company's financial position and results of operations.

FINANCIAL INSTRUMENTS

Financial assets within the scope of IAS 39 - *Financial Instruments: recognition and measurement* are classified as financial assets at fair value through profit or loss, loans and receivables or available-for-sale ("AFS"), as appropriate. The Company determines the classification of its financial assets at initial recognition.

Financial instruments classified at fair value through profit or loss and financial assets classified as AFS are recognized on the trade date, which is the date that the Company commits to purchase or sell the asset.

The Company has classified its financial instruments as follows:

Fair value through profit or loss	Loans and receivables	Available-for-sale	Other financial liabilities	Derivatives
• Cash and cash equivalents	• Accounts receivable • Loans and other receivables included in "Investments and intangibles" • Promissory note receivable	• Other portfolio investments included in "Investments and intangibles" • Third-party-produced equity film investments	• Accounts payable and accrued liabilities • Long-term debt • Other long-term financial liabilities included in "Other long-term liabilities"	• Derivatives that are part of a cash flow hedging relationship

Financial assets at fair value through profit or loss

Financial assets at fair value through profit or loss are carried at fair value. Changes in fair value are recognized in other income (expense) in the consolidated statements of income and comprehensive income.

Loans and receivables

Loans and receivables are initially recognized at fair value plus transaction costs. They are subsequently measured at amortized cost using the effective interest method less any impairment. Receivables are reduced by provisions for estimated bad debts which are determined by reference to past experience and expectations.

Financial assets classified as AFS

Financial assets that are not classified as at fair value through profit or loss or as loans and receivables are classified as AFS. A financial asset classified as AFS is initially recognized at its fair value plus transaction costs that are directly attributable to the acquisition of the financial asset. AFS financial instruments are subsequently measured at fair value, with unrealized gains and losses recognized in OCI and accumulated in accumulated other comprehensive income ("AOCI") until the investment is derecognized or determined to be impaired, at which time the cumulative gain or loss is reclassified to the consolidated statements of income and comprehensive income and removed from AOCI. AFS equity instruments not quoted in an active market where fair value is not reliably determinable are recorded at cost less impairment, if any, determined based on the present values of expected future cash flows.

Other financial liabilities

Financial liabilities within the scope of IAS 39 are classified as other financial liabilities. The Company determines the classification of its financial liabilities at initial recognition.

Other financial liabilities are measured at amortized cost using the effective interest rate method. Long-term debt instruments are initially measured at fair value, which is the consideration received, net of transaction costs incurred. Transaction costs related to the long-term debt instruments are included in the value of the instruments and amortized using the effective interest rate method.

Derecognition

A financial asset is derecognized when the rights to receive cash flows from the asset have expired, or when the Company transfers its rights to receive cash flows from the asset and the associated risks and rewards to a third party. The unrealized gains and losses recorded in AOCI are transferred to the consolidated statements of income and comprehensive income on disposal of an AFS asset.

A financial liability is derecognized when the obligation under the liability is discharged or cancelled or expires.

Determination of fair value

Fair value is defined as the price at which an asset or liability could be exchanged in a current transaction between knowledgeable, willing parties, other than in a forced or liquidation sale. The fair value of instruments that are quoted in active markets is determined using the quoted prices where they represent those at which regularly and recently occurring transactions take place. The Company uses valuation techniques to establish the fair value of instruments where prices quoted in active markets are not available. Therefore, where possible, parameter inputs to the valuation techniques are based on observable data derived from prices of relevant instruments traded in an active market. These valuation techniques involve some level of management estimation and judgment, the degree of which will depend on the price transparency for the instrument or market and the instrument's complexity.

The Company categorizes its fair value measurements according to a three-level hierarchy. The hierarchy prioritizes the inputs used by the Company's valuation techniques. A level is assigned to each fair value measurement based on the lowest level input significant to the fair value measurement in its entirety. The three levels of the fair value hierarchy are defined as follows:

Level 1 – Unadjusted quoted prices at the measurement date for identical assets or liabilities in active markets.

Level 2 – Observable inputs other than quoted prices included in Level 1, such as quoted prices for similar assets and liabilities in active markets; quoted prices for identical or similar assets and liabilities in markets that are not active; or other inputs that are observable or can be corroborated by observable market data.

Level 3 – Significant unobservable inputs that are supported by little or no market activity.

The fair value hierarchy also requires an entity to maximize the use of observable inputs and minimize the use of unobservable inputs when measuring fair value.

The fair values of cash and cash equivalents are classified within Level 1 because they are based on quoted prices for identical assets in active markets.

The fair value of portfolio investments measured at fair value are classified within Level 2 because even though the security is listed, it is not actively traded. The Company determines the fair value for interest rate swaps as the net discounted future cash flows using the implied zero-coupon forward swap yield curve. The change in the difference between the discounted cash flow streams for the hedged item and the hedging item is deemed to be hedge ineffectiveness and is recorded in the consolidated statements of income. The fair value of the interest rate swap is based on forward yield curves, which are observable inputs provided by banks and available in other public data sources, and are classified within Level 2.

The fair value of the 4.25% Senior Unsecured Guaranteed Notes ("2020 Notes") are classified within Level 2 because they are traded, however, in what is not considered an active market.

EARNINGS PER SHARE

Basic earnings per share are calculated using the weighted average number of common shares outstanding during the year. The computation of diluted earnings per share assumes the basic weighted average number of common shares outstanding during the year is increased to include the number of additional common shares that would have been outstanding if the dilutive potential common shares had been issued. The dilutive effect of stock options is determined using the treasury stock method.

CHANGES IN ACCOUNTING POLICIES

In December 2011, the IASB amended both IAS 32 - *Financial Instruments: Presentation* and IFRS 7 - *Financial Instruments: Disclosures* by moving the disclosure requirements in IAS 32 to IFRS 7 and enhancing the disclosures about offsetting financial assets and liabilities. The effective date of the amendments is for the Company's fiscal year commencing September 1, 2013. The Company has assessed the impact of these amendments and determined there is no impact on its consolidated financial statements.

4. ACCOUNTS RECEIVABLE

	2014	2013
Trade	168,969	152,911
Other	19,840	13,880
	188,809	166,791
Less allowance for doubtful accounts	5,800	2,489
	183,009	164,302

5. INVESTMENTS AND INTANGIBLES

	Intangibles	Investments in associates	Other	Total
Balance - September 1, 2012	13,452	20,438	8,500	42,390
Increase (decrease) in investment	10,690	(8,606)	7,887	9,971
Investment impairment	—	(3,399)	—	(3,399)
Equity loss in associates	—	(138)	—	(138)
Dividends from associates	—	(1,100)	—	(1,100)
Amortization of intangible assets	(4,416)	—	—	(4,416)
Fair value adjustment	—	(485)	152	(333)
Balance - August 31, 2013	19,726	6,710	16,539	42,975
Increase in investment	4,434	4,268	5,006	13,708
Investment impairment	—	(706)	—	(706)
Equity loss in associates	—	(1,685)	—	(1,685)
Amortization of intangible assets	(7,177)	—	—	(7,177)
Fair value adjustment	—	—	515	515
Balance - August 31, 2014	**16,983**	**8,587**	**22,060**	**47,630**

INTANGIBLES

Intangible assets are comprised of software, patents, customer lists, brand names, trade marks and digital rights. The Company expects the net book value of intangible assets with a finite life to be amortized by December 2020.

IMPAIRMENT OF LONG-LIVED ASSETS

At each reporting date, the Company assesses its long-lived assets, including property, plant and equipment, program and film rights, film investments, goodwill and intangible assets, for potential indicators of impairment, such as an adverse change in business climate that may indicate that these assets may be impaired. If any impairment indicator exists, the Company estimates the asset's recoverable amount. The recoverable amount is determined for an individual asset, unless the asset does not generate cash inflows that are largely independent of those from other assets, in which case the asset is assessed as part of the CGU to which it belongs. An asset's or CGU's recoverable amount is the higher of its fair value less costs to sell ("FVLCS") and its value in use ("VIU"). The determination of the recoverable amount in the impairment assessment requires estimates based on quoted market prices, prices of comparable businesses, present value or other valuation techniques, or a combination thereof, necessitating management to make subjective judgments and assumptions.

The Company records impairment losses on its long-lived assets when the Company believes that their carrying value may not be recoverable. For assets excluding goodwill, an assessment is made at each reporting date as to whether there is any indication that previously recognized impairment losses may no longer exist or may have decreased. If the reasons for impairment no longer apply, impairment losses may be reversed up to a maximum of the carrying amount of the respective asset if the impairment loss had not been recognized.

Goodwill

Goodwill is reviewed for impairment annually or more frequently if there are indications that impairment may have occurred.

Goodwill is allocated to a CGU or group of CGUs for the purposes of impairment testing based on the level at which management monitors it, which is not larger than an operating segment. The Company records an impairment loss if the recoverable amount of the CGU or group of CGUs is less than the carrying amount.

Refer to note 10 for further details on the Company's annual impairment testing for goodwill.

Broadcast licenses

Broadcast licenses are reviewed for impairment annually or more frequently if there are indications that impairment may have occurred.

Broadcast licenses are allocated to a CGU for the purposes of impairment testing. The Company records an impairment loss if the recoverable amount of the CGU is less than the carrying amount.

Refer to note 10 for further details on the Company's annual impairment testing for broadcast licenses.

Intangible assets and property, plant and equipment

The useful lives of the intangible assets with definite lives (which are amortized) and property, plant and equipment are confirmed at least annually and only tested for impairment if events or changes in circumstances indicate that an impairment may have occurred.

LEASES

The determination of whether an arrangement is, or contains, a lease is based on the substance of the arrangement at the inception date: whether fulfillment of the arrangement is dependent on the use of a specific asset or assets or the arrangement conveys a right to use the asset. Where the Company is the lessee, asset values recorded under finance leases are amortized on a straight-line basis over the period of expected use. Obligations recorded under finance leases are reduced by lease payments net of imputed interest. Operating lease commitments, for which lease payments are recognized as an expense in the consolidated statements of income and comprehensive income, are recognized on a straight-line basis over the lease term.

6. PROPERTY, PLANT AND EQUIPMENT

	Land	Broadcasting and computer equipment	Buildings and leasehold improvements	Furniture and fixtures	Other	Total
Cost						
Balance - September 1, 2012	5,539	155,009	104,666	20,210	3,732	289,156
Additions	–	11,505	2,161	810	–	14,476
Disposals and retirements	–	(25,642)	(726)	(2,233)	(1,269)	(29,870)
Balance - August 31, 2013	5,539	140,872	106,101	18,787	2,463	273,762
Additions	–	8,874	1,483	134	2,109	12,600
Acquisitions	–	783	–	37	80	900
Disposals and retirements	–	(4,414)	(154)	(383)	(92)	(5,043)
Balance - August 31, 2014	**5,539**	**146,115**	**107,430**	**18,575**	**4,560**	**282,219**
Accumulated depreciation						
Balance - September 1, 2012	–	97,826	17,906	8,825	1,319	125,876
Depreciation	–	16,545	5,791	2,541	118	24,995
Disposals and retirements	–	(25,286)	(567)	(2,227)	(201)	(28,301)
Balance - August 31, 2013	–	89,085	23,110	9,139	1,236	122,570
Depreciation	–	11,709	5,971	2,423	90	20,193
Impairments	–	–	1,240	–	–	1,240
Disposals and retirements	–	(4,886)	(123)	(369)	(24)	(5,402)
Balance - August 31, 2014	**–**	**95,908**	**30,198**	**11,193**	**1,302**	**138,601**
Net book value						
August 31, 2013	5,539	51,787	82,991	9,648	1,227	151,192
August 31, 2014	**5,539**	**50,207**	**77,232**	**7,382**	**3,258**	**143,618**

Included in property, plant and equipment are assets under finance lease with a cost of $28,297 at August 31, 2014 (2013 - $27,355) and accumulated depreciation of $19,080 (2013 - $16,764).

7. PROGRAM AND FILM RIGHTS

Balance - September 1, 2012	229,306
Additions	154,371
Transfers from film investments	17,793
Amortization	(168,883)
Balance - August 31, 2013	232,587
Additions	220,966
Transfers from film investments	6,984
Acquisitions (note 26)	77,539
Amortization	(207,639)
Balance - August 31, 2014	**330,437**

	2014	2013
Cost	967,159	710,824
Accumulated amortization	636,722	478,237
Net book value	330,437	232,587

The Company expects that 50% of the net book value of program and film rights will be amortized during the year ended August 31, 2015. The Company expects the net book value of program and film rights to be amortized by September 2019.

OTHER

Other is primarily comprised of investments in venture funds. These venture funds invest in early growth stage companies that are pursuing opportunities in technology, mobile media and consumer sectors.

INVESTMENTS IN ASSOCIATES

In assessing the level of control or influence that the Company has over an investment, management considers ownership percentages, board representation, as well as other relevant provisions in shareholder agreements. The Company exercises significant influence over the following investments which have been accounted for using the equity method and are included in investments in associates.

Fingerprint Digital Inc.

Fingerprint is a technology company providing a turnkey mobile solution to content creators and distributors seeking to link mobile offerings within one branded network. Its focus is educational gaming platforms for kids and their parents across any connected device.

Food Network Canada ("Food Network")

Food Network is a Canadian Category A specialty television network. This brand is the destination for Canadians for all things food-related and provides entertainment programming related to food and nutrition.

Food Network had been classified as an associated business based on management's judgment that the Company has, based on rights to board representation and other provisions in the shareholder agreement, significant influence despite owning only 19.9% of the voting rights. On April 30, 2013, the Company disposed of its interest in Food Network Canada, which had a carrying value of $11,388 on the disposition date (note 26).

KidsCo Limited

KidsCo Limited was an international children's television channel for preschoolers, children aged 6 to 10 and families. The channel was available in 18 languages and presented in over 100 territories on satellite, cable and IPTV platforms across Europe, Asia, Africa, Australia and the Middle East.

At August 31, 2013, the Company performed its annual impairment test for fiscal 2013 and determined that this investment was impaired based on expected future cash flows. As a result, an impairment charge was recorded in other expense (income), net of $3,399. On December 31, 2013, KidsCo ceased business and was wound up.

SoCast Inc. (formerly Supernova Interactive Inc.)

SoCast Inc. is a digital media company that develops and creates software service platforms, including its social relationship management platform for entertainment companies.

The following amounts represent the Company's share in the financial position and results of operations of the associates:

As at August 31,	2014	2013
Assets	8,926	7,025
Liabilities	339	315
Net assets	8,587	6,710

For the year ended August 31,	2014	2013
Revenues	320	13,620
Expenses	2,005	13,758
Net loss for the year	(1,685)	(138)

8. FILM INVESTMENTS

The following table sets out the continuity for film investments, which include the Company's internally produced proprietary film and television programs, acquired distribution rights and third-party-produced equity film investments:

	Total
Balance – September 1, 2012	67,847
Additions	63,670
Tax credit accrual	(21,969)
Transfer to program and film rights	(17,793)
Investment impairment	(3,722)
Amortization	(25,759)
Balance – August 31, 2013	62,274
Additions	47,774
Tax credit accrual	(19,801)
Transfer to program and film rights	(6,994)
Amortization	(19,808)
Balance – August 31, 2014	**63,455**

At August 31, 2014, the Company performed an impairment test on certain third-party-produced equity film investments and determined no impairments were present based on expected future cash flows. In 2013, an impairment charge was recorded in other expense of $3,722.

	2014	2013
Cost	953,238	925,885
Accumulated amortization	889,783	863,611
Net book value	**63,455**	**62,274**

The Company expects that 34% of the net book value of film investments will be amortized during the year ended August 31, 2015. The Company expects the net book value of film investments to be fully amortized by August 2023.

9. BROADCAST LICENSES AND GOODWILL

Broadcast licenses and goodwill are tested for impairment annually as at August 31, or more frequently if events or changes in circumstances indicate that they may be impaired. During the second and third quarters of fiscal 2014, the Company concluded that interim impairment tests were required for goodwill for the Radio segment and for broadcast licenses for certain Radio CGUs. As a result of these tests, the Company recorded goodwill and broadcast license impairment charges of $65.5 million and $17.5 million in fiscal 2014, respectively, as certain radio CGUs had actual results that fell short of previous estimates and the outlook for these markets was less robust.

At August 31, 2014, the Company performed its annual impairment test for fiscal 2014 and determined that there were no further impairments, other than those recorded in the second and third quarters of fiscal 2014, for the year then ended. The changes in the book value of goodwill were as follows:

	Total
Balance – August 31, 2012	646,045
Balance – August 31, 2013	646,045
Acquisitions (note 26)	354,963
Impairments (note 10)	(65,549)
Balance – August 31, 2014	**934,659**

The changes in the book value of broadcast licenses for the period ended August 31, 2014, were as follows:

	Total
Balance – August 31, 2012	520,770
Impairments	(5,734)
Balance – August 31, 2013	515,036
Acquisitions (note 26)	482,399
Impairments (note 10)	(17,451)
Balance – August 31, 2014	**979,984**

At August 31, 2013 the Company performed its annual impairment test for fiscal 2013. As certain CGUs had actual results that fell short of previous estimates and the outlook for these markets was less robust, impairment losses of $5,734 were recorded for certain Radio broadcast licenses.

Broadcast licenses and goodwill are located primarily in Canada.

10. IMPAIRMENT TESTING

At each reporting date, the Company is required to assess its intangible assets and goodwill for potential indicators of impairment such as an adverse change in business climate that may indicate that these assets may be impaired. If any such indication exists, the Company estimates the recoverable amount of the asset or CGU and compares it to the carrying value. In addition, irrespective of whether there is any indication of impairment, the Company is required to test intangible assets with an indefinite useful life and goodwill for impairment at least annually.

For long-lived assets other than goodwill, the Company is also required to assess, at each reporting date, whether there is any indication that previously recognized impairment losses may no longer exist or may have decreased.

The Company completes its annual testing during the fourth quarter of each fiscal year.

The test for impairment of either an intangible asset or goodwill is to compare the recoverable amount of the asset or CGU to the carrying value. The recoverable amount is the higher of an asset's or CGU's FVLCS and its VIU. The recoverable amount is determined for an individual asset unless the asset does not generate cash inflows that are largely independent of those from other assets or groups of assets (such as broadcast licenses and goodwill) and the asset's VIU cannot be determined to equal its FVLCS. If this is the case, the recoverable amount is determined for the CGU to which the asset belongs.

The Company has determined the VIU calculation is higher than FVLCS and therefore, the recoverable amount for all CGUs or groups of CGUs is based on VIU with the exception of two Radio CGUs.

In determining FVLCS, recent market transactions are taken into account, if available. If no such transactions can be identified, an appropriate valuation model is used. These calculations are corroborated by valuation multiples, quoted share prices for publicly traded subsidiaries or other available fair value indicators.

The VIU calculation uses cash flow projections generally for a five-year period and a terminal value. The terminal value is the value attributed to the CGU's operations beyond the projected period using a perpetuity growth rate. The assumptions in the VIU calculations are segment profit growth rates (for periods within the cash flow projections and in perpetuity for the calculation of the terminal value), future levels of capital expenditures and discount rates.

Segment profit growth rates and future levels of capital expenditures are based on management's best estimates considering historical and expected operating plans, strategic plans, economic considerations and the general outlook for the industry and markets in which the CGU operates. The projections are prepared separately for each of the Company's CGUs to which the individual assets are allocated and are based on the most recent financial budgets approved by the Company's Board of Directors and management forecasts generally covering a period of five years with growth rate assumptions over this period. For longer periods, a terminal growth rate is determined and applied to project future cash flows after the fifth year.

- The discount rate applied to each asset, CGU or group of CGUs to determine VIU is a pre-tax rate that reflects an optimal debt-to-equity ratio and considers the risk-free rate, market equity risk premium, size premium and the risks specific to each asset or CGU's cash flow projections.

The recoverable amount for the Radio segment group of CGUs' overall goodwill impairment test was based on VIU. In the third quarter of fiscal 2014, the Company recognized an impairment charge of $65,549 based on the conclusions stated in the preceding paragraph. The recoverable amount and carrying value of the Radio segment group of CGUs after the impairment charge is approximately $378,689.

Sensitivity to changes in assumptions

An increase of 50 basis points in the pre-tax discount rate, a decrease of 50 basis points in the earnings growth rate each year, or a decrease of 50 basis points in the terminal growth rate, each used in isolation to perform the Radio goodwill impairment test, would have resulted in additional goodwill impairment in the Radio segment of between $1,600 and $9,000. However, no material additional broadcast license impairments would arise.

The Company has completed its annual impairment testing of goodwill and intangible assets for fiscal 2014. There were no additional impairment losses to be recorded as a result of the testing. The Company also assessed for any indicators of whether previous impairment losses had decreased. No previously recorded impairment losses on broadcast licenses were reversed.

The carrying amounts of goodwill and broadcast licenses allocated to each CGU and/or group of CGUs are set out in the following tables:

Goodwill

	2014	2013
Television	760,760	412,764
Radio	174,099	233,281
	934,859	646,045

Broadcast licenses

	2014	2013
Television		
Managed brands	825,000	361,101
Other	7,424	7,424
Radio[1]	147,560	156,511
	979,984	515,036

[1] Broadcast licenses for Radio consist of all Radio CGUs combined. There is no individual Radio CGU that comprises more than 10% of the total broadcast licenses balances.

11. ACCOUNTS PAYABLE AND ACCRUED LIABILITIES

Accounts payable and accrued liabilities are comprised of the following:

	2014	2013
Trade accounts payable and accrued liabilities	86,023	70,552
Program rights payable	63,061	74,456
Film investment accruals	3,111	2,620
Dividends payable	15,578	14,358
Financing lease accruals	2,638	2,457
	170,411	164,443

- In calculating the VIU, the Company uses an appropriate range of discount rates in order to establish a range of values for each CGU or group of CGUs.

The pre-tax discount and growth rates used by the Company for the purpose of its VIU calculations performed for each of the following groups of CGUs in the following periods were:

	2014	2013
Television		
Managed brands		
Pre-tax discount rate	11% - 13%	11% - 13%
Earnings growth rate	4.3% - 13.6%	0% - 4.6%
Terminal growth rate	2%	2%
Other		
Pre-tax discount rate	11% - 13%	11% - 13%
Earnings growth rate	4.3% - 13.6%	0% - 4.6%
Terminal growth rate	2%	2%
Radio		
Pre-tax discount rate	13% - 15%	12% - 14%
Earnings growth rate	2.0% - 8.1%	5.0% - 7.1%
Terminal growth rate	2%	2%

If the recoverable amount of an asset is less than its carrying amount, the carrying amount of the asset is reduced to the recoverable amount and the reduction is recorded as an impairment loss in the consolidated statements of income and comprehensive income.

If the recoverable amount of the CGU or group of CGUs is less than its carrying amount, an impairment loss is recognized. The impairment loss is allocated first to reduce the carrying amount of any goodwill allocated to the CGU or group of CGUs and then to the other assets of the CGU or group of CGUs pro rata on the basis of the carrying amount for each asset in the CGU or group of CGUs. The individual assets in the CGU cannot be written down below their fair value less costs to sell, if determinable.

Except for goodwill, a previously recognized impairment loss is reversed only if there has been a change in the assumptions used to determine the asset's recoverable amount since the last impairment loss was recognized. The reversal is limited so that the carrying amount of the asset does not exceed its recoverable amount, nor exceed the carrying amount that would have been determined, net of depreciation or amortization, had no impairment loss been recognized for the asset in prior years. Such reversal is recognized in the consolidated statements of income and comprehensive income.

In the second quarter of fiscal 2014, the Company determined that there was a broadcast license impairment in two Radio CGUs in Ontario. For one CGU, the Company used VIU to determine the recoverable amount, which resulted in an impairment charge of $6,000, while the FVLCS was used for the second CGU, which resulted in an impairment charge of $2,000 that reduced the carrying value (primarily broadcast licenses) of these CGUs to their recoverable amount. The recoverable amount for the Radio segment group of CGUs' overall goodwill impairment test was based on VIU.

In the third quarter of fiscal 2014, operating results in the Radio segment fell below previous estimates made in the second quarter, as the Radio segment continued to experience a soft advertising market and rating challenges in some markets. As well, the overall radio advertising market experienced a year-over-year decline in the quarter and on a year-to-date basis, causing the Company to lower its cash flow projections to reflect a weaker near term outlook. As a result, the Company determined there was a broadcast license impairment in three Radio CGUs in Ontario and one in British Columbia, as well as a goodwill impairment in the Radio segment group of CGUs overall.

In the third quarter of fiscal 2014, for three CGUs, the Company used VIU to determine the recoverable amount, while the FVLCS was used for one CGU, which resulted in impairment charges totalling $10,691 (predominantly comprised of broadcast license impairments) that reduced the carrying values of these CGUs to their recoverable amount at the end of the third quarter. The recoverable amount of these CGUs after the impairment charges is $49,171.

12. PROVISIONS

The Company recorded restructuring charges of $3,930 (2013 – $4,424) primarily related to severance and employee related costs as a result of the business acquisitions and the related integration. The Company anticipates that these provisions will be substantially paid by fiscal 2015.

The continuity of provisions is as follows:

	2014	2013
Restructuring		
Balance, beginning of period	4,441	2,452
Additions	3,930	4,424
Payments	(3,076)	(2,435)
Balance, end of period	**5,295**	**4,441**
Long term portion	(630)	(1,094)
Total current restructuring provision	**4,665**	**3,347**
Legal claims	649	594
Total current provisions balance, end of period	**5,314**	**3,941**

13. LONG-TERM DEBT

	2014	2013
Bank loans	333,677	—
Senior unsecured guaranteed notes	550,000	550,000
Unamortized financing fees	(9,426)	(11,034)
	874,251	538,966

Interest rates on the balance of the bank loans fluctuate with Canadian bankers' acceptances and/or LIBOR. As at August 31, 2014, the weighted average interest rate on the outstanding bank loans and Notes was 3.9% (2013 – 4.3%). Interest on the bank loans and Notes averaged 4.2% for fiscal 2014 (2013 – 5.8%).

The banks hold as collateral a first ranking charge on all assets and undertakings of Corus and certain of Corus' subsidiaries as designated under the credit agreement. Under the facility, the Company has undertaken to comply with financial covenants regarding a minimum interest coverage ratio and a maximum debt to cash flow ratio. Management has determined that the Company was in compliance with the covenants provided under the bank loans as at August 31, 2014.

On February 3, 2014, the Company's credit agreement with a syndicate of banks was amended and restated. The principal amendment effected was the establishment of a two year $150.0 million term facility, maturing February 3, 2016, incremental to the existing $500.0 million revolving facility maturing February 11, 2017. The $150.0 million term facility was fully drawn on inception and the proceeds were used to reduce the amount drawn on the revolving facility. Both the term and revolving facilities are subject to the same covenants and security. Interest rates on both the term and revolving facilities fluctuate with Canadian prime rate, Canadian bankers' acceptances and/or LIBOR plus an applicable margin.

Contemporaneously with the amendment and restatement of the credit agreement, the Company entered into Canadian dollar interest rate swap agreements to fix the interest rate on $150.0 million at 1.375%, plus an applicable margin, to February 3, 2016. The fair value of Level 2 financial instruments such as interest rate swap agreements is calculated by way of discounted cash flows, using market interest rates and applicable credit spreads. The Company has assessed that there is no ineffectiveness in the hedge of its interest rate exposure. The effectiveness of the hedging relationship is reviewed on a quarterly basis. As an effective hedge, unrealized gains or losses on the interest rate swap agreements are recognized in OCI.

In the second quarter of fiscal 2013, the Company issued $550.0 million principal amount of 4.25% Senior Unsecured Guaranteed Notes due February 11, 2020 ("2020 Notes") and redeemed the existing $500.0 million principal amount of 7.25% Senior Unsecured Guaranteed Notes due February 10, 2017 ("2017 Notes") effective March 16, 2013.

The issuance of the 2020 Notes and redemption of the 2017 Notes resulted in the Company recording debt refinancing costs of $25.0 million in the second quarter of fiscal 2013, which included the early redemption premium of $18.1 million and the non-cash write-off of unamortized financing fees of $6.9 million related to the 2017 Notes.

On February 27, 2013, the Company's $500.0 million credit facility, available on a revolving basis, with a syndicate of banks was amended. The principal amendment was to extend the maturity date to February 11, 2017.

14. OTHER LONG-TERM LIABILITIES

	2014	2013
Public benefits associated with acquisitions	27,604	1,414
Unearned revenue	6,611	8,751
Program rights payable	71,926	20,735
Long-term employee obligations	34,451	30,343
Deferred leasehold inducements	16,052	15,414
Derivative fair value	72	—
Merchandising and trademark liabilities	11,021	13,486
Finance lease accrual	4,056	3,098
	171,793	93,241

15. SHARE CAPITAL

AUTHORIZED

The Company is authorized to issue, upon approval of holders of no less than two-thirds of the existing Class A shares, an unlimited number of Class A participating shares ("Class A Voting Shares"), as well as an unlimited number of Class B non-voting participating shares ("Class B Non-Voting Shares"), Class A Preferred Shares, and Class 1 and Class 2 Preferred Shares.

Class A Voting Shares are convertible at any time into an equivalent number of Class B Non-Voting Shares. The Class B Non-Voting Shares are convertible into an equivalent number of Class A Voting Shares in limited circumstances.

The Class A Preferred Shares are redeemable at any time at the demand of Corus and retractable at any time at the demand of a holder of a Class A Preferred Share for an amount equal to the consideration received by Corus at the time of issuance of such Class A Preferred Shares. Holders of Class A Preferred Shares are entitled to receive a non-cumulative dividend at such rate as Corus' Board of Directors may determine on the redemption amount of the Class A Preferred Shares. Each of the Class 1 Preferred Shares, the Class 2 Preferred Shares, the Class A Voting Shares and the Class B Non-Voting Shares rank junior to and are subject in all respects to the preferences, rights, conditions, restrictions, limitations and prohibitions attached to the Class A Preferred Shares in connection with the payment of dividends.

The Class 1 and Class 2 Preferred Shares are issuable in one or more series with attributes designated by the Board of Directors. The Class 1 Preferred Shares rank senior to the Class 2 Preferred Shares.

In the event of liquidation, dissolution or winding-up of Corus or other distribution of assets of Corus for the purpose of winding up its affairs, the holders of Class A Preferred Shares are entitled to a payment in priority to all other classes of shares of Corus to the extent of the redemption amount of the Class A Preferred Shares, but will not be entitled to any surplus in excess of that amount. The remaining property and assets will be available for distribution to the holders of the Class A Voting Shares and Class B Non-Voting Shares, which shall be paid or distributed equally, share for share, between the holders of the Class A Voting Shares and the Class B Non-Voting Shares, without preference or distinction.

EARNINGS PER SHARE

The following is a reconciliation of the numerator and denominator (in thousands) used for the computation of the basic and diluted earnings per share amounts:

	2014	2013
Net income attributable to shareholders (numerator)	**150,408**	159,895
Weighted average number of shares outstanding (denominator)		
Weighted average number of shares outstanding - basic	84,993	83,860
Effect of dilutive securities	334	330
Weighted average number of shares outstanding - diluted	**85,327**	84,190

The calculation of diluted earnings per share for fiscal 2014 excluded 12,618 (2013 – nil) weighted average Class B Non-Voting Shares issuable under the Company's Stock Option Plan because these options were not "in-the-money".

16. ACCUMULATED OTHER COMPREHENSIVE INCOME (LOSS)

	Unrealized Foreign currency translation adjustment	Unrealized change in fair value of available-for-sale investments	Unrealized change in fair value of cash flow hedges	Actuarial gains (losses) on defined benefit plans	Total
Balance - September 1, 2012	(1,065)	253	–	–	(812)
Items that may be subsequently reclassified to income:					
Amount	2,333	152	–	–	2,485
Income tax	–	(20)	–	–	(20)
	2,333	132	–	–	2,465
Items that will never be subsequently reclassified to net income:					
Amount	–	–	–	838	838
Income tax	–	–	–	(222)	(222)
	–	–	–	616	616
Transfer to retained earnings	–	–	–	(616)	(616)
Balance - August 31, 2013	1,267	366	–	–	1,653
Items that may be subsequently reclassified to income:					
Amount	1,720	515	(71)	–	2,164
Income tax	–	(69)	19	–	(50)
	1,720	446	(52)	–	2,114
Items that will never be subsequently reclassified to net income:					
Amount	–	–	–	(2,977)	(2,977)
Income tax	–	–	–	789	789
	–	–	–	(2,188)	(2,188)
Transfer to retained earnings	–	–	–	2,188	2,188
Balance - August 31, 2014	**2,987**	**832**	**(52)**	**–**	**3,767**

ISSUED AND OUTSTANDING

	Class A Voting Shares #	$	Class B Non-Voting Shares #	$	Total $
Balance – September 1, 2012	3,434,292	26,595	79,924,384	883,410	910,005
Conversion of Class A Voting Shares to Class B Non-Voting Shares	(4,000)	(31)	4,000	31	–
Issuance of shares under stock option plan	–	–	50,200	1,155	1,155
Issuance of shares under dividend reinvestment plan	–	–	1,134,666	26,731	26,731
Shares repurchased	–	–	(64,104)	(708)	(708)
Balance – August 31, 2013	3,430,292	26,564	81,049,146	910,619	937,183
Conversion of Class A Voting Shares to Class B Non-Voting Shares	(2,000)	(15)	2,000	15	–
Issuance of shares under stock option plan	–	–	259,500	5,465	5,465
Issuance of shares under dividend reinvestment plan	–	–	1,024,947	24,682	24,682
Balance – August 31, 2014	**3,428,292**	**26,549**	**82,335,593**	**940,781**	**967,330**

No Class A Preferred Shares, Class 1 Preferred Shares or Class 2 Preferred Shares are outstanding at August 31, 2014.

DIVIDENDS

The holders of Class A Voting Shares and Class B Non-Voting Shares are entitled to receive such dividends as the Board of Directors determines to declare on a share-for-share basis, as and when any such dividends are declared or paid. The holders of Class B Non-Voting Shares are entitled to receive during each dividend period, in priority to the payment of dividends on the Class A Voting Shares, a dividend which is $0.005 per share per annum higher than that received on the Class A Voting Shares. This higher dividend rate is subject to proportionate adjustment in the event of future consolidations or subdivisions of shares and in the event of any issue of shares by way of stock dividend. After payment or setting aside for payment of the additional non-cumulative dividends on the Class B Non-Voting Shares, holders of Class A Voting Shares and Class B Non-Voting Shares participate equally, on a share-for-share basis, on all subsequent dividends declared.

2014 Date of record	Date paid	Class A Voting Shares Amount paid	Class B Non-Voting Shares Amount paid
September 16, 2013	September 30, 2013	$0.084583	$0.085000
October 15, 2013	October 31, 2013	$0.084583	$0.085000
November 15, 2013	November 29, 2013	$0.084583	$0.085000
December 13, 2013	December 30, 2013	$0.084583	$0.085000
January 15, 2014	January 31, 2014	$0.084583	$0.085000
February 14, 2014	February 28, 2014	$0.090417	$0.090833
March 14, 2014	March 31, 2014	$0.090417	$0.090833
April 15, 2014	April 30, 2014	$0.090417	$0.090833
May 15, 2014	May 30, 2014	$0.090417	$0.090833
June 16, 2014	June 30, 2014	$0.090417	$0.090833
July 15, 2014	July 31, 2014	$0.090417	$0.090833
August 15, 2014	August 29, 2014	$0.090417	$0.090833
		$1.055834	**$1.060833**

The total amount of dividends declared in fiscal 2014 was $91,376 (2013 - $84,452).

On October 23, 2014 the Company declared dividends of $0.090417 per Class A Voting Share and $0.090833 per Class B Non-Voting Share payable on each of November 28, 2014, December 30, 2014 and January 30, 2015 to the shareholders of record at the close of business on November 14, 2014, December 15, 2014 and January 15, 2015, respectively.

17. DIRECT COST OF SALES, GENERAL AND ADMINISTRATIVE EXPENSES

	2014	2013
Amortization of program and film rights	207,639	168,883
Amortization of film investments	19,808	25,759
Other cost of sales	27,615	35,276
Employee costs	149,459	155,687
Other general and administrative	138,857	114,957
	543,378	500,562

18. INTEREST EXPENSE

	2014	2013
Interest on long-term debt	32,121	32,814
Imputed interest on long-term liabilities	14,698	10,279
Other	1,501	1,702
	48,320	44,795

19. OTHER EXPENSE (INCOME), NET

	2014	2013
Interest income	(722)	(1,091)
Foreign exchange loss	649	876
Equity loss of investees	1,685	623
Third-party-produced film investment write down	—	3,722
Investment in associates (recovery) impairment	(256)	3,399
Income from joint ventures	—	(12,093)
Increase in purchase price obligation (note 26)	3,336	—
Other	1,048	1,004
	5,740	(3,560)

27. COMMITMENTS, CONTINGENCIES AND GUARANTEES

LEASES

The Company enters into operating leases for the use of facilities and equipment. During fiscal 2014, rental expenses in direct cost of sales, general and administrative expenses totalled approximately $21,422 (2013 - $21,239). Future minimum rental payments payable under non-cancellable operating leases at August 31, are as follows:

	2014	2013
Within one year	25,430	24,428
After one year but not more than five years	97,722	88,888
More than five years	290,617	279,157
	413,769	392,473

The Company has entered into finance leases for the use of computer equipment and software, telephones, furniture and broadcast equipment. The leases range between three and five years and bear interest rates varying from 2.1% to 7.0%. Future minimum lease payments under finance leases together with the present value of the net minimum lease payments are as follows:

	2014		2013	
	Minimum payments	Present value of payments	Minimum payments	Present value of payments
Within one year	2,921	2,638	2,556	2,147
After one year but not more than five years	4,362	4,056	3,247	3,098
Total minimum lease payments	7,283	6,694	5,803	5,245
Less amounts representing finance charges	589	—	558	—
Present value of minimum lease payments	6,694	6,694	5,245	5,245

PURCHASE COMMITMENTS

The Company has entered into various agreements for the right to broadcast or distribute certain film, television and radio programs in the future. These agreements, which range in term from one to five years, generally commit the Company to acquire specific films, television and radio programs or certain levels of future productions. The acquisition of these broadcast and distribution rights is contingent on the actual delivery of the productions. Management estimates that these agreements will result in future program and film expenditures of approximately $61,711 (2013 - $53,997). In addition, the Company has commitments of $97 (2013 - nil) for future television script production.

The Company has commitments related to trade marks and certain other intangible rights until February 2021, for a total of approximately $16,641 (2013 - $19,942). The Company has certain additional annual commitments, some of which are contingent on performance, to pay royalties for trade mark rights. In addition, the Company has licenses and other commitments over the next five years to use specific software, signal and satellite functions of approximately $29,549 (2013 - $40,352). Generally, it is not the Company's policy to issue guarantees to non-controlled affiliates or third parties, with limited exceptions.

LITIGATION

The Company, its subsidiaries and joint ventures are involved in litigation matters arising out of the ordinary course and conduct of its business. Although such matters cannot be predicted with certainty, management does not consider the Company's exposure to litigation to be material to these consolidated financial statements.

OTHER MATTERS

Many of the Company's agreements, specifically those related to acquisitions and dispositions of business assets, included indemnification provisions where the Company may be required to make payments to a vendor or purchaser for breach of fundamental representation and warranty terms in the agreements with respect to matters such as corporate status, title of assets, environmental issues, consents to transfer, employment matters, litigation, taxes payable and other potential material liabilities. The maximum potential amount of future payments that the Company could be required to make under these indemnification provisions is not reasonably quantifiable, as certain indemnifications are not subject to a monetary limitation. As at August 31, 2014, management believed there was only a remote possibility that the indemnification provisions would require any material cash payment.

The Company indemnifies its directors and officers against any and all claims or losses reasonably incurred in the performance of their service to the Company to the extent permitted by law. The Company has acquired and maintains liability insurance for directors and officers of the Company and its subsidiaries.

B SALES TAXES

All companies operating in Canada need to understand how sales taxes apply to their particular business in their province or territory. Sales taxes may take the form of the Goods and Services Tax (GST), Provincial Sales Tax (PST), or Harmonized Sales Tax (HST). GST is levied by the federal government. PST is levied by the provinces, with the exception of Alberta, the Northwest Territories, Nunavut, and Yukon, where no PST is charged. Ontario, Nova Scotia, New Brunswick, Newfoundland and Labrador, and Prince Edward Island have combined the GST and PST into one Harmonized Sales Tax or HST.

A business is considered an agent of the federal and provincial governments and is therefore required to collect sales taxes on behalf of these governing bodies. Sales taxes apply to most goods and services, but some exceptions do apply, which will be discussed in this appendix. We will discuss the collection, payment, recording, and remittance of each of these types of sales taxes in the following sections.

LEARNING OBJECTIVE 1 ▶ Explain the different types of sales tax.

Types of Sales Taxes

GOODS AND SERVICES TAX

The GST is a federal sales tax on most goods and services provided in Canada. A business must register for the GST if it provides taxable goods or services in Canada and if it has revenues of more than $30,000 in any year. Businesses that have to register for the GST or decide to do so voluntarily are called registrants. Registrants can claim a credit—called an input tax credit (ITC)—for the amount of GST they pay or owe on purchases of goods or services against the GST they collect or are owed. GST returns are submitted quarterly for most registrants (monthly for large registrants) to the Canada Revenue Agency. The taxes are payable to the Receiver General for Canada, which is the collection agent for the federal government. We will discuss remittances of GST to the Canada Revenue Agency a little later in the appendix.

The GST applies at a rate of 5% on most transactions. Transactions subject to GST are called taxable supplies. There are two other categories of goods and services with respect to the GST:

1. zero-rated supplies, such as basic groceries and prescription drugs and
2. exempt supplies, such as educational services, health care services, and most financial services provided by financial institutions.

No GST applies to zero-rated or exempt supplies. However, businesses that supply zero-rated goods can claim input tax credits (ITCs) on the costs incurred to provide zero-rated goods. For example, assume that Jenna's Corner Grocery sells bananas to a customer. There is no requirement for Jenna to collect GST on the sale because bananas are a basic grocery item. However, the grocery store must pay for utilities to operate the store, and any GST paid on utility bills and other expenses can be claimed by Jenna against the sales of items such as bananas as an ITC.

HARMONIZED SALES TAX

The Harmonized Sales Tax or HST is a combined or harmonized tax. Provinces that adopt the HST combine their provincial sales tax rate with the federal GST rate and charge one combined rate on most goods and services. HST has the same regulations as GST; that is, HST is charged on taxable supplies, and no HST is charged on zero-rated and exempt supplies. In these provinces, the Receiver General for Canada is the collection agent for both the federal and provincial governments, reducing some of the administrative burden from the provinces. Similar to GST, HST returns are submitted quarterly for most registrants (monthly for large registrants). We will discuss remittances to the Canada Revenue Agency a little later in the appendix.

The provinces of Ontario, Nova Scotia, New Brunswick, Newfoundland and Labrador, and Prince Edward Island charge HST and they are referred to generally as participating provinces.

Illustration B-1 provides the GST/HST status of some typical goods and services.

▶ ILLUSTRATION
Examples of GST/HST status

Taxable Supplies	Zero-Rated Supplies	Exempt Supplies
Building materials	Prescription drugs	Used house
Ready-to-eat pizza	Uncooked pizza	Dental services
Two doughnuts	Six or more doughnuts	Insurance policy

The reason ready-to-eat pizza and two doughnuts have GST/HST added to the purchase price is because they are considered convenience items, which are taxable, and not basic groceries, which are not taxable.

PROVINCIAL SALES TAX

Provincial sales taxes are charged on retail sales of certain goods and services. There are only four provinces that charge a separate Provincial Sales Tax: British Columbia, Saskatchewan, Manitoba, and Quebec. In Quebec, it is referred to as Quebec Sales Tax or QST. For businesses that have sales transactions in several provinces, the amount of PST they need to charge will depend on where the goods are being shipped. Consequently, a business could have several PST payable accounts while operating out of a province where only HST applies to sales. For example, Rogers Communications Inc. sells telecommunications services and products throughout Canada and is headquartered in Toronto, Ontario. When a sale is made to a customer in Saskatchewan, Rogers charges that customer both GST and Saskatchewan PST. Rogers is then responsible for submitting any PST collected on Saskatchewan sales to the Saskatchewan provincial government.

Provincial sales taxes are remitted periodically to the Minister of Finance in each province, which is the collection agent for provincial governments. PST rates vary by province and can change with each provincial budget. Certain goods are exempt and therefore can be purchased with no PST, such as children's clothing, textbooks, and residential rent. Examples of exempt services that are not taxable include personal services such as dental and medical services. Because rates and exemptions vary by province, it is important when starting a business to check with provincial officials for details on how to calculate the provincial tax that must be applied to sales.

To summarize, four provinces—British Columbia, Manitoba, Quebec, and Saskatchewan—apply both PST and GST to the selling price of a taxable good or service. The provincial tax rates used by these four provinces vary but the GST is consistent at the rate of 5%. Five provinces charge a combined HST: New Brunswick, Newfoundland and Labrador, Nova Scotia, Ontario, and Prince Edward Island. Four provinces and territories charge only the GST: Alberta, the Northwest Territories, Nunavut, and Yukon. GST/HST is charged on sales of most products and services and PST is also charged on most products and services but with notable exceptions.

The rates of sales tax in each province and territory are shown in Illustration B-2.

Province/Territory	GST (HST) Rate[1]	PST Rate[3]
Alberta	5.0%	0.0%
British Columbia	5.0%	7.0%
Manitoba	5.0%	8.0%
New Brunswick	13.0%	N/A
Newfoundland and Labrador	15.0%[2]	N/A
Northwest Territories	5.0%	0.0%
Nova Scotia	15.0%	N/A
Nunavut	5.0%	0.0%
Ontario	13.0%	N/A
Prince Edward Island	14.0%	N/A
Quebec	5.0%	9.975%
Saskatchewan	5.0%	5.0%
Yukon	5.0%	0.0%

[1]These rates are in effect as of April 1, 2013, and are subject to change.
[2]Rate is effective January 1, 2016.
[3]These rates are current as of May 4, 2015, and are subject to change.

LEARNING OBJECTIVE **2** ▶ **Record sales taxes collected by businesses on goods and services.**

Sales Taxes Collected on Receipts

Sales taxes are collected by businesses from consumers on taxable goods and services. It is important to understand that sales taxes are not a source of revenue for a company. They are collected by a company on behalf of the federal and provincial governments. Consequently, collected sales tax is a current liability to the company until remitted to the respective government at regular intervals.

SERVICES

Now let's look at how service companies record sales taxes on the services they provide.

Services with PST

Assume that $250.00 of cleaning services were provided by a company in Manitoba for cash on July 24. These services are subject to both PST (8%) and GST (5%), and would be recorded as follows:

July 24	Cash	282.50	
	Service Revenue		250.00
	PST Payable ($250 × 8%)		20.00
	GST Payable ($250 × 5%)		12.50
	To record cleaning service revenue.		

A	=	L	+	OE
+282.50		+20.00		+250.00
		+12.50		

↑Cash flows: +282.50

Note that the revenue recorded is $250.00, and not $282.50. The service revenue recognized is exclusive of the GST and PST amounts collected, which are recorded as current liabilities.

Services with HST

Assume now that these same services were provided by a company in New Brunswick, where HST is 13%. The entry would be as follows:

A	=	L	+	OE
+282.50		+32.50		+250.00

↑Cash flows: +282.50

July 24	Cash	282.50	
	Service Revenue		250.00
	HST Payable ($250.00 × 13%)		32.50
	To record cleaning service revenue.		

MERCHANDISE

Entries are needed to record the sales taxes owed when merchandise inventory (goods) is sold, or to reduce sales taxes payable when merchandise inventory is returned.

Sales with PST

Assume that Staples sells $1,000 of office furniture, on account, in the province of Manitoba, where PST is 8% and GST is 5%. Staples uses a perpetual inventory system and the cost of the furniture to Staples is $800. Staples will make the following two entries to record the sale and the cost of the sale on May 20:

A	=	L	+	OE
+1,130		+50		+1,000
		+80		

Cash flows: no effect

A	=	L	+	OE
−800				−800

Cash flows: no effect

May 20	Accounts Receivable	1,130	
	Sales		1,000
	GST Payable ($1,000 × 5%)		50
	PST Payable ($1,000 × 8%)		80
	To record sale of merchandise on account.		
20	Cost of Goods Sold	800	
	Merchandise Inventory		800
	To record cost of goods sold.		

The merchandise inventory does not include any sales taxes that may have been paid when the company purchased the merchandise. We will learn more about that in the next section of this appendix. Under a periodic inventory system, the second entry would not be recorded.

Sales Returns and Allowances with PST

If the customer from the previous transaction returns $300 of the merchandise purchased from Staples on May 25 and the goods are returned to inventory, Staples entries to record the sales return would appear as follows (assuming an inventory cost of $240):

A	=	L	+	OE
−339		−15		−300
		−24		

Cash flows: no effect

A	=	L	+	OE
+240				+240

Cash flows: no effect

May 25	Sales Returns and Allowances	300	
	GST Payable ($300 × 5%)	15	
	PST Payable ($300 × 8%)	24	
	Accounts Receivable		339
	To record credit for returned merchandise.		
25	Merchandise Inventory	240	
	Cost of Goods Sold		240
	To record cost of merchandise returned.		

Note that the GST and PST payable accounts, rather than a receivable account, are debited, to indicate that this is a return of previously collected sales tax.

Under a periodic inventory system, the second entry would not be recorded.

Sales with HST

Assume now that Staples sells the same $1,000 of office furniture, on account, in the province of Ontario, where HST is 13%. Staples uses a perpetual inventory system and the cost of the furniture to Staples is $800. Staples will record the following two entries to record the sale and the cost of the sale on May 20:

May 20	Accounts Receivable	1,130	
	Sales		1,000
	HST Payable ($1,000 × 13%)		130
	To record sale of merchandise on account.		
20	Cost of Goods Sold	800	
	Merchandise Inventory		800
	To record cost of goods sold.		

A	=	L	+	OE
+1,130		+130		+1,000

Cash flows: no effect

A	=	L	+	OE
−800				−800

Cash flows: no effect

Notice that no PST account is used because provinces that adopt HST are essentially replacing GST and PST with one tax only, HST.

Under a periodic inventory system, the second entry would not be recorded.

Sales Returns and Allowances with HST

Assume the same $300 of merchandise was returned to Staples on May 25. Staples entries to record the sales return would appear as follows:

May 25	Sales Returns and Allowances	300	
	HST Payable ($300 × 13%)	39	
	Accounts Receivable		339
	To record credit for returned merchandise.		
25	Merchandise Inventory ($300 ÷ $1,000 × $800)	240	
	Cost of Goods Sold		240
	To record cost of merchandise returned.		

A	=	L	+	OE
−339		−39		−300

Cash flows: no effect

A	=	L	+	OE
+240				+240

Cash flows: no effect

Under a periodic inventory system, the second entry would not be recorded.

LEARNING OBJECTIVE 3 ▸ **Record sales taxes paid on the purchase of goods and services.**

Sales Taxes Paid on Payments

Businesses, similar to consumers, must pay the applicable PST and GST or HST charged by their suppliers on taxable goods and services.

PURCHASE OF MERCHANDISE FOR RESALE

When purchasing merchandise for resale, the treatment of the PST is different than that of the GST. In British Columbia, Manitoba, and Saskatchewan, PST is a single-stage tax collected from the final consumers of taxable goods and services. Consequently, wholesalers do not charge provincial sales tax to the retailer, which will in turn resell the merchandise, at a higher price, to the final consumer. By presenting a vendor licence number, retailers are able to buy merchandise for resale, exempt of the PST. In Quebec, however, QST is a provincial sales tax on most goods and services paid by both consumers and businesses alike.

Businesses in Canada must pay GST/HST on the purchase of merchandise but can then offset the GST/HST paid against any GST/HST collected. If a business is a registrant in Quebec, QST paid on most purchases can also be offset against any QST collected. Consequently, **when merchandise for resale is purchased, the GST/HST and QST paid by a business are not part of the inventory cost**. The GST/HST paid on purchases is debited to an account called GST or HST Recoverable and is called an input tax credit. The QST paid on purchases in Quebec is debited to an account called QST recoverable and is called an input tax refund (ITR).

Purchases with GST

The following is an entry to record the purchase of merchandise for resale in the province of Manitoba on May 4 at a price of $4,000, on account, using a perpetual inventory system:

A	=	L	+	OE
+4,000		+4,200		
+200				

Cash flows: no effect

May 4	Merchandise Inventory	4,000	
	GST Recoverable ($4,000 × 5%)	200	
	Accounts Payable		4,200
	To record merchandise purchased on account.		

As previously discussed, GST is not included in the Merchandise Inventory account, but is instead recorded as a receivable.

Under a periodic inventory system, the $4,000 debit would have been recorded to the Purchases account.

Purchase Returns and Allowances with GST

The entry to record a $300 return of merchandise on May 8 is as follows:

A	=	L	+	OE
−15		−315		
−300				

Cash flows: no effect

May 8	Accounts Payable	315	
	GST Recoverable ($300 × 5%)		15
	Merchandise Inventory		300
	To record the return of merchandise.		

Note that the GST Recoverable account is credited instead of the GST Payable account because this is a reduction of the previously recorded GST.

Under a periodic inventory system, the credit of $300 would have been recorded to the Purchase Returns and Allowances account.

To summarize, PST is not paid on purchases of merchandise for resale. GST paid on purchases is recoverable and recorded as a current asset in the GST Recoverable account. Purchase returns and allowances require an adjustment of GST only, since PST was not paid on the original purchase.

Purchases with HST

The following is an entry to record the purchase of merchandise for resale in the province of Prince Edward Island, where the HST rate is 14%, on May 4 at a price of $4,000, on account, using a perpetual inventory system:

A	=	L	+	OE
+4,000		+4,560		
+560				

Cash flows: no effect

May 4	Merchandise Inventory	4,000	
	HST Recoverable ($4,000 × 14%)	560	
	Accounts Payable		4,560
	To record merchandise purchased on account.		

The HST is not included in the Merchandise Inventory account but is instead recorded as a receivable.

Under a periodic inventory system, the $4,000 debit would have been recorded to the Purchases account.

Purchase Returns and Allowances with HST

The entry to record a $300 return of merchandise in the province of Prince Edward Island, where the HST rate is 14%, on May 8 is as follows:

May 8	Accounts Payable	342	
	HST Recoverable ($300 × 14%)		42
	Merchandise Inventory		300
	To record the return of merchandise.		

A	=	L	+	OE
−42		−342		
−300				

Cash flows: no effect

Note that the HST Recoverable account is credited instead of the HST Payable account because this is a reduction of the previously recorded HST.

Under a periodic inventory system, the credit of $300 would have been recorded to the Purchase Returns and Allowances account.

To summarize, HST paid on purchases is recoverable and recorded as a current asset in the HST Recoverable account.

OPERATING EXPENSES

The accounting treatment of sales taxes incurred on operating expenses depends on the type of sales taxes that the company is charged.

Operating Expenses with PST

Although PST is not charged on goods purchased for resale, it is charged to businesses that use taxable goods and services in their operations. For example, a business must pay GST and PST when it buys office supplies. As with all purchases made by a business that is a registrant, the GST is recoverable. (That is, it can be offset as an ITC against GST collected.) Because the PST is not recoverable, the PST forms part of the cost of the asset or expense that is being acquired.

The following is the entry for a cash purchase of office supplies on May 18 in the amount of $200 in the province of Saskatchewan, where PST is 5% and GST is 5%:

May 18	Supplies ($200 + $10* PST)	210	
	GST Recoverable ($200 × 5%)	10	
	Cash		220
	To record purchase of office supplies.		
*$200 × 5% = $10			

A	=	L	+	OE
+210				
+10				
−220				

↓ Cash flows: −220

In this situation, the cost of the supplies includes both the supplies and the PST. Because GST is recoverable, it does not form part of the asset cost.

This same purchase would be recorded as follows if it occurred in the province of Quebec, where QST is 9.975% and GST is 5%:

May 18	Supplies	200.00	
	GST recoverable ($200.00 x 5%)	10.00	
	QST recoverable ($200.00 x 9.975%)	19.95	
	Cash		229.95
	To record purchase of office supplies		

A	=	L	+	OE
+200.00				
+10.00				
+19.95				
−229.95				

↓ Cash flows: −229.95

Operating Expenses with HST

When HST is applied, it is treated in the same manner as GST. HST is recoverable and does not form part of the cost of the item purchased. The purchase of office supplies would be recorded as follows if it had occurred in the province of Ontario, where HST is 13%:

A = L + OE	May 18	Supplies	200	
+200		HST Recoverable ($200 × 13%)	26	
+26		Cash		226
−226		To record purchase of office supplies.		

↓ Cash flows: −226

Note that the type and amount of sales tax paid changes the amount recorded as the cost of office supplies in each province: $210.00 in Saskatchewan, $200.00 in Quebec, and $200.00 in Ontario.

PROPERTY, PLANT, AND EQUIPMENT

The PST and GST or HST apply to other purchases, such as the purchase of property, plant, and equipment, in the same manner as described in the Operating Expenses section above. All GST (or HST) paid is recoverable and is not part of the asset's cost. The PST, however, is part of the cost of the asset being purchased because it is not recoverable.

Property, Plant, and Equipment with PST

The following is the entry for the purchase of office furniture on May 20 from Staples, on account, for $1,000 plus applicable sales taxes in Manitoba, where PST is 8% and GST is 5%.

A = L + OE	May 20	Furniture ($1,000 + $80* PST)	1,080	
+1,080 +1,130		GST Recoverable ($1,000 × 5%)	50	
+50		Accounts Payable		1,130
		To record purchase of office furniture.		
Cash flows: no effect	*$1,000 × 8% = $80			

Because the PST is not recoverable, the cost of the furniture is $1,080, inclusive of the PST. Compare this entry made by the buyer to record the purchase with the entry made by the seller (Staples) to record the sale, shown earlier in this appendix. Both companies record accounts payable and accounts receivable in the same amount, $1,130. However, the seller records both GST and PST payable while the buyer records only GST recoverable.

In Saskatchewan, where PST is 5% and GST is 5%, the same entry would be recorded as follows:

A = L + OE	May 20	Furniture ($1,000 + $50* PST)	1,050	
+1,050 +1,100		GST Recoverable ($1,000 × 5%)	50	
+50		Accounts Payable		1,100
		To record purchase of office furniture.		
Cash flows: no effect	*$1,000 × 5% = $50			

Property, Plant, and Equipment with HST

In Ontario, where HST is 13%, the entry would be recorded as follows:

A = L + OE	May 20	Furniture	1,000	
+1,000 +1,130		HST Recoverable ($1,000 × 13%)	130	
+130		Accounts Payable		1,130
		To record purchase of office furniture.		
Cash flows: no effect				

As we have noted before, the type and amount of sales taxes paid change the amount recorded as the cost of the office furniture in each province: $1,080 in Manitoba, $1,050 in Saskatchewan, and $1,000 in Ontario.

| **LEARNING OBJECTIVE** | **4** | **Record the remittance of sales taxes.** |

Remittance of Sales Taxes

As mentioned in the introduction, businesses act as agents of the federal and provincial governments in charging and later remitting taxes charged on sales and services. For example, Staples, the seller of office furniture shown earlier in the appendix, must remit GST or HST to the Receiver General for Canada and PST to the Minister of Finance, where applicable. Notice that, even if Staples has not received payment from a customer buying on account before the due date for the remittance, the tax must still be paid to the government authorities. As a registrant, however, Staples will also benefit from claiming ITCs and recording a reduction in amounts payable from applying GST/HST on sales.

GST (OR HST)

When remitting the amount owed to the federal government at the end of a reporting period for GST (or HST), the amount of GST/HST payable is reduced by any amount in the GST (or HST) Recoverable account.

To illustrate, Quasar Company operates retail clothing stores in British Columbia. Quasar collects GST and PST from its customers upon each sale and pays GST on all purchases. In British Columbia, GST is 5% and PST is 7%. At the end of the quarter, October 31, 2017, Quasar had total sales of $400,000 during the quarter and reported the following account balances related to GST:

GST Recoverable	$12,000
GST Payable	$20,000

Quasar will complete its GST return, prepare the required journal entry, and pay the amounts owing.

The difference between GST Recoverable and GST Payable is remitted to the Canada Revenue Agency. The journal entry to record the remittance is as follows:

Oct. 31	GST Payable	20,000	
	GST Recoverable		12,000
	Cash		8,000
	To record remittance of GST.		

A = L + OE
−12,000 −20,000
−8,000

▼ Cash flows: −8,000

If Quasar Company were located in a province that had HST, the journal entry would be the same but the accounts would be titled HST Payable and HST Recoverable. If Quasar Company collected both GST and HST (because sales are made to multiple provinces), the entry would also be the same but the accounts would be titled GST/HST Payable and GST/HST Recoverable.

GST/HST returns require the registrant to report at specified dates, depending on the business's volume of sales. The amount of the sales and other revenue as well as the amount of GST/HST charged on these sales, whether collected or not, is reported on the return. The amount of the ITCs claimed is also entered to reduce the amount owing to the Receiver General. If the amount of GST/HST recoverable exceeds the amount of GST/HST payable, the return should be filed as soon as possible in order to ask for a refund. The entry to record the cash receipt from a GST/HST refund will be similar to the entry shown above, except that there will be a debit to Cash, instead of a credit. Quasar would report for the period of August 1 to October 31, 2017, and it would report its total sales of $400,000 in addition to GST charged and GST ITCs.

The above discussion of the remittance of GST/HST explains why all registrants need two general ledger accounts—a payable account and a recoverable account. The GST (or HST) Payable account is used to keep track of all GST or HST charged on sales and revenues. The second account, GST (or HST) Recoverable, is used to keep track of the GST/HST ITCs that have been paid on all of the business's purchases. Both amounts must be reported on the return. Failure by a business to capture the proper amounts of ITCs has a significant impact on income and on cash flows.

PST

The remittance of PST to the Minister of Finance of the applicable province is similar to that of GST/HST except that, since no credit can be claimed, the amount paid at the end of each reporting period is the amount of the balance in the PST Payable account.

Total PST collected by Quasar Company during the quarter ending October 31, 2017, is $28,000. The entry to record a remittance of PST is as follows:

A	=	L	+	OE
−28,000		−28,000		

↓ Cash flows: −28,000

Oct. 31	PST Payable	28,000	
	Cash		28,000
	To record remittance of PST.		

QST

The remittance of QST to the Minister of Revenue of Quebec is similar to that of GST/HST.

ROUNDING TAX AMOUNTS

Be careful when you record the amounts of taxes charged or claimed in the business accounts. Numbers must be rounded carefully. If the amount of the tax calculated on a credit sale is less than half a cent, the amount should be rounded down. If the amount of the tax as calculated comes to more than half a cent, the amount should be rounded up. For example, applying 13% HST on an amount of $49.20 would give you $6.396. The tax amount to be recorded must be rounded up to $6.40. On the other hand, if the sale is a cash sale, due to the abolition of the one-cent coin (the penny), the amount of the sale, including all taxes, must be rounded to the nearest five cents. Rounding might seem insignificant, but when a business has many transactions, the amounts can add up and the registrant is responsible to the government authorities for any shortfall created in error.

CONCLUSION

Sales tax law is intricate. It has added a lot of complexity to the accounting for most transactions flowing through today's businesses. Fortunately, computers that are programmed to automatically determine and record the correct sales tax rate for each good or service provided have simplified matters somewhat. Before recording sales tax transactions, however, it is important to understand all of the relevant sales tax regulations. Check the federal and provincial laws in your jurisdiction.

▶ Brief Exercises

Explain the different types of sales taxes. (LO 1) AP

BEB–1 List the various sales taxes in Canada and explain the main differences between the types. In what way are they alike to the consumer?

Record sales—perpetual inventory system—Quebec. (LO 2) AP

BEB–2 Record the sale on account, for $1,600, of merchandise costing $900 in the province of Quebec. Assume the company uses a perpetual inventory system. The QST is 9.975%. (Use QST payable for Quebec sales tax transactions.)

Record sales return—perpetual inventory system—Quebec. (LO 2) AP

BEB–3 Half of the shipment described in BEB–2 is returned because the incorrect sizes have been shipped. Record the return of merchandise on the seller's books.

Record sales and sales return—periodic inventory system—Quebec. (LO 2) AP

BEB–4 Record the sale in BEB–2 and the sales return in BEB–3 assuming the business uses a periodic inventory system.

BEB–5 Record the billing for $450 of services by D. R. Wong, dentist, in the province of British Columbia. Dental services are exempt from GST and PST.

Record exempt services— British Columbia. (LO 2) AP

BEB–6 Record the billing of accounting services of $700 for the preparation of personal income tax returns in the territory of Nunavut. GST is applicable on this service. Nunavut does not charge PST.

Record fees—Nunavut. (LO 2) AP

BEB–7 Record the purchase on account of $4,100 of merchandise for resale in the province of Manitoba, where the PST is 8%. The company uses a perpetual inventory system and the purchase is PST exempt.

Record inventory purchase— perpetual inventory system— Manitoba. (LO 3) AP

BEB–8 Record the return of $500 of the merchandise purchased in BEB-7.

Record purchase return— perpetual inventory system— Manitoba. (LO 3) AP

BEB–9 Record the purchase on account of $4,100 of merchandise for resale in the province of New Brunswick, where HST is 13%. The company uses a perpetual inventory system.

Record inventory purchase— perpetual inventory system— New Brunswick. (LO 3) AP

BEB–10 Record the return of $500 of the merchandise purchased in BEB-9.

Record purchase return— perpetual inventory system— New Brunswick. (LO 3) AP

BEB–11 Record the cash purchase of $600 of office supplies in the province of Saskatchewan, where PST is 5%.

Record purchase of supplies— Saskatchewan. (LO 3) AP

BEB–12 Record the cash purchase of $600 of office supplies in the province of Nova Scotia, where HST is 15%.

Record purchase of supplies— Nova Scotia. (LO 3) AP

BEB–13 Record the purchase on account of a $32,000 delivery truck in the province of Prince Edward Island, where HST is 14%.

Record purchase of vehicle— Prince Edward Island. (LO 3) AP

BEB–14 Record the purchase on account of a $32,000 delivery truck in the province of British Columbia, where the PST is 7%.

Record purchase of vehicle— British Columbia. (LO 3) AP

BEB–15 Record the purchase on account of $300 of office supplies and $5,000 of merchandise for resale in the province of Manitoba. The company uses a perpetual inventory system and the purchase of merchandise is PST exempt. The PST rate is 8%.

Record purchase of supplies and inventory—perpetual inventory system—Manitoba. (LO 3) AP

BEB–16 Record two payments: one cheque to the Receiver General for Canada for GST and one to the Minister of Finance of British Columbia for PST. The balances in the accounts are as follows: GST Payable $6,120, GST Recoverable $940, and PST Payable $8,570.

Record remittance of GST and PST—British Columbia. (LO 4) AP

BEB–17 Record the deposit of a cheque from the Receiver General for a refund of $690 following the filing of an HST return. The balances in the accounts are as follows: HST Payable $3,920 and HST Recoverable $4,610.

Record HST refund. (LO 4) AP

▶ Exercises

EB–1 Nebula Limited is a merchant operating in the province of Manitoba, where the PST rate is 8%. Nebula uses a perpetual inventory system. Transactions for the business are shown below:

Record purchase and sales transactions—perpetual inventory system—Manitoba. (LO 2, 3) AP

May 1   Paid May rent to the landlord for the rental of a warehouse. The lease calls for monthly payments of $7,300 plus 5% GST.

3   Sold merchandise on account and shipped merchandise to Marvin Ltd. for $25,000, plus applicable sales taxes, terms n/30, FOB shipping point. This merchandise cost Nebula $18,600.

5   Granted Marvin Ltd. a sales allowance of $800 for defective merchandise purchased on May 3. No merchandise was returned.

7   Purchased on account from Macphee Ltd. merchandise for resale for $11,000, plus applicable tax.

12   Made a cash purchase at Home Depot of a desk for the shipping clerk. The price of the desk was $600 before applicable taxes.

31   Paid the quarterly remittance of GST to the Receiver General. The balances in the accounts were as follows: GST Payable $7,480 and GST Recoverable $1,917.

Instructions

Prepare the journal entries to record these transactions on the books of Nebula Limited.

<table>
<tr><td>

Record purchase and sales transactions—perpetual inventory system—Alberta. (LO 2, 3) AP

</td><td>

EB-2 Refer to Nebula Limited in EB–1. Assume instead that the company operates in the province of Alberta, where PST is not applicable.

Instructions

Prepare the journal entries to record these transactions on the books of Nebula.

</td></tr>
<tr><td>

Record purchase and sales transactions—perpetual inventory system—Ontario. (LO 2, 3) AP

</td><td>

EB-3 Refer to Nebula Limited in EB–1. Assume instead that the company operates in the province of Ontario, where HST is 13%.

Instructions

Prepare the journal entries to record these transactions on the books of Nebula. Assume that the GST balances on May 31 are the balances in the HST accounts.

</td></tr>
</table>

EB-4 Triton Company is a retailer operating in the province of Manitoba, where the PST rate is 8%. Triton uses a periodic inventory system. Transactions for the business are shown below:

Record purchase and sales transactions—periodic inventory system—Manitoba. (LO 2, 3) AP

Nov. 1 Paid November store rent to the landlord. The lease calls for monthly payments of $5,500 plus 5% GST.
4 Purchased merchandise for resale on account from Comet Industries. The merchandise cost $8,000 plus applicable tax.
6 Returned $500 of merchandise to Comet Industries.
7 Sold merchandise on account to Solar Star Company for $10,000 plus applicable sales taxes, terms, n/30, FOB shipping point. The merchandise was shipped to Solar Star. The cost of the merchandise to Triton was $6,000.
12 Purchased a new laptop computer at Staples for the marketing manager. The price of the laptop was $1,200 before applicable taxes.
30 Paid the quarterly remittance of GST to the Receiver General. The balances in the accounts were as follows: GST Payable $2,520 and GST Recoverable $985.

Instructions

Prepare the journal entries to record these transactions on the books of Triton Company.

Record purchase and sales transactions—periodic inventory system—Alberta. (LO 2, 3) AP

EB-5 Using the information for the transactions of Triton Company in EB–4, assume now that Triton operates in the province of Alberta, where PST is not applicable.

Instructions

Prepare the journal entries to record these transactions on the books of Triton.

Record purchase and sales transactions—periodic inventory system—Ontario. (LO 2, 3) AP

EB-6 Using the information for the transactions of Triton Company in EB–4, assume now that Triton operates in the province of Ontario, where HST is 13%.

Instructions

Prepare the journal entries to record these transactions on the books of Triton. Assume that the GST balances on May 31 provided in EB–4 are the balances in the HST accounts.

Record transactions for services, equipment, and supplies—British Columbia. (LO 2, 3, 4) AP

EB-7 Leon Cheng is a sole proprietor providing accounting services in the province of British Columbia, where PST is charged at the rate of 7% and GST is at the rate of 5%. Transactions for the business are shown below:

June 1 Paid cash to a local courier for the delivery of documents to several clients. The invoice was for $200 plus GST and PST.
5 Paid $800 cash plus GST and PST to have the office painted. Use the Repairs Expense account.
10 Purchased photocopy paper for $250 from a local stationery store, on account. The store added the appropriate sales taxes to the purchase price.
13 Billed a client for accounting services provided. The fee charged was $4,700 and the appropriate sales taxes were added to the fee billed.
15 Collected $896 on account. This included accounting services of $800, GST of $40, and PST of $56.
22 Paid $720 cash plus applicable taxes to Air Canada for an airline ticket to Ottawa to meet with a client. Airfare is subject to both PST and GST.
30 Received invoice from BC Tel for telephone service for the month of June. The invoice is for $150 plus GST and PST.
30 Paid the quarterly remittance of GST to the Receiver General. The balances in the accounts were as follows: GST Payable $1,890.50 and GST Recoverable $741.60.
30 Paid the quarterly remittance of PST to the Minister of Revenue for the province of British Columbia. The balance in the PST Payable account was $2,640.00.

Instructions

Prepare the journal entries to record these transactions on the books of Leon Cheng's accounting business.

EB-8 Ruby Gordon, L.L.B. is a sole proprietor providing legal services in the province of Newfoundland and Labrador, where the HST rate is 15%. Transactions for the business are shown below:

Record transactions for services, equipment, and supplies—Newfoundland and Labrador. (LO 2, 3, 4) AP

June 8   Purchased equipment for scanning and printing on account at a cost of $1,500. The appropriate taxes were added to this purchase price.

     10   Purchased toner for the equipment for $100 cash from a local stationery store. The store added the appropriate taxes to the purchase price.

     12   Billed Lee Ltd. for legal services provided. The fee charged was $1,250 plus appropriate taxes.

     18   Paid cash of $220 plus applicable taxes to have a boardroom table repaired.

     22   Collected the Lee Ltd. account billed on June 12.

     30   Paid the quarterly remittance of HST to the Receiver General. The balances in the accounts were as follows: HST Payable $2,520.60 and HST Recoverable $820.45.

Instructions

Prepare the journal entries to record these transactions on the books of Ruby Gordon's legal practice.

EB-9 Refer to the data for Ruby Gordon, L.L.B. in EB-8. Assume instead that Ruby is operating her legal practice in Alberta and that on June 30 she paid a quarterly remittance of GST, as opposed to HST, to the Receiver General. Assume the balances were as follows: GST Payable $970.50 and GST Recoverable $315.55.

Record transactions for services, equipment, and supplies—Alberta. (LO 2, 3, 4) AP

Instructions

Prepare the journal entries to record these transactions on the books of Ruby Gordon's legal practice.

▶ Problems

PB-1 Mark's Music is a store that buys and sells musical instruments in Ontario, where the HST rate is 13%. Mark's Music uses a perpetual inventory system. Transactions for the business are shown below:

Record purchase and sales transactions—perpetual inventory system—Ontario. (LO 2, 3) AP

Nov. 2   Purchased three electric guitars from Fender Supply Limited, on account, at a cost of $900 each.

     4   Made a cash sale of two keyboards for a total invoice price of $2,600 plus applicable taxes. The cost of each keyboard was $675.

     5   Received a credit memorandum from Western Acoustic Inc. for the return of an acoustic guitar that was defective. The original invoice price before taxes was $700 and the guitar had been purchased on account. Mark's Music intends to return the defective guitar to the original supplier.

     7   One of the keyboards from the cash sale of November 4 was returned to the store for a full cash refund because the customer was not satisfied with the instrument. The keyboard was returned to inventory.

     8   Purchased supplies from a stationery store. The price of the supplies is $200 before all applicable taxes.

     10   Sold one Omega trumpet to Regional Band, on account, for an invoice price of $5,100 before applicable taxes. The trumpet had cost Mark's Music $2,850.

     13   Purchased two saxophones from Yamaha Canada Inc. on account. The invoice price was $1,900 for each saxophone, excluding applicable taxes.

     14   Collected $4,150 on account. The payment included all applicable taxes.

     16   Returned to Yamaha Canada Inc. one of the saxophones purchased on November 13, as it was the wrong model. Received a credit memorandum from Yamaha for the full purchase price.

     20   Made a payment on account for the amount owing to Fender Supply Limited for the purchase of November 2.

Instructions

Prepare the journal entries to record the Mark's Music transactions.

PB-2 Transaction data for Mark's Music are available in PB-1. Assume instead that the company operates in the province of British Columbia, where the PST rate is 7% and the GST rate is 5%.

Record purchase and sales transactions—perpetual inventory system—British Columbia. (LO 2, 3) AP

Instructions

Prepare the journal entries to record these transactions on the books of Mark's Music.

PB-3 Transaction data for Mark's Music are available in PB-1. Assume that the company uses a periodic inventory system instead of a perpetual inventory system and operates in the province of Ontario, where the HST rate is 13%.

Record purchase and sales transactions—periodic inventory system—Ontario. (LO 2, 3) AP

Instructions

Prepare the journal entries to record the Mark's Music transactions.

Record purchase and sales transactions—periodic inventory system—British Columbia. (LO 2, 3) AP

PB–4 Transaction data for Mark's Music are available in PB–1. Assume that the company uses a periodic inventory system instead of a perpetual inventory system and operates in the province of British Columbia, where the PST rate is 7% and the GST rate is 5%.

Instructions

Prepare the journal entries to record these transactions on the books of Mark's Music.

Record service transactions—Alberta. (LO 2, 3, 4) AP

PB–5 Manny Lee, L.L.B., is a lawyer operating as a sole proprietor in the province of Alberta. Alberta does not charge provincial sales taxes and the GST rate is 5%. Transactions for the business are shown below:

May 1 Signed a two-year lease for the office space and immediately paid the first and last months' rent. The lease calls for monthly rent of $1,650 plus applicable taxes.

4 Purchased furniture, on account, from George's Furniture at a cost of $4,100. The appropriate sales taxes were added to this purchase price.

5 Returned one chair to George's due to a defect. The cost of the chair before taxes was $800.

6 Billed a client for the preparation of a contract. The client was very pleased with the document and immediately paid Manny's invoice for fees of $2,500 plus taxes.

10 Purchased paper for the photocopier for $300 cash from a local stationery store. The store added the appropriate sales taxes to the purchase price.

13 Billed Manson Ltd. for legal services rendered connected with the purchase of land. The fee charged is $1,100 plus applicable taxes.

18 Paid George's for the furniture purchase of May 4, net of returned items.

19 Paid $22 cash to a local grocery store for coffee beans for the office coffee machine. Coffee beans are zero-rated grocery products for GST and HST purposes. Use the Office Expense account.

21 In accordance with the lease agreement with the landlord, Manny must pay for water supplied by the municipality. The water invoice was received and the services amounted to $150. No GST is charged for municipal water.

25 Collected a full payment from Manson Ltd. for the May 13 bill.

27 Completed the preparation of a purchase and sale agreement for Pedneault Inc. and billed fees of $600.

Instructions

(a) Prepare the journal entries to record these transactions on the books of Manny Lee's law practice.

(b) Determine the balances in the GST Payable and GST Recoverable accounts. Determine if the company must make a payment to the Receiver General or if it will apply for a refund. Record the appropriate journal entry.

Record service transactions—Ontario. (LO 2, 3, 4) AP

PB–6 Refer to Manny Lee's law practice in PB–5. Assume instead that Mr. Lee operates in the province of Ontario, where the HST rate is 13%.

Instructions

(a) Prepare the journal entries to record these transactions on the books of Manny Lee's law practice.

(b) Determine the balances in the HST Payable and HST Recoverable accounts. Determine if the business must make a payment to the Receiver General or if it will apply for a refund. Record the appropriate journal entry.

PRESENT VALUE CONCEPTS

Present value concepts are widely used by accountants when preparing financial statements. Under IFRS, these concepts are more widely applied than under ASPE. This appendix will explain the basics that you must be aware of to understand related topics in this text.

Simple and Compound Interest

Interest is payment for the use of money. It is the difference between the amount borrowed or invested (the principal) and the amount repaid or collected. The amount of interest to be paid or collected is usually stated as a percentage rate over a specific period of time. The rate of interest is generally stated as an annual rate.

The amount of interest involved in any financing transaction is based on three elements:

1. **Principal**: The original amount borrowed or invested
2. **Interest rate**: An annual percentage of the principal
3. **Time**: The number of periods that the principal is borrowed or invested

When calculating interest, it is important to know when and how to use simple or compound interest.

SIMPLE INTEREST

Simple interest is calculated on the principal amount only. It is the return on the principal for one period.

Simple interest is usually expressed as shown in Illustration PV-1.

| Interest | = | Principal (p) | × | Interest Rate (r) | × | Time (t) |

▶ ILLUSTRATION
Simple interest formula

For example, if you borrowed $1,000 for three years at a simple interest rate of 9% annually, you would pay $270 in total interest, calculated as follows:

$$\text{Interest} = p \times r \times t$$
$$= \$1,000 \times 9\% \times 3$$
$$= \$270$$

	Year 1		Year 2		Year 3		
	$90	+	$90	+	$90	=	$270

COMPOUND INTEREST

Compound interest is calculated on principal *and* on any interest earned that has not been paid or withdrawn. It is the return on (or growth of) the principal for two or more time periods. Compounding calculates interest not only on the principal but also on the interest earned to date on that principal, assuming the interest is left on deposit (that is, it is added to the original principal amount).

To illustrate the difference between simple and compound interest, assume that you deposit $1,000 in Last Canadian Bank, where it will earn simple interest of 9% per year, and you deposit another $1,000 in First Canadian Bank, where it will earn interest of 9% per year compounded annually. Also assume that in both cases you will not withdraw any interest until three years from the date of deposit. The calculations of interest to be received and the accumulated year-end balances are given in Illustration PV-2.

▶ **ILLUSTRATION** **PV-2**
Simple versus compound interest

LAST CANADIAN BANK				FIRST CANADIAN BANK		
Simple Interest Calculation	Simple Interest	Accumulated Year-End Balance		Compound Interest Calculation	Compound Interest	Accumulated Year-End Balance
Year 1 $1,000.00 × 9%	$ 90.00	$1,090.00		Year 1 $1,000.00 × 9%	$ 90.00	$1,090.00
Year 2 $1,000.00 × 9%	90.00	$1,180.00		Year 2 $1,090.00 × 9%	98.10	$1,188.10
Year 3 $1,000.00 × 9%	90.00 $270.00	$1,270.00		Year 3 $1,188.10 × 9%	106.93 $295.03	$1,295.03

$25.03 Difference

Note in Illustration PV-2 that simple interest uses the initial principal of $1,000 to calculate the interest in all three years. Compound interest uses the accumulated balance (principal plus interest to date) at each year end to calculate interest in the following year. This explains why your compound interest account is larger: you are earning interest on interest. For practical purposes, compounding assumes that unpaid interest earned becomes a part of the principal. The accumulated balance at the end of each year becomes the new principal on which interest is earned during the next year. Assuming all else is equal (especially risk), if you had a choice between investing your money at simple interest or at compound interest, you would choose compound interest. In the example, compounding provides $25.03 of additional interest income.

When borrowing or lending money, the lending agreement should always state whether interest will be calculated using the simple or compound method. If the compound method is used, the frequency of compounding must also be stated. The shorter the amount of time between compounding calculations (that is, the more frequent the compounding), the more interest will be earned.

Compound interest is used in most business transactions. Simple interest is generally applicable only to short-term situations of one year or less.

Action Plan
- Recall the formula for simple interest.
- Understand that compound interest means that interest is calculated on the principal plus any interest earned that has not been paid or withdrawn.
- Understand that the amount of simple interest will be different than the amount of interest calculated using compound interest.

BEFORE YOU GO ON...DO IT **1** ▶ **Calculate Simple and Compound Interest**

Shoto Company has borrowed $10,000 to complete some renovations to its office. The loan agreement indicates that the loan must be repaid in two years, with interest of 6%.

(a) Calculate the amount of simple interest Shoto will have to pay.
(b) Calculate the amount of compound interest Shoto will have to pay assuming annual compounding.
(c) Based on your answers to parts (a) and (b), is there a difference in the amount of interest Shoto would have to pay? If so, what is the difference?

Solution

(a) Simple interest
Interest = $10,000 × 0.06 × 2
= $1,200

(b) Compound interest

Compound interest calculation	Compound interest	Accumulated year-end balance
Year 1 Interest $10,000 × 0.06 × 1	$600	$10,600
Year 2 Interest $10,600 × 0.06 × 1	$636	$11,236
Total interest paid $1,236 ($600 + $636)		

(c) If the loan agreement specifies simple interest, Shoto will pay $1,200 in interest, but if the agreement specifies compound interest, Shoto will pay $1,236, a difference of $36.

Related exercise material: BEPV–1.

LEARNING OBJECTIVE **2** Calculate the present value of a single amount.

Present Value of a Single Amount

In the previous section on simple and compound interest, the initial principal was given. It was used to calculate the interest earned and the value of the investment at the end of three years. **The initial principal, invested at the beginning of year one, is the present value (PV) of the investment. The value of the investment at the end of three years is the future value (FV) of the investment.** In this section, we will discuss how to determine the present value of future cash flows.

PRESENT VALUE VARIABLES

The present value is the value today of a given amount to be paid or received in the future, assuming compound interest. The present value is based on three variables:

1. The *dollar amount* to be received (the future amount or future value)
2. The *length of time* until the amount is received (the number of periods)
3. The *interest rate* (the discount rate) per period

Present value calculations are used in measuring many items. For example, the present value of principal and interest payments is used to determine the market price of a bond. Determining the amount to be reported for long-lived assets, notes payable, and lease liabilities may also involve present value calculations.

Alternative terminology The discount rate is also referred to as the *effective rate* or the *imputed rate.*

The process of determining the present value is often referred to as **discounting the future cash flows**. The word "discount" has many meanings in accounting, each of which varies with the context in which it is being used. Be careful not to confuse the use of this term.

In the following section, we will show four methods of calculating the present value of a single future amount: present value formula, present value tables, financial calculators, and computer spreadsheets (specifically Excel).

Present Value Formula

To illustrate present value concepts, assume that you want to invest a sum of money today that will provide $1,000 at the end of one year. Assuming that the interest rate is 5%, what amount would you need to invest today to have $1,000 one year from now? The formula used to determine the present value of a single future amount is shown in Illustration PV-3.

$$\text{Present Value } (PV) = \text{Future Value } (FV) \div (1 + i)^n$$

▶ ILLUSTRATION **PV-3**
Present value of a single future amount formula

Where PV = present value
   FV = future value
   i = interest
   n = number of periods (this is similar to t in a simple interest calculation)

In applying this formula to calculate the present value (PV) for the above example, the future value (FV) of $1,000, the interest (discount) rate (i) of 5%, and the number of periods (n) of 1 are used as follows:

$$PV = \$1,000 \div (1 + 0.05)^1$$
$$= \$1,000 \div 1.05$$
$$= \$952.38$$

The variables in this situation are shown in the time diagram in Illustration PV-4.

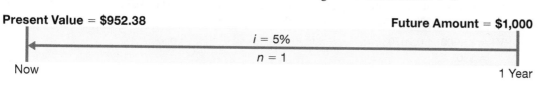

Present Value = $952.38   **Future Amount = $1,000**

$i = 5\%$

$n = 1$

Now   1 Year

▶ ILLUSTRATION **PV-4**
Time diagram for the present value of $1,000 discounted for one period at 5%

If the single future cash flow of $1,000 is to be received in *two years* and the interest (discount) rate is 5%, its present value is calculated as follows:

$$PV = \$1,000 \div (1 + 0.05)^2$$
$$= \$1,000 \div 1.1025$$
$$= \$907.03$$

The time diagram in Illustration PV-5 shows the variables used to calculate the present value when cash is received in two years.

▶ILLUSTRATION **PV-5**
Time diagram for present value of $1,000 discounted for two periods at 5%

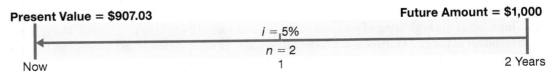

Present Value = $907.03 .... Future Amount = $1,000

$i = 5\%$

$n = 2$

Now .... 1 .... 2 Years

Present Value Tables

The present value may also be determined through tables that show the present value of 1 for *n* periods for different periodic interest rates or discount rates. In Table PV-1, the rows represent the number of discounting periods and the columns represent the periodic interest or discount rates. The five-digit decimal numbers in the respective rows and columns are the factors for the present value of 1.

TABLE PV-1
PRESENT VALUE OF 1
$$PV = \frac{1}{(1 + i)^n}$$

(n) Periods	1.5%	2%	2.5%	3%	3.5%	4%	5%	6%	7%	8%	9%	10%
1	0.98522	0.98039	0.97561	0.97087	0.96618	0.96154	0.95238	0.94340	0.93458	0.92593	0.91743	0.90909
2	0.97066	0.96117	0.95181	0.94260	0.93351	0.92456	0.90703	0.89000	0.87344	0.85734	0.84168	0.82645
3	0.95632	0.94232	0.92860	0.91514	0.90194	0.88900	0.86384	0.83962	0.81630	0.79383	0.77218	0.75131
4	0.94218	0.92385	0.90595	0.88849	0.87144	0.85480	0.82270	0.79209	0.76290	0.73503	0.70843	0.68301
5	0.92826	0.90573	0.88385	0.86261	0.84197	0.82193	0.78353	0.74726	0.71299	0.68058	0.64993	0.62092
6	0.91454	0.88797	0.86230	0.83748	0.81350	0.79031	0.74622	0.70496	0.66634	0.63017	0.59627	0.56447
7	0.90103	0.87056	0.84127	0.81309	0.78599	0.75992	0.71068	0.66506	0.62275	0.58349	0.54703	0.51316
8	0.88771	0.85349	0.82075	0.78941	0.75941	0.73069	0.67684	0.62741	0.58201	0.54027	0.50187	0.46651
9	0.87459	0.83676	0.80073	0.76642	0.73373	0.70259	0.64461	0.59190	0.54393	0.50025	0.46043	0.42410
10	0.86167	0.82035	0.78120	0.74409	0.70892	0.67556	0.61391	0.55839	0.50835	0.46319	0.42241	0.38554
11	0.84893	0.80426	0.76214	0.72242	0.68495	0.64958	0.58468	0.52679	0.47509	0.42888	0.38753	0.35049
12	0.83639	0.78849	0.74356	0.70138	0.66178	0.62460	0.55684	0.49697	0.44401	0.39711	0.35553	0.31863
13	0.82403	0.77303	0.72542	0.68095	0.63940	0.60057	0.53032	0.46884	0.41496	0.36770	0.32618	0.28966
14	0.81185	0.75788	0.70773	0.66112	0.61778	0.57748	0.50507	0.44230	0.38782	0.34046	0.29925	0.26333
15	0.79985	0.74301	0.69047	0.64186	0.59689	0.55526	0.48102	0.41727	0.36245	0.31524	0.27454	0.23939
16	0.78803	0.72845	0.67362	0.62317	0.57671	0.53391	0.45811	0.39365	0.33873	0.29189	0.25187	0.21763
17	0.77639	0.71416	0.65720	0.60502	0.55720	0.51337	0.43630	0.37136	0.31657	0.27027	0.23107	0.19784
18	0.76491	0.70016	0.64117	0.58739	0.53836	0.49363	0.41552	0.35034	0.29586	0.25025	0.21199	0.17986
19	0.75361	0.68643	0.62553	0.57029	0.52016	0.47464	0.39573	0.33051	0.27651	0.23171	0.19449	0.16351
20	0.74247	0.67297	0.61027	0.55368	0.50257	0.45639	0.37689	0.31180	0.25842	0.21455	0.17843	0.14864

When present value tables are used, the present value is calculated by multiplying the future cash amount by the present value factor specified at the intersection of the number of periods and the discount rate.

For example, if the discount rate is 5% and the number of periods is 1, Table PV-1 shows that the present value factor is 0.95238. Then the present value of $1,000 discounted at 5% for one period is calculated as follows:

$$PV = \$1,000 \times 0.95238$$
$$= \$952.38$$

For two periods at a discount rate of 5%, the present value factor is 0.90703. The present value of $1,000 discounted at 5% for two periods is calculated as follows:

$$PV = \$1,000 \times 0.90703$$
$$= \$907.03$$

Note that the present values in these two examples are identical to the amounts determined previously when using the present value formula. This is because the factors in a present value table have been calculated using the present value formula. The benefit of using a present value table is that it can be quicker than using the formula.

Table PV-1 can also be used if you know the present value and wish to determine the future cash flow. The present value amount is divided by the present value factor specified at the intersection of the number of periods and the discount rate in Table PV-1. For example, it can easily be determined that an initial investment of $907.03 will grow to yield a future amount of $1,000 in two periods, at an annual discount rate of 5% ($1,000 = $907.03 ÷ 0.90703).

Financial Calculators

Present values can also be calculated using financial calculators. Financial calculators have five distinctive keys on the numeric pad, usually in a row and in a different colour than other keys on the pad. The five keys correspond to the five possible variables that could be used in a present value calculation, as shown in Illustration PV-6.

▶ ILLUSTRATION **PV-6**
Financial calculator keys

Where:
    I/Y   = interest rate per period (some calculators use I/YR or i)
    N   = number of periods
    PV   = present value (occurs at the beginning of the first period)
    PMT = payment (an annuity, all payments are equal, and none are skipped)
    FV   = future value (occurs at the end of the last period)

To calculate the present value, **enter each of the other variable amounts and then press the corresponding key for that variable amount**. If an amount represents an outflow of cash, a negative value for the amount must be entered. Once the four known variables are entered, in any order, press the CPT (compute or equivalent key) and the PV variable key and the answer will appear on screen. When calculating the present value of a single future amount, enter zero for the annuity payment amount, followed by the PMT key. We will learn about annuity payments in the next section of the appendix.

Helpful hint Always begin by clearing the calculator.

For example, if you are calculating the present value of a single future cash flow of $1,000 to be received in two years and discounted at 5%, you would enter the data into the financial calculator as follows:

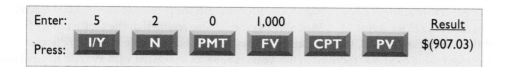

Note that the result is the same as with the present value formula and tables except the calculator shows $907.03 as a negative number. The reason the present value is a negative number is to demonstrate that an outflow (negative) of cash today of $907.03 will provide a future inflow (positive) of cash of $1,000.00 in two years using an annual interest rate of 5%.

Helpful hint The interest rate is entered as a whole number, not as a percentage. In this example, the 5% interest rate is entered as "5" and not ".05" or "5%".

The present value amounts calculated with a financial calculator can be slightly different than those calculated with present value tables. That is because the numbers in a present value table are rounded. For example, in Table PV-1 the factors are rounded to five digits. In a financial calculator, only the final answer is rounded to the number of digits you have specified in the viewing screen.

Computer Spreadsheets

Present value calculations can also be prepared very easily using a computer spreadsheet. For example, in Excel, use the insert function (fx) icon (commonly found at the top of the screen or near the cell content bar). Click on this icon and a pop-up screen will appear, allowing you to select a function. Select the category Financial then select the PV function. Another pop-up box will appear, allowing you to enter the necessary information. The terms are very similar to a financial calculator. A comparison is shown in the table below.

Present Value Variable	Excel Variable	Financial Calculator Key
Present value	PV	PV
Interest rate (or discount rate)	RATE	I/Y
Number of periods	NPER	N
Annuity payment amount	PMT	PMT
Future value	FV	FV

Excel will also ask for the type of annuity. For all of the calculations in this textbook, you should enter "0," which indicates that the payment is at the end of the period. You will learn about annuities with payments at the beginning of the period in other courses.

One difference between Excel and financial calculators is how the interest rate is entered. With Excel, a 5% interest rate is entered as either .05 or 5%. Similar to financial calculators, cash outflows should be entered as negative numbers. The PV formula can also be typed directly into a cell as follows: = PV(rate,nper,pmt,fv,type).

Continuing with the example shown previously, the following data should be used in the = PV(rate,nper,pmt,fv,type) formula in Excel:

RATE	.05
NPER	2
PMT	$0.00
FV	$1,000.00
Type	0

The result is a PV of $(907.03), which is the same as the result obtained using the financial calculator.

Summary of Methods

A major benefit of using a financial calculator or a spreadsheet is that you are not restricted to the interest rates or numbers of periods on a present value table. In Table PV-1, present value factors have been calculated for 12 interest rates and the maximum number of periods is 20. With a financial calculator, you could, for example, calculate the present value of a future amount to be received in 25 periods using any discount rate, such as 5.75%, which is not in the present value table.

Regardless of the method used in calculating present values, **a higher discount rate produces a smaller present value**. For example, using an 8% discount rate, the present value of $1,000 received one year from now is $925.93 versus $952.38 at 5%. You should also realize that **the further away from the present the future cash flow is, the smaller the present value**. For example, using the discount rate of 5%, the present value of $1,000 received in five years is $783.53 compared with $952.38 in one year.

BEFORE YOU GO ON...DO IT **Calculate the present value of a single amount**

Suppose you have a winning lottery ticket and the lottery commission gives you the option of taking $10,000 three years from now, or taking the present value of $10,000 now. If an 8% discount rate is used, what is the present value of your winnings of $10,000 three years from now? Show the calculation using one of (a) the present value formula, (b) Table PV-1, (c) a financial calculator, or (d) Excel functions.

(continued)

BEFORE YOU GO ON...DO IT (continued)

PV (?)   **$10,000**

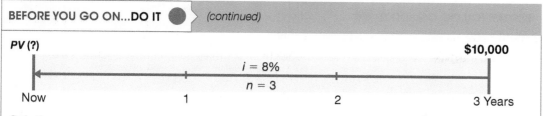

Now   1   2   3 Years

$i = 8\%$
$n = 3$

Solution

(a) Using the present value formula:

$$PV = \$10,000 \div (1 + 0.08)^3$$
$$= \$10,000 \div 1.259712$$
$$= \$7,938.32$$

(b) Using the present value factor from Table PV-1:
The present value factor for three periods at 8% is 0.79383

$$PV = \$10,000 \times 0.79383$$
$$= \$7,938.30$$

(c) Using a financial calculator:

Enter:	8	3	0	10,000			Result
Press:	I/Y	N	PMT	FV	CPT	PV	$(7,938.32)

(d) Using the Excel PV function, the data used in the = PV(rate,nper,pmt,fv,type) formula are:

RATE	.08
NPER	3
PMT	$0.00
FV	$10,000.00
Type	0

$$PV = \$(7,938.32)$$

Do It Again

Determine the amount you must deposit now in your savings account, paying 3% interest, in order to accumulate $5,000 for a down payment on a hybrid electric car four years from now, when you graduate. Show the calculation using one of (a) present value formula, (b) Table PV-1, (c) financial calculator, or (d) Excel functions.

PV (?)   **$5,000**

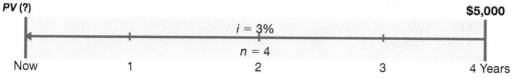

Now   1   2   3   4 Years

$i = 3\%$
$n = 4$

Solution

The amount you must deposit now in your savings account is the present value calculated as follows:

(a) Using the present value formula:

$$PV = \$5,000 \div (1 + 0.03)^4$$
$$= \$5,000 \div 1.125509$$
$$= \$4,442.43$$

(b) Using the present value factor from Table PV-1:
The present value factor for four periods at 3% is 0.88849.

$$PV = \$5,000 \times 0.88849$$
$$PV = \$4,442.45$$

(c) Using a financial calculator:

Enter:	3	4	0	5,000			Result
Press:	I/Y	N	PMT	FV	CPT	PV	$(4,442.44)

(continued)

Action Plan

- Note that $10,000 is the future value, the number of periods is three, and the discount rate is 8%.
- Recall that the present value of $10,000 to be received in three years is less than $10,000 because interest can be earned on an amount invested today (that is, the present value) over the next three years.
- Understand that the discount rate used to calculate the present value is the interest rate that would be used to earn $10,000 in three years if the present value is invested today.
- Remember that the answer obtained from the different methods will be slightly different due to rounding of the PV factors.
- Draw a time diagram showing when the future value will be received, the discount rate, and the number of periods.
- Note that $5,000 is the future value, $n = 4$, and $i = 3\%$.

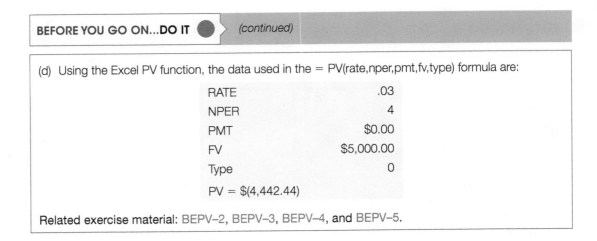

BEFORE YOU GO ON...DO IT (continued)

(d) Using the Excel PV function, the data used in the = PV(rate,nper,pmt,fv,type) formula are:

RATE	.03
NPER	4
PMT	$0.00
FV	$5,000.00
Type	0
PV = $(4,442.44)	

Related exercise material: BEPV–2, BEPV–3, BEPV–4, and BEPV–5.

LEARNING OBJECTIVE 3 Calculate the present value of an annuity.

Present Value of a Series of Future Cash Flows (Annuities)

The preceding discussion was for the discounting of only a single future amount. Businesses and individuals frequently engage in transactions in which a series of equal dollar amounts are to be received or paid periodically. Examples of a series of periodic receipts or payments are loan agreements, instalment sales, mortgage notes, lease (rental) contracts, and pension obligations. These series of periodic receipts or payments are called **annuities**. The **present value of an annuity** is the value today of a series of future receipts or payments, discounted assuming compound interest. In calculating the present value of an annuity, it is necessary to know (1) the discount rate (i), (2) the number of receipts or payments (n), and (3) the amount of the periodic receipts or payments (PMT).

CALCULATING THE PRESENT VALUE OF AN ANNUITY

To illustrate the calculation of the present value of an annuity, assume that you will receive $1,000 cash annually for three years, and that the discount rate is 4%. This situation is shown in the time diagram in Illustration PV-7.

▶ILLUSTRATION
Time diagram for a three-year annuity

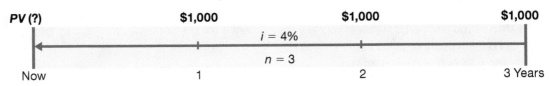

One method of calculating the present value of this annuity is to use the present value formula to determine the present value of each of the three $1,000 payments and then add those amounts as follows:

$$PV = [\$1,000 \div (1 + 0.04)^1] + [\$1,000 \div (1 + 0.04)^2] + [\$1,000 \div (1 + 0.04)^3]$$
$$= \$961.54 + \$924.56 + \$889.00$$
$$= \$2,775.10$$

The same result is achieved by using present value factors from Table PV-1, as shown in Illustration PV-8.

Future Value	×	Present Value of 1 Factor at 4%	=	Present value
$1,000 (one year away)		0.96154		$ 961.54
1,000 (two years away)		0.92456		924.56
1,000 (three years away)		0.88900		889.00
		2.77510		$2,775.10

▶ILLUSTRATION **PV-8**
Present value of a series of cash flows

Determining the present value of each single future cash flow, and then adding the present values, is required when the periodic cash flows are not the same in each period. But when the future receipts are the same in each period, there are other ways to calculate present value.

Present Value of an Annuity Formula

One way to calculate the present value of a series of equal periodic payments received at equal intervals is to use the present value of an ordinary annuity formula, as shown in Illustration PV-9.

$$PV = PMT\left(\frac{1 - (1 + i)^{-n}}{i}\right)$$

▶ILLUSTRATION **PV-9**
Present value of an ordinary annuity of 1 formula

In applying this formula to calculate the present value (PV) for the above example, the payment (PMT) of $1,000, the interest (discount) rate (i) of 4%, and the number of periods (n) of 3 are used as follows:

PV = $1,000 $[(1 - ((1 + 0.04)^{-3}) \div 0.04]$
= $1,000 × 2.775091$
= $2,775.09

Present Value Tables

The second way to calculate the present value of a series of equal periodic payments is to use a present value of an annuity table. Table PV-2 shows the present value of 1 to be received periodically for a given number of periods at different discount rates. You can see in Table PV-2 that the present value

TABLE PV-2
PRESENT VALUE OF AN ANNUITY OF 1

$$PV = PMT\left(\frac{1 - (1 + i)^{-n}}{i}\right)$$

(n) Periods	1.5%	2%	2.5%	3%	3.5%	4%	5%	6%	7%	8%	9%	10%
1	0.98522	0.98039	0.97561	0.97087	0.96618	0.96154	0.95238	0.94340	0.93458	0.92593	0.91743	0.90909
2	1.95588	1.94156	1.92742	1.91347	1.89969	1.88609	1.85941	1.83339	1.80802	1.78326	1.75911	1.73554
3	2.91220	2.88388	2.85602	2.82861	2.80164	2.77509	2.72325	2.67301	2.62432	2.57710	2.53129	2.48685
4	3.85438	3.80773	3.76197	3.71710	3.67308	3.62990	3.54595	3.46511	3.38721	3.31213	3.23972	3.16987
5	4.78264	4.71346	4.64583	4.57971	4.51505	4.45182	4.32948	4.21236	4.10020	3.99271	3.88965	3.79079
6	5.69719	5.60143	5.50813	5.41719	5.32855	5.24214	5.07569	4.91732	4.76654	4.62288	4.48592	4.35526
7	6.59821	6.47199	6.34939	6.23028	6.11454	6.00205	5.78637	5.58238	5.38929	5.20637	5.03295	4.86842
8	7.48593	7.32548	7.17014	7.01969	6.87396	6.73274	6.46321	6.20979	5.97130	5.74664	5.53482	5.33493
9	8.36052	8.16224	7.97087	7.78611	7.60769	7.43533	7.10782	6.80169	6.51523	6.24689	5.99525	5.75902
10	9.22218	8.98259	8.75206	8.53020	8.31661	8.11090	7.72173	7.36009	7.02358	6.71008	6.41766	6.14457
11	10.07112	9.78685	9.51421	9.25262	9.00155	8.76048	8.30641	7.88687	7.49867	7.13896	6.80519	6.49506
12	10.90751	10.57534	10.25776	9.95400	9.66333	9.38507	8.86325	8.38384	7.94269	7.53608	7.16073	6.81369
13	11.73153	11.34837	10.98318	10.63496	10.30274	9.98565	9.39357	8.85268	8.35765	7.90378	7.48690	7.10336
14	12.54338	12.10625	11.69091	11.29607	10.92052	10.56312	9.89864	9.29498	8.74547	8.24424	7.78615	7.36669
15	13.34323	12.84926	12.38138	11.93794	11.51741	11.11839	10.37966	9.71225	9.10791	8.55948	8.06069	7.60608
16	14.13126	13.57771	13.05500	12.56110	12.09412	11.65230	10.83777	10.10590	9.44665	8.85137	8.31256	7.82371
17	14.90765	14.29187	13.71220	13.16612	12.65132	12.16567	11.27407	10.47726	9.76322	9.12164	8.54363	8.02155
18	15.67256	14.99203	14.35336	13.75351	13.18968	12.65930	11.68959	10.82760	10.05909	9.37189	8.75563	8.20141
19	16.42617	15.67846	14.97889	14.32380	13.70984	13.13394	12.08532	11.15812	10.33560	9.60360	8.95011	8.36492
20	17.16864	16.35143	15.58916	14.87747	14.21240	13.59033	12.46221	11.46992	10.59401	9.81815	9.12855	8.51356

factor of an annuity of 1 for three periods at 4% is 2.77509. This present value factor is the total of the three individual present value factors, as shown in Illustration PV-8. (The difference of 0.00001 between 2.77509 and 2.77510 is due to rounding.) Applying this present value factor to the annual cash flow of $1,000 produces a present value of $2,775.09 ($1,000 × 2.77509).

Financial Calculators

The third method of calculating the present value of a series of periodic payments is to use a financial calculator and input the variables as follows:

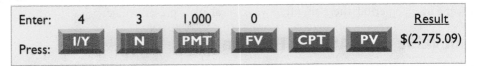

When using a financial calculator to calculate the present value of an annuity, you must also specify if the annual cash flow is at the end of each period or the beginning. In **an ordinary annuity, the payments are at the end of each period**, as in our example. In **an annuity due, the first payment starts immediately, at the beginning of the first period**. In this appendix and textbook, all of the annuity examples are ordinary annuities with the payments at the end of each period. Generally this is also the default setting on new calculators. But you should learn how to set your calculator for the two types of annuities. This will be slightly different for different calculators so you may need to check your calculator's user manual to learn how to switch between the two types of annuities.

Computer Spreadsheets

Using the Excel PV function, the data used in the = PV(rate,nper,pmt,fv,type) formula and the result for this example are:

RATE	.04
NPER	3
PMT	$1,000.00
FV	$0.00
Type	0

The result is a PV of $(2,775.09).

INTEREST RATES AND TIME PERIODS

In the preceding calculations, the discounting has been done on an annual basis using an annual interest rate. There are situations where adjustments may be required to the interest rate, the time period, or both.

Using Time Periods of Less Than One Year

Discounting, or compounding, may be done over shorter periods of time than one year, such as monthly, quarterly, or semi-annually. When the time frame is less than one year, it is necessary to convert the annual interest rate to the applicable time frame. Assume, for example, that the investment you made in Illustration PV-7 paid $500 semi-annually for three years instead of $1,000 annually. In this case, the number of periods (n) becomes 6 (3 years × 2 payment periods per year), and the discount rate (i) is 2% (4% × $^6/_{12}$ months).

If present value tables are used to determine the present value, the appropriate present value factor from Table PV-2 is 5.60143 (6 periods at 2%). The present value of the future cash flows is $2,800.72 (5.60143 × $500). This amount is higher than the $2,775.09 calculated in Illustration PV-9 because interest is calculated twice during the same year. Thus, interest is compounded on the first half-year's interest.

Limitations of Present Value Tables

As previously discussed, one of the limitations of the present value tables is that the tables contain a limited number of interest rates. This is particularly a problem when time periods of less than one year are used. For example, if the annual interest rate was 9% and the payments were semi-annual, you would need to use the present value factor for 4.5%, which has not been included in Tables PV-1 or PV-2 in this textbook due to space limitations. If the payments were quarterly, you would need to use 2.25%, which is also not in the PV tables.

You will likely find PV tables to be of very limited value in other courses or in your own life. Consequently, we highly recommend you learn how to use either a financial calculator or a computer spreadsheet to perform these calculations.

BEFORE YOU GO ON...DO IT **Calculate the present value of an annuity**

Corkum Company has just signed a capital lease contract for equipment that requires rental payments of $6,000 each, to be paid at the end of each of the next five years. The appropriate discount rate is 6%. What is the present value of the rental payments; that is, the amount used to capitalize the leased equipment? Show the calculation using one of (a) the present value of an annuity formula, (b) Table PV-2, (c) a financial calculator, or (d) Excel functions.

| PV = (?) | $6,000 | $6,000 | $6,000 | $6,000 | $6,000 |

i = 6%

n = 5

Now   1   2   3   4   5 Years

Solution

The present value of lease rental payments of $6,000 paid at the end of each year for five years, discounted at 6%, is calculated as follows:

(a) Using the present value of an annuity formula:
$$PV = \$6,000\ [(1 - ((1 + 0.06)^{-5}) \div 0.06]$$
$$= \$6,000 \times 4.212364$$
$$= \$25,274.18$$

(b) Using the present value factor from Table PV-2:
The present value factor from Table PV-2 is 4.21236 (5 periods at 6%).

$$PV = \$6,000 \times 4.21236$$
$$PV = \$25,274.16$$

(c) Using a financial calculator:

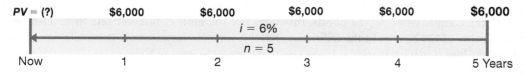

Enter:	6	5	6,000	0		Result
Press:	I/Y	N	PMT	FV	CPT PV	$(25,274.18)

(d) Using Excel functions and the PV formula = PV(rate,nper,pmt,fv,type):

RATE	.06
NPER	5
PMT	$6,000.00
FV	$0.00
Type	0

PV = $(25,274.18)

Related exercise material: BEPV–6, BEPV–7, and BEPV–8.

Action Plan

- Draw a time diagram showing when the future value will be received, the discount rate, and the number of periods.
- Note that each of the future payments is the same amount paid at even intervals; therefore, use present value of an annuity calculations to determine the present value (*i* = 6% and *n* = 5).

LEARNING OBJECTIVE **4** ▶ Calculate the present value of a bond.

Applying Present Value Concepts

CALCULATING THE MARKET PRICE OR PRESENT VALUE OF A BOND

The present value (or market price) of a bond is a function of three variables: (1) the payment amounts, (2) the length of time until the amounts are paid, and (3) the market interest rate, also known as the discount rate.

The first variable (dollars to be paid) is made up of two elements: (1) the principal amount (a single sum), and (2) a series of interest payments (an annuity). To calculate the present value of the bond, both the principal amount and the interest payments must be discounted, which requires two different calculations. The present value of a bond can be calculated using present value formulas, factors from the two present value tables, a financial calculator, or Excel.

It is important to note that **the interest rate used to determine the annual or semi-annual interest payments is fixed over the life of a bond**. This is the bond's contractual interest rate. The company issuing the bond chooses the specific interest rate before issuing the bonds. But investors may use a different interest rate when determining how much they are willing to pay (the present value) for the bonds. Investors are influenced by both general economic conditions and their assessment of the company issuing the bonds. **Investors use the market interest rate to determine the present value of the bonds.** In the following sections, we will illustrate how to calculate the present value of the bonds using a market interest rate that is equal to, greater than, or less than the contractual interest rate.

Market Interest Rate Equals the Contractual Interest Rate

When the investor's market interest rate is equal to the bond's contractual interest rate, the bonds' present value will equal their face value. To illustrate, assume there is a bond issue of 5-year, 6% bonds with a face value of $100,000 and on the issue date the market interest rate is equal to the contractual interest rate. Interest is payable **semi-annually** on January 1 and July 1. In this case, the investor will receive (1) $100,000 at maturity, and (2) a series of 10 $3,000 interest payments [($100,000 × 6%) × $^6/_{12}$ months] over the term of the bonds. The total number of interest periods is 10 (5 years × 2 payments per year), and the discount rate (i) is 3% (6% × $^6/_{12}$ months) per semi-annual interest period. The time diagram in Illustration PV-10 shows the variables involved in this discounting situation.

▶ **ILLUSTRATION**
Time diagram for the present value of a five-year, 6% bond paying interest semi-annually

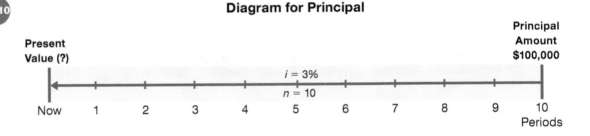

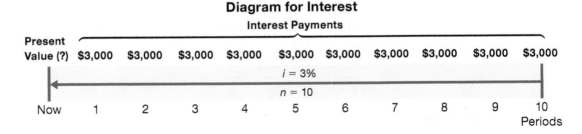

Present Value Tables. The calculation of the present value of these bonds using factors from the appropriate present value tables is shown in Illustration PV-11.

6% Contractual Rate and 6% Market Rate

Present value of principal to be paid at maturity
$100,000 × PV of 1 due in 10 periods (n) at 3% (i)
$100,000 × 0.74409 (Table PV-1) $ 74,409
Present value of interest to be paid periodically over the term of the bonds
$3,000 × PV of 1 due periodically for 10 periods (n) at 3% (i)
$3,000 × 8.53020 (Table PV-2)   25,591*

Present value of bonds $100,000

*Rounded

▶ILLUSTRATION 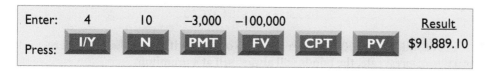 PV-11
Present value of bonds
(market rate equals contractual
rate)

Using a financial calculator or Excel functions would yield the same result. Thus, when the market rate is the same as the contractual rate, the bonds will sell at face value.

Market Interest Rate Is Greater Than the Contractual Interest Rate

Now assume that the market interest rate is 8%, not 6%. The future cash flows are again $100,000 and $3,000, respectively. **These cash flows are based on the bond contract and do not vary with the market interest rate.** But the market interest rate can and does vary, depending on investor expectations and current economic conditions. If the market interest rate is 8%, then the present value is calculated using this rate. In this case, 4% (8% × $6/12$ months) will be used because the bonds pay interest semi-annually. The present value of the bonds is $91,889, as calculated in Illustration PV-12.

6% Contractual Rate and 8% Market Rate

Present value of principal to be paid at maturity
$100,000 × PV of 1 due in 10 periods (n) at 4% (i)
$100,000 × 0.67556 (Table PV-1) $67,556
Present value of interest to be paid periodically over the term of the bonds
$3,000 × PV of 1 due periodically for 10 periods (n) at 4% (i)
$3,000 × 8.11090 (Table PV-2)   24,333*

Present value of bonds $91,889

*Rounded

▶ILLUSTRATION PV-12
Present value of bonds
(market rate greater than
contractual rate)

While it was necessary to use both PV tables (one for the semi-annual interest payment and one for the final payment of the bond principal) in the previous calculation, the financial calculator and Excel can both handle the two sources of cash flows in a single calculation. This is another major benefit of using a financial calculator or Excel compared with using present value tables or formulas.

Financial Calculators. If using a financial calculator, the interest payments and future repayment of principal should both be entered as negative numbers because they represent cash outflows. The result shown for the present value will then be a positive number, which is consistent with the fact that the company will receive cash when it issues a bond. The data entered for this example and the result are as follows:

Enter:	4	10	−3,000	−100,000		Result
Press:	I/Y	N	PMT	FV	CPT	PV	$91,889.10

Computer Spreadsheets. Similarly, if using Excel functions, the interest payments and future repayment of principal are entered as negative numbers in the PV formula = PV(rate,nper,pmt,fv,type). The data entered and the result are as follows:

RATE	.04
NPER	10
PMT	$(3,000.00)
FV	$(100,000.00)
Type	0
Result: PV = $91,889.10	

In this situation, the bonds will sell for $91,889, at a discount of $8,111. **If the market interest rate is greater than the contract interest rate, the bonds will always sell at a discount.** If investors determine that the bond's contract interest rate is too low compared to current market interest rates, they will compensate by paying less for the bonds. Note that they will still collect the full $100,000 at the maturity date.

Market Interest Rate Is Less Than the Contractual Interest Rate

On the other hand, the market rate might be lower than the contractual interest rate. In this case, the interest paid on the bonds is higher than what investors expected to earn. As a result, they will compensate by paying more for the bonds. To illustrate, assume the same information used in the previous example except that now the market interest rate is 5%. Using a market interest rate of 5% the present value will be calculated using 2.5% (5% × $^6/_{12}$ months) as the discount rate. The cash payments and number of periods remain the same.

Present Value Tables. In this case, the present value of the bonds is $104,376, as calculated in Illustration PV-13.

▶ILLUSTRATION
Present value of bonds
(market rate less than
contractual rate)

6% Contractual Rate and 5% Market Rate	
Present value of principal to be paid at maturity	
$100,000 × PV of 1 due in 10 periods (*n*) at 2.5% (*i*)	
$100,000 × 0.78120 (Table PV-1)	$ 78,120
Present value of interest to be paid periodically over the term of the bonds	
$3,000 × PV of 1 due periodically for 10 periods (*n*) at 2.5% (*i*)	
$3,000 × 8.75206 (Table PV-2)	26,256*
Present value of bonds	$104,376

*Rounded

Financial Calculator. If using a financial calculator, the data entered and the result are as follows:

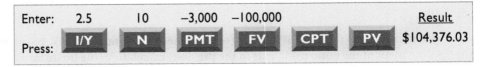

Enter:	2.5	10	−3,000	−100,000		Result
Press:	I/Y	N	PMT	FV	CPT PV	$104,376.03

If using Excel functions and the PV formula = PV(rate,nper,pmt,fv,type), the data entered and the result are as follows:

RATE	.025
NPER	10
PMT	$(3,000.00)
FV	$(100,000.00)
Type	0
Result: PV = $104,376.03	

These bonds will sell for $104,376, at a premium of $4,376. **If the market interest rate is less than the contractual interest rate, the bonds will always sell at a premium.**

The relationship between bond market price and interest rates is shown in Illustration PV-14.

Bond will sell at a *discount*	• Market interest rate is greater than the contractual interest rate.
Bond will sell at a *premium*	• Market interest rate is less than the contractual interest rate.

▶ILLUSTRATION PV-14
Relationship between bond market price and interest rates

BEFORE YOU GO ON...DO IT 4 ▸ **Calculate the present value of a bond issue**

Forest Lake Enterprises issued $1 million of 6-year, 4.5% bonds that pay interest semi-annually. The market rate of interest for the bonds at the issue date is 4%. What cash proceeds did Forest Lake Enterprises receive from the issue of the bonds?

Solution

1. Amount to be received at maturity is the face value of the bonds, $1,000,000
2. Semi-annual interest payment $22,500 ($1,000,000 × 4.5% × $^{6}/_{12}$ months)
3. Number of periods n = 12 (6 years × 2 payments a year)
4. Discount rate i = 2% (4% × $^{6}/_{12}$)

The cash proceeds that Forest Lake will receive from issuing the bonds is the present value of principal to be paid at maturity plus the present value of the interest payment paid periodically, calculated as follows:

Present value of principal to be paid at maturity:
$1,000,000 × 0.78849 (PV of 1 due in 12 periods
at 2% from Table PV-1) $ 788,490

Present value of interest to be paid periodically over the term of the bonds:
$22,500 × 10.57534 (PV of 1 due each period for 12 periods
at 2% from Table PV-2) 237,945

Present value of bonds $1,026,435*

If using a financial calculator, the data entered and the result are as follows:

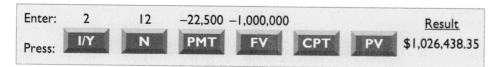

Enter: 2   12   −22,500 −1,000,000   **Result**
Press: I/Y   N   PMT   FV   CPT   PV $1,026,438.35

If using Excel functions and the PV formula = PV(rate,nper,pmt,fv,type), the data entered and the result are as follows:

RATE	.02
NPER	12
PMT	$(22,500.00)
FV	$(1,000,000.00)
Type	0

Result: PV = $1,026,438.35

*Note that the financial calculator and Excel results are the same amount but they are slightly different than the PV table calculation because the factors in the PV tables are rounded.

Related exercise material: BEPV–9 and BEPV–10.

Action Plan
• Note that Forest Lake Enterprises will be able to sell these bonds at a premium because the bonds pay higher interest (4.5%) than the current market interest rate (4%).
• Recall that the contractual interest rate is used to determine the interest payment; the market rate is used to determine the present value.
• Adjust the interest rates and number of periods for the effect of the semi-annual periods.
• Use Table PV-1 to determine the present value of the principal and Table PV-2 to determine the present value of the interest payments.
• You can instead use a financial calculator, remembering to enter the interest and principal payments as negative numbers.
• You can instead use Excel functions, entering the interest and principal payments as negative numbers.

Apply present value concepts to notes payable to calculate the periodic payments, the interest rate, or the number of periods.

USING PRESENT VALUE CONCEPTS WITH NOTES PAYABLE

Non-current notes payable are normally repayable in a series of periodic payments. Examples of non-current notes payable include unsecured notes, mortgages (which are secured notes on real property, such as a house), and loans (for example, student or car).

The present value of the note payable is the amount borrowed and thus typically doesn't need to be calculated as in the case of a bond payable. The future value of a note payable is zero because the note will be paid in full through the periodic payments, which include both interest and principal. Instead, present value concepts are often used with notes payable to determine one of the following three variables: (1) the payment amount, (2) the length of time until the amounts are paid (time to maturity date), or (3) the interest rate.

Calculating the Periodic Payment for a Note Payable

Payments for a non-current note payable may be fixed principal payments plus interest, or blended principal and interest payments. To illustrate these two types of payments, we will assume that Heathcote Company issues a five-year note payable, with an 8% interest rate, to purchase a piece of equipment costing $25,000.

Fixed Principal Payments Plus Interest. If we first assume that repayment is to be in fixed principal payments plus interest, paid annually, then the payment amount would be $5,000 ($25,000 ÷ 5 years) for principal plus 8% interest on the outstanding balance. Illustration PV-15 shows how the interest and periodic cash payment are determined for this note.

▶ ILLUSTRATION PV-15
Note payable instalment payment schedule with fixed principal payments plus interest

	(A)	(B)	(C)	(D)
			Fixed Reduction of Principal	Principal Balance
	Cash Payment	Interest Expense		
Interest Period	(B) + (C)	(D) × 8%	$25,000 ÷ 5	(D) − (C)
Start of Year 1				$25,000
End of Year 1	$ 7,000	$2,000	$ 5,000	20,000
End of Year 2	6,600	1,600	5,000	15,000
End of Year 3	6,200	1,200	5,000	10,000
End of Year 4	5,800	800	5,000	5,000
End of Year 5	5,400	400	5,000	0
Totals	$31,000	$6,000	$25,000	

Note that the periodic cash payment is a different amount each period because the interest is a different amount each year. Recall that an annuity, by definition, is an equal payment each period. That means we cannot use present value concepts introduced in this appendix to analyze the note. Instead we will focus on notes payable with blended payments, which are the same amount each period, in the following section of this appendix.

Blended Principal Plus Interest Payments. In the case of blended principal and interest payments, the periodic payment is an annuity and thus present value concepts can be used to calculate the amount of the annual payment. As long as four of the five present value amounts (present value, interest rate, number of periods, payments, and future value) are known, present value concepts can be used to calculate the one unknown.

Present Value Tables. If we divide the total loan amount of $25,000 by the present value factor for an annuity from Table PV-2 for $i = 8\%$ and $n = 5$, then we can determine that the annual payment is

$6,261.41 ($25,000 ÷ 3.99271). Illustration PV-16 shows the note payable instalment payment schedule using the annuity of $6,262.41 as the annual cash payment.

Interest Period	(A) Cash Payment	(B) Interest Expense (D) × 8%	(C) Reduction of Principal (A) − (B)	(D) Principal Balance (D) − (C)
Start of Year 1				$25,000.00
End of Year 1	$ 6,261.41	$2,000.00	$ 4,261.41	20,738.59
End of Year 2	6,261.41	1,659.09	4,602.32	16,136.27
End of Year 3	6,261.41	1,290.90	4,970.51	11,165.76
End of Year 4	6,261.41	893.26	5,368.15	5,797.61
End of Year 5	6,261.41	463.80	5,797.61	0
Totals	$31,307.05	$6,307.05	$25,000.00	

▶ILLUSTRATION **PV-16**
Note payable instalment payment schedule with blended principal plus interest payments

We can see from this illustration that the periodic blended payment of $6,261.41 is exactly the amount needed to pay the required interest plus the principal of the note in full by the end of year five.

Financial Calculators. If using a financial calculator to determine the periodic payment, the data entered and the result are as follows:

Enter: 8   5   25,000   0   Result
Press: I/Y   N   PV   FV   CPT   PMT $(6,261.41)

Computer Spreadsheets. If using the Excel PMT formula = PMT(rate,nper,pv,fv,type), the data entered and the result are as follows:

```
RATE                    .08
NPER                      5
PV              $25,000.00
FV                   $0.00
Type                      0
Result: PMT = $(6,261.41)
```

While the above three methods all provided the same periodic payment, the financial calculator and Excel functions are more useful because they can be used for any interest rate and any number of periods, not just those included in the PV table.

Calculating the Interest Rate for a Note Payable

There are several situations in which it may be necessary to calculate the effective interest rate. For example, sometimes businesses offer financing with stated interest rates below market interest rates to stimulate sales. Examples of notes with stated interest rates below market are seen in advertisements offering no payment for two years. As we have seen in the case of bonds, if the contractual or stated interest rate is less than the market or effective interest rate, then the present value of the loan will be less than the face value. With a zero-interest-rate note, the market or effective interest rate in the transaction must be calculated using present value concepts.

Present Value Tables. As an example, assume that a furniture retailer is offering "No payment for two years, or $150 off on items with a sticker price of $2,000." The implicit interest cost over the two years is $150, and the present value of the asset is then $1,850 ($2,000 − $150). From Table PV-1, the effective interest rate can be determined as follows:

PV ÷ FV = present value factor $1,850 ÷ $2,000 = 0.925

Looking at the $n = 2$ row of Table PV-1, this would represent an interest rate of approximately 4%. Most notes have an interest cost, whether explicitly stated or not.

Financial Calculator. Using a financial calculator will result in a more precise interest rate calculation. In this example, the data entered and the result are as follows:

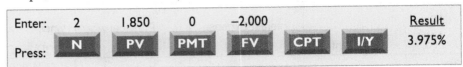

Enter: 2 N, 1,850 PV, 0 PMT, −2,000 FV, CPT, I/Y — Result 3.975%

Computer Spreadsheets. In the Excel RATE formula = RATE(nper,pmt,pv,fv,type), the data entered and the result are as follows:

NPER	2
PMT	$0.00
PV	$1,850.00
FV	$(2,000.00)
Type	0
Result: RATE = 3.975%	

Also note that the purchaser should record the furniture at a cost of $1,850 even if the purchaser chose the option of no payment for two years. In this case, the purchaser will recognize interest expense of $73.54 ($1,850 × 3.975%) in the first year and $76.46 [($1,850 + $73.54) × 3.975%] in the second year.

Canada Student Loans: Calculation of Time to Pay

The Canadian federal government, in an effort to encourage post-secondary education, offers loans to eligible students with no interest accruing while they maintain their full-time student status. When schooling is complete, the entire Canada Student Loan must be repaid within 10 years. Repayment of the loan can be at a fixed rate of prime plus 5%, or a floating rate of prime plus 2.5%. One calculation you might be interested in is how long it will take to repay your Canada Student Loan if you have a certain amount of money available to make monthly payments.

Let's assume that you attend school for four years and borrow $2,500 per year. Upon graduation, because there was no interest while you were a student, you have a total debt of $10,000. Also assume you have opted for a fixed rate of interest of 8% while repaying the loan. If you can pay $150 a month, will you be able to repay the loan within the 120 months (10 years × 12 months per year) allowed?

Present Value Tables. This particular example could not be done with the PV tables in this textbook because of the interest rate. Since we are making monthly payments, we must also use a monthly interest rate. The monthly interest rate of 0.6667% is less than the lowest percentage on the table and thus the table cannot be used.

Financial Calculator. Using a financial calculator, the data entered and the result are as follows:

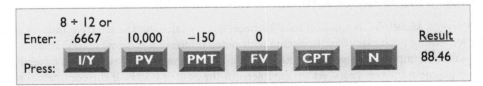

8 ÷ 12 or
Enter: .6667 I/Y, 10,000 PV, −150 PMT, 0 FV, CPT, N — Result 88.46

Note that, because you are making monthly payments, the annual interest rate of 8% must be adjusted to a monthly rate of 0.6667%. Also note that the payments are a negative number because they are a cash outflow. The present value is a positive number because it is equal to the amount borrowed, which was a cash inflow. The future value is zero because the loan will be fully paid at maturity.

The result of 88.46 means that you would need to make 89 monthly payments: the first 88 months at $150 per month, and the last month at a lesser amount for the remaining balance. This is less than 120 months, which means that you will be able to pay your student loan in the allowed period.

Computer Spreadsheets. The same result can be obtained using the Excel NPER formula = NPER(rate, pmt,pv,fv,type). The data entered and the result are as follows:

RATE	.08 ÷ 12 = .006667
PMT	$(150.00)
PV	$10,000.00
FV	$0.00
Type	0
Result: NPER = 88.46 periods	

BEFORE YOU GO ON...DO IT **5** **Calculate the periodic payment of a note payable**

You are about to purchase your first car for $25,000. You pay $1,000 cash and finance the remaining amount at an annual interest rate of 7% over a period of 48 months. How much is your monthly payment, assuming you make equal blended principal and interest payments each month?

Solution

1. Using a financial calculator, the data entered and the result are as follows:

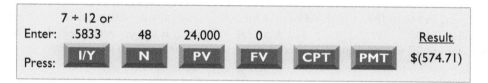

2. Using Excel functions, the formula is: = PMT(rate,nper,pv,fv,type).

RATE	.07 ÷ 12 = .005833
PMT	48
PV	$24,000.00
FV	$0.00
Type	0

Result: PMT = $(574.71)

Action Plan
- Use n = 48 and i = 0.5833% (7% ÷ 12 months), PV = $24,000, and FV = $0.
- The present value factors in the tables cannot be used because the interest rate is 0.5833% which is not available on Table PV-2.
- Use a financial calculator or Excel functions to calculate the payment.

Related exercise material: BEPV–11, BEPV–12, BEPV–13, BEPV–14, BEPV–15, BEPV–16, BEPV–17, BEPV–18, BEPV–19, and BEPV–20.

LEARNING OBJECTIVE **6** **Estimate the value of an asset using future cash flows.**

ASSETS: ESTIMATING VALUE IN USE USING FUTURE CASH FLOWS

In Chapter 9, you learned that companies are required to regularly determine whether the value of property, plant, and equipment has been impaired. Recall that an asset is impaired if the carrying amount reported on the balance sheet is greater than its recoverable amount. The recoverable amount is either the asset's fair value or its *value in use*. Determining the value in use requires the application of present value concepts. The calculation of value in use is a two-step process: (1) estimate future cash flows, and (2) calculate the present value of these cash flows.

Present Value Tables

For example, assume JB Company owns a specialized piece of equipment used in its manufacturing process. JB needs to determine the asset's value in use to test for impairment. As the first step in determining value in use, JB's management estimates that the equipment will last for another five years and that it will generate the following future cash flows at the end of each year:

Year 1	Year 2	Year 3	Year 4	Year 5
$9,000	$10,000	$13,000	$10,000	$7,000

In the second step of determining value in use, JB calculates the present value of each of these future cash flows. Using a discount rate of 8%, the present value of each future cash flow is shown in Illustration PV-17.

▶ **ILLUSTRATION** (PV-17)
Present value of estimated future cash flows of specialized equipment

	Year 1	Year 2	Year 3	Year 4	Year 5
Future cash flows	$9,000	$10,000	$13,000	$10,000	$7,000
Present value factor	0.92593	0.85734	0.79383	0.73503	0.68058
Present value amount	$8,333	$ 8,573	$10,320	$ 7,350	$4,764

The value in use of JB's specialized equipment is the sum of the present value of each year's cash flow, $39,340 ($8,333 + $8,573 + $10,320 + $7,350 + $4,764). If this amount is less than the asset's carrying amount, JB will be required to record an impairment, as shown in Chapter 9.

Financial Calculator

The present value method of estimating the value in use of a property, plant, and equipment asset can also be used for intangible assets. For example, assume JB purchases a licence from Redo Industries for the right to manufacture and sell products using Redo's processes and technologies. JB estimates it will earn $6,000 per year from this licence over the next 10 years. What is the value in use to JB of this licence?

JB expects to earn the same amount each year and uses 8% as the discount rate. If using a financial calculator, the data entered and the result are as follows:

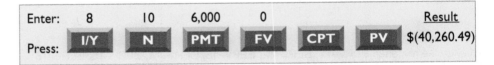

Computer Spreadsheet

The value in use of the licence can also be determined using Excel functions and the PV formula = PV(rate,nper,pmt,fv,type). The data entered and the result are as follows:

RATE	.08
NPER	10
PMT	$6,000.00
FV	$0.00
Type	0
Result: PV = $(40,260.49)	

Helpful hint The results using the financial calculator and Excel functions are negative because they represent the amount you should be willing to pay today to receive $6,000 per year for 10 years if the discount rate is 8%.

If the calculated value in use for the licence is less than the asset's carrying amount, JB will be required to record an impairment.

BEFORE YOU GO ON...DO IT	6	Calculate the value in use of an asset

You are attempting to estimate the value in use of your company's production equipment, which you estimate will be used in operations for another eight years. You estimate that the equipment will generate annual cash flows of $16,000, at the end of each year, for the remainder of its productive life, and that 9% is the appropriate discount rate. What is the value in use of this equipment?

Solution

The value in use is equal to the present value of the estimated annual future cash flows for the remaining life of the asset discounted at an appropriate discount rate.

Future annual cash flows:	$16,000
Number of periods:	8
Discount rate:	9%
Present value annuity factor ($n = 8, i = 9\%$):	5.53482
Present value:	$88,557 = $16,000 × 5.53482

Action Plan
- Identify future cash flows.
- Use Table PV-2 to determine the present value of an annuity factor for $n = 8$ and $i = 9\%$ and calculate the present value.
- Alternatively, use a financial calculator or Excel functions to solve.

If using a financial calculator, the data entered and the result are as follows:

Enter:	9	8	16,000	0		Result
Press:	I/Y	N	PMT	FV	CPT	PV	$(88,557.11)

If using Excel functions and the PV formula = PV(rate,nper,pmt,fv,type), the data entered and the result are as follows:

RATE	.09
NPER	8
PMT	$16,000.00
FV	$0.00
Type	0
Result: PV = $(88,557.11)	

Related exercise material: BEPV–21.

▶ Brief Exercises

BEPV–1 Determine the amount of interest that will be earned on each of the following investments:

	Investment	(i) Interest Rate	(n) Number of Periods	Type of Interest
(a)	$1,000	5%	1	Simple
(b)	$500	4%	2	Simple
(c)	$500	4%	2	Compound

Calculate simple and compound interest. (LO 1) AP

BEPV–2 Wong Ltd. is considering an investment that will return a lump sum of $600,000 five years from now. What amount should Wong Ltd. pay for this investment in order to earn a 4% return?

Calculate present value of a single-sum investment. (LO 2) AP

BEPV–3 Mohammed's parents wish to invest in a 10-year guaranteed investment certificate (GIC) in his name that will provide $10,000 to attend college. The investment pays 4% annually. How much must Mohammed's parents invest today to receive $10,000 10 years from now?

Calculate present value of a single-sum investment. (LO 2) AP

BEPV–4 Xin Su has been offered the opportunity to invest $44,401 now. The investment will earn 7% per year, and at the end of that time will return Xin $100,000. How many years must Xin wait to receive $100,000?

Calculate number of periods of a single investment sum. (LO 2) AP

BEPV–5 If Jin Fei invests $3,152 now, she will receive $10,000 at the end of 15 years. What annual rate of interest will Jin earn on her investment? Round your answer to the nearest whole number.

Calculate interest rate on single sum. (LO 2) AP

Determine present values.
(LO 2, 3) AP

BEPV–6 Using a financial calculator, answer the following:

(a) What is the present value of $25,000 due nine periods from now, discounted at 10%?
(b) What is the present value of $25,000 to be received at the end of each of six periods, discounted at 9%?

Calculate present value of an annuity investment. (LO 3) AP

BEPV–7 Tarzwell Ltd. is considering investing in an annuity contract that will return $25,000 at the end of each year for 15 years. What amount should Tarzwell Ltd. pay for this investment if it earns a 6% return?

Determine number of periods and discount rate. (LO 3) AP

BEPV–8 For each of the following cases, indicate in the chart below the appropriate discount rate (*i*) and the appropriate number of periods (*n*) to be used in present value calculations. Show calculations. The first one has been completed as an example.

	Annual Interest Rate	Number of Years	Frequency of Payments	(*n*) Number of periods	(*i*) Discount Rate
1.	6%	2	Quarterly	2 × 4 = 8	6% ÷ 4 = 1.5%
2.	5%	8	Semi-annually		
3.	7%	5	Annually		
4.	4%	3	Quarterly		
5.	2%	6	Semi-annually		
6.	6%	9	Monthly		

Calculate present value of bonds. (LO 4) AP

BEPV–9 New Line Railroad Co. is about to issue $100,000 of 10-year bonds that pay a 5.5% annual interest rate, with interest payable semi-annually. The market interest rate is 5%. How much can New Line expect to receive for the sale of these bonds?

Calculate present value of bonds. (LO 4) AP

BEPV–10 Assume the same information as in BEPV–9, except that the market interest rate is 6% instead of 5%. In this case, how much can New Line expect to receive from the sale of these bonds?

Determine unknown amounts in various present value situations. (LO 4, 5) AP

BEPV–11 Using a financial calculator, solve for the unknowns in each of the following situations.

(a) On June 1, 2017, Ada Diya purchases lakefront property from her neighbour, Josh Bello, and agrees to pay the purchase price in seven payments of $16,000 each. The first payment is to be made on May 31, 2018. (Assume that interest compounded at an annual rate of 7.35% is implicit in the payments.) What is the purchase price of the property on June 1, 2017?
(b) On January 1, 2017, Bakari Corporation purchased 200 of the $1,000 face value, 8%, 10-year bonds of Sterling Inc. The bonds mature on January 1, 2027, and interest is paid annually on December 31. Bakari purchased the bonds to yield 10.65%. How much did Bakari pay for the bonds?

Calculate payment on note. (LO 5) AP

BEPV–12 Marsdon Company receives a six-year, $50,000 note that bears interest at 8% from a customer. The customer will make annual blended principal plus interest payments at the end of each year. What is the annual payment that Marsdon will receive from its customer?

Calculate payment on note. (LO 5) AP

BEPV–13 Assume the same information as BEPV–12, except that the interest rate is 9% instead of 8%. What is the annual payment that Marsdon will receive from its customer?

Calculate effective interest rate on note. (LO 5) AP

BEPV–14 Phang Ltd. issues a six-year, $1,058,871 mortgage note on January 1, 2017, to obtain financing for new equipment. The terms provide for semi-annual instalment payments of $112,825. What is the effective interest rate on the mortgage note payable?

Calculate quarterly payments on note payable. (LO 5) AP

BEPV–15 The municipality of Lansdown issued a three-year, 5% mortgage note payable for $185,000 to finance the purchase of three salt trucks. The terms provide for equal quarterly blended principal plus interest payments. What are the quarterly payments on the note?

Determine how long to repay note. (LO 5) AP

BEPV–16 You have borrowed $18,000. If the annual rate of interest is 4%, how long will it take you to repay the note if you are making semi-annual blended principal plus interest payments of $1,702?

Calculate annual payments. (LO 5) AP

BEPV–17 You would like to purchase a car that costs $32,000, and the dealer offers financing over a five-year period at 3%. If repayments are to be made annually, what would your annual payments be?

Determine unknown amounts in various present value situations. (LO 5) AP

BEPV–18 Using a financial calculator, provide a solution to each of the following situations.

(a) Lisa Okoye owes a debt of $42,000 from the purchase of her new sport utility vehicle. The debt bears annual interest of 7.8% compounded monthly. Lisa wishes to pay the debt and interest in equal monthly payments over eight years, beginning one month from now. What equal monthly payments will pay off the debt and interest?
(b) On January 1, 2017, Celmira Jalloh offers to buy Dave Contee's used snowmobile for $8,000, payable in five equal annual instalments, which are to include 7.25% interest on the unpaid balance and a portion of the principal. If the first payment is to be made on December 31, 2017, how much will each payment be?

BEPV–19   As CFO of a small manufacturing firm, you have been asked to determine the best financing for the purchase of a new piece of equipment. If the vendor is offering repayment options of $10,000 per year for five years, or only one payment of $46,000 at the end of two years, which option would you recommend? The current market rate of interest is 8%.

Compare financing options. (LO 5) AN

BEPV–20   If the market rate of interest in BEPV–19 was 10%, would you choose the same option?

Compare financing options. (LO 5) AN

BEPV–21   Tsung Company signs a contract to sell the use of its patented manufacturing technology to Herlitz Corp. for 12 years. The contract for this transaction stipulates that Herlitz Corp. pays Tsung $21,000 at the end of each year for the use of this technology. Using a discount rate of 4%, what is the value in use of the patented manufacturing technology?

Calculate value in use of a patent. (LO 6) AP

Company Index

Subject Index